DICTIONARY OF AMERICAN BIOGRAPHY

AMERICAN
COUNCIL
* OF *
LEARNED
SOCIETIES
*

DICTIONARY OF

AMERICAN BIOGRAPHY

DICTIONARY OF AMERICAN BIOGRAPHY

UNDER THE AUSPICES OF THE
AMERICAN COUNCIL OF LEARNED SOCIETIES

EDITED BY
DUMAS MALONE

Steward—Trowbridge

VOLUME XVIII

CHARLES SCRIBNER'S SONS
NEW YORK
1936

Prompted solely by a desire for public service the New York Times Company and its President, Mr. Adolph S. Ochs, made possible the preparation of the manuscript of the Dictionary of American Biography through a subvention of more than $500,000 and with the understanding that the entire responsibility for the contents of the volumes rests with the American Council of Learned Societies.

CONTRIBUTORS TO VOLUME XVIII

Charles David Abbott	C. D. A.
Thomas P. Abernethy	T. P. A.
Adeline Adams	A—e. A.
Arthur Adams	A—r. A.
Franklin P. Adams	F. P. A.
James Truslow Adams	J. T. A.
Randolph G. Adams	R. G. A—s.
Raymond William Adams	R. W. A.
Nelson F. Adkins	N. F. A.
Cyrus Adler	C. A.
Robert Greenhalgh Albion	R. G. A—n.
William F. Albright	W. F. A.
Arthur N. Alling	A. N. A.
William H. Allison	W. H. A.
John C. Almack	J. C. A—k.
Russell H. Anderson	R. H. A.
Gertrude L. Annan	G. L. A.
Katharine Anthony	K. A.
John Clark Archer	J. C. A—r.
Raymond Clare Archibald	R. C. A.
Frank Collins Baker	F. C. B.
Preston A. Barba	P. A. B.
Lewellys F. Barker	L. F. B.
Gilbert H. Barnes	G. H. B.
James Barnes	J. B.
Claribel R. Barnett	C. R. B.
John H. Barnhart	J. H. B—t.
Harold K. Barrows	H. K. B.
Clarence Bartlett	C. B—t.
Ernest Sutherland Bates	E. S. B—s.
H. Y. Benedict	H. Y. B.
Elbert J. Benton	E. J. B.
Percy W. Bidwell	P. W. B.
William C. Binkley	W. C. B.
Glen A. Blackburn	G. A. B.
Arthur A. Blanchard	A. A. B.
Edith R. Blanchard	E. R. B.
Wyndham B. Blanton	W. B. B.
Willard Grosvenor Bleyer	W. G. B.
Bruce Bliven	B. B.
Ernest Ludlow Bogart	E. L. B.
Louis H. Bolander	L. H. B.
Charles K. Bolton	C. K. B.
Ethel Stanwood Bolton	E. S. B—n.
Robert W. Bolwell	R. W. B.
Beverley W. Bond, Jr.	B. W. B., Jr.
Sarah G. Bowerman	S. G. B.
Julian P. Boyd	J. P. B.
William A. Braun	W. A. B.

Carl Bridenbaugh	C. B—h.
Jessica Hill Bridenbaugh	J. H. B—h.
Jean Lambert Brockway	J. L. B.
Alfred Mansfield Brooks	A. M. B.
C. A. Browne	C. A. B.
Robert Bruce	R. B.
Oscar MacMillan Buck	O. M. B.
Solon J. Buck	S. J. B.
F. Lauriston Bullard	F. L. B.
C. C. Burlingame	C. C. B.
Edmund C. Burnett	E. C. B.
C. Pauline Burt	C. P. B.
Henry J. Cadbury	H. J. C.
James M. Callahan	J. M. C.
Alfred Copeland Callen	A. C. C.
Henry Seidel Canby	H. S. C—y.
Zechariah Chafee, Jr.	Z. C., Jr.
Henry S. Chapman	H. S. C—n.
E. Clowes Chorley	E. C. C.
Robert C. Clark	R. C. C.
Robert Glass Cleland	R. G. C.
D. A. Clippinger	D. A. C.
Hugh McD. Clokie	H. M. C.
Frederick W. Coburn	F. W. C.
Hobart Coffey	H. C.
Esther Cole	E. Co.
Melvin E. Coleman	M. E. C.
E. Merton Coulter	E. M. C.
Isaac J. Cox	I. J. C.
Esther Crane	E. Cr.
Katharine Elizabeth Crane	K. E. C.
Avery O. Craven	A. O. C.
William J. Cunningham	W. J. C.
Edward E. Curtis	E. E. C.
Robert E. Cushman	R. E. C.
Stuart Daggett	S. D.
Arthur J. Daley	A. J. D.
Tenney L. Davis	T. L. D.
Edward H. Dewey	E. H. D.
Z. C. Dickinson	Z. C. D.
Irving Dilliard	I. D.
Charles A. Dinsmore	C. A. D—e.
Frank Haigh Dixon	F. H. D.
William E. Dodd	W. E. D.
Elizabeth Donnan	E. D.
Dorothy W. Douglas	D. W. D.
William Howe Downes	W. H. D.
Stella M. Drumm	S. M. D.
Edward A. Duddy	E. A. D.

Contributors to Volume XVIII

CLYDE AUGUSTUS DUNIWAY	C. A. D—y.
WILLIAM FREDERICK DURAND	W. F. D.
WALTER A. DYER	W. A. D.
EDWARD DWIGHT EATON	E. D. E.
WALTER PRICHARD EATON	W. P. E.
EVERETT E. EDWARDS	E. E. E.
ABRAM I. ELKUS	A. I. E.
THOMPSON C. ELLIOTT	T. C. E.
ELIZABETH BRECKENRIDGE ELLIS	E. B. E.
ELMER ELLIS	E. E—s.
EPHRAIM EMERTON	E. E—n.
WILLIAM M. EMERY	W. M. E.
MARGARET SITTLER ERMARTH	M. S. E.
JOHN O. EVJEN	J. O. E.
HUNTER D. FARISH	H. D. F.
HALLIE FARMER	H. F.
ETHEL WEBB FAULKNER	E. W. F.
WALTER R. FEE	W. R. F.
GUSTAV JOSEPH FIEBEGER	G. J. F.
MANTLE FIELDING	M. F.
JAMES KIP FINCH	J. K. F.
MARY ELIZABETH FITTRO	M. E. F.
JOHN C. FITZPATRICK	J. C. F—k.
ALEXANDER CLARENCE FLICK	A. C. F.
JOHN E. FLITCROFT	J. E. F.
JEREMIAH D. M. FORD	J. D. M. F.
DOUGLAS S. FREEMAN	D. S. F.
JOHN C. FRENCH	J. C. F—h.
PAUL H. FURFEY	P. H. F.
ESSON M. GALE	E. M. G.
WILLIAM A. GANOE	W. A. G.
CURTIS W. GARRISON	C. W. G.
F. LYNWOOD GARRISON	F. L. G.
HAZEL SHIELDS GARRISON	H. S. G—n.
GEORGE HARVEY GENZMER	G. H. G.
JOHN LAWRENCE GERIG	J. L. G.
W. J. GHENT	W. J. G.
EDGAR L. GILCREEST	E. L. G.
LEONIDAS CHALMERS GLENN	L. C. G.
GEORGE W. GOBLE	G. W. G.
ARMISTEAD CHURCHILL GORDON, JR.	A. C. G., JR.
DOROTHY GRAFLY	D. G—y.
CHARLES GRAVES	C. G.
HENRY S. GRAVES	H. S. G—s.
VIRGINIA GEARHART GRAY	V. G. G.
FLETCHER M. GREEN	F. M. G.
DOROTHY GREENWALD	D. G—d.
ANNE KING GREGORIE	A. K. G.
MARTHA GRUENING	M. G.
GURNEY C. GUE	G. C. G.
SIDNEY GUNN	S. G.
CHARLES W. HACKETT	C. W. H.
LE ROY R. HAFEN	L. R. H.
HORACE H. HAGAN	H. H. H.
EDWIN H. HALL	E. H. H.
J. G. DER. HAMILTON	J. G. deR. H.
TALBOT FAULKNER HAMLIN	T. F. H.
JOSEPH MILLS HANSON	J. M. H.
EDWARD ROCHIE HARDY, JR.	E. R. H., JR.
ALVIN F. HARLOW	A. F. H.
FREEMAN H. HART	F. H. H.
MARY BRONSON HARTT	M. B. H.
DOREMUS A. HAYES	D. A. H.
GEORGE H. HAYNES	G. H. H.
ELIZABETH WILTBANK HEILMAN	E. W. H.
ROBERT HERRICK	R. H.
JOHN HAYNES HOLMES	J. H. H.
ROLAND MATHER HOOKER	R. M. H.
WALTER HOUGH	W. H.
JOHN TASKER HOWARD	J. T. H.
ARCHER B. HULBERT	A. B. H.
EDWARD HUNGERFORD	E. H.
WILLIAM O. INGLIS	W. O. I.
RAY W. IRWIN	R. W. I.
JOSEPH JACKSON	J. J.
RUSSELL LEIGH JACKSON	R. L. J.
EDNA L. JACOBSEN	E. L. J—en.
M. C. JAMES	M. C. J.
THEODORE D. JERVEY	T. D. J.
W. L. G. JOERG	W. L. G. J.
EDWIN LEE JOHNSON	E. L. J—on.
JOSEPH E. JOHNSON	J. E. J.
RUFUS M. JONES	R. M. J.
H. DONALDSON JORDAN	H. D. J.
GEORGE MORROW KAHRL	G. M. K.
KATHARINE AMEND KELLOCK	K. A. K.
LOUISE PHELPS KELLOGG	L. P. K.
FREDERICK P. KEPPEL	F. P. K.
JOHN KIERAN	J. K.
FISKE KIMBALL	F. K.
JAMES GORE KING, JR.	J. G. K., JR.
RICHARD R. KIRK	R. R. K.
FRANK J. KLINGBERG	F. J. K.
ALBERT C. KNUDSON	A. C. K.
RALPH S. KUYKENDALL	R. S. K.
LEONARD W. LABAREE	L. W. L.
ROBERT LA FOLLETTE	R. L-F.
J. H. LANDMAN	J. H. L.
WILLIAM CHAUNCY LANGDON	W. C. L.
CONRAD H. LANZA	C. H. L.
KENNETH S. LATOURETTE	K. S. L.
WILLIAM LAWRENCE	W. L.
ANNA LANE LINGELBACH	A. L. L.
GEORGE W. LITTLEHALES	G. W. L.
ELLA LONN	E. L.
HENRY NOBLE MacCRACKEN	H. N. M.
HOWARD McCLENAHAN	H. McC.
ROGER P. McCUTCHEON	R. P. M.
JOSEPH McFARLAND	J. McF.
WALTER M. McFARLAND	W. M. M.
ALEXIUS McGLANNAN	A. M.
REGINALD C. McGRANE	R. C. M.
DOUGLAS C. McMURTRIE	D. C. M.
T. F. McNEILL	T. F. M.
HELEN TAFT MANNING	H. T. M.

Contributors to Volume XVIII

Asa Earl Martin	A. E. M.
Karen Martin	K. M.
William R. Maxon	W. R. M.
Franklin J. Meine	F. J. M—e.
Clarence W. Mendell	C. W. M—l.
A. Howard Meneely	A. H. M.
Newton D. Mereness	N. D. M.
George P. Merrill	G. P. M.
Frank J. Metcalf	F. J. M—f.
Harvey C. Minnich	H. C. M.
Broadus Mitchell	B. M.
Carl W. Mitman	C. W. M—n.
Harriet Monroe	H. M.
Robert E. Moody	R. E. M.
John Hill Morgan	J. H. M.
Richard B. Morris	R. B. M.
Jarvis M. Morse	J. M. M.
Sidney G. Morse	S. G. M.
Harry W. Mountcastle	H. W. M.
Kenneth B. Murdock	K. B. M.
I. William Nachlas	I. W. N.
William Allan Neilson	W. A. N.
John Herbert Nelson	J. H. N.
Lowry Nelson	L. N.
H. Edward Nettles	H. E. N.
Allan Nevins	A. N.
A. R. Newsome	A. R. N.
Franklin T. Nichols	F. T. N.
Jeannette P. Nichols	J. P. N.
Robert Hastings Nichols	R. H. N.
Roy F. Nichols	R. F. N.
Alexander D. Noyes	A. D. N.
Grace Lee Nute	G. L. N.
Robert B. Osgood	R. B. O.
Victor H. Paltsits	V. H. P.
Scott H. Paradise	S. H. P.
Henry Bamford Parkes	H. B. P.
Charles O. Paullin	C. O. P.
James H. Peeling	J. H. P.
Henry F. Perkins	H. F. P—s.
Hobart S. Perry	H. S. P
Frederick T. Persons	F. T. P.
James M. Phalen	J. M. P—n.
Francis S. Philbrick	F. S. P.
Paul Chrisler Phillips	P. C. P.
Ulrich B. Phillips	U. B. P.
David deSola Pool	D. deS. P.
John M. Poor	J. M. P—r.
Alden L. Powell	A. L. P.
Julius W. Pratt	J. W. P.
Samuel C. Prescott	S. C. P.
Henry F. Pringle	H. F. P—e.
Charles McD. Puckette	C. M. P.
Richard J. Purcell	R. J. P.
Arthur Hobson Quinn	A. H. Q.
Charles Henry Rammelkamp	C. H. R.
James G. Randall	J. G. R—l.
P. O. Ray	P. O. R.

J. Fred Rippy	J. F. R.
Frank H. Ristine	F. H. R.
Donald A. Roberts	D. A. R.
Burr Arthur Robinson	B. A. R.
Henry Morton Robinson	H. M. R.
Herbert Spencer Robinson	H. S. R.
William A. Robinson	W. A. R.
James Grafton Rogers	J. G. R—s.
Eugene H. Roseboom	E. H. R.
Lois K. M. Rosenberry	L. K. M. R.
Marvin B. Rosenberry	M. B. R.
Henry Kalloch Rowe	H. K. R.
William Sener Rusk	W. S. R.
Verne Lockwood Samson	V. L. S.
M. G. Seelig	M. G. S.
Roy W. Sellars	R. W. S.
James Lee Sellers	J. L. S.
Robert Francis Seybolt	R. F. S.
George Dudley Seymour	G. D. S.
Harry Shaw, Jr.	H. S., Jr.
William Bristol Shaw	W. B. S.
William E. Shea	W. E. S—a.
Owen L. Shinn	O. L. S.
Lester B. Shippee	L. B. S.
Richard H. Shryock	R. H. S.
Wilbur H. Siebert	W. H. S—t.
Marian Silveus	M. S.
Francis Butler Simkins	F. B. S.
Theodore Sizer	T. S—r.
David Eugene Smith	D. E. S.
Edward Conrad Smith	E. C. S.
Fred M. Smith	F. M. S.
Warren Hunting Smith	W. H. S—h.
William Roy Smith	W. R. S.
F. W. Sohon	F. W. S.
Torald Sollmann	T. S—n.
Herbert Solow	H. S.
James P. C. Southall	J. P. C. S.
E. Wilder Spaulding	E. W. S.
Oliver L. Spaulding, Jr.	O. L. S., Jr.
Thomas M. Spaulding	T. M. S.
Charles Worthen Spencer	C. W. S
Robert E. Spiller	R. E. S.
Harris Elwood Starr	H. E. S.
Bertha Monica Stearns	B. M. S.
George M. Stephenson	G. M. S.
Wendell H. Stephenson	W. H. S—n.
Wayne E. Stevens	W. E. S—s.
Helen R. Steward	H. R. S.
George R. Stewart, Jr.	G. R. S., Jr.
Randall Stewart	R. S.
Witmer Stone	W. S.
Carl G. Stroven	C. G. S.
Edna Swenson Suber	E. S. S.
Lionel M. Summers	L. M. S.
William W. Sweet	W. W. S.
Carl B. Swisher	C. B. S.
Charles S. Sydnor	C. S. S.

Contributors to Volume XVIII

Thomas E. Tallmadge . . . . T. E. T.
Frank O. Taylor . . . . . . F. O. T.
William A. Taylor . . . . . W. A. T.
Charles Hiram Thayer . . . . C. H. T.
Charles M. Thomas . . . . . C. M. T.
Irving L. Thomson . . . . . . I. L. T.
Willard Thorp . . . . W. T.
Edward Larocque Tinker . . E. L. T.
Charles C. Torrey . . . . . . C. C. T.
Robert B. Tunstall . . . . . R. B. T.
Alonzo H. Tuttle . . . . . . A. H. T.
George B. Utley . . . . G. B. U.
William T. Utter . . . . . . W. T. U.
Robert W. G. Vail . . . . . R. W. G. V.
John G. Van Deusen . . . . J. G. V-D.
Carl Van Doren . . . . . . C. V-D.
Henry R. Viets . . . . . . H. R. V.
Harold G. Villard . . . . . H. G. V.
Eugene M. Violette . . . . . E. M. V.
Albert T. Volwiler . . . . . A. T. V.
Alexander J. Wall . . . . . A. J. W.
Margaret F. Washburn . . . M. F. W.
Francis P. Weisenburger . . . F. P. W.
Allan Westcott . . . . . . A. W—t.

William H. Weston, Jr. . . . W. H. W., Jr.
George F. Whicher . . . . . G. F. W.
A. Curtis Wilgus . . . . . A. C. W.
James F. Willard . . . . . J. F. W.
Amelia Williams . . . . . . A. W—s.
Mary Wilhelmine Williams . M. W. W.
Samuel C. Williams . . . . . S. C. W.
Tyrrell Williams . . . . . T. W.
H. Parker Willis . . . . . H. P. W.
Samuel Williston . . . . . . S. W.
William H. Wilmer . . . . . W. H. W.
James Southall Wilson . . . J. S. W.
George B. Winton . . . . . G. B. W.
Clark Wissler . . . . C. W.
George Edward Woodbine . . G. E. W.
Maude H. Woodfin . . . . . M. H. W.
Carl R. Woodward . . . . . C. R. W.
George Woolsey . . . . . . G. W.
C. P. Wright . . . . C. P. W.
Walter L. Wright, Jr. . . . . W. L. W., Jr.
James Ingersoll Wyer . . . J. I. W.
Kimball Young . . . . K. Y.
Harold Zink . . . . H. Z.
Adolf Edward Zucker . . . . A. E. Z.

DICTIONARY OF

AMERICAN BIOGRAPHY

Steward—Trowbridge

STEWARD, IRA (Mar. 10, 1831–Mar. 13, 1883), labor leader, was born in New London, Conn. At nineteen he went from Boston to Providence, R. I., and served an apprenticeship as a machinist under the twelve-hour system. Within a year he was agitating for shorter hours and was finally dismissed by the Draper Machine Company, for which he worked, because of "his peculiar views." In the fall of 1863, as a delegate to the convention of the International Union of Machinists and Blacksmiths in Boston, he secured the passage of a resolution that for the first time demanded an eight-hour labor law; he also secured large appropriations from his own union and the Boston Trades' Assembly for legislative lobbying. Henceforth, Steward and the eight-hour movement were one.

His insistence upon legislation in contrast to purely economic action by the unions sprang from his wish to reach the masses of the unskilled, whose low living standard constantly threatened the more advanced. He proposed to work through the existing political parties and to begin by endeavoring to secure an eight-hour day upon all government work. He labored indefatigably, appearing before every session of the Massachusetts legislature, contributing constantly to reform papers, making innumerable speeches, and organizing state and local eight-hour leagues. At the time of his death he was president of both the Boston Eight-Hour League and the National Ten-Hour League. Among Steward's influential co-laborers was Wendell Phillips [q.v.], who in 1869 helped establish the Massachusetts Bureau of Labor Statistics, the first in the country. Under Steward's friend, George E. McNeill [q.v.], as deputy chief, assisted by Steward's extremely able wife (Mary B.), the bureau published pioneer work on the condition of woman and child wage-earners. Largely at its instance, Massachusetts in 1874 passed the first effective ten-hour law for women and children. Meanwhile, with the disbanding of the army after the Civil War, a number of eight-hour laws of the all-inclusive Steward type were pushed through various legislatures—six of them by 1867; but their opponents had so hedged them about with restrictions that they proved unenforceable. Steward opposed Greenbackism, as well as the formation of a separate labor party, but believed in the solidarity of labor and an ultimate socialistic state. In 1878 he and his followers, McNeill and young George Gunton [q.v.], joined with leading American members of the Marxian International Workingmen's Association to form the International Labor Union, the first large-scale attempt in America to organize the unskilled.

In 1878 Steward's wife died and he was "completely unnerved." For a number of years he had been planning a book to be entitled "The Political Economy of Eight Hours." Abandoning the post he had held since the early seventies as inspector at the Boston custom-house, he began to live upon the kindness of friends, ostensibly to write, but the book never materialized. In 1880 he moved to Plano, Ill., and married his cousin, Jane (Steward) Henning, a woman of considerable means. In March of 1883 he died there, aged only fifty-two. He left his unfinished notes to George Gunton who, finding them too fragmentary to put into shape for the press, published instead his own first book, *Wealth and Progress* (1887). For this action he was bitterly blamed by Steward's disciples. The original Steward manuscript is now in the library of the State Historical Society of Wisconsin. Like all Steward's writings, the fragments are keen and epigrammatic. Of published work, aside from articles in the *Daily Evening Voice* (Boston), the *Labor Standard,* and other papers, Steward left only one pamphlet, *A Reduction of Hours an Increase of Wages* (1865). It was republished together with the longest fragment from the manuscript collection, "The Power of the Cheaper over the Dearer," in *A Documentary History of American Industrial Society* (vol. IX, 1910), edited by J. R. Commons and others.

Steward's philosophy was strikingly novel for his day. He held that shorter hours develop leisure-time wants, hence a demand for higher wages; higher wages force the introduction of labor-saving machinery and better technique; these make possible mass production, which, to be stabilized, requires mass purchasing power. Mass purchasing power must be protected against the down drag of the unemployed by progressively shortening hours of labor in accordance with an index of unemployment. In the long run, effective regulation requires the cooperation of the leading industrial nations, which, in the 1860's, Steward considered ripe for an eight-hour limit. Ultimately, the working class would be able to buy the capitalist out—the abundance of its accumulations forcing down his interest rate —and thus inaugurate socialism. It was at this point that George Gunton broke away from his master and developed his own conclusion of a happy ending for capitalism, contending that higher wages would indeed result but also greater concentration of business and permanently increasing profits to present owners. Steward's influence in the labor movement suffered an eclipse when the body of American labor turned its back upon politics.

[*Chicago Daily Tribune,* Mar. 14, 1883; *Boston Commonwealth,* Mar. 24, 1883; *Comrade,* Dec. 1901; *American Federationist,* Apr., May 1902; J. R. Commons and others, *Hist. of Labour in the U. S.* (1918), vol. II; D. W. Douglas, "Ira Steward on Consumption and Unemployment," *Jour. of Pol. Econ.,* Aug. 1932.]

D. W. D.

STEWARDSON, JOHN (Mar. 21, 1858–Jan. 6, 1896), architect, was born in Philadelphia, the eldest child of Thomas and Margaret (Haines) Stewardson. His great-grandfather, Thomas, had emigrated from Westmoreland, England, to Philadelphia in 1789 and died in Newport, R. I., in 1841. The boy went first to private Philadelphia schools and, from 1873 to 1877, to Adams Academy at Quincy, Mass. He entered Harvard College with the class of 1881. At the end of two years he went to Paris and began his architectural study in the Atelier Pascal. He entered the École des Beaux Arts in 1881 and remained there but one year. During these three and a half years he spent all his leisure time in traveling over

France and sketching indefatigably. Upon his return to Philadelphia in 1882 he entered the office of T. P. Chandler. Working there and in other architects' offices until 1885, he rapidly became known for his ability and charm. In the meantime he had become acquainted with Walter Cope [*q.v.*], who like him was a pioneer in bringing into the garish and anarchic American architecture of the eighties a new taste, refinement, poise, and knowledge, and in 1886 they formed a partnership and entered on the career that was destined to be so important in improving the architecture of Philadelphia and the educational design of the whole country (see sketch of Cope). During this all-too-brief association of ten years, Stewardson found time for much additional travel, which undoubtedly vivified and stimulated the firm's output. He traveled in Italy and Belgium in 1888 and in England in 1894. It was on this later trip that he became so charmed with the brickwork of St. John's College in Cambridge that the University of Pennsylvania designs, then under way in the office, were changed from stone to brick stone-trimmed—the tower of the dormitory group there bears the date 1895.

He was one of those architects who are primarily artists. His many water colors, rich yet delicate, reveal the sensitiveness of his taste, which kept its basic romanticism from becoming sentimental or mawkish. Even his three years in Paris seem only to have deepened his love for the varied and fluid forms of Gothic, especially English Gothic, architecture, at a time when other Americans were being made over into good, bad, or mediocre classicists. The choir screen of St. Luke's Church in Philadelphia (erroneously attributed solely to Cope but chiefly the work of Stewardson) shows his sure Gothic sense; and the quietness of the Bryn Mawr College work and the directness of Blair Hall at Princeton University still set them off in contrast to the extravagances of much later work beside them. He had a love for people of all kinds that amounted to social genius and was attested by the many expressions of grief at his untimely death, alike from friends, office mates, and architects all over the country. In 1897 his friends collected a fund that was given to the University of Pennsylvania to endow a traveling fellowship under the auspices of the school of architecture, the Stewardson Fellowship. He was a fellow of the American Institute of Architects, one of the founders, and president, 1885–86 and 1891–92, of the T-Square Club. He was a member of the Episcopal Church. Tall and thin, he had always a passion for outdoor life of all kinds. He loved dogs and horses and rode a great deal, in the course of visits of inspection to works being carried on in the Philadelphia suburbs as well as for pleasure. He liked boating and skating. On a winter afternoon he went skating on the Schuylkill with some friends. In the late dusk he was separated from them; and there was heard the sound of breaking ice, and a cry, then silence. This accident seemed the more tragic because of his approaching marriage.

[Information from his brother, Emlyn Stewardson, his sister, M. M. Stewardson, and his former colleague, James P. Jamieson; manuscript of address of R. Clipston Sturgis, June 16, 1917, at the unveiling of a memorial tablet to Cope and Stewardson in Blair Hall, Princeton, in possession of Emlyn Stewardson and of author; *Third Report of . . . Class of 1881 of Harvard College* (1887); *Fifth Report . . . of 1881* (1898); *Brickbuilder,* Jan. 1896; *Am. Arch. and Building News,* Jan. 11, 1896.]   T. F. H.

STEWART, ALEXANDER PETER (Oct. 2, 1821–Aug. 30, 1908), Confederate soldier, chancellor of the University of Mississippi, was born of Scotch-Irish ancestry in Rogersville, Tenn., the son of William and Elizabeth (Decherd) Stewart. At the age of seventeen he was appointed to the United States Military Academy, graduating in 1842. He was commissioned second lieutenant in the 3rd Artillery, but after being stationed a little over a year at Fort Macon on the coast of North Carolina, he was recalled to West Point to serve as assistant professor of mathematics. In May 1845 he resigned from the army, and on Aug. 7 of that year was married to Harriet Byron Chase, of Trumbull County, Ohio. From that time until the Civil War he was professor of mathematics and natural and experimental philosophy in Cumberland University at Lebanon, Tenn., and in Nashville University.

Although a Whig who had voted against secession, Stewart volunteered early and was made a major in the Confederate army. He soon distinguished himself, especially while in command of the heavy artillery at Columbus, Ky., and at the battle of Belmont. In consequence he was commissioned brigadier-general in Cheatham's division at the battle of Shiloh, and served with this division in the Kentucky campaign and the retreat toward Chattanooga. On June 2, 1863, he was advanced to the rank of major-general and was placed in command of a division of Hardee's corps. After participating in the fighting at Chattanooga and Chickamauga, his division took part in the campaign from Dalton to Atlanta, and he was made lieutenant-general on June 23, 1864, after Gen. Leonidas Polk was killed. Stewart was wounded in the battle of Mount Ezra Church near Atlanta. At the close of the war he was in North Carolina commanding the Army of the Tennessee.

After the war he turned for a second time from military to civil life and resumed his professorship in Cumberland University. Early in 1870 he made his only excursion into the field of business by going to St. Louis, Mo., to become secretary of the St. Louis Mutual Life Insurance Company. In 1874 he was elected chancellor of the University of Mississippi. His experience as a teacher, his prestige as a lieutenant-general, and his strong character were all needed, for the future of the university was not promising and attendance was decreasing. In private, the university students continued to refer to him as "Old Straight," the nickname first used by his soldiers during the war, both because of his military bearing and because of the impartial decisions which he strictly enforced during his twelve-year administration. Resigning in 1886, he spent the next four years partly in traveling and partly in the home of his son in St. Louis. When the Chickamauga and Chattanooga National Military Park was created in 1890, Stewart was appointed by President Harrison as the Confederate member of the controlling board of three commissioners. Taking his duties with characteristic seriousness, he moved to the reservation, supervised the laying out of roads and the placing of monuments, and had actual custody of the park for some years. In 1904 his health began to fail and two years later he moved to Biloxi, Miss., where he spent the last two years of his life. He performed his duties as park commissioner by correspondence. He was survived by his three sons, and is buried in Bellefontaine Cemetery in St. Louis.

[*Who's Who in America,* 1908–09; G. W. Cullum, *Biog. Reg. . . . Officers and Grads. U. S. Mil. Acad.* (1891); *War of the Rebellion: Official Records,* see Index; *Confed. Mil. Hist.* (1899), vol. I; *Confed. Veteran,* Sept. 1908, Jan. 1909; *Hist. Cat. of the Univ. of Miss., 1849–1909* (1910); New Orleans *Times-Democrat,* St. Louis *Globe-Democrat,* and *Chattanooga News,* Aug. 31, 1908.]   C. S. S.

STEWART, ALEXANDER TURNEY (Oct. 12, 1803–Apr. 10, 1876), merchant, son of Alexander and Margaret (Turney) Stewart, was born in Lisburn, County Antrim, Ireland, of Scotch Protestant parents in modestly comfortable circumstances. His father died shortly after or before the birth of Alexander, and the latter at an early age was placed under the care of his maternal grandfather. The boy was bright, orderly, and careful, and the grandfather, intending to fit him for the ministry, placed him in an academy in Belfast. After his grandfather died, young Stewart, not predisposed toward clerical duties but with no definite notion as to a career, decided to visit America. He reached New York, perhaps in 1820, bearing letters of introduction to several prominent persons, and for some months lived a quiet and rather studious life. For a short time he taught in a private school. He returned home to claim an inheritance, which amounted to $5,000 or more in American money. He had intended investing this in Ireland, but it is said that an American friend urged him to go into trade in New York, specifically advising him to import Irish laces. He knew little of business, but decided to follow the advice, and so invested about $3,000 in laces, returned to New York, and late in the summer of 1823 opened a small shop on lower Broadway in a room measuring twelve by thirty feet. Shortly he moved to a larger store, and soon afterward to another.

From the first he displayed not only a canniness in observing the market and the fashions, but an exactitude in method which was uncommon at the period. During the business depression of 1837 and thereafter, he bought at auction many stocks of merchants who had failed, and made good profits on them. In 1846 he built a marble-faced building at Broadway and Chambers Street, in which he installed both wholesale and retail dry-goods business (Stokes, *post,* vol. V). In 1850 he extended the building to Reade Street, and now had the largest establishment in the city. He had gained a large trade among wealthy and fashionable folk, and his business again rapidly outgrew its quarters. In 1862 he completed a new building of steel and stone, eight stories high, covering the entire block between Ninth and Tenth Streets, Broadway and Fourth Avenue, and costing nearly $2,750,000, and there opened what was then the largest retail store in the world. His wholesale department remained in the older building at Chambers Street. Stewart's enterprises had now become colossal for their day, and would have been remarkable at a much later date. In his new store some 2,000 persons were employed, and the current expenses were about $100,000 a year. The total sales of his wholesale and retail stores for the three years preceding his death were $203,000,000. During the Civil War, when he had large Army and Navy contracts, his annual income averaged nearly $2,000,000. In carrying on this huge business, he always paid cash for purchases, though he sold on credit, as did other merchants. He built or acquired a controlling interest in numerous mills in New England, New York, and New Jersey, manufacturing cotton, silk, and woolen goods, blankets, ribbons, thread, and carpets. For the buying of foreign merchandise, he installed offices and warehouses in several cities of England, in Ireland, Scotland, France, Germany, and

Switzerland. At his death he also owned the Grand Union Hotel and a retail store at Saratoga Springs, the Metropolitan Hotel, the Globe Theater, Niblo's Garden, and other enterprises in New York City. He was a shrewd trader and a strict disciplinarian. Some of his methods of dealing with employees, notably a system of money fines for lapses, were regarded as rigid and harsh, but he drove no one harder than he drove himself. There was much criticism of him during his life, the most justifiable being of a wage policy that was low even for his time, and acridity is seen in editorial comment after his death. However, he gave largely to charity at times; he sent a shipload of provisions to Ireland during the famine of 1847, and brought the vessel back loaded with immigrants, for many of whom he found work in America. During the Civil War he offered to give to the Sanitary Commission as much as Cornelius Vanderbilt did. Vanderbilt, piqued by this challenge, raised his subscription two or three times until at length he and Stewart each drew a check for $100,000. Stewart sent a shipload of flour to France after its war with Prussia in 1871, and in the same year gave $50,000 to the Chicago fire sufferers. In 1862 he gave $10,000 for the relief of English cotton mill operatives. At the time of his death he was erecting a building intended to supply working women and girls with board and lodging at cost; but the building later became the Park Avenue Hotel. Stewart's greatest semi-altruistic enterprise was the purchase of Hempstead Plains on Long Island, where he built the "model town" of Garden City for persons of modest means. He was appointed secretary of the treasury by President Grant in 1869 and confirmed, but was barred by the section of the law of Sept. 2, 1789, prohibiting the holding of the post by a man engaged in business (1 *Statutes at Large,* 67). A bill was introduced to repeal the section, and Stewart offered to turn his business over to trustees and donate its profits to charity during his incumbency, but action was indefinitely postponed. Meanwhile, George S. Boutwell was appointed to the post "to fill a vacancy."

Shortly after the Civil War Stewart erected a mansion on Fifth Avenue which was long regarded as the finest in America. There he gave sumptuous dinners and receptions, at which there were guests ranging from diplomats and millionaires to struggling artists and musicians. Stewart was a small, wiry, active man with sharp features, keen blue eyes, and reddish-sandy hair; he was always carefully dressed. He was survived for ten years by his wife, the former Cornelia Mitchell Clinch, whom he married on Oct.

16, 1823. On Nov. 7, 1878, the coffin containing his remains was stolen from the family vault in St. Mark's churchyard and held for reward, which was paid in 1880; the reinterment was at Garden City.

[Obituaries and editorials in *N. Y. Times*, Mar. 6–12, 1869, Apr. 11–14, 1876, Oct. 26, 1886; *Evening Post* (N. Y.), Apr. 10, 11, 13, 1876; *Sun* (N. Y.), Apr. 11–14, 1876; *Frank Leslie's Illustrated Newspaper*, Apr. 22, 1876; *Harper's Weekly*, Apr. 29, 1876; *Harper's New Monthly Magazine*, March 1867; A. T. Stewart Scrap Book, N. Y. Pub. Lib.; I. N. Phelps Stokes, *The Iconography of Manhattan Island*, vols. V, VI (1918–28); C. H. Haswell, *Reminiscences of an Octogenarian of the City of N. Y.* (1896); M. H. Smith, *Sunshine and Shadow in N. Y.* (1868); *The Posthumous Relatives of the Late Alex. T. Stewart. Procs. before the Surrogate. Extracts from Newspapers, etc.* (1876); New York City tax records; and Burial Certificate No. 234,380.]   A. F. H.

STEWART, ALVAN (Sept. 1, 1790–May 1, 1849), lawyer, abolitionist, was born in South Granville, N. Y., the son of Uriel Stewart, who five years after the boy's birth moved to Westford, Chittenden County, Vt. Alvan attended district school and in 1809 entered the University of Vermont, leaving there in 1812 to teach in Canada. After a visit home he was arrested as a spy in Schoharie County, N. Y., and upon his release went to Cherry Valley, Otsego County, N. Y., where he taught school and studied law. In 1815 he journeyed as far West as Paris, Ky., and there spent a year teaching and studying. He then traveled in the South for a time, finally returning to Cherry Valley, where he was admitted to the bar. About 1832 he moved to Utica. Here he acquired a considerable reputation as a lawyer and was regarded as a most formidable adversary before a jury (Proctor, *post*, p. 220). Originally a Democrat, he became an aggressive protectionist, and in 1828 published a pamphlet, *Common Sense*, opposing Jackson on the tariff question.

In 1834 he joined the newly organized American Anti-Slavery Society, and at once took the lead in establishing abolitionist organizations in New York. In 1835 he issued a call for a convention, which assembled at Utica on Oct. 21, and formed the New York State Anti-Slavery Society. During the next few years, as the society's president, he labored incessantly, collecting money, organizing auxiliaries, and making speeches. These speeches, characterized by a wildfire humor and a vivid, if somewhat exuberant, imagination, earned for him the title of humorist of the anti-slavery movement. He aspired to another title, however, that of constitutionalist to the cause. Basing his argument upon the due process clause of the Constitution, he contended that slaves were deprived of their freedom with-

out due process of law, and that slavery itself was therefore in violation of the Constitution. This view he attempted to persuade the American Anti-Slavery Society at its 1838 meeting to adopt. It so outraged William Jay [*q.v.*], son of the great jurist, that he withdrew from the society; and though Stewart won over to his views a majority of the delegates, he was unable to convince the two-thirds necessary to amend the anti-slavery creed.

As president of the New York State Anti-Slavery Society, he took the position that the national society had no jurisdiction within the bounds of his organization. In the 1838 convention of the latter he proposed that agents of the national society be excluded from all the state auxiliaries, and the proposal was adopted. Furthermore, at the New York State Society headquarters, he opposed the pledging of contributions to the support of the national society. "A dollar spent at Utica," he told his constituents, "is worth three spent at New York." Erratic, independent, and intractable by nature, he placed himself at the head of the faction opposed to the operations of the American Anti-Slavery Society. More than any other abolitionist except William Lloyd Garrison [*q.v.*] he was responsible for the disruption of the national movement, which occurred in 1840.

At an early date Stewart had urged separate political anti-slavery organization. In 1840 he joined with Myron Holley [*q.v.*], the leading political abolitionist, in calling an anti-slavery political convention, which met in Albany, on Apr. 1, with Stewart as presiding officer. This convention organized the Liberty Party and nominated James G. Birney [*q.v.*] for president and Stewart for governor of New York; but in the subsequent campaign, Birney received only a few thousand votes and Stewart a few hundred. Disgusted with the outcome of political action, he returned to private life. He still served as president of the diminished New York society, and on occasion he donated his services as counsel for the slave. Before the supreme court of New Jersey, in a test case arranged by local abolitionists, he challenged the constitutionality of slavery with eloquence (*A Legal Argument before the Supreme Court of the State of New Jersey . . . for the Deliverance of Four Thousand Persons from Bondage*, 1845). In his early years he "was quite too much given to his cups," but later became an advocate of total abstinence and an effective temperance lecturer (Beardsley, *post*, pp. 159, 169). In 1835 he published *Prize Address for the New York City Temperance Society*. His wife was Keziah Holt of Cherry Valley, N. Y., by whom he had five children, three of them dying young. In 1860 *Writings and Speeches of Alvan Stewart on Slavery* was published by his son-in-law, Luther R. Marsh.

[*The Friend of Man* (Utica, N. Y.), 1835–42; *Emancipator* (N. Y. and Boston), 1833–42; Bayard Tuckerman, *William Jay and the Constitutional Movement for the Abolition of Slavery* (1893); Levi Beardsley, *Reminiscences* (1852); L. B. Proctor, *The Bench and Bar of N. Y.* (1870); G. H. Barnes, *The Anti-Slavery Impulse* (1933); D. S. Durrie, *A Geneal. Hist. of the Holt Family in the U. S.* (1864); *N. Y. Tribune,* May 3, 1849; *Oneida Morning Herald,* May 4, 1849.]

G. H. B.

STEWART, ANDREW (June 11, 1791–July 16, 1872), congressman from Pennsylvania, was born on his father's farm in German Township, Fayette County, Pa., the eldest son of Abraham and Mary (Oliphant) Stewart. Both parents were natives of Pennsylvania; the father had removed to Fayette County from York County, and the mother from Chester County before their marriage in 1789. Andrew attended the local schools, helping to defray expenses by working on a farm, teaching school, and working as a clerk in a store. He studied law in Uniontown, and on Jan. 9, 1815, he was admitted to the Fayette County bar. From 1815 to 1818 he was a member of the state House of Representatives. In 1818 he was appointed federal attorney for the western district of Pennsylvania, a position he held until his election to Congress in 1820. Believing the protective tariff and internal improvements to be the mainstays of the prosperity of the country as well as of Pennsylvania, he took up the cudgels in their behalf. He was returned to Congress continuously until 1828, when his support of Adams against Jackson led to his defeat. He was reëlected in 1830 and 1832 but was again defeated in 1834. In 1842 he was elected as a Whig, and after three terms he declined a renomination. In 1848 he was a candidate for the nomination for vice-president; and because of illness he was obliged to decline an appointment as secretary of the treasury in President Taylor's Cabinet. In 1870 he ran for Congress as a Republican but was defeated.

His speeches in Congress in defense of the protective tariff and advocating internal improvements received considerable attention; many of them were printed in full in Whig newspapers; and editions amounting to several hundred thousand copies were published in pamphlet form. Of these a collection, *The American System. Speeches on the Tariff Question, and on Internal Improvements, Principally Delivered in the House of Representatives of the United States* (1872), is perhaps the most important. He was so zealous an advocate of protection that he was known to

his contemporaries as "Tariff Andy." Tall and of vigorous build his personality lent weight to his arguments, which, not devoid of humor, are set forth in plain and understandable terms and evidence an exhaustive knowledge of his subject. Among specific enterprises that he supported were the Cumberland road, the Chesapeake and Ohio Canal, and the Pittsburgh, Connellsville, and Baltimore railroad. He was a director in the Chesapeake and Ohio Canal Company. Besides his political interests he conducted an extensive private business in building and real estate; he erected and managed a blast furnace and numerous saw and flour mills; and he rebuilt a glass factory. He owned considerable property in Uniontown, on some of which he erected tenant houses; and the real estate that passed through his hands has been estimated at eighty thousand acres. In 1825 he married Elizabeth, the daughter of David Shriver of Cumberland, Md., superintendent of the eastern division of the National Road. They had six children. Stewart Township, in eastern Fayette County, was named for him.

[*Memoirs of John Quincy Adams,* vols. VII–XII (1875–77), ed. by C. F. Adams; *Biog. Dir. of the Am. Cong.* (1928); *History of Fayette County, Pennsylvania* (1882), ed. by Franklin Ellis, pp. 363, 595, 775; James Hadden, *A Hist. of Uniontown* (1913), pp. 775–778; *Biographical and Portrait Cyclopedia of Fayette County* (1889), ed. by J. M. Gresham; *Pittsburgh Commercial* and the *Pittsburgh Gazette,* July 17, 1872.]

S. J. B.

STEWART, CHARLES (July 28, 1778–Nov. 6, 1869), naval officer, was born in Philadelphia, Pa., and died at Bordentown, N. J. He was the son of Charles and Sarah (Ford) Stewart, who some years prior to the American Revolution emigrated from Belfast, Ireland, to Philadelphia. The elder Charles Stewart pursued a seafaring life, and at the time of his death, in 1780, appears to have been master of a merchant vessel. His widow, left with slender funds at her disposal, subsequently had great difficulty in providing for her eight children. Charles, the youngest, soon turned to the sea, securing, at the age of thirteen, employment as a cabin boy in the merchant service. During the next few years he rose through the successive grades until he became master of a merchantman.

When the dispute between the United States and France occurred, young Stewart entered the navy. On Mar. 9, 1798, he was commissioned lieutenant and began a cruise in West Indian waters aboard the frigate *United States.* On July 16, 1800, he received command of the schooner *Experiment,* which soon captured two armed French vessels, recaptured a number of American merchantmen, and, through an error in identity, badly crippled a Bermudian privateer. The

Experiment also provided convoy, and, near the end of the cruise, rescued a large number of women and children who had been shipwrecked after fleeing from the negro uprising in Santo Domingo. After returning to Norfolk in 1801, Stewart was for a time in charge of the frigate *Chesapeake,* but in 1802 went to the Mediterranean as first officer of the frigate *Constellation.* At the end of a year he was again in America. Receiving command of the brig *Siren,* he returned to the Mediterranean, where he participated in the destruction of the *Philadelphia* after its capture by the Tripolitans; engaged in maintaining a strict blockade of Tripoli; and distinguished himself in the numerous assaults upon the enemy during August and September 1804. At the close of the War with Tripoli he proceeded with the squadron under the command of Commodore John Rodgers, 1773–1838 [*q.v.*], to Tunis for the purpose of quieting that regency. The desired settlement was soon effected, and Stewart, commissioned captain, Apr. 22, 1806, returned to the United States. During a portion of the years 1806 and 1807 he was engaged in supervising the construction of gunboats at New York, and until the outbreak of the War of 1812 participated in commercial enterprises which took him to the East Indies, the Mediterranean, and the Adriatic.

At the outset of the struggle with Great Britain he urged a vigorous use of the navy. He soon received command of the brig *Argus* and the sloop-of-war *Hornet*; then, in December 1812, became commander of the *Constellation.* A superior British force kept the frigate confined at Norfolk, and during the summer of 1813 Stewart took charge of the *Constitution,* then being refitted at Boston. With her he subsequently made a brilliant record. On a cruise beginning in December 1813 he destroyed several British vessels, and in April of the following year returned to Boston after evading a strong blockading squadron. In December 1814 he again slipped out of the harbor. On this second cruise, while in the vicinity of the Madeira Islands, he separated and captured two British warships—the small frigate *Cyane* and the sloop-of-war *Levant.* A British squadron eventually recaptured the *Levant,* but Stewart succeeded in bringing the *Cyane* to the United States. In consequence of these achievements he received a great ovation from the people of New York, a sword of honor from the legislature of Pennsylvania, and a gold medal from Congress.

Stewart's service during the remainder of his life was varied. In 1816 he was given command of the ship of the line *Franklin,* and during the following year sailed to the Mediterranean,

where he commanded a squadron until 1820. He subsequently served, until 1824, as commodore of a squadron in the Pacific; was a naval commissioner during the years 1830–32; and at various times (1838–41, 1846, 1854–61) had charge of the navy yard at Philadelphia. By act of Congress, Mar. 2, 1859, he was made "senior flag officer" (an office created for him in recognition of his distinguished and meritorious service). In 1862 he became rear-admiral on the retired list, and thereafter lived in his country house, "Old Ironsides," at Bordentown. On Nov. 25, 1813, while the *Constitution* was being refitted, he had married Delia Tudor, sister of Frederic Tudor [*q.v.*], and a member of an affluent and socially prominent Boston family. Two children from this union survived their father: Delia Tudor and Charles Tudor Stewart. The latter became a successful civil engineer and lawyer; the former married John Henry Parnell, and became the mother of Charles Stewart Parnell, eminent Home Rule advocate in the British Parliament.

With respect to person, Stewart has been described as about five feet nine inches in height, well proportioned, and prepossessing in appearance. He has been unstintedly praised for his coolness and courage in times of stress; for his broad and vigorous mentality, for his fund of information on a wide range of domestic and foreign subjects; and for his conversational abilities, which made him a favorite at social gatherings.

[*Stewart Clan Mag.,* Oct. 1930–31; *Biog. Sketch and Services of Commodore Charles Stewart* (1838); E. S. Ellis, "Old Ironsides," *Chautauquan,* July 1898; John Frost, *Am. Naval Biog.* (1844); Charles Morris, *Heroes of the Navy in America* (1907); C. J. Peterson, *The Am. Navy . . . and Biog Sketches of Am. Naval Heroes* (1858); Thomas Sherlock, *The Life of Chas. Stewart Parnell* (1881); William Tudor, *Deacon Tudor's Diary* (1896); *Pub. Ledger* (Phila.), Nov. 8, 1869.]

R. W. I.

STEWART, EDWIN (May 5, 1837–Feb. 28, 1933), naval officer, was born in New York City, son of John and Mary (Aikman) Stewart, and a younger brother of John Aikman Stewart [*q.v.*]. His father, a native of Lewis, in the Hebrides, had come to America from Stornoway, Scotland, when a boy. Edwin attended Phillips Academy, Andover, Mass., and later entered Williams College, preparatory to the study of law. His college work was interrupted by the Civil War, however, and though he received the degree of A.B. from Williams with the class of 1862, he joined the navy Sept. 9, 1861, as assistant paymaster.

He served first in the *Pembina* in the Port Royal campaign and, after promotion to paymaster Apr. 14, 1862, in the *Richmond.* West

Gulf Squadron, in operations on the Mississippi and at the battle of Mobile Bay. After the war, he was in the *Michigan* on the Great Lakes, 1865–68; fleet paymaster in the *Hartford,* Asiatic Squadron, 1872–75; and then for several years chiefly at New York, where in 1880–83 he was an inspector of provisions and clothing. Following duty in the *Lancaster,* European Squadron, he returned to New York as chief pay officer, and through his reports was largely instrumental in accomplishing the reform by which naval purchases, hitherto made by several bureaus, were centralized in a new bureau of supplies and accounts. He was appointed paymaster general, with the rank of commodore, and head of the bureau on May 16, 1890, and, with reappointments in 1894 and 1898, held this important post throughout the period of the Spanish-American War and up to his retirement for age May 5, 1899. He had been made pay director, then the highest rank of his corps, Sept. 12, 1891, and on May 5, 1899, he was made rear admiral. Secretary of the Navy John D. Long commended highly the work of Stewart's bureau, declaring that it was "performed with the most gratifying efficiency and promptness" (*Annual Reports of the Navy Department for the Year 1898,* I, 42). In his own report (*Ibid.,* pp. 665–670) Stewart remarked that his bureau had carried on the work of three army departments—pay corps, quartermaster general, and commissary—and that despite wartime expenditures amounting in 1898 to $11,422,640, the prices paid "were in most cases no higher, and in many cases lower, than before the commencement of hostilities." Notable in his handling of wartime supply problems was the use of refrigerator ships with both the Cuban and Philippine forces, and his pre-war memorandum anticipating the needs of Dewey's squadron. The latter prompted the departmental order of Apr. 6, 1898, enabling Dewey to purchase within forty-eight hours the collier *Nanshan* and supply ship *Zafiro* at Hongkong and load them with five months' stores.

After his retirement Stewart lived in Washington, D. C., until 1901, and later at South Orange, N. J., where he died in his ninety-sixth year, the oldest officer on the navy list. His burial was in Arlington Cemetery. He was commander of the District of Columbia Commandery, Military Order of the Loyal Legion, in 1900, and in 1913–17 was vice commander-in-chief of the Legion's national organization. He was twice married: first, Aug. 24, 1865, to Laura S. Tufts of Andover, Mass., who died Feb. 3, 1875, during his absence on the Asiatic station; and second, May 17, 1877, to Susan Maria, daughter of Edward Estabrook of Platteville, Wis. He had two sons by each marriage, three of whom survived him, one of them a naval officer.

[L. R. Hamersly, *The Records of Living Officers of the U. S. Navy and Marine Corps* (7th ed. 1902); *Fiftieth Anniv. Report of the Williams College Class of '62* (1913); *Who's Who in America,* 1920–21; *Army and Navy Reg.,* Mar. 4, 1933; *Army and Navy Jour.,* May 6, 1899; *Sun* (N. Y.), Feb. 28, 1933; *N. Y. Times,* Mar. 1, 1933.]   A. W—t.

STEWART, ELIZA DANIEL (Apr. 25, 1816–Aug. 6, 1908), humanitarian, advocate of temperance, was the daughter of James Daniel, a Southerner, and Rebecca (Guthery) Daniel. Her grandfather, Capt. John Guthery, an officer of the Revolution, founded Piketon, Ohio, where Eliza was born. She was orphaned at the age of twelve, and after being educated in Ohio seminaries, she earned her living by teaching school for many years. In 1848 she married Hiram Stewart, who died a few months later. During the Civil War she gathered and sent sanitary supplies to the Union armies and visited the sick soldiers, who gave her the name "Mother" Stewart, by which she was commonly known. She helped form the first woman's suffrage organization in 1869 in Springfield, Ohio, where she then lived, and was elected president. She was also active in charity work in Ohio, and was a member of the first national board of charities.

Her first and greatest interest, however, was in the fight against strong drink. In 1858 she became a charter member of the Good Templar Lodge founded in her home town, and until her death she campaigned with voice and pen against the use of liquor. Her most effective work began on Jan. 22, 1872, when she lectured on temperance in Springfield. Shortly afterwards she published in a city paper an appeal to women signed "A Drunkard's Wife." In 1872 and again in 1874, she made an eloquent and successful plea in court in a suit of a drunkard's wife against a saloon keeper, gaining wide publicity for her cause. She arranged temperance mass meetings in Springfield and other cities and in 1873 held prayer meetings in saloons, acting upon a suggestion of Dioclesian Lewis [*q.v.*], who had come West to investigate Mother Stewart's work. Under her leadership the praying "Crusade" against the drinksellers spread throughout the state and closed many drinking places—which soon opened, convincing her of the need for greater organization to secure outlawry of the liquor traffic. In December 1873 she had formed a Woman's League in Osborne, Ohio, the first organization in the Women's Christian Temperance Union movement. The next month she was made president of the new Springfield Union; then came county organization; and soon afterwards she formed in Ohio the first state W. C. T. U. She was a leader in the rapid extension of the work into other Northern states, and in 1878 she traveled widely in the South, organizing both white and colored women. She spent five months in 1876 in Great Britain, lecturing and holding prayer meetings, which opened the "Whisky War," and resulted in the organization of the British Women's Temperance Association and the Scottish Christian Union.

In 1891 she represented the National W. C. T. U. at the World's Convention of Good Templars held in Edinburgh, and in 1895 she attended the World's W. C. T. U. Convention in London and made the opening speech. She spent the last five years of her life at Hicksville, Ohio, where she died. In addition to various articles on temperance, she wrote two books: *Memories of the Crusade* (1888), and *The Crusader in Great Britain* (1893). Mother Stewart had much personal charm, and was an original and forceful speaker. She was of medium height and ample figure, with a firm, kindly face set with piercing black eyes.

[Consult Mrs. Stewart's own works; *Who's Who in America*, 1903–05; C. C. Chapin, *Thumb Nail Sketches of White Ribbon Women* (1891); E. P. Gordon, *Women Torch-Bearers* (2nd ed., 1924); *Cyc. of Temperance and Prohibition* (1891); F. E. Willard and M. A. Livermore, *Portraits and Biographies of Prominent Am. Women* (copr. 1901); *Union Signal*, Aug. 13, 27, 1908; *Ohio State Jour.* (Columbus), Aug. 8, 1908.]   M. W. W.

STEWART, GEORGE NEIL (Apr. 18, 1860– May 28, 1930), physiologist, the son of James Innes and Catherine (Sutherland) Stewart, was born at London, Ontario, whither his parents, emigrants from Caithness, Scotland, had gone to engage in the fur trade with the Indians. After a few years, they returned to the towns of Wick and Lybster in Scotland on the North Sea, where his father engaged in the herring industry. The head-master of the village school became interested in the boy and prepared him for Edinburgh University. He matriculated in 1879, at the age of nineteen, and remained for seven years, receiving successively degrees in arts, M.A. in 1883, with honors in mathematics; in science, B.S. in 1886 and D.Sc. in 1887; in medicine, C.M. and M.B. in 1889, and M.D. in 1891; and finally, LL.D., *honoris causa*, in 1920. During his first year at Edinburgh, he served as assistant in physics to Tait, and it may be presumed that this contact with the brilliant and scholarly physicist fixed his taste for exact and experimental science and thus determined the cast of his life work. In Tait's laboratory he started his first research, and the application of physics to biology domi-

nated his earlier and much of his later investigations.

In the winter of 1886 he went to Berlin to work on electro-physiology, under the renowned Emil Du Bois-Reymond, and from 1887 to 1889 he served an excellent apprenticeship in practical teaching as demonstrator of physiology, including histology and biochemistry, at Manchester, under William Stirling. He held the George Henry Lewes scholarship in physiology at Cambridge from 1889 to 1893, and was one of the group of brilliant young investigators who worked under the guidance of Sir Michael Foster and laid the foundations and established the traditions that are the glory of British physiology. He worked chiefly on the velocity of blood flow, on temperature regulation, and on the cardiac nerves. He also took the recently established course in public health, and secured the degree of D.P.H. at Cambridge in 1890. From 1891 to 1894 he served also as external examiner in physiology at the University of Aberdeen, and thus kept in contact with medical teaching.

He came to America in 1893 as an instructor at Harvard under Bowditch, and in 1894 was appointed to the chair of physiology at Western Reserve University, Cleveland, Ohio. To this, his first independent post, he gave nine of his best years. He supplemented his admirable didactic instructions with "practical exercises" by the students, to an extent which had not been deemed feasible before, especially with mammalian experiments, and which had a profound and lasting influence on the teaching of the subject in America. He incorporated his presentation of physiology in a textbook, *A Manual of Physiology* (1896), which was widely used and reached an eighth edition in 1918. Stewart continued his investigations, at first chiefly on circulation time, and then on the electric conductivity of the blood and hemolysis, as an approach to the problem of cell permeability. In 1903 he accepted the invitation to become the successor of Jacques Loeb [*q.v.*] as head of the department of physiology at the University of Chicago. He welcomed especially the new opportunity of teaching graduate students in physiology. His own investigations in this period were on cerebral anemia, resuscitation, and the respiratory center.

In 1907, friends of Western Reserve University established the H. K. Cushing Laboratory of Experimental Medicine, with the double purpose of promoting the experimental investigation of disease, and of attracting Stewart back to Cleveland. He accepted the invitation and headed this laboratory until his death. From 1910 to 1915 he devised and applied a calorimetric method of measuring the blood flow, suitable for clinical use. Between 1916 and 1923, he worked intensively on the epinephrine output of the adrenal glands, with the assistance of J. M. Rogoff. Their experiments led to the conclusion that the epinephrine output is not sufficient to perform the functions of a fight-and-fright hormone which had been attributed to it. From 1924 to 1927 they investigated the course of the removal of the adrenal glands, and proved that these effects are due entirely to deficiency of the adrenal cortex. They showed that life is prolonged by pregnancy, and in 1927 definitely established the efficiency of extracts of adrenal cortex. The results of these investigations were summarized in 1926 in the eleventh Mellon lecture (*Archives of Internal Medicine,* June 1929). Up to the time of his death, they were engaged in the purification of these extracts, to increase their safety for clinical use.

Although he lived in the United States for thirty-seven years Stewart remained a British citizen. He was a prodigious worker, with a brilliant intellect, keen penetration, sound judgment, and an infinite respect for facts. A rapid thinker, he had the power of vivid and lucid presentation, based upon broad culture and deep learning, a sense of human values and a quick and apt humor. During the later years of his life he was handicapped by the developments of pernicious anemia, to which he finally succumbed at Cleveland. He was survived by three sons, a daughter, and his widow, Louise Kate (Powell) Stewart, to whom he had been married on Sept. 20, 1906.

[J. J. R. Macleod, *Nature,* June 28, 1930; Torald Sollmann, *Bull. Acad. Med.* (Cleveland), July 1930; *Science,* Aug. 15, 1930; J. M. Rogoff, *Collected Papers H. K. Cushing Lab. Experimental Med.,* Western Reserve University, vol. IX (1927–31); *Cleveland Plain Dealer,* May 29, 1930.] T. S—n.

STEWART, HUMPHREY JOHN (May 22, 1854–Dec. 28, 1932), organist, composer, was born in London, England, the son of Humphrey Stark of Reading, Berks County. At the age of eleven he began his career as chorister and organist, and until 1886 played the organ in various London churches. He matriculated in New College, Oxford, in 1873 and obtained the degree of B.Mus. in 1875. It is not known just when or why he changed his name to Stewart, but he did so some time between 1875 and 1886, when he came to the United States. He went immediately to San Francisco, Cal., where he became the organist at the Church of the Advent. During the following years he occupied similar positions at Trinity Church, and at the First Unitarian Church. In 1901 he was engaged for a number of organ recitals at the Pan-American Exposi-

tion, Buffalo, N. Y., and after this engagement went to Boston, where for two years he was organist of Trinity Church. He then returned to California, and from 1902 to 1914 was organist of St. Dominic's in San Francisco. In 1915 he was appointed official organist of the Panama-Pacific International Exposition in San Francisco, and from that time until his death he served as municipal organist of San Diego. In this position he gave almost daily recitals on the organ at Balboa Park, the first out-door organ in the world. Owing to the ideal climate, the recitals were seldom interrupted by rain, and the series offered from 250 to 300 concerts each year. In 1919 the programs presented 2270 selections by 385 composers.

As a composer Stewart achieved his greatest distinction for his choral work, "The Hound of Heaven." For the Bohemian Club of San Francisco he composed the music for four of the annual "Grove-Plays"—*Montezuma* (1903), *The Cremation of Care* (1906), *Gold* (1916), and *John of Nepomuk* (1921). Other important works are *The Nativity,* an oratorio (1888); *His Majesty,* a comic opera (1890); *The Conspirators,* an operetta (1900); two orchestral suites, *Montezuma* (1903), and *Scenes in California* (1906); a mass in D minor (1907); a mass in G (1911); a romantic opera, *Bluff King Hal* (1911); and *Requiem Mass* (1919), dedicated to the pope. In addition to these major works he composed songs, shorter choruses, pieces for violin, organ, and piano, and incidental music to several plays. He received many honors, and was awarded a number of prizes. He was a founder of the American Guild of Organists and in 1899 was awarded the gold medal of that organization for an anthem. In 1907 two of his choral works won prizes, one from the Chicago Madrigal Club and the other from the Pittsburgh Male Chorus. He was accorded the official flag of the City of New York "for distinguished ability as a recital organist" in 1921, and in 1930 received from Pope Pius XI the decoration of Commander of the Holy Sepulchre. He died in San Diego, and was survived by a daughter. Elson (*post,* p. 257) called him "the leading musical reviewer of the Pacific coast."

[*Who's Who in America,* 1932–33; *Alumni Oxonienses,* vol. IV (1888); J. T. Howard, *Our Am. Music* (1931); L. C. Elson, *The Hist. of Am. Music* (rev. ed., 1925); Rupert Hughes, *Am. Composers* (rev. ed., 1914); *Musical America,* Jan. 10, 1933; *Grove's Dict. of Music and Musicians, Am. Supp.* (1930); C. A. McGrew, *City of San Diego* (1922), vol. II; *San Francisco Chronicle,* Dec. 29, 1932.] J. T. H.

STEWART, JOHN AIKMAN (Aug. 26, 1822–Dec. 17, 1926), banker, was born in New

York City. His father, John Stewart, was a native of the island of Lewis, in the Hebrides; his mother, Mary (Aikman) Stewart, was born in New York; Edwin Stewart [q.v.] was a younger brother. John attended the common schools and completed what was then called the "literary and scientific course" at Columbia College in 1840. He then took up civil engineering, being a member of the staff which surveyed the line of the New York, Lake Erie & Western Railroad in 1840–42. In 1842 he was appointed clerk of the board of education of New York City, and held the post for eight years. From 1850 to 1853 he was actuary of the United States Life Insurance Company, and is credited with having brought some new ideas into the insurance business.

Late in 1852, when he was only thirty years old, he laid before John Jacob Astor, Royal Phelps, Peter Cooper, and other prominent New York business men a plan for a novel banking institution which should serve largely in a fiduciary capacity. They saw merit in it and agreed to become stockholders; thus was born, early in 1853, the United States Trust Company. Stewart served as its secretary until the end of 1864. He was then elected president and held that office for thirty-eight years, retiring in 1902 to become chairman of the board of trustees, in which position he continued until his death. He had a personal acquaintance with all the Presidents of the United States from Lincoln to Coolidge. He was a trusted financial adviser to President Lincoln, and served as assistant treasurer of the United States under him in 1864–65. He again rendered valuable service to the country in 1894, during Cleveland's administration, when the gold reserve was dangerously depleted.

Stewart was a trustee of Princeton University from 1868 until his death, and, as senior trustee, served as president pro tempore of the University from October 1910, when Woodrow Wilson resigned to become governor of New Jersey, until the spring of 1912, when John Grier Hibben was chosen president. He did much for benevolence, education, and religion, was long a trustee of the John F. Slater Fund for the education of the freedmen of the South, and was one of the oldest and most zealous promoters of the American Bible Society. He was twice married: first, in 1847, to Sarah Yule Johnson of New York, who died in 1887; and second, Nov. 25, 1890, to Mary Olivia Capron of Baltimore, Md. His second wife, a son by his first marriage, and a daughter survived him. He gave up his daily attendance at his office in his latter years, but visited it frequently and kept in close touch with the business until shortly before his death in New York City, at the age of 104. He was slightly deaf, but read without spectacles and retained his mental faculties until the end.

[Who's Who in America, 1926–27; Who's Who in New York, 1907; N. Y. Herald, Aug. 26, 1921; Trust Companies, June 1921; N. Y. Times and World (N.Y.), Dec. 18, 1926; N. Y. Herald Tribune and Wall Street Jour., Dec. 18, 21, 1926; records of the United States Trust Company; information concerning first marriage from John A. Stewart, Jr.]   A.F.H.

STEWART, PHILO PENFIELD (July 6, 1798–Dec. 13, 1868), missionary, college founder, inventor, was born in Sherman, Conn., the son of Philo and Sarah (Penfield) Stewart, and a descendant of Alexander Stewart who came to New London, Conn., from Ireland about 1719. At the age of ten, because of his father's death, Philo was sent to live with his grandfather Penfield in Pittsford, Vt., and when fourteen years old was apprenticed to an uncle in Pawlet, Vt., to learn harness making, serving for seven years, with the highly prized privilege of attending Pawlet Academy for three months each year. He early showed much mechanical aptitude.

Being attracted to Christian service, in 1821 he accepted appointment by the American Board of Commissioners for Foreign Missions as an assistant missionary among the Choctaws at Mayhew, Miss. He made the journey of nearly 2,000 miles on horseback, carrying his entire outfit in a pair of saddle-bags, preaching along the way, and completing the journey at an expense to the Board of ten dollars. At the mission he superintended its manual labor, taught the boys' school, and conducted services on Sunday in various Indian settlements. Ill health took him back to Vermont in 1825, but he returned in 1827, bringing several new workers. One of these, Eliza Capen from Pittsford, Vt., he married in 1828.

His wife's impaired health necessitated their leaving the mission in 1830 and Stewart in 1832 joined his fellow student of Pawlet Academy days, John J. Shipherd [q.v.], then pastor of a church in Elyria, Ohio. Both were ardently religious and born reformers. Together they evolved the plan of a community and school where their ideas could be realized. Stewart was especially attracted by the thought of a school combining study and labor with such economy that students might defray all their expenses. The result of their efforts was the founding of Oberlin. Together they selected a tract of forest land, about nine miles from Elyria, on which Oberlin now stands. During Shipherd's absence of several months in New England to acquire title to this land and seek funds and colonists, the Stewarts were with the Shiperd family in Elyria. Stewart occupied himself in perfecting a cookstove, undertaken originally to meet a need in Mrs. Shipherd's kitchen, the manufacture of which he hoped might yield substantial income to the projected school. At the same time he had general supervision of the work at Oberlin, meeting and encouraging the colonists as they came from the East. When the school was opened in 1833, the Stewarts took charge of the boarding hall. They had pledged themselves to the service of the "Institute" for five years, with no compensation beside their living expenses. For the first year Stewart was also treasurer and the general manager; but, disagreeing with his associates in his opposition to radical abolitionism and to the admission of negro students (R. S. Fletcher, "Oberlin, 1833–1866," MS.), he resigned in 1836 and returned to the East.

He now tried to perfect a planing mill which had been projected at Elyria, but the financial crash of 1837 ruined the undertaking and he came into financial straits. Making his home in Troy, he returned to the stove project, which proved so successful that in thirty years more than 90,000 stoves were sold. The patent for the "Oberlin stove," granted June 19, 1834, he had deeded to the Oberlin Collegiate Institute. Other patents were issued to him on Sept. 12, 1838, Apr. 12, 1859, and Apr. 28, 1863. His attempt to found a school in Troy was unsuccessful, as was also a water-cure establishment with an original system of gymnastics which he tried to establish. In their prosperous days the Stewarts adhered strictly to their former simplicity of living. They maintained great interest in Oberlin and made contributions to its work.

[*Stewart Clan Mag.*, Dec. 1924; J. H. Fairchild, *Oberlin, the Colony and the College* (1883); D. L. Leonard, *The Story of Oberlin* (1898); *A Worker and Worker's Friend: P. P. Stewart, as a Mechanic, Teacher, and Missionary* (1873), apparently written by his wife; *Troy Daily News*, Dec. 14, 1868; information as to certain facts from Prof. R. S. Fletcher, Oberlin, Ohio.]
E. D. E.

STEWART, ROBERT (Jan. 31, 1839–Oct. 23, 1915), missionary, was born in Sidney, Ohio, the son of Dr. James Harris and Jane Abigail (Fuller) Stewart, and a descendant of George Stuart who settled in Pennsylvania at Marietta on the Susquehanna about 1717. Robert attended the public schools of Allegheny and the academies of Shirleysburg and Glade Run, Pa. In 1859 he graduated with first honors from Jefferson College, and in 1865 completed the course at the Allegheny United Presbyterian Theological Seminary. The following year, Nov. 9, he was ordained by the First Ohio Presbytery. For

some time he served churches of his denomination at Ashland, Savannah, and Dayton, Ohio, and at Davenport, N. Y.; from 1872 to 1878 he was professor of exegetics and homiletics in the Newburg (N. Y.) Theological Seminary; and from June 1879 until November 1880 he edited for his Church the *Evangelical Repository* and *Sabbath School Helps*.

As a member of the Board of Foreign Missions of the United Presbyterian Church he visited India and Egypt in 1880 as a special commissioner, and decided to join the India Mission. Returning to the United States, he was commissioned by the Board the following year and set sail for India on Nov. 5, 1881. In Cairo, Egypt, on Dec. 1, he was married to Eliza Frazier Johnston, of St. Clairsville, Ohio. From 1883 until 1892 he was in charge of the Christian Training Institute and principal of the Theological Seminary in Sialkot, Punjab, teaching in the latter institution Biblical languages, theology, and church history, and preparing translations for educational use. From 1892 until the latter part of 1900 he was in the United States engaged chiefly in writing. In November 1900 he returned to India, and at Jhelum, Punjab, where the Seminary was then located, he remained, except for a brief furlough in 1909–10, during the rest of his life, serving as senior professor and carrying forward the work of translation. In December 1901 he was a delegate to the Alliance of Reformed Churches in India, and in December 1902 a member of the India Decennial Missionary Conference (Madras).

By 1891 he had ready for the press translations into Urdu (Punjabi) of Philip Schaff's *Ante-Nicene Christianity*, W. D. Ralston's *Talks on Psalmody*, R. H. Pollock's *The Saviour's Claim*, and other works. During his extended furlough in America he published his *Life and Work in India* (1896), a comprehensive and authoritative account of missionary activities in India. During his latter term of service in India he issued a translation (Urdu) of the Psalms. Among his other numerous works were, in English, *Filled with the Spirit* (1896), *Ancestors and Children of Colonel Daniel Fisher and His Wife Sybil Draper* (1899), *Apostolic and Indian Missions Compared* (1903), *Colonel George Steuart and His Wife Margaret Harris, Their Ancestors and Descendants* (1907), *Hinduism Historically Considered* (n.d.); in Urdu, an introduction to the books of the New Testament (1909), a Protestant catechism, and a translation of W. D. Killen's work on the Apostolic Church. His death, in his seventy-seventh year, occurred at Sialkot.

[A sketch of Stewart appears in his *Colonel George Stewart* (1907); see also his *Life and Work in India* (1896); *Biog. and Hist. Cat. of Washington and Jefferson Coll.* (1902); *Reports of the Board of Foreign Missions of the United Presbyterian Church,* 1881–92, 1900–15; *Who's Who in America,* 1914–15; *United Presbyterian,* Oct. 28, 1915.]   J. C. A—r.

STEWART, ROBERT MARCELLUS (Mar. 12, 1815–Sept. 21, 1871), railroad president, governor of Missouri, was born at Truxton, Cortland County, N. Y., the son of Charles and Elisabeth (Severance) Stewart. At Truxton he obtained an academic education, and then taught school and studied law. The lure of the West drew him to Louisville, Ky., and finally to St. Joseph, Mo., where he settled in 1840. Here he soon developed a satisfactory law practice, and in 1845 was chosen a delegate to the Missouri constitutional convention. The following year he was elected to the state Senate, where he served until 1857. He inaugurated and financed the preliminary survey of the Hannibal & St. Joseph Railroad, became its attorney, and by lobbying at Washington obtained a grant of some 600,000 acres of choice federal land for his company. About 1854 he was chosen the first president of the corporation, and he saw the road practically completed before the opening of the Civil War, although it did not begin operation until 1867.

After Trusten Polk [*q.v.*] resigned the governorship of Missouri (in February 1857) Stewart was elected (in August) to that office as an anti-Benton Democrat. His opponents charged, and it was not denied, that he effectively used his position as head of the railroad company to gain votes in this campaign. As governor he stressed the material interests of the state, especially favoring a liberal policy toward railroad development. The problem of "bleeding Kansas" also absorbed much of his attention. In January 1859 the state assembly, at his request, voted him $30,000 with which to protect the western border of Missouri against a "band of thieves, robbers and midnight assassins" (*Messages and Proclamations, post,* III, 232) from Kansas. When the secession issue grew hot, Stewart took middle ground by upholding the Crittenden compromise proposals. He asserted, however, that Southerners had a right to take their slaves into Kansas territory. In an attempt to please the other camp he ridiculed "nullification, secession, disunion and all radical Southern fire-eating propositions" (Stevens, *post,* II, 398). In his final message to the legislature (Jan. 3, 1861) he straddled the issue by asserting that: "Missouri will . . . hold to the Union so long as it is worth an effort to preserve it. . . . She cannot be frightened . . .

by the past unfriendly legislation of the North, nor dragooned into secession by the restrictive legislation of the extreme South" (*Messages and Proclamations, post,* p. 144). After he retired from the governorship, he was elected a delegate to the state convention "to consider the . . . relations between the Government of the United States . . . and the Government and people of the State of Missouri" (*Journal and Proceedings of the Missouri State Convention,* 1861, p. 3), and veered round to his true convictions by taking a strong stand for the Union. He did not, however, favor coercing the seceding states.

Stewart edited the *St. Joseph Journal* until 1863 when Gov. Hamilton R. Gamble [*q.v.*] gave him a commission to recruit a brigade of Union men, but because of his excessive drinking General Halleck relieved him of his command (Rutt, *post,* p. 339). Except when his mind was clouded by alcohol, Stewart was an able executive. He was tall and handsome, with dark hair. He died unmarried, in St. Joseph, at the age of fifty-six.

[*The Am. Ann. Cyc.* . . . *1871* (1872); W. B. Davis and D. S. Durrie, *An Illustrated Hist. of Mo.* (1876); Lucien Carr, *Missouri: A Bone of Contention* (1888); J. F. Severance, *The Severans Geneal. Hist.* (1893); H. L. Conard, *Encyc. of the Hist. of Mo.* (1901), vol. VI; W. B. Stevens, *Missouri: The Center State* (1915), vol. II; *The Messages and Proclamations of the Govs. of the State of Mo.,* vol. III (1922); files of the *St. Joseph Journal;* C. L. Rutt, *The Daily News' Hist. of Buchanan County and St. Joseph, Mo.* (1898); personal notes from Mrs. Mary L. Crane, a grandniece of Governor Stewart.]   H. E. N.

STEWART, WILLIAM MORRIS (Aug. 9, 1827–Apr. 23, 1909), lawyer, United States senator, was the eldest son of Frederick Augustus Stewart and his wife, Miranda Morris. From his birthplace, Galen, Wayne County, N. Y., his parents moved during his childhood to Trumbull County, Ohio. He spent three years in Farmington Academy (Ohio), and then returned to New York State, where he taught mathematics in the Lyons high school. Intending to study law, he entered Yale College in September 1848, but left early in 1850, lured by the discovery of gold in California. Reaching San Francisco in May, he engaged in mining in Nevada County, Cal. When he had accumulated about $8,000, he abandoned mining and began the study of law in the office of John R. McConnell, Nevada City, and was admitted to practice in 1852. The next year he was elected district attorney and wrote the first rules and regulations for quartz mining in Nevada County. In 1854 he served as acting attorney-general of the state, and formed a law-partnership in San Francisco with Henry S. Foote [*q.v.*], ex-governor of Mississippi, whose daughter, Annie Elizabeth, he married in the spring of the following year. Three daughters were born to them.

In 1856, Stewart moved to Downieville, Sierra County, Cal., but the discovery three years later of silver mines in Nevada drew him to Virginia City and Carson City, where his energy, resourcefulness, and knowledge of mining law and practice brought him to the front. During four years of complicated litigation he successfully defended the interests of the original claimants to the famous Comstock Lode, and received $500,000 in fees. He was president for a number of years of the Sutro Tunnel Company, founded by Adolph H. J. Sutro [q.v.]. Winning fame as a specialist in mining law, he was retained by some of the largest mining companies in the West.

With characteristic energy he threw himself into the turbulent politics of the nascent state of Nevada. In 1861 he was elected to the territorial council, and two years later to the constitutional convention, serving as chairman of the judiciary committee, but he led the forces that defeated the adoption of the proposed constitution because of a taxation provision obnoxious to the dominant mining interests. The following year, upon the admission of Nevada into the Union, Stewart was elected to the United States Senate as a Republican, remaining in that body until March 1875. During these years he was instrumental in securing the defeat of the proposed sale of mineral lands on the public domain to help pay the Civil War debt, and the passage of the mining laws of 1866 and 1872, which recognized and confirmed the rights of miners according to their rules and regulations. At first he supported President Johnson and his reconstruction measures, but eventually advocated Johnson's impeachment and voted for his conviction. In 1869 he was the author of the Fifteenth Amendment to the federal Constitution in the form in which it was finally adopted. Pacific railroad projects naturally received his hearty support. In 1871 he was offered, but declined, appointment to the Supreme Court (Reminiscences, p. 250). Returning to Nevada in 1875, he devoted the next dozen years to his mining interests and lucrative law practice.

In 1887 he was again elected to the Senate and served there continuously until 1905. He was perhaps the first member of either house to propose federal appropriations for the reclamation of Western arid lands. In 1891, with seven other Republican senators, he fought on the side of the Democrats to prevent the enactment of the Lodge Force Bill. His most distinguished efforts, however, were directed toward the re-

monetization of silver. In 1888 he was a delegate to the Republican National Convention and drafted the currency plank in the party platform. Incensed at what he regarded as Republican abandonment of this plank, he declined election as a delegate to the National Convention of 1892 and joined the Silver party; and, as a member of that party, was reëlected to the Senate in 1893 and 1899. He constantly denounced the "crime of 1873," and bitterly fought the repeal (1893) of the silver-purchase clause of the Sherman Silver Act of 1890. With the fervor of an apostle, he edited and published (in Washington, 1892–98) a weekly newspaper, first called the Silver Knight and later the Silver Knight-Watchman (see Reminiscences, p. 321). After the nomination of Bryan upon a free-silver platform in 1896, he counseled the Populist and Silver party leaders to indorse Bryan, which they did. Later, when the unexpected discoveries of new sources of gold had convinced him that the silver question was disposed of, he returned to the Republican party, indorsed McKinley in 1900, and vigorously attacked Bryan's silver speeches in that campaign. At the expiration of his term in 1905, he declined reëlection, returned to Nevada, and spent his last years at his newly established home in Bullfrog.

With John T. Boyle he was employed as counsel for the Roman Catholic prelates of California in the controversy with the Mexican government over the Pious Fund of the Californias, and as senior counsel for the claimants presented one of the winning arguments before the Permanent Court of Arbitration at The Hague in 1902 (W. L. Penfield, "The 'Pious Fund' Arbitration," North American Review, December 1902). He was a lifelong friend and adviser of Leland Stanford [q.v.], and was one of the first trustees of Stanford University. He accumulated several large fortunes which quickly disappeared, much going for charitable and educational purposes. Though no orator, he was a clear and impressive speaker. Possessed of unlimited self-confidence, colossal self-assertion, unflagging energy, and indomitable perseverance, he was a striking product of the mining frontier. Over six feet tall, of erect and massive figure, with long flowing beard and silvery hair, he was one of the most picturesque and rugged characters ever known in Washington. His first wife was killed in 1902 in an automobile accident at Alameda, Cal., and in the fall of 1903, at Atlanta, Ga., he married Mary Agnes (Atchison), widow of Theodore Cone. In 1908 Reminiscences of Senator William Morris Stewart was published under the editorship of George R. Brown.

[The *Reminiscences* and *Obit. Record Grads. Yale Univ.*, 1909, give the year of Stewart's birth as 1825, but the *Biog. Dir. Am. Cong.* (1928), *Who's Who in America*, 1908–09, and E. M. Mack, *post*, in both thesis and article, give 1827. The fullest account of his public life is Effie M. Mack, "Life and Letters of William Morris Stewart, 1827–1909" (unpublished dissertation, Univ. of Cal.) ; the author had access to Stewart's private papers and many letters are quoted at length. A shorter account by the same author appears in *Proc. of the Pacific Coast Branch of the Am. Hist. Asso.* (1930), pp. 185–92. See also Alonzo Phelps, *Contemporary Biog. of California's Representative Men* (1881) ; O. T. Shuck, *Representative and Leading Men of the Pacific* (1870) ; Eliot Lord, "Comstock Mining and Miners," *Monograph of the U. S. Geol. Survey*, vol. IV (1883) ; *The Call* (San Francisco), Apr. 24, 1909; and *San Francisco Chronicle*, Apr. 24, 1909.]

P.O.R.

STEWART, WILLIAM RHINELANDER (Dec. 3, 1852–Sept. 4, 1929), capitalist, philanthropist, was born in New York City. His parents, Lispenard and Mary Rogers (Rhinelander) Stewart, were descendants of some of New York's oldest families. Young Stewart was educated by tutors and in the private schools of Dr. Anthon and Dr. Charlier. He then entered the Columbia University Law School, where he was graduated in 1873. After several years' practice of law with the firm of Platt, Gerard & Buckley, he gave up the profession and devoted his time thereafter to the management of estates as executor and trustee, and to philanthropic work.

Appointed by Gov. Alonzo B. Cornell [*q.v.*] as commissioner for the first judicial district on the state board of charities, May 31, 1882, he served with that organization for forty-seven years; from 1894 to 1903 and from 1907 to 1923 he was president of the board. Upon his retirement in March 1929, Gov. Franklin D. Roosevelt wrote: "Your record is unique in the annals of the State's history, both in length of time and in the variety and scope of your activities" (*New York Times*, Sept. 5, 1929, p. 29). In regard to juvenile reformatories, he believed in "abandoning a system based upon punishment and retribution" and substituting "one which would provide for proper classification, open grounds for play and exercise, proper industrial and scholastic education, and care of the boys and the girls in separate institutions" (*Report of the State Board of Charities*, 1929, pp. 1–2). In 1898 he was elected president of the National Conference of Charities and Corrections, and received its gold medal in recognition of his services. In 1900 he organized the New York State Conference of Charities and Corrections, of which he was elected president in 1903. In 1910 he founded the New York City Conference of Charities and Corrections. He was for several years chairman of the state commission for the establishment of Letchworth Village, a farm colony for the feeble-minded. During his presidency of the state board of charities, his public duties, which included much traveling among the state institutions, occupied at least half his time and sometimes more; those who knew him and his work testified that for much of his labor he received no emolument.

In 1889 he conceived the idea of building the Washington Arch in Washington Square at the end of Fifth Avenue, New York. He was treasurer of the committee appointed to further the project, did much towards raising funds, and in 1895 formally presented the Arch to Mayor Strong in a public ceremony. In 1894, after the Lexow Committee investigation of New York's city government, Stewart had been one of the Committee of Seventy who labored for the overthrow of Tammany Hall and the election of Mayor William L. Strong and a reform administration. The last task which he undertook was that of completing the tomb of General Grant on Riverside Drive, and at the time of his death he had collected $100,000 (including a substantial donation of his own) of the $400,000 needed. Meanwhile, on the business side, he was president of the Rhinelander Real Estate Company from 1908 until 1929 and a director in two banks and several corporations. He was also a member of many scientific and other learned societies. On Nov. 5, 1879, he married Annie M. Armstrong of Baltimore, by whom he had three children, one of whom died young. She divorced him, Aug. 24, 1906, and was afterward twice married. Besides a number of pamphlets and magazine articles, Stewart wrote two books, *The Philanthropic Work of Josephine Shaw Lowell* (1911), and *Grace Church and Old New York* (1924). He died in New York City.

[*Who's Who in America*, 1928–29; *N. Y. Times*, May 4, 5, 1895, on occasion of the dedication of the Washington Arch; *The Washington Arch: its Conception, Construction and Dedication* (1895) ; *N. Y. Times* and *N. Y. Herald Tribune*, Sept. 5, 6, 1929; annual reports of N. Y. State Board of Charities and Corrections, 1882–1929; *N. Y. Biog. and Geneal. Record*, July 1893.]

A.F.H.

STICKNEY, ALPHEUS BEEDE (June 27, 1840–Aug. 9, 1916), lawyer, railway builder, was born in Wilton, Me., the son of Daniel and Ursula Maria (Beede) Stickney, and a descendant of William Stickney who came to Boston in 1637 and two years later settled in Rowley, Mass. Educated in common schools and academies of Maine and New Hampshire until he was eighteen, he then began the study of law in the office of Josiah Crosby in Dexter, Me. His preparation was somewhat delayed by school-teaching which he was obliged to undertake in order to earn money, but in 1862 he was admitted to the bar, and moved to Minnesota, where he practised law until 1869.

Railroad building was just beginning in Minnesota and neighboring states, and in 1869 Stickney moved to St. Paul, gave up practice, and became connected with railroad enterprises. His first great undertaking, in 1871, was the St. Paul, Stillwater & Taylor's Falls Railroad—later a part of the Chicago, St. Paul, Minneapolis & Omaha system—which he served for several years as vice-president, general manager, and chief counsel. In 1879 he became superintendent of construction of the St. Paul, Minneapolis & Manitoba Railway, which subsequently became part of the Great Northern, and the following year was general superintendent of about 500 miles of the Canadian Pacific Railway. In 1881 he organized and built the first section of the Wisconsin, Minnesota & Pacific Railroad, and in 1881–82 he was vice-president of the Minneapolis & St. Louis Railway. In 1883 he organized and began the construction of the Minnesota & Northwestern Railroad, serving as president until its union with the Chicago, St. Paul & Kansas City in 1887, and then as president of the consolidated road. This office he held until 1892, when he was elected chairman of the board of directors. In that capacity he reorganized the road as the Chicago Great Western Railway, of which he was president from 1894 to 1900 and chairman of the board of directors from 1892 to 1908. When bankruptcy came in 1908 he was appointed receiver. In 1909 he retired from active work.

In his administration of the Chicago Great Western, Stickney endeavored to apply ideas both as to financing and operation which were novel in the United States. These he set forth in a book entitled *The Railway Problem* (1891). Following the English practice, he endeavored to raise the money for financing the road from the stockholders, and to reorganize it without a funded debt. In this way the stock would represent a real investment and would have first claim on surplus earnings, instead of being junior to a heavy mortgage. This scheme, admirable as it would be in periods of depression when fixed charges become insupportable, met two difficulties: in the first place, investors did not buy the railway stock offered, and in the second place, the earning power of the road did not increase as rapidly as had been estimated. The result was that the floating debt grew to unmanageable proportions, reaching $10,653,000 by January 1908, when the road was forced into the hands of a receiver. This experience seemed

to show that the Stickney plan of a bankruptcy-proof railroad was not proof against insufficient earnings, and that the general creditors could put a road in the hands of a receiver as effectively as could the owners of defaulted bonds.

In the actual operations of the Chicago Great Western Stickney applied methods that were in advance of his time. Assuming that carefully analyzed statistics of past records could be made the basis for the formulation of definite policies, he worked out methods of operation and maintenance and applied them ruthlessly. It is difficult to reach a definite conclusion as to the efficacy of these methods, for the road was exposed to the severest competition, and its officials, apparently, did not always carry out the Stickney plans wholeheartedly. Stickney himself charged in 1909 that many of the railroads had resumed the practice of rebating under such subterfuges as that of allowing large claims for overcharges and damages presented by favored shippers. The charges resulted in an investigation by the Interstate Commerce Commission, before which Stickney laid a plan for revising the rate laws so as to make such practices impossible. This was set forth in a pamphlet entitled *Railway Rates* (1909).

Stickney did much to develop the Northwest, encouraging settlers to come thither and persuading Eastern and European capitalists to make investments there. During his railroad career he acquired extensive outside interests, one of the chief of which was the St. Paul union stockyards and packing houses, which he built in 1882. He was twice married: first, in October 1864 to Kate W. H. Hall of Collinsville, Ill.; and second, in 1901, to May Crosby. By his first wife he had seven children. He died at his home in St. Paul.

[M. A. Stickney, *The Stickney Family* (1869); *Who's Who in America*, 1916–17; *Railway Age Gazette*, Aug. 18, 1916; *N. Y. Times*, Aug. 10, 1916; *St. Paul Dispatch*, Aug. 9, 1916.]   E. L. B.

STIEGEL, HENRY WILLIAM (May 13, 1729–Jan. 10, 1785), "Baron von Stiegel," ironmaster, glassmaker, townbuilder, about whose eccentricities and grandiose manner of living in Pennsylvania many stories, true and apocryphal, have been told, was born near Cologne, Germany, the son of John Frederick and Dorothea Elizabeth Stiegel, and the eldest of six children. His father died in 1741. Nine years later Heinrich Wilhelm, his mother, and his brother Anthony sailed from Rotterdam in the *Nancy* and arrived at Philadelphia on Aug. 31, 1750. After a year or two in Philadelphia, the mother and brother settled in Schaefferstown, and Heinrich apparently secured employment with Jacob Huber, ironmaster, near Brickerville, Lancaster County. On Nov. 7, 1752, he married Huber's daughter, Elizabeth, who died Feb. 13, 1758. Two daughters were born to them. About three months after his wife's death, in partnership with Charles and Alexander Stedman of Philadelphia, he bought his father-in-law's property, added to it, and named it Elizabeth Furnace. On Oct. 24 of the same year he married Elizabeth Hölz of Philadelphia, who bore him one son. On Apr. 10, 1760, he became a British citizen, taking the name of Henry William Stiegel. The soubriquet "Baron" was doubtless given him because of his lordly manner of living.

At Elizabeth Furnace he made six-plate and ten-plate stoves and all sorts of iron castings, including kettles for potash and soap works, and stoves, kettles, and other equipment for the West Indies sugar-makers. Thousands of acres of woodland were purchased, tenant houses were erected, and by 1760 Stiegel was one of the most prosperous ironmasters in the country. He built another residence there, as well as stores, a mill, and a malt house. In 1760 he purchased another forge, which he named Charming Forge, near Womelsdorf, Berks County, selling a half interest in it to the Stedmans in 1763. On Sept. 20, 1762, he acquired from the Stedman brothers a third interest in 729 acres of land in Lancaster County, laid out the town of Manheim, built and sold houses, and conducted a real estate boom. Here in 1763 he began to build himself a third large mansion, which had in it a chapel and on its roof a platform for performances by the band of musicians he had organized among his workmen.

In 1763–64 he went to England, visited London and Bristol, and is said to have brought back with him a number of skilled glass makers. Upon his return early in 1764 he began the erection of a glass manufactory at Manheim, meanwhile experimenting in the making of bottles and window glass at Elizabeth Furnace. The first glassmaking at Manheim was begun in November 1765, and by 1767 the plant was in full operation. In 1769 he built a second factory there, known after 1772 as the American Flint Glass Manufactory, where glass was made until 1774. He had agents for the sale of his products in Philadelphia, Boston, New York, Baltimore, and numerous smaller towns in Pennsylvania and Maryland. At the Manheim works, in addition to window and sheet glass, was made the beautiful Stiegel glassware that is now eagerly sought by collectors . . . bottles, funnels, water lenses, retorts, flasks, measures, drinking glasses,

scent bottles, and toys . . . some of it engraved or enameled, in white, light green, deep emerald, olive, wine, amethyst, and the blue that was a favorite of the day. Thin and light in weight, with a brilliant surface and uniform color, it has great beauty of form and, as it was made largely by hand, an exquisite variety in proportion. The Metropolitan Museum of Art, New York, contains the large Hunter Collection, and there is a good one in the Pennsylvania Museum of Art, Philadelphia.

Though Stiegel was one of the wealthiest men in Pennsylvania, he was careless and happy-go-lucky, with a self-confidence so great that he could scarcely envisage the possibility of failure, and he wasted much of his substance both in extravagant living and in over-ambitious business ventures. A passionate lover of music and a connoisseur of beauty as well as mechanically skilful, he has been described as cursed with the "ironic gift of too great facility." Certainly his career was a meteoric one. Apparently prosperous enough in 1770–71, he began to suffer hard times in 1772, and in 1773 instituted a lottery in hope of recouping his fortunes. By 1774 he was obliged to sell his property (much of which he had mortgaged for the sake of his glass factories), became a bankrupt, and in the later months of the year spent some weeks in a debtor's prison. From that time his fortunes declined rapidly, and his hopes vanished. For a while he had a more or less self-assumed position as caretaker at Elizabeth Furnace and then was employed there by the new owner as foreman. In 1779, partially dependent on his brother, he turned country schoolmaster and music teacher at Brickerville and Schaefferstown, with an interval as clerk at the Reading Furnaces, Berks County. When his wife died in Philadelphia in 1782, she was buried there for lack of funds to bring her body to Schaefferstown. Three years later Stiegel himself died in poverty at Charming Forge, then in the hands of his nephew, and was buried in an unmarked grave.

[In the record of the ship Nancy, given in facsimile in R. B. Strassburger, Pa. German Pioneers (1934), vol. II, 155 C, Stiegel signed his name as Henderick Willem Stiegel. F. W. Hunter, Stiegel Glass (1914), contains by far the best biog. of Stiegel and includes a bibliog., geneal., lists of deeds, employees, purchasers of glass, etc. See also T. P. Ege, Hist. and Geneal. of the Ege Family . . . 1738–1911 (1911); W A. Dyer, Early Am. Craftsmen (1915); Rhea M. Knittle, Early Am. Glass (copr. 1927); Mrs. N. H. Moore, Old Glass, European and Am. (1924); F. W. Hunter, "Baron Stiegel and Am. Glass," Bull. Met. Museum of Art, Dec. 1913; Nat. Soc. Colonial Dames of America, Pa. Soc., Forges and Furnaces in the Province of Pa. (1914); A. S. Brendle, Henry William Stiegel (1912); and J. T. Faris, The Romance of Forgotten Men (1928), a popular account. Many of Stiegel's ledgers, daybooks, journals, etc., are in the colls. of the Hist. Soc. of Pa.]

W. A. D.

STILES, EZRA (Nov. 29, 1727 o.s.–May 12, 1795), scholar, Congregational clergyman, president of Yale College, was born in North Haven, Conn., then a part of New Haven, where his father, Isaac, was for more than thirty-five years pastor of the Congregational church. He was a descendant of John Stiles who emigrated from England and settled in Windsor, Conn., in 1635. Ezra's mother, Kezia, daughter of the Rev. Edward Taylor of Westfield, Mass., died five days after the child's birth, and the following year his father married Esther, daughter of Samuel Hooker, Jr., of Hartford. Prepared at home, Ezra was ready for college at the age of twelve, but did not enter until 1742, when he enrolled at Yale College. Here he distinguished himself in all branches of learning but showed special fondness for mathematics, astronomy, and Biblical history. After his graduation, in 1746, he remained in New Haven, devoting himself to intellectual pursuits, particularly to the study of theology, and on May 30, 1749, was licensed to preach by the New Haven Association of Ministers. The week before, he had been appointed tutor at Yale.

For six years he filled this position with more than ordinary acceptability, but his time and thought were by no means confined solely to its duties. His mental equipment and abilities as a speaker were such that he was the natural choice for orator on important public occasions. In 1750 he delivered the funeral oration in honor of Governor Jonathan Law [q.v.]; in 1753, an oration in memory of Bishop Berkeley; and in 1755, one in compliment of Benjamin Franklin during his visit to New Haven. All these were in Latin. Franklin, in 1749, had sent an electrical apparatus to Yale, and Stiles had engaged in some of the first electrical experiments carried on in New England. The two became friends and corresponded for the remainder of Franklin's lifetime. During his tutorship Stiles had doubts as to the advisability of his entering the active ministry. From childhood he had been of frail constitution, but an even more important reason for his hesitation was uncertainty of mind as to some of the dogmas of the Christian religion. Accordingly, he studied law and in November 1753 was admitted to the bar. His attitude toward religion at this time was not due to disbelief, but rather to an intellectual honesty which would not permit him to accept anything as true until thorough investigation had convinced him of its verity. A long and patient study of the Scriptures, carried on with every help available,

at length brought him to a firm belief in the truth of revelation. His openness of mind is evinced by the fact that during visits to Newport, Boston, New York, and Philadelphia in 1754, he attended Quaker meetings and Episcopal, Reformed Dutch, and Roman Catholic services, in order to acquaint himself at first hand with the merits of different forms of worship. Several invitations to settle in the ministry came to him, and attempts were made to draw him into the Anglican communion, the Episcopalians of Stratford, Conn., urging him in January 1755 to succeed Dr. Samuel Johnson [q.v.] as their rector. He was disposed to continue the practice of law, but when in the early summer of 1755 the Second Congregational Church of Newport, R. I., called him to become its pastor, the attractiveness of that town with its foreign contacts—it was then a shipping center of importance—its Redwood Library, the prospect of leisure for study, his love of preaching, and the advice of his father and friends led him to accept. Resigning his tutorship, he was ordained and installed there on Oct. 22, 1755. On Feb. 10, 1757, he married Elizabeth, daughter of Col. John Hubbard of New Haven.

During the many years Stiles resided in Newport his interests and activities were amazingly varied. In 1756 he became librarian of the Redwood Library and continued as such as long as he remained in the town. He sought information on all manner of subjects, and his correspondence with prominent people at home and abroad was voluminous. Visitors to Newport of any importance inevitably found their way to his door. In 1765, upon the recommendation of Franklin, the University of Edinburgh conferred on him the degree of doctor of divinity. Although he was an ardent antiquarian, his interest in contemporary conditions was almost equally keen, and he gathered and recorded a great variety of statistics. His taste for scientific inquiry remained; he made observations of the comet of 1759 and of the transit of Venus ten years later, studied other natural phenomena, and carried on experiments in chemistry. Recognized as probably the most learned man in New England, he was made a member of the American Philosophical Society on Jan. 26, 1768, and in 1781 was elected a councilor. Having neglected Hebrew in college, in 1767, when forty years old, he set to work acquiring a thorough knowledge of that language; he also studied Arabic, Syriac, and Armenian, becoming for his day a very competent orientalist. Subsequently, he took a few lessons in French and was soon perusing works by French authors. When he began his diary,

January 1769, he was working on an ecclesiastical history of New England and British America, which he left incomplete. He was much interested in promoting the manufacture of silk and recorded in his diary, June 4, 1771: "I have now Three Thous^d Silkworms hatched." Based on his experiments and investigations in this field, he wrote "Observations on Silk Worms," a sizable manuscript which has been preserved. He found time, also, to supervise the early education of his children: "Ezra," he records in his diary, Jan. 9, 1769, "began to learn hebrew about this time, Æt. 10." He did not neglect the Bible or permit any of his family to do so. Reviewing his fidelity in this respect at a much later date, July 21, 1793, he wrote: "Besides read^g in course privately in my Study, I read thro' the Bible in my Fam^y at Morning Prayers from 1760 to 1791, Eight times, or once in 4 years. My Fam^y have had full opport^y of being acquainted with the sacred Contents of the Bible.'

In spite of his varied intellectual pursuits and the hours spent in writing, he performed his ministerial duties with the utmost conscientiousness. In 1771 he made 926 pastoral calls and the following year, 1030. He gave much attention, also, to catechising the children. The spiritual welfare of the many slaves in Newport—Stiles himself owned one whom he later set free—was a matter of concern to him. On Feb. 24, 1772, he wrote: "In the Evening a very full and serious Meeting of Negroes at my House, perhaps 80 or 90: I discoursed to them on Luke xiv, 16, 17, 18, . . . They sang well. They appeared attentive and much affected." He was on intimate terms with the Jews of Newport, frequently attending their synagogue, and had friendly relations with Christian denominations other than his own. With Rev. Samuel Hopkins [q.v.], pastor of the First Congregational Church, he cooperated cordially, though he was not in sympathy with many of the views of that noted theologian. To President Clap of Yale he wrote protesting against the removal of deistical books from the college library, urging the vanity of trying to suppress such writings and the danger of suppressing truth. "The only way is," he maintained, "to come forth into the open field and dispute the matter on an even footing" (Holmes, post, p. 79). For the Church of England in America, however, he had no liking. "It is grievous to think," he complained, "that when our Pious Ancestors came over into this Land when an howling wilderness, to enjoy ye Gospel in ye purity & simplicity of it y^t the Chh of England should thrust it self in among us" (Diary, I, 125). Later, he declared that as he had observed it in New England, it was "inspired with a secular principle, unanimated with the Love of Jesus so much as with the Love of Dignities & Preeminence, making the Chh. an asylum for polite Vice & Irreligion" (Ibid., II, 113).

While in Newport he had an important part in the founding of Rhode Island College (Brown University). As early as January 1762 he had been considering the possibility of a third New England college, and when James Manning [q.v.] came to Rhode Island in the summer of 1763 with a project for establishing a Baptist institution of learning, Stiles gave it his support. It was agreed that the new college should be under Baptist control but that representatives of other denominations should have a share in its management. The work of drawing up a charter was committed to Stiles, since he was regarded by the Baptists as better fitted for that task than any of their own members. Accordingly, he prepared a document which provided for a board of thirty-five trustees, nineteen of whom were to be Baptists, seven Congregationalists, five Friends, and four Episcopalians; and a board of twelve Fellows, eight of whom were to be Congregationalists. The trustees were to elect the president, but practically all other control of the institution was left to the Fellows, subject to the sanction of the trustees. The charter was approved by the committee in charge of the project, but Providence Baptists in the Rhode Island Assembly objected to it on the ground that it provided for an essentially Congregational college, and Stiles was charged with playing a trick on the Baptists, though, as a matter of fact, they were given the final decision in all matters. Before the charter was granted by the Assembly, however, it was so changed as to insure a majority of Baptists on both the board of trustees and the board of Fellows. Stiles was named as one of the original Fellows but declined the office. In 1765 he was again elected and again he declined.

He was a stanch advocate of American rights and liberties, and prophesied that British oppression would force the colonies to declare their independence. Writing to Benjamin Franklin, Oct. 23 and Nov. 6, 1765, he said that he disapproved of the Stamp Act, but that after it was passed he remained loyal and had nothing to do with the mob violence that resulted in the resignation of the Newport stamp officer. Charges that he encouraged violence, he ascribed to the Episcopalians, who disliked him. When the Revolution broke out, however, he gave it wholehearted support. He followed its course with intense interest, and recorded in his diary much valuable information, including accounts of movements and battles, often illustrated by maps.

The Revolution brought to an end what was probably the happiest period of his life. Fearing that Newport would fall into the hands of the British, many of the inhabitants fled elsewhere for safety. On Oct. 10, 1775, Stiles wrote: "How does this Town sit solitary that was once full of People! I am not yet removed, altho' three quarters of my beloved Chh & Congregation are broken up and dispersed" (*Diary*, I, 624). In March 1776 he took his family and goods to Dighton, Mass., where he resided about fourteen months, supplying the church there and making occasional visits to Newport and other places. In the meantime, he was asked to take charge of churches in Taunton, Mass., and Providence, R. I.; Dr. Charles Chauncy, 1705–1787 [*q.v.*], also invited him to become his assistant in the work of the First Church, Boston. In May 1777, at the request of the First Church, Portsmouth, N. H., he removed to that town, but the following September was elected president of Yale College. It was some months before he made up his mind to accept. He had no illusions about the office: "At best," he wrote, "the Diadem of a President is a Crown of Thorns" (*Ibid.*, II, 209), and he was not disposed to occupy the seat of authority until he was sure of "sitting as easy in the Chair, as such a Cella Curulis would admit of" (*Ibid.*, II, 226). Finally, in March 1778 he signified his acceptance and on July 8 he was installed as president and as professor of ecclesiastical history. It is significant of the affection in which he was held by his Newport parishioners that they were unwilling to dismiss him and that he remained technically their pastor until May 18, 1786.

The unsettled state of the country during Stiles's presidency of Yale made his position an especially difficult one; furthermore, the funds of the college were practically exhausted. Stiles nevertheless carried the institution through the period with reasonable success. In addition to his administrative duties he bore a heavy burden of teaching, giving instruction in Hebrew, ecclesiastical history, philosophical and scientific subjects, and, for a time, in theology. He loved academic forms and ceremonies and introduced them whenever occasion permitted. An amusing incident of his New Haven career was occasioned by the support he gave to a dancing master. He permitted about seventy-five students to attend his classes and three of his own children as well. This, he says, produced "a great Combustion" and after "Violent Proceed^gs" the dancing master had to leave town (*Diary*, III,

10–11, 15). The most notable event of his administration was a change in the college charter, whereby several of the state officials were made *ex officio* members of the corporation with all the rights of the original Fellows, and certain financial aid from the state was secured. He preached often and took an active part in ecclesiastical matters; he was also the first president of the society for the abolition of slavery formed in Connecticut in 1790.

He died of "bilious fever," at his home in New Haven, in his sixty-eighth year, after a few days' illness. His first wife had died on May 29, 1775, having borne him two sons and six daughters, of whom one son, Isaac, and four daughters survived him; Isaac was lost at sea a few months after his father's death; a daughter, Ruth, was the mother of Ezra Stiles Gannett [*q.v.*]. On Oct. 17, 1782, Stiles married Mary (Cranston) Checkley, widow of William Checkley and daughter of Benjamin Cranston of Newport.

The almost incredible amount of work that Stiles accomplished was carried on in spite of physical handicaps. His son-in-law, Abiel Holmes [*q.v.*], describes him as "a man of low and small stature; of a very delicate structure; and of a well proportioned form. . . . The delicacy of his frame requiring a special care of his health, he was prudently attentive . . . to its preservation. . . . Having carefully studied his own constitution, he was generally his own physician. By regulating his diet, exercising daily in the open air, and using occasionally a few simple medicines, he was, by the divine blessing, enabled, with but very small interruptions, to apply himself assiduously to study, and to discharge the various duties of public and of domestic life" (*Life, post*, pp. 349, 350). Although he wrote much, he published little. A few of his sermons appeared in printed form, among them *The United States Elevated to Glory and Honor* (1783), an election sermon preached at Hartford, May 8, 1783; and his *History of Three of the Judges of King Charles I* was issued in 1794. Stiles bequeathed some of his manuscripts to Abiel Holmes, who in 1798 published, with many extracts from them, *The Life of Ezra Stiles, D.D., LL.D.* To his successor in the presidency of Yale College he also bequeathed a large number of manuscripts. From these have been printed *The Literary Diary of Ezra Stiles, D.D., LL.D.* (3 vols., 1901), and *Extracts from the Itineraries and Other Miscellanies of Ezra Stiles . . . with Selections from His Correspondence* (1916), both edited by Franklin B. Dexter [*q.v.*], and both of much historical value. Manuscripts more recently presented to Yale College are published in *Letters & Papers of Ezra Stiles* (1933), edited by Isabel M. Calder.

[Besides sources mentioned, see J. L. Kingsley, "Life of Ezra Stiles," in Jared Sparks, *The Lib. of Am. Biog.*, vol. XVI (1847) ; F. B. Dexter, *Biog. Sketches Grads. Yale Coll.*, vol. II (1896) ; W. B. Sprague, *Annals of the Am. Pulpit*, vol. I (1857) ; H. R. Stiles, *The Stiles Family in America* (1895) ; W. E. Channing, *A Discourse Delivered at the Dedication of the Unitarian Congregational Church in Newport, July 27, 1836* (1836) ; G. A. Kohut, *Ezra Stiles and the Jews* (1902) ; W. C. Bronson, *The Hist. of Brown Univ.* (1914) ; Ebenezer Baldwin, *Annals of Yale Coll.* (1831) ; T. D. Woolsey, *An Hist. Discourse* (1850) ; A. P. Stokes, *Memorials of Eminent Yale Men* (1914), vol. I ; *Atlantic Mo.*, Aug. 1844. Constance Rourke, in *Trumpets of Jubilee* (1927), pp. 5–11, gives a gay and not too reverent appreciation ; C. D. Ebeling, in *Amerikanisches Magazin* (Hamburg), I (1795), 172–73, publishes an obituary and tells of Stiles's kindness in sending him an account of early Connecticut history.]   H. E. S.

STILES, HENRY REED (Mar. 10, 1832–Jan. 7, 1909), physician, genealogist, historian, was born in New York City. His father, Samuel Stiles, head of a bank-note engraving company, was descended from John Stiles, one of four brothers who emigrated from Bedfordshire, England, to Windsor, Conn., in 1635. His mother was Charlotte Sophia (Reed), daughter of Abner Reed, to whom Samuel had been apprenticed to learn engraving.

Stiles studied for one year at the University of the City of New York and in 1849 entered Williams College as a sophomore. Ill health interrupted his studies and he did not graduate, but a quarter of a century later Williams granted him an honorary degree (1876). In 1855 he graduated from the Medical Department of the University of the City of New York, and also from the New York Ophthalmic Hospital. He practised medicine for a few months, first in New York City and then in Galena, Ill. During 1856, after his marriage (Jan. 31) to Sarah Woodward, he edited the *Toledo Blade*. For the next two years he was a partner in the firm of F. C. Brownell of Hartford and New York, publishers of educational books and the *American Journal of Education*. In 1857, when ill health made it inadvisable for him to apply himself closely to business, he began tracing the genealogy of his family among the early records of Windsor, Conn. The history of the ancient town soon engrossed him. From the records of town acts, tax lists, registers, old wills, petitions, letters, journals, newspapers, and church records, as well as from the memories of aged inhabitants, he collected a mass of historical and genealogical material which he published in a volume of a thousand pages, *The History of Ancient Windsor, Connecticut* (1859). Largely made up of extracts from old documents, this *History* is not a readable narrative, but as a source book of

genealogical and historical fact it is extremely valuable. A new edition, revised and greatly enlarged, *The History and Genealogies of Ancient Windsor, Connecticut* (2 vols.), appeared in 1891.

Stiles's interest in publishing the vital statistics, public documents, and personal papers of early New England and New York, begun thus casually, persisted throughout the remaining fifty years of his life and occupied fully half of his time. He compiled and published *A History of the City of Brooklyn* (3 vols., 1867–70), *The Stiles Family in America: Genealogies of the Connecticut Family* (1895), and *The History of Ancient Wethersfield, Connecticut* (2 vols., 1904) based on the collections of Sherman W. Adams ; he assisted in compiling and edited *Letters from the Prisons and Prison-ships of the Revolution* and *Account of the Interment of the Remains of American Patriots Who Perished on the British Prison-ships,* both in the Wallabout Prison-Ship Series (1895) ; *The Civil, Political, Professional and Ecclesiastical History . . . of the County of Kings and the City of Brooklyn* (1884) ; *Joutel's Journal of La Salle's Last Voyage, 1686-7* (1906), and the genealogies of several families ; and contributed articles to historical periodicals and biographical series. He was editor of the *Historical Magazine* from January to June 1866, and of the *New York Genealogical and Biographical Record* from 1900 to 1902. His genial, kindly manner, enthusiasm, and industry enabled him to interest others in the preservation of valuable historical material and made him a successful organizer and officer of historical and genealogical societies.

He carried on his professional career somewhat intermittently, practising medicine until 1863 and holding minor public medical offices from 1868 until 1877 when he took charge of the Dundee (Scotland) Homeopathic Dispensary and, for the first time, occupied himself solely with medical work. His health failed after four years here and he returned to New York City, where he maintained a consulting practice which gave him considerable time for historical compilation. From 1888 until his death he conducted a sanatorium at Hill View on Lake George, New York.

[Stiles's own publications : *The Stiles Family in America* (1895), Preface to *The Hist. of Ancient Windsor, Conn.* (1859), and *The Hist. and Geneals. of Ancient Windsor, Conn.* (1891), II, 712–14 ; T. A. Wright, "Henry Reed Stiles," *N. Y. Geneal. and Biog. Record,* Apr. 1909 ; *Brooklyn Daily Eagle,* Jan. 9, 1909.]
V. L. S.

STILL, ANDREW TAYLOR (Aug. 6, 1828–Dec. 12, 1917), founder of osteopathy, was born in Jonesboro, Va., the son of Abram and Martha Poage (Moore) Still. His father, a Methodist preacher, removed his family in 1834 to New-market, Tenn., and then to Macon County, Mo., to Schuyler County, Mo., and in 1845 back to Macon County. Young Andrew during this period led a typical frontiersman's life, gaining what education he could from local schools. On Jan. 29, 1849, he married Mary M. Vaughn. Four years later, he removed with her to Waka-rusa Mission, Kan., where she died in 1859. He devoted himself to farming, doctoring Indians, and studying anatomy on the bodies of dead Indians, obtained by grave snatching (*Autobiography, post*, p. 94). According to his own account, he took a course of medicine in the Kansas City School of Physicians and Surgeons, and fought with John Brown in the border warfare. In October 1857 he was elected as the Free-State candidate to the territorial legislature from Douglas and Johnson counties. On Nov. 15, 1860, he married Mary E. Turner. Enlisting in 1861, he obtained a captain's commission in 1862, and later in the same year, a major's commission in the Kansas militia.

On his return from the war, he was stimulated by a desire to aid alcoholic and drug addicts, who in their plight, appealed in vain to so-called regular doctors. He meditated over this and allied topics until, finally, the truth dawned on him "like a burst of sunshine" that he was "approaching a science by study, research, and observation" (*Autobiography, post*, p. 95). This great truth was reënforced by the personal tragedy of losing three children in an epidemic of cerebro-spinal meningitis in 1864, a tragedy that impelled him to the conclusion that "all the remedies necessary to health exist in the human body . . . they can be administered by adjusting the body in such condition that the remedies may naturally associate themselves together, hear the cries, and relieve the afflicted" (*Ibid.*, p. 100). On this doctrine he built and for twenty-five years sustained osteopathy, which, however, has been influenced also by other practitioners, by state laws, and by the development of general scientific knowledge and practice. He attempted to introduce the new system in Baker University of Baldwin, Kan., but met with so much opposition and ridicule that, in 1875, he removed to Kirksville, Mo., where he developed a considerable practice, in which he used both drugs and osteopathy. Up to 1892, he moved about a good deal, from Kirksville to Henry County, Mo., to Hannibal, to Macon, and finally back to Kirksville, all the while practising and spreading the teachings of osteopathy. As aids in this work,

he had three sons and a daughter, a quack pile doctor, and a lightning-rod peddler, all of whom he had indoctrinated in the new science and art (*Autobiography, post*, pp. 144–45). On Oct. 30, 1894, he incorporated the American School of Osteopathy in Kirksville, Mo. One year after the founding of the school, he vigorously assaulted the doctrine of healing drugs with his assertions that he was "as much afraid of Dover's powders as a darkey is of a skeleton. If I should give calomel, I would do it with my eyes shut, and keep them shut for nine days, so uncertain would I be as to results" (*Autobiography, post*, p. 288). In 1894 he also established the *Journal of Osteopathy*. From this time up to his death, he busied himself with teaching at the school, writing for the journal, and treating patients who came in numbers to consult him. In 1897 he published privately his *Autobiography* (revised ed., 1908), dictated to Mrs. Annie Morgan, as amanuensis (p. 172). He also published *Philosophy of Osteopathy* (1899), *The Philosophy and Mechanical Principles of Osteopathy* (1902), *Osteopathy, Research, and Practice* (1910).

[*Autobiog., ante*, indispensable for understanding Still and the beginnings of osteopathy; C. P. McConnell, *Clinical Osteopathy* (1917), esp. for development and present status of osteopathy; D. W. Wilder, *The Annals of Kan.* (new ed., 1886), p. 193; articles on "A. T. Still" and "Osteopathy," in *Encyc. Am.* and *Encyc. Brit.* written by practitioners of osteopathy; Morris Fishbein, *The Medical Follies* (1925), destructively critical; correspondence with the editor of the *Jour. of the Am. Osteopathic Asso.*]   M. G. S.

STILL, WILLIAM (Oct. 7, 1821–July 14, 1902), reformer, negro leader, was the son of Levin Steel, a former Maryland slave, who had gone North after purchasing his freedom. Subsequently, Levin was joined by his wife Sidney and their children, who had been recaptured by slave-hunters upon their first attempt to escape. To thwart further pursuit the family changed its name to Still—the mother also discarding the name Sidney for that of Charity—and settled among the sparsely inhabited pine lands at Shamong, Burlington County, N. J. Here William was born, the youngest of eighteen children. From an early age he worked on his father's farm, and his educational opportunities were few. In 1841 he left home and three years later moved to Philadelphia. In 1847 he married Letitia George by whom he had two sons and two daughters. The same year he became a clerk in the office of the Pennsylvania Society for the Abolition of Slavery.

Deeply impressed by his own family's experience, Still as clerk did all that lay in his power to help runaway slaves to freedom. Nineteen out of every twenty escaped slaves that passed through Philadelphia stopped at his house. In the decade 1851–61 he was the chairman and corresponding secretary of the Philadelphia branch of the Underground Railroad. The experiences of all those who had successfully fled from bondage he jotted down carefully, and in 1855 he made an extended tour through Canada to ascertain how the slaves that had made their way were faring. His *The Underground Railroad,* published in 1872, is one of the best accounts of how runaway slaves made their way to freedom. In 1859 he sheltered John Brown's widow and daughter when they passed through Philadelphia on their way to visit the leader of the Harpers Ferry raid before his execution. After the outbreak of the Civil War Still resigned as clerk and embarked first in the stove and then in the coal business. In February 1864 he was appointed post sutler at Camp William Penn for colored soldiers near Philadelphia. Methodical in his habits, he prospered in his business ventures.

Always intent on promoting the welfare of his race, in 1861 Still helped organize and finance a social, civil and statistical association to collect data about the colored people. Previous to this, in a remarkably well-expressed letter written on Aug. 30, 1859, to the *North American and United States Gazette,* he had begun a campaign against the regulation of the Philadelphia street car lines compelling all persons of color to ride on front platforms. This resulted in the Pennsylvania legislature ending this discrimination in 1867. Still's course during this controversy was bitterly assailed in colored circles so that he defended his attitude in a public address afterwards published in pamphlet form (*A Brief Narrative of the Struggle for the Rights of the Colored People of Philadelphia in the City Railway Cars,* 1867). The same procedure he followed in 1874 when he became unpopular among his own people by supporting the Democratic candidate for mayor of Philadelphia, publishing *An Address on Voting and Laboring.* In reporting against the establishment of a colored men's bank in Philadelphia he again displayed courage and independence. He served on the Freedmen's Aid Commission and was made a member of the Philadelphia board of trade. A devout Presbyterian he became superintendent of one of the denomination's Sunday schools in 1880 and the same year he founded the first colored Young Men's Christian Association. In welfare work he helped manage homes for aged colored persons and for destitute colored children; and also an orphan asylum for the children of negro soldiers and sailors.

[*Underground Railroad Records* (1886), a third edition of Still's book, contains a sketch of the author; see also *Appletons' Ann. Cyc. . . . 1902* (1903); W. J. Simmons, *Men of Mark* (1887); J. W. Gibson and W. H. Crogman, *The Colored American* (1902), pp. 490–98; *Pub. Ledger* (Phila.), July 15, 1902; A. S. Norwood, "Negro Welfare Work in Phila. as Illustrated by the Career of William Still," unpublished thesis, Univ. of Pa.]

H. G. V.

STILLÉ, ALFRED (Oct. 30, 1813–Sept. 24, 1900), physician, was born in Philadelphia, son of John and Maria (Wagner) Stillé and elder brother of Charles Janeway Stillé [*q.v.*]. He attended good preliminary schools and spent some time at Yale College, but left as the result of the "conic section rebellion" to transfer to the University of Pennsylvania, where he was graduated A.B. in 1832, A.M. in 1835, and M.D. in 1836. Fourteen years later he received the degree of M.A. from Yale, and was then enrolled as a member of the college class of 1832. Upon graduating in medicine he became house physician at "Blockley," now the Philadelphia General Hospital. Here he had the opportunity to study the typhus cases brought to the hospital during the epidemic of 1836 under Dr. William Wood Gerhard [*q.v.*], whose observations of these same cases led him to proclaim typhus as fundamentally different from typhoid fever. After a short service, however, Stillé resigned to spend two and a half years in study in Europe, a considerable part of the time in Paris, where he was profoundly influenced by Louis.

Returning to Philadelphia, he served as resident physician in the Pennsylvania Hospital, 1839–41, and then entered upon private practice. From 1849 to 1877 he was a visiting physician to St. Joseph's Hospital. In 1845 he began to lecture on pathology and the practice of medicine for the Philadelphia Association for Medical Instruction, and continued until 1851. In 1854 he was elected to the chair of practice of medicine in the Pennsylvania Medical College, continuing until 1859. In 1864 he succeeded the elder William Pepper [*q.v.*] as professor of the theory and practice of medicine in the University of Pennsylvania, holding this office until 1883, when he retired and was made professor emeritus. At this time he gave his valuable medical library to the University.

Stillé's first important writing, and the first American book on the subject, *Elements of General Pathology,* appeared in 1848. In 1860 he published *Therapeutics and Materia Medica* (1860). Probably his most striking literary production, written in collaboration with Professor John M. Maisch [*q.v.*], was the *National Dispensatory* (1879), an enormous work of 1628 pages. Of his numerous monographs and papers,

Epidemic Meningitis or Cerebro-Spinal Meningitis, published in 1867, is still looked upon as classic. He was president of the Philadelphia County Medical Society in 1862, one of the founders of the Philadelphia Pathological Society and its president from 1859 to 1862, one of the founders of the American Medical Association, its first secretary, and its president in 1871, a fellow of the College of Physicians of Philadelphia and its president in 1883.

Stillé was born and educated, lived, taught, and died in Philadelphia. He was always a proponent of higher standards of education. As a professor he was a perfect type of the old school —highly cultured and purely didactic. His high sense of morality and dignity can be divined from the closing sentence of his valedictory address: "Only two things are essential; to live uprightly, and to be wisely industrious." His lectures, scientifically correct, were polished literary essays, read to his classes year after year without addition or alteration. They were entirely lacking in inspiration, and since he had no connection with any hospital to which he could take his students, he could hold no clinics or ward classes by which to compensate for their deficiencies. In his later years he was a strikingly handsome old gentleman with delicate, sensitive, well-chiseled features, long white hair that curled about his collar, and a full white beard of considerable length. His appearance was venerable, benevolent, and patriarchal. He began to manifest the infirmities of age in his sixties and retired from his professorship and other activities at seventy, to live for seventeen years more, a recluse in his own home, where only a few friends visited him. He died in his eighty-seventh year, almost forgotten.

In 1841 he had married Caroline Barnett, who afforded him brief companionship and then acquired a mental disease from which she suffered for many years. After her death, he married, in June 1899, Katharine A. Blackiston of Chestertown, Md., who survived him, and according to instructions contained in his will published a small volume entitled *Fragments* (1901), composed of excerpts from his writings and letters. By his first marriage there were two sons and a daughter.

[C. W. Burr, "A Sketch of Alfred Stillé," *Univ. Medic. Mag.,* Jan. 1901; William Osler, "Memoir of Alfred Stillé," *Trans. Coll. of Phys. of Phila.,* 3 ser. XXIV (1902), pub. also in *Univ. of Pa. Medic. Bull.,* June 1902; E. E. Salisbury, *Biog. Memoranda Respecting . . . the Class of 1832 in Yale Coll.* (1880); *Obit. Record Grads. Yale Univ.,* 1901; J. W. Jordan, *Colonial Families of Phila.* (1911), vol. II; Katharine Blackiston Stillé, *Fragments* (1901); J. W. Croskey, *Hist. of Blockley* (1929); *Pub. Ledger* (Phila.), Sept. 25, 1900.]   J.McF.

STILLÉ, CHARLES JANEWAY (Sept. 23, 1819–Aug. 11, 1899), educator and historian, brother of Alfred Stillé [*q.v.*], was the son of John and Maria (Wagner) Stillé. His father was a descendent of Oloff Stillé, one of the Swedish settlers on the Delaware, who, arriving in 1641, established a home near Upland, now Chester, Pa., and later moved to Passyunk. His descendants were successful merchants in Philadelphia. Stillé's mother was descended from the Rev. Tobias Wagner of Reading, Pa., member of a Lutheran family in Württemberg, who emigrated to Pennsylvania in 1742.

Charles prepared for Yale College at a school conducted by the Rev. Dr. Steele at Abington, Pa., and the Edge Hill School near Princeton, N. J. He entered Yale in 1835, and upon graduation in 1839 delivered a valedictory oration, *The Social Spirit* (1839), which showed the ideals and ethical standards that were to characterize his life and writings. After studying in the office of Joseph Reed Ingersoll, he was admitted to the bar. His interests led him, however, rather to develop his taste for history and literature, in pursuance of which he visited Europe repeatedly.

During the Civil War he published a pamphlet entitled *How a Free People Conduct a Long War* (1862), drawing a comparison between the current conflict and the long struggle of Great Britain against the French Revolution and Napoleon; unusually free from harshness, it was pervaded with enlightened patriotism, and half a million copies of it were distributed. He was asked to serve as a member of the United States Sanitary Commission and as corresponding secretary of its Executive Committee, and had much to do with the success of the great "Sanitary Fair" held in Philadelphia in 1864, at which $1,000,000 was raised for the work of the Commission. After the war he published *History of the United States Sanitary Commission* (1866). These activities taught him, he said, "to look upon important public questions in a large and liberal way" (*Reminiscences of a Provost,* p. 4) and thus prepared him for the responsibilities that soon came to him. Without having had previous experience in teaching, he was appointed in 1866 to the professorship of English literature and belles-lettres in the University of Pennsylvania. When he assumed his duties, the course of study in the college was substantially that of a century before, and the only gift of money the institution had received in over eighty years was one of $5,000. With characteristic zeal Stillé began at once to advocate the establishment of elective courses of study, which in

1867 were introduced into the upper classes of the college.

In 1868 he became the tenth provost of the University of Pennsylvania. His inaugural address, *The Claims of Liberal Culture in Philadelphia* (1868), presented the needs of the University as the center of the higher education of the community. The twelve years of his administration proved his unusual qualities as an educational leader and a practical executive. It was not easy to find support for his projects in the self-perpetuating Board of Trustees, long established in set grooves of action, yet he succeeded in obtaining their approval for marked changes. He aroused the interest of the community, enlisted the cordial cooperation of the faculty, and won the devoted affection of the students. New departments—of science (1872), music (1877), and dentistry (1878)—were created. Through the Provost's persistent efforts the city was induced in 1870 to sell on reasonable terms ten acres of land in West Philadelphia, where adequate facilities could be provided for the expansion of the University. There the cornerstone of College Hall, the first of the new buildings, was laid on June 15, 1871. The following year the city made a grant of five and a half acres for the erection of University Hospital, which was opened in 1874. Untiring in his efforts to put the University upon a sound financial basis, Stillé fell short of his high aim, but nevertheless he did obtain, among other gifts, the endowment of the Towne Scientific School, the John Welsh Chair, and the Bloomfield Moore scholarships for women, as well as a sum to found the Tobias Wagner Library. A notable means adopted for bringing the University into closer relationship with the city was the establishment of scholarships for graduates of the Philadelphia public schools. The extraordinary progress begun in his administration initiated the great expansion that was to continue under his immediate successors.

Stillé resigned the provostship in 1880 for reasons which he set forth in *Reminiscences of a Provost, 1866–1880* (n.d.); disagreeing with the board of trustees, he contended that the Provost should be a member of the board, that powers of discipline over students should be vested in the faculty, and that a great, united effort should be made to put the University finances on a stable basis. In 1881 he retired also from the John Welsh professorship, of which he was the first incumbent, and thereafter devoted himself to historical studies. In addition to a number of pamphlets, he published *Studies in Mediaeval History* (1882); *The Life and Times of John Dickinson* (1891); and *Major-General Anthony Wayne and the Pennsylvania Line in the Continental Army* (1893). On his second visit to Sweden, in 1888, he discovered the whereabouts of the records of the Swedish colonists on the Delaware. Abstracts of these, in translation, he afterwards presented to the Historical Society of Pennsylvania, of which he was president for eight years (*Pennsylvania Magazine of History and Biography,* January 1892). The Gloria Dei Church of Philadelphia, founded by Swedish Lutherans, deeply interested him and became the beneficiary of one-third of his residuary estate. On Apr. 21, 1846, he had married Anna Dulles, who survived him. They had no children but adopted Mrs. Stillé's niece as their daughter; she died in 1896. Stillé's death occurred at Atlantic City, N. J.

[Besides Stillé's *Reminiscences* mentioned above, see *Proc. Hist. Soc. of Pa. on the Death of Charles Janeway Stillé* (1900); *Obit. Record Grads. Yale Univ.,* 1900; J. W. Jordan, *Colonial Families of Phila.* (1911), vol. II; J. B. McMaster, *The Univ. of Pa. Illustrated* (1897); G. E. Nitzsche, *Univ. of Pa.* (1916); H. M. Lippincott, *The Univ. of Pa.* (1919); *Public Ledger* (Phila.), Aug. 12, 1899.]   A. L. L.

STILLMAN, JAMES (June 9, 1850–Mar. 15, 1918), banker and capitalist, was born at Brownsville, Tex. His parents, Charles and Elizabeth Pamela (Goodrich) Stillman, both came from families long settled at Wethersfield, Conn. Thither in 1703 had gone George Stillman, the first of the line in America, who had settled in Hadley, Mass., in 1690. Charles Stillman, as a young cotton merchant, had ventured into the Rio Grande valley before the Mexican War, settling at Matamoros, Mexico, and later at Brownsville on the Texas side of the river, where he acquired large tracts of land. About 1855 or 1856 the boy was brought to Connecticut and there he got his early schooling. Before the Civil War the family settled in New York City. During the war James continued his studies in private schools at Cornwall-on-Hudson and Sing Sing (now Ossining), N. Y. At sixteen he went to work with the mercantile firm, Smith, Woodward & Stillman, of which his father had long been a member and which had traded in cotton during the war. Young Stillman consorted with older men and in particular gained much from consultation with Moses Taylor [*q.v.*], the president of the National City Bank.

Charles Stillman having been forced by impaired health to retire from business, the son early assumed many responsibilities of the family's head. On June 14, 1871, he married Sarah Elizabeth Rumrill. She bore him three sons and two daughters, all of whom survived him; separated from him in 1894, she was not mentioned in his will. In 1872 Stillman received from his father a power of attorney. He became a member of the cotton firm, which enjoyed prosperity over a long period. As his surplus gradually increased and his outside investments were expanded, he naturally formed contacts with financiers and industrialists. In the directorate of the Chicago, Milwaukee & St. Paul Railway he met William Rockefeller [q.v.], then one of the magnates of the petroleum industry. The friendship between the two men, beginning in 1884, lasted throughout Stillman's lifetime. Both of Stillman's daughters married sons of Rockefeller.

Personally known to only a few of his business associates and not at all to the general public, Stillman reached and passed his fortieth year. One of his early ambitions he had achieved; he held a directorship in the National City Bank. On the death of Moses Taylor in 1882 his son-in-law, Percy R. Pyne, had succeeded to the presidency of that institution. In his final illness Pyne's choice for his own successor was Stillman, who was promptly elected by the directors in 1891. Everything Stillman did on assuming the office indicated adherence to the code and practice of Taylor, his first mentor in finance. The bank's reserves were increased far beyond the technical requirements. Gold accumulated in its vaults and the huge surplus caught the attention of conservative business men. Deposits grew with the surplus (in a few years they more than quadrupled) and the National City rose from the second to the first rank among Wall Street institutions. While it was being built up through the application of old and tried banking principles, it became a leader in a new field, as the foremost bank in the service of the great industrial and financial combines that marked the last decade of the nineteenth century and the first of the twentieth. Early in that era of consolidation Stillman allied himself with the Standard Oil group of financiers headed by H. H. Rogers [q.v.] and William Rockefeller. In 1899 the sales of stock of the Amalgamated Copper Company and the Consolidated Gas Company of New York were both conducted by the National City, although even Wall Street gasped when a national bank engaged in such promotions. The copper operation, designed to secure a monopoly, proved disastrous and became notorious (John Moody, *The Truth about the Trusts*, 1904, pp. 3–44). Stillman also developed close relations with E. H. Harriman [q.v.] in western railroad operations. There was considerable rivalry between the Harriman-Stillman-Rockefeller-Schiff group and the Morgan-Hill combination until

1907, when a greater "community of interest" developed.

In connection with the money panic of that year, Stillman, though overshadowed in the popular mind by J. P. Morgan [q.v.], was one of the more influential leaders, being particularly notable for his advocacy of the support of weaker New York banks by the stronger. (For an interesting contrast between Stillman and Morgan, see Corey, *post*, p. 260.) Two years later he retired from the presidency of the bank, retaining the chairmanship of the board of directors, and for several years passed most of his time in France, where he was able more fully to gratify his esthetic tastes. In the World War he identified himself fully with the Allied cause, giving generously from his private fortune in support of French effort. Late in 1917 he returned to America and for a few months devoted himself to the management of the bank while its president was busy in Washington. On Mar. 15, 1918, in New York City, he died of heart disease. His estate, valued at $50,000,000, went to his family (will in *New York Times*, Mar. 24, 1918). Much had been given to public causes during his lifetime; but in the main such gifts had been successfully concealed. The man's unusual reticence and hatred of publicity may have hidden even from associates his real character. There were those who thought they detected, beneath an affected hardness of manner, a vein of emotionalism, but he gave the general impression of coldness.

[Edgar Stillman, *1654–1903, Hist. and Genealogy of George Stillman, 1st, and His Descendants* (1903), following another line, but giving information about original American ancestor; H. R. Stiles, *The Hist. of Ancient Wethersfield, Conn.* (1904), II, 667–84; Anna R. Burr, *The Portrait of a Banker: James Stillman, 1850–1918* (1927), a highly uncritical biography, reviewed by Edwin Le Fevre, in *Saturday Rev. of Literature*, Nov. 26, 1927; John Moody, *The Masters of Capital* (1919); Lewis Corey, *The House of Morgan* (1930); J. K. Winkler, *The First Billion. The Stillmans and the National City Bank* (1934), undocumented, popular, and critical; F. A. Vanderlip, "From Farm Boy to Financier," *Saturday Evening Post*, Dec. 22, 1934, Jan. 19, Mar. 30, 1935; obituaries in N. Y. newspapers, Mar. 16, 1918.]   W. B. S.

STILLMAN, SAMUEL (Feb. 27, 1737, o.s.–Mar. 12, 1807), Baptist clergyman, was born in Philadelphia, Pa. The family moved to Charleston, S. C., where Samuel attended Rind's Academy and studied theology for one year under the Rev. Oliver Hart, pastor of the Baptist church with which he had united. He was ordained on Feb. 26, 1759, and preached for two years at James Island, in the vicinity of Charleston. In May 1759 he was married to Hannah Morgan, of Philadelphia, and they had fourteen children, only two of whom survived their father. Conditions of health led him northward and for two years he lived at Bordentown, N. J., where he supplied two churches. He received the honorary degree of Master of Arts from the College of Philadelphia in 1761, and the same degree, *ad eundem,* that same year from Harvard, and from Brown in 1769. The last-named University conferred on him the degree of Doctor of Divinity in 1788.

In 1763 Stillman visited Boston, where he was engaged by the Second Baptist Church as assistant pastor. After about a year he was called to the pastorate of the First Baptist Church, a position he retained for the rest of his life. He was installed on Jan. 9, 1765, by a council to which only "orthodox," *i.e.,* Congregational, churches were invited. At that time the First Baptist Church was not in very amicable relations with other Baptist churches; but, except with the Second Church, from which a number of members withdrew to follow Stillman, better relations were soon established. He brought his church into the Warren Association and became one of the outstanding leaders in that influential organization, in spite of the facts that the first half of his pastorate was very definitely handicapped by the strained relations with the Second Baptist Church. By the time he settled in Boston he was already interested in the movement to found Rhode Island College (Brown University), and was named among the original trustees in 1764. A year later, he became a fellow of the College, retaining the position for life. He was in constant association with James Manning and Hezekiah Smith [*qq.v.*], and his influence penetrated the religious and educational interests of the Baptists of New England for forty years.

He early acquired a reputation for intellectual ability. His preaching, prevailingly Calvinistic and evangelical, was not unmindful of the application of fundamental gospel principles to the public life of the day. One of his early sermons in Boston, *Good News from a Far Country* (1766), had its inception in the repeal of the Stamp Act. The General Court invited him to preach the annual election sermon in 1779 when the most vital public concern was the policy of the constitutional convention. Stillman frankly argued the necessity of inserting in the constitution of the state a Bill of Rights and provision for the separation of church and state, since only by this procedure could the sacred rights of conscience be secured. The citizens of Boston elected him as one of their twelve delegates to the convention for the ratification of the federal Constitution, and, on the first observance of Independence Day after the institution of the new government, they requested him to preach the anniversary sermon. In 1808 his addresses were published under the title *Select Sermons on Doctrinal and Practical Subjects.* He was an active proponent of the Baptists and other dissenters in the famous Pittsfield case of 1779, but this was merely a continuation of his activities as chairman of the Baptist Committee on Grievances.

[In a funeral discourse preached by Dr. Thomas Baldwin, reference is made to Stillman's diary, but it does not seem to be extant. This discourse gives numerous biographical facts as does N. E. Wood, *The Hist. of the First Bapt. Ch. of Boston* (1899). There is a brief sketch in Stillman's *Select Sermons* (1808). David Benedict, in his *Gen. Hist. of the Bapt. Denomination* (2 vols., 1813), gives facts much used in the later sketches. See also *Hist. Cat. of Brown Univ., 1764–1914* (1914). Wm. Cathcart, ed., *The Bapt. Encyc.* (1881), adds little, but Wm. B. Sprague, *Annals Am. Pulpit,* vol. VI (1860), gives a detailed list of his published works, chiefly sermons, and personal recollections by two of his contemporaries.]   W. H. A.

STILLMAN, THOMAS BLISS (May 24, 1852–Aug. 10, 1915), chemist, educator, was born at Plainfield, N. J., the son of Dr. Charles Henry and Mary Elizabeth (Starr) Stillman. His early schooling at Plainfield was supplemented by studies at the grammar school of Madison University, Hamilton, N. Y., and at Alfred University, Alfred, N. Y. In 1870 he entered Rutgers College, from which he graduated in 1873 with the degree of B.S. He then pursued a special course in analytical chemistry at Rutgers, where he also assisted in teaching this subject.

In the spring of 1874 he was appointed chemistry assistant to Prof. A. R. Leeds of the Stevens Institute of Technology, Hoboken, and two years later went abroad to study analytical chemistry under the celebrated Dr. R. Fresenius at Wiesbaden, Germany. Here he remained two years, then, declining the offer of a position as instructor by Fresenius, returned to the United States and opened an analytical laboratory in New York City in 1879. He also became consulting chemist of the Sawyer-Mann Electric Light Company, associate editor in the science department of the *Scientific American,* and manager of the assay department of the *Mining Record.* In 1882 he resumed his connection as assistant to Professor Leeds at Stevens Institute, performing post-graduate studies for which he received the degree of Ph.D. in 1883. In 1886 he was appointed professor of analytical chemistry at Stevens and in 1902, upon the death of Professor Leeds, became head of the chemical department with the title of professor of engineering chemistry.

In addition to his work as a teacher, Stillman

conducted an outside consulting practice, serving as chemical expert to various municipalities in their water-supply problems, of which subject he had made a special study. He took also an active interest in the improvement of the milk supply of cities, and for a number of years was chemist to the Medical Milk Commission of Newark, N. J. In connection with his teaching and his consulting practice he published *Engineering Chemistry, a Manual of Quantitative Chemical Analysis for the Use of Students, Chemists and Engineers* (1897), a standard work which has gone through six editions and has long been used as a college textbook and practical treatise. In 1909 Stillman retired from his professorship at Stevens in order to devote all his time to consulting and chemical engineering practice. He became senior member of the firm of Stillman & Van Siclen, chemical experts, in New York. In 1911 he was appointed city chemist of Jersey City and Bayonne, a position which he continued to occupy until his death, four years later.

In addition to his *Engineering Chemistry,* Stillman published *Examination of Lubricating Oils* (1914) and was the author of more than thirty journal articles relating to chemical analysis and various chemical engineering subjects. He patented several processes, for manufacturing fertilizers, illuminating gas, *et cetera,* and attracted considerable attention by the "synthetic" dinner which he gave at the Hotel Astor, New York, on Feb. 21, 1906, at which he prepared many courses of the menu from synthetic products. He was a member of the American Chemical Society, American Electro-Chemical Society, American Institute of Mining Engineers, and chemical societies in Germany, Great Britain, and France. Though a man of genial disposition, he had a capacity for hard work. In 1881 he married Emma L. Pomplitz of Baltimore, Md., who survived him with three children.

[*Stevens Indicator,* Oct. 1915, with portrait and bibliog.; *Jour. Industrial and Engineering Chemistry,* Sept. 1915; B. P. Starr, *A Hist. of the Starr Family of New England* (1879); *N. Y. Times,* Aug. 11, 1915.]
C. A. B.

STILLMAN, THOMAS EDGAR (Mar. 23, 1837–Sept. 4, 1906), lawyer, was born in New York City, the son of Alfred and Elizabeth Ann (Greenough) Stillman. He successively attended public school No. 2, in New York City, the Free Academy of New York, and Alfred Academy (now Alfred University) at which latter institution he finished his secondary education and completed two years of college work. In 1857 he entered Madison College (now Colgate University), Hamilton, N. Y., where he attained a creditable scholastic record, graduating two years later. He remained in Hamilton for the next three years, studying law in the office of Joseph Mason, later county judge and member of Congress. Under the tutelage of Mason, his brother Charles Mason, who subsequently became a judge of the New York court of appeals and was then a justice of the New York supreme court, and David J. Mitchell, a prominent attorney, he received a thorough training for the profession. During this period he took part locally in Lincoln's campaign of 1860. Having been admitted to the bar in 1862, Stillman moved to New York, where, after a brief period of independent legal activity, he joined the firm of Barney, Butler & Parsons as managing clerk. Shortly afterwards he was admitted as junior partner, Barney and Parsons withdrew, and Thomas H. Hubbard [*q.v.*] joined the firm, which from 1874 until the date of Stillman's retirement in 1896, was known as Butler, Stillman & Hubbard.

Beginning his career in the field of commercial and general practice, Stillman soon began to give special attention to admiralty problems, gradually forging to the front of the admiralty bar by his able handling of important suits pertaining to this branch of jurisprudence. The first of these litigations was the case of the *Circassian* (*Fed. Cas.* No. 2723) in which he unraveled the tangled skein of legal troubles so successfully as to establish his reputation as an admiralty lawyer. Following that of the *Circassian* he took part in many maritime *causes célèbres,* some of which established new principles of American maritime law, such as those of the *Scotland* (105 *U. S.,* 24), the *Pennsylvania* (19 *Wallace,* 125), and the *Atlas* (93 *U. S.,* 302). From his admiralty practice Stillman passed into the field of corporation law, especially as it concerned railroads, and thus gravitated naturally into corporation management. This he first undertook in connection with the administration of the Mark Hopkins estate, valued in the neighborhood of $19,000,000, part of which represented substantially one-fourth ownership of the Southern Pacific Company. In fact, during his later years Stillman gradually withdrew from the practice of law to devote more time to corporate affairs, becoming president of the San Antonio & Aransas Pass Railway Company (1893–1900) and director of the Southern Pacific Company, of the United States National Bank, and of many minor companies.

From the personal standpoint Stillman appears to have led a well-rounded and active existence, passing an exceptionally happy family life with his wife, the former Charlotte Elizabeth Greenman, whom he had married on Jan. 10, 1865, and enjoying the society of a wide circle of friends. He was a man catholic in his tastes, with a wide interest in literature, art, and history,—public spirited, kindly, and charitable. Following his retirement from active business he devoted much of his time to travel, spending every summer in Europe. It was while traveling through France that he met his death as the result of injuries sustained in an automobile accident. He was survived by four daughters.

[T. H. Hubbard, "Memorial of Thomas Edgar Stillman," in *Asso. of the Bar of the City of N. Y.—1907* (1907), abridged in *Report . . . Am. Bar. Asso.,* 1908; *N. Y. Times, N. Y. Tribune,* and *World* (N.Y.), Sept. 5, 1906.]   L. M. S.

STILLMAN, WILLIAM JAMES (June 1, 1828–July 6, 1901), artist, journalist, and diplomat, was born in Schenectady, N. Y., the son of Joseph and Eliza Ward (Maxson) Stillman. After graduating from Union College in 1848, he studied landscape painting in New York during part of the next winter under Frederick Edwin Church [*q.v.*], and in December 1849 sailed for England, where, during his brief stay, he met J. M. W. Turner and began his long friendship with John Ruskin. In 1851 or 1852, after his return to America, he joined Kossuth and was sent to Hungary on a special mission, which, owing to Kossuth's incompetence in giving directions, failed. After a brief stay in France he opened a studio in New York and became art critic for the *Evening Post.* In January 1855 he founded the *Crayon: A Journal Devoted to the Graphic Arts, and the Literature Related to Them.* Although it was a literary success (numbering among its contributors James Russell Lowell), Stillman at the end of 1856 severed his connection with the paper because of financial difficulties and ill health. Through the *Crayon,* however, he had formed valuable acquaintances among the *literati* of Cambridge and Concord, and he now removed to Cambridge, where for a time he continued his landscape painting and was instrumental in forming the Adirondack Club, whose roster included the names of Emerson and Agassiz. In 1860 he was again in Europe pursuing his art and enjoying the company of Dante Gabriel Rossetti and Ruskin. Soon after the outbreak of the Civil War he became American consul at Rome (appointment confirmed, Feb. 19, 1862), where he and his wife, Laura Mack, whom he had married on Nov. 19, 1860, lived until 1865. At that time he received a consular appointment to Crete, and there soon found himself in the midst of the Cretan insur-

rection of 1866. He at once sided with the Cretans, but by his kindness to the natives he so incurred the enmity of the pasha that his own life and that of his family were much endangered. By 1868 the strain had become so great that he abandoned the consulate and removed to Athens, where his wife died the following year. He soon settled in London. For the next few years he engaged in literary pursuits. In 1871 he married Marie Spartali, daughter of the Greek consul-general in London. In 1875 he set out for Herzegovina, then on the point of insurrection, as a volunteer correspondent for the London *Times,* and he soon extended his activities into Montenegro and Albania. He spent much of his remaining life in the employ of the *Times* as a special correspondent, with his residence in Rome. In 1898 he retired on a pension and removed to Surrey, where three years later he died.

As a landscape painter, he had quite exhausted his enthusiasm by 1860, although during the ten preceding years he exhibited pictures at the National Academy and was elected an associate of that body in 1854. The critical influence of Ruskin, whom he regarded with utmost reverence, seems in a measure to have run counter to Stillman's native artistic bent and may have helped to silence his genius. But his ultimate abandonment of painting was probably due to the fact, as he himself hints, that his theoretic knowledge of his art surpassed his executive ability. His literary work reflects both his honesty and versatility. Of himself he once wrote that he had never published a book except from a desire to contribute to human knowledge. For *Old Italian Masters Engraved by Timothy Cole* (1892) he wrote the biographical and descriptive material; and for *Venus & Apollo in Painting and Sculpture* (1897), a series of handsome reproductions from photographs, he produced an introduction and notes. His interest in art and archaeology found further expression in *The Acropolis of Athens* (1870), a splendid group of illustrations from photographs taken by Stillman himself; in *On the Track of Ulysses* (1888); in the *Report of W. J. Stillman on the Cesnola Collection* (1885); and in letters appended to the first and second annual reports of the Archaeological Institute of America. Many autobiographical data went into the making of such historical works as *The Cretan Insurrection of 1866-7-8* (1874), *Herzegovina and the Late Uprising* (1877), *The Union of Italy, 1815–1895* (1898), and *Francesco Crispi: Insurgent, Exile, Revolutionist, and Statesman* (1899). As an essayist he is to be remembered as the author of *Poetic Localities of Cambridge* (1876) and

The Old Rome and the New and Other Studies
(1898). His love of animals, of whose immortality he was firmly convinced, was responsible
for two charming narratives, *Billy and Hans*
(1897) and *Little Bertha* (1898). In 1901 appeared *The Autobiography of a Journalist.*

An innate spirit of inquiry led him ever to seek
fresh fields of thought as well as endeavor. Hostile in early life to the teachings of evolution, he
ultimately accepted the scientific creed of Darwin. And he so far freed himself from the dogmas of Calvinism as fully to accept the tenets of
Spiritualism, although deprecating the professional medium. "Perhaps his material prosperity and success might have been more signal,"
wrote the London *Times* when he died, "had his
tastes and gifts been fewer. Certainly his life
would have been less full, and the man less engaging."

[W. J. Stillman, *The Autobiog. of a Journalist* (2
vols., 1901); *Who's Who in America,* 1899–1900;
Sophie S. Martin, *Mack Geneal.* (1903), vol. I; cats.
of the exhibitions of the Nat. Acad. of Design, 1851–
58; C. E. Norton, ed., *Letters of James Russell Lowell*
(2 vols., 1894), *passim;* H. E. Scudder, *James Russell
Lowell* (2 vols., 1901), *passim;* obituaries in *Evening
Post* (N. Y.), July 8, and *Times* (London), July 9,
1901.]   N. F. A.

STILWELL, SILAS MOORE (June 6,
1800–May 16, 1881), lawyer and writer on financial topics, was born in New York City, the
fifth of six children of Stephen and Nancy
(Moore) Stilwell. He was descended from
Nicholas Stillwell [*sic*], who was in Manhattan as early as 1645 and may have been in Virginia previously. Stephen Stilwell, a merchant
and veteran of the Revolution, moved his family
in 1804 to Glasco, Ulster County, N. Y., where
he bought a glass factory and iron foundry.
After investing heavily in Western lands, he
went bankrupt in 1810. Silas entered Woodstock Free Academy, but left at the age of
twelve to become a clerk in a New York hardware store. Two years later he went West to
work with land surveyors. At twenty-two he
was a member of the Tennessee legislature, soon
afterward moved to Virginia, and in 1824 was
admitted to the bar. He practised successfully
for several years and served as member of the
House of Burgesses. In 1828 he returned to
New York where he continued his political activities. Elected in 1829 to the Assembly on
the National Republican ticket, he served three
terms, 1830–33. The demands of the new Workingman's Party enlisted his sympathy, particularly the abolition of imprisonment for debt. On
this issue, says Thurlow Weed (*post*), Stilwell
staked his political future, and as a result of his
efforts the Stilwell Act, abolishing the penalty,

was passed in 1831. In 1834 he ran, unsuccessfully, for lieutenant-governor on the ticket headed by William H. Seward [*q.v.*]. Two years
later, as candidate for alderman in New York
City he was successful and as chairman of an
evenly divided board he exercised great authority in appointments.

Banking reform next attracted him. Disapproval of Jackson's withdrawal of government
deposits from the Bank of the United States
caused Stilwell to break with his party and join
the Whigs. On his interest in the revision of
banking laws in New York State has been based
the claim that he was the author of the Free
Banking Law of 1838. A pamphlet which he
published at this time, however, *A System of
Credit for a Republic, and the Plan of a Bank
for the State of New-York* (1838), shows that
what he had in mind was radically different from
the plan adopted. The election of Harrison to
the presidency brought Stilwell into touch with
national politics. He is said to have refused a
cabinet post because of his large losses in the
panic of 1837, but President Tyler appointed him
United States marshal for the southern district
of New York in 1841 and sent him on a special
mission to The Hague.

Stilwell's claim to authorship of the National
Banking Act is not recognized by historians of
American banking. During 1861 and 1862 he
was in Washington, where he was in close contact with Secretary Salmon P. Chase [*q.v.*] and
with Edward Jordan, solicitor of the treasury.
He prepared a pamphlet, published by the government, *A System of National Finance: Notes
Explanatory of Mr. Chase's Plan of National
Finance* (1861), and worked with Jordan on a
preliminary draft of the banking bill, but his
contribution to the Act as it finally emerged
seems to have been less important than that of
Elbridge Gerry Spaulding [*q.v.*] and Samuel
Hooper (Helderman, *post,* pp. 136–42). From
1861 to 1872 he wrote articles on financial topics for the *New York Herald* under the pseudonym Jonathan Oldbuck. He published in 1866
a lecture, *National Finances: A Philosophical
Examination of Credit,* and in 1879, *Private History of the Origin and Purpose of the National
Banking Law.* In later life he changed parties a
second time, becoming again a stanch Democrat.
A romantic episode in his career was his courtship of Caroline Norsworthy, the daughter of a
rich New York merchant and landowner, whom
he married in defiance of parental wishes. She
brought him a considerable fortune and with
what he had himself acquired he was regarded
at one time as a rich man. He had four children,

three of whom survived him. After his wife's death he became deeply interested in Spiritualism and prepared the manuscript of a book in its defense. He died in New York City.

[Dewitt and Lamont Stilwell, *Hist. and Geneal. Record of One Branch of the Stilwell Family* (1914); J. E. Stilwell, *The Hist. of Lieut. Nicholas Stilwell* (1929) and *The Hist. of Capt. Nicholas Stilwell and His Descendants* (1930); D. S. Alexander, *A Pol. Hist. of the State of N. Y.*, vol. I (1906); F. W. Seward, *Autobiog. of Wm. H. Seward . . . with a Memoir of His Life* (1877); *Autobiog. of Thurlow Weed* (1883), ed. by H. A. Weed; *A Report of Two Interviews with the Hon. Silas M. Stilwell* (1874); A. M. Davis, "The Origin of the National Banking System," in *Reports of the National Monetary Commission*, vol. XXXV (1910), being *Sen. Doc. 582*, 61 Cong., 2 Sess.; L. C. Helderman, *National and State Banks* (1931); *N. Y. Herald*, May 17, 1881.]   P. W. B.

STILWELL, SIMPSON EVERETT (Aug. 25, 1849–Feb. 17, 1903), scout, peace officer, best known as "Jack" Stilwell, was born in Tennessee, the son of William and Clara Stilwell. While he was still a youth the family moved to Missouri and afterward to eastern Kansas. At the age of fourteen he left school and joined a wagontrain for Santa Fé, and for several years remained in New Mexico. On June 18, 1867, at Fort Dodge, Kan., he engaged for his first service as a scout, and on Aug. 28, 1868, he joined Maj. G. A. Forsyth's company of fifty scouts, operating from Fort Wallace in search of hostile Indians. On Sept. 17, on the Arikaree Fork of the Republican River, this company was suddenly surrounded by a force of 900 Cheyennes and Sioux, under Roman Nose, and a desperate battle followed, continuing until the arrival of a relief force eight days later. On the first night, Stilwell, with a companion, crept through the hostile cordon, and three days later reached Fort Wallace with the news. For this exploit he became famous. During the next thirteen years, enrolled under the names Simpson E. Stilwell, J. E. Stilwell, and Jack Stilwell, he was irregularly employed as a scout, serving under Custer, Miles, Mackenzie and others, and was often detailed to exceptionally hazardous ventures. His scouting service ended on Jan. 22, 1881. On hearing that his brother Frank, who had become an outlaw in Arizona, had been shot to death by Marshal Wyatt Earp at Tucson in March 1882, he started for the scene to avenge the killing, but it seems that on learning the facts of the case he quietly returned.

For a time he was a United States deputy marshal at the Cheyenne-Arapaho agency, in the present Oklahoma. On the opening of Indian territory to settlement, he made his home at El Reno, where he was elected a police judge. In 1894 he was appointed a United States commissioner, with station at Anadarko, and was re-appointed in 1897. In the meantime he had studied law and had been admitted to the bar. His health failing, he resigned his post on Nov. 10, 1898, and accepted an invitation from William F. Cody [*q.v.*] to move to the new town of Cody, Wyo. On Jan. 14, 1899, he was again appointed a United States commissioner. He was cared for in his last years on the ranch of "Buffalo Bill," and died at Cody. He had been married, at Braddock, Pa., on May 6, 1895, to Esther Hannah White, who survived him. In his scouting days he was slight and lithe, though later he became somewhat corpulent. His intelligence, daring, and resourcefulness are highly praised by all his commanders. He had an excellent command of Spanish and a workable knowledge of most of the languages of the plains Indians. He was modest in manner, and, as a rule, reticent of speech.

[J. E. Stilwell, *Hist. of Capt. Jeremiah Stilwell . . .* (1931), vol. IV of the *Stilwell Geneal.*; G. A. Custer, *My Life on the Plains* (1874); G. A. Forsyth, *Thrilling Days in Army Life* (1900); N. A. Miles, *Personal Recollections* (1896); R. G. Carter, *The Old Sergeant's Story* (1926); D. L. Spotts, *Campaigning with Custer* (1928); H. W. Wheeler, *Buffalo Days* (1925); service record from the Quartermaster-General's Office; information from his widow, Mrs. Carl Hammitt, Cody, Wyo., and from Dan W. Peery, Oklahoma City; *N. Y. Herald*, Sept. 21, 1902.]   W. J. G.

STIMPSON, WILLIAM (Feb. 14, 1832–May 26, 1872), naturalist, was born in Roxbury, Mass., the son of Herbert H. and Mary Ann (Brewster) Stimpson. His early education was in the common schools of Boston, and in his sixteenth year he entered the upper class of the Boston High School, from which he was graduated in July 1848. At an early age William became interested in natural history. The possession of a copy of *Report on the Invertebrata of Massachusetts* (1841), presented to him by the author, Augustus A. Gould [*q.v.*], laid the foundation for a strong friendship between the distinguished conchologist and the young naturalist, and this connection brought him to the notice of Jean Louis Rodolphe Agassiz [*q.v.*], from whom he received great encouragement. His parents were desirous that he should go into business and his excursions to the seashore and other nature pursuits were looked upon as a waste of time. As a compromise he was permitted to study civil engineering, but his employer reported that he was more interested in hunting land snails than in surveying, and advised that the boy be permitted to enter upon a career more in accord with his inclinations. Accordingly, he was allowed to enter the Boston Latin School in 1848. The following summer he went on a fishing smack to Grand Manan, collecting and studying the marine animals of that region and later was associated with the workers in Agassiz's laboratory. Through the aid of friends he received an appointment as naturalist to the North Pacific Exploring Expedition in 1852, and all parental opposition to his career as a naturalist was finally removed. He spent four years with the expedition, and returned to the United States in 1856 to begin the classification of the immense amount of material gathered during these fruitful years. His headquarters were in the Smithsonian Institution, Washington, D. C. Nine years were thus occupied, in the course of which he visited Europe to collect comparative data, making many friends among European scientists. The results of his work were published in 1907 as volume XLIX of the *Smithsonian Miscellaneous Collections.*

Stimpson was called to the directorship of the Chicago Academy of Sciences in 1865 by his friend, Robert Kennicott [*q.v.*], while the latter was away upon the expedition to Alaska and the Yukon from which he never returned. Here, in a new building believed to be fire-proof, Stimpson assembled his great collection of manuscripts, drawings, and material loaned by institutions and collectors from many parts of the world. The Smithsonian collections, those of Louis François de Pourtalès [*q.v.*], and specimens from many eastern naturalists, were placed at his disposal. Priceless volumes in large number were loaned for his study, and manuscripts in preparation as well as some ready for publication were here assembled. It is probable that, previous to this time, no single depository contained as much valuable scientific material as did the Chicago Academy of Sciences in the latter part of 1871, when, in the great fire of October, the building and its treasures were destroyed. All that was left of William Stimpson's life work were some pieces of mound-builder pottery. From this tragic blow he never recovered. He had long been a sufferer from weakness of the lungs and his attempt to study the Gulf Stream with the Coast Survey in 1871–72 completely broke his health. He died at Ilchester, Md., scarcely eight months after his loss through the Chicago fire.

Stimpson's works were written in Latin, a noteworthy accomplishment in his day. He published many papers on mollusca and crustacea, among them being *A Revision and Synonymy of the Testaceous Mollusks of New England* (1851), *The Crustacea and Echinodermata of the Pacific Shores of North America* (1857); *Notes on North American Crustacea* (1859); *Prodomus Descriptionis Animalium Evertebratorum* (1857–60); *Researches upon the Hydro-*

biinæ and Allied Forms, Smithsonian Miscellaneous Collections, vol. VII (1865). He was honored by membership in the National Academy of Sciences in 1868, and in many other scientific societies, both at home and abroad. At his death he was survived by his wife, Annie Gordon, of Ilchester, Md., to whom he had been married on July 28, 1864, and several children.

[W. H. Dall, "Some American Conchologists," *Proc. of the Biological Soc. of Washington,* vol. IV (1888); *Proc. Chicago Acad. Sci.,* 1872; *Am. Naturalist,* vol. VI (1872); *Chicago Tribune,* June 12, 1872.]

F. C. B.

STIMSON, ALEXANDER LOVETT (Dec. 14, 1816–Jan. 2, 1906), expressman and author, was born in Boston, Mass., the son of Lovett and Sally (Fisher) Stimson. His father was a dancing master. Little is known of Stimson's early youth, but in 1840 he was in Georgia, working as a rodman on the survey of the Georgia Railroad under his elder brother, John K. Stimson, a civil engineer. During his stay in Georgia he studied law. Now and then in those earlier years he had a try at the newspaper business—in New York, in Boston, and in New Orleans—but did not remain in it for long periods. It gave him an itch for writing, however, and throughout life he produced articles and stories in large numbers for various periodicals. In 1846 he took a position as clerk in the New York office of Adams & Company, an express company, and this determined his future career. In 1850 he and his brother John launched an express line of their own, Stimson and Company's New Orleans and Mobile Express, operating by steamboat from New York to New Orleans and Mobile, but it was soon absorbed by Adams & Company.

In 1852 Stimson founded a magazine devoted to this youthful business, the *Express Messenger,* the first journal of its kind, and operated it as proprietor and editor for several years. It was during this period that he manifested his greatest literary activity. He wrote a history of the Mercantile Library Association of Boston and his two longest pieces of fiction, *Easy Nat; or The Three Apprentices* (1854), later republished as *New England Boys* (1856), and *Waifwood* (1864), a novel. In 1858 first appeared the work by which he is best known, his *History of the Express Companies: and the Origin of American Railroads.* It reappeared in 1881, largely rewritten, as *History of the Express Business, Including the Origin of the Railway System in America, and the Relation of Both to the Increase of New Settlements and the Prosperity of Cities in the United States.* His idea, originated in 1851, that express companies might act as purchasing agents, led to the development of order and commission departments in express companies. During the Civil War he served as representative of the Adams Express Company at various places in the South. Later he was with Wells Fargo & Company and the American Express Company. For several years in the latter part of his life he was attorney for the National Express Company. During this time he continued to write frequent articles for newspapers and express periodicals. His wife was Mary Jerome of Syracuse, N. Y., whom he married in New York City in 1844. She died in 1881. Stimson died in 1906 at Glens Falls, New York, where he had been living for six years. He was survived by one son.

[See *Express Gazette*, Jan. 1881, Jan. 15, 1906; Stimson's *Hist. of the Express Business* (1881), which contains a number of references to his own career; and obituary in *Glens Falls Morning Post*, Jan. 3, 1906. His death is recorded in the Vital Statistics Bureau, Albany, N. Y. Information has been supplied by the American Antiquarian Society.]   A. F. H.

STIMSON, LEWIS ATTERBURY (Aug. 24, 1844–Sept. 17, 1917), surgeon, was born in Paterson, N. J., the son of Henry Clark and Julia Maria (Atterbury) Stimson. On his father's side he was descended from John Stimson who emigrated from England and settled in Watertown, Mass., in 1635; on his mother's from Elias Boudinot, 1740–1821 [*q.v.*]. When he was barely fifteen he entered Yale College, the baby of his class. After graduation in 1863, he visited Europe. In 1864 he entered the Union army as a captain and rendered excellent service, but was invalided home near the end of the war with a severe typhoid fever that nearly ended his career. He soon entered his father's banking office, becoming a member of the New York stock exchange. On Nov. 9, 1866, in Paris, France, he married Candace T. Wheeler, daughter of Thomas M. Wheeler of New York. Having acquired a keen taste for a scientific life he began to study medicine in 1871, for the most part in Paris but with a year in the Bellevue Hospital Medical School, where he took the degree of M.D. in 1874. He then began practice in New York. In 1875 he won the James Wood prize with a paper entitled *Bacteria and Their Influence upon the Origin and Development of Septic Complications of Wounds* (1875), which showed the influence of his association with Louis Pasteur in Paris. In 1876, appointed visiting surgeon to the Presbyterian Hospital, he was one of the first in America to use antiseptics and to operate by the Lister spray method. He became visiting surgeon to Bellevue Hospital in 1879. He was professor of physiology (1883–85), professor of

anatomy (1885–89), and professor of surgery (1889–98) in the Medical College of the University of the City of New York (later New York University). In 1898 he became professor of surgery in the Cornell University Medical College, a position he held until his death. With Dr. William Mecklenburg Polk he was instrumental in founding this college and in securing an endowment and a building from Oliver Hazard Payne [*qq.v.*], his friend and classmate at Yale. In 1889 he resigned from the Presbyterian Hospital to become surgeon to the New York Hospital and its Chambers Street branch, where he gained much of his experience in traumatic surgery that formed the basis of his best-known book, *A Practical Treatise on Fractures and Dislocations* (1899), a classic in the subject. He also published *A Manual of Operative Surgery* (1878); *Clinical Lectures on Surgery* (1878), from the French of Léon Gosselin; *The Growth of a People, a Short Study in French History* (1883), from the French of Paul Lacombe; and edited *The Principles of Surgery and Surgical Pathology* (1894), from the German of Hermann Tillmanns. He was a much-admired and respected teacher. He was regent of the state of New York, 1893–1904, a member of the Société de Chirurgie of Paris, a founder of the New York Surgical Society, and a member of the New York Academy of Medicine.

The death of his wife, by whom he had a son and a daughter, occurred early in his surgical career (June 1876). Overwhelmed by this loss, he survived it "by years of constant grinding work." Sailing his 87–foot schooner yacht, *Fleur-de-Lys*, which he used for trips to Norway, Iceland, Labrador, and the Mediterranean, was his keenest pleasure. In *The Cruise of the Fleur-de-Lys in the Ocean Race* (1905) he describes the race for the Kaiser's Cup, in which he came in seventh at Falmouth. He was a man of fine presence and strong personality, and his reserve and self-restraint, once penetrated, showed a warm friendly nature. His convictions were clear and strongly held and expressed; he fought his opponents hard, but without venom or malice. On Sept. 17, 1917, he was out on the Shinnecock Hills, near his summer home, in full vigor, when death overtook him suddenly.

[L. E. and A. L. de Forrest, *The Descendants of Job Atterbury* (1933); F. A. Virkus and A. N. Marquis, *The Abridged Compendium of Am. Geneal.*, vol. I (1925); *Who's Who in America*, 1916–17; *Obit. Record Grads. Yale Univ.* (1918); E. L. Keyes, in *Civil War Memories of Lewis A. Stimson* (1918); D. B. Delavan, *Early Days of the Presbyterian Hospital, New York* (priv. printed, 1926); *Surgery, Gynecology, and Obstetrics*, Apr. 1927; and obituary in *N. Y. Times*, Sept. 18, 1917.]   G. W.

STINESS, JOHN HENRY (Aug. 9, 1840–
Sept. 6, 1913), jurist, was born in Providence,
R. I., the son of Philip Bessom and Mary
(Marsh) Stiness. His grandfather, Samuel
Stiness of Marblehead, is said to have fought
in the Revolution and later to have taken part in
the War of 1812. His father was a manufacturer
of screws. He received his education in Providence at the old University Grammar School,
and in Brown University, 1857–59. For two
years he taught grammar school, intending to
return to college, but when the Civil War began
he enlisted in the Union army. Appointed second lieutenant in the 2nd New York Artillery,
he served a year and a half, part of the time as
adjutant, and also as judge advocate. He was
discharged because of illness in November 1862.
Since a boyhood experience as page in the Rhode
Island General Assembly, he had made up his
mind to become a lawyer. Without returning to
the university to finish his course, in January
1863 he began the study of law in the office of a
Providence firm. In 1865 he was admitted to the
bar and made marked progress from the start.
He was married on Nov. 19, 1868, to Maria Williams, and had a son and a daughter, both of
whom survived him. In 1874 he became a Republican member of the state House of Representatives, and was chairman of the committee
to appoint a successor to the retiring Senator
William Sprague of Rhode Island. In the long-
continued contest which resulted in the election
of Gen. Ambrose E. Burnside he played an active part. On Apr. 13, 1875, he was elected a
member of the supreme court of Rhode Island,
an office which he occupied with distinction for
twenty-nine years, twenty-five years as associate, and four as chief justice. His retirement
from the bench occurred in 1904. That same
year he became Republican nominee for representative in Congress, but was defeated in a
close election.

Outside his legal activities, he had many interests. He was particularly devoted to the concerns of the Episcopal Church of Rhode Island
and served it in various capacities. An authority
on canon law, he acted as counsel for the church,
notably so in the trial of Algernon Sidney Crap-
sey [*q.v.*] for heresy. In 1897 he was appointed
by the governor on a commission to revise the
state constitution, and, since that formidable task
dragged on, was again appointed to a similar
commission in 1912. He was awarded two honorary degrees by Brown University, and in 1897
he was elected a fellow. A lover of books and a
keen student of history, he collected a fine library, and was the author of various articles and
pamphlets on law and Rhode Island history.
Among the better known are *Two Centuries of
Liquor Legislation in Rhode Island* (1882), *A
Century of Lotteries in Rhode Island* (1896),
and *Civil Changes in the State* (1897). He was
a ready, effective speaker and a genial raconteur. His outstanding characteristic was his
extraordinary quickness and clarity of thought.
His success on the bench was largely due to his
ability to strip a case of its confusing features
and to penetrate swiftly to the essential issues.
The same clearness of expression was evident
in his writing.

[See *Who's Who in America*, 1912–13; *Proc. R. I.
Hist. Soc. 1913–14* (1914); *The Biog. Cyc. of Repre-
sentative Men of R. I.* (1881), p. 566; *Providence
Daily Jour.*, Oct. 11, 1904; obituary in *Providence
Sunday Jour.*, Sept. 7, 1913. His opinions as judge
are to be found in 11–26 *R. I. Reports*.]   E. R. B.

STIRLING, LORD WILLIAM [See ALEX-
ANDER, WILLIAM, 1726–1783].

STITH, WILLIAM (1707–Sept. 19, 1755),
historian, minister, and third president of the
College of William and Mary, was born in Virginia, the son of Capt. John Stith of Charles
City County and Mary (Randolph) Stith, the
daughter of William Randolph of "Turkey Isl-
and," Henrico County, and the grand-daughter
of William Randolph [*q.v.*]. After attending the
grammar school attached to William and Mary,
of which his mother had become matron following her husband's death, he matriculated at
Queen's College, Oxford, on May 21, 1724. There
he is entered on the register as seventeen years
old and, by an error, the son of John Stith "of the
Virgin Islands." On Feb. 27, 1727/28 he received his B.A. degree from the university, was
ordained a minister of the established church,
and on Apr. 12, 1731, having received the King's
Bounty for clergymen to Virginia, returned to
Williamsburg. "The Visitors and Governors of
the College" elected him master of the grammar
school, Oct. 25, 1731, and the next day he qualified for the office by assenting to the Thirty-nine
Articles and by taking the customary oath *de
fideli administratione*. Concomitantly with this
position, he acted as chaplain to the House of
Burgesses. Several of his sermons before that
body were published at its request, *A Sermon
Preached Before the General Assembly* (1745/
46), *The Sinfulness and Pernicious Nature of
Gaming* (1752), and *The Nature and Extent of
Christ's Redemption* (1753). In July 1736, supported by indorsements from Governor Gooch
and Commissary Blair, he was called to the
charge of Henrico Parish, in Henrico County,
where he remained for sixteen years, marrying

Stith

meanwhile, on July 13, 1738, his first cousin Judith, the daughter of Thomas Randolph of "Tuckahoe," Henrico County, by whom he had three daughters.

In his leisure hours at the glebe near Varina he composed the only completed portion of his *History of the First Discovery and Settlement of Virginia* (Williamsburg, 1747; London, 1753), the earliest important secondary account of the colony from its beginnings through 1624 and one that has influenced most subsequent interpretations of the history of Virginia under the London Company. Although drawing upon John Smith's and Beverley's narratives for parts of his own—Smith's writings he considered "confused," but "of unquestionable Authority, for what is related, whilst he staid in the Country" (preface)—Stith, with systematic scholarship, likewise scrutinized the official records of the company, which were made accessible to him by William Byrd, and the public papers collected by his uncle, Sir John Randolph. His sympathies are strongly with the Sandys-Southampton faction in their defense of the company's chartered rights against the "arbitrary Proceedings and unjust Designs" (*Ibid.*) of James I; but as his case is built around the partisan and somewhat varnished Virginia court minutes his findings are necessarily one-sided. Significant and penetrating, nevertheless, is his consciousness of the importance of Virginia's early history and traditions, while his sturdy outspokenness against regal usurpations is an earnest of the developing spirit of American independence.

Late in 1751, having been chosen minister of St. Ann's, he resigned from his Henrico pastorate; but before his resignation became effective he succeeded his brother-in-law William Dawson as president of the College of William and Mary and qualified on Aug. 14, 1752. As a consequence of his having opposed Governor Dinwiddie's pistole levy for land grants, he was not appointed commissary to the Bishop of London and member of the governor's council as his predecessors had been. During his presidency, however, he served also as minister of York-Hampton parish, in York County. His brief administration was uneventful, save for the meeting of the clergy at the college in 1754, which resulted in providing a fund for the families of deceased clergymen.

[L. G. Tyler, *Williamsburg* (1907); W. F. Craven, *Dissolution of the Virginia Company* (1932); *William and Mary College Quart.*, esp. Apr. 1897, p. 244, Oct. 1898, pp. 99, 123, Jan. 1913, p. 185; L. W. Burton, *Annals of Henrico Parish* (1904), ed. by J. S. Moore; *Alumni Oxonienses* (1888), ed. by Joseph Foster, vol. IV.]   A. C. G., Jr.

Stobo

STOBO, ROBERT (1727–*c.* 1772), soldier, was born and reared in Glasgow, the sole heir of William Stobo, a merchant. His mother was the daughter of James Mitchell of Balmore, descended from the family of the earls of Montrose. Stobo is said to have entered the University of Glasgow (*Memoirs, post,* p. 14), but after a brief time emigrated to Virginia where, as a merchant, he enjoyed the patronage of Governor Dinwiddie, and as a genial member of society gained considerable personal popularity. A captain in the Virginia militia, he fought with Washington at Fort Necessity, July 3, 1754, and was held as a hostage by the French under the terms of capitulation which were later violated by both parties. Convinced that he was no longer on parole, he dispatched secretly by Indians two letters to Washington containing a map and a description of Fort DuQuesne and urging immediate attack. The letters were carelessly circulated, and the French, hearing of their contents, refused to release Stobo and confined him in Quebec. One of his letters was captured by the French in Braddock's baggage, whereupon Stobo was tried for treason and on Nov. 8, 1755, sentenced to be executed. This sentence was never confirmed, however, and after several unsuccessful attempts he succeeded in escaping, with Lieut. Simon Stevens and others. After a hazardous thirty-eight days' flight down the Saint Lawrence River during April, May, and June 1759, he reached the British forces at Louisbourg. He immediately joined the expedition against Quebec, and from July 10 until Sept. 7, when he returned to General Amherst with dispatches, he ably assisted Wolfe, leading the attack on Pointe aux Trembles, and pointing out the Foulon where Wolfe later landed for the ascent to the Plains of Abraham.

In November he returned to Virginia, there to receive a vote of thanks of the House of Burgesses, a gift of £1,000, and his back pay as a major—a commission voted him while he was a prisoner in Canada (*Journals of the House of Burgesses of Virginia, 1758–1761,* 1908, pp. 150–52). After a brief visit to England, he returned to join Amherst, who on Pitt's recommendation commissioned him a captain in the 15th Regiment of Foot with which he served until 1770 in Canada, the West Indies, the Lake region, and England. On June 4, 1767, he purchased land on Lake Champlain apparently with the intention of settling there. He returned with his regiment to England, however, in July 1768, and before the end of August had made the acquaintance of Tobias Smollett, who wrote a very generous letter recommending him to David

Hume (E. S. Noyes, *The Letters of Tobias Smollett, M.D.*, 1926, pp. 103–04). After 1770 his name disappeared from the Army List. About this time, Washington made repeated efforts to find him, in order to purchase his claim to 9,000 acres of land on the Ohio River, due him as land bounty for military services. In the absence of records, it may be conjectured either that Stobo died in England or that he returned to America, settling on Lake Champlain or on the Little Kanawha River in what is now West Virginia.

Although Stobo played no large rôle in the events in which he participated, his adventurous career has formed a basis for romantic narrative. Some years after his death, *Memoirs of Major Robert Stobo of the Virginia Regiment* (1800) was published in London. In Sir Gilbert Parker's *The Seats of the Mighty* (1896), he appears as Robert Moray (Robert Stobo in the first version, a serial in the *Atlantic Monthly,* beginning March 1895); and he was probably the model for Tobias Smollett's great Scotch character Lismahago in *The Expedition of Humphry Clinker* (1771).

[*Memoirs of Major Robert Stobo* (1854), ed. by N. B. Craig, a reprint of the London edition of 1800, often incorrect; B. M. Nead, *Some Hidden Sources of Fiction* (1909); J. C. Fitzpatrick, *The Writings of George Washington*, vols. I, III (1931); S. M. Hamilton, *Letters to Washington and Accompanying Papers*, vols. I (1898), III (1901); E. B. O'Callaghan, *Docs. Rel. to the Colonial Hist. of the State of N. Y.*, vol. X (1858); *Rapport de l'Archiviste de la Province de Québec*, 1920–21, 1922–23, 1923–24, 1924–25, 1928–29; *Bulletin des Recherches Historiques* (Lévis), Oct. 1903, May–June 1908, Dec. 1925; *An Hist. Jour. of the Campaigns in North America for the Years 1757 . . . 1760 by Capt. John Knox* (3 vols., 1914–16), ed. by A. G. Doughty; *Journal du Marquis de Montcalm . . . de 1756 à 1759* (1895), ed. by H. R. Casgrain; *A Jour. of Lieut. Simon Stevens* (1760); J. M. Le Moine, *Maple Leaves* (Quebec), 4 ser. (1873), 6 ser. (1894), 7 ser. (1906); Stobo's letters describing Fort Duquesne in *Minutes of the Provincial Council of Pa.*, VI (1851), 141–43, 161–63; and his map in *Pa. Archives*, II (1853), 146.]   G. M. K.

STOCKBRIDGE, HENRY (Sept. 18, 1856–Mar. 22, 1924), jurist, the descendant of John Stockbridge who emigrated from England about 1635 and settled in Scituate, Mass., and son of Henry Smith Stockbridge [*q.v.*] and Fanny E. (Montague) Stockbridge, was born in Baltimore, Md., and was always identified with that city. He was the nephew of Levi Stockbridge and the cousin of Horace Edward Stockbridge [*qq.v.*]. He went to OverLea School near Catonsville, to Williston Seminary, Easthampton, Mass., and graduated from Amherst College in 1877. He received the LL.B. degree from the law school of the University of Maryland the following year. The succeeding January he was taken into partnership in his father's law office and remained in active practice until his eleva-

tion to the bench. In 1882 he received the appointment as examiner in equity in the Baltimore courts and served six years. He also found time for some political writing for the *Morning Herald* in 1882–83 and during 1887–88 for editorial articles for the *Baltimore American.* He was married on Jan. 5, 1882, to Helen M. Smith of Hadley, Mass. They had two sons. In 1888 he won the congressional seat from Isidor Rayner [*q.v.*] after a stubborn fight, in which, for the first time since the Civil War, the Republicans of Baltimore City elected a representative to Congress, and he served one term. He was a member of the state Republican committee for two years and gave his advice in the formulation of party strategy during the nineties. He accepted the position of commissioner of immigration for Baltimore from 1891 to 1893, a non-salaried position involving the organization of the service. In 1896 he became associate judge of the supreme bench of Baltimore. In April 1911 the Democratic governor, Austin Crothers, appointed him to the court of appeals, and the following fall he was elected with virtually no opposition. Failing health prevented the completion of his fifteen-year term, and he withdrew from active work in December 1923. His opinions from the bench (*Md. Reports,* 115–45) reveal the extent of his legal erudition, his perception of justice, his capacity for clarity of statement and for logical application of the rules of law and evidence —qualities that have made them a guide for other jurists. His associates recognized in him the sturdiness, energy, thrift, and conscientiousness characteristic of his New England strain, while his deep conservatism aroused the antagonisms of organized labor.

His judicial duties did not debar him from manifold other activities. He lectured at the University of Maryland from 1899 to 1914; he served as regent of the university from 1907 to 1920, as president of the board of trustees of the endowment fund from 1905 to his death, and as provost for a brief period in 1912. Trustee of Enoch Pratt Free Library for many years, member of innumerable learned societies, he was particularly active in patriotic organizations. He directed the efforts of the Society of the Sons of the American Revolution to the Americanization of immigrants, himself preparing an excellent handbook on the subject. Under congressional charter he became one of the incorporators and chairman of the Maryland branch of the Red Cross. He served with such distinction as a member from Maryland on the commission on uniform state laws that he was made president from 1920 to 1922. He had a long and useful connection with the Maryland Historical Society. For many years active in the Congregational Church, he withdrew his membership and became a member of the Presbyterian Church.

[Scrapbook in possession of his wife; M. P. Andrews, *Tercentenary Hist. of Md.* (1925), vol. III; E. F. Cordell, *Univ. of Md.* (2 vols., 1907); L. R. Meekins, *Men of Mark in Md.* (1910), vol. II; C. H. Forrest, *Official Hist. of the Fire Department of . . . Baltimore* (1898); *Md. Hist. Mag.*, June 1924; *Biog. Record of the Alumni . . . of Amherst College*, vol. II (1901), ed. by W. L. Montague; *Report of the Eighteenth Ann. Meeting of the Am. Bar Asso.* (1895); J. M. Smith, *Hist. of . . . Sunderland, Mass.* (1899); *Minute Man*, June 1924; *Baltimore American*, Mar. 23, 1924; *Sun* (Baltimore), Mar. 12, 1911, Mar. 23, 1924.]   E. L.

STOCKBRIDGE, HENRY SMITH (Aug. 31, 1822–Mar. 11, 1895), lawyer, was born in North Hadley, Mass., the brother of Levi Stockbridge [*q.v.*] and the son of Abigail (Montague) and Jason Stockbridge, a farmer of considerable wealth and a man of sufficient influence to serve in the state legislature in 1835 and 1836. He was the descendant of John Stockbridge who emigrated from England about 1635 and settled in Scituate, Mass. After spending his early years on the farm, the boy entered Amherst College, where he graduated in 1845. Instead of returning to his native environment, he went immediately to Baltimore and studied law in the office of Coleman Yellott. Admitted to the bar in 1848, he soon formed a partnership with Silas Morris Cochran, which was dissolved only when the latter was elected in 1861 to the court of appeals. On Aug. 31, 1852, he married Fanny E. Montague of Sunderland, Mass., by whom he had one son, Henry Stockbridge [*q.v.*]. His nephew was Horace Edward Stockbridge [*q.v.*]. In the twelve years before the Civil War, when the Murray Institute was a flourishing forum in Baltimore, he first attracted attention as a leader in its proceedings. Originally a member of the Whig party, after its dissolution he acted with those opposed to the Know-Nothing party. In 1859 he offered himself as a Reform candidate for the state legislature and led the ensuing contest for the seats of the city representatives. A certain degree of victory crowned his efforts, for in the closing days of the session the election was held a nullity. He also served as counsel for William G. Harrison in the latter's congressional contest for the seat of Henry Winter Davis. His earliest inclination toward the Republican party was manifested in his vote for Frémont in 1856. From the outbreak of the Civil War he proved a stanch Unionist. In 1862 he was appointed by Gov. Augustus W. Bradford one of the commissioners of the draft, and he served as a special district attorney for the war department. In 1864 he entered the Maryland legislature, where he became chairman of the committee on the judiciary. In this position he drafted the bill to summon the constitutional convention of that year. When that body convened, he was made chairman of its judiciary committee and thus obtained opportunity to contribute largely to the form of the constitution that abolished slavery in Maryland. He took the stump afterward to insure its adoption. He was made a vice-president of the Republican National Convention in 1868. Active participation in politics lapsed then until 1879, when he accepted the post of chairman of the Republican state committee, where he continued to serve until 1883.

During all these years of political activity he pursued an active private practice. In 1865 he served by appointment as judge of the Baltimore County court. In 1867 he failed to be elected to the court of appeals. For a time he was counsel for the Freedmen's Bureau of Maryland and fought the cause of colored children in the cases arising from apprentice laws that threatened to evade the emancipation clause. What might be termed his extra-professional activities were varied and important. For many years he was first vice-president of the Maryland Historical Society and chairman of its publication committee. From its beginning he served as president of the West Baltimore Improvement Association. He served on the board of trustees of Howard University, was the first governor of the Society of Colonial Wars, and helped to erect the Humphrey Moore Institute, which proved a life-long interest.

[*The Biog. Cyc. of Representative Men of Md. and the District of Columbia* (1879); C. H. Forrest, *Official Hist. of the Fire Department of Baltimore* (1898); *Report of the Eighteenth Ann. Meeting of the Am. Bar Asso.* (1895); *Biog. Record of the Alumni . . . of Amherst College*, vol. I (1883), ed. by W. L. Montague; Sylvester Judd, *Hist. of Hadley . . . Also Family Geneal.* by L. M. Boltwood (1905); L. E. Blauch, "Education and the Maryland Constitutional Convention, 1864," *Md. Hist. Mag.*, Sept. 1930; *Baltimore American, Sun, Morning Herald,* and *Baltimore News,* Mar. 12, 1895.]   E. L.

STOCKBRIDGE, HORACE EDWARD (May 19, 1857–Oct. 30, 1930), agricultural chemist, college president, and agricultural editor, son of Levi [*q.v.*] and Joanna (Smith) Stockbridge, was born and passed the first ten years of his life on his father's farm at Hadley, Mass., one of the largest in the Connecticut Valley. His father, the first professor of agriculture in the Massachusetts Agricultural College at Amherst and later its president, moved to Amherst in 1867. Horace prepared for college in the public schools and in 1874 entered the Massachusetts Agricultural College, graduating with the degree of B.S. in 1878. He then did graduate work at Boston University for two years, and, following in his father's footsteps, specialized in agricultural chemistry.

In the summer of 1880 he was employed for a short time in the United States Department of Agriculture under Dr. Harvey W. Wiley, chief of the division of chemistry. In 1881 he was appointed instructor in the Massachusetts Agricultural College. The following year he went to Germany to study at the University of Göttingen, where he received the degree of Ph.D. in 1884, being the first graduate of an American agricultural college to be awarded it. He then returned to the Massachusetts Agricultural College as associate professor of chemistry but almost immediately thereafter was selected by the Japanese government as one of the Americans to undertake the higher education of the Japanese students in that country. Accordingly, in the spring of 1885, having received an appointment as professor of chemistry and geology at the Imperial College of Agriculture and Engineering, he went to Sapporo, Japan. From 1887 to 1889 he was also chief chemist to the Japanese government. Along with other activities he began extensive agricultural experiments, some of which had important results. After four years' service he was given a six-month leave of absence at full pay, with the privilege of resigning at the end of that time. Before going to Japan he had married, on Mar. 30, 1885, Belle Lamar of Americus, Ga. On account of their children they decided that it was best to take up their residence again in the United States.

Soon after his return, Stockbridge accepted the appointment of director of the Indiana Agricultural Experiment Station at Lafayette. He organized the work but remained there only a few months, resigning in 1890 to accept the presidency of the North Dakota Agricultural College and directorship of the experiment station, both of which institutions were yet to be established. He selected the location, named the entire faculty and staff, and planned the buildings. Resigning in 1894, he moved to Americus, Ga., to give his personal attention to the old Sumter County plantation which he had purchased a few years earlier. He also became interested in a Florida orange grove, and in 1897 the trustees of the Florida Agricultural College and Experiment Station offered to create a department in that institution expressly for him. Thus persuaded to undertake work there, he remained as professor of agriculture and director of state farmers' institutes until 1902. He also

served as secretary of the Florida state agricultural society and Florida state fair.

In the summer of 1906 he became agricultural editor of the *Southern Ruralist,* published in Atlanta, Ga. This position he held for sixteen years, meanwhile continuing to operate his plantation in Sumter County. During 1916–17 he served as president of the Farmers' National Congress. He refused to support the second Liberty Loan in 1917, because he objected to increased second-class postal rates, and Secretary of the Treasury William G. McAdoo published a letter of rebuke to him (*New York Times,* Oct. 8, 1917). In 1918 he was a trustee of the University of the South, Sewanee, Tenn. Resigning from the *Southern Ruralist* in 1922, he became editor of the *Southern Farm and Dairy,* which position he held until his retirement from work on account of failing health. He was the author of *Rocks and Soils* (1888, 1895, 1902), *Land Teaching, a Handbook of Soils, Gardens, and Grounds* (1910), and numerous reports and magazine articles. In politics he was a Republican and was treasurer of the Georgia Republican campaigns, 1920–24. For many years, until his health compelled him to withdraw, he was successively warden and vestryman of St. Philip's Cathedral, Atlanta, and served in many benevolent and religious activities connected with the Episcopal diocese. He died and was buried in Atlanta, survived by his wife, three sons, and a daughter.

[*Gen. Cat., Mass. Agriculture Coll.* (1886); *Who's Who in America,* 1930–31; *Am. Agriculturist,* July 1890; *Atlanta Constitution,* Oct. 31, 1930, and *Boston Transcript,* Oct. 30, 1930.] C. R. B.

STOCKBRIDGE, LEVI (Mar. 13, 1820–May 2, 1904), agriculturist, educator, was born in Hadley, Mass., son of Deacon Jason and Abigail (Montague) Stockbridge and elder brother of Henry Smith Stockbridge [*q.v.*]. The responsibilities of the home farm early fell to him. After the district school he had attended Hopkins Academy, and his keen intellectual curiosity drove him to spend his evenings and rainy days in further study. For several winters he taught the district school and in the local Lyceum trained himself as a speaker and writer. Seeing clearly the need of improved farming methods and of greater knowledge of underlying scientific principles, he studied the works of Liebig, of Lawes and Gilbert, and of Johnson, and while still a young man, won for himself more than local repute as a pioneer in agricultural experiment.

His active interest in civic and political affairs brought about his election as a representative in the Massachusetts legislature in 1855,

1870, 1883, and as state senator in 1865–66. From 1869 to 1891 he served continuously as cattle commissioner, winning distinction by his vigorous and determined work in the control of contagious disease. For twelve years a member of the State Board of Agriculture, he was a powerful advocate of agricultural education and was associated from its earliest inception with the work of securing an agricultural college for the state.

When the Massachusetts Agricultural College took form at Amherst in 1867, he became its farm superintendent and instructor in agriculture. The public trials of plows and mowing machines which he conducted drew entries from manufacturers in all parts of the country, and did much for the improvement of farm implements. His years of experience as farmer and business man served him well in shaping for the students a course of instruction combining classroom lectures with practical work on the farm, a plan for which no pattern existed and few textbooks were available. Friend and counselor to "his boys," he won the respect and affection of all students. Tall, spare, bearded, with keen, compelling eye, he blended in his speech the English of the King James Bible with the forceful pungency of Yankee diction. Not only did many students receive from him aid in completing the college course, but even the College itself was at least once carried through a financial crisis by money raised on his personal notes.

As professor of agriculture from 1869 to 1880, and as president of the College, 1880–82, he carried out investigations on the origin of dew, on the value of the soil mulch, and, with the second lysimeter in the country, on the leaching of plant food from the soil. His most important publications, dealing with these investigations, were "Experiments in Feeding Plants," (*Thirteenth Annual Report of the Massachusetts Agricultural College*, 1876), and "Report to the Directors of the Massachusetts Experiment Station" (*Sixteenth Annual Report . . .*, 1879). His experiments with fertilizers led to the publication of the Stockbridge Formulas, the first effort by any agricultural investigator to compound for each crop a fertilizer which should contain nitrogen, phosphoric acid, and potash as well, in the required proportion. The first $1,000 received for the use of his name in the manufacture and sale of these fertilizers was used for the experimental work which laid the foundation for the later establishment of the Massachusetts Experiment Station.

Resigning from the College in 1882, Stockbridge was made honorary professor of agriculture. His activity in all town matters continued, however, until the end of his life. A firm believer in cooperative enterprise, he led in the organization of the Amherst Grange (1873), and of the Grange Store (1877). He was selectman during the years 1870, 1883–87, and 1889–90, was assessor for many years, and was many times moderator of town meeting. He married, first, Jan. 20, 1841, Syrena Lamson, who died in 1850; second, Nov. 4, 1853, Joanna Smith, who died in February 1882; and third, Oct. 23, 1883, Elizabeth (Ashcroft) Strong, who survived him. His son, Horace Edward Stockbridge [*q.v.*], also won distinction in agriculture, as investigator, writer, and editor.

[Private papers of Levi Stockbridge, in Mass. State College Hist. Collection; reports of the Mass. State Board of Agric., 1859–74; reports of the Mass. Agric. Coll., 1866–82; W. H. Bowker, *A Tribute to Levi Stockbridge* (1904), address at memorial exercises, Amherst, repr. in part in *Levi Stockbridge and the Stockbridge Principle of Plant Feeding* (1911); L. B. Caswell, *Brief Hist. of the Mass. Agric. Coll. . . . 1917* (n.d.); F. P. Rand, *Yesterdays at Mass. Agric. Coll.* (1933); J. M. Smith, *Hist. of the Town of Sunderland, Mass.* (1899), p. 461; *Springfield Republican* and *Greenfield Recorder*, May 4, 1904; *Amherst Record*, May 11, 1904.]   C. H. T.

STOCKDALE, THOMAS RINGLAND (Mar. 28, 1828–Jan. 8, 1899), congressman from Mississippi, the sixth child of William and Hannah (McQuaid) Stockdale and a grandson of James Stockdale who came to America at the close of the Revolution, was born on a farm near West Union Church, in Greene County, Pa. After overcoming economic obstacles in securing an education, he graduated from Jefferson (now Washington and Jefferson) College in 1856. In the same year he went to Mississippi, where he supported himself by teaching and devoted his spare time to reading law. This he did with such diligence that he was able to complete the two-year law course of the University of Mississippi in one year, graduating and being admitted to the bar in 1859. He began to practise at Holmesville, Pike County, in the southern part of the state. The young Pennsylvanian must have found a satisfactory place for himself in Mississippi before 1861, for upon the outbreak of the Civil War in April of that year he enlisted as a private in the Quitman guards. Before the close of the war, transferring from the infantry to the cavalry, he rose to the rank of lieutenant-colonel. Most of his service was in Mississippi. In May 1865, he was paroled from the army of Gen. N. B. Forrest [*q.v.*] and returned to his law practice at Holmesville. On Feb. 13, 1867, he married Fannie Wicker, the daughter of a planter of Amite County.

During the reconstruction period Stockdale

continued to ally himself with the native white people of Mississippi. In 1868 he represented Mississippi in the National Democratic Convention. The next year, now a resident of Lawrence County, he ran for the state Senate but with all the other Democrats of the county suffered defeat. During the campaign he spoke in opposition to Gov. J. L. Alcorn [q.v.], but most of his hearers were negroes and gave him scant attention. In 1872 and 1884 he was a presidential elector on the Democratic ticket. In 1886 he was elected to Congress, and served continuously for eight years (Mar. 4, 1887–Mar. 3, 1895). In the House he continued in his allegiance to the South, and used the fact of his Northern birth and education to drive home several telling blows in the course of sectional discussions. While not fluent, he spoke with rugged common sense and some humor. On May 5, 1888, he made a speech on the tariff, in which he pointed out that much of the burden of protection fell, in the form of increased cost of living, upon the negroes in agricultural work (*Congressional Record,* 50 Cong., I Sess., App., pp. 82–88). This argument was a unique weapon for a Southern representative to wield against Northern defense of the tariff. At the end of four terms in Congress he was defeated for renomination, but found some solace in being appointed, in 1896, an associate judge of the state supreme court, to complete a term which expired in May 1897. Two years later he died at his home in Summit, where he had resided for many years. A son and a daughter survived him.

[*Biog. Dir. Am. Cong.* (1928); *Pubs. Miss. Hist. Soc.,* vol. XI (1910); *Biog. and Hist. Memoirs of Miss.* (1891), vol. II; Dunbar Rowland, *Mississippi* (1907), vol. II; *Biog. and Hist. Cat. of Washington and Jefferson Coll.* (1902); *Hist. Cat. of the Univ. of Miss.* (1910); *Daily Democrat* (Natchez, Miss.), Jan. 10, 1899.]
C. S. S.

STÖCKHARDT, KARL GEORG (Feb. 17, 1842–Jan. 9, 1913), Lutheran clergyman, was born at Chemnitz, Saxony, the eldest of the four children of Julius Adolf and Rosalie (Liebster) Stöckhardt. His father, a distinguished chemist and teacher, was descended from five generations of Lutheran pastors, and in his only son the clerical instincts welled up with renewed force. He studied theology, 1862–66, at the universities of Erlangen and Leipzig, became an active member of the Christian (non-duelling) student corps, Wingolf, and, after taking his theological examinations, waited seven years for an appointment. Meanwhile, he taught till 1870 in a girls' school at Tharandt, studied for short terms at Berlin and Marburg, assisted for a few trying months of 1870 at the Église des Billettes in Paris, served as chaplain in the hospitals of Sedan, and latterly

became a teacher in the Gymnasium at Erlangen, at the same time holding a repetent's position in the University. Finally, in October 1873, he was made deacon of the State Church congregation at Planitz, near Zwickau, probably because it was thought that his zeal and orthodoxy would check the influence of Friedrich K. T. Ruhland, the Missouri-trained leader of the Saxon Free Church, who was pastor of St. John's in Niederplanitz. The easy-going ways of the State Church were utterly repugnant to Stöckhardt's nature, however; he was soon at loggerheads with his ecclesiastical superiors and with the greater part of his parish; and in 1876 he quit the State Church amid a blaze of polemics and joined Ruhland's party. He founded a paper, *Die Freikirche,* to continue the argument and, having charged the State Church with apostasy, was soon indicted for libel and blasphemy. At this juncture C. F. W. Walther [q.v.] came to his rescue, and in the early autumn of 1878 Stöckhardt left Germany to become pastor of Holy Cross Church, St. Louis, Mo. Some months later he was tried and convicted *in absentia* and sentenced to eight months in jail, but in 1891 and again in 1909 he revisited his old home and even preached from his old pulpit without molestation.

His thirty-four years in St. Louis, interrupted only by a severe illness in 1900–01 and by the two trips to Germany, were busy, happy, and rich in achievement. He was pastor of Holy Cross until 1887 and professor in Concordia Theological Seminary, in which he had given instruction in Biblical exegesis since 1879, from 1887 until his death. His literary productions included *Die Kirchliche Zustände Deutschlands* (1892); *Das Schlachtfeld von Sedan: Erinnerungen aus dem Kriegsjahr* (1914); three volumes of sermons—*Passionspredigten* (2 vols., 1884) and *Adventspredigten* (1887); and a series of exegetical works—*Kommentar über den Propheten Jesaia, Kap. I–XII* (1902), *Die Biblische Geschichte des Alten Testaments* (1896), *Die Biblische Geschichte des Neuen Testaments* (1898); *Kommentar über den Brief Pauli an die Römer* (1907); *Kommentar über den Brief Pauli an die Epheser* (1910); *Kommentar über den Ersten Brief Petri* (1912); *Ausgewählte Psalmen Ausgelegt* (1915); and numerous contributions to the periodicals and other publications of the Missouri Synod. He was editor, also, with E. W. Kähler, of Vol. X, *Die Catechetische Schriften* (1892), of the St. Louis edition of Luther's works. Within the limits set by his adherence to the old Lutheran doctrines of plenary inspiration and his consequently too simple view of the problems of date and authorship, Stöckhardt was a Biblical scholar of no mean stature, and his commentaries on Romans, Ephesians, and First Peter are masterpieces of their anachronistic kind. Frequent homiletic, devotional, and polemical passages enhance the interest and practical usefulness of his work, which still continues to shape the teaching and preaching of the Missouri Synod. Stöckhardt was twice married: in 1873 to Anna König of Tharandt, who died in 1898; and in 1901 to Mary Kohne of Pittsburgh, who survived him. He had two sons by adoption. His death came, without warning, of an apoplectic stroke.

[See Otto Willkomm, *D. Th. Georg Stöckhardt: Lebensbild eines deutsch-amerikanischen Theologen* (Zwickau, 1914); three articles by W. H. T. Dau, in *Theol. Quarterly* (St. Louis), Apr., July 1913, Jan. 1914; Franz Pieper, obituary and funeral address, *Der Lutheraner* (St. Louis), Jan. 21, 1913; *St. Louis Globe-Democrat*, Jan. 10, 1913. For Stöckhardt's father see the article by B. Lepsius, *Allgemeine Deutsche Biographie*, vol. XXXVI (Leipzig, 1893).]   G. H. G.

STOCKTON, CHARLES G. (Aug. 27, 1853–Jan. 5, 1931), physician, was born at Madison, Lake County, Ohio, the son of Charles Lewis and Sarah (Shaver) Stockton and a descendant of Richard Stockton who was in Flushing, L. I., in 1656, through his son Richard who settled at Princeton, N. J. His father, a practising physician, moved his family to Northampton County, Va., where the boy was educated in the local schools. Later, he attended Westfield Academy at Westfield, N. Y., and then took his medical courses at the University of Buffalo, graduating in 1878. He began practice in Buffalo, early specializing in diseases of the gastro-intestinal tract. In 1883 he was appointed professor of materia medica and therapeutics in the medical department of Niagara University, transferring in 1887 to the chair of medicine and clinical medicine at the University of Buffalo, which post he held until 1918, when he became professor emeritus. He attained an exceptional success as a practitioner of internal medicine and became one of the foremost consultants in the country. When in 1901 President McKinley was shot in Buffalo, Stockton was called in consultation and participated in the care of the dying President. During the greater part of his professional career he served on the medical staff of the Buffalo General Hospital and for years he was consultant physician at the Buffalo City Hospital and the state Hospital for Crippled and Deformed Children.

In addition to professional societies, he belonged to the American Society for the Advancement of Science, the Washington Academy of Sciences, the Buffalo Society of Natural Sciences, the Buffalo Society of Artists, and the Buffalo Historical Society. He contributed much to the literature of his specialty. In 1903 he published *Diseases of the Stomach,* a translation from the German of Franz Riegel, and was himself the author of *Diseases of the Stomach and Their Relation to Other Diseases* (1914). He was the editor of *Selected Papers, Surgical and Scientific, from the Writings of Roswell Park* (1914), containing "Roswell Park: A Memoir" written by Stockton and published in the *Buffalo Historical Society Publications* (vol. XXII) in 1918. The bulk of his writings appeared as journal literature and contributions to various systems of medicine. Among the latter were J. C. Wilson and A. A. Eshner, *An American Text-book of Applied Therapeutics* (1896); A. L. Loomis and W. G. Thompson, *A System of Practical Medicine* (4 vols., 1897–98); G. M. Gould, *A Cyclopedia of Practical Medicine and Surgery* (1900); and the *Oxford Medicine* (6 vols., 1920–21), edited by H. A. Christian and Sir James Mackenzie. A personal friend of Dr. William Osler [*q.v.*], he wrote the introduction to the section on diseases of the digestive apparatus for Osler's *Modern Medicine, Its Theory and Practice* (7 vols., 1907–10). He was also a contributor to *Nelson Loose-leaf Medicine.* He was a pioneer in his conception of social medicine, and his presidential address before the state medical society in 1910 was prophetic of the changes in medical practice which have taken place since that time. For years he was surgeon, with the grade of major, of the 74th Infantry, New York National Guard. During the World War he was chief of advisory boards of a district covering western New York. On Nov. 23, 1875, he married Mary L. Taylor of Westfield, N. Y. He died suddenly at his home in Buffalo from the rupture of an abdominal aortic aneurism.

[T. C. Stockton, *The Stockton Family* (1911), gives Stockton's middle name as Gleason, but a letter from Stockton himself in the Cat. Div., Lib. of Cong., states that "Charles G." was his baptismal name. For biog. data see *Jour. Am. Medic. Asso.,* Jan. 24, 1931; *N. Y. State Jour. of Medicine,* Feb. 15, 1931; *Who's Who in Am. Medicine* (1925); *Who's Who in America,* 1930–31; *Buffalo Evening News,* Jan. 6, 1931.]
J. M. P.—n.

STOCKTON, CHARLES HERBERT (Oct. 13, 1845–May 31, 1924), naval officer, was a descendant of Richard Stockton who was in Flushing, Long Island, in 1656. Charles was born in Philadelphia, the son of Rev. William Rodgers Stockton, an Episcopalian clergyman, and Emma Trout (Gross) Stockton. After schooling at the Germantown Academy and the Freeland Academy (Collegeville, Pa.), he was appointed in November 1861 midshipman at the Naval Academy, then located at Newport, R. I.

In 1864 he saw his first active service, on board the *Macedonian* during her pursuit of the Confederate steamers *Florida* and *Tallahassee*. After his graduation in the following year he was ordered first to the *Dacotah,* then to the *Chattanooga,* and finally to the *Mohican,* in which he sailed for the Pacific, where he served three years. In the meantime he had been promoted ensign (1866), master (1868), and lieutenant (1869). In 1870 he joined the *Congress* and made an extensive cruise embracing the West Indies, the coast of Greenland, and the Mediterranean. In 1874–75, on board the *Swatara,* he made a voyage around the world, assisting on the Asiatic Station with the observations of the transit of Venus. After a year at the Hydrographic Office in Washington he was sent in 1876 to the *Plymouth* of the North Atlantic Squadron and served on board her until 1879, when he was ordered to the New York navy yard. The summer of 1880 he spent at the Torpedo Station, Newport, and in November was made a lieutenant commander.

From 1882 to 1885 he was again in the Pacific, this time serving as the executive officer of the *Iroquois* and taking part in the suppression of a riot on shore at Panama as commander of a battalion of seamen. A pamphlet entitled *Origin, History, Laws, and Regulations of the United States Naval Asylum,* which he compiled while attached to the Bureau of Yards and Docks, was published by the Navy Department in 1886. In the summer of 1887 and 1888 he lectured at the Naval War College, Newport, and in the latter year he served on the commission that located the Puget Sound navy yard, Bremerton, Wash. In 1889–91 he commanded the *Thetis* and made a cruise with the whaling fleet in Bering Sea and the Arctic Ocean. On his return home he was assigned to special duty at the Naval War College. While there he attained a proficiency in international law which led to his lecturing on that subject during several summers. In 1898–1900 he was president of the College. In 1898 he prepared and arranged for publication a book entitled *International Law: A Manual Based upon Lectures Delivered at the Naval War College by Freeman Snow,* and in 1904 his paper on the "United States Naval War Code" and his volume *International Law: Recent Supreme Court Decisions and Other Opinions and Precedents* were issued.

In the meantime he had been promoted commander (April 1892) and captain (July 1899) and had served on the Asiatic Station as commander of the *Yorktown* (1895–97). In 1901–03 he commanded on that station in the battleship *Kentucky,* and in 1903–06 he served as naval attaché in London, having a small part in the work of the Alaska Boundary Commission. On Jan. 7, 1906, he was promoted rear admiral. While holding that rank he was president of the board of inspection and survey and also of the naval examining and retiring boards and commander of a special service squadron sent to Bordeaux, France, for the Maritime Exposition. He was retired on Oct. 13, 1907.

Stockton's usefulness by no means came to an end with his retirement from the navy. In 1908–09 he was first delegate at the Declaration of London Conference. From 1910 to 1918 he served, without salary, as president of the George Washington University during a crucial period in the history of that institution. The university was reëstablished on a new site, its fiscal affairs were systematized, and the number of students was doubled. For more than a decade he lectured at the university on international law. In 1911 a new edition of the manual on international law was published, and in 1914 he brought out his standard work, *Outlines of International Law.* He also continued to add to his special studies in this field various articles contributed to periodicals.

A devout member of St. John's Episcopal Church in Washington, Stockton found time to act as vestryman and committeeman and in other administrative capacities. He was twice married: on June 23, 1875, to Cornelia A. Carter of New York, who died on July 1, 1876; and on Nov. 23, 1880, to Pauline Lentilhon King, also of New York. He had a daughter by his first wife and a son and daughter by his second. The Admiral was of robust constitution, stocky, a little below average stature—a friendly and genial man who throughout a long life was always adding to his attainments.

[Record of Officers, Bureau of Navigation, Washington, 1864–93; Navy Registers, 1862–1907; Marcus Benjamin, *Charles Herbert Stockton: An Eminent Churchman* (1925); *Who's Who in America,* 1924–25; T. C. Stockton, *The Stockton Family of N. J.* (1911); *Army and Navy Jour.,* June 14, 1924; *Evening Star* (Washington), June 1, 1924.]   C.O.P.

STOCKTON, FRANK RICHARD (Apr. 5, 1834–Apr. 20, 1902), novelist and story-writer, was born in Philadelphia, Pa., the third of nine children of William Smith and Emily (Drean) Stockton. The Stockton family, descended from Richard Stockton who came to Long Island before 1656, had been conspicuous and influential in New Jersey since the seventeenth century, and another Richard Stockton [*q.v.*] had been a signer of the Declaration of Independence. William Smith Stockton of the Burlington branch, though a layman, was eminent in Methodist affairs, a leader in the schism which resulted in the Methodist Protestant Church, and a voluminous writer on theological subjects. In secular matters he was a temperance advocate and an abolitionist. His son by an earlier marriage, Thomas Hewlings Stockton, was a clergyman of their denomination, chaplain in turn of both houses of Congress. The children of Emily Drean Stockton, who had been born in Leesburg, Loudoun County, Va., inclined less to theology than to literature. John Drean Stockton, at first a steel-engraver, was editor and later a proprietor of the *Philadelphia Post*. A sister, Louise Stockton (Aug. 12, 1839–June 12, 1914), a writer of children's stories, also was associated with the newspaper, as was, in some unidentified capacity, their brother Francis Richard, who seems always to have been called Frank R. Stockton.

The most talented of the three, unwilling to study medicine as his father desired him to, after his graduation at eighteen from the Central High School in Philadelphia Frank chose to learn wood-engraving, for which before the days of photo-engraving there was a large demand. He worked at his craft, in Philadelphia and New York, until 1866 and possibly later. On Feb. 20 of that year, Stockton, who then had an office in New York, patented an engraving tool of which he said: "The object of my invention is to furnish a graver by means of which both sides of a line is cut at the same time and by the same tool" (quoted from the original letters patent). He is said to have been an expert craftsman, but his wood-engravings for the *Poems* (1862) of his clerical half-brother are undistinguished. Stockton had won prizes for writing while still at school. Having married Marian Edwards Tuttle, of Amelia County, Va., in 1860, he published the same year a pamphlet called *A Northern Voice for the Dissolution of the United States of North America*. But while he remained a wood-engraver, what he wrote was, on the whole, hardly more than so much text for pictures. In 1867 he contributed to the *Riverside Magazine for Young People* the stories collected in 1870 as *Ting-a-Ling,* and he followed this with the abundantly illustrated *Round-About Rambles in Lands of Fact and Fancy* (copyright 1872).

He began to write for *Hearth and Home* in 1869, served for a few months on the staff, and became a frequent contributor to *Scribner's Monthly* (afterwards the *Century Magazine*). When in 1873 the *St. Nicholas Magazine* was founded, under the editorship of Mary Elizabeth Mapes Dodge [*q.v.*], Stockton was made assist-

ant editor. In this post he remained until 1881, when he retired from editing to live entirely by writing. As editor he had been primarily a writer. His experiences with *Hearth and Home* had led him to compile, in collaboration with his wife, a straightforward handbook on *The Home: Where It Should Be and What to Put in It* (1873). By his colleagues of *Scribner's* and *St. Nicholas* he had been, it appears, regarded as amusing, eccentric, and gifted, and encouraged to write for both magazines. During these years he published *What Might Have Been Expected* (1874), *Tales Out of School* (1875), *Rudder Grange* (1879), *A Jolly Fellowship* (1880), *The Floating Prince and Other Fairy Tales* (1881).

The quick success of *Rudder Grange,* of which an episode had appeared in *Scribner's* five years before, and others since, determined Stockton's subsequent career. At forty-five he was almost entirely unknown except for his stories for children, of which the *Ting-a-Ling* tales were as admirable as the later *Floating Prince* and *The Bee Man of Orn and Other Franciful Tales* (1887) were to be. After 1880 he wrote largely for adults, out of the vein of absurd invention which he had discovered that he had and that the public liked in him. He followed *Rudder Grange* with two sequels, *The Rudder Grangers Abroad* (1891) and *Pomona's Travels* (copyright 1894), as he followed his masterpiece *The Casting Away of Mrs. Lecks and Mrs. Aleshine* (copyright 1886) with *The Dusantes* (copyright 1888), and *The Adventures of Captain Horn* (1895) with *Mrs. Cliff's Yacht* (1896). He said that he valued Defoe and Dickens most among "all who have created fiction" ("My Favorite Novelist and His Best Book," *Munsey's Magazine,* June 1897). But Stockton had the blunt verisimilitude of Defoe no more than he had the huge exuberance of Dickens or the moral earnestness of either of them. However circumstantial Stockton might be, his imagination worked in a world of cheerful impossibility, as easygoing as a fairy-tale or a Gilbert and Sullivan opera.

His novels are, in effect, loose-knit comic operas in prose without music. Even when the scenes are plausibly localized and the characters ostensibly actual, the stories have a farcical irresponsibility. In *Rudder Grange* the heroine, elaborated from a maid in Stockton's own household, marries a man who is shaking with ague, spends part of her honeymoon as a guest in a lunatic asylum and later has a child to which her mistress gives so much time that her master hires another child to occupy himself with. The Rudder Grangers live for a time in a canal boat.

They leave their house for a tent on their own estate, and then take refuge in the house, which has been deserted by the tenants, who have moved into the tent. In *The Casting Away of Mrs. Lecks and Mrs. Aleshine,* two middle-aged women, also studied from actual persons whom Stockton knew, are shipwrecked in the Pacific, paddle their way in life-preservers, using oars as if they were brooms, to a deserted island on which they find a comfortable house, and there live much as they would do at home, each week depositing in a ginger jar a sum for board and lodging from which they subtract a charge for doing the housework. When Stockton's invention is at its most fantastic his manner is at its gravest. He is Sindbad and Munchausen lying about domestic adventures as roundly as about events at the end of the earth. Though *Rudder Grange* established his reputation, and *Mrs. Lecks and Mrs. Aleshine* was without much doubt the top of his achievement, he made his chief stir in the world with the short story "The Lady or the Tiger?" which first appeared in the *Century* in November 1882 and furnished the title to a volume of stories in 1884. It owed its vogue to its posing of a dilemma which started insoluble arguments. Would a barbaric princess, forced to a decision by her father, give her lover up to another lady who must marry him or to a tiger which would certainly destroy him? Stockton ingeniously set the problem and stubbornly refused an answer. The chattering debate which the story roused became a nuisance and a handicap to Stockton, who could neither equal the invention nor live it down. Yet such other stories by him as "The Transferred Ghost" (1882), "The Remarkable Wreck of the 'Thomas Hyke'" (1884), "A Tale of Negative Gravity" (1884), and in general the stories in his own collection called *A Chosen Few* (1895) are almost equally ingenious. He survives by them, by one or two novels, and by some of his stories for children.

Stockton was the principal humorist of the genteel tradition during the 1880's. In the midst of all the crowding issues of the decade he remained gaily aloof, letting his lively fancy go its happy way in many books, some of them dictated while he lay at ease in a hammock. Though attached by his profession to New York, where his slight, limping figure and his swarthy face were always welcomed by his few close friends, he lived most of his later life in suburban New Jersey, at Nutley and at Convent Station. At the latter he was a neighbor of the congenial Arthur Burdett Frost [*q.v.*], Stockton's own favorite among his illustrators. His last three years he passed at a house which he had bought in West

Virginia not far from Harpers Ferry. He was as sharp-eyed for Virginia singularities, for example in *The Late Mrs. Null* (1886), as for those he studied with greater variety in New Jersey. Always a traveler, he was one of the earliest Americans to write about the charms of Nassau in the Bahamas ("An Isle of June," in *Scribner's,* November 1877); his *Personally Conducted* (1889) was devoted to European travel. "The Lady or the Tiger?" was made into an operetta by Sydney Rosenfeld (Wallack's Theatre, May 7, 1888) and *The Squirrel Inn* (1891) into a play with the help of Eugene W. Presbrey, who produced it in 1893 (Theatre of Arts and Letters). Neither of them had notable success. Stockton's best book outside his fiction, *Buccaneers and Pirates of Our Coasts* (1898), handles a grim subject in a spirit both comic and romantic, as does *Kate Bonnet; The Romance of a Pirate's Daughter* (1902). A collected edition of his fiction, *The Novels and Stories of Frank R. Stockton,* was published in twenty-three volumes, 1899–1904. He died in Washington, D. C., survived by his wife. There were no children.

[Stockton lived reticently and has not been made the subject of the biography he deserves. A memorial sketch by his wife, prefixed to the posthumous volume, *The Captain's Toll-Gate* (1903), which also contains a bibliog., is the chief source of information but is lacking in detail. There are accounts of his editorial years in W. W. Ellsworth, *A Golden Age of Authors* (1919), R. U. Johnson, *Remembered Yesterdays* (1923), and L. F. Tooker, *The Joys and Tribulations of an Editor* (copr. 1924). See also T. C. Stockton, *The Stockton Family* (1911); C. C. Buel, in *Century,* July 1886; Julius Chambers, in *Author,* July 15, 1891; obituary in *N. Y. Times,* Apr. 21, 1902. The present account is based in part upon personal information, with particular indebtedness to Walter L. Pforzheimer.]

C. V–D.

STOCKTON, JOHN POTTER (Aug. 2, 1826–Jan. 22, 1900), senator, attorney-general of New Jersey, was born at Princeton, N. J. The son of Commodore Robert Field Stockton [*q.v.*] and Harriet Maria (Potter), he came of a distinguished line. After graduating from the College of New Jersey in 1843, he read law in the office of his cousin, Richard Stockton Field [*q.v.*], and was licensed as attorney in 1847 and admitted to the bar in 1850. His family connections brought him numerous opportunities for advancement. He was appointed one of the commissioners to revise and simplify legal procedure in New Jersey, and later he became reporter of the court of chancery, publishing *Reports of Cases . . . in the Court of Chancery, and on Appeal, in the Court of Errors and Appeals of . . . New Jersey* (3 vols., 1856–60). While his father's influence was at its height he secured from President Buchanan, June 15, 1858, appointment as minister resident to the Papal States. During the Civil War he conducted a law practice at Trenton and, as a Democrat, made his first serious attempt to enter politics. In 1862 he was sufficiently prominent to report at the state Democratic convention the resolutions extending to the Administration support in the "speedy suppression of the rebellion by all Constitutional means" but objecting to the suspension of the writ of *habeas corpus,* to the restriction of freedom of speech and of the press, and to the emancipation of slaves.

Three years later Stockton's election as United States senator gave rise to a celebrated contest. In the New Jersey legislature the Democrats and Union Republicans were so closely matched that the houses could organize only after a series of compromises. Stockton was elected on Mar. 15, 1865, but not until the legislature in joint session had substituted for the majority rule one making a plurality of votes sufficient to a choice. His right to his seat was promptly challenged, but the issue was not settled for a year. On Mar. 26, 1866, the judiciary committee of the United States Senate reported in his favor by a vote of 22 to 21, Stockton himself casting the decisive vote; but upon further protests, the next day he withdrew his vote and the committee unseated him, 23 to 21. The case attained great notoriety throughout the nation and led to a considerable pamphlet war. If Stockton, a Democrat, had retained his seat, the Senate might not have overridden President Johnson's veto of the Civil Rights Act. Indignant at the alleged flouting of New Jersey's sovereignty, the legislature—of which the Democrats had by now obtained control—attempted ineffectively to withdraw New Jersey's ratification of the Fourteenth Amendment, and the federal Congress was moved to regulate for the first time the election of senators (Act of July 25, 1866). In 1869 Stockton was again a candidate, and this time was elected without a question, but at the end of his term (1875), despite public respect for his name and family, he was superseded by another Democratic leader, Theodore Fitz Randolph [*q.v.*]. His hopes for the governorship were disappointed by the choice of Gen. G. B. McClellan [*q.v.*], and he had to be contented with the post of attorney-general, which from 1877 he held for twenty years.

Contemporaries describe Stockton as a convincing speaker, with a melodious voice and facile diction. His dignified manner does not seem to have been suited, however, to the increasingly urban Democracy of New Jersey, and he was further handicapped by residence in Mercer County whereas the party strength lay in the northeastern counties. Thus, although he continued to take part in state politics, he was never a determining factor, and he held his place largely through family influence. After retiring from office in 1897, he practised law in Jersey City. He married Sarah Marks and had two sons and a daughter, all three of whom survived him.

[C. M. Knapp, *N. J. Politics during the Period of the Civil War and Reconstruction* (1924); W. E. Sackett, *Modern Battles of Trenton,* vol. I (1895); C. P. Smith, "Personal Reminiscences" (MS. in N. J. State Lib.); John Whitehead, *Judicial and Civil Hist. of N. J.* (1897); T. C. Stockton, *The Stockton Family of N. J.* (1911); *Biog. Dir. Am. Cong.* (1928); *N. Y. Times,* Jan. 23, 1900.]					H. M. C.

STOCKTON, RICHARD (Oct. 1, 1730–Feb. 28, 1781), lawyer, signer of the Declaration of Independence, son of John and Abigail (Phillips) Stockton, was born at Princeton, N. J., whither his grandfather, also Richard, had removed in 1696 and acquired a large tract of land. The first of his line in America was his great-grandfather, another Richard, who was in Flushing, L. I., as early as 1656. John Stockton was for many years presiding judge of the court of common pleas of Somerset County, N. J., and a liberal patron of the College of New Jersey, being largely instrumental in securing its removal from Newark to Princeton. Richard Stockton received his preparatory education at the academy conducted by the Rev. Samuel Finley [*q.v.*] in Nottingham, Md., and entered the College of New Jersey at Newark, from which he was graduated in 1748. He took up the study of the law in the office of David Ogden [*q.v.*] of Newark, was licensed in 1754 as an attorney, in 1758 as a counselor, and in 1764 as a sergeant. In the course of a decade he built up a large practice and became generally recognized as one of the most eloquent members of the bar in the middle colonies. Among his legal protégés who received their training in his busy office were Elias Boudinot, William Paterson, and Joseph Reed [*qq.v.*].

For some years Stockton had little time or inclination for politics. In a letter to Joseph Reed in 1764, he stated his position: "The publick is generally unthankful, and I never will become a Servant of it, till I am convinced that by neglecting my own affairs I am doing more acceptable Service to God and Man" (Reed, MSS., *post,* I, 47). Shortly afterward, however, he was drawn into public affairs. As a trustee of the College of New Jersey, he was requested by the board in 1766 to tender the presidency to John Witherspoon [*q.v.*], then residing at Paisley near Glasgow. Received in London by the King and the Marquis of Rockingham with every mark of respect and given the freedom of the city of Edinburgh at a public dinner (*New York Journal or General Advertiser,* June 4, 1767), he was yet unable at first to persuade Mrs. Witherspoon to consent to her husband's accepting the call. Undaunted, however, Stockton wrote his wife: "I have engaged all the eminent clergymen in Edinburgh and Glasgow to attack her in her intrenchments and they are determined to take her by storm, if nothing else will do" (Hageman, *post,* I, 80). Finally, after prolonged negotiations, in which the aid of young Benjamin Rush [*q.v.*] was enlisted, Mrs. Witherspoon yielded and Stockton's mission was successful (V. L. Collins, *President Witherspoon,* 1925, I, 72–81). Stockton always maintained a close attachment to his alma mater, was one of its chief financial advisers throughout his lifetime, and held the opinion that great changes would occur when the colleges had "thrown into the lower House of Assembly men of more foresight and understanding than they now can boast of" (Reed MSS., Oct. 8, 1764).

On his return home in 1767 he immediately took a prominent rôle in provincial politics. In 1768 he was appointed to the Council, which position he retained until the end of the royal government. A year later, during the rioting directed against lawyers because of the costs, abuses, and multiplicity of law suits, he took a vigorous stand and brought about the resumption of orderly judicial process in Monmouth County (Smith, *post,* p. 40). In 1774 he was commissioned one of the justices of the supreme court. Such leisure time as he enjoyed in this period was devoted to the improvement of his extensive landed estate, "Morven," at Princeton, where he bred choice horses and cattle and gathered art treasures and a considerable library.

His early position on the differences between the colonies and the mother country had been that of a moderate. In 1764 he suggested, as the readiest solution of the troubles, the election of some able Americans to Parliament (W. B. Reed, *Life and Correspondence of Joseph Reed,* 1847, I, 30), but a year later, during the controversy over the Stamp Act, he maintained positively that Parliament had no authority over the colonies (Keasbey, *post,* I, 308). Under date of Dec. 12, 1774, he drafted and sent to Lord Dartmouth "An Expedient for the Settlement of the American Disputes," in which he "suggested substantially a plan of self-government for America, independent of Parliament, without renouncing allegiance to the Crown" (Nelson, *post,* p. 429). Immediate measures would have to be taken, he averred, or else there would be an

"obstinate, awful and tremendous war" (T. B. Myers, *post,* pp. 176–77; *Historical Magazine,* November 1868, p. 228). This appeal is regarded as having been the basis, in part at least, of the petition of the Continental Congress to the King, July 8, 1775 (Justin Winsor, *Narrative and Critical History of America,* vol. VI, 1887, p. 108 n.). He was elected to the Continental Congress, June 22, 1776, and took his seat six days later in time to hear the closing debate on the Declaration of Independence. During his attendance at the subsequent sessions his name was brought forward by his friends at home as a candidate for governor, and on the first ballot in the legislature (Aug. 30, 1776) the votes were equally divided between Stockton and William Livingston [*q.v.*]. The next day Livingston was chosen governor and Stockton first chief justice of the new state, which position he declined, preferring for the time being the more active career in Congress.

During the summer and fall of 1776 Stockton served on numerous important committees of Congress. On Sept. 26 he was appointed with George Clymer [*q.v.*] to visit the northern army. Writing from Saratoga, Oct. 28, he reported that the New Jersey soldiers were "marching with cheerfulness, but great part of the men barefooted and barelegged. . . . There is not a single shoe or stocking to be had in this part of the world, or I would ride a hundred miles through the woods and purchase them with my own money" (Peter Force, *American Archives,* 5 ser. II, 1851, pp. 561, 1256, 1274). During his absence on this journey, Nov. 23, he was appointed as one of a committee "to devise . . . measures for effectually reinforcing General Washington, and obstructing the progress of General Howe's army" (*Journals of the Continental Congress,* vol. VI, 1906, p. 975). Before he could reach Princeton, however, the enemy had invaded New Jersey. He placed his family in the home of a friend, John Covenhoven, in Monmouth County, for safety, but while there was betrayed by Loyalists, dragged in bitterly cold weather to Perth Amboy, and confined in jail. Removed subsequently to New York, he was imprisoned and subjected to indignities which provoked a formal remonstrance from Congress (Jan. 3, 1777), and efforts to secure his exchange. His release found him in shattered health, his beautiful estate wantonly pillaged, and his fortune greatly depleted. He remained an invalid until his death at Princeton, Feb. 28, 1781, in his fifty-first year.

Stockton married Annis Boudinot, a talented poetess, the sister of Elias Boudinot who in 1762 married Stockton's sister, Hannah. Of Stockton's two sons, the elder, Richard [q.v.], became eminent at the bar, and of his four daughters, the eldest, Julia, married Dr. Benjamin Rush.

[Sources include: *New Jersey Gazette,* Mar. 7, 1781; Samuel Stanhope Smith, *A Funeral Sermon on the Death of the Hon. Richard Stockton* (1781); John Sanderson, *Biog. of the Signers to the Declaration of Independence,* vol. III (1823); R. S. Field, *The Provincial Courts of N. J.* (1849); W. A. Whitehead, "Sketch of the Life of Richard Stockton," *Proc. N. J. Hist. Soc.,* 2 ser. IV (1877); T. B. Myers, in *Orderly Book of Sir John Johnson during the Oriskany Campaign, 1776-77* (1882), pp. 173-78; William Nelson, in "Documents Relating to the Colonial History of the State of New Jersey," *Archives of the State of N. J.,* 1 ser. X (1886), 427-30 n.; E. Q. Keasby, *Courts and Lawyers of N. J.* (1912), I, 307-09; T. C. Stockton, *The Stockton Family of N. J.* (1911); J. F. Hageman, *Hist. of Princeton* (2 vols., 1879); letters of Stockton among the Reed MSS. in the N. Y. Hist. Soc. and the Green MSS. at Princeton Univ. Charges by William Gordon, *The Hist. of the Rise . . . of the U. S.* (1788), II, 300, that Stockton's defeat for the governorship was due to his refusal to furnish horses for public use are stoutly denied by other writers (see Hageman, *ante,* I, 118-19, and references there given).]   R. B. M.

STOCKTON, RICHARD (Apr. 17, 1764-Mar. 7, 1828), lawyer, politician, gentleman farmer, son of Richard [q.v.] and Annis (Boudinot) Stockton, was born at the family estate, "Morven," near Princeton, N. J. He was tutored privately and attended the College of New Jersey, where he graduated in 1779 and received a master's degree in 1783. At this time the young man expressed his determination to retire to "Morven" which he had inherited and there attend to his books, cultivate friendship, and be untroubled by the affairs of the world (Richard Stockton to Walter Stone, May 26, 1783). After studying law in Newark with his uncle, Elisha Boudinot, however, he was admitted to the bar in 1784 and by 1792 was able to write that he was "engaged in all the causes of importance to come on at the Supreme Court" (Stockton to Robert Watts, Aug. 17, 1792). In 1804 and 1805 he was arguing before the United States Supreme Court the case of *Graves and Barnewall* vs. *Boston Marine Insurance Company* (2 *Cranch,* 419). In the meantime he had served a short time in 1788 as treasurer of the College of New Jersey and in 1791 became one of its trustees, a position in which he was active until his death.

On Nov. 2, 1796, he was elected by the New Jersey legislature to fill the unexpired term of United States Senator Frederick Frelinghuysen [q.v.], who had resigned. In the Senate (Nov. 12, 1796-Mar. 3, 1799) he was an energetic supporter of Federalist principles. In January 1801 he was tendered by President Adams the position of circuit judge under the projected judiciary act (*The Works of John Adams,* vol. IX,

1854, p. 94), but declined the offer, probably because of his interest in the governorship of his state. Later the same year he became the Federalist candidate for that office, but was defeated by Joseph Bloomfield [q.v.], the candidate of the Democratic element. In 1802 he and Bloomfield received an equal number of votes; the tie was unbroken and there was no election. In 1803 and in 1804 he was the Federalist candidate and was again defeated.

In 1812 New Jersey Federalists temporarily improved their political position and Stockton was elected from the second district to the federal House of Representatives (1813-15). Strongly opposed to the second war with Great Britain, believing its declaration to have been an act of "political insanity," he was conspicuous in his opposition to the policies of the administration. He demonstrated his sympathy for the British point of view on impressment and urged that the "idle doctrine of free trade and sailors' rights" be dismissed. He prophesied that no treaty of peace would alter any of the maritime rights previously claimed by England; and when the treaty was negotiated, he considered it "a mere tub to the great whale" and "hardly worth a vote" (Stockton to David Daggett, Dec. 30, 1815).

Stockton was interested in the development of the steamboat, in the building and improvement of canals, and in undeveloped land investments. He owned large tracts in North Carolina and Oneida County, N. Y. Tall and stout, dignified to the level of haughtiness, he commanded respect by his appearance and ability; the younger members of the bar knew him as "the old duke" (Elmer, *post,* p. 414). He expressed his legal opinions and political views in logical, well phrased sentences. The federal Constitution he considered an ark of safety for personal liberty; and in his judgment it had not been improved by a single one of its amendments (Stockton to Rufus King, May 4, 1824). In 1820 he received eight votes from Massachusetts Federalists for the vice-presidency. In 1827 he was appointed a member of the New Jersey commission to settle the long-standing dispute with New York over the eastern boundary of the state. He died the following year at "Morven." Stockton was married to Mary Field of Burlington County, N. J., and Robert Field Stockton [q.v.] was one of their nine children.

[Letters scattered among the collections of the Lib. of Cong., Hist. Soc. of Pa., Princeton Univ., N. J. Hist. Soc., N. Y. Pub. Lib., N. Y. Hist. Soc., and Yale Univ.; L. Q. C. Elmer, *The Constitution and Govt. of the Province and State of N. J.* (1872); *Northern Monthly Mag.,* Sept. 1867; J. F. Hageman, *Hist. of Princeton and Its Institutions* (1879), vol. I; W. R.

Fee, *The Transition from Aristocracy to Democracy in N. J., 1789–1829* (1933); *Biog. Dir. Am. Cong.* (1928); *Gen. Cat. Princeton Univ.* (1908); T. C. Stockton, *The Stockton Family of N. J.* (1911); "Letters from Richard Stockton to John Rutherfurd . . . in 1798," *Proc. N. J. Hist. Soc., 2 ser.* III (1874); *True American* (Trenton, N. J.), Mar. 8, 1828.]

W. R. F.

STOCKTON, ROBERT FIELD (Aug. 20, 1795–Oct. 7, 1866), naval officer, was born in Princeton, N. J., the fourth of the nine children of Richard, 1764–1828 [*q.v.*] and Mary (Field) Stockton. He was of the fifth generation from Richard Stockton, an English Quaker who came to Flushing, Long Island, before 1656 and whose son Richard moved to New Jersey in 1696. Robert's grandfather was Richard [*q.v.*], the Signer, and his father, "Richard the Duke," an eminent lawyer and United States senator and representative. At the age of thirteen Robert entered the College of New Jersey, where he excelled in mathematics, languages, and elocution. On Oct. 1, 1811, he was appointed midshipman and ordered to the *President,* the flagship of Commodore John Rodgers [*q.v.*], with whom he was closely associated throughout the War of 1812 —in the cruises of the flagship in the North Atlantic, in the construction of the *Guerrière* at Philadelphia, and in the military operations in defense of Washington and Baltimore. In these last-named operations, for his services as aide-de-camp, he was commended by Rodgers in official dispatches to the department. On Dec. 9, 1812, he was promoted to a lieutenancy, having previously served as master's mate.

In the war with Algiers, 1815, Stockton as first lieutenant of the *Spitfire* participated in the capture of two Algerine warships. In 1816 he began a tour of duty in the Mediterranean that lasted four years, during which he served first on board the *Washington,* 74, flagship of the squadron, and later on the *Erie,* of which vessel he was successively second lieutenant, executive officer, and commander. Always sensitive about points of honor, he enlivened his duties in the Mediterranean by fighting two duels, one with a British officer and the other with an American midshipman. Much interested in the American Colonization Society, Stockton in 1821 conveyed on board the *Alligator* to the west coast of Africa Dr. Eli Ayres, agent for the society, and obtained by means of a treaty with the native kings a new site for the agency, Cape Mesurado, later Liberia. On this cruise he captured several small French slavers and, after a sharp engagement, the Portuguese letter of marque *Mariana Flora.* The legality of this capture was sustained by the United States Supreme Court (11 *Wheaton,* 1–57), Justice Story delivering the opinion and Daniel Webster representing the captor. In 1822, while employed in suppressing piracy in the West Indies, he made prize of or chased ashore several small vessels at Sugar Key. In 1823–24, when stationed with a surveying party on the Southern coast, he was married to Harriet Maria Potter of Charleston, S. C., who bore him nine children—three sons and six daughters; John Potter Stockton [*q.v.*] was his second son. In 1827–28 he was again employed with surveying duties.

Inheriting in the latter year the family homestead "Morven" at Princeton, N. J., he lived there, on leave of absence or furlough from the navy, for a decade, engaged in civilian pursuits. He invested his private fortune in the Delaware & Raritan Canal, serving as its first president, and in the Camden & Amboy Railroad. In behalf of these enterprises he visited Europe and furthered them in many other ways. He imported blooded horses from England and engaged in racing, one of his horses winning a stake of $10,000. He organized the New Jersey Colonization Society and became its first president. Taking an active part in New Jersey politics, he supported John Quincy Adams for a time, but later allied himself with Andrew Jackson and became one of the General's most intimate friends.

In 1830 Stockton was promoted master-commandant and in 1838, captain. Returning to active service in the latter year, he sailed for the Mediterranean in command of the *Ohio,* the flagship of the squadron. He made a study of the naval architecture and establishments of England and especially interested himself in a plan for a steamship for the American navy. In 1840, while on a furlough, he took part in the Presidential election of that year, speaking in most of the New Jersey counties in behalf of William H. Harrison. In 1841 he refused the offer of President Tyler to make him secretary of the navy. After assisting in the construction of the steamer *Princeton,* named for his home town, he became her first commander, 1843–45. He was in command of her when, during an excursion down the Potomac, one of her guns burst, killing among others Abel P. Upshur [*q.v.*], secretary of state, and Thomas W. Gilmer [*q.v.*], secretary of the navy. A court of inquiry exonerated him of blame for the accident. He was chosen by the President to convey to the Texan government the resolution of the American government providing for annexation.

War with Mexico now being imminent, in October 1845 he was ordered to proceed to the Pacific in the *Congress* and reinforce the American Squadron there, an assignment of duty which was destined to mark the climax of his naval career. Ambitious, self-confident, impulsive, eager to take the initiative, he was not likely to miss an opportunity for distinction. On July 15, 1846, he arrived at Monterey, Cal., the war having already begun, and on the 23rd he relieved Commodore J. D. Sloat [q.v.]. On the same day he issued a dashing proclamation to the Californians, now generally regarded as an unfortunate document. Assuming command of the land operations, he enrolled the Bear Flag battalion of John C. Frémont [q.v.] as volunteers of the American army and proceeded to conquer Southern California. After taking possession of Santa Barbara he sailed for San Pedro, where he arrived on Aug. 6. A week later, the combined forces of the navy and army entered Los Angeles and raised the American flag. On Aug. 17 he issued a proclamation declaring California a territory of the United States, and proceeded to organize a civil and military government, assuming for himself the title of governor and commander-in-chief. He placed the Mexican coast south of San Diego under blockade and planned for himself an expedition inland from Acapulco to the city of Mexico, but was forced to abandon this ambitious design on account of the recapture of Los Angeles by the Mexicans. Early in January 1847 the combined forces of Stockton and Gen. S. W. Kearney [q.v.], after fighting the battles of San Gabriel and Mesa, repossessed Los Angeles and ended the war on California soil. Soon thereafter Stockton was superseded. Returning overland, he arrived in Washington in October. On May 28, 1850, he resigned from the navy.

Elected to the United States Senate as a Democrat from New Jersey, Stockton served from Mar. 4, 1851, to Jan. 10, 1853. During his brief term he introduced a bill providing for the abolition of flogging in the navy and urged adequate harbor defenses, making speeches on both subjects. From 1853 until his death he was president of the Delaware & Raritan Canal Company. He espoused the American Party and was considered as a possible candidate for the presidency in 1856. He was delegate to the Peace Conference held in Washington early in 1861. Hopeful and buoyant, warm-hearted and generous, he possessed strong religious sentiments.

[Record of Officers, Bureau of Navigation, Washington, 1809–58; Navy Reg., 1815–50; S. J. Bayard, A Sketch of the Life of Com. Robert F. Stockton (1856); T. C. Stockton, The Stockton Family of N. J. (1911); R. G. Cleland, A Hist. of Cal.; The Am. Period (1922); H. H. Bancroft, Hist. of the Pacific States, vol. XVII (1886); J. H. Smith, The War with Mexico (1919); Sen. Exec. Doc. 31, 30 Cong., 2 Sess.; R. W. Neeser, Statistical and Chronological Hist. of the U. S. Navy (1909); M. A. DeW. Howe, Figures of the Past (1926); J. E. Watkins, The Camden and Amboy Railroad (n.d.); N. Y. Tribune, Oct. 9, 1866.] C.O.P.

STOCKTON, THOMAS HEWLINGS (June 4, 1808–Oct. 9, 1868), Methodist Protestant clergyman, was one of the outstanding figures in the early history of his denomination. The son of William Smith Stockton and his first wife, Elizabeth Sophia (Hewlings), he was the eldest of a brilliant family of whom Frank R. Stockton [q.v.], his half-brother, was one of the younger members; he was born at Mount Holly, N. J., and his childhood was passed near Philadelphia. His career was determined by the religious interest of his father. The latter, an influential layman in the Methodist Episcopal Church, took a leading part in protesting against the arbitrary policy then prevailing among the bishops; and in 1828 he withdrew from the Methodist denomination with those reformers who later organized the Methodist Protestant Church.

This controversy, occurring during Thomas Stockton's formative years, not only turned him from the Methodist ministry, but provoked a hatred of sectarianism which influenced his entire career. At the age of nineteen he enrolled in Jefferson Medical College; but, disliking the profession of medicine, he cut short his training, and after an unproductive essay in literary work for periodicals, he entered the ministry of the newly organized Methodist Protestant Church. In 1830 he declined the editorship of the new denominational paper, the *Methodist Protestant,* recommending his friend Gamaliel Bailey [q.v.] instead. Two years previously he had married Anna Roe McCurdy, by whom he had eleven children (*Poems,* p. 300).

During the first years of his pastoral service, which were spent in northern Maryland, he discovered a capacity for pulpit oratory which was as unexpected as it was gratifying. His sermons were neither learned nor profound, but their style was graceful and literary, and they reflected the lovable spirit of the man himself. His reputation rapidly increased. When only twenty-five years of age, he was elected chaplain of the House of Representatives, an office which, except for one short interval, he filled until 1836.

Once more in the regular ministry, at Baltimore, Stockton became involved in the rising anti-slavery controversy. In 1838 he was again elected editor of the church paper, but when told that it should publish nothing on the subject of slavery, he resigned and removed to Philadelphia, where he preached to non-sectarian congregations for nine years, to the end that "professors of religion shall learn to live less for self and sect, and more for 'Christ and the Church'" (*Poems*, p. 306), but at the end of this time he returned to the Methodist Protestant denomination. During the remainder of his career, he alternately withdrew from his denomination and returned to it, meanwhile organizing independent, non-sectarian congregations. This he did in Cincinnati, in Baltimore, and again in Philadelphia. During these years, however, he attained a national reputation. In the capacity of chaplain of the Senate, in 1863, he conducted the religious services at the dedication of the Gettysburg national cemetery, when Lincoln made his immortal address. At the time of his death, in 1868, he was considered one of the greatest pulpit orators of his day.

Nothing that Thomas Stockton said or wrote long survived his death. His collected poems, *Floating Flowers from a Hidden Brook* (1844), and *Poems* (1862), are graceful and pleasing, but not inspired. His essays and controversial works, *The Bible Alliance* (1850), *Ecclesiastical Opposition to the Bible* (1853), and *The Book Above All* (1871), are without the charm and spirit that made his spoken words so memorable to his hearers. His one volume of collected addresses, *Sermons for the People* (1854), is, as Stockton himself said, not a learned book, "for the simple reason—which I greatly regret, though not without excuse—that there is no learning in the author himself" (*Sermons,* Preface, p. vii). It was only as minister to his congregations that in his day he touched greatness.

[Stockton's works, esp. autobiographical notes appended to his *Poems* (1862); T. C. Stockton, *The Stockton Family of N. J.* (1911); J. G. Wilson, *Life, Character, and Death of Rev. Thomas H. Stockton* (1869); Alexander Clark, *Memory's Tribute to the Life, Character and Work of Thomas H. Stockton* (1869); T. H. Colhouer, *Sketches of the Founders of the M. P. Church* (1880); A. H. Bassett, *A Concise Hist. of the M. P. Church* (1882); E. J. Drinkhouse, *Hist. of Meth. Reform . . . in the M. P. Church* (1899); *Public Ledger* (Phila.), Oct. 12, 1868.]

G. H. B.

STOCKWELL, JOHN NELSON (Apr. 10, 1832–May 18, 1920), mathematical astronomer, was born at West Farms, Northampton, Mass., the son of William Stockwell, a farmer, and his wife, Clarissa Whittemore. He was a descendant of William Stockwell, born at Thompson, Conn., about 1744, whose forebears had emigrated from England to New England at the beginning of the eighteenth century. After residing in West Farms for seven years the family moved to Ohio. John, the fifth of eight children, was sent to live on a farm with an uncle in Brecksville, Ohio, when he was eight years of age. In the kitchen of his uncle's house there hung the usual almanac,

in which it was stated that there would be a total eclipse of the moon on Nov. 24, 1844. This awesome event so thrilled the twelve-year-old lad that he then and there resolved to learn how to predict such phenomena. He had never heard of astronomy, and the opportunities for any formal education in that wilderness were limited, but during the winter months when the farm duties were few he studied all the almanacs he could find, solved many of the arithmetical problems proposed in a weekly periodical, the *Dollar Magazine,* and mastered an old arithmetic which fell into his hands. About this time he read of the discovery of the planet Neptune in 1846, and was inspired to begin alone to study algebra, geometry, and trigonometry, with the result that in an amazingly short time he seems to have mastered much of these subjects and even some of the calculus also. In Denison Olmsted's *Compendium of Astronomy* (1839), and also in the books of Thomas Dick, occasional references to Laplace and the *Traité de Mécanique Céleste* awakened the curiosity of the young scholar and he decided to order it through a book firm in Cleveland, Ohio. To his consternation he found not one but four stupendous tomes filled with the hieroglyphics of Laplace and, to add to his dilemma, a bill for forty dollars instead of five. He finally paid the bill by working on the farm, and then, by innate ability alone, mastered the great work. He was at the time twenty years of age.

In 1852 he published his first work, *The Western Reserve Almanac of the Year of our Lord, 1853.* For a short time, thanks to the offer of Benjamin A. Gould, 1824–1896 [*q.v.*], he worked as a computer in the longitude department of the United States Coast Survey and also in the United States Naval Observatory. A chance acquaintance with Leonard Case, 1820–1880 [*q.v.*], who had become interested in the Brecksville farmer-astronomer, led to Stockwell's appointment to the first chair of mathematics and astronomy at the Case School of Applied Science from 1881 to 1888. He was also chairman of the faculty. Both Mr. Case and Dr. Gould aided greatly in promoting his career, the former contributing considerable financial assistance toward his private researches after he resigned from his position at the Case School. He received honorary degrees from Western Reserve University, was a fellow of the American Association for the Advancement of Science, and a member of a number of scientific societies. His chief contributions, made over a period of seventy years, dealt with the theory of the moon's motion or with the computation of eclipses. One of his outstanding works was a *Memoir on the Secular Variations of the Elements of the Orbits of the Eight Principal Planets,* Smithsonian Contributions to Knowledge Series, volume XVIII (1873). In his last years he proposed, in *Ocean Tides* (1919), a theory of the tides in which he took issue with the accepted theory.

He was married on Dec. 6, 1855, to Sarah Healy, a foster-daughter of the Brecksville uncle. From this long and happy union there were born six children. Stockwell was a natural mathematician. His clear, analytical, and methodical mind enabled him to solve almost any mathematical problem in astronomy to which he turned his attention. Personally he was modest, genial, and gentle, and his life was one of extreme simplicity.

[Personal recollections of the writer; *Who's Who in America,* 1920–21; T. J. J. See, "Historical Notice of John Nelson Stockwell," *Popular Astronomy,* Dec. 1920; C. S. Howe, biographical sketch in *Science,* Jan. 14, 1921; *Cleveland Plain Dealer,* May 19, 1920.]

H. W. M.

STODDARD, AMOS (Oct. 26, 1762–May 11, 1813), lawyer, soldier, acting governor of Louisiana, was born in Woodbury, Conn., the eldest son of Anthony and Phebe (Reade) Stoddard, fourth in descent from the Rev. Solomon Stoddard [*q.v.*], and fifth in descent from Anthony Stoddard who arrived in Boston about 1639. When Amos was a few months old, his father moved to Lanesborough, Mass. In childhood the boy developed a retentive memory and was able to repeat prayers or sermons which he had just heard. Some of his Puritan ancestors had been clergymen of note, but Amos, as a frail boy less than seventeen, longed to join the Continental Army. Gathering the dirt under his heels to increase his height so that Baron Steuben would not reject him, he enlisted in the infantry in June 1779. Later he became a matross in the artillery and served until the close of the war. In spite of exposure and hard campaigns, his health improved so greatly that when mustered out, a six-foot youth, he could march forty miles a day without fatigue.

In 1784 he became assistant clerk of the supreme court of Massachusetts, living in the home of Charles Cushing in Boston, where he wrote, studied, and read 150 volumes in a year. He served as a commissioned officer in the suppression of Shays's Rebellion, returning late in 1787 to his clerkship and the study of law. In 1791 he went to England. To him has been attributed *The Political Crisis: or, A Dissertation on the Rights of Man,* published in London in that year (Willis, *post*). While in England he investigated his lineage, but failed to clear the title of his

American relatives to the ancestral acres in Kent.

Returning to America, he was admitted to the Massachusetts bar in 1793, and opened an office at Hallowell in the District of Maine. He represented Hallowell in the Massachusetts legislature in 1797. He was in demand as an occasional speaker and several of his orations and addresses were published. After serving two years in the Massachusetts militia he returned to the United States Army in 1798, as a captain in the 2nd Regiment of Artillerists and Engineers, and in 1807 became a major.

When Louisiana was purchased, Stoddard was commissioned first civil and military commandant of Upper Louisiana, to serve until Congress enacted laws for its government. As the agent and commissioner of France, Mar. 9, 1804, in a ceremony at St. Louis, he received Upper Louisiana in the name of France from the Spanish governor, and raised the French flag. On the next day, with equal formality, he assumed the government in the name of the United States (*Missouri Historical Society Collections,* vol. VI, 1931, p. 320). Following Jefferson's instructions, he made practically no changes in the government and personnel. He kept the peace, was sparing in his gifts to the Indians but entertained others lavishly, and had marked success in destroying prejudice and in conciliating the inhabitants (*Governors Messages and Letters: Messages and Letters of William Henry Harrison,* vol. I, 1922, p. 170). He emphasized the importance of archives. He had previously exposed some fraudulent practices in regard to land grants. When he was relieved of civil authority, Sept. 30, 1804, the representatives of the several districts of Louisiana wrote of his "exemplary dispensation of justice" and of their "regret in parting" (*Missouri Historical Society Collections,* vol. III, 1908–11, p. 144). Assigned to duty in Lower Louisiana, he continued to gather all available information concerning the history and geography of the country, believing that if more were known concerning it, opposition to the purchase would cease. He incorporated this material in *Sketches, Historical and Descriptive, of Louisiana* (1812). During the War of 1812 he did notable work in preparing and subsequently defending Fort Meigs against attack. He was wounded during Procter's siege, and died of tetanus. He never married.

[Sources include Amos Stoddard MSS., Mo. Hist. Soc., also three letters, N. Y. Hist. Soc.; F. L. Billon, *Annals of St. Louis* (1886); Wm. Cothren, *Hist. of Ancient Woodbury, Conn.,* vol. I (1854); F. B. Heitman, *Hist. Reg. and Dict. U. S. Army* (1903), vol. I; *Mass. Soldiers and Sailors of the Rev. War,* vol. XV (1907); E. H. Nason, *Old Hallowell on the Kennebec*

(1909); J. W. North, *The Hist. of Augusta* (1870); C. and E. W. Stoddard, *Anthony Stoddard . . . a Geneal.* (1865); Wm. Willis, *A Hist. of the Law, the Courts, and the Lawyers of Me.* (1863); J. T. Scharf, *Hist. of St. Louis City and County* (1883), vol. I; Louis Houck, *A Hist. of Mo.* (1908), vol. II. A manuscript autobiography in private possession contains no additional facts of significance.]   H. R. S.

STODDARD, CHARLES WARREN (Aug. 7, 1843–Apr. 23, 1909), author, was born at Rochester, N. Y., the third of six children of Samuel Burr Stoddard and Harriet Abigail (Freeman) Stoddard of Lee, Mass. His father, a paper manufacturer and later a merchandise broker, was a descendant of the Rev. Solomon Stoddard [*q.v.*]. In 1855 the family moved to San Francisco. Returning to the East in the clipper ship *Flying Cloud,* which rounded Cape Horn, Charles attended an academy in western New York, 1857–59, and then rejoined his family in California, where he soon became a clerk in a book store. His first published poem appeared anonymously in 1861, and during the next two years his verse, under the pseudonymn of "Pip Pepperpod," was printed regularly in the *Golden Era,* to which Samuel Langhorne Clemens and Francis Brett Harte [*qq.v.*] were also contributors. Under the persuasion of Thomas Starr King [*q.v.*] he attended the preparatory division of the College of California (later merged with the University of California) at Oakland from 1863 until the fall of 1864, when, in poor health, he went to the Hawaiian Islands. Upon his return to San Francisco he contributed to the *Californian,* and in 1867 his *Poems* appeared, edited by Bret Harte. In the same year he ended his quest for religious satisfaction by becoming a Roman Catholic.

During the next twenty years he traveled widely. Between 1868 and 1873 he made two trips to Hawaii and one to Tahiti, which furnished material for his *South-Sea Idyls* (1873), reprinted in London as *Summer Cruising in the South Seas* (1874). In 1873 he went to Europe as traveling correspondent for the *San Francisco Chronicle,* and in London also served for a short time as secretary to Mark Twain. He lived in England and Italy for three years, made a year's tour of Egypt and the Holy Land in 1876–77 (recounted in *Mashallah!,* 1881, and *A Cruise under the Crescent,* copyright 1898), and then returned to the United States. After two years in San Francisco, he lived in Hawaii, 1881–84, where he wrote *A Troubled Heart* (1885), the story of his conversion. He was professor of English at the University of Notre Dame, February 1885 to June 1886, and lecturer on English literature at the Catholic University of America, Washington, D. C., 1889–1902.

When he was ordered to resign his position at the university in 1902, he tried to support himself in Washington for a year by writing. His health broke down, however, and he went to live with friends in Cambridge, Mass. In 1905, being in receipt of an annuity from Mrs. Bellamy Storer, and receiving a commission from the *Sunset Magazine* to write a series of articles on the California missions, he returned to San Francisco. Disappointed in the changed city of his youth, however, he soon removed to Monterey and there, accessible to only a few close friends, spent the remainder of his life.

He is remembered chiefly for his *South-Sea Idyls,* one of the few books that capture successfully the spirit of the South Seas. His other South Sea books, *The Lepers of Molokai* (copyright 1885), *Hawaiian Life* (1894), and *The Island of Tranquil Delights* (1904), though little known, contain some of his best writing. Among his other books are *The Wonder-Worker of Padua* (copyright 1896), *In the Footprints of the Padres* (1902), *For the Pleasure of His Company* (1903), his only novel, and *Exits and Entrances* (copyright 1903). His poems were collected by Ina Coolbrith as *Poems of Charles Warren Stoddard* (1917). In the charm and informality of his writing there is reflected the personal charm that won him innumerable friends and led Mark Twain to hire him less for his usefulness as a secretary than for his company. A man of great sweetness, kindliness, and gentleness, with a gift of whimsical humor, he is said to have had a wider friendship among literary folk than any one else in his day.

[See *Who's Who in America,* 1908–09; Charles and E. W. Stoddard, *Anthony Stoddard . . . a Geneal.* (1865); *Cath. Encyc.,* vol. XIV (copr. 1912); *Charles Warren Stoddard's Diary of a Visit to Molokai in 1884* (1933); G. W. James, in Stoddard's *Apostrophe to the Skylark* (copr. 1909), *Ave Maria,* May 22, 1909, and *Nat. Mag.,* Aug. 1911; Theodore Bentzon, in *Ave Maria,* May 15, 1909 (reprinted from *Revue des Deux Mondes*); Francis O'Neill, in *Cath. World,* July 1915; W. D. Howells, "The Editor's Easy Chair," *Harper's Monthly Mag.,* Dec. 1917; Thomas Walsh, in *Nation,* Oct. 4, 1922; Yone Noguchi, in *Nat. Mag.,* Dec. 1904; Joaquin Miller, in *Overland Monthly,* Oct. 1895; H. M. Bland, *Ibid.,* Apr. 1906; Charles Phillips, *Ibid.,* Feb. 1908; Barnett Franklin, *Ibid.,* June 1909; H. M. Bland, "Charles Warren Stoddard and His Place in Am. Literature," *Univ. of Cal. Chronicle,* Oct. 1909; obituary in *San Francisco Chronicle,* Apr. 25, 1909. Letters and other manuscript material are in the possession of *Ave Maria,* Notre Dame, Ind.; Mrs. J. Makee-Crawford, Berkeley, Cal.; Mrs. Finlay Cook, San Francisco; and the Bishop Museum, Honolulu, Hawaii. A biog. of Stoddard is being prepared by Carl G. Stroven, Univ. of Hawaii.]   C. G. S.

STODDARD, DAVID TAPPAN (Dec. 2, 1818–Jan. 22, 1857), missionary among the Nestorians in Persia, was born at Northampton, Mass., the son of Solomon and Sarah (Tappan)

Stoddard. His father, a lawyer and a member of the General Court, was a great-grandson of the Rev. Solomon Stoddard [*q.v.*] who was pastor of the church at Northampton for fifty-seven years and one of whose daughters was the mother of Jonathan Edwards. On his mother's side, David was a nephew of Arthur, Benjamin, and Lewis Tappan [*qq.v.*], and was related to Benjamin Franklin. He was named for a great-uncle who was professor of divinity at Harvard; his older brother, Solomon, won distinction as a Latinist. It is thus not surprising that David was a youth of promise and predisposed to both scholarship and religion. His mother hoped that he would enter the ministry and gave him careful religious instruction. As a boy he was active physically, although never robust, and was interested in mechanics. He studied at Round Hill School, Northampton, and in 1834, vivacious and attractive, entered Williams College as a sophomore. After a year there he transferred to Yale, where he graduated in 1838. As a student he developed a great interest in the natural sciences, making some of his own instruments, and in 1838–39 he was a tutor in Marshall College and in Middlebury College. During his first year at Yale, however, a profound religious experience had decided him to enter the ministry, and therefore, declining invitations to teach science in two Western colleges, he entered Andover Theological Seminary in 1839. Transferring after a year to Yale, he was a tutor there, 1840–42, meanwhile studying theology. He was licensed in 1842 in western Massachusetts, having some difficulty because of his adherence to the "New Haven theology," then regarded as heretical by the Calvinists of the older school, and was ordained in New Haven, Jan. 27, 1843.

At the time of his religious awakening in 1836, Stoddard had thought of becoming a missionary. That purpose, half forgotten, was reawakened in 1842 by contact with the Rev. Justin Perkins [*q.v.*], on furlough from Persia. Accordingly, in 1843, after his ordination and his marriage (Feb. 14) to Harriette Briggs, he went to Northwestern Persia under the American Board of Commissioners for Foreign Missions as a missionary among the Nestorians. In Oroomiah (Urmia), he was placed at the head of the chief school for boys conducted by his mission, and continued in charge after the school was moved to Seir. He also preached among the Nestorian churches. Persistently unwell, however, he returned in 1848 to the United States in an effort to regain his health. On the way, at Trebizond, his wife died. While in America he spoke extensively on missions, and for a time was in charge of two publications of his board, the *Dayspring* and the *Journal of Missions*. After the death of Mary Lyon [*q.v.*], in 1849, the trustees of Mount Holyoke Seminary approached him with a view to the possibility of his succeeding her as the head of that institution. His heart was in Persia, however, and in 1851 (after his marriage on Feb. 14 to Sophia Dana Hazen, who for several years had been a member of the staff of Mount Holyoke) he returned to resume his headship of the seminary at Seir. He was also in charge of a church ten miles away and did a great deal of preaching there and elsewhere.

Stoddard was a student of the Turkish and Persian languages and became something of an expert in Syriac. He aided Perkins in the translation of the New Testament into modern Syriac and prepared "A Grammar of the Modern Syriac Language, as Spoken in Oroomiah, Persia, and in Koordistan," published in the *Journal of the American Oriental Society* (vol. V, 1855–56). He was also the author of an arithmetic for the Nestorians, published by his mission. He continued his interest in the natural sciences, and through his knowledge of astronomy won the respect of some of the scholars of his district. He died at Seir, of typhus contracted while on a journey to Tabriz on business for his mission.

[J. P. Thompson, *Memoir of Rev. David Tappan Stoddard, Missionary to the Nestorians* (1858); F. B. Dexter, *Biog. Notices Grads. Yale Coll., Supp. to Obit. Record* (1913); C. and E. W. Stoddard, *Anthony Stoddard . . . a Geneal.* (1865); D. L. Tappan, *Tappan-Toppan Geneal.* (1915); ann. reports, Am. Board of Commissioners for Foreign Missions; *Missionary Herald*, vols. XL–LIII, *passim*, and obituary, June 1857.]   K.S.L.

STODDARD, ELIZABETH DREW BARSTOW (May 6, 1823–Aug. 1, 1902), novelist, poet, the wife of Richard Henry Stoddard [*q.v.*], was born in Mattapoisett, Mass., the second of nine children of Wilson and Betsey (Drew) Barstow. Her paternal ancestors came from Yorkshire, England, the first-known, William Barstow, having settled in Hanover, Mass., in 1649. He and his male descendants were shipbuilders, always prominent in their several localities, and frequently wealthy. Elizabeth attended school in Mattapoisett and was later sent to several educational institutions in New England, among them the Wheaton Female Seminary at Norton, Mass. From the first she showed a disinclination for prescribed study, although she read avidly. The works of Addison, Steele, Dr. Johnson, Fielding, Smollett, Sterne, and Sheridan she found in the library of her friend, the Rev. Thomas Robbins [*q.v.*] of Mattapoisett.

Through Rufus Wilmot Griswold [*q.v.*], indirectly, she met Stoddard, and after a short courtship she and the poet went to New York and were there married, probably in December 1851. They first lived in Brooklyn, then successively on East Thirteenth, East Tenth, and East Fifteenth streets, Manhattan. She and her husband were hospitable, and their home was ever a meeting-place for people of literary tastes. After her marriage, fostering a natural inclination and encouraged by her husband, she began to write. Short stories, poems, and sketches from her pen began to appear infrequently in the *Atlantic Monthly,* the *Knickerbocker, Harper's New Monthly Magazine, Appleton's Journal,* and other publications. In 1862 her first novel, *The Morgesons,* appeared. This was followed by *Two Men* (1865), *Temple House* (1867), both fiction; *Lolly Dinks's Doings* (1874), a book for children; and her collected *Poems* (1895). With her husband she edited several books of minor importance. As a writer Mrs. Stoddard was in advance of her time. Her novels, praised for their verisimilitude by Hawthorne and by Leslie Stephen, were realistic, even photographic, in detail in a day when the literature in vogue was either romantic or didactic and consciously ethical. The scene of each is laid in New England, and the characters are mainly the grim, determined folk of the author's girlhood. Although each of the works was twice reprinted, they were never really popular. In addition to the fact that they were out of the fashion and that they appeared when the Civil War and its consequences occupied the minds of everyone, they had many glaring faults. The humor was grim, the organization poor; a fertile imagination clogged the pages with plots and details. Mrs. Stoddard seemed never to feel the need for ordered expression and as a result her work is inchoate and without form. She had a certain narrative skill but an undisciplined technique. Her poetry, less popular with all and less important to her than her fiction, is a direct personal revelation. Uneven, careless in structure, it nevertheless burns with the intensity characteristic of the writer, and its morbidity of thought unfailingly reveals the frustration of her hopes and desires. Unsatisfied from childhood, she found little in her later life to lift her from morbidity: both her fiction and poetry were criticized severely; her husband was forced to poorly remunerated journey-work and subsequent ill-health; all three of her children met with an untimely death. A frail, nervous, highly imaginative woman, she was something of an angular individualist. Her tongue was sharp, and she frequently made enemies by its injudicious use. Nevertheless, those of her many acquaintances who understood her life knew her as a woman of kindliness and intelligence, with some literary talent, an apt critical judgment, and keen, tart, conversational power.

[*Who's Who in America,* 1901–02; R. H. Stoddard, *Recollections, Personal and Literary* (1903); *Mattapoisett and Old Rochester, Mass.* (copr. 1907); Mary Moss, in *Bookman,* Nov. 1902; obituary in *N. Y. Times,* Aug. 2, 1902.]   H.S., Jr.

STODDARD, JOHN FAIR (July 20, 1825–Aug. 6, 1873), educator and textbook writer, third of six children of Phineas and Marilda (Fair) Stoddard, traced his descent, through Solomon Stoddard [*q.v.*], from Anthony Stoddard of Boston, who emigrated to America from the west of England about 1639 and whose illustrious progeny included Jonathan Edwards and William Tecumseh Sherman [*qq.v*]. Born on a farm in Greenfield, N. Y., where he received his early education, he attended Montgomery Academy in Orange County, and the Nine Partners' School in Dutchess County, and by the time he was sixteen was teaching a district school. His major interest was mathematics, and the young teacher prepared and tried out in manuscript a textbook following the Pestalozzian trend made popular by Dana Pond Colburn [*q.v.*]. Encouraged by Prof. David Perkins Page [*q.v.*] of the State Normal College, Albany, N. Y., from which he was graduated in 1847, he published this as *The American Intellectual Arithmetic* in 1849. Its immediate success led to the preparation of a long series of mathematical works, some in collaboration with W. D. Henkle. Their popularity is shown by the fact that "up to 1860, 1,-500,000 copies had been issued, and the annual sales exceeded 200,000" (Greenwood and Martin, *post,* p. 852). Some of them were still in print in revised form in 1912. Stoddard's books gained from the ascendant theory of disciplinary values, which made arithmetic an "educational" as well as a practical subject. "That *Intellectual Arithmetic,*" he said, "properly taught, is better calculated, than any other study, to *invigorate* and *develope* these [reasoning] faculties of the mind *cannot admit* of a doubt" (*The American Intellectual Arithmetic,* 1850, p. v). Sensible and helpful teaching suggestions were presented in these books, and in the *Report of the Commissioner of Education for the Year 1897-98, The American Intellectual Arithmetic* (revised edition, 1866) is rated as one of the very best mental arithmetics published.

Stoddard was an educator of eminence as well as a textbook writer. He headed Liberty Normal Institute (1847–51), the University of

Northern Pennsylvania (1851–54), and the Lancaster County Normal School (1855–57), all in Pennsylvania. He purchased the property of the closed University of Northern Pennsylvania and opened it as a teachers' college in April 1857. Within a month the buildings were destroyed by fire, but that fall he established the Susquehanna County Normal School at Montrose, which had an attendance of some three hundred, mostly teachers, for the next two years. In 1857 he was elected president of the Pennsylvania State Teachers' Association. He was a frequent speaker at teachers' institutes, fervently advocating higher standards in the profession.

With all his other activities, he continued his studies in higher mathematics. In 1853 he had received the degree of A.M. from the University of the City of New York (later New York University), and his removal to New York City in 1859 was partly due to his wish to make use of metropolitan facilities for advance study. He was principal of Grammar School No. 10 for several years. In 1864, in ill health, he retired to his birthplace, Greenfield, N. Y., where he continued writing and revising textbooks, and speaking at teachers' institutes. On Oct. 18, 1865, he married Eliza Ann, daughter of George W. and Eliza Platt. They had one daughter. In 1867 they moved to New Jersey, where they lived for the rest of Stoddard's life. He died at Kearny of what was called nervous consumption.

[Charles and E. W. Stoddard, *Anthony Stoddard of Boston, Mass., and His Descendants* (1865); Eliza P. Stoddard, *In Memoriam: Obituary and Addresses of the Late Prof. John F. Stoddard* (1874), with portrait; J. M. Greenwood and Artemas Martin, in *Report of the Commissioner of Educ. for the Year 1897–98* (1899); art. on Stoddard in "Pa. Educ. Biogs.," *Am. Jour. of Educ.*, Dec. 1865; W. S. Monroe, *Development of Arithmetic as a School Subject* (1917), p. 99; *The Am. Ann. Cyc.*, 1873; obituary in *Newark Daily Advertiser*, Aug. 6, 1873.]   E.W.F.

STODDARD, JOHN LAWSON (Apr. 24, 1850–June 5, 1931), lecturer and writer, was born at Brookline, Mass., the son of Lewis Tappan Stoddard and his second wife, Sarah H. (Lothrop) Stoddard, a nephew of David Tappan Stoddard [*q.v.*], and a descendant of the Rev. Solomon Stoddard [*q.v.*] of Northampton. After attending public school in Boston he entered Williams College, from which he graduated in 1871. He spent the next two years at the Yale Divinity School, but his increasing unorthodoxy led him to abandon the ministry and take up an instructorship in the classics in the Boston Latin School, 1873–74. After two years of foreign travel, chiefly in Greece, Palestine, and Egypt, and some further teaching, he entered in 1879 upon his highly successful career as a

public lecturer. A pioneer in the use of the stereopticon, during the next eighteen years he traveled widely, visiting, as he said, "nearly every part of the habitable globe," and each winter delivered a series of illustrated lectures in the larger American cities, descriptive of European, Oriental, and American cities, life, and scenery. In this period he also published *Red-Letter Days Abroad* (1884); *Glimpses of the World* (1892), a volume of photographs with explanatory text; and a *Portfolio of Photographs* (copyright 1894), issued in sixteen weekly instalments. Broadly advertised by his speaking tours, which had made his name a household word, a series of ten volumes, *John L. Stoddard's Lectures*, first published in 1897–98, with five supplementary volumes in 1901, had an extensive and long-continued sale. His *Famous Parks and Buildings* (1899) and *Beautiful Scenes of America* (1902) catered similarly to the popular taste for pictures and light information. In April 1897 he retired and made his home in New York. He had been married, Dec. 24, 1877, to Mary Hammond Brown of Bangor, Me., and had a son, born in 1883, who also became a writer of distinction. Some five years later he became estranged from his wife, and on Aug. 15, 1901, after being divorced, he was married to Ida M. O'Donnell of Barnesville, Ohio. During subsequent years, spent chiefly in retirement abroad, he selected *The Stoddard Library; A Thousand Hours of Entertainment with the World's Great Writers* (12 vols., 1910), with an accompanying handbook published in 1915.

His European home was first in a villa at Meran in the Austrian Tyrol, then from about 1906 until 1914 on Lake Como, Italy, and afterwards until his death on a larger estate near Meran. Love for the Tyrol and its people, as well as his own strongly independent habits of thought, drew him during the World War into sympathy with the Central Powers, a feeling that finds expression in his pamphlet *Why Is It?*, published by the German-American Defense Committee in 1915, in *America and Germany* (1916), and in *La Decadence de l'Angleterre* (Berne, 1917). In religion he had been for many years a free thinker, but his harrowing wartime experiences in a frontier province and his suffering from typhus fever in 1917 inclined him toward Catholicism. In 1922, with his wife, he became a member of the Roman Catholic Church. Thereafter he gave his time almost wholly to religious study and writings, the latter including *Christ and the Critics* (2 vols., 1926–27), a translation of Dr. Hilarin Felder's *Jesus Christus; The Theology of Saint Paul* (2 vols., 1926–

27), from the French of Fernand Prat; *The Evening of Life* (1930), from the French of Louis Baunard; and *Yesterdays of an Artist-Monk* (copyright 1930), from Willibrord Verkade's *Die Unruhe zu Gott*. A volume of his verse, *Poems,* appeared in 1913, his *Rebuilding a Lost Faith* in 1921, and his *Twelve Years in the Catholic Church* (1930) just before his death in his Italian home. He is remembered far less for these later writings than for his extraordinary popularization, both on the platform and in published form, of the travel lecture which combined a wealth of pictures with entertaining accounts of strange people and scenes. Unlike the modern travelogue, however, which often degenerates into a mere running comment on the motion picture film, these lectures were prepared beforehand with the utmost care. Their success was even more a matter of delivery. By natural gifts and long training Stoddard was an excellent speaker, and from the moment his slender, erect figure appeared on the platform his audience was won by his eloquence and personal magnetism.

[Charles and E. W. Stoddard, *Anthony Stoddard . . . a Geneal.* (1865); *Who's Who in America,* 1930–31; *Obit. Record Soc. of Alumni Williams Coll.,* Apr. 1932; "Originator of the Modern Travel Lectures," *Hampton's Mag.,* Oct. 1910; G. E. Chase, in *Libraries,* May 1931; J. A. Walsh, in *Cath. World,* Oct. 1931; obituary in *Boston Transcript,* June 5, 1931.]

                                   A. W—t.

STODDARD, JOHN TAPPAN (Oct. 20, 1852–Dec. 9, 1919), chemist and teacher, was a native of Northampton, Mass., the son of William Henry and Helen (Humphrey) Palmer Stoddard, a nephew of David Tappan Stoddard [*q.v.*]. He was of the seventh generation of Stoddards in America, a direct descendant of Anthony who emigrated from England to Boston in 1639, and of Anthony's son, Solomon [*q.v.*], who moved to Northampton to become the forebear of the large number of Stoddards prominent in its affairs from its settlement to the present (1932). The Northampton Stoddards were all well educated, some at Yale, some at Harvard, and those of later date at Amherst College. For the most part they were ministers and educators, men of loyalty and strength of purpose.

John Tappan Stoddard received the degree of A.B. from Amherst College in 1874, and the following year served as assistant principal of the Northampton high school. During the years 1876 to 1878 he studied in Germany, working under Hans Hübner at Göttingen and receiving the degree of Ph.D. in 1877. His dissertation, *Über Anhydrobenzamidotoluylsäure und über eine neue Ketonbase,* was published at Göttingen in the same year. In 1878 he returned to North-

ampton and became associated with Smith College, serving as professor of physics (1878–81) and as professor of physics and chemistry (1881–97). In 1897 he became the first chairman of the department of chemistry, and this post he held with distinction until the time of his death. He went to Smith College at a time when modern ideas of technical laboratory training were first being introduced into American colleges and universities. With the vision and imagination always characteristic of him, he soon introduced these at Smith and supervised the very considerable expansion of the department of chemistry. The chemistry building, renamed Stoddard Hall after his death, was erected two years after he assumed the headship of the department and was planned with so much foresight that a generation later it was still considered adequate in every way for scientific research.

He was the author of four textbooks, all of which went through several editions and were widely used: *An Outline of Qualitative Analysis* (1883), *Quantitative Experiments in General Chemistry* (1908), *Introduction to General Chemistry* (1910), and *Introduction to Organic Chemistry* (1914). In addition he contributed research articles to the *Journal of the American Chemical Society.* An enthusiastic billiards player, he was also the author of a unique book, *The Science of Billiards with Practical Applications* (1913); and as a result of experiments in photography, he published an article on "Composite Photography" in the *Century Magazine* (March 1887). His contributions to teaching and to science found less expression in his publications, however, than in his personal contacts with colleagues and students and in the practical projects committed to his direction. A man of foresight and of personal charm, he was a very considerable influence in the early history of Smith College. On June 26, 1879, he married Mary Grover Leavitt of Northampton; they had two sons and one daughter. He died at his home in Northampton.

[J. McK. Cattell, *Am. Men of Science* (2nd ed. 1910); *Bull. of Smith Coll., Ann. Report,* 1919–20; *Daily Hampshire Gazette* (Northampton), Dec. 9, 1919; *Celebration of the Quarter-Centenary of Smith Coll.* (1900); Solomon Clark, *Antiquities, Historicals, and Grads. of Northampton* (1882); H. J. Kneeland, *Some Old Northampton Homes* (pamphlet, 1909); Charles and E. W. Stoddard, *Anthony Stoddard . . . a Geneal.* (1865); Frederick Humphreys, *The Humphreys Family in America* (1883); *Who's Who in America,* 1918–19; *Boston Transcript,* Dec. 9, 1919.]

                                   C.P.B.

STODDARD, JOSHUA C. (Aug. 26, 1814–Apr. 3, 1902), inventor, was born in Pawlet, Rutland County, Vt., the son of Nathan Ashbel and Ruth (Judson) Stoddard, and a descendant of the Rev. Solomon Stoddard [*q.v.*]. After obtaining a common-school education in his native town Joshua worked on his father's farm for many years, engaging in bee culture and the production of honey. This occupation he pursued with ordinary success throughout his life, particularly in Worcester, Mass., where he resided for well over half a century. He was something of a poet, lived in constant expectation of the end of the world according to the ingenious calculations of the "timists," and possessed considerable mechanical skill and ingenuity. In the course of his life he was granted sixteen patents, most of which were for improvements in horse-drawn hay rakes.

One invention, however, quite distinct from the rest, brought him much renown but no financial reward. This was a steam calliope, for which he received a patent on Oct. 9, 1855. It was based upon the conception that the bells of the whistle by the vibration of whose thin edges the sound of the steam whistle is produced, could be so arranged as to render accurately the diatonic scale in music. After experimenting for a number of years he succeeded in constructing a series of bells on which seven notes of the octave could be played by steam, and invented a delicate valve for the admission of steam to the whistles. His calliope consisted of a steam chest on top of which were a number of valve chambers (according to the number of whistles) having double poppet valves, and over each valve was a whistle of its own particular tone. A stem passed from each valve through the steam chamber to the outside, by which stem the valve could be opened and shut by the slightest pressure. A long cylinder with pins driven into it was so placed that when it was revolved the pins pressed on the valve stems and thus blew the whistles to play a tune. The ingenious part of the cylinder, however, was the use of pins of different shapes, whereby notes of varying lengths—whole, half, quarter, eighths, and even dotted notes—could be produced. Stoddard later made other improvements so that an organ or piano keyboard could be used in playing the instrument.

Late in 1855 he organized, in Worcester, the American Steam Music Company and began manufacturing instruments for use on steamboats, locomotives, and in circuses. The company held its first marine exhibit in August 1856 in the waters around New York, having fitted up an instrument on the side-wheel tugboat *Union.* This instrument was later placed permanently on the passenger boat *Glen Cove.* In 1858 the *Armenia,* in passenger service on the Hudson, was equipped with a 34-whistle, keyboard calliope, which continued in use until 1870. Gradually instruments were installed on other vessels both in Eastern and mid-Western waters, and one or two were sold to circuses. Stoddard was an unworldly man with practically no business judgment and in less than five years was pushed out of the organization no better off than before making his invention.

Subsequently, he devised his hay-raking machines, for which he received patents, Aug. 6, 1861, Sept. 27, 1870, and Jan. 10, 1871. These were made under his name and widely used for many years. On Jan. 22 and Aug. 12, 1884, he received patents for improvements in fire escapes, and on Mar. 12, 1901, a patent for a fruit-paring machine; but nothing came of them. He was married on Jan. 23, 1845, at Canaan, N. Y., to Lucy Maria Hersey, and at the time of his death in Springfield, Mass., was survived by two sons.

[C. and E. W. Stoddard, *Anthony Stoddard . . . a Geneal.* (1865); *Springfield Republican,* Apr. 4, 1902; J. H. Morrison, *Hist. of Am. Steam Navigation* (1903); Patent Office records.]   C. W. M—n.

STODDARD, RICHARD HENRY (July 2, 1825–May 12, 1903), poet, critic, editor, was born at Hingham, Mass., the son of Reuben and Sophia (Gurney) Stoddard. On his paternal side he was a descendant of John Stodder who had emigrated to Hingham and received there a grant of land in 1638. His ancestors had followed the sea for several generations, and his father had risen, through hard work, from the rank of ordinary seaman to that of master and part-owner of the *Royal Arch,* on which he was lost when Stoddard was but a child of two or three. He seems to have been the one person who might have influenced the child's later literary pursuits, for in letters which he wrote his wife while he was away on voyages, signed interchangeably "Reuben Stodder" and "Reuben Stoddard," he exhibited a certain amount of untrained literary ability. The Gurneys were an uneducated and improvident family who, at the time Stoddard was a child, were principally employed as operatives in cotton mills throughout New England. After her husband's death Stoddard's mother made her home first with her husband's family and then with her own people, moving with them from one factory town to another. In the *Christian Parlor Book* (February, October 1851, and February 1852) and in *Recollections, Personal and Literary* (1903) Stoddard writes rather pathetically of his chaotic and squalid early life. His mother was a restless and lonely woman who, although she attempted to apply herself to her child's education, had neither the intelligence nor the emotional stability to give him much aid. After a few years in Hingham and in Abington, the ancestral home of the Gurneys, mother and son moved to Boston, where Stoddard ran about as a street urchin, while his mother was engaged in making rough clothes for the sailors who entered Boston harbor. She married again, another sailor, and with her husband and the ten-year-old child moved to New York in the autumn of 1835. Here Stoddard attended school for a few years, learning little, but reading cheap reprints of Burns, James Beattie, Cowper, and Shakespeare. At the age of fifteen he was compelled to begin to contribute to the support of the family. He thus became successively an errand boy, a shop boy, a legal copyist, "a sort of factotum" in the office of a short-lived journal, a bookkeeper, and at the age of eighteen an iron moulder.

It is difficult to understand how one with such a background could have entered upon literature as a profession. His mother and his step-father had been unsympathetic towards advanced learning and too poor even to provide their son with good books to read. But Stoddard, unschooled as he was, early began to cultivate his love for literature and literary figures. He assiduously studied the English masters and by 1845 had begun to write. He was the typical figure of the literary climber. He worked at his task of iron moulding uncomplainingly, buoyed up by the thought of friendly conversation with book-loving companions at night, and he sought out such men as Dr. Ralph Hoyt, Park Benjamin [q.v.] and Lewis Gaylord Clark [q.v.]. From them and the books he studied so earnestly he learned much of the history and forms of English poetry. His early verse appeared in such magazines as the *Rover,* the *Home Journal,* the *Southern Literary Messenger,* the *Knickerbocker,* the *Union Magazine,* and *Godey's Lady's Book.* In 1849 he brought out, at his own expense, his first volume, *Foot-Prints,* of which one copy (now in the Library of Congress, Washington, D. C.) was sold before Stoddard repented of his amateurish attempts and burned the whole edition. The poems are frankly imitative of Keats and Wordsworth. He was married, probably in December 1851, to Elizabeth Drew Barstow of Mattapoisett, Mass. [see Elizabeth Drew Barstow Stoddard], a high-strung, temperamental woman who had a genius for conversation and some gift for writing. In the same year he brought out *Poems,* which was favorably reviewed, a much more finished work than *Foot-Prints.* In 1853 he received through the intervention of Nathaniel Hawthorne [q.v.], with

whom he had scraped up an acquaintance, an appointment as inspector of customs in the New York custom house, a position which he held until 1870. During his seventeen-year tenure of this office he wrote constantly. From 1860 to 1870 he was a literary reviewer for the *World* (New York). After his discharge from customs duty he became for some three years a confidential secretary to Gen. George Brinton McClellan [q.v.] in the docks department; in 1877 he was appointed city librarian, a political position involving the handling of municipal books, which he held for nearly two years. From 1880 until his death he was the literary editor of the *Mail and Express.* During this latter period of his life he was engaged in several editorial ventures, notably as editor of the *Aldine,* a short-lived journal, and the Bric-à-Brac and Sans-Souci Series. In 1880 appeared *The Poems of Richard Henry Stoddard,* a collected edition, and ten years later *The Lion's Cub; with Other Verse.* A fair sample of his editorial work is *English Verse* (1883), done in collaboration with W. J. Linton. In 1903 there appeared his *Recollections, Personal and Literary,* edited by Ripley Hitchcock, with an introduction by E. C. Stedman.

Stoddard was not in any sense a great poet. His ear was faulty, his powers of imagination were limited, but he often felt keenly and deeply the emotions which he expressed. Some of his poems have undoubted charm; still others are indisputably powerful, as, for example, his tribute to William Cullen Bryant, "The Dead Master," and his *Abraham Lincoln: An Horatian Ode* (1865). He was one of the first in America to deal with Oriental themes (*Poems,* 1852, and *Songs of Summer,* 1857). Nevertheless, he was clearly imitative in most of his verse; many of his poems echo trite sentiments and express feeble emotions. In the field of criticism, however, he did much able work. By constant study he made himself one of the most learned critics of his day, and though his critical work often shows mistaken judgment or even personal bias, as in the case of Poe, it is on the whole remarkably accurate and painstaking, considering that most of it was designed as mere hackwork. As an editor he was careful and comparatively sound in his judgment, although the appeal of much that he edited was distinctly popular (over 60,000 copies of the Bric-à-Brac Series were sold in eighteen months).

When his reputation became assured, about 1870, his home assumed the aspects of a literary salon. He has been described as the "Nestor of American literature," and indeed for over thirty years his home was one of the most important centers of New York's cultural life. He served as a link between the older writers—Poe, Hawthorne, Lowell, Longfellow, Bryant, all of whom he had known—and the later writers of his own day—Bayard Taylor, Edmund Clarence Stedman, George Henry Boker, Thomas Buchanan Read, Paul Hamilton Hayne, and Herman Melville [*qq.v.*]. Widely popular, Stoddard received the poetic effusions of hundreds of poetasters from all over the land, but, although he was genial, he was none the less firm and unswerving in his literary judgment. He hated sham and vigorously condemned as he wholeheartedly praised; his remarks on Bohemianism, for example, were vitriolic. His conversation was vigorous and quite often profane. Withal he was a brave figure of a man, often railing at fate but going ahead methodically and painstakingly, dropping many caustic comments on life by the way. His friends understood and loved him, and the Authors Club dinner given him in 1897 was one of the most brilliant and sincere tributes ever offered a literary man.

In the later years of his life, as the result of rheumatism in childhood, two cataracts, and an attack of paralysis, he was an almost helpless invalid. A variety of other circumstances had combined as well to embitter him. His unfortunate early life, the poor royalties from his work and from his wife's novels, the early death of two children, a sorrow crowned by the death of his third son, Lorimer, the gifted playwright, followed within the year by Mrs. Stoddard's death—all served to drive him towards a madness from which only his beloved books and faithful friends saved him. Yet he remained unswerving in his devotion to literature and the literary life.

[The chief biog. source is Stoddard's *Recollections, Personal and Literary* (1903), with a rather full list of his works. See also *Who's Who in America*, 1901–02; A. R. Macdonough, in *Scribner's Monthly*, Sept. 1880, the best single article on Stoddard; S. A. Allibone, *A Crit. Dict. of Eng. Literature*, vol. II (1870), for a full bibliog. and references to reviews; obituary in *N. Y. Times*, May 13, 1903. Stoddard's lib. is in the possession of the Authors Club of N. Y. Many of his MSS. are in the possession of Mrs. Ripley Hitchcock of N. Y., and there are large colls. of his letters in the libraries of Cornell Univ. and the Am. Antiquarian Soc.]

H. S., Jr.

STODDARD, SOLOMON (September 1643–Feb. 11, 1728/29), Congregational clergyman, baptized in Boston, Mass., Oct. 1, 1643, when about four days old, was one of the fifteen sons of Anthony Stoddard, who settled in Boston in 1639, and of Mary, sister of Sir George Downing and niece of Gov. John Winthrop [*q.v.*]. He studied with Elijah Corlet of Cambridge, and graduated from Harvard in 1662. From 1667 to

1674 he was librarian of the college, being the first to hold that office. During this period, in 1667, for reasons of health, he went as chaplain to the Congregationalists in Barbados, on the invitation of ex-Governor Searle. In 1669 he returned to Boston and was about to sail for England when he was invited to preach at Northampton, Mass. He went thither in November, and in March 1670 the town called him to the pastorate of the church. He accepted in February 1672, was ordained on Sept. 11 of that year, and held the pastorate until his death. In March 1670 he married Esther Mather, widow of his predecessor, the Rev. Eleazar Mather and daughter of the Rev. John Warham of Windsor; they had twelve children, among whom were Col. John Stoddard (1681–1748), member of the governor's council and commander-in-chief of the western division of Massachusetts, and Esther, mother of Jonathan Edwards [*q.v.*], who in 1727 was ordained associate pastor of the Northampton church.

Stoddard accepted the Half-Way Covenant, proposed by the synod of 1662, by which persons not sufficiently advanced in grace to qualify for full membership in the church could secure baptism for their children; at some period, before 1677, he introduced into his church the practice, usually called "Stoddardeanism," of allowing professing Christians to take the communion and enjoy other privileges of full membership, even when they were not certain that they were in a state of grace. "My business," he said "was to answer a case of Conscience, and direct those that might have Scruples about Participation of the Lords-Supper, because they had not a work of Saving Conversion, not at all to direct the Churches, to admit any that were not to rational charity true Believers" (*An Appeal to the Learned*, pp. 2, 3). He advocated this practice in the Reforming Synod of 1679, persuading that body to make a mere profession of faith and repentance and not a relation of a personal experience of grace the requisite for church membership. Subsequently, he engaged in controversy with Increase Mather [*q.v.*], defending "Stoddardeanism" in *The Doctrine of Instituted Churches* (1700), *The Inexcusableness of Neglecting the Worship of God, under a Pretence of Being in an Unconverted Condition* (1708), and *An Appeal to the Learned* (1709). For a century most of the churches in western Massachusetts accepted Stoddard's view of church membership. Edwards, however, rejected it, and though this resulted in his dismissal from Northampton in 1750, his influence caused it to be gradually abandoned.

Stoddard published nineteen other sermons and pamphlets. He attacked the belief that "every particular Congregation is absolute and independant" (*The Doctrine of Instituted Churches,* quoted by Trumbull, *post,* II, 59), advocating a national church governed by a synod. He also argued that the clergy should have more power than had been customary in New England, believing that the laity should be allowed only the right of electing their ministers. He was sternly opposed to long hair, wigs, extravagance in dress, and excessive drinking, being partly responsible for the sumptuary laws of 1676, and attacking the aforementioned and other wicked practices in *An Answer to Some Cases of Conscience Respecting the Country* (1722). He urged ministers to speak frequently of hellfire, declaring that "if Sinners don't hear often of Judgement and Damnation, few will be converted." His views on this subject are developed in *The Efficacy of the Fear of Hell to Restrain Men from Sin* (1713), and in *A Guide to Christ* (1714). He took great interest in politics; for half a century he was the most influential person in western Massachusetts, and his letters to Boston, especially during the Indian wars, strongly affected the policy of the government. As minister he was very successful, promoting revivals of religion in Northampton in 1679, 1683, 1712, and 1718. He dominated his congregation, receiving from malcontents the nickname of "Pope." Personally, he was tall and dignified, and was an impressive conversationalist in any company. Not so learned as the Mathers, he was more forceful as a writer and more original as a thinker. As an ecclesiastical statesman he was unrivaled in his generation.

[*A Report of the Record Commissioners Containing Boston Births, Baptisms, Marriages and Deaths, 1630–1699* (1883), p. 16; Charles and E. W. Stoddard, *Anthony Stoddard of Boston, Mass., and His Descendants; a Geneal.* (1865); J. R. Trumbull, *Hist. of Northampton, Mass.* (2 vols., 1902); W. B. Sprague, *Annals Am. Pulpit,* vol. I (1857); J. L. Sibley, *Biog. Sketches Grads. Harvard Univ.,* vol. II (1881); Williston Walker, *The Creeds and Platforms of Congregationalism* (1893); "Stoddardeanism," *New Englander,* July 1846; "Diary of Samuel Sewall," *Mass. Hist. Soc. Colls.,* 5 ser. vols. V–VII (1878–83); *Boston Weekly News Letter,* Feb. 20, 1729.]   H. B. P.

STODDARD, WILLIAM OSBORN (Sept. 24, 1835–Aug. 29, 1925), author, inventor, secretary to President Lincoln, was born in Homer, N. Y., the son of Prentice Samuel Stoddard by his first wife, Sarah Ann (Osborn). He was a descendant of Ralph Stoddard, who was in Groton, Conn., as early as 1695. William received his early education in private schools and at Homer Academy. From 1849 until 1853 he worked in his father's book and publishing shop

at Syracuse. In 1858 he received the degree of A.B., *cum laude,* from the University of Rochester.

That same year he became affiliated with the *Central Illinois Gazette* at West Urbana, Ill., his name first appearing as joint editor of this weekly paper in August 1858. At West Urbana (now Champaign), Stoddard met Abraham Lincoln, and although reared in New York as a disciple of William H. Seward, he was instantly won by Lincoln's personality. The young editor worked ceaselessly for Lincoln's election in the Illinois senatorial campaign of 1858 and he was one of the first Illinois editors to suggest him for the presidency. In the *Atlantic Monthly* (February 1925), he recounts his efforts in the spring of 1859 to awaken interest in Lincoln as a candidate, saying: "In all the long list of possible presidential candidates, the name of Lincoln had not been spoken of in any newspaper publication that I knew anything about." He then quotes from two articles which appeared in the *Gazette* advocating Lincoln's candidacy, the implication being that both were published in the spring of 1859. The first article, a personal item, did appear in the *Gazette* on May 4, 1859, and in this appears the assertion: "No man in the West . . . stands a better chance [than Lincoln] for obtaining a high position among those to whose guidance our ship of state is to be entrusted." The second article, however, an editorial entitled "Who Shall Be President?" did not appear in the *Gazette* until Dec. 7, 1859. In spite of Stoddard's belief to the contrary, he was not the first editor to put Lincoln forward as a candidate. The *Olney Times* (Olney, Ill.) came out in his behalf on Nov. 19, 1858, and on Dec. 16, 1858, the Chicago *Press and Tribune* published an editorial reprint from the Reading, Pa., *Berks and Schuylkill Journal* in which Lincoln was suggested for the presidency.

Stoddard worked vigorously for Lincoln in the campaign of 1860, and in recognition of his services, Lincoln, in 1861, appointed him as a secretary to sign land patents. In April of the same year, with Lincoln's permission, he enlisted as a private for three months' service in the United States Volunteers. Upon his discharge, he was appointed an assistant private secretary to Lincoln, with the task of sorting out for the waste basket the scores of letters received from office seekers, "blackguards," and "lunatics." Except for occasional help from department clerks, John George Nicolay, John Hay [*qq.v.*], and Stoddard attended to all of the clerical work at the executive office during the early part of Lincoln's administration. Stoddard relates the "queer kind of tremor" that came over him as he copied from "Abraham Lincoln's own draft of the first Emancipation Proclamation" (*Atlantic Monthly*, March 1925, p. 337).

An ardent opponent of slavery, he was active in organizing in 1862 the Union League of America. In September 1864 he was appointed United States marshal of Arkansas, resigning this position in 1866 because of ill health. After 1866, he became engaged in journalistic activities and in telegraphic, manufacturing, and railway enterprises, obtaining nine patents for mechanical inventions. From 1873 to 1875 he served as a clerk in the department of docks, New York City. In all, Stoddard wrote over one hundred books, among which were: *Abraham Lincoln* (1884); *The Lives of the Presidents* (10 vols., 1886–89); *Inside the White House in War Times* (1890); and *The Table Talk of Lincoln* (1894). His books for boys, some seventy-six in number, were perhaps his greatest literary successes. On July 25, 1870, he married Susan Eagleson Cooper of New York, by whom he had five children. He spent the later years of his life at Madison, N. J., where he died.

[In addition to Stoddard's writings, see E. W. Stoddard, *Ralph Stoddard of New London and Groton, Conn., and His Descendants* (1872); *Gen. Cat., Univ. of Rochester* (1911); *Who's Who in America, 1924–25*; *N. Y. Times*, Aug. 30, 1925; *The Americana Annual* (1926); *The New International Year Book . . . 1925* (1926). Information as to certain facts was supplied by W. O. Stoddard, Jr.]   A. L. P.

STODDART, JAMES HENRY (Oct. 13, 1827–Dec. 9, 1907), actor, was born in Barnsley, Yorkshire, England, one of a family of ten. His father was James Henry Stoddart, a provincial actor from Scotland; his mother was Mary (Pierce) Stoddart of Yorkshire. In appearance, however, the son always suggested very strongly the Scotch side of his ancestry. The elder Stoddart had been for many years connected with the Theatre Royal, Glasgow, and all five of his sons became actors. James Henry began as a child of five and as a youth acted with the American star, Charlotte Cushman, in Glasgow, playing a gypsy boy in *Guy Mannering*. In 1854 he made a hazard of new fortunes and came to New York, where James William Wallack engaged him as a member of his company. He remained in Wallack's company for two years and then joined Laura Keene [*q.v.*]. In 1859 he was at the Winter Garden, where Dion Boucicault was the stage manager and Joseph Jefferson [*qq.v.*] the leading player. There he played Lafourche in the famous production of Boucicault's *The Octoroon*. From 1864 to 1866 he was at the Olympic, where he played Moneypenny in *The*

Long Strike. In 1867 he went back again to Wallack's Theatre on Broadway at Thirteenth Street, and in 1875, after two unsuccessful seasons of touring as the star in *The Long Strike*, joined the company of Albert Marshman Palmer [*q.v.*] at the Union Square Theatre. He remained with this famous organization for two decades, moving with it to the Madison Square Theatre and playing in almost all the dramas to which it gave life. Consequently, he was identified at one time or another with most American actors of his period and with the works of many rising American playwrights, including Bronson Crocker Howard and Augustus Thomas [*qq.v.*]. One of his famous rôles was that of Pierre Michel in *Rose Michel*. Another, which illustrated his versatility and his sympathy with the newer drama of local color, was that of Colonel Preston in Augustus Thomas' play, *Alabama*. Here, in spite of his Scotch ancestry, he gave a convincing performance, carefully composed and natural in execution, of an old-school Southerner. The year 1896 found him playing in a melodrama, *The Sporting Duchess*, and on Jan. 30 the company held a celebration and gave him a loving cup in honor of his sixty-three years on the stage. Though, in all conscience, his career had been a long one, it was not till five years later that, for the second time, he became a star, and for the first time a successful one. During the season of 1901–02, at the Republic Theatre, New York, he played Lachlan Campbell in a dramatization of the then popular story by Ian Maclaren (John Watson), *Beside the Bonnie Briar Bush*. He had waited long, and worked hard, for his honors. As the proud, stern, self-contained father in this play, tender, true, and deeply religious, torn between a sense of justice and paternal love, he not only created an authentic Scotch atmosphere but displayed a power and pathos that captured the public. He was still playing this rôle when he was stricken with paralysis in April 1905 in Galt, Ontario. He died in 1907 at his home in Sewaren, N. J. In 1902 he published his *Recollections of a Player*. His wife was Matilda (Phillips) Conover, whom he met and married, Oct. 28, 1855, when both were playing with Lester Wallack. They had two sons, one of whom died young, and a daughter.

Stoddart was so striking in appearance, especially in later life, that disguise was impossible, and he applied his skill to fitting his own personality to a part. Tall and slender, wiry of frame, with an extraordinarily wide mouth and wide-set, penetrating blue eyes, he had the face and figure of some old Scotchman carved out of rock and heather. But it was a face and figure oddly appealing, and Stoddart knew how to make the most of it, both for humor and pathos. He could play with a light touch, and he could strike deep. Till his final illness, he scarcely ever lacked employment in the best companies, and for fifty years was a valued and beloved figure on the American stage.

[*Who's Who in America,* 1906–07 ; J. H. Stoddart, *Recollections of a Player* (1902) ; *N. Y. Tribune,* Jan. 28, 31, 1896 ; G. C. D. Odell, *Annals of the N. Y. Stage,* vols. VI, VII (1931) ; obituaries in *N. Y. Times, Evening Post* (N. Y.), Dec. 10, 1907 ; Locke Coll., in N. Y. Pub. Lib., and Shaw Coll., Widener Lib., Harvard Univ.]   W. P. E.

STODDART, JOSEPH MARSHALL (Aug. 10, 1845–Feb. 25, 1921), editor and publisher, the son of Joseph M. and Elizabeth (Fahnestock) Stoddart, was born in Philadelphia, Pa., where his father was a dry-goods merchant. After a period in the public schools of his native city, he was sent to the Port Royal Academy, Frankford, also in Philadelphia. At the age of sixteen he was placed with the publishing firm of J. B. Lippincott & Company, Philadelphia, and remained there thirteen years, though in the last year of the Civil War he served two enlistments of three months each. In 1874 he left to become a publisher on his own account. In that year he published *Out of the Hurly Burly,* the first book of the humorist, Charles Heber Clark [*q.v.*], which became instantly popular and was a remarkable financial success. Stoddart is credited with "discovering" Clark; certainly he induced that author to continue with other laughable volumes, of which *Elbow Room* (1876), is best remembered. The first illustrations made by Arthur Burdett Frost [*q.v.*] appeared in *Out of the Hurly Burly.*

Stoddart was both keen and enterprising. Learning that a new edition of *The Encyclopædia Britannica* (the ninth) was on the eve of publication, he made an arrangement by which he received advance sheets that permitted him to begin reprinting the great work of reference in America simultaneously with its reprinting in Great Britain. This was continued from 1875 until the twenty-five volumes were completed in 1884. In the meantime he began the publication of *Stoddart's Encyclopædia Americana* (4 vols., 1883–89), a "companion" to the *Britannica,* written by American contributors and treating for the first time those American subjects neglected by the Edinburgh publication. When in 1878 Gilbert and Sullivan's comic opera, *H.M.S. Pinafore,* became a great success, he saw the value of publishing in the United States the words and scores of that and future productions by the gifted pair. On friendly terms with Richard D'Oyly

Carte, the London manager, he obtained the American rights and for some years remained the American representative of Gilbert and Sullivan. It was through his influence that the world première of *The Pirates of Penzance* took place in New York City on Dec. 31, 1879. The next year's opera was *Patience.* Through Stoddart's appreciation of novelty and publicity, Oscar Wilde, representative of the esthetic movement satirized in the opera, was brought to the United States to lecture in the cities where the opera was sung. Stoddart gave personal attention to Wilde's tour and published for him his reprint of Rennell Rodd's poems, under the title supplied by Wilde, *Rose Leaf and Apple Leaf* (1882), with an introduction and dedication by Wilde. It was the most sumptuous and artistically produced volume, as well as the daintiest, that had been produced in the United States up to that time. In 1877–79 he brought out a new three-volume edition of John Fanning Watson's *Annals of Philadelphia,* enlarged by Willis Pope Hazard. From 1880 to 1882 he issued *Stoddart's Review,* but in the latter year it was sold and consolidated with the *American* (Philadelphia).

About 1889 or 1890 he returned to the J. B. Lippincott Company to take over the management of *Lippincott's Monthly Magazine,* which immediately responded to his magic touch, improving in attractiveness and increasing in circulation. Amélie Rives's *The Quick or the Dead?,* her first novel, written at Stoddart's suggestion, appeared in that magazine, as did Rudyard Kipling's *The Light That Failed,* Conan Doyle's "The Sign of the Four," which resulted in the whole series of Sherlock Holmes stories, and Oscar Wilde's *The Picture of Dorian Gray.* Stoddart was also the first to encourage Sir Gilbert Parker. Subsequently he went to Collier's and became the editor of *Collier's Weekly.* He was editor of the *New Science Review,* 1894–95, and finally in 1900 edited the *Literary Era,* a monthly published by Henry T. Coates. Failing health in 1903 caused him to return to his home at Elkins Park, just outside of Philadelphia, where he died in 1921. He married in 1869 Isabella Herkness (d. 1900), daughter of Alfred Morris Herkness. He was survived by four children.

[*Who's Who in America,* 1903–05 ; obituary in *Evening Bull.* (Phila.), Feb. 26, 1921 ; other data from J. Alfred Stoddart, a son, and from personal knowledge.]   J. J.

STODDERT, BENJAMIN (1751–Dec. 17, 1813), first secretary of the navy, was born in Charles County, Md., the grandson of James Stoddert, a surveyor who emigrated from Scotland to La Plata, Md., about 1650. His father, Thomas Stoddert, was a lieutenant in the Maryland militia of the French and Indian War. His mother, Sarah (Marshall) Stoddert, was the daughter of Thomas Marshall of "Marshall Hall." The Revolutionary War began just as he was finishing his apprenticeship as a merchant, and he joined a Pennsylvania Regiment under Thomas Hartley [q.v.] in January 1777 with rank of captain. When his regiment was united to John Patton's in 1779 he found himself outranked by the new officers. In consequence he resigned on Apr. 16 (Letter of Apr. 16, 1779, in Papers of the Continental Congress, Library of Congress, no. 78, vol. XXI, folio 39). On Sept. 1, he was unanimously elected secretary to the board of war. He held this arduous post until Feb. 6, 1781, when he resigned (*Ibid.*, folios 17, 21). On June 17, 1781, he married Rebecca Lowndes, the daughter of Christopher Lowndes, a merchant at Bladensburg, Md. She died about 1800 leaving eight children, one of whom became the mother of Richard Stoddert Ewell and Benjamin Stoddert Ewell [qq.v.]. With shrewd business instinct, he decided to begin his mercantile career in Georgetown, Md., at that time a small place with only one trifling retail shop. Because of its central location and shipping facilities Georgetown soon sprang into astonishing prominence as a port, and the firm that Stoddert had entered, Forrest, Stoddert, & Murdock, had a great share of the Potomac trade with branches established by Uriah Forrest at London and Bordeaux (Stoddert to John Templeman, undated, Library of Congress). Jointly or singly he purchased great tracts of land in what is now the District of Columbia and erected a charming dwelling in Georgetown overlooking the Potomac. Soon he came to know General Washington, first in a business way by furnishing supplies to his nephews. Stoddert's sagacity and business sense were later employed by the president in the first delicate and critical moves toward establishing the federal capital. With William Deakins, Jr., he was asked to purchase, privately, blocks on important sites at a price lower than the government could command. After the site of the federal city had been fixed the business was made public, and these lands were ceded to the government. Stoddert's signature is found on the deed from the original proprietors (Washington Papers, Library of Congress, Jan. 21, 1785, Oct. 24, 1792; Letter Book, Vol. XIII, pp. 48, 118, 121, 122, 124–26). In order to handle these extensive realty transactions, the Bank of Columbia was organized in January 1794 with Stoddert as an incorporator and, later, president.

In the well known crash through excessive speculation, several years later, he probably lost heavily.

It was his highly successful mercantile career and stanch Federalism that caused him to be made secretary of the navy. Following the declination of George Cabot [q.v.], President Adams appointed Stoddert on May 18, 1798, and three days later he was confirmed as the first secretary. The choice has been generally conceded as a most fortunate one in a critical time. The so-called naval war with France was imminent, and the navy was pitifully weak. By heroic measures some fifty ships were acquired in the next two years, and a fleet was built up under celebrated commanders with about six thousand men in service. After the "war," he recommended reduction and replacement by thirteen frigates and twelve 74-gun ships. With characteristic thoroughness and foresight he also drafted the bill for the government of the marine corps, began construction of the naval hospital at Newport, and began the work of locating docks and of establishing navy yards. The latter were not contemplated by Congress but maneuvered by a masterpiece of loose-construction on the ground that the yards already rented were too small for the 74-gun ships Congress had authorized. On the advice of Joshua Humphreys [q.v.] and of his captains, Stoddert purchased ground at Washington, Gosport, Va., Portsmouth, N. H., Charlestown, Mass., Philadelphia, and Brooklyn. This was virtually all carried out in 1800 and early in 1801, before the new administration could rescind it. He stayed on at the request of Jefferson until April 1801.

The remaining twelve years of his life were filled with pecuniary embarrassments that distracted and embittered him. Georgetown commerce was on the wane, owing, as he believed, to the European wars, which diverted to larger ports such a share of the carrying trade that it sucked in the local produce trade from smaller places (Stoddert to Templeman, *ante*). Jefferson's embargo, and finally the War of 1812, seemed to him to cap the climax of his suffering, and he died heavily in debt (Stoddert to James McHenry, eight letters, 1801–1812, Library of Congress; advertisements in *Daily National Intelligencer* of Washington, Jan. 31, Feb. 10, Feb. 21, 1814).

[Papers of the Continental Cong., Washington Papers and Letter Books, and Stoddert Coll. in Lib. of Cong.; H. S. Turner, "Memoirs of Benj. Stoddert," *Columbia Hist. Soc. Records*, vol. XX (1917); W. B. Bryan, *A Hist. of the National Capital*, vol. I (1914); C. O. Paullin, "Early Naval Admin. under the Constitution," *U. S. Naval Institute Proc.*, vol. XXXII, no. 3 (1906); G. W. Allen, *Our Naval War with France*

(1909); *Jour. of the Continental Cong.*, vol. IX (1912) ed. by Gaillard Hunt, XIV (1909) ed. by W. C. Ford; *The Works of John Adams*, vol. X (1856), ed. by C. F. Adams; *National Intelligencer* (Washington), Dec. 24, 1813.]   C. W. G.

STOECKEL, CARL (Dec. 7, 1858–Nov. 1, 1925), philanthropist, patron of music, was born in New Haven, Conn., the son of Gustave Jacob Stoeckel and his wife, Matilda Bertha Wehner. The elder Stoeckel was a Bavarian musician who came to the United States in 1848, and became an instructor and professor of music at Yale University from 1855 to 1894. He was the first head of the Yale School of Music. Carl was educated at the Thomas School and the Hopkins Grammar School at New Haven, and with private tutors in America and in Europe. He was married on May 6, 1895, on the Isle of Wight, England, to Ellen Battell Terry, the daughter of Robbins Battell, jurist and philanthropist, of Norfolk, Conn. After their marriage Stoeckel and his wife made their home in Norfolk where they became patrons of art and music in a manner that exerted an influence on the development of musical life not only in their own community but throughout the country as well. Stoeckel founded the Litchfield County University Club in 1896, and in 1904 provided funds for the publication of books pertaining to Litchfield County to be written by members of the Club. Mrs. Stoeckel was instrumental in founding the Norfolk Glee Club, a chorus of mixed voices, in 1897, and two years later Stoeckel brought about the formation of the Litchfield County Choral Union, with a nucleus of the Norfolk Glee Club and the Winsted Choral Union. Three neighboring organizations were subsequently admitted to membership: the Salisbury Choir (1905), the Canaan Choral Society (1906), and the Torrington Musical Association (1906).

For the first seven years the concerts of the organization were devoted to choral works with orchestral accompaniment, but in 1907 concerts consisting exclusively of orchestral music were added to the festivals, held annually in June. The first festivals were held in the armory at Winsted, but from 1906 they were given in the "Music Shed," which Stoeckel erected for the purpose on his Norfolk estate. Until they were discontinued in 1923 the festivals represented an ideal in community expression, and in mutual cooperation and participation. Although guided and financed by the founders, the choral union and the festivals belonged to the members of the union. The concerts brought to Norfolk distinguished guests from America and Europe, and, commencing in 1908, eminent composers were commissioned to write works for perform-

ance at the festivals. By 1922 sixteen prominent composers had been commissioned for one or more works each. The Norfolk festivals inevitably reflected Stoeckel's personality, yet he constantly fought to keep them from exploiting either himself or any other individual. He resented particularly any reference to Norfolk as the "American Bayreuth," for he felt that Bayreuth had been founded for the glorification of one man, Richard Wagner. Before his death at his Norfolk home, Stoeckel edited and printed for free distribution two volumes of *The Correspondence of John Sedgwick* (1902–03). He also purchased the birthplace and farm of John Brown at Torrington, Conn., and presented it to the John Brown Association.

[*Who's Who in America*, 1924–25; J. H. Vaill, *Litchfield County Choral Union* (2 vols., 1912), and *The Litchfield County Univ. Club* (1931); *Waterbury American* (Waterbury, Conn.), Nov. 7, 1925; *N. Y. Times*, Nov. 15, 1925.]   J. T. H.

STOEK, HARRY HARKNESS (Jan. 16, 1866–Mar. 1, 1923), mining engineer, educator, was born in Washington, D. C., the son of Jacob F. and Susan (Lear) Stoek. He attended the public schools of Washington, graduating from the Central High School in 1883, and entered Lehigh University. During his college years he gave his summer vacations to practical work in geology and engineering. He graduated with the degree of B.S. in 1887, and with that of Engineer of Mines in 1888. He began his professional experience immediately as an assistant engineer for the Susquehanna Coal Company, Wilkes-Barre, Pa., doing mine surveying, engineering office work, and experimental work on the frictional resistance of mine-car wheels. In January 1890 he was called back to Lehigh as instructor in mining and geology, and at the close of the college year 1892–93 was appointed assistant professor of mining engineering and metallurgy at Pennsylvania State College. In this capacity he served until January 1898.

From teaching he now turned to technical journalism, becoming managing editor and later editor in chief of *Mines and Minerals* (Scranton, Pa.). His editorial work, his "Questions and Answers" department, his technical articles —for which he gathered material first-hand on visits to mining districts all over the country— made his name known throughout the mining world. He also wrote, or revised and edited, many of the mining instruction pamphlets of the International Correspondence Schools, Scranton. It is difficult to overestimate his influence on coal-mining education, for his writings were a veritable Bible for the men in the industry. In addition, he gave lectures on coal mining at

Yale, Pennsylvania State College, and Brooklyn Polytechnic Institute, prepared a chapter on the Pennsylvania anthracite coal field for the *Twenty-second Annual Report of the United States Geological Survey* (1902), and for the Carnegie Institution of Washington prepared an "Economic History of Anthracite" as a part of the "Economic History of the United States" which the Institution had projected.

In October 1909, Stoek relinquished the editorship of *Mines and Minerals* to accept a call from the University of Illinois to organize a department of mining engineering. Within three years he had drawn up a curriculum, built a laboratory, and initiated a large-scale program of research. His indefatigable labor and tireless energy resulted in a department which, while never large from the standpoint of student enrollment, was outstanding in the quality of its instruction and in the character and productivity of its research work. He served as its head until his death in 1923. One of his great interests was the vocational education of miners. In Pennsylvania he had seen the results of such education, offered both in the pages of his magazine and in night schools. Through his initiative the Illinois Miners' and Mechanics' Institutes were organized, under the department of mining engineering of the University, and began their work in January 1914. At this time he published a comprehensive bulletin, *Education of Mine Employees* (1914). During the summer of that year he visited England and the Continent, making a study of mining methods and of mining education, collegiate and vocational.

From 1910 until the reorganization of the state department of mines in 1917, he served as a member of the Mining Investigation Commission and as member and secretary of the Illinois Mine Rescue Commission. He was active in the affairs of the American Institute of Mining and Metallurgical Engineers, the American Mining Congress, the International Railway Fuel Association, and the Coal Mining Institute of America. He was a consulting engineer for the United States Bureau of Mines, and made many private reports and investigations on such subjects as the valuation of coal properties, coal storage, and mine safety. His numerous writings are found in the technical press, in the bulletins of the Engineering Experiment Station of the University of Illinois, and in the proceedings of engineering societies. They cover almost every phase of coal mining. It has been said that "To him, more than to any man of his generation, belongs the honor of changing coal mining from a rule-of-thumb trade to an engineering science"

(Dean E. A. Holbrook, in "Memorial Exercises," *post*).

Stoek was married to Miriam Ricketts of Wilkes-Barre, on Dec. 20, 1894. Death came to him suddenly, in Urbana, in his fifty-eighth year. His wife and son had died some years before; one daughter survived him. In 1926 a bronze tablet by Lorado Taft, commemorating Stoek's life and work, was unveiled in the College of Engineering Library at the University of Illinois.

[*Trans. Am. Inst. Mining & Metallurgical Engineers*, vol. XXIX (1923); *Coal Age*, Mar. 8, 1923; *Coal Mine Management*, Mar. 1923; *Jour. Western Soc. of Engineers*, Apr. 1923; *Who's Who in America*, 1922–23; "Memorial Exercises and Presentation of Tablet in Honor of Professor Harry Harkness Stoek, May 2, 1926," (MS. in Coll. of Engineering, Univ. of Ill.); personal acquaintance.]   A. C. C.

STOEVER, MARTIN LUTHER (Feb. 17, 1820–July 22, 1870), educator, author, was born in Germantown, Pa. After his graduation in 1838 from Pennsylvania (now Gettysburg) College, he became a teacher at Jefferson, Frederick County, Md., being deterred from entering the Lutheran ministry by a slight hesitancy in his speech. In the autumn of 1841 he was recalled to Gettysburg and spent the rest of his life there, as principal of the Academy, 1842–51, and as professor in the College after 1844, teaching history, 1844–56, and Latin, 1851–70. He was acting president in 1850 between the administrations of Charles Philip Krauth and Henry Louis Baugher [qq.v.]. On June 14, 1850, he married Elizabeth McConaughy of Gettysburg, who with their son, William Caspar, survived him. He was secretary for a number of years of the General Synod of the Evangelical Lutheran Church in the United States, was one of the editors, 1857–61, of the *Evangelical Review,* and was sole editor and proprietor, 1862–70. Articles from his pen appeared in every issue but two of its entire career, 1849–70. Though himself of the school of S. S. Schmucker [q.v.], he kept the pages of the *Review* open to contributors of every degree of orthodoxy and printed many literary essays, thereby making the journal both a theological and a cultural influence. In his travels in behalf of the College and the Church, he gathered information for a series of "Memoirs of Deceased Lutheran Clergymen," eighty-three in all, ranging from the shadowy figures of the early eighteenth-century pioneers to his own elder contemporaries. He supplied the bulk of the Lutheran material for W. B. Sprague's *Annals of the American Pulpit* and published separately a *Memoir of the Life and Times of Henry Melchior Muhlenberg* (1856) and a *Memorial of Rev. Philip F. Mayer* (1858), besides a few occasional addresses. He was accurate in his statement of facts and rescued not a few good men from oblivion, but his fondness for Latin quotations and his desire to improve every opportunity for edification sometimes interfered with the biographical intention. A daguerreotype shows him a stocky Pennsylvania German, with a broad, benign countenance rising moonlike above a thicket of beard. His kindness and hospitality were proverbial. He was a member of the United States Sanitary Commission. During the battle of Gettysburg he and his wife filled their house on the Square with wounded soldiers and turned their yard into a field kitchen with food and drink for every comer. After the Confederate retreat three Union officers emerged uncaptured from behind the cider barrels in the cellar. He declined calls to several educational institutions, the last offer of this kind—a tender of the presidency of the University of Nebraska—coming while his body awaited burial. He died in Philadelphia, while visiting relatives, after an illness of two days, and was buried in Germantown.

[J. G. Morris, *Fifty Years in the Luth. Ministry* (1878); E. S. Breidenbaugh, *The Pa. Coll. Book 1832–82* (1882); C. B. Stover and C. W. Beachem, *The Alumni Record of Gettysburg Coll. 1832–1932* (1932); S. G. Hefelbower; *The Hist. of Gettysburg Coll. 1832–1932* (1932); *The Press* (Phila.), July 25, 1870.]

G. H. G.

STOKES, ANSON PHELPS (Feb. 22, 1838–June 28, 1913), merchant, banker, publicist, son of James Boulter and Caroline (Phelps) Stokes and brother of William Earl Dodge Stokes [*q.v.*] and Olivia Egleston Phelps Stokes [*q.v.*], was born in New York City, where shortly before 1800 his grandfather, Thomas Stokes, coming from London, had settled as a merchant. On his mother's side, he was the grandson of Anson Greene Phelps [*q.v.*], and a descendant of George Phelps who emigrated from Gloucestershire, England, to Dorchester, Mass., about 1630. His immediate ancestors were noted, not only for their business ability, but also for their religious, civic, and philanthropic interests. Thomas Stokes had been one of the thirteen founders of the London Missionary Society, and after coming to the United States was an active supporter of the American Bible Society, the American Tract Society, and the American Peace Society. James Boulter Stokes was one of the founders of the Association for Improving the Condition of the Poor, and a trustee of other charitable institutions. Anson Phelps, also, was a man of pronounced piety and a promoter of benevolent enterprises.

When scarcely more than a boy, having received a good elementary schooling, Anson Phelps Stokes entered the employ of Phelps, Dodge & Company, a mercantile establishment founded by his grandfather. In 1861 he became a partner and also a member of the firm of Phelps, James & Company, Liverpool. On Oct. 17, 1865, he married Helen Louisa, daughter of Isaac Newton Phelps. Withdrawing from Phelps, Dodge & Company in 1879, with his father and his father-in-law he organized the firm of Phelps, Stokes & Company, bankers. Three years later, however, after the death of his father, he closed out the business. In 1895 he organized the Woodbridge Company, and in 1902, the Haynes Company, realty corporations, which constructed and operated office buildings in New York City. He was an official of the Ansonia Clock Company, Ansonia, Conn., a director of several banks and of the Liverpool and London and Globe Insurance Company.

Stokes continued the family tradition of public service, devoting much time and energy to problems of the day and to the work of benevolent institutions. A vigorous advocate of free trade and civil service reform, he was a founder and first president of the Reform Club, and the vice-president of the Nineteenth Century Club, a local organization for the consideration of social and political problems. In their early days he was one of the most active members of the Civil Service Reform Association and of the Free Trade League. A foe of Tammany Hall, he was chairman of a committee of seventy in 1887 which conducted a campaign in opposition to the election of Col. John R. Fellows, Tammany candidate for district attorney. Some years earlier he had refused the Democratic nomination as candidate for Congress, and in 1888 he declined President Cleveland's offer to name him minister to Austria. An ardent anti-imperialist, he was an incorporator and president of the National Association of Anti-Imperialist Clubs, and in 1900 he presided and spoke at the great Bryan anti-imperialist meeting at Madison Square Garden, New York. He made a study of the currency and trust problems and published *Joint-Metallism* (1894) and *Dangers of the Proposed Paper Money Trust* (1898). The former, which went through five editions, proposed a "plan by which gold and silver together, at ratios always based on their relative market values, may be made the metallic basis of a sound, honest, self-regulating and permanent currency, without frequent recoinings, and without danger of one metal driving out the other." His official connections with charitable organizations were numerous, and he was an early supporter of the first tuberculosis sanatorium in the United States, established by Dr. Edward L. Trudeau [*q.v.*] at Saranac, N. Y. He helped to found the Metropolitan Museum of Art, and was himself a collector of paintings and books, his library of Americana being especially notable.

Fond of outdoor activities, he made frequent trips to England to hunt with the Quorn and Pytchley hounds. As a youth he went abroad on the clipper ship *Dreadnought,* studying navigation under the captain, and ever after he was an enthusiastic sailor. He owned successively three schooner yachts, was a member of the New York Yacht Club, and in 1882–83 was its vice-commodore. His experiences and observations on two of his sailing trips are recorded in *Cruising in the West Indies* (1902, 1903) and *Cruising in the Caribbean with a Camera* (1903). He was a member of the Society of Naval Architects and Marine Engineers, New York, and of the Institution of Naval Architects, England, and was the inventor of a centerboard, patented Mar. 31, 1903, and of a globular floating battery for coast defense, patented Apr. 7 of the same year. He was also an enthusiastic promoter of fresh-water sailing in Upper Saint Regis Lake, where, on Birch Island, he had a camp. In 1898 an accident while he was riding near his country home at Lenox, Mass., resulted in the loss of one of his legs. At the time of his death in New York City, fifteen years later, he was survived by four sons and five daughters.

[*Stokes Records* (3 vols., 1910), prepared by Stokes and privately printed for the family; *Evening Post* (N. Y.), June 30, 1913; Patent Office records; *Who's Who in America,* 1912–13; O. S. Phelps and A. T. Servin, *The Phelps Family of America* (1899), vol. II; information from a son, Anson Phelps Stokes.] H. E. S.

STOKES, CAROLINE PHELPS (1854–1909). [See STOKES, OLIVIA EGLESTON PHELPS, 1847–1927.]

STOKES, MONTFORT (Mar. 12, 1762–Nov. 4, 1842), senator from North Carolina, governor, was born within the limits of what was then Lunenburg County, Va., the eleventh child of David Stokes, a planter and a member of the county court, and of Sarah (Montfort) Stokes. He was probably the descendant of Christopher Stokes who emigrated from England before 1624 and settled in Warwick County, Va., where he became a member of the House of Burgesses. Joseph Montfort Street [*q.v.*] was a nephew. Although the details of his service are in doubt, it is certain that Stokes served in the Revolutionary War. After the war he was a planter near Salisbury, N. C. From 1786 to 1791 he was a clerk of the state Senate, and for some years

thereafter clerk of the superior court of Rowan County. In 1804 he was elected to fill a vacancy in the federal Senate but declined the office. In the following year he was elected by the General Assembly a trustee of the University of North Carolina, an office he retained until 1838; and he was repeatedly chosen as a presidential elector on the Democratic ticket. About 1812 he removed to Wilkesboro and, during the War of 1812, served as a major-general of the state militia. Again elected a federal senator to fill a vacancy and reëlected for the full term, he served from Dec. 4, 1816, to Mar. 3, 1823. Active in the long struggle of the western counties to obtain more adequate representation, he was president of the convention that met at Raleigh in November 1823 to attempt constitutional reform. He sat in the state Senate in 1826 and in the House of Representatives in 1829 and 1830. In 1830 he was elected governor as the candidate of the western element in opposition to Richard Dobbs Spaight [*q.v.*]. He was married twice, first to Mary, the daughter of Henry Irwin. She died some years after their marriage. Later he married Rachel, the daughter of Hugh Montgomery of Salisbury, who survived him. A son, Montfort S. Stokes, served with distinction in the Mexican and Civil wars and was mortally wounded at Mechanicsville in 1862. On July 14, 1832, while still governor, Stokes was appointed by President Jackson one of the three commissioners to report on conditions in the present state of Oklahoma. When the legislature met, Nov. 19, following, he resigned and early in February 1833 was at Fort Gibson in the Indian Territory. On the conclusion of his two-year term he was appointed to another Indian commission, and in March 1836 became sub-agent for the Cherokees, Senecas and Shawnees. A year later, on the grant of a full agency to the Cherokees, he was placed in charge. Untiring in his labors, he strove to maintain at least a semblance of peace and order in what was then perhaps the most turbulent section of the Union. At the end of his term, in 1841, however, President Tyler refused him a reappointment. A post as register of the land office of Fayetteville, Ark., for which he did not qualify, was offered, and two months before his death the sub-agency for the Senecas, Shawnees, and Quapaws was given him, which he consented to fill. He died at Fort Gibson and was buried with military honors.

[L. C. Bell, *The Old Free State . . . Lunenburg County and Southside, Va.* (1927), vol. II; *Biog. Directory of the Am. Congress* (1928); J. H. Wheeler, *Hist. Sketches of N. C.* (1851), vol. II, and *Reminiscences and Memories of N. C.* (1884); Grant Foreman, *Pioneer Days in the Early Southwest* (1926); *Va. Mag. of Hist. and Biog.,* July 1898; W. K. Boyd, *Hist. of N. C.,* vol. II (1919); J. P. Arthur, *Western N. C.* (1914); *The State Records of N. C.*, vols. X, XVIII, XX–XI (1890–1903); *The Legislative Manual . . . of N. C. . . . 1874* (1874); K. P. Battle, *Sketches of the Hist. of the Univ. of N. C.* (1889); *Jour. of the Senate and House of Commons of . . . N. C. . . . 1832–33* (1833), pp. 143–46 for his resignation; *Jour. of the Exec. Proc. of the Senate of the U. S.*, vols. IV–VI (1887); *Ark. State Gazette* (Little Rock), Dec. 7, 1842.]   W. J. G.

STOKES, OLIVIA EGLESTON PHELPS (Jan. 11, 1847–Dec. 14, 1927) and Caroline Phelps Stokes (Dec. 4, 1854–Apr. 26, 1909), philanthropists, were born at Clifton Cottage, on the East River near 30th Street, New York, the sixth and the youngest of the ten children of James Boulter and Caroline (Phelps) Stokes. Their father was a wealthy banker, real estate owner, and philanthropist; their mother was a daughter of Anson Greene Phelps [*q.v.*]. Two of their brothers were Anson Phelps Stokes and William Earl Dodge Stokes [*qq.v.*]. The sisters were devoted to each other, were much alike in character and interests, cooperated on many philanthropic projects, and, since neither of them married, were seldom separated. They were educated at home, but Caroline also attended Miss Porter's School in Farmington, Conn., for several years. They were members of the Presbyterian Church but in later years felt drawn more and more to the liturgical worship and devotional life fostered by the Episcopal Church. After their father's death in 1881 they traveled extensively in the United States and Europe, visited Palestine, and in 1896 made a trip around the world. They both had a taste for writing, Caroline producing a novel, *Travels of a Lady's Maid* (1908), Olivia the *Letters and Memories of Susan and Anna Bartlett Warner* (1925), an unpublished memoir of her sister, and three small books of devotion. From both sides of their family they inherited strong religious feeling and many active philanthropic interests. Out of their ample fortune they made innumerable gifts to religious, educational, charitable, and other public enterprises. Among their principal benefactions were St. Paul's Chapel of Columbia University, Woodbridge Hall at Yale University, the chapel of Berea College, Dorothy Hall at Tuskegee Institute, the chapel at Yale in China, the gymnasium at the Constantinople Woman's College, Caroline Cottage at the New York Colored Orphan Asylum, the Haynes Memorial Gates at the First Church Cemetery in Hartford, Conn., the open-air pulpit at the Cathedral of St. John the Divine in New York, and the public library at Ansonia, Conn. They contributed with equal generosity to many other institutions. The welfare of the Indian, the negro, the poor whites of the South, and the slum-dwellers of New York were their most abiding concern, and with her residuary estate Caroline endowed the Phelps-Stokes Fund for their care. Olivia became the chief patron of the Fund. At the turn of the century Caroline's health began to decline, and she spent the rest of her life at Redlands, Cal., where she died in 1909 in her fifty-fifth year. Olivia survived her by more than eighteen years, dying at her winter residence in Washington, D. C., in her eighty-first year.

[T. J. Jones, *Educational Adaptations: Report of Ten Year's Work of the Phelps-Stokes Fund, 1910–1920* (1920); J. H. Dillard and others, *Twenty Year Report of the Phelps-Stokes Fund, 1911–1931* (1932); A. P. Stokes, *Stokes Records* (privately printed, 1910); O. S. Phelps and A. T. Servin, *The Phelps Family of America* (2 vols., 1899); Anna B. Warner, *Some Memories of James Stokes and Caroline Phelps Stokes: Arranged for Their Children and Grandchildren* (printed for the family, 1892); Olivia E. P. Stokes, "The Story of Caroline Phelps Stokes" (387–page typescript; copy in office of Phelps-Stokes Fund, 101 Park Ave., New York); obituaries in *N. Y. Times*, Apr. 28, 1909, and *N. Y. Herald Tribune*, Dec. 15, 1927.]   G. H. G.

STOKES, ROSE HARRIET PASTOR (July 18, 1879–June 20, 1933), American radical, was born in the small Jewish settlement of Augustowo, Suwalki, Russian Poland. She was the daughter of Jacob and Anna (Lewin) Wieslander but her father died when she was very young and her mother soon remarried, giving the child her step-father's name of Pastor. They were desperately poor. When Rose was three they moved to London, settling in the Whitechapel slums. There for a time she attended the Bell Lane Free School where Israel Zangwill was once a pupil and later a teacher. When she was eleven her people emigrated to America, settling in Cleveland, and for the next twelve years she helped support the increasing family—six other children were born—by her earnings in a cigar factory. Although her formal schooling was ended, her mind was constantly active and rebellious. She read, wrote, and studied at night; some of her poems were published in the New York *Jewish Daily News*; and in 1903 she went to New York as a feature writer for this paper. Some five months after her arrival she interviewed the young millionaire James Graham Phelps Stokes—son of Anson Phelps Stokes [*q.v.*]—who was living at the University Settlement on the East Side and was interested in socialism. Out of this interview, which she wrote up with high praise for Mr. Stokes and his views, grew the romance which culminated in their marriage, July 18, 1905.

For some years both were active supporters of the Socialist Party, the Intercollegiate Socialist Study Society, and other radical movements, but in 1917 estrangement began between them over the World War. Both withdrew from the Socialist Party on July 9, 1917, after its adoption of the St. Louis Platform condemning American participation in the war, but after a few months Rose Pastor Stokes rejoined the party, and from that time was increasingly identified with its left wing and with those factions that eventually helped to found the American Communist Party. In 1918, she was sentenced to ten years in prison under the Espionage Act, for a letter written to the *Kansas City Star* denouncing the United States government as allied with the profiteers, but the sentence was reversed on appeal (*Stokes vs. U. S.*, 264 *Fed. Reporter*, 18) and eventually the government dropped the case. In the course of this trial she made the *apologia* for her views which has since become famous: "For ten years I have worked and produced things necessary and useful for the people of this country and for all those years I was half starved. . . . I worked at doing useful work and never had enough. But the moment I left the useful producing class—the moment I became part of the capitalistic class which did not have to do any productive work in order to exist—I had all the vacations I wanted, all the clothes I wanted. I had all the leisure I wanted—everything I wanted was mine without my having to do any labor in return for all I had received." (*In the United States Court of Appeals, 8th Circuit, No. 5255: Rose Pastor Stokes, Plaintiff in Error vs. United States of America; Brief for Plaintiff in Error*, pp. 15, 16.)

The breach between wife and husband widened, and on Oct. 17, 1925, the latter was granted a divorce. Although Rose retained his name throughout her life, she never accepted any alimony from him, and lived from this time in poverty. She was several times arrested in the years that followed for picketing in strikes and taking part in radical demonstrations, and on one of these occasions it was revealed that some time in 1927 she had remarried. Her second husband was Isaac Romaine, a private language teacher and a Communist. In 1930 it was found that she was suffering from cancer, which Communists claimed had its inception when she was clubbed by police in a riot in December 1929, and she now became more than ever a symbol and a martyr. Liberal and radical friends raised funds to send her on a trip to Russia and also, on two occasions, to a German clinic for treatment, but she died in Frankfurt-am-Main in 1933.

Among her writings are a propaganda play, dealing with feminism and labor conditions, *The Woman Who Wouldn't* (1916); a translation with Helena Frank, *Songs of Labor* (1914), by the Yiddish poet, Morris Rosenfeld; and an autobiography, unpublished at the time of her death. Her contribution, however, was emotional rather than intellectual; she has been remembered not so much for anything she wrote or said, as for the ardor and sincerity with which she embraced the cause of rebel workers everywhere and acted in accordance with her convictions.

[The papers of Rose Pastor Stokes were turned over before her death to Samuel Ornitz, who plans to publish the autobiography. This sketch is based on *Who's Who in America*, 1918–19; *N. Y. Tribune*, Apr. 16, July 19, 1905; *Kansas City Star*, Mar. 17, 20, May 20–23, 1918; *N. Y. Times* (see Index) July 1917, Feb.-June 1918, May 1919, Oct. 1920, Sept., Nov., 1921, Oct. 1925, Apr., Nov. 1926, Feb. 1929, June 21, 1933; *Daily Worker* (N. Y.), June 21, 1933; reminiscences of personal friends.]   M.G.

STOKES, WILLIAM EARL DODGE (May 22, 1852–May 19, 1926), hotel owner and capitalist, was born in New York City, the son of James Boulter and Caroline (Phelps) Stokes. He was a brother of Anson Phelps Stokes, Caroline Phelps Stokes, and Olivia Egleston Phelps Stokes [*qq.v.*]. He graduated at Yale in 1874 and became a bank clerk, later entering his father's banking firm, Phelps, Stokes & Company. Inheriting a fortune said to have amounted to $11,000,000 at his father's death, he retired from the banking business and for a number of years increased his fortune by shrewd real estate transactions in New York City. He was in those years one of the largest operators in realty in the district west of Central Park and did much to build up that quarter of the city. He was also one of the pioneers in the introduction of asphalt street paving into New York. Meanwhile he acquired mineral and timber lands in Rockingham County, Va., and built the Chesapeake Western Railway, a short railroad, from Elkton, Va., through Harrisonburg to these undeveloped lands. He had begun breeding racing horses on his Patchen Wilkes Farm, Lexington, Ky., and he gave thousands of dollars in prizes, mostly to boys and girls in Virginia, to encourage the breeding of the best poultry stocks. His enthusiasm for good blood later led him to write a book, *The Right to Be Well Born* (1917), in which he set forth his views on eugenics, based upon his experience in stock-breeding, and urged that the registration of the pedigrees of human beings be required by law. In 1906–07 he built the Hotel Ansonia, a huge, ornate, and highly successful structure at Broadway, 73rd and 74th Streets, New York City, and operated it until his death. Shortly after it was completed, the City Health Department summoned him to court for keeping hogs and geese, said to be fine blooded stock, on its roof, and forced him to remove them.

On Jan. 5, 1895, in New York City he married Rita Hernandez de Alba de Acosta, a beautiful Cuban heiress, who obtained a divorce in 1900, was re-married and divorced, and later became engaged to Percy Stickney Grant [*q.v.*]. There was one son by the marriage, who at first remained in his mother's care, but a few years later was returned to his father on the payment to his mother, it is said, of a million dollars. On Feb. 11, 1911, Stokes married Helen Elwood of Denver, Colo., by whom he had a son and a daughter. That same year, in a quarrel with two chorus girls, he was shot and painfully wounded. He grew more and more eccentric with age, and during his latter years his time was largely occupied in litigation. He brought suit against his second wife for divorce in 1919; she retorted with a counter-suit, and for the better part of four years their complicated actions were in the courts, the sensational charges and testimony furnishing much public entertainment through the newspapers. Because of certain testimony introduced in the case, Stokes was tried for conspiracy and subornation of perjury, but was acquitted. The wife finally obtained a legal separation and a large settlement. At the time of his death in New York City in 1926 there were damage suits pending against him, demanding in all about $8,000,000, practically the whole amount of his fortune, but most of these were subsequently dropped. He was survived by his three children.

[See O. S. Phelps and A. T. Servin, *The Phelps Family of America* (1899), vol. II; *Yale Univ. Obit. Record of Grads.* (1926); *World* (N. Y.), June 8, 1911, and May 20, 1926; obituaries in *Sun* (N. Y.), May 19, *N. Y. Times* and *N. Y. Herald-N. Y. Tribune*, May 20, 1926. New York newspapers and court records, 1919–24, supply many details as to his litigation with his wife, his attorneys, and others, and give sidelights on his character and career.]   A. F. H.

STONE, AMASA (Apr. 27, 1818–May 11, 1883), railroad builder, capitalist, philanthropist, was born on a farm in Charlton, Mass., the son of Amasa and Esther (Boyden) Stone, and a descendant of Simon Stone who settled in Watertown, Mass., in 1635. Amasa's education was confined to that afforded by the local town school. At seventeen he began to learn the carpenter's trade in Charlton, and three years later moved to Worcester. His was a non-technical non-scientific age and he progressed rapidly from carpentry into the fields of the contractor and the bridge-builder.

In 1840 with his brother-in-law, William Howe [*q.v.*], inventor of a wooden truss, he secured the contract to build the first railroad bridge over the Connecticut River at Springfield. Two years later, the firm of Boody, Stone & Company, contractors, acquired the patent rights to the Howe truss and entered upon a notable record of bridge building. On Jan. 13, 1842, Stone married Julia Ann Gleason of Springfield. In 1844 he became superintendent of the New Haven, Hartford & Springfield Railroad. Opportunities in Ohio, where dependence on canals and turnpikes was holding back development, lured him to the new West. In 1849, with Stillman Witt and Frederick Harbach, he contracted to build the Cleveland, Columbus & Cincinnati Railroad, first unit of the Big Four, and after its completion he became successively superintendent and president, with his home in Cleveland.

An industrial empire was in the making south of the Great Lakes; Cleveland was one of its centers; and Amasa Stone was one of the empire builders. He obtained the contract to build the Chicago & Milwaukee Railroad as well as the Cleveland, Painesville & Ashtabula Railroad. Of the latter he was president for thirteen years before it was merged in the Lake Shore & Michigan Southern, Jan. 1, 1869. For a time he was managing director of the new system. His interests expanded to include mines, iron and steel, banking and communications. As an officer of the Lake Shore Railroad, Stone recognized the South Improvement Company's system of rebates for a privileged list of oil refining companies, thereby saving the oil refining industry in Cleveland, but at the expense and embitterment of those producers less fortunate (Ida M. Tarbell, *The History of the Standard Oil Company*, 1904, I, 47, 277). The Lake Shore Railroad was his pride, but it was also his undoing. As president in 1863 he had insisted on using the Howe truss, with iron rather than wooden timbers, in designing the long bridge at Ashtabula, though warned by engineers that such a bridge would not be safe. After eleven years of service the bridge collapsed, carrying to destruction a train-load of people. He was blamed for an experiment "which ought never to have been tried" (verdict of coroner's jury, quoted in Dennett, *post*, p. 101). Under the weight of charges —many of them unfair—and the strain of sleepless nights, his health broke, and five and a half years later he ended his own life.

In business Stone was never able to endure a subordinate position. His friends saw a man of strong physique, courteous, kindly, unassuming, but when he passed beyond the fireside he became the dominant, even domineering, type of the business world. A life of struggle, achievement, and command made him so. Shortly before the end he made his greatest benefaction. He became interested in the project of moving Western Reserve College from Hudson to Cleveland and transforming it into an urban university, and for that purpose gave a half-million dollars. One of his daughters married John Hay [*q.v.*] and the other Samuel Mather [*q.v.*].

[The only satisfactory appraisal of Stone's place in history is in Tyler Dennett, *John Hay* (1933); in addition see John Hay, *Amasa Stone* (n.d.), which memoir appears also in *Mag. of Western Hist.*, Dec. 1885; *Report of the Joint Committee Concerning the Ashtabula Bridge Disaster, under Joint Resolution of the Gen. Assembly* (1877); *Cleveland Plain Dealer*, May 12, 1883; J. G. Bartlett, *Simon Stone Geneal.* (1926).]

E. J. B.

STONE, BARTON WARREN (Dec. 24, 1772–Nov. 9, 1844), frontier evangelist, who seceded from the Presbyterian denomination and was a leader in the establishment of churches designated by the name Christian, was the son of John and Mary (Warren) Stone. He was born near Port Tobacco, Md., reared in Pittsylvania County, Va., and in 1790, with the intention of becoming a barrister, he entered the academy at Guilford, N. C., conducted by Rev. David Caldwell [*q.v.*]. Converted under the influences created in that vicinity by the preaching of James McGready [*q.v.*], he became in 1793 a candidate for the ministry in the Orange Presbytery and put himself under the tutelage of Rev. William Hodge. Confused and depressed by the theology he encountered, he went to his brother's home in Oglethorpe County, Ga., and soon became teacher of languages at the seminary of the Methodist preacher, Hope Hull, in Washington, Ga. Returning to North Carolina in 1796, he was licensed by the Orange Presbytery. After itinerant preaching in Tennessee, he took charge of the churches at Cane Ridge and Concord, Bourbon County, Ky., and was ordained in 1798, accepting the Confession with the proviso "so far as I can see it consistent with the word of God" (*Biography, post,* p. 30), for some of the doctrines of Calvinism still troubled him. On July 2, 1801, he married Elizabeth, daughter of Col. William and Tabitha (Russell) Campbell.

The Great Revival, which had a notable manifestation at Cane Ridge, brought the conservative and "New Light" forces of the Presbyterian Church into sharp conflict. As a result, in September 1803, Stone and four others withdrew from the Synod of Kentucky and formed the Springfield Presbytery. They issued a three-fold "Apology," setting forth in detail their reasons for this act, the second section of which was written by Stone. The following year, convinced that there is no authority in the New Testament

for such an ecclesiastical organization, they dissolved the presbytery, signed its "Last Will and Testament," and agreed to acknowledge no name but Christian and no creed but the Bible. The remainder of Stone's life was spent chiefly in evangelical work and the establishment of churches. For the remarkable growth of the movement in Kentucky and Ohio he was largely responsible. His wife having died in 1810, he married, Oct. 31, 1811, her cousin, Celia Wilson Bowen, daughter of William and Mary Bowen. Some two years later they settled in Lexington, in which place and afterwards in Georgetown Stone taught school in connection with his religious activities. In 1826 he started a paper called the *Christian Messenger.* He had met Alexander Campbell [*q.v.*] in 1824 and formed a warm regard for him, although they were not in entire theological agreement. With the growth in Kentucky of the Disciples of Christ, as the Campbellites were called, Stone urged cooperation with them. At a conference held in his church at Lexington on Jan. 1, 1832, the Christians and Disciples agreed to act as one, and Rev. John T. Johnson, a Disciple, became co-editor of the *Christian Messenger.* A complete amalgamation never took place, however, and a religious body known as Christian persisted. Stone would never sanction the abandonment of that designation, but "This union, . . ." he declared, "I view as the noblest act of my life" (*Biography, post,* p. 79). In 1834 he moved to Jacksonville, Ill.; he continued, however, to edit the *Messenger* and to carry on evangelistic work. His tendency to theological speculation occasioned controversial pamphlets and led to his being denounced as a Unitarian. His own publications include: *Atonement* (1805), *A Reply to John P. Campbell's Strictures on Atonement* (1805), *An Address to the Christian Churches in Kentucky, Tennessee, and Ohio, on Several Important Doctrines of Religion* (1814; 2nd ed., corrected and enlarged, 1821), and *Letters to James Blythe, D.D., Designed as a Reply to the Arguments of Thomas Cleland, D.D., Against My Address, 2d ed., . . . on the Doctrine of the Trinity, the Son of God, Atonement . . .* (1824). The Rev. Thomas Cleland, Presbyterian, had attacked Stone in *The Socini-Arian Detected* (1815), and in *Letters to Barton W. Stone Containing a Vindication Principally of the Doctrines of the Trinity, the Divinity and Atonement of the Saviour* (1822); in 1825 he published *Unitarianism Unmasked; . . . A Reply to Mr. Barton W. Stone's Letters to the Rev. Dr. Blythe.* Stone died at the home of his son-in-law, Capt. S. A. Bowen, in Hannibal, Mo., and his remains were buried in the Cane Ridge, Ky., graveyard. By his first marriage he had had five children; by the second, six.

[*The Biog. of Eld. Barton Warren Stone, Written by Himself* (1847); C. C. Ware, *Barton Warren Stone* (1932); J. R. Rogers, *The Cane Ridge Meeting-house* (1910); C. C. Cleveland, *The Great Revival in the West* (1916); Lewis and R. H. Collins, *Hist. of Ky.* (2 vols., 1874); J. H. Garrison, *The Story of a Century* (1909); W. T. Moore, *A Comprehensive Hist. of the Disciples of Christ* (1919); N. S. Haynes, *Hist. of the Disciples of Christ in Ill.* (1915); A. W. Fortune, *The Disciples in Ky.* (1932); M. T. Morrill, *A Hist. of the Christian Denomination in America* (1912); W. E. Garrison, *Religion Follows the Frontier* (1931).]   H. E. S.

STONE, CHARLES POMEROY (Sept. 30, 1824–Jan. 24, 1887), soldier, was born at Greenfield, Mass., the son of Dr. Alpheus Fletcher Stone and Fanny (Cushing) Stone, widow of George Arms. He was a descendant of Gregory Stone who settled in Watertown, Mass., in 1635. Graduating at West Point in 1845, he served with the siege train throughout Scott's campaign in Mexico. Resigning in 1856, being then a first lieutenant, he was employed by a private association as chief of a commission for the exploration of the Mexican state of Sonora. His *Notes on the State of Sonora* was published in 1861.

On Apr. 16 of that year he was mustered into service as colonel, District of Columbia Volunteers; he was reappointed to the regular army as colonel, 14th Infantry, in July, and in August was appointed brigadier-general of volunteers, both commissions antedated to May. His reputation stood high, and he had every prospect of a brilliant career, until the disaster at Ball's Bluff, near Leesburg, Va., Oct. 21, 1861. With the recklessness common in brave but inexperienced officers, Col. Edward D. Baker [*q.v.*] involved a regiment of Stone's command in a skirmish with the Confederates under Gen. Nathan G. Evans [*q.v.*], which resulted in numerous casualties and Baker's death. The public was seized with a "victim-hunting mania" (Blaine, *post*, I, 382), and as Baker was a senator many of his colleagues were eager to avenge his death upon somebody. Their choice was Stone. Hints of incompetency were succeeded by whispers of treason. The display of credulity and cruelty which followed was hardly surpassed even in the World War. An investigator could solemnly set down, for example, the statement of a witness that he had heard the Confederate adjutant general say that General Evans said that Stone was a fine man and a gentleman. It is recorded that Stone "is too well spoken of in Leesburg to be all right" (War Department records). The Joint Committee on the Conduct of the War heard many witnesses, but refused their names to Stone, refused him their testimony, refused to

tell him what acts were charged against him. He was arrested at midnight, Feb. 8, 1862, and conveyed to Fort Lafayette, rising from the waters of New York harbor, where he was held in solitary confinement for fifty days. On the representations of his physician he was then transferred to Fort Hamilton, on land, where he was still kept in solitary confinement but was allowed to exercise under guard. His appeals to the War Department to know the charges against him were unanswered. Shame at last began to stir in Congress, though not in the War Department. He was released, Aug. 16, 1862, in reluctant compliance with an act of Congress, general in terms, but passed with this particular case, in mind. The Joint Committee, the Secretary of War, and General McClellan have mutually blamed each other for the imprisonment. There is guilt enough for all.

Stone was left unemployed until May 1863, when he was sent to General Banks, at the latter's request, and served under him at Port Hudson and in the Red River campaign. On Apr. 4, 1864, for no cause stated or now known, he was mustered out of his volunteer commission and as a colonel of the regular army was again left unemployed. He was finally assigned to the Army of the Potomac; but, sick and despairing, he resigned from the army, Sept. 13, 1864. From 1865 to 1869 he was engineer and superintendent for the Dover Mining Company, Goochland County, Va. From 1870 to 1883 he served in the Egyptian army, becoming chief of staff and lieutenant-general. After his return home he was chief engineer for a year of the Florida Ship Canal Company. Later, he was constructing engineer for the foundations of the Statue of Liberty in New York harbor. He was twice married: first, to Maria Louisa Clary, daughter of Gen. Robert E. Clary; and, second, to Annie Jeannie Stone, daughter of John H. Stone of Louisiana. He died in New York City.

[J. G. Bartlett, *Gregory Stone Geneal.* (1918); *War of the Rebellion: Official Records (Army)*; *Battles and Leaders of the Civil War* (4 vols., 1887–88); J. G. Blaine, *Twenty Years of Congress*, vol. I (1884); *Report of the Joint Committee on the Conduct of the War*, pt. 2, 1863; *Speech of Hon. J. A. McDougall . . . on the Arrest of Gen. Stone, and the Rights of the Soldier and Citizen* (1862); *Eighteenth Ann. Reunion, Grads. U. S. Mil. Acad.* (1887); G. W. Cullum, *Biog. Reg., Officers and Grads. U. S. Military Acad.*, vol. II (1891); *N. Y. Tribune*, Jan. 25, 1887; unpublished records in the War Dept.; for a hostile view, J. D. Baltz, *Hon. Edward D. Baker* (1888).]   T. M. S.

STONE, DAVID (Feb. 17, 1770–Oct. 7, 1818), representative and senator from North Carolina, was born at "Hope," the family home, near Windsor, N. C. He was the son of Elizabeth (Williamson) Hobson Stone and Zedekiah Stone, who is said to have been a native of Massachusetts and a descendant of Gregory Stone, an English emigrant to Watertown, Mass., about 1635. Zedekiah Stone was a prosperous planter in Bertie County, N. C., and won distinction for his political activity during and after the Revolution. The boy was educated at the College of New Jersey (Princeton), where he was graduated in 1788. He studied law in Halifax under William Richardson Davie [q.v.] and was admitted to the bar in 1790. He was at once elected to the House of Commons from Bertie County and served four terms. On Mar. 13, 1793, he was married to Hannah Turner of Tennessee, who bore him five children. In 1794 he became a judge of the superior court but served only four years. Elected to the federal House of Representatives, he served from Mar. 4, 1799, to Mar. 3, 1801, and was a member of the first standing committee of ways and means. He was a brilliant man of great personal charm and magnetism, and of much independence of character. Generally he acted with the Republicans and voted to repeal the Sedition Act. In 1800 he supported Jefferson and voted for him in the House in 1801. Elected to the federal Senate in 1801, he continued to support Jeffersonian policies, and in the Chase impeachment he voted "guilty." He spoke seldom and, while regarded as able, was never a leader. He was defeated for reëlection by Jesse Franklin [q.v.]; but the same legislature made him again a judge, and he resigned to accept. Two years later he was elected governor and served two terms from 1808 to 1810. In 1811 and 1812 he was again a member of the House of Commons and at the latter session defeated Jesse Franklin for the federal Senate. Taking his seat in 1813, he declined to vote for some of the important war measures of the administration, and thereby aroused so much feeling in North Carolina that he was censured by the legislature in December 1813. The newly elected legislature being also hostile, he resigned in 1814, filing with the governor an eloquent defense of his course, which met with the approval of the Federalists in the state. After his retirement he removed to Wake County, where the rest of his life was spent cultivating his plantation. In June 1817 he was married to his second wife, Sarah Dashiell, who survived him.

[S. A. Ashe, Biog. Hist. of N. C., vol. IV (1906); Biog. Directory Am. Cong. (1928); J. G. Bartlett, Gregory Stone Geneal. (1918), footnote p. 132; The Papers of Archibald D. Murphy (2 vols., 1914), ed. by W. H. Hoyt; Raleigh Register, Oct. 9, 1818.]

J. G. deR. H.

STONE, DAVID MARVIN (Dec. 23, 1817–Apr. 2, 1895), editor and publisher, was born in Oxford, Conn., the youngest of five children of a physician, Noah Stone, and his wife, Rosalind (Marvin) Stone. He was a descendant of John Stone who emigrated from England in 1639 and settled in what later became Guilford, Conn. He attended the village schools until he was fourteen, when he began earning his own living. After working hours he studied Latin and Greek by himself and at seventeen became a school teacher. In 1842 he found a place as clerk in a dry-goods house in Philadelphia and was employed there until the firm failed, seven years later. Meanwhile he had been writing correspondence for the Dry Goods Reporter of New York, and this led to his being offered the editorship of the magazine early in 1849. Though he was successful as an editor he could not agree with the owner of the paper and resigned later in the year. He then obtained a reporter's job on the New York Journal of Commerce, which, during the forty-four years that followed, became a veritable reflection of his own personality. During his earlier years with the Journal he was engaged in many other activities. For a time he edited the Ladies' Wreath, a popular magazine. At various times he contributed a weekly financial review to the New York Observer and conducted a similar department in Hunt's Merchants' Magazine. A Sunday-school novel from his pen entitled Frank Forrest was published in 1850 and ran through many editions. He also wrote many articles and stories for other publications. After the death of David Hale [q.v.], editor of the Journal of Commerce, much of his work fell upon Stone's shoulders. At the beginning of the Civil War, Gerard Hallock [q.v.], the principal owner of the paper, dictated a conciliatory policy towards the seceding states which became so offensive to the government that the Journal was forbidden the use of the mails and Hallock was forced to retire from its ownership. Stone and William Cowper Prime [q.v.] proposed taking it over, and learned that under their management it would be permitted to continue. In 1864 the Journal, together with other New York newspapers, was made the victim of a serious hoax, when a bogus "proclamation of the President" was delivered to it—supposedly from the New York Associated Press—and published. The editors of the World and the Journal of Commerce were ordered arrested and the papers suppressed; but it was quickly discovered that they had been the victims and not the perpetrators of the trick, and the papers were resumed. In 1866 Stone became editor-in-chief of the Journal, and in 1884 he bought out Prime's interest in the paper. In 1869 he was elected president of the New York Associated Press, the pioneer news-gathering agency of America. He held the latter position for almost twenty-five years, retiring only when the association was merged with the United Press.

As head of the *Journal of Commerce,* Stone became one of the best known editors in New York. Endowed by nature with a big, powerful body and perfect eyesight (he never wore spectacles), the amount of work he performed was prodigious. He remarked in 1889 that he had not had a whole day's absence from his office in twenty-nine years. During his latter years he had no editorial assistant and wrote with his own hand about three hundred editorial articles a month, covering a wide range of subjects. Frequently a lay sermon was found among the rest, for Stone was a prominent church and Sunday-school worker in Brooklyn, and delivered hundreds of lectures upon the life of Christ and other religious subjects. He retired from the *Journal of Commerce* in 1893 and died two years later in Brooklyn. His wife, the former Delia Charlotte Hall of Wallingford, Conn., whom he married on Sept. 7, 1841, died on Oct. 19, 1887. There were no children.

[W. L. Stone, *The Family of John Stone* (1888); *Jour. of Commerce,* Apr. 4, 1895, and Sept. 29, 1927; Victor Rosewater, *Hist. of Coöperative News-Gathering in the U. S.* (1930); obituaries in *N. Y. Herald, N. Y. Times,* and *World* (N. Y.), Apr. 3, 1895; information from friends and associates of Stone; burial records in Oxford, Conn., and Greenwood Cemetery, Brooklyn, N. Y.]   A.F.H.

STONE, ELLEN MARIA (July 24, 1846–Dec. 13, 1927), missionary and lecturer, was born in Roxbury, Mass., and died in Chelsea, Mass. She was a descendant of Gregory Stone who emigrated to Watertown, Mass., in 1635. Her father and her mother, Benjamin Franklin Stone and Lucy Waterman (Barker) Stone, were religiously minded, she was named for a missionary, and at her baptism her mother dedicated her to that calling. She graduated from the grammar and high schools of Chelsea and in 1866–67 taught there. From 1867 to 1878 she was on the editorial staff of the *Congregationalist.* Then, as the result of a deepening religious purpose, she offered herself to the American Board of Commissioners for Foreign Missions, was accepted, and was assigned to Samakov, Bulgaria. About 1883 she was transferred to Philippopolis, also in Bulgaria, and there for more than ten years she spent much of her time visiting women in their homes. Soon, too, she began a training class to prepare Bible-women

to do similar work. For a time she was in charge of the mission's school for girls, and in 1885, in the course of the uprising in which Eastern Rumelia was united to Bulgaria, she ministered to sick and wounded soldiers in Sofia. In 1898, after a furlough in the United States, she was assigned to Saloniki and placed in charge of the evangelistic work for women in that area. Her new duties involved a great deal of travel, most of it through rural and mountainous districts.

It was in connection with these journeys that there unexpectedly came upon her the great adventure of her life, which suddenly lifted her name from obscurity and for a time made it known throughout much of the civilized world. On Sept. 3, 1901, while on one of her regular tours, she and her party were attacked by brigands. She and Katerina Stephanova Tsilka, an American-educated Bulgarian who was attached to the mission, were held captive and a large ransom was demanded. The American Board felt that it could not pay the sum without encouraging the kidnapping of other missionaries, but with the indorsement of President Theodore Roosevelt and his secretary of state, a popular appeal for funds was made throughout the United States. A sum of about $66,000 was collected and after skilful negotiations paid to the brigands, and on Feb. 23, 1902, the two women were released. That spring Miss Stone returned to the United States. While her name was long retained on the staff of her mission, she never resumed her residence in the Near East. Instead, she traveled widely in America, telling the story of her captivity. Later, she became a lecturer of the Woman's Christian Temperance Union, for the most part speaking on missionary subjects. She also spent a great deal of time in Washington, attempting to obtain the passage by Congress of an appropriation which would reimburse those who had contributed to her ransom. Her account of her captivity, "Six Months Among the Brigands" (*McClure's Magazine,* May–July, September 1902), was her only published writing which obtained wide circulation.

[Manuscript files of the Am. Board of Commissioners for Foreign Missions; annual reports of the same, 1879–1908; *Missionary Herald,* Nov., Dec. 1901, Jan., Mar., Apr. 1902, Feb. 1928; *Who's Who in America,* 1916–17; "Repayment of Ransom of Ellen M. Stone," *House Report 807,* 62 Cong., 1 Sess.; *Boston Transcript,* Dec. 14, 1927; J. G. Bartlett, *Gregory Stone Geneal.* (1918).]   K.S.L.

STONE, GEORGE WASHINGTON (Oct. 24, 1811–Mar. 11, 1894), Alabama jurist, was born in Bedford County, Va., the son of Micajah and Sarah (Leftwich) Stone. His grandfather, Micajah, had settled in Virginia before the Revolution. When George was seven years old the family migrated to Lincoln County, Tenn., where the father became a planter in comfortable circumstances. The boy was educated in the schools which were available in the local community and studied law in the office of James Fulton at Fayetteville, Tenn. Going to Alabama to take his bar examination, he was admitted to the bar in May 1834. He practised in Sylacauga and in Talladega until 1843, when he was appointed judge of the circuit court to fill out an unexpired term. In December of the same year he was elected by the legislature for the six-year term. In 1849 he resigned to resume his law practice, opening a new office in Hayneville, Ala.

In 1856 he was elected associate justice of the supreme court of Alabama and was reëlected in 1862. During the reconstruction period he was retired from the bench and practised in Montgomery. After the restoration of home rule in the state, he was appointed associate justice by Governor Houston. He held the office by appointment from 1876 to 1880, when he was elected to it for a term of six years. In 1884 he was appointed chief justice by Governor O'Neal. From 1886 until his death he held the office by election.

Stone served half a century on the bench of Alabama and twenty-five years of that time he sat on the supreme bench. He was not only learned in the law, but he had a judicial mind, and he was noted for the amount of labor he gave to preparing his decisions. His expression was clear and vigorous and his decisions were regarded as models of correct judicial style. When he came to the bench both the law and its administration were in a chaotic state in Alabama. The standards had not been high before the Civil War and the demoralization resulting from war and reconstruction had increased the confusion. Stone set himself to bring some sort of order into the judicial system of the state. He stood for a vigorous administration of criminal law and rigid honesty in the administration of civil law. He aided in the preparation of the Revised Penal Code in 1865 and was able to introduce some improvements into it. As chief justice for a quarter of a century he handed down more than two thousand decisions and through them materially improved the quality of judicial work. He was an earnest advocate of judicial reform. He opposed the separate courts of law and equity which existed in Alabama and the probate courts with their judges untrained in the law. He was not able, however, to win popular support for the reform of either of these conditions during his lifetime. Stone died in Montgomery in his eighty-third year. He had been three times married:

Dec. 16, 1834, to Mary Gillespie of Franklin, Tenn.; Sept. 4, 1849, to Emily Moore of Lowndes County, Ala.; Feb. 8, 1866, to Mary E. (Harrison) Wright of Lowndes County. He was survived by his third wife and several children.

[Stone's opinions may be found in 28–29 and 53–101 *Ala. Reports*; for general sources, see T. M. Owen, *Hist. of Ala. and Dict. of Ala. Biog.* (1921), vol. IV; Willis Brewer, *Ala., Her Hist., Resources, War Record and Public Men* (1872); *Memorial Record of Ala.* (1893), vol, II; William Garrett, *Reminiscences of Public Men in Ala., for Thirty Years* (1872); G. W. Stone, "Judicial Reform," *Proc. . . . Ala. State Bar Assoc.*, 1889; D. T. Blakey, "Hon. George W. Stone," *Ibid.*, 1895; "Half a Century on the Bench," *Ibid.*, 1893; "Memorial," 100 *Ala. Reports*, ix–xx; *Daily Reg.* (Mobile, Ala.), Mar. 13, 1894.]   H. F.

STONE, HORATIO (Dec. 25, 1808–Aug. 25, 1875), sculptor, the second child of Reuben and Nancy (Fairchild) Stone, was born at Jackson, Washington County, N. Y. When his father, who preferred work on the farm chores, failed to encourage his early interest in wood carving, the boy left home and did not communicate with his family until later years. Between 1841 and 1847 he practised as a physician in New York. Increasingly he turned to sculpture, however, especially after his removal in 1848 to Washington, where he had studios variously in the northwest section of the city, at the Navy Yard, and in the sub-basement of the Capitol building. During the Civil War, from Sept. 21, 1862, until his honorable discharge Sept. 20, 1865, he served as a contract surgeon with the Union forces. He was stationed at the Patent Office General Hospital and at the Columbian College Hospital, both in Washington, at West's Buildings General Hospital, Baltimore, and at Fort Delaware, Del. In 1864 he published *Freedom,* a small volume of poems containing besides the title piece, "Eleutheria," set to music by George Henry Curtis as a cantata, and "Day." The style is sonorous, if not turgid, and the sentiment inevitably seeks the point when America is sung as the climax of creation's travail. He was active in the organization of the Washington Art Association, which had among its objects the establishment of a national art gallery and the preservation of historic monuments, and in 1857 became its president. A year later there appeared his *Inaugural Address . . . and an Address on National Art.* It was as a result of the work of the Washington Art Association that the art commission of 1859 was appointed by President James Buchanan, and that in 1860 the National Gallery of Art was incorporated.

Four of Stone's works are preserved in the Capitol—his bust of Chief Justice Roger Brooke Taney, his statues of Alexander Hamilton (1864) and Senator Edward Dickinson Baker of Oregon (1874), and his masterpiece, a statue of John Hancock (1856), all in marble. The Hamilton (see Glenn Brown, *History of the United States Capitol,* vol. II, 1903, plate 291) shows the dramatic pose and careful details of the current style, but with a unity and simplicity that one likes to think also marked the doctor's efforts as surgeon if they did not his prose and poetry. His other works include busts of Hamilton and Jefferson, said to be copies of Jean Antoine Houdon's, a statue of Jefferson, and a bust and a statue of Thomas Hart Benton. He is said to have made a pair of bronze doors in New York and, more plausibly, to have executed the stone for his mother's grave (in the Jackson cemetery), carved in Italy and showing the three Marys at the tomb. Exhibitions of his works were held at the National Academy of Design in New York City in 1849 and in 1869. He never married. His personality is recalled as one of charm and versatility. At least twice during his career he visited Italy, and it was at Carrara that he died.

[*Art Jour.* (N. Y.), Nov. 1875; C. E. Fairman, *Art and Artists of the Capitol of the U. S. A.* (1927); obituary in *N. Y. Times,* Sept. 24, 1875; date of death and other information from H. E. Cole, Executive Department, Division of the Budget, Capitol, Albany, N. Y., and Adjutant-General C. H. Bridges, Washington, D. C.]
W. S. R.

STONE, JAMES KENT (Nov. 10, 1840–Oct. 14, 1921), educator and Roman Catholic priest, was born in Boston, Mass., the son of Dr. John Seely Stone [*q.v.*] and his second wife, Mary Kent (1807–1901). He was prepared for college at E. S. Dixwell's Latin School in Cambridge and entered Harvard in 1856 but did not graduate until 1861. At the conclusion of his freshman year he traveled in Europe for a time while perfecting himself in modern languages, and in 1860–61 studied at the University of Göttingen, where he became a good student, a skilled Alpine climber, and a disciple of German academic methods. After teaching for a while in Dixwell's Latin School, he enlisted as a private in the Union army, was advanced to a lieutenancy in the Second Massachusetts Volunteers, experienced hard fighting at Antietam, and was retired in January 1863. Appointed an assistant professor of Latin in Kenyon College, Gambier, Ohio, in January 1863, he studied theology, took orders in the Protestant Episcopal Church, and in 1867, after holding chairs in Latin and mathematics, became president of the college. In the meantime he had been married on Aug. 26, 1863, to Cornelia Fay, daughter of Harrison Fay, by whom he had three daughters.

His married life was happy, and his social relations with students and faculty were pleasant; but high church leanings in a low church atmosphere brought a conflict with the local bishop and the school of divinity that led him to resign. Called to the presidency of Hobart College at Geneva, N. Y., in 1868, he was happier as a "primitive Catholic" under Bishop Arthur Cleveland Coxe [*q.v.*], a high churchman. The death of his wife on Feb. 15, 1869, brought intense grief and months of solitude. After commencement, 1869, he resigned his presidency and on Dec. 8, 1869, apparently under no Catholic influences beyond an intimate knowledge of the Tractarian Movement, he was received into the Roman Catholic Church by Father Winand Michael Wigger [*q.v.*] of Madison, N. J. Though the Fays, who were concerned about the Stone children, took steps to have Stone committed to an asylum, his father stood in the way. Meanwhile Stone wrote his polemical volume, *The Invitation Heeded* (1870), which was compared by friendly critics to Newman's *Apologia* and went through several editions and into several foreign tongues. Desirous of becoming a priest, he declined a professorship at Georgetown College and joined the Paulists. On Dec. 21, 1872, he was ordained a priest by Archbishop John McCloskey [*q.v.*] and in 1874 became a master of novices. Finally, making a tragic sacrifice which he alone could gauge, he permitted the adoption of his two surviving daughters by Michael J. O'Connor (1820–90) and his wife, childless philanthropists of San Rafael, Cal.

He was now in a position to withdraw from the Paulists, and in 1876 he joined the more severe Congregation of the Passion at Pittsburgh, Pa. As Father Fidelis of the Cross, he took his final vows on Aug. 11, 1878, and found a welcome anonymity. In 1881, after some time in the Roman mother-house on Celian Hill, he was sent to establish his congregation in Argentina, where in his twelve years he founded several monasteries, was instrumental in building Holy Cross Church (Buenos Aires), and journeyed forbidding distances over the pampas giving missions. There were brief interims when he labored for his congregation in Paraguay, 1883; attended a general chapter in Rome, 1884; laid the foundation stone of the Passionist Church of San Luis in Valparaiso, Chile, 1886; visited the United States, 1885 and 1889, where he saw his children and preached at the opening of the Catholic University in Washington; and brought missionaries from Rome, 1891, to extend his work. After preaching throughout the United States, 1894–97, even in the Appleton Chapel at Harvard, he was elected consultor to the general and stationed at Rome. At the end of his term he became provincial consultor in the United States, 1899; master of novices, 1902; and provincial, 1905–08. Again he was sent to South America as provincial. Theodore Roosevelt [*q.v.*], impressed with the refined austerity and bearing of Father Fidelis, whom he met in Buenos Aires, said that at his entrance "you heard the clink of the saber" (Smith, *post,* p. 364). In 1911 Fidelis was commissioned to inaugurate the Passionist congregation in Brazil, where he erected foundations at São Paulo and Curitiba. In 1914 he was assigned to Mexico but was unable to enter the country under Carranza. Until 1917 he served in Cuba and in negro missionary work in Corpus Christi, Tex. At that time, upon the invitation of D. E. Hudson, C.S.C., he went to Notre Dame University to write an autobiographic sequel to his early volume under the title, *An Awakening and What Followed* (1920). Retired at the Passionist monastery in Chicago, he continued to work until shortly before his death, when he returned, in a sense, to the old family life with his two daughters at San Mateo, Cal.

[W. G. and Helen G. Smith, *Fidelis of the Cross, James Kent Stone* (1926); Felix Ward, C. P., *The Passionists, Sketches Hist. and Personal* (1923); G. F. Smythe, *Kenyon College, Its First Century* (1924); *The Am. Cath. Who's Who* (1911); review in *Cath. World,* Nov. 1870; "A Convert's Experiences of the Catholic Church," *Contemporary Rev.,* June 1900; *Fifth Report, Harvard Coll. Class of 1861* (1892); J. T. Morse, Jr., in *Harvard Graduates' Mag.,* Dec. 1921; death notice in *San Francisco Chronicle,* Oct. 15, 1921.]

R. J. P.

STONE, JOHN AUGUSTUS (Dec. 15, 1800– May 29, 1834), playwright and actor, was born in Concord, Mass., the youngest of four children of Joshua and Sarah (Avery) Stone. His father was a cabinet-maker, a descendant of Gregory Stone who came from England in 1635 and settled in Watertown, Mass. His early life is obscure, but he probably made his début at the Washington Garden Theatre, Boston, as Old Norval in *Douglas,* and he seems to have specialized in old men's parts, like Old Hardy in *The Belle's Stratagem,* in which he made his first appearance in New York, at the City Theatre in Warren Street, July 10, 1822. In the same year he married Mrs. Amelia (Greene) Legge, an actress in the same company, who is better known in the history of the stage as Mrs. Stone, and who later married Nathaniel Harrington Bannister [*q.v.*]. He appears at the new Chatham Garden Theatre in 1824, and there on Nov. 4 his first play, *Restoration; or, The Diamond Cross,* was performed, Stone playing Diego. It has disappeared, but it was evidently a romantic play, with Spanish characters. After he had filled en-

gagements at the Bowery and the Chatham and at Niblo's Garden in 1828, his most important play, *Metamora; or, the Last of the Wampanoags,* was produced at the Park Theatre on Dec. 15, 1829, with Edwin Forrest [*q.v.*] as Metamora. Forrest had offered a prize of $500 and half the proceeds of the third night for the "best Tragedy, in five acts, of which the hero, or principal character shall be an aboriginal of this country" (*Critic,* Nov. 22, 1828). The committee of award, headed by William Cullen Bryant [*q.v.*], selected from among the fourteen plays submitted the Indian drama. It provided Forrest with one of his most popular parts and brought him thousands of dollars, none of which, however, were shared by the author. Forrest never permitted the publication of his successes, so that *Metamora* exists now only in a manuscript fragment, limited to the part of Metamora, in the Edwin Forrest Home for Aged and Infirm Actors in Philadelphia. From this and contemporary accounts, it is clear that the play provided Forrest with an appealing character, King Philip, the son of Massasoit, who defends his people against the English aggression and finally kills his wife, Nahmeokee, to save her from falling into the hands of the whites, dying himself from the bullets of his foes. While not the first Indian play, *Metamora* started the great vogue of the aboriginal drama and established the stage convention for the Indian dialect, a curious mixture of Ossian and the real Indian speech.

When Stone left New York for Philadelphia is not clear. His one extant play was published there in 1827, *Tancred; or, The Siege of Antioch,* a chronicle play, laid in the Christian camp before Antioch in 1097, in which Tancred triumphs over the wiles of the Grecian emperor and the sultana. But on Mar. 23, 1831, he acted at the Park Theatre in New York at his benefit, when his *Tancred, King of Sicily* was performed (evidently, judging from the cast, a totally different play from the earlier *Tancred*). Its first production had been on Mar. 16. And when *The Demoniac; or, The Prophet's Bride* was played at the Bowery on Apr. 12, 1831, he played Taher Ben Yhudah in what must have been an oriental drama. He next revised James Kirke Paulding's *The Lion of the West,* in which James Henry Hackett [*qq.v.*] had been acting since April 1831 the part of Nimrod Wildfire. Since both original and revision have disappeared, it is hard to assign Stone's share, but apparently he wrote a new play, a melodramatic comedy, in which Nimrod Wildfire from Kentucky straightened out all the complications. Beginning Nov. 14, 1831, at the Park, it became one of Hackett's famous parts. Stone wrote another play for Forrest, *The Ancient Briton,* produced first at the Arch Street Theatre, Philadelphia, Mar. 27, 1833. It was an historical tragedy, the action beginning about 60 A.D. in the mountains of Wales, during the reign of Nero, while Suetonius was general of the Roman forces. Boadicea defeats the Romans but afterwards commits suicide. The Britons were painted like the Indians in *Metamora.* Of other plays, like *Fauntleroy; or, The Fatal Forgery* and *La Roque, the Regicide,* attributed to Stone, little is known but the titles. A prize play for George Handel Hill [q.v.], *The Knight of the Golden Fleece, or, The Yankee in Spain,* was produced posthumously at the Park Theatre, Sept. 10, 1834. Charles Durang, who knew Stone, describes him as "a small man, slight in figure, but genteel." He was evidently of a despondent nature, or he may have been made so by the discouraging conditions of the stage. On May 29, 1834, he threw himself off the Spruce Street Wharf in Philadelphia into the Schuylkill River. He was survived by his widow and two sons. Forrest erected a handsome tombstone to his memory, in Machpelah Cemetery, with the inscription "Erected to the Memory of John Augustus Stone, Author of Metamora, By His Friend Edwin Forrest."

[Dates of birth and death are given on authority of the town clerk of Concord and the manuscript diary of William Wood, the Philadelphia manager, in the lib. of the Univ. of Pa. The *Pennsylvanian* (Phila.), May 31, 1834, however, gives the date of death as May 28. Stone's biog. must be gathered from Charles Durang, "The Phila. Stage," 3 ser., ch. 25, in *Sunday Despatch* (Phila.), beginning July 8, 1860; J. N. Ireland, *Records of the N. Y. Stage* (2 vols., 1866–67); James Rees, *The Life of Edwin Forrest* (1874); W. R. Alger, *Life of Edwin Forrest,* vol. I (1877); G. C. D. Odell, *Annals of the N. Y. Stage,* vols. III, IV (1928); R. D. James, *Old Drury of Phila.* (1932). See also J. G. Bartlett, *Gregory Stone Geneal.* (1918). For a portrait, see O. S. Coad and Edward Mims, Jr., *The Am. Stage* (1929). For dramatic criticism, see A. H. Quinn, *A Hist. of the Am. Drama from the Beginning to the Civil War,* vol. I (1923).]

A. H. Q.

STONE, JOHN MARSHALL (Apr. 30, 1830–Mar. 26, 1900), governor of Mississippi, was born at Milan in west Tennessee, the son of Asher and Judith (Royall) Stone, both natives of south-side Virginia. He was the descendant of Joshua Stone who settled in Prince Edward County, Va., early in the eighteenth century. When John was eleven years old his father died leaving the mother with nine children to struggle against poverty. As a result, the boy's education was restricted to the common schools, but in spite of this he first earned his living as a school teacher. Then he was a clerk on a Tennessee River steamboat running from the Ohio to Eastport, Miss. After settling for a time at Eastport, he became in 1855 station agent at the neighboring town of Iuka. With the opening of the Civil War, he became captain of the Iuka Rifles in the 2nd Mississippi Infantry, and in the spring of 1861 his company reached Virginia. He participated in most of the important battles in that state during the next four years and was wounded, though not severely. His ability and bravery obtained his advancement to the rank of colonel in the brigade commanded by Joseph R. Davis [q.v.]. At times, as during the Wilderness fighting, he was in charge of the brigade. Early in 1865 he was captured in North Carolina, while leading some Mississippi recruits to Virginia. Released from Johnson's Island in July 1865, he returned to his railroad agency at Iuka. There, on May 2, 1872, he married Mary Gilliam Coman. After their two children died in infancy, three of Stone's nieces were adopted.

After serving his political apprenticeship in several local offices, he was elected to the state Senate and, reëlected, he served from 1870 to 1876. Chosen by acclamation president *pro tempore* of that body, he became acting-governor of Mississippi on Mar. 29, 1876, after the forced resignation and removal of Gov. Adelbert Ames and Lieut.-Gov. A. K. Davis. The next year he was elected governor. The activities of his administration were chiefly devoted to reorganizing the government on the basis of control by the native white people of the state and to abolishing the extravagances of the recent Carpetbag government. In addition, the Mississippi Agricultural and Mechanical College (now Mississippi State College) was established, and a state board of health was created, which at once performed valiant service during the severe yellow-fever epidemic of 1878. He opposed the popular demand for the establishment of a railroad commission. Nevertheless, under his successor, Gov. Robert Lowry [q.v.], the commission was formed, and Stone was appointed a member in 1884. In 1889 he was again elected governor. Once more economy in state affairs was necessary owing to the panic of the early 'nineties. As his first administration marked the return of power to the white race, so his second gave a constitutional basis for the perpetuation of white control in the provisions of the constitution of 1890. Popular approval, which has sometimes approached reverence, for this document has brightened the halo about the name of Stone. Since the constitution of 1890 added two years to the terms of those holding state office, he served a six-year term, from 1890 to 1896. Nine months before his death he was made president of the Agricultural and Mechanical College.

He was an able administrator, and he was a man of substantial character who was above suspicion in all his public life. These facts, coupled with the length of his service, largely explain the great respect in which his administrations are held. Furthermore, his régime appeared in an excellent light in contrast with the corruptions of the Reconstruction period, and the fear of a return of those hardships kept the political leaders of Mississippi in a state of unusual harmony.

[Dunbar Rowland, *Mississippi* (1907), vol. II; *Biog. and Hist. Memoirs of Miss.* (1891), vol. II; Robert Lowry and W. H. McCardle, *A Hist. of Miss.* (1891); *Pubs. Miss. Hist. Soc.*, esp. vol. XII (1912); *Commercial Appeal* (Memphis), Mar. 27, 1900, Mar. 1, 1931.]
C. S. S.

STONE, JOHN SEELY (Oct. 7, 1795–Jan. 13, 1882), Protestant Episcopal clergyman, educator, was the ninth child of Ezekiel and Mary (Seely) Stone, and sixth in descent from William Stone—fourth son of the Rev. Samuel Stone of Hereford, England—who sailed from London to New England on May 20, 1639, and was one of the founders of Guilford, Conn. Born and brought up in West Stockbridge, Berkshire County, Mass., John shouldered his musket in 1814 and marched to the defense of Boston.

He graduated from Union College, Schenectady, N. Y., in 1823, and entered the General Theological Seminary, New York City. On Jan. 4, 1826, in St. Mark's Church, New York, he was ordered deacon by Bishop Hobart, and on Jan. 7, 1827, in Hartford, Conn., was ordained priest by Bishop Brownell. He was a tutor in Greek and Latin at Hobart College, 1825–27, and then became rector of St. Michael's Church, Litchfield, Conn. He was subsequently rector of All Saints Church, Frederick, Md., 1828–29; Trinity Church, New Haven, Conn., 1830–32; St. Paul's Church, Boston, 1832–41; Christ Church, Brooklyn, 1842–52; and St. Paul's Church, Brookline, Mass., 1852–62. In 1862 he was appointed professor of theology in the Philadelphia Divinity School, where he served until 1867. In that year he became the first dean and professor of systematic theology of the newly founded Episcopal Theological School, Cambridge, Mass. Retiring from that office and active service in 1876, he lived in Cambridge until his death, some six years later.

As a pastor, Stone was sympathetic, cheerful, and transparent as a child. As a dean he was more successful as a friend of the students than as an administrator. Young men felt and responded to his love of truth, his simplicity of nature, and his intellectual and moral courage. He was an eloquent preacher and a leader of thought in the Evangelical school of his Church. Hold-

ing firmly to the standard of the Reformation, justification by faith, he sympathized with the orthodox rather than the advanced school of New England theology. Ecclesiastically, he was one of those who opposed the Tractarian Movement of Oxford and the teachings of Pusey and Newman in regard to the Sacraments, defining the visible Church of Christ as "a congregation of faithful men, in which the pure word of God is preached, and the Sacraments duly administered according to God's Ordinance."

Stone published *Memoir of the Life of the Rt. Rev. Alexander Viets Griswold* (1844); *The Mysteries Opened* (1844), republished as *The Christian Sacraments* (1866); *Lectures on the Institution of the Sabbath* (1844), republished as *The Divine Rest* (1867); *The Church Universal* (1846), republished as *The Living Temple* (1866); and *A Memoir of the Life of James Milnor, D.D.* (copr. 1848). On May 2, 1826, he married Sophie Morrison Adams, by whom he had five children, of whom only two were living when his wife died. On Sept. 5, 1839, he married Mary Kent, a daughter of Chancellor James Kent [*q.v.*] of New York. She was born in Albany, May 19, 1807, and died in Boston, Jan. 10, 1901. Of the children of this second marriage, the eldest, James Kent Stone [*q.v.*], after serving as president of Kenyon and Hobart colleges, was received by the Roman Catholic Church in 1869 and as a Passionist father, under the name Fidelis of the Cross, became a devoted missionary. Another son, Henry, died in service in the Civil War; a daughter, Elizabeth, was the wife of the Rev. Alexander V. G. Allen [*q.v.*], professor of ecclesiastical history in the Episcopal Theological School at Cambridge.

[G. Z. Gray, *John S. Stone, A Memorial Sermon* (1882); W. G. and H. G. Smith, *Fidelis of the Cross, James Kent Stone* (1926); C. L. Slattery, *Alexander Viets Griswold Allen* (1911); *Churchman*, Jan. 21, 1882; *Church Almanac*, 1883; *Boston Transcript*, Jan. 14, 1882; personal acquaintance.]
W. L.

STONE, JOHN WESLEY (July 18, 1838–Mar. 24, 1922), lawyer, jurist, and member of Congress from Michigan, was born at Wadsworth, Ohio, the son of Chauncey and Sarah (Bird) Stone. His father, a farmer, was a cooper by trade and a Methodist preacher; he was descended from Simon Stone, an emigrant from England, who was in Watertown, Mass., as early as 1635. John attended the district schools of Wadsworth, and a small academy at Spencer, Ohio. About 1856 the family moved to Allegan County, Mich., where Stone taught school in winter and in summer split rails and helped clear the new farm.

In 1859 he commenced the study of law with

Silas Stafford, an attorney in Plainwell, and the following year was elected clerk of Allegan County. Continuing the study of law, he was admitted to the bar in 1862. In the same year he was reëlected county clerk and served until 1864, when he was chosen prosecuting attorney. He was prosecutor for Allegan County until 1870. Meanwhile, in 1865 he formed a law partnership with Dan J. Arnold of Allegan, which continued until 1873, when Stone was elected circuit judge of the twentieth judicial district, comprising the counties of Allegan and Ottawa. He resigned this office on Nov. 1, 1874, and removed to Grand Rapids, where he became junior member in the firm of Norris, Blair & Stone.

From 1877 to 1881 Stone served as member of Congress from the fifth congressional district, then resumed the practice of law in Grand Rapids in partnership with Nathaniel A. Earle. Later these two formed a partnership with Edward Taggart. Early in the administration of President Harrison, Stone was offered but declined an appointment as governor of Washington Territory. In 1882 he was appointed United States attorney for the western district of Michigan, which office he held for four years, meantime forming a partnership with his assistant Wesley W. Hyde.

Stone's business had often taken him to the Upper Peninsula, and in 1887 he decided to move to Houghton, because of the financial opportunities offered by that rapidly developing country. He practised law in Houghton from 1887 to 1890 with the firm of Stone & Gray; in 1890 was elected circuit judge of the twenty-fifth judicial district, composed of the counties of Marquette, Delta, Menominee, Dickinson, and Iron, and the following year transferred his residence to Marquette. He held the office of circuit judge until Dec. 31, 1909, and the next day took his seat on the bench of the supreme court of the state, to which he had been elected in the preceding spring. He served on the supreme court until his death, twelve years later, at Lansing. Except for a few short breaks, his public service in the state of Michigan extended over a period of more than sixty years.

Tall, slender, with a ruddy complexion, Judge Stone was a distinguished figure. He was invariably even-tempered, and an indefatigable worker, even during his late years. His opinions as a member of the supreme court appeared in 159–217 *Michigan Reports*. They were, for the most part, excellently written, some of them models of brevity and conciseness, and all showing a keen analytical mind, wide learning, and a sound knowledge of the law. He was married,

May 2, 1861, to Delia M. Grover of Allegan, Mich., who died Jan. 25, 1902. To this marriage seven children were born.

[J. G. Bartlett, *Simon Stone Geneal.* (1926); *Who's Who in America*, 1922–23; *Biog. Dir. Am. Cong.* (1928); *Mich. Biogs.* (Mich. Hist. Com., 1924), vol. II; C. B. Howell, *Mich. Nisi Prius Cases ... Biog. Sketches of the Judges of Mich.* (1884); G. I. Reed, *Bench and Bar of Mich.* (1897); *Detroit Free Press*, Mar. 25, 1922; personal letters from the family of Judge Stone.]
                                                    H. C.

STONE, LUCY (Aug. 13, 1818–Oct. 18, 1893), reformer and pioneer in the woman's rights movement, was born near West Brookfield, Mass. Her mother was Hannah (Matthews) Stone. Her father, Francis Stone, was a descendant of Gregory Stone who emigrated from England to Massachusetts Bay in 1635. Francis Stone was a well-to-do farmer and tanner who believed that men were divinely ordained to rule over women. Hannah, his wife, meek and docile, accepted this view; but Lucy, when still very young, became resentful of woman's lot. Upon discovering that the Bible seemed to uphold male domination she wanted to die. Soon, however, she began to suspect the man-made translations of the Scriptures and decided to study Greek and Hebrew to find out whether they were correct. Though her brothers were sent to college, her father was shocked when she expressed a wish to go, and he would give her no financial aid. Therefore, she determined to educate herself, and when sixteen began to teach district school at a dollar a week, "boarding around." For several years afterward she continued to teach, except for short periods at Quaboag Seminary in Warren, Mass., the Wesleyan Academy in Wilbraham, Mass., and at Mount Holyoke Female Seminary. During this time her hostility towards the existing status of women increased, for she learned that, because of her sex, she had no vote in the Congregational Church in West Brookfield of which she was a member. Finally, in 1843 she had enough money to start work at Oberlin College and registered there. For the first two years she helped eke out her expenses by teaching and by manual labor, but in her third year her father relented and came to her aid. At college she was looked upon as a dangerous radical, for she was an ardent abolitionist, was uncompromising on the question of woman's rights, and, under the influence of the brimstone sermons of Charles Grandison Finney [*q.v.*], became Unitarian in religion. In August 1847 she was graduated at Oberlin College.

A few weeks later she gave her first public address on woman's rights, from the pulpit of her brother, William Bowman Stone, at Gardner,

Mass. The following year she began to lecture regularly for the Anti-Slavery Society, but she urged the elevation of woman whenever pretext offered. After two or three years most of her time was given to free-lance lecturing on the rights and wrongs of her sex, and she traveled over much of the country delivering her message. Possessed of rare eloquence and a singularly beautiful voice, she was, as Elizabeth Cady Stanton said, "the first person by whom the heart of the American public was deeply stirred on the woman question" (Blackwell, *post,* p. 94). In 1850 she headed the call for the first national Woman's Rights convention, which was held at Worcester, Mass., and had much to do with arranging for the later conventions, which took place annually. She published the proceedings at her own expense. She had intended never to marry, in order that she might give all of her energies to the cause of woman's rights, but on May 1, 1855, she became the wife of Henry Brown Blackwell [*q.v.*], after he had offered to devote his life to the same cause. He kept his word. In connection with their marriage they drew up a joint protest against the legal disabilities of women that was given wide publicity. Lucy Stone felt that a woman's abandonment of her name upon taking a husband was symbolical of her loss of individuality, so she kept her own name after marriage, merely substituting the title Mrs. for Miss.

Following her marriage her labors for woman's rights continued and broadened. For a time the family lived in New Jersey, and there, in 1858, she let her household goods be sold for taxes and used the incident for a written protest against taxation without representation. When the Fourteenth Amendment to the federal Constitution was pending, she and her husband strove, in vain, to win suffrage for women through getting the word "male" struck from the bill. In 1866 when the American Equal Rights Association was formed she was made a member of the executive committee. In 1867, partly through her efforts, the New Jersey Woman Suffrage Association was organized, with her as president. For two months of the same year she and her husband campaigned in Kansas in behalf of amendments to the state constitution for extending suffrage to women and to negro men. In 1868, while still living in New Jersey, they helped organize the New England Woman Suffrage Association. Soon they removed to Boston to aid the woman movement in Massachusetts. Just at this time a split, over program and methods, occurred in the American Equal Rights Association, and in its place de-

veloped the National Woman Suffrage Association and the American Woman Suffrage Association. She helped form the latter, which concentrated on gaining suffrage by states. Twenty years later, upon the initiative of Alice Stone Blackwell, her daughter, the two organizations were united as the National American Woman Suffrage Association, and she was placed on the executive committee. She raised most of the money with which the *Woman's Journal* was founded in 1870. Two years later she and her husband assumed the editorship and were in charge of it for the remainder of their lives. Under their direction the publication became a tower of strength to the cause of woman's rights. Meanwhile she was the leading spirit in the Massachusetts Woman Suffrage Association, which she and her husband helped organize in 1870, and in the New England and the American associations; and she likewise gave much individual time to lecturing and drafting bills and to legislative hearings in the interest of a better status for women. She delivered her last lecture for the cause to which she devoted her life in connection with the World's Columbian Exposition at Chicago in 1893. Shortly afterward her health began to fail from an internal tumor. At her home in Boston she died, urging her daughter, Alice Stone Blackwell, to "make the world better" (Blackwell, *post,* p. 282). Her funeral, said a friend, was like a coronation (*Ibid.,* p. 285). She was short of stature but well built; her cheeks were rosy throughout life; her nose was broad and tip-tilted, adding to her expression of good nature and approachableness; her eyes were bright gray; her mouth, strong and kindly; and she had an abundance of dark brown hair, which had whitened very little when she died. She possessed unusual personal magnetism, but she had not much sense of humor. Ruggedly honest in acts and words, modest, unselfish, and fearless, she was kind in her human relationships, even to her opponents, and was very fond of children. She died at her home in Dorchester, Mass.

[Some letters in Lib. of Cong., but most of papers in possession of daughter, Alice Stone Blackwell; A. S. Blackwell, *Lucy Stone, Pioneer of Woman's Rights* (copr. 1930), "Lucy Stone, New Jersey Pioneer Suffragist," *The Civic Pilot,* Jan. 1923, and "Three Pioneer Women," in *Alpha Phi Quarterly,* Jan. 1927; *History of Woman Suffrage* (6 vols., 1881–1922), ed. by E. C. Stanton, S. B. Anthony, M. J. Gage, and I. H. Harper; J. G. Bartlett, *Gregory Stone Geneal.* (1918); *Boston Evening Transcript,* Oct. 19, 1893; *N. Y. Tribune,* Oct. 22, 28, 1893.]   M. W. W.

STONE, MELVILLE ELIJAH (Aug. 22, 1848–Feb. 15, 1929), journalist, was born at Hudson, Ill., second of the six sons of the Rev.

Elijah and Sophia Louisa (Creighton) Stone. His father was a Methodist Episcopal clergyman "on circuit," who supplemented his clerical income by manufacturing tools for saw mills; he was a descendant of Simon Stone who emigrated from England in 1635 and settled at Watertown, Mass. After attending the public schools in Chicago Stone became a newspaper reporter on the *Chicago Republican* but soon acquired an interest in an iron foundry. On Nov. 25, 1869, in Chicago, he married Martha Jameson McFarland, daughter of John Stuart McFarland, by whom he had two sons and a daughter. When the great Chicago fire of 1871 wiped out his foundry, he went back to newspaper work. In 1875, with two partners, he organized the first penny daily, the *Chicago Daily News,* launching an experimental issue on Christmas day. In 1881 with Victor Fremont Lawson [*q.v.*], whose partner he had become, he started a morning edition. Seven years later he sold out his interest in the papers to Lawson. After several years of European travel, he turned to banking and for a time was president of the Globe National Bank. He was also treasurer of the Chicago Drainage Canal, and president of the Citizens' Association and of the Civil Service Reform League.

In 1893 he was persuaded to become general manager of the Associated Press of Illinois, incorporated by the Western Associated Press when it refused a place in the merger of the New York Associated Press (founded 1848) and the United Press. He immediately contracted with the Reuter Telegram Company, Ltd., of Great Britain and its allied associations in other European countries for the exclusive right to use their news in the United States. When the United Press went into receivership in 1897, most of its papers joined the Associated Press; others formed the Publishers' Press, which later combined with the Scripps-McRae service to form the United Press Associations. In 1898 the supreme court of Illinois ruled that the Associated Press was bound to furnish its reports to any newspaper which applied for them (*Inter-Ocean Publishing Company* vs. *Associated Press,* 184 *Illinois Reports,* 438). This was fatal to the cooperative plan of the self-governing association, and in September 1900 the organization was dissolved in Illinois but simultaneously reorganized in New York under a statute permitting formation of corporations not for profit. This Stone headed as general manager and secretary until he retired in 1921, establishing in these years a number of important journalistic principles. He sedulously fostered the cooperative principle upon which the organization was

based, widely copied by such news agencies as the Canadian Press and the Shimbun Rengo Sha of Japan. He proved that news could be gathered and distributed free from partisanship and editorial bias, and without thought of monetary profit, a distinct departure from previously accepted practices, which had made press associations commercial in character. He also asserted that there was little true appeal to readers in episodic sensationalism and held that the news columns should mirror what he called the "substantial activities of the people," whether the actors in them were great or humble. Under his management there was fought through the federal courts to the Supreme Court of the United States a case which in 1918 established the legal principle that news is a commodity and that in it a property right exists (*International News Service* vs. *Associated Press,* 248 *United States Reports,* 215). On successive trips abroad he established Associated Press bureaus in the principal European capitals and persuaded chancelleries of the Old World to open their news sources to American correspondents.

His greatest personal triumph came in connection with the Russo-Japanese War of 1904–05. After going to Saint Petersburg (later Leningrad) and persuading Czar Nicholas II to remove the censorship from Russian press dispatches, he was influential in preventing the failure of the peace parley between the two countries at Portsmouth, N. H., in August 1905. Learning that the czar had instructed his plenipotentiaries to withdraw when the Japanese made demands for indemnity, he communicated with Pres. Theodore Roosevelt [*q.v.*] and with Emperor Wilhelm II of Germany, urging that pressure be brought to bear on both parties. The upshot was that Tokio withdrew its demand for a money payment, the czar authorized further negotiations, and peace followed. Stone's part in this was so confidential, however, that it was not known for some years. In 1921 his autobiography, *Fifty Years a Journalist,* appeared. He died in New York, survived by his wife and daughter, and was buried in the National Cathedral at Washington, D. C. He has been described as a man "of a constructive mind, remarkable executive powers, and a most frank, engaging, and delightful personality" (*Nation, post,* p. 274), and as "true and kindly, eminently interested in his work and his duty" (*Times,* London, quoted in *New York Times,* Feb. 18, 1929).

[J. G. Bartlett, *Simon Stone Geneal.* (1926); *Who's Who in America,* 1928–29; "*M.E.S.*" *His Book* (1918); Victor Rosewater, *Hist. of Coöperative News-Gathering in the U. S.* (1930); "'M.E.S.,'" *Nation,* Mar. 6,

1929; *N. Y. Times*, Feb. 16, Mar. 24, Mar. 31, 1929; records of the Associated Press.]   M. E. C.

STONE, RICHARD FRENCH (Apr. 1, 1844–Oct. 3, 1913), physician and editor, was born near Sharpsburg, Bath County, Ky., the son of Samuel and Sally (Lane) Stone. Samuel Stone, grandson of Josiah Stone, an English immigrant to Virginia, was a member of the Kentucky legislature and brigadier-general in the state militia. He moved his family to Putnam County, Indiana, in 1851, and there Richard received his early education in the public schools and in Bainbridge Academy. He taught school and studied medicine under Dr. J. B. Cross of Bainbridge for four years, and in 1863 entered Rush Medical College in Chicago. After one year he was appointed a medical cadet in the Union army and assigned to duty at Madison, Ind. He was shortly transferred to Philadelphia, Pa., where he served successively in three large military hospitals and attended the medical department of the University of Pennsylvania, from which he graduated in 1865. During the following year he served as acting assistant surgeon at camps at Key West and Cedar Keys, and in the post hospital at Monticello, Fla. He resigned from the military service in April 1866 and returned to Indiana, where he practised at New Albany, at Carpentersville, and finally at Bainbridge. In 1879 he participated in the founding of the Central College of Physicians and Surgeons, at Indianapolis, in which he held the chair of materia medica, therapeutics, and clinical medicine from 1880 until he resigned in 1886. After 1880 he lived in Indianapolis. At various times he was on the medical staffs of the Indianapolis City Hospital and City Dispensary (1882), the Marion County Asylum, and the Indiana Institute for the Education of the Blind. He took a lively interest in the activities of the Grand Army of the Republic and in local Democratic politics. He was a member of the pension bureau examining-board at Indianapolis, 1885–95, and in 1895 was appointed surgeon-general of the state militia with the grade of colonel. He contributed occasional papers to journal literature, perhaps the most notable being "Etiology of Specific Disease" (*Journal of the American Medical Association*, July 16, 1892), a discourse in opposition to the idea of the bacterial causation of disease. In 1885 he published *Elements of Modern Medicine*, and in 1894 his *Biography of Eminent American Physicians and Surgeons*, with a second and enlarged edition in 1898. This work required the labor of years. Though the sketches are often ill chosen, and in the case of living men largely autobiographical, it remains one of the best available sources of information for the biographer of American medical men.

In his earlier professional career Stone was a general practitioner who did some surgery and more obstetrics with creditable skill. His many outside activities, however, took toll of his clientele, and in his later years he added real estate promotion to a precarious practice, with scant success in either. He died in his office, probably a suicide, from asphyxiation by gas. An associate described him as being quiet and reserved, marked by a diffidence that interfered seriously with any activities involving public contacts. He was married on Nov. 24, 1869, to Matilda C. Long, daughter of Dr. William Long of New Maysville, Ind., by whom he had one son.

[R. F. Stone, *Eminent Am. Physicians and Surgeons* (1894), with portrait; H. A. Kelly and W. L. Burrage, *Am. Medic. Biogs.* (1920); Samuel Earp, in *Indianapolis Medic. Jour.*, Oct. 15, 1913; obituary in *Indianapolis Star*, Oct. 4, 1913, with portrait.]
                    J. M. P.—n.

STONE, SAMUEL (July 1602–July 20, 1663), Puritan clergyman, the son of John Stone, a freeholder of Hertford, England, was baptized in Hertford on July 30, 1602. In 1620 he matriculated as a sizar from Emmanuel College in the University of Cambridge, where he received the B.A. degree in 1623. The year before, he took holy orders at Peterborough and resided in Aspen, Essex, at the home of Richard Blackerby. There he studied divinity, Bible exegesis, and Hebrew until his appointment as curate at Stisted, Essex. He held this curateship from June 13, 1627, to Sept. 13, 1630, when he was suspended for nonconformity. Through the influence of Thomas Shepard [*q.v.*] he then obtained the Puritan lectureship at Towcester in Northamptonshire. There he met Thomas Hooker [*q.v.*] and with him emigrated to Newtown (Cambridge) in New England as colleague minister in place of John Cotton [*q.v.*]. Eminently practical, he selected the site of Hartford, Conn., negotiated its purchase from the Indians and removed there in 1636. The town was probably named in honor of his birthplace. His first wife died in 1640. After Hooker's death, in 1647, he remained sole minister of the Hartford church until his own death. Although his godliness was especially revealed "in frequent *Fastings*, and exact *Sabbaths*," he possessed "a certain Pleasancy" and a "most ready Wit" (*Magnalia, post,* III, 117). He represented his church at the New England synods of 1637, 1643, and 1646–48. As chaplain under John Mason [*q.v.*], he served through the Pequot War of 1637. On occasion he examined those accused and ministered to those convicted of witchcraft and even gave advisory opinions in civil cases. Apparently he was the "Rev. Mr. Stone" who accompanied Governor Winthrop of Connecticut to England in 1661 (*Haerlemse Saterdaeghse Courant* of Sept. 17, 1661, *New York Historical Society Collections*, 2 ser., I, 1841, 456). He found time to write a "Confutation of the Antinomians" and "A Body of Divinity," neither of which he published, and *A Congregational Church Is a Catholike Visible Church Or an Examination of Mr. Hudson* (1652).

The latter part of his life was embittered by a violent controversy with a party in his church led by William Goodwin, the ruling elder. Although its origin, as Cotton Mather tartly stated, "has been rendred almost as obscure as the Rise of *Connecticut* River" (*Magnalia, post,* III, 177), it is difficult to avoid the conclusion that personal friction between Stone and Goodwin both originated and prolonged the controversy. Qualifications for baptism, church membership, and the rights of the brethren were the main points at issue. Stone believed that the essence of Congregationalism was *"a speaking* Aristocracy *in the Face of a silent* Democracy" (*Ibid.,* 118). Although his ideas of church government approached Presbyterianism more than Independency, he was steadfastly supported by a majority. In this controversy, which deeply influenced religious life throughout New England, Stone's conduct was not above reproach; yet he consistently and conscientiously acted according to his own precepts. Upon his death at Hartford his inventory was £563. His will mentioned his second wife Elizabeth Allen, to whom he was married in 1641, and five of his children.

[Unpublished MSS. in possession of Mass. Hist. Soc.; Cotton Mather, *Magnalia Christi Americana* (1702), Book III, 62, 116–18; John and J. A. Venn, *Alumni Cantabrigienses,* pt. I, vol. IV (1927); Wm. Urwick, *Nonconformity in Herts* (1884), 518 ff.; John Winthrop, *The Hist. of New England* (1825), ed. by James Savage; *Conn. Hist. Soc. Colls.,* vol. II (1870); J. H. Trumbull, *The Memorial Hist. of Hartford County, Conn.* (1886), I, 262, 280; G. L. Walker, *Hist. of the First Church in Hartford* (1884), ch. vii; Sylvester Judd, *Hist. of Hadley* (new ed. 1905); Thomas Shepard, "Memoir of his own Life," in Alexander Young, *Chronicles of . . . Massachusetts* (1846); W. DeL. Love, *The Colonial Hist. of Hartford* (1914); James Savage, *A Geneal. Dict.,* vol. IV (1862), pp. 207–08; *Dict. Nat. Biog.*]   F. T. N.

STONE, THOMAS (1743–Oct. 5, 1787), signer of the Declaration of Independence, was born on "Poynton Manor," Charles County, Md., the eldest son of David and Elizabeth (Jenifer) Stone and the great-great-grandson of William Stone, 1603–1660 [*q.v.*]. He received a classical education from a Scotch school-master and then went to Annapolis, where he studied law in the office of Thomas Johnson [*q.v.*]. After his ad-

mission to the bar in 1764, he went to Frederick to practise. He married Margaret Brown in 1768. Perhaps some of the £1,000 dowry was used to buy land near Port Tobacco, Charles County, where the family removed about 1771 and built "Habre-de-Venture," one of the most beautiful examples of colonial architecture in Maryland. In 1774, when the legality of the poll tax for the support of the clergy was tested, he was one of the sheriff's lawyers against Thomas Johnson, Samuel Chase, and William Paca [*qq.v.*], who were later to be his colleagues in Congress. Although his sympathies were entirely with the colonists when the break with England came, he always seems to have favored a milder course than many of his fellow representatives. He took his seat in the Continental Congress on May 13, 1775, and, except for a part of the year 1777 when he declined reëlection, he served until October 1778. His most important work was on the committee that framed the Articles of Confederation. Since, just a few days before the Declaration of Independence was voted upon, permission was given by Maryland to her delegates to vote as they thought best, he voted for the Declaration and signed it. He is the least known of the Maryland signers partly because he seldom spoke either in Congress or the Maryland Senate, and few of his letters have been preserved. He appeared, however, to have hated the thought of war and in September 1776 spoke in favor of treating with Lord Howe for peace (Burnett, *post,* II, 74, footnote).

Elected state senator for a five-year term in 1776 and reëlected twice he represented Charles County in the first three Senates, but he died before he completed his third term. He was one of the Maryland commissioners appointed to confer with those from Virginia over jurisdiction of the Chesapeake Bay. He opposed the movement for the issuance of paper currency and wrote to Washington for advice on the subject. Washington replied on Feb. 16, 1787, that if he were in the Maryland legislature, he would be decidedly against it and gave a number of reasons (*Writings of Washington,* IX, 1835, ed. by Jared Sparks, 231–32). This letter was reprinted frequently during the period of wildcat banking to show the opinion of the first president. Stone was also elected to the Congress of the Confederation in 1783 and took his seat on Mar. 26, 1784. He served as chairman of Congress for a few days toward the close of the session but declined reëlection and resumed his law practice. Although elected to the Constitutional Convention in Philadelphia, he declined to serve on account of the illness of his wife, who died in June

1787. Overcome with grief, he gave up his work and died four months later in Alexandria, Va., while waiting for a boat to take him to England. Three children survived him.

[Raphael Semmes Coll. in possession of Md. Hist. Soc., Baltimore; J. T. Scharf, *Hist. of Md.* (1879), II, 235–37; John Sanderson, *Biog. of the Signers to the Declaration of Independence* (1827), IX; H. E. Hayden, *Va. Geneal.* (1891); *Archives of Maryland*, vols. XI, XII (1892–93); E. C. Burnett, *Letters of Members of the Continental Cong.*, vol. II (1923).]

M. E. F.

STONE, WARREN (Feb. 3, 1808–Dec. 6, 1872), surgeon and physician, was born at Saint Albans, Vt., the youngest child of Peter and Jerusha (Snow) Stone, and a descendant of Simon Stone, who emigrated to New England in 1635 with his brother Gregory. His early education was limited, but he later studied assiduously under private tutors. He began his medical work at Keene, N. H., under Dr. Amos Twichell, and subsequently studied under Elisha Bartlett and Willard Parker [qq.v.] at Berkshire Medical Institution, Pittsfield, Mass., where he secured the degree of M.D. in December 1831. He settled in West Troy, N. Y., in 1832, but in October, as few opportunities for practice arose, he sailed from Boston for New Orleans on the brig *Amelia*. Storms and epidemic cholera caused the ship to be beached near Charleston, S. C., on Folly Island, where Stone labored among the sick until he himself contracted cholera. Arriving in December, sick, poor, friendless, he came to a New Orleans desolated by its first cholera epidemic. During his years in the city he was to serve through eighteen epidemics of cholera and yellow fever. After securing a supernumerary position in Charity Hospital, he served as assistant surgeon (1834–35), as resident surgeon (1835–39), and as visiting surgeon (1839–72). For many years he was consulting physician at Hôtel Dieu. In 1839, with Dr. William E. Kennedy, he founded the Maison de Santé, one of the earliest private hospitals in America. Here in 1841 he lost his eye from an infection following an operation. During his years on the staff of the Medical College of Louisiana (later Tulane University) from its opening in 1834 until his retirement in 1872, Stone rose from the position of acting demonstrator of anatomy (1834) to that of professor of surgery (1839–72). Though he lectured with earnest, long-remembered emphasis, he was a discursive, not a systematic, lecturer, often talking on unannounced subjects, and as a teacher of surgery he was too erratic to do full justice to his professorship. During the Civil War, Stone, who was an enthusiastic friend of Jefferson Davis [q.v.], in spite of his Northern birth accepted a

Confederate commission and was appointed surgeon general of Louisiana. His incorrigible spirit brought him into conflict with the Federal military authorities in New Orleans, and at one time he was confined in Fort Jackson.

He has been called the "great commoner" of his profession in the South (Gross, *post*, p. 101), where his kind and winning, if somewhat blunt, manners won him great popularity and inspired unbounded confidence in his ability. Although he met emergencies with ingenuity and quickness, he was not what his contemporaries would have called a brilliant operator. He believed in the prompt opening and draining of suppurating joints, the frequent use of nourishment and stimulants, and the combination of codliver oil and phosphate of lime for use in diseases of the nutritive functions ("Phosphate of Lime in Scrofula and Other Depraved States of the System," *New Orleans Monthly Medical Register*, Oct. 1, 1851). Moreover, he was the first to resect part of a rib to secure permanent drainage in cases of empyema; he reported in 1850 the first successful cure for traumatic vertebral aneurism by open incision and packing ("A Case of Traumatic Aneurism," *New Orleans Medical and Surgical Journal*, Jan. 1850); he made the first cure of an aneurism of the second portion of the subclavian artery by digital compression upon the third portion; and he was the initial user of silver wire for the ligation of the external iliac ("Ligature of the Common Iliac Artery for Aneurism . . .," *Ibid.*, Sept. 1859). His fame was rather the result of his work than of his publications, though he published a number of articles, most of them in the *New Orleans Medical and Surgical Journal*, of which he was co-editor for a short time (1857–59). In 1868 appeared *Clinical Memoranda* and *Notes from the Lectures of Dr. Warren Stone*, edited by his son.

He was a man of unusual height and weight, with a large, rugged head and strong features. His pithy conversation was anecdotic and stimulating, and some of his sayings are still remembered. His quiet charity was not limited to professional services. He died in New Orleans of diabetes mellitus. In 1843 he had married Malvina Dunreith Johnson of Bayou Sara, who with a daughter and two sons survived him.

[J. G. Bartlett, *Simon Stone Geneal.* (1926); S. E. Chaillé, in *Medic. News* (N. Y.), Mar. 15, 1902; editorials in *New Orleans Medic. and Surgical Jour.*, July 1845, Mar. 1849, Jan. 1851; S. D. Gross, *Autobiog.* (1887), vol. II, pp. 100–01, 104–06; *A Century of Am. Medicine: 1776–1876* (1876), ed. by E. H. Clarke, etc.; A. B. Miles, in *Trans. Southern Surgical and Gynecological Asso.*, vol. VII (1895) and in *New Orleans Medic. and Surgical Jour.*, May 1895; F. B. J. Romer, in *New Orleans Medic. and Surgical Jour.*, Jan. 1875; R. F. Stone, *Biog. of Eminent Am. Physi-*

cians and Surgeons (1894); H. A. Kelly and W. L. Burrage, *Am. Medic. Biogs.* (1920); Edmond Souchon, in *Trans. Am. Surgical Asso.*, vol. XXXV (1917); F. W. Parham, in *Surgery, Gynecology, and Obstetrics,* Dec. 1923; obituary in *Nat. Republican,* Dec. 8, 1872.]

V. G. G.

STONE, WARREN SANFORD (Feb. 1, 1860–June 12, 1925), trade-union official, was born on a farm near Ainsworth, Iowa, the son of John and Sarah (Stewart) Stone. His paternal grandfather was an emigrant from Holland. At fifteen, after a farm boyhood with little schooling, he was able to enter Washington Academy nearby. He remained there for three years, an eager student, contributing to his own support by doing odd jobs, and then spent a year at Western College, Toledo, Iowa. In the fall of 1879 he went to work as a locomotive fireman on the Chicago, Rock Island & Pacific Railroad. At Agency, Iowa, on Oct. 15, 1884, he was married to Carrie E. Newell. Six months earlier, on becoming an engineer, he had joined the Brotherhood of Locomotive Engineers. He was soon afterward made secretary-treasurer of his local division and after a time was chosen as chairman of the Brotherhood's general committee of adjustments. His special talent as a negotiator won many decisions for the men, and he came to be well known throughout the organization. In August 1903, on the death of Peter M. Arthur [q.v.], he was chosen grand chief of the Brotherhood, a post he retained until his death. On taking office he faced a critical situation. Wages were low, living costs were rising, and the organization was losing membership. After a careful study of conditions, he formulated a plan for bettering wages and reducing hours by dealing with the railway managers through regional groups and carrying one contest to a finish before taking up another. The first struggle, with the Western group, was brought to a victorious conclusion in 1906; the second, with the Southeastern group, was settled in 1908. A bitter contest followed in 1912 with the Eastern group, the representatives of fifty-two powerful roads, who at first refused concessions. At a critical moment in the dispute the United States commissioner of labor and the presiding judge of the United States commerce court proposed mediation, and after hearings that lasted for five months a satisfactory compromise was reached. In the same year Stone succeeded in establishing a pension system in the Brotherhood, which was followed, nine years later, by a system of widows' pensions, the first in the history of American labor. In 1916 he led the railway unions in their successful fight for the passage of the Adamson Bill. In 1923, during the shopmen's strike, he

intervened by drawing up a plan for settlement which brought the strike to an end. He was active in the movement which resulted in the founding, in October 1919, of *Labor,* the weekly organ of the railway unions. In the following year he brought the Brotherhood into the banking business, and at the time of his death the organization owned or controlled twelve banks and eight investment companies. In the spring of 1925 his health failed. He died at his home in Cleveland, survived by his wife. There were no children.

Stone's manner was genial, though bounded by a reserve that seemed to forbid a too close approach. By some he was thought to be domineering and obstinate. He differed from most trade-unionists in believing the compulsory closed shop unnecessary. He favored a greater degree of collectivization of industry and was a zealous advocate of the plan devised by Glenn Edward Plumb [q.v.] for the cooperative ownership of the railways. He also favored independent political action and was one of the leaders in the movement to bring labor to the support of LaFollette in the presidential campaign of 1924. He seems to have had no political ambitions and is said to have twice rejected a cabinet post. Much of the work he did for his organization is permanent. Under his control the Brotherhood increased in membership by 137 per cent. and greatly multiplied its resources. The vast financial structure he built up began to sag after his death, however, and suffered a series of disasters. His last days were troubled by a controversy which arose with the American Federation of Labor over the fact that a subsidiary corporation of the Brotherhood refused to pay union wages to its employees in the West Virginia mines. The matter had not been settled at the time of his death.

[*Who's Who in America,* 1924–25; *The New International Year Book,* 1925; *Locomotive Engineers Jour.,* July 1925; obituaries in *Cleveland Plain Dealer* and *N. Y. Times,* June 13, 1925.]

W. J. G.

STONE, WILBUR FISK (Dec. 28, 1833– Dec. 27, 1920), Colorado pioneer and jurist, the son of Homer Bishop and Lucy (Lindley) Stone, was born in Litchfield, Conn. He came of English stock, being a descendant of William Stone, one of the founders of Guilford, Conn. When he was six years old the family moved west, settling successively in New York, Michigan, Indiana, and Iowa. At eighteen he left the Iowa farm and went to Indiana where, after two years at the academy in Rushville, he attended Asbury University (later De Pauw) and Indiana University. He took the degree of A.B. at Indiana in 1857 and the degree of LL.B. in 1858.

During his college days he wrote essays and made contributions to various newspapers, and while studying law he acted as instructor in Greek and Latin at the university. For a year he served as editor of the *Daily Enquirer* at Evansville, Ind. He then began the practice of law. In the fall of 1859 he went to Omaha on legal business and was detained through the winter. There he served on the *Nebraskian* and, being able to write shorthand, reported the proceedings of the territorial legislature.

Meeting a number of returning "Pike's Peakers," he decided to go to the new gold country in the spring of 1860. He arrived in Denver after a six-weeks trip by ox team, followed the mining rush to South Park, and spent the winter at Cañon City, where he drafted the code for the first people's court of that section. He was elected a member of the legislature of Colorado in 1862 and 1864, and he served as assistant United States district attorney, 1862–66. In the winter of 1865–66 he returned to Indiana, and in February 1866 married Sarah Sadler of Bloomington, by whom he had two sons. Returning to Colorado, he and his wife settled at Pueblo, where Stone engaged in the practice of law, acted as an editor of the *Chieftain,* Pueblo's first newspaper, and in 1868 served as district attorney for the third (southern) judicial district. He was a promoter of the Denver & Rio Grande Railway, acting for some time as its attorney, and was instrumental in bringing the Atchison, Topeka, & Santa Fé Railroad to Pueblo. In 1875–76 he took a prominent part in drafting the constitution of the state of Colorado. He moved in 1877 to Denver, where he lived for the rest of his life. In October 1877, when a vacancy occurred in the state supreme court, he was nominated and elected without opposition. He served until January 1886 and then for nearly three years was judge of the criminal court at Denver. When Congress in 1891 created the court of private land claims to determine Spanish and Mexican land titles in the Southwest, he was appointed one of the five judges. His knowledge of Spanish and his association with Spanish-Americans of southern Colorado qualified him especially well for service on this unique court. He was sent by his colleagues to study the archives in Spain and to procure evidence in the famous Peralta case, involving a claim (later proved fraudulent) to over 12,000,000 acres of land in Arizona. When the work of the court was completed in 1904, he resumed private practice and spent much time in travel abroad. He was United States commissioner in the federal district court at Denver during the last five years of his life. During his twenty-six years of judicial service he won a name for clearness, impartiality, and integrity. He was an entertaining public speaker, his addresses being characterized by sparkling humor, and he wrote numerous articles for newspapers and magazines. The last work appearing under his name was a large *History of Colorado* (4 vols., 1918), of which he was consulting editor. He was an active member of the Episcopal Church.

[See J. M. Lindly, *The Hist. of the Lindley, Lindsley-Linsly Families*, vol. II (1924); *Who's Who in America*, 1916–17; W. F. Stone, ed., *Hist. of Colo.* (1918), vol. II, pp. 182 ff.; J. C. Smiley, *Semi-Centennial Hist. of the State of Colo.* (1913), vol. II, pp. 8–13; W. N. Byers, *Encyc of Biog. of Colo.* (1880); *Hist. of the City of Denver* (1901); T. F. Dawson, "Scrapbooks of Newspaper and Mag. Clippings," vol. LXV, pp. 21–31, in colls. of State Hist. Soc. of Colo.; H. D. Teetor, in *Mag. of Western Hist.*, Apr. 1889; *Report Colo. Bar Asso., 1921*, vol. XXIV, p. 166; obituary in *Rocky Mountain News*, Dec. 28, 1920. Information has been supplied by Stone's son. Stone's opinions as justice of the Colo. supreme court appear in 3–8 *Colo. Reports.* For the Peralta case see *Certificacion de ún Expediente, etc., etc., sobre los Bienes del difunto Don Miguel Nemecio Silva de Peralta de la Córdoba, etra.* (2 vols., 1892), in the Colls. of the State Hist. Soc. of Colo.]

L. R. H.

STONE, WILLIAM (c. 1603–c. 1660), third proprietary governor of Maryland, was born in Northamptonshire, England. He emigrated to Virginia sometime before 1628 and in 1633 served as justice of Accomac County, the name then applied to the entire eastern shore of Virginia. It was later called Northampton, possibly by Stone for his birthplace. He served as sheriff of Northampton for a term in the forties. He married Virlinda Cotton, the sister of William Cotton, a prominent minister. They had seven children. When Leonard Calvert [*q.v.*], governor of Maryland, died and designated a Roman Catholic, Thomas Greene, as his successor, Lord Baltimore soon removed Greene, placed him on the Council in August 1648, and appointed William Stone governor. Stone was a member of the Church of England but had non-conformist connections and sympathies. He brought thirty-three people with him to Maryland and received a grant of 5,000 acres "lying west of Nanjemi Creek on the Potomac."

He took a special oath when he came into office, in which he promised not to "trouble molest or discountenance any Person whatsoever in the said Province professing to believe in Jesus Christ and in particular no Roman Catholick for or in respect of his or her Religion" (*Archives, post,* III, 210). The Maryland Toleration Act, which is worded quite similarly, was passed by the Assembly on Apr. 21, 1649. The Governor's Council was reorganized with an equal number of Catholics and Protestants, and several Puritans were members of the Assembly. When Stone visited Virginia late in 1649 and left Greene in charge of the Maryland government, Greene at once proclaimed Charles II to be rightful heir to the English throne. Although Lord Baltimore and Stone both disavowed this act as soon as they heard of it, nevertheless, it aroused Puritan suspicion. In 1650 a commission was appointed by Parliament to reduce Virginia to Parliamentary authority. Construing its instructions to include Maryland, the members of the commission arrived at St. Mary's in 1652 and demanded that the Governor and Council be loyal to the Commonwealth of England and that all writs and warrants be issued in the name of the Keepers of England. When Stone agreed to the first but not the second, since according to his oath all writs had to be issued in the name of the Lord Proprietary, he was deprived of his commission. He was, however, reinstated a few months later when he decided to give in on the point (*Archives, post,* III, 275). The next year he found himself in trouble with the Puritans of Providence (now Annapolis) because he had imposed certain oaths upon them and had removed some Puritan officials. In vain they sent two petitions for aid to Virginia. However, at Lord Baltimore's command, Stone issued two proclamations, one that henceforth all writs would be issued in the name of the Lord Proprietary and another charging the commissioners with leading the people in rebellion against the proprietor. Then the commissioners returned, reinforced with Puritans from Providence and Patuxent, and again forced Stone to resign. When the news of this second surrender reached Lord Baltimore, he wrote Stone a letter demanding that he return to his duties. Stone gathered a small force and met the Puritans in the Battle of the Severn on Mar. 25, 1655. He was badly defeated, wounded, and captured. After the battle he was sentenced to death by a council of war but was saved by some of his friends among the Puritans. The Baltimore forces did not regain power until 1657 under Gov. Josias Fendall [*q.v.*]. Stone was a member of his Council. He died at his estate in Charles County.

[Raphael Semmes Colls. in possession of Md. Hist. Soc., Baltimore; *Archives of Maryland*, vols. I, III (1883, 1885); *Narratives of Early Maryland* (1910), ed. by C. C. Hall; J. H. Latane, "The Early Relations of Maryland and Virginia," *Johns Hopkins Univ. Studies in Hist. and Pol. Sci.*, 13 ser., vols. III, IV (1895); J. T. Scharf, *Hist. of Md.* (1879), vol. II; J. L. Bozman, *The Hist. of Md.* (1837), vol. II.]   M. E. F.

STONE, WILLIAM JOEL (May 7, 1848–Apr. 14, 1918), representative in Congress, gov-

ernor of Missouri, United States senator, was born in Madison County, Ky. His father, William Stone, was a Virginian by birth, and his mother, Mildred Phelps, a Kentuckian. The boy worked on his father's farm and attended a rural school until he was fifteen years of age, then went to stay with a married sister at Columbia, Mo., where he attended the state university for three years and in 1867 entered the law office of his brother-in-law, Squire Turner.

He was admitted to the bar in 1869, and two years later settled at Nevada, Vernon County, Mo. From 1872 to 1874 he was prosecuting attorney of Vernon County. In 1884 he was elected to the lower house of Congress on the Democratic ticket, and served three terms. Going to Washington as a moderate reformer, he opposed corruption in big business and was instrumental in exposing several fraudulent railroad claims to lands in the Northwest. In 1892 he was elected governor of Missouri. Problems connected with the panic of 1893 absorbed the greater part of his attention as governor. He successfully managed the financial difficulties of the state and when strikes and other industrial disturbances occurred he was able to handle the situation without resort to military force. Upon retiring from the governorship in 1897 he practised law in St. Louis, but kept a dominant influence in political affairs, and in 1903 was chosen to succeed George G. Vest in the United States Senate. Now far more conservative, he served here continuously until his death.

Few equaled and probably none excelled Stone as a practical politician. When the state was rocked (1902–03) by the "boodling" exposures of Joseph W. Folk [*q.v.*], the name "Gum-Shoe Bill" was awarded to Stone by foes, and even accepted by friends, for his adroitness in avoiding charges of political corruption. Besides all but holding the state Democratic party in the hollow of his hand for twenty-five years, he was prominent in the national councils of the party, being a member of the National Committee from 1896 to 1904, and its vice-chairman during the last four years of that period. He was an ardent admirer and a follower of the principles of William Jennings Bryan.

In the United States Senate, Stone, as a faithful partisan, voted for the railroad rate regulation laws of 1906, filibustered against the Aldrich-Vreeland currency bill in 1908, and opposed the Payne-Aldrich tariff bill in 1909. During Wilson's administration he became the ranking member of the Finance Committee, and in the critical year of 1914 succeeded to the chairmanship of the important committee on Foreign

Relations. In this position he successfully steered to ratification the Bryan peace and arbitration treaties. He received a storm of criticism early in 1917 as one of the "little group of willful men" who blocked President Wilson's Armed Ship Bill (*New York Times,* Mar. 5, 1917).

In the crisis of March-April 1917 Senator James A. Reed warned Stone: "It is the decree of fate, war will be declared. A vote against it will mean your political ruin. You are old and you have no property." Stone, with deep feeling, replied: "I know what it means to me. I know this war is coming. I know the people are aflame with . . . battle. . . . But would you have me consider my personal welfare in a case that involves the lives of millions of men . . . ? I cannot vote to send our boys into this conflict" (*Memorial Addresses, post,* p. 74). Nevertheless, as the war went on he gave wholeheartedly his thought and energy to the success of the American forces. He became deeply depressed by the reverses of the Allies early in 1918, and this emotional strain no doubt hastened his end.

Stone was looked upon as being a man's man, and a good mixer. Although he was an able and successful lawyer, he failed to accumulate wealth. He was not a church member, but he stood high in several fraternal orders. On Apr. 2, 1874, he married Sarah Louise Winston, by whom he had three children.

[*The Messages and Proclamations of the Govs. of . . . Mo.,* vol. VIII (1926) ; *Hist. of Vernon County, Mo.* (1911), vol. II ; A. J. D. Stewart, *The Hist. of the Bench and Bar of Mo.* (1898) ; H. L. Conard, *Encyc. of the Hist. of Mo.* (1901), vol. VI ; *William Joel Stone : Memorial Addresses Delivered in the Senate* (1919) ; *Who's Who in America,* 1916–17 ; *Biog. Dir. Am. Cong.* (1928) ; Lincoln Steffens, "Enemies of the Republic," *McClure's Mag.,* Apr. 1904 ; "The Bourbon Democrat Who Holds the Senate Reins on Foreign Affairs," *Current Opinion,* Feb. 1916 ; "Mr. Stone Hears from the Country," *Lit. Digest,* Mar. 24, 1917 ; *Washington Post* and *St. Louis Globe-Democrat,* Apr. 15, 1918.]

H. E. N.

STONE, WILLIAM LEETE (Apr. 20, 1792–Aug. 15, 1844), journalist and historian, was a descendant of John Stone and of William Leete [*q.v.*], both among the first settlers of Guilford, Conn. The second of eleven children of Rev. William Stone, a Yale Congregationalist who served three years in the Revolution "with a Hebrew Bible and the whole works of Josephus in his knapsack" (W. L. Stone, Jr., "Life," *post,* p. 10), and of Tamson (Graves) Stone, he was born at New Paltz, N. Y. His father retired to a farm on the upper Susquehanna and young Stone grew up in a frontier atmosphere, but he had a good training in Latin, Greek, and Puritan theology from his strong-willed parent. This frontier-classical schooling was apparently all

the formal education he secured. In 1809 he walked forty miles in a single night to offer himself as apprentice to the editor of the *Cooperstown Federalist;* he was accepted and remained for three years. In 1813 he purchased the Federalist *Herkimer American,* having for his journeyman Thurlow Weed [*q.v.*]. In 1814 Stone sold this paper and bought the *Northern Whig* at Hudson. By his marriage, Jan. 31, 1817, to Susannah Pritchard Wayland, daughter of Rev. Francis Wayland of Saratoga Springs and sister of Francis Wayland [*q.v.*], later president of Brown University, he acquired a literary adviser, and while at Hudson he edited two literary periodicals, the *Lounger* and the *Spirit of the Forum.* In 1816 he purchased the *Albany Daily Advertiser,* which was merged with the *Albany Gazette;* two years later his business failed and he became editor of the *Mirror,* Hartford, Conn., a journal formerly "vigilant and spicy" in its defense of Federalism, but under Stone's editorship harmlessly literary. Here he formed a literary club which edited a weekly magazine, *The Knights of the Round Table.*

His influence as an editor increased after 1821, when he became one of the proprietors of the *New York Commercial Advertiser.* He was one of the first to champion the cause of Greek independence; though a Federalist, he was a personal friend of DeWitt Clinton [*q.v.*] and zealously fought for the Erie Canal, writing on request *Narrative of the Festivities Observed in Honor of the Completion of the Grand Erie Canal* (1825) ; and as a "high Mason" he stepped forth as a mediator in the Anti-Masonic outburst following the disappearance of William Morgan [*q.v.*], writing *Letters on Masonry and Anti-Masonry* (1832), which evidently aimed at (but failed to obtain) wide circulation because of a strict impartiality designed to conciliate both sides. He ridiculed Frances Wright [*q.v.*] and women's rights, spoke sarcastically of extension of the suffrage, and advocated emancipation of slaves by Congress. An unwavering Federalist editor, he frankly admitted in 1829 that he had reached the top of his profession. He was director of the Institution for the Deaf and Dumb, for some time a school commissioner, and in 1843–44 superintendent of the commons schools of New York City.

Throughout his life he was interested in the early history of his region. In *Tales and Sketches* (2 vols., 1834) he published an account of his own pioneer experiences and of Revolutionary traditions; "Uncle Tim and Deacon Pettibone" and "Dick Moon, the Peddlar," both of which appeared in *The Atlantic Club-Book* (2 vols.,

1834), were rather stereotyped reporting of New England rusticity and asceticism; "The Mysterious Bridal," in *Tales and Sketches,* reprinted in *The Mysterious Bridal and Other Tales* (3 vols., 1835), portrays a typical colonial New England Thanksgiving with such success that Chancellor Kent thought it deserved a place beside *Bracebridge Hall.* Another New England sketch, "Mercy Disborough; a Tale of the Witches" (in *Tales and Sketches*), deals with legends of the regicides, wherein Stone's ancestor, Governor Leete of Connecticut, appears to good advantage. In 1833 appeared *Matthias and His Impostures,* an account of remarkable deceptions occurring in New York, and in 1836, *Maria Monk and the Nunnery of the Hôtel Dieu,* after Stone had gone to Montreal to investigate charges made by a "silly and profligate woman." A social satire, *Ups and Downs in the Life of a Distressed Gentleman* (1836), and *Letter to Dr. A. Brigham, on Animal Magnetism* (1837) came next. Meanwhile, gathering great stores of manuscripts and books, Stone set out to write a history of the Iroquois, beginning with *Life of Joseph Brant—Thayendanegea* (1838). This was followed by *Life and Times of Red Jacket* (1841). Seven chapters of the life of Sir William Johnson had been completed at the time of the author's death; the work was finished by his son, William L. Stone, Jr. [*q.v.*]. Three volumes, *The Poetry and History of Wyoming* (1841), *Uncas and Miantonomoh* (1842), and *Border Wars of the American Revolution* (1843), were by-products of his chief interest. A result of still greater value was the creation in 1838 of the New York State Historical Agency for the transcribing of the documents in European archives later published by J. R. Brodhead [*q.v.*]. Stone's most lasting contribution was in awakening an interest in the state archives, though in his own day his greatest influence was exerted in the field of journalism. Stone had only the one son, but adopted his sister's son, William Henry, who changed his name to William Henry Stone.

[Stone's great mass of MSS. and books was scattered, a part going to the Fort Ticonderoga Museum. The best biographical sketch is that by his son, "Life and Writings of Col. William Leete Stone," in *The Life and Times of Sa-go-ye-wat-ha, or Red Jacket* (ed. of 1866), pp. 9–101. See also W. L. Stone, Jr., *The Family of John Stone* (1888); F. B. Dexter, *Biog. Sketches Grads. Yale Univ.,* vol. IV (1917), for sketch of the Rev. William Stone; journal of a trip from New York to Niagara, *Buffalo Hist. Soc. Pubs.,* vol. XIV (1910); J. D. Hammond, *The Hist. of Political Parties in the State of N. Y.* (1842), I, 452–53; *Autobiog. of Thurlow Weed* (1884), ed. by Harriet A. Weed; *Correspondence of James Fenimore Cooper* (2 vols., 1932); *N. Y. Tribune,* Aug. 17, 1844. Laughton Osborn, *The Vision of Rubeta* (1838), satirizing in verse Stone's exposé of the charges of Maria Monk, is an intelligent and valuable commentary and, portraying Stone as domineering and opinionated, provides a good corrective for the life by W. L. Stone, Jr.]   J. P. B.

STONE, WILLIAM LEETE (Apr. 4, 1835–June 11, 1908), journalist, historian, was the only child of William Leete Stone [*q.v.*], the well-known historian, and Susannah Pritchard (Wayland). He was born in New York City and received his early education there and in Saratoga Springs, his mother's home, to which she returned in 1844 after his father's death. Under his uncle, President Francis Wayland [*q.v.*], he entered Brown University in 1853 and received his degree five years later, John Hay being a classmate with whom he carried on a correspondence for years. The year 1856 he spent in Germany learning the language for the purpose of translating memoirs of German participants in the American Revolution. He took a course at the Albany Law School, was admitted to the bar, and practised his profession in 1860–63 at Saratoga Springs.

Literary work proved to be more inviting than the law, however, and he accepted the city editorship of the *New York Journal of Commerce,* 1864–67. As his father's literary executor, he completed in 1865 *The Life and Times of Sir William Johnson* for which his father had written the first seven chapters. The next year he wrote a guidebook, *Saratoga Springs,* and "Life and Writings of Col. William Leete Stone" in a reprint of his father's *Life . . . of Red Jacket.* In 1867 appeared his translation, *Letters and Journals Relating to the War of the American Revolution,* from the papers of the wife of General Riedesel, followed by *Memoirs and Letters and Journals of Major General Riedesel* (2 vols., 1868), and much later by *Journal of Capt. Pausch* (1886) and *Letters of Brunswick and Hessian Officers during the American Revolution* (1891). Meanwhile his printing shop in New York had succumbed to the panic of 1872 and the *College Review,* 1870–74, of which he was editor and proprietor, had proved to be unprofitable. He therefore obtained (1872) a position in the Customs House in New York which he held for many years. With an assured income, he devoted himself to historical projects. As one of the incorporators and secretary of the Saratoga Monument Association in 1871 he worked indefatigably. When the corner stone of the monument was laid on Oct. 17, 1877, he delivered an address and subsequently wrote *History of the Saratoga Monument Association* (pamphlet, 1879). During the Centennial of 1876, he was appointed historian for New York State. His interest in the Revolution resulted in the publication—in addition to the translations previously mentioned—

of *The Campaign of Lieutenant General John Burgoyne* (1877); *Memoir of the Centennial Celebration of Burgoyne's Surrender at Schuylerville* (1878); *The Orderly Book of Sir John Johnson* (1882); *Ballads and Poems Relating to the Burgoyne Campaign* (1893); and *Visits to the Saratoga Battle-Grounds 1780–1880* (1895). He found time also to write a *History of New York City* (1868); *Reminiscences of Saratoga and Ballston* (1875); the third supplement (1881) to Dowling's *History of Romanism*; a genealogy, *The Family of John Stone* (1888); *The Starin Family in America* (1892); several chapters in J. G. Wilson's *The Memorial History of the City of New York* (4 vols., 1891–93); and *Washington County, New York* (1901). He wrote articles for newspapers, historical journals, and genealogical and biographical encyclopedias, and left unfinished a history of the Six Nations and a life of George Clinton.

Although an editor and compiler rather than a creative historian, Stone won a creditable place among American literary men. Mayor Strong designated him one of a committee which supervised the publication of the *Records of New Amsterdam* (7 vols., 1897). He was an original trustee of the New York State Historical Association. Shortly before his death Governor Higgins appointed him a member of the commission for the Hudson-Fulton celebration in 1909. He was interested in reforms, education, sports, and public affairs, but was not ambitious for public honors. With a genial disposition and a ready wit, he was a welcome guest in a wide circle. He married, June 1, 1859, Harriet Douglas Gillette of Cleveland, Ohio, and they had six children, two of whom died in infancy. During the latter part of his life he lived at Jersey City Heights, N. J., and Mount Vernon, N. Y.

[A short autobiography to 1888 is included in *The Family of John Stone*, published that year. See also *Proc. N. Y. State Hist. Asso.*, vol. VIII (1909); *Publisher's Weekly*, June 20, 1908; *N. Y. Times*, June 12, 1908. Most of Stone's papers are in the possession of his wife at Mount Vernon, N. Y. His Brown University papers and correspondence with John Hay are at Providence, R. I. His historical library is in the Fort Ticonderoga Museum.]   A. C. F.

STONE, WILLIAM OLIVER (Sept. 26, 1830–Sept. 15, 1875), portrait painter, was born at Derby, Conn., the youngest of three children of Frederick William and Ellen (Stone) Stone. He was a descendant of William Stone who emigrated from England in the company of William Leete [*q.v.*] and settled in Guilford, Conn., in 1639. His grandfather, Leman Stone, was an important citizen of Derby, whose mansion house, the "Castle," in what is now East Derby,

near the confluence of the Housatonic and Naugatuck rivers, served both as residence and warehouse, the dock at the waterside enabling vessels from the West Indies to discharge their cargoes and store them in this building. William Oliver presumably received his early education in the Derby public schools. He became a pupil of Nathaniel Jocelyn [*q.v.*] of New Haven in the late forties, went to New York in 1854, and soon became a popular and successful portraitist. In 1859 he became an Academician and exhibited regularly at the National Academy of Design from then until the time of his death. Occasionally he sent portraits to the Royal Academy exhibitions in London, where they were well hung. Though his most successful portraits were those of women and children, "rich in color and graceful in treatment" (H. T. Tuckerman, *Book of Artists*, 1867, p. 399), he was always desirous of painting portraits of men and "expected to produce some notable masterpieces in this respect," an ambition that was fairly fulfilled. His best portrait of a man was generally considered to be that of the editor of the *New York Herald*, James Gordon Bennett, while one of his most charming portraits of women was that of Mrs. Hoey. His portrait of Miss Rawle has been shown at the Metropolitan Museum, New York. The New York Historical Society owns his portrait of Thomas Jefferson Bryan; the Union Club, New York, that of Howell L. Williams, and the National Academy of Design that of John Whetton Ehninger. Among his other subjects were Cyrus West Field, the Rev. Henry Anthon, William Wilson Corcoran, the founder of the Corcoran Gallery in Washington, Bishop Abram Newkirk Littlejohn of Long Island, and Bishop William Ingraham Kip of California. Though he was a prolific painter and in one year sent nine pictures to the Academy, his workmanship was of a distinctly superior order. In certain examples it reminds one not a little of the rugged style and admirable modeling of some of Sir Henry Raeburn's heads. Considering his popularity and the number of his works, it is surprising that he is among the least known of the portrait painters of his day. He died in Newport, R. I., at the age of forty-five. He was married early, before leaving his native place, and had one daughter, Louise, who married a man named Ingalls and lived with her father.

[W. L. Stone, *The Family of John Stone* (1888); Samuel Orcutt and Ambrose Beardsley, *The Hist. of the Old Town of Derby, Conn.* (1880); H. W. French, *Art and Artists in Conn.* (1879); *Boston Transcript*, Aug. 11, 1926; *Art Journal*, Nov. 1875; obituaries in *N. Y. Tribune*, Sept. 17, and *Derby Transcript*, Sept. 24, 1875; information from Emma E. Lassey, Derby Pub. Lib.]   W. H. D.

STONEMAN, GEORGE (Aug. 8, 1822–Sept. 5, 1894), soldier, governor of California, was born at Busti, Chautauqua County, N. Y., the eldest of ten children of George and Catherine (Cheney) Stoneman. He was a descendant of Richard Stoneman, who came to New Berlin, N. Y., after the Revolution. He received his preparatory education at an academy in the neighboring village of Jamestown and was appointed a cadet at the United States Military Academy where he was graduated in 1846. He was commissioned brevet second lieutenant in the 1st Dragoons (now the 1st Cavalry) and was detailed as quartermaster of the "Mormon Battalion," a volunteer unit which formed part of General Kearny's expedition to California. He served in the Southwest until 1855, having risen to the rank of captain in the newly organized 2nd (now 5th) Cavalry. At the opening of the Civil War he was in command at Fort Brown, Tex. Refusing to surrender to Gen. D. E. Twiggs, his immediate superior, who had cast in his lot with the Confederacy, he escaped with part of his command, and was assigned to temporary duty at the cavalry school at Carlisle, Pa. On May 9, 1861, he was promoted major in the 1st (now 4th) Cavalry, and later in the month was in command of the advance across the Long Bridge from Washington to Alexandria. He then served in West Virginia on the staff of General McClellan, who, when he took command of the armies, made him chief of cavalry of the Army of the Potomac with the rank of brigadier-general of volunteers. After the Peninsular campaign of 1862 he was assigned to command the 1st Division, III Corps, and in November of the same year took command of the corps as major-general of volunteers, serving with it through the Fredericksburg campaign. For gallantry in this battle he received the brevet rank of colonel in the regular army.

When Hooker took command of the Army of the Potomac he formed his cavalry into a separate corps of more than 10,000 men and gave the command to Stoneman. At the opening of the Chancellorsville campaign he sent him with most of this force to make a great raid toward Richmond and to operate against Lee's rear. This operation continued from Apr. 13 to May 2 and caused great alarm in Richmond; but since the main army was unsuccessful at Chancellorsville it had no influence upon the course of the campaign. In July 1863 Stoneman became chief of the Cavalry Bureau in Washington, but the next winter he joined the western armies, commanding the XXIII Corps. He was promoted lieutenant-colonel of the 3rd Cavalry in the regular army on Mar. 30, 1864. In April he was assigned to the cavalry corps of the Army of the Ohio, and with this command took part in the Atlanta campaign. Sherman sent him with his corps to break the railway at Jonesboro near Atlanta, and at Stoneman's request these orders were broadened to include also a raid by part of his force to release the prisoners of war at Macon and Andersonville. Early in August he was cut off at Clinton, Ga. He held the attention of the enemy, with one brigade, and was finally forced to surrender, but the rest cut their way back to the army with heavy loss. He remained a prisoner of war until he was exchanged and returned to duty in October. In December he made another raid, with considerable success, into southwestern Virginia, later operating in east Tennessee and the Carolinas in cooperation with Sherman. He received the brevet ranks of brigadier-general and major-general in the regular army in March 1865, and commanded in Petersburg and Richmond for the next four years. He became colonel of the 21st Infantry upon muster out of the volunteer service, joined that regiment in Arizona, and commanded it and the Department of Arizona until his retirement for disability in August 1871.

He then established himself near Los Angeles on his magnificent estate, "Los Robles" (see Archduke Ludwig Salvator, *Eine Blume aus dem Goldenen Lande,* 1878, pp. 214, 215). In 1883 he resigned his commission in the army to accept the Democratic nomination for governor of California. He was elected by a large majority and served until 1887. As a railway commissioner from 1879, he had opposed the increasing power of the Pacific railways in state affairs and in business, and had gained a strong popular following. He continued the same policies as governor, particularly in regard to railway taxation matters. He also favored legislation encouraging irrigation projects. These policies, involving highly controversial issues, made his administration a stormy one; the legislature was twice in extra session, and generally in deadlock over his recommendations. In 1891, by special act of Congress, he was restored to the army list as colonel, retired. At the end of the war he had married Mary Oliver Hardisty, of Baltimore, Md. She, with their four children, survived him when he died in Buffalo, N. Y. He was buried with military honors at Lakewood, on Chautauqua Lake, N. Y.

[Information from the family; G. E. Cullum, *Biog. Reg. . . . U. S. Mil. Acad.* (1891); D. N. Couch, obituary article, *Ann. Reunion, Asso. Grads., U. S. Mil. Acad., 1895* (1895); J. H. McClintock, *Arizona* (1916), vol. III; William Bushong, *The Last Great Stoneman*

Raid (1910); T. H. Hittell, *Hist. of Cal.*, vol. IV (1897); *Buffalo Courier*, Sept. 6, 1894.]   O. L. S., Jr.

STORER, BELLAMY (Aug. 28, 1847–Nov. 12, 1922), congressman from Ohio, diplomat, was born at Cincinnati, Ohio, the son of Bellamy and Elizabeth (Drinker) Storer, and the descendant of William Storie, who with his father Augustine Storr, emigrated from England about 1636 and died in Dover, Me. Bellamy was the nephew of David Humphreys Storer and the cousin of Francis Humphreys Storer and Horatio Robinson Storer [qq.v.]. He was educated in the common schools of Cincinnati, in a private school at Boston, and in Harvard College, where he received the A.B. degree in 1867. In 1869 he graduated from the law school of Cincinnati College, commenced practising law in his native city, and was appointed assistant attorney for the southern federal district of Ohio, 1869–70. With Charles P. Taft [q.v.] he edited the first volume of the *Cincinnati Superior Court Reporter* (1872). His standing in Cincinnati was enhanced by his marriage on Mar. 20, 1886, with Maria (Longworth) Nichols, the widow of George Ward Nichols [q.v.] and aunt of Nicholas Longworth, 1869–1931 [q.v.]. A lifelong Republican, he was elected to the Fifty-second and Fifty-third congresses, Mar. 4, 1891–Mar. 3, 1895, serving on the committee on interstate and foreign commerce during both congresses and on the foreign affairs committee in the Fifty-third Congress. He took very little part in congressional debates and his only considerable utterance regarding foreign affairs was an attack upon the administration's policy in Hawaii (*Congressional Record*, 53 Cong., 2 Sess., pp. 1948–52).

An admirer of William McKinley, he helped both in the gubernatorial campaign in Ohio and later in the presidential campaign of 1896. His reward, an appointment on May 4, 1897, as minister to Belgium, seems to have been disappointing (*Selections from the Correspondence of Theodore Roosevelt and Henry Cabot Lodge*, 1925, I, p. 254), but in view of the fact that both he and his wife were Roman Catholics, the appointment was a logical one. He had been received into the Roman Catholic Church on Oct. 4, 1896. After two years of quiet usefulness at Brussels he was appointed on Apr. 12, 1899, to be minister to Spain. There he successfully handled such post-war problems as the return to Spain of Spanish prisoners of the Filipinos and the release of Cuban political prisoners in Spain. On Sept. 26, 1902, he was appointed by Theodore Roosevelt, a friend of himself and his wife, to be ambassador to Austria-Hungary. According to the Austrian foreign minister Storer became "*persona gratissima*" at the Austrian Court and the Emperor "spoke of him in terms of the highest consideration and personal esteem" (American chargé d'affaires *ad interim* at Vienna to the secretary of state, Mar. 22, 1906, Dispatches from Austria in the department of state). It was therefore a matter of some regret at Vienna when Storer was summarily removed from his position on Mar. 19, 1906. From Storer's *Letter . . . to the President and the Members of his Cabinet, November, 1906* (1906) it appears that the President, who had asked Storer to urge upon the Pope the claims of Archbishop Ireland to a cardinalate, had come to fear the political consequences of having his name involved in church controversies and had therefore rebuked both the Ambassador and Mrs. Storer for undue activity in ecclesiastical matters. The Storers failed to respond to the President's letter; the Ambassador's resignation was requested, and he was removed before his resignation had had sufficient time to reach Washington.

Storer returned to his practice in Cincinnati. During the World War he aided the Belgian relief work in Cincinnati, and during the winter of 1914 to 1915, which he spent at Rome, he organized a bureau of inquiry to handle the large correspondence addressed to the Pope regarding missing soldiers. The work of the bureau was continued at his expense until the end of the war. He died at Paris and was buried at Marvejols, France.

[M. L. Storer, *In Memoriam Bellamy Storer* (1923); *Who's Who in America*, 1922–23; *Harvard College Class of 1867. Secretary's Report*, no. 3 (1870), no. 8 (1887), no. 10 (1897); Malcolm Storer, *Annals of the Storer Family* (1927); *Papers Relating to the Foreign Affairs of the U. S.*, 1897–1906; some unprinted material in the department of state.]   E. W. S.

STORER, DAVID HUMPHREYS (Mar. 26, 1804–Sept. 10, 1891), obstetrician and naturalist, was born in Portland, Me., the son of Woodbury and Margaret (Boyd) Storer. His father, a descendant of Augustine Storr, who emigrated from England to Boston in 1636, was chief justice of common pleas at Portland. After his graduation from Bowdoin College in 1822 and from the Harvard Medical School in 1825, he was apprenticed, as was the custom of the time, to the leading surgeon of Boston, John Collins Warren, 1776–1856 [q.v.]. In practice, he soon began to confine his work to obstetrics, and in this branch of medicine he became eminent both as a practitioner and as a teacher. Dissatisfied with the four months' winter term offered at the Harvard Medical School in 1839, Storer, Oliver Wendell Holmes [q.v.], and Edward Reynolds, under the leadership of Jacob

Bigelow, started the Tremont Street Medical School, Boston, which held courses throughout the year and flourished until the Harvard school was reorganized. At that time (1854) Storer became professor of obstetrics and medical jurisprudence, and carried on the work of his predecessor, Walter Channing [q.v.]. He served the school until 1868, acting as dean from 1854 to 1864. Popular as a teacher, he was much beloved as the dean. He did much to advance obstetrics in the United States, especially in relation to the work of the American Medical Association. His sound views on medical jurisprudence were clearly outlined in his discourse, *An Address on Medical Jurisprudence: Its Claims to Greater Regard from the Student and the Physician* (1851), before the Massachusetts Medical Society. He was, moreover, a lover of books, and it was through his efforts that over 10,000 volumes of medical works were collected for the Boston Public Library and later added to the Boston Medical Library after its founding in 1875.

It is as a naturalist and collector, however, that Storer is best remembered. He began collecting coins at an early age and is said to have made a bargain with all the toll gatherers of the Boston bridges and the keepers of sailors' boarding-houses in his efforts to obtain odd coins, shells, and rare fishes. He joined the Boston Society of Natural History in early manhood, immediately after it was founded in 1830, and contributed many papers to its proceedings. He collected and described the *Mollusca* of Massachusetts, and issued in 1837 a translation of L. C. Kiener's work on shells, *General Species and Iconography of Recent Shells, Comprising the Massena Museum, the Collection of Lamarck, the Collection of the Museum of Natural History, and the Recent Discoveries of Travelers.* His collection is now at Bowdoin College. When appointed on a committee for the natural history survey of Massachusetts, he reported on fishes and reptiles in *Ichthyology and Herpetology of Massachusetts* (1839), a work he later expanded as *A History of Fishes in Massachusetts* (1867), a "land-mark in the ichthyological literature of the country" (Scudder, *post*, p. 391). His *A Synopsis of the Fishes of North America* (1846), hurriedly written, is of less value. A conservative, faithful worker, he often spent the hours from five to breakfast-time in the museum of the Natural History Society, attended to a large obstetrical practice during the day, lectured at the Harvard Medical School, and sought the fish-wharves for strange specimens. For thirty-five years he is said never to have missed being at his desk, as medical examiner for an insurance company, when the clock struck noon. For many years he served on the staff of the Massachusetts General Hospital (1849–58) and the Lying-in Hospital (1854–68); he also acted as secretary to the Massachusetts Medical Society, founded the Obstetrical Society of Boston, and was a member of numerous scientific bodies. On Apr. 29, 1829, he married Abby Jane Brewer, sister of Thomas Mayo Brewer [q.v.]. Of their five children, Horatio Robinson Storer and Francis Humphreys Storer [qq.v.] became scientists of note. Storer's open, brilliant countenance and friendly eye have been finely shown in Frederick Porter Vinton's portrait in the Boston Medical Library.

[Malcolm Storer, *Annals of the Storer Family* (1927); H. A. Kelly and W. L. Burrage, *Am. Medic. Biogs.* (1920); G. C. Shattuck, O. W. Holmes, and others, in *Boston Medic. and Surgical Jour.*, Mar. 24, 1892; *Trans. Am. Gynecological Soc.*, vol. XVI (1891); *Jour. Am. Medic. Assoc.*, Oct. 3, 1891; T. F. Harrington, *The Harvard Medic. School* (1905), vol. II; S. H. Scudder, in *Proc. Am. Acad. Arts and Sci.*, vol. XXVII (1893); J. C. White, in *Proc. Boston Soc. Nat. Hist.*, vol. XXV (1892); "List of Pub. Writings of David Humphreys Storer," in Bowdoin Coll. Lib., *Bibliog. Contributions*, no. 2, Aug. 1892; obituaries in *Boston Transcript* and *Boston Herald*, Sept. 11, 1891.]
H. R. V.

STORER, FRANCIS HUMPHREYS (Mar. 27, 1832–July 30, 1914), chemist, was born at Boston, Mass., the second son of David Humphreys Storer [q.v.] and Abby Jane (Brewer) Storer. He was a brother of Horatio Robinson Storer and a first cousin of Bellamy Storer [qq.v]. He received his early education in the schools of Boston, and in 1850 entered the Lawrence Scientific School of Harvard University. His zeal and proficiency in chemistry attracted the attention of Prof. Josiah Parsons Cooke [q.v.], and for two years (1851–53) he was Cooke's assistant, at the same time teaching a private class in chemical analysis at the Harvard Medical School. In 1853 he accepted an appointment as chemist with the United States North Pacific exploring expedition, and visited the principal islands of the Atlantic and Pacific oceans. On his return he completed his chemical course, receiving the degree of B.S. from Harvard in 1855. After two years (1855–57) in Europe, where he studied with Robert W. Bunsen at Heidelberg, Theodor Richter in Freiberg, Julius Stöckhardt in Tharand, and Émile Kopp in Paris, he became chemist of the Boston Gas Light Company, a position which he retained until 1871. He made daily tests of the gas furnished by the company to consumers, conducted miscellaneous scientific researches upon the composition and illuminating power of coal and gas (see *American Journal of Science,* Nov. 1860, p. 420), and in addition (1857–65) maintained a private analytical and consulting laboratory.

With his fellow chemist, Charles William Eliot [*q.v.*], later president of Harvard, he began in 1860 a series of publications upon "The Impurities of Commercial Zinc" (*Memoirs of the American Association of Arts and Sciences,* vol. VIII, pt. 1, 1861) and other chemical subjects. These early chemical contributions, which included important research upon volatile hydrocarbons with Cyrus Moors Warren [*q.v.*], were published in the *Memoirs* and *Proceedings of the American Academy of Arts and Sciences,* in Silliman's *American Journal of Science* (for which Storer also wrote many abstracts and reviews upon technical chemistry) and in the *Répertoire de Chimie Pure et Appliquée,* of which he was American editor for a number of years. His interest in the field of pure chemistry during this period is exemplified by the publication of his first book, *First Outlines of a Dictionary of the Solubilities of Chemical Substances* (1864), a reference work of great value. In 1865 he gave up his consulting practice to accept the professorship of general and industrial chemistry at the newly organized Massachusetts Institute of Technology, where Eliot was professor of analytical chemistry and metallurgy. Having no books suitable for their work of instruction, Eliot and Storer together published *A Manual of Inorganic Chemistry* (1867) and *The Compendious Manual of Qualitative Chemical Analysis* (1868), both of which were extensively used for a long period. In 1867 Storer spent several months abroad in order to study the chemical exhibits at the Paris exposition and to investigate European processes of chemical industry.

The alliance with Eliot, which had been more closely cemented by Storer's marriage on June 21, 1871, to Eliot's sister, Catherine Atkins Eliot, continued to be of importance to his career. Among the first acts of Eliot's administration at Harvard was the organization of the Bussey Institution, a school of agriculture and horticulture, in which Storer was appointed professor of agricultural chemistry. In 1871 he became dean of the Institution as well and continued in these two offices until his retirement in 1907. It was during this period that he performed his most important work, chemical research upon soils, fertilizers, forage crops, cereals, fruits, vegetables, wood, and other products, most of the results being published in over fifty contributions to the *Bulletin of the Bussey Institution,* volumes I–III. This journal, founded and edited by Storer, was the forerunner of numerous later publications upon scientific agriculture. His vast knowledge of all phases of agricultural chemistry is best exemplified in the publication of his most important work, *Agriculture in Some of Its Relations with Chemistry* (1887), the two volumes of which were subsequently enlarged to three. This work, which ran through seven editions, "rendered special service because of its timeliness, appearing when the vast store of information it contained was very inaccessible" (*Experiment Station Record,* Nov. 1914, p. 698). His other publications include *A Cyclopaedia of Quantitative Chemical Analysis* (2 vols., 1870–73), *Elementary Manual of Chemistry* (1894), and *Manual of Qualitative Analysis* (1899), both of the latter with W. B. Lindsay. After his retirement at the age of seventy-five, he continued to maintain a deep interest in chemical instruction and research, though he no longer had a productive part in them. The genial nature of his personality and his friendly appreciation of the work of other contemporary American agricultural chemists, such as Samuel William Johnson and Eugene Woldemar Hilgard [*qq.v.*], are revealed in his books and letters.

[*Who's Who in America,* 1914–15; Benjamin Silliman, Jr., *Am. Contributions to Chemistry* (1874); *Harvard Grads.' Mag.,* Sept. 1914; L. W. Fetzer, in *Biochemical Bull.,* Mar. 1915, with bibliog.; C. W. Eliot, in *Proc. Am. Acad. Arts and Sciences,* vol. LIV (1919); *Industrial and Engineering Chemistry,* June 1924; *Jour. Chemical Educ.,* Jan. 1925; Storer's unpublished correspondence with H. W. Wiley; obituary in *Boston Transcript,* July 30, 1914.]   C. A. B.

STORER, HORATIO ROBINSON (Feb. 27, 1830–Sept. 18, 1922), gynecologist and medical numismatist, was born in Boston, Mass., the son of David Humphreys Storer [*q.v.*] and Abby Jane (Brewer) Storer, the latter a descendant of Governor Thomas Dudley [*q.v.*] of the Massachusetts Bay Colony. He was a brother of Francis Humphreys Storer and a first cousin of Bellamy Storer [*qq.v.*]. He graduated from Harvard College in 1850, having studied under Jean Louis Rodolphe Agassiz and Asa Gray [*qq.v.*], both close friends of his distinguished father. He went with Jeffries Wyman [*q.v.*] to Labrador in the summer of 1850 and furnished a report on the fishes of that region, *Observations on the Fishes of Nova Scotia and Labrador, with Descriptions of New Species* (1850), for the Boston Society of Natural History. After taking the degree of M.D. in 1853 at the Harvard Medical School, he studied abroad for two years in Paris, London, and Edinburgh. In Edinburgh he served as private assistant to Sir James Y. Simpson, who was then using chloroform as a general anesthetic. On his return to Boston he assisted W. O. Priestley in editing the *Obstetric Memoirs* *of James Y. Simpson* (2 vols., 1855–56) and introduced the use of chloroform in obstetrics to his father and Walter Channing [*q.v.*]. Moreover, he soon established a specialty, gynecology, not hitherto recognized as a distinct branch of medicine, and in 1869 was one of the founders of the *Journal of the Gynecological Society of Boston,* the first publication devoted exclusively to diseases of women. In 1865 he was appointed professor of obstetrics and medical jurisprudence in the Berkshire Medical College at Pittsfield, Mass., where he taught until the school closed two years later. He also attended the Harvard Law School, from which he obtained the degree of LL.B. in 1868, in order to equip himself with legal knowledge that would aid him in his crusade against criminal abortions, begun as early as 1857. In connection with this he published numerous papers and books. Among these were *Criminal Abortion in America* (1860), the best of them; *Criminal Abortion* (1868) written with F. F. Heard; and others of a more popular nature, such as *Why Not? A Book for Every Woman* (1866) and *Is It I? A Book for Every Man* (1867), which sold into many thousands of copies. Other less important books are *On Nurses and Nursing* (1868), *The Causation, Course and Treatment of Reflex Insanity in Women* (1871), and *Eutokia: A Word to Physicians and to Women upon the Employment of Anaesthetics in Childbirth* (1863). For many years he delivered a popular course of lectures on diseases of women to physicians from a large part of the United States. He also lectured in California in 1871. He was visiting physician to the Boston Lying-in Hospital and a founder of the Boston Gynecological Society.

In 1872, after an infection received in the course of an operation, from the effects of which he never fully recovered, he retired from practice. He spent five years in Italy, where he wrote *Southern Italy as a Health Station for Invalids* (1875), and then returned to live in Newport, R. I., until his death at the age of ninety-two. During this time he became the world authority on medical medals and devoted himself to adding to his collection, over three thousand in number, which he later gave to the Boston Medical Library. The catalogue of the Storer collection and all other known medals of medical interest, written by Storer and edited by his son, was published after his death as *Medicina in Nummis* (1931). On July 12, 1853, he married Emily Elvira Gilmore (d. 1872), by whom he had a daughter and three sons. On Sept. 20, 1872, he married her sister, Augusta Caroline Gilmore, who died two years later in Italy, leaving a

daughter. His third wife was Frances S. Mackenzie, a nurse and founder of the Saint Elizabeth's Hospital in Boston, whom he married on Sept. 15, 1876. It was after this marriage that Storer became an ardent Roman Catholic. Of his three sons, one became a physician in Boston. A plaque by R. Tait McKenzie (1913) is an excellent likeness of Storer.

[*Who's Who in America,* 1922–23; Malcolm Storer, *Annals of the Storer Family* (1927), art. in *Harvard Grads.' Mag.,* Mar. 1923, and note in *Medicina in Nummis* (1931); J. M. Toner, *A Sketch of the Life of Horatio R. Storer* (1878), with bibliog.; *Boston Medic. and Surgical Jour.,* Oct. 5, 1922, and Jan. 25, 1923; obituaries in *Boston Herald* and *Boston Transcript,* Sept. 19, 1922.]   H. R. V.

STOREY, MOORFIELD (Mar. 19, 1845– Oct. 24, 1929), lawyer, author, publicist, was born in Roxbury, Mass., the son of Charles William and Elizabeth (Moorfield) Storey. Both his parents were of colonial stock, his earliest paternal ancestor having come to Ipswich about 1635. About 1800 the spelling of the name was changed to agree with the spelling of an English branch of the family with which relationship was assumed. Storey attended the Boston Latin School and Harvard College, receiving the degree of A.B. from the latter institution in 1866, and proceeding to its law school. In October 1867, however, he was offered the position of clerk to the United States Senate committee on foreign relations, in effect the office of secretary to its chairman, Charles Sumner [*q.v.*], and, as the duties of this post were considered technically equivalent and superior as training to the methods usual at that time of preparing for the practice of law, he accepted it. As a result he was closely connected in an official capacity with the attempt to impeach President Andrew Johnson [*q.v.*]. In May 1869 he left Washington to study law in the office of Brooks and Ball in Boston, also securing an appointment as clerk in the office of the district attorney of Suffolk County. He qualified as a member of the bar on Aug. 28, 1869, and in October, when the position of assistant district attorney fell vacant, he was promoted to that office. From June 1871 until October 1873 he practised law with his father; he then returned to the office of Brooks and Ball as a partner. The firm he joined was regarded as the most active one in Boston in the practice of commercial law, and he quickly acquired a reputation that eventually grew to be international in range. Firms with which he was associated as a leading member were in the front rank for nearly fifty years. His own branch was the management of litigation, in which he was conspicuously successful, but his office also achieved high repute for the value of its opinions and the thoroughness with which its instruments were drafted. He once stated that he could remember only one instance in which an opinion given by his office as to the validity of bonds was overruled, and that was by a Texas decision that overruled nearly every lawyer in the country and had to be corrected by the legislature.

Though he was eminently successful as a lawyer, in politics he usually met with failure, indifference, or a success that earned him much dislike and suspicion and little in the way of gratitude or popularity. He was a crusader against political corruption, and because he attributed it to them, he attacked Benjamin Franklin Butler and James Gillespie Blaine [*qq.v.*], even opposing a memorial statute to Butler years after his death, and leading the Mugwumps in their desertion of Blaine for Cleveland in 1884. He was a leader in the Anti-Imperialist League that opposed United States ownership of the Philippines; he espoused the cause of the colored people (*Guinn* vs. *United States, 238 United States Reports,* 347; *Buchanan* vs. *Warley,* 245 *United States Reports,* 60; *Moore* vs. *Dempsey, 261 United States Reports,* 86), and defended the rights of the American Indian. He served many years (1877–88, 1892–1910) on the Board of Overseers of Harvard, and successfully opposed the granting of honorary degrees to Governor Butler and President McKinley. In 1900 he dallied with the possibility of running for president or vice-president on the third party ticket, and when that came to nothing, he was a candidate for Congress as an independent, but received only a few votes. He wrote something like eighty pamphlets or articles, and innumerable public letters, in addition to seven books, which include *Charles Sumner* (1900), *Ebenezer Rockwood Hoar* (1911) with E. W. Emerson, *The Reform of Legal Procedure* (1911), *Problems of Today* (1920), and *The Conquest of the Philippines* (1926). With the exception of some that were legal, historical, or biographical, most of his writings were on subjects on which feeling ran high or in which only a minority was interested. But not all his opinions, even when they were severely critical, were neglected or coldly received, for a speech before the American Bar Association in 1894 on the inefficiency and corruption of American legislatures made such a favorable impression that he was elected president of the organization the next year, and he was on the conservative side in the controversy over Nicola Sacco and Bartolomeo Vanzetti [*qq.v.*].

Though he was often called a Puritan, he did not deserve that designation if being a Puritan means, as some say it does, frantic striving to abolish everything the dour cannot trust themselves to indulge in moderately or to practise gracefully, for he lacked neither social nor intellectual accomplishments, and he had a sense of the ridiculous, which the true Puritan never has. He advocated unpopular causes effectively, being a good lawyer, and, though he may have attached more importance to the abstract than to the actual, he was honest and courageous in public affairs. He unquestionably exerted considerable influence on the development of commercial law in America. On Jan. 6, 1870, in Washington, D. C., he married Gertrude Cutts, who died in 1912. There were five children, four of whom, with grandchildren and great-grandchildren, survived him. He died in Lincoln, Mass., and was buried in Mount Auburn Cemetery.

[*Who's Who in America,* 1926–27; M. A. DeWolfe Howe, *Portrait of an Independent, Moorfield Storey, 1845–1929* (1932); J. T. Morse, in *Harvard Grads.' Mag.,* Mar. 1930; J. W. Allen, in *Am. Bar Asso. Jour.,* Feb. 1930; obituary in *Boston Transcript,* Oct. 25, 1929.]

S.G.

STOREY, WILBUR FISK (Dec. 19, 1819–Oct. 27, 1884), newspaper editor, the son of Jesse and Elizabeth (Pierce) Storey, was born on a farm near Salisbury, Vt., where his grandfather, Solomon, a native of Norwich, Conn., had settled during the Revolution. After attending the local schools until he was twelve, Wilbur spent five years in the office of the Middlebury *Free Press* learning the printing trade. Then for a year and a half he was a compositor on the *New York Journal of Commerce,* and in 1838 he migrated to Indiana, where he published two short-lived newspapers, the *Herald* at La Porte, and the *Tocsin* at Mishawaka. Subsequently, after a brief experience as proprietor of a drug store, he moved to Jackson, Mich., where he read law for two years and established a new paper, the *Patriot,* which he sold upon his appointment as postmaster by President Polk. Removed from office by President Taylor, he again became a druggist. He attracted some attention in the Michigan constitutional convention of 1850 and his activities in politics led to his appointment as state prison inspector.

The significant part of his journalistic career began in 1853, when he bought an interest in the *Detroit Free Press* (established in 1831), of which he later became sole owner. He enlarged the paper and on Oct. 2, 1853, began the publication of a Sunday edition to take the place of the Monday issue. Under his direction the *Free Press* came to be regarded as one of the leading

Democratic newspapers in the West. In 1861, from Cyrus H. McCormick [*q.v.*], he purchased the *Daily Chicago Times* (established in 1854 in the interests of Stephen A. Douglas), bringing with him a large part of the staff of the *Free Press* when he took possession on June 8, 1861. Changing the title to *Chicago Times* (June 20), he continued the paper as a Democratic organ. After the Emancipation Proclamation, he ceased to favor the prosecution of the Civil War and bitterly assailed President Lincoln, with the result that the *Times* came to be regarded as a radical "copperhead" sheet. Finally General Ambrose E. Burnside [*q.v.*], commander of the Department of the Northwest, ordered its suppression because of its "repeated expression of disloyal and incendiary sentiments" (*War of the Rebellion: Official Records, Army,* 1 ser., XXIII, 381). On June 3, 1863, Union soldiers took possession of the plant; part of the issue of that day was destroyed, and the issue for the following day did not appear at all. This attempt to stifle the *Times* aroused vigorous protests from loyal citizens who regarded its suppression as an unwarranted interference with the freedom of the press. Lincoln promptly revoked Burnside's order, and the *Times* resumed publication on June 5. Its circulation and advertising increased after its brief suspension, and by the close of the Civil War it had become one of the most prosperous of the Chicago daily papers. After 1868 it was independent in politics.

When the great fire of 1871 destroyed the five-story plant erected in 1866, Storey was tempted to retire, but with improvised equipment the *Times* resumed publication on Oct. 18, 1871, and he decided to continue it, providing a new fireproof building which was completed in 1873. In 1877 he demonstrated his characteristic enterprise in gathering news by establishing a news bureau in London to get the latest reports of the progress of the Russo-Turkish War. In 1878 he went abroad, hoping to restore his failing health, but suffered a stroke and had to be brought home. His active career ended in that year, although he lived until 1884, being adjudged of unsound mind during the last year of his life. At the time of his death the *Times* was valued at a million dollars. He was married three times: in 1847 to Maria Isham of Jackson, Mich., whom he later divorced; about 1870 to Mrs. Harriet Dodge, who died in 1873; and on Dec. 2, 1874, to Eureka (Bissell) Pearson, who survived him.

Storey, unlike Greeley, Bowles, and Dana, was not primarily an editorial writer, but rather an executive who directed the news and editorial policies of his paper. In the emphasis which he constantly placed on the importance of news and in the vigor and fearlessness of the *Times's* editorial attacks, he seems to have been influenced by the elder James Gordon Bennett and the *New York Herald.* Like Bennett he kept aloof from his fellow citizens and engendered no little hostility on the part of the men whom his paper denounced.

[Nine-column obituary in *Chicago Times,* Oct. 28, 1884, written apparently by an associate of many years; A. T. Andreas, *Hist. of Chicago* (3 vols., 1884–86; F. W. Scott, "Newspapers and Periodicals of Ill., 1814–79," *Ill. Hist. Colls.,* vol. VI (1910); *The Biog. Encyc. of Ill.* (1875); *Encyc. of Biog. of Ill.,* vol. II (1894); H. P. Smith, *Hist. of Addison County, Vt.* (1886); *Chicago Tribune,* Oct. 28, 1884.]   W. G. B.

STORROW, CHARLES STORER (Mar. 25, 1809–Apr. 30, 1904), engineer, was a son of Thomas Wentworth and Sarah Phipps (Brown) Storrow. His mother was of old New England stock, as was his paternal grandmother, Ann (Appleton), who in 1777 married Capt. Thomas Storrow of the British army, then a prisoner of war. They subsequently lived in England, the West Indies, and Canada, but returned to Boston in 1795, where Thomas Wentworth Storrow became a successful merchant. Charles was born while his parents were temporarily residing in Montreal, Canada, but in his early childhood the family returned to Boston, where he began to go to school. Soon, however, his father removed the family to Paris, France, where the boy attended a private school. He returned to New England, however, to receive his college preparation at the Round Hill School, Northampton, Mass., and graduated from Harvard, first in his class, in 1829. In his senior year he began the study of civil engineering with Loammi Baldwin [*q.v.*], and some months after his graduation, entered the École National des Ponts et Chaussées in Paris. After two years here he spent some time studying engineering works in France and Great Britain.

Upon his return to Boston in 1832 he became an engineer with the Boston & Lowell Railroad, then just beginning construction. He directed the running of the first train, drawn by the locomotive *Stephenson* from Boston to Lowell and return, May 27, 1835, and upon completion of the road the following year became its manager. In addition to his work in this capacity, he investigated the quantity of water utilized by the Lowell mills, and in 1835 he published a *Treatise on Water-Works*—something of a pioneer in its field. Ten years later he resigned his railroad position to become engineer, treasurer, and agent for the Essex Company at Lawrence, Mass. Showing broad appreciation of the work before him, he planned wisely for the long future. He laid out the city, designing the canals, designating the mill sites, and building several mills. From his own design he built the large masonry dam across the Merrimac River, a pioneer structure which is still in excellent condition in use after nearly a century has elapsed. In 1853, when Lawrence was incorporated as a city, he was made its first mayor.

Storrow's work at Lawrence brought him into close association with Abbott Lawrence [q.v.], who was president of the Essex Company, and when the latter, in 1847, took steps toward the formation of the Lawrence Scientific School at Harvard, he tried to persuade Storrow to assume charge of the school as professor of engineering. Storrow declined this position, however, not desiring to leave his work at Lawrence. In 1860, though maintaining his connection with the Lawrence enterprise, he established his home in Boston. He served in 1861 as engineer member of the state commission on the drainage of the Sudbury and Concord meadows, and in 1862, as consulting engineer, went to Europe to study tunnels for the Hoosac Tunnel Commission, in his report, dated Nov. 28, 1862, advising the Commission upon plans and methods for the construction of the tunnel. At the age of eighty he retired, resigning his position with the Essex Company. His eminent services to engineering were recognized by his professional brethren in his election (1893) to honorary membership in the American Society of Civil Engineers. He was also a fellow of the American Academy of Arts and Sciences.

On Oct. 3, 1836, Storrow married Lydia Cabot Jackson, daughter of Dr. James Jackson [q.v.] of Boston. They had four daughters and three sons, one of whom was James Jackson Storrow [q.v.]. Storrow died in his ninety-sixth year, at Boston.

[*Proc. Am. Acad. Arts and Sci.*, vol. XL (1905); *Proc. Am. Soc. Civil Engineers*, vol. XXX (1904); *Engineering News*, Feb. 16, 1893, May 5, 1904; John Wentworth, *The Wentworth Geneal.* (1878), I, 513–14; M. B. Dorgan, *Hist. of Lawrence, Mass.* (1924); *Boston Transcript*, May 2, 1904.]   H. K. B.

STORROW, JAMES JACKSON (July 29, 1837–Apr. 15, 1897), lawyer, was born in Boston, Mass., the son of Charles Storer Storrow [q.v.], the engineer who planned and built the industrial city of Lawrence, Mass., and of Lydia Cabot (Jackson), daughter of the Boston physician, Dr. James Jackson [q.v.]. He attended Phillips Academy, Andover, for four years and entered Harvard in the fall of 1853. There he distinguished himself in literary and mathematical studies, was an editor of the *Harvard Magazine,* and at graduation was chosen class orator. Though naturally quiet and studious, all his life he loved the outdoors. At Lawrence, where he lived until 1860, he rowed on the Merrimac; and at Cambridge he was on the Harvard crew. He graduated with the degree of A.B. in 1857, read law in the office of Elias Merwin, and spent a year in the Harvard Law School. He was admitted to the bar in February 1860, and soon made a reputation for ability, notably in the copyright case of 1869, *Lawrence* vs. *Dana et al.* (4 *Clifford*, 1; 15 *Federal Cases*, 26). For many years he had been in and about the shops at Lawrence. There his strong mechanical bent was stimulated which resulted in his devoting himself to patent law as his life work. On Aug. 28, 1861, he married Annie Maria Perry, a granddaughter of Commodore Oliver Hazard Perry [q.v.]. They had two sons and a daughter, all of whom survived him. James Jackson Storrow, Jr. (1864–1926), became a leader in civic and industrial life in Boston and New England. Mrs. Storrow died on Mar. 9, 1865, and on Sept. 12, 1873, he married Anne Amory Dexter of Brookline, who survived him. There were no children by the second marriage.

Beginning in 1878 Storrow was associated with Chauncey Smith [q.v.] as counsel for the Bell Telephone Company and its successors in the great litigation in the federal courts over the validity of the Bell telephone patents, which comprehended some 600 cases and lasted to 1896. Storrow's work in this litigation showed again and again his legal genius. He was masterly in his clear analysis of evidence, in his unerring discrimination of tangled issues, and in his cogent presentation of their merits. He frequently performed extraordinary feats of legal presentation, as in his oral argument before the United States Supreme Court in the Telephone Appeals (126 *U. S.,* 1 *The Telephone Cases*), published in 1887 as a bulky volume: *Supreme Court of the United States, October term, 1886;* . . . *Oral Argument on the Bell Patents . . . Jan. 24 to Feb. 8, 1887.* Another instance was his disposal of the claims of Antonio Meucci during an oral argument at New Orleans, Feb. 6, 1886; while he was still speaking the opposing attorneys interrupted him to withdraw that line of defense (*American Bell Telephone Company et al.* vs. *National Improved Telephone Company et al.;* 27 *Federal Reporter,* 663). Storrow allowed himself little diversion, even in the family circle, though he had a wide range of general interests. Even on mountain-climbing expeditions he often spent much time in thought. Such unremitting concentration demanded its penalty of him.

In 1895 Storrow took a purely personal interest in the Venezuela boundary question. In June his friend, Richard Olney [q.v.], became secretary of state. Knowing the thoroughness with which Storrow studied any question, Olney suggested to Señor Don José Andrade, the Venezuelan minister at Washington, that Venezuela retain Storrow in addition to its official adviser, William L. Scruggs [q.v.], to represent that government before the commission appointed by President Cleveland to determine the true boundary line. Storrow went to Caracas, Venezuela, and saw President Joaquin Crespo and his cabinet, who were so impressed that Secretary Olney's suggestion was forthwith adopted. Storrow's brief for Venezuela was published in the London *Times* on July 21, 1896. This was arranged unofficially by Olney through the able assistance of Henry White and had much to do with the change in attitude of the British government and its consent to submit the controversy to arbitration. Storrow went to Venezuela again in 1897 to submit to President Crespo and the Venezuelan legislature the protocol for an arbitration treaty agreed upon by Señor Andrade and Sir Julian Pauncefote and secured its approval. After his return Storrow went to Washington. On Apr. 15, 1897, while going through the new Library of Congress building, he suffered a heart attack from which he died. His body was brought back to Boston for a funeral in Trinity Church and then taken to Newport, R. I., for burial.

[J. J. Storrow Collection, Am. Telephone Hist. Lib., New York City; C. H. Swan, Narrative History of the Litigation on the Telephone Patents (MS., 1903); *Papers Relating to the Foreign Relations of the U. S. ... 1895* (1896), pt. II; Allan Nevins, *Henry White; Thirty Years of Am. Diplomacy* (1930); Henry James, *Richard Olney and His Public Service* (1923); Richard Olney, Address on James J. Storrow, Oct. 30, 1897 (Typed MS. in Lib. of Cong.); *Evening Star* (Washington, D. C.), and *Boston Evening Transcript*, Apr. 16, 1897; O. P. Dexter, *Dexter Genealogy, 1642–1904* (1904), p. 116; E. C. and J. J. Putnam, *The Hon. Jonathan Jackson and Hannah (Tracy) Jackson. Their Ancestors and Descendants* (1907); H. G. Pearson, *Son of New England, James Jackson Storrow, 1864–1926* (1932); information from the family, especially the grandson, James J. Storrow, III.]   W. C. L.

STORRS, RICHARD SALTER (Feb. 6, 1787–Aug. 11, 1873), Congregational clergyman, for sixty-two years pastor in Braintree, Mass., was the third in family descent of a distinguished line of Congregational ministers, whose combined service extended from 1763 to 1900. His grandfather was Rev. John Storrs (1735–1799), a graduate of Yale, a tutor there, and a chaplain in the Revolution; his father, Richard Salter Storrs (1763–1819), was for nearly thirty-four years pastor in Longmeadow,

Mass.; his son, also Richard Salter Storrs [q.v.], carried on the family tradition by a pastorate of more than fifty years at the Church of the Pilgrims, Brooklyn, N. Y. They were the descendants of Samuel, son of Thomas and Mary Storrs of Nottinghamshire, England, who emigrated to Barnstable, Mass., in 1663. On his mother's side, also, Richard 2nd was of ministerial stock. She was Sarah Williston, daughter of Rev. Noah Williston of West Haven, Conn.

Richard was born in Longmeadow, but when he was four years old, his grandfather Williston requested that the child be given to him and reared as his own. The parents consented and the boy's youth was spent in West Haven under a rigorous Puritanical tutelage. Prepared by his grandfather, he entered Yale in 1802; but after a year there he was compelled by ill health to withdraw. Returning now to his father's home, Longmeadow, he engaged in outdoor work, and later taught schools in West Suffield, Conn., Longmeadow, and West Haven, Conn. While in the last-named place he met Lyman Beecher [q.v.] of East Hampton, L. I., who persuaded him to go to that town and take charge of Clinton Academy. During his stay there he had the stimulating experience of living in Beecher's household. An interesting example of one phase of his work survives in *A Dialogue Exhibiting Some of the Principles and Practical Consequences of Modern Infidelity* (1806), which he prepared for a student exhibition; in 1932 it was reprinted in the *Magazine of History* (vol. XLV, Extra No. 180). He reëntered Yale in 1806 but soon transferred to Williams College, from which he graduated in 1807. He then studied theology with Rev. Aaron Woolworth of Bridgehampton, L. I., was licensed by the Suffolk Presbytery, supplied churches in Smithtown and Islip, and in May 1809 entered Andover Theological Seminary, graduating the following year. After six months' missionary work in Georgia as agent of the American Education Society, he was ordained and installed, July 3, 1811, as pastor of the First Congregational Church, Braintree, Mass.

Thenceforth, for considerably more than half a century, he was one of the conspicuous figures of New England Congregationalism. Stanchly orthodox, he energetically opposed the Unitarian movement and was one of the first Massachusetts preachers to refuse to exchange with any clergyman suspected of being unsound in the faith. Although not wholly in sympathy with political abolitionism, he boldly denounced slavery, and a discourse of his, *American Slavery and the Means of Its Removal*, was published in

1844. He was among the early promoters of Sunday schools and temperance societies, and served as secretary of the American Tract Society (1820–25) and director of the American Education Society (1821–30). He was especially interested in home missionary work, was for years an official of the Massachusetts Missionary Society, and during a five-year leave of absence from his church (1831–36) he went up and down New England as a missionary agent. In 1816 he became an editorial writer for the *Recorder* (later the *Boston Recorder*), established the year before, and served for eight years; from 1850 to 1856 he was an editor of the *Congregationalist*. As a director of the Doctrinal Tract Society (later the Congregational Board of Publication) he prepared many works for the press. His own contributions to periodicals were numerous, and in addition to sermons, he published *Memoir of the Rev. Samuel Green* (1836). A typical representative of the old-school New England clergy, severe but friendly, fearless in reproof and denunciation, burning with zeal to promote the spiritual welfare of the land, he was regarded with both awe and affection by his parishioners, and held in high esteem by leading men of his time. He was married first, Apr. 2, 1812, to Sarah Strong Woodhull, who died Apr. 4, 1818; second, Sept. 16, 1819, to Harriet Moore, who died July 10, 1834; and third, Oct. 18, 1835, to Anne Stebbins, who survived him.

[Charles Storrs, *The Storrs Family* (1886); Calvin Durfee, *Williams Biog. Annals* (1871); *Gen. Cat. of the Theological Seminary, Andover, Mass., 1808–1908*; W. S. Pattee, *A Hist. of Old Braintree and Quincy* (copr. 1879); E. A. Park, *A Sermon . . . at the Funeral of Rev. Richard Salter Storrs, D.D.* (1874); *Boston Transcript*, Aug. 12, 1873.]   H. E. S.

STORRS, RICHARD SALTER (Aug. 21, 1821–June 5, 1900), Congregational clergyman, for more than fifty years pastor of the Church of the Pilgrims, Brooklyn, N. Y., was the third of that name and the fourth in line of descent to gain distinction in the ministerial calling. His father was Rev. Richard Salter Storrs [*q.v.*] and his mother, Harriet (Moore) Storrs. Born in Braintree, Mass., he prepared for college at the academy in Monson, Mass., and graduated from Amherst in 1839. For the next two years he taught; first, at Monson, and later, at Williston Seminary, Easthampton, Mass. Abandoning an earlier intent to qualify for the bar after a year in the law office of Rufus Choate, he entered Andover Theological Seminary in 1842 and graduated in 1845. He was immediately called to the Harvard Congregational Church, Brookline, Mass., where, Oct. 22, he was ordained. On the first day of that month he had

married Mary Elwell Jenks, daughter of Rev. Francis and Sarah (Phillips) Jenks, and a niece of Wendell Phillips. He had served hardly a year in his first parish when his abilities as a preacher led to his being called to the recently organized Church of the Pilgrims, Brooklyn, N. Y. Here, during a pastorate that covered the entire last half of the nineteenth century, he was a leading citizen, rivaling in influence and public esteem his contemporary, Henry Ward Beecher. When in 1869 he was called to the Central Church, Boston, more than a hundred of Brooklyn's most prominent men petitioned him to remain. On the fiftieth anniversary of his pastorate, at a gathering in the Academy of Music, he was presented with a medal in recognition of his civic services. A discourse, *The Church of the Pilgrims,* which he delivered and published in 1886, sets forth not only the growth of that organization but also the changes that had taken place about it during the past four decades. Many of those affecting the religious, educational, and philanthropic life of the city he had furthered. He was a corporate member of the Brooklyn Institute of Arts and Sciences, and one of its board of trustees; he was one of the foremost advocates of the movement that resulted in the establishment of Packer Collegiate Institute; he organized the great Sanitary Fair held in February 1864; he was president of the Long Island Historical Society; and in 1889 he served as park commissioner. For the city with whose growth and enrichment he was so long associated he had a jealous affection which made him a vigorous opponent of its consolidation with New York. As an orator he had a country-wide reputation, being popular as a lyceum lecturer, and acceptable at institutions of learning. While he cannot be credited with independent scholarship, his learning was comprehensive and his memory extraordinary. His appearance was "statuesque," and his discourses, enlivened with striking imagery, flowed forth in long, melodious sentences. The diversity of their content is suggested by such titles as "Libraries of Europe," "Climate and Civilization," "John Wycliffe and the First English Bible," "The Muscovite and the Ottoman." Many of his lectures appeared in pamphlet form and some are contained in *Orations and Addresses* (1901). Among his publications, also, are: *The Constitution of the Human Soul* (1857); *Conditions of Success in Preaching Without Notes* (1875); *The Divine Origin of Christianity Indicated by Its Historical Effects* (1884); *Bernard of Clairvaux, the Times, the Man and His Work* (1892). Theologically, "A more orthodox minister has not maintained the faith once delivered to the saints in our time than he" (Cuyler, *post,* p. 1416). From 1848 to 1861 he was one of the editors of the *Independent;* from 1888 to 1897 president of the American Board of Commissioners for Foreign Missions; and in 1895–96, president of the American Historical Association. He was also a trustee of Amherst College. His death occurred at his home in Brooklyn, and he was survived by three of four children.

[Charles Storrs, *The Storrs Family* (1886); *Obit. Record Grads. Amherst Coll. . . . 1900* (1900); *Gen. Cat. of the Theolog. Sem., Andover, Mass., 1808–1908; The Congregational Year-Book,* 1901; *Who's Who in America,* 1899–1900; T. L. Cuyler, in the *Independent,* June 14, 1900; *Congregationalist,* June 14, 1900; *Brooklyn Daily Eagle,* June 6, 7, 8, 1900; *Brooklyn Times,* June 6, 8, 1900.]   H. E. S.

STORY, ISAAC (Aug. 7, 1774–July 19, 1803), poet and miscellaneous writer, was the second son and second child in a family of eleven born to the Rev. Isaac and Rebecca (Bradstreet) Story of Marblehead, Mass. He was graduated from Harvard College in the class of 1793 and studied law. After a brief residence in Castine, Me., 1797–99, he settled in central Massachusetts, first in the town of Sterling, later in Rutland. He was hardly established in his profession, however, when he died, unmarried, in his twenty-ninth year, while visiting his parents at Marblehead. An obituary attributed to his cousin, the noted Joseph Story [*q.v.*], characterized him as: "In his manners bland, social and affectionate; in his disposition, sportive and convivial; in his morals, pure, generous, and unaffected; in his mind, vivacious, refined, and facetious" (*Salem Register,* July 25, 1803).

Isaac Story's literary career was closely patterned after that of Joseph Dennie, Royall Tyler, David Everett [*qq.v.*], and other young lawyers who wrote moral essays, political squibs, and light verse for the newspapers in the large leisure of waiting for professional employment. The current fashion of using pseudonyms makes the identification of his contributions difficult. Two of his juvenile poems, *Liberty* (1795) and *All the World's a Stage* (1796), both signed "The Stranger," were printed by William Barrett of Newburyport, Mass. For Barrett's *Political Gazette,* and later for the *Farmer's Museum* of Walpole, N. H., Story wrote a series of essays under the caption, "From the Desk of Beri Hesdin"; these were modeled on Dennie's "Lay Preacher" papers, but were more serious in tone and conventional in substance. He also contributed essays signed "The Traveler" to the *Columbian Centinel* of Boston and had some editorial connection with Daniel S. Waters' *Castine Gazette* (later the *Castine Journal and Eastern*

Advertiser), but what he wrote for the latter journal has not been determined. There survive in print *An Eulogy on the Glorious Virtues of the Illustrious Gen. George Washington* (Worcester, 1800), and *An Oration, on the Anniversary of the Independence of the United States of America* (Worcester, 1801). Three publications, *An Epistle from Yarico to Inkle* (Marblehead, 1792), which is in the main a reprint of a poem published in London in 1736, *The Barber's Shop: Kept by Sir David Razor* (Salem, n.d.), and *Original and Select Poems, By the Stranger* (Albany, 1827) have been erroneously ascribed to Story. Three manuscript books of his poems, with some letters and miscellaneous prose, are preserved in the library of Harvard University. He was best known for his verses signed "Peter Quince," in imitation of the burlesque odes of "Peter Pindar" (John Wolcot, 1738–1819). They were written originally for the Newburyport *Political Gazette,* but when that paper was discontinued in 1797, Story transferred the series to the *Farmer's Museum.* In 1801 a collection of them was published in Boston under the title, *A Parnassian Shop, Opened in the Pindaric Stile; By Peter Quince, Esq.* Besides many pieces of topical wit and political satire directed against Democrats of all descriptions, the volume contains some serious patriotic, moral, and sentimental poems. The verse is facile, but no longer sparkles.

[The date of birth, which is sometimes given as Aug. 25, is taken from *Vital Records of Marblehead, Mass.,* vol. I (1903). See also Perley Derby and F. A. Gardner, *Elisha Story of Boston* (1915); H. M. Ellis, "Joseph Dennie and His Circle," *Univ. of Tex. Bull., Studies in English, No. 4* (1915); G. A. Wheeler, *Hist. of Castine, . . . Me.* (1875); A. P. Peabody, "The Farmer's Weekly Museum," *Proc. Am. Antiquarian Soc.,* n.s., vol. VI (1890); E. A. and G. S. Duyckinck, *Cyc. of Am. Lit.* (1856), vol. I; obituary in *Salem Register,* July 25, 1803.]   G. F. W.

STORY, JOSEPH (Sept. 18, 1779–Sept. 10, 1845), jurist, eldest of the eleven children of Elisha and Mehitable (Pedrick) Story, was born in Marblehead, Mass. His father had seven children by an earlier marriage. Descended from another Elisha Story, who arrived in Boston from England about 1700, Joseph had forebears of some influence and position in colonial New England. Before the War of the Revolution his paternal grandfather, William Story, had held the office of registrar in the court of admiralty. His own father, who became a physician and surgeon of considerable reputation, had been associated with the Sons of Liberty and was one of the "Indians" who took part in the Boston Tea Party. His mother's father was a wealthy merchant of Marblehead and a Loyalist.

Story received the best education that the

times and the place afforded. He was one of the first pupils to attend the newly established academy at Marblehead. A misunderstanding with the master of the school caused him to leave the academy in the fall of 1794 with his preparation for college still incomplete. It was prophetic of the tremendous industry and power of concentration with which he was later to amaze the legal world by producing volume after volume of commentaries in rapid succession, that Story, just turned fifteen and almost alone and unaided, should not only have finished his preparatory studies, but further should have made himself sufficiently acquainted with the subjects covered by the college freshman class for the first six months, to pass the examinations and to become a regularly enrolled student in Harvard at the close of the January vacation in 1795. In his college career he was confessedly a grind: "I was most thoroughly devoted to all the college studies, and scarcely wasted a single moment in idleness. I trace back to this cause a serious injury to my health. When I entered College I was robust and muscular, but before I left I had become pale and feeble and was inclined to dyspepsia" (*Miscellaneous Writings*, p. 16). He was graduated from Harvard in 1798, being rated second to William Ellery Channing who led the class.

He returned to Marblehead and began the study of law in the office of Samuel Sewall, then a member of Congress and later chief justice of the supreme court of Massachusetts. Though by general acclaim he still ranks as the foremost of American legal writers, Story acquired the foundations of his legal knowledge by means and methods which would be anathema to the educators of today. As in the case of office students in all generations, he was left largely to his own devices and thrown back upon his own resources —perhaps not a handicap to one of his studious habits. For months at a time he not infrequently devoted fourteen hours a day to study. The scarcity of American reports—there were then only five or six volumes available—made it necessary for him to depend upon treatises, some of them already very old. He tells us that he read Blackstone with pleasurable comprehension, but that his next assignment, Coke on Littleton, proved so difficult that he wept bitterly over the failure of his first unsuccessful attempts to understand it. After mastering Littleton he turned to Saunders' *Reports* and the study of special pleading, developing such an interest in this branch of the law as to make it for several years his favorite subject. While still in Sewall's office he read through "that deep and admirable work

upon one of the most intricate titles of the law, Fearne on Contingent Remainders and Executory Devises" (*Ibid.*, p. 20). Apparently it was not until after he had begun the actual practice of law that he became acquainted with the *Year Books* and the early English reports that followed them.

On the appointment of Sewall to a judgeship, Story left his office and went to that of Samuel Putnam in Salem. This change probably accounts for the fact that on his admission to the bar, at the July term of the common pleas in Essex County, 1801, he opened his own office in that town. He began his career as a practising lawyer under circumstances that were neither auspicious nor pleasant. Story himself was an avowed Republican; the bench and bar of eastern Massachusetts were, practically without exception, Federalists. At first he was made to feel this political difference pointedly; was, as he says, "excluded from those intimacies which warm and cheer the intercourse of the profession" (*Ibid.*, p. 22). However, during his second year at the bar his practice began to grow. It increased, until at the time of his appointment to the Supreme Court of the United States some ten years later, it was, if we may believe his own statement, as extensive and lucrative as that of any lawyer in the county.

His participation in politics and public affairs began early in his career. He was chosen by Marblehead to deliver the eulogy on the death of Washington (published, 1800). In 1803 he was appointed to the station of naval officer for the port of Salem, but this appointment he declined. The next year he delivered the annual Fourth of July oration in Salem (published, 1804). He was Salem's representative in the legislature of Massachusetts in 1805 and again in 1806 and 1807. A memorial, relative to the infringements of the neutral trade of the United States, and addressed to the President and Congress in behalf of the inhabitants of Salem, was drawn up by him in January 1806 (*Ibid.*, p. 43). This same year, as chairman of the committee appointed to make a report on the matter, he was largely responsible for the act of the legislature raising the salaries of the judges of the supreme court of Massachusetts. In his time, as for a long time afterwards, there was no court of equity in Massachusetts. During the session of the legislature in 1808 he moved the appointment of a committee to take under consideration the establishment of a court of chancery. He was made chairman of the committee and drew up an exhaustive report in favor of the creation of such a court. The report was not accepted, but it is part of the history of Story and equity. Together with Chancellor Kent he will always be remembered as the founder of the system in the United States; in 1842 he drew up the rules of equity practice for the United States Supreme Court and the circuit courts; his *Commentaries on Equity Jurisprudence* (14th ed., 3 vols., 1918), and his *Commentaries on Equity Pleading* (10th ed., 1892), are still in use.

In the fall of 1808 he was elected a member of Congress to fill the vacancy caused by the death of Jacob Crowninshield. He remained in Congress for one session only, until Mar. 3, 1809, and declined to become a candidate for reëlection. The reasons for this refusal, as he later gave them, were that a continuance in public life would be incompatible with his complete success at the bar, and that obedience to party projects required too much sacrifice of opinion and feeling. That he was unwilling to sacrifice his own opinions for the sake of his party, during even his short stay in Congress, is shown by his attitude toward the Embargo, which, he had become convinced, had failed of its object and should be abandoned. Jefferson accused him of being responsible for the repeal of the Embargo—"I ascribe all this to one pseudo-Republican, Story" (P. L. Ford, *The Writings of Thomas Jefferson*, IX, 1898, p. 277). In another matter also he was openly in disagreement with his party. In January 1809 he offered a bill providing for a committee to inquire into the expediency of building up the United States navy. Such a plan was contrary to the principles of the Republican party, and the bill did not pass. On leaving Congress he was once more elected a member of the Massachusetts legislature; he was made speaker of the House of Representatives in January 1811, and again in May of the same year. After his elevation to the Supreme Court, though his interest in political affairs continued unabated, he made it a rule to take no active part in politics. The only recorded exception to this rule was his appearance at a town meeting in Salem, December 1819, where his animosity to slavery and the slave trade led him to speak strongly against the Missouri Compromise. It was this same feeling and subject which had inspired his sensational charge to the grand jury of the circuit court earlier in the year, for which he was taken to task by the newspapers of the day (*Life and Letters*, I, 336–48). The same hatred of slavery showed itself again some three years later (May term, 1822) in his opinion, much-discussed at the time, in the case of the alleged slave-runner *La Jeune Eugénie* (2 *Mason*, 409).

But even after he became a judge, Story was active in the field of public or semi-public usefulness. In August 1813, he delivered in Salem a eulogy at the burial of Captain James Lawrence who had been killed in the fight between the *Chesapeake* and the *Shannon*. He served as president of the Merchants' Bank of Salem from 1815 till 1835, and as vice-president of the Salem Savings Bank from 1818 till 1830. He was elected a member of the Board of Overseers of Harvard College in 1819, and in 1825 he became a fellow of the Corporation. In 1820 he drew up for the merchants of Salem a long memorial addressed to Congress asking that certain restrictions on commerce be removed (published, 1820); in this same year he was elected a delegate from Salem to the convention called to revise the constitution of Massachusetts. During the next year he found time to prepare and deliver a scholarly address before the members of the Suffolk bar on the progress of jurisprudence. Among his *Miscellaneous Writings* are to be found two other addresses which in the case of any one other than Story would be considered matters of major importance: a remarkable legal argument made in 1825 before the Board of Overseers of Harvard College (against the claims of the professors and tutors of the college that none but resident instructors could be chosen for fellows of the corporation), and the annual oration before the society of Phi Beta Kappa at Harvard in 1826. In this same busy period he drew up the Crimes Act of 1825, usually attributed to Daniel Webster, who carried it through Congress; in 1816 he had drawn up his bill to extend the jurisdiction of the circuit courts (*Life and Letters*, I, 293). He was one of the organizers of the Essex Historical Society, and a member of the board of trustees of Mount Auburn Cemetery from 1831 until his death.

On Nov. 18, 1811, shortly after he had passed his thirty-second birthday, Story was appointed an associate justice of the Supreme Court of the United States. By his panegyrists much has been made of the fact that he was the youngest person ever to be appointed to this position. It should be remembered, however, that Madison had already tried to honor with the position three other men in succession, all of them at that time more prominent than Story—Levi Lincoln, formerly in Jefferson's cabinet, who declined; Alexander Wolcott of Connecticut, whom the Senate refused to confirm; and John Quincy Adams, then minister at St. Petersburg, who preferred to remain there. Madison then turned to Story, at the suggestion, it is said, of Ezekiel Bacon, a congressman from Massachusetts. Though the salary of $3,500 was only slightly more than half of his professional income, Story at once accepted the office, motivated, he said, by the honor, the permanence of the tenure, and especially by "the opportunity it will allow me to pursue, what of all things I admire, juridical studies" (*Life and Letters,* I, 201). At this time the judges of the Supreme Court exercised also a circuit court jurisdiction. Story's circuit took in Maine, New Hampshire, Massachusetts, and Rhode Island. The illness and infirmities of his predecessor, William Cushing, had led to a vast accumulation of cases on the docket. By an early decision (*United States* vs. *Wonson,* 1 *Gallison,* 5) Story reversed the former practice of the circuit court of allowing appeals from the district court to the circuit court in jury cases at common law. By this ruling 130 cases were at once stricken from the docket. But the respite thus gained was of short duration. The War of 1812 gave the crippled shipping interests of Story's maritime circuit a chance to recoup their losses by turning to privateering. Soon his court was flooded with cases involving admiralty and prize law, subjects at that time but little understood, and depending on principles which were then neither well defined nor established. His decisions in these cases, the result of broad study on his part, first put the admiralty jurisdiction of the federal courts on a sound basis. What was perhaps the most famous of these cases, decided in 1815 (*De Lovio* vs. *Boit,* 2 *Gallison,* 398), was long afterwards referred to by a justice of the Supreme Court in these words, "The learned and exhaustive opinion of Justice Story, . . . affirming the admiralty jurisdiction over policies of marine insurance has never been answered, and will always stand as a monument of his great erudition" (*Insurance Company* vs. *Dunham,* 11 *Wallace,* 35). In 1816 William Pinkney [*q.v.*], who was considering the request of the government to go as minister to Russia, offered Story his law practice in Baltimore. Though this was estimated to be worth $20,000 a year, and though Congress had just refused to raise the salaries of the federal judges, Story, still far from the affluence which he later enjoyed, declined Pinkney's offer.

Many of the opinions written by Story as a justice of the Supreme Court impress us, even today, by their remarkable breadth of learning; some of them are elaborate to a degree; in some there is a marked tendency to range over the whole field in any way involved, and widely beyond the mere facts and law necessary for a judgment in the particular case. This tendency, natural to him, and unquestionably of great advantage in the writing of the commentaries, can hardly be said to enhance his reputation as a judge. Yet not a few of his opinions had important legal and constitutional results; many of them that no longer attract attention were of the most vital interest in their day. Among the latter class was (1815) his famous dissenting opinion in the case of the *Nereide* (9 *Cranch,* 388, 436), in which he, disagreeing with Marshall and the majority of the court, argued against the ruling that a neutral might lawfully put his goods on board a belligerent ship for conveyance. Unknown to the court until shortly thereafter, Lord Stowell had just decided a British case of similar nature on the basis of the very rule for which Story had contended. At about this same time Story was assigned the writing of the opinion in *Green* vs. *Liter* (8 *Cranch,* 229), presumably because no one of his colleagues had the necessary knowledge of the now almost obsolete old real actions adequately to discuss the principles of the writ of right on which the case was based. It has been called the "most prominent and elaborate opinion delivered by him at this time" (*Life and Letters,* I, 260), but it shows no great depth of historical legal learning, especially of the period when the writ of right was the supreme action in English law. One of the most important opinions in his whole career was delivered in 1816 in the case of *Martin* vs. *Hunter's Lessee* (1 *Wheaton,* 304), which decided that the appellate jurisdiction of the Supreme Court could rightfully be exercised over the state courts, "an opinion which has ever since been the keystone of the whole arch of Federal judicial power" (Charles Warren, *The Supreme Court in United States History,* 1922, vol. I, 449). Another opinion, extremely important in contemporaneous (1822) international politics, was that in the case of the *Santissima Trinidad* (7 *Wheaton,* 283); this held that a prize captured by a ship which had been guilty of a violation of American neutrality, and brought into a United States port, should be given back to the original owner. The constantly increasing extent of admiralty jurisdiction claimed by the federal courts, in the development of which claim Story had played a major part, had aroused a feeling of hostility among some of the inland states, which saw, or thought they saw, some phases of their common law jurisdiction menaced in inland waters. This feeling was allayed (1825) by Story's opinion in the case of the *Thomas Jefferson* (10 *Wheaton,* 428), which held that the admiralty jurisdiction of the federal courts did not extend beyond waters affected by the ebb and flow of the tide. A case which moved the country mightily at the time, 1841, was that of the *United States* vs. *Schooner*

Amistad (15 *Peters,* 518). A cargo of negroes on the *Amistad,* a slave-runner, had gotten control of the ship and murdered the officers; on being brought into port by a vessel of the United States navy they were claimed as slaves by certain Spaniards; the question before the court was whether or not the negroes were entitled to their freedom. Story's decision, for the court, held that they should be freed and sent back to Africa. Story's opinion in another case famous in its time (1844) because of its religious ramifications, *Vidal* vs. *Philadelphia* (2 *Howard,* 127), was so far approved by the court as a whole that he could later write to Kent that "not a single sentence was altered by my brothers, as I originally drew it" (*Life and Letters,* II, 469). It held valid the will of Stephen Girard who had bequeathed to Philadelphia several millions of dollars to found a college for poor white children, but on the condition that no ecclesiastic of any kind, or on any pretence or for any purpose, should ever be allowed to enter the institution. That opinion of Story which is today best known and most often read is doubtless his learned and powerful dissenting opinion in *Charles River Bridge* vs. *Warren Bridge* (11 *Peters,* 420, 583). It was one of three dissenting opinions, all on questions of constitutional law, which he wrote during the 1837 term. The opinion of the court as a whole seemed to Story to destroy the sanctity of contracts and to be immoral. His own opinion won the approval of many, if not most, of the best lawyers in the country; Webster called it his "ablest and best written opinion" (*Life and Letters,* II, 269).

It has been said that in the Supreme Court Story was dominated by John Marshall. In refutation of this statement one of the latest of Story's biographers has prepared the following succinct set of facts: Story wrote opinions in 286 cases in the Supreme Court; of these 269 are reported as the opinion of the court or of a majority; three were concurring opinions and fourteen dissenting opinions; he wrote four dissenting opinions on questions of constitutional law, one being in the lifetime of Marshall; in the only case (*Ogden* vs. *Saunders*) in which Marshall was in a minority on a question of constitutional law, Story and Duval concurred with him in the question upon which he wrote the opinion; Story wrote the opinion of the majority of the court in five cases in which Marshall dissented; in four of the cases in which he dissented in Marshall's life, the latter wrote the opinion of the majority (W. D. Lewis, ed., *Great American Lawyers,* III, 1907, p. 150). Marshall died in 1835. Story was generally regarded as the logi-

cal successor to his position, and Marshall before his death is said to have favored that choice (*Life and Letters,* II, 210). Soon after Marshall's death, Story himself had protested as only a man alive to a probability would be likely to protest, that he had never for a moment imagined that he would be thought of, that he was "equally beyond hope or anxiety" (*Ibid.,* II, 201). Today we can see that there was no likelihood of his receiving the appointment. He was out of sympathy with Jackson, personally and politically. The President, on his part, could say no good word for what he called "the school of Story and Kent"; he had already referred to Story as "the most dangerous man in America" (*Ibid.,* II, 117). Within the year Roger B. Taney was appointed to fill Marshall's place.

In 1828 the Royall Professorship of Law at Harvard, then vacant, had been offered to Story. He declined it on the ground that he feared that an increase of duties at his age might seriously interfere with his health. But in the very next year Nathan Dane, after talking the matter over with Story, established a new professorship of law, with the understanding, and on the explicit condition, that the first occupant of the chair should be Story. He was elected to the position in June of that year, accepted it, and in September moved permanently from Salem to Cambridge. For the rest of his life the Law School was one of his chief interests. In a very real sense he may be regarded as its founder; along with his colleague J. H. Ashmun, who had accepted the Royall Professorship, and together with Tapping Reeve and James Gould [*qq.v.*] of the Litchfield Law School, he was one of the pioneers in law-school, as contrasted with office, instruction for those who are starting a legal education. His opening class at the law school numbered eighteen students; before he died his reputation and personality had brought the annual enrollment to almost 150. Through his efforts the permanent funds of the school were increased and the library was built up and expanded. His ability as a teacher seems to have been no less marked than his skill as an organizer, and this in spite of the fact that his own knowledge of the law had been acquired without benefit of teacher. But by far the most important fact in connection with Story's association with the Law School lies in another field. In establishing his professorship Dane had stipulated that a number of formal lectures in certain named branches of the law should be prepared, delivered, and revised for publication by the professor on his foundation. This did not fit into Story's scheme of teaching, for he wrote out no formal lectures, but taught by a method of informal discussion. So in place of publishing a series of lectures, he devised the plan which resulted in his well known *Commentaries.*

The continuing importance and reputation of these has almost obscured the fact that they were by no means Story's only legal treatises. Much writing of the same general nature had already come from his pen. As early as 1805 he had published, with valuable notes, *A Selection of Pleadings in Civil Actions.* At about the same time he undertook the task of making a digest of American law similar to, and supplementary to, Comyns' *Digest.* Though the project was finally abandoned, three large volumes in manuscript gave evidence of his endeavor. In 1809 he brought out a new edition of Chitty's *A Practical Treatise on Bills of Exchange and Promissory Notes,* and in the next year one of Charles Abbott's *A Treatise on the Law Relative to Merchant Ships and Seamen,* with annotations and references to American decisions. This work he reëdited in 1829. He was the editor of an annotated edition of Lawes's *A Practical Treatise on Pleading in Assumpsit* (1811). He was the writer of many of the elaborate notes in Wheaton's *Reports* (*Life and Letters,* I, 282–83). In 1828 he published in three volumes *Public and General Statutes Passed by the Congress of the United States, 1789–1827.*

The *Commentaries* themselves followed one another in quick order. *Bailments* appeared in 1832; *On the Constitution,* in three volumes, in 1833; *The Conflict of Laws* in 1834; *Equity Jurisprudence,* in two volumes, in 1836; *Equity Pleading* in 1838; *Agency* in 1839; *Partnership* in 1841; *Bills of Exchange* in 1843; *Promissory Notes* in 1845. That one man, with few precedents to depend upon, should have written these voluminous works on exact, technical legal subjects, within the space of a little more than twelve years, seems incredible—and even more incredible when it is considered that during the same period he performed in full his work as a law teacher and as a judge, the latter requiring attendance on the court at Washington and circuit-court duty as well. Add to all this the fact that within the same interval he published *The Constitutional Class Book* (1834), prepared and delivered a long discourse on Marshall (before the Suffolk bar, 1835), drafted the Bankruptcy Act of 1841, contributed nearly a score of articles on legal subjects to the *Encyclopedia Americana* (*Life and Letters,* II, 26–27), and we have an example of industry in legal scholarship that has yet to be equaled. The success of the *Commentaries* was widespread and immediate. Some

of them (*Bailments, Equity Jurisprudence*) went into third editions even during the short space of his remaining years. The financial returns from his books are said to have reached the then lofty figure of $10,000 per annum. Through his decisions, and his correspondence with some of the leading British jurists, Story was well known in England before his *Commentaries* appeared; with the translation of some of his works, notably *On the Constitution* and *The Conflict of Laws,* into French and German, he now acquired a truly international reputation. But, unlike more modern representatives of his type, he never went abroad, and never received any honorary degrees from foreign universities. At home he had already been honored with several.

Story's predominant personal characteristic was probably his unusual power of conversation. His son says that the father, a chronic dyspeptic at thirty-two, was practically unable to take physical exercise, apparently because of lack of time and interest, and that "his real exercise was in talking" (*Life and Letters,* II, 106). Poetry played a not inconsiderable part in his life. He read it habitually and wrote verse more or less throughout his life. The motto of the *Salem Register* was written by him and gives a good idea of his general style:

"Here shall the Press the People's right maintain,
Unawed by influence and unbribed by gain;
Here Patriot Truth her glorious precepts draw,
Pledged to Religion, Liberty, and Law."

Before 1804 he had the temerity to publish a long and youthful effusion, *The Power of Solitude* (1802?), written at a time when "his leisure moments were employed in writing love songs, full of rapturous exaggerations or sentimental laments" (*Life and Letters,* I, 100). Later on he repented of this act and bought up all the copies of the book that he could find. But there still remain a few copies to attest the wisdom of his efforts to destroy them. He was fond of music, drawing, and painting. His favorite novelist was Jane Austen. As a result, he tells us, of observing the intellectual attainments of the girls in the mixed classes which as a boy he attended at Marblehead Academy, he was an active champion for the higher education of women. Like many of the other leading men of eastern Massachusetts at that time he was a Unitarian. The picture of him given us by his son (*Life and Letters,* II, 552) is that of a man five feet eight inches tall, with a well-knit figure; active, restless, and nervous in his movements; with thick auburn hair in his youth, but bald in his later years save for a thick mass of silvery hair on the back of his head; his blue eyes were lively and his mouth was large and expressive.

Story died on Sept. 10, 1845. He had been married first to Mary Lynde Oliver on Dec. 9, 1804. She died in June of the next year. On Aug. 27, 1808, he married Sarah Waldo Wetmore, daughter of Judge William Wetmore. Of the seven children of this marriage only two survived him. One of these, Louisa, married George T. Curtis [*q.v.*]; the other was William Wetmore Story [*q.v.*], the sculptor.

[W. W. Story, ed., *Life and Letters of Joseph Story* (2 vols., 1851), is indispensable. Tinged with hero worship and pride of family, it is nevertheless reliable. Next in importance are *The Miscellaneous Writings of Joseph Story* (1852). Prefaced by a remarkable autobiographical letter written by Story in 1831, this book contains many of his addresses, and a number of book reviews of such substance as to be entitled to rank as essays. The best recent account of Story is that by William Schofield, in W. D. Lewis, ed., *Great American Lawyers*, III (1907). It is especially good for a discussion of the meaning and importance of some of Story's judicial opinions. On this matter the *Life and Letters*, and Charles Warren, *The Supreme Court in U. S. History* (3 vols., 1922), should also be consulted. For Story's connection with the Harvard Law School see, in addition to the *Life and Letters*, Charles Warren, *Hist. of the Harvard Law School* (1908), vols. I, II. Two funeral orations by men who were intimately acquainted with Story have been published: Simon Greenleaf, *A Discourse Commemorative of the Life and Character of the Hon. Joseph Story* (1845); Charles Sumner, *The Scholar, the Jurist, the Artist, the Philanthropist* (1846). See also *The Centennial Hist. of the Harvard Law School, 1817–1917* (1918); Perley Derby and F. A. Gardner, compilers, *Elisha Story of Boston and Some of His Descendants* (1915); and obituary in *Boston Daily Advertizer*, Sept. 12, 1845. Story's decisions in the Supreme Court will be found in Cranch's *Reports*, Wheaton's *Reports*, Peters' *Reports*, and Howard's *Reports*; his decisions upon his circuit are reported by Gallison, Mason, Charles Sumner, and W. W. Story, 13 vols. in all. The last editions of the *Commentaries* are as follows: *Bailments* (9th, 1878); *On the Constitution* (5th, 1891); *Conflict of Laws* (8th, 1883); *Equity Jurisprudence* (14th, 1918); *Equity Pleading* (10th, 1892); *Agency* (9th, 1882); *Partnership* (7th, 1881); *Bills of Exchange* (4th, 1860); *Promissory Notes* (7th, 1878).]

G. E. W.

STORY, JULIAN RUSSELL (Sept. 8, 1857–Feb. 23, 1919), portrait painter, was born at Walton-on-Thames, Surrey, England, youngest of the four children of William Wetmore Story [*q.v.*] and Emelyn (Eldredge) Story. He was educated at Eton and at Brasenose College, Oxford, where he received the degree of B.A. in 1879. A letter from William Wetmore Story to James Russell Lowell, written in 1864, mentions the younger Story's early determination to be an artist and the father's intention to let him reach his own decision in the matter (Henry James, *William Wetmore Story and his Friends*, 1903, vol. II, p. 147). Later Robert Browning writes the family of his admiration of an early exhibit by the young man at the Grosvenor Gallery in London (*Ibid.*, p. 279). Gifted with his parents' charm of manner, trained under Frank Duveneck [*q.v.*] in Florence and under Gustave Rodolphe

Boulanger and Jules Joseph Lefebvre in Paris, he became in later years a portrait painter of distinction, in whose work technical mastery was combined with charm of color and handling. In 1891 he married Emma Eames, a celebrated opera-singer, from whom he was divorced in 1907. In 1909 he married Elaine (Sartori) Bohlen of Philadelphia, Pa., who with three children survived him. For many years he centered his activities at Vallombrosa, Italy, travelling to Paris, London, and America as occasion required. Later he divided his time between Italy and Philadelphia, finally giving up the villa at Vallombrosa a few years before his death. He belonged to clubs in Florence, London, New York, and Philadelphia, and to the societies of portrait painters in Paris and London. In 1906 he became an associate of the National Academy. He received a third class medal and honorable mention at the Paris Salon of 1889, a gold medal at Berlin in 1891, and silver medals at expositions in Paris (1890), Buffalo (1901), and San Francisco (1915). In 1900 he became a chevalier of the Legion of Honor.

Story went through the usual transitions from Salon compositions ("The Entombment of Christ," Peabody Institute, Baltimore, Md.), historical compositions ("Mlle. Sembreuil," Pennsylvania Academy of the Fine Arts, Philadelphia), and realistic illustration ("Laboratory of Clinical Physiology at Saint Lazare") to portraiture à la mode in the larger cities of Europe and America. His masterpiece in this last field is probably his "Madame Emma Eames" in the Cincinnati Art Museum, Cincinnati, Ohio. Other portraits are to be seen in Philadelphia, where for a time Story was commissioned to portray many of the leaders of business and professional life and their wives. Story's style varies considerably with his subject. The observer notes his vigorous drawing, his conscientious modelling, his increasing boldness of handling and of lighting, and his ability to use color of the higher ranges without disintegration. His composition is invariably soberly satisfactory, his feeling for textures delightful. Less brilliant than his friend, John Singer Sargent [*q.v.*], he perhaps less frequently exploited the possibilities of mere technical virtuosity. He died in Philadelphia and was buried from the Church of St. Luke and the Epiphany.

[The date of birth has been supplied by the librarian of the National Academy of Design. See *Who's Who in America*, 1918–19; Mary E. Phillips, *Reminiscences of William Wetmore Story* (1897); *Am. Art Ann.*, vol. XVI (1919); obituaries in *Am. Art News*, Mar. 1, and *Pub. Ledger* (Phila.), Feb. 25, 1919. There are brief references in Samuel Isham, *The Hist. of Am. Painting* (1905); Henri Sylvestre, Jr., *The Marvels in Art of the Fin de Siècle* (1893), vol. II; G. W. Sheldon, *Recent Ideals of Am. Art* (1888). *Who's Who in Philadelphia,* 1925, inaccurate in details, contains a portrait.]

W. S. R.

STORY, WILLIAM EDWARD (Apr. 29, 1850–Apr. 10, 1930), mathematician, eldest son of Isaac and Elizabeth B. (Woodberry) Story, was born at Boston, Mass., and was descended from Elisha Story, who came from England to Boston about 1700. Joseph Story [*q.v.*], associate justice of the United States Supreme Court for many years, was a brother of his grandfather; and his great-grandfather, Dr. Elisha Story of Bunker Hill, was one of the "Indians" of the Boston Tea Party. After graduation from Harvard in 1871, Story spent three and a half years in European study, particularly with the mathematicians Weierstrass and Kummer at Berlin and with C. G. Neumann at Leipzig, where he received the degree of Ph.D. in 1875 with a dissertation entitled *On the Algebraic Relations Existing between the Polars of a Binary Quantic* (1875). After spending the year 1875–76 as tutor in mathematics at Harvard, he went to the Johns Hopkins University, where he was at first associate in mathematics and then associate professor until 1889. The first seven years of this period were the most notable in the history of American mathematics up to that time, because of the presence at Baltimore of J. J. Sylvester [*q.v.*], through whose influence the *American Journal of Mathematics* was founded, with Sylvester as editor-in-chief and Story as "associate editor in charge" (1878–82). In this journal he published most of his mathematical papers, but others appeared in *Proceedings of the London Mathematical Society* (vol. XXIII, 1892), *Mathematische Annalen* (vol. XLI, 1893), *Zeitschrift für Physikalische Chemie* (vol. LXXI, 1910), *Proceedings of the American Academy of Arts and Sciences* (vol. XL, 1904), *Transactions of the American Mathematical Society* (January 1907), *The London, Edinburgh and Dublin Philosophical Magazine* (July 1910), and the *Official Report . . . of the New England Association of Colleges and Preparatory Schools* for 1903. He founded, edited, and published the *Mathematical Review* at Worcester, Mass., between 1896 and 1899, but only 208 pages, in two numbers and part of a third, were actually issued. He was also joint editor (1899) of *Clark University, 1889–1899,* the decennial celebration volume.

From 1889 until 1921, when he became professor emeritus, Story was professor at Clark University. Twelve doctoral dissertations in the fields of geometry and algebra were completed under his direction. He was elected a fellow of the American Academy of Arts and Sciences (1876) and of the National Academy of Sciences (1908), and served as president of the Mathematical Congress at the World's Columbian Exposition, Chicago (1893), and of the Omar Khayyam Club of America (1924–27). His admirable address before this club in 1918, *Omar Khayyàm as a Mathematician,* was printed privately in book form, with Story's portrait, in 1919, and reprinted in *Twenty Years of the Omar Khayyàm Club of America* (1921). Among the eighty men listed as the chief research mathematicians of the United States in 1903, Story was ranked by his colleagues as fifteenth (*American Men of Science,* 5th ed., 1933, p. 1269). His interest in mathematical bibliography led him to accumulate a catalogue comprising tens of thousands of hand-written cards in 156 drawers and 35 boxes, now the property of the library of the American Mathematical Society (see its *Bulletin . . . Catalogue,* 1932). He was married June 20, 1878, to Mary Harrison of Baltimore, and they had one son.

[*Eleventh Report of the Class of 1871 of Harvard Coll.* (1921); *Vita* in Story's Leipzig dissertation, mentioned above; Perley Derby, *Elisha Story of Boston and Some of His Descendants* (1915); F. I. Virkus, *The Abridged Compendium of Am. Geneal.,* I (1925), 218–19; Florian Cajori, *The Teaching and Hist. of Mathematics in the U. S.* (1890); Story's own account of his research, in *Clark Univ., 1889–1899* (1899), pp. 71–73, 546–47; J. C. Poggendorff's *Biographisch-Literarisches Handwörterbuch . . . der exacten Wissenschaften,* vols. III (1898), IV (1904), V (1926); *Harvard Grads. Mag.,* June 1930; *Who's Who in America,* 1928–29; *Springfield Daily Republican,* Apr. 11, 1930.]

R. C. A.

STORY, WILLIAM WETMORE (Feb. 12, 1819–Oct. 7, 1895), sculptor, essayist, and poet, was born in Salem, Mass., the second son and sixth child of Joseph Story [*q.v.*] and Sarah Waldo (Wetmore) Story. When Story was ten years old, the family moved from Salem to Cambridge, where he was prepared for college by William Wells and had James Russell Lowell [*q.v.*] for constant companion, Charles Sumner [*q.v.*] for intimate family friend and boyhood hero, and Thomas Wentworth Higginson [*q.v.*] for youthful admirer. Higginson later recalled Story as "a sort of Steerforth" among his fellows. In Lowell's *Fireside Travels,* dedicated to Story in 1864, the opening essay, "Cambridge Thirty Years Ago," reminiscent of Washington Allston, Margaret Fuller Ossoli, and Harriet Martineau, describes the boy's environment. In 1838 he received the degree of A.B. and in 1840 the degree of LL.B. from Harvard. The genius for friendship and for concentrated work in varied lines which marked his entire life was exerting itself at this time as he began the practice of law, first with the firm of Hillard and Sumner, and later with his brother-in-law, George Ticknor Curtis [*q.v.*]. He was a leading member of the "Brothers and Sisters," and a little later of the group which met at the home of George Ripley [*q.v.*] for the discussion of literary and esthetic problems. Long an amateur of the various arts, he now combined the exacting duties of a law practice and the preparation of volumes in the field of jurisprudence with painting, modelling, and music, to which he devoted himself in his spare time. Moreover, he delivered the Phi Beta Kappa poem at Harvard in 1844, while the *Boston Miscellany* and Lowell's short-lived *Pioneer* carried poems and essays by him. Among his legal publications were two textbooks which long maintained their place as standards, *A Treatise on the Law of Contracts Not under Seal* (1844) and *A Treatise on the Law of Sales of Personal Property* (1847), and several volumes of reports. His *Poems* appeared in 1847, followed by a second volume with the same title, dedicated to Lowell, in 1856. He also served as commissioner in bankruptcy, and commissioner for the United States courts in Massachusetts, Maine, and Pennsylvania, and reporter for the United States circuit court for the district of Massachusetts. Due in part to such incessant labor, he suffered a severe attack of brain and typhoid fever, from which he had hardly recovered when his distinguished father died in 1845 and the turning point of his career occurred.

On the death of Judge Story the trustees of Mount Auburn Cemetery proposed the erection in the chapel of a marble statue of their late colleague, to be paid for by public subscriptions, and nominated young Story as sculptor. To equip himself for this commission he left for Italy in the fall of 1847, with his wife, Emelyn Eldredge of Boston, whom he had married on Oct. 31, 1843, and his two small children. On his return to America his sketch was accepted. During the eight months of his stay he prepared for the press the *Life and Letters of Joseph Story* (2 vols., 1851), followed later by an edition of *The Miscellaneous Writings of Joseph Story* (1852). Back in Italy, he completed the statue of his father. Another year in America followed, devoted to both his vocation and his avocation. But he finally gave in to the claims of sculpture and, settling in Rome (1856), devoted his chief efforts to that art. "My mother," he later recalled, "thought me mad and urged me to pursue my legal career, in which everything was open to me, rather than take such a leap in the dark. But I had chosen, and I came back to Italy, where I

have lived nearly ever since" (James, *post*, vol. I, p. 32). The choice of Washington Allston under analogous stress, leading to stagnation in Cambridge, that of Lowell, leading to the Court of St. James's as ambassador, and that of the younger Henry James, Story's sensitive biographer, leading eventually to British citizenship, provide alluring contrasts and, along with Story's nostalgia for European culture, help to clarify a significant phase of American adolescence. The winter he spent listening to law lectures in Germany during his years of wavering, subsequent seasons in England and visits to France, and, much later, life in the Engadine, varied by occasional visits to America, suggest the breadth of background against which the sculptor moved. But in 1856 the burden of proof was still on Story. Indeed, the corner was not turned until the International Exhibition in London in 1862, when the "Cleopatra" (a replica of which is in the Metropolitan Museum, New York City) and the "Libyan Sibyl" (in the National Gallery of Art, Washington, D. C.) placed Story, at least in English eyes, in the forefront of Anglo-American sculpture. The considerations that Story won this position without the rigor of the usual technical training, that the reputation he achieved in his own day has not been maintained in the following century, and that he might have gone farther in law or in poetry if he had stayed in America are all beside the point. The main significance of his career is that of one whose versatility and charm enabled him to cross cultural boundaries to the advantage of the peoples concerned.

An apartment in the Palazzo Barberini in Rome became the center from which radiated the influence of the Storys. Their most celebrated contact was with the Brownings, with whom they were in almost daily intimacy until the death of Elizabeth Barrett Browning. Nathaniel Hawthorne [*q.v.*] rewarded Story for permitting his shy presence in his studio by describing the "Cleopatra" in *The Marble Faun* with such power that the public ever since has seen the fire of the novelist rather than the cool accuracy of the sculptor. During a childhood illness of Story's daughter, we read of Thackeray's and Hans Christian Andersen's being drafted for the amusement of the little convalescent. Charles Eliot Norton [*q.v.*], Mrs. Gaskell, Walter Savage Landor, Lady William Russell, Richard Monkton Milnes, Russell Sturgis [*q.v.*], and John Lothrop Motley [*q.v.*] add further distinction to the list of the close friends of the Storys. Only in the unforgotten death of their six-year-old son, Joseph Story, do they seem to have suffered a major grief. Without being in any direction a genius, Story learned the secret of happiness by the wise development of his many talents.

As a sculptor Story sought to give internal validity to his figures. He chose subjects of dramatic interest and, in so far as his smooth surfaces and careful accessories permitted, he expressed their inherent passion. Yet his approach to his conceptions was fundamentally an intellectual one, and he perhaps never learned to sacrifice what he knew about the subject to the demands of plastic creation. "Saul" (1863), reminiscent of Michelangelo's "Moses," "Medea" (1864), a center of interest at the Centennial Exposition in Philadelphia, and now in the Metropolitan Museum, "Salome" (1870), "Jerusalem in her Desolation" (1873), now in the Pennsylvania Academy of the Fine Arts, Philadelphia, and "Alcestis" (1874) represent, with the "Sibyl" and "Cleopatra," the most successful of the ideal figures. The fact that now and then he treated the same subject in both sculpture and poetry, and that in the case of "Cleopatra" at least he succeeded better in verse indicates the weakness of his plastic expression. Of his portrait figures, the seated "George Peabody" in London, in bronze, of which a replica was erected in Baltimore, and the dignified statues of John Marshall and Joseph Henry in Washington are the most adequate, while his last work, the stone for the grave of his wife in Rome, provides one of the few instances of that intensity, the lack of which in many other works causes them to miss immortality. Sumner, near the close of the Civil War, urged Story to become the sculptor of free America. When one recalls the Farragut and Sherman and Shaw and Lincoln of Augustus Saint-Gaudens, one realizes how fruitless was the request. Story's interest in sculpture, rather than his sculpture, is of importance.

A collection of essays gathered from the *Atlantic Monthly* and elsewhere, *Roba di Roma,* appeared in 1862 and long remained the outstanding appreciation of the spirit of contemporary Italy. Later came *Vallombrosa* (1881), *Fiammetta; a Summer Idyl* (1886), and *Excursions in Art and Letters* (1891). The *Graffiti d'Italia* (1868), containing "Ginevra da Siena," "Cleopatra," and "Giannone," despite the echoes of the forms of Browning and the felicities of Lowell, represents Story's most sustained poetry. Mention should also be made of his widely influential letters to the London *Daily News* (Dec. 25, 26, 27, 1861), reprinted as *The American Question* (1862), in which he debated and upheld the validity of the Federal position on union and emancipation. Several of his plays, usually prepared for private theatricals, reached the public in printed form, and a treatise on *The Proportions of the Human Figure* was published in 1866. Honors included doctorates from Oxford and from Bologna, and decorations from the governments of Italy and France. When he visited America in 1877 he was widely entertained in Boston and New York as America's outstanding representative of the arts. Mrs. Story's death in 1894 marked the end of his active career. He lived only until the following year, dying at the home of his daughter, Madame Edith Story Peruzzi, wife of the Marquis Simone Peruzzi di Medici, at Vallombrosa, Italy. He was buried beside his wife and son in the Protestant Cemetery at Rome, "il simpatico Americano." The two surviving sons continued their father's devotion to the arts, Thomas Waldo in sculpture and Julian Russell [*q.v.*] in painting.

[Henry James, *William Wetmore Story and His Friends* (2 vols., 1903); Mary E. Phillips, *Reminiscences of William Wetmore Story* (1897); Lorado Taft, *The Hist. of Am. Sculpture* (1903); W. J. Clark, *Great Am. Sculptures* (1903); *Passages from the French and Italian Note-Books of Nathaniel Hawthorne* (2 vols., 1872); *The Letters of Elizabeth Barrett Browning* (2 vols., 1897); C. R. Post, *A Hist. of European and Am. Sculpture* (1921), vol. II; obituary in *Evening Post* (N. Y.), Oct. 8, 1895.]   W. S. R.

STOTT, HENRY GORDON (May 13, 1866–Jan. 15, 1917), electrical engineer, was born in the Orkney Islands, the son of the Rev. David Stott and Elizabeth Jane Dibblee. Prepared in part by his father, he attended Watson Collegiate School, Edinburgh, proceeding thence to the College of Arts and Sciences at Glasgow, where he completed the course in mechanical engineering and electricity in 1885. During the previous year he had been employed by the Electric Illuminating Company of Glasgow, and upon graduation he became assistant electrician on board the steamship *Minia* of the Anglo-American Telegraph Company, principally engaged in repairs to cable lines. During his four and a half years with this organization he conducted experiments resulting in improved methods of cable repair and "was identified with the 'duplexing' of the United States Cable Company's main cable (2,750 knots), the longest duplex cable in the world" (*Transactions, post,* LXXXI, 1776).

After about a year as assistant engineer of the Brush Electric Engineering Company, Bournemouth, England, and another in a similar capacity with Hammond & Company, engaged in the construction of a power plant and an underground cable line at Madrid, Spain, he came to the United States in 1891 to construct the underground cable and conduit system for the Buffalo Light & Power Company. His performance of this task led to his appointment as engineer of the company, in which connection, during the ensuing decade, he had an active part in the industrial development of Buffalo. Among the notable projects for which he was responsible was the Wilkerson Street power plant, which he designed and executed. In 1901 he removed to New York City to become superintendent of motive power for the Manhattan Railway Company, assuming charge of the organization of the operating force, the construction of the power plant in Seventy-fourth Street, substations, and transmission lines. Retained in the same position after the amalgamation of the Manhattan system with the Interboro Rapid Transit Company, he supervised the construction of the Fifty-ninth Street power plant and the design, construction, and operation of the power-generating stations of the distributing system of the gigantic Interboro company, which controlled subway, elevated, and surface lines of New York City.

Stott was an active participant in the affairs of numerous professional societies; he was president of the American Institute of Electrical Engineers (1907–08), vice-president of the American Society of Mechanical Engineers (1912–14), a director of the American Society of Civil Engineers (1911), and vice-president and trustee of the United Engineering Society (1911). To the *Transactions* of a number of these bodies he contributed papers revealing an unusual capacity for minute analysis of engineering problems. Among them were "Locating Faults in Underground Distribution Systems" and "The Distribution and Conversion of Received Currents" (*Transactions of the American Institute of Electrical Engineers,* vol. XVIII, 1902); "Power Plant Economics" (*Ibid.,* vol. XXV, 1907); "Notes on the Cost of Power" (*Ibid.,* vol. XXVIII, pt. 2, 1910); "Test of a 15,000 Kilowatt Steam-Engine Turbine Unit," with R. J. S. Pigott (*Ibid.,* vol. XIX, pt. 1, 1911). He was in the front rank of both electrical and mechanical engineers and with his technical qualifications combined an extraordinary executive ability—a power of inspiring the confidence of his employees and of bringing out their best efforts. He early became a United States citizen. On July 22, 1894, he married Anna Mitchell, who with a son and a daughter survived him. He was an active member of the Protestant Episcopal Church of New Rochelle.

[*Who's Who in America,* 1916–17; *Proc. Am. Inst. Elec. Engineers,* Feb. 1917; *Jour. Am. Soc. Mech. Engineers,* Feb. 1917, with portr.; *Trans. Am. Soc. Civil Engineers,* vol. LXXXI (1917); *Power,* Jan. 23, 1917, pp. 121, 132; *Cassier's Mag.,* Apr. 1906; *N. Y. Times,* Jan. 17, 1917.]   B. A. R.

STOUGHTON, EDWIN WALLACE (May 1, 1818–Jan. 7, 1882), lawyer, was born in Springfield, Windsor County, Vt., the son of Thomas P. Stoughton by his first wife, Susan (Bradley) of Windsor, Vt. He was descended from Thomas Stoughton who came with his brother Israel to Dorchester, Mass., about 1630 and some ten years later settled in Windsor, Conn. What formal academic training Edwin had he received at local schools and at a neighboring academy. At eighteen he forsook his father's homestead and went to New York City to seek his fortune at the bar so that he might capitalize his eloquence and his analytical thinking. In May 1837 he commenced the study of the law in the office of Philo T. Ruggles, but soon became a clerk in the offices of Seeley & Glover, with the privilege of using the firm's library for reading and study. He eked out his meager salary by contributing to magazines, writing for *Hunt's Merchants' Magazine* in 1839 and later for the *New World.* His literary efforts displayed an understanding of current events, history, and economics, together with a fairly lucid literary style. In 1840 he was admitted to the bar.

Stoughton constituted his own law firm. His practice was confined largely to court-room work, and his legal renown was won chiefly in a series of patent suits. Notable among these were the Charles Goodyear patent cases (76 *U. S.,* 788), the Woodworth planing-machine cases, the Ross Winans eight-wheel car patent cases, the Wheeler & Wilson sewing machine cases, and the Corliss steam-engine patent case. He appeared for the United States and New Jersey in *U. S.* vs. *Callicott* (14,710 *Federal Cases*), when the defendant was convicted of malfeasance in the Internal Revenue office; and was retained by William M. Tweed as an adviser, but took no active part in Tweed's defense.

In early life Stoughton was a War Democrat, but when his party publicized complaints respecting the use of the federal troops made by President Grant in Louisiana he defended the President, and thenceforth his sympathies were with the Republican party. He became a personal friend of President Grant and accepted his request to become a member of a commission of leading Republicans and Democrats which was to report on the controversial Hayes-Tilden election of 1876 in the state of Louisiana. He went to New Orleans and personally observed the canvassing of votes by the Returning Board. Subsequently he was one of those who represented the Republican cause before the Electoral Commission, arguing, in two addresses, that Congress could not go behind the decision of a state and that the election certificate must be accepted if the proper state authorities signed it. The commission accepted this legal reasoning and honored all the disputed Republican electoral votes. He contributed an article entitled "The 'Electoral Commission' Bubble Exploded" to the *North American Review,* September-October 1877.

As a reward for his services, President Hayes appointed Stoughton envoy extraordinary and minister plenipotentiary to Russia, Oct. 30, 1877. Because of ill health, he left St. Petersburg on leave of absence early in 1879, but failed to recover his strength in southern Europe and returned to New York, resigning his post in July of that year. Less than three years later he died, in New York, of Bright's disease and dropsy. He was married, Mar. 3, 1855, to Mary Fiske, a widow, but left no children

[H. R. Stiles, *The Hist. and Geneals. of Ancient Windsor, Conn.,* II (1892), 736; *N. Y. Tribune, N. Y. Times, N. Y. Herald,* Jan. 8, 1882; *Papers Relating to the Foreign Relations of the U. S.,* 1878, 1879; *Medico-Legal Journal* (N. Y.), Dec. 1883; *Encyc. of Contemporary Biog. of N. Y.,* vol. I (1878); G. W. Fuller, *Descendants of Thomas Stoughton* (1929); *In Memory of Edwin Wallace Stoughton: Report of a Meeting of the Bar of the Courts of the State of N. Y., and of the U. S. for the Second Circuit . . . Jan. 13, 1882;* Letter *of Judge Black to Mr. Stoughton, Reply to Stoughton's Defence (?) of the Great Fraud* (1877).]

J.H.L.

STOUGHTON, WILLIAM (Sept. 30, 1631–July 7, 1701), colonial magistrate, was the second son of Israel Stoughton, who came to New England about 1630, was one of the founders of Dorchester, and became one of the largest landowners in the Massachusetts Bay Colony. Israel was a brother of John Stoughton, rector of Aller, Somerset, and step-father of Ralph Cudworth, the Cambridge neo-platonist. It is probable that William was born in England. After graduating from Harvard College in 1650, he went to England to continue his studies at Oxford, where he became a fellow of New College and received the degree of M.A. on June 30, 1653. He was curate at Rumboldswyke, Sussex, in 1659. Ejected from his fellowship at the Restoration (1660), he returned to Massachusetts in the summer of 1662. He preached for several years in the Dorchester church and was paid for his services, but repeatedly declined to become pastor there or at Cambridge. In 1668 he preached an election sermon in which he asserted that "God sifted a whole Nation that he might send Choice Grain over into this Wilderness" (*New Englands True Interest; . . . A Sermon,* 1670, p. 19).

Stoughton served as an assistant of Massachusetts Bay, 1671–86; as a commissioner of the United Colonies, 1674–76, 1680–86; and as judge of various courts. With Peter Bulkeley he represented Massachusetts before the King in the controversy over the Mason claims, 1676–79, and by adopting the conciliatory attitude he deemed necessary in these negotiations greatly displeased the radical element in Massachusetts. In 1681 Stoughton and Joseph Dudley [*q.v.*] were appointed, at their own suggestion, to examine land titles in the Nipmuck country—a profitable service, since each agent received a liberal portion of the land ceded by the Indians as the result of the investigation. As a stanch political friend of Dudley, Stoughton declined office in 1684 and 1686, when the former failed of reëlection to the office of assistant.

When Dudley became president of the temporary government established in 1686 after the revocation of the charter, he appointed his adherent deputy president. Apparently a loyal servant of the King—except when the interests of the Crown conflicted with his own interests as a landholder or the interests of Harvard College, of which he was one of the most generous native benefactors (Sibley, *post,* p. 319)—Stoughton was on the council of Gov. Edmund Andros [*q.v.*]; but when rebellion came he signed an address of the magistrates advising the Governor to deliver the fort to the revolutionists, and in 1690 he signed a paper drawn up by members of the former council denouncing Andros' acts while governor. Named lieutenant-governor May 1692 under Sir William Phips [*q.v.*], he became acting governor on the latter's departure for England in 1694, and was the active head of the government thereafter until his death, except from May 1699 to July 1700, when Governor Bellomont was in Boston.

Stoughton was chief justice of the court of oyer and terminer which tried the Salem witchcraft cases in 1692, and by his insistence on the admission of "spectral evidence," as well as by his overbearing attitude toward the accused, the witnesses, and the jury, was largely responsible for the tragic aspect they assumed (Phips to the Earl of Nottingham, *Calendar of State Papers, Colonial Series, America and West Indies, January 1693–14 May 1696,* 1903, p. 30; Robert Calef, *More Wonders of the Invisible World,* 1700). He seems never to have repented (Calef, *op. cit.;* Hutchinson, *post,* II, 61), and his refusal to yield to feelings of compassion after most others had become enlightened indicates his essentially cold, proud, and obstinate nature. It is notable, however, that his part in the witch-craft delusion did not damage him in the eyes of his contemporaries, and that he died respected as one of the most eminent citizens of the colony.

[Sources include: *Records of the First Church at Dorchester . . . 1636–1734* (1891); *A Report of the Record Commissioners of . . . Boston*, no. 21 (1890); Joseph Foster, *Alumni Oxonienses*, vol. IV (1892); Edward Calamy, *An Abridgment of Mr. Baxter's Hist. of His Life and Times* (2nd ed., 1713), vol. II; A. G. Matthews, *Calamy Revised* (1934); "The Diaries of John Hull," *Trans. and Colls. Am. Antiq. Soc.*, vol. III (1857); N. B. Shurtleff, *Records of the Gov. and Company of the Mass. Bay*, vols. IV–V (1854); Thomas Hutchinson, *The Hist. of the Colony of Massachuset's Bay*, vol. I (1765), the most favorable treatment; R. N. Toppan, *Edward Randolph; Including His Letters and Official Papers*, vols. III–VI (1899–1909); W. H. Whitmore, *The Andros Tracts*, vol. I (1868); *Calendar of State Papers, Colonial Series, America and West Indies, 1701* (1910), p. 164; *Proc. Mass. Hist. Soc.*, 2 ser. I (1885); J. L. Sibley, *Biog. Sketches Grads. Harvard Univ.*, vol. I (1873); J. W. Dean, "William Stoughton," *New Eng. Hist. and Geneal. Reg.*, Jan. 1896; J. G. Palfrey, *Hist. of New England*, vol. III (1864), a severe judgment; C. W. Upham, *Salem Witchcraft* (1867), vol. II, and Emory Washburn, *Sketches of the Judicial Hist. of Mass.* (1840), the last two being more severe than Palfrey in their judgments of Stoughton. A writer in *Putnam's Mag.*, Sept. 1853, attributing to the Chief Justice an act of repentance resembling that of Samuel Sewall [*q.v.*], has apparently confused the two men.]   S. G. M.

STOW, BARON (June 16, 1801–Dec. 27, 1869), Baptist minister, was named in honor of Baron Steuben, but the middle name was early dropped from use. The first of five children of Peter Stow, a native of Grafton, Mass., and Deborah (Nettleton) Stow of Killingworth, Conn., he was born at Croydon, N. H. About 1809 the family moved to a farm in the adjacent town, Newport, where the boy attended district school, read avidly, and was marked as a student of promise. When he was sixteen, the death of his father threatened to hold him to the farm, but his interest lay elsewhere. He united with the Baptist church at Newport, being baptized Dec. 31, 1818, and immediately turned toward the ministry. After preparation in the academy at Newport, in September 1822 he was admitted to Columbian College, Washington, D. C. Here he made contacts with teachers and fellow students which became important for his later career. Although his health was not robust, he completed his course in a little over three years, being appointed valedictorian at his graduation, December 1825.

He had already devoted considerable time to editorial work on the *Columbian Star*, the weekly journal of the Triennial Convention, and from Jan. 28, 1826, until the summer of 1827 he was the editor of that periodical. An unfortunate episode of this editorial experience was his publication of insinuations against Luther Rice [*q.v.*].

Rice's counter-blast in a local Washington newspaper, the *Daily National Journal*, Nov. 9, 1826, led to immediate action by the First Baptist Church (manuscript records, Nov. 10, 1826), but the matter was cleared up commendably by a statement of regret in an agreement which both men signed.

On Sept. 7, 1826, Stow had married Elizabeth L. Skinner of Windsor, Vt. In the summer of 1827 he went to Portsmouth, N. H., where he was ordained on Oct. 24. Here he developed the methods of religious work which characterized his entire ministry. His preaching was distinctly evangelistic, with very direct appeal to the individual. He was constant in pastoral visitation even when increasingly tasks for the larger religious community were placed upon him. With John Newton Brown [*q.v.*] he had an indeterminable part in the production of the New Hampshire confession of faith. The most distinguished period of his career was his pastorate of the Second or Baldwin Place Church in Boston, where he succeeded his college roommate, Dr. James D. Knowles. Installed there in November 1832, he entered upon a pastoral and preaching ministry of marked power. Changes in the northern part of the city, where the church was located, and dissatisfaction with results, felt more by Stow himself than by his parishioners, led to his resignation in May 1848. In October of that year, he began an almost equally significant pastorate at the Rowe Street Baptist Church which continued until early in 1867.

Of an especially sensitive temperament, he was frequently physically incapacitated; trips to Europe in 1840–41 and in 1859 brought physical recuperation and enrichment of his mental powers. He refused many calls to other pastorates, to secretarial positions, and to the presidencies of at least three colleges. He was actively associated with the foreign missions enterprise and was one of the leaders in its reorganization by the Northern Baptists in 1845. Although of irenic disposition—well illustrated in his *Christian Brotherhood* (1859), a forceful plea for Christian union—he possessed strong feelings which occasionally dominated him and led to some trying experiences. He wrote prolifically for the religious press, including two brief works on missionary history prepared especially for the Sunday School library and a devotional book, *Daily Manna for Christians* (1843), which was much read. With Samuel F. Smith [*q.v.*] he edited *The Psalmist* (1843), which was for several decades the hymnal most widely used by American Baptists.

[J. C. Stockbridge, *A Model Pastor: A Memoir of of the Life and Correspondence of Rev. Baron Stow, D.D.* (1871) ; memorial discourses in R. H. Neale, *The Pastor and Preacher* (1870) ; *The Bapt. Encyc.* (1883) ; records of the First Baptist Church, Washington, D. C.; *Boston Transcript*, Dec. 28, 1869.]   W.H.A.

STOWE, CALVIN ELLIS (Apr. 26, 1802–Aug. 22, 1886), educator, was born in Natick, Mass., the son of Samuel and Hepzibah (Biglow) Stow. He added the final "e" to the family name after his graduation from college. He was a descendant of John Stowe who settled in Roxbury, Mass., and took the freeman's oath in 1634. When he was six years old, his father, the jovial village baker, died, leaving his widow in poverty. At twelve, the boy was apprenticed to a paper maker. He prepared for college at Gorham Academy, Gorham, Me., and entered the class of 1824 at Bowdoin College. Franklin Pierce [*q.v.*] was a classmate and William Pitt Fessenden [*q.v.*] was in the class above them. Graduating with valedictory honors, Stowe remained for a year as librarian and instructor. In 1825 he entered Andover Theological Seminary. During his senior year he made a translation from the German of Johann Jahn which was subsequently published as *Jahn's History of the Hebrew Commonwealth* (Andover 1828, London 1829) ; the following year he was editor of the *Boston Recorder*. In 1829 he revised and edited with notes *Lectures on the Sacred Poetry of the Hebrews,* a translation by G. Gregory from the Latin of Robert Lowth.

In 1831 he became professor of Greek in Dartmouth College. The following year he married Eliza, daughter of Rev. Bennet Tyler [*q.v.*] of Portland, Me., and in 1833 was called to the chair of Biblical literature in Lane Theological Seminary, Cincinnati, Ohio. His wife died in 1834, and on Jan. 6, 1836, he married Harriet Elizabeth (see Harriet Elizabeth Beecher Stowe), daughter of Lyman Beecher [*q.v.*], president of the Seminary. While in Cincinnati Stowe was actively interested in the improvement of the common schools, regarding such improvement as the great need of the West. The College of Teachers in Cincinnati was founded in 1833 largely through his influence. He published in 1835 *Introduction to the Criticism and Interpretation of the Bible.* In 1836 the state of Ohio appointed him commissioner to investigate the public school systems of Europe, especially of Prussia. For this congenial task he was given every facility in England and on the Continent. Returning in 1837, he published his famous *Report on Elementary Instruction in Europe,* a copy of which the legislature put into every school district of the state. It was reprinted by the legislatures of Massachusetts, Pennsylvania, Michigan, and other states, in *Common Schools and Teachers' Seminaries* (1839), and in E. W. Knight, *Reports on European Education by John Griscom, Victor Cousin, Calvin E. Stowe* (1930).

In 1850 Stowe accepted a call to the chair of natural and revealed religion at Bowdoin. Two years later he went to Andover Theological Seminary as professor of sacred literature. In 1853, 1856, and 1859, he visited Europe with his wife, whose *Uncle Tom's Cabin,* published in 1852, occasioned the enthusiastic reception which was accorded them, especially in England. Failing health caused him to resign the Andover professorship in 1864, and Hartford, Conn., became the family home. In 1866 the Stowes began spending their winters at Mandarin, Fla., on the St. John's River, where they took oversight of the religious welfare of the neighborhood. In 1867 he published *Origin and History of the Books of the Bible.* He was at home in many languages, ancient and modern. A man of large frame and wearing a patriarchal beard, he was a child in financial and practical matters. He was a born story-teller and his tales of the characters he knew in his boyhood furnished much of the local coloring for his wife's *Old Town Folks.* Early in their married life, he urged his wife to enter upon a literary career, and his enthusiasm was her constant encouragement. He always carried with him pocket editions of the Greek New Testament and Dante's *Divina Commedia;* they were under his pillow throughout his last illness.

[*New England Hist. and Geneal. Reg.,* Apr. 1856; *Vital Records of Natick* (1910) ; *Gen. Cat. of Bowdoin Coll.* (1912) ; Nehemiah Cleaveland, *Hist. of Bowdoin Coll.* (1882), ed. by A. S. Packard; *Congregationalist,* Aug. 26, Sept. 2, 1886; C. E. Stowe, *Life of Harriet Beecher Stowe* (1889) ; C. M. Rourke, *Trumpets of Jubilee* (1927) ; *Boston Transcript*, Aug. 23, 1886.]   E.D.E.

STOWE, HARRIET ELIZABETH BEECHER (June 14, 1811–July 1, 1896), author and humanitarian, was born in the town of Litchfield, Conn. Her father, Lyman Beecher [*q.v.*], was the pastor of the Congregational Church and a stern Calvinist. A vigorous, enthusiastic man, he was accustomed to work off his surplus energies by shoveling sand from one pile to another in the cellar of his house. He was fond of music and played the violin. An upright piano, which he had brought from New Haven, was borne into the house with as much reverence, said his daughter, as if it had been "the ark of the covenant."

Roxana Foote, the minister's first wife and the mother of eight children, died when her daughter Harriet was only four. She had been a mill girl of the type made famous by Lucy Larcom and her friends. She had read Samuel Richardson's *History of Sir Charles Grandison* in her girlhood days and a copy of it lay on the parlor table of the Beecher home. Shy and diffident, she could never lead the services in the weekly women's prayer meetings. "She never spoke in company or before strangers without blushing," said Harriet (Fields, *Life and Letters, post,* p. 13). Her wish was that all of her sons should become ministers—a wish that was fulfilled with one exception by Harriet's six brothers.

The future author of *Uncle Tom's Cabin,* although brought up in New England, numbered among her childhood friends members of the negro race. Candace, her mother's washerwoman, and Dinah, the servant at Aunt Harriet Foote's were destined to appear again and again among the author's favorite characters. The motherly colored woman, Candace, who was so devoted to the memory of her dead mistress, left a strong impression on the mind of little Harriet. The children turned to her for comfort in their sorrow and bereavement. They stood somewhat in awe of their new stepmother, Harriet Porter, who soon came from Portland, Me., and seemed to them extremely fine and elegant.

Harriet's education, like that of most Puritan children, was two-thirds religious. At the age of eleven she wrote a composition on the subject: "Can the Immortality of the Soul be Proved by the Light of Nature?," and chose to defend the negative. When her paper was read aloud at the school exhibition, her father praised it without knowing it was hers. "It was the proudest moment of my life," she said in after years. A contrast to her father's orthodox theology was furnished by her uncle, Samuel Foote, a seafaring man and a frequent visitor at the Beecher home. Uncle Sam, as he was called, had been to the ends of the earth and was a romantic figure in the eyes of his niece. He sometimes insisted that Turks were as good as Christians, and Catholics as good as Protestants, and he could argue so skilfully that the minister was hard put to it to defend his own view. The poetry of Byron, which Harriet read before her teens, likewise made a strong impression on her. Her father talked a great deal about the English poet, whom he admired while he also condemned him. On Byron's death, he preached a sermon which Harriet long remembered.

Like her elder sister Catherine, Harriet was unable to accept her father's Deity unquestioningly. A great deal of doubt and conflict accompanied her conversion at the age of fourteen. Years of morbid introspection darkened her girl-

hood and left their traces on her maturity. All her writings testify to a life-long preoccupation with the problem of religion. Even in her fiction the conflict between faith and doubt forms an ever-present theme. Somewhat late in life she attended the Episcopal Church with her daughters who were Episcopalians. The loss of a beloved son caused her to become interested in spiritualism, and she corresponded on the subject with Elizabeth Barrett Browning.

Up to the age of thirteen, when she was sent to Hartford to attend a school for girls, her most intimate companion had been her brother Henry Ward [*q.v.*]. "Harriet and Henry come next," wrote the second Mrs. Beecher, describing her step-children, "and they are always hand in hand." Hand in hand, they went to the dame school where they learned to read. The sympathy thus founded lasted all their lives. Hand in hand they waged their great battle against slavery. When Beecher was in England speaking for the cause, he awoke one morning so hoarse that he could scarcely use his voice. "I will speak to my sister three thousand miles away," he said, and called out, "Harriet." With this his voice returned and he made that day one of his most famous speeches (Annie A. Fields, *Memories of a Hostess,* 1922, p. 268). His sister adored him. "He is myself," she wrote to George Eliot during the Beecher trial. "I know you are the kind of woman to understand me when I say that I felt a blow at him more than at myself" (C. E. and L. B. Stowe, *post,* p. 291).

In October 1832 the family moved to Cincinnati, where Dr. Beecher had been called to be the head of the Lane Theological Seminary and where his daughter Catherine [*q.v.*] established the Western Female Institute. Her uncle Samuel Foote also joined the colony. Harriet liked her new environment and wrote cheerful letters home. Employed as a teacher in her sister's school, she still found time to try her hand at divers kinds of writing. For the first time she began to unfold the more playful and imaginative side of her nature. She wrote sketches for the *Western Monthly Magazine* and received a prize of fifty dollars for a story—"Prize Tale, a New England Sketch"—which appeared in the issue of April 1834, and was separately printed under that title. It was subsequently reprinted in *The Mayflower* (1843) as "Uncle Tim" and again reprinted in *The Mayflower* (1855) with the name of the leading character and the title changed to "Uncle Lot." Her marriage, Jan. 6, 1836, to Calvin Ellis Stowe [*q.v.*], professor of Biblical literature in her father's seminary, put an end for the time being to her career of authorship. Except for a few tales and sketches, published in *The Mayflower,* she produced almost nothing until 1852. These, however, convinced her husband that she must be "a literary woman" and he urged her strongly to write, and also to drop the E from her signature.

Altogether, she spent eighteen years in Cincinnati. It was a period of much poverty and hardship but rich in observation and experience which she afterwards turned to good account in her tales and novels. There six of her seven children were born and one of them was buried. She lived through the cholera epidemic of 1849, to which her baby was a sacrifice. She visited a Kentucky plantation and saw the life of the slaves in their cabins. To the impressions thus gained were added, however, those of her brother who had seen New Orleans and ascended the Red River. Her father's seminary was a hotbed of anti-slavery sentiment; one of the most extreme advocates of Abolitionism, Theodore D. Weld [*q.v.*], was an early student there. Mrs. Stowe and her brother Henry, then editor of a newspaper, became deeply interested in the cause. Her letters confirm her son's statement that she "was anti-slavery in her sympathies, but she was not a declared abolitionist" (C. E. Stowe, *post,* p. 87). When the press of J. G. Birney [*q.v.*] was destroyed by a mob she was more concerned about the violation of private rights and mob violence than defense of abolitionism. It was not until her return to New England in 1850 during the discussion over the Fugitive Slave Law, that her anti-slavery feeling became intense.

In 1850 Stowe was called to a professorship in Bowdoin College, Brunswick, Me. On her way thither Mrs. Stowe stopped in Brooklyn for a visit with her brother who had become the popular pastor of Plymouth Church. "Henry's people," she wrote her husband, "are more than ever in love with him, and have raised his salary to $3,300 and given him a beautiful horse and carriage worth $600." To the Stowes, who were extremely poor at this time, more so in fact than they were ever to be again, this seemed like unexampled prosperity. By all accounts the family arrived in Brunswick at the nadir of their fortunes. A visit to her brother, Edward Beecher [*q.v.*], fanned her sentiments on slavery to white heat. Edward thundered from his Boston pulpit against the Fugitive Slave Law and his wife wrote to Mrs. Stowe, who had just borne her seventh child, "Now, Hattie, if I could just use the pen as you can, I would write something that would make this whole nation feel what an accursed thing slavery is." To this Mrs. Stowe replied, "As long as the baby sleeps with me nights, I can't do much at anything; but I will do it at last. I will write that thing if I live" (Fields, *Life and Letters, post,* p. 130). When she told her brother Henry that she had begun her story, he answered heartily, "That's right, Hattie! Finish it, and I will scatter it thicker than the leaves of Vallombrosa" (C. E. and L. B. Stowe, *post,* p. 288).

The outcome of her endeavor was *Uncle Tom's Cabin, or Life Among the Lowly,* first published as a serial (June 5, 1851–Apr. 1, 1852) in the *National Era,* an anti-slavery paper of Washington, D. C. She gives two accounts of the origin of this book (see Fields, *Life and Letters, post,* pp. 130 ff., 147, 164–65). In one instance, she states that she wrote the pages which describe the death of Uncle Tom in Brunswick and read them to her little boys. In the other, she says that she wrote the passage in Andover and read it to her husband. Both accounts agree in stating that the first part of the book ever committed to writing was the death of Uncle Tom. She wrote this at one sitting and when her supply of writing paper gave out, finished it on some scraps of brown paper taken from a grocer's parcel. She then composed the earlier chapters and sent them to the *National Era,* which paid her $300 for the serial. The Boston publisher who had contracted for the book rights protested that she was making the story too long, but she replied that she did not write the book; it wrote itself. It was finally brought out by John P. Jewett [*q.v.*] on Mar. 20, 1852, in two volumes, with a woodcut of a negro cabin as the frontispiece.

Although no one had expected the work to be popular or successful, ten thousand copies were sold in less than a week. Within a year the sales amounted to three-hundred thousand. It was generally supposed that Mrs. Stowe had made a fortune out of it, but her returns were far below what they should have been. She received a royalty of ten per cent. on the American sales but not a penny for the dramatic rights, although *Uncle Tom's Cabin* was one of the most popular plays ever produced on the American stage. The English circulation, which reached a million and a half, was a triumph of pirated editions. The young man who worked at Putnam's and sent the book to England received five pounds for his trouble (*The Times Literary Supplement,* London, July 8, 1926, p. 468).

The hero of *Uncle Tom's Cabin* is a colored man, a slave, who passed from the ownership of a Kentucky planter to that of a New Orleans gentleman and thence to that of a cotton planter on the Red River. In Colonel Shelby, St. Clare, and Simon Legree, the author depicted three types of Southern slave-owners. Uncle Tom's first master was drawn from a benevolent planter of the same name, whom Mrs. Stowe had known in Kentucky. St. Clare was an idealized portrait and still lives in fiction as the type of a gracious, high-bred gentleman. Simon Legree, who caused the death of Uncle Tom, was likewise destined to survive as a historic villain. The patience and piety of the humble hero and the spiritual beauty of the child Eva were drawn from cherished ideals peculiar to the author. In the death of little Eva and the martyrdom of Uncle Tom, the author reached the high notes of her pathos; but the struggle of George and Eliza for freedom and their final achievement of it through flight to Canada was probably the most popular feature of the book. In the description of George Harris as a freeman, the style rises to eloquence.

Mrs. Stowe had not foreseen the storm of wrath which *Uncle Tom* was to evoke. In the South her name was hated. A cousin living in Georgia told her that she did not dare to receive letters from her with her name on the outside of the envelope, and the *Southern Literary Messenger* declared the book a "criminal prostitution of the high functions of the imagination," saying that the author had "placed herself without the pale of kindly treatment at the hands of Southern criticism" (December 1852, pp. 721–31; October 1852, pp. 630–38). While Mrs. Stowe had feared the abolitionists would find the work too mild, they proved at last to be its only partisans. From all sides she was attacked and the accuracy of her facts questioned. Her reply to this criticism was *A Key to Uncle Tom's Cabin* (1853). Much of the material was collected after *Uncle Tom's Cabin* was written, though the defense was announced as containing the facts on which the story was based (Rourke, *post*, p. 100). From the popular point of view, this book was a complete failure. As a defense, it was hardly more successful. It failed to disprove the charge that there were errors of fact in her earlier work, and its indictment of slavery was far less powerful. Its polemics added nothing to the pathos of her novel.

From the first there was some discussion of the literary value of *Uncle Tom's Cabin*. Her critics thought she owed a great deal to her subject. As a romance and a picture of American manners, however, it undoubtedly deserves high rank. Mrs. Stowe apparently had a fondness for the South. While she hated it for being on the side of slavery, she portrayed its atmosphere with fire and sympathy. She was the first American writer to take the negro seriously and to con-

ceive a novel with a black man as the hero. Although it was written with a moral purpose, the author forgot the purpose sometimes in the joy of telling her tale. The influence of Sir Walter Scott, whom she had read in girlhood, and of Charles Dickens, her great contemporary, is clearly visible.

Mrs. Stowe had her first inkling of the fame she had acquired when she went to buy a seat for Jenny Lind's concert and found there were no more. Otto Goldschmidt, the singer's husband, hearing that the author of *Uncle Tom's Cabin* had been turned away, immediately sent tickets with the compliments of his wife. The English abolitionists paid her every honor. When she went to visit England soon after the appearance of the book, people thronged the docks to have a glimpse of her. Lord Shaftesbury composed an address of welcome on behalf of the women of England, a great demonstration was held at Stafford House in her honor, and the Duchess of Sutherland presented her with a gold bracelet in the form of a slave's shackle. One hundred thousand copies of her second antislavery novel, *Dred, A Tale of the Great Dismal Swamp* (1856), were sold in England in less than a month. She met Lord Palmerston, Charles Dickens, and other celebrities of the English world. A considerable sum was collected for her anti-slavery work in America. On the proceeds of her literary ventures, she made two subsequent visits to England and toured the Continent with her family. Among her friends were Lady Byron, George Eliot, and the Ruskins. Her friendship with Lady Byron led to Mrs. Stowe's spectacular contribution to the Byron controversy several years later, when she published in the *Atlantic Monthly* (September 1869) "The True Story of Lady Byron's Life." In this article she charged Lord Byron, on the alleged authority of Lady Byron, with having had a guilty love for his sister, Mrs. Leigh. For the second time, Mrs. Stowe became the focus of a public storm, and for the second time she appeared in print with a detailed argument in her own defense, renewing and elaborating in *Lady Byron Vindicated* (1870) the charge of incest against Byron and adding that a child had been born of the union. The feeling aroused against her in England was intense. Charles Dickens wrote to James T. Fields: "Wish Mrs. Stowe was in the pillory" (Annie A. Fields, *Memories of a Hostess,* p. 191). She had precipitated a bitter controversy which was to last for years. Even those who believed the story could not understand her action. She was accused of scandalmongering and a desire for notoriety (see *American Mer-*

cury, April 1927). Mrs. Stowe could not be judged by ordinary standards, however. Her interest in the case was sincere and conscientious. The life of Byron had always had a strong fascination for her. Like her father, she admired his genius while she mourned his faults. Since Lyman Beecher had once preached a sermon on Byron's life and character, his daughter saw no harm in writing a book on the same subject. It was to her a public question, like that of slavery, and she handled it in the same indomitable spirit.

As a writer, Mrs. Stowe was exceedingly industrious. Already past forty when she published her first book, she continued to pour forth a steady stream of fiction. Throughout the high excitement that followed *Uncle Tom,* the distraction of her trips to Europe, the removals of her family from one home to the other, she kept up her literary industry. The *Atlantic Monthly,* the New York *Independent,* and the *Christian Union,* of which her brother Henry was the editor, contained regular contributions from her pen. For nearly thirty years, she wrote on the average almost a book a year. Following *Uncle Tom's Cabin* and *Dred,* she turned to her New England background. In *The Minister's Wooing* (1859), *The Pearl of Orr's Island* (1862), and *Oldtown Folks* (1869), she pictured types and scenes familiar in her girlhood. For the last named, perhaps "the richest and raciest" of her novels, she drew largely on her husband's reminiscences, as she did also in writing *Sam Lawson's Oldtown Fireside Stories* (1872). In *Poganuc People* (1878) she described her early childhood. The originals of most of her characters were close at hand and can often be identified. Sometimes she did not even disguise the names. A comparatively recent critic declares that "the autobiographical material that fills her later work . . . is much more than autobiography; it is intimate history of New England. . . . As the historian of the human side of Calvinism she tempered dogma with affection." He adds, "She could bring her soul under discipline but not her art. . . . The creative instinct was strong in her but the critical was wholly lacking" (Parrington, *post,* II, 372, 375, 376). In addition to her numerous novels, she published with her sister Catherine *Principles of Domestic Science* (1870) and *The New Housekeeper's Manual* (1873); she also issued a volume entitled *Religious Poems* (1867), containing "Still, still with Thee, when purple morning breaketh," which became a popular hymn. An edition of her works in sixteen volumes, *The Writings of Harriet Beecher Stowe,* appeared in 1896.

After the Civil War she bought a home in Florida, where she spent most of the years that remained to her. Her old age was not prosperous, for she was not a good business woman, and her husband was, if possible, more impractical than she. Her son and grandson tell us that she invested ten thousand dollars in a scheme for raising cotton on a Florida plantation and that all of this was lost. She had previously spent large sums on a house in Hartford which, when built, proved unsuitable for use. While writing *Oldtown Folks,* she was obliged to live on advances from her publishers, because her investments, amounting to thirty-four thousand dollars, were entirely unremunerative. The *Christian Union,* her brother's paper, cost her considerable sums. Even at the height of her prosperity, she was never free from money worries. The modest place at Mandarin where she spent her declining years was at last sold for a song.

The life-time of Mrs. Stowe almost spanned the nineteenth century. Born and bred to womanhood in Puritan New England, she spent her first maturity at a Western outpost. When her family went to Cincinnati in 1832 they traveled by stage-coach and steamboat, and hogs still ran about the dusty city streets. She lived to speed by railway through the Middle West and give readings from her stories on Lyceum platforms. On her wedding journey she had traveled through Ohio in a stage-coach. On her lecture trips she went over the same ground by express train. The World's Fair at Chicago found her, as she would have said, "still this side of spirit-land"; but that great blast of progress could no longer rouse her. She had the rare experience of waking up one morning and finding herself famous. Her brother Edward wrote to her and warned her against pride. It was not necessary. The daughter of Lyman Beecher could not be corrupted by success. She remained herself through all vicissitudes—earnest, whimsical, devoted. From her childhood, she was preoccupied and absent-minded, not hearing what was said to her and making funny blunders. This tendency increased with her advancing years. A full decade before her death, she lapsed into a dreamy state which lasted to the end. When they brought her a gold medal, she thought it was a toy.

[The standard biogs. are C. E. Stowe, *Life of Harriet Beecher Stowe, Compiled from Her Journals and Letters* (1889); A. A. Fields, *Life and Letters of Harriet Beecher Stowe* (1897); and C. E. and L. B. Stowe, *Harriet Beecher Stowe, the Story of Her Life* (1911). Joseph Sabin and others, *Bibliotheca Americana,* vol. XXIV (1933–34) lists her writings before 1860, including translations, and contemporary works on *Uncle Tom's Cabin.* J. F. Rhodes, *Hist. of the U. S. from the Compromise of 1850,* vol. I (1893), describes the reception of *Uncle Tom's Cabin* at home and abroad.

See also A. A. Fields, *Authors and Friends* (1896); V. L. Parrington, "The Romantic Revolution in America, 1850–1860," *Main Currents in Am. Thought*, vol. II (1927); C. M. Rourke, *Trumpets of Jubilee* (1927); L. B. Stowe, *Saints, Sinners, and Beechers* (1934); *Boston Transcript*, July 1, 1896.]   K.A.

STRACHEY, WILLIAM (fl. 1606–1618), historian and first secretary of the Virginia colony, was descended from the honorable and ancient Strachey family of Essex. He appears not to have been the son of William who married Mary Cook (as is sometimes stated), but of John Strachey, whose son William was baptized in Saffron Walden church, Mar. 16, 1567/8. There are other conjectures which point towards him as the William Strachey who matriculated at Emmanuel College, Cambridge, in 1588 (John and J. A. Venn, *Alumni Cantabrigienses,* pt. 1, vol. IV, 1927, p. 172); who married Frances Foster, 1588, and had a son William; and who died in 1634. It is known that he wrote verse, little of which was published, that he was a friend of the poet Donne, and that Thomas Campion praised—overgenerously, to judge from surviving specimens—his poetic gifts in an epigram wherein he termed Strachey "my old boon companion" (*sodalis*). His writings attest that he was a pious anti-papist, a man of considerable culture and learning, a keen, scientific, and dependable observer, as well as the master of a prose style which, if at times pedantic, possesses dignity and power and occasionally eloquence; while it may be assumed from knowledge of the other incumbents of the Virginia secretaryship that he was considered one of the most prominent citizens of the colony, of competent fortune, superior talents, and experience in public affairs. In the dedication to Bacon (some time after July 11, 1618) of his *Historie of Travaile,* Strachey designates himself "one of the Graies-Inne Societe," but his name does not appear in the index to Joseph Foster's *Register of Admissions to Gray's Inn* (1889). Save that he contributed a second-rate sonnet to the commendatory verses of Ben Jonson's *Sejanus* (1604), there is little specific fact bearing on his career prior to the summer of 1606, when he accompanied Sir Thomas Glover to Constantinople as secretary (*Times Literary Supplement,* London, July 3 and 24, Aug. 7, 1930). His friendly intercourse with Sir Henry Lello, whom Glover had gone to supplant as ambassador, so enraged his employer that Strachey was soon dismissed, returning considerably aggrieved to England.

His name next appears among the grantees under King James's second charter to the London Company of Virginia, to which he paid a £25 subscription. On June 2, 1609, he sailed for Virginia; but his ship, the *Sea Adventure* (having aboard both the new governor, Sir Thomas Gates [*q.v.*], and Sir George Somers, admiral of the little fleet), became separated from the others in a severe storm late in July and was wrecked on the Bermudas. There the party wintered, constructing two small vessels, and on May 23, 1610, reached Jamestown, to find matters so desperate that only the opportune arrival of Lord De La Warr [*q.v.*] prevented the abandoning of the colony.

De La Warr appointed Strachey to his council, as secretary and recorder, and when Gates left for England in July he carried with him two interesting papers from the secretary's pen. One was De La Warr's dispatch (obviously drawn up by Strachey) to the patentees in England, announcing his arrival, the safety of the shipwrecked party, and the state of the colony (Major, *post*); the other was Strachey's more detailed letter to an "excellent lady," which was repressed by the Company in consequence of its outspoken account of the settlement and was first printed by Samuel Purchas in 1625 as "A True Reportory of the Wracke, and Redemption of Sir Thomas Gates . . ." (*Purchas His Pilgrimes,* vol. IV; reprinted in *Hakluytus Posthumous or Purchas His Pilgrimes,* vol. XIX, 1906). In manuscript, however, it furnished material both for *A True Declaration of the Estate of the Colonie in Virginia* published by the patentees in 1610 (reprinted in Peter Force, *Tracts,* vol. III, 1844) and for Shakespeare's play *The Tempest* (C. M. Gayley, *Shakespeare and the Founders of Liberty in America,* 1917, pp. 40–76; R. R. Cawley, "Shakespeare's Use of the Voyagers in *The Tempest,*" *Publications of the Modern Language Association of America,* vol. XLI, 1926).

Late in 1611 Strachey returned to London, where at his "lodging in the blacke Friers" he edited the first written code of laws for the Virginia settlement, *For the Colony in Virginea Brittania: Lavves Diuine, Morall, and Martiall* (1612; reprinted in Force, *Tracts,* vol. III), the military part based on Dale's enlargement of the *Lawes for governing the Armye in the Lowe Countreyes* and the civil code being his own compilation. The tract entitled *The Proceedings of the English Colonie in Virginia,* by "W. S.," printed at Oxford the same year and long attributed to Strachey, even to the point of confusing it with his *True Reportory,* is now recognized as the work of the Rev. Dr. William Symonds, who had delivered the sermon *Virginea Britannia* to the prospective colonists in April 1609 at Whitechapel (Gayley, *ante,* p. 74). Before the close of 1613 (Major, *post,* pp. 5, 140) Strachey completed the first two books of his most ambitious literary undertaking, *The Historie of Travaile into Virginia Britannia, Expressing the Cosmographie and Comodities of the Country, Togither with the Manners and Customes of the People,* and inscribed the manuscript to Sir Allen Apsley. Neither Apsley nor the Virginia Committee encouraged him to publish (although it has been said that the *Historie* induced Apsley to advise the Pilgrim emigration to America), nor did he meet with better success five or six years later when he inscribed it afresh to Francis Bacon. In consequence, the work remained unfinished and, until its publication by the Hakluyt Society in 1849 (R. H. Major, editor), was overlooked by writers on Virginia; yet it is a highly authoritative work and probably the most ably written of the contemporary histories of the region, valuable alike for its ethnological account of the Virginia Indians and—so far as it goes—for its commentary on early American discoveries and settlements. Of the author's subsequent career, nothing is known.

[Major's comments in Strachey's *Historie* (1849); P. A. Bruce, *Institutional Hist. of Va. in the Seventeenth Century* (1910), vol. II; H. L. Osgood, *The Am. Colonies in the Seventeenth Century,* vol. I (1904); *Mass. Hist. Soc. Colls.,* 4 ser. I (1852), reprinting accounts of the Roanoke and Sagadahoc colonies from Strachey's *Historie; Wm. and Mary Coll. Quart. Hist. Mag.,* Jan., July 1896, Jan. 1902; Alexander Brown, *The Genesis of the U. S.* (2 vols., 1890).]

A. C. G., Jr.

STRAIGHT, WILLARD DICKERMAN (Jan. 31, 1880–Dec. 1, 1918), diplomat, financier, and publicist, was born at Oswego, N. Y., the son of Henry H. and Emma May (Dickerman) Straight, both of English stock. Henry Straight, an instructor in natural science at Oswego Normal School, and after 1883 in the Cook County Normal School at Normal Park, Ill., died in 1886 of tuberculosis. From 1887 to 1889 his widow taught in the Girls' Normal School in Tokyo, Japan. She returned to the United States in 1889 and died in 1890, also of tuberculosis. Willard and his sister Hazel were then adopted jointly by Dr. Elvire Rainier and Miss Laura Newkirk, of Oswego. Willard was educated in the Oswego public schools, the Bordentown (N. J.) Military Institute, and Cornell University, where he studied architecture and was graduated in 1901, with the degree of B. Arch.

In November of that year, he went to China to take a post in the Imperial Maritime Customs Service. He remained in this service until the Russo-Japanese War, when he went to Korea (Chosen) as a correspondent for Reuter's News Service. There he was soon made vice-consul and secretary to the American minister to Seoul (Keijo). In 1906, he served for a few months as secretary to the American Legation in Cuba but in the same year he returned to the Orient as consul-general at Mukden (Monkden). From November 1908 to June 1909 he was acting chief of the Division of Far Eastern Affairs in the Department of State. In 1909 he returned to the Orient as a representative, first of a group of American bankers, and then of a similar international group, interested in developing railways in Manchuria and the northern part of China proper. Through the political opposition of Russia and Japan, this scheme failed.

Straight thereupon played an important part in the attempt at an international loan to the Chinese government by a consortium of bankers (see sketch of Jacob Henry Schiff). Shortly thereafter, the Chinese Revolution took place and, in 1912, Straight left the Orient forever. On Sept. 7, 1911, he had married Dorothy Whitney, daughter of William C. Whitney [*q.v.*], the well-known Wall Street capitalist. On his return to New York, he planned to study law with the purpose of ultimately practising in the field of international law; but, in the meantime, he continued the association, as Far-Eastern expert, with J. P. Morgan & Company which had grown out of his work for the bankers in the Orient. In 1915 he was persuaded to accept a post as third vice-president of the American International Corporation, formed to facilitate American participation in foreign developments in engineering, railroads, and industrial projects, and in public finance. In the previous year, he had signalized his interest in public affairs by making possible, in cooperation with his wife, the publication of a weekly journal, *The New Republic.* He had previously been greatly attracted by the book, *The Promise of American Life* (1909), by Herbert D. Croly and had sought the acquaintance of the author. The idea of establishing the paper grew spontaneously out of one of their conversations, and Croly became its chief editor. In 1915, Straight's keen interest in the Orient found a definite outlet in the creation of the monthly magazine first called the *Journal of the American Asiatic Association* and later, radically changed in form, called *Asia.* During these years he was also a guiding spirit in the American Asiatic Association, the American Manufacturers' Export Association, and India House, a club in New York started to encourage foreign trade.

With the entrance of the United States into the World War, Straight promptly volunteered for service and was commissioned as major attached to the Adjutant General's office. On Oct. 29, 1917, he was put in charge of organizing the overseas administration of the War Risk Insurance Bureau. In one month and sixteen days, he and his handful of assistants arranged a canvass of 250,000 American soldiers and persuaded them to sign up for insurance to the value of more than $1,000,000,000. Thereafter, he became a student in the staff college at Langres, France. At the beginning of June, he was placed in charge of liaison for the III Corps. He distinguished himself by preparing a liaison manual which was adopted almost *in toto* for the American Expeditionary Force. He died in Paris on Dec. 1, 1918, of influenza and pneumonia.

Willard Straight was a man of varied talents. His many published drawings and sketches show his decided artistic ability. He also had unusual native gifts as a writer. He made remarkable progress in a short time in studies of Oriental languages, history, and politics. That he had noteworthy capacity as an executive and leader of men is shown by the series of responsible posts he held while still in his late twenties and early thirties.

[H. D. Croly, *Willard Straight* (1924); Louis Graves, *Willard Straight in the Orient* (1922), reprinted from "An American in Asia," *Asia*, Sept. 1920–May 1921; "Willard Straight," in *New Republic*, Dec. 7, 1918, pp. 163–64; obituary in *N. Y. Times*, Dec. 2, 1918; *Who's Who in America*, 1918–19; E. D. and G. S. Dickerman, *Dickerman Genealogy. Descendants of Thomas Dickerman . . .* (1922).]   B. B.

STRAIN, ISAAC G. (Mar. 4, 1821–May 14, 1857), naval officer and explorer, son of Robert Strain and Eliza (Geddes) Strain, was born in Roxbury, Pa. He entered the navy as a midshipman, Dec. 15, 1837, and first saw service in the West Indies and on the Brazilian coast. In 1842 he was ordered to the naval school at Philadelphia, which he attended for nearly a year. He then secured leave of absence from the navy for the purpose of conducting an exploring expedition into Brazil. This expedition, partly financed by members of the Academy of Natural Sciences of Philadelphia, was not entirely successful, and in 1844 Strain joined the *Constitution* at Rio de Janeiro and served on her in the East Indies. In 1848 he served on the west coast of Mexico in the *Ohio* in the vicinity of Mazatlán and Guaymas. That summer, following the close of the war with Mexico, while the *Ohio* lay anchored at La Paz, Lower California, Strain landed and explored the peninsula as far as the time allotted him would allow. Early in the winter of 1848–49 he took passage in the *Lexington* for New York but obtained permission to leave his ship at Valparaiso. From there he crossed the

continent to Buenos Aires, embodying his observations in a book, *Cordillera and Pampa, Mountain and Plain: Sketches of a Journey in Chili and the Argentine Provinces in 1849* (1853). He was lent to the Interior Department (Jan. 23, 1850) to serve on the Mexican Boundary Commission, and in 1853 volunteered to conduct an exploration of the Isthmus of Darien between Caledonia Bay on the Caribbean and the Gulf of San Miguel on the Pacific, to determine the possibility of a ship-canal across the isthmus by that route. The privations and sufferings endured by his party, as well as his own energy and fortitude, brought him into public notice. In his report to the Department he declared this route to be "utterly impracticable" (*Report of the Secretary of the Navy, 1854*, n.d., p. 426). In the summer of 1856 he joined the expedition in the steamer *Arctic* under Lieut. Otway H. Berryman to ascertain by soundings the possibility of a submarine telegraph cable between the United States and Great Britain. Never recovering from the effects of the hardships of the Darien expedition, he died at Aspinwall (later Colón), Panama.

Though he never attained a higher rank than lieutenant, nor ever commanded a ship, his restless ambition led him to seek occasion to explore unknown lands and won him the recognition of his superiors. By the secretary of the navy, James Cochran Dobbin, he was called "an accomplished and enterprising officer" (*Ibid.*, p. 384). Though nine lives were lost in the Darien expedition, he met disaster with unflinching courage; English naval officers at Panama considered the conduct of his command the "perfection of military discipline." He was a corresponding member of the Historical and Geographical Institute of Brazil, the American Ethnological Society of New York, and the Academy of Natural Sciences of Philadelphia. Besides his *Cordillera and Pampa* he wrote *A Paper on the History and Prospects of Interoceanic Communication by the American Isthmus* (1856).

[Extensive search has failed to reveal Strain's middle name. See *Proc. Acad. of Nat. Science of Phila.*, vol. II (1846); J. T. Headley, *Darien Exploring Expedition under the Command of Lieut. Isaac G. Strain* (1885); U. S. Navy Dept. Registers, 1837–57; manuscript log of U.S.S. *Ohio*, 1847–48; *Exec. Doc. 34*, 31 Cong., 1 Sess., for report of Mexican Boundary Commission; *Report of the Secretary of the Navy, 1856* (n.d.), pp. 466–68; U. S. Navy Dept. Archives; Nathan Crosby, *Ann. Obit. Notices of Eminent Persons . . . 1857* (1858); *Springfield Pioneer* (Springfield, Ohio), Dec. 25, 1835; *Springfield Weekly Republic*, Dec. 24, 1841, and June 12, 1857.]   L. H. B.

STRANAHAN, JAMES SAMUEL THOMAS (Apr. 25, 1808–Sept. 3, 1898), capitalist, civic leader, was born at Peterboro, Madison County, N. Y., a son of Samuel and Lynda (Josselyn) Stranahan, and a descendant of James Stranahan who emigrated to Scituate, R. I., probably in 1725. His parents (both of Scotch-Irish stock) had come from Connecticut to the Mohawk Valley as pioneers. When James was eight years old his father died; his mother re-married, and he spent the remainder of his boy-hood on the farm of his step-father, John Down-er. So well did he avail himself of the country schools in the neighborhood that long before he was twenty-one he was a schoolmaster himself. A year at Cazenovia Seminary completed his formal education, but he had mastered enough of the elements of land surveying to enable him to set up in that calling, then fairly remunerative in a new country. During the thirties, while Stranahan was a wool merchant at Albany, Ger-rit Smith [q.v.], the wealthy abolitionist, who had known him at Peterboro, interested him in the development of some of his Oneida County properties, and particularly in the promotion of the village of Florence as a manufacturing cen-ter. A term as assemblyman at Albany in 1838 gave Stranahan an insight into legislative meth-ods that was to serve him well forty years later.

In 1840 he went to Newark, N. J., and became a successful railroad contractor. He was one of the earliest operators on a large scale to take railroad stock in payment for construction work. After four years he transferred his activities to Brooklyn, N. Y., then a city of less than 100,000, where harbor improvements known as the At-lantic Basin and Docks had been projected. He entered into this enterprise with great energy and enthusiasm, bringing it to ultimate suc-cess, although it was twenty-six years before a dividend could be paid on the corporation stock. Meanwhile he invested in East River ferries and came to be known as one of Brooklyn's public-spirited and substantial citizens. His election to Congress as a Whig in 1854 came after a defeat as candidate for mayor. Yet his lasting reputa-tion was to be won as a servant of the city rather than of the nation. As president of the Brooklyn park board (1860–82) he was largely responsible for the creation of Prospect Park at a time when few American public men saw the importance of public parks in municipal development. Much of the time he worked almost single-handed. His services were recognized in an unusual way dur-ing his lifetime by the dedication on June 6, 1891, of a statue of him by Frederick William MacMonnies, erected through public subscrip-tion. Hardly less significant was his early and persistent espousal of the plans for the original East River Bridge. In 1883, the year in which

he presided at the formal opening of the bridge, he pledged support of the Greater New York consolidation plan, which involved the loss of Brooklyn's identity as a city and ran counter to the cherished ideas of some of his co-workers and friends. He was seventy-five when he set out to win over Brooklyn for consolidation; he was ninety when the goal was finally reached, and he was hailed as one of the fathers of the greater city. He was twice married: first, on May 4, 1837, to Mariamne Fitch (d. 1866) of Oneida County, N. Y., and second to Clara Cornelia Harrison, author of *A History of French Paint-ing* (1888). He died at Saratoga, N. Y., sur-vived by his wife and one of the three children of his first marriage.

[H. R. Stiles, *Geneals. of the Stranahan, Josselyn, Fitch, and Dow Families in N. Am.* (privately printed, 1868), and *A Hist. of the City of Brooklyn,* vol. III (1870); *Biog. Directory of the Am. Cong., 1774–1927* (1928); *An Account of the Dinner by the Hamilton Club to Hon. James S. T. Stranahan, ... Dec. 13, 1888* (1889); ann. reports of the Commissioners of Prospect Park, 1861–67, Brooklyn Park Commissioners, 1868–82; obituary in *Brooklyn Daily Eagle,* Sept. 3, 1898.]
W. B. S.

STRANG, JAMES JESSE (Mar. 21, 1813–July 9, 1856), leader of the Mormon sect known by his name, was born in Scipio, N. Y., the son of Clement and Abigail (James) Strang. He seems to have been named Jesse James for his mother's father, but in 1831–32 reversed the or-der (Quaife, *post,* p. 2). In February 1816, the family settled near Hanover, Chautauqua Coun-ty, N. Y. After a period of bad health, Strang in his early youth began to show precocious intel-lectual interests, though, aside from a period at the Fredonia Male Academy, his formal educa-tion was spasmodic. For the most part he was a moody, introspective lad, although his member-ship in the church of his parents and his attendance at the popular debating societies did something to socialize him. In spite of a strict religious background in his Baptist home, his reading of the works of Volney, Paine, and Shelley led to a lively skepticism. After a season or two of teaching he studied law and was ad-mitted to the bar in October 1836. In the same year he married Mary Perce. Besides practising law he served as postmaster at Ellington, N. Y., from 1838 to 1843. For two years he also owned and edited the Randolph *Herald.*

It was not until 1843, after the family had moved to Burlington, Wis., to settle near his wife's people, that Moses Smith, husband of the sister of Strang's wife and an ardent Mormon, interested him mildly in the new sect. Stimu-lated by Aaron and Moses Smith, in February 1844 he made a trip with the former to Nauvoo,

Ill., more out of curiosity than enthusiasm for the new gospel. Yet under the influence of Joseph and Hyrum Smith the erstwhile "cool Philosopher" (Quaife, p. 201), as Strang had often dubbed himself, became an ardent convert. Learning that the Prophet was laying plans to move out of Illinois, Strang enthusiastically suggested the advantages of Wisconsin. On June 27, the day when Joseph Smith was killed by a mob at Carthage, Ill., Strang claims to have had a visitation from the angels of God, who ordained him to be ruler of the Mormons in the Prophet's place. To bolster this claim, Strang exhibited a letter alleged to have been written by Smith in which he instructed Strang to found an ecclesiastical unit of the Mormon church in Wisconsin and further gave a premonition of his own death and named Strang as his prophetic successor. In the struggle of various factions for control of the church after Smith's death this vision and the letter were the subject of heated dispute. In spite of the power of opposing factions, Strang drew around him at Voree, Wis. (near Burlington), a group of followers including Apostle John E. Page and Patriarch William Smith, the Prophet's brother.

Strang made an unsuccessful attempt to win the support of converts in the eastern states and especially in Great Britain, and for some years the little colony at Voree barely kept going in the face of internal dissension and economic hardship. In this period, 1844–47, Strang poured out a number of revelations, reported finding sacred plates, which he translated, and gave out creedal pronunciamentos including instructions to found a communistic order, to build a temple, and to erect a home for him at the expense of the Saints. Under the influence of one of his followers, John C. Bennett, he also established the Order of the Illuminati, in effect a secret society sworn to support him and his organization even though they ran counter to the laws of the civil government. Strang decided in 1847 to remove his followers to the Beaver Islands, in the northern waters of Lake Michigan. But it was not until 1849, when the city of St. James was established on Big Beaver Island, that the success of the new venture was assured. In the face of Gentile opposition and the rigors of the wilderness he established his new Zion, and on July 8, 1850, with proper divine revelations to support the project, he was crowned King. His religious "kingdom" was patterned on *The Book of the Law of the Lord,* which he alleged was an ancient Mosaic document given him by divine powers for translation.

Strang held or controlled the principal local offices, and he was twice (1852, 1854) elected member of the Michigan state legislature. Through measures sponsored by him the civil government of the northern Michigan counties was thoroughly organized for the first time. When recourse to mob action failed, his enemies resorted to lawsuits in their efforts to drive him out. The most famous of these court actions was brought in Detroit in May and June 1851, by George C. Bates, then United States district attorney, who charged Strang and his chief henchmen with counterfeiting, robbing the mails, and trespassing on federal lands. The Whig press, because of his political affiliation with the Democrats, flayed him unmercifully, but in spite of public agitation against him he was acquitted. Although at the outset of his sectarian venture Strang had been violent in his opposition to the polygyny or spiritual wifery practised among the Nauvoo Mormons, in 1850 he announced a revelation proclaiming plural marriage to be a divinely appointed institution. His followers, for the most part, accepted this *volte-face,* but poverty and the lack of available unmarried women prevented its extensive practice. Strang himself had four polygynous wives. While the growing economic strength of the Mormon colony in competition with the Gentile communities was a factor, it was dissension within his own ranks which brought about his assassination and the brutal dispersal of his people at the hands of a mob stimulated by various apostates. Dr. Hezekiah McCulloch, a trusted adviser of Strang who had broken with him, appears to have planned his death. On June 16, 1856, Strang was shot down by Alexander Wentworth and Thomas Bedford as he was about to board the armored steamer *Michigan.* He was removed to Voree, where he died on July 9. "With Strang's death died his Church" (Quaife, p. 179), for he steadfastly refused to name a successor, although he knew he would never recover.

Strang was intellectually one of the most able of the early Mormon leaders. He was fearless and capable in debate, an effective orator, and a lucid journalist. In dealing with his followers, although an absolute dictator, he was good-natured, kind, and self-confident. In fact, because of his success in vanquishing opposition both from within his Church and from his enemies without, his sense of power at the end of his life amounted almost to a megalomania. His own works, especially *The Book of the Law of the Lord* (1856), and *Ancient and Modern Michilimackinac, . . .* (1854), give an excellent picture of his kingdom and his struggle with the Gentiles. Other writings were *The Diamond* (1848), and *The Prophetic Controversy* (1854).

[M. M. Quaife. *The Kingdom of Saint James* (1930); H. E. Legler, "A Moses of the Mormons," *Publications Parkman Club* (Milwaukee), nos. 15–16 (1897); Orrin Poppleton, "The Murder of King Strang," *Hist. Collections . . . Made by the Mich. Pioneer and Hist. Soc.,* vol. XVIII (1892); C. J. Strang, "A Michigan Monarchy," *Ibid.*; *Detroit Free Press,* July 13, 1856; O. W. Riegel, *Crown of Glory: The Life of James Jesse Strang,* was announced for publication in the fall of 1935.] K. Y.

STRATEMEYER, EDWARD (Oct. 4, 1862–May 10, 1930), writer of juvenile fiction, was born in Elizabeth, N. J. His father, Henry Julius Stratemeyer, who came from Germany in 1848 and in 1849 joined the California gold rush, returned to New Jersey to settle the affairs of a brother who had died. Later he married his brother's widow, Anna (Seigel) Stratemeyer, by whom he had two sons and a daughter, and established himself as a tobacconist in Elizabeth. Stratemeyer attended the public schools of Elizabeth and after his graduation from high school had private tutoring in rhetoric, composition, and literature. For several years, while he worked as a clerk in a tobacco store owned by his step-brother, he tried to write stories modeled on those of William Taylor Adams ("Oliver Optic") and Horatio Alger [*qq.v.*]. In 1888 he sold his first story, "Victor Horton's Idea," to *Golden Days for Boys and Girls,* a weekly published in Philadelphia, for seventy-five dollars, and definitely decided upon a career as a writer of books for boys. After 1890 he lived in Newark, N. J., where until about 1896 he owned and managed a stationery store. In March 1891 he was married to Magdalene Baker Van Camp of Newark.

From 1891 to 1893 he wrote six serial stories for Frank A. Munsey's *Argosy.* In 1893 he became editor of *Good News,* a weekly magazine for boys, to which he contributed many stories during the years 1893–95; in 1895 he edited *Young People of America,* and in 1896 ran a periodical of his own called *Bright Days,* at first a monthly, later a weekly. By this time he had adopted the pen name of Arthur M. Winfield. His first book, *Richard Dare's Venture; or, Striking Out for Himself,* appeared in 1894 as the first volume of the Bound to Win Series, and about 1896 he began to give all his time to the writing of full-length stories in series. The first of these to gain him popularity was the Old Glory Series, which began with the success of *Under Dewey at Manila* (1898). In 1899 he started the Rover Boys' Series for Young Americans, most popular of all his work, of which the thirtieth volume was published in 1926. Under

the name of Captain Ralph Bonehill he wrote the Flag of Freedom Series (1899–1902), the Mexican War Series (1900–02), the Frontier Series (1903–07), and the Boy Hunters Series (1906–10), and others, as well as numerous separate volumes. In 1906 he founded the Stratemeyer Literary Syndicate in New York City and employed many writers of juvenile fiction to elaborate plots which he supplied into book-length stories. Under this plan were produced the Tom Swift and Motor Boys Series for boys and the Bobbsey Twins for young children, which rivalled some of his own series in popularity. Stratemeyer, who was a very methodical and industrious man, spent a great deal of time studying and collecting data for his books and wrote steadily throughout his life, amply realizing his early ambition to sell a million copies of his books. His total output was over one hundred and fifty books, and he was the originator of over six hundred others. His stories, which frequently depict preparatory school and college life, are full of action and none-too-plausible adventure; there is little attempt at character-drawing. Stratemeyer died in Newark of pneumonia. He was survived by his wife and his two daughters.

[*Who's Who in America,* 1928–29; G. W. Browne, in *Writer,* Mar. 1902; *Proc. N. J. Hist. Soc. . . . . 1930,* vol. XV (n.d.); *Fortune,* Apr. 1934; *N. Y. Times,* May 13, 1930 (editorial); *Newark Evening News,* June 4, 1927, and May 12, 1930 (obituary); information from a daughter, Edna C. Stratemeyer, 171 North Seventh St., Newark, N. J..　　　　　E. S. S.
　　　　　　　　　　　　　　　　　　　R. W. B.

STRATON, JOHN ROACH (Apr. 6, 1875–Oct. 29, 1929), clergyman and reformer, was born in Evansville, Ind., the son of Julia Rebecca (Carter) and Henry Dundas Straton, a Baptist preacher of rigorous orthodox faith. He was a student at Mercer University, from 1895 to 1898 and was professor of oratory and interpretation of literature there in 1899. He attended the Southern Baptist Theological Seminary, in Louisville, Ky., where he was ordained in 1900 and graduated in 1902. After teaching two years, 1903–05, in Baylor University at Waco, Tex., he became pastor of the Second Baptist Church in Chicago. In 1908 he went to the Seventh Immanuel Church in Baltimore, Md. From 1913 to 1917 he was minister of the First Baptist Church in Norfolk, Va. In 1918 he accepted the pastorate of the Calvary Baptist Church in New York City.

The frankness with which he assailed the excesses of the years after the World War was in itself enough to attract immense public attention; but this was accentuated by sensational methods of public appeal that precipitated feverish controversy. He preached on cabaret orgies, the ouija board, and the Elwell murder mystery. He made a tour of the tenderloin district, and on an Easter Sunday, in 1920, denounced the whiskey drinking, soliciting, and dancing he had seen. He attended the Dempsey-Carpentier prize-fight and used his experience as the basis of a furious pulpit denunciation of the sport. He attacked the atheists and forced trial of a suit against Charles L. Smith, president of the American Association for the Advancement of Atheism, for sending annoying literature through the mails. Repeatedly he conducted exciting revival services. These activities, sustained with immense vitality and resource, made him a figure of first-class local importance. In his later years, he became a national figure as well. His evolution debates with Charles Francis Potter carried his name and word to all parts of the land (see his *The Famous New York Fundamentalist—Modernist Debates, the Orthodox Side*, 1925). On the death of William Jennings Bryan, he assumed undisputed leadership of the Fundamentalist forces. Bitter controversy with Gov. Alfred E. Smith led him into the presidential campaign of 1928, and for weeks, in the blasting heat of summer, he toured the Southern states in opposition to the "wet," Catholic, Tammany standard-bearer of Democracy. Among the books he published were, *The Menace of Immorality in Church and State* (1920), *The Gardens of Life* (1921), and *The Old Gospel at the Heart of the Metropolis* (1925).

He was in appearance and temper the typical Protestant zealot. His lean, handsome face had a granite-like quality of grim and terrible resolution. His tall, spare, and powerful figure quivered with nervous energy, yet was held taut in masterful control. A fine voice gave wings to a natural eloquence, carefully trained to full effectiveness. His mind, set like hardened cement by early domestic and educational influences, became impervious to later impressions of thought and life. He read widely and more than once confounded his opponents by unexpected knowledge of facts; but these facts were held at arm's length like stones to be broken by the hammers of controversy, never received into his mind like food to be digested and absorbed. He was less intolerant and more tender than his critics imagined; if he appeared stern and unrelenting, it was because of his dogmatic assurance of the rightness of his position. His superb showmanship, which included early use of the radio and constant resort to newspaper publicity, was as sincere as it was ingenious and occasionally vulgar; it was motivated not by self-seeking but

by shrewd understanding of the popular mind and determination to capture that mind at any cost for the causes he had at heart. An ironic humor, a genuine courage, a fierce scorn of consequences armored him against storms of public ridicule. There was comfort, also, in the unshakable loyalty of hosts of followers. It is doubtful, however, if he ever suspected the vicarious enjoyment of wickedness he supplied in sermons that gave his hearers the nearest thing to indulgence in what he denounced. The severity of his campaign exertions, following upon the strain of his New York ministry, led to a paralytic stroke. He died at a sanitarium in Clifton Springs, N. Y., survived by his wife, formerly Georgia Hillyer of Atlanta, Ga., to whom he was married on Nov. 2, 1903, and by four sons.

[*Who's Who in America*, 1928–29; *New Republic*, Nov. 13, 1929; *N. Y. Times*, esp. Oct. 30, Nov. 7, 1929.]
                    J. H. H.

STRATTON, CHARLES SHERWOOD (Jan. 4, 1838–July 15, 1883), midget, better known as General Tom Thumb, was born at Bridgeport, Conn., of English colonial stock, the third of the four children of Sherwood Edwards Stratton, a carpenter, and his wife, Cynthia (Thompson). The other members of the family were of normal stature, but Charles stopped growing when six months old, and until he entered his teens he remained two feet one inch tall and weighed only fifteen pounds. Later he grew to a height of three feet four inches, and good living ultimately increased his weight to seventy pounds. In the fall of 1842 P. T. Barnum [*q.v.*], staying overnight in a Bridgeport hotel, heard of the local dwarf, drove a quick bargain with the parents, taught the boy to dance, sing, tell stories, and strut the stage in various guises, advertised him as "General Tom Thumb, a dwarf eleven years of age, just arrived from England," and put him on exhibition in his New York museum. Under Barnum's tutelage the bashful boy was turned into a pert, graceful entertainer. He had a ready wit and a good sense of showmanship, was healthy and symmetrically formed, cheerful, lively, and winning. He became at once a celebrity; money flowed into Barnum's coffers; and when the two departed for England Jan. 18, 1844, accompanied by a tutor and the General's parents, the New York municipal brass band and some 10,000 people thronged to the wharf to see them leave.

In England Barnum achieved even greater success with his protégé than in the United States. Starting with a letter of introduction from Horace Greeley to the American minister, Edward Everett, he conducted his publicity campaign until it attained its climax in an invitation to Buckingham Palace. Queen Victoria, then twenty-five years old, was amused and charmed by the General, and thereafter his tour of England and of the Continent was a triumphal progress. One of his performances was an impersonation of Napoleon, which was much admired by the Duke of Wellington and which Louis Philippe, at his own request, was also privileged to see. When Stratton returned to the United States in 1847 his European acclaim had increased his popularity. He toured the country and visited Cuba, but in 1852 or thereabouts he retired to his native town. Subsequently he made several visits to Europe and in 1872 a trip around the world. Sometimes he traveled under Barnum's management, sometimes under his own. Barnum appears to have been his one intimate friend.

In 1862 he met another one of Barnum's dwarfs, Lavinia Warren (Oct. 31, 1841–Nov. 25, 1919) of Middleboro, Mass., whose full name was Mercy Lavinia Warren Bumpus. While they were Barnum's week-end guests at Bridgeport, he proposed marriage to her and was accepted. The wedding was celebrated in Grace Episcopal Church, New York, Feb. 10, 1863; and the New York newspapers in their efforts to report the event adequately almost forgot the Civil War. The Strattons' one child, a daughter, died in early childhood. In his youth Stratton had evinced more than his share of Yankee thrift and acquisitiveness. He had a sharp eye for a first mortgage and owned considerable real property in Bridgeport. Later he joined the Masons and cultivated a taste for expensive cigars and rather more expensive horses and yachts. He died unexpectedly, on his estate in Middleboro, Mass., of an apoplectic stroke. When his affairs were settled, it was found that his wealth had been all but completely squandered. He was buried at Bridgeport, where there is a monument to his memory. His widow married an Italian dwarf with a Papal title, Count Primo Magri.

[H. R. Stratton, *A Book of Strattons* (2 vols., 1908–18), is authority for day of birth, given by Barnum as Jan. 11. See also *An Account of the Life, Personal Appearance, Character, and Manners of Charles S. Stratton, the American Man in Miniature* (London, 1844); *Life and Travels of Thomas Thumb, in the U. S., England, France, and Belgium* (copr. 1849); *Adventures of Mr. and Mrs. Tom Thumb, at Home and Abroad* (1863); *Sketch of the Lives . . . of Charles S. Stratton . . . and His Wife Lavinia Warren* (London, 1865); Sylvester Bleeker, *Gen. Tom Thumb's Three Years' Tour around the World* (1872); M. R. Werner, *Barnum* (1923); P. T. Barnum, *Struggles and Triumphs: or, The Life of P. T. Barnum* (2 vols., 1927), ed. by G. S. Bryan; *N. Y. Tribune*, July 16, 1883.]   G. H. G.

STRATTON, SAMUEL WESLEY (July 18, 1861–Oct. 18, 1931), creator of the Bureau of Standards, was born on his father's farm at Litchfield, Ill., the son of Samuel and Mary B. (Webster) Stratton. From early youth the son shared in the farm labor, and from boyhood he showed the keenest interest in mechanics. He attended the schools of his native township, and, after working for two years to earn money for further education, he entered the University of Illinois in 1880 as a special student. He quickly decided to undertake the four-year course in Mechanical Engineering. Earning his way from year to year, he received the degree of Bachelor of Science in 1884 and engaged in special research problems. In 1885 he was appointed instructor in mathematics in the university; but his work was soon confined to physics alone, and he became professor of physics in 1891. In 1891 he was asked to establish and take charge of a new course in electrical engineering. In 1892 he became assistant professor of physics at the newly organized University of Chicago, where he remained until 1901. While there he became associated with Michelson on his investigation on the speed of light, planned and supervised construction of the Ryerson laboratories, and gave much attention to the application of physics to engineering. From college days he had always maintained a deep interest in military affairs and on taking up his work in Chicago joined the naval militia and rose to the rank of lieutenant-commander. As head of this organization, he entered the naval service during the Spanish-American War in 1898, with the rank of lieutenant. His unit was assigned to the *Texas*.

Two years later, in 1900, through the instrumentality of the assistant secretary of the treasury, Frank A. Vanderlip, who had been one of his close college friends at Illinois, he was asked by the secretary of the treasury, Lyman J. Gage, to prepare a report for a proposed bureau of standards. The bill authorizing the establishment of the bureau was drawn by him, with the existing office of weights and measures as a nucleus, and the many hearings and demonstrations before the congressional committee were skilfully handled by him and won acceptance and generous support. The bill was passed in 1901 and the bureau of standards became an actuality. On the insistence of Gage, he became its first director. His vision of the usefulness of such a bureau was so clear that he was never seriously handicapped by the limitations of function expressed in the organic act, and from the beginning the work of the bureau expanded greatly in scope and usefulness. In 1903 the bureau was transferred to the department of commerce, thereby making possible a greater opportunity for emphasizing and assisting in the prosecution of research as an aid to commerce and industry. He and the bureau became important factors in the international conference on weights and measures, as well as in manifold advisory committees for the better development and standardization of basic industries. He had the gift of obtaining first the confidence and then the cooperation of industrial leaders and men of vision and high character in many technical fields. Under his direction the bureau grew to be a great research center. With the advent of the World War the service he rendered the government, both personally and through the bureau, was invaluable. The reputation attained by the bureau of standards, not only in American industry but also in the world, is in reality largely due to this man, who picked his lieutenants with rare judgment and gave them the credit for work that was often to a great degree the product of his own logical thinking and carefully organized experimentation. He made it a rule to give the credit to the younger men who collaborated with him on problems which greatly interested him. This policy dated from his university experience, where he was the junior worker and received too little consideration for the part he took in the research work. Largely on account of this generosity only a small number of scientific papers appeared under his name, aside from his annual bureau reports and such official reports as "Metric System in Export Trade" (*Sen. Doc. 241*, 64th Cong., 1 Sess., 1916). Notable among his scientific papers are "A New Harmonic Analyser" published with Michelson in the *Philosophical Magazine* (Jan. 1898) and "Metrology in Relation to Industrial Progress" in the *Journal of the Franklin Institute* (Oct. 1912).

While at the bureau, he never lost interest in technical education, and when he was invited to become the president of the Massachusetts Institute of Technogoly in 1923 he accepted, in the belief that he could render a special service both to the Institute because of his knowledge of the needs of industry, and to American industry by participating actively in the training of men of the type who would become the leaders in the industrial fields. He felt strongly that technical schools should render an increasing service to industry and to the public through basic instruction and through emphasis on research in both pure and applied science, and during his presidency worked with these ends in view. For many years the position of president of the Institute had made exacting and almost impossible demands on the energies of its incumbent. In 1930 a reorganization of administrative policy was

effected, whereby he became chairman of the corporation, and Karl T. Compton was elected to the office of president. Thus two men shared the many and varied responsibilities that one had always borne hitherto. This arrangement was of brief duration, however, for Stratton died suddenly, while in the act of dictating a eulogy of his friend Edison, who had died earlier that same day. He had never married.

Unusually modest and often unassertive to the point of shyness, he had qualities that greatly endeared him to a very wide circle of devoted friends. He was a man of strong personality, of forceful character, and of unswerving loyalty. His mind was a storehouse of specialized knowledge in many fields, textiles, china and glass, antique furniture, and mechanical devices of every sort, as well as the latest technical advances in physics and engineering. Throughout his life he found particular enjoyment in constructing with his own hands pieces of scientific apparatus, or cabinets and articles of furniture, and whether working with wood or metal his technique and attention to detail were complete and faultless. In this avocation he not only found relief from the greater problems and cares incident to his office, but his work expressed that striving for exactness and high quality, even to perfection, which characterized his life. He was a member of several of the learned societies, chairman of the international conference on weights and measures, and a chevalier and an officer of the French Legion of Honor. Many honors came to him from universities at home and abroad. He was awarded the Cresson Medal of the Franklin Institute and the Public Service Medal of the National Academy. With A. Lawrence Lowell, president of Harvard University, and Judge Robert Grant he was appointed on a commission to advise the governor of Massachusetts in the case of Bartolomeo Vanzetti and Nicola Sacco [*qq.v.*] and signed the report of the committee in the *Decision of Gov. Alvan T. Fuller in the . . . appeal of Bartolomeo Vanzetti and Nicola Sacco* (1927).

[*Technology Rev.*, Nov. 1931; *Science*, Oct. 30, 1931; *Record and Index of the Am. Soc. of Mechanical Engineers*, 1931; *Who's Who in America*, 1930–31; *Boston Evening Transcript*, Oct. 18, 1931; personal acquaintance.]   S. C. P.

STRAUS, ISIDOR (Feb. 6, 1845–Apr. 15, 1912), merchant, was born at Otterberg, Rhenish Bavaria. His parents, who were first cousins, were Lazarus and Sara (Straus) Straus. His father came to the United States in 1852 and settled at Talbotton, Ga., where in the fall of 1854 he was joined by his wife and four children, Isidor, Hermina, Nathan [*q.v.*], and Oscar Solomon [*q.v.*]. Isidor was educated at the Collins-worth Institute in Talbotton. In 1871 he married Ida Blun of New York, who bore him four sons and three daughters. Since the outbreak of the Civil War frustrated his ambition to prepare for the United States Military Academy at West Point, he became a clerk in his father's store. In 1863 he went to Europe as secretary to John E. Ward of Savannah, Ga., on a commission to purchase supplies for the Confederacy; as the blockade of Southern ports rendered this futile, however, he worked in a shipping office at Liverpool, England, in 1864. He also dealt in Confederate bonds and sold cotton acceptances, and returned to New York in 1865 with some $12,000. With the help of this capital his father and he formed the crockery firm of L. Straus & Son (later L. Straus & Sons) in New York, which in 1874 took over the crockery and glassware department of R. H. Macy and Company. In 1888 Isidor and his brother Nathan were admitted to partnership in Macy's, and in 1896 they became its sole owners, developing it into the biggest department store in the world. They also built up the Brooklyn department store of Abraham & Straus. Straus was a vice-president of the chamber of commerce of the state of New York, director of several banks, the first president of the New York Crockery Board of Trade, president of the New York Retail Dry Goods Association, and a member of the World's Fair Commission in New York.

He was a warm friend of President Cleveland and took an active part in the campaign which resulted in Cleveland's reëlection in 1892. It is said that he was invited to become postmaster general, but declined the honor. It was due to his influence that Cleveland set himself squarely behind the gold standard and called Congress in extra session (Aug. 7, 1893) for the repeal of that clause of the Sherman Act of 1890 which compelled the Treasury to make monthly purchases of silver bullion for monetary purposes. Straus remained a Gold Democrat, losing his party enthusiasm when his party adopted the Free Silver platform under Bryan's leadership. He was strongly opposed to the protective tariff. At a special election in 1893, he ran for Congress on the issue of the Wilson Tariff Bill and was elected by a large plurality. He served from Jan. 30, 1894, to Mar. 3, 1895, declining renomination. He also declined to be considered for the Democratic nomination for mayor of New York in 1901 and 1909. His philanthropic activities were many. He was president of the Educational Alliance, "the people's palace" of New York's congested East Side, from its organization

(1893) until his death, a vice-president of the J. Hood Wright Memorial Hospital, a trustee and treasurer of the Montefiore Home from its establishment in 1884, a trustee of the Birkbeck Company, and a member of the American Jewish Committee from its inception. He was keenly interested in the Jewish people.

He and his wife, a woman of sweetness and strength, were passengers on the S.S. *Titanic* on its ill-fated maiden voyage across the Atlantic. When the order was given for women and children to take to the life-boats, Mrs. Straus would not leave her husband. Straus was strongly urged to take a place in the boats with her, but refused to do so as long as any women remained on board. Mrs. Straus declined to be separated from her companion of forty years, so the aged couple went down with the ship. Straus's was a strong individuality, compounded of keen insight, sound judgment, high integrity, candid statement, and high executive powers. He was a man of simple tastes, democratic accessibility, and cordial large-heartedness.

[*Who's Who in America*, 1912–13; *Biog. Directory of the Am. Cong., 1774–1927* (1928); *Nineteenth Ann. Report, 1911: The Educ. Alliance ... N. Y.* (1912); Edward Hungerford, *The Romance of a Great Store* (1922); O. S. Straus, *Under Four Administrations: From Cleveland to Taft* (1922); *Am. Hebrew and Jewish Messenger*, Apr. 26, 1912; *N. Y. Herald*, Apr. 16–21, 1912; *N. Y. Times, N. Y. Tribune, World* (N. Y.), *Evening Post* (N. Y.), Apr. 15–21, 1912.]

D. deS. P.

STRAUS, NATHAN (Jan. 31, 1848–Jan. 11, 1931), philanthropist, was born in Otterberg, Rhenish Bavaria, son of Lazarus and Sara (Straus) Straus, and brother of Isidor and Oscar Solomon Straus [*qq.v.*]. In 1852 his father emigrated to the United States, where two years later he was joined by his wife and their four children. Nathan was educated in Talbotton, Ga., in a log cabin school and the Collinsworth Institute. After the Civil War the family moved to New York, where in 1866 Nathan joined his father's firm of L. Straus & Son. By 1888 he had become one of the owners of R. H. Macy and Company. It was he who originated, among other things, the depositors' account system, rest rooms, medical care, and a cost-price lunchroom for the employees of the store. He retired from active concern with business in 1914. On Apr. 28, 1875, he married Lina Gutherz, a woman of cultured mind, who shared unwearyingly in all his philanthropies. He was park commissioner in New York City (1889–93) and president of the board of health (1898). In 1894 he refused the Democratic nomination for mayor.

His philanthropies were numerous and of wide scope. In the panic winter of 1892–93 he distributed food and 1,500,000 buckets of coal for five cents each. In the following winter he issued over two million five-cent tickets for coal or food or lodging, and established lodging houses providing bed and breakfast for five cents. In 1892 he began a campaign for pasteurization of milk, in which he had to combat public ignorance and indifference, professional prejudice, commercial greed and political corruption, but which led ultimately to the compulsory pasteurization of milk in most cities. In 1891, 241 of every thousand babies born in New York City died before their first birthday, but of 20,111 babies who received his pasteurized milk during four years only six died. By 1909 the death rate of children under five had been halved, largely as a result of milk pasteurization. Straus continued to open milk depots at his personal cost, until in 1920 he had 297 milk stations in thirty-six cities in the United States and abroad. In 1909 he established in his cottage in Lakewood, N. J., the pioneer tuberculosis preventorium for children. In 1911 President William Howard Taft appointed Straus sole delegate from the United States to the Third International Congress for the Protection of Infants, held in Berlin. The first International Child's Congress under the auspices of the League of Nations (August 1925) officially recognized his work. Layman though he was, without pretensions to medical knowledge, he lives in the annals of medicine as a pioneer in public health.

As the years went on philanthropy became his ruling passion. Never a man of great wealth, he deliberately reduced his fortune through his gifts, and responded munificently to every campaign for relieving primary needs. In his devotion to Palestine his Jewish soul found its most complete expression. For the last fifteen years of their lives he and his wife lived with this as the dominant interest in their lives, and in the last two decades of his life he gave nearly two-thirds of his fortune to Palestine. In 1912 he established there a domestic science school for girls, a factory for men, a health bureau to fight malaria and trachoma, and a free public kitchen, which he made into a permanent foundation. Later he opened a Pasteur Institute, child-health welfare stations (through the Women's Zionist Organization, Hadassah), and the monumental Nathan and Lina Straus Health Centers in Jerusalem and Tel Aviv. In 1927, when almost an octogenarian, he journeyed to Jerusalem for the fourth time and laid the cornerstone of its health center, at the entrance to which his inscription in English, Arabic, and Hebrew proclaims that it is for all inhabitants of the land, Christian, Moslem, and Jew. The bloody rioting of the Arabs of Palestine in August 1929 robbed both him and his wife of the joy of life, and hastened the death of Lina Gutherz Straus (May 4, 1930). Less than a year later, shortly before his eighty-third birthday, Straus died in New York City, survived by two sons and one daughter.

In 1923 he was chosen by popular vote as the citizen who had done most for public welfare during the quarter of a century in which Greater New York had existed. In 1930 the National Institute of Social Sciences awarded him a gold medal in recognition of his distinguished and wide-spread social service rendered in behalf of humanity. The distinctiveness and originality of his character lay in the fact that he responded equally to the keen, sound judgments of his vigorous mind, and to the undisciplined spontaneity and impulsiveness of his tender heart. A deeply feeling Jew whose humanity transcended creed and race, he has been described as "a man of exalted spirituality, and firm convictions of righteousness in public and private affairs, . . . with a heart overflowing with human sympathy and understanding" (*The American Jewish Year Book, post*, p. 154). Taft summed up the popular judgment when he said, "Dear old Nathan Straus is a great Jew and the greatest Christian of us all" (*Ibid.*, p. 152). Foreign born, he was a passionate lover and servant both of America and of Palestine. He was a practical visionary, a fighting philanthropist, a belligerent pacifist, a lover of all men, yet capable of strong dislikes, an idealist, yet a hearty lover of the good things of life.

[*Who's Who in America*, 1930–31; Lina G. Straus, *Disease in Milk* (2nd ed., 1917); *Jewish Tribune*, Feb. 2, 1923; *New Palestine*, Feb. 3, 1928; D. deSola Pool, in *The Am. Jewish Year Book*, vol. XXXIII (1931), pp. 135–154; Edward Hungerford, *The Romance of a Great Store* (1922); J. W. Wise, *Jews Are Like That!* (1928); obituary in *N. Y. Times*, Jan. 12, 1931.]   D. deS. P.

STRAUS, OSCAR SOLOMON (Dec. 23, 1850–May 3, 1926), lawyer, diplomat, and author, was born in Otterberg, Rhenish Bavaria, the third son of Lazarus and Sara (Straus) Straus, whose other two sons, Isidor and Nathan [*qq.v.*], achieved fame as merchants and philanthropists. After emigrating to the United States in 1854, the family settled first in Talbotton and Columbus, Ga., and later in New York City. Oscar studied at private schools, at Columbia College, from which he was graduated in 1871, and at the Columbia law school, where he obtained his degree in 1873. After being associated for a short time with the law firm of Ward, Jones & Whitehead, he established a law partnership with James A. Hudson and Simon Sterne. In 1881, however, he gave up law and became a partner in L. Straus & Sons, merchants in china and glassware.

It is as a diplomat that he makes his chief claim to historical fame. A progressive Democrat in politics, he first drew the attention of President Cleveland, who, at the instance of Henry Ward Beecher [*q.v.*], named him minister to Turkey (appointment confirmed, Dec. 21, 1887), a post that he held until 1889. Here his diplomatic tact and zeal enabled him to obtain concessions for American interests in Turkey, chiefly of an educational and religious nature. At the same time he won the admiration of the sultan to such a degree that he was invited to arbitrate between the Turkish government and Baron Maurice de Hirsch in a matter concerning the building of railroads. In 1898 he was again appointed to the post at Constantinople (appointment confirmed June 3, 1898) by President McKinley, whom he had supported because of McKinley's opposition to the Free Silver pledge of the Bryan Democrats. His tactful and successful work at the Sublime Porte again won him the commendation of the State Department. He resigned at the close of 1900. During the presidency of Theodore Roosevelt, he was frequently called upon to give his advice on matters of national and international importance. In 1902 he was appointed a member of the Permanent Court of Arbitration at The Hague, and was subsequently reappointed in 1908, 1912, and 1920. In December 1906 (appointment confirmed, Dec. 12) Roosevelt named him secretary of commerce and labor, a post he held until Mar. 4, 1909. As secretary his chief problems were those of Japanese immigration and naturalization. In 1909, under William Howard Taft, he went once more to Turkey, this time as the first American ambassador to the Ottoman Empire (appointment confirmed, May 17, 1909). Again he distinguished himself by obtaining special securities for American interests in Turkey, notably in the exemption of foreign religious, educational, and benevolent institutions from supervision by the Turkish authorities; and in the special sanction to American colleges to own property in their own names. It is worthy of note that his service under both Democratic and Republican administrations made him one of the earliest American career diplomats.

When he resigned his mission to Turkey in December 1910, it was only to throw himself more actively into the arena of national politics, which was at that time agitated by the Taft-Roosevelt split and the emergence of the Progressive party. As nominee for governor he headed the Progressive ticket in New York State, and, while the party went down generally to defeat at the polls, his own popularity was so great that he ran ahead not only of his ticket but even of Roosevelt himself. In 1913 he travelled through North Africa and Europe, the better to acquaint himself with foreign affairs. In 1915 he was appointed chairman of the New York Public Service Commission by Gov. Charles S. Whitman. He was a member of the League to Enforce Peace, and by interviewing many influential persons in London and Paris he actively assisted Wilson in his successful attempt to incorporate a League of Nations in the Versailles treaty. He was a persuasive and eloquent speaker not only by virtue of the enthusiasms that animated him but by the possession of a literary skill that he showed at an early age. Throughout his career he made many polished addresses. His published writings include *The Origin of Republican Form of Government in the United States* (1885), *Reform in the Consular Service* (1894), *The American Spirit* (1913), *Roger Williams, The Pioneer of Religious Liberty* (1894), and his autobiographical memoirs, *Under Four Administrations: From Cleveland to Taft* (1922).

Both the tradition of his family and his own inclinations led him to make many efforts in behalf of his co-religionists. When he met Baron Maurice de Hirsch he discussed with him plans for the amelioration of the lot of the Russian Jews. As one of a committee, he presented to President Harrison a description of their sad circumstances. In 1903, when the Kishinev pogroms outraged the civilized world, he discussed with President Roosevelt the note that was later sent to the Russian government, and aided in the collection of funds for the relief of the destitute. During the Russo-Japanese Treaty of 1905, he met with Count Sergius Witte to discuss the question of the Jews in Russia. When in Turkey he conferred with Dr. Theodor Herzl and took up with him the Zionist movement, of which Dr. Herzl was founder. At the Peace Conference in Paris he assisted in providing for the safeguarding of the Jewish minorities in Europe. He was active during and after the World War in the American Jewish Committee, the Jewish Welfare Board, and the Joint Distribution Committee. He was founder (1892) and first president of the American Jewish Historical Society, and a patron and friend of numerous other Jewish organizations. In private and in public life he was singularly charming. On Apr. 19, 1882, he was married to Sarah Lavanburg, who with two daughters and a son survived him. Towards the latter part of his life he was frequently ill, but he always remained a dynamo of energy. When he died in New York City he was mourned as an outstanding public citizen.

[O. S. Straus, *Under Four Administrations: From Cleveland to Taft* (1922); *Who's Who in America,* 1924–25; James Creelman, *Israel Unbound* (1907); W. W. Howard, *Oscar S. Straus in Turkey* (1912); Cyrus Adler, in *The Am. Jewish Year Book,* vol. XXIX (1927); Peter Wiernik, *Hist. of the Jews in America* (1912); Paul Masserman and Max Baker, *The Jews Come to America* (1932); obituary in *N. Y. Times,* May 4, 1926.]   A. I. E.

STRAUS, SIMON WILLIAM (Dec. 23, 1866–Sept. 7, 1930), banker, realty financier, was born at Ligonier, Ind., the son of Frederick William and Madlon (Goldsmith) Straus. His father, a native of Rhenish Prussia, was the founder and head of the Citizens' Bank of Ligonier; later he went to Chicago and started a mortgage and loan business. Young Simon attended the public schools of Chicago and Hughes High School in Cincinnati, Ohio, and in 1884 entered his father's business in Chicago, which was then known as F. W. Straus & Company. On Apr. 25, 1893, he married Hattie Klee of Pittsburgh, Pa. In 1898, his father having retired, he assumed the presidency of the business, the name of which had been changed to S. W. Straus & Company. He continued as president until two years before his death, when he became chairman of the board. As the business grew, branches began to be established in other cities, and in 1915 Straus removed his office and home to New York, the branch there having become the most important of the chain. He was a pioneer in promoting the building of skyscrapers and originated the idea of real estate bonds used to finance a building project, his company floating the first issue of that sort of paper in 1909. Between that time and his death his company financed building by that method to the extent of more than a billion dollars, and did a huge business in the sale of mortgages and securities. The Straus Company supplied money for some of the greatest office buildings, apartment buildings, and hotels in New York and Chicago, among them the Chrysler Building, New York, the tallest building in the world at the time of its completion, and the Chanin Building. At the time of Straus's death, the company had branches in fifty cities. Its $4,000,000 building in New York boasted one of the handsomest banking rooms in America, while the Chicago office of the company was a thirty-two story building costing $12,000,000.

In 1911 Straus founded the Franklin Trust and Savings Bank of Chicago, and in 1928 the Straus National Bank and Trust Company of Chicago, acting as president of both until his death. He took over and became the first president of the Ambassador hotels in New York and elsewhere. As early as 1927 he became aware that the saturation point in building in New York was near and urged caution, but was not heeded. He encouraged thrift among his employees by adding bonuses to their savings accounts. He founded the American Society for Thrift in 1914, was its president for several years, and was active in the International Congress for Thrift, 1915, at the San Francisco Exposition. He also wrote many articles for newspapers and magazines on thrift, and gave advice as to lending and borrowing on mortgages. In 1920 he published *History of the Thrift Movement in America.* He became noted as a bitter opponent of tipping, but found after some years of effort that opposition was useless. Always eager to help the laborer and the middle-class employee, in 1928 he worked out and arranged to finance an employee-management plan for a large plumbing-fixture corporation in Chicago in the hope of bringing the idea of employee-management into the building industry. He gave liberally of his time and money to philanthropy in both America and Europe. In recognition of his charitable work in France, the French government in 1927 conferred on him the Cross of the Legion of Honor. He died in New York City, survived by his wife and three daughters.

[*Who's Who in America,* 1930–31; obituaries in *N. Y. Times, World* (N.Y.), and *N. Y. Herald Tribune,* Sept. 8, 1930.]   A. F. H.

STRAWBRIDGE, ROBERT (*d.* August 1781), one of the earliest apostles of Methodism in America, was born in Drummersnave (now Drumsna), near Carrick-on-Shannon, County Leitrim, Ireland. His father, a farmer in comfortable circumstances apparently, was also named Robert, and there was at least one other son, Gilbert. The younger Robert came under Methodist influences and was converted. His championship of the doctrines and ways of Methodism aroused violent opposition from his neighbors, and he removed to Sligo, where he joined a Methodist society. During the next few years he seems to have lived in several different places, preaching and working as a house-builder. Meanwhile, he married a woman whose maiden name was Piper.

Sometime between 1759 and 1766, he emigrated to Maryland and settled on Sam's Creek, Frederick County. Upon the year of his arrival depends the answer to the long-debated question whether to him or to Philip Embury [*q.v.*] belongs the honor of having formed the first Methodist Society and built the first Methodist meeting house in America. The dates of Embury's achievements are not disputed, and the burden of proof rests upon Strawbridge's supporters. A review of the evidence leaves a disinterested person convinced that unless new facts are discovered, while there is a reasonable doubt of Embury's priority, that of Strawbridge cannot be established. It is certain, however, that he was the earliest apostle of Methodism in Maryland, and that his influence was a considerable factor in its establishment in America. Soon after his arrival he began to preach, meetings were held in his house, a small society was formed, and a log meeting house erected about a mile from his home. He lived on Sam's Creek for about sixteen years, ministering there and making preaching tours in eastern Maryland and across the borders into Virginia, Delaware, and Pennsylvania, his farm and family being cared for in the meantime by neighbors. As a result of his activities, many were converted, some of whom later became preachers, and a number of societies were formed. During the later years of his life his home was in the upper part of Long Green, Baltimore County, on a farm the use of which had been given him by Capt. Charles Ridgely.

Henry Boehm [*q.v.*], in his *Reminiscences* (*post,* p. 19) writes: "I heard Strawbridge preach at my house in 1781. . . . He was a stout, heavy man, and looked as if he was built for service. My father was much pleased with him and his preaching. He was agreeable company, full of interesting anecdotes." He is traditionally regarded as having been "generous, energetic, fiery, versatile, somewhat intractable to authority, and probably improvident" (Stevens, *post,* p. 42). When Wesley's missionaries came to America in the fall of 1769, Strawbridge was at first inclined to cooperate with them and to conform to the English forms of Methodist procedure. He visited Joseph Pilmore [*q.v.*] in Philadelphia not long after his arrival, and was there again the following year, when he preached in St. George's Chapel. In 1773 he and his Maryland associates deeded at least six meeting houses to trustees to hold for John and Charles Wesley and such persons as should be "appointed at the yearly conference of the people called Methodists in England." Although he was not present at the first American Methodist Conference, held in Philadelphia, July 11, 1773, he was appointed to the Baltimore circuit along with Francis Asbury and two others, but his

name does not appear on the Conference minutes after 1775. Probably the reason for this fact is to be found in his unyielding attitude on the question of administering the Sacraments. Strawbridge was a lay preacher, but no doubt because of the limited opportunities for receiving the Sacraments in the sections where he labored, he had himself administered them before Wesley's missionaries had arrived. The first American Conference, however, decreed that the lay preachers must strictly avoid "administering the ordinances of baptism and the Lord's Supper." The Conference probably knew that Strawbridge would be obdurate, for, according to Asbury, it made an exception in his favor, but with the proviso that he should do so only "under the particular direction of the assistant" (*Journal of Rev. Francis Asbury,* 1852, I, 80). Strawbridge would not be bound by any such condition. He "appeared to be inflexible," Asbury wrote, "He would not administer the ordinances under our directions at all" (*Ibid.,* pp. 82–83). The last years of his life, therefore, he continued his circuit work independently, preaching around Baltimore, at Sam's Creek, and at Bush Chapel, Harford County. While on one of his itineraries in 1781 he became ill and died at the house of Joseph Wheeler, near Towson. He was buried not far from his own home and later his remains were removed to Mount Olivet Cemetery, Baltimore. He had six children, three of whom died early. So great was Asbury's resentment of Strawbridge's behavior that his reference to the latter's death (*Ibid.,* I, 431) was neither fair nor kind: "He is now no more: upon the whole, I am inclined to think that the Lord took him away in judgment, because he was in a way to do hurt to his cause; and that he saved him in mercy, because from his deathbed conversation he appears to have had hope in his end."

[For the Embury-Strawbridge controversy consult *Meth. Quart. Rev.,* July 1856; John Atkinson, *The Beginnings of the Wesleyan Movement in America* (1896); report of the Joint Commission on the Origin of Am. Methodism in *Jour. of the Twenty-Seventh Delegated Gen. Conf. of the M. E. Church,* 1916; *Meth. Rev.,* Jan., May 1928. See also William Crook, *Ireland and the Centenary of Am. Methodism* (1866); Nathan Bangs, *A Hist. of the M. E. Church* (3rd ed., vol. I, 1844); Henry Boehm, *Reminiscences, Hist. and Biog. of Sixty-four Years in the Ministry* (1865); Abel Stevens, *A Compendious Hist. of Am. Methodism* (1867); W. B. Sprague, *Annals of the Am. Pulpit,* vol. VII (1859); W. J. Townsend, H. B. Workman, and George Eayrs, *A New Hist. of Methodism* (2 vols., 1909); P. N. Garber, *The Romance of Am. Methodism* (1931); W. W. Sweet, *Methodism in Am. Hist.* (copr. 1933).]   H.E.S.

STRAWN, JACOB (May 30, 1800–Aug. 23, 1865), cattleman and farmer, was of English-

Welsh descent, the sixth and youngest child of Isaiah and Rachel (Reed) Strawn, who were Quakers. His great-grandfather, Lancelot Straughan, had settled in Pennsylvania in the first decade of the eighteenth century. Jacob was born and spent his first seventeen years on his father's farm in Somerset County, Pa. Attending the district school for a few months each winter, he received a meager education. In 1817 he moved with his parents to central Ohio. After working for his father until 1819, he settled on a nearby farm and began farming and dealing in live stock for himself. In 1828 he bought 395 acres of land about four miles southwest of Jacksonville, Ill. Moving to this farm in May 1831, he began the operations which earned for him the title of "cattle king," extending his holdings in Morgan, Sangamon, and LaSalle counties until he held over twenty thousand acres, chiefly in two tracts.

Except for the first few years, when he raised wheat and engaged in milling and butchering, he devoted his Illinois land to timber, pasture, and corn. In 1854 he raised 2,900 acres of corn, all of which was fed to stock, and owned 2,000 cattle, 700 hogs, and more than a hundred horses and mules. Later he was reputed to have fattened more than five thousand cattle in one year. He introduced into Illinois the practice of feeding shock corn to cattle. He bred few cattle, preferring to buy, fatten, and sell. On horseback he scoured central and southern Illinois, Missouri, and the settled parts of Iowa for feeder cattle which he drove to his Illinois farms. Here they were fattened for the markets in the East, New Orleans, and St. Louis. For several years he largely controlled the cattle market at St. Louis. On one occasion, to thwart a conspiracy of buyers to break his hold on that market, he sent agents out on all the roads leading into the city and bought all incoming herds. He broke the combination in two days and had no more difficulty of that kind. After 1850 he began to confine himself largely to grazing and feeding and to market more of his cattle at home.

In the last few years of his life he curtailed his operations. Possessed of a powerful physique and a strong constitution, he was an active man, spending most of his time outdoors, much of it in the saddle. He believed in hard work and in frugal, simple living, despised show, was plain in dress and rough in speech. He was scrupulously honest, prompt in his dealings, sympathetic toward those in distress, had a strong sense of honor, and commanded universal respect. Although he made no profession of religion, he was sympathetic toward it. He ab-

stained from the use of tobacco and liquor, and declined to serve the latter to his harvest workers. He was a Whig and a Republican, but sought no office. During the Civil War he actively supported the Union and aided in relief work among Union troops. In 1819 he married Matilda Green, daughter of John Green, a Baptist minister of Licking County, Ohio. She died in 1831 after having borne seven children. The following year he married Phoebe Gates, daughter of Samuel Gates of Greene County, Ill. By this marriage he had five sons and a daughter. He was buried in the Diamond Grove Cemetery, Jacksonville, Ill.

[*Prairie Farmer*, Nov. 1854, Oct. 4, 1860, Sept. 2, 1865; *Valley Farmer*, May 1859; *Quincy Whig*, July 3, 1854; *The Biog. Encyc. of Ill.* (1875); *History of Morgan County, Ill.: Its Past and Present* (1878); C. M. Eames, *Historic Morgan and Classic Jacksonville* (1885); *Encyc. of Biog. of Ill.*, vol. I (1892); Newton Bateman and Paul Selby, *Biog. and Memorial Ed. of the Hist. Encyc. of Ill.* (1915), vol. II; *Jour. Ill. State Hist. Soc.*, Apr. 1925; L. M. Glover, *Discourse Occasioned by the Death of Jacob Strawn, the Great Am. Farmer* (1865); Ellwood Roberts, *Old Richland Families* (1898); C. V. Roberts, *Early Friends Families of Upper Bucks* (1925); information from Samuel Clark, Princeton, Ill.]   R. H. A.

STREET, ALFRED BILLINGS (Dec. 18, 1811–June 2, 1881), lawyer, poet, librarian, was born in Poughkeepsie, N. Y., the son of Randall Sanford Street and Cornelia (Billings) Street. His immigrant ancestor, the Rev. Nicholas Street, came to Massachusetts between 1630 and 1638 and settled at Taunton, whence his progeny went via Connecticut to New York just before the Revolution. His father, a general in the state militia, served in the War of 1812, was twice district attorney of the second judicial district of New York, and, 1819–21, served as Democratic congressman for the fourth New York district. Alfred attended the Dutchess County Academy until the family's removal in 1825 to Monticello, N. Y., where after finishing his schooling he read law in his father's office. He was admitted to the bar and, although the law had little attraction for him, he practised at Monticello until his removal to Albany in 1839. There he set up a law office and for years maintained a sort of connection with the law, but literature, and particularly poetry, soon claimed him. He had indeed written poetry much earlier. His "A Winter Scene" and "A Day in March" were printed in the *Evening Post* (New York) during his fifteenth year (Griswold, *post*, p. 395). In Albany, where he had social standing, congenial companions, and access to books, his literary talents were encouraged and enlarged. On Nov. 3, 1841, he married Elizabeth, daughter of Smith Weed of Albany, by whom he had one son. From 1843 to 1844 he was editor of the *Northern Light,* a pretentious literary journal sponsored by a group of prominent citizens of Albany headed by John Adams Dix [*q.v.*]. To it Street contributed twelve poems, and eight articles of some length. He was director of the New York State Library from 1848 to 1862, and continued as law librarian until June 1868. While these posts may have been procured by his friends more in recognition of his renown as a poet than for competence as a librarian, yet he took his directorship seriously, was diligent and attentive, and produced less work of his own while he was librarian than before or after. During these years he wrote *The Council of Revision of the State of New York: Its History* (1859) and compiled *A Digest of Taxation in the States* (1863).

His best known books are *The Burning of Schenectady* (1842), and *Frontenac* (1849), a vigorous historical poem of seven thousand lines, of which a London edition was also issued in 1849. Two books, "Lake and Mountain or Autumn in the Adirondacks" and "Eagle Pine, or Sketches of a New York Frontier Village," said to have been prepared for the press (Allibone, *post*), seem never to have been published. In 1845 *The Poems of Alfred B. Street* appeared. Separately printed occasional poems are *Our State* (1849), *Burgoyne* (1877), *Knowledge and Liberty* (1849), *In Memoriam: President Lincoln Dead* (1870). The poems usually found in anthologies are "The Gray Forest Eagle," which is a spirited patriotic lyric, "Lost Hunter," "The Settler," and the more pretentious "The Burning of Schenectady" and "Frontenac." Street's literary place among American poets has been described as "the same as that generally assigned to Dryden among English poets,—one of the first of the second class" (Allibone, *post*). Primarily a poet of nature, he found his themes in the forests, mountains, and lakes of New York state. His work was marked by close and accurate observation, fidelity of description, directness, and occasionally by animation and vigor. Though he was diffuse, repetitious, sometimes over-minute, his verse scarcely deserves the neglect into which it has fallen. Some of his poems were translated into German, and they were well received in England. Disraeli paid tribute to his "originality and poetic fire"; Poe praised him as a descriptive poet (Allibone, *post*). But critics never noted in him imagination, inspiration, fancy, or high artistry. He was plain in person, taste, and attire; small, mild-mannered, a recluse to the borders of eccentricity.

[H. A. and M. A. Street, *The Street Geneal.* (1895); R. W. Griswold, *The Poets and Poetry of America* (1843); William Hunt, *The Am. Biog. Sketch Book* (1848), pp. 97–101; S. A. Allibone, *A Critical Dict. of Eng. Lit.*, vol. II (1870), with a full list of titles, and references to reviews and critical comments; E. A. and G. L. Duyckinck, *Cyc. of Am. Lit.* (1875), vol. II, p. 434; F. L. Mott, *A Hist. of Am. Mags.* (1930); reviews of Street's poems in *U. S. Mag. and Democratic Rev.*, Jan. 1846, pp. 76–77, and *Am. Rev.*, Apr. 1846, pp. 425–41; memoir in *Bentley's Miscellany*, vol. XXV (1849), pp. 563–66; obituaries in *Albany Argus* and *Albany Evening Jour.*, June 3, 1881.]   J.I.W.

STREET, AUGUSTUS RUSSELL (Nov. 5, 1791–June 12, 1866), leader in art education and in the study of modern languages, and, at the time of his death, "the most munificent benefactor of Yale College since its foundation," was born and bred in New Haven, Conn. He was the eldest of the five children of Titus Street (1758–1842), a prosperous New Haven merchant, and Amaryllis (Atwater) Street, and a descendant of the Rev. Nicholas Street, who came from England to Taunton, Mass., between 1630 and 1638, and later removed to New Haven. He was graduated from Yale in 1812. As he became a confirmed invalid during his student days his college life was singularly uneventful. He was, however, one of the eighteen members of the Phi Beta Kappa Society and one of the twenty-six of the Linonian Society. After graduation he studied law with Judge Charles Chauncey of New Haven but never practised that profession. For a number of years he was a silent partner in the bookselling and publishing firm of Hezekiah Howe & Company of New Haven, and in 1827 he was treasurer of the New Haven Tontine Company, which maintained a hotel facing the Green. He was later the builder and owner of the famous New Haven House and the adjoining property. On Oct. 29, 1815, he married Caroline Mary (b. 1790), the elder daughter of William Leffingwell (1765–1834), a wealthy resident of New Haven. The young couple settled quietly in New Haven and reared a family of girls, whose education their father carefully guided. After the death of Titus Street, the whole family resided in Europe for five years, their travels extending to Greece and Egypt. This gave Street "ample time for study and close observation . . . leading to [the] reflection upon the advantages of a thorough European culture, and the need of rounding out our ordinary American education by the study of the modern languages and the cultivation of the aesthetic arts" (Hoppin, *post,* vol. II, p. 146).

A number of years after his return to New Haven he began a series of notable gifts to Yale in the fields of modern languages and the arts.

These benefactions, which included the establishment of the Titus Street Professorship of Ecclesiastical History and a scholarship in the theological department, began in 1855 with a partial endowment of a professorship of modern languages, which he completed in 1863. During the first century and a quarter, though there had been some instruction, there was no official recognition of modern languages by the college. The first Street Professor of Modern Languages was appointed in 1864. In the same year Street made another important gift. The Trumbull Gallery, the earliest art museum connected with a college or university in America, had been maintained at Yale since 1832. Street now came forward with an offer to erect at his expense a building for a school of the fine arts. The building, designed by Peter Bonnett Wight [q.v.] in the Venetian Gothic style made popular by Ruskin's *The Stones of Venice,* was completed in 1866 shortly after the donor's death, his will having provided for its completion and partial endowment. It was in Street Hall, as it was known, that the important collection of paintings made by James Jackson Jarves [q.v.] was deposited, later to become the possession of the college. After her husband's death Mrs. Street endowed a professorship of painting in fulfillment of his plans, and later one of drawing. In the autumn of 1866 the college corporation created the Yale School of the Fine Arts, founded and partially endowed by the Streets, one of the earliest art schools in the country connected with an institution of higher learning. The "admission of pupils of both sexes" was specified by the donor, thus opening the doors of Yale to women for the first time.

The Streets lived for a dozen or more years in a fine house at the corner of Chapel and Temple Streets but in 1855 lent it to their eldest daughter, who had become the second wife of Rear Admiral Andrew Hull Foote [q.v.]. Later the lonely couple, who survived all seven of their daughters, lived in rooms in the New Haven House. Mrs. Street, who was very popular among Yale undergraduates, continued to live in the New Haven House until her death, at the age of eighty-seven, on Aug. 24, 1877. She built the Street Home for poor girls in Middletown, Conn., and in her will left a considerable sum for a variety of charitable purposes, among them funds for promoting the cause of Protestantism in Mexico. She was buried beside her husband in the Grove Street Cemetery.

[See records of the United Church and First Congregational (Center) Church, New Haven, Conn.; H. A. and M. A. Street, *The Street Geneal.* (1895), where, however, birth and marriage dates are given incorrectly; *Yale Coll. in 1868* (n.d.); F. B. Dexter, *Biog. Sketches Grads. Yale Coll.,* vol. VI (1912), *A Cat. . . . of the Portraits, Busts, etc. Belonging to Yale Univ.* (1892), and *A Selection of the Miscellaneous Hist. Papers of Fifty Years* (1918); *Obit. Record Grads. Yale Coll. . . . 1866* (1866); J. F. Weir, "Yale School of the Fine Arts," and J. M. Hoppin, "Augustus Russell Street," in *Yale Coll.* (2 vols., 1879), ed. by W. L. Kingsley; E. V. Meeks, in *Yale Alumni Weekly,* Nov. 4, 1932; N. P., in *Yale Courant,* June 27, 1866; obituaries in *Daily Register* (New Haven), June 12, *New Haven Daily Morning Jour. and Courier,* June 13, and *Columbia Weekly Register* (New Haven), June 16, 1866; minutes of the Yale Corporation, copies of the wills of Street and his wife, letters, inventories, deeds of property, etc. in the office of the treasurer at Yale. Portraits of Street, his wife, and his father-in-law are at Yale.]   T. S—r.

STREET, JOSEPH MONTFORT (Dec. 18, 1782–May 5, 1840), editor and Indian agent, was born in Lunenburg County, Va., the son of Anthony Waddy and Mary (Stokes) Street and the grandson of John Street of Bristol, England, who settled in New Kent County, Va., early in the eighteenth century. His father was a prosperous planter, a member of the county court, and vestryman of Cumberland Parish, and his mother was the sister of Montfort Stokes [q.v.]. In Richmond he met John Wood, a newspaper man of doubtful reputation from New York, with whom he entered into what Wood later described to Henry Clay as an "ardent friendship" such as "frequently entails misery on those who are the slaves of such a strong passion" (letter of Oct. 9, 1806, Clay Papers, vol. I, no. 75). On July 7, 1806, they began to publish the *Western World* in Frankfort, Ky. A Federalist sheet, it was active in instigating the investigations that proved Benjamin Sebastian [q.v.] guilty of taking a Spanish pension, retired John Brown [q.v.] to private life, and forced Aaron Burr [q.v.] to appear before a grand jury in Kentucky twice in 1806. It also accused Harry Innes [q.v.] of corrupt intrigue, and Innes sued Street for libel. Another libel suit, begun by Christopher Greenup [q.v.], was discontinued upon Street's public retraction. Street was everywhere the object of vituperation and revenge. Challenged to a succession of duels, after demonstrating beyond doubt both his courage and his skill, he refused to fight again and announced that he would merely file further challenges and publish them in proper order. As he grew more intimate, personally and politically, with Humphrey Marshall and Joseph H. Daviess he became estranged from Wood, who accused him of swindling him out of the money invested in the paper and in 1807 withdrew. Street continued to publish the *Western World* for a time but then lost control. The paper declined in popularity, partly through the bitterness of its criticism of the federal government and of the administration of foreign affairs and partly through the changes that came over Kentucky with growing prosperity. He was married, on Oct. 9, 1809, to Eliza Maria (Posey) Thornton, the daughter of Thomas Posey [*q.v.*]. On May 9, 1811, he executed a deed of trust to John Posey conveying more than 6,000 acres of land, six negroes, four horses, two cows, and household furniture in trust for her (Innes Papers, vol. XVIII, no. 40, 2/3 way through vol.). When, a little more than a year later, he lost the suit for libel brought by Innes and was ordered to pay heavy damages, he made the plea that the amount ordered was entirely beyond his means and sought an accommodation (see Innes sketch).

In these circumstances he took his wife and baby son, the first of fourteen children, to the western frontier. During the summer of 1812 he built a log house at Shawneetown, Ill., where he was active in local politics and became a brigadier-general of militia. In 1827 he was appointed Indian agent to the Winnebago at Prairie du Chien. He was later at Rock Island, again at Prairie du Chien, and the last months of his life near the present Agency City, Iowa. Without comprehending the essential difficulties or possibilities of the Indian problem he maintained cordial relations with his wards and was active in defending them. He sought, unsuccessfully, in 1827 to remove Henry Dodge [*q.v.*] and the other squatters at the lead mines reserved by treaty to the Winnebago. He caused the arrest of Jean Brunett in 1829 for cutting timber on Indian lands and was himself forced to pay a fine for exceeding his authority. In 1838 he undertook, again unsuccessfully, to prevent fraud in disbursing monies to the Winnebago under a commission composed of Simon Cameron [*q.v.*] and James Murray. He was hopeful that westward removal would help the Indians and advocated mission schools, training in agriculture and industrial crafts, division of land in severalty, and the curtailment of the influence of the fur traders. He rendered valuable service to the government in the Black Hawk War, keeping the Winnebago neutral and, after the capture of Black Hawk [*q.v.*], persuading them to deliver the prisoner to the federal army. He died near the present Agency City, Iowa.

[Issues of the *Western World* in Harper Library, Univ. of Chicago, through the courtesy of Winifred Ver Nooy, Chicago; Street letters and papers in Hist., Memorial and Art Department of Iowa, Des Moines, in Wis. State Hist. Lib., Madison, and in files of the Indian office, Washington, D. C.; Clay Papers and Harry Innes Papers, esp. vols. XVIII, XXII, in Lib. of Cong.; *Annals of Iowa*, Apr. 1901, Jan. 1921, Apr. 1927; "The Edwards Papers," *Chicago Hist. Soc. Colls.*, vol. III (1884), ed. by E. B. Washburne; W. B. Street, "General Joseph M. Street," *Annals of Iowa*, July–Oct. 1895; I. M. Street, "Joseph M. Street's Last Fight with the Fur Traders," *Ibid.*, Oct. 1929; George Wilson, "A Neglected Kentucky Hero," *Register of the Ky. Hist. Soc.*, Sept. 1906; R. G. Thwaites, "The Ohio Valley Press," *Proc. Am. Antiquarian Soc.*, n.s., XIX (1909); L. C. Bell, *The Old Free State . . . Hist. of Lunenburg County* (1927), vol. II, p. 338; Wm. Meade, *Old Churches* (1857), vol. I; H. A. and M. A. Street, *The Street Geneal.* (1895); *Wm. and Mary College Quart.*, Apr. 1928; *Va. Mag. of Hist. and Biog.*, Apr. 1904, p. 422.]   K. E. C.

STRICKLAND, WILLIAM (*c.* 1787–Apr. 6, 1854), architect, engineer, engraver, was born of humble parents in Philadelphia. His father, John, was a carpenter who during William's boyhood worked for Benjamin H. Latrobe [*q.v.*], and through this connection the son came to the notice of Latrobe, from whom he received his professional training. In 1807 he accompanied his father to New York, where the latter was engaged in the remodeling of the Park Theatre, and here learned something of scene painting. Upon his return to Philadelphia, finding at the moment little demand for his services as an architect, he set himself up "as a sort of artist in general" (Kane, *post*, p. 29), selling landscapes when he could, painting scenery, making designs for carpenters and plasterers. He became a competent engraver and aquatinter, executed a number of plates for the *Port Folio* and the *Analectic Magazine*—chiefly dealing with scenes and episodes of the War of 1812— and made fourteen engravings from the drawings of David Porter [*q.v.*] to illustrate Porter's *Journal of a Cruise Made to the Pacific Ocean . . . 1812, 1813, and 1814* (2 vols., 1815). He was not an educated man in any formal sense, but by nature he was endowed with a remarkable visual memory, good reasoning powers, and a skilful hand. That he was one of those men who can undertake successfully almost any kind of work is evidenced by his varied achievements in the fields of architecture and engineering.

In the former field, he is remembered as an outstanding exponent of the Greek Revival in America, which had its first monument in the Bank of Pennsylvania, designed by his preceptor, Latrobe. Judge John Kintzing Kane [*q.v.*], who delivered an obituary oration on Strickland before the American Philosophical Society, which had elected him to membership in 1820, characterized his taste as disciplined in the severe harmonies of Grecian architecture, adding that he became a purist in art as he grew older, caring less and less for decoration. This fact is illustrated by the contrast between his first building, the Masonic Temple, Philadelphia (so-called Gothic, 1810), and his later, coldly severe, Custom House, still standing. The latter, built for the Bank of the United States and com-

Strickland

pleted in 1824, was modeled on the Parthenon. Strickland had a more graceful side, however, which appears in his Merchants' Exchange (1834), likewise in Philadelphia. This delightful building is unique because of its colonnade curved on plan, and because it is crowned with a copy of the Choragic Monument of Lysicrates. Colonial and early Federal architecture, harking back to Rome by way of England, France, and the Italian Renaissance, was committed to domes, but the Greek Revivalists could not use the dome, that most precious property of their predecessors, because there was no precedent for it in Greek architecture. Strickland substituted the Monument of Lysicrates, and has been called the inventor of this happy expedient (Tallmadge, *post*). Among his other Philadelphia buildings were the first United States Custom House (1819), the New Chestnut Street Theatre (1822), St. Stephen's Church, a Jewish synagogue, the Friends' Lunatic Asylum, the United States Naval Asylum (1827), and the United States Mint (1829). In 1828 he designed a restoration, in wood, of the original steeple of the State House (Independence Hall); he designed the marble sarcophagus of Washington at Mount Vernon and certain alterations in Washington's tomb (1837), and at the time of his death was engaged on the Tennessee capitol, Nashville, beneath which distinguished work of the period he was buried.

Concurrently with his architectural work, he was engaged in numerous significant engineering enterprises. In 1824 he made a reconnaissance for the Chesapeake and Delaware Canal. In 1825, taking with him his young assistant, Samuel Honeyman Kneass [*q.v.*], he went to Great Britain for the Pennsylvania Society for the Promotion of Internal Improvement, to investigate canals, roads, railways, and bridges, and upon his return made a report asserting that railroads were bound in time to supersede the canals then being built so extensively. This view was considered altogether too impracticable for the Society to accept, and accordingly Judge Kane rewrote the last paragraphs of Strickland's report before publication (Kane, *post*, p. 30). Upon his return to the United States, Strickland became engineer for the Pennsylvania State Canal. He designed and built the Delaware Breakwater, begun in 1829, for the United States government, and in 1835 he made the survey for a railroad between Wilmington, Del., and the Susquehanna River. He was subsequently one of the editors of *Public Works of the United States of America* (London, 1841), a folio atlas of plates, and its accompanying vol-

Stringfellow

ume, *Reports, Specifications and Estimates of Public Works in the United States of America* (1841). Other publications of his include the important *Reports on Canals, Railways, Roads, and Other Subjects Made to "The Pennsylvania Society for the Promotion of Internal Improvement"* (1826); *Address upon a Proposed Railroad from Wilmington to the Susquehanna* (1835); and *Tomb of Washington at Mount Vernon* (1840).

[Memorial address by J. K. Kane, *Proc. Am. Philosophical Soc.*, vol. VI (1859); Joseph Jackson, *Early Phila. Architects and Engineers* (1923), and *Encyc. of Phila.*, vol. IV (1933); J. T. Scharf and Thompson Westcott, *Hist. of Phila.* (3 vols., 1884); Wm. Dunlap, *A Hist. of the Rise and Progress of the Arts and Design in the U. S.* (3 vols., 1918), ed. by F. W. Bayley and C. E. Goodspeed; T. E. Tallmadge, *The Story of Architecture in America* (copr. 1927); A. F. Harlow, *Old Towpaths* (1926); F. A. Cleveland and F. W. Powell, *Railroad Promotion and Capitalization in the U. S.* (1909); *Republican Daily Banner and Nashville Whig*, Apr. 8, 1854.]   A. M. B.

STRINGFELLOW, FRANKLIN (June 18, 1840–June 8, 1913), Confederate Scout, was born at "The Retreat" near Raccoon Ford, Culpeper County, Va., where his father, Rittenhouse, and grandfather, Robert, had lived and played the rôle of planter for many years. His mother was Anne (Slaughter) Stringfellow, a member of another family of local distinction. He was named Benjamin Franklin Stringfellow but was usually known as Frank. He was sent to school first in Albemarle County and then at the Episcopal High School of Alexandria. From Alexandria he went to Shuqualak, Noxubee County, Miss., where he became teacher of Latin and Greek in the Stanton School. Drawn back to Virginia by the intense excitements of the spring of 1861, he sought to enter the Confederate army. Delicate in health and weighing only ninety-four pounds, his applications were several times rejected. However, on May 28, 1861, he attained the status of a private in the Powatan troop, 4th Virginia Cavalry, and rendered distinguished service as a courier in the battle of Bull Run, which led to his assignment to the staff of Gen. J. E. B. Stuart, who asked his appointment to a captaincy the next year. After the battle of Gettysburg he was attached to the staff of Gen. Robert E. Lee for secret scout service, whence he rose to the rank of chief of scouts in the Army of Northern Virginia. Small and wiry of stature, he sometimes entered the lines of the enemy as a woman, moved about under different disguises, hid himself under brush heaps at night near Union headquarters and managed to read army orders before they were issued and to forward the information to General Lee. His services were many and extraordinary and all but caused the defeat of General Grant in the battle of the Wilderness in 1864. He was many times a prisoner within the Union lines, from which he escaped again and again with valuable information. Detained as a spy in the Old Capitol prison in 1865, he managed to escape just before the assassination of Lincoln and, having stopped on his way home at the house of Mrs. Mary E. Surratt, he was naturally in some danger and hurried away to Canada, where he remained some years. When the excitements of 1865 and 1866 calmed he returned to Fairfax County, Va., where he married Emma Frances Greene, the daughter of James Greene, and took up his residence at "Wakefield," in the vain hope that the old planter life of his boyhood might be renewed. They had six children.

Being of a most religious nature, he studied theology at the Episcopal Seminary in Virginia and was graduated in 1876. For thirty years he served different parishes as a clergyman in the Episcopal church; and toward the end of the century he became one of the most popular public lecturers in the South, using the amazing experiences of his scout life for his themes. He held audiences spellbound for two hours at a time rehearsing the hairbreadth escapes from enemy headquarters, his services as a spy in Washington City, and his inventiveness when the enemy seemed about to make an end of him. His closing years were spent as rector of Saint John's Church, Mechanicsville, in Louisa County, not far from the scenes of his wartime exploits.

[Personal letters from Jefferson Davis, Robert E. Lee, and J. E. B. Stuart, published in an undated pamphlet *War Reminiscences*; *War of the Rebellion: Official Records* (Army), 1 ser., XI, pt. 2, XXIX, pt. 1; XXXIII, XXXVI, pt. 3; P. A. Bruce, *Brave Deeds of Confederate Soldiers* (copr. 1916); W. A. R. Goodwin, *Hist. of the Theological Seminary in Va.* (1924), II, 154; L. S. Watkins, *The Life of Horace Stringfellow* (1931), esp. pp. 104–06, 125–28, 148–51; *Geneal. and Hist. Notes on Culpeper County, Va.* (1900), comp. by R. T. Green; information from his grandson, Frank Stringfellow Barr, University of Virginia; the author heard him deliver some of his lectures.] W. E. D.

STRINGHAM, SILAS HORTON (Nov. 7, 1797–Feb. 7, 1876), naval officer, son of Capt. Daniel Stringham and Abigail (Horton) Stringham, was born in Middletown, N. Y. He entered the navy as a midshipman, Nov. 15, 1809, serving first in the frigate *President* under Commodore John Rodgers, 1773–1838 [*q.v.*]. In this ship he participated in the *Little Belt* affair, and during the War of 1812 took part in the engagement with the *Belvidera*. During the second war with Algiers he served in the brig *Spark* in Commodore Isaac Chauncey's squadron, returning

to the United States in 1818. While on this station he distinguished himself during a storm near Gibraltar by going to the rescue of a capsized French brig. Though he and his men rescued the crew, he was unable to return to port and was blown off Algeciras, where his boat capsized, and one of his own men and two Frenchmen were drowned. He was an officer in the *Cyane* when in 1820 she convoyed the *Elizabeth,* the vessel that carried the first settlers to Liberia. For the next two years he served on the African coast, assisting in the suppression of the slave trade. Two slavers were captured, one American from Baltimore and one Spaniard. With these two ships under his command he captured two more slavers, all of which he brought to New York, where they were condemned as prizes. He spent the next two years as executive officer of the *Hornet* in the West Indies in operations against the pirates. There the pirate schooner *Moscow* and other vessels were captured. From 1823 until the opening of the Mexican War his naval career was quite uneventful, but in 1847 he was given command of the ship-of-the-line *Ohio,* and in her took part in the bombardment of Vera Cruz, being present at the capitulation of the city. For a short time he commanded the Brazilian squadron and from 1853 to 1855 was in command of the Mediterranean squadron with the ill-fated *Cumberland* as his flagship.

In March 1861 he was summoned to Washington to confer with Gideon Welles, secretary of the navy, regarding the relief of Fort Sumter. Welles wrote, "Whilst there were doubts and uncertainty on every hand as to who could be trusted, I knew Commodore Stringham to be faithful, and . . . selected him to assist me in matters of detail. With him I communicated freely and fully in regard to the condition of Sumter . . ." (*Diary of Gideon Welles, post,* p. 5). Stringham made definite plans for the relief of the beleaguered garrison but was forced to give them over. He took command of the Atlantic blockading fleet, May 13, 1861, and planned a combined naval and military expedition against the forts at Hatteras Inlet, N. C., guarding Pamlico Sound. Stringham himself took command of the attacking fleet, supported by Gen. Benjamin F. Butler in command of the land forces. The bombardment began on Aug. 28, 1861, and the two forts capitulated the following day. It was the first great naval victory of the war. In compliance with orders, Stringham returned with his fleet to Hampton Roads. Though the Northern press criticized him severely for not advancing with his fleet into Pamlico Sound, it was proved that his vessels drew too much water to advance further, and that, moreover, his orders were to return to Hampton Roads. Wounded by this criticism, however, and irritated by a rebuke from the Navy Department for allowing vessels to slip through the blockade, he asked on Sept. 16, 1861, to be relieved of his command. He was made rear-admiral on the retired list the following year, and for the last two years of the war served as commandant of the Boston navy yard. His expedition against the Hatteras forts was ably planned and admirably conducted, not a single Union man being lost. In relieving him of his command Welles expressed high appreciation of his patriotism and zeal. After his retirement from the service he spent his declining years in Brooklyn, N. Y. In 1819 he married Henrietta Hicks, by whom he had four daughters.

[The date of birth is from G. F. Horton, *The Hortons in America* (1929), ed. by A. H. White. See also L. R. Hamersly, *The Records of Living Officers of the U. S. Navy* (4th ed., 1890); U. S. Navy Dept. Registers; *War of the Rebellion: Official Records* (*Navy*); manuscript Log of U. S. S. *Ohio*, 1847–48; *Diary of Gideon Welles* (1911), vol. I, pp. 5–12; *Private and Official Correspondence of Gen. Benjamin F. Butler* (5 vols., 1917); J. T. Headley, *Farragut and Our Naval Commanders* (1867); *Army and Navy Jour.*, Feb. 12, 19, 1876; and obituary in *N. Y. Times*, Feb. 8, 1876. Information has been supplied by Stringham's grand-daughter.]   L. H. B.

STRINGHAM, WASHINGTON IRVING (Dec. 10, 1847–Oct. 5, 1909), mathematician, was born in Yorkshire Center (later Delevan), N. Y., the youngest of nine children of Henry and Eliza (Tomlinson) Stringham. He was a descendant in the fourth generation of Jacob Stringham, of Huguenot ancestry. In 1865 he went to Topeka, Kan., where he studied in the preparatory department of Lincoln (later Washburn) College, and between 1867 and 1873 spent three years in the college itself, interrupting his college course at intervals to work at sign-painting and bookkeeping. In 1873 he entered Harvard College, and in 1877, at the age of thirty, he graduated with the degree of A.B. At Harvard he came under the influence of Benjamin Peirce [*q.v.*] and was initiated by him into the mysteries of the relatively new branch of quaternions. Upon his graduation from Harvard he was appointed to a fellowship in the Johns Hopkins University, where he studied for three years under James Joseph Sylvester [*q.v.*], taking the degree of Ph.D. in 1880. It was during this period that he contributed to the *Proceedings of the American Academy of Arts and Sciences* (vol. XIII, 1878) his first piece of original work, "Investigations on Quaternions." While he was working at Johns Hopkins he also contributed to the *American Journal of Mathematics*, then almost the sole medium in the United States for mathematical papers of distinctly high quality, three important memoirs: "Some General Formulæ for Integrals of Irrational Functions" (June 1879), "The Quaternion Formulæ for Quantification of Curves, Surfaces, and Solids and for Barycentres" (September 1879), and "Regular Figures in n-dimensional Space" (March 1880). After leaving Johns Hopkins he spent two years, 1880–82, at Leipzig, which Felix Klein was then making one of the mathematical foci of Europe, on the Parker fellowship of Harvard. He was thus among the early pupils of two men, Peirce and Klein, whose influence upon American mathematics was destined to be so marked in the quarter of a century which followed. Leaving Germany, he became professor of mathematics in the University of California (1882), where he remained until his death, and where he was active in setting a high standard of scholarship. He married on June 28, 1888, Martha Sherman Day, great-grand-daughter of Jeremiah Day [*q.v.*].

He was a frequent contributor to the *American Journal of Mathematics*, the *Transactions of the American Mathematical Society*, the *Proceedings of the American Association for the Advancement of Science*, and the publications of various other learned bodies. He was vice-president of the American Mathematical Society (1906) and a member of its council (1902–05). His books were not so important as his contributions to mathematical periodicals. He revised the English algebra of Charles Smith, *Elementary Algebra for the Use of Preparatory Schools* (New York, 1894), but the work was too scholarly for general use in the United States at that time. In 1893 there appeared his *Uniplanar Algebra: Being Pt. 1 of a Propaedeutic to the Higher Mathematical Analysis*, a part of which had already been published (1891) as a synopsis of a course of university extension lectures given in San Francisco during the winter of 1891–92. The work, however, was not well adapted to the classroom. He died at Berkeley at the age of sixty-two years, survived by his wife, two daughters and a son.

[*Who's Who in America*, 1908–09; *Harvard Coll. Class of 1877: Seventh Report, June 1917* (n.d.), with bibliog.; W. T. Reid, in *Univ. of Cal. Chronicle*, Jan. 1910; M. W. Haskell, *Ibid.*; W. C. Jones, *Illus. Hist. of the Univ. of Cal.* (1895); obituary in *Los Angeles Times*, Oct. 6, 1909.]   D. E. S.

STROBEL, EDWARD HENRY (Dec. 7, 1855–Jan. 15, 1908), diplomatist, was the son of Caroline Lydia (Bullock) and Maynard Davis Strobel. He was born in Charleston, S. C., where his great-grandfather had settled about a century earlier. His father, a bank cashier, died in 1868, after losing all his money in Confederate bonds. In spite of such discouraging circumstances, Strobel entered Harvard College and graduated in 1877. Graduating from the Harvard Law School in 1882, he was admitted to the New York bar in 1883 and for a time practised law in New York City. He decided, however, that the legal profession was overcrowded and turned to the field of international affairs. He wrote for the Cleveland campaign *Mr. Blaine and His Foreign Policy: An Examination of His Most Important Dispatches While Secretary of State* (1884), and in August 1885 Cleveland appointed him secretary of the legation at Madrid. He served until March 1890, acting as chargé d'affaires about one-third of the time. He made two important visits to Morocco, in which his diplomatic ability was strikingly demonstrated. He was third assistant secretary of state, 1893 to 1894, when he was appointed minister to Ecuador. In December of the same year he became minister to Chile. His comprehensive report on *Resumption of Specie Payments in Chile* (1896) was regarded as a timely and authoritative document on the currency question. Before leaving Santiago in 1897, at the request of France and Chile he acted as arbitrator of the Fréraut claim, with such satisfactory results that the French government made him an officer in the Legion of Honor in 1898, and in 1899 he was appointed counsel for Chile before the United States and Chilean claims commission at Washington. Returning to the United States he published *The Spanish Revolution, 1868-1875* (1898), for which he had gathered material at Madrid. The same year he was appointed Bemis Professor of International Law in the Harvard Law School.

In 1903 he became general adviser to the government of Siam, with the rank of minister plenipotentiary. He sailed in October 1903 for Paris, where the French foreign office and the Siamese minister were negotiating a treaty. The treaty was signed on Feb. 13, 1904, and he carried it with him to Bangkok. Almost immediately he gained the confidence and affection of the Siamese people to a remarkable degree. He accomplished the abolition of licensed gambling, which not only had a tremendous hold upon the people but furnished the government with a substantial revenue, and worked out a compensating system of land-tax laws and import duties. He effected a revision of the harbor regulations, a task necessitating skilful negotiations with the treaty powers, reorganization of the telegraph and pos-

tal services, extension of the government railways, the abolition of debt slavery, revision of the penal code, and improvement of the courts. New treaties favorable to Siam were concluded with Italy and Denmark. Siam's first foreign loan was negotiated in Paris and London, establishing her international financial standing. In November 1905 the King bestowed upon him the highest honor in Siam, the Grand Cross of the Order of the White Elephant. A month later he left Siam for a year's leave of absence in America. While visiting Egypt on the way, he was stricken with a grave illness, a streptococcic infection, apparently resulting from an insect's sting. He was removed to Paris and then to the United States. On Jan. 2, 1907, making light of his illness, he sailed again for Siam. He reached Bangkok the first of March, and although confined to his bed and suffering much pain he mustered all his energies to the task of negotiating a new treaty with France, which was signed on Mar. 23. This settled issues that had been a source of irritation between Siam and France for decades, and for the first time relations between the two nations were on a stable and friendly basis. The French government made him a grand officer of the Legion of Honor. He died in Bangkok at the beginning of the next year. He had never married.

[Letters in Lindsay Swift Correspondence, in Widener Lib., Harvard Univ.; official correspondence in archives of the state department; sketch by Lindsay Swift, *Harvard Graduates' Mag.*, March 1908 and briefer note in *Harvard College Class of 1877, Seventh Report* (1917); *Harper's Weekly*, Mar. 21, 1908; *American Jour. of International Law*, Jan. 1908; *Who's Who in America*, 1906–07; *Proc. Mass. Hist. Soc.*, vol. XLIX (1916); *Boston Evening Transcript*, Jan. 16, 18, 1908; *Boston Globe*, Jan. 16, 1908.]   I.L.T.

STROMME, PEER OLSEN (Sept. 15, 1856–Sept. 15, 1921), journalist and author, the third of the thirteen children of Ole and Eli (Haugen) Olsen, was born in Winchester, Wis. His grandparents had emigrated to America from Norway. At the age of thirteen he was sent to Luther College, Decorah, Iowa, and was graduated with the A.B. degree in 1876. He studied theology at Concordia Seminary in St. Louis, Mo., from 1876 to 1879, and was ordained to the Lutheran ministry. He served Norwegian congregations near Hendrum, Minn., and on the Dakota side of Red River from 1879 to 1881, in Ada, Minn., 1881 to 1886, and near Nelson, Wis., 1886 to 1887. While at Ada, he was also superintendent of schools of Norman County. He taught for one year at St. Olaf College, Northfield, Minn., and then he turned to journalism. He edited *Norden*, a Norwegian weekly, published in Chicago, from 1888 to 1890, and again in 1892. In the interval he made his initial visit to Norway, followed from time to time by ten other visits to Europe, including two journeys around the world as press correspondent in 1906 and 1910. In 1892 he bought and edited the *Superior Posten,* Superior, Wis., but soon gave it up to accept the headship of an academy at Mount Horeb, Wis. In 1894 he did journalistic work for the *Milwaukee Journal,* and from 1895 to 1898 edited the *Amerika,* a Norwegian weekly published in Chicago. From 1898 to 1900 he was on the editorial staff of the *Minneapolis Times,* covering especially the Minnesota state legislature. He did editorial work on the *Politikken* and the *Vor Tid,* Minneapolis periodicals, in 1904–05. In 1909 he was editor of the *Eidsvold,* a Norwegian magazine issued at Grand Forks, N. D., and, from 1911 to 1918, of the *Nordmanden,* published in the same city. He also wrote for the *Decorah Posten,* Decorah, Iowa, the *Daily News* and the *Skandinaven,* of Chicago.

Stromme was a Democrat and from time to time published campaign literature, organized democratic societies, and delivered political addresses for his party. In 1898 he ran on the Democratic ticket in Wisconsin for the office of state treasurer, but failed to be elected. He was a popular lecturer on Norwegian culture and literature, subjects to which he was deeply devoted. He was an unusually effective platform speaker, of fluent speech and ready wit, tall, and Viking-like, with a rugged, jovial face. His memory for poetry was phenomenal and he possessed a museum of telling mimicry. He was known as the Mark Twain among Norwegian Americans. His best contribution to fiction was *Hvorledes Halvor blev Prest* (1893), an excellent description of the early period of the Norwegian-Americans immigration. *Unge Helgesen* (1906) does not match it in literary value. He compiled a *Compend of Church History* (1902), and wrote discriminatingly about Mark Twain and Waldemar Ager, journalist and novelist, for *Symra,* a literary magazine. A volume of his poems, *Digte,* was published in 1921.

Stromme was a translator of ability. He received a prize for his translation of Aasmund Vinje's "Fedraminne." In 1909 he translated Gustav Frenssen's *Jörn Uhl* (1901) into English and stories by Byron A. Dunn and Stanley Waterloo into Norwegian. His most careful work was the translation into English of *Laaches Husandagtsbog,* a Norwegian devotional classic, under the title *Laache's Book of Family Prayer* (1902). In 1918 he translated J. W. Gerard's *My Four Years in Germany* (1917) into Norwegian. His memoirs, *Erindringer,* published in

book form in 1923, first appeared in the *Nordmanden,* and contain descriptions of hundreds of contemporaries whom the author learned to know in his busy, colorful career, as a student, minister, schoolman, author, lecturer, campaigner, newspaper man, and traveler, and is a highly creditable contribution to cultural history. Stromme was married to Laura Marie Eriksen, of Lansing, Iowa, on Nov. 12, 1879. She and six children survived him.

[*Who's Who in America,* 1920–21; *Who's Who Among Pastors in all the Norwegian Luth. Synods of America* (rev. ed. 1928); Stromme's memoirs, *Erindringer* (1923); *Luther Coll. Through Sixty Years* (1922); *Wis. State Jour.,* Sept. 15, 1921.]   J. O. E.

STRONG, AUGUSTUS HOPKINS (Aug. 3, 1836–Nov. 29, 1921), theologian, born at Rochester, N. Y., was the son of Alvah and Catharine (Hopkins) Strong and a descendant of John Strong who came to Massachusetts in 1630 and was subsequently one of the founders of Northampton. Alvah Strong was for years publisher of the *Rochester Democrat,* and Augustus, after preparatory studies at Rochester Collegiate Institute, had one year of business experience in that newspaper's office. He graduated from Yale College in 1857 and from Rochester Theological Seminary in 1859, then spent a year at the University of Berlin and in travel.

Returning to America, he was ordained to the Baptist ministry at Haverhill, Mass., Aug. 3, 1861. He served as pastor of the First Baptist Church of Haverhill, 1861–65, and of the First Baptist Church of Cleveland, Ohio, 1865–72. Here he acquired a reputation as a scholarly preacher, possessing keen theological discernment. Among his parishioners was Mr. John D. Rockefeller, whose daughter later married Strong's eldest son. In 1872 Strong was chosen president of Rochester Theological Seminary and professor of Biblical theology, succeeding Ezekiel Gilman Robinson [*q.v.*] in both positions. He served actively in his double rôle until 1912, when he retired with the title of president emeritus. Vigorous minded, affable, yet somewhat awe-inspiring, Strong has been ranked with William Newton Clarke, Alvah Hovey [*qq.v.*], and George W. Northrup as one of the four most influential Baptist theological teachers of his period. He represented the dogmatic tradition but, like the others, encouraged his students to pursue their own researches in the entire realm of truth. His method provided a large place for historical theology, but he was probably less influential than Clarke in promoting historical research in the Biblical field. The most liberal period of his career was probably the decade centering about the turn of the century.

Aside from his classroom teaching, he had wide influence through his theological writings. His *Systematic Theology* (1886), much enlarged in the three-volume edition of 1907–09, found its way into many a minister's library, as did his *Philosophy and Religion* (1888) and *Christ in Creation and Ethical Monism* (1899). Two volumes entitled *Miscellanies* (vols. I and II, 1912) gathered up various papers and addresses, historical and theological; of more popular interest were six other published works: *The Great Poets and Their Theology* (1897); *One Hundred Chapel-Talks to Theological Students* (1913); *Union with Christ* (1913); *Popular Lectures on the Books of the New Testament* (1914); *American Poets and Their Theology* (1916); and *A Tour of the Missions, Observations and Conclusions* (1918). This last book, the result of a world tour of Baptist mission fields made by Strong and his wife in 1916–17, is an evidence of his lifelong interest in the foreign mission movement. Considerably more than a hundred of his students went to the foreign fields; he served as president of the American Baptist Missionary Union from 1892 till 1895; on many occasions his counsel was sought, and he was often called upon for missionary sermons and addresses.

His educational influence was not limited to the administration of his own seminary. From 1884 to 1918 he served as trustee of Vassar College, from 1906 to 1911 being chairman of the board. Perhaps his greatest contribution to the cause of education was his share in starting the movement which resulted in the establishment of the new University of Chicago. Having long felt the inadequacy of opportunity for higher education under Baptist auspices, he conceived of the organization of a true university in New York City, with opportunities for research such as did not exist at that time, although Columbia University was soon to provide them. He tried to interest Mr. John D. Rockefeller in the plan and printed a pamphlet setting forth the importance of university education and pointing out the tendency in Europe and in America toward the great centers of population as the foci of educational enterprise. He received many responses, and these, with the pamphlet, he laid before Mr. Rockefeller, with whom he also discussed the matter during a trip to Europe. Furthermore, it was Strong who introduced William Rainey Harper [*q.v.*] to Mr. Rockefeller, having previously characterized Harper as the greatest organizer among American Baptists. Thus, while his own project was not adopted and Thomas W. Goodspeed and Frederick T. Gates [*qq.v.*] were undoubtedly chiefly responsible for securing Mr.

Rockefeller's support for the refounding of the University of Chicago, Strong seems to have been the man who first inculcated the university idea in Mr. Rockefeller's mind (F. T. Gates, in *Fourth Annual Meeting of the American Baptist Education Society,* 1892). Strong was a founder of the Rochester Historical Society and its president in 1890. He was married on Nov. 6, 1861, to Harriet Louise, daughter of Eleazer Savage; she died in 1914, and on Jan. 1, 1915, he married Marguerite Geraldine, daughter of Gerrit van Ingen and widow of John Jay Jones. She, with four daughters and two sons of his first marriage, survived him.

[*The Record* (Rochester Theological Seminary), May 1912, and supplement to issue of May 1922; unpublished autobiographic account of the effort to establish a Baptist university in New York; J. H. Strong, "Augustus Hopkins Strong," *Rochester Hist. Soc. Pubs.,* vol. I (1922); *Yale Univ. Obit. Record,* 1922; T. W. Goodspeed, *A Hist. of the Univ. of Chicago* (1916); *Who's Who in America,* 1920–21; B. W. Dwight, *The Hist. of the Descendants of Elder John Strong* (2 vols., 1871); *Democrat and Chronicle* (Rochester, N. Y.), Nov. 30, 1921.]   W. H. A.

STRONG, BENJAMIN (Dec. 22, 1872–Oct. 16, 1928), banker, was born at Fishkill on Hudson, N. Y., the son of Benjamin and Adeline Torrey (Schenck) Strong, and a descendant of John Strong who emigrated to Massachusetts in 1630 and in 1659 settled in Northampton. His grandfather, Oliver Smith Strong, had been a merchant in New York, while his father had experience in the management of railroad properties and in financial administration. Graduating from the high school of Montclair, N. J., at eighteen, he entered upon duty with the firm of Jesup, Paton & Company (later Cuyler, Morgan & Company), private bankers of New York. In 1901 he became assistant secretary in the Atlantic Trust Company, and in 1903 secretary of the newly organized Bankers' Trust Company. He married in 1895 Margaret Guitton Le Boutillier (d. 1905), daughter of John Le Boutillier of New York. On Apr. 10, 1907, he married Katherine Converse, a daughter of E. C. Converse, from whom he was divorced in 1920. After serving as vice-president, on Jan. 1, 1914, he became president of the Bankers' Trust Company, but soon he was appointed governor of the Federal Reserve Bank of New York, organized in 1914.

This selection was unexpected, for Strong had been active in the movement which aimed to secure the adoption of what was known as the Aldrich Bill (the banking reform plan proposed under the authority of the National Monetary Commission) and had supported the congressional campaign against the Federal Reserve

Act. Assuming office, he found the country convulsed by the early financial difficulties attendant upon the World War and the government desirous of hastening the organization of the Reserve institutions. Though he sharply opposed the hasty opening of the Federal Reserve banks, a peremptory order issued by the secretary of the treasury, W. G. McAdoo, compelled their opening on Nov. 16, 1914. The Federal Reserve Bank of New York took root slowly, most of the local institutions being opposed to it. Following the entrance of the United States into the war, however, it grew rapidly and was for years largely occupied with the financing of the successive issues of Liberty Bonds, in harmony with policies formulated in Washington. After the close of the World War there was an active movement in New York financial circles for the broadened use, in securities operations and in foreign trade, of the new funds growing out of the war profits of American industry and the inflowing tide of gold. Although Strong had from the first opposed the introduction and development of the "open-market powers" of the Federal Reserve system, he now perceived their great possibilities and began to use them. His object, explained in a memorandum written at the end of 1924, was to produce in that year of recession a condition of "easy money," designed to foster business activity and to raise commodity and security prices (Burgess, *post,* p. 256). Later, the Federal Reserve system was unable to cope with the outburst of speculation which reached a climax in 1929, though Strong had advocated a credit pressure which might have averted the ultimate collapse (*Ibid.*, pp. xxii–xxiii). During its earlier stages his policy probably assisted some of the European countries to facilitate, by international credit expansion, a premature movement toward the restoration of the gold standard. Its ultimate fruits, however, were slow in maturing. Strong paid frequent visits abroad and came to be regarded by many foreigners as the real head of the Federal Reserve system. Meanwhile he had drawn nearer to his end, partly owing to tuberculosis, a disease which he had contracted in 1916. During the post-war period frequent leaves of long duration necessitated his entrusting the management of the bank to others, though he had never been willing to give up control, and at the time of his death in October 1928 he had been absent from active work several months. A man of positive and dominant personality, he died in New York City, survived by his two sons and three daughters.

[B. W. Dwight, *The Hist. of the Descendants of Elder John Strong, of Northampton, Mass.* (1871), vol. I; *Who's Who in America,* 1928–29; W. R. Burgess,

ed., *Interpretations of Federal Reserve Policy in the Speeches and Writings of Benjamin Strong* (1930), with biog. sketch and reports of Strong's testimony before committees of the Senate and the House of Representatives, 1922–28; unpublished minutes and docs. of the Federal Reserve Board, 1914–28; obituaries in *N. Y. Evening Post,* Oct. 16, and *N. Y. Times,* Oct. 17, 1928; information from family in regard to certain dates.]

H. P. W.

STRONG, CALEB (Jan. 9, 1745–Nov. 7, 1819), lawyer and Federalist statesman, was born in Northampton, Mass., the son of Caleb Strong, a tanner, and Phebe (Lyman). He was fifth in descent from John Strong, who emigrated to Massachusetts in 1630, settling ultimately in Northampton. Prepared by Rev. Samuel Moody of York, he entered Harvard College, graduating in 1764 with highest honors. On his way home he contracted smallpox, which permanently impaired his sight, but after family help in reading law, and study under Joseph Hawley [*q.v.*], he was admitted to the bar in 1772. Chosen a selectman of Northampton the same year, he served from 1774 throughout the Revolution on the town's committee of safety. He sat in the General Court of 1776 and thenceforward for twenty-four years he served as county attorney. A delegate to the Massachusetts constitutional convention of 1779, he was a member of its drafting committee. He sat in 1780 on the last Massachusetts Council to wield the executive power. The same year he declined a seat in the Continental Congress, becoming a state senator and serving until 1789. In 1783 he declined, for pecuniary reasons, an appointment to the supreme judicial court.

Strong represented Massachusetts in the Federal Convention of 1787, sharing modestly in its work till August, when he was called home by illness in his family. Although favoring a stronger Union, he upheld democratic town-meeting principles, advocating low salaries and annual elections of representatives. He desired one rank and mode of election for the houses of Congress; yet, to conciliate the small states, he voted for the vital compromise which accorded them equal representation in the Senate. He opposed a council of revision; preferred a choice of the president by Congress to the institution of the electoral college; and moved successfully that the House alone should originate money bills, though the Senate might amend them. A leading Federalist in the Massachusetts ratifying convention, he was active and persuasive. Chosen senator from Massachusetts in 1789, he drew a four-year term. He was active in framing the Judiciary Act and served on numerous committees which drafted other formative laws—legal, financial, and miscellaneous. Forming, with

Oliver Ellsworth and Rufus King [*qq.v.*], an Administration bulwark in the Senate, he was chosen in 1791 to report Hamilton's plan for a national bank. After his reëlection in 1793, he actively urged a mission to England and supported Jay's Treaty. In 1796 he resigned and resumed private law practice.

Four years later, on the eve of Jeffersonian victory in the nation, the Massachusetts Federalists chose Strong as their candidate for governor. He consistently shared his party's views, but without its domineering temper and asperities. Of simple, engaging manner, he was conciliatory toward friend and opponent. He was a sober Calvinist withal, guided by duty, deliberate and firm in judgment, and the Massachusetts electorate found him transparently responsible, fair-minded, true to trust. Far more popular than his party, he defeated Elbridge Gerry [*q.v.*] in 1800, and continued governor by annual election throughout the prosperous, politically quiet years of Jefferson's first term. His popularity withstood the steady Democratic trend even after 1804, when Massachusetts chose Jeffersonian electors. Narrowly elected a seventh successive time in 1806, though with a Democratic legislature, he was finally defeated in 1807 by James Sullivan [*q.v.*]. Strong refused nomination in 1808, but in 1812, when war was near and Gerry governor, he consented again to run. Barely winning, despite the "gerrymander" which redistricted the state in Democratic interests, he was moderate in countering Gerry's proscription of Federalist officials.

Congress declared war against Great Britain, June 18, 1812. New England, fearing commercial ruin, opposed hostilities from the start. On June 26, Strong proclaimed a public fast because of war "against the nation from which we are descended" (Niles' *Weekly Register,* Aug. 1, 1812, p. 355), and the Massachusetts House asked public disapproval of the war in town and county meetings. Secretary of War Eustis requested Strong to order part of the militia into federal service, and General Dearborn twice made requisition for these troops. Strong, however, believed that he, as governor, should decide whether the Constitutional exigency existed which empowered the president to call out state militia, and that the militia must remain under state officers. The supreme judicial court, acting through Chief Justice Parsons, and Justices Sewall and Parker, sanctioned these views. Supported by his Council, Strong decided no exigency existed, and refused to furnish the troops.

His general order of July 3, 1812, required the militia to keep in instant readiness for state defense. On Aug. 5, believing the exigency of "foreign invasion" now existed, he ordered a small force into federal service for the defense of eastern Maine, to Chief Justice Parsons' disgust (W. H. Sumner, *A History of East Boston,* 1858, p. 738). The war dragged on and Massachusetts, led by Strong and the legislature, steadily hung back. Federal troops were sent elsewhere. In 1814 the British occupied eastern Maine, threatening coastal Massachusetts, and on Sept. 6, Strong called out the militia, independently of the national government. On his query, Secretary of War Monroe stated that its expenses would not be reimbursed. Addressing a special session of the legislature he had called, Oct. 5, Strong now held that the people of Massachusetts had been deserted by the United States and must take measures for self-preservation (*Niles' Weekly Register,* Oct. 29, 1814, p. 113). The legislature, controlled by extreme Federalists, promptly provided for a state army, apart from the militia; and for the calling of a New England convention to further mutual defense and eventual reshaping of the Federal compact. On Oct. 17 it invited the other New England states to this conference, and two days later chose delegates, Connecticut and Rhode Island quickly following suit. Strong approved the calling of the Hartford Convention, which met Dec. 15, and, with the legislature, approved its report; but the Massachusetts commissioners appointed pursuant to this report reached Washington along with the news of peace.

Strong had thought the first British peace conditions reasonable, including concessions by Massachusetts of territory and fisheries, and he blamed the American negotiators for rejecting them (Henry Adams, *History of the United States,* vol. VIII, 1891, p. 288). The winter of peace found Massachusetts' independent defense crippled, the Boston banks now refusing credit to the state as they had to the nation. Throughout the war Massachusetts, openly yearning for peace, had failed to cooperate with the Union, though remaining within it. Proceeding with measured care, Strong represented the attitude of his state, preventing overt disunionist acts but obeying the letter, not the spirit, of federal obligation.

Annually elected governor from 1812, he refused renomination in 1816, and retired. A humane, religious man, even-tempered, conscientious, moderate, he adhered through life to carefully thought out views. Some of these are set forth in his published speeches: *Patriotism and Piety: The Speeches of His Excellency*

Caleb Strong, Esq., to the Senate and House of Representatives . . . and Other . . . Papers from 1800 to 1807 (1808), and *The Speech of His Excellency Governor Strong, Delivered before the Legislature . . . October 16, 1812; with the Documents . . .* (1812). His wife, Sarah Hooker, whom he had married Nov. 20, 1777, died in 1817. Strong himself died in Northampton suddenly, of angina pectoris, survived by four of his nine children.

[H. C. Lodge, *A Memoir of Caleb Strong* (1879), also printed in *Proc. Mass. Hist. Soc.*, vol. I (1879), supersedes Alden Bradford's *Biog. of the Hon. Caleb Strong* (1820). See also Appendix to Joseph Lyman, *Sermon . . . at the Interment of Hon. Caleb Strong* (1819); B. W. Dwight, *The Hist. of the Descendants of Elder John Strong of Northampton, Mass.* (2 vols., 1871); *The Records of the Federal Convention of 1787* (3 vols., 1911), ed. by Max Farrand; H. V. Ames, *State Documents on Federal Relations Number 2: State Rights and the War of 1812* (1900); S. E. Morison, *The Life and Letters of Harrison Gray Otis* (2 vols., 1913); *Biog. Dir. Am. Cong.* (1928); *Boston Daily Advertiser*, Nov. 11, 1819. Some letters are in the Pickering Papers, Mass. Hist. Soc., Boston (see "Historical Index to the Pickering Papers," *Mass. Hist. Soc. Colls.*, 6 ser., vol. VIII, 1896).]

J. G. K., Jr.

STRONG, CHARLES LYMAN (Aug. 15, 1826–Feb. 9, 1883), mining engineer, was born at Stockbridge, Vt., the eldest child of David Ellsworth and Harriet (Fay) Strong and a descendant of Elder John Strong, who came from England in 1630, was an early settler of Windsor, Conn., and in 1659 removed to Northampton, Mass. David Strong was a merchant and farmer. Charles attended public schools in Stockbridge and Williston Academy, but his father's death defeated his plans for a college education. In 1842 he went to New York City, where he obtained employment as a book-keeper and remained some eight years.

About 1850 he went to San Francisco, as confidential clerk of Wells & Company of New York, to establish a bank for that firm. Most of his records were destroyed in the great fire of 1851, and he himself suffered severe injuries in attempting to save them; but after his recovery he settled all the institution's accounts from memory, and his settlements were subsequently upheld by the courts. In 1852 he became a partner in the firm of LeCount & Strong, booksellers and publishers (1854–55) of *The Pioneer,* edited by Ferdinand Cartwright Ewer [*q.v.*], the first literary periodical in California. To house the enterprise Strong built the first four-story brick building on the Pacific Coast, and for its use manufactured the first gas. He subsequently spent a small fortune in hunting for codfish as well as salmon in Puget Sound, but in 1860 abandoned the fisheries to become the first superintendent of the Gould & Curry mine at Virginia

City, Nev., one of the great bonanzas of the Comstock Lode. The owners, possessed of a source of seemingly inexhaustible wealth, desired a reduction works that would outrival anything of the kind ever before constructed anywhere. Giving free reign to his ideas, Strong built and equipped a magnificent structure, surrounded by beautifully landscaped grounds, at a cost of nearly a million dollars. This mill was used for a few years, but was then superseded by one more economical and efficient to maintain and operate. Little thought was given to economy in those early prosperous days on the Comstock, because the stockholders' demands for large dividends could be met by increasing ore production, despite the high cost and excessive waste of over-rapid and careless reduction. While superintendent of the Gould & Curry mine, Strong had seven or eight mills at times and as many as 1,000 men under him. He made daily visits to the widely scattered company works, on horseback or driving a rapid four-in-hand, and at night attended to his records and correspondence. Possessed of strong will and a keen sense of justice, he was an able director of men. Foremen said that they received more help from the few instructions he gave without alighting from his carriage than from other superintendents in half a day. Instead of bringing suit against those who attempted to secure part of the great wealth of the company's property by working spurs on their lode, he advocated pushing the mining work from the main ore-body out to the opponents' ground, thus proving the company's property rights. This policy often prevented litigation, or if not, facilitated successful defense.

Strong's strenuous program was too much for him, and early in 1864, his health broken from overwork, he retired, to spend several years in travel. About 1867 he purchased a ranch in the San Gabriel Valley, near the present Whittier, Cal., where he gave some attention to orange growing. About 1874, however, he returned to mining, developing mines and erecting mills in California, Arizona, and Nevada, but the strain of work and worry, in futile efforts to save a gold-mining venture at Auburn, Cal., in which he and his friends were interested, proved too great for him to stand, and in 1883 he committed suicide. He was survived by his wife, Harriett Williams (Russell) Strong [*q.v.*], whom he married Feb. 26, 1863, and by four daughters. It is said that when Nevada was first admitted as a state he was offered but declined a nomination as governor and that he later declined to become a candidate for the United States Senate. He has sometimes been credited with a share in the development of the cyanide process for extracting the precious metals from low-grade ores, but that he had any significant share in it is very unlikely, since the process was not successfully applied commercially until several years after his death.

[B. W. Dwight, *The Hist. of the Descendants of Elder John Strong* (2 vols., 1871); E. E. Olcott, "Charles L. Strong," in *Engineering and Mining Jour.*, Feb. 16, 1884; J. S. McGroarty, *Hist. of Los Angeles County* (1923), vol. III; Eliot Lord, "Comstock Mining and Miners," *Monographs of the U. S. Geol. Survey*, vol. IV (1883); *Mining and Scientific Press*, Feb. 24, 1877; *Daily Examiner* (San Francisco), Feb. 10, 1883; *Evening Bulletin* (San Francisco), Feb. 10, 1883.]   B. A. R.

STRONG, HARRIET WILLIAMS RUSSELL (July 23, 1844–Sept. 16, 1926), horticulturist, engineer, civic leader, the fourth daughter of Henry Pierrepont and Mary Guest (Musier) Russell, was born at Buffalo, N. Y. In 1852, in the hope of improving the health of their mother, who was threatened with invalidism, the family crossed the plains to California, but after living for a time in that state moved to Nevada, where the father served for a time as state adjutant-general.

Harriet was educated by private teachers and in Miss Mary Atkins' Young Ladies Seminary in Benicia, Cal. On Feb. 26, 1863, at Virginia City, Nev., she married Charles Lyman Strong [*q.v.*], then engaged as superintendent of the Gould & Curry Mining Company in exploiting the Comstock Lode. Four daughters were born of this union. In 1883 Strong committed suicide, leaving to his widow a considerable estate, but for eight years she was obliged to defend her claims to it in the courts against her husband's former partners. During the progress of this litigation she began a long and active career as horticulturist, engineer, and public citizen. From her ranch near Whittier came the white pampas plumes which so prominently figured in the presidential campaign of the "Plumed Knight," James G. Blaine, in 1884. On the same ranch she planted 150 acres to walnut trees, being a pioneer in the walnut industry in California. Her walnuts received numerous awards, including a silver medal at the Paris exposition of 1900, and brought her another fortune. Her name is intimately connected with the development of irrigation, and she was among the first, if not the first, to advocate the conservation of water by building storage dams near the source of mountain streams. On Dec. 6, 1887, she patented a design for a series of dams in river channels for the storage of water for irrigation and flood control and later, Nov. 6, 1893, she secured a patent for impounding debris and water in hydraulic mining. For this invention she received two medals at the World's Columbian Exposition, Chicago, in 1893. She was also one of the early advocates of the conservation of the flood waters of the Colorado River for irrigation, the safety of the Imperial Valley, and the development of hydro-electric power. With her daughters she organized a water company and sank a number of artesian wells, but sold the enterprise after a few years. She subsequently sank several successful oil wells.

In addition to her business activities, she played an important part in the political, civic, and cultural life of California. She was a founder of the Ebell Club and the Hamilton Club of Los Angeles, and for many years was first vice-president of the Los Angeles Symphony Orchestra. She was vitally interested in the education of women, especially in that type of education which would enable them to care for their own economic interests and to meet the problems of the business world. She was a member of the Republican party and took an active part in its affairs, national as well as local. The editor of *Southern California Business* wrote of her: "For many years she was probably the most active figure among women in the entire Southland in civic work of every description" (*post*, p. 26). She met her death in an automobile accident on the way from Los Angeles to her ranch near Whittier. Three of her four daughters survived her.

[J. S. McGroarty, *Hist. of Los Angeles County* (1923), vol. III; *Southern California Business* (official organ of the Los Angeles Chamber of Commerce), Nov. 1926; Bertha H. Smith, "Harriet W. R. Strong: Walnut Grower," *Sunset*, Apr. 1911; *Los Angeles Times*, Sept. 17, 1926.]   R. G. C.

STRONG, JAMES (Aug. 14, 1822–Aug. 7, 1894), Biblical scholar, born in New York City, was the son of Thomas Strong, an emigrant from England, and his wife, Maria (Peers), member of a Dutch family of New York State. His parents died when he was very young, and with his only brother he was brought up in the Episcopal Church by an aunt and his maternal grandmother. Abandoning his plan to study medicine because of uncertain health, he prepared for college at Lowville Academy and, having been converted under Methodist influences, entered Wesleyan University, Middletown, Conn., where he graduated in 1844 as valedictorian of his class. For the next two years he taught ancient languages in Troy Conference Academy, Poultney, Vt., and here met Marcia Ann Dustin of Middlebury, whom he married July 18, 1845.

The year after his marriage, Strong withdrew for a time from teaching, though he continued his studies in the ancient languages. Buying property and establishing a home in Flushing, he became interested in the building of railroads on Long Island and served as president of the Flushing Railroad Company for some two years prior to the opening of its road in 1854. He was also active in civic affairs, being a justice of the peace for several years and president of the corporation of the village of Flushing in 1855. Meanwhile, in addition to his business activities he published *A New Harmony and Exposition of the Gospels* (1852), epitomes of Hebrew and Greek grammar, Sunday School question books, and several other works. In 1858 he became professor of Biblical literature in Troy University, serving until his return to Flushing in 1863, part of the time as acting president. During this period he published *Theological Compend* (1859).

In 1867 Drew Theological Seminary was established at Madison, N. J., and the following year Strong was elected to its chair of exegetical theology, from which he retired as professor emeritus only a year before his death. It was during his twenty-seven years in this professorship that he accomplished most of his enormous amount of literary work. Before going to Troy University he had begun work with Dr. John M'Clintock [*q.v.*] on the monumental *Cyclopædia of Biblical, Theological, and Ecclesiastical Literature* (10 vols., 1867–81), of which only three volumes were published before his colleague's death. Strong completed this work and edited the Supplement, in two volumes (1885–86). To *The Exhaustive Concordance of the Bible* (copyright 1890), he gave long years, and it still stands as a monument of labor and painstaking accuracy. He edited the sections on Daniel (vol. XIII, 1876) and Esther (vol. VII, 1877) in the Schaff edition of J. P. Lange's *Commentary on the Holy Scriptures*; was the author of *Irenics* (1883), *The Tabernacle of Israel in the Desert* (1888), *The Doctrine of a Future Life* (1891), *Sketches of Jewish life in the First Century* (1891), *The Student's Commentary . . . on . . . Ecclesiastes* (1893), *The Students' Commentary . . . The Book of Psalms* (published posthumously, 1896), and many lesser works; and contributed frequently to religious periodicals.

Strong's great enthusiasm was the interpretation of the Bible, to which he brought independence of judgment and immense learning, including a profound knowledge of Greek, Hebrew, and the other Semitic languages. He traveled extensively in the Orient and acquainted himself with the latest developments in archeological re-

search. He was also at home in the French and German literature pertaining to this field. His position was conservative: he stoutly defended the Mosaic authorship of the Pentateuch and the accuracy of the Mosaic account of creation, contended that there was but one Isaiah, and supported the Pauline authorship of the Epistle to the Hebrews; in all this, however, he was actuated not by blind obedience to the traditional, but by conviction based on his own studies. He was a member of the Old Testament Company of the American Committee for the Revision of the Bible, and a member of the Palestine Exploration Society. As a teacher, he was at his best; he could treat the Bible in its broad outlines, or turn to the most exhaustive and microscopic examination of particular words and phrases. His manner in the classroom was vigorous and dogmatic, yet often revealed tenderness and wit. Although a trainer of ministers, he insisted on remaining a layman and as such had great influence in bringing about lay representation in the General Conference of the Methodist Episcopal Church. He himself was lay delegate to the General Conference of 1872. For several years he lectured at the Chautauqua Assembly, and he was attending a summer institute for ministers at Round Lake, N. Y., as instructor in Greek and lecturer on the Holy Land, at the time of his death. His funeral was held at Round Lake and he was buried at Flushing. His wife and four of their six children survived him.

[H. A. Buttz, "Prefatory Memoir," in Strong's *Student's Commentary . . . The Book of Psalms* (1896); *Alumni Record of Drew Theol. Sem.* (1926); *Appletons' Ann. Cyc. . . . 1894* (1895); E. S. Tipple, *Drew Theol. Sem. 1867–1917* (copr. 1917); *N. Y. Tribune*, Aug. 8, 1894; manuscript sketch by a daughter, Miss Emma Strong, Oxford, Md.]   O. M. B.

STRONG, JAMES HOOKER (Apr. 26, 1814– Nov. 28, 1882), naval officer, was born in Canandaigua, N. Y. His father, Elisha Beebe Strong, first judge of common pleas of Monroe County, N. Y., was descended from John Strong who came to New England with his father, John, in 1630, and died in Windsor, Conn., in 1698; his mother was Dolly Goodwin, daughter of Capt. James Hooker, of Windsor, Conn. In 1827 Strong entered the seminary at Chittenango, N. Y., the "Polytechny," and on Feb. 2, 1829, was appointed a midshipman in the navy. No berth being available for him, he continued his studies in the "Polytechny," but on Mar. 18, 1831, joined the U.S.S. *Lexington*, Commander Silas Duncan. The following winter he participated in an expedition which broke up an establishment on the Falkland Islands maintained by one Louis Vernet, who had confiscated three American ships and held their crews. Since Vernet acted under Argentinian authority, the affair caused an international imbroglio. Strong's service from that time until the Civil War was uneventful. On Mar. 1, 1861, he was given command of the *Mohawk* and was ordered to the Gulf of Mexico, where he was stationed for a year. In 1862 he commanded the steamer *Flag* in the South Atlantic Blockading Squadron, and the following year the *Monongahela*. In October 1863, with the *Monongahela, Owasco,* and *Virginia* under his command, he convoyed an expedition of nine thousand men under Gen. Nathaniel P. Banks [q.v.] to the mouth of the Rio Grande. Brownsville, Corpus Christi, Aransas Pass, and Fort Esperanza at Pass Cavallo were captured. On Nov. 17 he landed troops at Mustang Island, and shelled a shore battery which quickly surrendered.

The *Monongahela* under Strong was in the attacking column at Mobile Bay, Aug. 5, 1864, and after the passage of Fort Morgan, Commander Strong sheered out of line without orders and ordered full speed ahead for the Confederate ram *Tennessee,* striking her a glancing blow and pouring a full broadside of 11-inch shot into her, which had but little effect. On signal from Farragut he rammed her a second time and was about to strike her again when the *Tennessee* surrendered. The iron prow and cutwater of the *Monongahela* were carried away by the force of the collisions, and she was pierced twice by shells from the *Tennessee*. Strong's Civil War record was admirable, his conduct of the Banks expedition eliciting high praise from Banks himself, and from Major-General Dana. His plucky attack on the *Tennessee* kept her from destroying the weaker vessels of the Union fleet, and materially aided in compelling her surrender. He was mentioned favorably in Admiral Farragut's report of the battle.

After the war Strong served for two years as inspector of the Brooklyn Navy Yard, and in 1868–69 commanded the steam-sloop *Canandaigua* in the European Squadron. He was lighthouse inspector from 1871 to 1873, and the following year was in command of the South Atlantic Station. He was commissioned rear admiral on Sept. 25, 1873, and was retired on Apr. 25, 1876. He married Maria Louisa Von Cowenhoven of Long Island in 1844, by whom he had a daughter and a son who became a naval officer. He died in Columbia, S. C.

[For biog. data see B. W. Dwight, *The Hist. of the Descendants of Elder John Strong* (2 vols., 1871) ; L. R. Hamersly, *The Records of Living Officers of the U. S. Navy and Marine Corps* (4th ed., 1890) ; *Army and Navy Jour.,* Dec. 2, 9, 1882 ; *N. Y. Tribune,* Nov. 29, 1882 ; *News and Courier* (Charleston, S. C.), Nov. 29, 1882. For the Falkland Islands affair, see Julius Goebel, *The Struggle for the Falkland Islands* (1927) ; *Niles' Weekly Reg.,* Apr. 28, May 12, 1832 ; log of the *Lexington,* 1831–32, and letters of Commander Silas Duncan (MSS. in Navy Dept.). For Strong's Civil War Service, see *Battles and Leaders of the Civil War* (1887–88), vols. III, IV ; A. T. Mahan, *The Gulf and Inland Waters* (1883) ; F. A. Parker, *The Battle of Mobile Bay* (1878) ; log of the *Monongahela,* 1863–64 (MS., Navy Dept.) ; *Official Records of the Union and Confed. Navies,* 1 ser. IV, XIII, XIV, XVI, XVII, XX–XXII.]   L. H. B.

STRONG, JAMES WOODWARD (Sept. 29, 1833–Feb. 24, 1913), Congregational clergyman, college president, son of Elijah Gridley and Sarah Ashley (Partridge) Strong and brother of William Barstow Strong [q.v.], was born in Brownington, Vt. A descendant of John Strong of Plymouth, England, who came to Massachusetts in 1630 on the ship *Mary and John* and was later one of the founders of Northampton, he inherited much of the piety and austerity of his Puritan ancestors. Since the family patrimony had been lost as a result of the panic of 1837, James was subjected to the discipline of labor for his education and support. After attending the common schools, he found work in a printing office, was subsequently employed in a Burlington book store, and then taught a country school. His family joined the stream of migration to the West in 1851, settling in Beloit, Wis., to have the advantages of life in a college town. Three years in the preparatory department, varied with intervals of teaching school, enabled him to enter the freshman year of Beloit College in 1854. In spite of ill health, the necessity of earning his expenses by divers means, and weakness of vision which made him dependent upon the help of a reader for studying, the ambitious youth was valedictorian of his class in 1858.

He had always expected to enter the ministry, having been imbued with this purpose by his mother. Friends and classmates enabled him to go to Union Theological Seminary, taking notes of lectures and reading for him until his marriage to Mary Davenport in 1861, when she became his reader. After graduation in 1862 he was for two years pastor in Brodhead, Wis., and then became pastor of Plymouth Congregational Church in Faribault, Minn.

Here he came into contact with other Congregationalists who were seeking to establish in Minnesota "a second Oberlin or Beloit." He served as a trustee of Northfield College, in the village of Northfield, from its organization in 1866 until he was persuaded to become its first president in 1870, undertaking to develop it from a feeble preparatory school into a standard college. Encouraged by many gifts from Minnesota friends of the project, he resorted to New England—prolific source of educational benefactions from Eastern kinsmen to Western pioneer institutions. Philanthropic purses were promptly opened to him, one donor (William Carleton) attaching his name to the college by a single gift of $50,000. For thirty-three years President Strong—"in person," said the *Hartford Courant* in 1875, "slightly built, sinewy, energetic, and a very clear and interesting speaker"—labored to win suport for his non-sectarian Christian college, and led devoted teachers and trustees to the realization of collegiate visions after patterns set by their forebears. Never discouraged, even by periods of financial stringency and depression or by his own ill health and impaired vision, he persisted until he built Carleton into a standard college of liberal arts, with a foundation in the way of equipment and endowments upon which his successors could build still more adequately. He retired in 1903, living in Northfield as president emeritus until his death there ten years later.

[D. L. Leonard, *The Hist. of Carleton Coll.* (1904), esp. pp. 166–73; M. M. Dana, *The Hist. of the Origin and Growth of Carleton Coll.* (1879); Warren Upham, *Congreg. Work of Minn., 1832–1920* (1921); Warren Upham and Rose B. Dunlap, *Minn. Biogs.* (1912); B. W. Dwight, *The Hist. of the Descendants of Elder John Strong* (2 vols., 1871); *Addresses Delivered at the Quarter Centennial Anniv. of Carleton Coll.* (1895); *Alumni Cat. of the Union Theol. Sem. in the City of N. Y.* (1926); *Who's Who in America*, 1912–13; *Minneapolis Journal*, Feb. 24, 1913; MSS. and papers at Carleton College.]   C. A. D—y.

STRONG, JOSIAH (Jan. 19, 1847–Apr. 28, 1916), clergyman, social reformer, author, was born in Naperville, Ill., the son of Josiah and Elizabeth C. (Webster) Strong, and a descendant of Elder John Strong who came to Massachusetts in 1630, settling first in Dorchester and ultimately in Northampton. In 1852 his parents moved to Hudson, Ohio, then the site of Western Reserve College. From this institution Josiah was graduated in 1869 and at once entered Lane Theological Seminary in Cincinnati.

He began his professional career in 1871 at Cheyenne, Wyo., where he was ordained (Sept. 8) and installed as pastor of a Congregational church. Ten days before (Aug. 29), at Chardon, Ohio, he had married Alice Bisbee, daughter of Charles and Cordelia (Packard) Bisbee. The next eighteen years were a restless period in which a man of fine efficiency, ardent spirit, and ever-widening social interest and vision sought with feverish intensity the field appointed for his labors. He was everywhere successful, but nowhere satisfied. Thus after only two years in Cheyenne he returned to Western Reserve College to serve as chaplain and instructor in theol-

ogy. Three years later he accepted a call to a pastorate in Sandusky, Ohio. In 1881 he became a secretary of the Congregational Home Missionary Society, for the work in Ohio, Kentucky, West Virginia, and western Pennsylvania. In 1884 he returned again to the parish ministry as head of the Central Congregational Church in Cincinnati.

With the publication of his book, *Our Country,* in 1885, came the turning-point of Strong's career. This work had its origin in a small manual of the same title, issued years before by the Congregational Home Missionary Society, which he had been asked to revise and bring up to date; but in performing the task, Strong made the book his own through his clear and forceful style, his ample collection of new material, his first-hand Biblical knowledge, and his ardent social and spiritual idealism. As it came afresh from his hands, *Our Country* was a pioneer sociological treatise, already radical in its emphasis on the dangers of over-accumulation and concentration of capital, its sympathy with the discontents of labor, and its challenge to the church for concern with social problems. The book created a sensation. It was translated into foreign languages, Oriental as well as European, and reissued in new and revised editions in America. It made Strong a national figure, brought him repeated requests for lectures and speeches, and was the occasion of his appointment as secretary of the American Evangelical Alliance.

Josiah Strong had now found himself. He understood his message and his mission, both of which he stated in his second book, *The New Era,* which was published simultaneously in the United States and England in 1893, and, like its famous predecessor, had instant circulation of wide dimensions. In this volume the author laid down the principle that the teachings of Jesus center in the concept of "the Kingdom" as an ideal society here and now upon the earth. Jesus came to found this "Kingdom." The Christian church exists to extend it, to purify and perpetuate it. This purpose requires an organization commensurate with the task—a federation which shall overleap or absorb competing denominations, and direct their power to the solution of civic and industrial problems by generating a primary enthusiasm for human welfare.

Strong hoped to find or make such an organization in the Evangelical Alliance, but that society proved to be too conservative in its ideas, too pietistic in its practices. In 1898, therefore, he resigned his office and founded his own organization, the League for Social Service, which was reorganized in 1902 as the American Institute for Social Service. The history of the Institute is the record of his life work. He was tireless as a writer and lecturer. Active in the service of every constructive and beneficent public cause, he labored unceasingly to awaken the churches to a recognition of their social responsibility and to unite them in common labors for the common good. Passionate in his prophetic zeal, he was statesmanlike in his ingenious devising of practical methods of action. The "Safety First" movement, for example, was his original conception, and the American Museum of Safety one of the chief developments of the Institute. The Federal Council of the Churches of Christ in America, in the establishment of which he was an active participant, was to no small extent the fruit of his example. A born missionary, he went to England in 1904 and organized the British Institute of Social Service. Five years later (in 1909–10) he visited South American countries in the interest of the Institute idea and of the "Safety First" movement. His books written during this period include *The Twentieth Century City* (1898), *Religious Movements for Social Betterment* (1900), *Expansion under New World Conditions* (1900), *The Times and Young Men* (1901), *The Next Great Awakening* (1902), *Social Progress: A Yearbook* (1904–06), *The Challenge of the City* (1907), *My Religion in Every-Day Life* (1910), *Our World: The New World Life* (1913) and *Our World: The New World Religion* (1915), the first two of four projected volumes. He also edited *The Gospel of the Kingdom,* a monthly begun in October 1908, and published numerous sermons, addresses, and pamphlets.

Josiah Strong was tall and vigorous—a handsome man, with shining eyes. Passionate in his idealistic zeal and consecration, he was saved from fanaticism by abundant sanity, ripe scholarship, unfailing good nature, and unshakable confidence in his fellow men. With Francis G. Peabody, Washington Gladden, John Graham Brooks, and Walter Rauschenbusch, he was a pioneer and prophet of that social Christianity whose advent marks the most important chapter of recent religious history. He died in his seventieth year, after a prolonged and painful illness.

[B. W. Dwight, *The Hist. of the Descendants of Elder John Strong* (1871), vol. I; *Who's Who in America,* 1916–17; *New Church Rev.,* Jan. 1922; *Outlook,* May 10, 1916; *N. Y. Times,* Apr. 29, May 8, 1916; personal acquaintance.]   J. H. H.

STRONG, MOSES McCURE (May 20, 1810– July 20, 1894), surveyor, lawyer, legislator, was born at Rutland, Vt., son of Moses and Lucy Maria (Smith) Strong and a descendant of Elder John Strong, who emigrated to America

in 1630 and settled first at Dorchester, Mass., later at Northampton. His father was a lawyer and land-holder. After attending grammar school in Castleton, Vt., Strong went first to Middlebury College (1825–28) and then to Dartmouth, from which he graduated in 1829. He studied law in an office and at the law school at Litchfield, Conn., and was admitted to the bar in 1831. On July 31, 1832, he was married to Caroline Frances Green, daughter of Dr. Isaac Green of Windsor, Vt., by whom he had four children. After practising law in Rutland, Vt. (1831–36), and serving as deputy surveyor general of Vermont for one or two years, Strong went to Wisconsin in 1836, opened a law and land office at Mineral Point, and in 1837 became United States surveyor, assigned to the survey west of the Mississippi River. His native ability and thorough training made him prominent in territorial affairs. He was United States attorney for the territory of Wisconsin (1838–41), was instrumental in establishing the capital at Madison, and was elected a member of the territorial council to fill a vacancy in 1842 and for a full term of four years in 1843. While he never entirely gave up the practice of law, it was for many years subordinated to his other interests. He was a member of the constitutional convention of 1846 and became a member of the Assembly in 1850, when he served as speaker, and again in 1857. In the early fifties he became interested in the promotion of railway construction in Wisconsin, as a result, it is said, of a very long and uncomfortable coach journey from Milwaukee to Mineral Point. For six or seven years he was active in promoting and organizing railway and associated enterprises, but he also gave much time to mining, lumbering, and real estate development.

He was a man of heavy, stocky frame and strong features, quick and energetic in his movements. In disposition he was quiet, reserved, and somewhat withdrawn, but generous almost to a fault. Much given to thinking things out for himself, both in the practice of law and in connection with his other interests, he looked more to the rationale than to the language of opinions and dissertations, and he devoted himself assiduously to any matter that won his attention. He had a hasty temper which he controlled admirably, but that and his inability to surrender his convictions and adapt himself to the moods of the populace prevented him from winning public favor. He was active in establishing the Protestant Episcopal Church in Mineral Point, and at the time of his death was chancellor of the diocese of Milwaukee. He has been described as reasonable, fair-minded and unfailingly constant in his opinions and attachments (*Wisconsin Reports, post*). He died at Mineral Point, where he had lived since 1837.

[B. W. Dwight, *The Hist. of the Descendants of Elder John Strong* (1871), vol. II; H. P. Smith and W. S. Rann, *Hist. of Rutland County, Vt.* (1886), p. 911; A. M. Hemenway, *The Vt. Hist. Gazetteer,* vol. I (1868), pp. 1–10; J. R. Berryman, *Hist. of the Bench and Bar of Wis.* (2 vols., 1898); M. M. Strong, *Hist. of the Territory of Wis.* (1885), pp. 356, 387–88, 512; "Strong and Woodman Manuscript Colls. in Wis. State Hist. Lib.," *State Hist. Soc. of Wis. Bull.* . . . *No. 78,* Nov. 1915; 90 *Wis. Reports,* lix; obituary in *Milwaukee Jour.,* July 20, 1894; information from Strong's grand-daughter, Anna Strong Parkinson.]

M. B. R.

STRONG, THEODORE (July 26, 1790–Feb. 1, 1869), mathematician, descended from Elder John Strong who in 1630 emigrated from England to Massachusetts, was born at South Hadley, Mass., the second son of a Congregational minister, Joseph Strong, and his wife Sophia, daughter of the Rev. John Woodbridge. Prepared for college by his uncle, Col. Benjamin R. Woodbridge, Theodore graduated in 1812 at Yale, where his father and both grandfathers had graduated before him. He was immediately appointed tutor in mathematics at Hamilton College, then just organized, and in 1816 he was there made professor of mathematics and natural philosophy, a post which he held until he accepted a similar position at Rutgers College, New Brunswick, N. J., in 1827. Here he remained until he became professor emeritus in 1861. From 1839 to 1863 he was vice-president of Rutgers.

Strong was the author of scores of brief mathematical communications. His first paper, "Demonstrations of Stewart's Properties of the Circle," was published while he was still an undergraduate, in *Memoirs of the Connecticut Academy of Arts and Sciences* (vol. I, pt. 4, 1816). Other communications appeared in Gill's *Mathematical Miscellany,* Silliman's *American Journal of Science,* Runkle's *Mathematical Monthly, Proceedings of the American Academy of Arts and Sciences,* and *Proceedings of the American Philosophical Society.* Of his two books, *A Treatise on Elementary and Higher Algebra* (1859) and *A Treatise on Differential and Integral Calculus* (1869), the latter was in the press at the time of his death. Both works possessed many original features, but since these were not always improvements, and the arrangements were defective, the texts were unsuited for the classroom.

Strong became a fellow of the American Academy of Arts and Sciences in 1832 and of the American Philosophical Society in 1844; in 1863 he was one of the fifty incorporators of the National Academy of Sciences, to which he communicated five papers (1864–67). From the world point of view he made to mathematics no contribution of moment, and he was not in the same class with certain other Americans, such as Nathaniel Bowditch and Benjamin Peirce [*qq.v.*], but he was a vitalizing force in academic councils and a successful teacher, endowed with "remarkable geniality and unfailing kindness . . . childlike faith and simplicity, and tender bearing" (resolution of the Rutgers Faculty, 1869). On Sept. 23, 1818, he married Lucy Dix, daughter of Capt. John Dix of Boston, Mass., and by her had two sons and five daughters. One of the daughters became the wife of John W. Ferdon, Congressman from New York, and another became the mother of John C. Van Dyke [*q.v.*], long professor of the history of art at Rutgers College.

[B. W. Dwight, *The Hist. of the Descendants of Elder John Strong* (2 vols., 1871), portr.; *Memorial of Theodore Strong* (1869); J. P. Bradley, *Memoir of Theodore Strong* (1879), printed also in *Nat. Acad. Sci. Biog. Memoirs,* vol. II (1886); *A Hist. of the First Half-Century of the Nat. Acad. of Sci.* (1913); *Proc. Am. Acad. Arts and Sci.,* vol. VIII (1873), with bibliog.; *Am. Portrait Gallery with Biog. Sketches,* vol. III (1877); J. C. Poggendorff, *Biographisch-Literarisches Handwörterbuch,* vol. III (1898); *Cat. of the Officers and Alumni of Rutgers Coll.* (1916); Florian Cajori, *The Teaching and Hist. of Mathematics in the U. S.* (1890), p. 398; *Obit. Record Grads. Yale Coll.,* 1869; death notice in *N. Y. Tribune,* Feb. 3, 1869.]

R. C. A.

STRONG, WALTER ANSEL (Aug. 13, 1883–May 10, 1931), journalist and publisher, was born in Chicago and identified with its interests all his life. His parents were Dr. Albert Bliss Strong, a skilful Chicago physician, and Idea (Cook) Strong; he was descended from Elder John Strong who came to Massachusetts on the *Mary and John* in 1630. When Walter was fifteen years old his father died, leaving the family without financial resources, but, with assistance from a relative supplementing his own earnings, the boy succeeded in putting himself through high school and an engineering course at Lewis Institute. Later he took a law course at John Marshall Law School, Chicago. Entering Beloit College, supporting himself in part by working on a Beloit newspaper, he graduated in 1905 with the degree of B.A.

Returning to Chicago, Strong established connection with the *Chicago Daily News* as an audit clerk, soon becoming auditor and later business manager, which post he held at the time of the death, in August 1925, of Victor F. Lawson [*q.v.*], editor and publisher. Disposition of the paper was, under Lawson's will, left in the hands of his executor, John J. Mitchell, president of the Illinois Merchants Trust Company, and in December 1925 the *Daily News* was bought for $13,500,000 by a group headed by Strong, who had bent every effort to insure its continued control by those who would maintain the previous owner's high ideals and carry on his policies. Even before Lawson's death Strong had recognized the need of a new plant, and as soon as he became head of the *Daily News* he began plans for a new building. The site selected utilized for the first time in Chicago's history air rights over a railroad, the building being constructed, in part, over tracks of the Chicago & Northwestern, and on June 8, 1929, the *Daily News* moved to its imposing new quarters. In the reorganization a stock company was formed, Strong acquiring a majority of the stock and continuing to be the controlling stockholder until his death.

He was early interested in radio broadcasting and in 1922 the *Daily News,* largely through his influence, purchased half interest in a local station and became the first newspaper in Chicago, and one of the first in the country, to operate a radio station. In 1930 the station (WMAQ) was organized as a separate corporation, Strong becoming chairman of the board of directors. As a result of his efforts, a plan for pensioning *Daily News* employees after a certain number of years, and for protecting them with insurance during their lifetime, was evolved and put into operation. His interests extended widely into national organizations connected with newspaper publishing. He either had been or at the time of his death was a director of the Audit Bureau of Circulations, the American Newspaper Publishers Association, and the Associated Press. He was chairman of the board of the Advertising Federation of America—to which organization he gave much time hoping through it to improve standards of advertising throughout the country. He was an ardent supporter of the Boy Scout movement, a member of the Episcopal Church, serving for years as vestryman, and active in the community interests of Winnetka, the Chicago suburb of which he was a resident. For years he was a trustee of Beloit College. He had an essentially constructive mind; combined vision, business sagacity, and creative energy; possessed tremendous vitality and moral courage, and although only forty-seven at the time of his sudden death, had reached the front rank of the newspaper world through sheer force of personality, ability, and character. On Apr. 14, 1913, he married Josephine Haviland Webster, daughter of Towner Keeney Webster

of Evanston, Ill. Five children were born to them.

[*Chicago Daily News,* May 11, 1931, and succeeding days; nearly all metropolitan papers of the country, May 11, 1931; *Who's Who in America,* 1930–31; B. W. Dwight, *The Hist. of the Descendants of Elder John Strong, of Northampton, Mass.* (2 vols., 1871).]

G. B. U.

STRONG, WILLIAM (May 6, 1808–Aug. 19, 1895), justice of the Supreme Court, was born in Somers, Conn., the eldest of eleven children of William Lighthouse Strong and Harriet (Deming) Strong. He was descended from John Strong, who came from England to Dorchester, Mass., in 1630 and settled finally in Northampton. He attended schools in Monson and Plainfield, Mass., and then entered Yale College, from which he received the B.A. degree in 1828 and that of M.A. three years later. While teaching in various Connecticut towns, and in an academy in Burlington, N. J., he read law, and he studied for some months in the Yale Law School. He was admitted to the Philadelphia bar in October 1832 (J. H. Martin, *Martin's Bench and Bar of Philadelphia,* 1883, p. 315), but almost immediately entered practice in Reading. Everybody there spoke German; he mastered that language, gained universal respect, and as a lawyer attained an acknowledged preëminence. Also active in civic affairs, he was twice elected as a Democrat a representative in Congress, serving from 1847 to 1851. In 1857 he was elected for a fifteen-year term on the supreme court of Pennsylvania, and served with great distinction until he resigned in 1868, apparently because of the inadequacy of his income. He then practised in Philadelphia.

His nomination by President Grant as an associate justice of the Supreme Court of the United States was transmitted to the Senate on Feb. 7, 1870, and was confirmed, after strong opposition, on the 18th (*Journal of the Executive Proceedings of the Senate of the United States of America,* vol. XVII, 1901, pp. 359, 369; Warren, *post,* II, 518). He was precipitated into the critical controversy over the Legal Tender Act of Feb. 25, 1862. Among the supreme courts of fifteen states that had held the act constitutional was that of Pennsylvania (1866, *Shollenberger* vs. *Brinton, 52 Pennsylvania State Reports,* 9), with the concurrence of Strong, who was a stanch Unionist and acted with the majority of his court during the war years in sustaining the national government. In *Hepburn* vs. *Griswold* (8 *Wallace,* 603) the question of its constitutionality was directly raised before the United States Supreme Court. This case was argued, the Court's decision agreed upon, and the form of the opinion settled before the nominations of Strong and Joseph P. Bradley [*q.v.*] on Feb. 7. The decision, however, was announced on that day, Chase and three Democratic colleagues holding the act unconstitutional and three Republicans dissenting. Immediate steps were taken to insure a reargument, and this resulted in an outright reversal on May 1, 1871 (*Knox* vs. *Lee*, 12 *Wallace*, 457), Strong writing the majority opinion. There had been procedural steps without precedent; the new justices perhaps had been indiscreetly active; and there had been an undignified dispute among the justices in open court, on a motion for reargument, as to alleged agreements regarding the Hepburn decision. Whether the reversal, at least so promptly and by a vote of 5 to 4, was itself a mistake, is a question upon which lawyers greatly differ. The charge was promptly made, and has often been repeated, that the President "packed" the Court to insure a reversal. When the chief justiceship was vacated by Taney's death, Lincoln had frankly declared that he wanted a successor, who would "sustain what has been done in regard to emancipation and the legal tenders," and that necessarily a man of known opinions must be chosen (G. S. Boutwell, *Reminiscences of Sixty Years in Public Affairs*, 1902, vol. II, 29). Strong was considered by him as Taney's successor, and Chase, who was appointed, as secretary of the treasury had been responsible for the passage of the Legal Tender Act by Congress and might have been expected to uphold it. How Grant felt is shown by his later statement to Hamilton Fish (*Political Science Quarterly*, Sept. 1935, p. 351). He knew Strong's attitude and thought he knew Bradley's, and, while requiring no declaration of them, desired that the Legal Tender Act be upheld. Strong and Bradley were certainly the leading lawyers of their circuit, from which precedent required that at least one new justice be drawn; and weeks before the Hepburn decision was pronounced Strong was Grant's first choice for the vacancy created by the resignation (effective Feb. 1, 1870) of Justice Robert C. Grier [*q.v.*]. The Secretary of the Treasury revealed years later that he knew of the decision in advance (Boutwell, *Reminiscences*, II, 209), but there is no certain evidence that anybody else did. For a time at least, the case greatly impaired the Court's prestige, but Strong's position was wholly consistent with his record.

Strong remained a power in the counsels of the Court. Among many important cases on which he wrote the opinion of the Court were one on the Confiscation Act (*Bigelow* vs. *Forrest*, 9

Wallace, 339); the case of the state freight tax (15 *Wallace*, 232); *Tennessee* vs. *Davis* (100 *United States*, 257), concerning the powers of the federal courts within the states; and several of the leading cases on civil rights—(*Blyew* vs. *United States*, 13 *Wallace*, 581; *Strauder* vs. *West Virginia*, 100 *United States*, 303; *Ex Parte Virginia*, *Ibid.*, 339). Possessed of remarkable powers of analysis and exposition, and unusually sound judgment, he is generally regarded as one of the truly great judges of the Court in its long history. Upon his resignation (Dec. 14, 1880) the members of the bar of the Court expressed their appreciation of "the large and varied learning, the wide experience, the strong intellectual force, the rigid impartiality" that had characterized his service (102 *United States*, ix–x). He enjoyed in remarkable degree the affection and reverence of the people of Pennsylvania; and Senator George F. Hoar, intimately acquainted through three decades with most members of the Supreme Court, believed that in purity and integrity of character he was comparable perhaps to John Jay alone among his predecessors (Bradley, *post*, p. 58).

Strong was a member of the Electoral Commission of 1877. After his retirement he lived in Washington. An offer by President Hayes of the secretaryship of the navy was declined (*New York Tribune*, Aug. 20, 1895). He taught law in the Columbian (later George Washington) University in that city, and gave in the Union Theological Seminary of New York *Two Lectures upon the Relations of Civil Law to Church Polity, Discipline, and Property* (1875?). An ardent Presbyterian, and for many years probably the most prominent lay member of that church, he was long president (1883–95) of the American Sunday School Union, vice-president (1871–95) of the American Bible Society, and president (1873–95) of the American Tract Society. Of many public addresses there survive *An Eulogium on the Life and Character of Horace Binney* (1876); and a paper on *The Growth and Modifications of Private Civil Law* (1879). After his retirement he published his views on "The Needs of the Supreme Court" (*North American Review*, May 1881).

Strong was married on Nov. 28, 1836, to Priscilla Lee Mallery of Easton, Pa., who before her death in 1844 bore him two daughters and a son. On Nov. 22, 1849, he married Rachel (Davies) Bull of Churchtown, Pa., widow of Levi Bull; by her he had two daughters and two sons. Three daughters survived him. He was athletic, fond of outdoor sports and hunting, and sociable in his tastes.

[Strong's opinions are in *Pa. State Reports*, vols. XXX–LIX, and *U. S. Reports*, vols. LXXVI–CII. For the Legal Tender Cases, see H. L. Carson, *The Supreme Court of the U. S. Its History* (1892), II, 441–57; Moorfield Storey and E. W. Emerson, *Ebenezer Rockwood Hoar* (1911), pp. 198–202; Charles Warren, *The Supreme Court in U. S. History* (1926 ed.), II, ch. xxxi; G. F. Hoar, *Autobiography of Seventy Years* (1903), I, 284–88; Charles Bradley, ed., *Miscellaneous Writings of the Late Joseph P. Bradley* (1902), pp. 45–74, with the contemporary statement of the five justices who reversed *Hepburn* vs. *Griswold*; C. B. Swisher, *Stephen J. Field* (1930), pp. 174–97; P. G. Clifford, *Nathan Clifford* (1922), pp. 281–85; A. B. Hart, *Salmon Portland Chase* (1899), pp. 389–412; Sidney Ratner, "Was the Supreme Court Packed by General Grant?" *Pol. Science Quart.*, Sept. 1935. More personal materials are in Carson, *supra*, II, 461–63; B. W. Dwight, *The History of the Descendants of Elder John Strong* (1871), II, 1047–48; *Obit. Record of Grads. of Yale Univ. Deceased During . . . Year Ending . . . June, 1896*, pp. 353–54; obituaries in *N. Y. Tribune* and *N. Y. Times*, Aug. 20, 1895.] F.S.P.

STRONG, WILLIAM BARSTOW (May 16, 1837–Aug. 3, 1914), railroad official, was born at Browning, Orleans County, Vt., the son of Elijah Gridley Strong and Sarah Ashley (Partridge) Strong, and a brother of James Woodward Strong [*q.v.*]. He was a descendant of John Strong who was in Massachusetts in 1630 and settled first at Dorchester, later at Northampton. He attended public schools at Beloit, Wis., and graduated in 1855 from Bell's Business College of Chicago, Ill. He began railroad work as a station agent and telegraph operator at Milton, Wis., in March 1855. During the next twelve years he was employed by the Milwaukee & St. Paul Railroad (later the Chicago, Milwaukee & St. Paul) or by roads which became part of the St. Paul system. In 1867 he left the St. Paul to serve as general western agent of the Chicago & Northwestern Railway with headquarters at Council Bluffs, Iowa. He served as assistant general superintendent of the Chicago, Burlington & Quincy Railroad at Burlington, Iowa (1870–72), was assistant general superintendent of the enlarged Burlington system, which later included the Burlington & Missouri River Railroad in Iowa (1872), and became general superintendent of the Michigan Central Railroad (1874). In 1875 he returned to the Burlington as general superintendent.

In 1877 he was invited to take active direction of the extension program of the Atchison, Topeka & Santa Fé Railroad as vice-president and general manager, and his reputation depends, in the main, upon his success in transforming this small western railroad into a system of importance. The Santa Fé, when he took charge of the property, operated 786 miles of line, nearly all in Kansas; in 1889 when he resigned the presidency, which he had held since 1881, the mileage of the system was about 6,960

miles, and the Santa Fé ranked as one of the country's largest lines. The systematic expansion which he directed consisted of construction through Kansas to Colorado, connection with the Pacific coast by construction, lease, or traffic agreements, connection with the Gulf coast, and connection with Chicago. The Santa Fé was unsuccessful, however, in an attempted development in Colorado, and built competitive lines in Kansas which were probably ill-advised. Public opinion was tremendously impressed by the resources that Strong commanded during the period of his presidency, and by the energy and skill with which he directed Santa Fé affairs. This high regard for his capacity is shared by later students of Western railroad history, although the heavy cost of the new construction which he carried through, joined with the recession in general business that occurred in 1887 and 1888, compelled his company to reorganize in 1889. At that time, although he was reëlected president, the arrangements did not prove satisfactory, and he presently resigned. Comment at the time characterized him as an "honest, honorable, large hearted man, a born leader, an executive whose field is large affairs, and a practical railway manager of the highest ability" (*Railway Age, post*, p. 568). After he left the Santa Fé he took up his residence on a farm near Beloit and did not again return to railroad work, although at Beloit he was for a time president of a local bank and took some part in other business enterprises. He married Abby Jane Moore of Beloit on Oct. 2, 1859. At the time of his death, which occurred at Los Angeles, Cal., where he spent his last seven years, he was survived by one daughter and two sons.

[B. W. Dwight, *The Hist. of the Descendants of Elder John Strong, of Northampton, Mass.* (2 vols., 1871); *Who's Who in America*, 1914–15; R. E. Riegel, *The Story of the Western Railroads* (1926); G. D. Bradley, *The Story of the Santa Fe* (1920); Stuart Daggett, *Railroad Reorganization* (1908); *Railway Age*, Aug. 30, 1889; *Railway Age Gazette*, Aug. 7, 21, 1914; obituary in *Times* (Los Angeles), Aug. 4, 1914.] S. D.

STRONG, WILLIAM LAFAYETTE (Mar. 22, 1827–Nov. 2, 1900), merchant, mayor of New York City, was born in Richland County, Ohio. His father, Abel Strong, was of New England descent; his mother, Hannah (Burdine) Strong, a native of Pennsylvania. His father died when William was thirteen, and soon afterward he began work as a clerk in a country store to aid in the support of his mother and four other children. After working in a store in Mansfield, Ohio, in 1853 he went to New York with the fixed determination of making a fortune, an ambition in which he succeeded so well that at his death he was a millionaire. His first position in New York was that of clerk in the wholesale dry-goods house of L. O. Wilson & Company, the business which he followed throughout his adult life. After sixteen years as an employee he considered himself financially ready to launch his own business, and at forty-two established the firm of W. L. Strong & Company, which from the first was greatly successful. He was also president of the Central National Bank and of the Homer Lee Bank Note Company, vice-president of the New York Security and Trust Company, and a director in other banks, insurance, and railroad companies.

An ardent Republican, he served for long periods as president of the Union League and the Business Men's Republican Association, but sought public office only twice. In 1882 he ran for Congress unsuccessfully. In 1894, following exposures by the Lexow Committee of corruption in New York's city government, the "Committee of Seventy" (representing clubs and other organizations standing for civic betterment) selected Strong as its non-partisan candidate for mayor, and he was elected by a large majority over the Tammany Hall candidate. He had scarcely been inaugurated, however, when he began to be troubled by dissensions among his supporters, and his whole incumbency was beset by difficulties such as few mayors have encountered. His sole idea was to conduct his office in behalf of good government and without regard to political considerations. But the various elements which had brought about his election fought for precedence and for the appointment of their candidates to office, and Strong's political inexperience, his unwillingness to bargain in matters of right and wrong, kept him in stormy weather all through his single term. So unpleasant were his experiences that he positively refused to consider a renomination in 1897, and said that he would never again offer himself for public office. Nevertheless, under him the city was honestly governed for the first time in many years, and in some departments there was great improvement in efficiency. Two of his memorable appointments were those of Theodore Roosevelt [q.v.] as police commissioner and Col. George E. Waring as street commissioner, under whose régime the city had the cleanest streets yet known in its history. The New York and East River Bridge, the consolidation of the New York Public Library, and other large projects were begun during his administration. As a result of Strong's independent attitude, he and Thomas Collier Platt, the Republican boss, became enemies, and after his own term expired

Strong supported Seth Low [qq.v.], the Independent candidate for mayor, as against the Republican nominee, though he still considered himself a Republican. At his death in 1900 he was survived by his wife, the former Mary Aborn of Orange, N. J., a son, and a daughter.

[See *Who's Who in America*, 1899–1900; *Nat. Mag.*, Nov. 1891; T. C. Quinn, in *Munsey's Mag.*, Jan. 1895; *N. Y. Tribune*, Oct. 6, 1894, Dec. 31, 1897, and Nov. 3, 1900; obituaries in *Evening Post* (N. Y.), Nov. 2, and *N. Y. Herald, N. Y. Times, World* (N. Y.), Nov. 3, 1900. Much material is to be found in N. Y. newspapers during the municipal campaign of 1894, and during Strong's administration, 1895–97.]   A. F. H.

STROTHER, DAVID HUNTER (Sept. 26, 1816–Mar. 8, 1888), soldier, writer, illustrator, son of Col. John and Elizabeth Pendleton (Hunter) Strother, was born at Martinsburg in what is now West Virginia. The Strothers, since their arrival in Virginia from Northumberland, England, about 1650, had been a family of soldiers. David's grandfather fought in the Revolutionary War, his father in the War of 1812, David himself in the Civil War, and one of his sons in the Spanish-American War. He was educated at the Old Stone Schoolhouse in Martinsburg, and at Jefferson College, Canonsburg, Pa., studied art in Philadelphia, and continued his studies in France and Italy during the years 1840–43.

On his return to America in 1844 he began making drawings for magazines. He illustrated the 1851 edition of *Swallow Barn,* by his cousin John P. Kennedy [q.v.], who had assisted him in his artistic endeavors. Next he made the drawings for *The Blackwater Chronicle* (1853), by Pendleton Kennedy, a brother of John P. Kennedy; this book has sometimes been attributed to Strother himself. In December 1853 he contributed to *Harper's New Monthly Magazine* an article called "The Virginian Canaan," in which he gave an account of a visit to the Blackwater region of Randolph County. This was the first of a series of sketches dealing with life in the South which, with numerous pen drawings, appeared from time to time in *Harper's* under his pseudonym, "Porte Crayon." In 1857 some of these sketches were gathered into a volume, *Virginia Illustrated, by Porte Crayon,* containing 138 pen drawings. At this time Strother was one of the highest-paid contributors to *Harper's,* having a roving commission to travel and write for the magazine. Three characteristic series of articles, appearing at irregular intervals, were "North Carolina Illustrated" (1857), "A Winter in the South" (1857–58), "A Summer in New England" (1860–61).

At the outbreak of the Civil War, Strother, a

Unionist, offered his services to the North, and because of his knowledge of the Shenandoah Valley and his skill with the pen was assigned to the topographical corps. He served at different times on the staffs of Generals McClellan, Banks, Pope, and Hunter, went through thirty battles unwounded, and received one promotion after another until his resignation in September 1864. After the close of the war, he was brevetted brigadier-general. He now made his home at Berkeley Springs, W. Va., devoting his time to literature and art. During the years 1866–68 he contributed to *Harper's* a series of articles entitled "Personal Recollections of the War, by a Virginian," based on his diary and pen sketches made on the battlefields. Between 1872 and 1875 he contributed to the same magazine a series on "The Mountains," but by this time a change in the literary taste of the reading public had reduced the demand for writings of the sketchbook and diary type. He was appointed United States consul-general in the city of Mexico in 1879, returned to West Virginia in 1885—making his home at Charles Town—and at the time of his death was writing a book on the Mexicans. In 1849 he married Anne Wolfe, by whom he had a daughter, Emily, who married John Brisben Walker [*q.v.*]; in 1861 he married Mary Hunter, by whom he had two sons.

Strother's writings are in the Irving tradition —slow-moving, humorous, picturesque accounts of people and places, with numerous quotations from other writers. Illustrated with copious pen drawings, they preserve a record of the old South, portraying such places as Hot Springs, White Sulphur Springs, and the University of Virginia as they appeared in the fifties and sixties of the nineteenth century.

[H. T. Tuckerman, *The Life of John Pendleton Kennedy* (1871); *Library of Southern Literature*, vol. XI (1909); T. C. Miller and Hu Maxwell, *W. Va. and Its People* (1913), III, 1098–99; F. B. Heitman, *Hist. Reg. and Dict. U. S. Army* (1903), vol. I; *N. Y. Times* and *N. Y. Tribune*, Mar. 9, 1888.]   F. M. S.

STRUBBERG, FRIEDRICH ARMAND (Mar. 18, 1806–Apr. 3, 1889), novelist, was born in Cassel, Germany, the son of Heinrich Friedrich and Frederique Elise (Marville) Strubberg. The father was one of the foremost tobacco merchants in Germany. Although his vast business was greatly hampered by the Napoleonic embargo, his son was given the best instruction that wealth could afford. Nor was his physical education neglected. Especially was he trained to ride and shoot—accomplishments which later proved to be of great advantage. In 1822 Fritz Strubberg entered one of the large mercantile houses in Bremen as an unsalaried clerk, to fit himself for a business career, but after four years he became involved in a duel in which he wounded his adversary and found it wisest to flee. To the German youth of that day there could be only one destination: America, where he remained for the next three years, making extensive journeys for various mercantile houses. A financial crisis in his father's affairs led him to return to Germany late in the autumn of 1829, and when the business passed finally into other hands at the end of the thirties he once more set out for America. He studied for two years in the medical school at Louisville, Ky., receiving the M.D. degree, then journeyed down the Mississippi River to Memphis, and finally made his way to the extreme frontier of Texas where he settled on the Leona River, eighty hours from the nearest settlement. As Dr. Schubert, a name he assumed when he fled for the frontier after having killed his adversary in a second duel in New York, he spent a few happy years at his fortress on the Leona, but in time other pioneers settled there and he sought new fields.

He spent one of the most interesting years of his adventurous career as physician and colonial director of the *Mainzer Adelsverein,* organized in 1843 by a group of German noblemen to aid and conduct German emigrants to Texas. Of these activities he writes at length in the two volumes of *Friedrichsburg, die Colonie des deutschen Fürsten-Vereins in Texas* (1867). Later he responded to the urgent appeal for physicians in Arkansas which was being devastated by smallpox, cholera, and fevers. Here he was stung in the eye by a poisonous insect and his sight endangered. He sailed for France in 1854 to consult eye specialists and the eye was eventually saved but his vision was impaired. Strubberg henceforth remained in Germany, his only sister having attracted the wanderer to his native Cassel. He was married on June 5, 1866, to Antoinette Rosine Henrietta Sattler, the love of his early days in Bremen. Shortly afterwards his wife suffered a relapse into a mental disability which caused her death in an asylum. Strubberg suffered this experience silently, and later seems to have tried to conceal the fact of his marriage.

His fascinating personality and his abilities as a raconteur made him a welcome figure among the friends of his youth. Urged to put his adventures into literary form, Strubberg, now more than fifty years old, entered upon that career which made him one of the most widely read novelists of the day. His first work, *Amerikanische Jagd-und Reiseabenteuer aus meinem*

Leben in den westlichen Indianergebieten (1858), was well received and reached seventeen editions, the last in 1933. He centered his entire interest and energy upon his literary work and let his lively imagination draw upon his long career in America as an inexhaustible source of literary material. Under the pen name of Armand there followed in rapid succession more than fifty volumes of fiction. Among the most important of his works must be mentioned *An der Indianer-Grenze* (4 vols., 1859), in which American border life is graphically depicted; *Alte und neue Heimath* (1859), an important contribution to the cultural history of the Germans in America; *Scenen aus den Kämpfen der Mexicaner und Nordamerikaner* (1859); *Sklaverei in Amerika* (3 vols., 1862), an epic of the negro; and *Carl Scharnhorst* (1863), a tale of the adventures of a German boy, a youthful Leatherstocking, on the Western frontier. *Carl Scharnhorst* passed through twelve editions and still occupies a prominent place among the juvenile books in German literature. In 1885 the novelist moved from Cassel to the little Hessian town of Gelnhausen where he died and lies buried.

[Otfrid Mylius, "F. A. Strubberg," *Kölnische Zeitung,* Aug. 18, 1889; W. Bennecke, "Aus Armands Leben," *Hessenland,* May 2, 1889; Ludwig Fränkel, biographical article in *Allgemeine Deutsche Biographie,* vol. XXXVI (1893); P. A. Barba, *The Life and Works of Friedrich Armand Strubberg* (1913), in the Americana Germanica Series.]   P. A. B.

STRUDWICK, EDMUND CHARLES FOX (Mar. 25, 1802–Nov. 30, 1879), physician, was born near Hillsboro, N. C., the son of William Francis Strudwick, who had served as a member of Congress in 1796–97, and of Martha (Shepperd) Strudwick. He began the study of medicine under a local physician, James Webb, and received the M.D. degree at the University of Pennsylvania in 1824. He remained in Philadelphia two years, practising in the alms house, and then returned to take up practice at Hillsboro in 1826. In the next year he was married to Ann E. Nash, the daughter of Frederick Nash [*q.v.*]. They had five children. While engaging in a general practice, he became particularly interested in surgery and proved to be unusually skilful in this field. He performed scores of operations for cataract, by the old needle method, without the loss of an eye, and he was also noted as the leading lithotomist in his state. This did not mean, however, that he became a specialist in the modern sense; indeed in courage, skill, and devotion to his patients he represented the best type of the heroic "country doctor."

Like many physicians of his time, he took an active interest in public affairs, was one of the first directors of the North Carolina Railroad, and was an active Whig in politics. He remained a "Union man" until 1860, when a visit to Alabama convinced him that, regardless of right or wrong, North Carolina must inevitably side with her sister states "in resisting the coercion of the North." He presided over the first war meeting held at Hillsboro on Apr. 14, 1861, supported the Confederacy most loyally thereafter, and was financially ruined as a result. Refusing to take advantage of bankruptcy proceedings, he surrendered everything to his creditors and took up life anew in a two-room cottage. In his later years he was made the first president of the revived Medical Society of the State of North Carolina. He continued his practice until the day of his death, which was occasioned by accidental poisoning with atropine.

[*Biog. Sketch of Dr. Edmund Strudwick* (1879?); Frank Nash, *Edmund Strudwick: Man and Country Doctor* (1927); *Fourteen Distinguished Physicians and Surgeons: Brief Sketches of Eminent Men for whom Duke Hospital Wards are Named* (1931); *The Papers of Thomas Ruffin,* vols. I–III (1918–20), ed. by J. G. deR. Hamilton; *Daily Charlotte Observer,* Dec. 2, 1879; personal information from Mrs. Ann Strudwick Nash, a grand-daughter, of Raleigh, N. C.]
R. H. S.

STRUVE, GUSTAV (Oct. 11, 1805–Aug. 21, 1870), German-American publicist, political agitator, and soldier, was born in Munich, the son of the Russian diplomat Johann Gustav von Struve and Friederike Christine Sibille, *née* von Hockstetter, of a Swabian noble family. He attended preparatory schools in Munich and Karlsruhe, and from 1824 to 1826 studied law in Göttingen and Heidelberg. He accepted a post as secretary of the Oldenburg legation at Frankfurt, but soon found himself at odds with the stuffy diplomacy of the Metternich period. For a while he became a judge in Jever and afterwards settled as lawyer in Mannheim. He published a work on constitutional law, *Ueber das positive Rechtsgesetz* (1834), and one on current politics, *Briefwechsel zwischen einem ehemaligen und einem jetzigen Diplomaten* (1845), which earned him a short jail sentence because he accused Metternich of treason. The same thing happened shortly afterward because of another of the many pamphlets which he issued during the forties. In 1843 he founded the *Zeitschrift für Phrenologie* and published *Phrenologie in und ausserhalb Deutschland,* at the same time lecturing on the subject at Heidelberg and Mannheim. He agitated against capital punishment and advocated that phrenologists be put in charge of prisons.

In 1845 he became editor of a political journal,

Das Mannheimer Tageblatt, and when he proved too radical for the owners he founded his own, the *Deutscher Zuschauer,* and began the agitation for a German republic culminating in the Revolution of 1848. He was instrumental in calling the popular mass meeting at Offenburg in Baden, on Mar. 19, 1848, in which the revolutionary demands were formulated. He was elected a member of the *Vorparlament* but left this body when it proved too meek and impatiently organized an armed band of 300 men to cooperate with Friedrich K. F. Hecker [*q.v.*] for the establishment of a republic. After a clash with government troops he was arrested at Säckingen, and released on condition that he emigrate to Switzerland. After a short time he returned with 200 men to support Franz Sigel [*q.v.*], but they were again defeated at Freiburg, and Struve fled to Switzerland where he made preparations for renewed fighting. In September 1848 he appeared at Lörrach, proclaimed the republic of Baden, seized public treasuries, and took the field with 4000 men. He was again defeated by regular troops and condemned to five years of penal servitude for treason but was freed from prison by a mob. When the ephemeral republic under Brentano collapsed he fled again to Switzerland, was expelled to England, and finally emigrated to America in 1851.

He settled on Staten Island, but his efforts at journalism and play-writing did not prove successful. A wealthy German brewer by the name of Biegel invited him to live on his estate at Dobbs Ferry on the Hudson for the purpose of writing a history of the world from a democratic point of view; Struve considered this *Weltgeschichte* (1852–60), in nine volumes, his *magnum opus.* His main thesis was that tyranny and repression are detrimental to economic and cultural progress—America's progress in the nineteenth century he considered due to freedom from restrictions as much as to natural resources. Greatly interested in education, Struve was very active in promoting the German public schools of New York City. He edited the socialist periodical *Die Sociale Republik* in 1858 and 1859, and worked for the cooperation of labor groups in New York and Philadelphia. In 1856 he supported Frémont against Buchanan and in 1860 ardently worked for the election of Lincoln, for, like all the "Forty-eighters," he was a strong opponent of slavery. In 1861, at the age of fifty-six years, he entered the Union army as a private in the 8th German Volunteer Regiment under Louis Blenker, soon advancing to the rank of captain. He was discharged, however, in November 1862, because he protested against the appointment of Prince von Salm-Salm as Blenker's successor against the wishes of the entire regiment.

In 1863, his wife, Amalie Düsar, to whom he had been married in 1845, died, and he returned to Germany. He settled in Coburg where he was married to a Frau von Centener. He continued to publish various works, chiefly on America and on the Revolution. An autobiographical work, *Diesseits und Jenseits des Oceans,* appeared in 1863. Lincoln appointed him consul to the Thuringian states, but that government declined his appointment because his radical writings had involved him in renewed difficulties. In 1869 he settled in Vienna, where he died. He was survived by his second wife, and two of his three daughters by his first wife. Descriptions of Struve's character and even personal appearance differ from adulation to sarcastic belittlement. As a nineteenth century disciple of Rousseau and Robespierre he combined the noblest humanitarian intentions with opinionated impracticability. There seems to be general agreement that he utterly lacked qualities of leadership, but that he possessed idealism and tenacious courage.

[Information from Dr. Heinz Struve, Leipzig; *Allgemeine deutsche Biographie,* vol. XXXVI (1893); Friedrich von Weech, *Badische Biographieen* (rev. ed., part II, 1881); Gustav Struve, *Diesseits und Jenseits des Oceans* (1863); Karl Heinzen, *Erlebtes* (1864); *Allgemeine Zeitung* (Munich), Aug. 27, 1870.]

A. E. Z.

STRYKER, MELANCTHON WOOLSEY (Jan. 7, 1851–Dec. 6, 1929), Presbyterian clergyman and college president, descended from Jan Strÿcker who came to New Amsterdam in 1652, was the son of the Rev. Isaac Pierson Stryker, a presbyterian clergyman, and his wife, Alida Livingston Woolsey. Born in Vernon, N. Y., he had his schooling near by, at Rome. He spent three years in Hamilton College, and after a year's work in the New York City Y.M.C.A., returned to college and graduated in 1872. He studied for a year in Auburn Theological Seminary, preached the next year in Bergen, N. Y., then returned to Auburn, where he graduated in 1876. On May 30 of this year he was ordained and installed as pastor of Calvary Presbyterian Church, Auburn. Thence two years later he went to the First Presbyterian Church of Ithaca, N. Y., where he ministered until 1883. After two years in the Second Congregational Church of Holyoke, Mass., in 1885 he became pastor of the Fourth Presbyterian Church, Chicago. In his seven years there he attracted attention by his eloquent preaching.

Called to the presidency of Hamilton College

in 1892, he held that office for twenty-five years. In addition to performing his administrative work, he was pastor of the college church and taught classes in Biblical subjects and ethics. The college was in a precarious position when Stryker became its head, but his inspiring personality provided the needed leadership. He won influential friends for the institution and procured large additions to its funds. During his presidency important buildings were erected, so that the college was better equipped for instruction and living. The faculty was enlarged and strengthened. While intellectually progressive, Stryker stood for college education of the traditional type, aiming at general culture, in a time when different tendencies were strong. With his energetic nature, his broad culture, and his telling speech he affected all parts of the life of the college, leaving it better in every way than he found it, and relatively secure for the future.

Stryker was much interested in hymnology and church music. In his pastorates he strove to improve congregational singing, and in Hamilton College he trained the choir. He wrote and translated many hymns, none of which, however, have come into general use. He edited several hymnals: *Christian Chorals* (1885), *Church Song* (1889), *Choral Song* (1891), *College Hymnal* (1897, 1913), *Christian Praise* (1920). His own hymns are included in these collections. All his life he wrote verse, which was uneven and often labored and obscure, but contained passages of real beauty. Eight volumes were issued, among them *Hymns and Verses* (1883), *The Song of Miriam* (1888), *Lattermath* (1895), *Vesper Bells* (1919), *Embers* (1926). He published also *Psalms of Israel in Rhymed English Meter* (1915) and an edition of *Dies Irae* containing the Latin text and five metrical translations (1892). He was much in demand as a preacher and public speaker. A strong Republican, he frequently made campaign speeches. Some of his public utterances appeared in *The Well by the Gate* (sermons, 1903), *Baccalaureate Sermons, 1893–1905* (1905), and *Hamilton, Lincoln and Other Addresses* (1896). Out of his teaching came *Ethics in Outline* (1923) and textbooks in Biblical introduction.

After his retirement from the presidency of Hamilton in 1917, he lived at Rome, N. Y., until his death, serving as trustee of the college. He was married on Sept. 27, 1876, to Clara Elizabeth Goss of Auburn, N. Y., who survived him with two sons and three daughters. Stryker's adventurous, warm-hearted character and handsome appearance made him an impressive presence everywhere, and an enduring memory.

[*Hamilton College Bulletin*, Apr. 1930; W. S. Stryker, *Geneal. Record of the Strÿcker Family* (1887); *Gen. Biog. Cat. Auburn Theological Seminary* (1918); John Julian, *A Dict. of Hymnology* (1891); *Who's Who in America*, 1928–29; *N. Y. Times*, Dec. 7, 1929.]   R. H. N.

STUART, ALEXANDER HUGH HOLMES (Apr. 2, 1807–Feb. 13, 1891), congressman, secretary of the interior, was born at Staunton, Va., the son of Archibald Stuart [*q.v.*] and Eleanor (Briscoe) Stuart and the great-grandson of Archibald Stuart, a Scotch-Irish emigrant to Pennsylvania about 1727. He was educated at the academy in Staunton, at the college of William and Mary, and later at the University of Virginia, where he was graduated in 1828. During the same year he was licensed to practise law and began his professional career in Staunton. The Whig party soon claimed his support. As a champion of Henry Clay, he took a leading part in the Young Men's National Convention, which assembled at Washington in 1832. In 1836 he began a service of three years in the Virginia House of Delegates and made himself conspicuous as a champion of internal improvements. In a report of 1838 he proposed a comprehensive system of communications that would have linked the different parts of the state commercially (*Substance of the Remarks of Mr. Stuart of Augusta on the . . . General System of Improvement*, 1838). Though the plan as a whole was defeated, some of his proposals were carried into effect. In 1841 he became a member of the federal House of Representatives. There he was one of the few Southerners who supported Adams in his opposition to the "gag rule," and, when Clay broke with President Tyler, Stuart took the side of the former. Retiring from Congress in 1843, he did not again hold office until President Fillmore appointed him secretary of the interior in 1850. He was largely responsible for organizing the department as it had not been done by his predecessor (Robertson, p. 55). In 1853 he again retired to private life, but continued to take an active interest in politics. When the Whig party disintegrated and the American party was formed upon its ruins, he espoused the new cause and in 1856 published a series of letters, the "Madison" letters (Robertson, *post*, pp. 59–162), which came to be looked upon as an authoritative exposition of the doctrines of the party. The next year he was elected to the state Senate and served until the outbreak of the Civil War. He was chairman of a legislative committee which drew up a report on John Brown's raid (*Ibid.*, App. 1, pp. 383–405). In the document, New England abolitionism was roundly denounced, and the righteousness of the

Northern attitude in regard to slavery was questioned.

He was a member of the Virginia convention of 1861, and, while not denying the right of secession, he condemned the move as inexpedient, accurately foretold its dire consequence, and opposed it as long as opposition was practicable. During the war, his sympathy was with his section, but his age obviated his taking an active part in the struggle. Immediately after the surrender, he took the leading part in assembling a popular meeting in Augusta County looking toward the reëstablishment of peaceful relations with the Union. In 1866 he published a pamphlet, *The Recent Revolution, It's Causes and It's Consequences.* In 1870 he was instrumental in the creation and active in the work of the "committee of nine" that went to Washington and persuaded Congress and the President to permit Virginia to exclude clauses from the "Underwood constitution," which would have disfranchised the leading elements in the white population of the state and perpetuated "carpetbag" ascendency. The restoration of home rule to Virginia was, therefore, largely his work (C. G. Bowers, *The Tragic Era,* 1929, p. 277). In 1865 he was elected to Congress but was not permitted to take his seat. In 1873 he consented to serve once again in the House of Delegates but retired on account of his health at the end of three years. Throughout the period he advocated the payment of Virginia's pre-war debt. In 1876 he became rector of the University of Virginia, served until 1882, and again from 1884 to 1886. From 1871 to 1889 he served as a trustee of the Peabody education fund. In this capacity he urged upon the federal government the desirability of its contributing to the education of the negroes (Robertson, *post,* App. 3, pp. 462–78). In 1888 he published *A Narrative of the Leading Incidents of the Organization of the First Popular Movement in Virginia in 1865 to Reëstablish Peaceful Relations . . . and of the Subsequent Efforts of the "Committee of Nine"* . . . (also, Robertson, *post,* App. 2, pp. 406–61).

In person, Stuart was over six feet tall, handsome and dignified, serious but affable. On Aug. 1, 1833, he married his cousin, Frances Cornelia Baldwin, the daughter of Briscoe G. Baldwin of Staunton. They had nine children.

[A. F. Robertson, *Alexander Hugh Holmes Stuart* (1925); H. H. Simms, *The Rise of the Whigs in Va.* (1929); A. C. Cole, *The Whig Party in the South* (1912).]
T. P. A.

STUART, ARCHIBALD (Mar. 19, 1757–July 11, 1832), Revolutionary soldier, legislator, jurist, was for many years a prominent leader of the conservative wing of the Jeffersonian Democrats in his state. He was the son of Alexander and Mary (Patterson) Stuart and the grandson of Archibald Stuart, an Ulster Scotsman, who emigrated to Pennsylvania about 1727. Archibald was born near Staunton in the Valley of Virginia, which was then a frontier area. His preliminary education was received in the Augusta Academy. For some time during the Revolution he was a student at the College of William and Mary, where he played a prominent part in Phi Beta Kappa and was offered the chair of mathematics. He fought under his father at Guilford Court House and served in the Yorktown campaign. After the Revolution he studied law with Thomas Jefferson and then began the extensive practice that carried him to nearly every county in the Valley as well as to many outside of that section.

His political career began in 1783 with his election to the Virginia House of Delegates from Botetourt County. Very soon he stood out as one of the leaders in that body in the formative period between the Revolution and the organization of the new government in 1789. He aligned himself with Madison in the championing of such measures as the reform of the state court system, the payment of British debts, the various measures that made for religious liberty, the opening of the James River for navigation, the repudiation of paper money, and the reorganization of the federal and state governments. It is significant that he championed most ardently the two of these movements that were the most difficult to accomplish, that is, the reform in the state court system and the reorganization of state government. Both were eventually realized. After playing a prominent part in the ratification of the new federal Constitution in 1788, he was inactive in politics for nearly a decade, except for membership on the Virginia-Kentucky Boundary Commission in 1795. At the turn of the century he was a member of the state Senate, a leader in the passage of the Virginia Resolutions. From 1800 until just before his death he was a judge of the general court of Virginia. He was a presidential elector for the Jefferson Democrats from 1800 to 1824. In 1828 he supported Adams and thus indicated his strong inclination toward the conservative wing of his old party. From the earliest days of his political career he was an aristocrat who wanted to be a democrat but was uncertain whether the populace could be trusted. To both Madison and Jefferson he was an able lieutenant, and in each he found a warm personal friend. Jefferson designed the substantial home he built in Staunton,

Va., in the later years of the eighteenth century and in which Stuart's grand-daughter still (1935) lives. In May 1791 he married Eleanor Briscoe, the daughter of Gerard Briscoe of Frederick County, Va. Alexander Hugh Holmes Stuart [*q.v.*] was their son.

[H. G. Grigsby, "The Hist. of the Va. Federal Convention of 1788," *Va. Hist. Colls.*, new series, vol. X (1901); *Washington and Lee Univ. Hist. Papers*, vol. II (1890); A. F. Robertson, *Alexander Hugh Holmes Stuart* (1925); collections of correspondence, particularly the Breckenridge Papers in Lib. of Cong.]

F. H. H.

STUART, CHARLES (1783–1865), abolitionist, was born in Jamaica, the son of a British army officer, and spent his boyhood in various military posts. He was given his elementary education by his mother, a Scotch Presbyterian of the strictest Calvinistic stamp, and was sent to Belfast, Ireland, for his academic training. At the age of eighteen he secured a lieutenant's commission in the British East India Company's forces, with which he served for thirteen years, resigning with the rank of captain on a pension of $800 a year. He then migrated to America, received a grant of land on Lake Simcoe in upper Canada where he lived intermittently for some years, served as justice of the peace, and published *The Emigrant's Guide to Upper Canada* (1820). For part of the time he taught school during the winters and distributed Bibles and religious tracts at his own expense during his vacations. In 1824, when he was principal of a boys' academy in Utica, N. Y., he met Theodore D. Weld [*q.v.*], then a youth of fifteen, and conceived for him a regard "more than a father's affection for his first born" (Weld-Grimké *Letters, post*, II, 557). The next year both Stuart and Weld were converted as a result of the preaching of Charles G. Finney [*q.v.*], joined the "holy band" of Finney's assistant revivalists, and accompanied him for much of the next two years in the mighty revivals which he conducted in western New York.

Stuart sent Weld to Oneida Institute in 1827 to prepare for the ministry, and, after another year in Finney's "holy band," sailed to England in order to take part in the movement to abolish slavery in the British West Indies. At his own expense he traveled through the provinces as lecturing agent, and wrote pamphlets for the anti-slavery press. His tract, *The West India Question: Immediate Emancipation Safe and Practical* (1832, often reprinted), was one of the most famous pamphlets in the British propaganda. His most distinguished service, however, was in connection with the campaign of the American Colonization Society which was begun in 1830 to secure British support for their cause.

Against the "malignant jesuitry" of the colonization program Stuart penned a succession of pamphlet philippics, of which *Prejudice Vincible* (subsequently published with James Cropper's *A Letter to Thomas Clarkson*, 1832) was the most devastating. By the winter of 1831 he had turned not only the leading abolitionists but also the British public against the colonization cause.

Meanwhile Stuart had rendered invaluable service to anti-slavery beginnings in America. From the first he had imbued his disciple, Theodore Weld, with anti-slavery principles; and in the spring of 1831, when Arthur and Lewis Tappan [*qq.v.*], the New York philanthropists, called a council of reformers to plan an "American National Anti-Slavery Society" on the British model, it was Stuart's abolition doctrine which Weld expounded to the council. Indeed, for several years after the American Anti-Slavery Society had been organized, his pamphlet, *The West India Question*, was the approved statement of its abolition creed. Other notable anti-slavery tracts, among the scores he wrote, were *Is Slavery Defensible from Scripture?* (1831) and *A Memoir of Granville Sharp* (1836). More than any other man, Stuart brought the impulse of the British anti-slavery movement to the rising agitation in America.

In 1834 Stuart returned to the United States and, as the American Anti-Slavery Society's agent but at his own expense, lectured in Ohio, Vermont, and New York, suffering considerable mob violence at times, but courageously maintaining his course. In 1838 he visited the West Indies, where he studied the workings of emancipation, reporting his findings both to the American and to the British anti-slavery press. He returned from this mission in 1840, in time to attend the world anti-slavery convention at London. During the next two years he spoke and collected funds in England for those American abolitionists who had separated from the faction of William Lloyd Garrison [*q.v.*]. At the world anti-slavery convention of 1842, the British philanthropists with whom he had so long been associated united to do him honor. Stuart had also done pioneer work in England and Scotland in behalf of the American temperance movement, and he was subsequently instrumental in America in organizing relief for the sufferers in the Irish potato famine. In the main, however, his work was done, and he retired about 1842 to his property on Lake Simcoe, where he lived until his death.

[An autobiog. sketch and numerous letters in the Weld MSS., in private hands; notices of his labors in the anti-slavery reports and periodicals of England

and America; *Letters of Theodore Dwight Weld, Angelina Grimké Weld, and Sarah Grimké* (2 vols., 1934), ed. by G. H. Barnes and D. L. Dumond; G. H. Barnes, *The Anti-Slavery Impulse, 1830–1844* (1933); W. P. and F. J. Garrison, *William Lloyd Garrison* (4 vols., 1885–98).]

G. H. B.

STUART, CHARLES BEEBE (June 4, 1814–Jan. 4, 1881), engineer and author, was born at Chittenango Springs, Madison County, N. Y., the son of Henry Y. and Deborah Stuart. He began his professional career at the age of eighteen, under Jonathan Knight [*q.v.*] on the Baltimore & Ohio Railroad. Between 1833 and 1840 he was engaged on various lines under construction in northern New York; in 1840 he was chief engineer of the New York & Erie, and in 1842 became chief engineer of the line between Batavia and Rochester, now part of the New York Central. During six years' residence in Rochester he served twice as city surveyor, laying out Mount Hope Cemetery; he also located what became the Rochester and Niagara Falls branch of the New York Central, and a part of the line of the Great Western Railway of Canada, proposing to connect the two roads by a railway suspension bridge over the Niagara River two miles below the Falls. His scheme was generally considered impractical until the bridge was nearly ready for the passage of trains; among engineers only Charles Ellet, Jr., John A. Roebling, Edward W. Serrell [*qq.v.*], and Samuel Keefer believed that it could be accomplished. In November 1847, however, Stuart, as director of the American and Canadian bridge companies, contracted with Ellet for the construction of such a railroad and carriage bridge over the Niagara; work was commenced in the spring of 1848, and, after Ellet's resignation, was completed by Roebling in 1855.

In 1849 Stuart was state engineer and surveyor of New York, and in October of that year entered the service of the United States government as engineer in charge of the Brooklyn dry docks, which had been under construction since 1842 under the supervision of many different distinguished engineers. This task he completed in August 1851. Meanwhile, Dec. 1, 1850, he had been appointed engineer-in-chief of the United States Navy, a position he held until his resignation on June 30, 1853. In this capacity he wrote the specifications for the California floating sectional dry dock, which was constructed in New York under his supervision and shipped to San Francisco early in 1852. He was subsequently associated with Edward W. Serrell in the engineering firm of Stuart, Serrell & Company. In the middle fifties he became interested in Iowa railroads and as president of the

Iowa Land Company was concerned with the laying out of Clinton, Iowa. He was also financially interested in a railroad in Georgia, and in 1860 was consulting engineer for a projected railroad in Texas.

Upon the outbreak of the Civil War, he raised a regiment of engineers which was mustered into service at Elmira, Aug. 15, 1861, as Colonel Stuart's Independent Regiment, New York Infantry, subsequently the 50th New York Engineers. This regiment served with the Army of the Potomac in the construction of fortifications and bridges, participating in many engagements from the siege of Yorktown, Apr. 5–May 4, 1862, to the end of the war; Stuart, however, resigned his commission in June 1863 because of impaired health, and was honorably discharged.

Besides being an accomplished engineer, he was an effective writer. "Few makers of books have done so much themselves worthy of an enduring record; and still fewer have written a narrative, in which their own deeds figure largely, with so much modesty and good taste" (*New York Tribune,* quoted in "Press Notices," p. 15, *Naval and Mail Steamers*). Among his published works, besides numerous engineer's reports, were *The Naval Dry Docks of the United States* (1852); *The Naval and Mail Steamers of the United States* (1853); and *Lives and Works of Civil and Military Engineers of America* (1871), a valuable source of information concerning his eminent predecessors and contemporaries.

Stuart was married twice: first, at Glens Falls, N. Y., July 2, 1836, to Sarah Maria Breese, who died at Schenectady, Sept. 28, 1838; and second, at Tioga Point, Pa., Apr. 17, 1841, to Frances Maria Welles, who with two daughters and a son survived him. Two sons born of the first marriage and one born of the second died in infancy. At the time of his death Stuart was chief engineer of the Conotton Valley Railroad, then being built from the coal-fields in Carroll County to Cleveland, Ohio. He died at Cleveland of senile gangrene following a sprained ankle.

[*N. Y. Times,* Jan. 5, 1881; *Frank Leslie's Chimney Corner,* Feb. 8, 1873; F. M. Bennett, *The Steam Navy of the U. S.* (1896); *Trans. Am. Soc. Civil Engineers,* X (1881), 195 ff.; autobiog. material in Stuart's own writings; copy of record from family Bible, through the courtesy of the Veteran's Administration.]

B. A. R.

STUART, CHARLES MACAULAY (Aug. 20, 1853–Jan. 26, 1932), Methodist clergyman, educator, editor, was born in Glasgow, Scotland, the son of Lewis and Mary (Home) Stuart. Coming to the United States in youth, he spent a few years in business and then entered Kalamazoo College. Here, under the influence of two

Methodist ministers, Lewis R. Fiske and William X. Ninde, he decided to enter the ministry, and upon his graduation in 1880 he became a student in Garrett Biblical Institute. During his theological course he served as student pastor of the church at River Forest, Ill. In 1883 he graduated from Garrett, was received into the Detroit Conference of the Methodist Episcopal Church, and became pastor of the Fort Street Church in that city. On Oct. 10 of the same year he married Emma Rachel Littlefield, daughter of a fellow minister. To their great sorrow they had no children.

In 1885 Stuart became associate editor of the *Michigan Christian Advocate,* an independent Methodist journal under the control of the Detroit Conference. His gifts as a writer attracted the attention of Dr. Arthur Edwards, editor of the *Northwestern Christian Advocate,* Chicago, and in 1886 Stuart was called to become assistant editor of that important weekly. Here he served for ten years with ability and distinction. From 1896 to 1909 he was professor of sacred rhetoric in Garrett Biblical Institute, but in 1909, upon the sudden death of David D. Thompson, was recalled to the *Northwestern Christian Advocate* as its editor. After some three years in this post, he was elected to a professorship of Christian ethics and the philosophy of religion at Wesleyan University, Middletown, Conn., and almost at the same time was chosen president of Garrett Biblical Institute, to succeed Charles J. Little [*q.v.*]. After some hesitation Stuart chose the latter position, and from 1911 to 1924, when he became president emeritus, performed a notable work in the development of Garrett.

During his administration many changes were made both in the educational program and in the physical equipment of the institution. The burning of the principal dormitory in 1914 and the large increase in the number of students made a building program a necessity. With energy and foresight Stuart entered upon a plan of expansion which eventually resulted in the erection of a notable group of buildings, the center of the group being the Charles Macaulay Stuart Chapel. As an administrator Stuart was always kind and considerate, laying no claim to unusual executive ability, but nevertheless succeeding in maintaining a spirit of confidence and cooperation within the faculty and student body.

Among his other activities, he served his church as secretary of the joint hymnal commission which produced the *Methodist Hymnal* (1905), now in use in both branches of Episcopal Methodism. He was also three times the representative of the Rock River Conference in the General Conference of the Methodist Episcopal Church. His output of books was not large, but they all possess literary distinction and grace of expression. The most notable of his works are perhaps *The Vision of Christ in the Poets* (1896) ; *The Story of the Masterpieces* (1897) ; *In Memoriam: Charles Joseph Little* (1912) ; and *The Manifold Message of the Gospel* (1913). As a speaker he had grace and charm and was in considerable demand. He died at La Jolla, Cal.

["Charles Macaulay Stuart: A Memorial," *Garrett Biblical Inst. Bull.,* June 1932 ; *Who's Who in America,* 1930–31 ; *Minutes of the Rock River Conference,* 1932 ; *Hist. Cat. . . . Kalamazoo Coll. and Kalamazoo Theol. Sem.* (1903) ; *Northwestern Christian Advocate* (Chicago), Feb. 4, 1932 ; *Chicago Daily News,* Jan. 27, 1932.]
W. W. S.

STUART, GILBERT (Dec. 3, 1755–July 9, 1828), painter, was born in the township of North Kingstown, Kings (later Washington) County, in His Majesty's Colony of Rhode Island and Providence Plantations. The often repeated statement that he was born in Narragansett is incorrect without the explanation that "Narragansett" at that time was merely a popular name for "the Narragansett Country," the vague territory west of Narragansett Bay and, after 1677, south of East Greenwich. (See S. G. Arnold, *History of the State of Rhode Island and Providence Plantations,* 2 vols., 1859–60.) His father, Gilbert Stuart, a millwright and a native of Perth, Scotland, emigrated to Rhode Island to engage in the manufacture of snuff and was married in Newport on May 23, 1751, to Elizabeth, a daughter of Albro Anthony, a substantial land owner of Middletown, R. I. In partnership with Edward Cole and Dr. Thomas Moffatt, both of Newport, Stuart erected at the junction of the Mattatoxet stream and the Pattaquamscott tidal river a two-story building with gambrel roof, the snuff mill occupying the lower and the dwelling the two upper stories. In the northeast bedroom of the building, which is still (1935) standing, Gilbert Stuart was born. He was baptized by the Rev. James MacSparran in St. Paul's, "the Old Narragansett Church," on Palm Sunday, Apr. 11, 1756. The manufacturing venture failing, the elder Stuart in 1761 sold his interest in the mill, and the family moved to Newport, where they lived "next to Mr. Abraham Redwood" in a house satirically referred to by Stuart in later life as "a hovel on Bannister's Wharf," evidently in the rear of what is now 341–45 Thames St. There Stuart attended the school founded by Nathaniel Kay, collector of customs under Queen Anne, who bequeathed to Trinity Church in 1734 a fund "to teach ten poor boys their grammar and the mathematics gratis" (G. C. Mason, *An-*

nals of Trinity Church, Newport, R. I., 1698–1821, 1890, p. 28). According to Benjamin Waterhouse [*q.v.*], who was also at this school (*Monthly Anthology,* November 1805), Stuart early evidenced a talent for drawing. Waterhouse says that he copied pictures when he was but thirteen years old and a little later attempted to draw portraits in black lead (Dunlap, *post,* vol. I, p. 197). About 1769 a mediocre Scotch artist, Cosmo Alexander, came to Newport and painted portraits of some of its residents, among others Dr. William Hunter, a friend of the Stuart family. Stuart became his pupil and received what has been described as training in drawing and in the "groundwork of the palette" (*Ibid.,* p. 198). After going to Edinburgh with Alexander, who died there on Aug. 25, 1772 (Whitley, *post,* p. 8), he attempted to support himself by his art and, failing, is said to have worked his way home in 1773 or 1774 on a collier bound for Nova Scotia. We know little concerning the two years following Alexander's death except that he busied himself in painting, some of his clients coming from a colony of cultivated Jews settled in Newport, and in studying music, in which he was also talented. In this period shortly before the Revolution it was apparent that the American colonies, for the time being, were no place in which to practise the painter's art, and in June 1775 Stuart, alone, with little money and but one letter of introduction, sailed for London, determined to enter upon a painter's career. It is possible that he stopped in Philadelphia on the way, for an entry in the account books of Joseph Anthony, his uncle, shows a loan to Stuart in July 1775.

He reached London probably in November 1775 and, according to his daughter Jane, "went into cheap lodgings," sought clients, and occasionally painted portraits "at prices so low as scarcely to give him bread" ("The Youth of Gilbert Stuart," *Scribner's Monthly,* Mar. 1877, p, 642). There is a well authenticated story that he obtained employment as organist in a church in Foster Lane, probably Saint Vedast's. Although the church records rarely mention the names of the deputy organists, William Duncombe, who gave Saint Vedast's its organ in 1774, undertook either to "play himself or to find an able performer in his place" (letter to the author from the Rev. Andrew Freeman, Standish Vicarage, Stonehouse, Gloucester), and it is probable that Stuart eked out the slender earnings from his profession in this way. Stuart's classmate, Waterhouse, had spent a year in Scotland studying medicine and in the summer of 1776 removed to London to attend Saint Thomas' and Guy's hospitals. There he found Stuart lodging in York Buildings (Buckingham Street, Strand) with one picture on his easel, a family group painted for Alexander Grant. Stuart moved to Gracechurch Street to be near Waterhouse, and the two youths devoted one day a week to rambling about London and visiting its sights and picture galleries. Even at this early period, Stuart neglected his work and was in constant money difficulties. Finally, unable to support himself, he wrote Benjamin West, 1738–1820 [*q.v.*], a letter in which he described himself as "just arriv'd att the age of 21," "without the necessarys of life," his "hopes from home Blasted & incapable of returning thither," and asked West's help (facsimile in J. H. Morgan's life in Park, *post,* vol. I, p. 29). Upon the immediate response of West, at this time the leading figure in historical painting in England, with a studio that was a meeting place for the fashion of the day, Stuart moved to 27 Villiers St., not far from West's house in Newman Street, and became his pupil; later, probably in the summer of 1777, he became a member of West's household and remained with him for nearly five years.

He contributed one portrait to the Royal Academy exhibition in 1777, three in 1779, two in 1781, and four in 1782. By 1781 his work was attracting the favorable attention of the London critics, but in 1782 his famous "Portrait of a Gentleman Skating" (a full length of his friend William Grant of Congalton) brought him prominently to the attention of the public, and some time after the close of the exhibition he took rooms at No. 7 Newman St. It is probable that he continued to assist West for a time thereafter, but he seems to have received many commissions at once and in 1783 sent nine portraits to the Exhibition of the Incorporated Society of Artists, of which he became a member in December 1783. A list of his patrons for the next five years makes it clear that he had a large share of fashionable patronage at prices, Dunlap says, "equal to any, except Sir Joshua Reynolds and Gainsborough." John Boydell, the leading print seller of London, engaged him to paint fifteen portraits of contemporary painters and engravers, including Reynolds and West, from which plates were engraved and the prints sold by Boydell to the public. He exhibited for the last time in the Royal Academy of 1785. His address at this time is given as New Burlington Street, where he occupied a house at a rent of a hundred guineas (Whitley, *post,* p. 51). Here, according to tradition, he entertained lavishly, hiring a French chef, engaging professional musicians, and often performing himself, and it was here that he brought his bride, Charlotte Coates, daughter of a physician of Reading, Berkshire, after their marriage on May 10, 1786. The match had been opposed by the Coates family, but it seems to have been a happy one. Of the twelve children born of the union, the second son, Charles Gilbert, who died at twenty-six, and Jane, the youngest daughter, inherited some of their father's ability. Jane Stuart excuses the extravagances of her father's London life on the ground that his fine clothes, his costly establishment, and his many entertainments were required by a fashionable clientèle—a conclusion which does not necessarily follow.

Stuart's rise during these twelve years in London can be fully measured only when it is remembered that he spent most of the first twenty years of his life under unfavorable conditions, that he had had no teacher but Alexander and few, if any, great paintings to copy, that his environment provided very little stimulus, and that he had only a small circle to appreciate his gifts. Yet at nineteen, alone, inexperienced, without resources or friends, he had courage enough to travel from the Colonies to London, seeking his fortune in a calling where influence and favor were half the battle. Within five years after becoming West's pupil he was able to begin an independent career; within five years more he had become one of the leading portrait painters of London—and this in the London of Ramsay, Reynolds, Romney, and Gainsborough, at a time when portrait painting had reached the highest point attained by British art. Such distinction would have been sufficient to crown the work of a lifetime, yet it was achieved by Stuart before he reached the age of thirty-two.

In 1787, however, he had left England for Ireland. According to Jane Stuart, he went at the request of the Duke of Rutland, then lord lieutenant of Ireland, to paint his portrait, and entered Dublin on the day of the funeral of the duke (*Scribner's Monthly*, Mar. 1877, p. 645), who died on October 24. What really formed his determination to leave London when the full tide of success apparently had set in, may never be known; but it seems most probable that his improvidence and utter lack of business sense forced the change, since at the time imprisonment for debt was usually the end of reckless living. Mention of Stuart's name disappears from contemporary newsprints and periodicals in the summer of 1787, and his new-found prosperity apparently had utterly collapsed. Yet, whatever may have been the conditions determining his move, in Dublin again he was most successful. He painted the portraits of many of those prominent in political, social, and professional life, and was without a competitor worthy the name. He resided for a time in Pill Lane, Dublin, and later moved to Stillorgan, a suburb. Inordinately fond of social pleasures and delighted with the polished manners and the hospitality of Irish society which suited his genial temperament so well, he repeated his London life. His daughter says that Stuart "entered too much into these convivialities" and that her mother could never be induced to talk upon these Irish experiences, as it gave her "pain to remember anything associated with reckless extravagances, or what she called his folly" (*Ibid.*).

Stuart sailed for New York late in 1792 or early in 1793, and painted the portrait of the owner of the ship, one John Shaw, in payment for his passage. He is quoted as saying that he returned to his native land hoping to make a fortune by painting portraits of Washington: "I calculate upon making a plurality of his portraits, whole lengths, that will enable me to realize; and if I should be fortunate, I will repay my English and Irish creditors" (Herbert, *post*, p. 248). He also expected to profit through the sale of prints from a plate made from a portrait of Washington. He leased a studio on Stone, near William Street, and Dunlap, who was then living in New York, wrote that all who were distinguished by office, rank, or attainment availed themselves of his talents. Late in November 1794 he moved to Philadelphia, then the seat of the federal government, and opened a painting room on the south-west corner of Fifth and Chestnut Streets. As he had great social gifts and made it his practice to associate with the leaders of intellect and fashion in each land in which he resided, it was natural that he should choose to go to Philadelphia, then the largest city in America, but from a letter to his uncle, Joseph Anthony, it is plain that his immediate motive was to finish his uncle's portrait and to paint one of the President. The Philadelphia period is important by reason of the brilliant series of women's portraits which Stuart there completed; though it has always been conceded that he was a notable painter of old men, this group entitles him to high rank as a portrayer of women. His stay in Philadelphia will also be memorable because there he painted his first two life portraits of Washington. The first, a bust portrait, showing the right side of the face, known as the Vaughan Type, was painted in the late winter of 1795. "A list of the gentlemen who are to have copies of the portrait of the President of the United States" in Stuart's handwriting, dated Apr. 20, 1795, names thirty-two subscribers calling for thirty-nine "copies." Stuart received sittings, beginning Apr. 12, 1796, from Washington for his second life portrait, a life-size standing portrait, showing the left side of the face, eyes gazing right (left of spectator), right hand outstretched as if addressing an audience, which is known as the Lansdowne Type. His painting room was so thronged with visitors and patrons, however, that he was unable to finish his commissions, and in the summer of 1796 he moved to Germantown and fitted up the stone barn of the Wister mansion (now 5140 Main St.) as a studio. Here in the early fall of 1796, at the request of Mrs. Washington, the President sat for the third life portrait, bust size, showing the left side of the face, eyes front. This is the familiar "Athenaeum Head," unfinished as to the stock and coat, now in the Boston Museum of Fine Arts, which Stuart kept with him until his death. It is a highly idealized representation of Washington in his old age, when the loss of his teeth had changed not only the shape of his face but the expression as well. Following the seat of government to Washington in 1803, Stuart opened a studio at the corner of F and Seventh Streets, and for two years was fully occupied. He painted Jefferson, Madison, Monroe, William Branch Giles, and many others among the leaders, one contemporary writing that he was "all the rage" and "worked to death."

Sometime in the summer of 1805 he moved to Boston, where he lived for the remainder of his life. Here again he met with instant success. Charles Fraser [q.v.], the miniature painter, at the beginning of this period wrote that Stuart "had all the beauty and talents of Boston under his pencil" (A. R. and D. E. Huger Smith, *Charles Fraser*, 1924, p. 18). The remaining twenty-three years of his life in Boston ran true to form. He was overrun with commissions but, as he kept no books, "he did not know, at times, whether a picture he had finished had been paid for; so indifferent was he to all business matters" (Mason, *post*, p. 45). His health began to fail in 1825, and somewhat later symptoms of paralysis in his left arm depressed him greatly. He still continued to paint but with great difficulty. In the spring of 1828 he was attacked by gout, and on July 9, 1828, he died in his home on Essex Street. He was buried in Tomb 61 in the Central Burying Grounds on Boston Common, situated under the Mall which leads from Park Square to the Park Street Church. He died without a will. The inventory of his estate, which included an organ, eight "unfinished Sketches of Heads," household furniture, glass, china, etc., was valued at $375; his debts, which

were largely for household supplies, showed a deficit of $1,778 after the payment of five preferred claims, two of which were: "Paid for coffin and undertaker's bill . . . $36," and "Dr. Warren's bill for the last illness of deceased . . . $132" (probate records in Old Court House, Boston). He was survived by his wife and four of his daughters, Anne (Mrs. Stebbens), Agnes, Emma, and Jane Stuart, and as he left little but unfinished canvases, including the portraits of the President and Mrs. Washington, an exhibition of his work was held for their benefit at the Boston Athenaeum, which brought together 211 of his portraits.

There are several portraits of Stuart. The self-portrait of 1778 and the bust modeled by John Henri Isaac Browere [q.v.] from a life mask, which Jane Stuart called, "a most living and beautiful thing," best represent him in youth and old age. Of his most familiar likeness— the portrait by John Neagle [q.v.]— his daughter wrote that it was "utterly devoid of intellectual expression," and was considered "a positive caricature by his family and his intimate friends" ("Anecdotes of Gilbert Stuart," *Scribner's Monthly*, July 1877, p. 379). A contemporary writes of him: "In his person, Stuart was rather large, and his movements, in the latter part of his life, were slow and heavy, but not ungraceful. His manners had something of the formality of the old school. . . . He was sometimes a little fastidious and eccentrick; but never lost the manners of a gentleman on any occasion. . . . The lives and works of the great artists of all ages were familiar to him as his palett. He discoursed upon their excellences, defects, and peculiarities, as one who had read and examined them all most thoroughly. His eloquence was peculiar and attractive; his voice was strong and deep; his enunciation clear and distinct; and his countenance came in aid of his voice, for his features were bold and lion-like . . ." (Knapp, *post*, p. 196). In addition to Stuart's talents as a painter and musician, there are innumerable references to his gifts as a conversationalist. John Quincy Adams, whose character, education, and wide experience of the world rendered him no mean judge of men, wrote in his diary on Sept. 19, 1818, "I sat to Stuart before and after breakfast, and found his conversation . . . very entertaining. His own figure is highly picturesque, with his dress always disordered and taking snuff from a large, round tin wafer-box, holding, perhaps, half a pound, which he must use up in a day." Jane Stuart alludes to his irony and his keen sense of the ridiculous, but she and others stress his kindliness and benevolence. "Anything," she wrote, "like adverse fortune or neglected merit was sure to find a place in his regard" (*Ibid.*, p. 376). He was procrastinating and would only paint when in the mood, sometimes refusing a commission from distaste for the subject, sometimes for no apparent reason whatsoever. He failed even to answer the letter of the Pennsylvania Academy of the Fine Arts offering $1,500 for a replica of his Washington portrait of the Lansdowne Type, two and one-half times what he had been paid for the original, and he neglected the request of the authorities of the Pitti Palace, Florence, for his own portrait to add to its gallery of eminent artists. He was quick to take offense and impatient of any criticism of his work, often refusing to finish a portrait (for example, that of Prince Jerome Bonaparte) because of some fancied slight. If one of his portraits pleased him he often neglected to finish it, and had to be begged and cajoled into completing the canvas. While the artistic temperament is proverbially improvident and the mere pursuit of money rarely interests those gifted with unusual talents, still, in view of Stuart's ancestry, the poverty of his youth, his bitter experience in London, and his inability to order his early success there, it is difficult to understand why he never learned the lesson of prudence.

Stuart's palette, set in high key, often has been described, but West is quoted as having said, "It is of no use to steal Stuart's colors: if you want to paint as he does you must steal his eyes" (Mason, *post*, p. 39). It was Stuart's mastery of the use of what may be called transparent color which gave his portraits their lifelike and luminous effect, and it is in this quality that they stand supreme among American paintings. His chief object was always to paint his sitter so as to preserve the character and likeness of the individual. He had what Washington Allston [*q.v.*] described as "the faculty of distinguishing between the accidental and the permanent, in other words, between the conversational expression which arises from *manners* and the more subtle indication of the individual mind" (*Boston Daily Advertiser*, July 22, 1828). William Temple Franklin wrote Benjamin Franklin in 1784 that he had heard West say that Stuart "*'nails* the face to the canvas.'" Stuart's heads are well placed, powerfully and subtly modeled, and (when not on a panel) often so thinly painted as to show the web of the coarse English canvas, which he preferred, through the pigment. After completing the head he lost interest, and careless drawing will be found sometimes in the accessories. When criticized for this and for not paying more attention to the decorative side of

portrait painting, his reply was, "I copy the works of God and leave clothes to tailors and mantua-makers" (Mason, *post*, p. 38); yet when the whim took him he would with a few bold strokes paint a piece of lace to perfection, as if to show how simple it was to produce such an effect. While many of his portraits as compositions lack the decorative qualities of those of his British contemporaries, Stuart's heads, in their absence of flattery and in their scrupulous fidelity to nature, bring to mind those of the seventeenth-century Dutch painters. Early in his career Stuart said: "For my part, I will not follow any master. I wish to find out what nature is for myself and see her with *my own eyes*" (Dunlap, *post*, vol. I, p. 216). In this is the key to a full appreciation of his work. He left a reputation without rival in the United States, and the passing of the century since his death still finds his name first in the list of American portrait painters.

[Stuart's name sometimes appears as Gilbert Charles. For biog. material see, William Dunlap, *A Hist. of the Rise and Progress of the Arts of Design in the U. S.* (3 vols., 1918), ed. by F. W. Bayley and C. E. Goodspeed; G. C. Mason, *The Life and Works of Gilbert Stuart* (1879); Lawrence Park, *Gilbert Stuart, An Illustrated Descriptive List of His Works* (4 vols., 1926), with an account of his life by J. H. Morgan; W. T. Whitley, *Gilbert Stuart* (1932); J. H. Morgan and Mantle Fielding, *The Life Portraits of Washington and Their Replicas* (1931); J. D. Herbert, *Irish Varieties, for the Last Fifty Years* (1836); S. L. Knapp, *Lectures on Am. Lit.* (1829); J. H. Morgan, "Gilbert Stuart; Miniature Painter," *Antiques*, Oct. 1929, and "The Date of Stuart's Death, the Place of his Burial, and the Inventory of his Estate," *Ibid.*, Mar. 1934; W. G. Strickland, *A Dict. of Irish Artists* (2 vols., 1913); H. E. T., in *Bull. of the R. I. School of Design*, Oct. 1914, Jan. 1915; obituary notice in *Columbian Centinel*, July 12, 1828; probate records in Old Court House, Boston, Mass.]   J. H. M.

STUART, GRANVILLE (Aug. 27, 1834–Oct. 2, 1918), Montana pioneer, was of Scotch descent, the son of Robert and Nancy Currence (Hall) Stuart, and was born at Clarksburg, Va. (now W. Va.). In 1837 the family moved to Princeton, Ill., and a year later to the newly opened lands of the Black Hawk Purchase, in what is now Muscatine County, Iowa. With his brother James, young Stuart worked about the farm, hunted for game, and at times attended school. In the spring of 1852, the father, a returned Argonaut of '49, taking Granville and James with him, again set out for California, reaching the gold regions in September. All three became prospectors. The father went back to Iowa in 1853, and in June 1857 the sons, with nine companions, also set out for the East. On approaching Great Salt Lake they became alarmed at the hostility of the Mormons and turned north. In October they crossed the Continental Divide and entered Beaverhead Valley, in the present state of Montana. Proceeding to Deer Lodge Valley in April 1858, Granville and James, with two others, found gold and were thus among the early discoverers of the metal in that state. A journey to Fort Bridger followed, but in May 1861 the brothers were again in the valley, where they found more gold. A letter to a third Stuart brother, Thomas, then in Colorado, brought to the territory its first party of avowed prospectors in June 1862. On May 2 of that year Granville was married to Aubony (or Ellen), a Shoshone girl, who was to bear him nine children.

For some years Stuart followed the rush to the various new mining camps, engaging in many activities, but in 1867 he settled in Deer Lodge. With the growth of settlement he took a leading part in community affairs, and in 1871 was elected to the territorial council. In 1876 and in 1879 he was elected to the lower house, and in 1883 again to the council, being chosen president. Impressed with the practicability of cattle-raising on the open range, he organized, in 1879, the Davis, Hauser, and Stuart Company, of which he was made general manager. In the following year he placed a large herd in the Judith Basin. The experiment was for a time successful, but, by reason of overstocking the range and of losses suffered during the terrible winter of 1886–87, it ended in disaster. His Indian wife died in 1887, and in 1891 he was married to Isabel Allis Brown, a school-teacher. In the same year he was appointed state land agent. In 1894 President Cleveland appointed him minister to Uruguay and Paraguay, a post he retained for more than four years. In 1904 he became librarian of the Butte city library. His later years were spent in or near Missoula. In 1916 he was commissioned by the legislature to write a history of Montana, but it was not completed. He died at Missoula, and the body was interred at Deer Lodge. His wife and several children by his first marriage survived him.

Stuart was more than six feet tall, and somewhat gaunt of frame. His portrait reveals a finely formed head and a kindly, intellectual face. His manner was suave and courtly. He was a student, an observer, and an experimenter, and to the end his mind was alert and keen. Perhaps no one in the state more fully enjoyed the confidence and respect of his fellows. He was the first secretary of the Montana Historical Society, organized in Virginia City in 1864, and president from 1890 to 1895; in 1886–87 he was president of the Society of Montana Pioneers, for seven years president of the board of stock commissioners, and for sixteen years a school trustee. In 1865 he published *Montana As It Is,* a book important for its historical information and now exceptionally valuable by reasons of its rarity. His invaluable journals, with those of his brother James, were published in part, under the title *Forty Years on the Frontier,* in 1925.

[P. C. Phillips, ed., *Forty Years on the Frontier* (2 vols., 1925) ; articles and references throughout the *Contributions to the Hist. Soc. of Mont.*; *Montana Record-Herald* (Helena), and *Anaconda Standard,* Oct. 4, 1918 ; information from David Hilger, Helena.]

W. J. G.

STUART, HENRY ROBSON [See ROBSON, STUART, 1836–1903].

STUART, ISAAC WILLIAM (June 13, 1809–Oct. 2, 1861), historian and orator, was born in New Haven, Conn., one of nine children of Abigail (Clark) Stuart and the Rev. Moses Stuart [*q.v.*], who was then pastor of the First Church of Christ (Congregational) in New Haven. He was graduated from Yale in 1828. After teaching for a short period in the historic Hopkins Grammar School in Hartford, he became professor of Greek and Latin in South Carolina College, Columbia, S. C. Returning to Hartford in 1840, he made that city his home for the rest of his life, devoting himself to historical and antiquarian pursuits. He was for some years much interested in politics, being an admirer of Henry Clay and a believer in a protective tariff, and holding moderate views on the slavery question. He was a member of the Connecticut House of Representatives in 1844 and of the Connecticut Senate in 1845 and 1846. He achieved local fame as an orator and as a lecturer on historical subjects, and was much in demand as a speaker. In November 1834 in New York he married Caroline Bulkeley, by whom he had three daughters. From her father, Stephen Bulkeley, a wealthy merchant of Hartford, Mrs. Stuart inherited the ancient Wyllys estate in Hartford, on which stood the Charter Oak. Stuart died in Hartford. At his funeral, held in St. John's Church, Oct. 5, 1861, the Putnam Phalanx, of which he was a founder and first judge advocate, acted as a military escort.

He published a translation of an essay by J. G. Honoré Greppo, *Essay on the Hieroglyphic System of M. Champollion, jun.* (Boston, 1830), edited *The Oedipus Tyrannus of Sophocles* (New York, 1837), and wrote *Hartford in the Olden Time* (Hartford, 1853), originally contributed as a series of articles to the *Hartford Daily Courant* under the pen name of "Scaeva" and published under that name, *Life of Captain Nathan Hale, the Martyr-Spy of the American*

Revolution (Hartford, 1856), *Excursion of the Putnam Phalanx to Boston, Charlestown, and Providence, Oct. 4, 5, 6, and 7, 1859* (Hartford, 1859), and a *Life of Jonathan Trumbull, Sen., Governor of Connecticut* (Boston, 1859).

[*Obit. Record Grads. Yale Coll.* (1862); obituary in *Hartford Daily Courant*, Oct. 4, 1861; and gravestone in Cedar Hill Cemetery, Hartford.]   A—r A.

STUART, JAMES EWELL BROWN (Feb. 6, 1833–May 12, 1864), soldier, born on "Laurel Hill" plantation, Patrick County, Va., was of Scotch-Irish stock on the side of his father, Archibald Stuart, and on that of his mother, Elizabeth Letcher (Pannill), was of blood predominantly Welsh. Like his distant cousins, Archibald (1757–1832) and Alexander H. H. Stuart [*qq.v.*], he was descended from an earlier Archibald Stuart who settled in Pennsylvania in 1726 and moved to Virginia in 1738. His father was a member of the two Virginia constitutional conventions and served a term in the federal House of Representatives. The seventh of ten children, he received his early schooling at home and in Wytheville, Va., and attended Emory and Henry College, 1848–50. On July 1, 1850, he entered the United States Military Academy; he graduated No. 13 in a class of forty-six. He was a popular cadet, and was distinguished for his quiet, wholesome religion and, paradoxically, for his "almost thankful acceptance" of every challenge to a fight, even though he was often beaten.

Commissioned brevet second lieutenant in the Mounted Rifles in July 1854, he received regular commission Oct. 31, 1854, and in December joined his command in Texas. On March 3, 1855, he was transferred to the 1st United States Cavalry, and spent most of the subsequent six years in Kansas, where, on Nov. 14, 1855, after a whirlwind courtship, he married Flora, daughter of Col. Philip St. George Cooke. Three children were born of this marriage, a son and a daughter surviving him. Promoted first lieutenant Dec. 20, 1855, Stuart soon disclosed definite aptitude for outpost duty. During the summer of 1859 he came East, chiefly in the hope of selling to the war department the rights to a device he had invented for attaching the cavalry sabre to the belt (Patent No. 25,684; Oct. 24, 1859). While in Washington, in October, he was asked to ride in haste to "Arlington" with a sealed message for Col. R. E. Lee, who had been superintendent of the military academy for the last two years of his cadetship. Being accepted as Lee's aide, Stuart went with him to Harpers Ferry and there recognized "Osawatomie" (John) Brown, whom he had met in Kansas. Back on the frontier, Stuart on

Jan. 15, 1861, wrote Jefferson Davis asking that Davis procure for him "a position" in the "Army of the South." In March Stuart got leave for two months and, learning of the secession of Virginia, started for his native state. En route he mailed his resignation (dated May 3, accepted May 14) from the United States Army in which, Apr. 22, 1861, he had been promoted captain.

Because of the diarchy then prevailing, he was commissioned lieutenant-colonel of Virginia infantry, May 10, 1861, and captain of Confederate cavalry May 24, 1861. At Harpers Ferry, with about 300 horsemen, soon regimented as the 1st Virginia Cavalry, he successfully screened a wide front. At First Manassas he protected the Confederate left and, with a well-timed charge, contributed to the victory of July 21. He was made brigadier-general Sept. 21, 1861, and, though roughly handled in an unequal engagement at Dranesville, Va., Dec. 20, 1861, he organized an admirable outpost system and brought to high efficiency his cavalry, who, by the end of the year, numbered about 2,400 officers and men. Accompanying Joseph E. Johnston to the Peninsula, he did what seemed possible to cover the withdrawal of the army to the Chickahominy. From Lee, who had taken command June 1, 1862, he received on June 11 written orders to "make a secret movement to the rear of the enemy, now posted on the Chickahominy." In particular Lee wished to know whether the Federals occupied the watershed between the Chickahominy and the Totopotomoy, down which he intended to bring Jackson's Army of the Valley in a turning movement. The next day with 1,200 selected cavalry and a section of artillery, Stuart set out. He soon ascertained that McClellan's right did not extend across the watershed. He might then have turned back, but it was in his opinion the soundest prudence, as well as the more soldierly course, to make a complete circuit of the Federal army. When he reported to Lee on the 15th he brought with him 165 prisoners and 260 horses and mules. This operation was a model of its kind and involved the loss of one man only. Some critics have regarded it as a mistake because it warned McClellan of what was impending; but McClellan minimized its significance and did little to strengthen his exposed flank.

During the Seven Days' campaign, when he had under his command seven mounted regiments and the equivalent of four additional battalions, Stuart kept to the left of the attacking Confederate force, struck McClellan's base as it was being abandoned and, on the night of July 1, reached the vicinity of Malvern Hill after the battle of that day. On the 3rd, he seized Evelington Heights, which dominated the Federal camps at Harrison's Landing. Stuart's impetuosity led him to open fire with his solitary howitzer. General Franklin then moved out troops to occupy and to fortify the heights. Thus was thrown away the one chance of following up successfully the indecisive action of July 1. This, however, was not realized at the time and did not impair Stuart's reputation. On July 25 he was made major-general and in that grade was confirmed Sept. 27, 1862.

During the preliminaries of Second Manassas, all the cavalry of the army was placed under Stuart's orders. On the morning of Aug. 18 at Verdierville, he barely escaped capture but got personal revenge by raiding Pope's headquarters at Catlett's Station on the night of Aug. 22. Stuart next covered Jackson's movement to Bristoe Station and to Manassas Junction, and supported him most efficiently at Groveton. In the final fighting at Manassas and during the Maryland operations Stuart's conduct repeatedly won the praise of Lee. Following Lee's return to Virginia, Stuart on Oct. 9, 1862, set out across the Potomac with 1800 men and four guns to make a raid into Pennsylvania. He reached his objective, the bridge over the Conococheague at Chambersburg, but could not destroy the iron structure and had to turn back. Riding around the Federal army, he returned to Virginia via White's Ford on the morning of Oct. 12 and brought with him 1,200 Federal horses.

Stuart made the most of the popularity he gained by these spectacular achievements. For while his patriotism was above challenge, and his private life clean and beautiful, he had a lingering adolescent love of being dramatically conspicuous. He always rode a splendid horse—and rode so hard that no animal could long survive his galloping. His gray cloak was lined with red; in the lapel of his jacket was a red flower or ribbon love-knot; his hat was cocked on one side with a star of gilt that held a peacock's plume. In his camp there was music and dancing and much jollity, but never any drinking under Stuart's eye, any swearing in his presence, or any discoverable loose living. His tactical skill, though marked, was not startling or original and his strategic sense was not outstanding, but by the winter of 1862 his early aptitude for outpost service had developed into most extraordinary skill as an intelligence officer. Lee regarded Stuart as the "eyes of the army" and when he heard of Stuart's death said in a broken voice: "He never brought me a piece of false in-

formation" (R. E. Lee, Jr., *Recollections and Letters of General Robert E. Lee*, 1904, p. 125). Stuart had the good will of men as dissimilar as Jackson and Longstreet, and most of the younger men in the cavalry corps idolized him. Lee regarded him almost as a son and remarked after the war that Stuart was his ideal of a soldier. Stuart had, however, his bitter enemies, some of them in his own corps. They accused him of selfish disregard of the feats of his subordinates, of parading himself for admiration, and of claiming credit that belonged to others.

At Fredericksburg Stuart confounded his critics and vindicated all good opinions by his admirable employment of his artillery on the Confederate right; during the winter of 1862–63 he held the line of the Rappahannock with much skill, though the lack of forage already gave warning of later disaster. He gave Lee prompt notice of Hooker's movement across the Rappahannock at the beginning of the Chancellorsville operations, and then, under Lee's orders, he kept most of his troops concentrated, in complete disregard of Stoneman's raid against Lee's communications. He helped to find and to protect the roads of Jackson's march. After Jackson was wounded and A. P. Hill was temporarily incapacitated, Stuart was summoned to take command of the II Corps, and he handled it with skill, if perhaps without regard to losses, on May 3. The absence of even a hint that Lee considered him as Jackson's successor is indirect evidence, if negative, that Lee regarded him as indispensable at the head of the cavalry corps, which had been reorganized in brigades Nov. 10, 1862.

The Gettysburg campaign represents the most disputable chapter in the career of Stuart. He directed on June 9 the large, indecisive action of Brandy Station; and, as the advance continued, he was frequently engaged and with larger resources than he had at any time commanded. The general plan was that he was to hold the mountains till the Confederate infantry passed; then he was to cross the Potomac, make contact with Ewell's advanced column, and play his usual rôle in screening the army's movements and in collecting information and provisions. Stuart may have been spurred by recent criticisms in the press for failing to display initiative, not less than by his adventurous nature, to seek opportunity for some brilliant exploit. He proposed that he attempt to interpose the cavalry corps between the Federal army and Washington and then perform his mission in Pennsylvania. Lee assented but under conditions that he thought would give ample guarantee of Stuart's early presence on Ewell's flank in any event. Stuart was delayed by the presence of heavy Federal columns and did not pass the Potomac until the night of June 27–28. Inflicting such damage as he could on supply-trains and communications, he struck for Dover, Pa. Finding no Confederates there, he marched to Carlisle where, on the night of July 1, he received Lee's orders to report at Gettysburg. The next afternoon he rejoined the main army and, for the rest of the campaign, was ceaselessly active. In his report he claimed that he had performed a larger service than he could have rendered had he remained with the main army, which, he said, had Jenkins' large brigade available for outpost duty. Lee and all his senior lieutenants had, however, been groping in the dark because of Stuart's absence, and many asserted that Stuart had deprived his chief of victory by riding off on a bootless raid. There developed a heated controversy that has been revived at intervals ever since. The evidence probably permits of no more definite conclusion than that Lee's orders to Stuart, though somewhat vague, imposed an obligation to abandon the attempt to cross the Potomac east of Hooker's army should Stuart, in the attempt, meet with hindrance that would delay him. Stuart encountered such hindrance but impetuously determined to press on his adventure, doubtless in the belief that he could make up for the time he lost.

Never thereafter could Stuart be accused of failing to keep the commanding general informed of hostile movements. Except during the heaviest weather of winter, scouting was constant. Stuart himself preferred to live at an outpost and he perhaps found his highest excitement in lesser engagements. Among the most interesting of these were that of June 1863, in northern Virginia, the Auburn affair of Oct. 13–14, and the so-called "Buckland Races" of Oct. 19, 1863. The hard riding of the battles of 1863 almost destroyed the cavalry corps of the Army of Northern Virginia. Moreover, as the infantry was weakened, the cavalrymen often had to be called upon to dismount and to perform the same duty as infantry. Despite extravagant claims made concerning Stuart's contribution to the tactical employment of dismounted cavalry, it cannot be demonstrated that he initiated anything that had not previously been done in this respect.

With the approach of spring in 1864, it was plain that the cavalry could not undertake long operations on such forage as the quartermasters could provide. After Grant crossed the Rapidan May 4, 1864, Stuart, for a few days, by the full display of his skill was able to cover Lee's opera-

tions and to supply indispensable information concerning Federal movements. On May 9, however, Sheridan, with 12,000 sabres, made a wide detour and headed South from Spotsylvania for Richmond. Summoning all the men he could muster—approximately 4,500—Stuart demanded of the weak horses their last mile of endurance and contrived to get between Sheridan and Richmond at a place called Yellow Tavern. There, in a cruel clash, he turned off Sheridan's columns from the straight road to Richmond. In the action, however, Stuart himself, who had never been touched by a bullet or a sabre in all his combats of the war, was wounded (May 11, 1864) at close range by a dismounted Federal cavalryman. He died the next day in Richmond. He was buried in Hollywood Cemetery, Richmond, in which city an equestrian statue to him was erected in 1907.

[The records of Stuart's cadetship are among the MSS. of the Military Academy; his MS. reports and a fragmentary MS. diary of the cavalry corps are in the Confederate Museum, Richmond, Va. Virtually the whole of these is printed in *War of the Rebellion: Official Records (Army)*. The standard early biography is H. B. McClellan, *The Life and Campaigns of Major-General J. E. B. Stuart* (1885). This and some previously unpublished letters and family papers were made the basis of the very readable biography by J. W. Thomason, Jr., *Jeb Stuart* (1930). Of the books by Stuart's subordinates, among the most useful are: Heros von Borcke, *Memoirs of the Confederate War for Independence* (2 vols., 1866); Heros von Borcke and Justus Scheibert, *Die grosse Reiterschlacht bei Brandy Station* (1893); R. L. T. Beale, *History of the Ninth Virginia Cavalry* (1899); G. W. Beale, *A Lieutenant of Cavalry in Lee's Army* (1918); G. C. Eggleston, *A Rebel's Recollections* (1875); T. S. Garnett, *J. E. B. Stuart* (1907); J. E. Cooke, *Wearing of the Gray* (1867). The controversy over Stuart's conduct during the Gettysburg campaign has provoked numerous publications. These are listed, and the main outlines of the controversy are traced in App. III–1 of D. S. Freeman, *R. E. Lee* (4 vols., 1934–35), in which also, the relations of Lee to Stuart are set forth at length. A recent MS. memorandum by the historical section of Army War College admirably relates Stuart to the development of American cavalry tactics.]   D.S.F.

STUART, JOHN (c. 1700–Mar. 25, 1779), superintendent of Indian affairs for the southern district, was a native of Scotland who emigrated to America about 1748. He is said to have campaigned with his brother Francis against the Spaniards in Florida. In 1757 he was commissioned captain in the South Carolina provincials by Gov. William Henry Lyttleton [q.v.]. He married Miss Fenwick, of a prominent Carolinian family, and in 1759 a son was born who was to win fame in the Peninsular War and become Lieut.-Gen. Sir John Stuart. After the capture of Fort Loudon by the Cherokee under Oconostota [q.v.], Stuart was spirited away by Attakullaculla (Little Carpenter) whom he sent back to promote peace. In 1762 he was appointed superintendent of Indian affairs for the southern district, with a salary of £1,000 and £3,000 for Indian presents and other expenses. In 1772 he built a beautiful house in Charlestown, now Charleston, which is still (1935) standing, and he acquired a plantation on Lady's Island. At first he was without definite powers and a staff, and he was subservient to the governors, who had largely handled Indian affairs themselves. Following the proclamation of 1763, he became responsible to the secretaries of state in England, though still cooperating with the governors and commander-in-chief. During the summer and autumn of 1764 he was in the Floridas, and in October he was included in East Florida's Council by Gov. James Grant. In 1765 he utilized the "Plan for the Future Management of Indian Affairs," emanating from the Lords of Trade, to obtain full imperial status for his department. In November 1765 he and Governor Grant met the Creeks at Fort Picolata, East Florida, where peace was assured and boundaries were defined. In December 1766 Stuart was informed by Lord Shelburne that he had adopted the new plan too quickly in West Florida, and that his expenses were running above all expectation and proportion (*The New Régime*, 1916, ed. by C. W. Alvord and C. E. Carter, p. 451). In order to strengthen his authority Stuart suggested to Lord Hillsborough his appointment on the councils of all colonies within his district, and in April 1770 *mandamuses* were received by the governors of Virginia and of the provinces southward naming Stuart "councillor extraordinary" to advise them and their boards on Indian affairs. Thus the superintendent was able during the next five years to extend his influence widely. His predecessor's expenditures seem not to have exceeded £1,500 sterling a year, but his had increased steadily on account of numerous congresses and the lavish distribution of Indian presents. In 1768 they had been fixed at £4,000. By 1776 they had reached the "imperial" figure of £19,000, and they continued to mount until his death. During the rest of the British régime they were kept down to about £3,900.

Early in June 1775 his arrest was ordered by the assembly of South Carolina on the charge of attempting to incite the Catawba and Cherokee in the British interest. Fleeing from Lady's Island to Savannah and thence to St. Augustine, he remained until his death a refugee in the Floridas. His management of the southern tribes was much hampered by Revolutionary developments to the northward and was subject to the plans of British commanders operating in the south. Early in 1776 his wife and her daughter were restricted to their Charlestown home and

allowed £100 a month in currency from his estate, which had been sequestered. Later Mrs. Stuart managed to escape. To carry into effect Sir William Howe's directions about the management of the Indians, Stuart removed to Pensacola in July 1776. In February 1778 he sent two of his deputies to prepare the Cherokee and Seminole for action when summoned. He also organized three companies of refugees, one of which he dispatched to stop the rum traffic at Mobile. In March he posted two parties of whites and Indians on the Mississippi in compliance with Lord George Germain's warning of a possible invasion by that route. Nevertheless, James Willing's expedition surprised Natchez on Mar. 20 and compelled its neutrality. Another mischance, despite instructions, was the failure of the Indians to cooperate on the frontiers with Col. Archibald Campbell's expedition to Georgia in the winter of 1778. While under the severe censure of the British government for these reasons and the prodigious increase of his expenses, Stuart died at Pensacola.

[W. H. Siebert, "Loyalists in East Fla.," *Pubs. Fla. State Hist. Soc.*, no. 9 (2 vols., 1929) with citations esp. to Public Record office, London; Helen L. Shaw, *British Admin. of the Southern Indians, 1756–1783* (1931); P. M. Hamer, "John Stuart's Indian Policy during the Early Months of the Am. Rev.," *Miss. Valley Hist. Rev.*, Dec. 1930; G. B. Jackson, "John Stuart," *Tenn. Hist. Mag.*, Sept. 1917; Edward McCrady, *The Hist. of S. C. under the Royal Government* (1899); *Ga. Hist. Soc. Colls.*, vol. III (1873), pp. 189, 251; *The Correspondence of Gen. Thomas Gage*, vols. I, II (1931–33), ed. by C. E. Carter; "Observations of Supt. John Stuart and Gov. James Grant of E. Fla. on the Proposed Plan of 1764 for the Future Management of Indian Affairs," *Am. Hist. Rev.*, July 1915; W. H. Mohr, *Federal Indian Relations* (1933).]   W. H. S—t.

STUART, JOHN TODD (Nov. 10, 1807– Nov. 28, 1885), Illinois lawyer and congressman, though prominent in his own right is chiefly remembered as the friend, first partner, and political mentor of Abraham Lincoln [*q.v.*]. Among the prime factors of his life were his Scotch-Irish ancestry, his Kentucky background, and his Southern traditions. Born near Lexington, Ky., he came of substantial family, his father, Robert Stuart, being a Presbyterian minister, formerly of Virginia, who became the first professor of languages in Transylvania University. His mother, Hannah Todd, was the daughter of Gen. Levi Todd; he was thus a cousin of Mary Todd Lincoln [*q.v.*]. He graduated from Centre College, Danville, Ky., in 1826, was licensed as an attorney in 1827, and in 1828 made the rough journey on horseback to Springfield, Ill., then a small frontier village, where he opened a law office. He enlisted as a private in the Black Hawk War, was elected major, served in the same battalion as Lincoln, and, like Lincoln, reënlisted after discharge. Follower and admirer of Henry Clay, he soon became the leading spirit among the Whigs of the Sangamon region. After serving in the state legislature (1832–36), he sought election to Congress. He was defeated in the congressional election of 1836; but in 1838 he defeated Stephen A. Douglas in a contest which was spectacular and wholly remarkable. It was a rough frontier election in which the candidates used "veritable stumps, ox carts, . . . barrels, [or] the canal dump . . ." for platforms (Stevens, *post*, p. 317); and so close was the race that Stuart won by a majority of 36 in a total vote of over 36,000. Reëlected in 1840, he served four years in Congress (1839–43), being a member of the important committee on territories. On Oct. 25, 1837, he married Mary Virginia Nash of Jacksonville, Ill. There were six children of this union.

As a lawyer Stuart first practised independently, then (1833–37) in partnership with Henry E. Dummer. He had notably befriended Lincoln, with whom he had served in the legislature, the two men being described as "congenial spirits" who "seemed inseparable" (Angle, *post*, p. 17); and in April 1837 the *Sangamo Journal* announced the firm of Stuart and Lincoln at "Office No. 4, Hoffman's Row, up stairs." This partnership, which was most influential in Lincoln's life, lasted until 1841; in 1843 Benjamin S. Edwards and in 1860 C. C. Brown were added to the firm. Meanwhile, Stuart was again elected to public office, serving in the state Senate, 1848–52. He was typical of that group of old-line Whigs who opposed the Republican party: he supported Bell in 1860 and, while steadfastly loyal to the Union, became during the war an active opponent of the Lincoln administration, whose emancipation policy he abominated. This circumstance led to a striking result in 1862 when as Democratic candidate for Congress he defeated the administration candidate, Leonard Swett, in the President's own district. Seeking reëlection in 1864, however, he was defeated by Shelby M. Cullom. He continued his law work long after the war and found time for active connection with such enterprises as the Springfield City Railway Company, the Bettie Stuart Institute (a school for girls), the Illinois Watch Company, the building of the state house, and the Lincoln monument association, of which he was president.

Stuart was tall, sturdy, and strikingly handsome. The law was his life work: entering the profession as a mere youth he practised with distinction for over fifty years. He discouraged frivolous litigation, putting soundness of argument, clarity of statement, and honesty, above cleverness. His personal relationships were of the finest. When opposing Lincoln during the war he was careful to say: "Difference in political opinion since 1856 has in no wise diminished my respect for the man or the . . . confidence I have ever had in his . . . integrity" (Angle, 39). Vigorous in old age, he was steadily at work until a week before his death.

[Paul M. Angle, *One Hundred Years of Law: An Account of the Law Office Which John T. Stuart Founded* . . . (1928); A. J. Beveridge, *Abraham Lincoln: 1809–1858* (2 vols., 1928); *Biog. Dir. Am. Cong.* (1928); J. M. Palmer, *The Bench and Bar of Ill.* (1899), I, 187–90; C. C. Brown, "Major John T. Stuart," *Trans. Ill. State Hist. Soc.*, 1902, pp. 109–14; H. E. Pratt, "The Repudiation of Lincoln's War Policy in 1862," *Jour. Ill. State Hist. Soc.*, Apr. 1931; F. E. Stevens, "Life of Stephen A. Douglas," *Ibid.*, Oct. 1923–Jan. 1924; Joseph Wallace, *Past and Present of . . . Springfield* (2 vols., 1904), I, 44–45; *Chicago Legal News*, Dec. 5, 1885; *Chicago Daily Tribune*, Dec. 1, 1885.]
J.G.R—l.

STUART, MOSES (Mar. 26, 1780–Jan. 4, 1852), clergyman and Biblical scholar, was born at Wilton, Conn. His father, Isaac Stuart, a descendant of Robert Stewart, who was in Norwalk, Conn., about 1660, was a farmer; his mother, Olive (Morehouse) Stuart, who possessed somewhat more education than her husband, exercised a decisive influence in interesting her son in books. He learned to read at the age of four and exhibited unusual intelligence in childhood. In his fifteenth year he was sent to an academy at Norwalk, Conn., where he made a brilliant record. He entered the sophomore class at Yale in May 1797, and two years later was graduated at the head of his class, having done particularly well in mathematics. For the first year after his graduation he taught in an academy at North Fairfield (later Easton), Conn. During part of the following year he was principal of a high school at Danbury, which he left in order to continue his study of law in Newtown. He was admitted to the bar at Danbury in 1802, but, having received an appointment for two years as tutor at Yale, he never practised law. At Yale he became interested in religion, owing to the influence of President Timothy Dwight, 1752–1817 [*q.v.*], and in 1803 he was licensed to preach. Ordained to the ministry on Mar. 5, 1806, he became pastor of the First Church of Christ (Congregational) in New Haven, where he rapidly achieved a considerable reputation as a preacher. Less than four years later, though he knew no Hebrew, he was called to the professorship of sacred literature at Andover Theological Seminary, Andover, Mass., and was inaugurated on Feb. 28, 1810.

At that time there was probably no native-born

American who knew enough Hebrew to teach it properly. Biblical studies were entirely neglected, and the minister who showed too much interest in European Biblical scholarship was suspected of heterodoxy. (See Stuart's "Letter to the Editor, on the Study of the German Language," *Christian Review,* September 1841, p, 448.) He began at once to study Hebrew seriously and wrote a short Hebrew grammar which he circulated among his students in manuscript. In 1821 he imported a font of Hebrew type and printed a larger Hebrew grammar, the first to appear in America. Since no compositor was able to handle it, he had to set most of the type himself. In eight years he was able to add fonts of type for eleven oriental scripts. Having mastered Hebrew, he attacked the study of German. While it was hard to convince theologians and clergymen of the value of Hebrew, it was much more difficult to induce them to study German scholarly literature. Indeed, it was twenty years before Stuart's fight for the recognition of the importance of German scholarly work can be said to have triumphed. His translations include *A Greek Grammar of the New Testament* (1825), from the German of Georg Benedikt Winer, done with Edward Robinson, 1794–1863 [*q.v.*], and *Hebrew Grammar of Gesenius as Edited by Roediger* (1846), also from the German. In a series of elaborate commentaries (published 1827–52) on *Hebrews, Romans, Revelation, Daniel, Ecclesiastes,* and *Proverbs,* he showed in detail how German scholarship had revolutionized the field of Biblical studies. Among his most important other books are his *Letters to the Rev. Wm. E. Channing Containing Remarks on His Sermon Recently Preached and Published at Baltimore* (1819), *Letters on the Eternal Generation of the Son of God, Addressed to the Rev. Samuel Miller, D.D.* (1822); *Elements of Interpretation; Translated from the Latin of J. A. Ernesti* (1822), and *Critical History and Defence of the Old Testament Canon* (1845). Altogether he published almost forty books and brochures, a remarkable achievement when it is realized that he was the first American theologian to become favorably known abroad, and that the quality of his work was sufficiently good to deserve an encomium from Friedrich A. G. Tholuck.

His mental energy was enormous. Indeed, it was so far ahead of his physical stamina that he was obliged to restrict himself to four hours of study and writing a day, during which he refused to permit any interruption. He was extremely gifted as a teacher and lecturer, and exerted a remarkable influence through his students. He

taught more than 1,500 ministers, and some seventy men who later became professors or presidents of colleges. In 1848 he resigned his chair, but he continued his studies and wrote several more books. Four years later he died of an illness which was said to be influenza accompanied by typhoid fever. In 1806 he had married Abigail, daughter of James Clark of Danbury, by whom he had four sons and five daughters. One of his sons was Isaac William Stuart; Austin Phelps [*qq.v.*] was twice his son-in-law. Calvin Ellis Stowe [*q.v.*] of Andover, who knew him well, describes him as "tall, muscular, and lean; with a sharp and eager face and with rapid, nervous movements" (Sprague, *post*).

[E. A. Park, *A Discourse Delivered at the Funeral of Professor Moses Stuart* (Boston, 1852); William Adams, *A Discourse on the Life and Services of Professor Moses Stuart* (New York, 1852); W. B. Sprague, *Annals of the Am. Pulpit,* vol. II (1857), pp. 475–81; F. B. Dexter, *Biog. Sketches Grads. Yale Coll.,* vol. V (1911); A. P. Stokes, *Memorials of Eminent Yale Men* (1914), vol. I; J. G. Davenport, and Sarah Stuart Robbins, in *Conn. Mag.,* 1907, no. 1; S. A. Allibone, *A Critical Dict. of Eng. Lit.,* vol. II (1870), for bibliog. and list of reviews; Leonard Woods, *Hist. of the Andover Theological Sem.* (1885); *Gen. Cat. of the Theological Seminary, Andover, Mass., 1808–1908* (1909), with portrait; death notice in *Daily Evening Transcript* (Boston), Jan. 5, 1852.]   W.F.A.

STUART, ROBERT (Feb. 19, 1785–Oct. 29, 1848), fur trader, was the son of John and Mary (Buchanan) Stuart, and was born in Callander, Perthshire, Scotland. Except that he received a good common-school education, little is known of his youth. In 1807 he arrived in Montreal to join his uncle, David Stuart, then an agent of the North West Fur Company, and sometime later entered the fur company's service. In the spring of 1810 he met Wilson Price Hunt [*q.v.*], who had gone to Montreal to complete the organization of John Jacob Astor's Pacific Fur Company, and following the example of his uncle he became a partner in the new organization. Arriving in New York, he took lodgings in Brooklyn, where he met Elizabeth Emma Sullivan, to whom three years later, on July 21, 1813, he was married. On Sept. 6 of that year he took passage on the *Tonquin* with the expedition for the Columbia. From the time of the arrival on Mar. 25, 1811, Stuart was active and efficient in the affairs of the colony. In the summer of 1812 he was chosen by the partners as a courier to carry dispatches overland to Astor, and on June 29, with six companions, one of whom was Ramsay Crooks [*q.v.*], he left Astoria. After a perilous journey, attended by extreme privation and suffering, over a route which in considerable part had never before been seen by white men, the little party arrived in St. Louis on Apr. 30, 1813.

From St. Louis Stuart hurried on to New

York, where the dispatches were delivered. Astor employed both men, Stuart for several years serving as a traveling agent in the East, and later as Crooks's assistant at Mackinac. About 1820, on the transfer of Crooks to New York, Stuart succeeded him, and for the next fourteen years he remained as the head of the American Fur Company for the upper lakes region. A man of great executive ability, energetic, politic, and shrewd, he managed the organization's affairs with signal success, being particularly interested in 1824 in lobbying for high duties for blankets and guns for trading purposes. For a short time after Astor's retirement and Crooks's assumption of the presidency of the reorganized company in 1834, he appears to have remained at Mackinac, but in 1835 he established a home in Detroit. Here he invested heavily in real estate, and with ample time on his hands busied himself in civic, educational, and church affairs. In 1837 and again in 1839 he was director of the Detroit poor. In 1840 he was appointed by the governor to fill a vacancy as state treasurer—an office which he held for more than a year, and, from early in 1841 to Apr. 14, 1845, he was superintendent of Indian affairs for Michigan. Business in connection with the project of constructing a canal from Lake Michigan to the Illinois River took him, in the fall of 1845, to Chicago, where he became the secretary of the Canal Company's trustees. Here, three years later, he was seized with a sudden illness, from which he died. The body was returned to Detroit for burial. His widow, two daughters, and three sons survived him. His son David became a prominent attorney in Detroit, a representative in Congress, and, as a soldier in the Civil War, attained the rank of brigadier-general.

Stuart is described by a contemporary as "a severe man in all things," including family discipline and religious observance (Palmer, *post,* p. 537). At Mackinac he had come under the influence of the Presbyterian missionary, the Rev. William M. Ferry, who seems to have converted him from a state of complete indifference to religion to one of zealotry, and tamed considerably the hot-headedness which, on one occasion, led him to fracture the skull of a worker who became unruly. He became deeply concerned about many of the questions of his time. Though opposed to outright abolition of slavery, he was a friend and helper of runaway slaves; he was an advocate of justice to the Indian, of temperance, of better educational facilities, of adequate relief for the poor. The characterization made of him as a "severe man," however, is not borne out by his letters, especially those to Crooks, which re-

veal in him a warm-hearted friendliness and an engaging playfulness of mood.

[*Michigan Pioneer Colls.,* vol. III (188:), pp. 52–56; Friend Palmer, *Early Days in Detroit* (1906); Leo C. Lillie, *Historic Grand Haven and Ottawa County* (1931); Silas Farmer, *The Hist. of Detroit* (2nd ed., 1889), vol. I; E. O. Wood, *Historic Mackinac,* 2 vols. (1918); *Wis. Hist. Soc. Colls.,* vols. XIX, XX (1910–11); Kenneth W. Porter, *John Jacob Astor, Business Man,* 2 vols. (1931); *Daily Free Press* (Detroit), Nov. 1, 1848. The account of the journey from Astoria is given in Stuart's journal and traveling memoranda as printed in Philip A. Rollins' *The Discovery of the Oregon Trail* (1935), and is summarized in Washington Irving, *Astoria* (1836), and in H. M. Chittenden, *The Am. Fur Trade of the Far West,* 2 vols. (rev. ed., 1935).]

W. J. G.

STUART, ROBERT LEIGHTON (July 21, 1806–Dec. 12, 1882), sugar refiner, philanthropist, was born in New York City, one of the two sons of Kinloch and Agnes Stuart, who had arrived in America the year before from Edinburgh, Scotland. The father was a confectioner in a small way on the lower West Side of the city. He prospered moderately and at his death in 1826 he left to his wife and sons a profitable business, which seems to have been conducted in the widow's name until Robert reached his majority.

In 1828 Robert and his younger brother, Alexander, formed a partnership under the name of R. L. and A. Stuart, which lasted for half a century. They continued the candy business until 1856 but for the greater part of the time the chief activity of the firm was the refining and marketing of sugar. In 1832 they began the use of steam, then a new agency in sugar-refining processes. At first the capacity of their plant did not exceed 3,000 pounds a day, but a new building opened in 1835 enabled them to quadruple their product; fifteen years later the output was raised to over 40,000,000 pounds annually, valued at $3,000,000. During the succeeding twenty years the industry yielded good profits, but in the early seventies the Stuarts faced the necessity of introducing much new and costly machinery and of building refineries on the water front if they were to withstand competition. Rather than take such risks with their capital, they preferred to retire from the field.

With the beginning of their business prosperity the brothers had entered on a program of systematic giving to Presbyterian benevolences. From 1852 to 1879 (the year of Alexander's death) they gave in this way well over $1,000,-000, including large sums to the Presbyterian Hospital, Princeton Theological Seminary, and Princeton College. Robert was married in 1835 to Mary, daughter of Robert McCrea, one of the leading dry-goods importers and merchants of New York. She, too, was of Scotch Presbyterian ancestry and fully sympathized with her husband in all his religious and philanthropic activities. She also helped him to acquire an art collection of some distinction in its day. In the nine years of her widowhood she consistently carried on the Stuart tradition of generous giving. The outcome of the agitation for Sunday opening of museums, to which her husband had been opposed, constrained her, however, to withhold the funds over which she had stewardship from every institution adopting Sunday opening as a policy. Consequently, she revoked large bequests already made in her will to the American Museum of Natural History, of which her husband had been president (1872–81), and the Metropolitan Museum of Art. She had no children, and after her death more than $4,000,000 was distributed to various societies and institutions. The Stuart pictures and books went to the Lenox Library, later incorporated with the New York Public Library. By perpetual inhibition the room containing those collections is closed to the public on Sundays.

[Evening Post (N. Y.), Dec. 13, 1882; W. M. Mac-Bean, Biog. Reg. of St. Andrew's Soc. of the State of N. Y., vol. II (1925); George Wilson, Portrait Gallery of the Chamber of Commerce of the State of N. Y. (1890); H. F. Osborn, The Am. Museum of Natural Hist. (1910); P. L. Vogt, The Sugar Refining Industry in the U. S. (1908); J. L. Bishop, A Hist. of Am. Manufactures, II (1864), 593–94; H. M. Lydenberg, Hist. of the N. Y. Pub. Lib. (1923); N. Y. Times, Dec. 13, 1882; N. Y. Tribune, Jan. 1, 6, 1892.]   W. B. S.

STUART, RUTH McENERY (May 21, 1849–May 6, 1917), author, was the eldest of the eight children of James and Mary Routh (Stirling) McEnery of Marksville, Avoyelles Parish, La. Her father was born in Limerick, Ireland; her mother, of St. Francisville, La., was the daughter of Sir John Stirling, a Scotchman from Edinburgh. Plantation owners and professional and business men, the Stirlings and McEnerys and their kinsfolk were also active in affairs of state. From the age of three Ruth McEnery lived in New Orleans, where she attended both public and private schools and for several years taught in the primary grades. On Aug. 6, 1879, she married Alfred Oden Stuart, a cotton planter of Washington, Ark. She had one child, a son, who died in 1904. In 1883 her husband died, and she returned to New Orleans. She now began to turn to account a remarkably full and accurate knowledge of Southern "characters"—Louisiana Creoles, New Orleans trades- and market-people, plantation negroes, Arkansas "poor whites." Her first story appeared in the New Princeton Review in January 1888; her second, the characteristic "Lamentations of Jeremiah Johnson," in Harper's New Monthly Magazine, May 1888.

In the early nineties she moved to New York City. Between 1891 and 1917 she published more than twenty books, most of them collections of humorous short stories, sketches, and verses reprinted from Harper's, the Century Illustrated Monthly Magazine, and other magazines. These include A Golden Wedding and Other Tales (1893), Carlotta's Intended and Other Tales (1894); Solomon Crow's Christmas Pockets and Other Tales (copyright 1896); In Simpkinsville; Character Tales (1897); Napoleon Jackson, the Gentleman of the Plush Rocker (1902); The Second Wooing of Salina Sue, and Other Stories (copyright 1898); Aunt Amity's Silver Wedding, and Other Stories (1909); The Unlived Life of Little Mary Ellen (copyright 1910); and Daddy Do-Funny's Wisdom Jingles (1913). She also became well and favorably known as a public reader of her own compositions. Occasionally, for brief periods, she served as substitute editor of Harper's Bazar and other publications. Though always an industrious writer, she made many friends, for she possessed charm and sympathy, and her vivacious and witty conversation made her a delightful companion.

Her fiction was well received, not wholly, it may be thought, because the South had recently become an interesting literary subject, or because she wrote with a sometimes extravagant humor and with sentiment and optimism—rewarding the deserving, finding the long lost, and uniting the long separated. She was the first to describe the after-the-War plantation negro in his own social environment; she had a genuine affectionate sympathy for the originals of her characters; and she had an extraordinary skill in the use of the habitual locutions of her illiterate whites and blacks, a manner of speaking manifestly no one's invention, accurate in spirit and letter. While her plantation negroes are probably her most notable creations, her "Simpkinsville" people have contributed greatly to the gaiety of her books, and an Arkansas "poor white" story, Sonny (1896), has been her most popular work, and is very characteristic. Its chapters are monologues in dialect; its humor is of the laughter-provoking kind; and its people, if not lovable, are at least made likable by their author's affection for them.

[See Who's Who in America, 1916–17; E. L. Stevens, in Lib. of Southern Lit., vol. XI (1909), ed. by E. A. Alderman, etc.; The South in the Building of the Nation (copr. 1909), vol. XII, ed. by J. A. C. Chandler, etc.; Lib. of the World's Best Lit., vol. XXIV (1897), ed. by C. D. Warner; Candace Wheeler, in Harper's Bazar, Dec. 16, 1899, with portrait; Julia R. Tutwiler, in Bookman, Feb. 1904, with portrait; La. Hist. Soc. Pubs., vol. X (1918); G. W. Nott, in New Orleans Item, July 10, 1927; H. B. McKenzie, in Arkansas Gazette, Aug. 27, 1924; article by Kate Chopin reprinted in D. S. Rankin, *Kate Chopin and Her Creole Stories* (1932); editorial in *N. Y. Times* Bk. Rev., May 13, 1917; obituary in *Times-Picayune* (New Orleans), May 8, 1917. Biog. information has been supplied by a member of the McEnery family.]   R. R. K.

STUB, HANS GERHARD (Feb. 23, 1849–Aug. 1, 1931), Norwegian Lutheran clergyman, the son of Hans Andreas and Ingeborg Margrethe (Arentz) Stub, was born at Muskego, Wis., where his father, an emigrant from Norway in 1848, and one of the founders of the Norwegian Synod, was pastor. At the age of twelve Stub accompanied his father to Bergen, Norway, where he attended the Cathedral School from 1861 to 1865. Upon their return he attended Luther College, Decorah, Iowa, for one year and received the A.B. degree in 1866. From 1866 to 1869 he attended Concordia College, Fort Wayne, Ind., and then for three years the Concordia Theological Seminary, St. Louis, Mo. He was ordained in 1872 and for the next five years was a pastor in Minneapolis, Minn. He was professor in Luther Seminary at Madison, Wis., and later at Robinsdale, Minn., from 1878 to 1896, with the exception of one year of study at the University of Leipzig (1881–82). He served as pastor in Decorah, Iowa, from 1896 to 1900, doing part-time teaching in Luther College, and from 1900 to 1916 was again professor in Luther College. He was vice-president of the Norwegian Synod, 1905–11, and president, 1911–17. In 1906 he was a member of a group of Norwegian-Americans who made a voyage to Norway to attend the coronation of King Haakon VII and while there was decorated Knight of the Order of St. Olav.

Stub's name is linked with two achievements especially notable in the eyes of his constituents: the raising of an endowment fund of $250,000 for Luther College, and the merging of the Norwegian Synod, the Hauges Synod, and the United Norwegian Lutheran Church into the Norwegian Lutheran Church of America in 1917. He was president of the new body until 1925, when he resigned to become president emeritus. He, more than any other, was the effecter of this union, negotiations for which had been going on for eleven years. In 1914 he made another visit to Norway, this time bringing along a "memorial gift" gathered among Norwegians in America for presentation at the Centennial. Royalty again favored him in 1914 when he became Commander of the Order of St. Olav, and, in 1922, wearer of the Grand Cross, an insignia which he was wont to display. From 1918 to 1920 he was president of the National Lutheran Council, a temporary concession of ecclesiastical sectionalism in the East to the West. He preached the opening sermon at the Lutheran World Convention held in 1923 at Eisenach. He was joint or sole editor of *Evangelisk Luthersk Kirketidende,* 1889–1902, and of *Theologisk Tidsskrift,* 1899–1908, both uncompromisingly confessional-orthodox periodicals. He was the author of *Naadevalget* (1881); *Udvälgelsen* (1882), a defense of the Missourian doctrine of predestination and election; *Mod Frimureriet* (1882), an attack on Freemasonry; and *Kristofer Jansen og Ludvig Helger* (1894). He wrote on pioneer days, "Fra Fars og Mors Tid," for the periodical *Symra* in 1907. The surveys, *Hvad staar iveien?* (1911) and "Lidt af den nyere kirkehistorie iblandt os," in *Lutheraneren,* 1920–22, summarize local doctrinal conquests hoped for and achieved through ecclesiastical union. Numerous American institutions conferred honorary degrees on him.

Stub was married three times. His first wife, Diderikke Aall Ottesen, to whom he was married on Aug. 11, 1876, bore him two sons and died in 1879. He was married to Valborg Hovind, of Christiania, Norway, on July 31, 1884, and they had one son. She died in 1901, and, on Aug. 8, 1906, he was married to Anna Skabo, also of Christiania, who, with the three sons by former marriages, survived him when he died in St. Paul. Stub was the image of the aristocratic clergyman of Norway a century ago. His ways were gently condescending, his actions studied. He moved with ease and dignity in admiring circles who yearned for the authority and splendor of an ecclesiastical age gone by. He was a pulpit orator of ability, a theological professor reproductive but not creative, an organizer too prone to identify his doings with those of the Lord, as in the case of the merging of 1917, in which he saw a partial fulfilment of John 17:21.

[*Who's Who in America,* 1930–31; J. A. Bergh, *Den Norsk Lutherske Kirkes Historie i Amerika* (1914); *Luther Coll. Through Sixty Years* (1922); *Who's Who Among Pastors in all the Norwegian Luth. Synods of America* (rev. ed., 1928); *Lutheraneren,* Oct. 14, 1931; *Minneapolis Sunday Tribune,* Aug. 2, 1931.]
                                                J. O. E.

STUCK, HUDSON (Nov. 11, 1863–Oct. 10, 1920), Protestant Episcopal clergyman, archdeacon of the Yukon, was born in Paddington, London, England, the son of James and Jane (Hudson) Stuck. He attended Westbourne Park Public School and King's College, London. In 1885 he came to America and within three years was acting principal in the public schools of San Angelo, Tex. While in San Angelo he served as a lay reader in the Episcopal Church, and in 1889 he entered the Theological Department of the University of the South, Sewanee, Tenn. He was ordained priest in 1892 and became rector of

Grace Church, Cuero, Tex. In 1894 he was made dean of St. Matthew's Cathedral at Dallas, Tex., where he remained ten years, during this period establishing St. Matthew's Grammar School and a home for old people. He was a deputy to the General Conventions of the Protestant Episcopal Church in 1898, 1901, and 1913. Resigning from St. Matthew's in 1904, he became archdeacon of the Yukon under Bishop Peter Trimble Rowe, first missionary bishop of Alaska, and in this capacity served until the end of his life. He apparently never relinquished his British nationality.

Stuck's articles published in the *Spirit of Missions* in 1909 are interesting but conventional accounts of his work as a missionary; in 1920 he published *The Alaskan Missions of the Episcopal Church*. More noteworthy are his descriptions of the Yukon country. His *Ten Thousand Miles With a Dog Sled* (1914) and *Voyages on the Yukon and Its Tributaries* (1917) describe his travels at different seasons; the latter book was characterized by Cyrus C. Adams (*Geographical Review*, August 1920, p. 118) as "a fairly complete summary of Alaska, in most of its aspects." In 1913, with Harry P. Karstens, R. G. Tatum, and Walter Harper, he made the first complete ascent of Mount McKinley. In his descriptions of the achievement—an article in *Scribner's Magazine* (November 1913) and a book, *The Ascent of Denali* (1914), he urged that the native names of Denali, "the great one," and Denali's Wife be returned to Mount McKinley and Mount Foraker. In March 1919 the Royal Geographical Society bestowed the Back Grant upon him in recognition of his travels in Alaska and his ascent of Mount McKinley. He always regretted his lack of scientific training for exploration, but his careful observation was highly regarded by the scientific bodies before which he lectured and he was a fellow of both the Royal Geographical Society and the American Geographical Society. His last book, *A Winter Circuit of Our Arctic Coast* (1920), is the record of a journey—considered a greater *tour de force* than his ascent of Mount McKinley—made in the winter of 1917–18 when temperatures in the interior went down to —60°.

Stuck's writings reveal him as a warm and forceful character. The breadth of his culture is shown especially in *A Winter Circuit*, which deserves a place among belles-lettres. In all his books he stressed the peaceable and tractable nature of the Eskimos and Indians and stated his conviction that they are capable of considerable development. On the ground that the frontier of civilization always attracts the least desirable element of society, he pleaded for mission work in Alaska as a means of protecting the natives against unscrupulous adventurers and counteracting their detrimental influence by the influence of men of a higher type. Convinced of the civilizing power of books, he established a library in Fairbanks.

Stuck never married. He died at the home of Dr. Grafton Burke, Fort Yukon, Alaska, where St. Stephen's Hospital (since 1921 the Archdeacon Stuck Memorial Hospital) had been built largely through his influence. Two funds have been established in his memory: one of $25,000, given in part by Indians and other people in Alaska, to be used for medical work at Fort Yukon; the other, of $18,000, given to the University of the South.

[*Who's Who in America*, 1920–21; *Who's Who* (British), 1920; *Spirit of Missions*, Jan., July, Aug. 1921; *Churchman*, Oct. 23, 1920; *Geog. Rev.* (N. Y.), Apr. 1921; *Geog. Jour.* (London), Jan., Sept. 1914, Oct. 1918, Mar., Apr., July 1919, Jan. 1921; *Evening Star* (Washington, D. C.), Oct. 13, 1920; *Alaska Daily Empire* (Juneau), Oct. 12, 1920; information from the bishops of N. Y., La., and Tenn., from officials of the University of the South, from Dr. John W. Wood, Exec. Sec., Nat. Council, P. E. Church, and from other personal acquaintances; letters from a sister, Miss Caroline Stuck, Heathfield, Sussex, England.]

E. W. H.

STUCKENBERG, JOHN HENRY WILBRANDT (Jan. 6, 1835–May 28, 1903), theologian, sociologist, the son of Herman Rudolph and Anna Maria (Biest) Stuckenberg, was born at Bramsche, Hanover, Germany. His name before it was anglicized was Johann Heinrich Willbrand Stuckenberg. With his mother, three sisters, and one brother, he came to Pittsburgh, Pa., in 1839 to join his father and eldest sister, who had emigrated two years before. The family finally settled in Cincinnati, Ohio, where young Stuckenberg received most of his early schooling. He received his college and theological education at Wittenberg College, Springfield, Ohio, and was graduated with the A.B. degree in 1857 and the theological degree in 1858. He was pastor of a Lutheran congregation in Davenport, Iowa, for a year and then studied in the University of Halle, Germany, from 1859 to 1861. He was chaplain in the 145th Pennsylvania Volunteers from September 1862 to October 1863, served another congregation of the General Synod from 1863 to 1865 in Erie, Pa., and again went to Germany, where he studied from 1865 to 1867 in the universities of Göttingen, Tübingen, and Berlin. Pastorates in Indianapolis, Ind., and in Pittsburgh occupied him from 1867 to 1873, when he was made professor of exegesis in Wittenberg College. In 1880, for the third time, he went to Germany, this time to stay for fourteen years as pastor of the American Church in Berlin.

Stuckenberg derived unusual intellectual and social benefits from his Berlin pastorate, combining with extraordinary fruitfulness the duties of pastor, student adviser, lecturer, and author. He also enjoyed contacts with many of the faculty members of the university in Berlin, and was a member of the Philosophical Society of Berlin. He was a regular visitor to the large libraries, had access to all kinds of source material and professional periodicals, and was an indefatigable writer. Many of his articles are to be found in the *Evangelical Quarterly Review* (see particularly, January 1865, April 1867, July 1869), and the *Quarterly Review of The Evangelical Lutheran Church* (see January 1871, July 1876, April 1880, July 1886). He was for some time editor of the *Lutheran Quarterly* and of the *Evangelist,* and wrote for the *Andover Review* and the *American Journal of Theology.* His weightiest contributions appeared in a series of 200 articles in the *Homiletic Review* from 1884 to 1902, and for many years was in charge of its department of Christian sociology.

Among American writers, Stuckenberg's work in sociology places him beside Lester F. Ward [*q.v.*] as a pioneer in that field, although his treatment was largely philosophic while Ward was more concerned with natural scientific treatment. The problem of the state particularly attracted Stuckenberg. He made a particular study of international law, and was an ardent collector of maps, one of which was reproduced in 1895 in a New York paper as containing the key to the Venezuela territorial dispute. He was a champion of labor and in his later years lectured before many labor groups throughout the country. His most important books are: *Ninety-five Theses* (1868); *History of the Augsburg Confession* (1869); *Christian Sociology* (1880); *The Life of Immanuel Kant* (1882), the first biography of Kant in English; *Grundprobleme in Hume* (1885, pamphlet No. 13 of the 3rd Series issued by the Philosophical Society of Berlin); *The Final Science* (1885); *Introduction to the Study of Philosophy* (1888); *The Age and the Church* (1893); *Tendencies in German Thought* (1896); *The Social Problem* (1897); and *Introduction to the Study of Sociology* (1898). His *magnum opus* was *Sociology, The Science of Human Society* (2 vols., 1903).

Stuckenberg was a straight, tall, broad-shouldered man of commanding presence, quick of movement, fluent in speech, thoroughly at ease before his audiences. He was almost as well known in British circles as in American, his books re-

ceiving many elaborate and sympathetic reviews in leading English literary periodicals. He possessed a large library on theology, sociology, economics, political science, and philosophy, now in the library of Gettysburg College. He died in London, where he had gone to gather material for a new book. He was survived by his wife, Mary Gingrich, of Erie, Pa.; to whom he was married on Oct. 27, 1869. She was a leader in the Woman's Christian Temperance Union movement.

[A great amount of biographical material pertaining to Stuckenberg is now in the hands of the author of this sketch, by whom a biography is being prepared. Gettysburg College is in possession of his map collection. Besides the literature mentioned above, see *Who's Who in America,* 1901–02; *The New Schaff-Herzog Encyc. of Religious Knowledge,* vol. XI (1911); articles by S. G. Hefelbower in the *Luth. Observer,* Nov. 29, 1912; Harry E. Barnes in the *Luth. Quart.,* Oct. 1921, and C. T. Pihlblad in the *Ohio Sociologist,* Sept. 1928.]

J. O. E.

STUDEBAKER, CLEMENT (Mar. 12, 1831–Nov. 27, 1901), manufacturer of wagons and carriages, was of the fourth generation after Clement and Anna Catherine Studebecker, who arrived at Philadelphia in the ship *Harle* from Rotterdam on Sept. 1, 1736. They settled among their German brethren in what is now Adams County, Pa. John Studebaker, grandson of the immigrant, married Rebecca Mohler, a woman of exceptional character. Their fifth child and second son, Clement, better known throughout his life as Clem, was born on his father's farm at Pinetown, a few miles from Gettysburg, Pa. His father, having met with financial difficulties, moved his family and possessions, in wagons of his own manufacture, to Ashland County, Ohio, in 1836. Two years later his creditors dispossessed him of the one hundred and sixty acre farm he had bought, and he purchased a small tract where he was unsuccessful in a milling venture. He then rented a smaller patch and engaged in blacksmithing and wagon making.

Clem worked in his father's shop and on nearby farms and attended the district school. In 1850 he moved to the vicinity of South Bend, Ind., where he was engaged to teach the district school at fifteen dollars a month. Studying to make up the deficiencies in his own education, he successfully taught a winter and a spring term. In his free time he worked in a blacksmith shop for fifty cents a day. In the spring of 1852 he established, with his older brother Henry, the firm of H. & C. Studebaker. Their capital consisted of sixty-eight dollars and some blacksmith tools. In addition to doing ordinary blacksmith work, they made two wagons, the first of over three quarters of a million. The introduction of the railroad and the consequent development of agriculture in the Middle West increased the demand for wagons, and they supplied this demand with an excellent product. Quality was almost a fetish with them. The Studebakers' first notable advance came when they received a sub-contract for government wagons through George Milburn, Clem's future father-in-law. They sagaciously put the name of Studebaker on these and thus came to the notice of the government, which gave them many contracts. About 1857 Henry withdrew from the partnership. He was succeeded by another brother, John M., who had lately returned from California. In 1868 they organized the Studebaker Brothers Manufacturing Company with Clem Studebaker as its first president. Peter E. Studebaker joined his brothers at this time and, in 1870, established the company's first branch house at St. Joseph, Mo., to outfit emigrants crossing the plains. The youngest brother, Jacob F., joined them in 1870. The company thus formed became the largest manufacturer of horse-drawn vehicles in the world. Clem Studebaker was alive to the possibilities of self-propelled vehicles and began experiments with them in 1897. The manufacture of both electric and gasoline automobiles was begun by the company soon after his death.

Studebaker was in all respects an admirable character. He was a man of good judgment and high moral standards. Despite his limited formal education he maintained a home and social life of culture and refinement. Men of distinction, including Presidents Grant, Harrison, and McKinley, and leaders in industry, literature, and science were entertained in his home. His parents were German Baptists or Dunkers but he became a Methodist and an influence in the Church. He presented the congregation at South Bend with a church edifice. A strong Republican, he became prominent in party councils. As a delegate to the presidential convention of 1880 he was a member of the old-guard contingent that held out in vain for Grant. In 1888 he was again a delegate to the Republican National Convention. He represented Indiana at the Paris Exposition in 1878, the Centennial Exposition in Cincinnati in 1888, and the World's Columbian Exposition in Chicago in 1893. President Harrison appointed him a delegate to the Pan-American Congress in Washington in 1889. He was active in the educational activities of the Methodist Church, being for many years a trustee and for a time president of the Chautauqua Association, a member of the book committee which supervised the publications of the church, and a trustee and benefactor of De Pauw University. His first wife was Charity M. Bratt, by whom he had two children

who died in infancy. She died in 1863, and in 1864 he married Ann Milburn Harper, daughter of George Milburn of Mishawaka, Ind. To this union were born three children.

[Information furnished by C. A. Carlisle, including a manuscript life of Studebaker approved by the subject; *Ashland Times*, Oct. 13, 1897, containing autobiog. account read by Studebaker at a reunion at Ashland, Ohio, in 1897; *South Bend Daily Times*, Nov. 27, 1901; *Who's Who in America*, 1901–02; *Hist. of St. Joseph County, Ind.* (1880); *A Biog. Hist. of Eminent and Self-Made Men of the State of Ind.* (1880), vol. II; *Pictorial and Biog. Memoirs of Elkhart and St. Joseph Counties, Ind.* (1893); T. E. Howard, *Hist. of St. Joseph County, Ind.* (2 vols., 1907); I. H. Betz, "The Studebaker Brothers, the Wagon Builders of South Bend, Ind.," *Pennsylvania-German*, Apr. 1910; A. R. Erskine, *Hist. of the Studebaker Corporation* (1924); *Chicago Tribune*, Nov. 28, 1901; St. Joseph County, Ind., Marriage Record, V, 227.]   R. H. A.

STURGIS, RUSSELL (Oct. 16, 1836–Feb. 11, 1909), architect, critic, writer, was born in Baltimore, Md., the son of Russell and Margaret D. (Appleton) Sturgis. His father, then living temporarily in Baltimore, was a shipping merchant and a commissioner of pilots in New York City; he was a descendant of Edward Sturgis who was in Charlestown, Mass., in 1634 and was one of the first settlers of Yarmouth. Sturgis was educated in the public schools of New York and in the Free Academy of the City of New York (later the College of the City of New York), from which he was graduated with the degree of A.B. in 1856. After a year as a student in the office of Leopold Eidlitz [q.v.], he went to Munich for a year and a half of study. He was associated with Peter Bonnett Wight [q.v.] from 1863 to 1868, and then practised alone until about 1880. His architectural practice included several New York town houses, the Flower Hospital (New York), and three interesting "model tenements" in West Nineteenth Street, New York, besides many country houses throughout the East. These are usually in current versions of the popular Néo-Grec or Victorian Gothic styles. He designed four buildings—Farnam, Durfee, and Lawrance halls, and Battell Chapel—for Yale University between 1870 and 1885. By far the most interesting example of his work is the Farmers' & Mechanics' Bank, Albany, N. Y., unusually delicate in scale, its style based on French work of the period of Louis XII. But it was not Sturgis' architecture that made him famous.

Soon after leaving college, Sturgis and a few friends, founders of the Society for the Advancement of Truth in Art, published a serious little art magazine (1863–64) called the *New Path*. The articles by Sturgis were its backbone, and they already revealed his deep critical interest in his profession. In 1868 he wrote a *Manual* of the Jarves Collection of Early Italian Pictures in the Yale School of Fine Arts . . . A Brief Guide to the Study of Early Christian Art (New Haven), and he soon began to contribute to such magazines as the Nation frequent articles interpreting not only architecture but the whole field of art to the layman. From 1878 to 1880 he held a chair in architecture and the arts of design at the College of the City of New York. After four years abroad with his family, chiefly in Florence and Paris, he was for a brief period secretary to the municipal civil service board of New York, but the political complications of the position were not to his taste, and he soon resigned to devote himself almost exclusively to writing. In addition to serving as art editor for various encyclopaedias and dictionaries, he edited "The Field of Art" in Scribner's Magazine from 1897 until his death. He was co-author with Charles Eliot Norton [q.v.] of a Catalogue of . . . Ancient and Modern Engravings, Woodcuts and Illustrated Books, Parts of the Collections of C. E. Norton and R. Sturgis (1879), editor-in-chief of A Dictionary of Architecture and Building (3 vols., 1901–02), editor of Outlines of the History of Art (2 vols., 1904), and author of a series of books (1903–08) on the appreciation of architecture, sculpture, and painting. In 1904 he gave the Scammon lectures at the Art Institute of Chicago, which were published as The Interdependence of the Arts of Design (1905). Of his shorter brochures, The Etchings of Piranesi (1900) and Ruskin on Architecture (1906) deserve notice. The climax of his writing career was the ambitious A History of Architecture (4 vols., 1906–15), on which he was working at the time of his death and of which he completed only two volumes. In his articles on contemporary architects published by the Architectural Record in the Great American Architects Series he gave vivid expression to the architectural ideals of his day, and pointed out with a canny discrimination both its shortcomings and its achievements.

As a critic he was less profound than provocative and persuasive. He was animated by a sincere passion for beauty in the largest sense, and he had as background an unusually wide knowledge of the history and technique of the arts. He wrote well, in an easy, sometimes over-facile style that caught the public ear. Though his history is seldom original in point of view, it is the work of a true connoisseur, alert, sensitive, discriminating, a man of trained and generally sound taste. He was not without prejudices, for the precepts of Ruskin colored his views for his entire life. Thus he could only view with disgust the overwhelming swing of popular taste towards

Renaissance and classic eclecticism which characterized the end of the nineteenth century. Perhaps it was this hatred of the classic phase which made him so prophetically alert to rebellions against it. To him Louis Henri Sullivan [q.v.] seemed the bearer of a new light, and again and again he pointed to Sullivan's work, revolutionary as it was, as the most significant that was being done in America. His writing was perhaps the most important single factor in the artistic reawakening of the American people that characterized the early years of the twentieth century.

"Curious in viands and vintages," he was as much a connoisseur in living as in the field of art. And he looked the part, with his white hair and his distinguished beard and thin, sensitive nose. A student to the end of his life, he went out but little; he had, however, to compensate, a small circle of close friends—Robert Underwood Johnson, Montgomery Schuyler, Richard Watson Gilder [q.v.], William Crary Brownell [q.v.], and especially John La Farge [q.v.], his most sympathetic companion. He lived for many years at 307 East Seventeenth St., which was his office and study, and housed his magnificent library and collection of prints, and it was there he died. He had married, May 26, 1864, Sarah Marie, daughter of Danforth Newton Barney. They had three daughters and four sons, of whom one son died in infancy. Sturgis was a fellow of the American Institute of Architects, a member of the Architectural League of New York and its president, 1898–1902; a member and first president of the Fine Arts Federation of New York; and a trustee (1873–76) and corresponding secretary (1870–73) of the Metropolitan Museum of Art.

[R. E. Sturgis, Edward Sturgis of Yarmouth, Mass., 1613–1695, and His Descendants (1914); Who's Who in America, 1908–09; Who's Who in N. Y., 1907; E. P. Wheeler, in City Coll. Quart., Mar. 1909, with portraits; Montgomery Schuyler, in "The Field of Art," Scribner's Mag., May 1909; "Russell Sturgis's Architecture," in Architectural Record, June 1909; P. B. Wight, Ibid., Aug. 1909; obituaries in N. Y. Times and N. Y. Tribune, Feb. 12, 1909; information from Edward B. Sturgis, Sturgis' son.]   T.F.H.

STURGIS, SAMUEL DAVIS (June 11, 1822–Sept. 28, 1889), soldier, was born at Shippensburg, Pa., the son of James and Mary (Brandenburg) Sturgis, and a descendant of William Sturgis who came to Pennsylvania from Ireland about 1745. Samuel entered West Point, July 1, 1842, graduated July 1, 1846, and joined the 2nd Dragoons, with which he fought at Palo Alto and Resaca de la Palma. Before the battle of Buena Vista he volunteered for a reconnaissance which resulted in his capture but also in gaining essential information about the enemy. He remained a prisoner eight days. After the Mexican War he served in the West with the 1st Dragoons, in which he was promoted first lieutenant, July 15, 1853, and the 1st (now 4th) Cavalry, in which he was appointed captain, Mar. 3, 1855. At West Ely, Mo., July 5, 1851, he married Jerusha Wilcox, daughter of Jeremiah Wilcox of Akron, Ohio. He took part in an Indian campaign in New Mexico in 1855, the Utah expedition of 1858, and a campaign against the Kiowas and Comanches in 1860, after which he was charged with settling difficulties between white settlers and Indians on the "neutral lands" of the Cherokee border.

In 1861 he was in command at Fort Smith, Ark. All his officers resigned to join the Confederate army and the post was surrounded by hostile militia. Sturgis brought off his troops, however, with most of the government property under his care. He was promoted major, May 3, 1861. He fought at Wilson's Creek, succeeding to the command when Gen. Nathaniel Lyon [q.v.] was killed, and was appointed brigadier-general of volunteers with rank from Aug. 10, 1861, the date of the battle. He was in charge of the district of Kansas for a time and then commanded the defenses of the city of Washington until sent into the field for the second battle of Bull Run. He commanded a division of the IX Corps at South Mountain, Antietam, and Fredericksburg. At Antietam it was his division that carried the famous bridge, Sturgis himself leading the charge. He was transferred to the West with the IX Corps, and later had small commands in Tennessee and Mississippi, suffering a severe defeat by Gen. N. B. Forrest [q.v.] at Brice's Cross Roads (Guntown) in June 1864. Grant wrote to Stanton (Oct. 14, 1865): "Notwithstanding his failure at Guntown, Miss., I know him to be a good and efficient officer, far above the average of our cavalry colonels. From the beginning of the war he has suffered from having served in Kansas, and coming in contact with, and in opposition to, civilians, Senator Lane probably in the lead" (War Department records). He was mustered out of the volunteer army, Aug. 24, 1865, and went to duty as lieutenant-colonel of the 6th Cavalry, having been promoted Oct. 27, 1863. He became colonel of the 7th Cavalry, May 6, 1869, saw considerable service in Indian campaigns, was governor of the Soldiers' Home from 1881 to 1885, and retired in 1886. Criticism of his conduct at Brice's Cross Roads having been revived in 1882 he published *The Other Side as Viewed by Generals Grant, Sherman, and Other Distinguished Offi-*

cers, Being a Defence of his Campaign into N. E. Mississippi in the Year 1864. He died at St. Paul, Minn. His son, Samuel Davis Sturgis, Jr., became a major-general in the regular army in 1921.

[*War of the Rebellion: Official Records (Army)*; *Battles and Leaders of the Civil War* (4 vols., 1887–88); *Twenty-first Ann. Reunion Asso. Grads. U. S. Mil. Acad.* (1890); G. W. Cullum, *Biog. Reg. Officers and Grads. U. S. Mil. Acad.* (3rd ed., 1891), vol. II; *Army and Navy Jour.*, Oct. 5, 1889; *Pioneer Press* (St. Paul, Minn.), Sept. 29, 1889; unpublished records in the War dept.; information from son.]   T.M.S.

STURGIS, WILLIAM (Feb. 25, 1782–Oct. 21, 1863), merchant, only son of William and Hannah (Mills) Sturgis, was born in Barnstable, Mass. His father, a Revolutionary soldier, was a Cape Cod shipmaster of repute; his mother was a daughter of the Rev. Jonathan Mills of Harwich, Mass. Sturgis was a descendant of Edward Sturgis, who settled in Charlestown in 1634 and in Yarmouth, Mass., in 1638. He had but little schooling, and when only fourteen was employed in counting houses in Boston. On the death of his father in 1797 he shipped as a sailor before the mast. The boy studied navigation and used every means to advance himself in his calling. His voyages took him to the Northwest coast, where the ships bartered goods with the Indians for furs. Sturgis made a study of the Indian languages, became an adept trader, and cultivated friendly relations with the natives, among whom he was popular. At the age of nineteen, with less than four years' experience, he became master of the ship *Caroline*. His cruises sometimes led him into perilous situations, as when his ship *Atahualpa* battled with pirates off the Chinese coast in August 1809. In 1810 he formed a partnership with John Bryant as resident Boston merchants and in the fifty-three years of their association created an ample fortune. It has been said that more than half of the trade carried on from the United States with China and other countries of the Pacific coast from 1810 to 1840 was under their direction (Loring, *post*, p. 433). They also had dealings in nearly every quarter of the globe. Sturgis married in 1810 Elizabeth Marston Davis, daughter of John Davis, 1761–1847 [q.v.], judge of the United States district court. There were six children of this marriage, one son and five daughters.

For twelve years between 1814 and 1846 Sturgis was a member of the Massachusetts House of Representatives; he was a state senator in 1827 and 1836, and a member of the convention for revising the constitution of Massachusetts in 1820. He was president of the Boston Marine Society and a member of the Massachusetts Historical Society, to whose activities he made important contributions and to whose funds he was a liberal benefactor. He contributed $10,000 to the observatory in Cambridge, and erected in Mount Auburn Cemetery, Cambridge, a monument to Dr. Johann Gaspar Spurzheim, the phrenologist, who died in Boston in 1832. Distinguished for a highly cultivated intellect and a remarkably extensive knowledge, he was of almost Spartan simplicity in his personal habits. He was conspicuous for his firm yet liberal principles, and a high sense of honor. In October 1822 he contributed an article to the *North American Review*, "Examination of the Russian Claims to the Northwest Coast of America," and on Aug. 4 and 5, 1843, two articles on the *Somers* naval mutiny to the *Boston Courier*. During the controversy between the United States and Great Britain over the Oregon boundary, his personal acquaintance with the region and his familiarity with its history were of highest importance to the American government. His pamphlet, *The Oregon Question* (1845), presented a valuable discussion of the question, while his private correspondence with distinguished statesmen, both at home and abroad, is said to have had no small influence in bringing the controversy to an amicable and satisfactory issue (*Ibid.*, p. 458). He died in Boston, survived by his wife and three daughters.

[R. F. Sturgis, *Edward Sturgis of Yarmouth, Mass., 1613–1695, and His Descendants* (priv. printed, 1914); C. G. Loring, in *Proc. Mass. Hist. Soc.*, 1 ser., vol. VII (1864), pp. 420–73; card index of members of Mass. legislature, State Lib., Boston; obituaries in *New Eng. Hist. and Geneal. Reg.*, Apr. 1864, and *Boston Transcript*, Oct. 22, 1863.]   W. M. E.

STURTEVANT, BENJAMIN FRANKLIN (Jan. 18, 1833–Apr. 17, 1890), inventor, manufacturer, was born at Martin's Stream, Norridgewock, Me. He was the son of Seth and Hulda (Besse) Sturtevant and a lineal descendant of Samuel Sturtevant who emigrated to Plymouth in 1642 from Rochester, Kent, England. Sturtevant's parents were poor and his father was in ill health so that the boy had little opportunity for an education, being compelled to help in supporting the family by laboring on a farm. Desiring something better, he left home when he was fifteen and worked his way to Northbridge, Mass., and then back to Skowhegan, Me., where he entered a cobbler's shop and during the next eight years became a skilled shoemaker.

This confining employment injured his health, however, and in the hope of bettering his condition he turned his attention to the possibility of devising a machine to peg boots and shoes. Although he possessed no knowledge of mechanics

and had had no experience with machinery, he devised a crude model of a shoe-pegging machine in a few months. Proceeding immediately to Boston with the model but no money, he assigned one-half of his invention absolutely and the entire control of the remaining half to a local business man in return for a meager living wage. From 1857 to 1859 he was engaged in making improvements on the original machine, for which he secured five patents. Meanwhile, another patentee of a shoe-pegging machine, wholly worthless, met Sturtevant's backer and skilfully frightened him into believing that Sturtevant's ideas were infringements and open to possible lawsuits. As a result, Sturtevant lost his only financial support in addition to all rights in his patents, and was again penniless. He had not, however, divulged all of his ideas to his guarantor, and immediately turned his attention to peg-making machinery, realizing that any shoe-pegging machine was worthless without pegs. By December 1859 he had devised and patented (No. 26,627) a pegwood lathe which cut a spiral veneer from around a log, and by July 1862 (No. 35,902) the process and machinery for converting such veneer ribbons into pegs. This process involved drying the veneer, beveling one edge, which edge was then compressed and toughened (all by machinery of his invention) and the whole ribbon, usually 100 feet long, made into a roll ready for use in the shoe-pegging machines. Unfortunately, to obtain money for this work which consumed all of his time from 1860 to 1863, Sturtevant had to sell, bit by bit, most of the rights and other possible applications of these inventions, being able to retain for himself only such parts as applied to the production of shoe-pegs. One of the applications of his patents which he thus lost was for the manufacture of wooden toothpicks. Nevertheless, he secured enough capital to establish a ribbon pegwood manufactory at Conway, N. H., which was highly successful, having markets throughout the world.

The dust created by the buffing wheels in the early shoe factories was very annoying and about 1864 Sturtevant began considering ways and means of eliminating it. His solution of the problem was the invention of a rotary exhaust fan (patented Oct. 29, 1867) which within a comparatively short period he was supplying to the local trade in Boston. By applying the same mechanical features to the crude air blowers then existing he produced a greatly improved machine and developed so many new applications for it, such as pressure blowers, ventilating fans, and pneumatic conveyors, that he literally created a new industry. His business was at once successful and grew to such proportions that in 1878 he built a new plant at Jamaica Plain, Mass., which was the largest of its kind in the world. At the time of his death his manufactory produced over 5,000 blowers yearly and employed about 400 men. He gave liberally of the fortune he acquired to educational and religious institutions, contributing largely to Colby University, Vermont Academy, and Newton Theological Seminary. He was married at Norridgewock, Me., in 1852, to Phoebe R. Chamberlain and at the time of his death in Jamaica Plain was survived by his widow and two daughters.

[J. D. Van Slyck, *New England Manufacturers and Manufactories* (1879); W. B. Kaempffert, *A Popular Hist. of Am. Invention* (1924), vol. II; *Boston Daily Advertiser*, Apr. 18, 1890; *Boston Post*, Apr. 18, 1890; *Boston Transcript*, Apr. 17, 1890; Patent Office records; information from a son-in-law, W. V. Kellen, Esq.]
                 C. W. M—n.

STURTEVANT, EDWARD LEWIS (Jan. 23, 1842–July 30, 1898), agricultural scientist, the second of three sons of Lewis W. and Mary Haight (Leggett) Sturtevant, was born in Boston, Mass. The father traced his lineage to Samuel Sturtevant who landed at Plymouth in 1642, and the mother's family were Quakers who settled at West Farms, N. Y., about 1700. In Edward's childhood his parents died, leaving their sons to be reared by an aunt at Winthrop, Me., the father's birthplace. Having prepared for college at Blue Hill, Me., Sturtevant entered Bowdoin in 1859. To its classical course he was largely indebted for his ability as a writer and linguist. In 1861 he joined Company G, 24th Maine Volunteers, serving as lieutenant and captain until typhoid malaria contracted at Port Hudson compelled his return to Winthrop in 1863. He graduated from Bowdoin in that year and from the Harvard Medical School in 1866. He never practised medicine, but its training developed his interest in scientific research.

In 1867 the Sturtevant brothers purchased and began the development of "Waushakum Farm," near South Framingham, Mass., notable as the scene of "a series of brilliant experiments in agriculture which are still models in experimental acumen and conscientious execution" (Hedrick, in *Sturtevant's Notes, post*, p. 2). Their initial interest was a model dairy of Ayrshire cattle, based on stock which Sturtevant personally selected in Scotland. With his brother Joseph he prepared *The Dairy Cow: A Monograph on the Ayrshire Breed* (1875), long a standard work, and four volumes of the *North American Ayrshire Register* (South Framingham, 1875–80). His study of the physiology of milk and milk secretion was instrumental in gaining a general

audience for his research. For several years (1876–79) he was editor or coeditor of the *Scientific Farmer*. A lysimeter, the first in America, was erected at "Waushakum Farm" in 1875, and its records covering four years were presented at scientific meetings. His lifelong study of the history of edible plants resulted in many articles and books on the subject. To further this work he collected hundreds of books, including a valuable pre-Linnean library which, together with his herbarium and numerous notes, he presented to the Missouri Botanical Garden (catalogue in its *Seventh Annual Report*, 1896). His "Varieties of Corn" (*United States Experiment Station Bulletin*, no. 57, 1899) is an epitome of his twenty years' investigations of the maize plant. Among his practical achievements were the development of the Waushakum variety of yellow flint corn and the New Christiana muskmelon.

Sturtevant's eminence in agricultural research led to his being chosen the first director of the New York Agricultural Experiment Station at Geneva in 1882. During his administration he outlined the broad plans on which the work of the station has been developed, and assembled a small but notable corps of assistants. He was a leader in the movement for experiment stations and his objectives at Geneva were largely followed by the stations established under the Hatch Act of 1887.

In that year, having ample means, Sturtevant retired to his home at South Framingham to complete his historical study of edible plants. Beginning in 1893, he spent three winters in California in an unsuccessful attempt to secure relief from tuberculosis. His home life was singularly close and happy. He was married twice: on Mar. 9, 1864, to Mary Elizabeth Mann, who died in 1875, and on Oct. 22, 1883, to Hattie Mann, a sister of his first wife. By the first marriage he had two sons and two daughters, and by the second, one son. His eldest daughter, Grace, and his second wife supplied drawings for a number of his writings.

A man of small stature and nervous temperament, Sturtevant had an intensely active mind. He enjoyed analytical discussion and was always propounding new problems for solution. He was liberal with helpful suggestions to associates and to the scientific societies of which he was an active member. "He was not a great mingler with men, but he had a wide circle of friends and prized their friendship. Quiet by nature, a lover of his home and home life, he sought his greatest pleasures in his family, among his books or at his work" (Plumb, in *Proceedings, post*, p. 218). In 1919, more than two decades after his death

Sturtevant's Notes on Edible Plants was published under the editorship of U. P. Hedrick.

[Biog. sketch by U. P. Hedrick, and bibliog., in *Sturtevant's Notes on Edible Plants* (1919); U. P. Hedrick, *A Hist. of Agric. in the State of N. Y.* (1933); C. S. Plumb, in *Proc. of the Nineteenth Ann. Meeting of the Soc. for the Promotion of Agric. Sci.* (1898), in *Tenth Ann. Report Mo. Bot. Garden* (1899), with bibliog. and portrait, and in *Experiment Station Record*, vol. X (1898–99); W. C. Strong and B. P. Ware, in *Trans. Mass. Hort. Soc. for 1898* (1899); E. L. Sturtevant, "Joseph N. Sturtevant," *Scientific Farmer*, Feb. 1879; H. H. Wing, in L. H. Bailey, *Cyc. of Am. Agric.*, vol. IV (1909); L. H. Bailey, *Standard Cyc. of Hort.*, vol. III (1915); *Country Gentleman*, Aug. 4, 1898; *Bot. Gazette*, Sept. 1898; *Boston Transcript*, Aug. 1, 1898; G. N. Mackenzie, *Colonial Families in the U. S. A.*, vol. III (1912); correspondence with Miss Grace Sturtevant, Wellesley Farms, Mass.]   E. E. E.

STURTEVANT, JULIAN MONSON (July 26, 1805–Feb. 11, 1886), educator, Congregational clergyman, was born in Warren, Conn., second of the four children of Warren and Lucy (Tanner) Sturtevant. He was a descendant of Samuel Sturtevant who was in Plymouth as early as 1642. When Julian was eleven years old his father, financially distressed like so many other New England farmers by the economic consequences of the War of 1812, emigrated with his family to the Western Reserve, settling in what is now Tallmadge, Ohio. Here the boy attended an academy and in June 1822, with several companions, set out in a one-horse wagon for New Haven, Conn., to enroll at Yale College. Four years later he was graduated. He taught school in New Canaan, Conn., during the winter of 1826–27, and subsequently returned to Yale to study theology.

While a Divinity student he became one of the "Illinois Association" or "Yale Band," the members of which pledged themselves to devote their lives to the furtherance of religion and education in the West. On Aug. 27, 1829, he was ordained to the Congregational ministry at Woodbury, Conn., by the Association of Litchfield South, and four days later was married to Elizabeth Maria Fayerweather of New Canaan. She died on Feb. 12, 1840, and on Mar. 3 of the following year he married her sister, Hannah. By each he had five children. Shortly after his first marriage, with his friend and fellow member of the "Band," Theron Baldwin [*q.v.*], he left for the West. Settling at Jacksonville, Ill., he became the first instructor in Illinois College, which opened with an enrollment of nine on Jan. 4, 1830. With this institution he was connected for more than fifty-five years. From 1831 to 1844 he was professor of mathematics, natural philosophy, and astronomy. In the latter year he succeeded Edward Beecher [*q.v.*] as president and became also professor of mental science and sci-

ence of government. He served the college as president until 1876 and remained a member of the faculty until 1885.

For many years Sturtevant was one of the leaders in the religious and educational movements of the Middle West; in addition he took an influential part in the discussion of many important public questions. In religion, while by no means a radical, he represented a refreshingly independent and liberal point of view. In spite of many discouragements, he fought manfully to keep Illinois College free from narrow sectarian control and while president insisted upon a reasonable freedom in the discussion of theological matters. At the first National Council of Congregational Churches, held in Boston in 1865, he delivered the opening sermon. When the slavery question became an important issue in the West, while refraining from identifying himself with the radical abolitionists, he became a strong advocate of freedom. He was a friend of Abraham Lincoln, conferring and corresponding with him on the important issues of the day. When Richard Yates [*q.v.*], the war governor of Illinois, was about to depart for Altoona to attend the convention of loyal governors, he wrote to Sturtevant for advice; assuring him that such advice would have weight in determining his course (*Autobiography, post*, p. 299). During the Civil War, when attendance in the college had dropped to a low point, Sturtevant was sent to England, with the encouragement of Lincoln and armed with letters to prominent Englishmen, to win a more sympathetic support for the Northern cause.

Although not a prolific writer, he was in later life an occasional contributor to such periodicals as the *New Englander*, the *Congregational Review*, and the *Princeton Review*. Many of his addresses were published and he was the author of three books: a small but stimulating volume entitled *Economics, or the Science of Wealth* (1877); *The Keys of Sect* (1880), a discussion of sectarianism; and an autobiography, published ten years after his death. He died in Jacksonville, Ill.

[In addition to *Julian M. Sturtevant: An Autobiog.* (copr. 1896), ed. by his son, see *Quarter Century Celebration of Ill. Coll.: Hist. Discourse* (1855), by Sturtevant, and his "Address at the Semi-Centennial Anniversary of the Founding of Ill. Coll.," in the *College Rambler*, June 1879; also, *Obit. Record Grads. Yale Coll.*, 1886; C. H. Rammelkamp, *Ill. Coll.: A Centennial Hist.* (1928); G. F. Magoun, *Asa Turner, a Home Missionary Patriarch and His Times* (1889); *Daily Inter Ocean* (Chicago), Feb. 12, 1886.]   C. H. R.

STUTZ, HARRY CLAYTON (Sept. 12, 1876–June 25, 1930), automobile manufacturer, son of Henry J. and Elizabeth (Snyder) Stutz, was born on his father's farm at Ansonia, Ohio.

After receiving a public-school education he learned the machinist trade and upon finishing his apprenticeship at the age of twenty-one opened a small machine shop in Dayton, Ohio. The automobile, which was then beginning to appear on city streets, appealed to him strongly and he was one of the first residents of Dayton to secure and drive one. He kept himself informed as to its development while continuing to repair and manufacture farm pumping engines. In 1903 he made his first step into the automobile industry by accepting the management of the Lindsey-Russell Axle Company at Indianapolis, Ind. To enlarge his experience he subsequently worked for the G. & J. Tire Company and the Schebler Carburetor Company of Indianapolis. From 1906 to 1910 he was engineer and factory manager of the Marion Motor Car Company, and designed the first "underslung" pleasure car, which was manufactured by that company.

Toward the close of this period Stutz became associated with Henry Campbell, and the two organized the Stutz Auto Parts Company. The following year the partners organized the Ideal Motor Car Company to manufacture an automobile designed by Stutz. The completed car competed in the first five-hundred-mile Indianapolis Speedway race and finished in eleventh place. After continuing with his designing work for the succeeding two years, Stutz combined the Auto Parts Company and the Ideal Motor Car Company into the Stutz Motor Car Company, and served as president until 1919, when he disposed of his interests and joined with Campbell in the organization of the H. C. S. Motor Car Company of Indianapolis for the manufacture of inexpensive automobiles and taxicabs. It was during the six-year period from 1913 to 1919 that the Stutz automobile gained its greatest reputation, and between 1913 and 1915 Stutz cars were the leaders in most of the important automobile races. In 1924 Stutz abandoned the automobile field temporarily and devoted his attention to airplane engines; at the time of his death he was negotiating with airplane manufacturers for the use of a four-cylinder airplane engine of this design.

Stutz was greatly interested in sports, particularly in trap shooting, and was reputed to be one of the best shots in his section of the country. He was also a collector of sporting firearms and had one of the foremost collections in the United States. After disposing of his automobile interests he made his home in Orlando, Fla. He died in the night of June 25, 1930, in a hospital in Indianapolis, following an operation for appendicitis. He was twice married: on Oct. 25, 1898, to Clara M. Dietz of Dayton, from whom he was divorced; and in 1925 to Blanche Clark of Indianapolis, who with a daughter by his former marriage survived him.

[*Soc. of Automotive Engineers Jour.*, Sept. 1930; *Automobile Topics*, June 28, 1930; *Automotive Industries*, July 5, 1930; *Who's Who in America*, 1926–27; *N. Y. Herald Tribune*, *N. Y. Times*, and *Indianapolis Star*, June 27, 1930; information as to certain facts from daughter, Mrs. Emma Belle Horn.]

C. W. M—n.

STUYVESANT, PETRUS (1592–Feb. 1672), called Peter by the English, director-general of New Netherland, was a grandson of Johannes of Dokkum, in West Friesland, Netherlands, and a son of the Rev. Balthazar Johannes Stuyvesant, graduate of the University of Franeker, and his wife Margaretta (Hardenstein) Stuyvesant. His father was before 1619 the pastor of the Dutch Reformed Church at Scherpenzeel (now in West Stellingwerf), but in 1622 removed to Berlicum, in the classis of Franeker. The mother of Petrus having died in 1625, his father remarried in 1627, and was in a third pastorate at Delfzyl in Groningen from April 1634 until his death on May 26, 1637. Petrus had a sister Anna, who was married to Samuel Bayard, and he had two half-brothers and two half-sisters. He early entered a military career, serving his country at home and abroad and thus supplying the desires of his adventurous spirit. He was in the service of the Dutch West India Company in 1635 as a supercargo in Brazil. In 1643 he went to the Leeward Islands as governor of the Dutch possessions of Curaçao and adjacent islands, and in 1644 led an expedition against the island of St. Martin, making an attack in March and raising the siege on April 16. It was in this affair that Stuyvesant was shot in the right leg, which was afterward amputated and buried at Curaçao and not in Holland, as hitherto claimed (Stokes, *post*, VI, 64, under 1645). He returned to the Fatherland for recuperation and to have an artificial limb supplied, referred to afterwards as his "silver leg" on account of its adornments. He married on Aug. 13, 1645, Judith Bayard (1608–1687), in the Walloon Church of Breda, where her father, the Rev. Lazare Bayard, deceased, had been for years minister of that French Protestant congregation. She was a sister of Samuel Bayard of Amsterdam who had married Stuyvesant's sister Anna. Two sons were born in New Netherland of his marriage, Balthazar Lazarus (baptized May 27, 1647) and Nicholas William (1648–1698).

On Oct. 5, 1645, Stuyvesant appeared in person before the Zealand Chamber of the Dutch West India Company, "offering his services" and requesting speedy aid in his equipment to go to New Netherland (Stokes, IV, 105). On July 28, 1646, he was commissioned by the States-General as director-general of "New Netherland and the places situated thereabout, as well as the aforementioned islands of Curaçao, Buenaire, Aruba and the dependencies and appurtenances thereof" (*New York Historical Society Quarterly Bulletin,* Apr. 1926, p. 9), and on Christmas of 1646 his expedition of four vessels sailed out of the Texel to sea. Besides the soldiery, servants, traders, and adventurers there were on board a new body of officials for New Netherland, Stuyvesant's wife and his widowed sister Anna, with her three sons. Stuyvesant ordered the ships to stop first at Curaçao, whence, after a few weeks, they sailed to New Amsterdam; there the fleet anchored on May 11, 1647, amid great rejoicing of the commonalty. A few years later Stuyvesant's critics said his bearing on this occasion was "like a peacock, with great state and pomp" (Jameson, *post,* p. 342), and as thoughtless of others as if he were the Czar of Muscovy. But such charges need to be judged in the maze of political controversy and in comparison with other events. On May 27 he appointed a naval commander and a superintendent of naval equipments, and on June 6 provided to fit out a naval expedition against the Spaniards who were operating within the limits of the West India Company's charter. The first ordinance promulgated after his arrival at New Amsterdam for internal good order was on May 31 on the sale of intoxicants and on Sunday observance. He became a church-warden on July 22 and took up the reconstruction of the church in Fort Amsterdam. Son of a minister and son-in-law of another, he was himself a strict adherent of the Reformed Church and not liberal to other ideas in religion. This inclination, egged on by the clergy and the provincial council, led to the enactment of an ordinance on Feb. 1, 1656, forbidding "Conventicles and Meetings, whether in public or private" (Stokes, IV, 164) that were not according to the synod of Dort, principally directed against the Lutherans, but operative as well against Quakers and others. In June, the secular directors of the company at Amsterdam reproved Stuyvesant and urged leniency, but the general attitude against dissent in New Netherland remained throughout the Dutch régime.

In 1650 Stuyvesant's salary was 250 guilders monthly and a subsistence of 900 guilders per annum. On Mar. 12, 1650, the directors of the company conveyed to him their "Great Bouwery," or Farm No. 1, for 6,400 guilders, located at "about the present 5th to 17th Streets and

from the East River to an irregular line coinciding approximately with Fourth Avenue," New York City, known thereafter as "Stuyvesant's Bouwery" (Stokes, I, 34). In 1658 there was conveyed to him a town site on the East River (now State Street), then at the foot of the present Whitehall Street, upon which he erected a substantial mansion with gardens, owned in 1686 by Governor Dongan and named by him "The Whitehall." This was perhaps the finest residence in New Amsterdam.

Stuyvesant's career as director-general was marked by many progressive measures. He promoted intercolonial relations with the English, drove the Swedes from the Delaware, increased commerce, and by a variety of edicts sought to regulate internal affairs. His acts were often harsh and dictatorial. He was jealous of his official prerogatives. His idea of government was submission of the people to the official will. On Sept. 25, 1647, he instituted a Board of Nine Men to aid in promoting the general welfare and many good things were done for a time by this cooperation. But in 1649 the scenes were stormy. The commonalty sought and Stuyvesant opposed an independent municipal control at New Amsterdam. The people's representatives drew up a "Remonstrance" (*Vertoogh*) on July 28 to the States-General for redress of their grievances of many years (O'Callaghan, *post,* I, 271–318; Jameson, pp. 293–354). The people won their municipal government by proclamation of Feb. 3, 1653. But the inhabitants were as lax in public obligations to their city officials as they had been and continued to be toward the provincial authority.

After Stuyvesant's surrender of New Netherland to the English at his farm house on Aug. 27/Sept. 6, 1664, he withdrew from all public affairs. In 1665 he went to the Netherlands to defend his official conduct and upon his return to New York lived on his farm until his death at the age of eighty years. He was buried beneath the chapel he had erected on his farm in 1660. The site is now (1935) St. Mark's Episcopal Church, where a stone tablet in the eastern wall records his interment. In 1922 St. Mark's commemorated the two hundred and fiftieth anniversary of his death.

[Not much exists for a personal biography of Stuyvesant, though there is much on his official career in New Netherland. Bayard Tuckerman, *Peter Stuyvesant* (1893), has some interest, but is far from satisfactory. The genealogy is best in Mrs. Alma R. Van Hoevenberg's article, "The Stuyvesants in the Netherlands and New Netherland," in *N. Y. Hist. Soc. Quart. Bulletin,* Apr. 1926; it is based on new researches. For his career in New Netherland the best body of materials, drawn anew from original sources, is found in I. N. Phelps Stokes, *The Iconography of Manhattan Island*

(6 vols., 1915–28), and see vol. I, 25–113 for a summary of the acts of his official régime, contributed by the present writer to that work. See also *Collections of the N. Y. Hist. Soc.*, 2 ser., II (1849) ; E. B. O'Callaghan, *Documents Relative to the Colonial History of the State of N. Y.*, vols. I–III (1855–56) ; J. F. Jameson, *Narratives of New Netherland* (1909) ; Berthold Fernow, *The Records of New Amsterdam* (7 vols., 1907) ; E. T. Corwin, ed., *Ecclesiastical Records. State of N. Y.* (7 vols., 1901–16).]

V. H. P.

SUBLETTE, WILLIAM LEWIS (1799?–July 23, 1845), fur trader, merchant, the son of Philip and Isabel (Whitley) Sublette, was born in Lincoln County, Ky. The Sublettes were Huguenots who settled in Manakin-Town, Va. Col. William C. Whitley, the grandfather of William Sublette, was likewise a Virginian. With his family and friends Whitley accompanied his kinsman, George Rogers Clark, to Kentucky in 1772, and was engaged in close combat with Chief Tecumseh [*q.v.*] in the battle of the Thames, where both were killed. The Sublette name was conspicuous in the fur trade, five brothers being thus engaged. Milton, long known as one of the most enterprising and daring Indian traders, was second in prominence to William. The family moved to St. Charles, Mo., about 1818, where William served as constable. Lured by the advertisements of William Henry Ashley [*q.v.*] for "enterprising young men," William Sublette joined Ashley's expedition to the Rocky Mountains (Chittenden, *post*, I, 252). Citizens of St. Charles fitted him out with a rifle and buckskin suit, his sole possessions. He was with Ashley in the Arikara fight on June 2, 1823, and served as sergeant-major under Colonel Leavenworth in the attack upon the Arikara villages in August. Ashley formed a strong friendship for him, and after five years outfitted him for an expedition of his own. Sublette made a fortune, and with two former companions, Jedediah S. Smith [*q.v.*] and David E. Jackson, finally bought out Ashley. Part of the Oregon Trail was first known as Sublette's cut-off, and Sublette's trace.

The firm of Smith, Jackson, and Sublette took the first wagons over the difficult trail to the Rockies, a feat previously deemed impossible. The last rendezvous of this firm was held in the summer of 1830. They sold out their joint interests but retained their furs, cattle, and wagons. This wagon train and collection of furs was so large as to create a sensation on arrival at St. Louis in the fall. The same men ventured on an expedition to Santa Fé in 1831, when Smith was killed by Indians. In the summer of 1832 William Sublette went again to the Rocky Mountains, and was wounded in the famous fight at Pierre's Hole. In December 1832 he formed a

partnership with another of Ashley's men, Robert Campbell [*q.v.*]. This firm continued in business for ten years and was a serious competitor of the American Fur Company. Their principal trading posts were on the Platte River at the mouth of the Laramie, and on the Missouri near Fort Union. They had a large store in St. Louis. Sublette had a wigwam built in the rear of this store, where he maintained a family of Indians during his lifetime. He died in Pittsburgh, Pa., while on his way to Cape May in search of health. William Sublette was a bold, shrewd, character. He was appointed in 1841 to the staff of Gov. Thomas Reynolds of Missouri, with the rank of colonel, the title by which he was generally known. He was married on Mar. 21, 1844, to Frances Hereford of Tuscumbia, Ala. He filled several public stations, was a presidential elector for his district in 1844, and was a candidate for Congress. He is buried in St. Louis.

[Sublette Manuscripts in the Mo. Hist. Soc.; H. M. Chittenden, *Am. Fur Trade of the Far West*, 2 vols. (2nd ed. 1935) ; Ednah W. McAdams, *Ky. Pioneer and Court Records* (1929), p. 120 ; Census of Lincoln County, Ky., 1810 ; W. S. Bryan, and Robert Rose, *Hist. of the Pioneer Families of Mo.* (1876), p. 187 ; *Mo. Republican* (St. Louis), Oct. 19, 1830, Oct. 16, 1832, June 16, 1837 ; *Daily Mo. Republican*, Aug. 1, 1845.]

S. M. D.

SULLIVAN, GEORGE (Aug. 29, 1771–June 14, 1838), lawyer, congressman, was born at Durham, N. H. His parents were Gen. John Sullivan [*q.v.*] and Lydia (Worcester) Sullivan and he inherited the advantages of his father's prestige. He received a good education at Phillips Exeter Academy and Harvard College, graduating from the latter institution in 1790. He studied law in his father's office, was admitted to the bar, and began practice in Exeter, where he was henceforth a member of that remarkable local group of lawyers and politicians who exercised such an influence on the affairs of the state. A Federalist, he represented Exeter in the legislature (1805) and seemed to have a promising political career before him when the decline of Federalist strength began. He served one year as state attorney-general (1805–06), and in the reaction against the Jeffersonian policies which followed the Embargo, he was elected to the Twelfth Congress (1811–13). A single term in Washington offered no particular opportunity for distinction but he returned to New Hampshire well known as a stubborn opponent of Madison's foreign policies in general and of the War of 1812 in particular. His name appears at the head of a list of thirty-four congressmen who signed *An Address of Members of the House of Representatives . . . to Their Constituents, on the Subject of the War with Great Britain*

(1812), denouncing the war as contrary to all moral and prudential considerations. His speech delivered early in August 1812 at a convention of the Friends of Peace of Rockingham County was a scathing attack on President Madison, who according to the orator was responsible for American subserviency to French influence— "the greatest of all possible calamaties." This speech was printed and widely circulated by the Federalists and later proved embarrassing both to Sullivan and to Daniel Webster, who had headed the resolutions committee on that occasion.

During the war Sullivan served in the New Hampshire legislature (House, 1813–14; Senate, 1814–16). With the era of good feeling which followed, like many contemporaries he forgot the animosities of the earlier period. On Dec. 19, 1815, he began a period of almost twenty years of service as attorney-general, combining an extensive private practice with his public functions and retiring in 1835 when a statute required the incumbent of his office to give his entire service to the state. In 1817 he represented New Hampshire in the Dartmouth College Case, arguing with great eloquence and an imposing array of authority that the General Court had the right to alter and amend the college charter (Timothy Farrar, *Report of the Case of the Trustees of Dartmouth College against William H. Woodward*, n.d., pp. 70–104). While often grouped with Daniel Webster, Jeremiah Smith, Ichabod Bartlett, Jeremiah Mason, and other eminent New Hampshire lawyers of his time, Sullivan was probably inferior to these men in scope of legal attainments. "He relied too little on his preparation and too much upon his oratory, his power of illustration and argument" (J. M. Shirley, *The Dartmouth College Causes*, 1877, p. 29). He was, however, an extremely able leader of the bar, a most effective jury lawyer, and a man of integrity who exercised a salutary influence in the New Hampshire courts. He was twice married: on Aug. 6, 1799, at Exeter, to Clarissa Lamson, who died in 1824, having borne ten children; and on Jan. 14, 1838, to Philippa Call. He died in Exeter.

[C. H. Bell, *The Bench and Bar of N. H.* (1894) and *Hist. of the Town of Exeter, N. H.* (1888) ; E. S. Stackpole and Lucien Thompson, *Hist. of the Town of Durham* (2 vols., n.d.) ; W. J. Lamson, *Descendants of Wm. Lamson of Ipswich, Mass.* (1917), p. 87; *Biog. Dir. Am. Cong.* (1928) ; *Portsmouth Journal*, June 23, 1838.]
                                        W. A. R.

SULLIVAN, JAMES (Apr. 22, 1744–Dec. 10, 1808), statesman, fourth son of John and Margery (Browne) Sullivan, was born at Berwick, in the District of Maine, where his father taught school. After studying under his father, James

became a student in the law office of his brother John [*q.v.*] at Durham and there met Mehitable Odiorne, whom he married Feb. 22, 1768. The couple settled in a two-room house at Biddeford, but Sullivan soon prospered and moved to the new town of Limerick. Here he became king's counsel for York County and one of the most influential men in the District of Maine. He took a prominent local part in the early movement toward revolution and was a member of the Provincial Congress of Massachusetts and of numerous committees, including the Committee of Safety. In 1776 he was appointed a justice of the supreme court of Massachusetts and throughout the war continued to be returned as a member of the legislature.

In 1778 he moved to Groton, Mass. When the new state was organized in 1780 he was one of the committee to reorganize the laws. Two years later he resigned from the bench and in 1783 moved to Boston and was elected to Congress. On Jan. 26, 1786, his wife died, leaving six young children—among them William Sullivan [*q.v.*] —and on Dec. 31 he married Martha Langdon, sister of John and Woodbury Langdon [*qq.v.*]. During these years he was occupied largely with politics: holding public office, writing for the press, and active in the inner councils of his party. He advocated the adoption of the federal Constitution in letters signed Cassius, printed in the *Massachusetts Gazette*, Sept. 18–Dec. 25, 1787 (P. L. Ford, *Essays on the Constitution*, 1892). Toward the end of 1788 or in the beginning of 1789 he made a trip through the South, probably in the interest of Hancock, with a view to securing him the vice-presidency. In 1790 he resigned the position of probate judge, which he had held for a short time, and was made attorney-general of Massachusetts. In 1796 he was appointed agent to maintain the interests of the United States before the commissioners at Halifax who were to determine the disputed boundary line of Maine.

By this time Sullivan had become one of the most prominent lawyers in Massachusetts, with a large and very lucrative practice. In 1797 he ran for governor, but was defeated by the Federalist candidate. Ten years later, however, in June 1807, he was elected to the office. At this time occurred his controversy with Timothy Pickering [*q.v.*] in the course of which he refused to communicate Pickering's letter on the Embargo to the state legislature. A war of letters and pamphlets followed, on the eve of the election of 1808, and although Sullivan was reelected governor by a small majority, the election generally was a pronounced Federalist victory.

Sullivan was never a national leader, but he was throughout his career a man to be reckoned with as perhaps the richest, ablest, and most powerful of the Democrats, or Republicans as they were then called, in what was, for most of his life, Federalist territory. His writings for the press on contemporary issues, published under several pen names, were innumerable and carried great weight. Although he died in the governorship it is unlikely that if he had lived he would have risen to higher office. He was more than a mere politician, however, and was keenly interested in several fields of thought outside of politics. In 1801 he published *The History of Land Titles in Massachusetts,* a valuable work, and at that time was planning a history of Massachusetts criminal law. His interest in the history in America of his profession is, perhaps, his chief claim to intellectual distinction. He was one of the first members of the American Academy of Arts and Sciences, and one of the founders, for some years president, and a contributor to the early *Collections* of the Massachusetts Historical Society. In 1795 he published *The History of the District of Maine,* still valuable. He was also the author of *Observations upon the Government of the United States* (1791), a treatise on the suability of states, and is credited with having been influential in securing the adoption of the Eleventh Amendment to the Constitution. In 1792 he published *The Path of Riches: An Inquiry into the Origin and Use of Money; and into the Principles of Stocks and Banks,* and in 1801, *A Dissertation upon the Constitutional Freedom of the Press in the United States of America.* Both as citizen and capitalist he was interested in "public improvements" as then understood and he was the projector and for long president of the Middlesex Canal.

[T. C. Amory, *Life of James Sullivan* (2 vols., 1859); Henry Adams, *Hist. of the U. S.,* vol. IV (1890); Octavius Pickering and C. W. Upham, *The Life of Timothy Pickering* (4 vols., 1867–73), esp. vols. III, IV; *Interesting Correspondence between His Excellency Gov. Sullivan and Col. Pickering* (1808); T. C. Amory and G. E. Meredith, *Materials for a Hist. of the Family of John Sullivan of Berwick, New England* (1893); *New Eng. Hist. and Geneal. Reg.,* Oct. 1865; Geo. Folsom, *Hist. of Saco and Biddeford* (1830); *Columbian Centinel* (Boston), Dec. 14, 17, 1808.]

J. T. A.

SULLIVAN, JAMES EDWARD (Nov. 18, 1860–Sept. 16, 1914), promoter of amateur sports, was born in New York City, the son of Daniel and Julia (Halpin) Sullivan of County Kerry, Ireland. Springing from solid Irish stock not far removed from the soil, he grew up with a love for outdoor life and sports of every kind. His father was a foreman in the construction work of the New York Central Railroad, a man of little money and no pretensions. Sullivan's education was limited entirely to New York's public schools. He was determined to succeed, however, and was unwilling to drift into manual labor. Night study and voracious reading sharpened his quick mind. In 1878 he entered the publishing house of Frank Leslie [*q.v.*] and publishing and editing became his life work. The year before he had joined the Pastime Athletic Club, and thereafter athletics were his hobby.

He might have become a national champion in any one of a half dozen different sports but he preferred to compete in as many as he could. Even in track and field events, which he most enjoyed, the powerfully built Sullivan was an all-around man with a versatility quite comparable to the decathlon men of the present day. His best individual performance was winning second place in the Canadian half-mile championship of 1884. As a competing athlete he saw through the sham and hypocrisy of "amateurism" as it was exploited by the National Association of Amateur Athletes of America, which then ruled most amateur sports. Fired with the resolution to stamp out these athletic malpractices, in 1888 he and several others formed the Amateur Athletic Union of the United States. For one year there was a terrific sports war between the two organizations for control; but Sullivan, unswerving in purpose, had founded the Union on the rock of honesty. It survived and the National Association capitulated and disbanded. During the early days of the Union Sullivan paid most of the expenses himself, and until he died he was always an officer, serving as its secretary (1889–96), as president (1906–09), as secretary-treasurer (1909–14). In reality he was the first sports czar. He ruled with an iron hand. Technically there could be appeals from his decisions; actually there were none. Athletes, used to the slip-shod methods of the older organization, at first resented Sullivan's rigid discipline, but once they realized the deep sincerity of the man they swung to his side with enthusiasm.

He had a genius for organization and an almost prophetic vision of the recreational needs of the thousands of children and youths in large cities. It was he who suggested the founding of New York's Public School Athletic League, now the largest of its kind, and he was one of its incorporators. He also opened the first public playground and gymnasium in New York City in 1898. His fame was international and he was always appointed the American director of the various Olympic Games. President Theodore Roosevelt and President Taft named him as their personal representative at the Olympic

Games from 1906 to 1912. No other man had received such a distinction, and none has since. At each Olympic Games kings and princes decorated him. When the American Olympic team of 1906 returned from Athens the banners of greeting read, "Welcome home J. E. Sullivan and the American team." So zealous was he in his espousal of the amateur cause that he hesitated not a second in barring Jim Thorpe when the Indian was at the height of his Olympic glory; he was equally quick to bar Arthur Duffey, another hero. Even his own nephew, Timothy J. Sullivan, felt the force of his wrath and was declared a professional because of his participation in one basketball game that his uncle thought was not as strictly amateur as it might have been.

While he was fostering amateur sports, he continued his connection with Leslie's publishing house until 1889, when he resigned to become business manager and editor of the *New York Sporting Times,* which he bought in 1891. The following year he assumed the presidency of the American Sports Publishing Company. He held this position until his death, editing the hundreds of books known as "Spalding's Athletic Library." In 1882 he married Margaret Eugenie Byrne, who with two children, a son and a daughter, survived him.

[*Official . . . Handbook of the Amateur Athletic Union,* 1914; files and records of the Amateur Athletic Union of the United States; *N. Y. Times,* Sept. 17, 1914; *Who's Who in America,* 1914–15; information from associates and relatives.]   A. J. D.

SULLIVAN, JOHN (Feb. 17, 1740–Jan. 23, 1795), Revolutionary general and statesman, brother of James Sullivan [*q.v.*], was born at Somersworth, N. H., across the Salmon Falls River from Berwick, Me. His father, John Sullivan of Limerick, Ireland, and his mother, Margery Browne of Cork, had emigrated as redemptioners to Maine, about 1723; John is said to have bought Margery's freedom.

The younger John Sullivan studied law at Portsmouth under Samuel Livermore. In 1760, he married Lydia Worcester. An able, if somewhat litigious, lawyer, he was successful enough to maintain his family, which included two daughters who died in infancy and a daughter and three sons—one of them George Sullivan [*q.v.*]—who survived. In 1772 he was appointed major of the New Hampshire militia. He seems to have inherited an antipathy for England which led him to the patriot side in the American Revolution. Sent as delegate to the First Continental Congress in Philadelphia, he took his seat Sept. 5, 1774. By December he was back in New

Hampshire, in time to receive Paul Revere's warning of a British threat, whereupon he rallied a band that captured Fort William and Mary at the entrance of Portsmouth harbor, and appropriated above one hundred barrels of gunpowder. On May 10, 1775, he took his seat in the Second Continental Congress, by which body he was (June 22) appointed brigadier-general.

In July Sullivan joined Washington's army outside of Boston and was stationed with his brigade at Winter Hill. With the exception of trips to organize the defenses of Portsmouth in October 1775, he served through the siege of Boston, until the evacuation, Mar. 17, 1776. Then ordered to the Northern army, which was retreating from Canada after Montgomery's defeat at Quebec, he reached Chambly early in June, and upon the death of Gen. John Thomas [*q.v.*] succeeded to the command. Superseded by Horatio Gates [*q.v.*] in July, he went to Philadelphia and offered his resignation, but a personal conference with President John Hancock led him to withdraw it.

On Aug. 9, 1776, Sullivan was promoted to be major-general. He joined the main army and was stationed with his command on Long Island. In the battle of Aug. 27, he was captured by the British and taken before Lord Howe, who wished to send him with overtures of peace to the Americans. Having obtained Washington's permission, Sullivan went to Philadelphia. During the negotiations between Congress and Howe, Sullivan was exchanged for the British general, Richard Prescott. He then rejoined the American army in Westchester County, N. Y., shared in the retreat across the Jerseys, led the right column at Trenton, and pursued the British at Princeton. The winter of 1777 he spent in northern New Jersey, conducting various skirmishes against the British outposts.

In March 1777, Sullivan returned to New Hampshire to expedite the preparations for the ensuing campaign. On July 1 he joined Generals Nathanael Greene and Henry Knox [*qq.v.*] in threatening to resign if Congress persisted in elevating the newly arrived French officer, Du Coudray, over their heads. Congress demanded an apology, and suggested that otherwise they might be asked to resign. Neither apologies nor resignations were forthcoming, but Du Coudray was accidentally drowned Sept. 15. On Aug. 21 and 22, Sullivan led an expedition against the British posts on Staten Island, which, although conducted with spirit, failed of its objective. This failure coupled with the Du Coudray affair made him enemies in Congress who began to question his capacity. Meantime, he hurried his division to the south to join Washington in defending Philadelphia against Howe.

In September a proposition was made in Congress to suspend Sullivan from command, pending a court of inquiry into his conduct of the Staten Island affair. This matter was now complicated by violent criticism, on the part of delegate Thomas Burke [*q.v.*] of North Carolina, of Sullivan's conduct at Brandywine. Washington, however, refused to recall Sullivan, and the investigations exonerated him from blame. At the battle of Germantown he executed the movements assigned to him, and the American discomfiture on that occasion was due to the progress of the action elsewhere.

Sullivan spent the winter of 1777–78 at Valley Forge, and in the spring was directed to take the command in Rhode Island, with a view to driving the British from Newport. Everything depended on the active cooperation of the French army and fleet under D'Estaing. In August Sullivan threw his armies around Newport and began the siege. Lord Howe's British fleet appeared, and D'Estaing stood out to meet him. A storm scattered and injured both squadrons before any action was possible. D'Estaing's captains then counseled him to withdraw his fleet and army to Boston, which left Sullivan in an awkward position, with inferior forces. He withdrew to the north end of the island on which Newport stands, where the British attacked him on Aug. 29, 1778. In the following battle the British were severely repulsed, but since Lord Howe now reappeared, Sullivan's position was very dangerous, and during the night he withdrew his entire force, with baggage and artillery, to the mainland. It required all of Washington's tact and Lafayette's loyalty to smooth down the anger which Sullivan and his men exhibited at what they regarded as D'Estaing's desertion.

Sullivan remained at Providence until March 1779, when he was ordered to take an expedition into western Pennsylvania and New York to lay waste the Iroquois country. While a force, under Col. Daniel Brodhead [*q.v.*] made an independent raid up the Allegheny, another, under Gen. James Clinton [*q.v.*], marched from Canajoharie to join Sullivan near the New York-Pennsylvania line. On Aug. 29, thus reinforced, Sullivan completely routed the combined Indian and Loyalist forces, near modern Elmira, N. Y. After pursuing them through the length of the Finger Lake country, burning and harrying the countryside as far west as modern Livingston County, he returned with health so impaired that he was compelled to resign from the army (Nov. 30, 1779).

In 1780–81 he reappeared in Congress. At this time his brother Daniel, who was dying as a result of ill treatment received aboard one of the British prison hulks, brought to him a further overture of peace from the British. Sullivan himself flatly refused to have anything to do with the matter, but brought it to the attention of Luzerne, the French minister. Since Luzerne had loaned Sullivan money, this episode was dragged out after the latter's death to insinuate that he was a pensioner of the French, but the charge has been thoroughly refuted. In 1782 Sullivan was a member of the New Hampshire constitutional convention. From 1782 to 1786 he was attorney-general of New Hampshire, and during this period served also in the state Assembly, as speaker (1785). In 1786 he was elected president (governor) of the state, and during his tenure put down the paper-money riots with great firmness and moderation. He was reëlected president in 1787, acted as chairman of the New Hampshire convention of 1788 which ratified the federal Constitution, in the same year was again speaker of the Assembly, and in 1789 was made president for the third time. In September 1789 he was also appointed United States district judge of New Hampshire, a position which he held until his death at Durham in 1795. Descriptions of Sullivan's character reveal traits typical of his Irish ancestry: he was brave, hot-headed, oversensitive, fond of display, generous to a fault, usually out of money, and a born political organizer.

[T. C. Amory, *The Mil. Services and Pub. Life of Maj.-Gen. John Sullivan* (1868), supersedes sketch by O. W. B. Peabody in Jared Sparks, *The Lib. of Am. Biog.*, 2 ser. III (1844), but must be used in connection with O. G. Hammond, *Letters and Papers of Maj.-Gen. John Sullivan* (2 vols., 1930–31), being *N. H. Hist. Soc. Colls.*, vols., XIII and XIV. See also *New Eng. Hist. and Geneal. Reg.*, Oct. 1865; T. C. Amory and G. E. Meredith, *Materials for a Hist. of the Family of John Sullivan* (1893); *Provincial Papers . . . of N. H.*, vol. VII (1873); *State Papers . . . of N. H.*, vols. VIII (1874), X–XVII (1877–89); *Early State Papers of N. H.*, vols. XX–XXII (1891–93); E. C. Burnett, *Letters of Members of the Continental Congress*, vols. I–VII (1921–33); *Journals of the Continental Congress*; the various editions of Washington's writings; *Proc. Mass. Hist. Soc.*, 1 ser. IX (1867), XX (1884), 2 ser. I (1885). A. T. Norton, *Hist. of Sullivan's Campaign against the Iroquois* (1879), is superseded by *Jours. of the Mil. Exped. of Maj. Gen. John Sullivan against the Six Nations* (1887), ed. by G. S. Conover. See also *The Sullivan-Clinton Campaign in 1779: Chronology and Selected Docs.* (1929), and Louise W. Murray, *Notes from the Craft Coll. in Tioga Point Museum on the Sullivan Exped.* (1929). The various refutations of George Bancroft's ill-natured comments on Sullivan (*Hist. of the U.S.*, vols. IX, 1866, X, 1874) are gathered in *Gen. Sullivan not a Pensioner of Luzerne . . . with the Report of the N. H. Hist. Soc.* (1875).] R. G. A—s.

SULLIVAN, JOHN LAWRENCE (Oct. 15, 1858–Feb. 2, 1918), pugilist, was born in Boston, Mass. He inherited pugnacity from his father, Michael Sullivan of Tralee, Ireland, a fiery little laborer, small in stature. From his mother, whom he greatly resembled, a kindly giantess weighing 180 pounds, he derived his marvelous body and good nature. Even as a youth he displayed prodigious strength. Graduating from grammar school when he was sixteen, he found work as a plumber's assistant and later as a tinsmith. He was fond of sports and received several offers to engage in professional baseball.

A casual invitation to box in a Boston theatre when he was nineteen started him on his pugilistic career. His first blow knocked an opponent into the orchestra. For a year (1877–78) he gave boxing exhibitions in a variety show conducted by William Muldoon; twenty-five dollars was promised anyone who could last one round against him. Subsequent engagements gave him the reputation of being able to hit "hard enough to knock a horse down," and late in 1880 he issued a challenge, offering "to fight any man breathing, for any sum from $1000 to $10,000 at catch weights," adding, "This challenge is especially directed to Paddy Ryan." Ryan was the American champion and Sullivan had to show his powers in other contests before Paddy would meet him. A match was finally fought at Mississippi City, Miss., Feb. 7, 1882, with bare knuckles and on the turf, in which Sullivan knocked out the champion in the ninth round.

This victory made him a popular idol. Crowds flocked to see him on his journey North, and Boston, his home town, welcomed him with great acclaim, tendering him a reception in the Dudley Street Opera House. For the next ten years "The Boston Strong Boy" dominated the American prize ring and was one of the spectacular figures of the country. He was 5 feet 10½ inches tall, and when in condition weighed 180 pounds. His method of fighting was simply to hammer his opponent into unconsciousness. His hazel eyes, burning black with fury, and his blatant confidence seemed to paralyze his opponents. An habitué of saloons, he lived a riotous life, but even when not in condition was able to knock out his antagonists. He was ready to meet all comers, though his manager, Jimmy Wakely, barred the negro Peter Jackson. Flamboyantly patriotic, he had a fierce animosity for "foreign fighters." Among his engagements was one fought in Madison Square Garden, New York, Aug. 6, 1882, with the New Zealander Herbert Slade, "The Maori," whom he terrified and knocked out in three rounds. The Englishman Charlie Mitchell gave him the most trouble. In a fight in New York, May 14, 1883, Mitchell,

to the consternation of everyone including Sullivan, actually knocked the champion down. In the third round, however, the police interfered to save Mitchell's life. On Aug. 8, 1887, at the Boston Theatre, with high municipal officials present, Sullivan's admirers presented him with a $10,000 diamond-studded belt. In October of that year he went abroad, visiting England and Ireland, where he received frenzied ovations. He met the Prince of Wales at the Prince's request and treated him with the easy condescension he displayed toward American presidents and prelates with whom he became acquainted. A match between Sullivan and Mitchell took place, Mar. 10, 1888, on the estate of Baron Rothschild, at Chantilly, France. A fierce battle of some three hours was waged, at the end of which, much to Sullivan's chagrin, the fight was declared a draw. Both contestants were arrested. After a night in jail Sullivan posted bail of $1600 and fled the country. By 1889 he was a flabby wreck from dissipation, but William Muldoon trained him into condition, and on July 8, 1889, after seventy-five rounds under a glaring sun at Richburg, Miss., against Jake Kilrain, Sullivan was given the decision. This was the last bare-knuckle championship contest. A little more than three years later, Sept. 7, 1892, the clever, agile, hard-hitting James Corbett, in the twenty-first round, ended Sulivan's pugilistic career.

He had wasted a fortune; his diamond belt had gone for his debts. For several years he acted in various plays, touring the United States and visiting Canada and Australia; later he appeared in vaudeville. He opened a bar in New York and acquired an interest in a saloon in Boston. There was some talk of nominating him for Congress. Finally, in 1905, he reformed and became a temperance lecturer. He had married a chorus girl, Annie Bates, in 1883, but they soon separated. In 1908 he divorced her and married Kate Harkins of Roxbury (part of Boston), Mass., a boyhood sweetheart who had opposed his drinking and fighting. In 1912 they acquired a farm in West Abington, Mass. Five years later his wife died, and his last days were spent in poverty with an old sparring partner, George Bush, as a companion.

[In 1892 there appeared under Sullivan's name *Life and Reminiscences of a 19th Century Gladiator*. See also R. F. Dibble, *John L. Sullivan* (1925); William Inglis, *Champions off Guard* (1932); *Literary Digest*, Feb. 23, 1918; *N. Y. Tribune*, Feb. 8, 1882, July 9, 1889, Sept. 8, 1892; *N. Y. Times*, Feb. 3, 1918.]

W.O.I.

SULLIVAN, LOUIS HENRI (Sept. 3, 1856–April 14, 1924), architect, was born in Boston, Mass., the son of Patrick and Andrienne (List)

Sullivan. In looks, manner, and name he was an Irishman, but he referred to himself as of "mongrel origin." He placed great store on his genealogy, however, as a partial clue to his own personality. His father was a pure-blooded Celt, who from a waif became a wandering musician, and by grim pride and ambition advanced himself to the proprietorship of an academy of dancing in London, traveled, studied dancing in Paris, and visited Geneva. He sailed to Boston in 1847, opened a music and dancing academy there, and again prospered. According to his son, grace, rhythm, symmetry were his watchwords, and their consideration and practice obsessed his existence. In 1852 in Boston he married Andrienne List, a beautiful, highly emotional girl, of a strong personality, who had emigrated from Geneva with her parents in 1850. Her mother was French, but her father, Henri List, was pure German—an intellectual, said to have been educated for the priesthood but to have fled the convent for Geneva, where he taught school. Louis, the child of this Irish-French-German union, was self-willed, emotional, courageous, energetic. During his childhood, after a year or two with his grandparents, he spent winters with his father and mother at Boston, Newburyport, and Halifax, and summers with his grandparents at Wakefield, Mass., then called South Reading. In Boston he attended the public schools—the Brimmer school, the Rice school, and the English High School—and in his autobiography he gives great praise to a certain Moses Woolson, teacher in the English High School, who, he says, inculcated methods of thought, study, and work on which he relied through life. When in 1869 his father moved to Chicago in an effort to find a climate more lenient to the health of the mother, Louis was left with his grandparents. In this same year, at the age of thirteen, he determined to become an architect.

Two years later, owing to the death of his grandmother and the removal to Philadelphia of old Henri List, who had been his beloved counselor and companion, his home was once more broken up, and he moved to the house of a neighbor. At the end of the school year he passed the entrance examinations for the Massachusetts Institute of Technology, where in 1872 he entered the course in architecture under the tutelage of William Robert Ware [q.v.] and his romantic assistant, Eugène Létang, who was a graduate of the famous, almost mythical, École des Beaux Arts in Paris, regarded by Americans, chiefly because of deeds of its distinguished sons, Henry Hobson Richardson and Richard Morris Hunt

[qq.v.], as the miraculous fountain-head of all architectural knowledge, and the open sesame to success and renown in the practice of architecture. The study of academic architecture irked Sullivan, however, and he would desert the Greek and Roman orders to contemplate the recently completed Brattle Street Church tower in the virile and stimulating Romanesque as revived by Richardson. After a year there (1872–73) he decided that the Institute was no place for him, and his thoughts turned to Paris. Going to New York in the spring, he went to see Richard M. Hunt, bluff old autocrat, America's first and most distinguished eclectic, who was very kind to the boy, slapped him on the back, and told him to go to Paris. He did finally, but via Philadelphia and Chicago. In Philadelphia he tarried, working in the office of Furness and Hewitt. Here, as in all offices except Richardson's, the architectural vernacular was largely Victorian Gothic, which Sullivan aptly describes as "Gothic in its pantalettes." But the panic of 1873 left him without a job, and he betook himself to Chicago. The raw and unfinished city, rising from the ruins of the great fire, immediately captivated him. Here he stayed for a year, working principally in the office of Major William Le Baron Jenney [q.v.], afterwards to become famous as the first architect to utilize in a tall building a skeleton of metal as the basic element of its construction. At this time Sullivan's principal interest was engineering, and the Eads bridge, about to leap across the Mississippi, fired his imagination far more than any building he had seen. Still searching for the Holy Grail of his imagination, an underlying law for architecture, he set out for Paris in July 1874. Only six weeks intervened between his arrival and the examinations for entrance to the Beaux Arts. Sullivan laid out a schedule that demanded eighteen hours of study a day; at the end of a month, threatened with a collapse, he took a day off and recovered. He wore out three tutors, but passed his examination with éclat and then took a flying trip to Rome to verify, he says, Taine's description of Michelangelo's ceiling. A statement of his professor of mathematics kept ringing in his head, "—here our demonstrations shall be so broad as to admit of *no exception!*" That was what he must find for architecture—a rule that admits of no exceptions. His work at the Beaux Arts, most unfortunately, gave him no answer to his riddle, though his year in the atelier Vaudremer was filled with interesting experiences and youthful delight.

In a year he had returned to Chicago. After work in various offices, where he acquired a reputation as a remarkably skilful and rapid draftsman, in 1879 he entered the office of Dankmar Adler as a "probationary" partner; on May 1, 1881, the firm became Adler and Sullivan. The rise of the new firm was extremely rapid; in but a year or so its practice was exceeded by that of only one other in the city. The chief problem confronting the designer of large buildings in those days was to obtain more light for offices and to devise means for building ever higher, a problem essentially structural and economic which to Sullivan was of absorbing interest. Although he asserts that such buildings as the Borden Block, built in these early days, were a radical departure from their contemporaries, there is little to be seen in them that substantiates him. He designed in the vernacular, which was bad, a strange combination of Victorian Gothic, English "Eastlake," and French Néo-Grec. In the early eighties Chicago rushed headlong into Richardson's Romanesque revival, Sullivan along with John Wellborn Root [q.v.] and the rest, although he denies it. When the Auditorium Building, Chicago, was projected, Adler and Sullivan built a trial audience room, seating over six thousand, in the old Exposition Building, demonstrated their mastery of the problem of acoustics, and thereby won the contract for designing the new building. At the time of its building (1886–90), it was the city's greatest architectural monument, and the auditorium proper, only a part of a huge building devoted to the purposes of hotel and office building in addition, remains (1935) the greatest room ever built for the purpose of opera. It not only won the firm international recognition but also marked the critical crossing of the ways in the career of Louis Sullivan. Though the exterior was in the vernacular of the Romanesque revival, the fashionable style, the interior—designed, or at least detailed, after the exterior was completed—shows clearly the architect's break with the past and his embarkation on the unknown path of original design. In the meantime the practicability of skeleton construction had been demonstrated by Holobird and Roche in the Tacoma Building, Chicago. After a nervous breakdown that compelled a prolonged stay (1889–1900) in Ocean Springs, Miss., there followed a series of important buildings, designed by Sullivan in consistent adherence to the principles and peculiar forms set forth in the interior of the Auditorium, and accepting with enthusiasm the revolutionary principle of skeleton construction. Notable among these are the Wainwright Building, St. Louis, Mo., the first complete expression of his principles of construction combined with his original decorative treatment; the Transportation Building with its "Golden Arch," the sensation of the World's Columbian Exposition of 1893 and the formal introduction of Sullivan's new conception of architecture to the world; the Gage Building, Chicago, an almost perfect solution—structurally and architecturally—of the steel-constructed skyscraper; and the Getty Tomb, Graceland Cemetery, Chicago, a singularly beautiful and original architectural tour de force. Others are the Stock Exchange Building, the Schiller Theatre (later the Garrick), the Schlesinger and Mayer Building (later the Carson, Pirie, Scott & Company Building), all in Chicago; the Union Trust Building and the St. Nicholas Hotel, St. Louis; the Condict Building, New York, and the Guaranty Building, Buffalo, N. Y.

On July 1, 1899, Sullivan married Margaret Hattabough of Chicago, from whom he was divorced in 1917. There were no children. In 1900 he returned to Chicago, but with the death of Dankmar Adler in that same year his opportunity to do work on a large scale ceased. In addition to the fact that the clients of the firm were for the most part Adler's clients, Sullivan's haughty and uncompromising attitude turned away commissions, and his irregular and nonconforming mode of life did little to inspire confidence. The last years of his life, although beset by privations and harried by the triumph of eclecticism and the apparent defeat of his principles, were yet fruitful in many ways. He produced a series of small banks brilliant in design and rich in practical innovations, beginning with the National Farmers' Bank, Owatanna, Minn., and including the Merchants' National Bank, Grinnell, Iowa, and banks at Columbus, Wis., Cedar Rapids, Iowa, Lafayette, Ind., and Sidney, Ohio; a church, St. Paul's Methodist, at Cedar Rapids, and a residence or two. He also produced the twenty original drawings, unique in their beauty and importance, illustrating his philosophy of ornament (now in the possession of the Art Institute of Chicago), which were published as *A System of Architectural Ornament According with a Philosophy of Man's Powers* (1924), and he wrote in his last days his extraordinary *The Autobiography of an Idea* (1924).

The rule that would admit of no exception, the voice that cried *"Yea"* in thunder tones in the stillness of the Sistine Chapel, the Idea of which he wrote the autobiography was that "form follows function." The most grievous violation of this principle was the treatment of the skyscraper in Roman mode between the World's Columbian

Exposition and the World War. Most of Sullivan's energy was expended in pointing out the essentially modern function of the skyscraper, its peculiarly American character and unprecedented construction, and the proper form for its expression. The novelty of its steel skeleton construction, the vast opportunity that lay in truthfully expressing it, and the falsity inherent in the popular garment of Roman architecture with which it was clothed and concealed he dinned into the deaf ears of American architects until he became almost a nuisance. (See his *Kindergarten Chats on Architecture, Education and Democracy,* 1934, first published in the *International Architect and Builder* in 1901; "The Tall Office Building Artistically Considered," reprinted in *Western Architect,* January 1922; "The Young Man in Architecture," *Ibid.,* January 1925; and "The Chicago Tribune Competition," *Architectural Review,* February 1923.) The rise of Classicism or Eclecticism which followed the Chicago Exposition of 1893 was too strong, however, for Sullivan and his followers, the "Chicago School," to combat successfully at the time. But Sullivan, whose confidence in the ultimate outcome never failed, saw the turn of the tide in the overwhelming acclaim that greeted the second-prize design of Eliel Saarinen in the *Chicago Daily Tribune* competition of 1924.

Sullivan's permanent place in the roster of great architects is assured. Chronologically, at least, he is the father of Modernism in architecture—the Transportation Building at the World's Columbian Exposition anticipated by five years the Art Nouveau movement in Europe. He founded a school of architectural philosophy which has become almost universally accepted. He, more than any man, helped to make of the skyscraper America's greatest contribution to architecture. His original "Sullivanesque" style of architectural ornament, while too personal and complicated for popular acceptance, was yet a distinct and valuable contribution to the thesaurus of architecture, and his book, *The Autobiography of an Idea,* an intensely personal revelation, is a notable addition to American literature. On the back of the monolith in Graceland Cemetery erected to him by the architects and builders of Chicago is the following inscription: "By his buildings great in influence and power; his drawings unsurpassed in originality and beauty; his writings rich in poetry and prophecy; his teachings persuasive and eloquent; his philosophy where, in 'Form Follows Function,' he summed up all truth in Art, Sullivan has earned his place as one of the greatest architectural forces in America."

[The spelling of Sullivan's middle name is from *The Autobiog. of an Idea,* which contains a detailed account of his early life. See also *Who's Who in America,* 1922–23; memorial issue of *Western Architect,* June 1924; L. P. Smith and H. W. Desmond, in *Architectural Record,* July 1904; L. J. Millett, *Ibid.,* Oct. 1908; Montgomery Schuyler, *Ibid.,* Jan. 1912; A. N. Rebori, *Ibid.,* May 1916; F. L. Wright, *Ibid.,* July 1924; Fiske Kimball, *Ibid.,* Apr. 1925; Robertson Howard, in *Architectural Jour.,* June 18, 1924; *Am. Architect,* May 7, 1924; T. E. Tallmadge, *Ibid.,* Oct. 23, 1918, in *Building for the Future,* Oct. 1930, and *The Story of Architecture in America* (1927); G. H. Edgell, *The Am. Architecture of Today* (1928); and obituary in *Chicago Daily Tribune,* Apr. 15, 1924.] T. E. T.

SULLIVAN, LOUIS ROBERT (May 21, 1892–Apr. 23, 1925), physical anthropologist, was born in Houlton, Me., the son of James and Mary (Mitchell) Sullivan. He was graduated from Bates College, Lewiston, Me., in 1914, taught biology for a year in Tilton Seminary, Tilton, N. H., and then went to Brown University as assistant in biology under Prof. H. E. Walter. He was married on Nov. 24, 1915, to Bessie Pearl Pathers, of Lewiston, Me. In 1917 he was appointed assistant curator in physical anthropology at the American Museum of Natural History in New York City and associate curator in 1924. He received the Ph.D. degree from Columbia University in 1922. His first important scientific contribution was a study of race differences in the articulation of the lower jaw, but the World War soon called him from the laboratory. He was assigned to duty as first lieutenant in the anthropological division of the surgeon-general's office to assist in compiling data on drafted men. His special contribution to the study of these data was the determination of standard population areas in the United States, according to homogeneity in national and racial origins. The subsequent publication of studies has shown them to be fundamentally basic in relation to the geographical distribution of anthropological types. Later Sullivan was assigned to Camp Grant where he made a systematic anthropometric survey of all recruits, but unfortunately a fire in his quarters destroyed these records.

At this cantonment he suffered a severe attack of influenza which permanently impaired his health, but upon his return to the Museum in New York he began to plan new programs of research. He accepted with enthusiasm an opportunity to work at the Bernice P. Bishop Museum in Hawaii on an intensive study of native races in the island countries of the Pacific. His objective here was not only to study native adults but also to observe the growth of children, especially in Hawaii where race crossing was operating on a large scale. Unfortunately, steadily declining health made a change of climate necessary, so, after two years, he went to Tucson, Ariz. In this new environment he planned a study of race characters as observed among the Indians, Mexicans, and other types to be found in Arizona and neighboring states. He visited most of the United States Indian and public schools in the area, but, finally, when these data had been gathered, his vitality failed and he died at the age of thirty-three.

Notwithstanding the difficulties under which he labored, Sullivan published during his brief career twenty-five papers in anthropology, at least nine of which are considered contributions of importance. Though the bulk of the data gathered in Hawaii and the United States was left incomplete, his records were so clear and definite, his outlines for treatment so complete, that two major papers were subsequently issued, one covering the growth of children in Hawaii, the other the distinguishing face characters of North American Indians. A bibliography of his works appeared in the *American Journal of Physical Anthropology*, October–December 1925. In addition to these achievements Sullivan gave evidence of real genius in museum work particularly in dealing with the details of any exhibit demonstrating anatomical and race characteristics.

His scientific work was characterized throughout by originality and accuracy of observation. Almost from the start he set as his ultimate research objective the discovery of genetic relations among the known divisions of mankind, a problem that still remains peculiarly baffling. His scientific faith was in precise observation and originality in classification, believing that the consistent analysis of human qualitative characters such as particular forms of eye, ear, nose, lips, etc., rather than differences in measurement would point the way to genetic relations. Perhaps no other physical anthropologists possessed equal genius in setting up rating scales so that fruitful comparisons could be made, not only in the study of growth in size, but also in the establishment of race criteria. It is little short of a tragedy that Sullivan's early death barred the possible realization of the main objective in his life plan. Certainly his published work gave promise of at least a suggestive clarification of the race origin problem.

[J. M. Cattell, D. R. Brimhall, *Am. Men of Sci.* (3rd ed., 1921); *Gen. Cat. of Bates Coll.* (1915); *Anthropological Papers, Am. Museum of Natural Hist.*, vol. XXIII (1925); *Am. Anthropologist*, Apr.–June 1925; *Am. Jour. of Physical Anthropology*, Oct.–Dec. 1925.]
                                               C. W.

SULLIVAN, TIMOTHY DANIEL (July 23, 1862–Aug. 31, 1913), politician, the son of Daniel and Catherine (Connelly) Sullivan, was born in a New York City tenement. His father, a laborer, died when the boy was four years old, leaving the mother with half a dozen young children, and almost penniless. At seven or eight years of age Tim was on the street selling papers. He had only a few bits of primary schooling. Before he was fifteen he was making himself useful to the Tammany politicians in the Sixth Ward, the turbulent Five Points district, and thus he got his start in politics. He was scarcely twenty-one when he found a backer who set him up as a saloon keeper. A few years later he was either sole or part proprietor of six saloons. In 1886, at the age of twenty-three, he was elected to the state Assembly, and in the following year he married Helen Fitzgerald. In 1893 he was elected to the state Senate and served there until 1902. In 1892 he succeeded to the Democratic leadership of the Third Assembly District—the Bowery region—and before 1900 he was the uncrowned king of the lower East Side.

Besides his activities in the liquor business, he had interests in several successful theatres and as half owner of the Sullivan & Considine vaudeville circuit in the Western states. By 1898, outside of Brooklyn, no one could put on a boxing match in the State of New York save in clubs licensed by and paying tribute to Sullivan. He was likewise a leading member of a syndicate which levied tribute on gambling in New York City. The *New York Times* in articles beginning Mar. 9, 1900, charged that the annual takings of this ring were $3,095,000. Between 1900 and 1910 Sullivan was admittedly the most powerful politician in New York. He could have become dictator of Tammany Hall upon the retirement of Richard Croker [*q.v.*] in 1902 had he so desired, but his own position was more lucrative and more to his taste, so he worked for the appointment of his friend Charles W. Murphy [*q.v.*]. Known most commonly and affectionately to constituents as "Big Tim" or "The Big Feller," he was a handsome, jovial giant who distributed with a lavish hand a goodly percentage of the money which he was so shrewd in collecting through various channels. Vice and crime were carefully organized in his territory and paid graft to his machine, as did many lines of legitimate business, even to the pushcart peddlers. Nevertheless, there was probably never a leader so idolized by his constituents. It was said of him that he made millions and gave away millions. He gave a Christmas turkey dinner every year to from 5,000 to 7,000 poor men and derelicts, and presented each with a pair of stout shoes and socks. He was one of the most magnetic personalities ever known in American politics. An observer once remarked that his smile could adequately be described only by the word beautiful. When charged with grafting or partnership with crime and vice, he could arise in the Assembly or on a campaign rostrum, and by telling the story of his tenement boyhood and the sacrifices of his mother, reduce even hardened political opponents to tears.

He was elected to Congress in 1902, and re-elected in 1904, but he did not care for national politics, and retired in 1906. In 1908 he was again elected to the state Senate. His health was slowly failing, however, and in 1912, following the death of his wife and of his two favorite cousins and lieutenants, "Florrie" and "Little Tim" Sullivan, his mind began to give way. Nevertheless, he was elected to Congress that fall, though he made no campaign and did not even go to Washington to be sworn in. For a time he was confined in a sanitarium and later lived in a house belonging to his brother. On the night of Aug. 30, 1913, eluding observation, he wandered away. A train early next morning, a few miles from Eastchester, ran over the body of a man who, as the crew believed, was already dead. Strangely enough, the search for Sullivan continued while the body lay unidentified in a morgue for two weeks. Just as it was about to be sent to the potter's field it was identified by a policeman. The funeral was one of the most imposing ever seen in New York; it was estimated that 25,000 sincere mourners followed "Big Tim" to the grave. It was Sullivan who was responsible for Columbus Day becoming a legal holiday in New York, and for the law making the carrying of concealed weapons a felony.

[Newspaper literature on Sullivan is voluminous; see *N. Y. Herald*, Apr. 28, 1901, May 19, 1907, and Nov. 1, 1909; *World* (N. Y.), Oct. 27, 1901, June 14, 1903, and Feb. 16, 1913; *N. Y. Press*, Dec. 3, 1905, Sept. 29, 1912, and Nov. 17, 1912; *N. Y. Tribune*, Sept. 19, 1901; and all New York newspapers of Sept. 14, 15, 1913. Other sources include *Biog. Dir. Am. Cong.* (1928); G. K. Turner, "Tammany's Control of N. Y. by Professional Criminals," *McClure's Mag.*, June 1909; *Ten Months of Tammany* (1901), pub. by City Club of N. Y.; *Report of the Special Committee of the Assembly . . . to Investigate the Pub. Offices . . . of N. Y.* (5 vols., 1900); A. F. Harlow, *Old Bowery Days* (1931); M. R. Werner, *Tammany Hall* (1928); Harold Zink, *City Bosses in the U. S.* (1930); memorial addresses, *House Doc. 1177*, 63 Cong., 2 Sess.; *Proc. of the Legislature of the State of N. Y. on the Life . . . of Timothy D. Sullivan* (1914); *Current Lit.*, Dec. 1909; *Munsey's Mag.*, Dec. 1913.]
A. F. H.

SULLIVAN, WILLIAM (November 1774–Sept. 3, 1839), lawyer and writer, was born at Biddeford, Me., on the Saco River, son of James Sullivan [*q.v.*], later governor of Massachu-

setts, and Mehitable (Odiorne) Sullivan. Prepared for college by the Rev. Phillips Payson of Chelsea, Mass., he was graduated from Harvard with honors in 1792, studied law in his father's Boston office, and was admitted to the bar in 1795. On May 19, 1802 he married Sarah Webb Swan, daughter of Col. James Swan [*q.v.*]; to them ten children were born.

In Boston Sullivan proved himself an able lawyer and shared in the increasing fortunes of the growing city. During the early years of his practice he was frequently called upon to give legal advice to the selectmen (Boston Town Records, *passim*); in 1814 he served as fire ward, in 1821 he aided in drafting a charter for the city (Morison, *post*, II, 237). As chief marshal of the Boston Centennial Celebration in 1830, he left behind a characteristic letter addressed to the Chief Marshal of the Celebration of Sept. 17, 1930 (*Boston Transcript*, Jan. 23, 1926, pt. III).

He also played a prominent rôle in politics, despite his Democratic parentage allying himself with the Federalists. In 1804 he was elected to the Massachusetts General Court and thenceforth until 1830 was in almost continuous service as representative, senator, or member of the executive council of the state. In 1812 he was a member of the Federalist Convention in New York and of the Central Committee of Federalists in Massachusetts. Though not a delegate to the Hartford Convention, he was in sympathy with its actions and was sent with Harrison Gray Otis and Thomas H. Perkins [*qq.v.*] to carry to Washington the protest of the Massachusetts legislature which grew out of the report of that convention. Fourteen years later he joined with others to defend the convention against the charge brought by John Quincy Adams that the Federalists there present had advocated disunion (Henry Adams, *Documents Relating to New-England Federalism*, 1877, pp. 43–45, 63–91).

In 1829 his wife inherited a competence sufficient for the future needs of the family, making it possible for him to abandon the practice of law for the writing which had already become his greatest pleasure. His conviction that the permanence of the institutions of his country depended upon the spread of popular education induced him to prepare a series of "class books": *The Political Class Book* (1831); *The Moral Class Book* (1831); *Historical Class Book; (Part First) Containing Sketches of History . . . to . . . A.D. 476* (1833); *Historical Causes and Effects, from the Fall of the Roman Empire, 476, to the Reformation, 1517* (1838). In 1835 and 1836 he gave a series of historical lectures in Boston; these are preserved in manuscript in the Boston Public Library. In 1837 he brought out *Sea Life*. His most considerable work, *Familiar Letters on Public Characters and Public Events from the Peace of 1783 to the Peace of 1815* (1834), was republished in 1847 with notes and a sketch of the author by his son, under the title, *The Public Men of the Revolution*. He was in constant demand as a public speaker and a number of his occasional addresses were published. At his death he was described as a man of "most amiable and benevolent disposition, varied and extensive accomplishments" (*Boston Daily Advertiser*, Sept. 4, 1839). He was by all agreed to be hospitable, cheerful, of lively wit, sound sense, and great intelligence. His writing was simple and lucid—as he himself said, "not in the fashion of his day."

[Biog. sketch by J. T. S. Sullivan, in *The Pub. Men of the Revolution* (1847) ; MSS., Mass. Hist. Soc.; *New Eng. Hist. and Geneal. Reg.*, Oct. 1865, Oct. 1892; T. C. Amory, *Memoir of Hon. William Sullivan* (1879), pub. also in *Proc. Mass. Hist. Soc.*, vol. II (1880) ; *Col. Soc. of Mass. Pubs.*, vols. VII (1905), XVII (1915), XXVI (1927) ; J. T. Sargent, *A Discourse on the Death of William Sullivan* (1839) ; G. W. Warren, *The Hist. of the Bunker Hill Monument Asso.* (1877) ; T. C. Amory, *Life of James Sullivan* (2 vols., 1859) ; S. E. Morison, *The Life and Letters of Harrison Gray Otis* (2 vols., 1913).]   E. D.

SULLIVAN, WILLIAM HENRY (Aug. 9, 1864–Jan. 26, 1929), lumberman and civic leader, was born in Port Dalhousie, Ontario, Canada, the son of Timothy and Margaret (Sinnett) Sullivan; both parents were of Irish descent. The boy was educated in the public schools of St. Catharines, Ontario. While yet in his teens he went to Buffalo, N. Y., and followed there for a time the trade of a carpenter, which he had learned in Canada. Subsequently, he obtained employment in the Garretson furniture plant and soon became manager. In 1886 he was intrusted with the responsibility of building a sawmill for his employer, L. L. Garretson, who had bought a hardwood tract of 14,000 acres near Austin, Pa., and on the completion of this mill he was put in charge of its operation. Meanwhile, he had become acquainted with the Goodyears of Buffalo and for a while conducted some lumber mills for them at Galeton, Pa.

In 1902 the Goodyears decided to turn their attention to lumbering in the South and began acquiring extensive tracts of land in Washington and St. Tammany parishes in southeastern Louisiana and the adjoining counties of Pike and Marion in southern Mississippi. In 1906, having organized the Great Southern Lumber Company, they sent some representatives, including Sullivan, to select a site for a lumber mill. Largely at his suggestion, they finally decided upon a tract of land in Washington Parish,

La., along a stream called Bogue Lusa, which empties into the Pearl River. On this tract Sullivan directed the building of the largest sawmill in the world, with a capacity of 1,000,000 feet per day, and laid out a town which he named Bogalusa. He soon became vice-president and general manager of the company and organized other industries, such as a paper mill, a box and crate factory, and a turpentine and creosote plant, which were operated along with the lumber mill. His last project was the manufacture of California redwood lumber, an enterprise which was inaugurated at a cost of $1,000,000 and put into successful operation only a few days before his death. With the growth of the varied interests of the company, the town of Bogalusa developed rapidly into a thriving industrial community of about 14,000 people. As an executive, Sullivan planned on a large scale and with a view to permanence, mixing sentiment and good busines sense. He worked hard to make Bogalusa a beautiful and comfortable place in which to live and to preserve it from extinction through the exhaustion of the timber resources of the vicinity. He induced the company to reforest large tracts of its cut-over lands and encouraged other land owners in that region to do the same thing. His contribution to the development of the lumber industry of Louisiana into one of the leading industrial activities of the state was greater perhaps than that of any other single individual. He was also active in the development of farming interests and offered special inducements to farmers settling on the company's cut-over lands that were not reforested.

When the town was incorporated in 1914, Sullivan was elected mayor under the commission form of government and was continued in that office without opposition until his death. In all its civic and business activities he took a leading part. During the flood of 1927 he was one of the three principal advisers of Secretary of Commerce Hoover in the relief work of the Mississippi Valley and at Hoover's suggestion became the director of that work in Louisiana. He was of striking physical appearance—tall, large of frame, and well proportioned; he had a forceful personality, engaging manners, and inexhaustible energy. He was married twice: first, on Oct. 4, 1886, at Buffalo, N. Y., to Elizabeth Calkins, who died on July 11, 1918; and second, on Jan. 27, 1922, at Slidell, La., to Ella Rose Salmen, who died less than two months before his own death. Three children were born to the first of these unions and two to the second. In 1927 he was made a member of the military staff of Governor Simpson of Louisiana and from that time was popularly known by the title of colonel.

[*Times-Picayune* (New Orleans), the *New Orleans Item-Tribune,* and the *Bogalusa Sunday Times,* Jan. 27, 1929; *Lumber Trade Jour.,* Feb. 1, 1929; *Southern Lumberman,* Feb. 2, 1929; *Who's Who in La. and Miss.* (1918); Alcée Fortier, *Louisiana* (1909), vol. I; P. B. Carter, "Hist. of Washington Parish," *La. Hist. Quart.,* Jan. 1931; information from D. T. Cushing, general manager of the Great Southern Lumber Company.]   E. M. V.

SULLIVANT, WILLIAM STARLING (Jan. 15, 1803–Apr. 30, 1873), botanist, distinguished as America's foremost bryologist, was born at Franklinton, a frontier settlement near the present site of Columbus, Ohio, the eldest of four children of Lucas Sullivant, a Virginian, and Sarah (Starling) Sullivant. His father, having been commissioned by the federal government to survey this virgin region, had purchased a large tract along the Scioto River. Here young Sullivant grew up, self-reliant and notably sturdy of physique. He attended school in Kentucky, entered Ohio University at Athens, and was graduated from Yale College in 1823. His father's death in the same year obliged him immediately to assume management of the family properties in Ohio, so that he became at once a surveyor and engineer. Until late in life he engaged successfully in business affairs.

When about thirty Sullivant first became interested in botany. He studied the flowering plants and in 1840 published *A Catalogue of Plants, Native and Naturalized, in the Vicinity of Columbus, Ohio.* Shortly, however, he turned to the mosses, a difficult group requiring microscopic examination and thus well suited to his bent for scrupulously accurate and detailed study. His *Musci Alleghanienses* (2 vols., 1845–46) was accompanied by beautifully prepared specimens of the mosses and hepatics discussed, mostly of his own collecting in the southern Alleghanies. Next came two papers entitled "Contributions to the Bryology and Hepaticology of North America" (*Memoirs of the American Academy,* new ser., vols. III, 1848, and IV, 1849), illustrated by engravings. Far more important was his contribution to the second edition (1856) of Gray's *Manual* of a synoptical illustrated treatise upon the bryophytes. This was republished separately as *The Musci and Hepaticae of the United States East of the Mississippi River* (1856), and it laid the foundation for subsequent bryological studies in the United States. With the assistance of Leo Lesquereux [*q.v.*], Sullivant issued also in the same year the well-known exsiccati *Musci Boreali-Americani* in fifty uniform sets of about 360 specimens each. In 1865 he prepared a similar but larger

series of exsiccati which included many recent species from California, and he assisted C. F. Austin in publishing the classic *Musci Appalachiani* (1870) also. In the meantime he had published upon part of Charles Wright's Cuban mosses and upon important collections obtained by several governmental surveys, the most noteworthy result being an elaborately illustrated folio (1859) describing the mosses collected by the United States Exploring Expedition under Lieut. Charles Wilkes [*q.v.*]. Sullivant's greatest work, however, is the *Icones Muscorum* (1864), a thick imperial octavo volume with 129 illustrations in copperplate, being "figures and descriptions of most of those mosses peculiar to eastern North America which have not been heretofore figured." This publication placed him in the front rank of bryologists. A *Supplement* to it appeared the year after his death, which resulted from pneumonia. His bryological collections and books were bequeathed to Harvard University.

Sullivant was married, Apr. 7, 1824, to Jane Marshall, of Kentucky (a niece of Chief Justice Marshall), who died within a year. His second wife, Eliza Griscom Wheeler of New York, whom he married Nov. 29, 1834, was an acute bryologist who assisted in all his scientific work up to her death, Aug. 23, 1850. On Sept. 1, 1851, he married Caroline Eudora Sutton, who survived him. By the three marriages there were thirteen children. He is commemorated by the genus *Sullivantia,* a unique plant of the saxifrage family, which he himself discovered in Ohio.

[Data are mainly from a biog. memoir by his long-time friend Asa Gray, in Sullivant's *Icon. Musc. Suppl.* (1874), pp. 1–8, repub. in *Am. Jour. Sci.,* 3 ser., vol. VI (1873); *Proc. Am. Acad. Arts and Sci.,* vol. IX (1874); *Biog. Memoirs Nat. Acad. Sci.,* vol. I (1877). See also W. J. Youmans, *Pioneers of Science in America* (1896), pp. 394–401, esp. the concluding portion, as to admirable personal traits; and Joseph Sullivant, *A Geneal. and Family Memorial* (1874). For list of plant species named in Sullivant's honor, see article by Clara Armstrong in *Ohio Naturalist,* vol. I, pp. 33–35, Jan. 1901.]   W. R. M.

SULLY, DANIEL JOHN (Mar. 9, 1861–Sept. 19, 1930), cotton speculator, son of Abraham (or Abram) Charles and Jane Sully, was born in Providence, R. I. He attended the Norwich Free Academy and in his teens found his first employment as clerk in a coal merchant's office. On Oct. 1, 1885, he married Emma Frances Thompson, daughter of the manager of the great Knight cotton mills at Providence. Sully entered the employ of the Knight organization and became deeply interested in the production of raw cotton. Realizing the value of an intimate knowledge of the subject, he persuaded his employers to let him spend the better part of two years in the South in the study of the growing and marketing of cotton. He served with the Knight mills for some time longer, but his interest in manufacture was waning, and he was becoming more and more absorbed in the speculative feature of the cotton trade. He finally resigned and entered a brokerage office in Boston, where he spent four years, returning to Providence in 1891 to become a member of the brokerage firm of F. W. Reynolds & Company. Here he specialized in Egyptian cotton. American cotton production appeared to him to be a waning industry, and therefore, when he went to New York in 1902 and opened a brokerage office of his own, he was a pronounced "bull" in the market. Theodore Price, the dominant "bull" up to that time, had pushed the price of cotton up to nine cents but feared to attempt going further. At this point Sully practically took charge of the market. Steadily he bought and pushed the price upward. By May 1903 he was believed to have made a million dollars profit. He sold out most of his holdings and took his family for a brief trip to Europe. During his absence prices continued strong, and on his return he plunged into buying again. For the next few months he dictated the price of cotton. His operations not only covered the cotton markets of the South but extended to the exchanges of Liverpool and Alexandria, Egypt. As he completed his "corner" and prices climbed steadily upward, the public entered into the speculation on an unprecedented scale. Cotton finally rose to a few points above seventeen cents. Sully meanwhile was speculating in stocks, grain, and other commodities, and his credit was greatly extended. On Mar. 18, 1904, a panic seized the cotton market, and a drop of twelve to thirteen dollars per bale occurred, throwing Sully into bankruptcy. His liabilities were $3,000,000, and he could pay only fifty cents on the dollar. Next he took over a soap company and endeavored to establish an international organization, but this failed in 1908. His noted art collection was sold, and he was forced to turn his handsome seaside home at Watch Hill, R. I., into a summer boarding-house. This, too, was sold to pay debts in 1914, and he spent his later years in rather reduced circumstances. He died in Beverly Hills, Cal. He was survived by his wife, a son, and two daughters, one of whom was the first wife of Douglas Fairbanks, the actor.

[See *Who's Who in America*, 1920–21; *N. Y. Tribune*, Mar. 19, 1904; obituaries in *N. Y. Times, World* (N.Y.), and *N. Y. Herald Tribune* and in *Providence Journal*, Sept. 20, 1930; city records of Providence, R. I. The New York newspapers—especially *Commercial Advertiser*, and *Wall Street Journal*—during 1903 and 1904 are full of references to Sully's "corner" in cotton and to his failure.] A. F. H.

SULLY, THOMAS (1783–Nov. 5, 1872), painter, was born at Horncastle, Lincolnshire, England, the fourth child of Matthew and Sarah (Chester) Sully, who were actors. In 1792 the Sullys came to America with their family of four sons and five daughters, and settled in Charleston, S. C. Influenced largely by prudential motives they decided upon a business career for Thomas, and at the age of twelve he was placed with an insurance broker, who soon discovered that the boy's heart lay elsewhere and advised his father that he should be a painter. His artistic tastes were first stimulated by the influence of a schoolmate, Charles Fraser [q.v.], who instructed him in the "rudiments of the art," and later by his elder brother Lawrence (1769–1803), a miniature and device painter. For a time he was under the instruction of a Monsieur Belzons, the husband of one of his sisters, but as the two were temperamentally far apart Sully soon broke away from his French brother-in-law (c. 1799). Upon the invitation of his favorite brother, Lawrence, who had moved to Richmond, Va., he went to live with him and his wife, the former Sarah Annis of Annapolis, Md., and became his brother's pupil. The two brothers later decided to remove to Norfolk, and it was there on May 10, 1801, that Sully painted his first miniature from life, a likeness of his brother Chester. In this same year he painted "ten pieces valued at one hundred eighty dollars," and in the following year he achieved his "first attempt in oil colors," a small portrait of William Armistead. He began, early in his painting career, his methodical "Account of Pictures" (oftener spoken of as his "Register"), which suggests that he thought he had entered upon his rightful vocation and that he looked forward to a steady and increasing employment. On the pages of the "Register," ruled in columns, he entered the date on which a likeness was begun, the size of the picture, the sitter's name, with an occasional explanatory note, the price received, and the date of the completion of the picture. This record he continued until the end of his career.

The Sullys lived and worked together in both Richmond and Norfolk until the death of Lawrence Sully in Richmond in 1803. On June 27, 1805 (Hart, *post*, p. 13), Thomas married his widowed sister-in-law, whom with her three children he had supported for two years. She bore him six daughters and three sons. Of the sons one became an artist; another, Alfred Sully, a soldier and Indian fighter. The marriage was a happy one and the family life unusually harmonious. In November 1806, after several years of hard work and little remuneration, on the advice of Thomas Abthorpe Cooper [q.v], the distinguished actor, Sully removed to New York City. This proved a turning-point in his career, for he was introduced there to his patron's wide circle of friends, many of whom he painted. There are records of his having painted during this period John E. Harwood, Mr. Twaits, Mr. and Mrs. John Darley, all on Cooper's order, and later Mrs. Villars as "Lady Macbeth," and Mrs. Ann Brunton Warren of the Philadelphia Theatre. At the end of 1807 he had produced "pieces" to the number of seventy and listed his receipts at $3,203. The Embargo at the end of this year greatly injured his prospects, so that he was forced to paint a series of "thrift" portraits for thirty dollars each. He was fortunate, however, in meeting Gilbert Stuart [q.v.], then at the height of his fame (1807) and living in Boston. Allowed to stand by the great artist's chair while he painted, Sully relates that it was "a situation I valued more at that moment than I shall ever again appreciate any station on earth" (Dunlap, post, vol. II, p. 250). Stuart consented to criticize a portrait of Isaac P. Davis which Sully was engaged to paint, and the few words of praise from the great painter, "Keep what you have got, and get as much as you can" (Ibid., p. 251), came like a benediction to the younger man. Following his Boston visit, Sully determined to go to Philadelphia to live. He made a preliminary visit in 1807, when he painted a portrait of Miss Wilcocks, sister of his friend Benjamin Chew Wilcocks, and in 1808 settled in the city, which remained his home for the rest of his life. One of his letters of introduction was written by Washington Irving to Rebecca Gratz [qq.v.], whom he later painted. At this time he was receiving an almost ludicrously small sum for his work, fifty dollars being his regular price for a bust portrait, though a half-length sometimes brought him eighty dollars. Yet these likenesses from the hand of the still young painter had the quality of enduring art, and many of them will remain among the loveliest portraits of all time.

A great longing for improvement in his art and a desire for wider opportunities made Sully again contemplate a trip abroad which he had given up at the time of his brother's death. Wilcocks and six of his friends each promised to give two hundred dollars towards a proposed journey to England. In return Sully offered to make a copy of some one of the great masters for each of his six benefactors while he was abroad, a promise which, though it meant nine months

of incessant application and more than rigid economy, he scrupulously fulfilled. On May 17, 1809, he was admitted to American citizenship and on June 10 he set sail for England, landing five weeks later, July 13, 1809, in Liverpool. In two weeks' time he was painting in London. Among his letters of introduction was one from William Rawle to Benjamin West, 1738–1820 [qq.v.], who received him kindly and asked to see a sample of his work. Though West appeared to be impressed with the portrait of Charles King which Sully painted to show him, he questioned Sully's knowledge of the anatomy and structure of the head, and recommended the serious study of osteology and anatomy. Sully followed his advice with profit, and at the further suggestion of West, who had almost given up portrait painting in favor of historical pieces, he sought out and observed the work of the best portrait artists of the day. Particularly attracted by the portraits of Sir Thomas Lawrence, he made the painter's acquaintance and was introduced by him to many important people, some of whom became his sitters. Among these was the Kemble family. He painted the lovely Frances Anne Kemble [q.v.] at various times later on, sometimes as her natural self and sometimes in her acting rôles.

On Mar. 10, 1810, he set sail for home and on Apr. 24 once more resumed his brush in Philadelphia at 56 South Eleventh St. There he finished many head and bust portraits, and attempted some whole-length figures, the first being a composition piece after Schiller's play, The Robbers, which featured the portrait of William B. Wood as Charles de Moor. This picture was soon followed by another that attracted even greater attention, that of George Frederick Cooke in the rôle of Richard III. During the next succeeding years Sully painted portraits that showed him at his very best, and his reputation was soon firmly established as a "History and Portrait Painter." His income, while not large, was steadily increasing, and he was free from pecuniary anxieties. He joined the Pennsylvania Academicians, a body of artists looking to the then recently established Academy of the Fine Arts, and served on a committee for the management of the schools of the academy. In 1818, when the legislature of North Carolina asked him for two full-length portraits of Washington, he proposed instead that he paint an historical picture showing Washington crossing the Delaware to attack Trenton. When the picture was completed, however, it was so large (17'4" x 12'5") that it was not accepted, and Sully finally disposed of it for $500 to a frame-maker. It now hangs in the Boston Museum of Art. Another important composition was "The Capture of Major André." Sully left South Eleventh Street in 1812 for the Philosophical Hall, where he painted for the next ten years and opened a gallery of pictures to the public for twenty-five cents admission. Later he changed his address many times, finally settling about 1830 in a house near the corner of Fifth and Chestnut streets which belonged to Stephen Girard [q.v.]. There he made his home for the remainder of his life, about forty-four years. When in 1824–25 the Marquis de Lafayette paid his farewell visit to the United States, he was invited by six prominent gentlemen of Philadelphia to sit to Sully for his portrait. The picture, done in Washington (Sully, "Recollections of an Old Painter," *Hours at Home,* November 1869, p. 74), was apparently painted by subscription and was valued by the artist at six hundred dollars, but as the money was not immediately forthcoming Sully held the picture for some time, finally handing it over to the subscribers for about two hundred and fifty dollars. The finished picture now hangs in Independence Hall, Philadelphia. After Charles Willson Peale's death in 1827 and Gilbert Stuart's in 1828, Sully had no formidable rivals in his art, and in 1837 when he made his second visit to England and painted the young Queen Victoria from life he reached the summit of his fame.

It was in the high tide of his power that Sully determined upon his second visit to England. Several of the great painters who were alive at the time of his first visit had died, and it seemed a propitious time for an American artist with an established reputation to try his fortune in the English capital. Just on the eve of his departure he was commissioned by the Society of the Sons of Saint George in Philadelphia to "memorialize" Queen Victoria by a portrait to be owned by the society. When the queen's permission had been obtained, a painting-room was established in Buckingham Palace, and the first sitting for the head took place on Mar. 22, 1838. Blanche Sully, who had accompanied her father to England, usually sat for the queen's regalia, which weighed thirty or forty pounds. The original sketch for the head is owned by the Metropolitan Museum in New York; the finished picture, full length, belongs to the Society of the Sons of Saint George in Philadelphia. The visit was altogether a success. While awaiting the queen's pleasure Sully painted portraits of many distinguished people; he was elected to honorary membership in the Garrick Club for three months; and he and his daughter, who had established themselves at 46 Great Marlborough St., were the recipients of many delightful invitations. At the end of September 1838 he was in his Philadelphia studio once more. His prestige was even greater than before, and as he grew older he continued to command his field. At the age of seventy-five and even eighty years he was singled out by people of culture and discrimination who wished to have portraits painted. In his career he produced upwards of twenty-six hundred works, an average of thirty-seven for each year in which he painted, a notable example of industry. Many of the portraits, which include the most distinguished men and women of the day, are in the possession of the Pennsylvania Historical Society, the Pennsylvania Academy of the Fine Arts, the Metropolitan Museum, and the United States Military Academy at West Point. Mrs. Sully died on July 25, 1867 (Hart, *post,* p. 13), and it was his daughter Blanche who ministered to Sully during his last years. He died on Nov. 5, 1872, and was buried on Nov. 9 in Laurel Hill Cemetery, Philadelphia, where lie many of the Sully name. He is described by his contemporary, William Dunlap, as walking with the stride of a man of six feet, though he was not over five feet eight inches in height, and as having a face "marked with the wish to make others happy" (Dunlap, *post,* vol. II, p. 276). His whole life, indeed, was characterized not only by great consideration for others but by the utmost fairness and honesty. In 1873 *Hints to Young Painters and the Process of Portrait-Painting as Practiced by the Late Thomas Sully* was published. Sometimes called "the Sir Thomas Lawrence of America," he was undoubtedly influenced by the work of the older artist, especially in his delineation of women and of children, who are the embodiment of innocence and happiness, depicted with grace and charm. He was at his best when portraying the lovely women who flocked to his studio at the height of his success, but some of his portraits of men, such as his "Dr. Samuel Coates," are marked by an admirable firmness. Although occasionally his draftsmanship leaves something to be desired, he was always a master of color, and his paintings have a warmth and beauty seldom if ever surpassed.

[The date of Sully's birth is given variously as June 8 and June 19, 1783. See Edward Biddle and Mantle Fielding, *The Life and Works of Thomas Sully* (1921), with a complete list of Sully's paintings; C. H. Hart, *A Register of Portraits Painted by Thomas Sully 1801–1871* (1908); *Memorial Exhibition of Portraits by Thomas Sully* (1922), Pa. Acad. of the Fine Arts; William Dunlap, *A Hist. of the Rise and Progress of the Arts of Design in the U. S.* (3 vols., 1918), ed. by F. W. Bayley and C. E. Goodspeed, with many contemporary anecdotes; Henry Budd, "Thomas Sully," *Pa. Mag. of Hist. and Biog.,* vol. XLII (1918), p.

97; H. T. Tuckerman, *Book of the Artists* (1867); Samuel Isham, *The Hist. of Am. Painting* (1905); Suzanne La Follette, *Art in America* (1929), brief comment; J. D. Champlin and C. C. Perkins, *Cyc. of Painters and Painting,* vol. IV (1887); and obituary in *Press* (Phila.), Nov. 6, 1872. There are occasional references to Sully in Frances Anne Kemble, *Records of Later Life* (1882).] M.F.

SULZBERGER, CYRUS LINDAUER (July 11, 1858–Apr. 30, 1932), merchant, leader in Jewish affairs, civics, and philanthropy, was the son of Leopold and Sophia (Lindauer) Sulzberger and a first cousin of Mayer Sulzberger [*q.v.*]. Born in Philadelphia, he received his education at Central High School there. At the age of sixteen he was one of the founders of the Young Men's Hebrew Association of Philadelphia. In 1877 he removed to New York to become bookkeeper of the textile importing firm of N. Erlanger, Blumgart & Company, of which he became a member in 1891, president in 1902, and chairman of the board in 1929.

Although he won marked success in the business world, Sulzberger was best known for his constructive work in dealing with Jewish immigration when the great inrush of foreign peoples was a national problem, and for his activities in Jewish philanthropic endeavor. He was one of the organizers in 1900 and chairman from 1904 to 1909 of the Industrial Removal Office, an organization with branches in 108 cities in the United States, which endeavored to relieve the congestion of Jewish immigrants in New York City by aiding them to settle in other localities. His work in this field coincided with the peak years of immigration; in his statement and testimony before the Congressional Immigration Commission, Mar. 11, 1910, he was able to show that the Industrial Removal Office, in the period 1902–09, had sent 45,711 immigrants from New York City into 1,278 towns and cities ("Reports of the Immigration Commission," *Senate Document 764,* 61 Cong., 3 Sess., XLI, 194). A deep student of immigration problems, he was also an able spokesman for the continued liberalization of the laws governing entry into the United States, recognizing, while laboring to this end, the necessity of providing for the distribution and Americanization of immigrants. Besides his chairmanship of the Industrial Removal Office he was president (1903–09 and 1919–21) of the Jewish Agricultural and Industrial Aid Society, which helped in placing some 80,000 Jews on farms in the United States. In October 1910 Gov. Charles E. Hughes appointed him a member of the New York state commission on congestion of population, which presented a report in February 1911 recommending legislation to create a permanent commission on distribution of population; to provide for an inquiry into manufacturing in tenement homes; to inaugurate the annual publication of a directory of industrial opportunities to promote the spread of factories to a greater number of towns, and to furnish additional facilities whereby the state labor department might permanently spread the supply of laboring population to avoid excessive unemployment in congested communities. The commission also recommended the placing of public institutions outside city limits and definite measures to remove city dwellers to small land holdings and farms (*Documents of the Assembly of the State of New York . . . 1911,* vol. XXV, no. 34).

Sulzberger's activity in organized philanthropy included service as president of the United Hebrew Charities of New York (1908) and of the National Conference of Jewish Charities (1912–14), as member of the executive committee of the American Jewish Committee in 1907 and its secretary in 1914–15 when that organization collected vast sums for the relief of Jews overseas, and as trustee of the Federation for the Support of Jewish Philanthropic Societies of New York City (1919). He was a founder of the *American Hebrew* in 1879, and aided in the publication of *The Jewish Encyclopedia.* Despite his high responsibilities, he was a self-effacing man who preferred labor to the honor of office. With vigor and intelligence he applied a broadly social mind to philanthropy, and his constructive ideas supplied the motivation of many activities carried on in the names of others. A leader in civic reform, he ran for public office only once, as candidate for president of the Borough of Manhattan, New York City: on the unsuccessful Fusion ticket of 1903.

He married, May 13, 1884, Rachel Peixotto Hays, by whom he had five children. Two sons, with his wife, survived him. He died in New York City.

[*Am. Hebrew and Jewish Tribune,* May 6, 1932; *Who's Who in Am. Jewry,* 1928; *Who's Who in America,* 1932–33; *Jewish Encyc.,* vol. XI; *Am. Hebrew,* July 13, 1928; *Jewish Tribune,* July 13, 1928; *Am. Jewish Year Book, 1933–34* (1933); *N. Y. Times,* May 1, 1932; information from Dr. Cyrus Adler.] C.M.P.

SULZBERGER, MAYER (June 22, 1843–Apr. 20, 1923), jurist, scholar, was born in Heidelsheim, Baden, Germany, the son of Abraham and Sophia (Einstein) Sulzberger. He came of a family which had included a number of rabbinical scholars. His father, a minister and teacher in Heidelsheim, came to America as a result of the Revolution of 1848, settling in Philadelphia where a brother, Leopold, father of Cyrus L. Sulzberger [*q.v.*], had settled some ten years before. Mayer Sulzberger received the degree of A.B. from the Central High School of Philadelphia in 1859, attended a business college, worked as bookkeeper for a business concern, studied law in the office of Moses A. Dropsie [*q.v.*], and in 1865 was admitted to the bar. After thirty years of successful practice he was elected in 1895 a judge of the court of common pleas and served by reëlection until his retirement, Jan. 3, 1916, being president judge from 1902.

As a judge Sulzberger was penetrating, impartial, and witty. A few of his papers and addresses were printed: "Nominations for Public Office" (*Penn Monthly,* March 1881), presented at a meeting of the Philadelphia Social Science Association; "The Practice of Criminal Law" (*American Law Register,* June 1903); *Politics in a Democracy* (1910), address delivered at the Silver Jubilee of Temple University; two lectures on "Medical Jurisprudence" (*The Jeffersonian,* January and February 1915). He gave his law library to the court upon his retirement from the bench. He was subsequently a member of the committee to revise the constitution of Pennsylvania and of the Philadelphia Board of City Trusts.

Sulzberger as a young man was greatly influenced by the Rev. Isaac Leeser [*q.v.*] of Philadelphia, one of the prominent Jewish leaders of the day, and throughout his life he was active in Jewish welfare work and in the promotion of Jewish education and higher Jewish learning in America. He was a trustee of the Baron de Hirsch Fund (1884) and of the Mikveh Israel Congregation of Philadelphia; first president of the Young Men's Hebrew Association of Philadelphia in 1875, and president again in 1885. From 1865 he served actively on the board of the Jewish Hospital of Philadelphia, founded by his father, and he was also a trustee of the Jefferson Medical College. As president of the American Jewish Committee from 1906 to 1912 he took an active part in the movement that brought about the abrogation of the treaty of commerce with Russia in the latter year. He was offered appointment as minister to Turkey by President Harrison and as ambassador to Turkey by President Taft, but declined in both cases. He was secretary of the board of trustees of the short-lived Maimonides College, Philadelphia (1867–73); trustee of Gratz College, Philadelphia, from its foundation in 1897; a director of the Jewish Theological Seminary from 1901; an original governor of the Dropsie College for Hebrew and Cognate Learning; one of the founders of the Jewish Publication Society of America and chairman of its publication committee, 1888–1923; and a founder of the Oriental Club of Philadelphia. At a time when there was no important collection of Hebraica and Judaica in the United States he expended a considerable part of his income for the purchase of Hebrew manuscripts and incunabula and the assembling of a general Jewish library, which in 1902 he turned over to the Jewish Theological Seminary of America. He also collected Arabic, Ethiopic, and Samaritan manuscripts, which together with a small collection of Egyptian objects and Assyrian and Phoenician seals were presented to the Dropsie College.

In his youth, Sulzberger translated into English the dictionary of Hebrew authors of Azariah de Rossi and part of Maimonides' "Guide of the Perplexed," both translations being published serially in the *Occident,* and for a year after the death of Isaac Leeser he edited that periodical. The latter years of his life he devoted to a series of Biblical studies which resulted in the publication of four books: *The Am Ha-Aretz, the Ancient Hebrew Parliament* (1910); *The Polity of the Ancient Hebrews* (1912); *The Ancient Hebrew Law of Homicide* (1915); *The Status of Labor in Ancient Israel* (1923). After his retirement from the bench he became an honorary lecturer on Jewish jurisprudence and institutes of government in the Dropsie College. He died, unmarried, in his eightieth year.

[*Address of Hon. Norris S. Barratt . . . upon the Presentation . . . of the Portrait . . . of Hon. Mayer Sulzberger . . . also Proc. of the Law Asso. of Phila.* (1916); *Addresses Delivered in Memory of Mayer Sulzberger . . . May 30, 1923* (1924); *Am. Jewish Hist. Soc. Pubs.,* no. 29 (1925); L. E. Levinthal, *Mayer Sulzberger* (1927), with intro. by Robert von Moschizker; S. W. Pennypacker, *Autobiog. of a Pennsylvanian* (1918), pp. 241–42; H. S. Morais, *The Jews of Phila.* (1894); *Who's Who in America,* 1922–23; *Jewish Encyc.,* vol. XI; *The Am. Jewish Year Book,* vol. XXVI (1924); *Jewish Chronicle* (London), Apr. 27, 1923; *Jewish Exponent,* Apr. 27, May 4, 25, June 1, 1923; *Jewish Tribune,* Apr. 27, 1923; *Pub. Ledger* (Phila.), Apr. 21, 1923.]

C. A.

SUMMERS, GEORGE WILLIAM (Mar. 4, 1804–Sept. 19, 1868), congressman from western Virginia, was a prominent representative of his section in the struggle which resulted in the division of the state at the outbreak of the Civil War. He was born in Fairfax County, the youngest of ten children of Col. George and Ann Smith (Radcliffe) Summers and a great-grandson of John Summers who built the first cabin on the site of Alexandria. In 1813, however, his family moved to Kanawha County in the western part of the state (now W. Va.) and after the death of the father, in 1818, George William lived in Charleston with his mother and elder brother Lewis. After attending school here and

Washington College, Lexington, Va., he matriculated at Ohio University (Athens), where he graduated in 1826. He then began the study of law under his brother, and in 1827 was admitted to the bar.

Becoming active in politics, he was elected from Kanawha to the House of Delegates in 1830 and was reëlected in 1831, 1834, and 1835. During his first term, favoring the interest of the West against Tidewater policy, he tried to get an extension of the proposed Staunton and Potomac railroad to the Kanawha, but was defeated. In the legislative debates of 1831–32 he opposed slavery and suggested that the proceeds of public lands be used to effect emancipation. He was elected to the federal House of Representatives in 1841 and reëlected in 1843. In a speech of 1842 favoring a protective tariff he stated that diversities of soil, climate, products, and population within the United States were the true elements of strength and perpetual union rather than of opposing interests and conflicting policies. He was a thorough Unionist, holding that the Constitution and laws of the United States, and its treaties, are the supreme law of the land. In the state constitutional convention of 1850 he won distinction by a speech on the basis of representation, presenting the views of transmontane against tidewater Virginia. He was Whig candidate for governor in 1851 under the new constitution and in his campaign not only denied the right of secession but maintained the duty of the president to enforce federal laws in South Carolina should that state attempt to secede. His defeat by Joseph Johnson, the Democratic nominee, was due in part to charges that he was affiliated with abolitionists, or at least was too friendly toward the Methodists who were preaching abolition. In May 1852 he was elected judge of the 18th judicial circuit of Virginia, serving until his resignation, July 1, 1858, two years before the expiration of his term.

He was a member of the Peace Conference at Washington in the spring of 1861, and throughout the critical period before the war was an active Union man. As a delegate to the Richmond convention which passed the Virginia ordinance of secession he made a vigorous speech in support of the Union (*Speech of Honorable George W. Summers on Federal Relations . . . March 11, 1861*, 1861). He took no part in the organization of the "restored" state of Virginia, however, preferring to remain neutral, and thereafter he refused to accept any office, although he continued the practice of law until his death.

He died in Charleston and was buried on his Kanawha River farm.

On Feb. 14, 1833, he married Amacetta Laidley, daughter of John Laidley of Cabell County. Only one of his five children survived him.

[W. S. Laidley, *Hist. of Charleston and Kanawha County* (1911); *W. Va. Hist. Mag. Quart.,* July 1903; T. C. Miller and Hu Maxwell, *W. Va. and Its People* (1913), vol. III; *Bench and Bar of W. Va.* (1919), ed. by G. W. Atkinson; *The W. Va. Encyc.* (1929); D. L. Pulliam, *The Constitutional Conventions of Va. from the Foundation of the Commonwealth to the Present Time* (1901); *Biog. Dir. Am. Cong.* (1928); C. H. Ambler, *Sectionalism in Va. from 1776 to 1861* (1910) and *A Hist. of W. Va.* (1933); H. T. Shanks, *The Secession Movement in Va.* (1934); *Daily Nat. Intelligencer* (Washington, D. C.), Sept. 30, 1868.]

J. M. C.

SUMMERS, THOMAS OSMOND (Oct. 11, 1812–May 6, 1882), Methodist clergyman and editor, was born near Corfe Castle, Isle of Purbeck, Dorsetshire, England, the son of James and Sarah Summers. Left an orphan at the age of six, he was reared by his maternal grandmother and, later, by an aunt. The latter died when Thomas was sixteen, leaving him a small patrimony. About two years thereafter he decided to emigrate to the United States and in 1830 arrived in New York City.

His parents were rigid Calvinists and he had had a careful religious training but had received only the rudiments of a secular education. He was a good penman and accountant, however, and easily found employment. Pursuing theological studies because of an inherent interest in them, he finally discarded Calvinism and became a devout follower of John Wesley. Soon, both by inclination and the advice of friends, he was led to enter the ministry of the Methodist Episcopal Church. In 1835 he was admitted on trial to the Baltimore Conference; the following year he was ordained deacon, and in 1839, elder. From 1836 to 1839 he was stationed in Baltimore, and in the latter year was sent to West River, Md. Conscious of his meager education, he applied himself industriously to study. In spite of defective vision and the exacting demands of his ministry, he made rapid progress and in time his knowledge became cyclopedic.

In 1840 he went to Texas, where he undertook missionary work in Houston and Galveston, and was one of the founders of the Texas Conference. He became a member of the Alabama Conference in 1844 and the following year was one of its delegates to the General Convention at Louisville, Ky., which organized the Methodist Episcopal Church, South. Of this Convention he was secretary and he also served as assistant secretary of the first General Conference of the Church, which was held the succeeding year.

Thereafter until his death he was secretary of all its sessions. In 1846 he was made assistant editor of the *Southern Christian Advocate,* which position he held until 1850, when he was elected book editor of the Church. Its publication house was established in Nashville, Tenn., and from then on, except for a period during the Civil War which he spent at Tuscaloosa, Ala., that city was his home. In addition to performing the routine duties of his office, from 1851 to 1856 he was editor of the *Sunday School Visitor.* In July 1858 he assumed editorship of the *Quarterly Review of the Methodist Episcopal Church, South.* This suspended publication in 1861 and was revived in 1879, Summers being elected editor in October of that year. From 1868 to 1878 he was editor of the *Christian Advocate,* Nashville. He had little capacity for original writing and left few works of his own; but he revised, corrected, and compiled, with an industry that never flagged, a minute attention to details, and a memory that was well-nigh infallible. Among his publications were *Biographical Sketches of Eminent Itinerant Ministers* (1858) and *Commentary on the Gospels* (4 vols., 1869–72). He devoted much attention to hymnology and ritual, for which he had a natural fondness.

In 1875 Vanderbilt University opened its doors, and the following year Summers consented to add to his editorial responsibilities those of dean and professor of systematic theology. By the time of the meeting of the General Conference held at Nashville in May of 1882, his health had become much impaired. He was gratified by being made secretary once more, but a few days later he died. His lectures at Vanderbilt were edited by J. J. Tigert and published in 1888 under the title *Systematic Theology.* He had married in 1844 N. B. Sexton of Tuscaloosa, Ala., who with a son survived him.

[O. P. Fitzgerald, *Dr. Summers: A Life-Study* (copr. 1884), reviewed in *Meth. Rev.* (N. Y.), May 1885; Gross Alexander, *A Hist. of the Methodist Episcopal Church South* (1894); J. T. Acklen, *Tenn. Records: Tombstone Inscriptions and Manuscripts* (1933); John Wooldridge, *Hist. of Nashville, Tenn.* (1890); *Methodist* (N. Y.), May 20, 1882; *Daily American* (Nashville), May 6, 8, 1882; personal acquaintance.]
G. B. W.

SUMNER, CHARLES (Jan. 6, 1811–Mar. 11, 1874), United States senator, notable advocate of the emancipation of the slave and the outlawry of war, son of Charles Pinckney Sumner and Relief (Jacob) Sumner, was born in Boston, Mass. His father—a descendant of William Sumner, who had come to Dorchester from England about 1635—was graduated from Harvard College in 1796 and read law in the office of Josiah Quincy. For many years he served as

sheriff of Suffolk County. He was a man of sound learning, independent in thought and action, outspoken in condemnation of slavery, and so earnest an advocate of "equal rights" that he opposed the exclusion of negro children from the schools and the law prohibiting intermarriage of blacks and whites. At the Boston Latin School (1821–26), the intimates of Charles Sumner were Robert C. Winthrop, James Freeman Clarke, Samuel F. Smith, and Wendell Phillips. Disappointed in his ambition to secure an appointment to West Point, at the age of fifteen he entered Harvard College where he showed (1826–30) great aptitude for history, literature, and forensics.

In the Harvard Law School (1831–33) Sumner became the devoted pupil and friend of its most eminent professor, Joseph Story, and at the end of his studies was urged to join the staff as an instructor, but he preferred to try his powers in active practice. Before entering upon its routine he took an orientation journey to Washington, especially to attend sessions of the Supreme Court, upon which Story was then sitting. For weeks young Sumner enjoyed the privilege of sitting at table in friendly intercourse with Chief Justice Marshall and his colleagues. He heard Webster and Francis Scott Key clash as opposing counsel before the Supreme Court, and in the Senate listened to the "splendid and thrilling" eloquence of Clay. Nevertheless, he left Washington declaring that nothing he had seen had made him look upon politics "with any feeling other than loathing" (*Memoir,* I, 142). Upon return to his office the drab routine of practice proved little to his liking. He became a lecturer in the Harvard Law School, a frequent contributor to the *American Jurist,* and devoted much time to reviewing and revising legal textbooks. He came into close intimacy with Francis Lieber and with William Ellery Channing, who exercised a profound influence upon him, and he formed a deep and lifelong affection for Whittier, Longfellow, and Emerson.

At twenty-six, though he had made no assured start in his profession, to the dismay of his friends he borrowed money and broke away from the law office for an indefinite sojourn in Europe. He remained abroad more than two years. It was no holiday trip. In every land which he visited he was an eager student and close observer. This experience gave him facile command of French, German, and Italian, an understanding of European governments and jurisprudence, and an intimate acquaintance with many of the leaders in public life and in letters in England, France, and Germany. Upon his return to Boston he had the entrée to the city's most cultivated social and intellectual circles. But he found the work of the law office weary, stale, and unprofitable. "Though I earn my daily bread, I lay up none of the bread of life" (*Memoir*, II, 167). The one position which would then have satisfied his ambition was that of reporter of the Supreme Court. That appointment went to another, and Sumner brought himself to the verge of collapse by undergoing the heart-breaking drudgery of annotating Francis Vesey's *Reports of Cases . . . in the High Court of Chancery* (20 vols., 1844–45).

In 1845 Sumner was chosen as the orator for Boston's Independence Day celebration. The delivery of that oration proved a turning-point in his career. For the first time he faced a great assembly gathered to hear him. He now stood six feet four inches in height, and his strong face kindled with animation as he spoke. His voice was of great power, and he used it with skill. Of that brilliant audience not less than one hundred were in full military or naval dress uniform. With terse introduction, Sumner announced the theme of his oration: "What is the true grandeur of nations?" He then proceeded to lay down his thesis, putting it interrogatively: "Can there be in our age any peace that is not honorable, any war that is not dishonorable?" (*Works*, I, 9). The city's military and naval guests felt themselves "officially assailed by the speaker as well as personally insulted" (*Memoir*, II, 346) and were with difficulty restrained from leaving the hall while he was still speaking. Ex-Mayor Eliot, whom Webster called "the impersonation of Boston," commented: "The young man has cut his throat!" (Quoted by Wendell Phillips, in *Boston Daily Advertiser*, Mar. 13, 1877). That oration revealed to Sumner not less than to his friends that he could thrill and sway great audiences. It brought him into closer cooperation with leaders like Theodore Parker and John A. Andrew. For years thereafter no lecturer on the Lyceum platform was more welcome than Sumner.

In the annual address before the American Peace Society (1849) he made a strong plea for "a Congress of Nations, with a High Court of Judicature," or for arbitration established by treaties between nations (*Works*, pp. 262–67). When his boyhood friend, Congressman Robert C. Winthrop, voted for the Mexican War bill, Sumner wrote a succession of letters publicly accusing him of sanctioning "the most wicked [act] in our history" (*Works*, I, 322). Such imputations brought upon Sumner a storm of criticism. Winthrop declined further social relations

with him, and Boston's social autocrat, Ticknor, declared that Sumner was "outside the pale of society" (Haynes, *post*, p. 4).

From Sumner's office was issued the call for a convention of all citizens of the Commonwealth opposed to the nomination of Cass and of Taylor. In that convention, at Worcester on June 28, 1848, Sumner made the principal speech, and his denunciation of the conspiracy "between the lords of the lash and the lords of the loom" (*Works*, II, 81) increased the antipathy of the rich and conservative Whigs of Boston for him. He was put forward as a candidate for the United States Senate by a coalition of Free Soilers and Democrats, but his election was blocked for more than three months by the impossibility of securing a two-thirds majority in the House. Finally the deadlock was broken when in several towns the voters met in special meetings, legally called for that one purpose, and by formal vote instructed their representatives to support Sumner.

He entered the Senate on Dec. 1, 1851. By the great majority the compromise measures of 1850 were accepted as a finality. Only five days before the end of the nine months' session, Sumner gained the floor as a matter of right, to speak to an amendment which he had moved, that no allowance under the pending appropriation bill should be authorized for expenses incurred in executing the law "for the surrender of fugitives from service or labor; which said Act is hereby repealed" (*Works*, III, 94). For more than three hours he presented a tremendous arraignment of the Fugitive-slave Law. The galleries filled. For an hour Webster himself was an attentive listener, this being his last visit to the Senate chamber. Near Webster, while Sumner was speaking, sat Horace Mann, who wrote in his journal: "the 26th of August, 1852, redeemed the 7th of March, 1850" (Mary T. P. Mann, *Life of Horace Mann*, 1865, p. 381). In the debate Southern senators heaped angry derision upon Sumner's amendment. Only Chase and Hale took the floor in its support, and but four votes were given in its favor. Nevertheless, Chase declared that in American history Sumner's speech would mark the day when the advocates of the restriction of slavery "no longer content to stand on the defensive in the contest with slavery, boldly attacked the very citadel of its power in that doctrine of finality" which both political parties were endeavoring "to establish as the impregnable defense of its usurpations" (*Congressional Globe*, 32 Cong., 1 Sess., App., p. 1121).

Sumner was outspoken, both in the Senate and

in the Massachusetts convention, in opposition to the Kansas-Nebraska Bill. This brought him into greater disfavor with the Boston press and society, both dominated by conservative Whigs, whom he still further offended by presenting in the Senate "with pleasure and pride" petitions from New England clergymen protesting against the passage of that bill. In the debate upon the right of petition Southern senators who had hitherto been on friendly terms with Sumner poured contempt upon his "vapid rhetoric," charged him with repudiating his oath of office and with declaring his intention to disobey the Constitution, and denounced him as a "miscreant," a "sneaking, sinuous, snake-like poltroon." They urged his expulsion, but an informal poll showed that the requisite two-thirds vote could not be secured. Sumner declared that he had sworn to support the Constitution as he understood it. "Does he recognize the obligation to return a fugitive slave?" demanded Toucey. Sumner's reply was: "To that I answer distinctly, 'No.'" (June 28, 1854, *Congressional Globe*, 33 Cong., 3 Sess., p. 1559). Sumner's vindication of Massachusetts against attack and his courage in maintaining his own opinion won admirers in quarters where he had been held in slight regard.

Sumner had a large part in the organization of the Republican party. Resistance of influential Whigs to the formation of a new party with the main object of opposing the extension of slavery gave opportunity for the rapid growth of the Know-Nothing party, by the votes of whose oath-bound members some Massachusetts politicians, notably Henry Wilson and Nathaniel P. Banks, were enabled to climb to high office. Sumner scorned such association, and boldly denounced "a party which, beginning in secrecy, interferes with religious belief, and founds a discrimination on the accident of birth" (*Works*, IV, 80). Such defiant language led to some futile intriguing to prevent his reëlection.

At the opening of the new Congress, Dec. 5, 1855, hot debate began at once with the Senate's demand for documents relating to the struggle in Kansas. With sure prescience Sumner declared: "This session will not pass without the Senate Chamber's becoming the scene of some unparalleled outrage" (T. W. Higginson, *Contemporaries*, p. 283). Two days before he was to speak, he wrote to Theodore Parker: "I shall pronounce the most thorough philippic ever uttered in a legislative body" (*Memoir*, III, 439). When he began his speech, "The Crime against Kansas" (*Works*, IV, 137–256), the air was tense in the Senate chamber, for none of his hearers could doubt that blood would soon be

shed in the territory. Sumner denounced the Kansas-Nebraska Act as "in every respect a swindle . . . —no other word will adequately express the mingled meanness and wickedness of the cheat" (*Works*, IV, 155). Turning his attention to the senators who "had raised themselves to eminence on this floor by the championship of human wrongs," he characterized Butler as Don Quixote, paying his vows to a mistress who, "though polluted in the sight of the world, is chaste in his sight. I mean the harlot, Slavery." Douglas he described as "the squire of Slavery, its very Sancho Panza, ready to do its humiliating offices" (May 20, 1856, *Congressional Globe*, 34 Cong., 1 Sess., App. pp. 530–31). Of Mason, the author of the Fugitive-slave Law, he said: "He holds the commission of Virginia . . . of that other Virginia from which Washington and Jefferson avert their faces, where human beings are bred as cattle for the shambles" (*Ibid.*, p. 543). Writhing under Sumner's denunciation of the Kansas-Nebraska Bill as a "swindle," Douglas shouted: "Is it his object to provoke some of us to kick him as we would a dog in the street, that he may get sympathy upon the just chastisement?" (*Ibid.*, p. 545). Mason deplored the political necessity of tolerating in the Senate a man whose very presence elsewhere would be "dishonor," and "the touch of whose hand would be a disgrace" (*Ibid.*, p. 546). Sumner branded some of Douglas' statements as false, and rejoined: "No person with the upright form of man can be allowed, without violation of all decency, to switch out from his tongue the perpetual stench of personality. . . . The noisome, squat and nameless animal, to which I refer, is not the proper model for an American Senator" (*Ibid.*, p. 547). Sumner's brutal frankness may find some palliation in the fact that heretofore he and other anti-slavery leaders had been subjected to the most galling epithets. His speech gave great satisfaction to anti-slavery men throughout the North. Within a few weeks a million copies of it had been distributed.

Two days after his speech was delivered, at the end of the day's session Sumner, who had remained at his desk, heard his name called. Looking up he saw a tall stranger who said: "I have read your speech twice over carefully; it is a libel on South Carolina, and Mr. Butler, who is a relative of mine" (Sumner's testimony, *Works*, IV, 261)—and down upon the head of the defenseless man crashed a blow from a heavy walking stick. Pinioned by his desk, Sumner could not rise till he had wrenched it from its fastenings. Blow followed blow, till he fell bleeding and unconscious to the floor. The man guilty of this brutal assault was Representative Preston S. Brooks [*q.v.*] of South Carolina. From the North came an outburst of universal condemnation of the attack and expressions of deepest sympathy for its victim. Sumner's injury was far more serious than at first appeared. Twice he tried to resume his duties, only to find that he could not undertake even the lightest tasks. Haunted by "the ghost of two years already dead," he went to Europe in quest of health a second time, and subjected himself many times without anesthetic to the moxa, which his physician described as "the greatest suffering that can be inflicted on mortal man" (Dr. Brown-Séquard, quoted in *Memoir*, III, 564–65). Three and a half years had passed before he was sufficiently recovered to return to the Senate. Meantime he had been reëlected by the almost unanimous vote of the Massachusetts legislature.

Sumner found a new Senate in which Southern leaders were taking more aggressive ground than ever before. Jefferson Davis' resolutions, affirming the sanctity of slave property in the territories, were passed by a vote of two to one. Under these circumstances Sumner determined to attempt an "assault on American slavery all along the line" (*Memoir,* III, 606). In the debate on the bill for the admission of Kansas as a free state, in an impassioned speech, "The Barbarism of Slavery" (*Works,* V, 1–174), he proceeded to set forth his indictment of slavery in its social, moral, and economic as well as political aspects. Many of his friends doubted the wisdom and timeliness of such an utterance on the eve of a presidential election; but it proved of immense influence and was distributed broadcast by the Republican national committee.

In the months following the Republican victory in 1860, alone among the Massachusetts delegation in Congress Sumner opposed the state's being represented in the peace conference (February 1861) and he was unyielding to petitions signed by tens of thousands of Massachusetts citizens urging his support of the Crittenden Compromise. In October 1861, at the Massachusetts Republican convention, he was the first statesman of prominence to urge emancipation, insisting that the overthrow of slavery would make an end of the war. Throughout the following year in the Senate, in public addresses, and in conferences with the President he never ceased to press for emancipation. When the Proclamation was finally issued, no man had done more than Sumner to prepare public sentiment for its approval.

When the Republicans got control of the Senate in 1861, for the first time Sumner received a committee assignment worthy of his abilities: he was made chairman of the committee on foreign relations, a position for which he was preeminently fitted and in which he was destined to render invaluable service. Although Captain Wilkes's seizure of Mason and Slidell was hailed with wild enthusiasm and at first seemed to have official approval, Sumner at once declared: "They will have to be given up" (G. H. Monroe, in *Hartford Courant,* Nov. 22, 1873). By the President's invitation he came into conference with the cabinet, set forth the principles of international law involved in the case, and read letters which he had just received from Cobden and Bright. The next day, with suitable apologies, Seward informed the British minister that the envoys would be given up. Sumner's influence was undoubtedly potent both in effecting a peaceful solution and in reconciling the American people to the inevitable surrender. In his chairmanship of the committee on foreign relations he aided the Union cause by defeating or suppressing resolutions which would almost inevitably have involved the United States in war with France and with Great Britain.

Already in the second year of the war he began the struggle to secure for all citizens of the United States, regardless of race or color, absolute equality of civil rights. As early as February 1862, he announced his extravagant doctrine that the seceded states had abdicated all rights under the Constitution; as he later phrased it, they had committed suicide (*Congressional Globe,* 37 Cong., 2 Sess., pp. 736–37, 2189). He was insistent that the initiation and the control of reconstruction should be by Congress, not by the President. It was Sumner's influence more than that of any other, as Lincoln declared in a cabinet meeting on the last day of his life, that blocked the recognition of Louisiana which was the most vital point for reconstruction in accordance with the Lincoln plan. Despite Sumner's opposition to policies nearest to the President's heart, he treated him with the greatest personal consideration.

During the Johnson administration Sumner and Thaddeus Stevens [*q.v.*] were brought into a strange cooperation as the Senate and House leaders, respectively, of the opposition to the President's reconstruction policy. Sumner was intent upon securing equality of civil rights for the freedmen, while Stevens' main concern was to prevent the defeat of the Republican party by Democratic reënforcements from the Southern states. It was Sumner's persistence which led the Senate to add to the requirements for "re-admission" of the seceded states the insertion in their constitutions of a provision for equal suffrage rights for whites and blacks. In effect this act of Congress, passed over the President's veto, abolished all the Johnson governments in the South. Sumner has been justly criticized for insisting upon the immediate grant of the ballot to the freedmen. It should be remembered, however, that in his own plan federal law was to guarantee to the blacks not only the ballot but also free schools and free farmsteads. In the movement for the impeachment of Johnson, Sumner took a prominent part. His first impressions favorable to the President soon gave way to a settled conviction that he was the chief menace to the country. Sumner regarded impeachment as a political rather than a judicial proceeding; hence neither in the Senate nor elsewhere did he put any curb upon his denunciations of Johnson's "misdeeds," and his opinion, filed with those of eighteen of the thirty-five who voted for conviction, was the longest and most bitter of them all (*Works*, XII, 318–410). He declared he would vote, if he could, "Guilty, of all [the charges] and infinitely more" (*Ibid.*, XII, 401). In this document Sumner is seen at his worst. Lurid and furious invective largely took the place of argument. In his view, Johnson was the "enormous criminal" of the century.

By temperament, training, and experience President Grant and Sumner were antipathetic, and they soon came into antagonism. Sumner's opposition on constitutional grounds was largely responsible for the rejection of the nomination of Stewart for secretary of the treasury. Though Motley was named minister to England upon Sumner's recommendation, he was later removed. The President seemed to take no serious exception to Sumner's influence in preventing the ratification of the Johnson-Clarendon Convention, nor to his startling assertion of the United States' "national claims," amounting to billions of dollars, against Great Britain, owing to her concession of ocean belligerency to the Confederate States. The most violent clash developed over the President's pet project, the acquisition of Santo Domingo. Sumner's committee brought in an adverse report upon the treaties that had been negotiated by Grant's personal envoy. Motley's removal at this juncture seemed like retaliation. Grant persisted in urging annexation. Finally, in a scathing speech—made more exasperating by his entitling it "Naboth's Vineyard"—Sumner denounced the whole Santo Domingo project (*Works*, XIV, 89–130; see also, pp. 168–249).

While these controversies were in progress there came to Sumner one of the greatest griefs of his life, his demotion from the chairmanship of the committee on foreign relations. In distinguished qualifications for this position he was without a peer in public life. But the tension had become so great that Sumner was not on speaking terms with the President and the Secretary of State. His champions asserted that this was but "a flimsy pretext" and that "the San Domingo scheme was at the bottom of the whole difficulty" (Haynes, p. 366). A more reasonable explanation of the administration's pressure may have been a fear that his extraordinary views as to "national claims" against Great Britain would prove an obstacle to the adjustment which was then under negotiation. Though thus shut out from any official relations with the joint commission, Sumner was frequently consulted by its members, and was shown great consideration by the British commissioners, whose head told Sumner that without his speech "the treaty could not have been made and that he worked by it as a chart" (*Memoir*, IV, 491). Despite his demotion, Sumner not only gave his vote for the Treaty of Washington but made the principal speech in exposition and support of it (*Memoir*, IV, 489–90). It is clear that Sumner himself did not expect that the enormous sums suggested by him would actually be paid by Great Britain. He was reasonably satisfied with the result—that the new treaty, at least as construed by the United States, would secure an arbitral adjustment of all claims, whether individual or national, growing out of the cruisers' depredations. He considered this a most important advance in establishing the principle of arbitration, and predicted: "Great Britain will never, in any future wars, place herself in the predicament in which my speech demonstrated she was placed in the matter of the rebel cruisers" (Whipple, *post*, p. 209).

At the opening of the regular session of Congress in December 1872, Sumner introduced a bill which provided that, inasmuch as "national unity and good will among fellow-citizens can be assured only through oblivion of past difference, and it is contrary to the usage of civilized nations to perpetuate the memory of civil war," the names of battles with fellow-citizens should not be continued in the Army Register, or placed on the regimental colors of the United States (*Works*, XV, 255). Apparently as a penalty for his opposition to Grant in the preceding campaign a bill of precisely opposite intent was introduced in the House, passed and sent to the Senate, where both bills were temporarily laid on the table because of Sumner's illness. Meantime, in the Massachusetts legislature a report denouncing Sumner's bill as "an insult to the loyal soldiers of the nation" and as "meeting the unqualified condemnation of the people of the Commonwealth" was adopted (*Journal of the Extra Session of the House of Representatives of Massachusetts, 1872,* 1873, p. 54). Sumner was deeply grieved by this injustice. Forthwith Whittier took the lead in a movement to rescind this resolution of censure, and two years later by large majorities in both houses of a new legislature it was annulled (*Journal of the House of Representatives of Massachusetts, 1874,* 1874, pp. 131–35).

On Mar. 10, 1874, against his physician's advice, Sumner went to the Senate, for on that day his colleague was to report the rescinding resolution. His fellow Senators were generous in their expressions of congratulation and goodwill. That evening he was prostrated by a heart attack and the next day he died. His body lay in state in the rotunda of the Capitol, and the funeral services were held in Cambridge. On Oct. 17, 1866, at the age of fifty-five, he had married Mrs. Alice (Mason) Hooper, a young widow; but they separated within a year and later were divorced (Shotwell, *post,* pp. 557–58, 584–85).

At the end of the Civil War, it has been said that the two most influential men in public life were Abraham Lincoln and Charles Sumner (Rhodes, *post,* V, 55). Time has dealt very differently with them, for Sumner's figure has been crowded into the background. Unlike Lincoln, he outlived his best days. His most characteristic and beneficent labors belonged to the epoch closed by the war; their fruits were merged in its triumphs. His later years brought misfortunes in full train: domestic sorrow, racking illness, the loss of friends, and ceaseless struggle over the problems of reconstruction, with some of which he was little fitted to cope. In contrast with most other American leaders of comparable political influence, Sumner entered public life "at the top": when he took his seat in the Senate he had never held public office of any kind. By no effort, he found himself thrust forward as the champion of an unpopular cause. Throughout his many years in the Senate, the goal of his constant striving was "absolute human equality, secured, assured, and invulnerable." He judged every man and every measure by reference to that goal. That any slave could be happy or that any slave-owner could be humane seemed to him impossible. As years passed, he became more intolerant not only of opposition but also of dis-

sent. His arraignments of Johnson and of Grant were extravagant beyond all reason. When George William Curtis, discussing with him some public question, suggested: "But you forget the other side!" Sumner's voice "shook the room, as he thundered in reply: 'There is no other side!'" (C. E. Norton, ed., *Orations and Addresses of George William Curtis,* 1894, vol. I, 256). To a senator's argument that the Constitution gave no authority for action which Sumner was urging, his reply was: "Nothing against slavery can be unconstitutional!" (Haynes, p. 279).

At the end of the war, the senator who for many years had been most vehement in denouncing all owners of slaves as "slave-mongers" was not the man to deal most tactfully and discriminatingly with the reconstruction problems. There is a measure of justice in the comment: "He would shed tears at the bare thought of refusing to freedmen rights of which they had no comprehension, but would filibuster to the end of the session to prevent the restoration to the southern whites of rights which were essential to their whole concept of life" (W. A. Dunning, *Reconstruction, Political and Economic,* p. 87). Yet in his later years Sumner displayed a kindness of sympathy toward the impoverished and suffering people of the South, and a magnanimity (as in his battle-flag resolution) which Congress did not reach till a full generation had passed.

Despite Sumner's intense devotion to the one "cause" which he championed with a crusader's zeal, he was diligent in the routine work of a senator, and commanded respect in his discussion of such topics as money and finance, the tariff, postal regulations, and copyright. He was much concerned over the abuses of patronage, through presidential favoritism or "senatorial courtesy," and introduced a well-thought-out bill for civil service reform. But his great work was not in the framing of laws. His was, rather, the rôle of an ancient Hebrew prophet—the kindling of moral enthusiasm, the inspiring of courage and hope, the assailing of injustice. His fearlessness in denouncing compromise, in demanding the repeal of the Fugitive-slave Law, and in insisting upon emancipation made him a major force in the struggle that put an end to slavery. It was his magnanimity and pertinacity that held in check barbarous attempts at retaliation, whether in the grant of letters of marque and reprisal, in the treatment of Confederate prisoners, or in the seizure of unoffending citizens of foreign countries in return for wrongs inflicted upon Americans abroad. Throughout the great national crisis his service was of inestimable value in keeping the United States at peace with Great Britain and with France, when war with either of them would have meant the disruption of the Union.

[*The Works of Charles Sumner* (15 vols., 1870–83), mostly edited by him, were considered by him a faithful record of his career. The references in the text are to this edition. Another edition, with introduction by G. F. Hoar, is *Charles Sumner, His Complete Works* (20 vols., 1900). The Sumner collection in the library of Harvard Univ. contains 40,000 letters received by him. E. L. Pierce, *Memoir and Letters of Charles Sumner* (4 vols., 1877–93), contains whatever seemed significant to an intimate of thirty years but lacks sense of proportion. Shorter biographies are those by A. M. Grimké (1892), a negro lawyer of Boston, which is mainly a tribute of gratitude to a champion of the author's race; by Moorfield Storey (1900), an excellent summary by an eminent lawyer who was for several years Sumner's private secretary; by W. G. Shotwell (1910), eulogistic and discursive; and by G. H. Haynes (1909). Storey's biography may be supplemented by M. A. DeW. Howe, *Portrait of an Independent: Moorfield Storey, 1845–1929* (1932). Sumner's personality was set forth in eloquent orations by G. W. Curtis and Carl Schurz, published separately and in *A Memorial of Charles Sumner* (1874), and in essays by intimate friends: E. P. Whipple, *Recollections of Eminent Men* (1887); and T. W. Higginson, *Contemporaries* (1899). *Memorial Addresses on the Life and Character of Charles Sumner . . . Forty-Third Congress, First Session, Apr. 27, 1874* (1874) include the notable tribute by L. Q. C. Lamar, which made a profound impression in both North and South, and the discriminating appraisal by G. F. Hoar. There is an obituary in *Boston Evening Transcript*, Mar. 12, 1874. J. F. Rhodes, *Hist. of the U. S.* (7 vols., 1893–1906), contains many references. W. A. Dunning, in *Reconstruction, Political and Economic* (1907), and *Essays on the Civil War and Reconstruction* (1898), is severely critical of Sumner. More recent writers on Reconstruction, such as H. K. Beale, *The Critical Year* (1930), and G. F. Milton, *The Age of Hate* (1930) are even more severe. For Sumner's relation to the *Alabama* claims, see C. F. Adams, Jr., *Charles Francis Adams* (1900), and "The Treaty of Washington," in *Lee at Appomattox and Other Papers* (1902); J. B. Moore, *Hist. and Digest of the International Arbitrations to Which the United States Has Been a Party*, vol. I (1898), ch. XIV; D. H. Chamberlain, *Charles Sumner and the Treaty of Washington* (1902); J. C. B. Davis, *Mr. Sumner, the Alabama Claims, and Their Settlement* (1878). Sumner's own statement of the controversies with Grant and Fish is in his *Works*, IV, 254–76.]   G. H. H.

SUMNER, EDWIN VOSE (Jan. 30, 1797–Mar. 21, 1863), soldier, was born at Boston, Mass., the son of Elisha and Nancy (Vose) Sumner, and a descendant of William Sumner who came to Massachusetts about 1635 and settled at Dorchester. He was commissioned second lieutenant in the 2nd Infantry, Mar. 3, 1819, promoted first lieutenant, Jan. 25, 1823, and served in that regiment until he was appointed captain, Mar. 4, 1833, in the newly organized 1st Dragoons (now the 1st Cavalry). His service was chiefly on the frontier until the outbreak of the Mexican War, when he was appointed major of the 2nd Dragoons, June 30, 1846, and joined Gen. Winfield Scott's army in Mexico. Scott's

faith in Sumner was such that he wished to relegate the latter's senior, Col. William S. Harney [*q.v.*], for whom he had no liking, to an unimportant command in Taylor's army. In the end, both Harney and Sumner remained, but the relations between them were permanently strained. The regiment of Mounted Riflemen (now 3rd Cavalry) had just been organized, most of its officers being wholly without military training. It needed an exceptionally strong man to command it, and Sumner was detached from the dragoons for that purpose. His service throughout the campaign was distinguished, at first in command of the Mounted Riflemen and later of his own regiment. He was wounded at Cerro Gordo and received brevets for his conduct there and at Molino del Rey. He was promoted lieutenant-colonel of the 1st Dragoons, July 13, 1848, and colonel of the 1st (now 4th) Cavalry, Mar. 3, 1855. Meanwhile, in the summer of 1852, after the death of the civil governor, J. S. Calhoun, Sumner as military commandant of the region was acting governor of New Mexico.

In September 1855, under orders from General Harney, Sumner's regiment left Fort Leavenworth for Fort Laramie, to arrive there ready for a spring campaign, but after marching west four hundred miles he turned back to Leavenworth, declaring that to continue would sacrifice most of the horses. Harney preferred charges for disobedience of orders, but Sumner was supported by the War Department. As commander of the post at Fort Leavenworth in 1856 during the struggle between Free-Soilers and proslavery men for the control of Kansas, he attempted to preserve order, dispersing armed bands of partisans of both sides, and under the direction of Gov. Wilson Shannon [*q.v.*], the "pretended" Topeka legislature. In 1857 he was engaged in a campaign against the Cheyennes in Kansas and the following year he assumed command of the Department of the West, with headquarters at St. Louis.

Sumner was of Northern birth; his wife also was a Northerner: Hannah W. Forster, daughter of Thomas Forster of Erie, Pa., whom he married Mar. 31, 1822. There is no apparent reason why any one should suspect him of sympathy with secession—except, possibly, the marriage of his daughter to a Southerner, Armistead Lindsay Long [*q.v.*]—but such sentiment was strong in St. Louis, and it is suggestive that on Jan. 5, 1861, he wrote, in a personal letter to General Scott: "I have belonged to the general government over forty years, and I consider it my government, and so long as it lasts, the only government to which I owe fealty. As I view this obligation, I feel bound in honor to devote myself to the preservation of the Union." (Unpublished letter.) Scott's opinion is indicated by his selection of Sumner to accompany the president-elect to Washington. Sumner was appointed brigadier-general, Mar. 16, 1861. He commanded the II Corps in the Peninsular campaign, at South Mountain, and at Antietam. McClellan recommended his promotion, writing to the War Department of his "extreme gallantry" and of "the judgment and energy he displayed in saving the day at the battle of Fair Oaks," and he was accordingly appointed major-general of volunteers with rank from July 4, 1862. He commanded the right grand division at the battle of Fredericksburg, and was then relieved from duty with the Army of the Potomac at his own request. He died at Syracuse, N. Y., while on the way to his new command in Missouri. One son, Edwin Vose Sumner, Jr., became a brigadier-general in the regular army; and another, Samuel Storrow Sumner, a major-general.

[*War of the Rebellion: Official Records (Army)*; *Battles and Leaders of the Civil War* (4 vols., 1887–88); J. H. Smith, *The War with Mexico* (2 vols., 1919); W. S. Appleton, *Record of the Descendants of William Sumner* (1879); *Kan. Hist. Colls.*, vols. VIII (1904), XVI (1923–25); G. B. Grinnell, *The Fighting Cheyennes* (1915); P. G. Lowe, *Five Years A Dragoon* (1906); H. H. Bancroft, *Hist. of the Pacific States*, vol. XII (1888); F. A. Walker, *Hist. of the Second Army Corps in the Army of the Potomac* (1887); *Sen. Ex. Doc. No. 5, and No. 10* and *House Ex. Doc. No. 4* (pt. 2), 34 Cong., 3 Sess. (1856); *N. Y. Herald*, Mar. 22, 1863; unpublished records in the War Dept.]
          T.M.S.

SUMNER, INCREASE (Nov. 27, 1746–June 7, 1799), jurist, governor of Massachusetts, was born in Roxbury, Mass., son of Increase Sumner, a well-to-do farmer of colossal size and strength, and Sarah (Sharp) Sumner, daughter of Robert Sharp of Brookline and first cousin of John Adams' mother. He was descended from William Sumner who came to Massachusetts about 1635 and settled in Dorchester. Having prepared for college in the Roxbury grammar school (now Roxbury Latin school), he entered Harvard, where he was graduated with distinction in 1767. He then taught in the Roxbury school for two years, studying law meanwhile under Samuel Quincy, solicitor general of the province and loyalist brother of Josiah Quincy [*q.v.*] the patriot. After admission to the bar in 1770, Sumner opened an office in his Roxbury home. His practice soon became important and lucrative. He married, Sept. 30, 1779, Elizabeth, daughter of William Hyslop, a prosperous Boston merchant. She survived Sumner, leaving a son and two daughters.

Early in life he took from the arms of the Kentish Sumners the motto, *In medio tutissimus ibis,* and shaped his whole political career accordingly. Though he was mildly opposed to the British contentions, his only part in the Revolution was to serve as representative in the General Court, 1776–79; and as senator, 1780–82. He was a member of the constitutional convention whose work was rejected by the voters in 1778, and of the convention of 1779–80 that framed the Massachusetts constitution. In June 1782 the legislature elected him to Congress to fill a vacancy, but he never sat because in August he was appointed associate justice of the supreme judicial court of Massachusetts. The work of the judges needed much courage during the turbulent times when the new state government had just been set up and there was much hostility to the comomn law and those who enforced it. The judges, as Sumner's portrait shows, still wore their pre-Revolutionary black silk gowns with white bands, but despite Sumner's vigorous protest Chief Justice Dana, followed by the other justices, soon abandoned them, and they were not resumed until 1901. Sumner acquired a reputation as "a dispassionate, impartial, discerning, able and accomplished judge" (W. H. Sumner, *post*, p. 12). Since the judges did not habitually write out their decisions until 1804, no printed reports of his legal views exist, but the Massachusettts Historical Society possesses his manuscript notes of his cases. As a member of the Massachusetts convention of 1788 which ratified the federal Constitution, Sumner delivered several speeches, especially in support of biennial rather than annual elections of Congress. He remained a warm supporter of the new national government, replying to Fisher Ames's "I say it won't last" with, "Let us see how it works. Let us give it a fair trial" (*Ibid.*, p. 16).

Almost against his will, Sumner was put forward by the Federalists in 1796 as their gubernatorial candidate against Samuel Adams. There was little to recommend him in comparison with Adams, who was triumphantly reëlected. In 1797, Adams having retired, Sumner swept the state against the divided Democratic-Republican opposition of James Sullivan and Moses Gill, and was sworn in as governor on June 2, 1797, his tall and commanding figure a striking contrast to the gouty infirmity of Hancock, who had to be carried to the Council chamber in a chair, and to the bent old frame of Adams. Having inherited considerable property from his father-in-law, he entertained lavishly and drove a coach and four on all public occasions. His middle-of-the-road policy was just what Massachusetts needed to calm the dissensions aroused by the proposed French war and the Alien and Sedition Acts. "He had indeed 'united all hearts,' and his freedom from political bias made of him a refreshing and admirable contrast to the bitter actions and animosities of the politicians of that period" (Morse, *post*, p. 178). He was reëlected in 1798 and 1799 by overwhelming majorities, getting the unanimous vote of many towns. During his administration, Jan. 11, 1798, the government was removed to the new State House on Beacon Hill. His chief activities were in military affairs. He worked to increase munitions, obtain additional arsenals for the artillery, and fortify the sea coast of the state. He wore a uniform at all military ceremonies, despite the efforts of the bench and bar to dissuade him. At his third election in 1799 he was ill with angina, and he was sworn in on his death bed in Roxbury.

Sumner was a practical farmer, attending personally to his estates and much interested in advancing agriculture. His personality was impressive but kind. "He never . . . forgot his dignity in any place or circle, even in the moments of his greatest familiarity" (W. H. Sumner, *post*, p. 32). He was solid and judicious rather than brilliant. "In the analysis of his mind there is not to be found one extraordinary power, nor one mean quality" (Knapp, *post*, p. 94). He was given a public funeral and buried in the Granary Burial Ground in Boston.

[S. L. Knapp, *Biog. Sketches of Eminent Lawyers* (1821); W. H. Sumner, *Memoir of Increase Sumner . . . together with a Geneal. of the Sumner Family* (1854), reprinted from *New England Hist. and Geneal. Reg.*, April 1854; Eliphalet Porter, *A Sermon . . . Occasioned by the Death of . . . Increase Sumner* (1799); Abiel Holmes, *A Sermon Preached . . . After the Interment of . . . Increase Sumner* (n.d.); Peter Thacher, *A Sermon . . . at the Interment of . . . Increase Sumner* (n.d.); W. S. Appleton, *Record of the Descendants of William Sumner* (1879); A. E. Morse, *The Federalist Party in Mass.* (1909); Alden Bradford, *Hist. of Mass.*, vol. III (1829); J. S. Barry, *The Hist. of Mass.*, vol. III (1857); A. B. Hart, ed., *Commonwealth Hist. of Mass.*, vol. IV (1930); T. C. Amory, *Life of James Sullivan* (1859).]   Z. C., Jr.

SUMNER, JETHRO (*c.* 1733–March 1785), Revolutionary soldier, the son of Jethro and Margaret (Sullivan) Sumner, was born in Nansemond County, Va., where his grandfather, William Sumner, had become a freeholder about 1691. He served from 1755 to 1761 in the Virginia militia during the French and Indian War, rising to a lieutenancy and to the command of Fort Bedford in 1760. Prior to the autumn of 1764 he emigrated to North Carolina and was married to Mary, the daughter of William and Christian McKinnie Hurst, of Granville County.

She brought him a large inheritance and he established himself as a tavern-owner and planter at the seat of Bute (later Warren) County. With a fair education, military experience, business acumen, handsome physique, native ability, and attractive personality, Sumner rose to local prominence as justice of the peace in 1768 and as sheriff, 1772–77. He represented Bute County in the revolutionary provincial congress of August–September 1775, which elected him major of the minute-men of Halifax district. In November he went to the aid of the Virginia patriots near Norfolk; and, following his election on Apr. 15, 1776 by the fourth provincial congress as colonel of the third battalion of North Carolina continentals, he marched first to the lower Cape Fear, thence to aid in the successful defense of Charlestown in June. Later he joined Charles Lee, 1731–1782 [*q.v.*], on the projected expedition against Florida, but left it at Savannah in September to return to North Carolina for supplies. He led his battalion northward in the following spring and served in Washington's army through Brandywine, Germantown, and Valley Forge, until illness in the spring of 1778 compelled his return to North Carolina. During the summer he recruited for the continental battalions.

Elected brigadier-general by the Continental Congress on Jan. 9, 1779, Sumner led a brigade of newly recruited continentals to South Carolina and participated in the battle of Stono Ferry on June 20. For more than a year from July he was recruiting the North Carolina battalions. As commander of a brigade of militia in the southern piedmont region he assisted in the gallant defense of North Carolina against Cornwallis' invasion in the fall of 1780 until, in October, piqued by the elevation of General Smallwood to the command of the state forces, he declined further militia service. However, at General Greene's request, he offered his services again in February 1781; but General Caswell did not give him a militia command. Again he endeavored to raise troops until July, when he reinforced Greene with a brigade of three small battalions of raw continentals, who fought like veterans at Eutaw Springs on Sept. 8. During the remainder of the war, he was in charge of military forces in North Carolina. In 1783 he retired to the supervision of his tavern, his plantations, and his three minor orphan children. On Apr. 18, 1784, he presided at the meeting of the North Carolina Society of the Cincinnati in Hillsboro. With his strong constitution undermined by the exposures of war, he died at his home in Warren County between

Mar. 15 and 19, 1785. His possessions included approximately 20,000 acres and thirty-four slaves. Sumner was a brave and reliable officer, considerate of his soldiers, and a good disciplinarian. His creditable, varied, and continuous service throughout the war ranks him among the foremost of North Carolina patriots in the Revolution. His daughter, Jacky Sullivan Sumner, became the wife of Thomas Blount [q.v.].

[Colonial Records of N. C. (10 vols., 1886–90); State Records of N. C. (16 vols., 1895–1905); Jethro Sumner Papers, 1760–1784, in N. C. Historical Commission; Bute and Warren County Records; J. F. D. Smyth, A Tour in the U. S. A. (2 vols., 1784); Jours. of the House of Burgesses of Va.; S. A. Ashe, "Jethro Sumner," in S. A. Ashe, Biog. Hist. of N. C., vol. V (1906); K. P. Battle, "The Life and Services of Brigadier General Jethro Sumner," in The N. C. Booklet, Oct. 1908.]   A. R. N.

SUMNER, WILLIAM GRAHAM (Oct. 30, 1840–Apr. 12, 1910), educator, economist, publicist, and social scientist, was born in Paterson, N. J. His father, a Lancashire artisan, had emigrated from England to Paterson in 1836, and there married Sarah Graham, whose parents were also from Lancashire. Soon after his son's birth, Thomas Sumner, in the hope of bettering his condition, moved with his family westward, but after a period of wandering returned to the East and finally settled in Hartford, Conn., where for many years he was employed in the repair shop of the Hartford and New Haven Railroad Company. An uneducated workman, but a reader and thinker with intelligent views on social and economic questions, he exerted a lasting influence upon his son. Prepared in the public schools of Hartford, young Sumner entered Yale in 1859. Here he took high rank as a scholar and was known as a reserved, soberminded, self-reliant youth, independent in his thinking, who spent his spare time in general reading rather than in athletic or social activities. His sterling qualities, however, won him the lasting friendship of associates who were later prominent in the industrial and political affairs of the country. Through the aid of these, he went abroad after his graduation in 1863 for further study. From boyhood he had looked forward to entering the ministry, and he now prepared for that calling at Geneva, Göttingen, and Oxford. Returning to the United States, he was tutor at Yale from 1866 to 1869. During this period, Dec. 28, 1867, he was admitted to the diaconate of the Protestant Episcopal Church, and in 1869 he became assistant to Dr. E. A. Washburn, rector of Calvary Church, New York, where he was ordained priest, July 15, 1869. In addition to his clerical duties he helped to establish, and edited, The Living Church, an

able monthly published in the interests of the Broad Church party, which, however, survived but a year. He was also engaged at this time in translating and editing the second book of K. C. W. F. Bähr's "The Books of the Kings" in J. P. Lange's Commentary on the Holy Scriptures, the translation being published in 1872. In September 1870 he became rector of the Church of the Redeemer, Morristown, N. J., and on Apr. 17 of the following year he married Jeannie Whittemore Elliott, daughter of Henry Hill Elliott, a New York merchant, and Elmira (Whittemore) Elliott.

Sumner was an able preacher and performed scrupulously the other duties of his office, but his interest turned increasingly to public questions and matters of social and economic import, upon which he could not express himself freely in the pulpit. Accordingly, in 1872 he accepted a call to the newly created chair of political and social science at Yale University. In the service of this institution he spent the remainder of his life, though his fame and influence rapidly extended beyond its borders. His activities were varied. For three years (1873–76) he was one of New Haven's board of aldermen; for twenty-eight years (1882–1910) he was an active member of the Connecticut State Board of Education and contributed much to the improvement of the common school system; his utterances on public questions attracted wide attention and he was constantly importuned for addresses and magazine articles; he was the author of numerous books still regarded as authoritative; he carried on extended research into the origin of social institutions which give him rank among the foremost students in this particular field. His industry was prodigious. He worked long hours and seldom took a holiday. Not only did he cultivate all the social sciences, but as aids in his work he informed himself on such subjects as anatomy, biology, and even calculus. He had a good working knowledge of at least a dozen languages, familiarity with the most of them having been acquired after he was forty-five years old.

Outside activities, however, were never permitted to interfere with his college duties. He considered teaching his first business. Of large frame—always fastidiously dressed—fine head "magnificently bald," somewhat stern countenance, keen eye and "iron voice," thoroughly conversant with his subject and boldly independent in his treatment of it, he commanded the respect and confidence of his classes. He made everyday affairs his textbook, and beginning with these, set forth the underlying economic and social facts and principles with a freshness and vigor then and always rare in college teaching. Going straight to the heart of his subject, he stated the facts in plain and often epigrammatic language. Honest and fearless, despising gush and sentimentality, indifferent to tradition, he struck hard blows, never glossed over anything, and never spared anybody's feelings. Contemptuous of pedagogical methods, he was, nevertheless, one of the most effective teachers of his generation. His lecture room was crowded and no one at Yale was considered by the students really to have qualified for a degree if he had not been under Sumner. Instructors in other colleges visited his classroom, or wrote to him, seeking the secret of his success. In addition to teaching he did his full share of administrative work. He rebelled against the conservatism strongly entrenched at Yale when he went there, deplored the prominence given to the classics, and labored, against much opposition, to broaden the curriculum, especially by introducing scientific studies into the academic department. When President Noah Porter [*q.v.*] objected to Sumner's use of Herbert Spencer's *The Study of Sociology* as a textbook, he waged and won a vigorous fight for academic freedom, which through newspaper reports attracted wide attention.

As soon as he was free from the restrictions his clerical position imposed, Sumner at once proceeded to take up the cudgel against economic and political evils and in behalf of what he deemed sound governmental principles. This warfare he carried on through public addresses, but more particularly through essays published in various periodicals, so keen in analysis, flawless in logic, and full of fire that they attracted country-wide attention. Their very titles were such as to arrest attention—"The Absurd Attempt to Make the World Over," "That It Is Not Wicked to Be Rich; Nay, Even, That It Is Not Wicked to Be Richer Than One's Neighbor," "Protectionism, the —Ism Which Teaches that Waste Makes Wealth," "Prosperity Strangled by Gold," "The Delusion of the Debtors," "The Conquest of the United States by Spain." Practically every social question of the day is treated, and such underlying subjects as equality, rights, duty, and liberty are stripped of all their traditional and sentimental trappings and critically examined. Throughout his career he was an outstanding advocate of a sound monetary system, opposing free silver, bimetalism, and all inflationary expedients. For years, often almost single-handed, he fought protectionism, maintaining that as a prosperity measure it was economic quackery, and from a moral point of view,

pernicious. He deplored the agitation against "big business," regarding the evolution of trusts as a natural and expedient phenomenon, and vigorously opposed any infringement of the government upon the industrial field, maintaining that state interference could not be scientific, or even intelligent, and that the remedies would be worse than the disease. His arguments against socialism have been considered the most difficult to answer that have been put forth. He was long prominent among the leaders in civil service reform; in the days of the Spanish-American War he was one of the small and unpopular group of anti-imperialists. Though he is usually classed as an advocate of *laissez-faire,* it was only to what he called "empiricism," unintelligent experimentation and social panaceas, that he was opposed. That social conditions can be improved he firmly believed, but such improvement can come, he was convinced, only by scientific procedure carried on by thoroughly informed individuals. In a democracy, therefore, the right kind of education is of supreme importance. In all his aggressive presentation of these subjects, he was inspired by strong moral convictions, and with hatred of shams, loose thinking, sentimental motive, and especially of jobbery and injustice. He was especially solicitous for the "Forgotten Man," a term which he chose as the title for one of his public lectures (1883). By the "Forgotten Man," he meant the self-supporting and self-respecting person who has to bear the cost of all the political bungling and the social quackery. "I affirm that there is always somebody who pays, and that it is always the sober, honest, industrious, economical men or women, who attend no meetings, pass no resolutions, never go to the lobby, are never mentioned in the newspapers, but just work and save and pay" (*William Graham Sumner, post,* p. 287).

The most significant of Sumner's essays have been edited by Albert G. Keller and published under the titles: *War and Other Essays* (1911), *Earth Hunger and Other Essays* (1913), *The Challenge of Facts and Other Essays* (1914), and *The Forgotten Man and Other Essays* (copr. 1919). In 1924 *Selected Essays of William Graham Sumner,* edited by Keller and M. R. Davie, was issued. Among Sumner's more ambitious publications in the economic field were *A History of American Currency* (1874); *American Finance* (1875); *The Financier and Finances of the American Revolution* (2 vols., 1891); "Monetary Development," in *The First Century of the Republic* (1876), edited by T. D. Woolsey and others; "A History of Banking in the United States" (1896), being the first volume of *A His-*

tory of Banking in All the Leading Nations,
edited by A. W. Dodsworth. He also wrote three
biographies, aside from *The Financier,* which,
within the limits set by the author, rank among
the best that have appeared—*Andrew Jackson
as a Public Man* (1882), *Alexander Hamilton*
(1890), and *Robert Morris* (1892). One of his
most widely read publications, *What Social
Classes Owe to Each Other,* notable for its cold,
keen logic and pungency, appeared in 1883, and
has since been several times republished.

Having, as a young man, stormed his way
with incredible industry and vigor into the political economy and political science which he
was called to Yale to develop, he found himself
less and less satisfied, as the years passed and
he came more and more under the influence of
Herbert Spencer, to stay within the traditional
boundaries of these subjects. Economics and
politics were only a part of the picture; there
were also religion and marriage, alongside and
intricately interconnected with the economic and
political organizations. To see society truly, one
must view all of its institutions, not some of
them—and all of them in their interrelations.
Sumner's interest broadened into preoccupation
with a general science of society, so that in middle life he began to recede from economics,
eventually withdrawing his long-popular courses
in that subject and turning with eagerness and
vigor, despite broken health, toward anthropology and what he called "societology."

This venture involved the study of all the institutions of society in their evolution from the
simplest, primitive forms. Accordingly, he sub-
merged himself in the literature relating to these
and within ten to fifteen years had assembled a
large amount of classified material from the best
sources in a number of languages. Eventually
he started upon a treatise on the science of society; but, as he reduced his materials to order
and his conclusions to writing, he found himself forced to generalize, beyond and beneath institutions of all kinds, to the underlying stratum,
custom, out of which they all have developed.
When he was about two-thirds through a first
draft of his treatise, he arrived reluctantly at the
conviction that he had omitted an absolute essential, namely, the analysis of custom. He set aside
the manuscript and devoted several years to
work on this essential, emerging with that classic
of the science, *Folkways* (1907). He remarked
at the time of its publication that what he had
done on the science of society must now be rewritten in the light of the mores; his age and
illness made that task impossible.

The logical necessity felt by Sumner and met
by his conception and analysis of the folkways
and mores confronts any serious student of society's evolution. His *Folkways,* as is becoming
more evident every year, is a fundamental contribution to one and all of the social sciences.
Relatively minor, though exceedingly important
contributions, such as that of the aleatory element as the basis of religion, occur throughout
Sumner's studies in society's evolution. Furthermore, he is one of the very few "sociologists"
who have had the disposition and the industry to
eschew *a priori* reasoning and sentimentality in
favor of induction from arduously gathered facts.

Seventeen years after Sumner's death, his *Science of Society* (1927), with the mass of data he
had accumulated entirely sifted, and reclassified,
with much important evidence added, and with
the system he had outlined considerably revised,
was published in four volumes by his successor
at Yale, Professor Albert G. Keller. This joint
work is to be classed with *Folkways* as one of
the most important contributions yet made in the
field of social science. While it is impossible to
apportion the parts supplied by the two authors,
it is certain that the volumes preserve the spirit
of Sumner and contain his corrected and recor-
rected conclusions as to the nature and life of
human society. A popular abridgment by Keller,
Man's Rough Road, appeared in 1932. In 1934
a two-volume edition of the essays, entitled *Essays of William Graham Sumner,* edited by A.
G. Keller and M. R. Davie, was issued. It includes a number of hitherto unpublished essays
and a bibliography of writings and of leading
biographical articles.

In spite of physical handicaps Sumner kept at
his work with indomitable will until the end. On
Dec. 26, 1909, he went to New York to deliver
an address as president of the American Sociological Society. At the Murray Hill Hotel he
collapsed, and on Apr. 12 following he died in
the Englewood (N. J.) Hospital, survived by
his wife and two sons. His funeral was held in
Battell Chapel, New Haven, and he was buried
in Guilford, Conn.

[A bibliog. of his writings, prepared by M. R. Davie,
is in *The Forgotten Man and Other Essays* (copr.
1919); a sketch of his life, largely autobiographical,
appeared in *Popular Science Mo.,* June 1889, and is
reprinted in *The Challenge of Facts and Other Essays*
(1913); the most complete portrayal of his career,
based partly on family and other unprinted sources, is
H. E. Starr, *William Graham Sumner* (1925). See also
introduction to *War and Other Essays* (1919); A. G.
Keller, *Reminiscences (Mainly Personal) of William
Graham Sumner* (1933) and "The Discoverer of the
Forgotten Man," *Am. Mercury,* Nov. 1932; *N. Y.
Times,* Apr. 13, 14 (editorial), 1910; *New Haven Evening Register,* Apr. 13, 1910.]   H. E. S.

SUMTER, THOMAS (Aug. 14, 1734–June 1,
1832), Continental officer, guerrilla, senator, and

representative, was born near Charlottesville, Va. It is said that his father, William Sumter, was an English redemptioner of Welsh extraction who died when Thomas was very young, and that his mother, Patience, was a midwife, who lived to a great age. With little schooling, the boy worked in his father's mill, tended his mother's sheep, and went with wild youths on the campaigns of Braddock and Forbes. His most enlightening experience, perhaps, was in 1762, when, after serving as sergeant of Virginia troops against the Cherokees, he accompanied Henry Timberlake [q.v.] on a mission to the head men and visited England with Chief Outacity [q.v.]. He was lodged for debt in the Staunton jail, escaped, and in 1765 acquired lands near Eutaw Springs, S. C. Here he opened a crossroads store near Nelson's Ferry, became a justice of the peace, and in 1767 married Mrs. Mary (Cantey) Jameson, of an old and prominent South Carolina family; she was the widow of William Jameson.

Elected to the first and second provincial congresses, he served as captain with the mounted rangers under William Thomson [q.v.]; and during an arduous Cherokee campaign he was placed in the Continental service as lieutenant-colonel of the 2nd Regiment of riflemen (later the 6th). After campaigns in Georgia and Florida he resigned, on Sept. 19, 1778, a full colonel, and was in retirement when the British conquered South Carolina in 1780. Unlike most South Carolina leaders, he did not take protection, and when Tarleton raided and destroyed his home, he joined Whig refugees near Charlotte, N. C. Informally elected general, he established headquarters on Sugar Creek, and revived resistance so successfully that Lord Rawdon offered 500 guineas for his betrayal. Repulsed at Rocky Mount on July 30, 1780, he was successful at Hanging Rock on Aug. 6, but in cooperating with Gates he was overtaken by Tarleton at Fishing Creek on Aug. 18 and completely routed. Within a short time, however, he resumed operations, and on Oct. 6, 1780, was commissioned brigadier in command of South Carolina militia. At Fishdam Ford on Nov. 9 he escaped Wemyss' attempt to kidnap him, and on Tyger River on Nov. 20 he repulsed Tarleton in the well-fought battle of Blackstock's Hill, where he was severely wounded. For these achievements he received the thanks of Congress on Jan. 13, 1781. Declining activity until Feb. 16, 1781, he marched then for Granby, but finding the post had been warned, he went on a daring raid against Thomson's, Fort Watson, and Nelson's Ferry, and successfully returned to Sugar Creek.

In spite of the non-existence of the state government, Sumter now undertook to raise a dependable force of mounted state troops. With the sanction of Governor Rutledge and General Greene, he enlisted regulars for ten months' service, to be paid in negroes and plunder from Loyalists. The scheme, known as "Sumter's law," was successful in procuring a force, but it augmented civil war between Whig and Tory, and gave Sumter the name of plunderer. Without an open break with Greene, Sumter maneuvered to maintain his command as a separate unit until July 1781, when, having finally joined Greene, he led the "raid of the dog days" into the low country. Though causing Dorchester and Biggin to be evacuated, he was repulsed at Quinby, and then to Greene's consternation he disbanded for the summer and retired to North Carolina. In the ensuing campaign, therefore, Greene dismounted and diverted Sumter's force and stationed him at Orangeburg for police duty. Disgusted, Sumter resigned before March 1782, after serving as senator in the Jacksonboro Assembly. In 1783, he received the thanks of the South Carolina Senate, was voted a gold medal, and declined his election to the Continental Congress. He served many terms in the South Carolina House, and after legislative investigation at his own request of "Sumter's law" he was exonerated and asked to wind up accounts with the state troops. The legislatures of both North and South Carolina by enactment forbade state courts to entertain suits for losses under his scheme.

After the war, he founded the village of Stateburg, S. C., bred race-horses, was a charter member of the Santee canal company, and of the Catawba company, took out grants for more than 150,000 acres of land, and experimented with tobacco and cotton in an effort to find a staple to replace indigo. In the South Carolina convention to consider the federal constitution, he opposed ratification before Virginia could be heard from. As a member of the First Congress, his speeches voiced antifederalist fears, and he was among the last to be won to assumption. He was defeated in 1793 because of supposed speculation in government paper, but was reelected in 1796 and remained in the House until sent to the Senate in December 1801. A devoted Jeffersonian, yet among the few senators to oppose Jefferson, he was gratified by the appointment of his only son Thomas as secretary of legation to France, and later as minister to Portugal in Brazil. In December 1810 he resigned from the Senate, and for the next twenty-two years was harried by litigation and creditors, until the South Carolina legislature in 1827 granted him a moratorium for life from his debt to the bank of the state of South Carolina. Although a small man, Sumter's strength and agility were as remarkable as his longevity, and he rode horseback until the day of his death on his estate near Stateburg in his ninety-eighth year.

The most significant phase of Sumter's career was in the Revolution; his importance was out of all proportion to the small numbers he commanded. The popular uprising of which he was part was an essential factor in the climax at Yorktown. Known as the "Gamecock of the Revolution," and the most feared of the partisans, he kept the largest body of militia in the field and was the first to make them stand against British regulars. But with all his imagination for daring schemes, he seems to have lacked the capacity for attention to detail that would insure success. In war he was a politician, and in politics he was an old soldier. Adaptable and progressive, he acquired dignity as he advanced and might well be called a typical American of the frontier school. Fort Sumter, S. C., was named in his honor.

[Manuscript materials on Sumter are in the Library of Congress, the William L. Clements Library, the Wisconsin State Historical Library, and the New York Historical Library. A comprehensive bibliography is included in A. K. Gregorie, *Thomas Sumter* (1931). See also letters published in *Year Book City of Charleston, 1899, Pubs. South. Hist. Asso.*, Mar. 1907; Kate Furman's article, *Ibid.*, Sept., Nov. 1902; and the account of his funeral in the *Camden Jour.*, June 9, 1832.]   A. K. G.

SUNDERLAND, ELIZA JANE READ (Apr. 19, 1839–Mar. 3, 1910), lecturer, writer, reformer, and educator, was born on a farm near Huntsville, Ill., under pioneer conditions. Her Quaker father, Amasa Read of Uxbridge, Mass., died when Eliza was very young; her mother, Jane Henderson, an Ohioan of Scotch descent, was a woman of strong mind and character. After a short time at an Abingdon (Ill.) seminary, Eliza, then aged fifteen, began teaching a district school which had driven out a succession of men teachers, and she quickly tamed the rebellious pupils. Having earned enough money for further study, she entered Mount Holyoke Seminary in 1863, and was graduated two years later. Conditions at home prevented her from accepting an invitation to join the seminary faculty, and she took a position in the Aurora (Ill.) high school. In 1867 she was made principal, thus becoming one of the first women in the United States to head a public secondary school. Her gifts as an educator were quickly apparent. The institution became known as the "model school" of Illinois, and helped raise educational standards in the Middle West. In 1871 she gave up her position

to marry, Dec. 7, Jabez Thomas Sunderland, an Englishman who was pastor of a church in Milwaukee, Wis., and later was prominent in the Unitarian denomination. Subsequently, she taught in high school at Chicago and Ann Arbor, Mich., where her husband had charges. The family lived in the latter place for twenty years (1878–98) and she seized the opportunity to study at the University of Michigan, from which she received the degree of Ph.B. in 1889, and that of Ph.D. in 1892, specializing in philosophy. Her education was also widened by extensive travel in Europe, Palestine, and Egypt.

Her interests included all matters concerned with human betterment, especially temperance, the advancement of women, the improvement of education, and the elevation of religion. For many years she was probably the leading woman of Michigan in such activities. For a short time, while living in Chicago, she was associate editor of the *Illinois Social Science Journal* (1878); during residence in Hartford, Conn., she was a member of the city school board (1907–10), and several times addressed the state legislature in behalf of educational and other reforms. She was also chief organizer and first president of the Women's Western Unitarian Conference, and from 1886 to 1891 was a vice-president of the Association for the Advancement of Women. She was a speaker of force and eloquence, lecturing extensively and often preaching in Unitarian and Universalist churches. In 1893 she spoke in Chicago at the Congress of Women of the World's Columbian Exposition, and at the World's Parliament of Religions, her paper before the latter being considered one of the best on the program. Her chief interest was religion, which she regarded not as a matter of creed but of conscience and heart. She constantly worked for a broader and finer religious faith. Her wide, sympathetic spiritual insight was remarkable: she mothered University of Michigan students perplexed with religious problems; and she regarded with kindly understanding the monuments of ancient polytheism on the banks of the Nile.

Besides articles—mostly religious—in newspapers and magazines, she published a number of pamphlets, contributed "Importance of the Study of Comparative Religions" to *The World's Congress of Religions* (1894), and, in collaboration with her husband, wrote *James Martineau and His Greatest Book* (1905). She died in Hartford, Conn., where her husband had been minister of the Unity Church since 1907, survived by him and by two daughters and a son.

[*Who's Who in America*, 1910–11; *Eliza Read Sunderland; a Brief Sketch of Her Life: Memorial Ad-*

dresses (n.d.); F. E. Willard and M. A. Livermore, *Am. Women* (1897); M. K. Eagle, *The Cong. of Women . . . World's Columbian Exposition* (1894), vol. I; *Christian Reg.,* Mar. 10, 1910; *Chicago Tribune,* Sept. 16, 1893; *Hartford Courant,* Mar. 4, 1910.]

M. W. W.

SUNDERLAND, LA ROY (Apr. 22, 1804– May 15, 1885), abolitionist, was born in Exeter, R. I. He received a common-school education, was a student for a time at Day's Academy, Wrentham, Mass., and in 1826 was admitted into full connection by the New England Conference of the Methodist Episcopal Church. Though he was little more than five feet tall, the emotional intensity of his preaching style was such that his colleagues prophesied that he would become the greatest revivalist of his time; but Sunderland himself became increasingly doubtful as to the divine origin of his powers and in 1833 withdrew from the active ministry. Meanwhile, however, he had begun to further the anti-slavery cause among the Methodist ministers of New England. The initial document of this agitation, "An Appeal on the Subject of Slavery" (*Zion's Herald,* Extra, Dec. 5, 1834), was from his hand, and the first anti-slavery society in the Methodist Church was organized through his efforts. In 1836, when despite the active hostility of the church press, the board of bishops, and even the General Conference, the anti-slavery faction founded *Zion's Watchman* in New York City, he became its editor, to lead the van of Methodist abolitionism.

He continued to meet with opposition within the church. In six successive sessions of the New England Conference, of which he was still a member, presiding bishops and dignitaries from New York brought charges against him, ranging from slander to immorality. The General Conference went so far as to change its rules in order to make him amenable to ecclesiastical discipline, and he was unsuccessfully sued for libel in the courts. Finally, in 1842, he withdrew with other radicals from the Methodist Episcopal Church and signed their call for a new church, the Wesleyan Connection of America, without an episcopacy and on an anti-slavery basis.

Sunderland, however, did not join the new denomination. The bitterness of his persecution and the acerbity of his resistance had left their mark upon his loyalties. Moreover, he had long been convinced that his early success as a revivalist had been due solely to hypnotic powers. Conversion, he concluded, was a "natural," not a miraculous, phenomenon, and religion itself was a fraud. Caught up in the restless reformism of the forties, he supported successively Mesmerism, Grahamism, and faith-healing, and

invented a faith of his own, which he called Panthetism. During his last years he became a leading exponent of "infidelity." To the confusion of the orthodox, who had hoped for a death-bed scene of despair if not of repentance, he died cheerfully and courageously facing an end which to him had no hereafter. He had been married, but his wife left him some time before his death; an obituary mentions several grandchildren (*Christian Advocate,* June 4, 1885).

Sunderland was a prolific writer in many fields, but only his editorial writings and a few of his tracts had any significance: one published sermon, "This Life a Time of Probation" (first printed in the *Methodist Preacher,* September 1830); an early plea for theological education (*Methodist Magazine and Quarterly Review,* October 1834); and the famous "Appeal on the Subject of Slavery." His *Panthetism . . . An Essay Toward a Correct Theory of Mind* (1847), *Book of Psychology* (1853), *Book of Human Nature* (1853), and *Ideology* (1885), contain some autobiographical information and reveal the trend of his thought.

[Sources include *Zion's Herald,* 1823–42, and issues of Apr. 22, June 3, 1885; *Christian Advocate,* 1837–42, and issues of May 28, June 4, June 11, 1885; *Zion's Watchman,* 1836–43; James Mudge, *Hist. of the New England Conference* (1910); Sunderland's tracts and books. His *Book of Human Nature,* p. x, is authority for date of birth given above; *Christian Advocate,* May 28, 1885, gives May 18, 1802.]

G. H. B.

SURRATT, JOHN H. (b. 1844) [See BOOTH, JOHN WILKES, 1838–1865].

SURRATT, MARY E. (1820–1865) [See BOOTH, JOHN WILKES, 1838–1865].

SUTHERLAND, JOEL BARLOW (Feb. 26, 1792–Nov. 15, 1861), congressman, was born at Clonmel, Gloucester County, N. J., the son of Daniel and Jane Sutherland, Scotch immigrants. He attended common schools and graduated (1812) from the University of Pennsylvania Medical School, enlisted in the War of 1812 as assistant surgeon in the "Junior Artillerists of Philadelphia," and before the end of the war became a lieutenant-colonel of rifles in the state militia. While the conflict was still in progress he entered politics and was elected to the Pennsylvania Assembly as an insurgent Democratic-Republican three successive times, 1813–15. When war ardors had somewhat cooled, the voters forced him to return to medical practice and the none too pleasant duties of lazaretto physician at the port of Philadelphia. On Apr. 13, 1815, he married Mary Read.

He still thirsted for politics, however, and, concluding that law would aid him more than medicine in his striving, he studied law and was admitted to the bar, Mar. 30, 1819. In two years he was back in the legislature, serving in the lower house until 1825; during the last year of his service he was speaker. In 1822 and 1824 he had been defeated for Congress but in 1826 he was elected both to that body and to the state Senate. He sat in the Senate through one session and then resigned to enter Congress in December 1827. He retained his seat for five terms, interspersing periods in Washington with legal work in Philadelphia as deputy prosecuting attorney for the county, 1830, 1832, 1833, and associate judge of the court of common pleas, 1833–34. In 1835 he sent his resignation from Congress to the governor, to enter upon a longer term as judge of the common pleas, but for some reason the resignation did not take effect and he remained in the House. There as in the legislature he proved himself specially adept at persuading his fellow members in private conversation to vote for his measures, but he was also a good debater and skilful in parliamentary procedure. He wrote a *Manual of Legislative Practice and Order of Business in Deliberative Bodies* (1827), to be used in state legislatures, which went into a fifth edition as late as 1853, and a *Congressional Manual* (1839). In 1831 he received fifty-four votes in opposition to Andrew W. Stevenson, the successful candidate for speaker. As member and chairman of the committee on commerce he devoted himself to river and harbor development and to the promotion of Philadelphia projects, especially the navy yard and the Delaware Breakwater. Though he considered himself an enthusiastic Jacksonian, he was so loyal to Pennsylvania interests that he became an ardent protectionist and opposed Jackson on the Maysville road veto and the veto of the bill rechartering the United States Bank. Because of these heresies he was defeated in 1836 by another Democrat and when he ran again in 1838, on the Whig ticket, he was once more defeated.

No preferment came his way thereafter except indirectly, by the appointment of two of his sons to the army and marine corps and one to the civil service. He maintained a law practice, served on the board of trustees of Jefferson Medical College (latterly as its president), and was first president of the Society of the War of 1812. He seems to have been dynamic, brilliant, and impulsive without possessing much depth or a great amount of tact or good judgment.

[A son, Charles Sutherland, prepared *Memoir of Joel Barlow Sutherland* (n.d, n.p.). See also J. T. Scharf and Thompson Westcott, *Hist. of Phila.* (1884), vols. I, II; *Phila. Inquirer*, Nov. 18, 1861; *Biog. Dir. Am. Cong.* (1928). A number of his letters are in the Buchanan MSS. and the George Wolf MSS. in the Hist. Soc. of Pa.]

R. F. N.

SUTRO, ADOLPH HEINRICH JOSEPH (Apr. 29, 1830–Aug. 8, 1898), mining engineer, bibliophile, mayor of San Francisco, was born in Aix-la-Chapelle, Prussia, of Jewish parentage. His father, a cloth manufacturer, died in 1847, and the Prussian revolution of the following year ruined the business. Consequently his mother with her seven sons and four daughters emigrated to America in 1850, settling in Baltimore. Fired by the gold discoveries in California, Adolph set out for the Pacific Coast via Panama, and arrived in San Francisco in November 1851. For the next nine years he was engaged in mercantile pursuits in that city and in Stockton.

In 1860 he was drawn to Nevada by interest in the great bonanza strike. He established a quartz-reducing mill at East Dayton, where he worked over the tailings of other mills by a new process of amalgamation and thus laid the foundation of his later fortune. Impressed by the old-fashioned and inefficient mining methods then employed in the region of the Comstock lode, he conceived the idea of driving a tunnel ten feet high, twelve feet wide, and some three miles long, with lateral branches bringing the total length to over five miles, into Mount Davidson from Carson River to the Comstock lode, to provide ventilation, drainage, and an easy means of transporting men and materials to and from the mines. "He employed journalists to explain the advantage of the tunnel, civil engineers to examine the country and locate the line, and geologists to report on the mineral character of the Comstock lode and the country rock" (Hittell, *post*, p. 413). He then formed the Sutro Tunnel Company; obtained, on Apr. 4, 1865, a charter from the Nevada legislature; and persuaded mine owners to sign contracts to pay the company two dollars per ton for all ore mined after the opening of the tunnel for their use. A coterie connected with the Bank of California in San Francisco gave him their support and helped to get through Congress (July 25, 1866) an act which granted Sutro and his associates the right of way through the public lands crossed by the tunnel, and several incidental franchises.

Shortly thereafter Sutro's California supporters turned against him, their object being to get control of the tunnel and thereby reap the immense profits which were anticipated. With indomitable perseverance he first sought, in vain, the aid of New York capitalists; then, in 1867, he went to Europe and visited a dozen countries and their mines, studying their tunnels, consulting their engineers, and obtaining indorsement for his own plans. In 1868 he published *The Mineral Resources of the United States and the Importance and Necessity of Inaugurating a Rational System of Mining with Special Reference to the Comstock Lode and the Sutro Tunnel in Nevada.* In Europe and from subscriptions by enthusiastic Nevada miners, he secured the initial funds with which to begin work in October 1869. Nine years later, at a cost of about $6,500,000, including interest, the tunnel was completed to the Comstock lode, and its opening marked the beginning of a new era in western mining.

The project proved immediately and immensely profitable. In 1879 Sutro sold his interest and returned to San Francisco, where he invested his tunnel profits in real estate, at one time owning one-twelfth of the acreage in San Francisco city and county. In the early eighties he bought the Cliff House and a thousand acres of land in the vicinity fronting on the ocean—Sutro Heights. In 1892 he began construction of the enormous Sutro salt-water baths, costing nearly a million dollars, and forming, when completed, the finest bathing pavilion then in existence. In 1894 he was elected mayor of San Francisco on the Populist ticket, and during his two-year term was constantly in strife with the board of supervisors and the railways operating within the city.

Sutro was deeply interested in the beginnings of science and of the art of printing, and ransacked Europe for *incunabula* of printing and block engraving. He collected a library of over 200,000 rare volumes, mainly of scientific and technical works, about half of which were destroyed in the fire of 1906. The balance now forms a part of the San Francisco Public Library. Although giving away much in unostentatious charity, he left an estate valued at about $3,000,000, which was divided among the four daughters and two sons who survived him. His wife, Leah Harris, whom he married in 1856, had died in 1893.

[*San Francisco Chronicle,* Aug. 9, 1898, Apr. 4, 1933; *San Francisco Call,* Aug. 9, 1898; H. H. Bancroft, *Chronicles of the Builders,* IV (1892), 195–97; G. W. James, *Heroes of Cal.* (1910); E. K. Holmes, *Adolph Sutro* (1895); *San Francisco: Its Builders, Past and Present* (1913), I, 53–62; S. P. Davis, *The Hist. of Nev.* (1913), I, 399–405; J. P. Young, *San Francisco* (1912), I, 385–86, II, 570, 805; J. S. Hittell, *The Commerce and Industries of the Pacific Coast* (2nd ed., 1882), pp. 413–14; "Report of the Commission to Examine and Report Upon the Sutro Tunnel, in Nevada," *Sen. Ex. Doc. No. 15,* 42 Cong., 2 Sess. (1872).]

P. O. R.

SUTTER, JOHN AUGUSTUS (February 1803–June 18, 1880), adventurer and colonist, originally named Johann August Suter, was born in Kandern, Baden. The facts regarding his ancestry and early life are obscure; his own statements were untruthful and contradictory. His parents are said to have been Johann Jakob Suter, a paper manufacturer, and Christine Wilhelmine (Stoberin), daughter of a clergyman (Dana, *post,* pp. 1–2). A part of his youth was spent in the village of Rünenberg, Basel Canton, Switzerland; he is said to have attended the military academy at Neuchâtel (*Ibid.,* p. 3); it is certain that he was officially recognized as a Swiss citizen and that he served his time in the Swiss army, possibly attaining the rank of captain. In 1826 he married Anna (or Annette) Dübeld (or Dubelt), by whom he had three sons and a daughter. After a number of escapades, he decamped from Berne in the spring of 1834, made his way to Havre, and sailed for America. He landed in New York, journeyed to St. Louis, Mo., and may have settled for a time at St. Charles. In 1835 and again in 1836 he accompanied a trading party to Santa Fé. In 1838 he accompanied the Eells-Walker missionary party to Oregon, arriving at Fort Vancouver in October. Eager to reach California, and finding the land journey impossible at that season, he sailed for Honolulu and then for Sitka, whence he was enabled to reach San Francisco Bay on July 1, 1839. Four days later, at Monterey, he presented to Governor Alvarado a project for establishing a colony on the unknown frontier to the north. Alvarado empowered him to select a tract, with the promise that in a year's time a grant would be made. On the south bank of the American River, at its junction with the Sacramento, Sutter landed a small party about Aug. 16. Indians from the former missions were employed; land was cleared; irrigating ditches were dug; grain was sown, orchards and vineyards were planted, and in time a fortified post was erected. To his colony he gave the name of Nueva Helvetia. In June 1841, on a second visit to Alvarado, he was made a Mexican citizen, and a grant of eleven square leagues of land was given to him.

His success was phenomenal. He rapidly built up a vast baronial estate, and though nominally a Mexican subject was virtually the independent ruler of his domain. For military aid given to Governor Micheltorena an additional grant of twenty-two square leagues of land was given him (Feb. 5, 1845). About this time he began to be hailed as "General" Sutter. He befriended the early American settlers drifting into the country, and his settlement became the rallying place for those who favored an uprising against the Mexican government; but on June 14, 1846, Frémont, suspicious of his attitude, seized his fort. Later it was restored to him, and with the conquest of

Sutter

California his fortunes seemed secure. In 1849 he was a delegate to the convention which drafted the state constitution; he presided at its last session, and was a candidate for the governorship at the first election. His son, John A. Sutter, Jr., had joined him at the end of 1844 and in 1851 his wife and the remaining children followed.

Meanwhile, however, the discovery of gold on his estate, Jan. 24, 1848, had marked the beginning of his ruin. His workmen deserted him; his flocks and herds disappeared, and squatters settled upon his lands. By 1852 he was bankrupt. Later the United States Supreme Court, while invalidating his claim to the Micheltorena tract, confirmed the earlier grant, but he could not afford the litigation necessary to recover his property. In 1864, the California legislature voted him a pension of $250 a month, which was continued until 1878. In 1865 his homestead on the Feather River was destroyed by fire. Late in that year he went to Washington, where he submitted a petition to Congress. By 1871 he had established a home in the Moravian village of Lititz, Lancaster County, Pa., though he spent his winters in Washington. In 1876 and again in 1880 bills for his relief were favorably reported in the House of Representatives, and on June 11 of the latter year a joint resolution in his behalf was introduced in the Senate, but immediately ordered to lie on the table. A week later, at Mades' Hotel, he died. His widow survived him by seven months, dying on Jan. 19, 1881.

Sutter was short and fat, with a broad head, and, in his maturity, a bald crown fringed with flaxen, graying hair. His manner was genial and at times expansive. His character and attainments have been variously estimated. Bancroft, whose personal judgments were often extreme, concedes him no merit but kindliness, and says that he was without ability, honor, truthfulness, or respect for the rights of others. A recent biography of him, by Julian Dana, is fervently eulogistic. By reason of his unique career, his vicissitudes of fortune, and his long and futile struggle for justice, he remains one of the most appealing figures in American history.

[See the summary in H. H. Bancroft, *Hist. of Cal.* (1886), V, 738–40, and bibliog. data, *Ibid.*, IV, 122–39; T. J. Schoonover, *The Life and Times of Gen. John A. Sutter* (1895); *The Diary of Johann August Sutter* (1932), with Intro. by D. S. Watson; *A Nation's Benefactor: Gen'l John A. Sutter . . . An Appeal* (1880); "Petition of John A. Sutter," *Sen. Misc. Doc.* 38, 39 Cong., 1 Sess. (1866); *Memorial of John A. Sutter to the Senate and House of Representatives of the U. S.* (1876); J. B. Landis, "The Life and Work of Gen. John A. Sutter," *Papers Read before the Lancaster County Hist. Soc.*, vol. XVII, no. 10 (1913); W. H. Davis, *Seventy-five Years in Cal.* (1929); Julian Dana, *Sutter of Cal.* (1934); *Evening Star* (Washington, D. C.), June 19, 1880. Blaise Cendrars, *L'Or* (trans.

Sutton

as *Sutter's Gold,* 1926) is a highly romantic treatment. The day of Sutter's birth is given variously as Feb. 8, 15, 23, and 28, 1803.]   W. J. G.

SUTTON, WILLIAM SENECA (Aug. 12, 1860–Nov. 26, 1928), educator, was born in Fayetteville, Ark., the son of James Tillton and Francena Lavinia (Martin) Sutton. His father was a merchant; his mother, for many years, was a teacher in the preparatory department of the Arkansas Industrial University (now the University of Arkansas). From this young and struggling institution, Sutton received the bachelor of arts' degree at the early age of eighteen.

Intending to study law, he taught a country school for a year and discovered the vocation that had much the strongest appeal for him. For a year he was a school principal at Fayetteville, at the end of which time he became superintendent. In 1883 he went to Ennis, Tex., as principal; on June 12, 1884, he married Annie Blackman Erwin, by whom he had two children. He was made principal of the Houston high school in 1886 and in the following year succeeded to the superintendency of the Houston schools. In this office he served with conspicuous success until 1897, when he was called to the headship of the school of education in the University of Texas. Here he was dean and founder of the Summer School, 1898–1918, dean of education, 1909–28; and acting president, 1923–24. He was a skilful teacher and administrator and a leader in the broadening of the curriculum and degree requirements and in establishing intimate relations with the high schools through a system of affiliation.

His influence was felt throughout Texas. In connection with the State Teachers' Association, of which he was president in 1896, he worked for higher personal and professional qualifications in teachers, and for better support for all schools. He was effective in securing better school laws, and was the founder of a Conference on Education that for a series of years caused many leading citizens to take much greater and more informed interest in education. He was honest, constructive, far-seeing, tolerant, good-humored in debate. Hating class spirit and sectarianism, animated by a genuinely democratic sympathy, he could speak with a homely and friendly effectiveness. In collaboration with W. H. Kimbrough and W. H. Bruce, he prepared a series of arithmetics; with P. W. Horn, he wrote *Schoolroom Essentials* (copyright 1911). In 1913 he published *Problems in Modern Education,* and, between 1891 and 1924, about forty articles on a wide variety of topics. A prolonged and emaciating sickness clouded his last years. He is buried in the State Cemetery at Austin.

[F. Eby and others, *In Memory of William Seneca Sutton* (1930), a record of exercises dedicating Sutton Hall at the Univ. of Tex.; *Who's Who in America*, 1926–27; records of Texas Teachers' Asso. and the Univ. of Tex.; *Dallas Morning News*, Nov. 27, 1928.]
                                        H. Y. B.

SUZZALLO, HENRY (Aug. 22, 1875–Sept. 25, 1933), teacher and educational leader, began an address on the Anglo-Saxon tradition at a luncheon of the Pilgrims in London on May 29, 1931, with the statement that there was not a drop of Anglo-Saxon blood in his veins. Yet there was not a thought in his mind, he said, nor an aspiration in his heart, which was not a part of this same tradition, a tradition which was brought to him, the son of immigrants from the Adriatic, through the American system of public education. His paternal grandfather was a native of Herzegovina. His father, Peter, who was born in the Adriatic port town of Ragusa (now Dubrovnick), followed a family tradition by taking to the sea as a boy. Later he spent some years in the California gold fields. At forty he returned to Ragusa to marry a distant cousin, Anne Zucalo (another form of the family name) and took his bride back to California. After various vicissitudes, the family settled in San José, where Anthony Henry was born, the eighth of nine children, only four of whom lived to maturity.

The family had small means, and the boy had to work after school hours. His opportunity for a higher education was due in large measure to the kindly interest of two local business men, Emil and Jesse Levy, who gave him employment, encouraged him in his ambitions, and advanced money when necessary. His school record was not remarkable, partly owing to rather delicate health, partly to calls of outside work, and partly to lack of interest. At any rate, he was not admitted directly to Stanford University, newly established in the neighboring town of Palo Alto, but had first to complete the program of the local normal school, earning his way there and throughout the long period of his professional preparation by teaching. At Stanford, where he entered in the fall of 1895, Suzzallo found himself. The faculty was young and enthusiastic, and a high proportion of his fellow-students were destined to make their mark in later life. Despite the outside calls upon him, which included a year's leave of absence as principal of a rural school, his academic record was brilliant and he took an active part in student affairs. Although he had earlier wavered between medicine and the law, he was now in no doubt as to the future.

Practical success as a teacher and principal, and, it is said, conflict with unenlightened school authorities, had turned him definitely toward education as a profession.

Following his graduation in 1899 came full-packed years of combined teaching, educational administration, and further study. In the San Francisco public-school system, Henry Suzzallo (he had dropped the Anthony) rose rapidly to the deputy superintendency, serving in that capacity for five months of each year. This arrangement made it possible for him to rise meanwhile (1902) to an assistant professorship in education at Stanford, and to complete the requirements at Columbia University for the master's degree in 1902 and the doctor's degree in 1905. In 1907 he went to New York as adjunct professor of education at Teachers College, Columbia University, and two years later was promoted to the professorship of educational sociology. While holding this professorship he served for a time as acting dean of Teachers College. In addition to his regular teaching duties at Stanford and Columbia, he taught for shorter periods at other universities, including Chicago, California, and Yale.

In 1915 he was elected to the presidency of the University of Washington, at Seattle. The period of his tenure was one of rapid development for American state universities, and in this development Washington had its full share. Though standards of admission and graduation were steadily advanced, the enrollment was more than doubled during these years, and the number of degrees granted annually was nearly trebled. A general plan for campus development was adopted and ten academic buildings were erected, four of them by private gift. State support for general maintenance was more than trebled and the salary scale for professors doubled. Perhaps Suzzallo's outstanding contribution was his success in coordinating the services of the university with the needs of the state. He entered promptly into the life of the community. He became a member of the state Board of Education and served in many other capacities. With the entry of the United States into the World War, he was plunged in a new set of responsibilities. In June 1917 he became chairman of the state Council of Defense, later a representative of the Shipping Board in the Northwest, adviser to the War Labor Policy Board, and a wage umpire for the National War Labor Board at Washington. He was mediator and conciliator in more than fifty strikes affecting war efficiency. During an extended illness of the Governor, he was in fact, if not in title, the governor of the state.

The steps leading to his removal from the presidency of the University in 1926 are too complicated for recital here. The issues were personal and political rather than educational. Though both the state legislature and the University regents were involved in the controversy, the real issue lay between the recently elected governor, Roland H. Hartley, and Suzzallo. The two men had come into sharp conflict some years before, during the latter's war service and when the former was active in the lumber industry, over the question of the eight-hour day, and it is generally believed that this had much to do with the later difficulties. Suffice it to say that the Governor's action in removing him from office, after he had declined to resign without the filing of specific charges, aroused nationwide discussion, but never even threatened Suzzallo's standing as an educator or as a citizen. Certainly there was no lack of opportunity for him to serve elsewhere. On leaving Washington he was in constant demand. Though he could have chosen from a number of college and university presidencies, he preferred to return to his old chair at Teachers College. He also organized a study of graduate instruction throughout the United States. In 1927 he served as visiting professor of the Carnegie Endowment for International Peace at Vienna and Budapest, and spent some time in the land of his forefathers, Dalmatia. In 1929 he was called to Washington to act as director of the National Advisory Committee on Education, in charge of the preparation of a report to the president of the United States, financed by a grant of $100,000 from the Rosenwald Fund.

Suzzallo had, in 1919, become a trustee of the Carnegie Foundation for the Advancement of Teaching, and during 1926–27 had served as chairman of the board. Upon the retirement of Dr. Henry S. Pritchett in 1930, he was elected to the presidency of the Foundation. His position made him, *ex officio,* a trustee of the Carnegie Corporation, and in the three years which remained to him he became one of the most influential trustees of the larger foundation. The work of preparing the report of the National Advisory Committee carried on into the first months of his presidency (*Federal Relations to Education. Report of the National Advisory Committee on Education,* 2 parts, 1931). His next important task was the personal direction of a study of higher education in the state of California, which the state government had invited the Carnegie Foundation to make (*State Higher Education in California. Report of the Carnegie Foundation for the Advancement of Teaching,* 1932). The economic depression having meanwhile created a critical situation, he was called to make a study in several regions of the possibilities of drastic economies without loss of essential efficiency in the conduct of systems of higher education.

To follow the central thread of his career is not to tell the whole story. He was a man of wide-ranging interests, with quick enthusiasms and an instinctive readiness to do his full share of any work to be done. His boyhood days, spent in the beautiful Santa Clara Valley, with summer holidays by the sea at Monterey, bred in him a lifelong appreciation of beauty in all its forms. It is characteristic that his first graduate work was done in the field of esthetics, and that years later he was responsible for building up a department of fine arts at the University of Washington, and for stimulating a community interest in the arts in Seattle. After returning to New York in 1930, he played an active part in developing the art program of the Carnegie Corporation. He was always interested in political affairs, and unusually well-informed as to political conditions. If he could have satisfied the technical requirements as to residence, it is said that he would have been nominated and elected "reform" mayor of San Francisco in 1906. Later on he served as a member of the committee on plans and platforms of the Republican National Committee. His services in the Northwest were perforce largely political, though never partisan. He was deeply concerned with ethical and religious questions, but his interest was not of the type to fit any denominational pattern. Reared in the faith of his fathers, Roman Catholicism, he early found himself more in sympathy with Protestantism, but though he attended the services of the Episcopal Church, he never joined its membership. His marriage, Feb. 8, 1912, to Edith Moore, a graduate of the University of Chicago, inaugurated an unusually close companionship. Since there were no children Mrs. Suzzallo could accompany him on his journeys, and wherever his duties might temporarily call him she established a home.

Even an incomplete list of the organizations in which he played an active part will indicate something of the calls upon his time in addition to his regular professional responsibilities. In the field of education the institutions which he served, either as officer or member of the governing or advisory board, include the National Education Association, the American Council on Education, the Association of State Universities, the Institute of International Education, the American Association for Adult Education, the Educational Research Committee of the Commonwealth Fund, the Cleveland Conference. At different times he served as trustee of Stevens Institute of Technology, as visitor to the United States Naval Academy, as editor of the *Journal of Educational Sociology,* and was active in nursing, pharmaceutical, religious, and other vocational studies. He also rendered special advisory services to the Universities of Wyoming, Denver, and Omaha, to Colorado College, and to the systems of higher education in Georgia and Oregon. In 1900 he became editor of the Riverside Educational Monographs which now include more than seventy titles, and a little later, the editor of the Houghton-Mifflin Educational Classics (6 vols.). After leaving the University of Washington, he undertook the editorship-in-chief of Collier's *The National Encyclopaedia* (10 vols., 1932). Besides several textbooks and numerous articles of a professional and general character, he is the author of *Our Faith in Education* (1924).

While all these interests and activities took their toll, perhaps the heaviest inroads upon what should have been his leisure came from incessant invitations to lecture both on educational and upon more general subjects. His lectures took him all over the country, enlarged the circle of his friends, extended his influence, and contributed to his unusual knowledge of social and political conditions throughout the United States. But these excursions meant a steady depletion of his reserves of strength. It was not until after the successive and heavy demands of the National Advisory Committee on Education and the California study that he realized that his health had become seriously impaired. He was persuaded to devote the summer of 1933 to rest and relaxation in California. The lightening of the load had come too late, however; he and Mrs. Suzzallo started to make their return trip by way of Canada, but on the voyage to Seattle his heart showed disquieting symptoms. He was taken directly to the Seattle General Hospital upon landing, and six days later, on Sept. 25, 1933, he died in the city where he had achieved some of his signal successes and had suffered his greatest disappointment. Had he lived a few days longer, he would have heard of the adoption by the regents of the University of a resolution designating the central building of the campus as the Henry Suzzallo Library. Since the death of Charles W. Eliot, probably the closing of no educational career attracted such widespread attention or evoked such appreciative editorial comment.

The first results of the two major surveys to which he devoted himself so unreservedly were disappointing. He failed to obtain the unanimous support of the National Advisory Committee on Education, minority reports being filed by the heads of negro institutions and by Roman Catholic educators; and public and political attention was directed almost wholly to a reference in the majority report to the ultimate desirability of giving education a place in the president's cabinet, to the neglect of recommendations of more immediate significance. The influence of the report grew steadily, however, and has been shown in great improvements in the educational service for the Indians and in the merger of the hitherto independent Board of Vocational Education with the federal Office of Education. The immediate effect of the publication of the California study seemed to be to accentuate the conflict of authority and influence between the state Board of Education and the regents of the University, but since Suzzallo's death the legislature has followed one of its chief recommendations in the creation of the state Council for Educational Planning and Coordination. The recommendations of the Commission (Part Two of the California report), written by Suzzallo himself, provide what might be called a charter of higher education for the country as a whole; and both reports set forth basic principles and make suggestions as to the elimination of duplication and other desirable and practicable economies.

In the judgment of those who knew him best, Henry Suzzallo will be remembered as an outstanding figure in his generation, not as a scholar, though his scholarship was sound and he made important contributions to educational sociology—a new field in which his alert and agile mind played over a wide range; not as a teacher in the ordinary sense of the term, though his classrooms were always overcrowded; not as an administrator, though his accomplishments at Seattle and elsewhere were distinguished. It will be rather as a man of many talents, of broad sympathies and interests who retained to the end of his life the curiosities and enthusiasms of his youth. His ability to enter immediately into an understanding with those with whom he came into contact and to share with them his own interests and sympathies had much to do with the influence he exerted. It was said of him that he never taught a subject, but always a student, and that what he taught, not only in the classroom but also on the lecture platform and through his writings, was a broad social and intellectual tolerance and a realizing sense of the place of education in a modern democracy.

[*The Carnegie Foundation for the Advancement of Teaching. . . . Ann. Reports of the President and the Treasurer,* 1931–33; *Henry Suzzallo, 1875–1933* (1934).

report of memorial meeting at Teachers College, Dec. 18, 1933; for the Hartley controversy, *N. Y. Times,* Oct. 6, 7, 1926, and *Seattle Daily Times,* beginning Oct. 5, 1926; obituaries in *Seattle Daily Times,* Sept. 25, 1933; *Seattle Post Intelligencer* and *N. Y. Times,* Sept. 26, 1933; *School and Society,* Sept. 30, 1933; family papers and personal acquaintance.]   F. P. K.

SVERDRUP, GEORG (Dec. 16, 1848–May 3, 1907), theologian, educator, the son of Harald Ulrik and Karoline Metella (Suur) Sverdrup, was born at Balestrand near Bergen, Norway. His father was a clergyman and for many years a member of the Storthing; his uncle Johan was for a generation the leader of the political liberals in the Storthing and prime minister of Norway from 1884 to 1889. One of his brothers likewise was a member of the Storthing. He received a classical education in the Nissen Cathedral School in Christiania and was graduated in theology from Christiania University in 1871. He then studied Semitics in the University of Paris, where he came to know Sven Oftedal [*q.v.*], and visited several German universities. In 1874 he left Norway to become professor of theology in Augsburg Seminary, in Minneapolis, Minn., where he taught for thirty-three years. From 1876 he was president of the institution.

A conservative eclectic Lutheran, with wholesome liberal leanings, Sverdrup's special fields were the Old Testament and dogmatics. As a practical churchman—he had no desire to be ordained—he stressed "Spirit and Life" over against dead orthodoxy and congregational inactivity. His peculiar view in the field of church polity that the local church is the right form of the Kingdom of God was followed by the Norwegian Lutheran Conference, 1869–90, and specifically adopted by its heir, the Norwegian Lutheran Free Church, whose moderator he was for several years. These bodies thus deviated from the well-grounded doctrine of the Lutheran Church that church polity is an adiaphoron. To Sverdrup the state church conception of church, of ministry, and of ministerial education was highly objectionable. Through Augsburg Seminary he wished to resurrect what he claimed to be the New Testament idea of *ekklesia* and to educate a democratic ministry. He regarded the organized local congregation of believers as the only quantity entitled to the name of church. All other so-called ecclesiastical organizations such as council, synod, state church, were purely human. He stressed lay preaching as the chief charism, a complement to the public ministry, which he regarded as highly necessary, but not as a *jure divino* institution. In liturgy, he was a low churchman.

Sverdrup championed congregationalistic ideas, which he called "free church ideas," in the lecture room, on the floor of synod, and in the press. He was a brilliant lecturer, a keen dialectician, schooled in Plato and Hegel, a resourceful parliamentarian, and a writer of clear and forceful Norwegian, the preferred language of his church body. He was an able linguist of extraordinary training, and a scholar of the first water. He was joint editor of *Theologisk Kvartalskrift* from 1875 to 1881, and sole editor, 1877–81; joint editor of *Lutheraneren,* a church weekly, 1885–90; joint editor of its successor, *Luthersk Kirkeblad,* 1890–94; and editor of *Gasseren,* a monthly on foreign missions in Madagascar, 1900–07. His ecclesiastico-political organ was *Folkebladet,* a weekly newspaper to which he was a continuous contributor for a generation, being for some time part owner and editor. A considerable amount of the material contributed by Sverdrup to these periodicals and his introduction to the Old and New Testament are published in Sverdrup's *Samlede Skrifter i Udvalg,* edited by Andreas Helland (1909–12). Some of his sermons were published under the title *Aand og Liv* in 1897. He was active on many church boards, especially those handling foreign missions and deaconess work sponsored by Norwegian-Americans. Due to his influence they entered upon deaconess work in the West and missions in Madagascar.

Sverdrup was twice married: to Kathrine Elisabet Heiberg in 1874, and, three years after her death in 1887, to her sister Elise Susanna Heiberg. He was survived by his widow, five children of his first wife, and two of his second.

[*Who's Who in America,* 1906–07; Andreas Helland, *Augsburg Seminar gjennem femti aar 1869–1909* (1920); J. O. Evjen, *Veiledning i Den lutherske Frikirkes Principer* (1914), an article on Sverdrup in Herzog-Hauck, *Realencyklopaedie für protestantische Theologie und Kirche,* vol. XXIV (3rd ed., 1913), and one on the Lutheran Free Church in *Distinctive Doctrines and Usages of the General Bodies of the Evangelical Luth. Ch. in the U. S.* (4th ed., 1914); discussions in the papers: *Indremissionsvennen,* 1930–32, *Reform,* 1932–33, and *Skandinaven,* 1932–33. Consult also articles on Erik K. Johnsen, Friedrich A. Schmidt, and Hans G. Stub in the *Dict. of Am. Biog.; Minneapolis Tribune,* May 4, 1907.]   J. O. E.

SWAIN, CLARA A. (July 18, 1834–Dec. 25, 1910), pioneer woman medical missionary in India, was born in Elmira, N. Y., the youngest of the ten children of John and Clarissa (Seavey) Swain. When she was two years old her parents returned to their former home in Castile, N. Y., where she spent her early life. Her education, received chiefly in schools of the neighborhood, was broken by periods of teaching. Finally, when she was twenty-two or more, she secured a position in the public schools of Canandaigua, in the seminary of which town she had just finished a year's course. As a young girl she had shown aptitude for nursing, and though she continued to teach for some time, she all the while harbored the desire of becoming a physician. At length she began a three-year course of training in the Castile Sanitarium, under Dr. Cordelia A. Greene. Upon its completion she entered the Woman's Medical College in Philadelphia, from which she graduated in 1869.

Just at this time there was a call for a trained person who could inaugurate medical instruction and care for women in India. Appeal was made to the Woman's Medical College, and Clara Swain was recommended. Interested in religious work and an active member of the Methodist Episcopal Church, she consented to undertake the mission, and, sponsored by the Woman's Foreign Missionary Society of her denomination, she sailed from New York, with Isabella Thoburn [q.v.], on Nov. 3, 1869. On Jan. 20, 1870, she arrived in Bareilly, which was the seat of her labors for more than fourteen years, though from 1876 to 1879 she was in the United States because of ill health. She is said to have been the first fully accredited woman physician to be sent by any missionary society to the non-Christian world. She became associated with the girls' orphanage at Bareilly, and at once started a medical class of fourteen native girls, thirteen of whom in April 1873 passed examinations before two civil surgeons and a missionary and were granted certificates authorizing them to practise "in all ordinary diseases." She also carried on a large practice among the women and children of the city, treating them both at the mission and in their homes. In 1871 the Nawab of Rampore gave an estate adjoining the mission property as a site for a hospital for women. A dispensary building was completed in May 1873, and in January 1874 the first woman's hospital in India was opened. Miss Swain continued her work at Bareilly until March 1885, when at the request of the Rajah of Khetri, Rajputana, she became physician to the Rani and the ladies of the palace. She served in this capacity for more than ten years, spending an eighteen-month furlough in the United States (1888–89). In 1896 she returned to Castile, which was her home until her death. In 1906–08 she revisited India, primarily to attend the jubilee of the founding of the Methodist mission there in 1856. A collection of her letters entitled *A Glimpse of India* was published in 1909; it tells the story of her work and gives an interesting picture of various aspects of Indian life.

[In addition to the above, see Mrs. Robert (Charlotte L. R.) Hoskins, *Clara A. Swain, M.D.* (1912); Mrs. J. T. Gracey, *Medical Work of the Woman's Foreign Missionary Soc., M. E. Church* (1881); and *Eminent Missionary Women* (1898); J. S. Dennis, *Christian Missions and Social Progress*, vols. I, II (1897); *Christian Advocate* (N. Y.), Jan. 5, 1911. Exact date of birth was furnished by the Rev. D. F. Eggleston, Castile, N. Y.]

H. E. S.

SWAIN, DAVID LOWRY (Jan. 4, 1801–Aug. 27, 1868), governor of North Carolina, college president, was born in Buncombe County, N. C. His father, George Swain, a native of Massachusetts and a man of some learning and much intelligence, had gone South in 1785, and, after service in the legislature and a constitutional convention of Georgia, had moved to North Carolina. He was a hatter by trade, ran a small farm, and for many years was postmaster of Asheville. There he married a widow, Caroline (Lane) Lowry. David, the second child, was taught at home until he was fifteen, and was then sent to school in Asheville. He entered the University of North Carolina in 1821 but remained only four months, leaving to begin the study of law in Raleigh. He was admitted to the bar late in 1822 and on Jan. 12, 1823 (Ashe, *post*) married Eleanor H. White of Raleigh.

He represented Buncombe in the House of Commons from 1824 to 1827, and from 1828 to 1829, when he became solicitor of an eastern district. Within a year he was a superior court judge, and, after two years, was elected governor, the youngest in the history of the state. Re-elected twice, he served from 1832 until 1835. In the latter year he was a member of the constitutional convention and was elected president of the University of North Carolina. In 1857 he was made a commissioner of the sinking fund and in 1861 was sent by the legislature to Montgomery, Ala., as one of a commission to represent the state near the Confederate government. A Union Whig, he did not believe in secession, but, after the call for troops, accepted it as a necessity. In 1863 Gov. Zebulon Vance [q.v.] wished to appoint him to the Confederate Senate that he might "modify and soften the present violent and desperate temper of Congress," but he declined. Throughout the war he was the constant and invaluable adviser of the governor. In April 1865 he went as a special commissioner to meet General Sherman on his approach to Raleigh and arrange favorable terms for the surrender of the state, and on Apr. 13, he surrendered the keys of the capitol to Sherman when he entered the town. The next month he was summoned by President Johnson to advise him as to reconstruction, and during the three years following he was consulted constantly by the

President and by Gov. Jonathan Worth [*q.v.*]. Johnson appointed him to the board of visitors of West Point and secured for the University of North Carolina its share of the public land allotted under the Morrill Act, but Congressional reconstruction resulted in the displacement of the trustees and faculty of the University and in virtual heartbreak for Swain; soon afterwards he was injured in a runaway accident and died within ten days.

In North Carolina history Swain was a constructive figure of first rank. An excellent lawyer and judge, he performed his greatest service as legislator and governor, effectively pressing forward the cause of tax reform, public education, internal improvements, and amendment of the constitution to put an end to the dangerous sectional controversy then existing. He had acquired by 1832 remarkable personal influence, and his messages—dynamic, and charged with telling facts presented in vigorous style—aroused the state. He induced the legislature to call the constitutional convention of 1835, and in it he led the western forces, which were bent on reform. A skilful politician, he was fair, patient, tactful, and yet perfectly frank; to him more than to anyone else belongs the credit of what the convention accomplished. He desired that the constitution be entirely rewritten, but, that being impossible, he favored every liberal reform proposed, advocating complete religious toleration, the reform of the system of representation, and popular election of the governor. He opposed the disfranchisement of free negroes. He spoke but seldom, doing his chief work off the floor, but when he raised his voice the convention listened. Occasionally he was fiery in speech, as when he warned the convention, "Unless our demands are granted, unless our wrongs are righted, we will rise like the strong man in his unshorn might and pull down the pillars of the political temple" (Ashe, *post*, p. 450).

Swain was also a constructive figure in a quite different sphere of activity. His choice as president of the University aroused much feeling in the faculty, one professor acidly remarking that the people of the state, having elected Swain to every office in their gift, were now sending him to the University to be educated. The trustees were wise in their choice, however, for he proved an excellent executive. He was a shrewd and able business man and the funds of the institution under his management increased largely. The student body was multiplied more than fourfold, and by 1860 included representatives from every Southern state and many Northern ones. The faculty was strengthened and enlarged. He pop-

ularized the institution until the state for the first time felt a consciousness of ownership. Teaching constitutional and international law, history, and moral science, he proved a rare teacher; though unconventional he had a dynamic personality and inspired his students with passion for public service. He established the North Carolina Historical Society with headquarters at the University and began there a notable collection of historical material. He founded the *University of North Carolina Magazine* and by his own contributions and those which he secured made it unique among college publications. In 1854 he was appointed the state's agent for the collection of historical material and began the work which resulted years later in the publication of the *Colonial and State Records*. With Francis L. Hawks [*q.v.*] he projected a documentary history of the state, which project was stopped by the war. He published several valuable historical monographs, the best known being "The British Invasion of North Carolina in 1776" (*University of North Carolina Magazine,* May 1853). During the Civil War by heroic efforts he kept the University open, delaying the conscription of students and carefully husbanding its diminishing resources. The war swept away the endowment, however, and only Swain's resourcefulness made it possible for the institution to continue in operation until 1868.

He was tall and heavy with a grotesquely ugly figure and ungraceful carriage. His voice was harsh, hollow, and high-keyed, but these defects were soon forgotten in the charm of his conversation. In temperament he was cautious and politic; in manner, suave and mild; but, as his political career showed, he had an abundance of fighting spirit. He was a genuine liberal, and so wise in counsel that he was kept in close touch with public life by those who sought his advice.

[Z. B. Vance, *Life and Character of Hon. David Lowry Swain* (1878); R. D. W. Connor, *Ante-Bellum Builders of N. C.* (1914); S. A. Ashe, *Biog. Hist. of N. C.,* vol. I (1905); *Proc. and Debates of the Convention of N. C. . . . 1835* (1836); *N. C. Legislative Jours.*; K. P. Battle, *Hist. of the Univ. of N. C.* (1907); W. J. Peele, *Lives of Distinguished North Carolinians* (1898); *Daily North Carolina Standard* (Raleigh), Aug. 28, 1868; *New-England Hist. and Geneal. Register,* Oct. 1870; Swain Papers in possession of the Univ. of N. C.]   J. G. deR. H.

SWAIN, JAMES BARRETT (July 30, 1820– May 27, 1895), journalist, was the son of Joseph and Jerusha (Everts) Swain of New York City and a descendant of Jeremiah Swain who was living in Charlestown, Mass., as early as 1638. After the usual schooling and apprenticeship, his newspaper work was begun on the ephemeral Harrison organ, *The Log Cabin,* published by

Horace Greeley in 1840. While running a private printing establishment in the succeeding years, he found time to publish *The Life and Speeches of Henry Clay* (Greeley & McElrath, 1843), the "Life" consisting of an unimportant memoir in the first volume. After this he was successively owner of the *Hudson River Chronicle* (1844–49), a small sheet published at Sing Sing; assistant on Greeley's *New York Tribune*; independent printer; city editor on the fledgling *New York Times* (1852); then the *Times* correspondent at Albany, writing under the name of Leo. From 1855 to 1857 he turned for the moment to the very different occupation of state railroad commissioner—one of three—but meanwhile found time to establish the *Free State Advocate* (1856) and the *Albany Statesman* (1857) in the interests of Frémont, both short-lived publications. In 1860 he was again representing the *Times,* in Washington. One of his real accomplishments in the newspaper field was the introduction of the correspondent system, extensively used before the day of the great newsgathering agencies.

Caught in the tide of war, he received an appointment as second lieutenant, and later as first, with authority to raise a regiment of cavalry. By May 1862, the ranks of "Scotts 900," as he called it, officially known as the 11th New York, were filled, and, newly commissioned colonel (Apr. 30), he conducted it to Camp Relief at Meridian Hill, Washington, named in honor of his wife, Relief Davis Swain, whom he had married in 1842. One of his sons, Chellis, was a lieutenant under him. Odd jobs, such as guard duty and reconnoitering were about all the regiment or its detachments were permitted, and on Feb. 12, 1864, for obscure reasons, Swain was dismissed, the regiment moving to the Gulf under another command. In 1866 this dismissal was revoked, and he was given honorable discharge (Frederick Phisterer, *New York in the War of the Rebellion,* 1st ed., 1890, pp. 73 and 311; 3rd ed., 1912, II, 958).

On his return home, he was appointed in 1865 engineer-in-chief on the staff of Gov. Reuben S. Fenton [*q.v.*]. This appointment led to a rather bizarre adventure in rapid transit development. A welter of visionary suggestions were in the air, and after unsuccessful projects, first in 1866, and then with the Tweed group in 1871, Swain applied in 1872 for a charter for the Metropolitan Transit Company, which, after a struggle, he secured, with a stock authorization of five million dollars. His scheme provided for "a three deck highway. . . . The lowest level . . . to be a subway for freight, the next a slightly depressed

road for passenger traffic, and the third . . . an elevated structure from which passenger cars would hang suspended and be drawn by horses driven on the road below" (Walker, *post,* p. 103). The service was to extend from the Battery to Harlem River, with side lines. Though he was unsuccessful in soliciting capital with which to realize this dream, his wants were nevertheless supplied by the prosaic positions of weigher in the New York Custom House, 1867–71; Senate reporter for the *New York Tribune* and clerk of one of the Assembly committees in 1872. His fluctuating and varied life was rounded out by a return to his comfortable, four-page, Republican sheet, the *Hudson River Chronicle,* which he revived in 1876 and which ceased publication with his death.

[Obituary notices in the *N. Y. Tribune* and *N. Y. Times,* May 28, 1895; W. C. Swain, *Swain and Allied Families* (1896); T. W. Smith, *The Story of a Cavalry Regiment, "Scotts 900"* (1897); J. B. Walker, *Fifty Years of Rapid Transit* (1918); *U. S. Official Reg.,* 1871; N. Y. Senate and Assembly journals, 1872; J. T. Scharf, *Hist. of Westchester County, N. Y.* (1886), vol. II.]
C. W. G.

SWALLOW, GEORGE CLINTON (Nov. 17, 1817–Apr. 20, 1899), geologist, was born in Buckfield, Oxford County, Me., the son of Larned and Olive Fletcher (Proctor) Swallow, and a descendant of Ambrose Swallow, who emigrated from England to Chelmsford, Mass., about 1666. Though he was largely self-taught as a boy, he completed his preparatory studies at the New Yarmouth Academy and graduated in 1843 from Bowdoin College, Brunswick, Me., where he studied the sciences under Parker Cleaveland [*q.v.*]. Immediately after graduation he gave a course of lectures to the senior class of his college on botany as applied to agriculture and the mechanic arts. From 1843 to 1849 he was principal of Brunswick Female Seminary. In 1849 he was elected principal of Hampden Academy, Hampden, Me., and became a member of the state board of education. During this time he was also active as a public lecturer throughout many of the counties of the state, and in 1851 was elected to the professorship of geology, chemistry, and mineralogy in the University of Missouri at Columbia. Soon after going to Missouri he was influential in establishing state wide agricultural and mechanical associations. When the Missouri geological survey was established in 1853 he became state geologist and held the position until the survey was abolished in 1861. In 1865, as state geologist of Kansas, he surveyed the coal fields and showed the positions of the various geological formations of the state. His demonstration in 1858 of the existence of Permian rocks on the American continent led to a personal controversy of some bitterness with Fielding Bradford Meek [*q.v.*]. (For an account see Merrill, *The First One Hundred Years of American Geology, post,* pp. 368–70.) During 1867–70 he was engaged in mining operations in Montana. At the end of that time he was appointed professor of agriculture in the agricultural and mechanical college of the University of Missouri. He became dean in 1872 and professor of botany, comparative anatomy, and physiology in the medical school of the university. In 1882 he removed to Helena, Mont., to edit the *Daily Independent,* and later became state inspector of mines, 1888–90. Swallow was a handsome man of over six feet. He married on Mar. 17, 1844, Martha Ann Hill of Columbia, Mo. (d. 1898). They had a son, who died in childhood, and a daughter. Swallow died at the home of his daughter in Evanston, Ill.

An all-round scientist and a very close observer, Swallow succeeded in producing work up to the highest standard of the time in spite of the fact that he labored under unfavorable conditions. In his Kansas work he erred, perhaps, in making exact statements where only approximations were possible and in attempting too rapid explorations in obedience to an unreasonable public demand for immediate results, but in his Missouri work it is recognized that he made a remarkably able classification of the rocks involved and defined with general accuracy the distribution of the formations. Of the five reports published, the second (1854) is the one commonly accepted as his principal work.

[A. G. Baker, *Geneal. of the Swallow Family* (1910); *Obit. Record Grads. Bowdoin Coll. . . . 1899* (n.d.); G. P. Merrill, *The First One Hundred Years of Am. Geology* (1924), *Contributions to a Hist. of Am. State Geological and Nat. Hist. Surveys* (1920), and "Contributions to the Hist. of Am. Geology," in *Ann. Report of the Board of Regents of the Smithsonian Institution . . . 1904* (1906); Frederick Starr, in *Popular Sci. Monthly,* Mar. 1898; C. R. Keyes, in *Am. Geologist,* June 1900; biog. sketch and bibliog., *Ibid.,* July 1899.]   G. P. M.

SWALLOW, SILAS COMFORT (Mar. 5, 1839–Aug. 13, 1930), Methodist Episcopal clergyman, reformer, Prohibition candidate for president, was born near Wilkes-Barre, Pa., the son of George and Sarah Swallow. Because of the illness of his father, he assumed the management of the farm at the age of fourteen. By diligent labor and the practice of economy he obtained sufficient money to enter Wyoming Seminary at Kingston, Pa. After his graduation he taught a country school for five years, and then began the study of law in the office of Volney B. Maxwell of Wilkes-Barre. Before his admis-

sion to the bar, however, he decided to enter the ministry of the Methodist Episcopal Church, and after pursuing theological studies in the Susquehanna Seminary, Binghamton, N. Y., was admitted on trial by the East Baltimore Conference of his church in 1863. He began preaching on a circuit in central Pennsylvania at a salary of $100 a year. Twice during the Civil War, in 1862 and 1863, he served for brief periods in the Pennsylvania Emergency Volunteers. Throughout the war his religious work was seriously handicapped by his outspoken anti-slavery pronouncements and his support of the Union cause in a region where a considerable pro-slavery and anti-war sentiment prevailed. On one occasion his church was padlocked by disgruntled members. He married Rebecca Louisa Robins of Elysburg, Pa., Jan. 20, 1866, was ordained elder the following year, and during the next two decades served many pastoral charges in central Pennsylvania. Between 1892 and 1905 he was superintendent of the Methodist Book Rooms in Harrisburg and editor of the *Pennsylvania Methodist* and of the short-lived *Church Forum.*

From early manhood Swallow was an earnest advocate of moral and spiritual discipline which rivaled that of the Puritans of the seventeenth century. From the time when in 1864 he threw his tobacco box "over the house" and took a solemn vow that tobacco should never again enter his lips unless to save his life, "and then only on the written prescription of two full-fledged physicians," and when, two years later, on his honeymoon trip to Philadelphia he walked out of the only theatre which he had ever entered because John S. Clark in *She Stoops to Conquer* said "I'll be d—d," he was an uncompromising enemy in both word and action of the use of tobacco and liquor in all forms, of dancing, of roller-skating, and of secular amusements in general. The militant attitude which he assumed in his condemnation of these diversions made him many bitter enemies and involved him in a large number of personal controversies. During the late nineties he made the Republican machine in Pennsylvania a target for his thrusts. His persistent attacks upon prominent politicians resulted in the filing of charges of libel against him on several occasions and the divided allegiance of many Methodist ministers, who sought to divorce religion and politics. The controversy in the church reached an acute stage in the fall of 1901, when he was suspended from all ministerial duties and church privileges until the next annual meeting of the Central Pennsylvania Conference at Bellefonte, in March 1902. Although this body failed to sustain the charges of "lying and insubordination," it declared him "to be guilty of highly imprudent and unministerial conduct" and authorized the Bishop to administer a "public reproof" (*The Minutes of the Central Pennsylvania Annual Conference,* 1902, p. 60).

Meanwhile the "fighting Parson," as he was termed, was waging a valiant campaign against the firmly entrenched liquor interests of the state and nation. In 1896 he was elected a delegate to the Prohibition National Convention, and the next year he carried eleven counties in his candidacy for state treasurer, while in 1898 as the Prohibition candidate for governor he received some 130,000 votes. Six years later he became the nominee of his party for the presidency and polled 258,847 votes. (See his article, "The Prohibition Party's Appeal," *Independent,* New York, Oct. 13, 1904.) During the remainder of his life he devoted his whole time to preaching, writing, and lecturing. In 1909 he published a volume of reminiscences entitled *III Score & X or Selections, Collections, Recollections of Seventy Busy Years*; in 1920, a pamphlet, *Then and Now or Some Reminiscences of an Octogenarian*; and in 1922, a supplementary pamphlet, *Fourscore and More.* He died in 1930 at the age of ninety-one.

[Swallow's autobiog. writings; *Minutes of Conferences of the M. E. Church,* 1863 ff.; *Who's Who in America,* 1920–21; *Who's Who in Pa.,* 1904; *Phila. Inquirer,* Aug. 14, 1930; *N. Y. Times,* Aug. 14, 1930.]
A. E. M.

SWAN, JAMES (1754–July 31, 1830), financier, agent of the French Republic, was born in Fifeshire, Scotland. Emigrating to Boston in 1765, he became a clerk in a counting-house near Faneuil Hall. He early found his place among the radically patriotic youth of the city and became a member of the Sons of Liberty. He was a participant in the Boston Tea Party and was wounded twice at the battle of Bunker Hill. He attained the rank of major by the close of the Revolution and was later made a colonel. Married to Hepzibah Clarke of Boston (intention signified, Oct. 3, 1776), Swan abandoned active service and became a placeman, serving as secretary to the Massachusetts Board of War in 1777, as a member of the Massachusetts legislature in 1778, and then as adjutant-general of the commonwealth. He used an inheritance of his wife to live lavishly, to invest in Loyalist properties confiscated by the commonwealth, and to speculate in lands in Pennsylvania, Virginia, and Kentucky. In 1786 he purchased the Burnt Coat group of islands lying off the east coast of Maine, the largest of which bears his name.

Heavily in debt by 1787, Swan went to France to recuperate his fortunes. Assisted by his constant friend, Lafayette, he obtained remunerative contracts to furnish the French marine with naval stores and salt meat provisions, and in 1795 was able to make another profitable deal by which he gained control of the remainder of the United States debt to France, amounting to $2,024,899.93. Successful in gaining the appointment as agent of the French Republic, he outwitted his banking competitors, among whom were the American speculators, Gouverneur Morris and Robert Morris [*qq.v.*], the Boston banker, Daniel Parker, and the powerful bankers of the United States government at Amsterdam, Willink, Van Staphorst, and Hubbard, by his scheme for commuting the debt. By the congressional act of Mar. 3, 1795, it was made possible for American debt obligations to France to be exchanged for 4½ and 5½ per cent. United States domestic stock issued under authority of this act. Acting both as agent of the French Republic and as broker, Swan accepted American debt obligations from France in payment for supplies furnished or to be furnished the French marine, and in turn exchanged these for American domestic stock on which the interest rate was one-half per cent. higher. On June 15, 1795, the arrangement was closed, and the American foreign debt to France was transformed into a domestic one. Swan returned to the United States the better to direct these transactions and remained until 1798. Going back to France he engaged in further mercantile ventures which met with only varying success, and in 1808 he was cast into a debtor's prison in Paris where he died on July 31, 1830. Though he lived in some comfort on a stipend from his wife, he refused to have what he considered an unjust debt paid by her. His wife, son, and three daughters—one of them the wife of William Sullivan [*q.v.*]—remained in the United States during his twenty-two years of imprisonment. Swan published *A Dissuasion to Great-Britain and the Colonies, from the Slave-Trade to Africa* (1773), *National Arithmetick: or, Observations on the Finances of the Commonwealth of Massachusetts* (1786), and *Causes Qui Se Sont Apposées aux Progrès du Commerce entre la France et les États-Unis de l'Amérique* (Paris, 1790).

[*Proc. Mass. Hist. Soc.,* 1 ser., vol. XIII (1875), pp. 209–10, 2 ser., vol. IV (1889), pp. 46 ff.; Dispatches, France, vols. I–III, IIIa, and Miscellaneous Letters (1789–1800), MSS. in State Dept. Archives; French Archives Photostats, *Affaires Étrangères, Correspondance Politique États-Unis,* vols. XVIII–XXII, and the William Short Papers, Lib. of Congress; S. F. Bemis, in *Current Hist.,* Mar. 1926; H. W. Small, *A Hist. of Swan's Island, Me.* (1898).]
R. L–F.

SWAN, JOSEPH ROCKWELL (Dec. 28, 1802–Dec. 18, 1884), jurist, legal writer, was born at Westernville, Oneida County, N. Y., a descendant of John Swan, who resided successively in Stow and Lunenburg, Mass., and Peterborough, N. H., where he died about the time of the American Revolution. Joseph's parents, Jonathan and Sarah (Rockwell) Swan, were Quakers, the former a merchant. About 1813 the family moved to Aurora, N. Y., where the youth received his academic training and began the study of law. In 1824 he entered the law office of his uncle, Gustavus Swan, at Columbus, Ohio. Soon afterward he was admitted to the bar. From 1830 to 1835 he was prosecuting attorney of Franklin County, and in 1834 he was elected by the General Assembly a judge of the common pleas court; in 1841 he was reëlected. At the end of his term he returned to the practice of law in Columbus in partnership with John W. Andrews. In 1854 he was elected a judge of the supreme court of Ohio. He was an ardent abolitionist and his election by an unprecedented majority was due to a coalition of the anti-slavery element of all parties. He served on this court but one term (to November 1859) and, though he lived twenty-five years longer, he never again accepted a judicial office or engaged in active practice, but devoted his time to wide reading, particularly in the field of seventeenth-century English history, to extensive writing, and to civic and business enterprises. He also rendered much aid to legislative committees, which habitually called on him for help in drafting important legislation.

For one whose tenure on the supreme court bench had been so brief he enjoyed a high reputation as a judge. "He probably held as high a place in the estimation of the Bench, the Bar and the Public as has ever been reached by any one of the many distinguished men who have adorned our judicial history" ("In Memoriam," *post*, p. vi). The explanation for this great reputation is found in his opinion in a single case, *Ex parte Bushnell* (9 *Ohio State*, 78). It was sought in this case under a writ of *habeas corpus* issued from the supreme court of Ohio to override a judgment of the district court of the United States and to discharge from jail a prisoner who had been convicted and sentenced by that court for a violation of one of the sections of the Fugitive Slave Law. Gov. Salmon P. Chase declared that if the prisoner were discharged the armed forces of the state would be used to prevent his reimprisonment by the federal government. Swan as chief justice cast the deciding vote in the court, which held that the state could not interfere with the actions of the federal courts within the limits of their constitutional power and that the application for the prisoner's dis-

charge should be denied. Swan wrote the opinion, which has become a classic and given him a reputation for great judicial and moral courage. As a result of this opinion the Republican party then in state convention refused to renominate him. Nevertheless, he was later three times offered appointment to the supreme court to fill vacancies, and once, a nomination by the Republican party.

It is upon his work as a legal writer, however, that his fame most depends. He was author of *The Practice in Civil Actions and Proceedings at Law in Ohio, and Precedents in Pleading* (2 vols., 1845, 1850), and *Commentaries on Pleading under the Ohio Code, with Precedents of Petitions* (1861). The latter work was largely responsible for the acceptance of a broad interpretation of the civil code, in the spirit of the code itself and not in the technical spirit of the common law. He made four general revisions of Ohio statutes (1841, 1854, 1860, 1868). The book which gave him his greatest renown, however, was published as early as 1837. It was entitled *A Treatise on the Law Relating to the Powers and Duties of Justices of the Peace ... in the State of Ohio*, and has been called "probably the most useful book ever published in Ohio" (Andrews, *post*, p. ix). Swan himself prepared twelve editions and up to 1930 twenty-seven editions had appeared.

Swan held many important positions other than judicial. In 1850 he was elected a member of the constitutional convention, at which he was recognized as one of its most influential members. He also served as general solicitor of the Pittsburg, Cincinnati, St. Louis Railroad Company (1869–79) and president of the Columbus & Xenia Railway. He was married in 1833 to Hannah R. Andrews of Rochester, N. Y., who died in 1876. His own death occurred in Columbus, Ohio. He was survived by three sons and two daughters.

[A. L. Priest, "John Swan . . . and Descendants" (typescript, Lib. of Cong., 1934); J. W. Andrews, "Joseph Rockwell Swan—An American," *Columbus Dispatch*, Dec. 19, 1884, repr. in later editions of Swan's *Treatise*; "In Memoriam," 42 *Ohio State Reports*; G. I. Reed, *Bench and Bar of Ohio* (1897); *Ohio State Bar Asso. Reports*, vol. V (1885); *Ohio Law Jour.*, Dec. 27, 1884; *Ohio State Jour.* (Columbus), Dec. 20, 1884; *Cincinnati Enquirer*, Dec. 19, 1884.]

A. H. T.

SWAN, TIMOTHY (July 23, 1758–July 23, 1842), composer and compiler of psalm-tunes, was born in Worcester, Mass., the eighth of the thirteen children of William and Lavina Keyes Swan. He was a descendant of Thomas Swan, who settled in Roxbury, Mass., before 1681. After the death of his father he spent a few years as an apprentice in the family of a Mr. Barnes, a loyalist in Marlboro, but in 1775 he went to Groton, Mass., to live with a brother, a merchant. Later he went to Northfield, where he learned the trade of hatter. His musical education was limited to three weeks in a singing school, although he received some instruction upon the fife from a British musician. In 1782 he moved to Suffield, Conn., where he lived for nearly thirty years. On Apr. 10, 1784, he married Mary Gay, daughter of the Rev. Ebenezer Gay of Suffield. There were fourteen children, four of whom died while young.

During his apprenticeship Swan composed the tune "Poland," and this was followed by many other tunes for church hymns, which were used in manuscript in many parts of New England. It was his habit to compose his tunes while at work—first the melody, then the harmonic parts, a few notes at a time, until the composition was complete. Swan's music was very popular in its day. Oliver Brownson printed half a dozen tunes in his *Select Harmony* (1783), including "Poland," "Lisbon," and "Majesty"; Simeon Jocelin wrote for permission to use some of the tunes; in 1810 Daniel Read [*q.v.*] offered to purchase "China" and "London" for three dollars, and one correspondent wrote, "I must publish 'Flanders,' unless you absolutely forbid me." "China" was composed in 1790 and first sung in public in 1794 (notation in Swan's *New England Harmony*, 1801, in the Collections of the American Antiquarian Society, Worcester, Mass.). This Swan considered his best tune, and later bookmakers have concurred in this opinion, for it is the only one of his tunes that has retained a place in modern hymnals; it is usually set to the words of Watts' "Why do we mourn for dying friends?" He loved poetry, Burns being his favorite author, and he wrote considerable verse for the local paper, much of it in the Scottish dialect. About 1800 he published *The Songster's Assistant*, a thirty-six page pamphlet of songs in two parts, most of the music never before published. The following year, 1801, *New England Harmony,* a volume of 103 pages, was published at Northampton, and in 1803 *The Songster's Museum.* The latter was published anonymously, but much of its music, 204 pages of secular music, was furnished by Swan. The authorship of *The Federal Harmony* (not to be confused with another book of the same title issued the same year by Asahel Benham) is questionable, but it has been attributed to Swan (Charles Evans, *American Bibliography,* vol. VI, 1910, p. 384, and vol. VII, 1912, p. 268; H. P. Main, in *The Music of the Modern World,* 1895, edited by Anton Seidl), and it may have been the first of his publications.

Four editions of the book appeared between 1785 and 1792, all printed in Boston. It contains only two tunes known to be Swan's, "China" and "Lisbon." He died in Northfield, Mass.

[A sketch of Swan, said to have been revised by his daughter, appeared in *The Christian Parlor Book* (1855), pp. 137–38. A small book of original music, some correspondence, and other papers relating to Swan are in the Lib. of the Am. Antiquarian Soc., Worcester, Mass. See also Joseph Sabin, *Bibliotheca Americana,* vol. XXIV (1933–34), cont. by Wilberforce Eames and R. W. G. Vail; F. J. Metcalf, *Am. Writers and Compilers of Sacred Music* (1925); *Celebration of the Two Hundred and Fiftieth Anniversary of the Settlement of Suffield, Conn.* (1921), p. 172; J. H. Temple and George Sheldon, *Hist. of the Town of Northfield, Mass.* (1875); Joel Munsell, *Reminiscences of Men and Things in Northfield* (n.d.); *Am. Musical Rev.,* May 1852; *Musical Herald,* Oct. 1882; obituary in *Boston Daily Advertiser,* Aug. 5, 1842.]   F. J. M—f.

SWANK, JAMES MOORE (July 12, 1832– June 21, 1914), statistician, historian, executive secretary of the American Iron and Steel Association, was born in Westmoreland County, Pa., the son of George W. and Nancy (Moore) Swank. His ancestors, rigid Scotch-Irish Presbyterians on his mother's side and German Lutherans on his father's, had lived in Pennsylvania since early colonial days. In 1838 his parents moved to Johnstown. After attending Jefferson College in Canonsburg, Pa., for one year, he clerked in his father's store, taught school, read law, and edited a Whig newspaper. In 1869 he went to Washington to serve as clerk of the House committee on manufactures, of which his friend Daniel J. Morrell, afterwards president of the American Iron and Steel Association, was chairman. Two years later he became a clerk in the Department of Agriculture and specialized in statistics; within six months he became chief clerk. During this time he wrote *The Department of Agriculture: Its History and Objects* (1872), the first history of the department. In 1873 he was chosen secretary of the American Iron and Steel Association, with headquarters in Philadelphia, and from 1885 until 1912, when he retired, he was vice-president and general manager. During much of this time he also served as secretary of the Industrial League of America, an organization which used the same headquarters as the Association and had similar political aims. Swank's previous training and mental traits fitted him well for this work. During his first year he compiled a *Directory to the Iron and Steel Works of the United States,* of which seventeen editions were published. He was a pioneer in collecting and publishing data for the iron and steel industry, and gained an international reputation as a statistician. Under his editorship the bulletin of the Association became an informing and influential periodical, particularly in relation to tariff legislation.

It was fortunate for the iron and steel interests that they secured Swank's services in 1873, for the strength of the Republican party in Congress was waning and the enemies of the protective tariff were pointing to it as one of the major causes of the panic of 1873. To counteract such influences, protectionists turned to the newspapers, only to find that in the very sections they needed most to reach—the South and West—the newspapers were hostile. To reach the voters, therefore, well edited pamphlets were printed, and widely and methodically distributed under Swank's leadership. Not one contained a special plea for iron and steel. As bill after bill for the reduction of duties was introduced into Congress, Swank redoubled his energy. Between 1880 and 1882, over 1,000,000 tracts were distributed. After Cleveland's famous tariff message in 1887, Swank distributed in nine months 1,387,864 tracts, principally in the Northwest (*Bulletin of the American Iron and Steel Association,* Nov. 7 and 14, 1888, p. 333). He also played a prominent rôle in bringing about and maintaining close cooperation between eastern business men and the leaders of the Republican party. Now and then he saw to it that a friendly, hard-pressed member of Congress had sufficient campaign funds. When the representatives of the iron and steel interests appeared before committees of Congress, Swank often accompanied them, and ably and adroitly supplied facts, figures, and suggestions, which usually resulted in favorable tariff legislation. He did this so fairly and courteously that, although he went through innumerable bitter tariff contests, no aspersions were ever cast on his character. Andrew Carnegie once declared that iron and steel owed "an unpayable debt" to Swank (quoted in McPherson, *post,* p. 265). During the period in which he served the Association, he saw pig iron production in the United States increase from 2,560,- 963 to 29,726,937 gross tons and steel production from 198,796 to 31,251,303 tons; he also saw the fear of European competition pass away in this field and the protective principle become established.

In 1880, as special agent for the census office, he collected statistics for iron and steel manufacturing and wrote an historical sketch to accompany them (*Report on the Manufactures of the United States at the Tenth Census,* 1883, pp. 729–901). This led to his well-known work on *The History of the Manufacture of Iron in All Ages* (1884). He also published *The Industrial Policies of Great Britain and the United States*

(1876), an historical account with a spirited defense of the protective tariff principle as developed in the United States, *Introduction to a History of Ironmaking and Coal Mining in Pennsylvania* (1878), *Notes and Comments on Industrial, Economic, Political, and Historical Subjects* (1897), *Progressive Pennsylvania* (1908), and *Cambria County Pioneers* (1910). He died in Philadelphia, survived by his second wife, Anna Park (Linton) Swank.

[*Who's Who in America,* 1914–15; H. W. Storey, *Hist. of Cambria County, Pa.* (1907), vol. II, pp. 481–85; J. B. McPherson, in *Bull. Nat. Asso. of Wool Manufacturers,* Sept. 1913; *Monthly Bull. Am. Iron and Steel Institute,* Jan. 1913, p. 20; A. T. Volwiler, in *Am. Hist. Rev.,* Oct. 1930; Swank Papers, Cambria Free Lib., Johnstown, Pa., and obituary in *Pub. Ledger* (Phila.), June 22, 1914.]   A. T. V.

SWANN, THOMAS (*c.* 1806–July 24, 1883), mayor of Baltimore, governor, and congressman, was born in Alexandria, then a part of the District of Columbia, the son of Thomas Swann, a prominent lawyer of Washington, and Jane Byrd (Page). After attending the preparatory school of Columbian College in the national capital and subsequently the University of Virginia (1826–27), he studied law in his father's office. On Mar. 2, 1833, he was named by President Jackson as secretary of the commission to Naples to negotiate a settlement of spoliation claims.

Shortly after his return from this mission he married, in 1834, Elizabeth Gilmor Sherlock of Baltimore, and moved to that city to engage in business. Here, as the energetic and indomitable president of the Baltimore & Ohio Railroad Company, he first rose to prominence. Acquisition of a considerable amount of stock of the struggling railroad brought him to a director's seat in 1847, and in October 1848 to the presidency. By 1853, despite almost insuperable obstacles—the credit of the company was practically *nil,* the city of Baltimore and the state at large were extremely skeptical—he had succeeded in extending the railroad through some two hundred miles of thinly settled, mountainous country to reach the Ohio River. This object accomplished he felt free to resign, but almost immediately undertook the presidency of the Northwestern Virginia Railroad (now the Grafton-Parkersburg line of the Baltimore & Ohio), which had obtained its charter through his efforts. Had he chosen, he might have acquired a reputation as a master railroad builder; instead he preferred to pour his energies into political channels.

He first appeared as a candidate for mayor of Baltimore on the ticket of the Native American party in 1856. The election was attended with great disorder and terrorism, as was the next election in 1858, but on each occasion Swann was declared elected. Whatever the tactics by which he secured office, as mayor he employed his high order of executive ability and broad comprehension of the material interests of the city to render it a signal service. Among other improvements, he replaced the inefficient volunteer fire companies by a municipal department equipped with modern apparatus, installed the police and fire alarm telegraph system, introduced a street railway and by imposing a park tax as compensation for the franchise made it possible to beautify the city.

When the Civil War began, Swann, who had already emancipated his large group of slaves, took decided ground against secession and remained throughout the struggle an unwavering Unionist. In 1864 he was elected governor of Maryland by the Union party under the constitution of that year, though he did not take office until the expiration of his predecessor's term in January 1866, and served only three years. He supported the Lincoln and Johnson plans for reconstruction, but as the Radicals developed their plans he joined forces with Maryland Democrats to secure removal of disfranchisement. He made possible the overthrow of the Radical Republican machine at the election of 1866 when he replaced the Republican police commissioners against whom certain charges had been preferred by men of less radical stamp. As a result of this move the registration books were opened, oaths were not exacted, the franchise was effectively restored to many former Southern sympathizers, and the conservatives won the election. The Democratic legislature rewarded Swann in 1867 by electing him to the United States Senate, but after consultation with political leaders he declined the post because he feared that the radical lieutenant-governor, Christopher C. Cox, might undo what he had accomplished. He also thought he discerned a plot on the part of the radical senators in Washington to reject his credentials. With this decision he sacrificed his most cherished ambition. He was not denied service in Congress, however, for in 1868, though the angry Republicans made a special effort to defeat him, he was elected a representative on the Democratic ticket. Reëlected for four successive terms, he remained in the House for ten years, rising to the chairmanship of the committee on foreign relations and enjoying contacts which probably made these the most satisfying years of his life. At the close of his congressional career in 1879 he retired to his estate, "Morven Park," near Leesburg, Va. In June 1878, two years after the death of his first wife, he married Josephine (Ward) Thom-

son, daughter of Gen. Aaron Ward and widow of John Renshaw Thomson, a former senator from New Jersey. This marriage brought little joy to the aged statesman, however, for a separation soon occurred. A daughter of the first marriage became the wife of Mayor Ferdinand C. Latrobe of Baltimore.

[*Tercentenary Hist. of Md.* (1925), vol. IV; H. E. Buchholz, *Govs. of Md.* (1908); W. F. Coyle, *The Mayors of Baltimore* (1910); *Baltimore Past and Present* (1871), ed. by F. A. Richardson and W. A. Bennett; J. T. Scharf, *The Chronicles of Baltimore* (1874); F. R. Kent, *The Story of Md. Politics* (1911); Edward Hungerford, *The Story of the Baltimore & Ohio Railroad* (1928); *Biog. Dir. Am. Cong.* (1928); M. P. Andrews, *Hist. of Md.* (1929); *Baltimore American and Commercial Advertiser* and *The Sun* (Baltimore), July 24, 25, 1883.]
                                        E. L.

SWARTWOUT, SAMUEL (Nov. 17, 1783–Nov. 21, 1856), soldier, merchant, speculator, and politician, was born in Poughkeepsie, N. Y., a descendant of Tomys Swartwout, who emigrated from Amsterdam to New Netherland in 1652. He was the son of Abraham and Maria (North) Swartwout. From 1804 onwards he was closely connected with Aaron Burr, 1756–1836 [*q.v.*]. It was Swartwout who on Oct. 8, 1806, delivered to Gen. James Wilkinson [*q.v.*] the famous cipher letter from Burr which was to produce such a strong impression of Burr's treason. Swartwout was afterwards arrested in New Orleans on Wilkinson's order and sent to Washington for trial as an accomplice in Burr's schemes. The proceedings attracted wide attention, for on their outcome rested the fate of Burr (4 *Cranch*, 75, *Ex parte Bollman*, and Appendix). After his own trial and acquittal, Swartwout served as an important witness against Burr (*Annals of Congress*, 10 Cong., 1 Sess., Appendix, pp. 633, 678), but he steadfastly refused to acknowledge any treasonable purpose in the other's designs or in his own agency. After the trial he sought to provoke a duel with General Wilkinson and, when he failed, posted the general as a coward. He accompanied Burr from Richmond to Baltimore, helped him in his arrangements to sail to England, and preceded him to that country to prepare for his favorable reception. He also, it seems, proposed to open up trade with the Mississippi Valley through Mobile and Pensacola in contravention to Jefferson's embargo. Apparently he did not succeed in either policy, although he remained in England for some time after Burr's arrival (Williamson Papers, *post*, Feb.–May 1808, and *Swartwout Chronicles, post*, pp. 341–42). After serving in the War of 1812 as captain in the "Iron Grays," he was connected with his brothers, Robert and John, as a merchant. In 1814 he married Alice Ann Cooper, by whom he had a son who died young and a daughter.

From this time on his fortunes were bound up with those of Andrew Jackson. Commended to the general by his audacious challenge to Wilkinson, he worked hard, doubtless spurred on by Burr, to make Jackson a presidential possibility. His personal charm, his energetic efforts, and his unswerving loyalty brought him the appointment (Apr. 25, 1829) of collector of the port of New York, the most lucrative public office in Jackson's gift. Despite the warnings of Van Buren, who distrusted Swartwout's reputation for speculation (H. F. De Puy, *post,* pp. 25–27; J. C. Fitzpatrick, *post,* pp. 262, 263, 266), Jackson continued him in office, and Van Buren as president followed suit. Notwithstanding the demands of the position, Swartwout found time for extensive speculations in lands, canals, and railways. At the expiration of his term (Mar. 29, 1838) his accounts with the government remained unsettled, and the inevitable investigation of his office reached a climax in January 1839, when it was found that, beginning within a few months of his appointment, he had appropriated more than a million dollars of public funds (*Congressional Globe,* 25 Cong., 3 Sess., pp. 19, 20–21, and Appendix, pp. 31–35, 89–111). Swartwout had already attempted to meet his shortage by sailing to England (August 1838), where he hoped to dispose of certain valuable coal and iron lands. Failing, he remained abroad until 1841. Then, assured that he would not be prosecuted—his property had been surrendered to meet claims—, he returned to the United States and lived in retirement until his death in New York, Nov. 21, 1856.

[In addition to the sources for Aaron Burr, which are useful for Swartwout, see A. J. Weise, *The Swartwout Chronicles, 1338–1899* (1899); Williamson Papers, MSS. in Newberry Lib., Chicago, Ill.; R. C. McGrane, *The Correspondence of Nicholas Biddle* (1919); H. F. De Puy, "Some Letters of Andrew Jackson," *Proc. Am. Antiquarian Soc.,* n.s., vol. XXXI (1922); J. C. Fitzpatrick, "The Autobiog. of Martin Van Buren," *Ann. Report Am. Hist. Asso. . . . 1918,* vol. II (1920); *House Doc. 111,* 25 Cong., 2 Sess., vol. V, and *House Doc., 13,* 25 Cong., 3 Sess., vol. II; J. S. Bassett, *Correspondence of Andrew Jackson,* vols. III–IV (1928–31), vol. VI (1933); A. J. Beveridge, *The Life of John Marshall* (1919), vol. III; B. J. Poore, *Perley's Reminiscences* (2 vols., 1886); obituary in *N. Y. Tribune,* Nov. 24, 1856.]   I.J.C.

SWAYNE, NOAH HAYNES (Dec. 7, 1804–June 8, 1884), jurist, was born in Frederick County, Va. He was of Quaker ancestry, being a descendant of Francis Swayne who came with his family to America in 1710 and settled near Philadelphia. Noah was the youngest of nine children of Joshua Swayne, who died in 1808; his mother was Rebecca, daughter of John and Ann Smith of Chester County, Pa. At the age of thirteen he was sent to the Quaker academy of Jacob Mendenhall at Waterford, Va. Two years later he began the study of medicine with an apothecary and physician at Alexandria, but abandoned it upon the death of his teacher. Turning next to the law, he entered the office of John Scott and Francis Brooks at Warrenton, Va. Admitted to the bar in 1823, he immediately moved to Ohio on account of his opposition to slavery. Here he located for one year at Zanesville and then moved to Coshocton, where he began practice. His success was immediate. In 1826 he was appointed prosecuting attorney for Coshocton County and in 1829 was elected as a Jeffersonian Democrat to the state legislature. In 1830 he was appointed by President Jackson United States attorney for the district of Ohio, which position he held for nine years, making his home in Columbus, where he remained until his appointment to the United States Supreme Court. In 1832 he married Sarah Ann Wager of Harpers Ferry, Va. (now W. Va.). His wife owned slaves, but, sharing his views as to the evils of slavery, she emancipated them.

During the more than thirty years he practised in Columbus he took high rank at the Ohio bar and was employed in many important cases in both the state and federal courts. One of his noted efforts was his defense, in 1853, before the United States circuit court in Columbus, of William Rossane and others who were accused of the burning of the steamboat *Martha Washington* for the fraudulent purpose of procuring insurance. Aside from his practice during this period he was a member of a state fund commission charged at a critical period in the finances of the state with the management of the state debt; a member of a commission to settle a dispute between Ohio and Michigan over the state boundary; and a member of still another commission to study the need of a state institution for the care of the blind.

On Jan. 21, 1862, President Lincoln appointed him a justice of the United States Supreme Court, and the appointment was confirmed on Jan. 24. The reason for his appointment is a little difficult to determine. He had had no judicial experience and though prominent as a lawyer in central Ohio was not a national figure. Justice McLean, whom he was to succeed, was a close friend and had expressed the hope that Swayne would be his successor. His appointment was strongly urged by Governor Dennison of Ohio and by the entire Ohio delegation in Congress, including Senators B. F. Wade and John Sher-

Swayne Swayne

man. There seems to be no basis for the persistent tradition that President Lincoln got the names of J. R. Swan [q.v.] and Swayne confused and really meant to appoint the former, who had become a national figure on account of his great opinion in the *Ex parte Bushnell* case (9 *Ohio*, 77).

His career of nineteen years was altogether satisfactory, though not brilliant. Two other appointees of Lincoln, Samuel F. Miller and Stephen J. Field [qq.v.], surpassed him in influence and reputation. His most noteworthy opinions were those given in the cases of *Gelpcke* vs. *City of Dubuque* (68 *U. S.*, 175) and *Springer* vs. *U. S.* (102 *U. S.*, 586). In the former case he took issue with Miller, arguing that though it was the general practice of the Supreme Court to follow the latest adjudications of state courts in construing the laws and constitutions of the states, this practice could not be followed when it would result in a sacrifice of justice. This decision had much to do in establishing the doctrine set forth in *Swift* vs. *Tyson* to the effect that in the interpretation of contracts and other instruments of a commercial nature, the true interpretation is to be sought not in the discussions of the local tribunals, but in the general principles and doctrines of commercial jurisprudence (41 *U. S.*, 2). In *Springer* vs. *U. S.* (102 *U. S.*, 586), he wrote an able opinion upholding the constitutionality of a federal income tax, an opinion overruled in the later "Income Tax Cases," but still believed by many able lawyers to be the correct interpretation of the Constitution. During the time he sat on the bench he was the most nationalistic-minded member of the court. In his dissents in the famous cases of *Texas* vs. *White* (74 *U. S.*, 700) and *Hepburn* vs. *Griswold* (75 *U. S.*, 603) and in the Slaughter House Cases (83 *U. S.*, 36), he stood for a more nationalistic position than even the Supreme Court as then constituted was willing to sustain. Possessed of a robust health, during his entire service he was present at practically every session and conference of the court. "He came," said Chief Justice Waite, "from a large . . . practice at the Bar, and brought with him an unusual familiarity with adjudged cases, and settled habits of labor and research. As might be expected, he soon became one of the most useful members of the Court, and took an active and leading part in all its work" (103 *U. S. Reports*, xii).

On Jan. 25, 1881, at the age of seventy-six, he retired from the bench under the authority of the federal statute. For a year he lived in Washington but after the death of his wife moved to New York City, where a son, Wager Swayne

[q.v.], was engaged in the practice of law. Here he died, survived by four sons and one daughter. He was buried in Oak Hill Cemetery, Washington, D. C.

[N. W. Swayne, *The Descendants of Francis Swayne* (1921); *Am. Law Rev.*, July–Aug. 1884; *Ohio State Bar Asso. Reports*, vol. V (1885); 103 *U. S. Reports*, ix–xii; 118 *U. S. Reports*, 699–700; H. L. Carson, *The Supreme Court of the U. S.: Its Hist.* (1892), vol. II; *The Biog. Cyc. . . . of the State of Ohio*, vol. V (n.d.); *Mr. Justice Swayne* (n.d.), pamphlet prepared by his sons; *N. Y. Tribune* and *Evening Star* (Washington), June 10, 1884.]   A. H. T.

SWAYNE, WAGER (Nov. 10, 1834–Dec. 18, 1902), soldier and lawyer, was born in Columbus, Ohio, the son of Noah Haynes Swayne [q.v.] and Sarah Ann (Wager). He was graduated at Yale in 1856, after losing a year on account of serious illness, and at the Cincinnati Law School in 1859. Having been admitted to the Ohio bar he commenced the practice of law in partnership with his father, then a leading attorney in Columbus and later an associate justice of the United States Supreme Court.

On Aug. 31, 1861, he entered the army as major, 43rd Ohio Infantry, and was promoted lieutenant-colonel, Dec. 14, 1861. Until February 1862 the regiment was in training in Ohio. It then joined the army under Pope and took part in the actions at New Madrid and Island No. 10 which opened the upper Mississippi. Later it was present at the siege of Corinth; in the battle of Corinth, Oct. 4, 1862, Swayne, already known as an efficient regimental commander, displayed such distinguished courage in the face of threatened panic among the troops, that upon Gen. D. S. Stanley's urgent recommendation he received the award of the medal of honor, the highest American decoration for heroism in action. On Oct. 18, 1862, he was promoted colonel. He commanded a brigade of the XVI Corps, Army of the Tennessee, in the Atlanta campaign, the march to the sea, and the campaign of the Carolinas, attracting favorable notice from Gen. O. O. Howard [q.v.], a circumstance which had important consequences later. He was in action at Resaca, Dallas, Kenesaw, and Atlanta. At Rivers Bridge, S. C., he received a shell wound, Feb. 2, 1865, which caused the amputation of his right leg. He was appointed brigadier-general of volunteers in April, with rank from Mar. 8, 1865.

Later in that year he was selected by General Howard, then organizing the Freedmen's Bureau, as an assistant commissioner in charge of the bureau's operations in Alabama; he was also in military command, and in order that he might have appropriate rank was appointed, in May 1866, major-general of volunteers, with commission dated back to June 20, 1865. He was not finally mustered out of the volunteer army until Sept. 1, 1867. Meanwhile, he had been appointed, July 28, 1866, colonel in the regular army, for the newly organized 45th Infantry. His service in Alabama with the Freedmen's Bureau continued until January 1868, and was especially marked by the establishment of numerous schools, some of which are still in existence. He married Ellen, daughter of Alfred Harris of Louisville, Dec. 22, 1868. The drastic reduction of the regular army in 1870 required the removal of all officers suffering from any form of physical disability, and Swayne was accordingly placed on the retired list in July.

He took up the practice of law in Toledo, in partnership with John R. Osborn, also serving for some years as a member of the board of education. In 1881 he removed to New York, where, in partnership with John F. Dillon [q.v.] and others, he continued to practise law until shortly before his death. His firm acted as counsel for the Associated Press, the Western Union Telegraph Company, the Wabash Railway, and other important corporations. A distinguished lawyer and a successful commander of troops, Swayne was also a most public-spirited citizen, always interested in philanthropic activities, particularly church and educational work.

[N. W. Swayne, *The Descendants of Francis Swayne and Others* (1921); *War of the Rebellion: Official Records (Army)*; F. B. Heitman, *Hist. Reg. and Dict. U. S. Army* (1903), vol. I; G. M. Dodge, in *Loyal Legion, Commandery of N. Y., Circular No. 10* (1903); *Obit. Record Grads. Yale Univ.*, 1903; O. O. Howard, *Autobiography* (1907), vol. II; *Bureau of Refugees and Freedmen: Report of the Assistant Commissioner for Ala.* (1866, 1867); *The Biog. Encyc. of Ohio of the Nineteenth Century* (1876); *Who's Who in America,* 1899–1900; *N. Y. Times,* Dec. 19, 1902.]   T. M. S.

SWEENY, PETER BARR (Oct. 9, 1825–Aug. 30, 1911), politician, son of James and Mary (Barr) Sweeny, was born in New York City. His father was a saloonkeeper there and later engaged in the same business in Jersey City. In the latter place young Peter served as a waiter. He received some education at a parochial school and at Columbia College. Having studied law in the office of James T. Brady [q.v.], he was admitted to the bar and practised successfully. He soon became interested in politics, and was active on the Tammany General Committee in 1852. In 1854 he was in Albany with his uncle, Thomas J. Barr, a state senator, lobbying in the interest of city stage-coach franchises as against street railroads. Silent and reticent by nature, Sweeny could not speak in public, his preference being for secret or "gumshoe" methods. He was elected district attorney in 1857, but broke down in his first speech before a jury and was so humiliated that he resigned his position.

By the early sixties Tammany Hall was coming under the control of a small group of men, of whom Sweeny and William M. Tweed [q.v.] were the most important. It has always been asserted, and apparently upon good authority, that Sweeny was the real guiding intelligence of the "Tweed ring"; hence his initial B. was humorously supposed to stand for "Brains" or "Bismarck." In 1863 Tweed became grand sachem of the Tammany Society, but Sweeny was behind the throne, working secretly as always. They now began filling important city offices with their henchmen, and the members of the "ring" were soon absolute masters of the city. Tweed is said to have feared Sweeny. "Sweeny is a hard, over-bearing, revengeful man . . .," Tweed testified when a witness before a special committee of the board of aldermen in 1877. "We were so opposite and unalike that we never got along very well" (Lynch, *post,* p. 278). Of himself Sweeny said modestly, "I am not and never claimed to be a leader. . . . I am a sort of adviser. I try to harmonize the interests of the party" (*North American Review,* October 1874). Sweeny acquired the position of city chamberlain in 1866, and Tweed testified later that he "heard" that Sweeny paid $60,000 for the job (*Report of Special Committee, post,* pp. 105, 112). In 1867 he astonished the public by turning over to the city treasury $200,000 in interest on public funds which his predecessors in the office had considered their personal perquisite. By this shrewd move he set up a specious reputation for honesty. In 1869 he was appointed park commissioner by Mayor A. Oakey Hall [q.v.]. He was associated with James Fisk [q.v.], in the manipulation of Erie Railroad stock, he and Tweed being elected directors of the company and helping to force out Daniel Drew and Cornelius Vanderbilt [qq.v.]. He also dealt largely in street railroad franchises. In 1869, at a meeting in Sweeny's hotel room in Albany, it was decided that fifty per cent. for graft should be added to all bills rendered against the city and county (*Ibid.,* pp. 75–78). Later this percentage was greatly increased. The loot thus secured was to be divided into five parts, Tweed, Sweeny, Comptroller Richard B. Connolly, and Mayor Hall receiving one share each, while the fifth share was to be used for the bribery of smaller politicians. Sweeny's devious nature is seen in the fact that his share was always paid to him through his brother James, a city employee. When the "ring" was overthrown in 1871 Sweeny resigned his city offices and fled to

Canada and from there to France. As the trial of Tweed drew on, Sweeny offered, if guaranteed immunity from prosecution, to refund $400,000 which "his brother James" had gotten from New York City. This deal was consummated, and after several years' residence in Paris, Sweeny, still comfortably wealthy, returned to the United States and died in 1911 at Lake Mahopac, N. Y. He married Sara Augusta Dotherty and was survived by a son.

[*Evening Post* (N. Y.), Aug. 31, 1911; *N. Y. Times, World, N. Y. Herald, Sun*, Sept. 1, 1911; *Report of the Special Committee of the Board of Aldermen Appointed to Investigate the "Ring" Frauds, Together with the Testimony Elicited during the Investigation* (Board of Aldermen, Jan. 4, 1878, Doc. No. 8); *N. Y. Times* and *Harper's Weekly*, 1869–72; C. F. Wingate, "An Episode in Municipal Govt.," *North Am. Rev.*, Oct. 1874, Jan. 1875, July 1875, Oct. 1876; W. C. Gover, *The Tammany Hall Democracy of the City of N. Y. and the General Committee for 1875* (1875); Rufus Home, "The Story of Tammany," *Harper's Mag.*, Apr.–May 1872; A. P. Genung, *The Frauds of the New York City Govt. Exposed* (1871); M. R. Werner, *Tammany Hall* (1928); D. T. Lynch, *"Boss" Tweed* (1927); R. H. Fuller, *Jubilee Jim* (1930); A. B. Paine, *Thomas Nast: His Period and His Pictures* (1904); scrapbooks of newspaper clippings relating to N. Y. City politics, N. Y. Pub. Lib.; names of parents and date of birth from N. K. Averill, Esq., Lake Mahopac, N. Y., at whose home Sweeny died; name of wife from Mrs. Arthur Sweeny.]
                          A. F. H.

SWEENY, THOMAS WILLIAM (Dec. 25, 1820–Apr. 10, 1892), soldier, Fenian leader, was born in County Cork, Ireland, the son of William and Honora (Sweeny) Sweeny. He emigrated to the United States in 1832. About 1843 he joined the "Baxter Blues" of New York City, and in 1846 became second lieutenant of New York volunteers in the Mexican War. He was with General Scott from Vera Cruz to the capture of Churubusco, where he received a wound that necessitated the amputation of his right arm. Following the war, as lieutenant in the 2nd United States Infantry, Sweeny was engaged almost continuously in operations against the Yuma Indians of the Southwest or the Sioux of the Nebraska region until January 1861, when he was promoted captain and ordered to the federal arsenal at St. Louis.

After serving under Gen. Nathaniel Lyon [*q.v.*] in the capture of Camp Jackson, Sweeny was commissioned brigadier-general of the three months' Missouri volunteers, May 20, 1861, and sent with Franz Sigel [*q.v.*] into Southwest Missouri to prevent the junction of the state troops under Gen. Sterling Price and Gov. C. F. Jackson [*qq.v.*] with the Confederate army under Gen. Ben McCulloch [*q.v.*]. Sigel's rash attempt with 1,100 men to stop Jackson's 4,000 at Carthage resulted in a rout, and the expedition failed of its objective. On Aug. 14, 1861, four days after receiving a severe wound in the battle

of Wilson's Creek (McElroy, *post*, p. 183), Sweeny was mustered out of the Missouri volunteers, but he returned to the volunteer service as colonel of the 52nd Illinois on Jan. 21, 1862, and under Grant aided in the capture of Fort Donelson. He was given outstanding credit by Sherman for helping save the day at Shiloh, Apr. 6 (*Battles and Leaders, post*, I, 511), and rendered praiseworthy service in the battles of Corinth, Oct. 3–4, 1862, Kenesaw Mountain, June 27, 1864, and Atlanta, July 20–22, 1864. He was commissioned brigadier-general of volunteers Nov. 29, 1862, and was honorably discharged from the volunteer service in August 1865. As the result of a quarrel with his superior officer, Gen. G. M. Dodge, after the battle of Atlanta, Sweeny was arrested and court-martialed, but acquitted. On Dec. 29, 1865, he was dismissed from the army for absence without leave, but on Nov. 8, 1866, was reinstated. Although a quick thinker and an aggressive fighter, he apparently lacked coolness and sound judgment.

While out of the service he received much notoriety as the leader of the ill-starred Fenian raid on Canada in 1866. An ardent Irish partisan, he was made secretary of war of the "Irish Republic" when William R. Roberts [*q.v.*] was elected president by the Fenian Congress in 1865. With Roberts he urged that Canada be conquered as a step toward freeing Ireland, and in 1866, superintended the details of the invasion of June 1–2 at Niagara and the simultaneous attempts to cross the border at Potsdam, N. Y., and St. Albans, Vt. The "invasion" was a fiasco. Sweeny, with some others, was arrested by United States authorities but was soon released without trial, and thereafter his interest and influence in the Fenian movement declined. Following this interlude he returned to the regular army until his retirement in 1870 with the rank of brigadier-general. Sweeny was married twice: first, to Eleanor Swain Clark of Brooklyn, and second, to Eugenia Octavia Reagan of Augusta, Ga. He died at his home in Astoria, L. I., survived by his second wife, three sons, and a daughter.

[Sketch by a son, W. M. Sweeny, in *Am.-Irish Hist. Soc. Jour.*, vol. II (1899); Sweeny's report of the Fenian raid, *Ibid.*, vol. XXIII (1924); F. B. Heitman, *Hist. Reg. and Dict. U. S. Army* (1903), vol. I; *War of the Rebellion: Official Records (Army)*, 1 ser. III, XXXVIII (pts. 1–5); *Battles and Leaders of the Civil War* (4 vols., 1887–88); R. J. Rombauer, *The Union Cause in St. Louis in 1861* (1909); J. Fairbanks and Edwin Tuck, *Hist. of Greene County, Mo.* (1915), vol. I; T. L. Snead, *The Fight for Missouri* (1886); John McElroy, *The Struggle for Missouri* (1909); J. A. Macdonald, *Troublous Times in Canada: A Hist. of the Fenian Raids* (1910); C. P. Stacey, "Fenianism and the Rise of National Feeling in Canada," *Canadian*

Hist. Rev., Sept. 1931; *Army and Navy Jour.*, Apr. 16, 1892; *N. Y. Times*, Apr. 12, 1892; name of Sweeny's mother from his son, W. M. Sweeny.]   H. E. N.

SWEET, JOHN EDSON (Oct. 21, 1832–May 8, 1916), mechanical engineer, manufacturer, was the son of Horace and Candace (Avery) Sweet, and was born on his father's farm at Pompey, Onondaga County, N. Y. He was a descendant of John Sweet who settled in Salem, Mass., in 1631 (Smith, *post*, p. 19). Educated in the district school, he developed a mechanical turn, decided to learn a trade, and in 1850 went to Syracuse, N. Y., and apprenticed himself to a carpenter and joiner. In the winter of 1850–51 he found the opportunity to work in an architect's office and learned something of drawing and architecture; during another lull in carpentry he worked for an artist. He then engaged in designing and building until the Civil War, when he had charge of the construction of a hotel in Selma, Ala. Until 1867 he worked as a draftsman, pattern-maker, and designer in Syracuse, with the exception of a period (1862–64) when he worked for the Patent Bolt and Nut Company, Birmingham, England, which was engaged in building a nail-making machine he and his brother had invented. In 1867 he personally exhibited at the Paris Exposition a typesetting machine which he had designed. From 1868 to 1871 he was superintendent in a manufacturing plant, and then for two years engaged in bridge building in New York state. In 1873 he was appointed master mechanic and director of the machine shop of Sibley College, Cornell University, where he remained for six years. His method of instructing students in shop practice was to have them develop and construct tools and equipment for which there was need. Thus were made standard gauges, straight edges, squares, and angles, the gauges being made by the use of a measuring machine (the first of its kind in the United States), devised by Sweet and built by the students, which read to the 10/100th of an inch. Under Sweet's direction the students built, too, one of the earliest American-made Gramme dynamos and a straight line reciprocating steam engine designed by Sweet. In 1879 he resigned and returned to Syracuse, where in 1880 he organized the Straight Line Engine Company. From that time until his death he was the active head of the company, which enjoyed a worldwide reputation.

He was much respected by his students, his employees, and all others who knew him. He played a leading part in the formation of the American Society of Mechanical Engineers, of which he was president, 1883–84, and in 1914 received the John Fritz Medal—the highest award of the four national engineering societies —"for his achievement in machine design and for his pioneer work in applying sound engineering principles to the construction and development of the high-speed steam engine." He wrote *Things That Are Usually Wrong* (1906) and contributed many articles to technical journals and newspapers, beginning in the 1850's with a series of articles on architecture which ran for twelve years. He traveled extensively and carefully recorded his experiences. On Nov. 24, 1870, he married Caroline V. Hawthorne (d. 1887) of Fulton, N. Y.; on May 9, 1889, he married Irene A. Clark of Syracuse. He died in Syracuse and was buried there.

[*Who's Who in America*, 1916–17; A. W. Smith, *John Edson Sweet* (1925); *Am. Machinist*, May 18, 1916, pp. 871–72; *Trans. Am. Soc. Mech. Engineers*, vol. XXXVIII (1916), pp. 1321–28; *Mech. Engineering*, May 1927, p. 477; obituary in *N. Y. Times*, May 9, 1916.]   C. W. M—n.

SWENSSON, CARL AARON (June 25, 1857–Feb. 16, 1904), Swedish Lutheran clergyman, educator, author, politician, was born in Sugargrove, Pa., the son of Jonas and Maria (Blixt) Swensson. His father was a pastor in the Church of Sweden and came to the United States in 1856 to minister to his countrymen. He was one of the founders of the Augustana Synod, a branch of the American Lutheran Church. Under his father's influence Carl acquired such a profound love for his Swedish heritage that when he matriculated at Augustana College and Theological Seminary at Paxton, Ill., he had contempt for the English language and things American, but at the time of his graduation from college in 1877 and his ordination to the ministry two years later, he had obtained a better perspective and had become intensely American. After his ordination he served the Swedish Lutheran congregation at Lindsborg, Kan. He won the admiration of the Swedish pioneers in the Smoky Hill Valley, and became so attached to them that he retained his residence in Lindsborg until his death. Through his magnetic personality and unbounded energy and ambition he became an invaluable advertising agent for the community. He was instrumental in founding Bethany College there in 1881 and made Lindsborg the cultural center of the Swedish population in the Southwest. He became a power not only in the Augustana Synod but also in the General Council of the Evangelical Lutheran Church. He was the first of the American-born Swedish clergymen to rise to eminence and, unlike most of his brother pastors, won popularity in both Sweden and America.

The beginnings of Bethany College were not auspicious, and in the earliest years Swensson assumed the entire financial risk. In 1884, however, he succeeded in having the Kansas Conference of the Augustana Synod adopt the school, and it speedily rose to collegiate rank and added departments of commerce and music. The annual rendition of Handel's "Messiah" attracted thousands of music lovers and artists to Lindsborg every year, and the chorus organized by Swensson in 1881 has made the name of the town well-known. While he served as pastor and college president, 1889–1904, Swensson wrote four books: *I Sverige* (1891), *Åter i Sverige* (1898), *Vid hemmets härd* (1890), and *I morgonstund* (1903). He was editor of *Förgätmig-ej* in 1902, a publication setting forth the progress of Bethany College, and joint editor of *Korsbaneret*, 1880–85, *Ungdomsvännen*, 1880–87, and *Jubel-album*, 1893, a work commemorating the activity of the Augustana Synod. He was successively editor and publisher of the *Lindsborgs-Posten*, the *Lindsborg Record*, and *Pedagogen* and contributing editor of *Fosterlandet*. He was politically ambitious and was elected to the Kansas legislature in 1889. As a campaign spellbinder he was in great demand, being almost equally effective in both Swedish and English in presenting the cause of old-line Republicanism against the onslaughts of Democrats and Populists. He was delegate-at-large to the Republican National Convention in 1896. On Sept. 15, 1880, he was married to Alma Christina Lind, of Moline, Ill., who, with two daughters, survived him when he died suddenly in Los Angeles, Cal., where he was to participate in the dedication of a church.

[*Who's Who in America*, 1903–05; G. M. Stephenson, *The Religious Aspects of Swedish Immigration* (1932); Alfred Bergin, *Lindsborg efter femtio år* (1919); Ernst Skarstedt, "Läroverkspresidenten Carl Swensson," in *Prärieblomman: Kalender för 1905*, pp. 77–93; J. E. Floren, "Dr. Carl Aaron Swensson," in *Korsbaneret: Kristlig kalender för 1905*, pp. 175–193; *Trans. Kan. State Hist. Soc.*, vol. VIII (1904); *Topeka Daily Capital*, Feb. 17, 1904.]   G. M. S.

SWETT, JOHN (July 31, 1830–Aug. 22, 1913), educator, was born on a farm near Pittsfield, N. H., the son of Eben and Lucretia (French) Swett, and a descendant of John Swett who emigrated from Devonshire, England, to Massachusetts in 1642. He attended the district school (1837–43) and Pittsfield Academy (1844–47). After a few weeks of attendance at Pembroke Academy, he was granted a teacher's certificate by the Pembroke school board and put in charge of the Buckstreet school, where he taught during 1847 and 1848, paid at the rate of ten dollars a month by subscriptions. His second school was at West Randolph, Mass., 1849 and 1850. He was given a tempting offer for the next year, but "debarred from the college course by delicate health and chronic weakness" of one of his eyes, he resolved to go west to the gold mines. He arrived in San Francisco in a sailing vessel by way of Cape Horn, Jan. 31, 1853. After five months in the mining country near Marysville and several more on a ranch near San José, he returned to San Francisco and began teaching in the Rincon school, where he remained until 1862. On May 8, 1862, he was married to Mary Tracy, daughter of Judge Frederick P. Tracy, by whom he had two daughters and four sons. Elected state superintendent of public instruction in 1862, he entered upon his duties at a time when little had been done to establish educational standards in the state. During the five years in which he held office, he labored with marked success for an allocated state school tax, for a system of state teaching certificates, for the use of uniform textbooks throughout the state, and for the provision of adequate buildings and good teaching. He helped to establish a state teachers' organization, held teachers' institutes, and was active in the founding of the *California Teacher*, which was first issued in August 1863. In 1868 he became principal of the Denman grammar school for girls in San Francisco and remained in that position, with exception of the years 1870–73 when he was deputy superintendent of the city schools, until 1876. At that time he became principal of the Girls' High School, where he was very successful. In 1889, after having been forced to resign his principalship as a result of his sturdy opposition to political influences in the schools, he was elected city superintendent of schools by popular vote. He continued to be an active opponent of the spoils system of appointing teachers, and an advocate of professional training for teachers and permanent certification. In 1895 he retired to his farm near Martinez, Cal., but held a number of advisory educational positions during the next thirteen years. He died at his farm. He numbered among his intimate friends John Muir, William Keith, Henry George, and Joaquin Miller [*qq.v.*].

He published a few poems, and many addresses and magazine articles, among them three of an autobiographical nature—"My Grandmother's Kitchen" (*Pioneer Magazine*, January 1855), "The Old Schoolhouse" (*Ibid.*, June 1855), and "My Schools and Schoolmasters" (*Educational Review*, December 1901). Among his books are *Common School Readings* (1867), *A History of the Public School System of Cali-*

fornia (1876), *Methods of Teaching* (1880), *A Normal Word Book* (1879), *School Elocution* (1884), *American Public Schools* (1900), and *Public Education in California* (1911), which was partly autobiographical. His state reports were published in 1864–65, and 1866–67; his city reports annually from 1891 to 1894. He collaborated with William Swinton [*q.v.*] in a number of elementary school textbooks in English composition, grammar, and geography, and prepared several readers.

[In addition to *Pub. Educ. in Cal.* and the autobiog. articles referred to, see W. G. Carr, *John Swett, the Biog. of an Educ. Pioneer* (1933), and obituary in *San Francisco Examiner*, Aug. 23, 1913. Family papers are in the possession of Frank Swett, Hill-Girt Farm, Martinez, Cal.]   J. C. A—k.

SWIFT, GUSTAVUS FRANKLIN (June 24, 1839–Mar. 29, 1903), meat packer, was born on his father's farm near Sandwich, Mass., the ninth of twelve children, and the fifth son, of William and Sally Sears (Crowell) Swift. Through his father he was descended from William Swift (or Swyft) who settled at Sandwich on Cape Cod in 1637, and through his mother, from Elder William Brewster of the *Mayflower*. He attended the common school and at fourteen went to work for his brother, the village butcher. At sixteen, he made his first independent venture, buying a heifer which he slaughtered himself, and peddling the dressed meat from door to door. Before he was twenty he had begun to journey once a week to the cattle market at Brighton, where each time he bought and killed a steer, returning to Cape Cod and peddling his meat before the next market day. In 1859–60 he opened his first butcher shop, at Eastham, Mass.; this shop he soon turned over to a brother, establishing another in Barnstable. Energetic and ambitious, he subsequently opened meat markets in Clinton and Freetown, and from these centers sent meat wagons out daily over regular routes, thus serving a considerable territory. Meanwhile he had acquired a reputation as a shrewd judge of beef cattle and had built up a thriving business as a cattle dealer. In 1872 James A. Hathaway, a Boston meat dealer, took him into partnership to do the buying for the firm, and Swift, following the cattle market westward toward the source of supply, established his headquarters successively at Albany, at Buffalo, and in 1875 at Chicago.

At that time, beef consumed in the East was still shipped in the form of live cattle and slaughtered locally. The cost of feeding stock in transit, loss of condition from overcrowding, and the fact that freight was paid on the entire animal whereas some parts were considered unsalable made the process unduly wasteful, in Swift's estimation, and he determined to ship dressed beef. He sent his first carload to Boston in the late fall of 1877. Hathaway, afraid of the new project, dissolved the partnership, but Swift persisted in his efforts. Successful winter shipments of dressed beef had been made previously, but attempts at refrigeration for warm-weather shipment had not met with great success, and to Swift is largely due credit for the practical development of the refrigerator car. The engineer he employed designed a car in which there was a circulation of fresh air, chilled by passing over ice. This arrangement proved satisfactory, and an essential step toward a revolution in the meat industry of the world had been accomplished. The problem of refrigeration was only one of those confronting the Western packers, however. The Eastern consumers had to be convinced of the quality of Chicago beef; the railroads, enjoying revenue derived from carrying livestock, fought the change by excessive charges on shipments of dressed meat; the Eastern butchers resented the competition. Swift, with his intimate knowledge of the meat trade in New England, introduced his product and won cooperation by forming a series of partnerships with local butchers. For the transportation of his beef he negotiated with the Grand Trunk Railway, which, having carried few cattle, had no stockyards to be maintained along its route. His refrigerator cars, however, he was forced to build at his own expense.

When Swift went to Chicago, Nelson Morris and Philip D. Armour [*qq.v.*] were both established packers, and competition was keen. In the effort to cut costs, waste was eliminated wherever possible. Because cleanliness reduced loss through spoilage, Swift insisted on scrupulous cleanliness in his plant. He was a pioneer in the development of by-products from parts of the animal formerly thrown away—oleomargerine, glue, soap, fertilizer, and eventually pharmaceutical preparations. He put all his profits and all the money he could borrow into the expansion of his business, which in 1885 was incorporated as Swift & Company with a capital of $300,000, twenty months later was capitalized at $3,000,-000, and before his death, at $25,000,000. In his endeavor to secure a place for American beef in the British market, he himself made a number of trips across the Atlantic, and his hard-won success in Great Britain was followed by the establishment of distributing houses in Tokyo, Osaka, Shanghai, Hongkong, Manila, Singapore, and Honolulu. Additional packing plants were established in the newer cattle centers—St.

Swift

Swift

Louis, Kansas City, St. Joseph, Omaha, St. Paul, and Fort Worth. In 1902, with J. O. Armour and Edward Morris he formed the National Packing Company, a combination subsequently dissolved by court order.

Thrifty, industrious, rigidly honest, Swift was rigorous in his requirements both of himself and of his employees. He was unsparing in criticism, rarely gave praise, but was quick to recognize merit by promotion. He had a gift for training men; most of his executives, including his own sons, were brought up from the ranks. About 1900 he began to encourage his employees to buy stock in the concern. His attention was devoted almost entirely to his business until the last decade of his life, when his philanthropies began. He was one of the founders and chief supporters of St. James Methodist Episcopal Church, Chicago, and a liberal donor to the University of Chicago, Northwestern University, the Y. M. C. A., and other causes.

On Jan. 3, 1861, he married Annie Maria Higgins, who with nine of their eleven children survived him. He died in his sixty-fourth year, of an internal hemorrhage following an operation.

[G. H. Swift, *William Swyft of Sandwitch and Some of His Descendants* (1900); T. W. Goodspeed, *The University of Chicago Biog. Sketches*, vol. I (1924); L. F. Swift and Arthur Van Vlissingen, Jr., *The Yankee of the Yards: The Biog. of Gustavus Franklin Swift* (1927); E. N. Wentworth, *A Biog. Cat. of the Portrait Gallery of the Saddle and Sirloin Club* (1920); R. A. Clemen, *The Am. Livestock and Meat Industry* (1923); Charles Winans, "The Evolution of a Vast Industry," *Harper's Weekly*, Nov. 11, 1905–Jan. 13, 1906; H. C. Hill, "The Development of Chicago as a Center of the Meat-Packing Industry," *Miss. Valley Hist. Rev.*, Dec. 1923; *Report of the Federal Trade Commission on the Meat Packing Industry: Summary and Part I* (1919); *Cosmopolitan*, May 1903; *Northwestern Christian Advocate*, Apr. 1, 1903; *National Provisioner*, Apr. 4, 1903; *Butchers' Advocate* (Chicago), Apr. 1, 1903; *Chicago Daily Tribune*, Mar. 30, 1903.]
E. Co.

SWIFT, JOHN FRANKLIN (Feb. 28, 1829–Mar. 10, 1891), lawyer, diplomat, was born of poor parents in Bowling Green, Mo. When he was six or seven years of age, his family moved to Illinois, where they resided eight years before returning to Missouri. He received a very limtied education in the country schools, and at the age of eighteen went to St. Louis to learn the trade of tinsmith. In 1852 he started overland for San Francisco and became a produce merchant in that rapidly rising city. During his spare time he studied law and was admitted to the bar in 1857. In a short time he became a prominent lawyer and acquired considerable wealth. He was elected to the lower branch of the legislature in 1863, and became a leader of the anti-monopoly movement. In 1865 he was appointed register of the land office in San Fran-

cisco by President Lincoln, but resigned in 1866 to take an extended trip to Europe and the East. He returned in time to participate in the Grant presidential campaign of 1868. In 1873 he served again in the legislature, and the following year he ran unsuccessfully for Congress on the anti-monopoly ticket. He was an independent candidate for the assembly in 1877 and was elected with the indorsement of many Republicans although he failed to get the regular nomination of the party. About this time he gained considerable fame in the prosecution of J. J. Marks, state harbor commissioner, and in winning for the city of San Francisco the suits brought against it by the Spring Valley Water Company.

Throughout his career Swift was an outstanding opponent of the monopolistic corporations which figured so largely in California politics. He was author of the provisions in the California constitution which vested in county boards of supervisors authority to control and annually revise water-rates. In 1880 he was appointed member of a commission, with James B. Angell and William H. Trescot [qq.v.], to negotiate modifications of the Burlingame Treaty with China. As chairman of a committee appointed by an anti-Chinese convention of citizens at Sacramento, he drew up a very able anti-Chinese memorial to Congress. The same year he was nominated for governor by both the Republicans and the American (anti-Catholic) party, but he rejected the latter as an "unsolicited and undesired honor," emphatically repudiating the peculiar views of the American party (Davis, *post*, p. 530). This action may have cost him the election, as he was defeated by a few hundred votes.

In 1888, with Stephen Mallory White [q.v.], he was employed by the California legislature to assist the United States attorney-general in winning a decision before the United States Supreme Court sustaining the constitutionality of the Chinese Exclusion Act (*Chae Chan Ping* vs. *United States*, 130 *U. S.* 581). The same year he was a delegate-at-large to the Republican National Convention. Swift seems to have been prominently considered for a position in President Harrison's cabinet, but in March 1889, he was finally appointed United States minister to Japan where he died two years later. His remains were brought to San Francisco and buried with military honors in Lone Mountain Cemetery. His wife, the daughter of Col. W. G. Wood, of San Francisco, survived him. A fluent speaker and a ready debater, Swift was an exceptionally popular after-dinner speaker. He contributed to magazines and reviews and published two books: *Going to Jericho* (1868), an entertaining narrative of the author's trip to Palestine, and *Robert Greathouse* (1870), a novel depicting frontier life in Nevada during the bonanza era. From 1872 to 1888 he was a regent of the University of California.

[W. J. Davis, *Hist. of Pol. Conventions in Cal.* (1893); T. H. Hittell, *Hist. of Cal.*, vol. IV (1897); San Francisco *Evening Bull.*, Mar. 10, *San Francisco Chronicle*, and *Morning Call*, Mar. 11, 1891.]

P. O. R.

SWIFT, JOSEPH GARDNER (Dec. 31, 1783–July 23, 1865), soldier and engineer, a descendant of Thomas Swift who was in Dorchester, Mass., as early as 1634, and a brother of William Henry Swift [*q.v.*], was born on the island of Nantucket. His father, Foster Swift, a physician in private practice, had recently been surgeon on a naval vessel and from 1814 until his death in 1835 was an army surgeon; his mother was Deborah, daughter of Thomas Delano of Nantucket, of Huguenot ancestry. Swift was appointed on May 12, 1800, a cadet (apprentice officer) in the corps of artillerists and engineers and served at Newport, R. I., until transferred to West Point, N. Y., in October 1801. On Mar. 16, 1802, the United States Military Academy was formally established to provide for the training of cadets at that place instead of with their several organizations as formerly. At first there was no definite period of residence or course of study. Swift and one other, commissioned second lieutenants on Oct. 12, 1802, are regarded as the first graduating class.

The rapid expansion of the tiny American army gave Swift correspondingly rapid promotion. He was promoted first lieutenant of engineers, June 11, 1805, immediately after his marriage (June 6) to Louisa Margaret, daughter of James Walker of Wilmington, N. C. He became captain, Oct. 30, 1806; major, Feb. 23, 1808; lieutenant-colonel, July 6, 1812; and on July 31, 1812, at the age of twenty-eight, he was appointed colonel and chief engineer of the army. He was in the field with Gen. James Wilkinson's army in 1813 during the abortive invasion of Canada which is chiefly remembered for the battle of Chrystler's Fields, and received for his services the brevet rank of brigadier-general in February 1814. Later in that year he was in charge of the construction of the fortifications of the city of New York, undertaken as a result of the British raids in Chesapeake Bay and completed in great haste following the capture of Washington. The work was prosecuted by the voluntary labor of thousands of citizens. The grateful city presented a barge, a silver service, and a set of silver drawing instruments to Swift

and had his portrait painted for the City Hall.

In 1816 the government brought the French military engineer, Simon Bernard [*q.v.*], to the United States and placed him in practical charge of all fortification work, though without actual rank. Swift remained chief engineer of the army, but his activities did not extend much beyond the administration of the Military Academy, of which the chief engineer was then *ex officio* superintendent. Finding the situation intolerable, he resigned from the army, Nov. 12, 1818. He was surveyor of the port of New York until 1826, and then chief engineer of several railroads, including the Baltimore & Susquehanna, the New Orleans & Lake Pontchartrain, and the New York & Harlem. From 1829 to 1845 he was a civil engineer in government service, in charge of harbor improvement on the Great Lakes. He spent the latter part of his life at Geneva, N. Y. He was almost—perhaps quite—the first American engineer of distinction whose training was acquired wholly in the United States. On account of his influence over younger engineers, such as his brother-in-law, George W. Whistler, and William Gibbs McNeill [*qq.v.*], who looked up to him as their leader and model, he is an important figure in the history of his profession. Personally, he was "a pink-cheeked, chubby optimist, a handsome man, a hard and methodical worker" (personal letter from William Patten).

[See *The Memoirs of Gen. Joseph Gardner Swift* (1890), ed. by Harrison Ellery, being diaries from 1807 to 1865; C. B. Stuart, *Lives and Works of Civil and Military Engineers of America* (1871); G. W. Cullum, *Biog. Reg. . . . U. S. Mil. Acad.* (3rd ed., 1891), and *Campaigns of the War of 1812–15* (1879); B. J. Lossing, *The Pictorial Field Book of the War of 1812* (1868), for a good brief description of the New York fortifications, of which the N. Y. Hist. Soc. has the drawings; *N. Y. Herald*, July 27, 1865. Swift's military papers are at West Point. There are collections of his letters in the N. Y. Pub. Lib. and in the possession of his descendant, William Patten of Rhinebeck, N. Y.]

T. M. S.

SWIFT, LEWIS (Feb. 29, 1820–Jan. 4, 1913), astronomer, sixth of the nine children of Gen. Lewis and Anna (Forbes) Swift, was born at Clarkson, Monroe County, N. Y. He was descended from William Swift, who settled at Watertown, Mass., before 1634 and later moved to Sandwich, Mass. Because of an accident in his thirteenth year that permanently lamed him and incapacitated him for farm work, Swift attended Clarkson Academy for three years, walking two miles each day on crutches in order to do so. From 1838 to 1846 he helped to make horse rakes, an invention of his father's. He then became a lecturer on scientific subjects and in 1851 entered business at Hunt's Corners, Cortland

County, N. Y. Becoming interested in astronomy, he began about 1855 a survey of the heavens with a somewhat damaged 3-inch lens purchased for five dollars, for which he made an eyepiece and mounting. This lens being accidentally broken, about 1860 he purchased a 4½-inch lens made by Henry Fitz [*q.v.*]. With this telescope, mounted on a platform attached to his barn in Marathon, N. Y., where he was then living, he discovered his first comet (1862 III). In 1872 he entered the hardware business at Rochester, N. Y., and there, with his telescope stationed on the roof of a cider mill, he continued to search for comets. The necessity of removing optical parts when the telescope was not in use finally resulted in the breaking of the flint disk, which was replaced by one from Alvan Clark [*q.v.*] and his sons. Between 1884 and 1893 he appears in Rochester directories as astronomer at the Warner Observatory, built and supported by H. H. Warner of Rochester, manufacturer of proprietary medicines. Upon the failure of Warner's business in 1893, the instrumental equipment was moved to the observatory built by the inventor Thaddeus S. C. Lowe [*q.v.*] on Echo Mountain, Cal. Swift continued his work there until about 1901, when his failing health compelled his retirement to his earlier home at Marathon, N. Y., for the remainder of his life. He lived a simple, frugal life and was capable of great physical endurance. In exposition he was clear and direct, and to those seeking his counsel he was kindly and helpful. He was twice married, first to Lucretia Hannah Hunt on June 26, 1850, and second to Caroline Doane Topping on Aug. 24, 1864. He had two children by his first marriage and three by his second, the youngest of whom, Edward D. T. Swift, discovered comet 1894 IV.

Swift discovered twelve comets and over twelve hundred nebulae, and observed three total eclipses of the sun, those of 1869, 1878, and 1889. During the eclipse of 1878 he observed two objects at first thought to be intramercurial planets, about which a similar observation was made by James Craig Watson [*q.v.*]. Though Swift continued to maintain his conviction of the reality of his discovery, the observation was never confirmed. Among his publications are "Appearance of the Great Comet of 1858" (*Astronomical Journal,* Nov. 2, 1858), "Entdeckung eines neuen Cometen" (*Astronomische Nachrichten,* Nov. 19, 1889), "The Merope Nebula" (*Monthly Notices of the Royal Astronomical Society,* January 1882), "Double Meteors," (*The Sidereal Messenger,* August 1882), and "Observations on the Secondary Tail of the Pons-Brooks Comet" (*Ibid.,* February 1884). Besides cash prizes to-

taling over eleven hundred dollars he received for the discovery of comets three gold medals from the Vienna Academy of Sciences, a silver medal as part of the Lalande prize (1881), four bronze medals of the Astronomical Society of the Pacific, and the Jackson-Gwilt bronze medal of the Royal Astronomical Society (1897), of which he was the first recipient. He was a member of the British Astronomical Association, a Fellow of the American Association for the Advancement of Science, and a Fellow of the Royal Astronomical Society.

[G. H. Swift, *William Swyft of Sandwitch and Some of His Descendants* (1900); *Who's Who in America,* 1912–13; *Gen. Cat. Univ. of Rochester* (1911); Lewis Swift, in *Popular Astronomy,* Nov. 1901; bibliog. in *Cat. of Sci. Papers,* 4 ser., vol. XVIII (1923), comp. by Royal Soc. of London; E. E. Barnard, in *Astronomische Nachrichten, Band* 194, *Seite* 133; E. B. K., in *Monthly Notices of the Royal Astronomical Soc.,* vol. LXXIII, p. 219; obituaries in *Pubs. Astronomical Soc. of the Pacific,* Feb. 1913, and in *N. Y. Times,* Jan. 6, 1913.]   J. M. P—r.

SWIFT, LUCIUS BURRIE (July 31, 1844–July 3, 1929), civil service reformer, writer, lawyer, the seventh child of Stephen Swift and Content (Aber) Swift, was a descendant of William Swyft, of Essex County, England, who came to America about 1630. He inherited a Puritan training and grew up on a farm in Orleans County, N. Y., where a typical district school, Yates Academy, and a home with sufficient books and newspapers helped to develop his intellectual interests. After two years of service with the 28th N. Y. Infantry in the Civil War, he entered the University of Michigan and was graduated in 1870. Returning to Medina, N. Y., he studied law and came under the liberal influences of George Kennan [*q.v.*] and of Godkin's *Nation.* From 1872 to 1879 he served as principal and superintendent of schools at La Porte, Ind. Here he was married to Mary Ella Lyon, a teacher who had been graduated from Elmira College, Elmira, N. Y. No children were born to them.

Swift moved to Indianapolis to practise law in 1879 and became nationally known during the eighties and nineties for his untiring labors in behalf of civil service reform. As chairman of the Indiana Independent Committee of One Hundred he canvassed his state for Cleveland in 1880, and the next year, with Wm. D. Foulke, and others, organized the Indiana Civil Service Reform Association. In 1886 he conducted an exhaustive inquiry and published the results in *A Report Relating to the Federal Civil Service in Indiana* (1886). He exposed gross violations of the Pendleton Civil Service Act and the evils of the patronage system. He was subsequently invited to the White House for a conference, appeared also before a Senate committee, and participated in a national conference of civil service reformers in New York. His influence was in part responsible for the unfavorable attitude taken by the reformers towards Cleveland's earlier policies. Meanwhile, he was fearlessly fighting for civil service reform in his state. Without compensation, he took charge of a legislative inquiry into the Indiana Hospital for the Insane, and in his report revealed wholesale corruption and revolting treatment of patients. This report was an important factor in causing the defeat of the Democrats in 1886 and 1888, in the establishment by law of non-partisan boards of control, and in the introduction of the merit system for employees. In 1888 he and most of his fellow reformers supported Harrison for the presidency, but, disappointed again, they returned to support Cleveland in 1892.

Swift rejected fealty to party organization as a means of accomplishing desired results, and in fidelity to principle few men were more unswerving. True to his Puritan inheritance he was little influenced by abuse or ridicule, material rewards, or popularity. Assisted only by his wife, he began to edit and publish the *Civil Service Chronicle* in 1889. For eight years the *Chronicle* was one of the most influential periodicals devoted to civil service reform in the United States. By 1896, after Cleveland had added 42,511 positions to the classified civil service list, Swift felt that the *Chronicle* had served its purpose and he discontinued it. Throughout this struggle for good government he enjoyed the intimate friendship and encouragement of Theodore Roosevelt. During the World War, like most Americans, he firmly supported the Allied cause by making addresses and writing pamphlets, but without giving due weight to its shortcomings or the merits of Germany's case. In 1928 he published a booklet, *How We Got Our Liberties,* wherein he traced the long struggle of the Anglo-Saxon peoples for freedom and liberty and sought to increase appreciation of this heritage.

[Meredith Nicholson, "An American Citizen," *Scribner's Mag.,* Dec. 1922; W. D. Foulke, *Lucius B. Swift, A Biography, Ind. Hist. Pubs.,* vol. IX (1930); G. H. Swift, *William Swyft of Sandwitch and Some of His Descendants* (1900); *The Mich. Alumnus,* Sept. 14, 1929; *Indianapolis Star* and *Indianapolis News,* July 4, 1929.]   A. T. V.

SWIFT, WILLIAM HENRY (Nov. 6, 1800–Apr. 7, 1879), soldier and engineer, was born in Taunton, Mass. He was the son of Dr. Foster Swift and Deborah (Delano) Swift, and brother of Joseph Gardner Swift [*q.v.*]. Entering the United States Military Academy as a cadet in

August 1813, when he was not yet thirteen years old, he remained at West Point until December 1818, when he left to accompany the expedition of Maj. Stephen H. Long [*q.v.*] to the Rocky Mountains, being allowed, however, to retain his cadetship. He was commissioned second lieutenant of artillery, July 1, 1819, being ranked at the foot of his class because his academic course was incomplete; and promoted first lieutenant, Aug. 5, 1824. Although nominally an artilleryman he was employed constantly on engineering duties, working not only on defensive projects but also on river and harbor improvement along the Atlantic and Gulf coasts, on surveys for the Chesapeake & Ohio Canal, for a projected canal across the Florida peninsula, and for several railroads. The extensive internal improvements then being undertaken—railroads and canals—caused a greater demand for civil engineers than the profession could supply, and Swift's services, like those of some other military engineers, were lent by the government to private corporations for some time.

In August 1832 he was given the brevet rank of captain as an assistant topographical engineer and in July 1838 the actual rank, upon the creation of an independent corps of topographical engineers. The elaborate post route map constructed in 1830–32 was almost entirely his work. From 1833 to 1843 he was on duty with the Coast and Geodetic Survey, and from then until 1849 he was the principal assistant in the topographical bureau in Washington. He was responsible for the construction, at Black Rock Harbor, Conn., of the first skeleton iron tower lighthouse in the United States, having studied this design while in Europe on government business in 1840–41. He built a similar lighthouse on Minot's Ledge, near Cohasset, Mass., in 1847–48, which was carried away during the great storm of Apr. 16, 1851, probably on account of unauthorized loading beyond the limit for which it was designed. He resigned from the army, July 31, 1849, and became successively president of the Philadelphia, Wilmington & Baltimore Railroad, now a part of the Pennsylvania system, and of the Massachusetts Western Railroad, now the Boston & Albany. In 1845, while still in the army, he had been chosen president of the board of trustees of the Illinois & Michigan canal, an office which he continued to hold until 1871. He was a director of many corporations and the trusted financial adviser of Baring Brothers, of his brother-in-law, George W. Whistler [*q.v.*], and others. Of the occasional professional papers which he wrote, a report on the Chesapeake & Ohio Canal was published in

1846 and one on the railroads of Massachusetts in 1856. "He was a broad minded, shrewd, business-like individual, wise, helpful, always fair and scrupulously honest" (personal letter from William Patten). He was appreciative of books and art, visited and encouraged young James McNeill Whistler while yet an obscure artist in Paris, and advised the young man's mother to let him go on painting. He was twice married: first, in 1825, to Mary, daughter of Charles Stuart, British consul in New London, who died in November 1837; and second, in 1844, to Hannah, daughter of John Howard of Springfield, Mass. He died in New York.

[See *The Memoirs of Gen. Joseph Gardner Swift* (1890), ed. by Harrison Ellery; G. W. Cullum, *Biog. Reg. . . . U. S. Mil. Acad.* (3rd ed., 1891); *N. Y. Tribune*, Apr. 9, 1879. Some of Swift's professional papers were left to the Chicago Hist. Soc., and many of his letters are in the possession of William Patten of Rhinebeck, N. Y.]

T. M. S.

SWIFT, ZEPHANIAH (Feb. 27, 1759–Sept. 27, 1823), Connecticut jurist, was born in Wareham, Mass., the son of Roland, a descendant of William Swyft, who emigrated from England to America before 1638 and settled in Sandwich, Mass., and his wife, Mary Dexter. In childhood, he moved with his parents to Lebanon, Conn., where he was reared and schooled, partly by the famed Master Tisdale. Enrolling in a remarkable class which included Joel Barlow, Uriah Tracy, and Oliver Wolcott [*qq.v.*], he was graduated from Yale College with both the baccalaureate and master's degrees (1778, 1781). Thereupon, he read and actually studied law, and on admission to the bar established a practice in the town of Windham, Conn. Despite his lack of a military record, he was elected a representative to the general assembly, 1787–93, serving as clerk of the lower house for four sessions, and as speaker in 1792. As a Federalist, he sat for two terms in the lower house of Congress, 1793–97, and then returned to his practice and to the study of law. In 1800, as secretary to Oliver Ellsworth [*q.v.*] on his mission to France, his provincial outlook was greatly broadened and yet his national patriotism was intensified. On his return he was elected to the state council of the general assembly.

In the meantime, Swift stood forth as a stout opponent of slavery with the publication of *An Oration on Domestic Slavery, Delivered at the North Meeting-House in Hartford* (1791) in which America is described as "the only christian country where domestic slavery is tolerated in any considerable degree . . ." (p. 11). Two years later he published *The Correspondent; Containing the Publications in the Windham*

Herald Relative to the Result of the Ecclesiastical Council, Holden 1792, Respecting the Rev. Oliver Dodge which resulted in a war of pamphlets with the Rev. Moses C. Welch. This was followed by *A System of the Laws of the State of Connecticut* in two volumes (1795, 1796), the first American law text. It displayed a thoughtful philosophy of government as well as a thorough presentation of the constitutional and working government of the state. Elected by the general assembly, he commenced in 1801 a long term on the superior court. A moderate Federalist and a free-thinker in a Christian community, Swift escaped the usual Republican abuse although he was a supporter of the standing order and a firm upholder of the independence of the judiciary. He became chief justice of the court but after he sponsored the Hartford Convention and became a party to its deliberations, he was bracketed with the state rulers who must be dethroned, and, in 1819, after the completion of the Republican-Tolerationist revolution he ceased to be chief justice.

Honored for his service and political orthodoxy by Yale and Middlebury colleges, Swift retired to his legal researches. As far as Connecticut was concerned, a eulogist was quite correct in the appraisal: "No other individual has done so much towards reducing the laws to an intelligible system adapted to our habits and condition" (see Dexter, *post*). In 1810 he published a *Digest of the Law of Evidence, in Civil and Criminal Cases; And a Treatise on Bills of Exchange, and Promissory Notes,* and in 1816 he printed *A Vindication of the Calling of the Special Superior Court, at Middletown . . . for the Trial of Peter Lung* which arraigned legislative interference with the judiciary and defended his own conduct as chief justice. In his retirement, broken only by two years in the general assembly, 1820–22, he published a *Digest of the Laws of the State of Connecticut* (1822–23), of which the second volume came out posthumously. As this work was used rather generally throughout the country in legal instruction and as a guide for courts, it further increased the indebtedness of bench and bar to Connecticut's leading judicial scholar.

After the death of his first wife, Jerusha Watrous, of Colchester, in 1792, he was married on Mar. 14, 1795, to Lucretia Webb, the daughter of Capt. Nathaniel Webb, of Windham. A son by his first wife died in infancy. Of the seven children of the second the most distinguished was Mary A. Swift, author of *First Lessons on Natural Philosophy for Children* (2 volumes, 1833–1836). Swift died while visiting a son in Warren, Ohio, and was buried there.

[G. H. Swift, *Wm. Swyft of Sandwich and Some of His Descendants* (1900); S. E. Baldwin, "Zephaniah Swift," *Great Am. Lawyers*, vol. II (1907); F. B. Dexter, *Biog. Sketches of the Grads. of Yale Coll.*, vol. IV (1907); E. D. Larned, *Hist. of Windham County, Conn.*, vol. II (1880); *Proc. Am. Antiquarian Soc.*, Apr. 1887; memoir in Swift's *Digest of the Laws of the State of Conn.*, vol. II (1823); R. J. Purcell, *Conn. in Transition* (1918); *Encyc. of Conn. Biog.* (1917), vol. I; *Biog. Directory of the Am. Cong.* (1928); *Amer. Hist. Rev.*, July 1934; *Am. Mercury* (Hartford), *Conn. Courant*, Oct. 14, 1823.]   R. J. P.

SWING, DAVID (Aug. 23, 1830–Oct. 3, 1894), preacher, was the second of the two sons of David and Kerenda (Gazley) Swing. His father, who died of the cholera in 1832, was an Ohio River pilot, and David was born over a store kept by his uncle, on the Cincinnati riverfront. He was a descendant of Samuel Schwing who emigrated to America in 1752, settling finally in New Jersey; and, on his mother's side, of John Gazley who emigrated from England in 1715 and established himself in Dutchess County, N. Y. When the boy was about five years old his mother married James Hageman, a blacksmith of Reading, Ohio, who also had two children, and in 1840 the Hagemans and Swings made a home for themselves on a farm near Williamsburg, Clermont County, Ohio. Here, not unacquainted with hardships, a shy, homely, tender-hearted boy, quick of mind and sensitive to beauty, David grew up. Converted at a Methodist revival when he was fifteen, he joined the Presbyterian church. He graduated from Miami University, Oxford, Ohio, in 1852, and after studying Old School theology, and being repelled by it, under Dr. Nathan L. Rice [q.v.] of Cincinnati, he became in 1853 professor of Latin and Greek and principal of the preparatory department at Miami. He married Elizabeth Porter, daughter of an Oxford physician, who bore him two daughters and died of tuberculosis on Aug. 2, 1879.

Swing finished his theological training under a local pastor, but during the twelve or more years he was in Oxford his chief intellectual interest was in literature and history. He also supplied neighboring churches. In 1866 he was persuaded by a former pupil to accept a call to the Westminster Presbyterian Church, Chicago, which in 1868 united with the North Church under the name of the Fourth Church. In the fire of 1871, its place of worship, Swing's dwelling, and all his books and papers were destroyed. He conducted services in a hall and later in McVicker's Theatre until a new edifice, for which he raised funds in the East, was completed. The originality, liberal spirit, and practical helpful-

ness of his sermons were now attracting attention not only in Chicago but elsewhere; *The Alliance* (1873–82), of which Swing was an editor, printed one of his sermons each week, as did also the *Inter-Ocean* and the *Chicago Tribune*. In 1874 he published *Truths for Today*, a volume containing fifteen sermons. He had already been attacked on the ground of heterodoxy by Francis L. Patton [q.v.], professor in the Presbyterian Theological Seminary of the Northwest and editor of *The Interior*; his book involved him in a trial for heresy. In April 1874 charges against him were filed with the Chicago Presbytery. The trial, which aroused widespread interest, resulted in the verdict "not proved." Patton asked for an appeal to the Synod of Illinois, North. Averse to controversy and extended litigation, Swing withdrew from the presbytery, although he did not resign his pulpit until October 1875.

Leading citizens of Chicago at once took measures to establish a new down-town church, and in December 1875 Central Church was organized with about 500 members. It first occupied McVicker's Theatre, but in 1880 Central Music Hall, built primarily to provide a platform for Swing, was dedicated. Here until his death he preached to two or three thousand each week and through his published sermons spoke to countless more. Although he was homely and awkward, without oratorical gifts, an essayist rather than a preacher, his personal charm, his ethical enthusiasm, and his substitution of the truths revealed by human experience for the dogmas of speculative theology as a basis of faith and conduct had great effect. He was a devotee of beauty and had the mind of a poet rather than that of a logician, yet he was strongly pragmatic in method. His sermons and lectures had literary excellence and came from a richly furnished mind; his comprehension was sufficiently limited, however, to permit him to say that the studies of Darwin were "so unimportant that few care whether they are true or false" (*David Swing: A Memorial Volume*, post, p. 102). For years he was one of the institutions of Chicago, beloved by its inhabitants and sought out by visitors from near and far. Among the several volumes of his utterances published during his lifetime are a second series of *Truths for Today* (1876); *Motives of Life* (1879); *Club Essays* (1881, 1889; 4th ed., 1898), read before the Chicago Literary Club; *Sermons* (1874, 1884, 1895). After his death, which occurred in his sixty-fourth year, numerous selections from his sermons and addresses appeared.

[G. S. Swing, *Events in the Life and History of the Swing Family* (1889); J. F. Newton, *David Swing, Poet-Preacher* (1909), containing bibliog.; *David Swing: A Memorial Volume* (1894), ed. by Helen Swing Starring, a daughter, including biog. sketch, sermons, and tributes; *The Message of David Swing to His Generation* (1913), with introduction by N. D. Hillis; *Chicago Tribune, Chicago Herald*, Oct. 4, 8, 1894.]   H. E. S.

SWINTON, JOHN (Dec. 12, 1829–Dec. 15, 1901), journalist, social reformer, was born in Salton, near Edinburgh, Scotland, the son of William and Jane (Currie) Swinton, and the brother of William Swinton [*q.v.*]. In 1843 the family moved to Canada, settling in Montreal, and young Swinton shortly afterward began work as a printer's apprentice in the office of the Montreal *Witness*. Later the family moved to New York City. Swinton entered Williston Seminary, at Easthampton, Mass., in 1853, but after a time returned to typesetting. As a journeyman printer he traveled in the South and the Middle West. In 1856 he went to Kansas to take part in the free-state movement and became manager of the Lawrence *Republican*. The next year he was back in New York City, where for a time he studied both law and medicine. A casual contribution to the *Times* brought him to the attention of Henry J. Raymond [*q.v.*], who gave him employment. In 1860 he was made chief of the editorial staff of the paper, a place he retained for ten years. For the next five years he was variously employed. He had become deeply interested in the cause of the wage-workers and in the spring of 1874 took a conspicuous and daring part in the great labor demonstration at Tompkins Square which was broken up by the police. In the same year he was the candidate of the Industrial Political Party for mayor.

Despite his radicalism, Charles A. Dana [*q.v.*], who greatly admired his talent, gave him a place on the editorial staff of the *Sun*. Here he remained for the years 1875–83, becoming the chief of the editorial staff. In the meantime, in 1877, he had been married and had established a home in Brooklyn. His wife was Orsena (Fowler) Smith, the widowed daughter of Prof. Orson Squire Fowler [*q.v.*]. On Oct. 14, 1883, having retired from the *Sun*, he started *John Swinton's Paper*, a four-page weekly labor journal. It was a brilliantly written paper and attracted wide attention, but it was poorly supported by the wage-earners, and was even boycotted by the powerful Knights of Labor. On Aug. 21, 1887, broken in health and with all his savings exhausted, he published the last number. For a time he seems to have been idle and in distress, but Dana soon reëmployed him and he remained

with the *Sun* until the editor's death. In his later years he wrote for various publications and was the correspondent for five or six European newspapers. He died after an illness of ten days at his Brooklyn home. His wife survived him. They had no children.

In his later days, usually accompanied by his wife, Swinton was a familiar sight at labor and social reform gatherings; his large head, with its bushy shock of white hair flowing out from under a skull cap, his strong, expressive face, and dark, piercing eyes surmounted by great shaggy eyebrows, and his luxuriant iron-gray mustache made an unforgettable picture. He was an omnivorous reader and nothing escaped his interest. He was the author of several pamphlets. In 1880 he published a booklet, *John Swinton's Travels,* the record of a brief European trip with his wife, and fourteen years later he published *Striking for Life,* a work on the labor movement. He had no ordered philosophy. Though a friend and great admirer of Karl Marx, he was not a Socialist. An advocate of the utmost degree of organization for others, he played a lone hand. As a writer he was distinguished; he had a rare sense of word values, and both in vehement invective and in biting sarcasm he was a master of the language of opprobrium. With all his radicalism, he remained a fervently religious Scotch Calvinist. Raymond spoke of him as "the only man I ever knew who had no axes of his own to grind" (*New York Times, post*). He was a man of unblemished integrity.

[*Who's Who in America*, 1901–02; John H. Brown, *Cyc. of Am. Biog.* (vol. VII, 1903); Robert Waters, *Career and Conversation of John Swinton* (1902); *N. Y. Times, N. Y. Tribune*, the *Sun* (N. Y.), Dec. 16, 1901; recollections of the writer.]   W. J. G.

SWINTON, WILLIAM (Apr. 23, 1833–Oct. 24, 1892), war correspondent, author, was born at Salton, near Edinburgh, Scotland, the son of William and Jane (Currie) Swinton, and a brother of John Swinton [*q.v.*]. The family emigrated to Canada in 1843. Swinton received his preparatory education at Knox College, a Presbyterian school which later became one of the colleges of the University of Toronto. He entered Amherst College with the class of 1856 but remained for only part of his freshman year. In 1853 he married Catherine Linton of Canada and secured a position as teacher of languages in the Edgeworth Female Seminary at Greensboro, N. C. From 1855 to 1858 he taught in the Mount Washington Collegiate Institute in New York City, meanwhile preparing for the Presbyterian ministry. He had already done some successful magazine writing, and soon after securing a position with the *New York Times* in 1858, he definitely abandoned plans for a ministerial career. Early in the Civil War he was sent to the front as the *Times* special correspondent with the armies in the field, where his savage criticisms of leading generals kept him in bad grace with the authorities. In this matter he can hardly be said to have transgressed the ethical code of the newspapers of the time, but in some respects his conduct would not bear scrutiny at any time or under any circumstances. He sought to secure privileges by methods savoring of blackmail and to get information by means that may very gently be called undignified. Early in the Virginia campaign of 1864 one of Gen. U. S. Grant's staff officers unceremoniously pulled him out of the hiding place where he was listening to a conference between Grant and Gen. George G. Meade. The patience of the War Department was finally exhausted, and on July 1, 1864, an order was issued depriving him of privileges as a correspondent and forbidding him to remain with the army. During the next few years he published several books dealing with the war: *The Times Review of McClellan; His Military Career Reviewed and Exposed* (1864), *Campaigns of the Army of the Potomac* (1866), *The Twelve Decisive Battles of the War* (1867), *History of the New York Seventh Regiment During the War of the Rebellion* (1870).

In 1869 he became professor of English at the University of California, then just established on its new (but temporary) site at Oakland. President Daniel Coit Gilman's policies were so strongly opposed by Swinton that the latter's resignation in 1874—with that of one other professor—was necessary to the restoration of harmony in the faculty. Swinton then turned to writing school textbooks, with such success that a gold medal was awarded to him at the Paris exposition of 1878 and his royalties sometimes reached $25,000 a year. He produced geographies, spelling books, readers, grammars, histories of the United States and of the world—in short, he covered almost the whole field of juvenile human knowledge. He was a hard but highly erratic worker, and so careless in his financial habits that he was frequently pressed for money. At such times he was ready to dispose of valuable copyrights for a comparatively small sum in cash. He spent this period of his life in Brooklyn, N. Y., and there he died, survived by three sons and two daughters.

[See H. C. Graves, *Hist. of the Class of 1856, Amherst Coll.* (n.d.); R. S. Fletcher and M. O. Young, *Amherst Coll. Biog. Record* (1927); W. C. Jones, *Illus. Hist. of the Univ. of Cal.* (1901); W. W. Ferrier, *Origin and Development of the Univ. of Cal.* (1930); *Hist. Mag.,* Nov. 1869, pp. 295–98; obituary in *N. Y. Times,* Oct. 26, 1892. For Swinton's methods as war correspondent, see J. D. Cox, *Mil. Reminiscences of the Civil War* (1900), vol. I, pp. 76–78, and *Personal Memoirs of U. S. Grant,* vol. II (1886), pp. 143–45.]   T. M. S.

SWISSHELM, JANE GREY CANNON (Dec. 6, 1815–July 22, 1884), reformer and editor, was the daughter of Thomas and Mary (Scott) Cannon, Scotch-Irish Covenanters of Pittsburgh, Pa. She spent her youth in the new settlement of Wilkinsburg, to which her parents removed soon after she was born. At the age of three she began attending school; by the time she was ten she was aiding her widowed mother in earning a living; at fourteen she became active in the anti-slavery cause; before her fifteenth birthday she took charge of the only school in the village. After six years of teaching she married, Nov. 18, 1836, James Swisshelm, a young farmer of the neighborhood. In 1838 she accompanied him to Louisville, Ky., where he attempted, unsuccessfully, to establish a business, and she earned what she could as seamstress and teacher. Her hatred of slavery became an absorbing passion during this sojourn. Returning to Pennsylvania, she took charge of a seminary at Butler in 1840, and began to use her pen in defense of the rights of married women. Two years later she rejoined her husband on a farm, which she named Swissvale, near Pittsburgh. In the midst of domestic duties she continued to write, supplying stories and verses to the *Dollar Newspaper* and to *Neal's Saturday Gazette*. At the same time she contributed to the *Spirit of Liberty,* the *Pittsburgh Gazette,* and to the *Daily Commercial Journal* racy, vehemently written articles on abolition and the property rights of women.

In 1847 she used a legacy from her mother to establish the *Pittsburgh Saturday Visiter* (*sic*), a political and literary weekly, advocating abolition, temperance, and woman's suffrage, the first number of which appeared on Dec. 20. She edited this paper with such spirited audacity that she became widely known for her powers of denunciation. "Beware of sister Jane," contemporary editors said to each other. Most notable among her attacks was one that she published in 1850 upon Daniel Webster's private life. This, she loved to believe, ruined his chances for becoming president. In 1853 she published a volume called *Letters to Country Girls,* compiled from articles in the *Visiter*. In 1857 she sold her paper, separated permanently from her husband—who secured a divorce from her on the ground of desertion a few years later—and, accompanied by her only child, took up her residence in Minnesota. The following year she began the *St. Cloud Visiter*. A libel suit ended this publication in a few months. She at once established the *St. Cloud Democrat,* a Republican paper, which she conducted in her usual intrepid, intensely personal manner until 1863. During this time she lectured frequently throughout the state on political subjects.

In the midst of the Civil War she went to Washington, D. C., and while doing clerical work in a government office and assisting in a war hospital contributed to the *New York Tribune* and to the *St. Cloud Democrat.* During this period she became a warm personal friend of Mrs. Lincoln. In the course of Andrew Johnson's administration she started a radical paper called the *Reconstructionist.* In this she attacked the President with such violence that in 1866 he dismissed her from the government service. Returning to Swissvale, she made that place her home for the rest of her life. In 1880 she published *Half a Century,* an entertaining account of her life to the year 1865. Her extreme individualism made her a free lance in all her undertakings. She never worked happily in reform organizations, preferring always to forge her own thunderbolts. Her firm convictions, her powers of sarcasm, her stinging yet often humorous invective, and her homely, vigorous style made her a trenchant journalist.

[In addition to *Half a Century,* see L. B. Shippee, "Jane Grey Swisshelm: Agitator," *Miss. Valley Hist. Rev.,* Dec. 1920; *Minn. Hist. Soc. Colls.,* vol. XII (1908); S. J. Fisher, "Reminiscences of Jane Grey Swisshelm," *Western Pa. Hist. Mag.,* July 1921; B. M. Stearns, "Reform Periodicals and Female Reformers," *Am. Hist. Rev.,* July 1932; A. J. Larsen, *Crusader and Feminist: Letters of Jane Grey Swisshelm, 1858–1865* (1934); *N. Y. Times,* July 23, 1884.]   B. M. S.

SWITZLER, WILLIAM FRANKLIN (Mar. 16, 1819–May 24, 1906), journalist, historian, and politician, first of two sons of Simeon and Elizabeth (Cornelius) Switzler, was born on a farm in Fayette County, Ky. His father was a native of Virginia, his mother of Kentucky, and his paternal grandparents of Switzerland. His family moved to Fayette, Mo., in 1826, and William began his schooling in a log house. Later his father bought a farm near Franklin, Mo., on which the boy grew up. He supplemented his training at Mount Forest Academy by omnivorous reading, including law, which he practised three years. In 1841 he became editor of the oldest Missouri newspaper outside of St. Louis, the *Columbia Patriot,* then a Whig weekly (founded at Franklin in 1819 as the *Missouri Intelligencer*); this he purchased in December 1842 and renamed the *Missouri Statesman.* An ardent Whig editorially, he nevertheless saw

that Democratic news was faithfully reported. So well known were his remarkable memory and his insistence on accuracy that citation of the *Statesman* was freely accepted as proof. He served three terms in the Missouri legislature, being elected in 1846, 1848, and 1856, and supported progressive and anti-slavery measures. During the Civil War he was so strong a Unionist that a guerrilla band threatened his life. Although he served as delegate to the National Constitutional Union Convention (Democratic) in Baltimore in 1860, Lincoln appointed him secretary of state in the provisional government in Arkansas two years later. But the appointment did not alter his politics, and in 1864 he supported George Brinton McClellan [*q.v.*]. Democratic candidate for national representative in 1866 and 1868, he each time unsuccessfully contested the election of his opponent. He contended that Democratic voters had been disfranchised by the Missouri constitution of 1865, which he was chosen to help frame and whose adoption he vigorously opposed. He was also a delegate to the state constitutional convention of 1875 and drafted the section on education. He edited the *Statesman* until 1885, when President Cleveland appointed him chief of the bureau of statistics in the Treasury Department. For short periods he also edited newspapers in St. Joseph and Chillicothe, Mo., and from 1893 to 1898, the *Missouri Democrat* at Boonville.

Switzler was one of the best informed men of his time on the history of his state. His publications include the *Early History of Missouri* (1872), the section on history in C. R. Barns's *The Commonwealth of Missouri* (1877), *Switzler's Illustrated History of Missouri* (1879), *History of Boone County, Missouri* (1882), and *History of Statistics and Their Value* (1888). He also contributed to H. L. Conard's *Encyclopedia of the History of Missouri* (1906). His last years he spent writing a history of the University of Missouri. A founder of the first circulating library in Columbia, head of the lyceum there in the 1840's, and sponsor of its first brass band, he was in his last decade still working for local improvements. In 1849 he helped lead a movement opening the way for the founding of Christian College (1851), of which he was a trustee for many years, and the Baptist (later Stephens) College (1856). He was a good public speaker, and his bearded face was a familiar sight at fairs, dedications of covered bridges, and Fourth of July celebrations. He was a Presbyterian and a vigorous temperance leader. In his latter years he enjoyed the editorial rivalry of Edwin William Stephens [*q.v.*]. Survived by two sons and a daughter, Switzler died of the infirmities of age in his eighty-seventh year in Columbia. His wife, Mary Jane Royall, of Columbia, whom he married Aug. 31, 1843, died in 1879. He left his mark as the dean of Missouri journalists, and three years after his death the first building of the School of Journalism of the University of Missouri was named in his honor.

[N. T. Gentry, in *Mo. Hist. Rev.*, Jan. 1930; H. L. Conard, *Encyc. of the Hist. of Mo.* (1906); *Kansas City Star*, Feb 4, 1900; obituaries in *St. Louis Post-Dispatch* and *Columbia Daily Tribune*, May 24, and in *Kansas City Jour.*, May 25, 1906; *House Miscellaneous Doc. 14*, 41 Cong., 2 Sess.; information from Switzler's daughter, Mrs. J. S. Branham, and F. C. Shoemaker, both of Columbia, Mo.]   I. D.

SYKES, GEORGE (Oct. 9, 1822–Feb. 8, 1880), soldier, was born at Dover, Del., the son of William Sykes and the grandson of James Sykes, noted physician and governor of Delaware, 1801–02. Sykes received his early education in Dover and was sent to the United States Military Academy at West Point, N. Y., in 1838. He was graduated in 1842 as a second lieutenant, 3rd Infantry, and went immediately to Florida where he took part in the Seminole War. He was promoted to the rank of first lieutenant in 1846, served in the war with Mexico during the entire campaign from Vera Cruz to Mexico city, and was brevetted captain for gallant conduct at Cerro Gordo. After the war he served mostly in the Southwest.

At the outbreak of the Civil War Sykes became a major, and, at the first battle of Bull Run, he commanded a battalion of regulars which particularly distinguished itself by protecting the disordered retreat of the Federal troops. For this service he was appointed a brigadier-general of volunteers. In the spring of 1862, Sykes commanded a brigade, subsequently the 2nd Division, V Corps, composed mostly of regulars, in the Peninsular campaign in Virginia. He valiantly defended his position at the battle of Gaines's Mill, checking the Confederate attack until darkness enabled the Union army to be withdrawn. At Malvern Hill on July 1, 1862, he again assisted in repulsing the enemy. In the second Manassas campaign, Sykes's division, part of Porter's V Corps, experienced heavy fighting, especially on Aug. 30, but held its ground until ordered back. Sykes was only lightly engaged at Antietam and at Fredericksburg. Late in the year he was promoted to the rank of major-general. At Chancellorsville, while Stonewall Jackson was fighting the main Federal forces, Sykes operated towards Fredericksburg against Lee's army.

In the Gettysburg campaign Sykes commanded the V Corps. It did not arrive on the battle-field until July 2, when it was ordered to hold the Round Tops, threatened by an enemy attack. Severe fighting occurred in which Sykes bravely led his men to hold these hills for the Federal army. At a council of war that night, he advised remaining on the defensive for one more day. This plan was adopted by Meade. When the Confederates made their famous charge on July 3, he was not directly engaged, although his troops suffered from artillery fire. An opportunity existed after the repulse of the enemy for a counter-attack by the V Corps and there seems to have been some controversy between Sykes and Meade as to whether Sykes had been ordered to do this. Sykes denied that he had been so directed, but, in any case, the chance passed without being utilized. He was brevetted brigadier-general in the regular army for his conduct in this battle.

Upon the reorganization of the Army of the Potomac early in 1864, Sykes was relieved from the V Corps, and sent to Kansas, where he remained on unimportant duties until the end of the war. In 1866 he was mustered out of the volunteer service as a major-general and reverted to the rank of lieutenant-colonel, 5th Infantry, in the regular army. The rest of his service was mainly in the West. He became colonel of the 20th Infantry in 1868, and died at Fort Brown, Texas, while commanding that regiment. Serious illness and great suffering marred the last years of his life. His wife, Elizabeth, was the daughter of Robert Goldsborough of Cambridge, Md. Sykes as a general was excellent on the defensive, but he lacked initiative. He was nicknamed "Tardy George," but his tardiness was mental, not physical.

[*War of the Rebellion: Official Records (Army)*, 1 ser., vols. X, part 2, XI, parts 1, 2, XXVII, part 1 (1884–89); *Battles and Leaders of the Civil War*, 4 vols. (1887–88); G. W. Cullum, *Biog. Reg. . . . Officers and Grads., U. S. Mil. Acad.* (1891); article by Henry Coppee in *Ann. Reunion, Asso. Grads., U. S. Mil. Acad.* (1880); G. J. Cross, *The Battle-field of Gettysburg* (1866); J. T. Scharf, *Hist. of Del.* (1881), vol. I; *Galveston Daily News*, Feb. 10, 1880.]   C. H. L.

SYLVESTER, FREDERICK OAKES (Oct. 8, 1869–Mar. 2, 1915), painter, poet, was born in Brockton, Mass., only son and second child of Charles Fred and Mary Louise (Kilburn) Sylvester. His father, a fashioner of shoemaking tools and later a hardware merchant, belonged to a Plymouth family, while his mother was a descendant of a line of Provincetown seafarers. After graduating from high school in Fall River in 1888, Sylvester went to the Massachusetts Normal Art School. Completing his course in 1891, he was appointed assistant professor of drawing and painting in Newcomb College, Tulane University, New Orleans, La. On Christmas of that year he married Florence Isabel Gerry of Fall River. In September 1892 he became head of the drawing department in the Normal and High School, St. Louis, Mo., and he taught in the St. Louis school system until 1913, when long illness finally forced him to take a leave of absence. He resigned the next year. An early convert to Christian Science, he had become meanwhile (1901) one of the first teachers at the Principia, with whose development he was closely associated until his death.

The Mississippi River, which became his favorite subject for painting, first aroused Sylvester at New Orleans, where he painted waterfront objects. On removing to St. Louis he continued in this vein, and at the Louisiana Purchase and Portland expositions he received medals for studies of the Eads bridge. Later, omitting all signs of man and commerce, he began to record the simple majesty of the river's various moods, especially as revealed in the region of its towering palisades above Alton, Ill. His "unquestioned . . . place in the art of the Middle West" (*Christian Science Monitor*, Sept. 17, 1915) rests on the many canvases produced in his bluff-crest studio near Elsah, Ill., which afforded a particularly fine view of the broad river. He preferred quiet tones—pale greens, mild blues, gray and rose—but also employed the bolder hues of sunset and autumn foliage. Typical of his work is "The River's Golden Dream," which hangs in the City Art Museum, St. Louis. A collection has been assembled at the Principia, while there are other examples in the St. Louis public library, at the University of Missouri, Christian College, and in private hands. When not teaching or painting, Sylvester devoted himself to writing. Like his canvases, his books, *Verses* (1903) and *The Great River: Poems and Pictures* (1911), reveal the solace he found in the contemplation of nature. He took a leading part in the development of the art colony of St. Louis and was head of its Artists' Guild, 1907–08. Always frail, he died of tuberculosis in his forty-sixth year, survived by his widow, a daughter, and a son. As he requested, his body was cremated, and the ashes were scattered in the river which was his joy in art and life.

[See *Who's Who in America*, 1914–15; F. W. Ruckstull, *Great Works of Art and What Makes them Great* (1925); Clarence Stratton, in *Art and Progress*, Sept. 1913; Laura R. Way, in *School Arts Mag.*, Nov. 1912; John Finley, in *Scribner's Mag.*, Oct. 1912; *Bull. of the St. Louis Art League*, July 1915; *N. Y. Times*, Mar. 3, 1915; obituaries and editorial in *St. Louis Post-Dispatch*, Mar. 3 and 4, 1915. A thesis on Sylvester's life and work by Mrs. Lulu Guthrie Emberson is in the Univ. of Mo. lib. Clippings, notebooks, and MSS. are in the possession of Mrs. Sylvester and Warren Sprague, both of St. Louis, and the Principia.] I. D.

SYLVESTER, JAMES JOSEPH (Sept. 3, 1814–Mar. 15, 1897), mathematician, was born in London, the youngest of six sons of Abraham Joseph. In later years his eldest brother adopted the surname Sylvester, and the rest of the brothers followed suit. James attended a school for Jewish boys in London and finished with honor his preparation for the university at the Royal Institution, Liverpool. In 1831 he matriculated at St. John's College, Cambridge, but after 1833 "degraded" for two years, returning in 1836. He was second wrangler in the mathematical tripos of 1837, but because of his Jewish faith was barred from a degree, as well as from prizes and a fellowship. After the Test Act of 1872, he was awarded both bachelor's and master's degrees. In 1837 he succeeded William Ritchie as professor of natural philosophy at University College, London, where he taught for four years. In 1841 he was granted the degrees of B.A. and M.A. by the University of Dublin, and in the same year accepted a call to the chair of mathematics in the University of Virginia.

Sensitive, race-conscious, and unable to control his temper, he was ill-fitted to meet the provincial prejudice of some of his students and to handle disciplinary problems. On Feb. 24, 1842, after about three months of service, he resigned his professorship because of the refusal of the faculty to expel a student with whom he had had difficulty (Bruce, *post*, III, 73–76). Going first to Washington and then to New York, where he lived with his eldest brother, he endeavored unsuccessfully to get appointments at Columbia and at Harvard.

Returning to London, he was engaged in actuarial work from December 1844 until 1856; at the same time he studied law in the Inner Temple and on Nov. 22, 1850, was called to the bar. During this period he was closely associated with Arthur Cayley (see *Dictionary of National Biography*), seven years his junior, a gifted mathematician who had also been called to the bar. In 1855 Sylvester was appointed professor of mathematics in the Royal Military Academy at Woolwich, where he taught until he was retired in July 1870. He had been president of the London Mathematical Society in 1866, and in 1869 presided over the meeting of the mathematical and physical science section of the British Association. In 1876, upon the recommendation of Joseph Henry and Benjamin Peirce [*qq.v.*], he was called to the newly opened Johns Hopkins University in Baltimore. Here he rendered memorable service. "As a source of intellectual enthusiasm, Sylvester stood out above all his colleagues," wrote one of his associates (Franklin, *Gilman, post,* p. 213). The oldest member of the faculty, he brought to the new institution not only his reputation and ability as one of the greatest mathematicians of his time, but an infectious eagerness for intellectual endeavor which had a stimulating effect upon the whole university. Setting new standards for mathematical research in America, inspiring scores of future teachers and investigators, he gave a marked impetus to the development of his science in the United States. From the foundation of the *American Journal of Mathematics* by the University in 1878 until May 1884 he was its editor, giving it at once a distinguished place among the learned journals of the world. In December 1883 he resigned his chair to accept election as Savilian Professor of Geometry at Oxford, in which position he continued for the remainder of his life, although failing health caused him to retire from teaching in 1894. His death three years later followed an apoplectic stroke.

Sylvester has been characterized as "perhaps the mind most exuberant in original ideas of pure mathematics of any since Gauss" (*Collected Papers of Charles Sanders Peirce*, vol. IV, 1933, p. 506). His work was chiefly in the domain of analysis rather than in that of geometry. In particular he devoted his attention to the theory of numbers—including the partitions of numbers and the distribution of primes; to higher algebra, as in the completion of Newton's work on the number of imaginary roots in an algebraic equation; and—building upon the foundations laid by Boole and Cayley—to the theory of invariants, a subject in which he was recognized as preëminent. He was the recipient of many honors while he lived, and after his death the Royal Society of London gave his name to a triennial award—the Sylvester Medal —for the encouragement of research in pure mathematics, while the Johns Hopkins University in 1901, wishing to do signal honor to two of the greatest living scientists, Lord Kelvin and Simon Newcomb, awarded them each a medallion bearing Sylvester's portrait.

Many of his papers, which during his lifetime appeared in various learned journals, were gathered into *The Collected Mathematical Papers of James Joseph Sylvester* (4 vols., 1904–12), edited by H. F. Baker. In 1870 he published *The Laws of Verse,* in which from his own polished translations of certain odes of Horace and several German poems he illustrated the principle of "phonetic syzygy"—"the apt juncture of syllables." "The most interesting thing about it," says Prof. George Saintsbury, speaking of this little volume, "is the author's agreement, from almost the most opposite preparation and point of view conceivable, with Poe—an agreement which extends to the doctrine that accent *creates* quantity" (*A History of English Prosody*, 1910, III, 444–45). Most of Sylvester's original verse showed more ingenuity than poetic feeling. He was completely at home in English, French, German, Italian, Latin, and Greek; was very fond of music; though eccentric and often irritable had considerable humor; was vivacious in conversation, and greatly enjoyed society. He never married.

[H. F. Baker, "Biographical Notice," in *The Collected Mathematical Papers of James Joseph Sylvester,* vol. IV; *Who's Who* (British), 1897; Arthur Cayley, "James Joseph Sylvester," *Nature* (London), Jan. 3, 1889; G. B. Halsted, "Sylvester at Hopkins," *The Johns Hopkins Alumni Mag.,* Mar. 1916; D. S. Blondheim, "A Brilliant and Eccentric Mathematician," *Ibid.,* Jan. 1921; *Johns Hopkins Univ. Circulars,* vol. I (Apr. 1880), p. 38, vol. III (Jan. 1884), p. 31; P. E. Matheson and E. B. Elliott in *Dict. Nat. Biog.,* first Supp.; Alexander MacFarlane, *Lectures on Ten British Mathematicians of the Nineteenth Century* (1916); *The Hist. Reg. of the Univ. of Cambridge,* 1917; H. H. Bellot, *Univ. Coll., London, 1826–1926* (1929); P. A. Bruce, *Hist. of the Univ. of Va.,* vol. III (1921); D. C. Gilman, *The Launching of a University* (1906), pp. 65–70; Fabian Franklin, *The Life of Daniel Coit Gilman* (1901), and memorial address on Sylvester (1897), repub. in *People and Problems* (1908); P. A. MacMahon, in *Nature* (London), Mar. 25, 1897; *Science,* Apr. 16, 1897; M. Noether in *Mathematische Annalen,* vol. L (1898); D. E. Smith and Jekuthiel Ginsburg, *A Hist. of Mathematics in America before 1900* (1934); *N. Y. Times,* Mar. 16, 1897; R. C. Archibald, "Unpublished Letters of James Joseph Sylvester and Other New Information Concerning His Life and Work," *David Eugene Smith Presentation Volume* (*Osiris,* vol. I, 1936).]   D. E. S.

SYLVIS, WILLIAM H. (Nov. 26, 1828–July 27, 1869), reformer and labor leader, was born in the village of Armagh, Indiana County, Pa., the second son of Maria (Mott) and Nicholas Sylvis. His father, a wagon-maker and a Democrat, was very poor. The panic of 1837 scattered the family for a while, William going by contract to a neighbor through whom he gained a slight education, an interest in Whig politics, and an admiration for Henry Clay. In the Forest Iron Works, Union County, he learned the trade of iron moulding. After a period of wandering as a journeyman, he married Amelia A. Thomas, Apr. 11, 1852, and settled in Philadelphia. By this, and a second marriage in 1866 to Florrie Hunter of Hollidaysburg, Pa., he had five sons.

As a result of a strike in 1857, during which

he was elected shop secretary, he joined and was made recording secretary of an iron-moulders' union which had been organized in Philadelphia in 1855. Shortly afterward he initiated a resolution in the union advocating a national convention of iron moulders, and with the president of the local union signed a call for the first convention of the Iron-Moulders International Union, which was held in Philadelphia in July 1859. Sylvis' address to the iron moulders of America became the preamble to the constitution of the new union, and at its second convention, Jan. 10, 1860, in Albany, he was elected treasurer. When the Whig party ceased to exist, he became a Union Democrat and in 1860 supported Douglas. On Feb. 22, 1861, in Philadelphia, he called to order the national convention of workingmen opposed to war. After the Civil War had begun he helped recruit a company for the Union army, but declined the lieutenancy offered him and worked as a teamster in Washington for nine months.

In 1863, at Sylvis' instigation the moulders' organization reconvened in Pittsburgh with half the original number of delegates, and elected him president. Single-handed, he reorganized the war-shattered union. In his report to the Pittsburgh convention in 1864 he recommended the establishment of cooperative foundries and, borrowing an idea from the Machinists' and Blacksmiths' International, the formation of a national trades assembly. He was intimately associated with the activities resulting in the "Labor Congress" at Baltimore in 1866, the first meeting of the National Labor Union, and in 1868 was elected president of that body, thus becoming the representative of 600,000 organized workers. Shortly after his election he appointed a permanent lobbying committee of five to remain in Washington during the sessions of Congress.

With most of the purposes of the National Labor Union Sylvis was in complete accord: he favored the Labor Reform Party, cooperation, the monetary reforms of Edward Kellogg [q.v.], Greenbackism, the eight-hour day, arbitration of labor conflicts, support of "the sewing-women and daughters of toil in this land," tenement-house reform, more rigid enforcement of the apprentice system, the establishment of workingmen's lyceums, institutes, and reading rooms, and the reservation of public lands for bona fide settlers. In theory he opposed strikes, but in practice he led some of the first great struggles of American trade unions. He strongly urged affiliation with the First International and maintained a regular correspondence with its leaders.

He was, however, influenced more by the English cooperative movement.

For a year just after the Civil War Sylvis edited the *Iron-Moulders International Journal,* and about 1869 he became joint proprietor of the *Workingman's Advocate,* the official organ of the National Labor Union, published simultaneously in Chicago and Philadelphia. His writings, scattered but prolific, touched all the political and labor questions of the day. He was a competent orator and the best known labor leader of his time. Throughout his life he remained a Methodist and was active in the temperance movement. He was often prominently mentioned by the labor press for the vice-presidency on a Labor or Democratic ticket. He died at the height of his career, before he was forty-one.

[J. C. Sylvis, *The Life, Speeches, Labors, and Essays of William H. Sylvis* (1872); T. V. Powderly, *Thirty Years of Labor, 1859–1889* (1889); J. R. Commons and associates, *Hist. of Labour in the U. S.* (1918), vol. II; N. J. Ware, *The Labor Movement in the U. S. 1860–1895* (1929); *Public Ledger* (Phila.), July 29, 1869.]   H. S.

SYMMES, JOHN CLEVES (July 21, 1742– Feb. 26, 1814), pioneer, was born at Southold, Long Island, the son of the Rev. Timothy and Mary (Cleves) Symmes and the descendant of Zechariah Symmes who emigrated from England to Charlestown, Mass., in 1634. His education was fairly adequate, and for a time he taught school. In 1770 he settled in Sussex County, N. J., and in 1780 he removed to Morristown. Taking a leading part in Revolutionary activities in New Jersey, he became chairman of the committee of correspondence for Sussex County in 1774, and in 1775 he was appointed a colonel in the militia. He helped cover Washington's retreat through New Jersey in 1776, and from 1776 to 1779 he fought in a number of battles, notably at Monmouth and at Short Hills. As a member of the New Jersey convention in 1776, he was on the committee that drew up the new state constitution, and in 1776, 1780, and 1785 he was elected to the New Jersey legislative council. Also in 1776 he was on a commission to investigate the dissatisfaction among the New Jersey state troops at Ticonderoga. A year later he was elected an associate justice of the supreme court of New Jersey, a commission that was renewed in 1783. In 1778 he represented New Jersey at the New Haven convention to regulate prices.

He was elected a member of the Continental Congress from New Jersey in 1785 and was re-elected in 1786. As a member of Congress he speedily became interested in western colonization. The immediate impetus to action probably came from Benjamin Stites who, while trading along the Ohio, had been greatly impressed with the possibilities of the fertile region that stretched northward from that river, between the Miami and the Little Miami rivers. Stites pointed out the many possibilities of these lands, and Symmes made a trip down the Ohio in the spring of 1787, certainly as far as the falls (Louisville). With characteristic impulsiveness he proposed at first to found a settlement on the Wabash above Vincennes; but after due reflection he applied to Congress for 2,000,000 acres in the more accessible region between the two Miamis. On Oct. 3, 1787, Congress authorized a formal contract with him, but before it was signed he issued his "Trenton Circular," which outlined his terms for granting land and called attention to the resources and the favorable location of the proposed colony. On Feb. 19, 1788, Congress appointed him a judge of the newly erected Northwest Territory, and, after making the first payment for his land, he left in July for the western country, although not until Oct. 15, 1788, was he given a definite contract for 1,000,000 acres, the Miami Purchase. About four and a half months later, he founded a settlement at North Bend, the third one on his lands. Soon he was selling many warrants for lands; but collections were poor, and he could not meet the payments due under his contract. Jonathan Dayton and Elias Boudinot [qq.v.], both of whom were personally interested in the new colony, came to his aid, and the president issued a patent, on Sept. 30, 1794, for the 311,682 acres Symmes had actually paid for.

As a colonizer, he had the perseverance and qualities of leadership that eventually won success. Yet he was quarrelsome and exceedingly careless, issuing conflicting warrants and even selling lands outside his patent. As a result he was made a defendant in many lawsuits, and, when he died in Cincinnati, the bulk of his property had been dissipated. Nevertheless, he had planted an important colony, with its chief settlement, Cincinnati, perhaps the most important military and commercial outpost in the early West. As a jurist, he was not at all noteworthy, holding his appointments from influence, rather than from any reputation for profound legal knowledge. In his capacity of territorial judge he did not cooperate wholeheartedly with Gov. Arthur St. Clair [q.v.], and differences between the two were common. His first wife, Anna Tuttle of Southold, Long Island, left two daughters, one of whom became the wife of William Henry Harrison [q.v.]. Mrs. Mary Halsey of New Jersey was his second wife, and his third

wife was Susanna Livingston, the daughter of William Livingston [q.v.], of New Jersey.

[C. T. Greve, *Centennial Hist. of Cincinnati* (1904), vol. I; C. H. Winfield, *Life and Public Services of John Cleves Symmes* (1877), also in *N. J. Hist. Soc. Proc.*, ser. 2, vol. V, pp. 22–43 (1879); *The Correspondence of John Cleves Symmes* (1926), ed. by B. W. Bond, Jr.; *Western Spy* (Cincinnati), Mar. 12, 1814; *New-England Hist. and Gen. Register*, Apr. 1859; Memo. of Record of John Cleves Symmes during the Revolutionary War (in Symmes's handwriting), Clarke MSS. II fo. 3, Hist. and Phil. Soc. of Ohio, Cincinnati.]
B. W. B., Jr.

SYMONS, GEORGE GARDNER (1865–Jan. 12, 1930), landscape painter, better known as Gardner Symons, was born in Chicago, Ill., of Jewish descent. After studying at the Art Institute of Chicago, he was a student in Munich, London, and Paris. He returned to the United States in 1909 and took up his residence in Brooklyn, N. Y. He spent most of his life in New York but made frequent sketching trips to the Berkshire hills, the valley of the Deerfield River, Gloucester, Mass., Cornwall, England, to various parts of Europe, whither he went almost every year to paint, and to southern California. In the latter part of his life he did much of his work at his country home in Colrain, Mass. He specialized in winter landscapes. He won the Carnegie prize of the National Academy of Design in 1909 for his "Opalescent River" and in 1911 became an Academician. In 1912 the National Arts Club conferred on him a gold medal and a prize of $1000 for his painting of "The Sun's Glow and Rising Moon." He was awarded a bronze medal at the International Exposition, Buenos Aires, 1910; the third W. A. Clarke prize and Corcoran bronze medal, Corcoran Gallery of Art, Washington, D. C., 1912; and the Saltus medal for merit, National Academy of Design, 1913. At the inaugural exhibition of the Toledo Museum of Art, 1912, he exhibited "Rock-ribbed Hills of New England" and "Snow-clad Fields in Morning Light"; at the Carnegie Institute, Pittsburgh, 1913, "Breaking of the Winter Ice" and "November, Dachau, Germany"; and at the sixth annual exhibition of the Concord Art Association, Concord, Mass., "Morning Light." He died in Hillside, N. J., at the home of a brother-in-law. He was a member of numerous clubs and societies of artists both in the United States and abroad.

His "Snow Clouds" is in the Corcoran Gallery of Art, "The Winter Sun" in the Art Institute of Chicago. There are other examples of his work in art museums in Los Angeles, St. Louis, Toledo, Brooklyn, Pittsburgh, and in numerous other cities throughout the country. "Opalescent River," in the Metropolitan Museum of

Art, New York, a typical Symons painting, shows bright sunlight shining on the snow and floating ice in the river, with groups of trees and farm buildings beyond, and hills in the distance. His pictures, which have been praised for their strength and originality, are characterized as well by great sincerity and truth, and by a warm sympathy of imagination.

[*Who's Who in America*, 1928–29; Eugen Neuhaus, *The Hist. and Ideals of Am. Art* (1931); L. M. Bryant, *Am. Pictures and Their Painters* (1917); Mantle Fielding, *Dict. of Am. Painters, Sculptors, and Engravers* (1926); *America*, Feb. 26, 1910, pp. 526–28; *Art News*, June 20, 1925, and Jan. 25, 1930; *Century*, Mar. 1920; *Am. Art Ann.*, 1923; *Boston Transcript*, Feb. 1, 6, 1912, May 15, 1922, and Jan. 14, 1930.]   W. H. D.

SYMONS, THOMAS WILLIAM (Feb. 7, 1849–Nov. 23, 1920), military engineer, was born at Keeseville, Essex County, N. Y., the son of Thomas and Syrena (Eaton) Symons. After a year spent at the Michigan Agricultural College, Lansing, he secured an appointment to the United States Military Academy at West Point. Graduating at the head of his class in 1874, he was commissioned second lieutenant in the corps of engineers. After service at Willet's Point, N. Y., 1874–76, and with the survey expedition under Lieut. George M. Wheeler [*q.v.*], 1876–79, during which time, May 2, 1878, he was promoted first lieutenant, he was made engineer officer of the Department of the Columbia.

In the course of his varied duties in this position he made a survey of the Columbia River, the results of which were published (*Senate Executive Document 186*, 47 Cong., 1 Sess.). From Dec. 28, 1882, until June 7, 1883, he was on duty with the Mississippi River Commission, and from June 18 to Dec. 15, 1883, with the Mexican boundary survey. For the next few years, except for a very brief tour of duty in March 1885 at Hot Springs, Ark., he was in Washington, D. C., aiding in the construction of the Washington aqueduct and serving as assistant to the engineer commissioner of the District of Columbia. On June 2, 1884, he was promoted captain. From November 1889 to October 1895 he was stationed in Portland, Ore., in charge of important river and harbor works in the Portland district.

Transferred to Buffalo, he now began notable engineering projects on the Great Lakes. He had charge of the construction of the Buffalo breakwater, which, when completed, was the largest in the world. He was promoted major Mar. 31, 1896. During the following year he made a study of the problems involved in a project for a ship canal to open the Great Lakes to ocean shipping and published several reports.

From July 1898 to April 1903 he was engineer of the 10th Lighthouse District, which included the Great Lakes system (within United States territory) up to the outlet of Lake Huron. In 1899 Gov. Theodore Roosevelt of New York appointed him a member of the state canal commission, in which capacity he was a strong advocate of the construction of the New York State Barge Canal. In 1903 he was appointed to succeed Col. Theodore Bingham as superintendent of public buildings and grounds in Washington, D. C., and as military aide to President Theodore Roosevelt. By special act of Congress, Apr. 20, 1904, he was granted leave of absence from June 2 of that year to July 1908, during which time he served on the advisory board of consulting engineers which supervised the construction of the New York State Barge Canal of which he came to be known as the "Father." Unfortunately, this great project, although technically a fine example of engineering skill, proved to be of little economic value and a complete financial failure. Symons was appointed colonel on May 8, 1908, and was retired at his own request on July 28 of that year. Thereafter his residence was in Washington, where he died. On Oct. 12, 1884, he married Letitia V., daughter of Alexander Robinson of Philadelphia, by whom he had two sons and a daughter.

[G. W. Cullum, *Biog. Reg., Officers and Grads. U. S. Mil. Acad.* (3rd ed., 1891) and supplements; *The Centennial of the U. S. Mil. Acad.* (1904), vol. II; *Army and Navy Jour.*, Dec. 4, 1920; *The Military Engineer*, Jan.–Feb. 1921; N. E. Whitford, *Hist. of the Barge Canal of N. Y. State* (1921); "N. Y. State's White Elephant," *Independent*, Feb. 7, 1925; *Who's Who in America*, 1920–21; *Evening Star* (Washington), Nov. 23, 1920.]   J. K. F.

SYMS, BENJAMIN (1591?–1642?), planter and philanthropist, was probably born in England. His name was spelled variously, as Sim's, Simes, Sym, Symms, Syms, and Symes. He was reported in the census of Virginia in 1624/25 as thirty-three years old and living at Basse's Choice in what was later known as Isle of Wight County. Although he had paid for the passage of Joan Meatheart to America, intending to make her his wife, they quarrelled in May 1626, and he appeared against her at a court session held in James City on Oct. 11, 1627. The court decided that Joan should serve a certain John Gill for two years, in return for which service Syms should be paid 100 weight of tobacco and three years' service from the first man servant to arrive in the colony on any vessel. There is no indication that he ever married. In 1629/30 he was living in Jamestown.

Notwithstanding the meagerness of this account of his life, it is nevertheless true that he left a clear record to show that he was one of the earliest and probably the earliest inhabitant of any North American colony to bequeath property for the establishment of a free school. On Feb. 12, 1634/35, two years before the first possible date for the gift of John Harvard [*q.v.*] to the college that bears his name, he wrote a will leaving a farm of two hundred acres situated on the Poquoson River in Elizabeth City County, together with the milk and the increase of eight cows to provide a free school for the children of the parishes of Elizabeth City and Kiquotan (Hening, *post,* VI, 389–90). This will was confirmed by the General Assembly held at James City in 1642/43. A fund was established that provided for the Syms School until 1805 and then formed part of the endowment of Hampton Academy, often referred to as the Syms-Eaton Free School, until 1852, when a public school system was established. In 1933 it was reported as a fund of $10,100 and is still used by the public school commissioners to educate the children of the county. In a pamphlet of unknown authorship published in London in 1649, *A Perfect Description of Virginia* (*The Virginia Historical Register and Literary Advertiser,* Apr. 1849, p. 75), the author mentioned "a free school, with two hundred acres of land, a fine house upon it, forty milch kine" and wrote that "the benefactor deserveth perpetual memory; his name, Mr. Benjamin Symes, worthy to be chronicled."

[J. C. Hotten, *The Original Lists of . . . Emigrants* (1874); W. W. Hening, *Statutes at Large,* vol. I (1810), p. 252, vol. VI (1819), pp. 389–92; E. D. Neill, *Virginia Carolorum* (1886); *The Virginia Mag. of Hist. and Biog.,* Oct. 1893, Jan. 1894, July 1916, July 1920; *William and Mary College Quart.,* Oct. 1897; *The Syms-Eaton Free School* (n.d.), comp. by Mrs. F. M. Armstrong, lent through the courtesy of Robert M. Newton, Hampton, Virginia who also supplied information concerning the present fund; Esther Crane, "The Tercentenary of an Educational Bequest," *Elementary School Journ.,* Nov. 1934.]

E. Cr.

SYNG, PHILIP (Sept. 29, 1703–May 8, 1789), silversmith, son of Philip and Abigail (Murdock) Syng, was born in Cork, Ireland, where Philip Syng the elder, "Goldsmith and Gentleman," practised his craft. Setting out for America the family landed at Annapolis, Md., on Sept. 29, 1714. Whether they went at once to Philadelphia is not clear; they were established there by 1720. About 1723 the father, who had trained three of his sons in his work, left his family and business and returned to Annapolis to live and work to the end of his life. At the time of his father's departure Syng took over the shop that had been established on Market Street and began to build for himself the reputation of being

the finest craftsman of the family and one of the two finest that Philadelphia produced. The most noted example of his silverwork is the inkstand which he made for the Assembly of Pennsylvania in 1752 at a cost of £25 16s. This inkstand was used at the signing of the Declaration of Independence and of the Constitution, but its historical interest is not greater than its artistic merit. Besides the many pieces of Syng's plate that have come to light, there are a number of pieces of jewelry, simple in style but well designed. It is probable that Syng's mark, as distinguished from that of his father, consisted of his initials in Roman capitals enclosed in a rectangle, with a leaf below, or before and after (Maurice Brix, *List of Philadelphia Silversmiths . . . 1762 to 1850,* 1920, frontispiece).

He was early a member of Benjamin Franklin's Junto, and when popular interest turned to the "electrical rod" he was one of the two or three serious experimenters with Franklin, who wrote in 1747 to Peter Collinson in London that Syng had invented a machine that aided in the generation of electricity (A. H. Smyth, *The Writings of Benjamin Franklin,* vol. III, 1905, pp. 306, 310 n.). He was also an early member of the American Philosophical Society, of which he was treasurer, 1769–71; one of the grantees of the charter for the Philadelphia Library Company, which was established in a room on Pewter Platter Alley; and one of the twenty-four trustees who met in Roberts' Coffee-shop in 1750 to organize the College and Academy of Philadelphia, which eventually became part of the University of Pennsylvania. He was a warden of Philadelphia (1753) and for ten years its treasurer (1759–69), a member of the Provincial Commission of Appeals (1765), and a signer of the Non-importation Agreement (1765). He was also Junior Warden of the first Masonic Lodge in America and from 1747 to 1749 a vestryman of Christ Church. He and his wife, Elizabeth Warner, whom he married on Feb. 5, 1729/30, are said to have had twenty-one children (Conner, *post,* p. 3), most of them girls, and only one son, Philip, who died in his twenty-seventh year, learned his father's art. One of his grandsons was Philip Syng Physick [*q.v.*], the surgeon. At his death Syng left a property of some size, including several houses and a country place called Prince of Wales Farm.

[See P. S. P. Conner, *Syng, of Phila.* (1891); J. W. Jordan, *Colonial Families of Phila.* (1911), vol. I; Louise Manly, *The Manly Family* (1930); H. F. Jayne and S. W. Woodhouse, Jr., in *Art in America,* Oct. 1921; Clara L. Avery, *Early Am. Silver* (1930). For an account of the elder Syng, see J. H. Pleasants and Howard Sill, *Maryland Silversmiths* (1930), pp. 72–74.]

K. A. K.

SZOLD, BENJAMIN (Nov. 15, 1829–July 31, 1902), rabbi, was born at Nemiskert, County of Neutra, Hungary, the son of Baruch Szold, a farmer, and Chaile (Endler). His was the only Jewish family in the village. Early left an orphan, he was brought up by his uncles. He received his training in Hebrew and rabbinics from private tutors (becoming *Morenu* at the early age of fourteen), and later, at the Presburg Talmudical College. His studies in Vienna were cut short by the revolution. For the next five years he acted as tutor in private families. He gained his academic knowledge at Frankel's Rabbinical Seminary and the University at Breslau, Silesia. On Aug. 10, 1859, at Cziffer, near Tirnova, he married Sophie Schaar, who survived him, together with four of the eight children that were born to them. The last eight years of his life were beclouded by a painful ailment, but he retained his mental vigor to the end. He died at Berkeley Springs, W. Va.

While a student, he officiated in synagogues at Brieg, Silesia (1857), and at Stockholm, Sweden (1858). The latter position he surrendered to Dr. Lewisohn who had received a call from the Congregation Oheb Shalom of Baltimore, Md., and he went to Baltimore in Lewisohn's stead. Arriving in the United States on Sept. 21, 1859, he served that congregation until 1892, when he was elected rabbi emeritus. He steered it away from extreme reform tendencies, and prepared for it the more traditional prayer book *Abodat Yisrael* (1863), with a German translation. New editions appeared in 1864, 1865 (with an English translation), and, revised jointly by himself, Marcus Jastrow [*q.v.*], and Henry Hochheimer, in 1871 and subsequently. Under his saintly influence his congregation soon became known for its strict observance of the Sabbath. He aided in establishing charitable institutions of Baltimore, and devoted himself to helping Russian Jewish refugees. He was a convinced Zionist long before Herzl organized the Zionist movement. During the Civil War he stood out boldly against slavery in the face of excited popular opinion in Maryland. On one occasion, having been unable to induce either General Meade or President Lincoln to pardon a deserter, in reckless protest he held the hand of the condemned soldier while the firing squad of twelve muskets fired the volley which ended the man's life.

Besides writing a number of unpublished studies in the Bible and the Talmud, Szold published *The Book of Job with a New Commentary* (1886), which shows marked originality, especially in the attention paid to the exegetic value of the masoretic accents. He was the author of some textbooks, minor publications, and a commentary on the eleventh chapter of Daniel for G. A. Kohut's *Semitic Studies in Memory of Rev. Dr. Alexander Kohut* (1897); he also edited Michael Heilprin's *Bibelkritische Notizen* (1893). He was outstanding in scholarship, forceful in his natural eloquence, moderate in his religious views, sharing neither orthodox rigidity nor reform's radicalism. His sweet and sincere humanity made him a champion of the unfortunate, and won for him the esteem of Jew and Gentile alike.

[*Jewish Comment* (Balto.), Nov. 17, 1899, Aug. 1, 8, Oct. 3, 1902; *Jewish Exponent* (Phila.) and *Am. Hebrew* (N. Y.), Aug. 8, 1902; *The Jewish Encyc.* (ed. 1925), vol. XI; *Year Book of the Central Conference of Am. Rabbis*, vol. XIII (copr. 1904); *Deborah* (Cincinnati), vol. II (1902); Peter Wiernik, *Hist. of the Jews in America* (1931); Emanuel Hertz, *Abraham Lincoln: The Tribute of the Synagogue* (1927); *Allgemeine Zeitung des Judenthums*, vol. XXXIII (1869); *Sun* (Balto.), Aug. 1, 1902.]   D. deS. P.

TABB, JOHN BANISTER (Mar. 22, 1845–Nov. 19, 1909), poet and priest, was born at "The Forest," Amelia County, Va., the son of Thomas Yelverton and Marianna Bertrand (Archer) Tabb. His father was seventh in direct line from Humphrey Tabb who settled in Elizabeth City County, Va., in 1637. The family had reason to be proud of its fame in the colonial and Revolutionary history of the state. Tabb's boyhood was spent under the influence of the ante-bellum régime, his mother and a tutor giving him his first lessons. For poetry and music he showed an early aptitude and passion. Though his weak eyesight prevented his enlistment in 1861, in the second year of the Civil War he was allowed to go to England with an expedition dispatched to transport supplies for the Confederacy, and in London and Paris he touched briefly the world of letters and the arts. On his return to Charleston he was transferred to the *Robert E. Lee,* most daringly successful of the blockade runners, but because of illness was not on the ship when it later fell into Union hands in November 1863. In the spring of 1864 he carried dispatches on the *Siren* until its capture on June 4. Tabb sank his papers but was taken, court-martialed, and sentenced to prison at Point Lookout, Md. One circumstance brought him comfort in prison: he met there Sidney Lanier, whose flute he heard one day as he lay prostrated with fever. When release came in February 1865, Tabb found Richmond a capitulated city. Until support was unavoidably withdrawn, he studied music in Baltimore. He then taught at Saint Paul's School, Baltimore, and in 1870 for a few months at Racine College, Racine,

Wis. Though he was preparing for the Episcopal ministry, Catholicism had since 1862 increasingly attracted him. The conversion of his friend, Father Alfred Allen Curtis [*q.v.*], later bishop of Wilmington, hastened his turning, and on Sept. 8, 1872, he was baptized in the communion. Deciding to take priest's orders, he attended Saint Charles' College, Ellicott City, Md. (1872–75). It was not until 1881, however, that he entered Saint Mary's Seminary in Baltimore to complete his theological studies. He was ordained on Dec. 20, 1884. Meanwhile he taught at Saint Peter's Boys' School in Richmond, Va., and at Saint Charles', where, after his ordination, he conducted classes in English for the rest of his active life.

Father Tabb commenced poet when he was in the Confederate service. His first volume, issued privately in 1882 (Litz, *post,* p. 97), was experimental. His first widely known volume, *Poems* (1894), preceded by *An Octave to Mary* (1893), reached a seventeenth edition. By the time of publication of *Lyrics* (1897), the periodicals bought his poems eagerly. His reputation was further augmented, particularly in England, by *Later Lyrics* (1902), *The Rosary in Rhyme* (1904), and *A Selection from the Verses of John B. Tabb,* compiled by Alice Meynell in 1907. After his death appeared *Later Poems* (1910) and *The Poetry of Father Tabb* (1928), edited by F. A. Litz, which printed selections from manuscript volumes privately owned. The poems in *Child Verse* (1899) and *Quips and Quiddits* (1907) are trivialized by Tabb's love of punning and elfish humor. In spite of his admiration for the romantic poets, his verse bears little resemblance to theirs in form. His most intense lyric utterance suggests the epigrammatic crypticism of Emily Dickinson. His nature poetry is often merely fanciful, but his religious lyrics for their intensity invite comparison with those of the seventeenth-century metaphysical poets.

As a priest Father Tabb never aspired beyond his dear duty at the college. He mingled little with the world beyond the college and the city of Baltimore. To the last he called himself an "unreconstructed rebel" (*Ave Maria,* Aug. 2, 1930, p. 132). His pupils loved him devotedly, and were molded by his rich and paradoxical nature. Blindness shadowed the last years of his life, and general paralysis preceded his death.

[See *Who's Who in America,* 1908–09; F. A. Litz, *Father Tabb: A Study of His Life and Works* (1923); Jennie M. Tabb, *Father Tabb* (1922); Alice Meynell, "Father Tabb as a Poet," *Cath. World,* Feb. 1910; J. M. Cooney, in *Ave Maria,* Aug. 2, 9, 16, 1930; obituary in Baltimore *Sun,* Nov. 20, 1909. For the spelling of Tabb's middle name, see Litz, *op. cit.,* p. 273, n. 1.]
W. T.

TABOR, HORACE AUSTIN WARNER (Nov. 26, 1830–Apr. 10, 1899), bonanza king, was born at Holland, Vt., the son of Cornelius Dunham and Sarah (Farrin) Tabor. His early years were spent on the farm and at the village school. He was a stonecutter for eight years. In 1855 he joined a company of Free-Soil emigrants to Kansas and in 1856 and 1857 was a member of the Topeka legislature, returning to Vermont to marry on Jan. 31, 1857, Augusta Pierce, daughter of his former employer.

Unsuccessful as a farmer in Kansas, in 1859 he took wife and baby and joined the Pike's Peak gold rush. His first season of prospecting was barren of results, and his wife took in boarders to pay expenses through the winter. The next spring Tabor went to the headwaters of the Arkansas, where rich placers were found. Here he prospered, first as a miner, then as a merchant, until the diggings played out and his business dwindled. Soon, however, the black sand that had cluttered the sluice boxes was found to contain silver, and a new rush to the district set in. Tabor, continuing with his store, grubstaked needy prospectors, among them August Rische and George F. Hook, who in May 1878 discovered the body of silver ore which became the famous Little Pittsburgh Mine. On account of the grubstake, one third of the find came to Tabor. He bought up near-by prospects and they turned into rich mines. In that same year he became the first mayor of Leadville.

The silver stream that poured into his lap he spent with lavish hand. In the saloon he was prodigal; at gambling his stakes were high; no beggar went from him empty-handed. An opera house and gifts for civic and fraternal purposes were bestowed on Leadville. His bounty extended to Denver and was reflected in the Tabor Block and the magnificent Tabor Grand Opera House. His investments were important in transforming Denver from a town into a city and in determining the direction of its growth. His popularity made him lieutenant-governor of Colorado in 1879–83, and his money procured him a seat in the United States Senate (Jan. 27–Mar. 3, 1883), to complete an unexpired term. The conservative wife who had endured his poverty was put aside for a dashing young divorcée, Elizabeth (McCourt) Doe, to whom he was married secretly Sept. 30, 1882, and remarried publicly Mar. 1, 1883, with President Arthur as a guest of honor.

By now, however, as the money he put into

banks, real estate, and business buildings showed good returns, Tabor had turned to less conservative buying. Promoters were able to sell him worthless mines in Mexico and South America, timber lands in Central America, and railroads built on paper. Then the production of his mines decreased and the price of silver declined; to bolster weak holdings he mortgaged sound ones; and the crash of 1893 and the repeal of the Sherman Act left him bankrupt. Heroically but vainly he tried to recoup his losses. He was old and broken in 1898 when friends secured him appointment as postmaster of Denver, and the following year he died. One son of his first marriage and two daughters of his second survived him. His first wife had died in 1895; the second returned to Leadville and spent her last years in destitution in a shack beside the Matchless Mine; here on Mar. 7, 1935, she was found frozen to death.

[Interviews with Tabor and Mrs. Tabor (1884) and with their son Maxcy (1922), and the Dawson Scrapbooks, in the possession of the State Hist. Soc. of Colo.; *Hist. of the City of Denver* (1880); L. A. Kent, *Leadville* (1880); *Portr. and Biog. Record of the State of Colo.* (1899); W. N. Byers, *Encyc. of Biog. of Colo.* (1901); J. C. Smiley, *Semi-Centennial Hist. of the State of Colo.* (1913), vol. II, and *Hist. of Denver* (1901); *Biog. Dir. Am. Cong.* (1928); David Karsner, *Silver Dollar, the Story of the Tabors* (1932), containing much fictionized detail; H. D. Teetor, in *Mag. of Western Hist.*, Jan. 1889, pp. 268–73; G. F. Willison, *Here They Dug the Gold* (1931); L. C. Gandy, *The Tabors: A Footnote of Western Hist.* (1934); *Rocky Mountain News* (Denver), *Denver Republican, N. Y. Times,* and *Washington Post,* Apr. 11, 1899; *N. Y. Times,* Mar. 8, 1935.]   L. R. H.

TAFT, ALPHONSO (Nov. 5, 1810–May 21, 1891), judge, secretary of war, attorney-general, diplomat, was the first member of his family to achieve national prominence. Born on a farm in Townshend, Vt., he was the only child of Peter Rawson Taft and Sylvia Howard. The first American Taft was Robert, who was born prior to 1640, came from England, and was one of the Braintree men who formed Mendon, Mass., in 1667; the name may originally have been either Toft or Taffe. Efforts to trace the birthplace of Robert Taft have been unavailing, however. It has been assumed by genealogists that his forebears were Scotch or Irish. Sylvia Howard, Alphonso's mother, was also Scotch or Irish. The first of her line (then probably Hayward) settled near Braintree, Mass., in 1642. Robert Taft of Mendon was a carpenter and farmer. Alphonso was descended from his son Joseph, who was a captain in the militia. The descent continues through Peter, also in the militia, and Aaron Taft, Alphonso's grandfather, who moved from Massachusetts into Vermont and settled at Townshend in 1799. The Tafts

were people of substance and education, but were not wealthy. Aaron Taft studied at Princeton. Peter Rawson Taft, although largely self-educated, was a member of the Vermont legislature and judge of the probate and county courts of Windham County.

Until he was sixteen Alphonso Taft attended local schools. Then he taught school in order to have funds to study at Amherst Academy. In 1829 he entered Yale College and was graduated with honors four years later. He had decided to study law. He taught school, again for funds, at Ellington, Conn., for two years. While studying law he held a tutorship at Yale. He was admitted to the bar of Connecticut in 1838, but did not intend to remain in New England. Vermont, he wrote his father (July 22, 1837), "is a noble state to emigrate from"; and he joined the march westward. He rejected New York as a place to practise because of its "selfishness and dishonesty," because "money is the all in all" (Alphonso Taft to Fanny Phelps, Oct. 9, 1838). Instead, he selected Cincinnati where he thought an income of from $3,000 to $5,000 was possible, while the competition was less severe.

His success at the bar was prompt; by 1854 he had more business than he could handle. Among his important cases was a suit to set aside the will of Charles McMicken whereby $500,000 had been left to the City of Cincinnati for a free university. Taft defended the will and won (165 *United States,* 465). He also successfully upheld the constitutionality of a law by which the city issued $2,000,000 in bonds to complete the Cincinnati Southern Railroad (1 *Cincinnati Superior Court Reporter,* 121; 21 *Ohio State Reports,* 14). He was greatly interested in railroad development in Ohio and the Middle West, and was connected with traction line projects in Cincinnati. In 1865 he was appointed to the superior court of Cincinnati to fill a vacancy and was elected to that bench for two terms. He resigned to resume his law practice on Jan. 1, 1872, and in March 1876 was called to Washington by President Grant to become secretary of war; after less than three months he became attorney-general. These posts did not offer great opportunities; Grant went out of office in 1877. But Taft assisted, as attorney-general, in drafting a bill which created the commission to settle the Hayes-Tilden election.

Politically Taft was a conservative. "I know not," he wrote to Fanny Phelps (Apr. 3, 1841), "what could lead you to suppose me anything else than a Whig." But he attended, in 1856, a conference at Pittsburgh which preceded the birth of the Republican party. On two occasions, in 1875 and 1879, he was an unsuccessful candidate for the Republican nomination for governor of Ohio. In 1882 he was appointed minister to Austria-Hungary by President Arthur. On July 4, 1884, he was transferred to St. Petersburg, where he remained until August 1885. His diplomatic career, which typified in the main his whole career, was not distinguished. No major questions arose for settlement. Alphonso Taft's life was marked by integrity rather than daring. He had character rather than genius.

On Aug. 29, 1841, he was married to Fanny Phelps of West Townshend, Vt. Of this marriage there were five children, of whom three died in infancy. Charles Phelps [q.v.] and Peter Rawson survived. She died on June 2, 1852. On Dec. 26, 1853, he was married to Louisa (usually called Louise) Torrey of Millbury, Mass. They had five children, of whom four survived: William Howard [q.v.], Henry Waters, Horace Dutton, and Fanny Louise. Alphonso Taft died in California on May 21, 1891.

[The sketch is based almost wholly on the Alphonso Taft and William Howard Taft papers in the Lib. of Cong. They are very extensive. L. A. Leonard, *Life of Alphonso Taft* (1920), was obviously written at the behest of the family. In the Taft papers is a sketch of Alphonso Taft in manuscript form by Adolph Richter, an old law associate. For genealogical material see *Genealogy, a Weekly Journal of American Ancestry*, Apr. 13, 1912; Mabel T. R. Washburn, *Ancestry of William Howard Taft* (1908); *Taft Family Gathering Proceedings . . . August 13, 1874* (1874). See also *Obituary Record of Grads. of Yale Univ. Deceased from June 1890 to June 1900* (1900); obituary in *Times-Star* (Cincinnati), May 22, 1891.]   H. F. P—e.

TAFT, CHARLES PHELPS (Dec. 21, 1843–Dec. 31, 1929), lawyer, publisher, philanthropist, born in Cincinnati, Ohio, was the eldest son of Alphonso Taft [q.v.] and the latter's first wife, Fanny Phelps, and a half-brother of William Howard Taft [q.v.]. He went to the Cincinnati public schools, prepared for college at Phillips Academy, Andover, and was graduated from Yale in 1864, receiving the M.A. degree from that institution in 1867. Meanwhile, he studied law at Columbia University, received the LL.B. degree in 1866, and was admitted to the bar that year. He practised for a few months with his father in Cincinnati and then went abroad for further study at Heidelberg, where he was awarded the degree of J.U.D., and at the Sorbonne. He traveled extensively through Europe; an interest in painting and sculpture, there aroused, never left him.

From 1869 to 1879 he practised law in Cincinnati. On Dec. 4, 1873, he was married to Annie Sinton, daughter of David Sinton of Cincinnati. They had two sons and two daughters. In 1879 he and his father-in-law acquired a controlling interest in the Cincinnati *Times*, which was consolidated the next year with the *Star*, another afternoon paper, as the *Times-Star*. Taft, as editor and ultimately as sole proprietor, built it into a profitable newspaper property. This, with the management of a very large estate left by his father-in-law, consumed most of his time. He was also identified with Ohio utility companies and with Cincinnati real estate, and for several years was part owner of the Chicago and Philadelphia National League baseball clubs.

During his early years as a lawyer, he codified the school laws of his state and he was joint editor of *The Cincinnati Superior Court Reporter* for the years 1870–71 and 1872–73 (vols. I, II, 1872, 1873). A lifelong Republican, he sought public office on several occasions. In 1872 he was defeated for Congress. He served one term in Congress (1895–97), without special distinction. In 1909 he became a candidate for the senatorial nomination, but withdrew in order to avoid possible embarrassment to his half-brother, who was then president-elect. Though well-known in Cincinnati and Ohio, he was usually identified to the rest of the country as the brother of William Howard Taft, whose career, indeed, he played a large part in shaping. But for his advice and financial assistance, it is virtually certain that William Howard Taft would never have become president. Unwittingly, he was a factor in the break between his brother and Theodore Roosevelt. After his election in 1908, Taft wrote Roosevelt, "you and my brother Charley made that possible." In due time, as the breach widened, friends of Roosevelt twisted this to mean that greater credit had been given Charles P. Taft, and Roosevelt resented it. The truth is that the President was very grateful for all that his brother had done, but was careful to insist that without Roosevelt's aid it would not have been possible for Charles to help.

Charles P. Taft, the most cultured member of his distinguished family, made notable contributions to the esthetic life of his native community. In May 1927 he and his wife gave to the Cincinnati Institute of Fine Arts their private art collection, their homestead, and an endowment of one million dollars for the Cincinnati Symphony Orchestra. He also made substantial gifts to the Cincinnati Law School. He died on Dec. 31, 1929.

[This sketch is based on the private papers of C. P. Taft and W. H. Taft in the Lib. of Cong. See also Cincinnati *Times-Star*, Jan. 1, 1930, for an authorized obituary; *Bulletin of Yale Univ. Obituary Record of Graduates Deceased During the Year Ending July 1, 1930* (1930); L. A. Leonard, *Life of Alphonso Taft* (1920).]   H. F. P—e.

TAFT, WILLIAM HOWARD (Sept. 15, 1857–Mar. 8, 1930), president and chief justice of the United States, was of the third generation in his family to follow the law. His grandfather, Peter Rawson Taft, was a judge of the probate and county courts of Windham County, Vt.; and his father, Alphonso Taft [*q.v.*], served two terms on the superior court in Cincinnati, Ohio. Though born and brought up in Cincinnati, William Howard Taft belonged to New England rather than the Middle West. Beginning with Robert Taft, his ancestors on his father's side had dwelt in Massachusetts and Vermont since the seventeenth century. His mother was Louisa Maria Torrey (she signed herself Louise), the second wife of Alphonso Taft. Her ancestor, William Torrey of Combe, St. Nicholas, Somersetshire, England, emigrated to America in 1640, settled at Weymouth, Mass., and served as a clerk of the Massachusetts House of Deputies, a magistrate, and a captain of the militia. His descendant, Samuel Davenport Torrey, born at Mendon, Mass., on Apr. 14, 1779, married as his second wife Susan Holman, who was the mother of Lousia Maria Torrey (born Sept. 11, 1827).

William Howard had two half-brothers, Charles Phelps [*q.v.*] and Peter Rawson; there were two younger brothers, Henry Waters and Horace Dutton, and a sister, Fanny Louise. At twelve he was at the head of his class, at thirteen he entered the Woodward High School in Cincinnati, and at seventeen he was ready for Yale, where he matriculated in the fall of 1874. Taft did well at Yale. He delivered the class oration on his graduation in 1878, and was second in a class of 121. Then turning his face westward, he went back to Cincinnati where, in 1880, he received his law degree from the Cincinnati Law School and was admitted to the Ohio bar. He was a large, too good-natured young man with a tendency toward sloth which worried his father and his youngest brother, Horace. Thus he was rebuked by the former in the summer of 1879 for being at a boat race when he might have been handling a minor law suit. "As usual," wrote Horace to his mother, "he put the thing off until he had only two or three days to prepare in" (Apr. 19, 1885). This weakness for procrastination never really left Taft. He was constantly complaining, when in the White House, that he had not yet had time to prepare some speech and would have to get it in shape in too brief a time. On the other hand, the law was a rather casual mistress in the eighties. While studying, he also had time to serve as a court reporter for the *Cincinnati Commercial.*

Taft's first participation in politics also occurred in 1880 when, encouraged by his father to develop himself as a speaker, he did some spell-binding for the Republican state committee. That he was to follow his father into that party was, of course, foreordained. The next year he campaigned for Miller Outcault, candidate for prosecuting attorney of Hamilton County; his reward, when Outcault was elected, was a post as assistant. This was his first public office. In 1882 he learned that politics had an unsavory side. Appointed collector of internal revenue for Cincinnati in March, he was promptly subjected to demands that he oust four or five office holders, "the best men in the service." Their removal, he wrote his father, "will cause a very big stink" and he declined to do such "dirty work" (July 24, 1882). He resigned several months later, resumed the practice of law, and toured Europe. He took an active part in the campaigns of 1884, although he shared his father's disappointment in the nomination of James G. Blaine. By now he was a partisan, although not a machine, Republican. The Mugwump movement did not penetrate Ohio to any extent. So William and Charles Taft, possibly because they knew that their father's diplomatic career would terminate unless Blaine won, did their best for the Republican nominee. In addition, William was chief supervisor of the election in Cincinnati. "You must have had a hard struggle to keep . . . the Kentuckians from voting at our polls," wrote his father from St. Petersburg (Nov. 3, 1884). Taft had an interest greater than the campaign. This was a disbarment case against Tom Campbell, a local politician-lawyer (Duffy, *post,* pp. 9–12). Taft was appointed to the staff which conducted the case against Campbell in the summer of 1884. In January 1885 he made the opening address and spoke, according to his admiring young brother, for over four hours during which "the life, the interest, the logic, the facts and the eloquence did not fail for one minute" (Horace to Alphonso Taft, Jan. 11, 1885). In May he became engaged to Helen Herron, the daughter of John W. Herron of Cincinnati, "a woman who is willing to take me as I am, for better or for worse." They were married on June 19, 1886, and in the course of time had three children, Robert Alphonso, Helen, and Charles Phelps.

Taft ascended the bench, the place beyond all others where he was happy, for the first time in March 1887. Gov. Joseph B. Foraker appointed him to the superior court of Ohio for the unfinished term of Judge Judson Harmon, who had resigned. In April 1888 he was elected for a five-year term; this was the only office save the presidency which he achieved by popular vote. Few of the youthful judge's opinions were of legal importance. Then, as later, he had a weakness for verbosity in writing. His most important case, perhaps, was *Moores & Company* vs. *The Bricklayers' Union, No. 1, W. H. Stephenson, et al.* Moores & Company, building supply dealers, boycotted by the union, had been awarded $2,250 damages by a jury in the lower court. Taft wrote an exhaustive opinion in which he declared the boycott illegal and confirmed the damage award (*Weekly Law Bulletin and Ohio Law Journal,* Jan. 20, 1890). The ruling attracted wide attention and was one of the factors which caused labor so bitterly to oppose him in later years.

The star of Taft was rising. It was a placid star, not a comet, against the judicial and political sky. In 1889, although but thirty-two, he was discussed for associate justice of the Supreme Court, but refused to share "the very roseate view" of those who thought he might be appointed. "My chances of going to the moon and of donning a silk gown at the hands of President Harrison," he wrote his father, "are about equal" (Aug. 24, 1889). He received, instead, a post as solicitor-general at Harrison's hands and the stage of his activity was enlarged to include Washington, D. C., where he assumed office on Feb. 4, 1890. Apprehensive about his ability, he wrote his father that he had had no experience in the federal statutes, and that the prospect was "rather overwhelming." But he did well. Within a year he could report that he had argued eighteen cases in the Supreme Court and won fifteen (to Alphonso Taft, Feb. 9, 1891). In March 1891 Congress created a new judgeship for each circuit of the federal circuit court and Taft was mentioned for an appointment to the sixth, which covered Kentucky, Ohio, Michigan, and Tennessee. Mrs. Taft was opposed. "If you get your heart's desire," she wrote him that summer, "it will put an end to all your opportunities . . . of being thrown with big-wigs" (July 18, 1891). But Taft had small taste for big-wigs. Clearly, he was less ambitious than other members of the family. He did not mind being poor, he said, for people with small incomes were as happy as those with fortunes. For eight years, from Mar. 17, 1892, he served on the circuit court.

For a man of judicial tastes, who was also becoming a profound legal scholar, the appointment was ideal. Noting that there was "only one higher judicial position in the country," Taft continued to keep an eye on the Supreme Court. Meanwhile, the work was absorbing.

Many decisions related to labor, and Taft was to be damned for these in 1908 and 1912. The man and the jurist must be kept distinct in any attempt accurately to portray Taft's views on labor. A large element of conservative public opinion was exceedingly alarmed over the state of the nation in 1892. The Haymarket bombing of 1886 was still all too vivid. The Homestead riots were in a few months to make crimson the muddy Ohio River. Financial panic and breadlines were to follow in a year. That Taft, as a private citizen, shared the alarm of the respectable people is clear. In July 1894 the Pullman strike was raging in Chicago. "It will be necessary for the military to kill some of the mob before the trouble can be stayed," he wrote his wife. "They have only killed six . . . as yet. This is hardly enough to make an impression" (July 8, 1894).

His first major labor case as circuit judge was when P. M. Arthur, grand chief of the Brotherhood of Locomotive Engineers, ruled that the members of the organization would refuse to handle freight of the Toledo, Ann Arbor & North Michigan Railway, which had declined to raise wages. They were to refuse, that is, even if they worked only on connecting lines. Taft upheld a temporary injunction previously issued by himself against this order and was criticized, unjustly, on the mistaken theory that he had ruled against strikes (54 *Federal Reporter,* 730; Duffy, pp. 35–36). In the case of Frank M. Phelan, a lieutenant of Eugene Debs, he made his viewpoint clear. Phelan, during the Pullman strike, urged the employees of the Cincinnati Southern Railroad, in receivership and therefore under the jurisdiction of the federal court, to cease work. He was enjoined. When he violated the injunction he was sentenced by Taft to six months' imprisonment (62 *Federal Reporter,* 803). "I shall find him . . . guilty on [*sic*] conspiring unlawfully to tie up the road by a boycott" (W. H. Taft to Helen Herron Taft, July 11, 1894). The decision was handed down on July 13, 1894. At the same moment when, as a private citizen, Taft was voicing approval of Chicago bloodshed he declared, as a judge, that the employees of the Cincinnati Southern had a right to organize, join a union, conspire to strike, and conduct a strike. "They have labor to sell," he said. "If they stand together, they are often able . . . to command better prices . . . than when dealing singly with rich employers" (62 *Federal Reporter,* 817). But he felt that the employees of the Cincinnati Southern had, in this instance, no grievance. Phelan was part of a combination which was illegal. The boycott he sought was illegal (Duffy, pp. 39–45). Actually, Taft's position on the right of labor to organize was definitely in advance of the existing legal opinion of the day. He gave further evidence of his sympathy for the workingman in his decision (on which he was reversed by the Supreme Court) that an employer could not relieve himself from negligence in accident cases by requiring employees to agree to non-liability (79 *Federal Reporter*, 561; see also 176 *United States*, 498). In another case (96 *Federal Reporter*, 298) he ruled that employers could not plead contributory negligence on the part of employees where statutory safety provisions had been violated. While on the circuit bench, Taft also strengthened the Sherman anti-trust law. In 1898 he decided, in the Addyston Pipe Case, that a combination of manufacturers of cast-iron pipe was in restraint of trade and issued an injunction (85 *Federal Reporter*, 271; Duffy, pp. 49–51).

In 1899 Taft was asked by the "liberal element" of the Yale Corporation to consider election to the presidency of the university (H. W. Taft to W. H. Taft, Jan. 14, 1899). He answered that "two insuperable objections" made this impossible. The first was that he was a Unitarian and this would "shock the conservative element" of the alumni. The second was that he did not feel qualified for the post (W. H. Taft to H. W. Taft, Jan. 21, 1899). A far different assignment lay ahead. On Mar. 15, 1900, he resigned from the bench, at the instance of President McKinley, to become president of the Philippine Commission. For the first time he was to be an executive and administrator. The reputation he earned did much to advance him toward the presidency. Emotionally, he grew very much attached to the little brown inhabitants of the Philippine Islands and their welfare always remained close to his heart.

On his arrival early in June 1900, Taft concluded that "the back of the rebellion" was broken and that the first immediate necessity was to end military rule in the islands. He was not a sentimentalist; the Filipinos who persisted in lawlessness were, when caught, to be "either hung or banished in Guam" (W. H. Taft to B. I. Wheeler, Oct. 17, 1900). Executions were not necessary. Education, pacification of still rebellious natives, and settlement of the perplexing issue of the friars' lands were the immediate objectives of the Philippine Commission. Taft directed his efforts to these as soon as he had relegated the military command of the islands to a secondary position. The Philippines, under Spain, had to a large extent been ruled by friars.

That they had abused their authority was, when Taft arrived, a firm conviction of the Filipinos. Many of the friars had been slain in the insurrections prior to the war with Spain. Their lands had been confiscated by the Philippine Congress. Taft concluded that this was "a political and not a religious question" (W. H. Taft to J. J. Hooker, Jan. 7, 1901). Most of the surviving friars had fled the islands and Taft's conviction was that the Roman Catholic hierarchy must not insist on their return. A specific part of the problem was settlement for the 400,000 acres of land owned by the friars and, until the insurrection, rented to the natives. Taft desired to purchase these lands and sell them to the natives at fair prices (Duffy, p. 109). After prolonged negotiations, which included a journey to Rome and conferences, in June 1902, with Pope Leo XIII, an agreement was reached. Ultimately, the United States paid $7,200,000 for the friars' lands. Meanwhile, in July 1901, Taft had been made civil governor of the islands. Until January 1904, when President Roosevelt called him back to become secretary of war, he devoted himself with great energy to improving the economic status of the Philippines, to the building of roads and harbors, toward establishing limited self-government.

On two occasions while Taft was in the Philippines he was offered an appointment to the Supreme Court by President Roosevelt. He declined because he felt that his task had not been completed. He accepted the post of secretary of war on the ground that he could continue his supervision of the affairs of the islands. But this was only part of his work. Taking office on Feb. 1, 1904, he soon became a close adviser to the President. Roosevelt and Taft made an excellent team; the latter's easy-going conservatism counteracted the President's impulsive qualities. Taft became, in effect, the "trouble shooter" of the administration. He took on his too-broad shoulders the task of starting actual construction of the Panama Canal and hurried to the Canal Zone for that purpose. When Roosevelt left Washington for a vacation he made his secretary of war, to all purposes, secretary of state as well. Everything was all right, the President said, with Taft "sitting on the lid." In September 1906, Taft was rushed to Cuba to effect peace when a revolution threatened. Clearly, Taft had been revealing unusual talents as an administrator and even more as a conciliator. Soon after Roosevelt's declaration in 1904 that he would not run again, the name of Taft as a successor came to the front. His private letters show that he had no taste for the office, that he believed himself disqualified because of his labor decisions when on the bench. But Mrs. Taft and his brothers desired that he stand for the nomination (Pringle, p. 498). His private letters of protest grew weaker as 1905 advanced. Late in 1907 he received definite word that he was the chosen candidate of the President. He ran as Roosevelt's man. He was elected in November 1908 over Bryan by an electoral vote of 321 to 162 and a popular plurality of more than a million. He took office in March 1909. He was troubled, bothered, and harassed almost from the start.

With Roosevelt's cordial assent, Taft chose his own cabinet. Secretary of State Philander C. Knox, Attorney-General George W. Wickersham, and, to a degree, Charles Nagel, secretary of commerce and labor, were the members on whom Taft was to lean most. His advisory board was not distinguished for its strength. Like most such bodies, it represented compromise. It included no member of the insurgent wing of the Republican party and to that degree was reactionary. But it was not a "Wall Street" cabinet, either. Wickersham was to annoy the financial interests in New York by his trust prosecutions. Taft began his presidency with a divided party, although technically he had both houses of Congress behind him. His fatal error of political thought, as distinct from specific mistakes, was his belief that the Republican party could be continued in power without giving ground to its more liberal wing. At the start and on the specific advice of Roosevelt, he declined to join in the fight of the House insurgents on the autocratic powers of Speaker Joseph G. Cannon (W. H. Taft to W. A. White, Mar. 12, 1909). His real difficulty, of course, was that he did not possess his predecessor's great genius for guiding, sometimes confusing, public opinion. His honesty of purpose was stolid and plodding. He could not magnify minor issues. "There is no use trying to be William Howard Taft with Roosevelt's ways," he said, ". . . our ways are different" (Butt, *post*, I, 236). Roosevelt had zealously refrained from attempting tariff revision, thus avoiding an issue fraught with death to presidents. Taft promptly plunged into it.

Tariff revision was part of the general demand, more vocal in the Middle West and the West than in the East, for a more equal distribution of wealth. Roosevelt had stilled the outcry only partially. Now, in 1909, a wide segment of public opinion insisted that tariff revision downward would further control the trusts. So Taft called a special session of Congress. The House schedules, while not revolutionary,

marked real reductions. But the Senate, with Nelson W. Aldrich as the extreme high-tariff advocate, amended the bill almost beyond recognition. Taft effected many compromises and said, in a detailed explanatory letter of June 27, 1909, to his brother Horace, that "the Payne bill was a genuine effort in the right direction." "I am not a high-tariff man; I am a low-tariff man," he insisted (W. H. Taft to W. D. Foulke, July 15, 1909). Shortly afterward he wrote his wife that he would either beat the bill or get what he wanted. After the Payne-Aldrich bill was passed, the President felt that it was a distinct step forward, "the best bill that the party has ever passed" (W. H. Taft to R. M. Wanamaker, Nov. 24, 1909). This was not wholly untrue; the Payne-Aldrich act was of slight economic importance, but it did mark a recession of the Republican urge toward higher and higher duties. Taft agreed that he "could make a lot of cheap popularity by vetoing the bill" (W. H. Taft to Horace Taft, June 27, 1910). Instead, he made himself its defender, praised it too lavishly, and so reaped the unpopularity which the act itself received.

"I have had a hard time . . . I have been conscientiously trying to carry out your policies but my method of doing so has not worked smoothly," wrote Taft to Roosevelt as the latter prepared to return from his African jaunt (May 26, 1910). Taft's cup of woe was brimming. On the one hand, in his own party, he faced such insurgents as Senators LaFollette, Cummins, Dolliver, Bristow, Borah, Clapp, and Beveridge. On the other, he was threatened by the growing strength of the Democratic party, which was to take over the House in November 1910, and the imponderable strength of Woodrow Wilson as a possible Democratic nominee. Worse than all was the friction with Roosevelt, to whom the insurgents were appealing and who disapproved of Taft's action in dismissing Gifford Pinchot because of his charges against the secretary of the interior, Richard A. Ballinger [*q.v.*]. Yet there were many accomplishments to which Taft might have pointed with pride had he been more of a political leader and less judicial. By means of the Tariff Board he started the first scientific investigation of rates. He created the postal savings system. He was a sincere friend of conservation, despite subsequent accusations from the Progressives. He negotiated an agreement with Canada which meant relatively free trade between that country and the United States. He then secured ratification by Congress only to have Canada, at first enthusiastic for the measure, ultimately reject it. Deeply interested in international peace, he attempted to arrange treaties of arbitration with Great Britain and France. They were so amended by the Senate that Taft discontinued the effort to secure senatorial concurrence. Under Attorney-General Wickersham a series of vigorous prosecutions against trusts were started; as a "trust-buster" President Taft was, in fact, more active than Roosevelt. Among his other accomplishments were efforts toward economy and efficiency in government, the first step toward a federal budget; the appointment of a commission to investigate the question of additional safety and workmen's compensation legislation; the admission of New Mexico and Arizona as states.

The Roosevelt-Taft "break," so-called, was inevitable from the time that Taft's predecessor returned from Europe in the summer of 1910. But there is no specific incident from which it can be dated. In general, it was due to the complete antithesis between the two men. Taft believed in a government of laws, not of men. Roosevelt held the law lightly; he believed in a government of men or, more accurately, of a single man—himself. Roosevelt was a consummate politician, in contrast to Taft. He enjoyed the presidency. Taft's four years in the White House were probably the unhappiest of his life. He was not such a misfit as Roosevelt came to believe, but he had no taste for politics. His private letters reveal that he was discouraged early in his administration and did not believe he would be reëlected. On Sept. 6, 1911, he confessed to his brother Charles: "I am not very happy in this renomination and reelection business. I have to set my teeth and go through with it. . . . But I shall be willing to retire and let another take the burden." He grew more conservative as the years passed, leaning more and more on such men as Aldrich. Roosevelt, in evolving his New Nationalism, grew more radical. Finally, he called for the initiative and referendum and for the recall of judicial decisions. The last, in particular, made Taft recoil. The two men drifted; Taft toward the nomination which he had to accept from his party whether he wanted it or not, and Roosevelt toward a contest for that nomination. At the Republican National Convention in Chicago in June 1912, Taft was renominated by routine steam-roller methods and was accused by Roosevelt of having "stolen" the convention. Roosevelt organized the Bull Moose Party and the campaign, the most bitter since that of 1876, began. Taft's defeat was inevitable. "As a leader, I had to have confidence and hope, but in my heart I have long been making plans for my future," he wrote when

it was over (W. H. Taft to C. H. Clark, Nov. 9, 1912). He received only 8 electoral votes against 88 for Roosevelt and 435 for Wilson. He was condemned by contemporary historians as one of the most lamentable of White House failures, a greater failure even than Grant. The appraisal was not sound. Taft would under no conditions have been a great president, but the political situation between 1909 and 1913 was such that no Republican, even Roosevelt, could have been successful. Taft was unique in that he did not want the office and surrendered it gladly. "Politics makes me sick" is a phrase which beats like a minor refrain through his private letters when he was president. The office brought out all his worst traits: vacillation, irritability, a complete inability to lead. It obscured very real gifts: an excellent judicial mind, an integrity which was never clouded, great talent as an administrator, a wide and broad sympathy for human problems.

He retired in March 1913 to the campus of his beloved Yale as Kent Professor of Constitutional Law. During the World War he served as joint-chairman of the National War Labor Board. Then, on June 30, 1921, President Harding gratified his heart's desire by naming him chief justice of the United States. It is not impossible that his work as administrator of the nation's highest court was more important than his decisions. He found himself, in 1921, on a bench which was badly divided; out of 180 opinions handed down in 1921–22, dissents were expressed in forty-five cases—exactly one-fourth of the total. Moreover, the Court was behind in its work. Taft's private letters disclose his concern, in the matter of new appointments to the Supreme Court, that the number of dissents be cut down. Regarding one candidate he wrote that the jurist "is rather an off horse and dissents a good deal" (W. H. Taft to C. D. Hilles, Dec. 1, 1922). "It would be too bad," he continued, "if we had another on the bench who would herd with Brandeis . . . as Brandeis is usually against the Court." The Chief Justice, in this instance, was not objecting to the liberal views of Associate Justice Brandeis, but to the frequency of his dissents, whether liberal or conservative. This is not an implication, on the other hand, that Taft was not, on the whole, conservative in his interpretation of the law.

As president he had been "to a unique degree . . . interested in the effective working of the judicial machinery and conversant with the details of judicial administration" (see Frankfurter and Landis, *post*, pp. 156–58). As chief justice he immediately interested himself in finding some relief from the mass of litigation which was swamping the Supreme Court and the lower federal courts. His first accomplishment was authorization by Congress in 1922 for the creation of a conference of senior circuit judges, with the chief justice as its head. This introduced the first degree of coordination into the federal judicial system (*Ibid.,* pp. 241–54). Even more important was his part in effecting the passage of the act of Feb. 13, 1925. This was known as the Judges' Bill and, stripped of technicalities, it gave the Supreme Court a greatly increased discretion over the cases which came before it. It terminated certain classes of appeals as matters of right and made them reviewable only through the discretionary writ of certiorari. The Supreme Court now had time to give prompt action on questions of constitutionality and other cases of national significance (*Ibid.,* pp. 261–86). When he retired in February 1930, the business of the court was practically current.

The reputation of Taft for conservatism came, in part, from the so-called Child Labor Case and the Coronado Coal Company Case. The former (*Bailey* vs. *Drexel Furniture Co.*; 259 *United States,* 20) resulted from an attempt of Congress to control child labor by the imposition of a tax imposed on interstate products manufactured through its aid. This, Taft wrote, was an infringement on the rights of the states and not a proper use of the power to tax; "to give such magic to the word 'tax,' " he held, "would be to break down all constitutional limitation of the powers of Congress and completely wipe out the sovereignty of the States." The Coronado case (*United Mine Workers of America* vs. *Coronado Coal Co.*; 259 *United States,* 344) grew out of a strike in the Prairie Creek field in Arkansas in 1914. Property of the Coronado Coal Company was destroyed and action for damages against the United Mine Workers had resulted in a verdict for the company in a lower court. Taft wrote the opinion, denying federal jurisdiction since coal-mining was not interstate commerce, but holding that the union, even though unincorporated, could be sued under the antitrust laws; its funds, accumulated for conducting strikes, were subject to execution for unlawful acts committed during a strike. "The circumstances are such," said he, "as to awaken regret that, in our view of the federal jurisdiction, we can not affirm the judgment" (259 *United States,* 413).

The most important dissent by Taft was against the majority opinion of Justice Sutherland invalidating the law of 1918 which fixed a minimum wage for women in the District of Columbia (*Adkins* vs. *Children's Hospital*; 261 *United States,* 525). The majority of the Court held that the act did not deal with any business charged with the public interest or with any temporary emergency. But the Chief Justice held that a minimum wage law for women was constitutional because sweatshop wages did just as much to impair their health and morals as did long hours (see C. E. Hughes, *The Supreme Court of the United States,* 1928, pp. 209–10). Taft did not fulfill, however, this promise of leading the Court toward an increasingly liberal view in social and labor questions. It is clear that his duties as administrative officer of the Court gave him, as a general thing, no desire to dissent.

In so far as Taft sanctioned the control of commerce and industry he believed, his decisions show that supervision by the federal government was superior to that by the states. He agreed with the Court in nullifying the Kansas law creating a court of industrial relations, on the ground that the industries it proposed to control —and the act gave extraordinary powers to the court of industrial relations—were not affected with the public interest. It had never been supposed, he said "that the business of the butcher or the baker, the tailor, the woodchopper . . . was clothed with such a public interest that the price of his product or his wages could be fixed by State regulation" (Hughes, pp. 211, 221–22). But he was, in contrast, an advocate of broad federal powers under the commerce clause of the Constitution. The Supreme Court had already refused to limit the power of Congress; in 1905 Associate Justice Holmes had held that the packers were engaged in interstate commerce even though their actual business might be limited to the stockyards of Chicago. Taft extended this doctrine when he wrote the opinion upholding the stockyards act (*Stafford* vs. *Wallace*; 258 *United States,* 495). The packing and stockyards industry, he said, was national in scope and susceptible to federal regulation even to the point of letting the secretary of agriculture fix brokers' prices. Several other cases might be cited in which he further amplified this view. In the case of *Myers* vs. *United States* (272 *United States,* 52), the Supreme Court settled an ancient controversy by sustaining the presidential power to remove executive officers. Taft's opinion, it has been said, "will probably rank as one of his most important contributions to constitutional law" (*Proceedings of the Bar and Officers of the Supreme Court of the United States in Memory of William Howard Taft,* 1931, p. 37).

Yet Taft, a coordinator and conciliator all of his life rather than an advocate, was not a leader of judicial thought in the sense that Justice Holmes was a leader—or Justice Brandeis or Cardozo. The new Supreme Court building will remain as a permanent monument to his constructive talents; he was largely responsible for the congressional act under which it was built. On Feb. 3, 1930, bad health, due chiefly to heart disease, forced his retirement from the bench. He died in Washington on Mar. 8, 1930, and was buried in the Arlington National Cemetery.

Taft's published writings, outside of his legal opinions, were not important. Most of them were revised from public lectures. Among them might be mentioned: *Popular Government* (1913); *The Anti-Trust Act and the Supreme Court* (1914); *Ethics in Service* (1915); *Our Chief Magistrate and His Powers* (1916). Taft was not the type who would contribute very much to contemporary thought by his pen. He blazed few new trails, even in the law. He was thorough rather than original in his mental processes. The final decade of his life, as chief justice, was beyond any doubt the happiest. During it he was doing the work he loved. He was filling the post to which he had always aspired. Before he died, it is a safe assumption, his quadrennium in the presidency had faded like an evil dream into those mists which memory no longer penetrates.

[This sketch is based very largely on the William Howard Taft papers at the Lib. of Cong., which are open to students under certain restrictions. A critical biography is under preparation by Henry F. Pringle who has had free access to them. For Taft's decisions as superior court judge of Ohio see the files of *The Weekly Law Bulletin and Ohio Law Journal* (1887–1890). An adequate analysis of his services on the U. S. Circuit is in H. S. Duffy, *William Howard Taft* (1930); the cases can be found in *Federal Reporter*, vols. LI–CI. The Taft papers are voluminous for his periods as governor of the Philippine Islands, secretary of war, and president. They contain much source material on the campaign of 1912. His services in the reorganization of the Supreme Court are described in Felix Frankfurter and J. M. Landis, *The Business of the Supreme Court* (1928). His labor decisions are discussed by A. T. Mason, in *Univ. of Pa. Law Review*, March 1930. Secondary sources of value include: A. W. Butt, *Taft and Roosevelt: The Intimate Letters of Archie Butt* (2 vols., 1930); H. H. Kohlsaat, *From McKinley to Harding* (1923); Mrs. W. H. Taft, *Recollections of Full Years* (1914); C. W. Thompson, *Presidents I've Known and Two Near Presidents* (1929); W. A. White, *Masks in a Pageant* (1928); N. W. Stephenson, *Nelson W. Aldrich, A Leader in American Politics* (1930); H. L. Stoddard, *As I Knew Them* (1927); Samuel Gompers, *Seventy Years of Life and Labor* (2 vols., 1925); L. White Busbey, *Uncle Joe Cannon* (1927); C. M. Depew, *My Memories of Eighty Years* (1922); J. B. Foraker, *Notes of a Busy Life* (2 vols., 1916); *La Follette's Autobiography* (1913); T. B. Mott, *Myron T. Herrick, Friend of France* (1929); Harvey W. Wiley, *An Autobiography* (1930); H. F. Pringle, *Theodore Roosevelt, A Biography* (1931). For genealogy and other personal details, see Mabel T. R. Washburn, *Ancestry of William Howard*

Taft (1908); "The Ancestry of William Howard Taft," in *Genealogy*, Apr. 13, 1912; *Quarter-Centenary Record of the Class of 1878, Yale Univ.* (1905); *Bulletin of Yale Univ. Obituary Record* (1930), pp. 69–72.]

H. F. P—e.

TAGGART, THOMAS (Nov. 17, 1856–Mar. 6, 1929), politician, hotel proprietor, banker, the son of Thomas and Martha (Kingsbury) Taggart, was born in County Monaghan, Ireland, emigrated with his parents to the United States in 1861, and spent his childhood in Xenia, Ohio, where his father worked on a railroad. Forced by poverty at the age of twelve to find employment in a railroad restaurant, he studied at night and finally reached high school. Cleanliness, cordiality, and memory for names and tastes earned him a transfer to a restaurant in Garrett, Ind., in 1874 and in 1877 to one in Indianapolis.

Here he shortly became active in politics, starting as a precinct committeeman and later becoming a ward leader. From 1886 to 1894 he filled the lucrative office of auditor in Marion County. As chairman of the Democratic county committee he managed, in 1888, a highly successful campaign that brought him in 1892 the chairmanship of the state committee. During the years 1895–1901 he ably served three terms as mayor of Indianapolis, stressing governmental economy and reasonable enforcement of liquor laws and adding notably to the park system. In 1904 he supported the presidential candidacy of Alton B. Parker [q.v.] and as chairman of the Democratic National Committee directed the campaign. He remained a national committeeman until 1916. In 1908 he failed to control the Democratic state convention but at the national convention secured the nomination of John Worth Kern [q.v.] for the vice-presidency. Two years later, when the state convention was considering whom to select as candidate for the United States Senate nomination, Taggart withdrew in Kern's favor. In 1912 he placed Samuel M. Ralston [q.v.] in the governor's chair and, according to Chairman McCombs, played a vital part in nominating Woodrow Wilson.

During the years following 1912 Taggart exerted great political influence in Indiana, conferring frequently with the governor and Democratic members of the legislature and of Congress. At the death of Senator Benjamin F. Shively, in 1916, Governor Ralston appointed Taggart United States senator, in which capacity he served from Mar. 20 to Nov. 7. Despite newspaper ridicule, he displayed serious interest in Senate business and dealt some telling blows at "pork-barrel" legislation, but was defeated at the election to fill the unexpired term. In 1920 he again encountered defeat but in 1922 brought about the election of his friend Ralston. Taggart's greatest political disappointment occurred at the Democratic National Convention of 1924 when, after months of labor on his part and with what he considered victory within grasp Ralston withdrew as a candidate for the presidential nomination.

Taggart showed exceptional ability in the operation of the Grand and the Denison hotels in Indianapolis and in the management of the large resort hotel at French Lick. He also interested himself in mining and banking, serving as vice-president of the Fletcher-American Company and as chairman of the board of directors of the Fletcher-American National Bank—at the time one of the largest banks in Indiana. Endowed with remarkable vitality, unusually attractive personal characteristics, great capacity as an organizer, a keen sense of humor, genuine fondness for people, and contempt for vindictiveness, he attained more than average success in both political and business affairs. Inclined to be silent himself, he had little regard for oratory. He emphasized practical results, at times perhaps, with ruthlessness. His deep blue eyes, blonde complexion, conservative dress, and erect carriage made him physically distinctive. He was a crack shot, a good horseman, and a race-track enthusiast, with his own stables. On June 17, 1877, he married Eva D. Bryant of Garrett, Ind., and he was the father of six children, five of whom survived him. He died in Indianapolis.

[J. B. Stoll, *Hist. of the Ind. Democracy, 1816–1916* (1917); *Biog. Dir. Am. Cong.* (1928); *Who's Who in America*, 1928–29; *Outlook*, Mar. 29, 1916; files of the *Indianapolis News*; obituary in *Indianapolis Star,* Mar. 7, 1929; information as to certain facts from Miss Lucy Taggart.]   H. Z.

TAGLIABUE, GIUSEPPE (Aug. 10, 1812–May 7, 1878), inventor, instrument maker, was born in Como, Italy, the son of Caesar Tagliabue, founder of the great scientific instrument business of London, and grandson of Caesar Tagliabue of Como, Italy, who was one of the first persons in the world to make thermometers in quantity. Caesar Tagliabue, the second, was well established in London when his son Giuseppe was born and the latter, after obtaining an ordinary education and learning cabinet making in Italy, entered his father's establishment and there acquired the trade of thermometer maker. Upon completing his apprenticeship in 1829, Tagliabue, although only seventeen years old, left London and went to Rio de Janeiro to ply his trade. After spending two years there without experiencing any material benefit, he emigrated to New York with all his worldly possessions, which consisted of a bellows, a bundle of glass

tubing, a pan of tallow, and less than five dollars.

Renting a single room on Water Street directly back of 298 Pearl Street, he began making and selling thermometers. His business soon outgrew these limited quarters and he acquired a four-story house at 298 Pearl Street, which not only served as his store and workshop but for a time was his residence as well. For upwards of forty-seven years he carried on his trade, becoming one of the most prominent and successful instrument makers of the United States. To him came Kane and Hall, the Arctic explorers; Bache and Hilgard of the United States Coast and Geodetic Survey; Borden, the inventor of the process of condensing milk; and Havemeyer, the sugar refiner—all to secure the delicate instruments so necessary to their several undertakings. Besides his thermometers he made a great variety of hydrometers, including original forms and new adaptations to meet the changing manufacturing requirements. Many of the instruments used by the Geodetic Survey were constructed by Tagliabue and his hydrometer for the proving of whiskey was officially adopted by the United States revenue bureau. He was always enthusiastic about his work and gave considerably more attention to the excellence of his instruments than to the money he received. Between 1859 and 1871 he found time to perfect a few instruments of original design, which he had patented. These included a mercurial barometer; an apparatus for testing iron and coal; an instrument to determine the amount of water in a barrel of oil; a number of hydrometers; and an apparatus for determining the proof spirits in fermented mash. These inventions were ever a source of loving pride to him and were profitable as well. He was married twice; his second wife was Adelaide Arniboldi of New York City, who with their six children survived him. He died at his home in Mount Vernon, N. Y.

[Correspondence with C. J. Tagliabue Manufacturing Company; *N. Y. Daily Tribune,* May 8, 1878; Patent Office records.]   C. W. M—n.

TAIT, ARTHUR FITZWILLIAM (Aug. 5, 1819–Apr. 28, 1905), landscape and animal painter, was born at Livesey Hall, near Liverpool, England. After attending a country school at Lancaster, at the age of twelve he went to work in Agnew's picture store, Manchester. There he devoted himself to studying from casts at the Royal Manchester Institution and had an opportunity to see many of the best English pictures of the period. In art he was almost entirely self-taught. In 1850 he emigrated to the United States and settled in New York. He was made a member of the National Academy of Design in 1858, and was a member of the Artists' Fund Society and the Lotos Club. He made most of his studies from nature in the Adirondacks and elsewhere during the summer months, and in 1874 spent four months in Europe. He contributed numerous paintings to the exhibitions of the National Academy, among other things "A Duck and her Young" (1868), "Ruffed Grouse" (1869), "Woodcock Shooting" and "The Halt on the Carry" (1871), "Racquette Lake" (1873), and "Lake Trout" (1878). He was represented at the Centennial Exhibition, Philadelphia (1876), by "The Portage—Waiting for the Boats," painted in conjunction with James Mac-Dougal Hart [q.v.] His "Quail and Young," painted in 1856, is in the permanent collection of the Corcoran Gallery of Art, Washington, D. C. His "The Happy Family," dated 1855, was in the S. B. Fales collection, which was sold at auction in New York, 1881. His picture of a Gordon setter belongs to the Charles Stewart Smith collection. Many of his pictures of animals and birds were lithographed and widely circulated. He was a skilful academic painter who had a high reputation in his day in a community which had no very close acquaintance with the best of art at home or abroad, but his work shows little trace either of genius or of imagination. He died at his home in Yonkers, N. Y., survived by his wife and two sons.

[*Who's Who in America*, 1903–05; J. D. Champlin and C. C. Perkins, *Cyc. of Painters and Paintings* (4 vols., 1886–87); Clara E. Clement and Laurence Hutton, *Artists of the Nineteenth Century* (1879); cats. of the S. B. Fales coll. (1881), of the Corcoran Gallery of Art, Washington, D. C., of the Nat. Acad. Exhibition, N. Y., 1894; obituaries in *Am. Art. Ann.*, 1905–06, and *N. Y. Times*, Apr. 29, 1905.] W. H. D.

TAIT, CHARLES (Feb. 1, 1768–Oct. 7, 1835), jurist, United States senator, and scholar, the son of James and Rebecca (Hudson) Tait and cousin of Henry Clay, was born in Louisa County, Va. The Taits, who were of Scotch ancestry, had emigrated to Virginia during the seventeenth century. James, a planter of some means, settled in Elbert County, Ga., in 1783. Charles received some schooling in Virginia and in 1786–87 attended Wilkes Academy, Washington, Ga. About this time he was thrown from a horse, receiving an injury to his leg which necessitated its amputation. Early in 1788 he entered Cokesbury College, Abingdon, Md., where in September he was made an instructor. He left Cokesbury in 1794, and, having read law while teaching, was admitted to the bar at Elberton, Ga., in February 1795. A few weeks later he was made rector of Richmond Academy, Au-

gusta, Ga., where William H. Crawford [q.v.] became his associate.

He began the practice of law at Lexington, Ga., in 1798, Crawford joining him as partner the following year. Both were soon drawn into the political feud which grew out of the Yazoo land frauds. Tait became a prominent figure in the faction known successively as the Jackson, Crawford, and Troup party, the leaders of which had opposed the Yazoo sales, and which embraced the planter, professional, and Virginian elements in the state. The opposing faction was led by John Clark [q.v.]. Tait's friendship for Crawford and his somewhat moody and sensitive nature involved him in a number of controversies with Clark men. In 1802, after considerable provocation, he challenged Peter Lawrence Van Allen. In the meantime, however, Van Allen insulted Crawford, Tait's second, who killed him in a duel. A challenge to John M. Dooly the next year did not result in a duel. From 1803 to 1809 Tait served as judge of the superior court for the western district of Georgia. He incurred the special enmity of Clark through the performance of official duties and in 1806 Clark memorialized the Georgia legislature, asking that Tait be impeached for official misconduct. Although Tait was exonerated, Clark later attacked him in pamphlets and in 1807 assaulted him with a horsewhip.

In 1809 he was elected to the United States Senate to fill the vacancy resulting from the resignation of John Milledge [q.v.], a position which he held by reëlection until Mar. 3, 1819. His most conspicuous public service was rendered through untiring efforts in behalf of the navy during that critical period. Made a member of the Senate committee on naval affairs in 1812, he served as chairman from 1814 to 1818, in which capacity he secured an appropriation of $1,000,000 for the Navy. He aided in the formation of Alabama as a separate territory and in securing its admission to the Union. His Admission Bill (3 *U. S. Statutes at Large*, 489–92) made provision for a state university comparable with the best institutions of the country. Having offended his constituents by contending that he should be allowed a salary as representative, and having acquired a fortune through planting, he removed in 1819 to Claiborne, Monroe County, Ala. In May 1820 President Monroe appointed him first federal judge of the District of Alabama. Retiring in 1826, he devoted himself to planting on land he owned in Wilcox County and to scientific study. In 1828 he declined a mission to Great Britain (Tompkins, *post*, p. 29). Soon after settling in Alabama

Tait made known to the scientific world the "Claiborne beds," one of the notable Eocene deposits of the country (Lea, *post*, pp. 27–28). His scientific acquirements won for him membership in the American Philosophical Society in 1827 and in 1832 he was elected a corresponding member of the Academy of Natural Sciences of Philadelphia. He was twice married: first, Jan. 3, 1790, to Mrs. Anne (Lucas) Simpson, of Baltimore; second, in 1822, to Mrs. Sarah (Williamson) Griffin of Georgia. He was survived by one son.

[The Tait Papers, comprising letters and plantation jottings, are in the Ala. department of archives at Montgomery; for published sources, see Alma Cole Tompkins, *Charles Tait* (1910), in the Ala. Polytechnic Inst. Hist. Series, short but reliable; J. E. D. Shipp, *Giant Days, or the Life and Times of Wm. H. Crawford* (1909); U. B. Phillips, *Life and Labor in the Old South* (1929); Willis Brewer, *Ala.: Her Hist., Resources, War Record, and Pub. Men* (1872); Isaac Lea, *Contributions to Geology* (1833); T. M. Owen, *Hist. of Ala. and Dict. of Ala. Biog.* (1921); *Biog. Dir. Am. Cong.* (1928); P. A. Brannon, "Jour. of James A. Tait for the Year 1813," *Ga. Hist. Quart.*, Sept. 1924; John Clark, *Considerations on the Purity of the Principles of William H. Crawford . . . in Connexion with that of Charles Tait* (1823); *Mobile Daily Commercial Register and Patriot*, Oct. 16, 1835.] H. D. F.

TAKAMINE, JOKICHI (Nov. 3, 1854–July 22, 1922), chemist, industrial leader, was born in Takaoka, Japan, the son of Seichi and Yukiko Takamine. His father was a physician, as were many of his ancestors, and his early years were spent in an environment of scientific culture and the tradition of the Sumarai. His father, with admirable foresight, sent him, at the age of twelve, to Osaka that his studies might there include the English language. Later he pursued his studies in Kyoto and Tokio and was graduated at government expense from the college of science and engineering of the University of Tokio in 1879. His high scholarship caused him to be selected as one of twelve to be sent by the Japanese government for post-graduate study at Glasgow University and Anderson's College, 1879–81. During his summer vacations he visited various industrial plants to observe the manufacturing of soda and fertilizers. Returning to Japan in 1883, he entered the department of agriculture and commerce where his work was guided by his belief that chemical industries should first be developed not to compete with other nations but to foster agriculture and industry indigenous to Japan.

Takamine first visited the United States in 1884 as one of the Japanese commissioners to the international Cotton Centennial Exposition in New Orleans. Here he met and, in 1885, was married to Caroline Field Hitch, the daughter of Col. Eben Hitch. This event brought him finally to make the United States his adopted country. He then returned to Japan and was made chief of the division of chemistry in the department of agriculture and commerce, and, later, acting chief of the patent bureau. In 1887 he left the government service to develop the first superphosphate works in Japan, the Tokyo Artificial Fertilizer Company. Meanwhile in his private laboratory he had developed from a special type of fungus the potent starch-digesting enzyme, Takadiastase. In 1890 he was suddenly called to Chicago and Peoria, Ill., to apply this substance practically to the distilling industry. Fire, commercial opposition, and serious illness harassed him until, in 1894, the Takamine Ferment Company, which he had founded, was little more than a name. He moved to the vicinity of New York City to further the industrial development of Takadiastase. The production of the enzyme for medicinal use was taken over by Parke, Davis & Company, of Detroit, Mich., with whom, from that time on, Takamine was closely associated. The crowning achievement of his life was the isolation of adrenalin from the suprarenal gland in 1901. This was the first of all gland hormones to be discovered in pure form, and the value of the substance to medicine and surgery can scarcely be overestimated. It was discovered almost simultaneously by another scientist, whose work Takamine was quick to recognize.

Takamine's commercial and scientific interests broadened. Among other industries he aided in the development in Japan of dyes, aluminum fabrication, Bakelite, the electric furnace, and nitrogen fixation. Through his influence the Imperial Research Institute was established in Japan in 1913. Prosperity and honors came to him in abundance. He continued his private research in his laboratory at Clifton, N. J., and strove continually for better understanding between his native land and his adopted land. Remembering his own struggles, he delighted in aiding young men; young chemists were encouraged and employed by him; young artists studied painting and music in France and Italy with his financial and moral assistance. His advice was sought not only by the humble and poor but also by captains of industry, diplomats, ambassadors, and princes. His home on Riverside Drive in New York City presented an historical development of Japanese art, and his country home at Merriewold Park furnished an example of the best in Japanese landscape gardening. Both were centers of culture and offered gracious hospitality to a wide circle of friends.

Takamine was co-founder and president of the Japanese Association of New York and of the Nippon Club, and a member of the Lotos, Chemists, Bankers, Drug and Chemical, and New York Athletic clubs. He was honored by the Imperial University of Japan in 1899, 1906, and 1912, became a member of the Royal Academy of Science of Japan in 1913; he received the Fourth Order of the Rising Sun in 1915, and the Senior Degree of the Fourth Rank (Sho Shii) and the Third Merit (Kum Santo) in 1922. His wife and their two sons survived him at his death.

[Information from the family and Takamine's secretary; *Who's Who in America*, 1922–23; K. K. Kawakami, *Jokichi Takamine; A Record of his Am. Achievements* (1928); *Am. Jour. of Pharmacy*, Nov. 1901; *N. Y. Times*, July 23, 1922.]   F. O. T.

TALBOT, EMILY FAIRBANKS (Feb. 22, 1834–Oct. 29, 1900), philanthropist, was born in Winthrop, Me., the descendant of Jonathan Fayerbanke (variously spelled) who emigrated from England in 1633 and later settled in Dedham, Mass. Her parents, Columbus and Lydia (Tinkham) Fairbanks, were farming people in very moderate circumstances. The daughter's formal education was limited to that provided by the local schools, but her mother's strong character, unusual native intelligence and social interests had perhaps as great an influence in the daughter's education as any formal schooling. When Emily was sixteen years old she taught an unruly school in Augusta, Me., with great success, a success especially notable because her predecessors had not been able to finish out their terms. In 1854, while teaching in Baltimore, Md., she met Israel Tisdale Talbot [*q.v.*]. They were married on Oct. 29, 1856. In 1857 they went to Europe for a prolonged tour and on their return took up what was to be their permanent residence in Boston. They had six children, four of whom reached adult life. A fair was held in Boston in 1859 to assist the Homeopathic Medical Dispensary, and it was there that Mrs. Talbot's first public work took place. From that moment she cooperated with her husband. She had a large part in obtaining funds for the support of the Massachusetts Homeopathic Hospital and was appointed by the governor of Massachusetts a member of the first board of trustees of the state insane hospital at Westboro. In 1887 honorary associate membership in the American Institute of Homeopathy was conferred upon her. As secretary of the education department of the American Social Science Association she personally consulted with Charles Darwin, and together with Dr. William T. Harris gave real impetus to child study in the United

States. The education of her two daughters was a matter of absorbing interest to her, and in 1877, largely through her leadership and organizing power, the public Latin school for girls was established in Boston in order to give the facilities for college preparation to girls such as were open to boys. When her daughters were students in the college of liberal arts of Boston University, she became deeply interested in the efforts made by young women to obtain a college education in spite of lack of money. The practical result of this interest was the aid she gave in organizing the Massachusetts Society for the University Education of Women, of which she was a director for several years.

Her most important contribution in education was, however, her plan for the cooperation of the college women of the country in opening educational opportunities for women, in enabling women graduates to make the best use of their training through mutual deliberation and counsel, and in stimulating young women to attend colleges and universities and to undertake graduate work. It was from her suggestion made in October 1881 that the Association of Collegiate Alumnae was organized, an association which was one of the three charter members of the International Federation of University Women formed in 1919, and which in 1921, together with the Southern Association of College Women, became the American Association of University Women. She died at her summer home in Holderness, N. H., on the anniversary of her wedding day and of the birthday of her husband.

[Manuscript sketch by her daughter, Marion Talbot; Marion Talbot and L. K. M. Rosenberry, *The Hist. of the American Asso. of Univ. Women* (1931); L. S. Fairbanks, *Geneal. of the Fairbanks Family in America* (1897); *Boston Evening Transcript*, Oct. 31, 1900.]
                                        L. K. M. R.

TALBOT, ETHELBERT (Oct. 9, 1848–Feb. 27, 1928), bishop of the Protestant Episcopal Church, was born in Fayette, Mo., the son of John Alnut and Alice (Daly) Talbot. He was graduated from Dartmouth College in 1870, and from the General Theological Seminary, New York, in 1873. In that same year he was ordained deacon (June 29) and priest (Nov. 4), and became rector of St. James Church, Macon, Mo. Here, in addition to the work of the parish and neighboring missions, he founded a school, which grew into St. James' Military Academy. New buildings had recently been erected, and a separate girls' school established, when the General Convention of 1886 elected Talbot missionary bishop of Wyoming and Idaho. After some hesitation he left his work in Macon, and was consecrated on May 27, 1887.

Upon arrival in his diocese, he found only four clergy in each of the states it comprised. Within ten years he had built a cathedral at Laramie and thirty-eight churches, and had founded three schools, including a school for Indian girls, and a hospital. His summers were largely spent in preaching in mining camps and towns, and he traveled extensively in the East and even in the British Isles in behalf of his work. His experiences in the West are the basis of *My People of the Plains* (1906), a book which, without the loss of its serious character, is filled with anecdotes which support his reputation as a raconteur. In 1891 he was elected bishop of Georgia but declined; six years later, however, he was elected bishop of Central Pennsylvania and accepted. The people of his Western diocese saw him go with regret, non-churchmen as well as churchmen. He had been offered nominations for governor and senator and was regarded by all as "our bishop."

On Feb. 2, 1898, Talbot was enthroned in the pro-cathedral, the Church of the Nativity, South Bethlehem. He at once began to work towards the division of his unwieldy diocese, which project was accomplished by the erection of the Diocese of Harrisburg in 1904. Talbot continued in charge of the remaining area, which in 1909 took the name Diocese of Bethlehem. The number of communicants having doubled since his coming, each diocese was by now almost as strong as the original one had been. The project of an associate mission led to the opening of Leonard Hall, South Bethlehem, in 1908. This developed mainly, in accordance with a minor purpose in its foundation, as a residence for postulants for holy orders taking their college work at Lehigh University. In his later years, Bishop Talbot's attention was given increasingly to the growing industrial and foreign population of his diocese, social problems, and church unity. He served for some time as chairman of the General Convention commission on Christian unity. A contribution by him to a symposium, *The Problem of Christian Unity* (1921), recommends as "The Next Step" immediate organic unions between American Protestant bodies. Meanwhile, he had summed up his teaching in two books—*A Bishop among his Flock* (1914), addressed to the laity of his diocese; and *A Bishop's Message* (1917), addressed to the clergy. In 1914 he published *Tim; the Autobiography of a Dog,* a sentimental and humorous account of his daughter's bulldog.

In 1923 he obtained the assistance of a coadjutor, Bishop Frank W. Sterrett. By the death of Bishop Alexander C. Garrett of Dallas on Feb. 18, 1924, Talbot became senior diocesan, and presiding bishop of the Protestant Episcopal Church. He was the last to hold the office by seniority, since it was about to be changed from a formal and representative to an administrative post. In 1925 he presided at the General Convention, and Jan. 1, 1926, handed over the office to the first elected presiding bishop, John Gardner Murray [*q.v.*]. Rapidly aging, on Sept. 15, 1927, he resigned the administration of his diocese to Bishop Sterrett, and a few months later died. Successful as administrator, Talbot was loved as pastor and friend by both clergy and laity. In thought his position was a moderate, but definite, Anglicanism aiming at charity both within and without the Church. He had learned to combine breadth of sympathy with firmness of conviction in the days when he preached to "wild westerners" on "temperance, righteousness, and judgment to come." On Nov. 5, 1873, he married Dora Frances Harvey, of Roanoke, Mo., and he was survived by one daughter, at whose home at Tuckahoe, N. Y., he died.

[*My People of the Plains*; autobiog. address to Bethlehem Convention, pub. in its *Journal*, 1912; official reports in convention journals of Mo., Central Pa., and Bethlehem dioceses; *Living Church,* Mar. 1, 1924, Mar. 3, 1928; *Bethlehem Churchman,* Mar. 1928; *The Living Church Annual . . . 1929*; J. W. Miller, *Hist. of the Diocese of Central Pa.* (1909); *Who's Who in America,* 1926–27; *N. Y. Times,* Feb. 28, 1928.]   E. R. H., Jr.

TALBOT, HENRY PAUL (May 15, 1864– June 18, 1927), chemist, was born in Boston, Mass., the son of Zephaniah and Eliza Frances (Paul) Talbot. The Talbot family was one of the earliest to settle in Massachusetts. William Cushing and Silas Talbot [*qq.v.*] are among the distinguished ancestors. Henry Talbot's boyhood was spent in Holliston and Boston. He was graduated from the Holliston High School in 1881 and attended the Massachusetts Institute of Technology, receiving the degree of S.B. in 1885. For three years he served as assistant and instructor at the Institute, and then he spent two years at the University of Leipzig, majoring in organic chemistry under Wislecenus and taking courses in the new field of physical chemistry under Ostwald. He received the Ph.D. degree, *summa cum laude,* in 1890, and returned to the Institute of Technology, which he served continuously until his death, rising from the rank of an instructor to the headship of the departments of chemistry and chemical engineering, 1902–20, and of the department of chemistry, 1920–22. He was chairman of the faculty from 1919 to 1921, chairman of the administrative committee which conducted the affairs of the Institute following the death of Richard C. Maclaurin [*q.v.*], and dean of students from 1921 until his death.

He served as a member of the Advisory Board of the United States Bureau of Mines, Department of Gas Defence, in 1917. He published two textbooks of chemistry and numerous papers upon scientific and educational subjects. Talbot served, both as an officer and constant counselor, many professional organizations, the American Chemical Society, the Society for the Promotion of Engineering Education, the New England Society of Chemistry Teachers, and the American Academy of Arts and Sciences, with the same devotion that he served the Institute of Technology. As a teacher his presentation of his subject of analytical and inorganic chemistry was clear, logical, and inspiring. In the earlier days he conducted one of the first courses in physical chemistry given in an American institution. His personal interest in the students under his influence bore fruit in many of the careers of later leaders in education, research, and chemical industry. Talbot was always a friend to the furtherance of scientific research, but he was so absorbed in his main objective that he had little leisure to spend in research. As an administrator he went far in encouraging research, but always the education of students was the goal, and the research among members of the instructing staff was encouraged in so far as it contributed to their efficiency as educators. His greatest concern was with the traits which make the real teacher.

His comparatively early death, three weeks after undergoing a major operation, was a heavy loss to his associates and to the institution which he had so faithfully and ably served. On June 17, 1891, he married Frances E. Dukehart, of Baltimore, Md., who survived him. They had one son who died as a child.

[Personal acquaintance; correspondence with Mrs. Talbot; *Who's Who in America*, 1926–27; J. M. Cattell, D. R. Brimhall, ed., *Am. Men of Sci.* (3rd ed., 1921); articles by J. F. Norris in *Technology Rev.*, July 1927, and A. D. Little, *Industrial and Engineering Chemistry*, Aug. 1927; *Technology's War Record* (1920); *Boston Evening Transcript*, June 18, 1927.]

A. A. B.

TALBOT, ISRAEL TISDALE (Oct. 29, 1829–July 2, 1899), physician, was born at Sharon, Mass., the son of Josiah and Mary (Richards) Talbot, and a descendant of Peter Talbot who was in Dorchester, Mass., before 1677. He received a common-school education and at the age of eighteen went to Baltimore, Md., where he established a private school. Although the venture proved successful, Talbot soon returned to New England and continued his studies at South Woodstock, Conn., and later at Worcester Academy, Worcester, Mass. In

March 1851 he became a medical student in the office of Dr. Samuel Gregg of Boston, and subsequently pursued courses in the Tremont Street Medical School (which in 1858 was united with the Harvard Medical School) and at the Homœopathic Medical College of Pennsylvania (later the Hahnemann Medical College), from which he was graduated in 1853. Returning to Boston, he took additional courses at the Harvard Medical School and in 1854 received the degree of M.D. from that institution. The following fifteen months were spent in hospitals and medical schools of Europe.

From the early days of his practice in Boston he took a leading part in the organization activities of the homœopaths. In this work his wife, Emily (Fairbanks) Talbot [*q.v.*], whom he married Oct. 29, 1856, gave him able assistance. Largely through his efforts a charter was secured for the Massachusetts Homœopathic Medical Society and for a medical dispensary. Of the society Talbot was recording secretary from 1861 to 1866; vice-president in 1866; and president in 1867. He was also one of those instrumental in the opening in 1870 of a small hospital, which was the nucleus of the Massachusetts Homœopathic Hospital. Upon the establishment of the Boston University School of Medicine in 1873, he was appointed dean and professor of surgery. The establishment of the state hospital for the insane at Westboro, Mass., was in no small measure the result of his endeavors. He took a prominent part in the proceedings of the American Institute of Homœopathy, serving as its general secretary from 1866 to 1869, and its president in 1872. Its *Transactions* list approximately a hundred papers read by him at meetings of the Institute. From 1867 to 1873 he was an editor of the *New England Medical Gazette*. In his younger years he was fond of mountain climbing and in 1854 made an ascent of Mont Blanc, which is said to have been the second complete ascent of that mountain made by an American. He died in Hingham, Mass.

[T. L. Bradford, *Biog. Index of the Grads. of the Homœopathic Medic. Coll. of Pa.* (1918); T. C. Bradford, "Biogs. of Homœopathic Physicians," vol. XXXI (MS. Hahnemann Medic. Coll., Phila.); *Proc. Mass. Homœopathic Medic. Soc.*, vol. XIII (1900); *Trans. Thirty-fifth Session, Homœopathic Medic. Soc. of the State of Pa.* (1900); *Trans. Fifty-sixth Session Am. Inst. Homœopathy* (1901); *Medic. Student*, Jan. 1900; *Am. Alpine Jour.*, May 1935; *Boston Transcript*, July 3, 1899.]

C. B—t.

TALBOT, JOHN (1645–Nov. 29, 1727), Anglican clergyman, missionary, was born in Wymondham, Norfolk, England, the son of Thomas Talbot and Jane, daughter of Sir John Mede of Lofts, Essex. He was admitted sizar at

Christ's College, Cambridge, graduated B.A. in 1663/4 and M.A. in 1671, and was a fellow of Peterhouse from 1664 to 1668 when he admitted marriage and forfeited his fellowship. His wife was a daughter of Sir Arthur Jenney of Knotshall, Suffolk. Talbot was rector of a church in Icklingham, Suffolk, 1673–89; he seems to have visited Virginia about 1693 (Hills, *History of the Church in Burlington, post*, p. 35) ; and from 1695 to 1701 he was rector of the church at Fretherne, Gloucestershire.

On Apr. 28, 1702, he sailed from Cowes for the port of Boston as chaplain of the *Centurion*. With him were George Keith [*q.v.*] and Patrick Gordon, the first missionaries sent to the colonies by the Society for the Propagation of the Gospel in Foreign Parts. In Boston he preached a sermon at Queen's Chapel, June 28, and soon afterward was chosen by Keith as assistant in his missionary travels. On Sept. 18, 1702, he was appointed a missionary of the Society. Setting off with Keith on an intercolonial journey for the purpose of consolidating the Church of England forces on the northeastern seaboard, he preached at Philadelphia to assemblies so large that no church could be found to hold them, and had similar successes in New York and New Jersey. "We find," he wrote, "a great ripeness and inclination amongst all sorts of people to embrace the Gospel" (Hills, *Church in Burlington*, p. 27). With him he carried a "wallet full" of books explanatory of the doctrine and liturgy of the Church of England. He soon became convinced that America needed a bishop, "to visit all the churches, to ordain some, to confirm others, and bless all" (*Ibid.*), and thenceforward was untiring in his effort to secure an ecclesiastic qualified to perform these functions. There was strong objection in the Colonies to the project of an episcopate, however, as much political as ecclesiastical, and Talbot's continued efforts to set up the mitre were opposed on every side.

In 1704, upon the petition of the churchmen of Burlington in the Jerseys, he became rector of the newly built St. Mary's Church there, but in the same year when certain members of the clergy began to agitate for a suffragan bishop, he went to England to plead the cause before the Society, and again took up his residence in Fretherne until 1708, when he returned to America. Four years later the Society for the Propagation of the Gospel empowered Gov. Robert Hunter [*q.v.*] to prepare a residence for Talbot in Burlington, and an established bishopric loomed as a certainty. With the accession of George I, however, the old Jacobite-Hanoverian quarrels were reopened, and Talbot, asked to renew the oath of allegiance, refused. Governor Hunter immediately charged him with incorporating the Jacobites in the Jerseys, refused to grant him residence, and in 1716 accused him of omitting certain prayers from the liturgy. In 1720–23 Talbot visited England, where he presented another petition to the Society for the Propagation of the Gospel. He was now granted the interest from the legacy left by Archbishop Tenison for the support of a bishop in America or, until the appointment of such a bishop, the support of a deserving missionary (Hills, *op. cit.*, pp. 161–62; Perry, *post,* I, 550). The tradition that while in England Talbot received episcopal consecration clandestinely at the hands of a nonjuror (Hills, "John Talbot," *post*), rests upon very questionable evidence (Fulton, *post*). Returning to America in 1723, he reopened negotiations with Governor Hunter, and the two became reconciled. The following year, presiding at a convocation of clergy who upheld the action of the vestry of Christ Church, Philadelphia, in dismissing the Rev. John Urmiston, and later supplying the vacant pulpit himself, Talbot gained an enemy in Urmiston, who made complaint, insinuating that Talbot had assumed the rôle of bishop, and recalled the old accusation of Jacobite sympathies. Urmiston's charges were reported to the Society for the Propagation of the Gospel, and in October 1724 Talbot was removed for disaffection toward the government. In July 1725 he wrote the Society that he had learned indirectly that he had been dismissed for "exercising acts of jurisdiction" over his fellow missionaries, which charge he emphatically denied. He was not reinstated, however, although shortly afterward the visiting commissary of the Bishop of London wrote to England in his behalf, characterizing him as "a man universally beloved, even by the dissenters" (Tiffany, *post,* p. 198). About this time he married Mrs. Anne Herbert, who survived him. He died at the age of eighty-two and was buried in St. Mary's Church, Burlington.

[G. M. Hills, "John Talbot, the First Bishop in North America," *Pa. Mag. of Hist. and Biog.*, vol. III, no. 1 (1879), and *Hist. of the Church in Burlington, N. J.* (2nd ed., 1885) ; John and J. A. Venn, *Alumni Cantabrigienses*, pt. 1, vol. IV (1927) ; Francis Blomefield, *An Essay towards a Topographical Hist. of the County of Norfolk*, I (1739), 722; George Keith, *A Jour. of Travels . . . on the Continent of North America* (1706) ; A. L. Cross, *The Anglican Episcopate and the American Colonies* (1902) ; H. D. Evans, *An Essay on the Episcopate of the Protestant Episcopal Church in the U. S. A.* (1855) ; E. P. Tanner, *The Province of New Jersey, 1664–1738* (1908) ; W. A. Whitehead, *Docs. Rel. to the Col. Hist. of . . . N. J.*, 1 ser. IV (1882) ; Ernest Hawkins, *Hist. Notices of the Missions of the Church of England in the North American Colonies* (1845) ; John Fulton, "The Non-Juring Bishops in America," in W. S. Perry, *The Hist. of the Am. Episcopal Church*

(1885), vol. I; C. C. Tiffany, *A Hist. of the Protestant Episcopal Church in the U. S. A.* (1895).]   E. H. D.

TALBOT, SILAS (Jan. 11, 1751–June 30, 1813), naval officer, was born at Dighton, Bristol County, Mass., the ninth of fourteen children of Benjamin and Rebecca (Allen) Talbot. At the age of twelve he lost his father, a farmer. Learning the trade of a stone-mason, he soon abandoned it for sea-going and mercantile pursuits. In 1772 he was married to a Miss Richmond and settled in Providence, R. I., where he had purchased a house out of his own earnings. Some preliminary drilling with a band of volunteers recommended him as a military man to the Rhode Island government, and, on June 28, 1775, he was appointed captain in one of its regiments. Three days later he received a commission as captain in the Continental Army. After participating in the siege of Boston and aiding in the transporting of troops to New York, he obtained command of a fireship and made a spirited attempt to burn the warship *Asia*. This enterprise, though unsuccessful, brought him to the attention of Congress, which on Oct. 10, 1777, promoted him to the rank of major.

In the defense of Hog Island, in the Delaware River, Talbot was so severely wounded that he retired to Rhode Island on leave of absence, but in the summer of 1778 he again saw active service in the Rhode Island campaign of Gen. John Sullivan [q.v.]. Fitting out the *Hawke* he captured the *Pigot* in October, again exhibiting initiative and gallantry. On Nov. 14, Congress rewarded him with a promotion to a lieutenant-colonelcy and Rhode Island about the same time recognized his services with the gift of a sword. As commander of the *Pigot* and later of the *Argo,* both under the army, he cruised against the small enemy vessels that interrupted the American trade between Long Island and Nantucket and captured more than a dozen of them. In recognition of these exploits Congress made him a captain in the Continental Navy, on Sept. 17, 1779, but when he failed to obtain a ship commensurate with his rank he put to sea as commander of the privateer *General Washington.* He had taken but a single prize when he ran into the British fleet off New York and after a chase surrendered to the *Culloden,* 74 guns. For a time he was confined on board the famous *Jersey* prison ship at New York, but later was transported to England and confined in a prison. After undergoing many hardships and making several futile attempts to escape he was exchanged for a British officer and landed at Cherbourg, France, in December 1781. Obtaining pecuniary aid from Franklin, he sailed for America, but before reaching his destination the vessel on which he had taken passage was captured by a British privateer. The British captain, however, considerably put him aboard an English brig bound for New York.

The settlement of his claims against the government and a prize case before the Pennsylvania Admiralty led Talbot to spend much time in Philadelphia, where, after the death of his first wife, he was married to a Miss Morris, grand-daughter of Gen. Thomas Mifflin [q.v.]. Soon after his marriage he established himself as a farmer in Fulton County, N. Y., on a section of the forfeited estates of Sir John Johnson [q.v.]. In 1792–93 he was a member of the New York Assembly, and, in 1793–95, of the federal House of Representatives. On June 5, 1794, President Washington chose him third in a list of six captains of the new navy then under organization. Before the end of his term in Congress he entered upon the superintendency of the construction of the frigate *President* at New York. From 1796, when work on this vessel was suspended, until the outbreak of the naval war with France in 1798, he was without naval duties. On May 11, 1798, President Adams reappointed him captain, an unnecessary act that led to a long and bitter controversy between Talbot and Thomas Truxtun [q.v.] over their rank; the President supported Talbot.

As commander of the Santo Domingo station, 1799–1800, he made a rather uneventful cruise in the West Indies on board the *Constitution.* One exploit that he conceived led to the capture of the *Sandwich* in the Spanish harbor of Puerto Plata, Santo Domingo. This capture, being illegal, cost the captors dearly. At the end of the cruise Talbot was commended by the secretary of the navy for his services in protecting American commerce and for laying the foundation of a permanent trade with Santo Domingo. He resigned from the navy on Sept. 23, 1801, and died twelve years later in New York City. From his third wife, a Mrs. Pintard of New York, he was separated. From his first two marriages he had at least four children. He is described as tall, with attractive features, impulsive, and fearless.

[Bureau of Navigation, Records of Officers, 1798–1801; *An Hist. Sketch to the End of the Revolutionary War of the Life of Silas Talbot* (1803); H. T. Tuckerman, *Life of Silas Talbot* (1850), also published in *Mag. of Hist.,* Extra Nos. vol. XXX (1926), no. 120; G. W. Allen, *Naval Hist. of Am. Rev.* (2 vols., 1913), and *Our Naval War with France* (1909); *Proc. of U. S. Naval Institute* (1906); C. W. Goldsborough, *U. S. Naval Chronicle* (1824); *Jour. of Continental Cong.,* vol. IX (1907), XII (1908), XV (1909); *Judgements in the Admiralty of Pa.* (1789); New York *Evening Post,* June 30, 1813.]   C. O. P.

TALCOTT, ANDREW (Apr. 20, 1797–Apr. 22, 1883), soldier, engineer, son of George and Abigail (Goodrich) Talcott, was born in Glastonbury, Conn. He was a lineal descendant of John Talcott, one of the first settlers of Hartford. Entering the United States Military Academy in March 1815, he was graduated, second in his class, in July 1818, and made a brevet second lieutenant in the corps of engineers. Having been advanced through the intervening grades, he became captain on Dec. 22, 1830.

After serving as assistant engineer in connection with the construction of fortifications at Rouse's Point, N. Y., 1818–19, he was engineer and aide-de-camp to Gen. Henry Atkinson in the establishment of posts on the upper Missouri and Yellowstone rivers, 1820–21. For the next five years he was engaged in engineering work on fortifications in Virginia, Rhode Island, New York, and Delaware. From 1826 to 1828 he superintended the construction of the canal through the Dismal Swamp in Virginia, and from 1828 to 1834, the construction of Fort Monroe and Fort Calhoun, Hampton Roads, Va. He also served as astronomer in determining the boundary line between Ohio and Michigan, 1832–36; and as superintending engineer of improvements on the Hudson River, 1834–36.

In 1836 he resigned his commission in the army to engage in work as a civil engineer. The varied tasks he was now called upon to execute bear evidence of his complete mastery of his profession. He was chief engineer in charge of the western division of the New York & Erie Railroad, 1836–37; superintendent of the improvement of the delta of the Mississippi River, 1837–39; member of the commission for the exploration and survey of the northeast boundary of the United States, 1840–43; member of a board of naval officers and engineers for examining Portsmouth and Pensacola navy yards and projecting stone and floating docks, 1844–45; chief engineer of the Richmond & Danville Railroad, 1848–55; astronomer and surveyor for marking the northern boundary of Iowa, 1852–53; superintendent of repairs of the United States Mint in Philadelphia, 1855–56; chief engineer of the Ohio & Mississippi Railroad from Cincinnati to St. Louis, 1856–57. In December 1857 he began his last and most important work, the location and construction of the railroad from Vera Cruz to the city of Mexico. On this project he was engaged until March 1867, with the exception of a period in 1860–61 when work was suspended because of a reorganization of the company. During this period of suspension he was manager of the Sonora Exploring & Mining

Company and chief engineer of the state of Virginia. When he retired from the Mexican undertaking in 1867 on account of political changes, the difficult feat of engineering involved was nearing completion. After his retirement he traveled abroad and upon his return settled in Baltimore, moving later to Richmond, where he died.

Talcott was always interested in practical astronomy, and while working on the Michigan-Ohio boundary line devised a method of determining terrestrial latitudes through the observation of stars near the zenith, adapting the zenith telescope to the purpose. "Talcott's method" was first described in the *Journal of the Franklin Institute* (October 1838), and its adoption by the Coast Survey led to great improvements in the zenith telescope and to the utilization of the method in all the great United States government surveys. Talcott never claimed any credit for originality in his method; he simply considered it the best means of determining latitude from his knowledge of practical astronomy and with the instruments then available. Credit was given him by others, however, and he was elected a member of the American Philosophical Society and an honorary member of the Connecticut Association of Arts and Sciences. He was twice married: first, in April 1826, to Catherine Thompson of Philadelphia, who died in 1828 leaving no child; second, Apr. 11, 1832, at Norfolk, Va., to Harriet Randolph Hackley, by whom he had six sons and five daughters. Seven of these children survived him.

[S. V. Talcott, *Talcott Pedigree in England and America* (1876); G. W. Cullum, *Biog. Reg. Officers and Grads., U. S. Mil. Acad.*, vol. I (1891); Alfred Mordecai, in *Fourteenth Ann. Reunion, Asso. Grads., U. S. Mil. Acad.* (1883); W. L. Marshall, *Notes on Talcott's Method* (1893); *Daily Dispatch* (Richmond, Va.), Apr. 24, 1883.]   G.J.F.

TALCOTT, ELIZA (May 23, 1836–Nov. 1, 1911), missionary to Japan, was born in Vernon, Conn., the daughter of Ralph and Susan (Bell) Talcott. Her father was a pioneer manufacturer of Rockville, in the town of Vernon, and a descendant of John Talcott, one of the first settlers of Hartford; her mother's ancestry went back to Thomas Hooker, founder of Hartford Colony. Eliza studied in the school of Sarah Porter [*q.v.*] at Farmington, Conn., and also taught there. Later, she attended the Connecticut Normal School at New Britain and for several years was a teacher in both public and private schools.

In 1873 she sailed for Japan under appointment of the American Board of Commissioners for Foreign Missions, being one of its first woman missionaries to that country. She acquired the language quickly and was soon engaged in various activities. In 1875 she helped to found and became the first principal of Kobe House, a boarding school for girls which developed into Kobe College. In 1880 she became a touring missionary from Okayama as a center, enduring the hardships of primitive travel and difficult living conditions, mingling with the people both as nurse and as religious teacher. This work was interrupted in 1884 by her first furlough. Returning to Japan the following year, she became the evangelistic head and house mother of the Doshisha Nurses Training School at Kyoto. During the Chino-Japanese War of 1894 she was at Hiroshima, an unofficial visitor to the sick and wounded in the six military hospitals there, bringing such sympathy and encouragement that soldiers testified: "Her visits do us more good than the visits of the doctors." After an attack of cholera, she returned to the United States in 1900 on a furlough which was prolonged for a number of years because of the condition of her health. Sailing again for her field in 1900, she was detained for two and a half years in the Hawaiian Islands to assist in work among the Japanese who were settled there. When at length she reached Japan she took up the training of evangelistic workers at the Woman's Bible School at Kobe, where she remained until her death.

She was gentle and unassuming, yet she gave the impression of great strength. Her parish was the entire Empire and she probably exerted a greater Christian influence than any other foreigner of her time. She recognized good in religions other than her own and she had unbounded faith in human nature and charity toward the erring. Her command of the Japanese language was perfect and she had so mastered the intricacies of Japanese etiquette that she commanded the confidence and respect of all classes of people. One of the Chinese prisoners to whom she had ministered said: "She had within her a mysterious happiness which we could not understand. No amount of preaching could have made such an impression as her work and example."

[S. V. Talcott, *Talcott Pedigree in England and America* (1876); *Missionary Herald*, Jan. 1912; *Mission News*, Dec. 1911; *Life and Light for Women*, Jan. 1911, Jan., Apr. 1912; L. E. Learned, *Eliza Talcott, the Florence Nightingale of Japan* (Woman's Board of Missions, 1917); *Japan Weekly Mail* (Yokohama), Nov. 11, 1911.]   F. T. P.

TALCOTT, JOSEPH (November 1669–Nov. 11, 1741), colonial governor, was born in Hartford, Conn., the fourth son of Lieutenant-Colonel John Talcott and his first wife Helena (Wake-

man) Talcott. His grandfather, John Talcott, who emigrated to Boston in 1632, was one of the founders of Hartford and was descended from the Talcotts of Colchester and Braintree, Essex, England. Both his father and grandfather were influential men in the Connecticut colony and inculcated in him a tradition of public service. At the age of twenty-three he was chosen selectman of Hartford, a unique honor for one of his age. In 1697 he began his military career as ensign of the Hartford train-band; he soon rose to the position of lieutenant and then to that of captain. He was commissioned major of the 1st Regiment of Connecticut troops in 1710 and retained that rank until he became governor. In 1723–24 he campaigned successfully against the Indians; for this service he was rewarded by the Connecticut General Assembly with a special grant of £15. Although he had not received a college education, he became prominent as a judge. In May 1705 he was appointed justice of the peace for Hartford County. Later he became judge of the county court, and court of probate in Hartford County, and in 1721 was made judge of the superior court of the colony.

He entered colonial political life in October 1708 when he was elected deputy from Hartford to the General Assembly. In 1710 he was elected speaker of the House, and in the following year was elected to the upper chamber of the Assembly, becoming one of the assistants or magistrates of the colony. He served in this capacity until 1723, when he was elected deputy-governor. A year later Gov. Gurdon Saltonstall [*q.v.*] died, and Talcott was chosen by the Assembly to complete Saltonstall's unexpired term. From that time until his death he was annually elected governor of Connecticut by the freemen of that colony. He was the first governor of Connecticut who had been born in the colony, most previous governors having been born in England. His term of office, seventeen years, was the second longest in the entire history of Connecticut, being exceeded only by that of Gov. John Winthrop. From his early youth he devoted himself so faithfully to the service of Connecticut that he became one of the outstanding men of his generation in the colony. He subordinated his personal life to the interests of the colony, as is shown by the fact that at the time of his second wife's death, in order to avoid the suspension of a session of the Assembly, he remained at his post as presiding officer of the Assembly until all necessary legislation had been completed.

Talcott's first wife was Abigail Clark of Milford, Conn., whom he married in 1693. She died in 1705. On June 26, 1706, he married a widow, Eunice (Howell) Wakeman of Southampton, Long Island, who died May 25, 1738. He had three sons by his first wife, two sons and four daughters by his second. While not a brilliant man, Talcott was an able executive and had the power of making others carry out his orders. He had an abundance of good judgment and performed his duties as statesman and soldier to the entire satisfaction of the freemen of Connecticut. He was not a radical, nor even a liberal, being possessed of a profound distrust for any new or untried policies, a conservatism that was characteristic of the colonial Connecticut of his time.

[The date of Talcott's birth is given variously as Nov. 11 and Nov. 16. See *Conn. Hist. Soc. Colls.*, vols. IV–V (1892–96), "The Talcott Papers," ed. by Mary K. Talcott; S. V. Talcott, *Talcott Pedigree in England and America* (1876); C. J. Hoadly, *The Pub. Records of the Colony of Conn.* (15 vols., 1850–90), vols. IV–VIII.]   R. M. H.

TALIAFERRO, LAWRENCE (Feb. 28, 1794–Jan. 22, 1871), Indian agent, came of a prominent Virginia family. He was born at "Whitehall," King George County, Va., the fourth son in the large family of James Garnett and Wilhelmina (Wishart) Taliaferro of "Oakland," King George County. After an education under tutors he enlisted, on Aug. 5, 1812, in a volunteer company of light infantry. He served on several fronts and was promoted to a first lieutenancy. At the end of the War of 1812 he retained his rank and served with the 3rd Regiment at many frontier posts. In 1819 he was appointed by President Monroe to be Indian agent at the fort, now called Fort Snelling, that was about to be constructed at the mouth of the St. Peter's (now the Minnesota) River. At first he had charge of both Sioux and Chippewa Indians, but in 1827 the Chippewa of the Upper Mississippi were ordered by the war department to place themselves under the Sault Sainte Marie agency. The age-long feud between the Sioux and the Chippewa, and the enmity of the Sioux and the Sauk, Foxes, and Winnebago, made his position anything but a sinecure. His endeavors to keep peace between the tribes were earnest and often successful, for the Indians came to believe that the "Iron Cutter," as the agent was called, was their friend and protector. His efforts in the Indians' behalf produced almost constant strife between himself and the traders, all of whose efforts to bribe or oust him failed. The American Fur Company contracted against him an especial dislike and distrust, but even this great monopoly's efforts to have him removed

from office were unsuccessful, and in 1839 he was appointed for the sixth time.

In 1839 he resigned his post and left the Indian country, leaving a quarter-breed daughter Mary L., who had been born on Aug. 17, 1828, and was educated by him at a local mission school. She later married a former soldier at Fort Snelling named Warren Woodbury and lived in West St. Paul, Minn. In 1862 she was captured with many others by the Sioux in their uprising of that year and rescued after six weeks' captivity. An orphan niece was reared in the Taliaferro home almost as a daughter. By his wife, Eliza Dillon, who was the daughter of a hotel-keeper of Bedford, Pa., and who accompanied him to the St. Peter's agency after their marriage in the summer of 1828, he had no issue. Most of his time after 1840 was spent at Bedford, where mineral waters had attracted him early in life. On Mar. 14, 1857, he reëntered military service in the quartermaster department and served at San Antonio, Fort Leavenworth, Pittsburgh, and Bedford. In 1863 his name was put on the retired list. He was a member of the Masonic Order and a deacon in the Presbyterian Church at Bedford. In the Civil War he was an ardent Unionist, though earlier in life he had been a slaveholder. He died at Bedford, where his widow remained for some years.

[Autobiography in *Minn. Hist. Soc. Colls.*, vol. VI (1894); a large collection of his diaries, correspondence, and accounts, an affidavit by his daughter, and a letter by a Bedford neighbor, Maria L. Rupp, all in the possession of the Minn. Hist. Soc.; W. M. Babcock, "Major Lawrence Taliaferro, Indian Agent," in *Miss. Val. Hist. Rev.*, Dec. 1924; L. P. du Bellet, *Some Prominent Va. Families*, vol. II (1907).]   G. L. N.

TALIAFERRO, WILLIAM BOOTH (Dec. 28, 1822–Feb. 27, 1898), Confederate soldier, only child of Warner and Frances (Booth) Taliaferro, was born at "Belleville," his mother's family estate, in Gloucester County. Through his father he was descended from Robert Taliaferro, gentleman, an immigrant to Virginia as early as 1647. He graduated in 1841 at the College of William and Mary and studied law at Harvard. As a captain in the 11th United States Infantry, he distinguished himself in Mexico, being discharged in August 1848 with the rank of major. On Feb. 17, 1853, he married Sally N. Lyons, of Richmond, by whom he had eight children. He represented Gloucester County in the House of Delegates, 1850–53, was a Buchanan presidential elector in 1856, and took command of the militia at Harpers Ferry in November 1859 after the capture of John Brown.

Early in the Civil War, as colonel, Confederate States Army, he served brilliantly under

Jackson in western Virginia, but in January 1862, with the commanders of other regiments stationed in a bleak encampment at Romney, he signed a petition which ultimately reached the Secretary of War, asking that the troops be moved to a more favorable locality (*War of the Rebellion: Official Records, Army,* 1 ser., V, 1046 ff.). This action greatly incensed Jackson, but thanks to proved capacity, Taliaferro retained his chief's confidence. Appointed brigadier-general on Mar. 4, 1862, he led a brigade throughout the Valley campaign, contributing notably to the victories of McDowell, Winchester, and Port Republic. At Cedar Mountain, Aug. 9, after the death of General Winder, he was called to command Jackson's old division when it had been almost routed. Under "Stonewall's" eye he extricated his troops skilfully, earning the permanent command of this redoubtable division. Three weeks later, at Groveton, he was severely wounded and incapacitated, but at Fredericksburg again directed his troops in repulsing Meade's attack on Jackson's corps.

In February 1863 he was ordered to Savannah, but General Beauregard soon called him to Charleston, and he defended Battery Wagner, on Morris Island, during the memorable assault of July 18, when with fewer than twelve hundred men he repulsed 5,000 assailants (*Official Records,* 1 ser., XXVIII, pt. 1, pp. 415–21). Later, commanding on James Island for over a year, he baffled all efforts of the Federals to reach Charleston. Because he was a near relative, the Secretary of War, James A. Seddon [*q.v.*], hesitated to urge his promotion (*Ibid.,* XXXV, pt. 1, pp. 622–23), and he was not commissioned major-general until Jan. 1, 1865. In the meantime he commanded briefly in eastern Florida, and in December 1864 safeguarded the garrison of Savannah in escaping from Sherman. After evacuating James Island in February 1865, with Rhett's and Elliott's brigades he fought stubbornly at Bentonville, but surrendered with Johnston's army in April.

Following the war, he served again in the legislature, 1874–79, distinguishing himself in opposition to repudiation of the state debt. He was Grand Master of Masons in Virginia, 1876–77; judge of the Gloucester County court, 1891–97, and long a member of the boards of visitors of the Virginia Military Institute, the College of William and Mary, and other institutions of the state.

Six feet tall and full-bearded, Taliaferro was by tradition and character a Virginia gentleman and a leader, temperamentally akin to Washington and Lee. Like them, he fulfilled his obliga-

tions punctiliously. As a soldier, though denied opportunities for independent command, he frequently displayed high tactical abilities. In peace time a farmer-lawyer, he could not be tempted to abandon the rural life. The foremost men of the Old Dominion frequented his hospitable manor house, "Dunham Massie," where in the hallway hung a Confederate flag beneath which every visitor passed. Here he ended his days, and his body was buried in the cemetery of Ware Church, built by his ancestors in the seventeenth century.

[Besides the volumes of *Official Records* cited above, see 1 ser. II, XII, XXI, XLIV, XLVII; C. A. Evans, *Confed. Mil. Hist.* (1899), vol. III; "A Soldier Sleeps," *Richmond Dispatch,* Mar. 1, 1898; G. F. R. Henderson, *Stonewall Jackson* (1898); G. T. Beauregard, "The Defense of Charleston," *Battles and Leaders of the Civil War* (1887–88), IV, 1–23; and Taliaferro's article, "Jackson's Raid Around Pope," *Ibid.,* II, 501–11; W. B. McGroarty, *Geneal. Chart of the Taliaferro Family* (1926). Information as to certain facts has been supplied by W. T. L. Taliaferro of College Park, Md., a son, and T. S. Taliaferro, Rock Springs, Wyo., a nephew of W. B. Taliaferro.]   J. M. H.

TALLMADGE, BENJAMIN (Feb. 25, 1754–Mar. 7, 1835), soldier and congressman, was born at Brookhaven, N. Y., second of five surviving children of the Rev. Benjamin and Susannah (Smith) Tallmadge. He was descended from Thomas Talmadge who was an early settler of Southampton, Long Island. Tutored by his father, Benjamin entered Yale in 1769, although the authorities there would have permitted him to matriculate at an earlier date. He states in his autobiography that idleness and an attack of measles prevented his making a particularly brilliant record in college, but he also mentions the fact that when he received his degree in 1773 he spoke publicly at the commencement exercises (*Memoir, post,* pp. 1–6).

Soon after his graduation he became superintendent of the high school in Wethersfield, Conn., a position which he held until the outbreak of the Revolution. On June 20, 1776, he was appointed lieutenant and adjutant in Chester's Connecticut State Regiment; he displayed superior military abilities and rose rapidly in rank, becoming captain Dec. 14, 1776, major Apr. 7, 1777, and brevet lieutenant-colonel Sept. 30, 1783. He participated in the battles of Long Island (Aug. 27, 1776), White Plains (Oct. 28), Brandywine (Sept. 11, 1777), Germantown (Oct. 4), and Monmouth (June 28, 1778), besides many smaller engagements. One of the most notable of his military achievements was the capture and destruction of Fort St. George, Long Island, Nov. 22, 1780. For this service he received the thanks of Washington, and of Congress. During the years 1778–83 he was occupied largely with important secret service, carrying on a confidential correspondence with Washington. He had charge of Major André during the latter's imprisonment in 1780, and became deeply attached to the young English officer. "When I saw him swinging under the gibbet," he wrote, "it seemed for a time as if I could not support it" (*Memoir,* p. 57).

After the close of the Revolution, Tallmadge engaged successfully in commercial pursuits in Litchfield, Conn. In 1800 he was elected as a Federalist to the United States House of Representatives, and was continued in that office for eight terms (1801–17), declining in 1816 to stand for reëlection. As a member of Congress he served on numerous committees, and was for a time chairman of the committee on military affairs. Since he was widely recognized as a devout Christian, many petitions involving religious interests were submitted to him to be presented to the House (Hickok, *post,* pp. 18–19).

Tallmadge married first, Mar. 18, 1784, Mary Floyd of Mastic, L. I., daughter of William Floyd [*q.v.*], a signer of the Declaration of Independence; she died June 3, 1805, leaving five sons and two daughters, and on May 3, 1808, he married Maria Hallett of New York City, who survived him. In person he was of more than average height, was well-proportioned, and retained his military bearing throughout his later life. His manners were those of the polished gentleman; in his charities he was noted for liberality. He died in Litchfield.

[A. W. Talmadge, *The Talmadge, Tallmadge, and Talmage Geneal.* (1909) ; P. Hickok, *A Sermon Preached at the Funeral of Col. Benj. Tallmadge* (1835) ; *Memoir of Col. B. Tallmadge, Prepared by Himself, at the Request of His Children* (1858), repr. in 1904 ; F. B. Dexter, *Biog. Sketches Grads. Yale Coll.,* vol. III (1903) ; *Biog. Dir. Am. Cong.* (1928) ; F. B. Heitman, *Hist. Reg. of Officers of the Continental Army* (1914) ; H. P. Johnston, *The Record of Conn. Men in the Military and Naval Service during the War of the Revolution* (1889), and "The Secret Service of the Revolution," *Mag. of Am. Hist.,* Feb. 1882 ; P. K. Kilbourne, *Sketches and Chronicles of the Town of Litchfield, Conn.* (1859).]
R. W. I.

TALLMADGE, JAMES (Jan. 28, 1778–Sept. 29, 1853), lawyer and statesman, descended from Thomas Talmadge who emigrated to New England some time after 1630 and settled at Southampton, Long Island, about 1642, was born at Stanford, Dutchess County, N. Y., the son of Colonel James and Ann (Southerland) Tallmadge. During the Revolution the father was an ardent patriot and commanded a company of Dutchess County volunteers at Saratoga. James graduated from Rhode Island College (now Brown University) in 1798 and practised law at Poughkeepsie, becoming one of the leading lawyers in the state. He was also interested in agriculture, and owned a large farm in Dutchess County. A Democrat in politics, he attached himself to the group headed by Gov. George Clinton [*q.v.*], and for a time served as Clinton's private secretary. In 1813 he was appointed brigadier-general of the New York militia, but while on his way to take command of troops on the northern frontier became ill and was unable to proceed. Before the close of the war, however, he took command of troops for the defense of New York City.

From 1817 to 1819 Tallmadge served as a member of Congress, soon distinguishing himself in debate. On Feb. 15, 1819, he introduced a notable amendment to a bill regarding the admission of Missouri to statehood (*Annals of Congress,* 15 Cong., 2 Sess., I, 1170, 1203–14). His amendment was designed to prohibit the further introduction of slaves into Missouri and to provide for the gradual emancipation of those born there after the admission of the state. Approved by the House but defeated by the Senate, it precipitated a controversy which became nation wide. In the argument over Andrew Jackson's dramatic Seminole campaign of 1819, Tallmadge eloquently defended Jackson's conduct. With respect to American industry he urged more adequate protection against foreign competition. Refusing to accept renomination, he retired to private life until 1821, when he became a delegate to the New York constitutional convention. Three years later, as a member of the state legislature, he advocated a more popular method of choosing presidential electors, and, during the same session, successfully opposed the collection of tonnage duties on the Erie Canal. In 1825 he became lieutenant-governor, in which capacity he served creditably for two years.

The remainder of his life was crowded with non-political activities. From 1828 until his death he spent the summer months at his country seat in Dutchess County and the winters in New York City. He was one of the founders of the University of the City of New York (now New York University) and president of its council, 1834–46; he was also a founder of the American Institute of the City of New York, for the promotion of useful arts, and from 1832 until his death served almost continuously as its president. In 1838 he went to Europe, where he was received with marked distinction. While there he collected information for the Institute; secured the removal of certain useless quarantine restrictions which handicapped American trade in Northern Europe; and took steps to aid Russia in obtaining machinery for the manufacture of cotton products. In 1846 he again served as delegate to a New York constitutional convention. A number of his speeches, both political and non-political, were published in pamphlet form.

Tallmadge was a man of fine presence, polished manners, and broad sympathies. On Jan. 21, 1810, he married his second cousin, Laura Tallmadge, who died in 1834. Of several children born to this union, only one, Mary, survived. She married Philip Van Rensselaer, proprietor of the Metropolitan Hotel, New York, at which her father died.

[A. W. Talmadge, *The Talmadge, Tallmadge, and Talmage Geneal.* (1909); G. B. Andrews, *A Sermon Occasioned by the Death of the Honorable James Tallmadge* (1853); *Hist. Cat. Brown Univ.* (1914); *Biog. Dir. Am. Cong.* (1928); Isaac Huntting, *Hist. of Little Nine Partners . . . and Pine Plains, N. Y.* (1897); *N. Y. Daily Times*, Oct. 1, 1853; and *Poughkeepsie Eagle*, Oct. 8, 1853.]   R. W. I.

TALMAGE, JAMES EDWARD (Sept. 21, 1862–July 27, 1933), geologist, theologian, was born in Hungerford, Berkshire, England, the first son and second child of eight in the family of James Joyce Talmage and Susannah (Preater) Talmage. He attended the schools of the local district and in 1874 was the Oxford diocesan prize scholar. Two years later the family emigrated to the United States and settled in Provo, Utah, where James was a student of Brigham Young Academy (later University) from 1876 to 1882. He afterwards attended Lehigh University (1882–83), the Johns Hopkins University (1884), and Illinois Wesleyan University (1896). Until 1911, when he was ordained an apostle in the Church of Jesus Christ of Latter-day Saints, he devoted himself to teaching. He was successively professor of chemistry and geology in Brigham Young Academy (1884–88), president of the Latter-day Saints College, Salt Lake City (1888–93), and president of the University of Utah (1894–97), resigning in 1897 to devote his full time to the chair of geology, which he held until his resignation in 1907. After 1907 he carried on a private practice as consulting mining geologist. In 1897 he was a delegate from the Royal Society of Edinburgh to the International Geological Congress at Saint Petersburg (later Leningrad), Russia. He was a fellow of numerous scientific societies in Great Britain and the United States, a life associate of the Philosophical Society of Great Britain, and a life member of the National Geographic Society. On Dec. 7, 1911, he was appointed to the Council of the Twelve Apostles, and from that time until his death gave himself to the service

of the church. On June 14, 1888, he married Mary May Booth, daughter of Richard Thornton and Elsie (Edge) Booth, by whom he had four sons and four daughters. He was the author of numerous articles, sermons, addresses, and books on scientific and religious themes. Among the more important of his scientific books are *First Book of Nature* (1888), *Domestic Science: A Book for Use in Schools and for General Reading* (1891), *Tables for Blowpipe Determination of Minerals* (1899), and *The Great Salt Lake, Present and Past* (1900). Among his religious books are *The Articles of Faith* (1899), *The Story of "Mormonism"* (1907), *The Great Apostasy* (1909), *The House of the Lord* (1912), *Jesus the Christ* (1915), *The Vitality of "Mormonism"* (1919), and *Sunday Night Talks* (1931), first given as radio speeches.

He had unusual ability in expository writing and speaking, being skilful in verbal definition and in conveying delicate shades of meaning. His remarkable and capacious memory added greatly to his efficiency as a writer and speaker. His scholarly manner, his connections with learned societies, and his unusual ability as a teacher and expounder secured for him a prestige among his own people which has probably never been equaled by any other leader of this Church. He became their leading authority on technical theological questions, while his opinion on the relation of Church dogma to science probably outweighed that of all his compeers. Using his talents to justify and defend Mormonism, Talmadge expounded with great force his rationalisation of the creed, and skilfully arrayed and supported the *raison d'être* of the faith he and his family had embraced.

[*Who's Who in America*, 1930–31; J. M. Cattell and D. R. Brimhall, *Am. Men of Sci.* (3rd ed., 1921); Andrew Jenson, *Latter-Day Saint Biog. Encyc.*, vol. III (1920), pp. 787–89; M. J. Ballard, in *Improvement Era*, Sept. 1933; B. S. Hinckley, *Ibid.*, July 1932; R. S. Bennett, in *Latter-Day Saints Millenial Star*, July 28, 1932, Aug. 1933; J. F. Merrill, *Relief Soc. Mag.*, Sept. 1933; *Deseret News* (Salt Lake City), July 27–29, and *Salt Lake Tribune*, July 28, 1933.]   L. N.

TALMAGE, JOHN VAN NEST (Aug. 18, 1819–Aug. 19, 1892), missionary to China, was born on a farm in Somerville, N. J., the son of David and Catharine (Van Nest) Talmage, and a descendant of Thomas Talmadge who emigrated from England to Massachusetts some time after 1630 and settled at Southampton, Long Island, about 1642. John's father was a man of sterling character; he served several terms in the state legislature and for a time was high sheriff of Somerset County. His home was a deeply religious one, but its religion was of a happy and cheerful type; of the seven sons four entered the ministry, one of them being Thomas De Witt Talmage [*q.v.*]. John spent most of his boyhood at Gatesville, N. J., where his father kept a tollgate, and attended a private school at Boundbrook. He was active physically and something of a leader among his mates. Having prepared for college in the home of an elder brother, a pastor at Blawenburgh, N. J., he entered Rutgers as a sophomore, was graduated in 1842, and then went to the New Brunswick Theological Seminary, where he was graduated in 1845.

As a lad he had read the biographies of missionaries and while in college had continued to keep in touch with missionary literature. It was not surprising, therefore, that an address by a missionary, the Rev. Elihu Doty [*q.v.*], which Talmage heard while a student, should have led him to decide to give his life to that calling. On leaving the seminary he offered himself to the American Board of Commissioners for Foreign Missions, with which his denomination, the Dutch Reformed, then cooperated. The Board's financial condition precluded sending him immediately, and for two years he served as assistant pastor in the Central Reformed Church of Brooklyn, being ordained at Millstone, N. J., on Aug. 26, 1846. In 1847 he sailed for Amoy, China, and arrived only a few years after the first Chinese treaties with Western powers had opened it to foreign residence. There he spent the major part of the remainder of his life, most of the time making his home on the island of Kulangsu, on the opposite side of the harbor from the city. The first of his infrequent trips to America was in 1849, barely two years after his arrival in China, to escort a member of his mission who was being invalided home. Before returning he married, Jan. 15, 1850, Abby F. Woodruff. His second voyage home was in 1862, when, after the death of his wife, he felt that he must take his four children to the United States. While in America he pleaded with the General Synod of his church to permit the cooperation of its missionaries with those of the English Presbyterians in the formation of an independent Chinese church in Amoy and the adjoining territory, and published in 1863 *History and Ecclesiastical Relations of the Churches of the Presbyterian Order at Amoy, China*. At first defeated, he later won his point. In November 1864 he married Mary E. Van Deventer and soon afterward returned to Amoy.

Here he continued to contribute to the building of a growing Chinese church. He shared both in preaching and in teaching. He was

noted, too, for his literary achievements. In his student days he had shown himself so proficient in Hebrew and Greek that on graduating from the theological seminary he was urged to allow his name to be considered for a professorship of languages in that institution. In Amoy he gave much attention to developing a romanized form of writing the vernacular, to enable illiterate Christians quickly to read the Bible and other religious literature, and prepared a good deal of printed material in that medium. Included in this material are a primer (1852), a reader (1853), a version of *Pilgrim's Progress*, the Book of Ruth, and portions of the New Testament. In the closing years of his life he finished a dictionary of the Amoy dialect. Able, cheerful, hopeful, hard-working, persistent, in the course of nearly half a century in Amoy he made a profound impression upon the missionaries and the rising churches of that region. Ill, he returned to America in 1889 and spent his remaining years at Boundbrook, near his boyhood home.

[A. W. Talmadge, *The Talmadge, Tallmadge, and Talmage Geneal.* (1909); *Biog. Notices of Officers and Grads. of Rutgers Coll. Deceased during the Academical Year Ending in June, 1893* (1893); *Biog. Record, Theological Sem. of New Brunswick* (1912); J. G. Fagg, *Forty Years in South China: The Life of Rev. John Van Nest Talmage, D.D.* (1894); J. I. Good, *Famous Missionaries of the Reformed Church* (1903); Ann. reports of the Am. Board of Commissioners for Foreign Missions, 1848–58, and of the Board of Foreign Missions of the Reformed Church in America, 1857; E. T. Corwin, *A Manual of the Reformed Church in America* (1902); *Christian Intelligencer*, Aug. 24, 1892; *Christian Herald*, Sept. 7, 1892; *Brooklyn Daily Eagle*, Aug. 20, 1892.]   K. S. L.

TALMAGE, THOMAS DE WITT (Jan. 7, 1832–Apr. 12, 1902), clergyman, editor, and lecturer, was born near Boundbrook, N. J., the son of David and Catharine (Van Nest) Talmage, and a younger brother of John Van Nest Talmage [*q.v.*]. His father was a farmer and a tollgate keeper. Thomas De Witt attended a school in New Brunswick, and at nineteen entered the University of the City of New York, where he studied law. He did not graduate, for before he had completed his course he turned to the ministry, in which profession three brothers, a brother-in-law, and two uncles were already engaged. In 1862, however, the University awarded him the degree of A.M. He graduated from the New Brunswick Theological Seminary in 1856, and in the same year was ordained (July 26), a minister of the Dutch Reformed Church, installed in his first charge at Belleville, N. J., and married to Mary R. Avery of Brooklyn, N. Y. Called to Syracuse, N. Y., in 1859, he served there until 1862, when he went to the Second Dutch Reformed Church of Philadelphia. Shortly after settling there, his wife, by whom he had had two children, was drowned in the Schuylkill River, June 9, 1862, and the following year he married Sarah Whittemore of Greenpoint, Long Island, a young woman of considerable means.

When he took charge of the church in Philadelphia it was quiet and old-fashioned, and had no great influence; but Talmage's magnetic and rather sensational style of preaching soon began to draw large audiences, and the church prospered. He had a fine, erect figure, strong, clear-cut features and a winning manner, and he used many startling gestures and illustrations to rivet attention. His critics called him a pulpit clown and a mountebank, but there were thousands who admired and reverenced him. His reputation increased so rapidly that he had several calls to other churches, and in 1869 accepted an invitation to the Central Presbyterian Church of Brooklyn, N. Y., a church then torn by dissension. His success there, notwithstanding some caustic criticism in the metropolitan newspapers, was immediate and impressive, and he was soon drawing the largest audiences which assembled to hear any minister in America. To take care of the throngs which came to hear him, a new church called the Tabernacle was hastily built. The burning of this edifice on Sunday morning, Dec. 22, 1872, just before the hour for service, was one of the memorable fire disasters in Brooklyn's history. A new and greater Tabernacle was completed by January 1874, the congregation meanwhile occupying the Academy of Music. At the height of his fame, Talmage's sermons were published weekly in about 3,500 newspapers. He was one of the most successful lecturers of modern times, for many years delivering an average of fifty lectures annually. In 1879 he was accused before the Brooklyn Presbytery of "falsehood and deceit, and . . . using improper methods of preaching, which tend to bring religion into contempt." He was acquitted, though the vote of the court on some of the counts was close. He was keenly alive to the value of publicity and while on a tour of Palestine in 1889 arranged to baptize a man in the River Jordan. His second Tabernacle was destroyed by fire in 1889; a third was erected, and this also was burned, in May 1894. Momentarily discouraged, he announced that he would give up his pastorate and devote his time to evangelism. He changed his mind, however, and accepted a call to the First Presbyterian Church of Washington, D. C.

He had long been more or less interested in religious journalism, having edited the *Christian at Work* (1874–76) and *Frank Leslie's Sunday*

Magazine (1881–89), and in 1899 he resigned his Washington pastorate and devoted himself to conducting the *Christian Herald,* of which he had been editor since 1890. His second wife, who bore him five children, died Aug. 5, 1895, leaving him $200,000, and on Jan. 22, 1898, he married Eleanor (McCutcheon) Collier, the well-to-do widow of Charles W. Collier of Allegheny City, Pa., who survived him. Among his numerous published works were *Crumbs Swept Up* (1870); *The Abominations of Modern Society* (1872); *Sermons* (1872); *Points* (1873); *Old Wells Dug Out* (1874); *Around the Tea-Table* (1874); *Every-Day Religion* (1875); *The Night Sides of City Life* (1878); *The Masque Torn Off* (1880); *Mormonism* (1880); *High License* (1884); *Rum, the Worst Enemy of the Working Classes* (1886); *The Marriage Ring* (1886); *Social Dynamite* (1887); *The Key-Note of the Temperance Reform* (1890); *Twenty-five Sermons on the Holy Land* (1890); *The Marriage Tie* (1890); *From Manger to Throne* (1890). An autobiography, *T. De Witt Talmage as I Knew Him,* with concluding chapters by his widow, appeared in 1912, and in 1923 a compilation entitled *Fifty Short Sermons by T. De Witt Talmage* was published by his daughter, May Talmage.

[*Who's Who in America,* 1901–02; *North American and U. S. Gazette* (Phila.), and *Press* (Phila.), June 10, 1862; *World* (N. Y.), Jan. 28, 1894, Apr. 13, 1902; *N. Y. Times, N. Y. Herald, Sun* (N. Y.), *Brooklyn Eagle,* and *Washington Post,* Apr. 13, 1902; A. W. Talmadge, *The Talmadge, Tallmadge, and Talmage Geneal.* (1909); *Record of Proc. in the Talmage Case Before the Presbytery of Brooklyn* (1879); John Rusk, *The Authentic Life of T. De Witt Talmage* (1902); C. F. Adams, *The Life and Sermons of Rev. T. De Witt Talmage* (1902); *Life and Teachings of Rev. T. De Witt Talmadge, D.D.* (1902), memorial vol.; C. E. Banks, *Authorized and Authentic Life and Works of T. De Witt Talmadge* (1902).]   A. F. H.

TALVJ [See ROBINSON, THERESE ALBERTINE LOUISE VON JAKOB, 1797–1870].

TAMARÓN, PEDRO (d. Dec. 21, 1768), bishop of Durango, was a native of La Guardia in the archbishopric of Toledo, Spain. He was the domestic chaplain of Bishop Juan Joseph de Escalona y Calatayud of Carácas, Venezuela, with whom he came to America when very young. He studied at the University of Santa Rosa, Carácas, and there he received the doctor's degree and served as professor of canonical law. He obtained the curacy of the cathedral there and the ranks of teacher of divinity (*maestrescuela*) and precentor. In 1758 the king nominated him as bishop of Durango, and in the same year he took charge of the bishopric. Between 1759 and 1763 he personally visited the most remote provinces of his diocese, even proceeding to the north as far as the last pueblo of New Mexico before he returned to his capital, Durango. In New Mexico in 1760 Tamarón "had occasion at many points to administer severe reproof; and the friars, while making various excuses for their remissness, denying some of its worst results, and even promising reforms, did not claim the ability to communicate with their neophytes, except through interpreters. Charges of neglect in other matters, of oppressing the natives, of being frequently absent from their posts, and of undue fondness for trade are not supported by any evidence of this period . . ." (H. H. Bancroft, *History of Arizona and New Mexico, 1530–1888,* 1889, pp. 269–70). The bishop offered to print *confesionarios* in native languages, if the friars would write them. Some promises were secured and some correspondence was carried on concerning the matter, but nothing was effected down to 1763.

The diary which Tamarón kept of his episcopal tour is his most notable writing. It is entitled "Descripción del Obispado de Durango; ó Diario de la Santa Visita de toda aquella Diócesis, dedicado al Rey Ntro. Sr. D. Carlos III." A copy of the diary was sent to the king and the original was deposited in the ecclesiastical archives at Durango, where it was as late as 1883. The diary is a most detailed description of the bishopric, having been written with such thoroughness that there is no pueblo, hacienda, or ranch which is not described; in addition, distances and directions are recorded. Tamarón governed with ability and zeal until Dec. 21, 1768, when he died at the pueblo of Bamoa, Sinaloa.

[Brief sketches of Tamarón's life and work are to be found in Antonio de Alcedo, *Diccionario Geográfico-Histórico de las Indias Occidentales ó America,* vol. II (Madrid, 1787), p. 56; H. H. Bancroft, *Hist. of the North Mexican States and Texas,* vol. I (1884), pp. 594–95; J. M. Beristain de Souza, *Biblioteca Hispano Americana Septentrional,* vol. III (Mexico, 1821), pp. 169–70; and *Diccionario Universal de Historia y de Geografía,* vol. III (Mexico, 1853), p. 144, and vol. VII (Mexico, 1855), pp. 207–08.]   C. W. H.

TAMMANY (fl. 1685), was a chief of the Lenni-Lenape, or Delaware, Indians, whose name—sometimes appearing as Tamanend—may mean "affable" or "deserving." The known facts regarding his life are meager, and much that has been written about him is purely fanciful. It seems probable that his home was somewhere along the Delaware River, in the present Bucks County, Pa., but even the approximate time of his death is unknown. Tradition places him among those who welcomed William Penn on his arrival in America, Oct. 27, 1682. His name first appears in writing on a deed of June 23,

1683 (*Pennsylvania Archives,* 1 ser., vol. I, 1852, pp. 62–65), and later is found on several other documents. The most important record concerning him is in the minutes of a conference held on July 6, 1694, between the Provincial Council of Pennsylvania and a delegation of Indians (*Minutes of the Provincial Council of Pennsylvania,* vol. I, 1852, p. 447). At this conference Tammany made a speech in which he professed strong friendship for the whites. He seems, however, not to have been the principal chief, and there is no authentic contemporary mention of him during his fifteen years' contact with the whites which gives him exceptional standing for character or capacity.

The last contemporary mention of him is in 1698 (Gabriel Thomas, *An Historical and Geographical Account of the Province and Country of Pensilvania and of West-New-Jersey in America,* 1698). For more than seventy years following the records are blank. It is evident, however, that oral tradition kept his name in remembrance and gradually invested him with the noblest attributes. By 1771 he begins to emerge as a chieftain devotedly attached to the whites and endowed with every virtue and ability. His name appeared on calendars, and for a time, at several places in the central colonies, informal gatherings were held in his honor on May 1. The seething ferment that preceded the Revolution brought forth a number of organizations to oppose the St. George, St. Andrew, and St. David societies, and by many of the insurgent groups Tammany was adopted as the tutelary saint. He soon came to be regarded as a symbol of American resistance to British aggression. A predominantly Loyalist society, organized in Philadelphia on May 1, 1772, as the Sons of King Tammany, shifted its political attitude by Apr. 28 following and thereupon altered its name to Sons of Saint Tammany. In the days immediately following the Revolution the chieftain underwent another transformation and became the patron saint of those who stood for democracy and opposed aristrocracy and privilege. During the period a number of new Tammany societies were founded. Only one of these, the famous and powerful Society of Tammany, of New York City, founded in 1786 by William Mooney [*q.v.*], a Revolutionary veteran, and reorganized in 1789, was fated to endure.

[E. P. Kilroe, *Saint Tammany and the Origin of the Society of Tammany* (1913) is a careful inquiry into all the legends and historical sources.]   W. J. G.

TANEY, ROGER BROOKE (Mar. 17, 1777–Oct. 12, 1864), attorney general, secretary of the treasury, chief justice of the United States, was born on a tobacco plantation in Calvert County, in southern Maryland. His father, Michael Taney, was a member of a family of planters; the founder of this was another Michael Taney, who about 1660 had come to Maryland as an indentured servant but had died the possessor of considerable property in land and slaves. His mother, Monica (Brooke) Taney, was descended from another family of the landed aristocracy; her first American ancestor had come to Maryland in 1650 with fox hounds and other trappings indicative of gentlemanly status. During the years of his boyhood Roger Taney imbibed the culture and the accepted ideas of his class. After studying in local rural schools and with a family tutor he went to Dickinson College in 1792 and graduated in 1795. The production of tobacco being less profitable than formerly, and there being no land in the family holdings for Roger Taney, who was a second son, he was trained for a career at the bar and in politics. He read law in the office of Judge Jeremiah Townley Chase, of the Maryland general court, at Annapolis, and was admitted to practice in 1799. With the aid of his father and other gentlemen of Calvert County he was elected to the state legislature for the term of 1799–1800. His political career was checked in 1800, however, when national issues caused the defeat of many Maryland Federalists in state politics. He moved to Frederick in 1801, his enemies declaring that he had been laughed out of Calvert County for being an aristocrat. He lived in Frederick until 1823, achieving a position of prominence in the community, and conducting a growing and increasingly profitable law practice.

On Jan. 7, 1806, he married Anne P. C. Key, daughter of a well-to-do farmer, John Ross Key, and the sister of Francis Scott Key [q.v.]. Six daughters, and a son who died in infancy, were born to them. One daughter and his wife died in 1855; the others survived him. Despite his constantly poor health, and the necessity of diligent labor to support his growing family, and despite his lack of success as a candidate, Taney continued active in politics, and became prominent among the leaders of the Federalists of the state. He broke with the more prominent and wealthy Federalists in 1812, however, when they refused or granted reluctantly their support to the government in the conduct of the war with Great Britain, and became a leader of the dissenting faction who were derisively called "Coodies." Taney's position was indicated by the title "King Coody." The "Coodies" were in the minority in the party during the war, but ultimately the disloyalty of the extreme Federalists brought them into disrepute, and in order to maintain their control of the state legislature they had to make concessions to Taney's faction. As a result he was chosen in 1816 for a five-year term in the state Senate, where he ousted the opposing faction from control and dominated the Federalist party during the few years in which it continued to survive. His major interest, apart from the issues of party politics, seems to have been in laws to prevent the evils due to unsound currency and bad banking, and in laws to protect the rights of negroes in the state, whether freemen or slaves.

He moved in 1823 to Baltimore, where professional opportunities were greater, and where he was recognized as one of the most eminent members of the bar. He was a master of the technicalities of procedure, on which turned the disposition of many cases of the period, although he never resorted to cheap trickery and was noted for complete fairness to his opponents. He was tall and flat-chested, with broad and stooping shoulders. His face was long and his features were uneven. His voice was low and hollow. His style of delivery was one of simple and direct earnestness, however, and was highly effective in spite of the absence of the florid eloquence which was characteristic of the time. It provided the basis for the clarity and persuasiveness of many of his judicial opinions in later years. He seems to have taken cases whenever they were offered, and there is no evidence that he hesitated to serve clients whom he believed to be in the wrong.

The Federalist party having been virtually dissolved, Taney in 1824 gave his support to Andrew Jackson. When, after Jackson's defeat in that year, a party was organized to bring about his election in 1828 Taney was made chairman of the state central committee. He seems not to have desired appointment to federal office at this time. He had to keep up his extensive practice in order to maintain the income to which he had become accustomed, his health was too poor to justify added exertions, and he was already in a position of some honor, having been appointed attorney general of Maryland in 1827. In 1831, however, when President Jackson found it necessary to reorganize his cabinet, Taney accepted a recess appointment as attorney general of the United States. He took the oath of office on July 20, assuming also for a short time the duties of acting secretary of war, and was duly confirmed as attorney general in December.

Taney's most significant activities as a member of the Jackson cabinet had to do with the second Bank of the United States, now seeking from Congress the renewal of its charter. Taney had long been interested in banking and currency problems. He had been a director of a branch of a state bank in Frederick from 1810 to 1815; in 1818 he had successfully sponsored a bill to charter the Frederick County Bank, and he had been a director from 1818 to 1823. While a member of the state Senate he sponsored legislation to prevent the circulation of bank notes at less than their face value, and to prevent the deliberate depreciation of the value of the notes of rural banks for which Baltimore bankers and brokers were said to be in part responsible. At first he evidently regarded a national bank as a desirable instrument for regulating the currency, and perhaps for restraining the predatory activities of the more powerful banks chartered by the states. He voted with the minority against the bill to tax the notes of the Baltimore branch, which in 1819 was declared unconstitutional by the Supreme Court of the United States, speaking through Chief Justice Marshall in *McCulloch* vs. *Maryland*. The subsequent conduct of the Bank of the United States, however, was not such as he could approve. He was for several years counsel in opposition to it in a case in which he felt that the officers of the bank had been guilty of sharp and unethical practice. After he moved to Baltimore, as counsel for the Union Bank of Maryland he observed both the power and the tendency toward ruthlessness of the Bank of the United States. When he entered the Jackson cabinet he held the conviction that if the institution was to be rechartered it must be with definite limitations on its powers. He so advised the President, and when the friends of the bank attempted at the session of Congress of 1831–32 to force the enactment of a law granting a new charter, believing that Jackson would not dare oppose it just before a presidential election, Taney advised him to veto it. Jackson was persuaded, and when other members of his cabinet refused to aid him in the preparation of a veto message on the merits of the case he called Taney to aid in redrafting the document which had been begun by Amos Kendall [*q.v.*].

The message, containing a compact legal argument which was evidently prepared by Taney, embedded in dynamic political materials presumably arranged by Kendall and others, was reprinted in the Jackson papers all over the country, and became one of the outstanding documents in the ensuing campaign. The officers of the bank, in spite of the fact that the government itself held one-fifth of the stock, spent thousands of dollars of bank money in circulating speeches

of Daniel Webster and others in the attempt to block Jackson's reëlection on the bank issue. Jackson succeeded in spite of the opposition, and in the months which followed he and other enemies of the bank learned more fully how it had participated in the presidential campaign, and also how its president, Nicholas Biddle, had schemed to block the government program of paying off the national debt with funds deposited in the bank. Taney and others thereupon advised Jackson immediately to withdraw the government deposits from the Bank of the United States and place them in selected state banks.

Jackson considered the measure at length, and secured Taney's promise to accept the post of secretary of the treasury if William J. Duane [*q.v.*], who then held that position, should refuse to remove the deposits. Although admitting the strength of the argument in the "Paper read to the Cabinet," which had been largely redrafted by Taney and presented to the cabinet to justify the removal of the deposits, Duane refused to take the step. Jackson dismissed him, and on Sept. 23, 1833, by recess appointment, Taney became secretary of the treasury. Three days later he announced that on and after Oct. 1 government deposits would no longer be made in the Bank of the United States and its branches but in certain specified state banks.

During the ensuing nine months he set up a system of government depositories which continued to function in spite of the concentrated opposition of all the forces back of the Bank of the United States. For the part which he played Taney was labeled by Webster, Clay, and other friends of the bank as the "pliant instrument" of Andrew Jackson. Early historians accepted this political indictment as true. Further examination of the facts, however, reveals that Taney was fundamentally anything but pliant. He was tactful in his methods, it is true, as one who succeeded in influencing the conduct of Andrew Jackson had to be, but it is evident that from the beginning he labored persistently to curtail the power of an institution which he had come to regard as a menace to the country. He had a program for improving the currency which included doing away with small denomination notes altogether. Unfortunately for the program it required the cooperation of Congress and of the states, and it required also that he should remain in office. This he was unable to do. The enemy was so strong in the Senate that when, toward the end of the session, his appointment was presented for confirmation, it was rejected (June 24, 1834), and he was retired to private life. His attack upon the bank, however, had been decisive, and the institution was not rechartered.

On Jan. 15, 1835, doubtless as much as a political reward as in recognition of merit, Jackson nominated Taney for the position of associate justice of the Supreme Court. His enemies defeated the nomination by postponing it indefinitely (Mar. 3, 1835). On Dec. 28, Jackson nominated him for the position left vacant by the death of Chief Justice Marshall. Many changes had taken place in the Senate since the preceding session, and on Mar. 15, 1836, the appointment was confirmed in spite of Whig opposition. His accession to the chief justiceship did not bring into the decisions of the Supreme Court the petty politics which his enemies had feared. It did, however, result in the reversal of certain trends which characterized the work of his predecessor. During the Marshall régime the Supreme Court had curbed at various points the legislative activities of the states, and had exercised a jealous guardianship over contract rights, including those conferred by corporation charters. One of the first important questions with which Chief Justice Taney was faced was whether rights not specifically conferred by a charter could be inferred from the language of the document. Speaking for a majority of the court in *Charles River Bridge* vs. *Warren Bridge* (*36 United States*, 420), and against a powerful dissent by Justice Story, the spokesman of the Marshall group, he held that rights could not be so inferred, and that rights granted by charters were to be construed narrowly. "While the rights of private property are sacredly guarded," he declared, "we must not forget that the community also have rights, and that the happiness and well being of every citizen depends on their faithful preservation" (*36 United States*, 548). The decision reflected his experience with the predatory activities of corporations, and particularly of the Bank of the United States. The legal principle which he asserted became a permanent and valued fixture in American constitutional law.

The decision did not mean, however, that Taney planned, by interpretation, to devitalize the obligation of contract clause of the Constitution, as was shown by his opinion in *Bronson* vs. *Kinzie* (*42 United States*, 311), in which he held unconstitutional a state law interfering with the execution of mortgages. Neither did it mean that his decisions would always be uncompromisingly against corporations. In *Bank of Augusta* vs. *Earle* (*38 United States*, 519), he asserted the important principle that although a state might exclude from its borders the corporations of other states, the courts, in the absence of specific legislation to that effect, would observe the rule of comity and hold that it had not done so. The change from the old régime represented merely a modification of the assumption that unchecked centralization of power in the federal government and unqualified judicial benevolence toward private aggregations of wealth and power worked always for the good of the country.

Taney always felt that the commerce clause of the Constitution should be interpreted narrowly when the issue was whether it should be used to defeat state laws (see for example *License Cases*, *46 United States*, 504; and his dissent in *Passenger Cases*, *48 United States*, 283). His opinions on the subject rarely suggested a denial of federal power to regulate, but tended rather to oppose the use of the Constitution to prevent state regulation where regulation otherwise would not exist. In other words, he apparently had little sympathy for the régime of *laissez-faire* which the Constitution was being used to enforce upon the states. He concurred in some opinions of his brethren upholding state laws as police regulations, but he seems to have felt that the rights of the state ought to be protected without resort to a special doctrine of police powers, which was then in evolution. The states were sovereign within their sphere. That ought to be enough, in cases where they had not by the Constitution specifically surrendered their power to act. In dealing, on the other hand, with the related subject of the extension of admiralty laws to inland waters, and the jurisdiction of federal courts over cases arising there, he asserted a breadth of federal power which had not been claimed even by Marshall (see *The Propeller Genesee Chief* vs. *Fitzhugh*, *53 United States*, 443).

In many ways Taney showed great restraint in the exercise of power. He abandoned the custom of delivering political charges to grand juries summoned before the circuit court of the United States. In his dissenting opinion in *State of Rhode Island* vs. *State of Massachusetts* (*37 United States*, 657) he went to the extreme of denying the jurisdiction of the Supreme Court in suits between states to determine boundary lines when acting in their sovereign capacity. In *Luther* vs. *Borden* (*48 United States*, 1) he used the doctrine of political questions to justify a denial of jurisdiction in a case involving the question as to which of two organizations was the legitimate government of a state. Despite this typical restraint, he went to the verge of impropriety in publishing a dissenting opinion in a case involving the Bank of the United States in which he had not heard the arguments and turning in part upon his activities as attorney general (*Bank of the United States* vs. *United States, 43 United States,* 710; see the appendix, p. 745). Nor should the fact be obscured that during the Civil War he was a number of times at the point of defying the military and civil officers of the Federal government.

While slavery issues are usually overemphasized in brief accounts of Taney, his life is not to be understood without reference to these issues and to the broader ones of economic and cultural conflict between the North and the South. Taney had been brought up in an undiluted Southern agrarian atmosphere, and his life was permanently conditioned by it. Like many of his Southern neighbors he cooperated in projects for colonizing free negroes in Africa; he manumitted his own slaves and even purchased others to enable them to work out their freedom. But he concluded from observation that white and colored people, being what they were, could not satisfactorily live together in large numbers as equals, and that slavery was probably necessary as long as negroes remained in the country. He was convinced that the solution of the problem, at any rate, was to be arrived at only by the people who were in immediate contact with it, and not by Northern abolitionists who had no comprehension of its complexity. This attitude doubtless added strength to his belief that in general the courts ought scrupulously to guard the sovereignty of the states from federal encroachment—for the population dominated by Northern culture and interests was gaining rapidly over the population of the South, and must in time control the federal government.

In 1856 Taney expressed privately the belief that the South was doomed to sink to a state of inferiority, and that power would be exercised to gratify Northern cupidity and evil passions without reference to the principles of the Constitution. His feelings being what they were, it is not surprising that when, a few months later, one of his colleagues prepared to present in *Dred Scott* vs. *Sandford* (60 *United States,* 393) an unnecessary argument in favor of the constitutionality of the Missouri Compromise, he consented to discuss for the court from the opposing point of view this and other sectional issues which might easily have been avoided. He argued that　negro could not possess the rights of citizenship which entitled him to sue in a federal court, and that therefore the lower court, in the case at hand, had erred in taking jurisdiction. Since doubt had been expressed, however, as to

whether this phase of the question of jurisdiction could now legitimately be determined by the Supreme Court, he sought to strengthen his position by another argument demonstrating that the lower court had been in error in taking jurisdiction. This argument was based on the fact that a slave could not possess rights of citizenship permitting him to sue in a federal court. It was admitted that Dred Scott had been born a slave. Taney sought to demonstrate that he was still a slave, and that he had not, as contended, become free because of residence in territory made free by act of Congress, because Congress had never had the constitutional power to exclude slavery from the territories.

Thus under cover of a discussion of jurisdiction Taney passed upon questions which lay at the base of the heated controversy between the North and the South. That the case could have been decided on narrower grounds was made apparent at the time both by the dissenting opinions and by the diversity of the opinions of the judges who concurred in the judgment. With unprecedented bitterness Republican and abolitionist leaders attacked Taney and the majority of the court for deciding unnecessarily that Congress had no power to exclude slavery from the territories, and for comments made on the rights of negroes. They misrepresented Taney's opinion to make him say that the negro now had no rights which the white man was bound to respect. So effective was the use to which the decision was put that it played an important part in ensuing elections, and has commonly been regarded as one of the major causes of the Civil War. Taney's opinion was sharply criticized by Northern lawyers on the ground that many of his arguments were *obiter dicta.* They were such, however, only by a narrow definition of the term, and, it might be added, only in the sense that many of the much-lauded doctrines of Chief Justice Marshall, announced in the foundation cases of American constitutional law, were *obiter dicta.* Fundamentally it was their content, and not their status as *obiter dicta,* which provoked Northern hostility. As his predecessor had taken advantage of his position to promulgate doctrines to justify the establishment of the strong central government which he thought desirable, so Taney, by the use of different doctrines, had attempted to protect the weaker of two diverse cultures from being smothered by the stronger. It is true that he had wholly miscalculated the effects of the decision, and that it hastened rather than retarded the ultimate subjugation of the South. Nevertheless, his opinion is to be accurately explained only in terms of what he attempted to do.

He wrote two other opinions of major importance in connection with sectional issues. In discussing the constitutionality of the Fugitive-slave Law, in *Ableman* vs. *Booth* (62 *United States,* 506), he presented a penetrating analysis of the relations between the state and national governments which was to be accepted as a masterpiece and quoted time and again by his colleagues and successors in future years. Unhappily the crisis was too close at hand for a general calm appraisal of the opinion at the time when it was delivered. In *Ex parte Merryman* (*Federal Cases* No. 9,487) he delivered a brilliant defense of the rights of civilians in war time, only to make himself again the object of bitter denunciation. The private records of the period reveal on his part a complete lack of sympathy with the national government in the conduct of the war, and the belief that force should not have been used to prevent the South from leaving the Union. Hence it was that when he died in Washington, on Oct. 12, 1864, he was scorned by the war-frenzied masses.

Taney's personality and his private life were such as to lend an air of incongruity to the hatred he aroused. He was considerate of others, gracious, dependable. Owing to his low salary, his open-handed charity, and the heavy expenditures arising from the fact that he and other members of his family were semi-invalids, he was always near to a state of financial embarrassment. Yet he paid all debts with scrupulous care, and refused aid, even from his best friends. He long hoped to make a contribution to history by writing at length the story of the battles of the Jackson period, but although rough drafts of certain segments were left for posterity his poor health prevented the completion of his dramatic account. Like his ancestors for a number of generations, he was a Roman Catholic. He was devoted to his church, and was sincere, humble, and devout in participation in its forms of worship. He carried his religion into the performance of his professional tasks to the extent of beginning each day's work in court only after having privately spent a few moments in prayer. He was broadly tolerant, however, and not much concerned with matters of creed. His wife was a Protestant, and he refused to permit members of his church to press the claims of Catholicism upon her or his daughters. He deeply resented the Know-Nothing movement, in so far as it represented an attack upon members of his faith, but his wrathful private protests were for the most part defensive in character, and he never

attempted to carry war into opposing camps. Only on rare occasions, such as in some instances during the bank war, in two or three letters written after the Dred Scott decision, and certain letters dealing with the mistreatment of one of his daughters by her husband, do the records show that beneath his calm and courteous exterior was a fiery temper resembling that which had made it necessary for his father (1819) to flee from a charge of manslaughter.

With the passing of the years resentment against him has died down, and his character and his motives have come more and more to be understood. He has won the respect of thoughtful students even though they may not accept his point of view, and Charles Sumner's vindictive prophecy that his name should be "hooted down the page of history" seems certain to go unfulfilled. More and more, sentiment concerning him can be accurately embodied in the declaration of his successor, Charles E. Hughes, that "he was a great Chief Justice."

[Available sources include: Samuel Tyler, *Memoir of Roger Brooke Taney, LL.D.* (1872); B. C. Steiner, *Life of Roger Brooke Taney* (1922); C. B. Swisher, *Roger B. Taney* (1935); *The Unjust Judge. A Memorial of Roger Brooke Taney, Late Chief Justice of the United States* (1865); E. S. Corwin, "The Dred Scott Decision, in the Light of Contemporary Legal Doctrines," *Am. Hist. Review,* Oct. 1911, pp. 52–69; H. H. Hagen, "The Dred Scott Decision," in *Georgetown Law Journal,* Jan. 1927; and "Ableman vs. Booth," in *Am. Bar Asso. Journal,* Jan. 1931; a longhand manuscript in the Lib. of Cong. by Taney giving an account of the struggle with the Bank of the United States; J. M. Campbell, ed., *Reports of the Cases at Law and Equity and in the Admiralty Determined in the Circuit Court of the United States for the District of Maryland by R. B. Taney* (1871); Charles Warren, *The Supreme Court in United States History* (2 vols., rev. ed., 1926); Mrs. J. C. Lane, *Key and Allied Families* (1931); death notice and obituary, *Daily National Intelligencer* (Washington, D. C.), Oct. 13, 14, 1864. Taney's home in Frederick, Md., preserved as a museum, contains some of his furniture, pictures, clothing, and other items.]

C.B.S.

TANNEBERGER, DAVID (Mar. 21, 1728– May 19, 1804), organ builder, also known as Tannenberg and Tanneberg, was born on Count Nicholas von Zinzendorf's estate, Berthelsdorf, in Upper (Saxon) Lusatia, the son of Johann and Judith (Nitschmann) Tanneberger. His family belonged on both sides to the Unitas Fratrum, his parents emigrating to Berthelsdorf in 1726 from Zauchtenthal in Moravia. As one of John Nitschmann's colonists, Tanneberger landed at New York from the Moravian missionary snow, *Irene,* on May 12, 1749, and proceeded to Bethlehem, Pa., where he was married on July 15 to Anna Rosina Kerner (or Kern) of Ebersdorf, Upper Lusatia, who had come to America in the same company. Thirty other couples were married that day, which was long celebrated at Bethlehem as the anniversary of the "Great Wedding." He was a skilful joiner, had a notably good tenor voice, and played the violin. In 1757 John Gottlob Klemm of Dresden, Saxony, who had learned organ building in Germany, took him as helper to repair the Bethlehem church organ. This, the first American-built organ, had been constructed by Gustavus Hesselius [q.v.] in 1746 and installed by Klemm at Bethlehem, where it was overhauled in 1751 by Robert Harttafel, whose later life was spent at Lancaster, Pa. These men were the first American organ builders; Tanneberger became the most expert and renowned of them all and contributed substantially to the musical culture of his time. He and Klemm set up a shop at Nazareth but relocated it at Bethlehem in 1760. Records exist of Tanneberger's trips to various points in quest of suitable timber for their work. Two of their instruments have been identified, one built (1758) for the chapel of the Manor House (Nazareth Hall), the other (1759) for the Bethlehem church. In 1761 Tanneberger transported Hesselius' old organ to Lititz in Lancaster County and installed it there. Klemm died May 5, 1762, and in 1765 Tanneberger removed to Lititz and bought the "Pilgerhaus" for a home and workshop. Organs of his manufacture were in high repute and were shipped all over eastern Pennsylvania from his Lititz shop and even to such distant points as Albany, N. Y. (1767), Salem, N. C. (1798), Baltimore (1798), and Madison, Va. (1801). He made organs not only for Moravian but also for Reformed, Lutheran, and Roman Catholic churches. He also built pianos, which he sold for twenty-two pounds ten shillings. His wife, who had borne him three daughters and two sons, died in 1792; and in 1800 he married Anna Maria (Fischer) Hall Lange of Heidelberg, Pa., who had been twice a widow. His last organ was built in 1804 for Christ Lutheran Church at York. While installing it, Tanneberger suffered a paralytic stroke, fell from a bench or scaffold, and died a few days later. He was buried at York, the organ playing for the first time at his funeral. He was survived by his three daughters. John Philip Bachmann, his son-in-law, continued the business at Lititz for more than twenty years.

[J. W. Jordan, "Early Colonial Organ-Builders of Pa.," *Pa. Mag. Hist. and Biog.*, July 1898, and "Moravian Immigration to Pa., 1734–67," *Trans. Moravian Hist. Soc.*, vol. V (Nazareth, Pa., 1899); P. E. Beck, "David Tanneberger, Organ Builder," *Papers Read before the Lancaster County Hist. Soc.*, Jan. 8, 1926; A. R. Beck, "David Tannenberg," *Pa.-German*, July 1909, and "The Moravian Graveyards of Lititz, Pa., 1744–1905," *Trans. Moravian Hist. Soc.*, vol. VII (1906); J. M. Levering, *A Hist. of Bethlehem, Pa., 1741–1892* (Bethlehem, 1903); A. G. Rau, "A List of the Bohemian and Moravian Emigrants to Saxony," *Trans. Moravian Hist. Soc.*, vol. IX (1913); *Church Music and Musical Life in Pa. in the Eighteenth Cent.*, vol. II (1927), Pubs. Pa. Soc. Colonial Dames of America, no. 4.]

G. H. G.

TANNER, BENJAMIN (Mar. 27, 1775–Nov. 14, 1848), engraver, was born in New York City. Having early displayed a talent for drawing and designing, he was placed with Peter C. Verger, a French engraver in that city, to learn the art. Though he remained with Verger until he was of age, engravings signed by him as early as 1792 are known, and in 1795 he engraved six of the small folio plates that illustrate Paul Wright's *The New and Complete Life of Our Blessed Lord and Saviour Jesus Christ*. Upon the completion of his apprenticeship he set up for himself in his native city, but in 1799 he went to Philadelphia, where he lived for the rest of his life. Between the years 1800 and 1805, however, his name does not appear in the directories of that city. In 1800 he engraved a portrait of Washington for Mason L. Weems's *A History of the Life and Death, Virtues and Exploits of General George Washington* (1800), which was published by John Bioren, Philadelphia. On Sept. 6, 1806, he was married in Philadelphia to Mary Bioren, probably a daughter of the publisher (notice in *Poulson's American Daily Advertiser*, Sept. 10, 1806). To his younger brother, Henry Schenck Tanner [q.v.], he taught the art of engraving, and, since the latter was interested in geography, the two began in 1811 the business of map engraving and publishing in Philadelphia. In 1817 Tanner joined Francis Kearny and Cornelius Tiebout [qq.v.] in banknote engraving under the firm name of Tanner, Kearny & Tiebout. By 1818 he had organized a second firm —Tanner, Vallance, Kearny & Company— which occupied the same premises and engaged in general engraving. Of this firm, which existed until 1824, Tanner's brother was a member. About 1828 Tanner or his young brother —the credit is variously assigned—devised a check blank engraved in such a way as to prevent alteration without detection. In 1835 Tanner abandoned general engraving, and made the production of check and note blanks his business, printing his product under the trade name "stereograph." He retired in 1845 because of failing eyesight and carried on his business through an agency. Shortly afterward he was found to be suffering from an abcess of the brain. He went to Baltimore for treatment and died there at the house of his son on Nov. 14, 1848.

His early engraved work which was in the

line manner, was somewhat crude. Later he improved immeasurably, and engraved many fine plates in line and in stipple. Among his best plates were both portraits and historical subjects connected with the Revolution and the War of 1812, such as "Perry's Victory," "Capture of the *Macedonian*," and "Surrender of Cornwallis." He engraved many designs by John James Barralet, including an imperial folio plate in stipple of "Apotheosis of Washington" (1802), and "America Guided by Wisdom." His portraits were usually in stipple and his subject plates in line. In conjunction with William Satchwell Leney [*q.v.*] he engraved a royal folio portrait (1812) of Archbishop John Carroll of Baltimore. He also engraved maps and charts, among them one for a volume of maps supplementing John Marshall's *The Life of George Washington* (5 vols., 1804–07), and plates for some annuals. Among the plates for the 1802–03 edition of W. F. Mavor's *Historical Account of the Most Celebrated Voyages* were many engraved by Tanner. In the exhibition of the works of American engravers in the New York Public Library in 1928, he was represented by several plates.

[Frank Weitenkampf, *Am. Graphic Art* (1912); W. S. Baker, *Am. Engravers and Their Works* (1875); D. M. Stauffer, *Am. Engravers upon Copper and Steel* (2 vols., 1907), with supplementary vol. (1917) by Mantle Fielding; *One Hundred Notable Am. Engravers, 1683–1850* (1928), cat. of exhibition at N. Y. Pub. Lib.; death notices in *Pub. Ledger* (Phila.) and *Sun* (Baltimore), Nov. 16, 1848.]   J. J.

TANNER, BENJAMIN TUCKER (Dec. 25, 1835–Jan. 15, 1923), bishop of the African Methodist Episcopal Church, was born in Pittsburgh, Pa., the son of Hugh S. and Isabel H. Tanner. His father died before the boy had finished his schooling and he was compelled to meet his expenses at Avery College, Allegheny City, from 1852 until 1857, by working as a barber in his spare time. In 1856 he was converted and became a licensed preacher of the African Methodist Episcopal Church. The year following he entered Western Theological Seminary, where he remained until 1860 and was then ordained as deacon and elder. Obliged to decline an appointment to the Sacramento station in California on account of a lack of means, he served as a substitute preacher for a year or more for a Presbyterian church in the District of Columbia. After the outbreak of the Civil War he organized a Sunday school for the freedmen newly enlisted in the navy, and in April 1862 was installed as head of the Alexander mission in E Street, the first of its kind to be established in Washington by the

African Methodist Episcopal Church. Having become a member of the Baltimore Conference in 1862, he was appointed the following year pastor of a Georgetown church, and in 1866 was promoted to a pastorate in Baltimore. He resigned from this position to become the principal of the Conference school at Frederick, Md. At the General Conference of his Church held in Washington in 1868 he was made its chief secretary and at the same time editor of the *Christian Recorder*. In 1881 he attended the Ecumenical Conference in London and in 1884 left the *Christian Recorder* to become the editor of the *A. M. E. Church Review*, which periodical he had helped to found. In 1888 he was elected bishop and assumed charge of the first district of the denomination with headquarters in Philadelphia. In September 1901 he was a delegate to the Third Ecumenical Conference on Methodism. At the General Conference held in May 1908 he was relieved of his duties at his own request and retired on half pay, being the first African Methodist Episcopal bishop to be given a pension.

His published writings include *An Apology for African Methodism* (1867); *The Negro's Origin; and Is He Cursed of God* (1869); *An Outline of Our History and Government for African Methodist Churchmen* (1884); and *Theological Lectures* (1894). On Aug. 19, 1858, he married Sarah Elizabeth Miller by whom he had two sons and five daughters.

[W. J. Simmons, *Men of Mark* (1887); B. W. Arnett, *The Budget . . . of the African Methodist Episcopal Church* (1884); *Who's Who of the Colored Race* (1915); R. R. Wright, *Centennial Encyc. of the African Methodist Episcopal Church* (copr. 1916); *Who's Who in America, 1920–21*; *Public Ledger* (Phila.), Jan. 16, 1923; *N. Y. Times,* Jan. 16, 1923.]
                    H. G. V.

TANNER, HENRY SCHENCK (1786–1858), cartographer and statistical geographer, was born in New York City but removed in early life to Philadelphia, Pa., where he was first associated with his brother Benjamin [*q.v.*], an engraver, and later with his brother's firm of Tanner, Vallance, Kearny & Company. Although trained as an engraver he was endowed with that combination of scientific and artistic sense that spells the true cartographer and that led him ultimately to produce for his time the outstanding map representations of the territory of the United States, based on a critical study of the source material. He engraved the thirty-one maps in *A New and Elegant General Atlas Containing Maps of Each of the United States* (*c.* 1812), the frontispiece map in *Travels in the United States* (1912) by John Melish [*q.v.*], two-thirds of the maps in Melish's *A Military and Topographical Atlas of the United States* (eds. of 1813, 1815), and, with J. Vallance, Melish's fundamental *Map of the United States . . . With the Contiguous British & Spanish Possessions* (1816), of 60 miles to the inch. Accompanying the last of these was a text—*A Geographical Description of the United States* (1816)—that included a brief discussion of the source maps on which the compilation was based. This text, as well as the work on the map itself, cannot but have exerted a shaping influence on Tanner's thought.

But all these undertakings were merely a prelude to Tanner's greatest work. The underlying principles of uniformity of scale and foundation on primary source material are expressed in its title: *A New American Atlas; Containing Maps of the Several States of the North American Union, Projected and Drawn on a Uniform Scale from Documents Found in the Public Offices of the United States . . . and Other Original and Authentic Information* (5 pts., 1818–23). It consisted primarily of maps of the individual states or of state groups, all on the scale of 15 geographical (or 17⅓ statute) miles to the inch, which would be large for many states even in a modern atlas. It ran through numerous editions until at least 1839. No modern atlas of relatively equal merit is available to the American public today, and the first paragraph of Tanner's announcement in the first instalment, dated Philadelphia, July 10, 1818, might still well serve as a charter for American cartography after a lapse of considerably more than a century. After criticizing previous American maps of the United States for their failure both "to convey an adequate idea of the subject" and "to do justice to the improved state of Geographical Science in the United States," and those published in Europe for their defectiveness and incorrectness, he expresses the view that "the subject must be brought to maturity" in America, where "we possess the materials and skill sufficient to exhibit a topographical representation of the United States, infinitely superior, as it regards correctness and detail, and every way equal in style, to any European publication of the kind."

The compilation of the maps in the *New American Atlas* gave Tanner a mastery of the cartographic sources relating to the United States. This, together with the rapid appearance of new material, led him to plan a synoptic view of the whole country, and in 1829 he published a map entitled simply *United States of America,* 64 by 50 inches in size, on the scale of

exactly 1:2,000,000, or about 32 miles to the inch—practically twice as detailed as Melish's map of 1816. The selection of a so-called natural scale for the construction of the map—*i.e.,* an absolute scale expressing ratio in terms of size of the earth as against the universal practice of the time of utilizing relative scales expressing ratio in terms of conventional units of measure on the map itself, such as miles to the inch—throws an interesting sidelight on the scientific bent of Tanner's mind. Characteristically, also, during the compilation he addressed a circular letter inviting information as to recent surveys in the recipient's local region. He accompanied the map with a *Memoir on the Recent Surveys, Observations, and Internal Improvements, in the United States, With Brief Notices of the New Counties, Towns, Villages, Canals, and Rail Roads . . .* (Philadelphia, 1829), which is a model of a scientist's rendering of account. Tanner published many other maps, atlases, and guide books, and geographical compendia; the price list at the end of the 1829 *Memoir* enumerates no less than eighty items. Among these are his *A Map of the United States of Mexico, Constructed from a Great Variety of Printed and Manuscript Documents* (1825), on the scale of 85 miles to the inch; Robert Mills's *Atlas of the State of South Carolina* (Philadelphia, 1825), consisting of county maps engraved by Tanner on the relatively large scale of 2 miles to the inch; *A Description of the Canals and Rail Roads of the United States* (New York, 1840), *The American Traveller* (1834), and *The Central Traveller* (1840). In 1850 he returned to New York, where he died eight years later.

[Bibliog. data are to be found in P. L. Phillips, *A List of Geographical Atlases in the Lib. of Cong.* (4 vols., 1909–20) and *A List of Maps of America in the Lib. of Cong.* (1901); Joseph Sabin, *A Dict. of Books Relating to America,* vol. XXIV (1933–34); and the maps, atlases, and other pubs. of Tanner in the Lib. of Cong. and the Am. Geographical Soc. of N. Y. There is a critical appraisal in W. L. G. Joerg, "Henry S. Tanner of Phila.," *Annals Asso. Am. Geographers,* vol. XXV (1935).]

W. L. G. J.

TANNER, JAMES (Apr. 4, 1844–Oct. 2, 1927), lobbyist, United States pension commissioner, better known as "Corporal Tanner," was born at Richmondville, Schoharie County, N. Y., the son of Josiah and Elizabeth (Earle) Tanner and a descendant of William Tanner who settled in Rhode Island about 1679. He attended the district schools and became a teacher at the age of seventeen. In September 1861 he ran away from his father's farm to enlist in the 87th New York Volunteer Infantry. Promoted to be corporal, he took part in the Peninsular campaign in the spring of 1862 and in the battles of Warrenton, Bristoe Station, and Second Manassas (Bull Run). At Bull Run (Aug. 29–30, 1862) he received a wound necessitating amputation of both legs four inches below the knees. He recovered, learned to walk with artificial limbs, and studied stenography. Friends procured for him the post of under-doorkeeper of the New York Assembly and late in 1864 a clerkship in the War Department at Washington. He was summoned from his room next door to the house where Lincoln lay dying to take stenographic notes on the first examination of witnesses of the assassination.

After the close of the war he returned home, studied law in the office of Judge W. C. Lamont, and was admitted to the bar in 1869. He held various positions in the custom house at New York, 1869–77, and was tax collector of Brooklyn, 1877–85. In his spare time he was a candidate for political offices, appeared often on the lecture platform, and was active in the Grand Army of the Republic. While commander of the Department of New York in 1876, he caused the legislature to be deluged with petitions for the establishment of a soldiers' home. The successful outcome of this agitation gained him a place on the pension committee of the Grand Army, with the duty of lobbying before congressional committees. Republican campaign managers sent him on speechmaking tours of California and Oregon in 1886 and 1887, and of Indiana in 1888. His friends claimed that his efforts won for Benjamin Harrison the small margin of votes by which he carried Indiana.

Tanner's reward for this service was the post of commissioner of pensions in the new administration. Thankful that "at these finger tips there rests some power," he declared his intention of raising all pensions to at least four dollars a month, "though I may wring from the hearts of some the prayer, 'God help the surplus!'" (speech at Columbia, Tenn., May 10, as quoted in *New York Tribune*, May 11, 1889). He raised the disability ratings of many pensioners, in some cases without application on their part, and ordered the payment in lump sums of thousands of dollars accrued before the original application. Many of the beneficiaries were persons with political influence. The employees of the Pension Office, taking advantage of Tanner's administrative ineptitude, proceeded to give each other higher ratings. The number of new names on the pension rolls was also increased on the principle of giving "an appropriation to every old comrade that needs it" (quotation in the *Nation*, Aug. 1, 1889). After a few

months the secretary of the interior interfered for reasons of economy. Tanner insubordinately informed him that he alone was responsible for the Pension Office; but, receiving no official encouragement, he sent a letter of resignation to the president in September 1889, and retired to private life as a pension attorney.

President Harrison, in accepting the resignation, affirmed his belief in Tanner's personal honesty, and public opinion concurred. It is fairly obvious that Tanner's failure was due to his limited education and his lack of good administrative standards. In 1904 President Theodore Roosevelt appointed him register of wills of the District of Columbia; and the Grand Army of the Republic made him its commander-in-chief for the year 1905–06. He was married in November 1866 to Mero L. White of Jefferson, N. Y., and was survived by two sons and two daughters. He died in Washington, D. C.

[J. E. Smith, *A Famous Battery and Its Campaigns* (1892); H. R. Stiles, *The Civil . . . Hist. . . . of the County of Kings* (1884); W. E. Roscoe, *Hist. of Schoharie County, N. Y.* (1882); *Who's Who in America*, 1918–19; G. C. Tanner, *William Tanner, Sr., of South Kingstown, R. I., and His Descendants* (1910); W. H. Glasson, *Federal Military Pensions in the U. S.* (1918); Report of the Secretary of the Interior for 1889, *House Ex. Doc. 1* (pt. 5), 51 Cong., 1 Sess.; articles by D. L. McMurry, in *Miss. Valley Hist. Rev.*, June 1922 and Dec. 1926; *N. Y. Times, N. Y. Herald Tribune, Washington Post*, Oct. 3, 1927.]   E. C. S.

TAPPAN, ARTHUR (May 22, 1786–July 23, 1865), philanthropist, abolitionist, was born at Northampton, Mass., the eighth of eleven children of Benjamin and Sarah (Homes) Tappan. Benjamin and Lewis Tappan [qq.v.] were his brothers. Reared in a serious, pious household, he attended the town school until the age of fifteen, when he was given a clerkship with Sewall & Salisbury, hardware and dry-goods dealers in Boston. Here for a time he sat under the preaching of William Ellery Channing. He entered business for himself as a dry-goods importer at the age of twenty-one, establishing the firm of Tappan & Sewall in Portland, Me., with a nephew of one of his former employers. Some two years later he moved his business to Montreal, where he married Frances Antill, Sept. 18, 1810. To them were born two sons, one of whom died in infancy, and six daughters.

Returning to the United States after the outbreak of the War of 1812, Tappan struggled against difficulties for several years before, in 1826, he started his most successful enterprise— a silk jobbing firm in New York in which he was joined two years later by his brother Lewis. Although he met with various reverses, he came to be esteemed a wealthy man. He attributed his success to the fact that he charged a fixed uniform price for articles, a practice not then customary. "I had but *one price*," he said, "and sold for cash or short credit" (L. Tappan, *Life, post,* p. 70). Heavily overstocked in a period of falling prices, the firm of Arthur Tappan & Company was forced to close its doors during the panic of 1837, but in eighteen months its creditors had all been paid.

As soon as he began to accumulate wealth Tappan began "to reflect seriously upon his obligations as a STEWARD of the Lord" (*Life,* p. 62). He gave generously of his substance and of his time, strength, and executive ability, to a multitude of religious and humanitarian causes. He was a supporter of the American Sunday School Union, the American Bible Society, the American Tract Society, the American Education Society, and the American Home Missionary Society, and held office in most of these organizations. He was concerned in the movement for stricter Sabbath observance, the temperance crusade, and the fight against tobacco. In 1827 he founded the *New York Journal of Commerce* to provide the city with a daily newspaper free from "immoral advertisements" and regardful of the Sabbath, but it did not prove the moral force he had desired, and after a year he turned it over to his brother Lewis. He supported the effort made to suppress licentiousness and vice in New York and in 1831 was president of the New York Magdalen Society, which sponsored a sensational report exposing conditions in that city. Though for some years a member successively of the Presbyterian congregations of John Mitchell Mason and Samuel Hanson Cox [*qq.v.*], he was an active promoter of the free church movement in New York, and with his brother was instrumental in leasing the Chatham Street Theatre and subsequently building the Broadway Tabernacle for Charles Grandison Finney [*q.v.*]. He gave a scholarship to Andover Theological Seminary and paid the tuition of a large number of divinity students at Yale. He contributed toward the establishment of Kenyon College, Gambier, Ohio, of Auburn Theological Seminary, of Lane Theological Seminary, Cincinnati; and in 1835, after the withdrawal of most of the Lane students because of restrictions upon the discussion of slavery, gave $10,000 and made a private pledge of his entire income in order to secure the establishment of Oberlin College.

Moved by concern for the welfare of the negroes, he joined the American Colonization Society, but becoming convinced that its policy was wrong withdrew and united with those who were agitating for the abolition of slavery. He first became associated with William Lloyd Garrison [*q.v.*] in 1830 by paying a fine to free Garrison from prison in Baltimore, and subsequently helped support the publication of the *Liberator.* About 1831 he promoted an unsuccessful project to establish a college for negroes in New Haven. In March 1833 he took an active part in launching the *Emancipator* in New York; in October of the same year he helped form the New York City Anti-Slavery Society, and in December, the American Anti-Slavery Society, being chosen the first president of each. In 1835 he volunteered assistance to Prudence Crandall [*q.v.*], arrested for opening a school for negro girls at Canterbury, Conn., and in this connection financed the establishment in Windham County of the anti-slavery *Unionist,* under the editorship of C. C. Burleigh [*q.v.*].

In 1840, believing that Garrison would weaken the cause of abolition by his action in associating with it other movements, such as that for women's rights, Tappan with others withdrew from the American Anti-Slavery Society, formed a new organization—the American and Foreign Anti-Slavery Society, of which he was elected president—and founded a new journal, the *American and Foreign Anti-Slavery Reporter.* Convinced that slavery could be destroyed under the Constitution by political action, he supported the Liberty Party and its presidential candidate, James G. Birney [*q.v.*], and was instrumental in establishing in Washington the anti-slavery weekly, the *National Era.* Meanwhile, in 1846, distressed by the refusal of several of the missionary organizations he had aided to espouse the cause of abolition, he took part in founding the American Missionary Association, and remained a member of its executive committee until his death. After the passage of the Fugitive Slave Law of 1850 he declared his determination "in the fear of God" to disobey it, and continued to give all the aid within his power to escaping fugitives.

Tappan was never of strong constitution and throughout his mature years suffered from constant headache. He had no humor and was stern and severe, with himself as well as others. As a champion of unpopular movements, through most of his career he was subjected to violent criticism; his business was endangered; and he himself was threatened with kidnapping, assault, and assassination. Abuse and threats, however, for the most part he heard calmly and ignored. He had a certain rigidity in maintaining his principles, owing partly to his natural austerity of thought and partly to the position of eminence he attained as the financial backer of many reform movements. Though his money gifts were somewhat curtailed—to his great distress—by his failure about 1842 through ill-advised speculation in real estate, he kept up his active interest in reform until his death. In 1849 he purchased an interest in "The Mercantile Agency" established by his brother, but retired from all business some five or six years later and took up his residence in New Haven, where he died.

[D. L. Tappan, *Tappan-Toppan Geneal.* (1915); Lewis Tappan, *The Life of Arthur Tappan* (1870) ; C. W. Bowen, *Arthur and Lewis Tappan* (1883) ; J. A. Scoville ("Walter Barrett"), *The Old Merchants of N. Y. City*, vol. I (1863) ; G. H. Barnes, *The Anti-Slavery Impulse* (1933) ; W. P. and F. J. Garrison, *William Lloyd Garrison* (4 vols., 1885–89) ; Annie H. Abel and F. J. Klingberg, *A Side-Light on Anglo-American Relations . . . Correspondence of Lewis Tappan* (1927); D. L. Leonard, *The Story of Oberlin* (copr. 1898) ; Joseph Sturge, *A Visit to the U. S. in 1841* (1842) ; *N. Y. Herald,* July 25, 1865.]   F. J. K.

TAPPAN, BENJAMIN (May 25, 1773–Apr. 20, 1857), senator, jurist, anti-slavery leader, was born in Northampton, Mass., eldest of the seven sons of Benjamin and Sarah (Homes) Tappan. Among the other children of the family were the eldest sister, Sarah, who became the mother of David Tappan Stoddard [*q.v.*] and the much younger brothers Arthur and Lewis Tappan [*qq.v.*]. Their father, a goldsmith, later a dry-goods merchant, was descended from Abraham Toppan, who came from Yarmouth, England, to settle in Newbury, Mass., in 1637; their mother, of Irish Presbyterian stock through the paternal line, was also a grandniece of Benjamin Franklin. A public-school education for the younger Benjamin was followed by an apprenticeship to a copperplate printer and engraver, a voyage to the West Indies, brief study of portrait painting under the famous Gilbert Stuart, and then a thorough legal education under Gideon Granger [*q.v.*].

Admitted to the bar at Hartford, Conn., in his twenties, he became a first settler (1799) of what is now Portage County, Ohio. On Mar. 20, 1801, he was married in Wethersfield, Conn., to Nancy Wright (d. 1822), sister of John Crafts Wright, later a congressman from Ohio. Accompanied by his bride he returned to Ravenna, Ohio, where he became an aggressive force in local politics. Having served as a member of the state Senate, 1803–05, he moved in 1809 to Steubenville, where he continued the practice of law. He served as an aide to Major-General Elijah Wadsworth during the War of 1812 and as president judge of the 5th circuit of the court of common pleas, 1816–23. His decisions for 1816–19, published as *Cases Decided in the Courts of Common Pleas, in the Fifth Circuit of . . . Ohio* (1831), referred to as *Tappan's Reports,* were

the first law reports in the state. Failing to be reëlected (Tappan to E. A. Brown, Steubenville, Jan. 29, 1823; MS. in Ohio State Library), he returned to private practice. He then served as an Ohio canal commissioner.

An ardent Jacksonian, he was a presidential elector in 1832, and served as a federal district judge until his appointment, together with those of other Democrats, was rejected by the Senate in May 1834. In 1838, Thomas Morris [*q.v.*] having assumed a position as "the first abolition senator" (Smith, *post,* p. 24) that made him unacceptable to the Ohio Democracy, Tappan was chosen as his successor. The latter had long been known as an opponent of slavery "in all shapes except that of abolitionism" (*Cincinnati Gazette,* Dec. 27, 1838) ; hence his selection satisfied the anti-slavery Democrats. His law office was then intrusted to his partner, Edwin M. Stanton [*q.v.*].

In the Senate, Tappan refused to present abolition petitions from his constituents, asserting that Ohioans should not attempt to interfere with local institutions elsewhere and chiding women petitioners for leaving the home "to mix with the strife of ambition or the cares of Government" (*Ohio Statesman,* Feb. 10, 1840). He was an anti-bank Democrat and "as uncompromising upon hard money as the Rock of Gibraltar" (Matthias Martin to William Allen, quoted by Holt, *post,* p. 576). His agency in the publication in the New York *Evening Post* (Apr. 27, 1844) of Calhoun's proposed treaty for the annexation of Texas, which was being secretly considered, led to a severe censure by the Senate (*Senate Journal,* 28 Cong., 1 Sess., pp. 439ff.). Like his colleague Allen, in 1845 he refused to follow the instructions of the Whig legislature in opposition to Texas annexation. Remaining an anti-slavery man, on July 12, 1849, he presided at a Northwest Ordinance (Free Soil) political celebration at Cleveland, and in 1856 he cast his last presidential vote for Frémont.

A lawyer of eminent talents and consistently a man of democratic principles, "of an intractable disposition" (*American Union,* Apr. 22, 1857), and with a gift of sarcasm which he used on friend and foe, he held firmly to his independent convictions. His views on slavery and corporate privileges were deemed radical by many of his contemporaries and he was referred to as "the hoary-headed skeptic" (McLean MSS., Library of Congress) because of his blunt professions of religious heterodoxy. Exemplary in private life and scholarly in tastes, he devoted his last years to an interest in mineralogy and conchology. At his death in Steubenville he was survived by two sons, Benjamin and Eli Todd Tappan [*q.v.*], the latter born to his second wife, Betsy (Lord) Frazer (d. 1840), whom he had married in 1823.

[MSS., including an autobiography to 1823, are owned by J. K. Wright of New York; other Tappan MSS. are in the Lib. of Cong. Sketches are found in D. L. Tappan, *Tappan-Toppan Geneal.* (1915); *U. S. Mag. and Democratic Rev.,* June–July 1840; J. B. Doyle, *20th Century Hist. of Steubenville and Jefferson County, Ohio* (1910); *Biog. Dir. Am. Cong.* (1928). See also F. P. Weisenburger, "Ohio Politics during the Jacksonian Period" (unpublished dissertation, Univ. of Mich.); T. C. Smith, *The Liberty and Free Soil Parties in the Northwest* (1897); E. A. Holt, "Party Politics in Ohio, 1840–1850," *Ohio Arch. and Hist. Soc. Quart.,* July 1928, Jan.–Apr. 1929. The best obituary is in the *Evening Post* (N. Y.), Apr. 24, 1857. The Tappan family Bible, owned by Mr. Wright, and the *American Union* (Steubenville), Apr. 22, 1857, give Apr. 20, 1857, as the date of Tappan's death.]

F. P. W.

TAPPAN, ELI TODD (Apr. 30, 1824–Oct. 23, 1888), educator and author, was born in Steubenville, Ohio, the only child of Benjamin Tappan [*q.v.*] by his second wife, Betsy (Lord) Frazer. The boy was educated in the public schools of Steubenville, under private tutors, and in St. Mary's College, Baltimore, Md. Leaving without taking a degree, he began the study of law in 1842 under his father and his father's partner, Edwin M. Stanton [*q.v.*], and was admitted to the bar in 1846. He founded the weekly *Ohio Press,* Columbus, that same year, and was its editor for two years. He then practised law in Steubenville for seven or eight years. In 1852 he served as mayor. He began teaching in the public schools in 1857, and from March 1858 to June 1859 was superintendent.

This last experience fixed his life career, and he was thereafter engaged in educational work. He was professor of mathematics in Ohio University, 1859–60, and again 1865–68, and teacher of mathematics in Mount Auburn Young Ladies' Institute in the interval, 1860–65. He became president of Kenyon College, Gambier, Ohio, in 1869, serving until 1875 when he was made professor of mathematics and political economy in the same institution. As president he completed the chapel known as "Church of the Holy Spirit" and completely revised the curricula of the college. He was also a champion of common schools. As early as 1854, in lectures to teachers, he revealed an insight into school organization and methods of instruction which was in advance of his time. While he was professor in Mount Auburn Young Ladies' Institute he published *Treatise on Plane and Solid Geometry* (1864), based in large measure upon well known French and German textbooks, to supplement the widely used series of arithmetics and algebras by Joseph

Ray. He was the author of the history of school legislation in Ohio from the beginning to the Codification Act of 1873 which formed part of the state's exhibit at the Centennial Exhibition in Philadelphia, and he contributed many articles to educational journals. He was a member of the first Ohio state board of school examiners in 1864, was elected president of the Ohio State Teachers Association in 1866; became a charter member of the council of the National Educational Association in 1880, its treasurer in 1880–81, and its president in 1883. In 1887 he was elected commissioner of common schools of Ohio, in which office he died. He was a member of the Episcopal Church for many years.

Tappan married Lydia McDowell of Steubenville, Feb. 4, 1851. Two children were born to this union: a son, and a daughter, Mary, who married John Henry Wright [*q.v.*], later a professor at Harvard, and became a writer of some repute.

[D. L. Tappan, *Tappan-Toppan Geneal.* (1915); *Thirty-fifth Ann. Report of the State Commissioner of Common Schools . . . of Ohio . . . 1888* (1889); J. J. Burns, *Educ. Hist. of Ohio* (1905); *Ohio Educ. Monthly,* Dec. 1888; *Ohio State Journal* (Columbus), Oct. 24, 1888; J. B. Doyle, *20th Century Hist. of Steubenville and Jefferson County, Ohio* (1910); *The Biog. Cyc. and Portrait Gallery . . . State of Ohio* (1895); *Nat. Educ. Asso. Jour. of Proc. and Addresses,* 1889.]

H. C. M.

TAPPAN, EVA MARCH (Dec. 26, 1854–Jan. 29, 1930), author of anthologies, textbooks, and stories for children, was born in Blackstone, Mass., the daughter of Edmund March and Lucretia (Logée) Tappan. Her father, a graduate of Dartmouth College and pastor of the Free Baptist Church, was the descendant of Abraham Toppan, who emigrated with his family from Yarmouth, England, and was admitted a freeman of Newbury, Mass., in 1637. When she was six her father died, and for the remainder of her childhood she lived at various seminaries, where her mother taught. She received an A.B. degree at Vassar College in 1875. For the next twenty years she taught school, first at Wheaton Seminary, Norton, Mass., from 1875 to 1880, and later at Raymond Academy, Camden, N. J., where she was associate principal from 1884 to 1894. In 1895 she received an A.M. degree and a Ph.D. in 1896 from the University of Pennsylvania. The next year she became head of the English department of the English High School at Worcester, Mass. Seven years later, when she was the author of several school books of recognized merit, she gave up teaching to devote all of her time to writing.

She published her first book, *Charles Lamb, the Man and the Author,* in 1896. In 1900 she published her second, *In the Days of Alfred the Great,* and the next year three others: *In the Days of William the Conqueror, Old Ballads in Prose,* and *England's Story.* By using an informal, lucid style, picturesque details, and well planned, compact organization she realized an ambition, cherished since childhood, of writing books that children would love to read. For the remainder of her life, except for an occasional year that she devoted to the care of her aged mother, she continued to write reference and textbooks for use in grade and high schools. Many of these are histories: *Our Country's Story* (1902), *The Story of the Greek People* (1908), *Our European Ancestors* (1918), *The Story of Our Constitution* (1922). In some she tried to acquaint children with the social and political background of historical periods: *In the Days of Queen Elizabeth* (1902) and *In the Days of Queen Victoria* (1903). In others, such as *American Hero Stories* (1906) and *Old World Hero Stories* (1911), she sought to lay a foundation for the future study of biography. In a series of supplementary readers she provided interesting facts about agriculture and industry: *The Farmer and His Friends, Diggers in the Earth, Makers of Many Things,* and *Travelers and Traveling,* all in 1916. In *Ella, a Little Schoolgirl of the Sixties* (1923) she recounted her own childhood experiences. Her writing gave her the means of realizing a second long-cherished desire: to provide a home for her mother. She never traveled abroad and but rarely in America, preferring to remain with her mother, who was unable to travel. After her mother's death in 1911, her own established habits kept her at home reading and writing. She died at Worcester, Mass.

[Foreword by Eva March Tappan in Edward March Tappan, *The Words of a Man* (1914); D. L. Tappan, *Tappan-Toppan Genealogy* (1915); *Boston Transcript,* Jan. 30, 1930; *Who's Who in America,* 1928–29; correspondence with Miss Lillian E. Prudden, New Haven, Conn.]   V. L. S.

TAPPAN, HENRY PHILIP (Apr. 18, 1805–Nov. 15, 1881), clergyman, philosopher, first president of the University of Michigan, was born at Rhinebeck on the Hudson, N. Y., of mixed Dutch and Huguenot ancestry. His father, Peter Tappan, an officer in the Revolutionary army, was a descendant of Jurian Teunnisse ·Tappan, who emigrated from Holland to Manhattan in 1625. The Tappan family had intermarried with the Clintons, and Tappan's mother, Ann DeWitt, could trace her family back to a connection with the famous DeWitts, the rivals of the House of Orange. Henry Philip was the youngest of seven children. From the district

school he was sent to Greenville Academy, but in 1819 he was forced to leave because of family financial troubles. He resorted to teaching to earn money and two years afterward entered Union College, Schenectady, whence he graduated in 1825 with the degree of B.A. Deciding for the ministry, he next entered Auburn Theological Seminary and was graduated in 1827. On Apr. 17, 1828, he married Julia Livingston, daughter of Col. John Livingston of New York City, by whom he had a son and four daughters. He was ordained at Pittsfield, Mass., in September 1828 as minister of the Congregational Church. His ministerial career was cut short, however, by an infection of the throat which forced him to travel to the West Indies for his health. In 1832 he became professor of moral and intellectual philosophy in the newly established University of the City of New York (later New York University), and from that time devoted his energies to philosophy and the theory of education. Unfortunately, the new university was not well managed, financially or otherwise, and in 1837 Tappan was dismissed along with seven others who had signed a statement expressing lack of confidence in the administration. For a brief interval thereafter he was the head of a private seminary, a young ladies' school in Leroy Place, Bleecker Street, N. Y.

Meanwhile he had written and published several books on philosophy, which in those days was scarcely separable from theology. Jonathan Edwards, 1703–1758 [*q.v.*], had set the stage by his famous treatise on the freedom of the will, and it was this problem which Tappan essayed to reanalyze. He began his publications in 1839 with his *Review of Edwards's "Inquiry into the Freedom of the Will."* This was followed in 1840 by his *Doctrine of the Will Determined by an Appeal to Consciousness* and in 1841 by his *Doctrine of the Will Applied to Moral Agency and Responsibility.* Though he shows the influence of Victor Cousin, the famous eclectic French philosopher of the time, yet there are touches of genuine originality in his handling of the problems. Tappan argued for a generic principle of contingency of which the free will is an expression. This thesis was supported by an appeal to consciousness, because "the causes first and best known to us are ourselves." He also published *Elements of Logic* (1844). In 1852, when he had received recognition both at home and abroad, he was offered his former chair, but declined it for the presidency of the University of Michigan. Although Michigan was still a pioneer state, he saw there an opportunity to integrate the university with the whole educational system and to make of it something more than the college which had served up to this time to complete American education. In his views on education—expressed in *University Education* (1851)—he was influenced by the Prussian system, which he had been able to examine during a visit abroad. Being convinced that much more than the college was needed to lift American thought to a creative level, he was careful in his selection of professors and gathered around him several brilliant men. To his credit, also, goes the founding of the Detroit astronomical observatory. Unfortunately, minor conflicts arose over such a matter as the serving of wine in his home, for the temperance movement was strong and already fanatical. But the university continued to grow and to make innovations under his leadership. A new board of regents which came into office in 1858 was unsympathetic, and in June 1863, after about five years of increasing friction, Tappan was suddenly asked to resign. There were protests throughout the state, but the action was not reconsidered. It remains to be noted that within a few years the regents expressed regret, and that in June 1875 they passed resolutions recognizing Tappan's distinguished ability and services.

Tappan spent the remaining years of his life in Europe, chiefly in Germany and Switzerland, often visiting his daughter and his son-in-law, the famous astronomer, Francis Brünnow, in Ireland. He died abroad, survived by his wife and one daughter, and was buried on the slopes of Vevey facing Lake Geneva. Tappan was a man of striking personal appearance, fully six feet in height, with massive head and shoulders. While he was a very capable thinker in the field of philosophy, he seems to have been at his best as an educator; in this field he was a genuine pioneer whose work was characterized by foresight and by imagination.

[See W. R. Cutter, *Geneal. and Family Hist. of Southern N. Y. and the Hudson River Valley*, vol. I (1910); B. A. Hinsdale, *Hist. of the Univ. of Mich.* (1906); C. M. Perry, *Henry Philip Tappan* (1933); A. D. White, in *Mich. Alumnus*, Mar. 1903; H. S. Frieze, *A Memorial Discourse, on the Life . . . of Rev. Henry Philip Tappan* (1882); and obituary in *N. Y. Tribune*, Nov. 18, 1881. There is a coll. of Tappan's MSS. in the lib. of the Univ. of Mich.]   R. W. S.

TAPPAN, LEWIS (May 23, 1788–June 21, 1873), merchant, abolitionist, brother of Benjamin and Arthur Tappan [*qq.v.*], was born in Northampton, Mass., and grew up in the devout household presided over by his father, Benjamin, and his mother, Sarah (Homes) Tappan. He was educated in the town school and at the age of sixteen became an apprenticed clerk to a dry-goods importing firm in Boston. Here he sat for

a time under the preaching of William Ellery Channing, and in 1825, to the distress of his Calvinistic family, served as treasurer of the American Unitarian Association. Soon, however, he returned to Orthodox views, and by 1828 was writing pamphlets upholding Evangelical convictions against Unitarianism. The family Calvinism also appears in his *Memoir of Mrs. Sarah Tappan* (1834). Meanwhile, assisted by his employers, he had endeavored to set up a business of his own, but in 1828 he entered into partnership with his brother Arthur as a silk jobber in New York. In the same year he took over from Arthur the *New York Journal of Commerce*, but in 1831 sold it to David Hale and Gerard Hallock [*qq.v.*]. As credit manager of Arthur Tappan & Company he was an important factor in the prosperity of the firm in the years preceding the panic of 1837. Shortly thereafter he withdrew from the partnership, and in 1841, under the firm name of Lewis Tappan & Company, established "The Mercantile Agency," the first commercial-credit rating agency in the country. He conducted this enterprise with great success until 1849, when he retired to devote himself to the humanitarian labors which had become his chief concern. In deliberately planning to draw upon his accumulated capital for his support for the rest of his life he was acting upon theories regarding the use of wealth which he later set forth in a pamphlet entitled *Is It Right to Be Rich?* (1869).

Like his brother Arthur, Lewis Tappan from the time of his first business success was a supporter of the American Board of Commissioners for Foreign Missions and the American Bible Society. He was a promoter of the free church movement in New York, and with Arthur was instrumental in leasing the Chatham Street Theatre and building the Broadway Tabernacle for the revivalist Charles Grandison Finney [*q.v.*], and subsequently in sending Finney as professor of theology to Oberlin College. He was one of the founders of the New York Anti-Slavery Society and the American Anti-Slavery Society in 1833, and by his activities in behalf of abolition drew upon himself hate and obloquy; in July 1834 his house was wrecked by a mob, and his furniture burned. In 1839–41 he was the outstanding member of the committee which undertook to secure the freedom of the *Amistad* captives, successfully defended before the Supreme Court by John Quincy Adams [*q.v.*]. Although at first both Tappans worked with William Lloyd Garrison [*q.v.*], Lewis, like Arthur, repudiated Garrison when the latter proposed to attach other reforms to the cause of abolition, and with the resulting schism in the American Anti-Slavery Society in 1840, he took a leading part in forming the American and Foreign Anti-Slavery Society, of which he was the first treasurer. He was especially conscious of the international aspect of the American struggle and for this reason maintained a wide and frequent correspondence with sympathetic interests in England, especially with the British and Foreign Anti-Slavery Society. At the suggestion of John Quincy Adams, he attended the international anti-slavery convention in London in 1843 (*Memoirs of John Quincy Adams*, vol. XI, 1876, pp. 380, 405). Realizing that the attitude of Great Britain could have an almost decisive bearing on the outcome of the struggle in the United States, he discussed with his English friends such matters as the annexation of Texas, the position of the negro in the United States, Canada, and Liberia, the coastwise slave trade, and the attitude of the churches. Believing that slavery could be abolished within the Union, he worked to win the cooperation of churches and missionary societies. When the older foundations which he had supported, notably the American Board, declined to enlist in the fight for abolition, he helped to found and became treasurer of the American Missionary Association (1846), explicitly committed to the cause of the negro. After the passage of the Fugitive Slave Act in 1850, he became a supporter of the work of Alexander M. Ross, who traveled through the South helping slaves to escape by the Underground Railroad (W. H. Siebert, *The Underground Railroad*, 1898, p. 180; A. M. Ross, *Recollections of an Abolitionist*, 1867).

As the struggle in America reached its crisis, Tappan gradually adopted the view that slavery was illegal everywhere and could be abolished by the federal government in all the slave states under the terms of the Constitution. He thus came to favor a more radical method of action than that sponsored by the American and Foreign Anti-Slavery Society, and in 1855 resigned as corresponding secretary of that body to accept office in a new organization known as the Abolition Society. By now, however, age was beginning to limit his activity. As the need for anti-slavery agitation lessened, he gave more attention to the constructive work for negroes being undertaken by the American Missionary Association. In 1870 he published *The Life of Arthur Tappan*, and suffered a paralytic stroke just as the book went to press. Three years later he died, as the result of another stroke, at the age of eighty-five. He was married twice: first, Sept. 7, 1813, to Susanna Aspinwall, by whom

he had six children, and second, in 1854, to Mrs. Sarah J. Davis. The youngest of his five daughters married Henry Chandler Bowen [*q.v.*]. From 1856 Tappan was a member of Plymouth Church, Brooklyn, and his funeral sermon was preached by his pastor, Henry Ward Beecher.

[D. L. Tappan, *Tappan-Toppan Geneal.* (1915); C. W. Bowen, *Arthur and Lewis Tappan* (1883); J. A. Scoville ("Walter Barrett"), *The Old Merchants of N. Y.*, vol. I (1863); E. N. Vose, *Seventy-five Years of The Mercantile Agency, R. G. Dun & Co., 1841–1916* (1916); G. H. Barnes, *The Anti-Slavery Impulse* (1933); G. H. Barnes and D. L. Dumond, *Letters of Theodore Dwight Weld, Angelina Grimké Weld, and Sarah Grimké* (2 vols., 1934); A. H. Abel and F. J. Klingberg, *A Side-Light on Anglo-American Relations, 1839–1858, Furnished by the Correspondence of Lewis Tappan and Others with the British and Foreign Anti-Slavery Society* (1927); W. P. and F. J. Garrison, *William Lloyd Garrison* (4 vols., 1885–89); Joseph Sturge, *A Visit to the U. S. in 1841* (1842); *Am. Missionary*, Aug. 1873; *Harper's Weekly*, July 12, 1873; *N. Y. Times*, June 23, 1873.]　　　　F. J. K.

TAPPEN, FREDERICK DOBBS (Jan. 29, 1829–Feb. 28, 1902), banker, was born in New York City, one of eleven children of Charles Barclay and Elizabeth (Dobbs) Tappen. His father was a veteran of the War of 1812 and a colonel of the New York state militia. Tappen received his early education at the Columbia College Grammar School. For a year he was engaged as civil engineer on the Erie Railroad. In 1850 he became "specie clerk" at the National Bank of New York, whose title was subsequently changed to that of Gallatin National Bank. With this institution he was identified during the rest of his life, being chosen as its cashier in 1857 and serving as its president, 1868–1902. His part in the American finance of his day was of distinctive and notable character. He became known as the "banking dictator" who, in days before the creation of the Federal Reserve system and in the absence of any central banking institution in America, was invariably chosen by the New York banks, at times of financial panic, to prescribe and direct their united policy.

Tappen's view of the manner in which a formidable financial crisis should be met was based on close-range personal observation of the panic of 1857 and the Wall Street gold-market crisis of "Black Friday" 1869. The New York Clearing House Association, otherwise known as the New York Associated Banks, an organization originally formed merely to facilitate exchange of checks, had already come to exercise partial supervision over credit policies. On the outbreak of panic in 1873, Tappen was chairman of the clearing-house committee, and was at once made chairman of its special "loan committee." His first expedient was the adoption of "clearing-house certificates," a device whereby hard-pressed banks in the clearing house, instead of being required to pay their mutual debit balances in cash at a moment of panicky money-hoarding, were authorized to make such inter-bank payments in bills of credit bearing high interest rates, secured by banking collateral approved and accepted by the loan committee. This machinery was not wholly new, but 1873 was the first occasion on which it was applied in a financial panic of the traditional character. The powers exercised by Tappen in 1873 and afterward were, however, much larger than this. The emergency of that year was so critical, and general insolvency seemed so imminent, that virtual dictatorship was granted him. The principles on which he based his program, as afterward enunciated by him, were that the banks act together under dictatorial powers of the central committee; that no solvent bank be allowed to fail because of depletion of its cash reserve; that the money market be relieved, but in such a way and on such terms that the genuineness of an applicant's need for credit would be proved by his readiness to accept them. Exercising his special powers, Tappen met the panic emergency of 1873, when $26,265,000 clearing-house certificates were issued, and general suspension by banks and banking houses was averted; of 1884, when the issue was $24,915,000; of 1890, when it was $16,645,000, and of 1893, when it reached $41,490,000. On some of these occasions he was not even on the managing committee, yet was at once appointed head of a special loan committee which superseded all others. In each of these formidable crises, he determined personally the manner in which the "pooled" credit resources should be applied.

This remarkable uniformity of recourse to Tappen as dictator in a panic emergency was partly ascribed to his presidency of a relatively small New York bank, whereby he escaped professional jealousies. But it was far more directly a tribute to his promptness of decision, financial insight, courage, and unquestioned fairness and integrity. His banking associates, at the memorial meeting in 1902, described him as possessing "the rare gift of knowing when to act, how to act, and of persuading others to act with him"; of being able to "detect bad banking almost through the leather of a portfolio," and of being ready, if circumstances required, to "close a bank, under his power from this body, with less concern than he would show to give help where it is deserved." He was a man of great individual popularity, of frank and winning personality, so readily accessible that the office in which he did his work was visible at once to any

one entering the front door of the bank. He spoke French fluently, was fond of literature and music, and was an expert fisherman. He was director in several hospitals and charities, and an active churchman. He died in Lakewood, N. J. He was survived by his wife, Sarah A. B. Littell, whom he had married about 1859, and one daughter.

[*Who's Who in America*, 1901–02; obituary of Charles Barclay Tappen, in *N. Y. Tribune*, Apr. 21, 1893; *Year Book of the Holland Society of New York*, 1902, pp. 125–32; *Proc. of a Meeting . . . in Memory of Frederick D. Tappen at the Clearing House*, Mar. 10, 1902 (n.d.); W. J. Gilpin and H. E. Wallace, *N. Y. Clearing House Asso., 1854–1905* (1905); editorial in *Commercial and Financial Chronicle* (N. Y.), Mar. 8, 1902; obituaries in *N. Y. Tribune* and *N. Y. Herald*, Mar. 1, 1902.]   A. D. N.

TAPPER, BERTHA FEIRING (Jan. 25, 1859–Sept. 2, 1915), pianist, teacher, was born at Christiania, Norway, the daughter of Lars Olsen Feiring and Berthe (Iversen) Feiring. She was musically inclined from childhood and commenced her first studies in her native town with Johann Svendsen and Agathe Backer-Gröndahl. Later she went to Leipzig, Germany, where she was graduated from the conservatory of music in 1878. Three years later she came to the United States and became active as a teacher of piano and as a pianist, playing principally with chamber music groups, notably with Franz Kneisel [*q.v.*] and the Kneisel Quartet. From 1889 to 1895 she was a graduate teacher at the New England Conservatory of Music in Boston, Mass. In October 1895 she went to Vienna to study with Theodor Leschetizky and remained there until 1896 when she returned to the United States. She continued her career as a teacher and from 1905 to 1910 was an instructor of advanced piano pupils at the Institute of Musical Art in New York City. A number of her pupils, among them, Leo Ornstein, Newton Swift, and Abram Chasins, achieved distinction on the concert platform and as composers and teachers. As a teacher she possessed a keen perception of how much could be made of embryonic talent, and she always had an accurate idea of the technical equipment necessary for each pupil to achieve the goal she had set for him. Moreover, she was quick to realize how long she herself should teach each student and when he should go abroad for study to broaden his training and his imagination under new tutorship and in a new environment. She befriended and inspired her pupils; often she would take one of them to the Tapper summer home at Blue Hill, Me., for an entire season. She composed a number of piano pieces and songs and contributed articles to musical journals. Her most important published work was *Grieg's Piano Works* which she edited for the *Musician's Library* (2 volumes, 1908, 1909).

Bertha Feiring was married twice; first, to her piano instructor at the Leipzig conservatory, Louis Mass, and, second, on Sept. 22, 1895, to Thomas Tapper, musician, editor, and author of books on musical subjects. She died in Boston, where she had been taken following an illness at Blue Hill, and was buried at Canton, Mass. Her husband, a daughter, and a son by her previous marriage survived her.

[Information from the family; *Who's Who in America*, 1914–15; *Grove's Dict. of Music and Musicians, Am. Supp.* (1930); A. W. Kramer, "Bertha Feiring Tapper: Altruist," *Musical America*, Sept. 25, 1915; *Boston Evening Transcript*, Sept. 4, 1915.]

J. T. H.

TARBELL, FRANK BIGELOW (Jan. 1, 1853–Dec. 4, 1920), archaeologist, was born in West Groton, Mass., the son of John and Sarah (Fosdick) Tarbell. His father, a jeweler and watchmaker, traced his ancestry to Thomas Tarbell, who emigrated to America in 1647, lived for a time in Watertown, Mass., and later established a more permanent home in Groton. Tarbell first attended the district school of West Groton, and then studied at Lawrence Academy in Groton, 1865–68. After waiting a year he entered Yale College, where he received the degree of A.B. in 1873. He won many scholarships and prizes, and was valedictorian of his class, a member of Phi Beta Kappa, and an editor of the *Yale Literary Magazine*. Following his graduation he spent two years in Europe with a New York family and then returned to Yale as teacher and student. He received the degree of Ph.D. at Yale in 1879. He was tutor in Greek, 1876–82, and assistant professor of Greek and instructor in logic at Yale, 1882–87. During 1888–89 he served as annual director of the American School of Classical Studies at Athens; from 1889 to 1892 he was instructor in Greek at Harvard College and in 1892–93 went back to Athens as secretary of the American School. He returned to America to become a member of the faculty of the new University of Chicago. There he served as associate professor of Greek, 1892–93, and then as professor of archaeology from 1893 until 1918, when he retired from teaching and made his home in Pomfret, Conn. He died following an operation at New Haven on Dec. 4, 1920. He never married. He contributed many articles and reviews to journals, edited *The Philippics of Demosthenes* (1880), wrote *A History of Greek Art* (1896) and the descriptive matter for an *Illustrated Catalogue of Carbon Prints on the Rise and Progress of Greek and Roman Art* (1897), and in 1909 made a catalogue of the

bronzes in the Field Museum, Chicago. He was a member of the Society for the Promotion of Hellenic Studies and the Archaeological Institute of America, and served on the advisory council of the Simplified Spelling Board. At the time of his death he left a bequest to Yale College which is used for the support of instruction in classical archaeology.

Although he was one of the first among Americans to enter the field of classical archaeology and achieve distinction there, it is rather as a personality influencing students and colleagues that he will be remembered. He is described by one of his students at Yale as somewhat severe, formal, and distant in manner, yet able "'by sheer intellectual distinction and force of character" to exert the greatest personal influence upon those who studied under him, giving quite unconsciously an example of intellectual honesty and candor (William Lyon Phelps, quoted in Herrick, *post*, p. 59). Frail, shy, and reserved, with a New England frugality of speech that sometimes broke into brusqueness, he was incapable of even the casual insincerities of social intercourse, as he was incapable of any pretension. His love of beauty and his devotion to truth were seldom given expression in words. They made him, nevertheless, a fastidious and accurate scholar, marked him with an austere serenity of spirit and of bearing, and led him to follow consistently and unaffectedly, without defiance or compromise or harsh judgments, the path of his own ideals.

[C. H. Wight, *Thomas Tarbell and Some of His Descendants* (1907); *Who's Who in America*, 1920–21; *Hist. of the Yale Class of 1873* (n.d.); *Fifth Supp. to the Hist. of the Yale Class of 1873 ... 1926*; Robert Herrick, in *Univ. Record* (Univ. of Chicago), Jan. 1921; *Yale Univ. Obit. Record of Grads.* (1921), pp. 86–88; obituaries in *Am. Jour. of Archaeology*, Jan.–Mar. 1921, p. 85, and *Chicago Daily Tribune*, Dec. 6, 1920.]

R. H.

TARBELL, JOSEPH (c. 1780–Nov. 25, 1815), naval officer, was probably a native of Massachusetts. In December 1798 he was appointed a midshipman on the *Constitution* and served on board her during the naval war with France. He was with that ship when she captured the *Sandwich* and for a time was the prize-master of the prize. On Aug. 25, 1800, he was promoted lieutenant. Retained under the peace establishment of 1801, he was ordered to the *Essex*. In 1803 he sailed for the Mediterranean as a lieutenant of the *Constitution* and two years later returned home in the *President*. As one of the officers of Commodore Edward Preble [*q.v.*], he was included in the resolution of Congress of Mar. 3, 1805, expressing the thanks of that body for the gallantry and good conduct displayed in the attacks on Tripoli in 1804 (2 *U. S. Statutes at Large,* 346). After service at Havre de Grace, Md., on ordnance duty, he was made master of the Washington navy yard in 1806. In 1807 he joined the gunboat flotilla of Capt. Stephen Decatur [*q.v.*] and in the following year was a member of the court that tried Capt. James Barron [*q.v.*] after the *Chesapeake-Leopard* affair. On Apr. 25, 1808, he was commissioned master commandant. In 1810–11, as commander of the *Siren,* he helped to enforce the embargo at Charleston, S. C., and the suppression of the slave trade at New Orleans. In 1811 after preparing the *Hornet* for sea at Washington, he was ordered to take command of the *John Adams* at Boston. His principal service during the War of 1812 was performed at Norfolk where he commanded first the *Constellation* and later the gunboat flotilla. On June 20, 1813, fifteen gunboats under his command engaged the *Junon,* 38, and two other small frigates, becalmed at Hampton Roads, with a slight loss on each side. This was the chief event in his naval career. He remained with the flotilla until the end of the war, being promoted captain in July 1813. In 1808 he married Eliza Cassin, the daughter of a naval officer; he died in Washington, D. C., survived by his wife and their two daughters. In 1918 a torpedo-boat destroyer was named for him.

[Bureau of Navigation, Record of Officers, 1798–1817; Naval Archives, 1798–1815: Letters to Officers, Sps. of War, Appointments and Resignations, Nominations and Appointments, Officers' Letters and Captains' Letters; Niles' *Weekly Register,* July 3, 1813; Abel Bowen, *The Naval Monument* (1840); Theodore Roosevelt, *The Naval War of 1812* (1882); *Sen. Doc. 92, 26 Cong., 1 Sess.; Norfolk and Portsmouth Herald,* Dec. 1, 1815; *Daily National Intelligencer,* Nov. 27, 1815; Veterans' Administration, Pension Files, War of 1812; Probate Court Files, Washington, D. C.]   C. O. P.

TARBOX, INCREASE NILES (Feb. 11, 1815–May 3, 1888), author, clergyman, was born in East (later South) Windsor, Conn., the son of Thomas and Lucy (Porter) Tarbox, and a descendant of John Tarbox who was in Lynn, Mass., in 1639. Orphaned at nine, he lived with an uncle from 1825 to 1829, worked on a farm in East Windsor, and attended the common schools. At eighteen he began teaching in a district school. He attended the academy at East Hartford for a time in order to prepare for college and in 1839 received the degree of A.B. from Yale. After teaching for two years in the East Hartford academy, he served at Yale as tutor in Latin (1842–44) and studied in the Divinity School. He was graduated in 1844 and ordained in November of the same year at the Hollis Evangelical (later the Plymouth Con-

gregational) Church in Framingham, Mass., where he served until 1851. On June 4, 1845, he was married to Delia (or Adelia) Augusta Waters of Millbury, Mass., by whom he had a son and three daughters. He was a founder and one of the original editors (1849–51) of the *Congregationalist.* In 1851 he gave up his church in Framingham to become secretary of the American Education Society (reorganized in 1874 as the American College and Education Society), and from that time until 1884, when he retired, he devoted himself to the work of providing help to students preparing for the ministry. Possessed of a balanced judgment, and being by nature sympathetic and kindly, he was markedly successful in the work.

His literary interests, which were strong, manifested themselves in various ways. He wrote juveniles for Sunday schools, poems—sometimes devotional, sometimes mildly satirical—and numerous articles on historical, religious, and literary subjects, which appeared in the *Congregational Quarterly,* the *New Englander,* and other magazines. Among his books are *Missionary Patriots: Memoirs of James H. Schneider and Edward M. Schneider* (1867), *Life of Israel Putnam . . . Major-General in the Continental Army* (1876), and *Songs and Hymns for Common Life* (1885). He edited *Sir Walter Ralegh and His Colony in America* (1884), with a memoir, for the Prince Society, and the *Diary of Thomas Robbins, D.D., 1796–1854* (2 vols., 1886–87). From 1881 to 1888, as historiographer of the New England Historic Genealogical Society, he wrote numerous brief, careful memoirs of members of the society, as well as seven more extensive biographies, which appeared in the *New England Historical and Genealogical Register.* It is for such articles as these that he is best remembered. Without great importance individually, these notes and memoirs form when taken together an interesting and valuable record. What Tarbox said of another writer on genealogical subjects might be said with equal truth of him: "It is a most fortunate thing for the world at large, that a few men have such natural or acquired tastes for certain kinds of literary work, that they will do it, regardless of trouble or expense . . ." (*New Englander,* April 1876, p. 280). He himself may be credited with the "large share of 'love to being in general' " which he attributes to such writers. The benignity of his appearance was, it is said, "the true index of a real benignity of character" (Stiles, *post,* p. 749). He was gentle and sensitive, perhaps even over-sensitive, yet in matters of conviction firm and independent. He died in

West Newton, Mass., where he had lived since 1860, survived by two of his daughters. He was buried in Framingham.

[H. M. Dexter, in *New England Hist. and Geneal. Reg.*, Jan. 1890; H. R. Stiles, *The Hist. and Geneals. of Ancient Windsor, Conn.*, vol. II (1892); *Vital Records of Millbury, Mass.* (1903); *Obit. Records Grads. Yale Univ. . . . 1880–90* (1890); *Fourteenth Ann. Report . . . Am. Coll. and Educ. Soc. . . . May 21, 1888*; *Congregationalist*, May 10, 1888; death notice and obituary in *Boston Evening Transcript*, May 4, 1888.]
D. G—d.

TARR, RALPH STOCKMAN (Jan. 15, 1864–Mar. 21, 1912), geologist, geographer, teacher, was born in Gloucester, Mass. He was the son of Silas Stockman Tarr, a contractor, and Abigail (Saunders) Tarr, and a descendant of Richard Tarr, first settler of Rockport, Mass. After his graduation from high school in 1881, he attended the summer school of zoölogy at Salem and in the autumn entered Harvard as a special student at Lawrence Scientific School. His course was interrupted several times and he did not take his degree for ten years. In the meantime, however, he had done summer work under the zoölogists Alpheus Hyatt and Spencer F. Baird [*qq.v.*], had spent a winter in the Smithsonian Institution, and in the employ of the United States Geological Survey had carried on intensive investigations on Cape Ann, the results of which were used by Professor Nathaniel Southgate Shaler [*q.v.*] in his monograph *The Geology of Cape Ann* (1890), with the wholehearted acknowledgment that "the larger part of the field observations" had been made by his assistant. Tarr had also mapped glacial moraines in Massachusetts for the Survey, and had done geological field work in New Mexico, Montana, and Texas. In 1890 he returned to Cambridge as an assistant to Shaler, and completed his work for the degree of B.S. in 1891.

On Mar. 28, 1892, he married Kate Story of Gloucester, and later the same year was appointed assistant professor of geology at Cornell University. In 1906 he was made full professor and head of the department of physical geography. He organized the Cornell Greenland Expedition which went north on Peary's ship in 1896, and in 1909 and 1911 conducted the National Geographic Society's expeditions to Alaska. He also took advantage of the opportunities which the country near Ithaca offered him to study physiographic and glacial problems and drainage, and investigated the geological history of the Finger Lake region, making surveys and a complete areal study under the auspices of the United States Geological Survey. The year before his death he was given charge of the Cor-

nell seismographic station. He died in Ithaca, survived by his wife, a son, and a daughter.

Tarr was president of the Association of American Geographers (1911–12), foreign correspondent of the Geological Society of London, and a member of several other professional societies. He served on the International Committee on Glaciers, and was elected corresponding member of the Royal Geographical Society of Vienna shortly before his death. He was an associate editor of the *Bulletin of the American Geographical Society* from 1899 to 1911 and of the *Journal of Geography* from 1902 to 1912. He was the author of widely used textbooks, including *The Economic Geology of the United States* (1893), *Elementary Physical Geography* (1895), *First Book of Physical Geography* (1897), *Elementary Geology* (1897), the school geographies (1900) prepared in collaboration with Frank Morton McMurry, *New Physical Geography* (1904), and *College Physiography* (published posthumously in 1914). His professional publications include *The Physical Geography of New York State* (1902) and contributions to the Geological Survey dealing with the Yakutat Bay region in Alaska and the Watkins Glen region of New York. With Lawrence Martin he wrote *Alaskan Glacier Studies* (1914), awarded the gold medal of the Société de Géographie de Paris. Tarr also wrote scores of short scientific papers and geographical reviews and contributed a number of articles to *Johnson's Encyclopedia,* the *International Encyclopedia,* and the tenth edition of the *Encyclopedia Britannica.* His contributions to glaciology included studies of the relation of eskers, kames, and kettle holes to the ice sheet, the significance of hanging valleys and other features of glacial erosion, the nature of ablation moraine and of the through glacier, the rôle of earthquakes in glacial advance, and the cause of flowage in ice. He also verified, through his researches near the living glaciers in Greenland, Alaska, Norway, Spitzbergen, and the Alps, the deductions drawn from similar phenomena in far-removed regions of former glaciation. A contemporary authority said that Tarr's studies of the dislocation giving rise to the Alaskan earthquake of 1899 were "a most important addition to our knowledge of the relation of earthquakes and faults, with accompanying changes of level of the land in relation to the sea" (Woodworth, *post,* p. 37). His work on the peneplain, on extended rivers, and on rifting in granite, was also important.

[A. P. Brigham, in *Annals of the Asso. of Am. Geographers,* vol. III (1913); J. B. Woodworth, in *Bull. Geol. Soc. of America,* vol. XXIV (1913), with

bibliog.; Lawrence Martin, in *Zeitschrift für Gletscherkunde*, vol. IX (1914), with bibliog. of Tarr's writings on glaciers and glaciation by E. F. Bean; W. T. Hewett, *Cornell Univ., A Hist.* (1905), vol. II; *Cornell Alumni News*, Mar. 26, 1913; *Harvard Coll. Class of 1891, Secretary's Report*, No. 4 (1906), No. 5 (1911); *Who's Who in America*, 1912–13; *Am. Men of Science*, 1910; *N. Y. Times*, Mar. 22, 1912.]
K. M.

TASHUNCA-UITCO [See CRAZY HORSE, *c.* 1849–1877].

TASHRAK [See Zevin, Israel Joseph, 1872–1926].

TATHAM, WILLIAM (Apr. 13, 1752–Feb. 22, 1819), civil engineer and geographer, was born at Hutton-in-the-Forest, Cumberland, England, eldest son of the Rev. Sandford Tatham and his wife, a daughter of Henry Marsden of Gisborne Hall, Yorkshire (John and J. A. Venn, *Alumni Cantabrigienses*, pt. 1, vol. IV, 1927). Sent to Virginia in 1769 to seek his fortune, he became a clerk in the trading house of Carter & Trent, on James River. Early in 1776 he removed to the Watauga settlement in the Tennessee country, where he was employed in the mercantile establishment of John Carter. For a time he was clerk of the celebrated Watauga Association. He drafted the petition (July 5, 1776) of the inhabitants on the western waters praying for incorporation into the government of North Carolina (J. G. M. Ramsay, *The Annals of Tennessee*, 1853, pp. 134–38). Throughout the Revolution he served the American cause intermittently, taking part first in the defense of Fort Caswell-on-Watauga in July 1776, and last in the operations at Yorktown, October 1781.

In 1780, in collaboration with Col. John Todd of Kentucky, Tatham prepared a "History of the Western Country," which is said to have received the approbation of Jefferson. This work was never printed and the manuscript has been lost. After a brief mercantile venture in Philadelphia and a visit to Havana in 1783, Tatham returned to Virginia where he became clerk of the council of state. He studied law under Samuel Hardy, a member of the council, and subsequently under William R. Davie [*q.v.*] of North Carolina, and was admitted to the bar Mar. 24, 1784. He was a delegate from Robeson County in the general assembly of North Carolina in 1787, and was elected by that body a lieutenant-colonel of militia. After a visit to England, he was prevailed upon to organize a geographical department for Virginia, and in 1791 published *A Topographical Analysis of the Commonwealth of Virginia for 1790–91*.

Tatham returned in 1792 to the Tennessee country, where he practised law, mapped the region, and gathered considerable materials for its history. Visiting Spain in 1796 on a mysterious mission connected with affairs in the West, he was ordered to leave the country. Removing to London, he devoted much time to literary pursuits, contributing to magazines and publishing works on engineering and agricultural subjects: *A Plan for Insulating the Metropolis by a Canal* (1797); *Remarks on Inland Canals* (1798); *The Political Economy of the Inland Navigation* (1799); *An Historical and Practical Essay on the Culture and Commerce of Tobacco* (1800); *Auxiliary Remarks on an Essay on the Comparative Advantages of Oxen in Tillage* (1801); *National Irrigation* (1801); *Report on a View of Certain Impediments and Obstructions, in the Navigation of the River Thames* (1803); and *Navigation and Conservancy of the River Thames* (1803). In 1801 he was appointed superintendent of construction of the elaborate Wapping Docks in the Thames at London.

Returning to America in 1805, Tatham was engaged for some years in a survey of the coast from Cape Fear to Cape Hatteras. In that field he was a pioneer. He was an assiduous collector of manuscript maps and historical data, and his invaluable collection was offered for sale, without success, to Congress in 1806 and again in 1817. In his proposal of 1806 (*American State Papers, Miscellaneous*, I, 1834, pp. 457 ff.), Tatham was probably the first to define the functions of a national library for the United States (W. D. Johnston, *History of the Library of Congress*, 1904, I, 50). He spent about five years as draftsman and geographer in the Department of State at Washington, and in 1817 President Monroe gave him a comfortable position in the government arsenal on James River.

Tatham was the friend and correspondent of Jefferson and other statesmen of his times, and collaborated with Robert Fulton in the field of canalization. He was a man of brilliant parts and great versatility, but was eccentric and lacking in mental poise. He had become addicted to the use of intoxicants and in a moment of intemperance stepped in front of a gun about to be fired in a salute and was killed instantly. Papers he left and his conversation previously indicated that the act was deliberate. He was unmarried.

[S. C. Williams, "William Tatham, Wataugan," in *Tenn. Hist. Mag.* for Oct. 1921, also printed separately (1923) under same title; *Public Characters of 1801–1802* (1804); *The Ann. Biog. and Obituary for the Year 1820* (1820), pp. 149–68, an excellent sketch, with autobiog. material and a list of Tatham's publications; G. W. Munford, *The Two Parsons* (1884);

Calendar of Va. State Papers, vols. V, VI (1885–86); *The State Records of N. C.,* vols. XX (1902), XXIV (1905); *Schedule of Vouchers, Tending to Prove that William Tatham Has Served the U. S. Near Forty Years* (1815); *Gentleman's Mag.* (London), Apr. 1819; *Richmond Enquirer,* Feb. 23, 25, and autobiog. sketch, Mar. 2, 1819.]   S. C. W.

TATTNALL, JOSIAH (Nov. 9, 1795–June 14, 1871), naval officer, was born at the family estate "Bonaventure," a few miles below Savannah, Ga., the son of Josiah and Harriet (Fenwick) Tattnall. His paternal great-grandfather, who came to South Carolina in 1700, was of English and French stock; his mother was of English stock. He was left an orphan when he was nine years of age and in his tenth year was sent to London to be educated under the supervision of his maternal grandfather. He remained abroad six years. A few months after his return home he was, on Mar. 10, 1812, appointed midshipman. After a few weeks of instruction in the naval school of Andrew Hunter [*q.v.*] at the Washington navy yard he was ordered to the *Constellation,* which, because of the blockade, remained at Hampton Roads throughout the war. In the engagement of Craney Island, Va., on June 22, 1813, he received his first baptism of fire and was one of a party that waded out from shore to take possession of the barges of the enemy.

The following year, after assisting in conveying reinforcements to Lake Erie, he was sent to the *Epervier* at Savannah where he was stationed when the war ended. Continuing with this vessel when she was attached to the squadron of Stephen Decatur, 1779–1820 [*q.v.*], he participated in 1815 in the war with Algiers. He was promoted to the rank of lieutenant on Apr. 1, 1818, and soon afterwards joined the *Macedonian* at Baltimore and made an extensive cruise in the Pacific. At Valparaiso, offended by the remarks of an English naval officer depreciating the part of the United States in the late war, he challenged him and wounded him in a duel. A period of professional study at Partridge's military school at Norwich, Vt., was followed in 1823 by an uneventful cruise in the West Indies as first lieutenant of the *Jackal,* one of Commodore David Porter's vessels engaged in suppressing piracy in the West Indies. After a tour of duty in the Mediterranean, 1825–26, he was again in the West Indies, this time on board the *Erie.* At St. Bartholomew he commanded a boat expedition that captured the piratical privateer *Federal.* In 1829 he was in charge of a survey of the Tortugas reefs and keys off the Florida coast. In 1831–32 he commanded the *Grampus* during a cruise off the

Mexican and Texas coast for the protection of American commerce, a service marked by the capture of the Mexican schooner *Montezuma.* In 1837 he conveyed to Vera Cruz on board the *Pioneer* the Mexican general, Santa Anna, captured by the Texans at San Jacinto.

He was promoted commander in 1838 and soon was made commandant of the Boston navy yard. In 1840 he was associated with Matthew C. Perry [*q.v.*] in ordnance experiments. Service in the Mediterranean as commander of the *Fairfield* was shortly brought to an end by reason of differences with his commodore, and he subsequently commanded the *Saratoga* of the African Squadron, 1843–44. In the Mexican War he had a conspicuous part in the navy's operations on the east coast of Mexico. In charge of the mosquito division with the *Spitfire* as his flagship, he bombarded the city of Vera Cruz and the Castle of St. Juan d'Ulloa and exhibited great daring. In the capture of Túxpan the *Spitfire* was in the lead and began the action, her commander receiving a wound in the arm. Tattnall returned to the United States with his health impaired. His native state recognized his services in the war with a vote of thanks and the gift of a sword.

After two years at the Boston navy yard he was ordered to the *Saranac* and sent to Cuba to maintain American rights imperiled by a revolution. He next took command of the naval station at Pensacola. In the meantime he had been promoted captain from Feb. 6, 1850. Ordered to the *Independence,* he cruised in the Pacific during 1854–55, until a difference with his commodore over questions of discipline led to his return to the United States. Dismissing the charges against him, the department ordered him to the naval station at Sacketts Harbor, N. Y. On Sept. 17, 1857, he was detached from this duty and appointed to the command of the squadron on the East India station. His most important work there was in connection with the negotiation of new treaties with China by the Occidental powers. He placed every facility of the fleet at the disposal of the American envoy. When the British fleet was defeated in 1859 at the mouth of the Pei-ho River he gave aid to the British that under the circumstances violated the neutrality of the United States. In explanation of his conduct he quoted the adage "Blood is thicker than water." The American government upheld his acts and the British government expressed its thanks to President Buchanan. When late in life he was in need of funds some British officers subscribed a sum of money for his relief. In 1860 he returned to

San Francisco on the *Powhatan,* giving passage to a numerous embassy of Japanese officials. Soon afterwards he was again assigned to the command of the Sacketts Harbor naval station, his last duty as an officer of the American navy.

Although opposed to secession, Tattnall was loyal to his native state and resigned from the navy on Feb. 20, 1861, to accept the appointment of senior flag officer of the Georgia navy in the Civil War. In March he was made a captain in the Confederate States Navy and shortly took command of the naval defenses of Georgia and South Carolina, improvising a small fleet with the *Savannah* as flagship. In November in Port Royal Sound, he ineffectually opposed the superior Union fleet, and early in the following year cooperated with the Confederate army in the defense of Fort Pulaski. On Mar. 29, 1862, he succeeded Franklin Buchanan [*q.v.*] in command of the naval defenses in the waters of Virginia with the ironclad *Merrimac,* renamed the *Virginia,* as his flagship. Several times he attempted to effect an engagement with the *Monitor* but the latter declined the challenge. In May when Norfolk was abandoned, he burned the *Merrimac* to prevent her capture. Tattnall was severely criticized, but a court martial upheld his action. Returning to Savannah in April he again took command of the Georgia naval defenses until March 1863. After that his activities were confined to Savannah, where he remained until December 1864 when the city was occupied by Sherman. Destroying the public property in his charge, he retreated to Augusta and was captured with the army of General Johnston. He was paroled in May 1865.

In 1866 he took up his residence with his family near Halifax, Nova Scotia, where he lived for four years. In January 1870 he was appointed to the office of inspector of the port of Savannah, holding it until his death. On Sept. 6, 1821, he had been married to Harriette Fenwick Jackson, who, with several daughters and a son, survived him.

[Bureau of Navigation, Record of Officers, 1809–63; D. E. Huger Smith, "An Account of the Tattnall and Fenwick Families in South Carolina," *S. C. Hist. and Geneal. Mag.,* Jan. 1913; F. F. Starr, *The Edward Jackson Family* (1895); C. C. Jones, *The Life and Services of Comm. Josiah Tattnall* (1878); *War of the Rebellion: Official Records* (*Navy*), vol. VII (1898), XII (1901), XVI (1903); J. T. Scharf, *Hist. of the Confed. States Navy* (1887); R. W. Neeser, *Statistical and Chronological Hist. of the U. S. Navy* (1909); Tyler Dennett, *Americans in Eastern Asia* (1922); Horatio Bridge, *Jour. of an African Cruiser* (1845); articles by W. H. Shock, *United States,* May 1892, C. O. Paullin, *Proc. U. S. Naval Institute,* June 1911, E. S. Maclay, *Ibid.,* July–Aug. 1914; *Savannah Daily Republican,* June 15, 16, 17, 1871.]   C. O. P.

TAUSSIG, WILLIAM (Feb. 28, 1826–July 10, 1913), physician, business man, civic leader, was born in Prague, Bohemia, fourth among some fifteen children of John L. Taussig and Charlotte (Bondy), his wife. Hebrew blood ran in the veins of his father, a native of Prague who manufactured cotton goods on a small scale. Completing the classical course in the University of Prague at eighteen, William turned to the study of chemistry and three years later emigrated to New York. The next year found him in St. Louis, Mo., chemist for Charless, Blow & Company, frontier druggists. During the cholera scourge which swept the city in 1849 he distinguished himself by his fearlessness as apothecary at quarantine. A year later he received the degree of M.D. from the St. Louis Medical College and established himself for practice in nearby Carondelet, of which town he was elected mayor in 1852. On May 3, 1857, he married Adele Wuerpel of St. Louis, daughter of a German teacher who had quit the Rhineland in 1848.

On the reorganization, in 1859, of the St. Louis county court, an executive body, Taussig was elected one of the five reform members. Among his first official acts was a report on the application of U. S. Grant to be superintendent of county roads—unfavorable, because he was not sure of Grant's loyalty to the Union. In general, however, he administered so wisely the affairs of the county, torn as it was between two camps during the forepart of the Civil War, that he was reëlected in 1863 and designated presiding judge. Following the destruction of an insane asylum in Fulton, Mo., by marauders and the failure of the state to provide relief for the homeless unfortunates, he at personal risk took them to St. Louis where they were lodged first in St. Vincent Asylum and later in the city insane asylum, the cornerstone of which he laid in 1864. During the war he held the post of examining surgeon for drafted soldiers.

Compelled, through long illness, to give up the medical profession, he was appointed collector of internal revenue by Lincoln in January 1865, and was thereby led to a complete change of career. After resigning the collectorship (1866) he turned to banking, and was president of the Traders' Bank from 1866 to 1869. Following the liquidation of the bank, he became associated with the project to bridge the Mississippi at St. Louis, and soon became the manager, later president, of the bridge company. In this capacity he faced business problems almost as great as the structural problems which confronted the bridge's engineer, James Buchanan Eads [*q.v.*].

The bridge company and others growing out of it were merged in 1889 in the Terminal Railroad Association, of which Taussig remained president until his retirement in 1896. Through his judgment and foresight, and because of the confidence of railway executives in his integrity and impartiality, all railroads entering the city joined in the establishment of a single union station—a traffic reform of the first importance. The station built under his administration was the finest of its time.

When he died of pneumonia in his eighty-seventh year, he was still head of the bridge company, a director in the St. Louis Union Trust Company, a director of Washington University, president of the Self-Culture Hall and Tenement House associations, and active in the Ethical Society. In memory of his service as president of the St. Louis board of education a public school was named for him. He was survived by his widow, a daughter, and two sons. His body was cremated and the ashes placed in Bellefontaine Cemetery. In politics he was associated with Carl Schurz, B. Gratz Brown, William M. Grosvenor, Henry T. Blow, and Emil Preetorius [qq.v.] in promoting the Liberal Republican movement. A model citizen, a cultured gentleman, practical yet imaginative, industrious and generous—he long gave shoes and clothing to needy school children anonymously—he was unusually well fitted for meeting the problems that came with the rise of the city.

[*Who's Who in America*, 1912–13; Wm. Hyde and H. L. Conard, *Encyc. of the Hist. of St. Louis* (1899), vol. IV; C. M. Woodward, *A Hist. of the St. Louis Bridge* (1881); Taussig's own "Personal Recollections of General Grant," in *Mo. Hist. Soc. Pubs.*, vol. II, no. 3 (1903), and his "Development of St. Louis Terminals" in "Addresses of the St. Louis Commercial Club" (St. Louis Public Library); *St. Louis Globe-Democrat*, July 11, 1913 and July 23, 1922; information from a son, Prof. F. W. Taussig.]　　　　　　　　I. D.

TAWNEY, JAMES ALBERTUS (Jan. 3, 1855–June 12, 1919), representative in Congress from Minnesota, son of John E. and Sarah (Boblitz) Tawney, was born in Mount Pleasant Township, near Gettysburg, Pa. He is said to have been a descendant of John Tawney, who emigrated from England and landed at Baltimore about 1650. Leaving school at fourteen, he was trained by his father, a farmer and blacksmith, to follow in his footsteps; later he also learned the machinist's trade. After working in a machine shop in western Pennsylvania he went west and in 1877 established himself in Winona, Minn., where he worked at his trade, studied law by himself and in the office of Bentley and Vance, and was admitted to the bar (1882). He finished his legal training with a term in the law school of the University of Wisconsin (1882–83). At Winona he was married on Dec. 19, 1883, to Emma B. Newell. As in the case of many young lawyers, his legal work was a stepping-stone to politics. In 1890 he was elected to the state Senate; in 1892 he was chosen to represent the first district of Minnesota in Congress and continued to be reëlected until his defeat in 1910. From the beginning he was an old-line Republican. Unquestioned ability, regularity, and length of service secured for him a position on the committee on ways and means from 1895 to 1905, on the committee on insular affairs from December 1899, and, in 1905, the chairmanship of the committee on appropriations. He was one of the quintet, along with Joseph Gurney Cannon [q.v.], S. E. Payne, John Dalzell [q.v.], and J. S. Sherman, which dominated the House until the smash of 1910.

In his first session Tawney demonstrated his Republicanism by making an attack on the proposal to repeal the Federal Election Law, by advocating increased duties on barley (which gained for him the sobriquet of "Barley Jim"), and by bringing forward pension bills on every possible occasion. In 1897 he took a leading part in framing the Dingley Tariff, having especial care for the lumber interests of his state (Tawney Papers, *post*). He was, indeed, always considered especially tender toward lumber interests (Folwell, *post*, p. 250). A consistent protectionist, he was opposed to special favors for Cuban sugar, but he believed in free trade between the United States and Puerto Rico as a "permanent policy" (letter to A. T. Stebbins, Mar. 1, 1900, Tawney Papers, *post*), although he supported the Foraker Bill as a temporary expedient. He had a voice in dissuading Roosevelt from pressing revision of the tariff when the latter was inclined to urge a special session for the purpose (Theodore Roosevelt to Tawney, Nov. 10, 17, 1904, *Ibid.*). Tawney was more or less a national figure from his position in the House, and his notoriety, if not fame, was enhanced by a clash with Roosevelt over appropriations for the secret service division of the Treasury Department in 1908. Following Roosevelt's caustic reference to the matter in his annual message of 1908, the House, wounded in its *amour propre*, tabled that portion of the message as well as a special message explanatory of the passage, thus upholding Tawney, who had been mentioned by name and who defended himself and the committee from what were considered personal aspersions (*Congressional Record*, 60 Cong., 2 Sess., pp. 660–64). This episode brought almost immediate repercussions. A defender of the Payne-

Aldrich Tariff, Tawney further weakened his position with his constituents, already shaken by the brush with the President. William Howard Taft's defense of Tawney, along with the tariff act, in the famous Winona speech and Roosevelt's speech attacking him contributed to his defeat in the election of 1910. An appointment to the international joint commission on the United States–Canadian boundary provided him with a lame duck's refuge and the only political position he held until his death at Excelsior Springs, Mo., in 1919. He was survived by his wife and five of his six children.

[*Who's Who in America*, 1918–19; *Biog. Dir. Am. Cong.* (1928); Tawney Papers, in the Minn. Hist. Soc. colls.; W. W. Folwell, *A Hist. of Minn.*, vol. IV (1930); *Current Lit.*, Nov. 1909, pp. 477–78, 481; *Independent*, May 28, 1908, pp. 1185–90; *Am. Rev. of Revs.*, Jan. 1909, pp. 39–41; E. V. Smalley, *A Hist. of the Republican Party* (1896); H. F. Stevens, *Hist. of the Bench and Bar of Minn.* (2 vols., 1904); Theodore Christianson, *Minn.*, vol. III (1935), pp. 27–30; obituary in *Minneapolis Jour.*, June 12, 1919.]   L.B.S.

TAYLOR, ALFRED ALEXANDER (Aug. 6, 1848–Nov. 24, 1931), congressman, governor of Tennessee, the third of the nine children of Nathaniel Green and Emmeline (Haynes) Taylor, was born in Happy Valley, Carter County, Tenn. His ancestors on his mother's side were among the founders of the Watauga settlement in 1769, and were leaders in the establishment of the Watauga Association and in the government of the state of Franklin. His father, a graduate of the College of New Jersey (later Princeton), was a prominent lawyer, preacher, and Whig politician, who served both before and after the Civil War as representative in Congress from Tennessee. Educated at Duffield Academy, Elizabethton, Tenn., at Pennington Seminary, Pennington, N. J., and at Buffalo Institute (later Milligan College), Milligan, Tenn., Taylor served briefly under his father in Washington, studied law, and, following his admission to the bar in 1870, established himself in Jonesboro, Tenn. Turning to politics almost immediately, he served as a member of the lower House of the Tennessee legislature in 1875–76. Because of his ready wit and his ability as a speaker he made such a strong popular appeal as a Republican campaigner in the state election of 1882 that he was selected by his party as its candidate for governor in 1886 in a futile effort to prevent the nomination of his brother, Robert Love Taylor [*q.v.*] by the Democrats. The result was a unique and picturesque political campaign in which the two brothers canvassed the state in joint debate, attracting widespread attention more because of their ability as entertainers than because of the issues involved in the campaign.

Soon labelled "Alf" and "Bob" by popular fancy, they waged a bloodless "War of the Roses" in which the weapons were droll anecdotes, scintillating repartee, and a matching of their skill as fiddlers.

When "Bob" won the election, "Alf" returned to his law practice, and in 1888 was elected representative in Congress from the first Tennessee district, serving in this capacity from March 1889 to March 1895. Upon his retirement from Congress, he joined his brother in a lyceum lecture tour of the United States, and later divided his time between his law practice and frequent lecture engagements until the Republican landslide of 1920 brought his election to the governorship. After serving one term (1921–23) as governor, he was defeated for reëlection and retired to his home near Johnson City, Tenn., where he spent the remainder of his life. He was married on June 22, 1881, to Jennie Anderson of Buffalo Valley, Tenn., by whom he had ten children. He was survived by six sons and two daughters. On the whole his direct influence upon the political affairs of Tennessee was perhaps slight; but indirectly, through his close association with his more famous brother, he contributed much toward encouraging the rural voters of the state to assert themselves. In his old age he attributed the success with which he and his brother met to the fact that, "We played the fiddle, were fond of dogs, and loved our fellow men."

[*Who's Who in America*, 1930–31; *Biog. Directory of the Am. Cong.* (1928); D. M. Robison, *Bob Taylor and the Agrarian Revolt in Tenn.* (1935); DeLong Rice, *"Old Limber," or the Tale of the Taylors* (copr. 1921); P. D. Augsburg, *Bob and Alf Taylor* (1925); *Notable Men of Tenn.* (1905), ed. by John Allison; obituary in *Nashville Banner*, Nov. 25, 1931.]   W.C.B.

TAYLOR, ARCHIBALD ALEXANDER EDWARD (Aug. 27, 1834–Apr. 23, 1903), Presbyterian clergyman and educator, was born in Springfield, Ohio, the son of Edward Taylor, a physician, and Penelope Virginia (Gordon) Taylor. After attending the school of E. S. Brooks in Cincinnati, he studied seven years in Princeton, graduating from the College of New Jersey in 1854 and from the Theological Seminary in 1857. He then entered the ministry of the Old School Presbyterian Church, being licensed by the Presbytery of Cincinnati on June 17, 1857, and ordained by the Presbytery of Louisville on May 6, 1858. At ordination he was installed as pastor of the church at Portland, Ky., which he had been serving since September 1857. Subsequently, he was pastor of the First Church of Dubuque, Iowa (1859–65), the Bridge

Street Church of Georgetown, D. C. (1865–69), and the Mount Auburn Church of Cincinnati (1869–73). In 1870–71 he was editor of *Our Monthly.*

He was elected president of the University of Wooster, Ohio, in 1873, being the second to occupy that office. During the ten years of his incumbency he did his principal work, ably and successfully managing the affairs of the institution and holding influential relations with the students. His contribution to its development was acknowledged in 1902 by the naming of a new building Taylor Hall. While president he was also professor of Biblical instruction and apologetics. After his resignation of the presidency in 1883, he was absent from Wooster for two years, but returned in 1885 to serve for three years as professor of logic and political science. He was a trustee of the university from 1873 to 1902, and president of the board of trustees during the last seven of these years. In 1888 he became editor of *The Mid-Continent,* a Presbyterian weekly published in St. Louis, which position he held until 1891. For part of this time he was in charge of the Presbyterian church in Ferguson, Mo. From 1892 to 1899 he was pastor of Westminister Presbyterian Church of Columbus, Ohio. Thereafter he lived in Columbus in declining strength until his death. He had the unusual distinction of being five times moderator of his Synod, and he was four times a commissioner to the General Assembly, a member of the Presbyterian boards of education and church erection, and a director of Western and McCormick theological seminaries. He wrote numerous articles for religious periodicals, and published sermons and addresses and a volume of verse entitled *Claudia Procula and Other Verses* (1899).

Taylor was an unusually interesting and attractive personality. He had a fertile mind, with a good deal of poetic imagination. He was long remembered for his kindliness, cheerfulness, and good conversation. As pastor and teacher he showed a gift for winning the confidence of all sorts of people. His humor was abundant and lively—in the view of some, to a degree beyond what befitted a minister. He had a large library and read in many fields with fine appreciation. He was a hunter and fisherman and lover of the woods. On Aug. 2, 1858, at Freehold, N. J., he was married to Annie Vanderveer, who died in 1867; and on May 21, 1868, at Munson Hill, Va., to Lucy Eleanor Munson, who survived him as did also a son by his first wife and a daughter by the second.

[*Princeton Theological Sem., Necrological Report* (1904); *Who's Who in America,* 1901–02; *The Presbyterian* (Phila.), Apr. 29, 1903; *Ohio State Jour.*

(Columbus), Apr. 24, 1903; report of board of trustees of University of Wooster, in minutes of the Ohio Synod, 1903; information from College of Wooster (formerly University) and from Edward Taylor of Xenia, Ohio, a grandson.]   R. H. N.

TAYLOR, BAYARD (Jan. 11, 1825–Dec. 19, 1878), traveler, translator, man of letters, was born at Kennett Square, Chester County, Pa. His earliest American ancestor, Robert Taylor, had come from England with William Penn and had settled near Brandywine Creek. There the Taylors had remained purely English and strictly Quaker until John Taylor, grandfather of Bayard, married Ann Bucher, of a Swiss Mennonite family, and was expelled from meeting. John Taylor's son Joseph married Rebecca Bauer Way, of English and German stock. The Swiss and German strains, however, did not disturb the Quaker discipline of the household in which Bayard Taylor was brought up. The village of Kennett Square and the Taylor homestead, a mile away, were quiet, orderly, and—for him—dull. At fourteen he was told by a lecturing phrenologist, Thomas Dunn English [q.v.], that he would be a traveler and a poet. His poems, which he began to write as early as seven, were symptoms of his restlessness. Neither they nor his studies at Bolmar's Academy in West Chester and at the Unionville academy could satisfy his intense hunger for the world beyond his Quaker horizon. He wrote to John Sartain [q.v.] asking to be apprenticed as engraver. He was apprenticed instead to the printer of the West Chester *Village Record* at seventeen. Poetry helped him to escape. Having attracted the attention of Rufus Wilmot Griswold [q.v.], editor of *Graham's Magazine* and anthologist of the American ephemerides, Taylor was encouraged to publish his first volume of verse, *Ximena* (1844), and was enabled to get free of his apprenticeship. With money advanced by the *Saturday Evening Post* and the *United States Gazette* of Philadelphia for letters which he was to send back from his travels, he walked to Washington for a passport. In New York he was generously received by Nathaniel Parker Willis, and he made a conditional agreement with Horace Greeley [qq.v.] for letters on Germany to the *Tribune.* He sailed for Liverpool in July 1844 with his cousin Franklin Taylor and his friend Barclay Pennock.

Only nineteen, Bayard Taylor had already shown the energy, eagerness, and charm which were to clear every path before him and make him his age's young hero among travelers. With one or both of his companions he spent two years in Europe. After a turn in Scotland, he visited London, hurried to the Rhine and Heidelberg, and then settled down for six months in Frankfurt. By Leipzig, Dresden, Prague, he went on foot to Vienna, and later journeyed in the same way to Italy, where he stayed longest in Florence. He shipped to Marseilles, tramped to Paris, returned to London. Once more back in New York, he published his *Views Afoot* (1846), which had an introduction by Willis and which ran to six editions within the year and to twenty in nine years. Taylor had traveled like a penniless, well-behaved undergraduate, excitedly alive to all he saw. He wrote ingenuously and engagingly.

Editors and publishers hastened to work the vein he had revealed in himself. After a year in Phoenixville, Pa., where he bought, ran, and soon sold the *Gazette* (re-named the *Pioneer*), he left to try his luck in New York in December 1847. First the contributor of a weekly article to the *Literary World*, after January 1848 he was manager of the miscellaneous and literary department of the *New York Tribune*. He made friends with writers in both New York and Boston, and moved in mildly Bohemian circles, a poet in private, a journalist in public. The California gold rush took him, on a commission for the *Tribune*, to the Pacific. He sailed June 1849 by way of Panama, spent five months in California, enjoyed the high spirits and variety of the gold regions without minding the hardships or violence, crossed Mexico from Mazatlán to Vera Cruz, and was in New York again by March 1850. His *Eldorado* (1850) doubled his fame as a traveler. As poet he was that year invited to deliver the Phi Beta Kappa poem at Harvard, and he won a prize offered by P. T. Barnum for the best lyric to be sung by Jenny Lind on her appearance at Castle Garden.

Long in love with Mary Agnew of Kennett Square, Taylor was married to her on Oct. 24, 1850, that they might be together during the few months she had still to live. She died in December. Profoundly grieved, and exhausted from overwork, he left New York in August 1851 for more than two years of travel in Egypt, Abyssinia, Syria, Palestine, Turkey, India, China. At Shanghai he joined Commodore Matthew Calbraith Perry's squadron and spent the summer of 1853 as master's mate, writing an account of the Japanese expedition which by the rules of the service he was never allowed to publish. Returning to New York around the Cape of Good Hope, he told about his travels in *A Journey to Central Africa* (1854), *The Lands of the Saracen* (1855), and *A Visit to India, China, and Japan, in the Year 1853* (1855), and gave countless lectures to lyceum audiences. He never outlived these journeys. For the home-keeping Americans of that generation he remained a Marco Polo, masterfully familiar with incredible lands. In Whittier's "The Tent on the Beach" Taylor appears as the Traveler.

He himself, if not tired of travel, at least desired increasingly to be known as a man of letters. Habit, facility, and need of funds sent him again to Europe during 1856–58 and made him write *Northern Travel* (1858), *Travels in Greece and Russia* (1859), and *At Home and Abroad* (1860). But having married Marie Hansen, daughter of the Danish astronomer Peter Andreas Hansen, at Gotha in Oct. 27, 1857, Taylor gradually withdrew to a farm which he had bought near his native village and on which he built a house called Cedarcroft. It was a delusive retirement. When he established himself, with his wife and daughter, there in May 1860 he was still only thirty-five, full of vivacious impulses and cosmopolitan tastes. The neighborhood which he had come to remember as pastoral turned out to be as dull as ever. It bored him with its primness and disapproved of him, especially for his robust use and praise of alcohol. His chief country friends were the family of Horace Howard Furness, the elder [*q.v.*], at Wallingford twenty miles away. In spite of Taylor's pleasure in Cedarcroft it was a burden for him to maintain it and its open-handed hospitality. To the end of his life he was strained with anxiety and hackwork. During the Civil War he served for a time as correspondent of the *Tribune* at Washington. In May 1862 he went to Saint Petersburg (Leningrad) as secretary of legation under Simon Cameron, the new minister to Russia. Left in charge in September, Taylor had a hand in keeping Russia friendly to the Union, but he was not, as he hoped, chosen to succeed his chief. Once again at Cedarcroft in September 1863 he published a novel he had completed in Russia, *Hannah Thurston* (1863), and followed it with two others, *John Godfrey's Fortunes* (1864) and *The Story of Kennett* (1866). His novels were vigorously crowded with things he had experienced or observed in America, but they were without distinction. So were the poems with which, earlier and later, he filled more than a dozen volumes, among them: *Rhymes of Travel, Ballads and Poems* (1849), *A Book of Romances, Lyrics, and Songs* (1852), *Poems of the Orient* (1855), *The Poet's Journal* (1862), *The Picture of St. John* (1866), *The Masque of the Gods* (1872), *Lars: A Pastoral of Norway* (1873), *The Prophet* (1874), *Home Pastorals, Ballads and Lyrics* (1875), *The Echo Club and Other Literary Diversions* (1876),

Prince Deukalion (1878). Except in a song and a ballad or two, and the agile, amusing parodies of the *Echo Club,* he was diffuse and commonplace. Between 1863 and 1870 he gave himself up, with intervals of travel and necessary odd jobs, to his translation, in the original meters, of *Faust* (2 vols., 1870–71). He knew all of the first and most of the second part so well that he could often translate without consulting the text. This translation was to be the English *Faust.* Instantly applauded, it has ever since been looked upon as the best version, and has been extravagantly praised. But its fidelity and sonorousness should not be allowed to hide the fact that Taylor rendered *Faust* in the second-rate English poetry which was all he knew how to write.

His last years were full of honors. He held the position of non-resident professor of German literature at Cornell from 1870 to 1877 and gave occasional lectures at the university. He was chosen to write the Gettysburg Ode in 1869 and the Centennial Ode in 1876. His renown in Germany was immense. He planned to crown his life with a great biography of Goethe. Sent as minister to Germany in April 1878, he saw himself at last free to live and write as he desired. But he had worn himself out doing what he thought he did not want to do, and he died in December of the same year. His body, brought home, lay in state in the New York city hall and was buried in the Hicksite Cemetery in Longwood, Pa. There was hardly a poet in America who did not celebrate Taylor's death in generous verse. The brilliance of his life for years blinded men to the mediocrity of his actual achievement.

[Taylor's name is sometimes given as James Bayard Taylor, but he himself says that it was simply Bayard. In addition to his own travel books, which are full of autobiog., see Marie Hansen Taylor and H. E. Scudder, *The Life and Letters of Bayard Taylor* (2 vols., 1884) ; Marie Hansen Taylor and Lilian Bayard Taylor Kiliani, *On Two Continents* (1905) ; A. H. Smyth, *Bayard Taylor* (1896), an excellent biog., with thorough bibliog.; *The Cambridge Hist. of Am. Lit.*, vol. III (1921), pp. 38–43 ; A. R. Justice, *Descendants of Robert Taylor* (1925) ; obituary in *N. Y. Times,* Dec. 20, 1878. R. H. Conwell, *The Life, Travels, and Lit. Career of Bayard Taylor* (1881), is inadequate. Numerous references to Taylor are to be found in the memoirs and biogs. of almost all his contemporaries. Juliana Haskell, *Bayard Taylor's Translation of Goethe's Faust* (1908) exactingly studies the reputation and merits of the work for which he is best known.]

C. V–D.

TAYLOR, BENJAMIN FRANKLIN (July 19, 1819–Feb. 24, 1887), poet, journalist, lecturer, was born in Lowville, N. Y., the son of Stephen William and Eunice (Scranton) Taylor. His father in the last five years of his life was president of Madison (later Colgate) University, Hamilton, New York. Graduating from

Hamilton Literary and Theological Institute (later Madison University) in 1838, young Taylor went to Michigan seeking employment. After three years of hardship, fighting poverty and malaria, because of ill health unable to gain a foothold in that pioneer environment, he returned to New York and for several years taught school in Springville, Norwich, and other places. In 1845 he went to Chicago, where he soon became literary editor of the recently established *Chicago Daily Journal.* During the last two years of the Civil War he served as war correspondent for the *Journal,* and his realistic reports of the battles of Missionary Ridge, Lookout Mountain, and other engagements, widely copied by other papers, gave him a national reputation. These accounts were published under the title *Mission Ridge and Lookout Mountain, with Pictures of Life in Camp and Field* (1872). Severing his connection with the *Journal* in 1865, Taylor left Wheaton, Ill., where he had been living, and became a free-lance writer and lecturer, making his home at Laporte, Ind., Dunkirk and Syracuse, N. Y., and, for the last six years of his life, in Cleveland, Ohio. He wrote three travel books, *The World on Wheels* (1874), *Summer-Savory* (1879), and *Between the Gates* (1878), the latter describing a transcontinental trip by rail, *Attractions of Language* (1842), *January and June* (1854), and a novel, *Theophilus Trent* (1887), based on his early school-teaching experiences in Michigan, which was published shortly after his death. He was, however, best known and admired as a poet. His volumes of verse—*Old-Time Pictures and Sheaves of Rhyme* (1874), *Songs of Yesterday* (1875) and *Dulce Domum* (1884), all included in *Complete Poetical Works* (1886)—touched the popular fancy and taste, were widely quoted, and brought their author wide recognition. His themes, chiefly drawn from farm life, the rural home, the days of the spinning wheel and the singing school, expressed the sentiment of the common people. Although painfully diffident and shy and utterly lacking in oratorical graces, he was for years in demand as a lecturer and from early life to the end of his career was one of the most familiar platform figures in America. He contributed both prose and verse to the *Atlantic Monthly, Harper's Monthly Magazine, Scribner's Monthly,* and other magazines. He had the friendship of many prominent men of his day, and his writings were widely reviewed at home and abroad. Whittier especially praised his ability to reproduce the scenes of long ago.

Taylor was of medium height, thick-set, smooth-shaven in a bewhiskered era. He was a brilliant conversationalist, and had a cordial, sympathetic nature that won him friends. He was married at Brooklyn, Mich., on Sept. 2, 1839, to Mary Elizabeth Bromley (d. July 2, 1848), seventeen-year-old daughter of Isaac Bromley of Norwich, Conn. On June 7, 1852, he married Lucy E. Leaming, daughter of Daniel M. Leaming of Laporte, Ind. He died in Cleveland, Ohio, survived by his wife and two sons by his first marriage. He was buried beside his father in the University Cemetery at Hamilton, N. Y.

[See Erastus Scranton, *A Geneal. Reg. of the Descendants of John Scranton of Guilford, Conn.* (1855); V. A. Bromley, *The Bromley Geneal.* (1911); *Am. Biog., A New Cyc.*, vol. XI (1922), pub. by Am. Hist. Soc.; obituaries in *Chicago Evening Jour., Chicago Tribune,* and *Cleveland Plain Dealer,* Feb. 25, 1887. Some of Taylor's letters are in the possession of Mrs. Eleanor Gridley, Chicago, and much miscellaneous material has been collected by the pub. lib., Lowville, N. Y.]
G. B. U.

TAYLOR, BERT LESTON (Nov. 13, 1866–Mar. 19, 1921), author and newspaper columnist, was born at Goshen, Mass., the son of A. O. and Katherine (White) Taylor. He attended New York public schools and in 1881–82 was a student in the sub-freshman class of the College of the City of New York. His first newspaper affiliation was with a weekly in Plainfield, N. H., and the *Argus and Patriot,* Montpelier, Vt. In 1896 he went to Duluth, Minn., where he became editorial writer for the *News-Tribune.* He used to say that his editorials generally were of the "What-does-the-New-York-Sun-mean-by-the-following?" variety. From 1899 to 1901 he was on the staff of the *Chicago Journal,* editing a column of comments upon the day's news, miscellaneous verse, and editorial paragraphs, called "A Little About Everything." From that he went to the *Chicago Daily Tribune,* where he established the "A Line o' Type or Two" column. In 1903 he wrote a column called "The Way of the World" for the New York *Morning Telegraph,* and in 1904 joined the staff of *Puck,* of which he was assistant editor until 1909. Then, recalled by the *Chicago Tribune,* he revived, with tremendous success, his "A Line o' Type or Two," which he conducted uninterruptedly until a few days before his death. On Nov. 16, 1895, he married Emma Bonner of Providence, R. I., who with their two daughters survived him. He died in Chicago.

Taylor became widely known as B. L. T., which was his signature at the bottom of his daily columns. "A Line o' Type or Two" achieved the widest fame and the greatest literary distinction of all newspaper departments in any way similar—and that in Chicago, where

Eugene Field's "Sharps and Flats" and George Ade's "Stories of the Streets and of the Town" had preceded it and set standards for originality and literary excellence. A complete newspaper column in length, appearing six days a week, it contained editorial comment (not necessarily in harmony with the editorial policy of the paper), excerpts from the rural press, and Taylor's own highly polished satirical verse, which was more in the manner of Calverley and Gilbert than in the homely style of Eugene Field [*q.v.*]. The column surpassed Field's in the variety of topics treated, but it followed the day's news so closely, and its general content was so timely, that most of it was as perishable as the day's news itself. Taylor printed also the signed contributions of hundreds of persons who sent to his column clippings, verses, and paragraphs of every conceivable sort. His requirements were high, and it was considered a distinction to "make the Line," a goal that was achieved by some of the best known writers in the country, whose habit it was to sign merely their initials or pseudonyms. Taylor set a standard for newspaper columning in the United States that has been the inspiration and despair of dozens of newspaper writers.

In addition to many short stories he wrote *The Well in the Wood* (1904), a juvenile; *The Charlatans* (1906), a novel of musical life; and the libretto for a musical comedy, *The Explorers,* with music by Walter H. Lewis, produced in Chicago in 1902. His other books—*Line-o'-Type Lyrics* (1902), *A Line-o'-Verse or Two* (1911), *The Pipesmoke Carry* (1912), *A Line o' Gowf or Two* (1923), *Motley Measures* (1913), *The East Window, and the Car Window* (1924), *A Penny Whistle* (1921), and *The So-Called Human Race* (1922)—all were reprints from his column, as were two pamphlets, *The Bilioustine* (1901), a burlesque of Elbert Hubbard's the *Philistine,* and *The Book Booster* (1901), a satire on the *Bookman* and various aspects of book publishing.

[*Who's Who in America,* 1920–21; "'B. L. T.' by Himself," *Everybody's Mag.,* Oct. 1920; introductions to Taylor's posthumous books by F. P. Adams, in *A Penny Whistle,* Ring Lardner, in *Motley Measures* (1927 ed.), J. R. Angell, in *The East Window, and the Car Window,* H. B. Fuller, in *The So-Called Human Race,* and Charles Evans, Jr., in *A Line o' Gowf or Two; In Memory of Bert Leston Taylor* (1921), program of a pub. meeting, Blackstone Theatre, Chicago, Mar. 27, 1921; "The Lost 'Colyumnist,'" *Lit. Digest,* Apr. 9, 1921; *Poetry,* May 1921; obituary *Chicago Sunday Tribune,* Mar. 20, 1921; personal acquaintance.]
F. P. A.

TAYLOR, CHARLES FAYETTE (Apr. 25, 1827–Jan. 25, 1899), orthopedic surgeon, was born in Williston, Vt., the son of Brimage and Miriam (Taplin) Taylor, and was brought up on a farm. His early educational opportunities were few, and, though his decision to study medicine was made in his young manhood, it was not until he was twenty-eight years old that he was able to attend a course of lectures at New York Medical College during the summer and winter of 1855. He was married on Mar. 7, 1854, to Mary Salina Skinner. In 1856, when he was serving as apprentice to a physician in Burlington, Vt., he was invited by the professors of the University of Vermont, because of his proficiency, to stand for public examination and as a result was awarded the degree of M.D. Almost immediately he sailed for England to study curative exercises and the Swedish system of Per Henrik Ling. In 1857 he began practice in New York, where for a time he was associated with his older brother, Dr. George H. Taylor. In 1861 he published *The Theory and Practice of the Movement Cure,* an effort to express ideas he had absorbed in London, but he later said that he "soon got over that infliction" and afterwards began to think his own thoughts. He never lost his interest in the "movement cure," however, and always practised it on suitable cases, inventing many machines which increased the efficiency of this form of physical therapy.

Taylor's great achievement lay in devising, and then applying, a method to relieve and eventually to cure a previously incurable disease, a spinal lesion known as Pott's disease (later discovered to be due to an infection of the bone by the bacillus of tuberculosis). His interest in spinal disease had been excited by Dr. John Murray Carnochan [*q.v.*], but he had no remembrance of having observed a case before 1857. At that time, from the attitude of a patient, he made a correct diagnosis of spinal disease. His failure to relieve this and other cases made a tremendous impression upon him and led to his invention of "the spinal assistant," designed to give protection to the diseased vertebrae through the principle of fixed points for adequate support. Relief and eventual cures followed. Patients multiplied. Sound mechanical principle was served by accurate mechanical detail, and Taylor became the first great American surgeon-mechanic, planning and accurately fitting back braces and later many other types of orthopedic appliances for chronic bone, joint, and muscle lesions. But he was much more than a brace-maker. Early in his life he recognized the influence of mental states upon physical conditions, and he constantly practised what has been described as "a common sense psychotherapy" with the happiest results. He also established a dispensary, and gave his services and his goods to

the needy until his strength and his resources were threatened. Then with the help of rich friends and grateful patients he was instrumental in establishing the New York Orthopaedic Dispensary, from which developed the great New York Orthopaedic Dispensary and Hospital.

Possessed of great energy and an alert, inquiring mind, he was very modest at heart and felt throughout his life his lack of early education. He published significant articles as important in their time as their titles suggest: *Mechanical Treatment of Angular Curvature or Pott's Disease of the Spine* (1863), *Spinal Irritation or the Causes of Backache among American Women* (1864), *Infantile Paralysis* (1867), *Mechanical Treatment of Diseases of the Hip* (1873), and "Emotional Prodigality" (*Dental Cosmos,* July 1879). Tempted more than once to concentrate his practice on gynecology because of his success in handling gynecological cases and because of their large financial return, he chose the less lucrative field of orthopedic surgery, convinced of his ability to serve his fellows more completely in this branch of medicine. About 1882 his health weakened, and after traveling widely abroad he settled in southern California. He died in Los Angeles, survived by his wife and four children, one of whom, Henry Ling Taylor, became a well-known surgeon. He was a member of numerous medical and scientific societies, and received several medals in honor of his work.

[Taylor's personal reminiscences, written for his family in 1887; H. L. Taylor, in *Am. Medic. Biogs.* (1920), ed. by H. A. Kelly and W. L. Burrage, and in *Am. Physical Educ. Rev.,* Sept. 1899, with bibliog.; E. H. Bradford, in *Trans. Am. Orthopedic Asso.,* 1899, vol. XII (1899); *Pediatrics,* Mar. 1, 1899; J. G. Kuhns and R. B. Osgood, "Am. Explorers in Orthopaedic Surgery," *Crippled Child,* Dec. 1931; obituary in *N. Y. Tribune,* Jan. 26, 1899.]   R. B. O.

TAYLOR, CHARLES HENRY (July 14, 1846–June 22, 1921), journalist, of Colonial ancestry, the son of John Ingalls and Abigail Russell (Hapgood) Taylor, was born near the Navy Yard in which his father was employed and almost under the shadow of the Bunker Hill monument, in Charlestown, then a separate municipality, later a part of Boston, Mass. The eldest of seven children, he left high school at fifteen to become a wage earner in a Boston printing office; during the Civil War at the age of sixteen, he managed to enlist in a volunteer regiment in spite of one rejection due to defective vision, and when nearly seventeen he was wounded in the assault on Port Hudson, La. At eighteen he was setting type for the *Daily Evening Traveller* (Boston), and at nineteen he became a reporter for that paper and correspondent for the *New*

York Tribune, earning the latter appointment by his recognition of the news value of William Lloyd Garrison's anti-slavery valedictory. In 1869 Taylor became private secretary to Gov. William Claflin [*q.v.*], in 1872 a member of the legislature, and in 1873 clerk of the House and publisher of the *Boston Daily Globe.* The remainder of his life was completely invested in the newspaper which represented his character and became his monument.

The great fire of 1872 had destroyed his hopes for a ten-cent magazine, *American Homes,* which had attained a circulation of 40,000, when he accepted the renewed invitation to manage the *Globe,* just in time to be caught in the panic of 1873. The paper, founded in 1872, already had lost $100,000, and every week added a $1200 deficit. For grim determination and enormous industry Taylor's next four years can hardly be surpassed in American journalism. He often said he never was more than one jump ahead of the sheriff. His work day covered sixteen hours. His assets were such intangibles as intelligence, energy, and integrity. He scorned to pay any debts by bankruptcy. A sense of humor and his unfailing optimism sustained him. He mastered every phase of newspaper work, "Upstairs" and "Downstairs," in both newsroom and counting room. In 1877 he made the great change which brought success. The *Globe* came out as an independent Democratic daily, the price (originally four cents) was reduced, and special appeal was made for women readers. In three weeks the circulation leaped from 8,000 to 30,000. In October the *Sunday Globe* was started, followed five months later by a daily evening edition. Thereafter Taylor developed the paper as "a reflection of New England life and thought." He eschewed many popular metropolitan features, clung to numerous old-fashioned ways, specialized in neighborhood news. Intolerant of orthodox practices, he did some unusual stunts, as when on the day of Garfield's funeral, Sept. 27, 1881, he filled the entire front page with original poems written for the occasion by such writers as Oliver Wendell Holmes and Julia Ward Howe. That edition sold 40,000 extra copies. The remainder of Taylor's life is the record of the growth of a prosperous newspaper. He strove throughout to earn for it an established position as a family friend. Such sayings as "When you make a caricature of a public man make one that even his wife can laugh at" expressed his temper and policies. At the time of his death he was the dean of American journalists.

"General" Taylor, as he was called from his rank as a member of the staff of Gov. William Eustis Russell [*q.v.*], was a man of simple habits, with a genius for friendship. His love of the "newspaper game" continued to the end. He kept in rare degree the loyalty of his employees. He married on Feb. 7, 1866, Georgiana Olivia Davis, who died in 1919. Three sons and two daughters survived him.

[*Who's Who in America,* 1920–21; Warren Hapgood, *The Hapgood Family* (1898); James Morgan, *Charles H. Taylor: Builder of the Boston Globe* (1923); obituaries in *Boston Transcript,* June 22, and in *Boston Daily Globe* and *N. Y. Times,* June 23, 1921; personal interviews with friends and relatives.]   F.L.B.

TAYLOR, CHARLOTTE DE BERNIER (1806–Nov. 26, 1861), entomologist, the daughter of William Scarbrough [*q.v.*] and of Julia (Bernard) Scarbrough, was born in Savannah, Ga. She attended Madam Binze's School in New York City and toured Europe after she was graduated. Upon her return to Savannah she was married to James Taylor, of the mercantile firm of Low, Taylor & Company, on Apr. 27, 1829. They had two daughters and one son. Possessed of leisure and means, Mrs. Taylor began, in the thirties, seriously to cultivate an interest which she had early acquired in entomological studies. There were few formal opportunities for study in this field in the United States, and undoubtedly she was largely self-trained. Her writings indicate that she was widely read and possessed contemporary agricultural and zoölogical works but was not familiar with the progress of research in agricultural chemistry. In a word, she was a naturalist rather than a laboratory scientist. Living in a society dominated by plantations she became especially interested in the insect life associated with the staple crops of the southern seaboard. She conducted patient and exact observations of the insect parasites of the cotton plant for over fifteen years before attempting to write on the subject. She employed magnifying glasses of some power but probably did not use the compound microscope. She made excellent drawings of the various parasites, though her accompanying sketches of plant forms were not so reliable.

During the fifties, she began publishing her findings in a number of American periodicals, her most important articles appearing in *Harper's New Monthly Magazine.* She imparted to her articles a literary charm somewhat unusual in the zoölogical literature of the period. Her understanding of the agricultural significance of entomological studies was also extraordinary in a day when agricultural writers were largely preoccupied with problems of soil exhaustion (see "Insects Belonging to the Cotton Plant," *Harper's New Monthly Magazine,* June 1860).

From the observation of the parasites of the cotton plant, her interests extended to the wheat parasites, and she called attention to the economic necessity for their systematic destruction (*Ibid.*, December 1859). A detailed study of the anatomy and natural history of the silk worm led her to predict a revival of the silk-raising industry in the United States (*Ibid.*, May 1860). Perhaps her most ambitious zoölogical study was that on the anatomy and natural history of spiders (*Ibid.*, September 1860). She revealed a remarkable skill of observation and knowledge of the general literature on the subject. Despite its literary quality and its emphasis upon the utilitarian there is little evidence that her work modified contemporary agricultural practice or later scientific investigations. It may be that the appearance of her articles in general literary journals rather than in scientific publications caused them to be neglected by subsequent investigators.

Mrs. Taylor was a woman of great personal charm. On the approach of the Civil War, she left Savannah for England and was thereafter cut off not only from friends but from her income as well. While on the Isle of Man in 1861, she began to write, but never completed, a work picturing life on a plantation. She is said to have suffered from pulmonary tuberculosis and died on the Isle of Man.

[S. A. Allibone, *A Critical Dict. of Eng. Literature and British and Am. Authors,* vol. III (1871); information from Mr. William Harden, of the Georgia Historical Society of Savannah.]   R. H. S.

TAYLOR, CREED (1766–Jan. 17, 1836), judge, law teacher, born apparently in Cumberland County, Va., was the son of Samuel and Sophia Taylor. As a lad he supplemented meager educational opportunities by service in the clerk's office of Cumberland County, first under Col. George Carrington, Jr., a well-informed lawyer, and later under Miller Woodson, a man of local prominence, allied by marriage to the large body of descendants of Baron Christopher de Graffenried, landgrave of North Carolina. Taylor, probably about 1797, married Woodson's daughter, Sally, who has come down in Virginia annals as a *grande dame* of her day. They had no children but adopted five, three of them the children of Taylor's nephew. Leaving the clerk's office, Taylor entered upon the practice of law and soon attained a position of importance, with a high reputation as an advocate. From "Needham," his estate in Cumberland County, named for his wife's English ancestors, he conducted an extensive correspondence, some of which survives. With the Randolphs of "Bizarre," especially, he

maintained a lifelong intimacy, and he sponsored the entrance into public life of John Randolph of Roanoke [*q.v.*].

In 1788 Taylor served in the House of Delegates, and from 1798 to 1805 in the state Senate, being speaker of that body in his last two terms. He represented Virginia on commissions to settle the Kentucky and Tennessee boundaries. On Nov. 2, 1805, he was named a judge of the general court, and on June 14, 1806, was appointed chancellor of the superior court of chancery for the Richmond district to succeed Chancellor Wythe. The appointment was unanimously confirmed by the General Assembly at its next session. In 1813 the Lynchburg district was added to his jurisdiction. He continued to reside at "Needham," notwithstanding some controversy on that subject, and retained his chancellorship until the abolition of the separate courts of chancery in 1831. Many of his decisions on points of practice were included with the official reports of decisions by the supreme court of appeals (*Hening and Munford's Reports,* vols. I, II, IV).

He participated in the establishment of the town of Farmville, and in plans for a canal connecting the waters of the Roanoke and Appomattox rivers, and was one of the commissioners to choose a site for the University of Virginia. His principal avocation, however, consisted in the conduct, at "Needham," of a law school at which many Virginia lawyers received their training. His correspondence shows that he had considered a similar project in 1810, but it was not until 1821 that the school was opened, with Taylor as "patron." He contemplated publishing in four volumes a journal of the school and of the moot-court attached to it, which with its appendices would constitute a complete form-book for the Virginia lawyer. This purpose was in large part frustrated by the discontinuance of the publication after the appearance of the first volume; but from that volume we may draw a favorable impression of the school, which was commended to the public by Jefferson, Madison, and Marshall. In methods, the school was characteristic of its day. The influence of the apprentice training system was not spent, procedural questions were emphasized, and the aim was to produce practitioners rather than legal scholars.

A leading figure in the Anti-Federalist movement of 1800, Taylor was nominated as a presidential elector; and on the adoption of the statewide system for choosing electors he presided over the election held in Richmond for the purpose of organizing the state. An old Republican of the school of Randolph and John Taylor of

Caroline, he favored Monroe for president over Madison in 1808. But gradually, doubtless influenced by the demands of his judicial position, he seems to have withdrawn from the political scene. His latter years were troubled by financial cares and declining health. A discriminating obituary at the time of his death (*Richmond Enquirer*, Jan. 28, 1836) described Taylor's public services as "less splendid than useful," but spoke of his private character in terms of eulogy.

[For source material consult E. G. Swem, *Va. Hist. Index*, vol. II (in preparation); MS. copies of Taylor's correspondence in Va. State Lib. (Archives Division); *Journal of the Law School and of the Moot Court Attached to It*, vol. I (1822), by Creed Taylor; E. G. Swem and J. W. Williams, *A Register of the Gen. Assembly of Va.*, *1776–1918* (1918); J. J. Casey, *Personal Names in Hening's Statutes at Large* (1896); *The Enquirer* (Richmond), June 17, 24, 1806; *Richmond Enquirer*, June 27, 1823, Jan. 28, 1836; *Constitutional Whig*, Mar. 5, 1824; Richmond *Whig and Public Advertiser*, Jan. 26, 1836. As to the controversy concerning his residence when chancellor, see *Journal of House of Delegates* (1817), p. 86, and *Journal of the Senate* (1817), p. 114. For thumb-nail sketches see *Sketches and Recollections of Lynchburg* (1858), by the Oldest Inhabitant (Mrs. Margaret C. A. Cabell); R. H. Early, *Campbell Chronicles and Family Sketches* (1927); H. M. Woodson, *Hist. Genealogy of the Woodsons and Their Connections* (1915); T. P. de Graffenried, *Hist. of the de Graffenried Family* (1925). Striking portraits of Taylor and his wife by C. B. J. Fevret de Saint-Memin are in the possession of his great-grandniece, Ellen Glasgow, of Richmond, Va. For the law school, see A. M. Dobie, "A Private Law School in Old Virginia," *Va. Law Review*, June 1930.]

R. B. T.

TAYLOR, EDWARD THOMPSON (Dec. 25, 1793–Apr. 5, 1871), chaplain of seamen making port in Boston, was born at Richmond, Va. Left an orphan so young that he had but the dimmest recollections of his parents, he was given a home by a woman about whom he seems to have remembered hardly more, for at the age of seven he left her and went to sea as a cabin boy. After ten years spent chiefly on shipboard, being ashore in Boston, he experienced an old-fashioned conversion in a Methodist chapel of which the Rev. Elijah Hedding [*q.v.*] was in charge. In 1812 he went to sea again, on the privateer *Black Hawk*, which was captured by a British man-of-war, and Taylor presently found himself in a prison at Halifax. Not relishing the prayers for the King read by the prison chaplain, the American captives successfully petitioned the commandant to let them provide their own chaplain, and Taylor was requisitioned to pray for them and to preach.

Upon his release, he returned to Boston and became a peddler for an Ann Street junk-dealer. Although he was illiterate, his religious fervor and unusual natural gifts led the quarterly conference of the Bromfield Street Methodist Church to license him to preach, and as he traveled about

the country he combined exhorting with the collecting of rags and the selling of tin ware. A widow in Saugus, Mass., offered him a home if he would care for her farm. He accepted the proposition, and the widow taught him to read. Holding meetings regularly in a schoolhouse of the town, and preaching occasionally elsewhere, he exerted a powerful influence upon people by his blunt, fearless honesty, his quickness of wit, his lively imagination, and his picturesque language. Impressed with his capabilities, a merchant, Amos Binney, sent him to Wesleyan Academy, Newmarket, N. H., but he was badly out of place there and remained only six weeks. In 1819 he was admitted to the New England Conference of the Methodist Episcopal Church on trial and later into full connection. On Oct. 12 of that year, he married Deborah D. Millett of Marblehead, Mass.

The first ten years of his ministry were chiefly in towns lying along the coast. Nowhere was he so much at home as among seamen. Late in 1829 some Methodists formed the Port Society of Boston to further the moral and religious welfare of sailors, and the following year established the Seamen's Bethel. Taylor was immediately chosen as the one uniquely fitted to be its minister. He soon won the admiration and affection of all classes, and in 1833 a building costing $24,-000 was erected for him, largely through the activities of Unitarian merchants and ministers. Here for more than forty years Father Taylor, as he came to be affectionately called, walked "the quarter deck," more like a sea captain in appearance than a parson, but admittedly one of the greatest American preachers of his generation. Harriet Martineau, Charles Dickens, Emerson, and Walt Whitman have all left tributes to his uniqueness and power, and the sermon of Father Mapple in Herman Melville's *Moby Dick* is obviously a portrayal of Taylor's manner of preaching. Emerson said of him: "He is the work of the same hand that made Demosthenes, Shakespeare, and Burns, and is guided by instincts diviner than rules" (*Journals, post*, III, 431). His sermons were full of the imagery and language of the sea, of pathos and sarcasm, of humor and striking similes, of hope and denunciation—all unpremeditated and delivered with unstudied dramatic effect. "I am . . . no man's copyist," he declared; "I go on my own hook,—shall say what I please" (Haven and Russell, *post*, 1904, p. 260); but his utterances were seldom resented. Sailors knew he was their stanch friend; others, of whatever rank, had to give place to them in the Bethel, which was commonly crowded to the "hatches"; they trusted him implicitly and firmly believed that his prayers for them must be answered, so full of impassioned pleading were they. A Methodist always, he was affectionately tolerant toward all, and radiated a wholesome joyousness and faith. He was noted for his epigrammatic sayings, and his blunt honesty. Daniel Webster, for whom he had great admiration, he characterized as the best bad man he ever knew. Of his friend Emerson he declared: "[He] is the sweetest soul God ever made; but he knows no more of theology than Balaam's ass did of Hebrew grammar" (*Ibid.*, p. 337). In his labors he was loyally helped by Mother Taylor, who cared for his secular affairs and saved him from giving away quite all his money to those in need. He made three trips to Europe, the last as chaplain on the *Macedonia*, laden with supplies for starving Ireland. Survived by four of his six children, he died at his home in Boston.

[*Minutes of the Ann. Conferences of the M. E. Ch.* (1871); James Mudge, *Hist. of the New England Conference of the M. E. Ch., 1796–1910* (1910); Gilbert Haven and Thomas Russell, *Father Taylor, the Sailor Preacher* (1871); reprinted with much supplementary material in *Life of Father Taylor* (1904); Harriet Martineau, *A Retrospect of Western Travel* (1838), vol. II; Charles Dickens, *Am. Notes for General Circulation* (1842); Walt Whitman, in *Century*, Feb. 1887; J. R. Dix, *Pulpit Portraits of Distinguished Am. Divines* (1854); E. W. Emerson and W. E. Forbes, *Journals of Ralph Waldo Emerson* (10 vols., 1909–14), *passim*; *New Eng. Quart.*, Oct. 1935; *Boston Transcript*, Apr. 5, 1871.]   H.E.S.

TAYLOR, FRANK WALTER (Mar. 8, 1874–July 27, 1921), illustrator, painter, was born in Philadelphia, Pa., the son of Frank Hamilton and Margaret (Johnston) Taylor. His father was an artist well known for drawings of old Philadelphia. Taylor attended Friends' School and studied at the Pennsylvania Academy of the Fine Arts, where he won a traveling scholarship in 1896 that enabled him to visit the principal art centers of Europe and, for a time, to settle in Paris, where he studied independently. In 1898 he opened his own studio in Philadelphia. Desiring to paint, he was, nevertheless, thrown into illustration as a ready means to earn a livelihood. During a long association with Charles Scribner's Sons, 1904–08, he illustrated Scribner books, and articles, stories, and poems for *Scribner's Magazine*. Especially noteworthy were his pictures for a special edition (1905) of Henry Van Dyke's *Fisherman's Luck*. Mary R. S. Andrews' *The Perfect Tribute* (1906), F. Hopkinson Smith's *The Veiled Lady* (1907), and Mary A. K. Waddington's *Château and Country Life in France* (1908). He also contributed illustrations to numerous popular magazines. For a time he was instructor in illustration at the Art Stu-

dents' League, New York, and at the School of Design for Women, Philadelphia. In 1921 he was appointed instructor in illustration at the Pennsylvania Academy of the Fine Arts. He contributed to international exhibitions in Rome, London, and Paris as well as in America, and in 1915 he won the special gold medal of honor for illustration at the Panama-Pacific Exposition, where he exhibited illustrations and charcoal portraits. His draftsmanship was distinguished, and his drawings had a velvety richness that was the result of his mastery of the charcoal medium. Whether he used black and white or color, he pitched his work in rather a low key. His friend Joseph Pennell [*q.v.*] described him as "the last of the American illustrators."

His other work includes many sketches of out-of-the-way places, the result of his anual trips abroad, as well as a series of sketches of the Thames. He was especially fond of France, and an admirer of Gaston La Touche and Pierre Auguste Renoir. He also produced portraits in oil and in charcoal, chiefly of artists, whom he preferred as subjects. Among his sitters were Joseph Pennell; John McLure Hamilton, the painter; George Arliss and Otis Skinner, actors; and R. Tait McKenzie, the sculptor. During the World War he was one of a group of Philadelphia artists who gave their services to aid government loan campaigns. Shortly before his death he contemplated a different type of illustrating, and was engaged on preliminary sketches for new editions of Oscar Wilde's *Ballad of Reading Gaol* and Whitman's *Leaves of Grass*. He also devoted more time to portraiture and to pictorial rendering of constructive drawings for architects. Among his last works was a series of nudes in chalk and charcoal.

He is represented in the Pennsylvania Museum and School of Industrial Art, the Free Library of Philadelphia, the Pennsylvania Academy of the Fine Arts, the University of Nebraska, the Rhode Island School of Design, the New York Public Library, the Society of Illustrators, New York, the Metropolitan Museum of Art, and the Library of Congress, Washington, D. C. He died in Ogdensburg, N. Y. He was survived by his wife, Elsie Carleton Megary, whom he had married on Apr. 19, 1917. There were no children.

[*Who's Who in America*, 1920–21; Joseph Pennell, in Cat. of Memorial Exhibition, M. Knoedler and Company, Jan. 1922; *Arts and Decoration*, Mar. 1922; *Pub. Ledger* (Phila.), July 28 (obituary), Aug. 28, Nov. 13, 1921; information from Taylor's wife, J. H. Chapman, and Albert Rosenthal.]   D. G—y.

TAYLOR, FRED MANVILLE (July 11, 1855–Aug. 7, 1932), economist, was born at Northville, Mich., the son of the Rev. Barton S. and Marietta (Rowland) Taylor. After his collegiate training in Northwestern University (A.B. 1876, A.M., 1879) he was teacher and principal in the Winnetka High School, Winnetka, Ill. (1876–78), and then became professor of history and politics at Albion College, Albion, Mich., where he taught from 1879 to 1892. On July 15, 1880, he married Mary Sandford Brown of Ann Arbor, Mich., by whom he had two sons and two daughters. In 1888 he received the degree of Ph.D. from the University of Michigan. Here his talents were recognized by such men as the professor of political economy, Henry Carter Adams [*q.v.*], and in 1892 Taylor began the teaching of economics at Michigan which occupied him until his retirement in 1929. He was assistant professor of political economy, 1892–93; junior professor, 1893–1904; professor, 1904–20; and professor of economics, 1920–29. After 1906, when he published *Some Chapters on Money,* and began to print the leaflets which grew into his *Principles of Economics* (1911), he devoted himself chiefly to studies in general economic theory. The earlier phase of his development had promised a goodly volume of publications of high quality, in spite of his frail health and heavy teaching load. His thesis, *The Right of the State to Be* (1891), together with several articles of that period, was very favorably received by leading critics, and by 1898 he had also earned an enviable reputation as an authority on currency and banking. His writings in this field refined Gresham's Law, and subjected the topics of circulation and qualities of monetary standards to penetrating analysis. He also did pioneer work on some relations between money and prices—for example, on the contrast in effects between changes in quantity of money, and changes in costs and demands of goods. His output of writings was restricted, however, and withheld from the wider public, by his too severe self-criticism.

His studies in money, moreover, were crowded into the background as he became preoccupied with general economic theory and with incessant revisions of his *Principles,* which reached its ninth edition in 1925. In form this book is a college text, entirely undocumented, containing some pedagogical novelties modeled upon natural science texts, and deliberately excluding "literary" style. It became, however, much more than an elementary text. During many years Taylor conducted his quizmasters and other advanced students through most of the subtleties of theoretical literature, firing their enthusiasm for his handling of these points, so that they carried his reputation abroad, and all this took effect upon the book. It far surpassed his modest hope "to restate the generally accepted doctrine, in a manner more organic and self-consistent than is usual" (Taylor to F. A. Hayek, Feb. 18, 1930). He integrated, perhaps more successfully than any predecessor, the influences of cost and demand (under all their aspects) in economic functioning. Other important contributions include his exposition and critique of "the present economic order of individual exchange-cooperation," and his overhauling of the theories of imputation, rent, capital, profit, and outputs in relation to variable inputs. Though he argued against most of the practical proposals inspired by socialists, his lifelong study of their literature left many imprints upon his *Principles,* and his last essay, the presidential address to the American Economic Association, 1928, dealt with some abstract features of "The Guidance of Production in a Socialist State" (*American Economic Review,* March 1929). He died in Pasadena, Cal., where he had lived since his retirement.

[Sources include *Who's Who in America,* 1930–31; *Northwestern Univ. . . . Alumni Record of the Coll. of Liberal Arts* (1903), ed. by C. B. Atwell; *Mich. Alumnus,* Apr. 22, 1933; obituary in *N. Y. Times,* Aug. 9, 1932; personal acquaintance. A bibliog. of Taylor's writings is being prepared for publication. Fragments of his letters and other unpub. papers are in the lib. of the Univ. of Mich.]   Z. C. D.

TAYLOR, FREDERICK WINSLOW (Mar. 20, 1856–Mar. 21, 1915), efficiency engineer, inventor, was born in Germantown, Philadelphia, Pa., the youngest child of Franklin and Emily Annette (Winslow) Taylor. He was a descendant of Samuel Taylor, who settled in Burlington, N. J., in 1677. His father was a lawyer, more interested, however, in literature than law; his mother was an ardent abolitionist and a coworker with Lucretia Mott [*q.v.*] in this cause. Taylor received his early education from his mother. In 1872, after two years of schooling in France and Germany, followed by eighteen months of travel in Europe, he entered Phillips Exeter Academy at Exeter, N. H., to prepare for the Harvard Law School. Though he graduated with his class two years later, his eyesight had become in the meantime so impaired that he had to abandon further study, and between 1874 and 1878 he worked in the shops of the Enterprise Hydraulic Works, a pump-manufacturing company in Philadelphia, learning the trades of pattern-maker and machinist. In the latter year he joined the Midvale Steel Company, Philadelphia, as a common laborer. In the succeeding twelve years he not only rose to be chief engineer (1884), but in 1883, by studying at night, obtained the degree of M.E. from Stevens Institute of Technology, Hoboken, N. J. On May 3, 1884, he married Louise M. Spooner of Philadelphia. His inventions during these years effecting improvements in machinery and manufacturing methods were many, the outstanding one being the design and construction of the largest successful steam hammer ever built in the United States (patent No. 424,939, Apr. 1, 1890). After three years (1890–93) as general manager of the Manufacturing Investment Company, Philadelphia, operators of large paper mills in Maine and Wisconsin, he began a consulting practice in Philadelphia—his business card read "Systematizing Shop Management and Manufacturing Costs a Specialty"—which led to the development of a new profession.

Behind this lay Taylor's years of observation and study of manufacturing conditions and methods. From these he had evolved a theory that, by scientific study of every minute step and operation in a manufacturing plant, data could be obtained as to the fair and reasonable production capacities of both man and machine, and that the application of such data would, in turn, abolish the antagonism between employer and employee, and bring about increased efficiencies in all directions. He had in addition worked out a comprehensive system of analysis, classification, and symbolization to be used in the study of every type of manufacturing organization. For five years he successfully applied his theory in a variety of establishments, administrative and sales departments as well as shops. In 1898 he was retained exclusively for that purpose by the Bethlehem Steel Company, Bethlehem, Pa. In the course of his work there he undertook, with J. Maunsel White, a study of the treatment of tool steel which led to the discovery of the Taylor-White process of heat treatment of tool steel, yielding increased cutting capacities of 200 to 300 per cent. This process and the tools treated by it are now used in practically every machine shop of the world. While he was at Bethlehem, too, Taylor's ideas regarding scientific management took more concrete form. Being convinced of the results that would be attained if these principles should be generally adopted throughout the industrial world, he resigned from the Bethlehem Steel Company in 1901, returned to Philadelphia, and devoted the remainder of his life to expounding these principles, giving his services free to anybody who was sincerely desirous of carrying out his methods. While he met with many unbelievers among both employers and employees, he lived to see his system widely applied. In 1911 the Society to Promote the Science of Management (after his death renamed the Taylor Society) was established by enthusiastic engineers and industrialists throughout the world to carry on his work.

Among Taylor's contributions to the technical journals were "A Piece-Rate System" (*Transactions of the American Society of Mechanical Engineers,* vol. XVI, 1895), an exposition of the principles on which his system of management was subsequently based, and "Shop Management" (*Ibid.,* vol. XXIV, 1903), which was translated and published in almost every country of Europe. An active member of the American Society of Mechanical Engineers, he served as vice-president in 1904–05 and as president in 1906, when he delivered as his presidential address his exhaustive monograph "On the Art of Cutting Metals" (*Ibid.,* vol. XXVIII, 1907). In 1911 he published *The Principles of Scientific Management,* and submitted to Congress a report entitled " 'Taylor System' of Shop Management" (*House Report 52, 62* Cong., 1 Sess.). In addition to these publications he was joint author with Sanford E. Thompson of two works on concrete, *A Treatise on Concrete, Plain and Reinforced* (1905) and *Concrete Costs* (1912). He received about one hundred patents for various inventions during his lifetime. For his process of treating high speed tool steels he received a personal gold medal at the Paris exposition in 1900, and was awarded the Elliott Cresson gold medal that same year by the Franklin Institute, Philadelphia. He was much interested in amateur sports, particularly tennis, and with Clarence M. Clark won the doubles championship of the United States at Newport, R. I., in 1881. He died in Philadelphia of pneumonia, survived by his widow and three adopted children.

[Kenelm Winslow, *Winslow Memorial,* vol. II (1888); *Who's Who in America,* 1914–15; F. B. Copley, *Frederick W. Taylor, Father of Scientific Management* (2 vols., 1923); *Trans. Am. Soc. Mech. Engineers,* vol. XXXVII (1916); *Frederick Winslow Taylor, A Memorial Vol.* (1920); obituary in *Pub. Ledger* (Phila.), Mar. 22, 1915; Patent Office records.]

C. W. M—n.

TAYLOR, GEORGE (1716–Feb. 23, 1781), ironmaster, signer of the Declaration of Independence, was born probably in northern Ireland of a good family. He had some education, for when he arrived in Pennsylvania, about 1736, he became a clerk in the Warwick Furnace and Coventry Forge in Chester County, and later manager. He was married in 1742 to Mrs. Anne Taylor Savage, who died in 1768. About 1754 he moved to Durham, in Bucks County, where he and a partner had leased a furnace, and during the remainder of his life his business interests lay largely there. After 1763 he lived much of the time at Easton, in Northampton County, which became the scene of his political activities. In October 1764, he was elected to the provincial assembly, and was returned annually for the next five years (*Pennsylvania Gazette,* Oct. 4, 1764, *et passim*). He was a member of the minority proprietary party and bitterly opposed a royal government and its chief advocate, Franklin (*Votes and Proceedings of the House of Representatives of the Province of Pennsylvania,* volume V, 1775, pp. 379 ff.). Unlike John Dickinson [*q.v.*], Taylor's opposition arose from his western radicalism. His attitude toward imperial affairs at this time was evinced by his membership on the committeee that drew up instructions for delegates to the Stamp Act congress.

After a politically inactive or unsuccessful interval of four years, he reappeared as chairman of a meeting of the principal inhabitants of the county protesting against closing the Boston harbor and favoring an intercolonial congress; six men, including Taylor, were named a Committee of Correspondence. He did not attend the conference of deputies in Philadelphia in July, but his absence was probably not due to lack of sympathy, for he went to the similar convention in January 1775. The following July he was elected to a colonelcy in the Bucks County militia and although he never saw active service he retained the title. Sent again to the assembly by Northampton in October 1775, he served with distinction on many important committees and helped draft instructions for delegates to Congress in November. Although a member of the second Committee of Safety from October 1775 to July 1776, he rarely attended. His membership in the too conservative assembly doubtless explains his absence from the radical conference of committees of June 1776, and from the usurping convention which grew out of it. His views, however, are indicated by his appointment by the latter body as delegate to the Continental Congress on July 20, in the place of one of several Pennsylvanians who had refused to approve the Declaration of Independence. He signed the engrossed copy of that document on Aug. 2, or thereafter, but took no other part in the activities of Congress, except to represent it, with George Walton [*q.v.*], at a conference with Indians at Easton in January 1777. He evidently quit Congress soon afterward. In March he was elected from Northampton to the new Supreme Executive Council of Pennsylvania, but because of illness he served only six weeks and then retired from active public affairs. He had been a moderate radical, whose attitude was largely provincial, and whose interest in politics was never absorbing.

Taylor had two legitimate children and five natural children by his housekeeper, Naomi Smith. Of the former, the daughter died in childhood and the son predeceased his father, leaving a large family.

[Source material for Taylor's life is scarce, and there is no complete, accurate, secondary account. The sketch in John Sanderson, *Biog. of the Signers to the Declaration of Independence,* vol. IX (1827), is not trustworthy. A substantially accurate article, with much new material, by Warren S. Ely is published in *Bucks County (Pa.) Hist. Soc. Pubs.,* vol. V. See also J. B. Laux, "The Lost Will of George Taylor, the Signer," *Pa. Mag. of Hist. and Biog.,* Jan. 1920 ; E. C. Burnett, *Letters of Members of the Continental Cong.,* vol. II (1923) ; W. C. Ford, ed., *Jour. of the Continental Cong.,* vol. VII (1907), see index volume.]   J.E.J.

TAYLOR, GEORGE BOARDMAN (Dec. 27, 1832–Sept. 28, 1907), Baptist clergyman, missionary, author, was born in Richmond, Va., the son of the Rev. James Barnett Taylor [*q.v.*] and Mary (Williams), and was named in honor of the early missionary to Burma, George Boardman. He was graduated from Richmond College in 1851, taught a year in an old-field school in Fluvanna County, and then went to the University of Virginia for three years. He had early joined the Baptist Church and while at the University preached regularly to a rural congregation. He was ordained to the ministry in Charlottesville and in 1855 became pastor of the Franklin Square Baptist Church in Baltimore. Here in 1857–58 he assisted Dr. Franklin Wilson in editing the *Christian Review.* Leaving Baltimore in November 1857 to become pastor of the Baptist Church in Staunton, Va., he was married on May 13, 1858, to Susan Spotswood Braxton, of Fredericksburg, daughter of Carter Braxton and Elizabeth Teackle Mayo. She was a bright, devout, tender woman with the heritage of the Virginia aristocracy, and gave her husband heartening companionship and help until her death in Rome, Mar. 7, 1884. Of their eight children, two sons and two daughters survived their parents. Through the years of his ministry in Staunton Taylor taught in several schools in the city and wrote a number of books for Sunday school libraries—notably a series called the Oakland Stories—to supplement a dwindling salary in the support of a growing family. With the outbreak of the Civil War he was elected captain of a company of home guards in Staunton and for a time was chaplain of the 25th Virginia Regiment in Stonewall Jackson's command.

For two years (1869–71) he was chaplain at the University of Virginia and in the summer of

1870 he went with his brother Charles on a tour through England, France, and Italy. In this same year he published a historical novel, *Walter Ennis,* depicting the struggles of the Baptists for religious liberty in eighteenth-century Virginia. From the University he returned to his pastorate in Staunton, and here, in 1872, at a meeting of the Baptist General Association of Virginia there was launched the Memorial Movement to raise $300,000 for the endowment of Richmond College, which his father had helped to found. Taylor bore a large share in this campaign and on release from his church traveled in the North collecting funds.

While engaged in this effort he was appointed by the Foreign Mission Board of the Southern Baptist Convention as missionary to Rome, to continue the work recently undertaken in that city. Reaching his post in the summer of 1873 he found that the mission consisted of a day and night school among the poor, a discharged evangelist, and a missionary who was released the week after his arrival. The rest of his life was given to an unremitting effort to spread the Baptist faith in Roman Catholic Italy. In 1878 he dedicated a chapel in Rome and returned to the United States to raise the money to pay for it. Occasional furloughs home, the longest in 1885–87 when he again served for two years as chaplain of the University of Virginia, were the only interruptions in his thirty-four years of missionary work. He saw Baptist congregations grow up in many of the cities of Italy and numerous native preachers go out from the theological school he had helped establish in Rome. At this school he continued to teach systematic theology, in spite of frail health and increasing deafness. In 1906 he had a fall, breaking a small bone in his hip; he remained cheerful in spirit, but after this accident his strength declined, and the following year he died. He was buried beside his wife, in Rome, in the Protestant Cemetery.

In 1872 Taylor published *Life and Times of James B. Taylor.* His most notable book, designed to promote the cause of Protestant missions, was *Italy and the Italians* (1898), a friendly and well-informed survey of the land, its history, its art, its religion and its people. During his last two years he was a member of the commission for the revision of the Italian New Testament (for the British and Foreign Bible Society), and shortly before his death he published in Italian a textbook of systematic theology.

[Files of the Foreign Mission Board, Southern Baptist Convention, Richmond; works by Taylor's son, George Braxton Taylor: *Life and Letters of Rev. George Boardman Taylor, D.D.* (1908); *Southern Bap-*

tists in Sunny Italy (1929), and *Va. Baptist Ministers: Fifth Ser.* (1915); W. S. Stewart, *Later Baptist Missionaries and Pioneers,* vol. I (1928); *Who's Who in America,* 1906–07; *Religious Herald* (Richmond), Oct. 3, 1907).]

M. H. W.

TAYLOR, HANNIS (Sept. 12, 1851–Dec. 26, 1922), lawyer, scholar, and diplomat, was born in New Bern, N. C., the son of Susan (Stevenson) and Richard Nixon Taylor, merchant. He was the grandson of Mary (Hannis) and William Taylor, who had emigrated before the Revolution from Paisley, Scotland to North Carolina. He attended Lovejoy's school at Raleigh, Dr. Wilson's school in Alamance County, and in 1867 entered the University of North Carolina, from which he withdrew at the end of a year because of his father's financial reverses. He began the study of law in an office at New Bern and after the removal of his family in 1869 to Mobile, Ala., continued the study in that city in the offices of Anderson and Bond. Admitted to the bar in 1870 he practised at Mobile until 1892, achieving prominence in his profession as solicitor for Baldwin County, as counsel in certain well-known cases (such as the Louisiana Lottery Case, *Ex parte Rapier,* 143 *United States,* 110, which was argued before the United States Supreme Court), and as president of the Alabama Bar Association (1890–91). On May 8, 1878, he married Leonora, daughter of William A. LeBaron of Mobile, Ala. There were three sons and two daughters, all of whom survived him.

He was appointed by President Grover Cleveland on Apr. 8, 1893, American minister to Spain. His four years at Madrid were critical ones for Spanish-American relations, and he seems to have conducted the many difficult negotiations entrusted to him with credit. He inherited such troublesome controversies as the settlement following the exclusion of missionaries from the Caroline Islands, and the Mora claim for indemnity for confiscations by the Cuban government which dated from early seventies and which was settled in 1895 largely through Taylor's efforts. After the termination of the commercial reciprocity agreement with Spain by the passage of the tariff act of 1894, he obtained preferential treatment for certain American exports to Cuba and Puerto Rico. The outbreak of further disorders in Cuba in 1895 led to friction between the two governments. Taylor protested the arrests of numerous American citizens or the confiscation of their property by Cuban authorities. His negotiations were often successful, as when in 1895 the Spanish government expressed regret that a gunboat off the Cuban coast had fired on the American ship *Alliança;* and when Americans on the *Competitor,* condemned to be executed for landing arms in Cuba, were granted a new trial.

After his return from Madrid Taylor turned to the practice of his profession, with headquarters in Washington, and to scholarship. In 1902 he served as special counsel for the United States before the Spanish Treaty Claims Commission, and in 1903 was junior American counsel before the Alaska Boundary Tribunal. He lectured on legal subjects in several Washington institutions, George Washington University, Georgetown University, and National University, served in 1906–07 as associate editor of the *United States Law Review,* and wrote prolifically. His first important work, *The Origin and Growth of the English Constitution* (2 vols., 1889–98), brought him wide recognition as a student of legal institutions. The book was, however, marred by certain defects, such as a tendency to digress, reliance upon questionable authorities, and consequent inaccuracies. He occasionally invited criticism by defending a thesis generally recognized as untenable, as when, in *The Science of Jurisprudence* (1908) and in *The Origin and Growth of the American Constitution* (1911), he credited Pelatiah Webster with virtual joint authorship of the federal Constitution; this thesis he had already stated in his *To The Congress of the United States: A Memorial in Behalf of the Architect of Our Federal Constitution, Pelatiah Webster* (n.d.). His other writings included: *A Treatise on International Public Law* (1901); *Jurisdiction and Procedure of the Supreme Court* (1905); *The Constitutional Crisis in Great Britain* (1910); *Why the Pending Treaty with Colombia Should be Ratified* (1914); *Due Process of Law and the Equal Protection of the Laws* (1917); and *Cicero . . . A Commentary on the Roman Constitution* (1916). In his vitriolic pamphlet, *A Review of President Wilson's Administration* (n.d.), he announced that although he had supported Wilson in 1912 he would vote for Hughes in 1916.

[T. M. Owen, *Hist. of Ala.* (1921), IV, 1649; Erwin Craighead, *Mobile: Fact and Tradition* (1930); *Register of the Dept. of State,* esp. for the years 1893, 1897; *Papers Relating to the Foreign Relations of the U. S.,* vols. for 1893–97 (1894–98); State Dept. records; critical reviews of three of his books in *Am. Hist. Review,* Jan. 1899, pp. 348–51; Jan. 1909, pp. 329–31; Oct. 1911, pp. 162–64; *Who's Who in America,* 1922–23; obituary in *Evening Star* (Washington, D. C.), Dec. 27, 1922; data concerning ancestry from his daughter, Mrs. Reid Hunt of Boston.]   E. W. S.

TAYLOR, HARRY (June 26, 1862–Jan. 28, 1930), soldier, was born at Sanbornton Bridge, now Tilton, N. H., the son of John Franklin and Lydia J. (Proctor) Taylor, and a descendant of Nathan Taylor who was in Massachusetts about

1690. He attended public schools, the New Hampshire Conference Seminary, and the United States Military Academy from which he was graduated in 1884 as a second lieutenant of engineers. His early career in the army was concerned with river and harbor developments on both the Atlantic and Pacific coasts, except for one year, 1888–89, during which he was assistant professor of mathematics at the Academy. His long service in civil engineering did not change until 1903, when he was sent to the Philippines to command a battalion of engineer troops. Two years later he returned to the United States to construct defenses and to improve navigation at the east entrance of Long Island Sound. In 1911 he was called to Washington as assistant to the chief of engineers of the United States army. He was promoted to the rank of colonel in 1915 and was placed in charge of the harbor work about New York City and along the Hudson River.

In May 1917 he was selected to be chief engineer of the American Expeditionary Force in France. He sailed the same month as a member of General Pershing's staff, with only two captains and three clerks to assist him in organizing abroad the extensive engineering forces which would be needed. He selected and prepared plans for ports for the debarkation of American armies. He inspected, planned, and constructed bases and training camps for the two million American soldiers in France. He assumed the management of certain French railroads, built connecting lines, and improved equipment—a task which he completed with remarkable efficiency and speed. In addition to construction, his duties as chief engineer required the procurement and placement of an enormous mass of engineering supplies for troops in modern warfare. This included equipment for offensive and defensive gas warfare, searchlights, trench tools, material for wire entanglements and for mining, explosives for destroying similar works of the enemy, and the training of troops to use them. An elaborate forestry service was organized to obtain the immense quantity of lumber needed. As American troops took over parts of the front the engineering department, under Taylor, built water systems for them, provided electricity, constructed roads, and performed many miscellaneous duties. Schools were opened for training recently appointed engineer officers in their duties. When the spring campaigns of 1918 started the original force of five assistants had been increased to 31,000 officers and men, and Taylor had become a brigadier-general.

In September 1918 Taylor returned to the United States to be once more assistant chief of engineers at the War Department. In June 1924 he succeeded to the office of major-general and became chief of engineers. In the two years during which he occupied this position, the engineering project at Muscle Shoals, Ala., was practically completed, and under his supervision, large and important improvements were made on the Ohio, Missouri, and Mississippi rivers. He was retired in 1926 and died at his home in Washington, D. C. On Oct. 30, 1901, he had been married to Adele Austin Yates, who, with their two children, survived him. For his work during the war he received the Distinguished Service Medal.

[War diary of General Taylor, manuscript in War Department files; *Who's Who in America*, 1928–29; W. L. Proctor, *A Geneal. of Descendants of Robert Proctor* (1898); M. T. Runnels, *Hist. of Sanbornton, N. H.*, vol. II (1881); G. W. Cullum, *Biog. Reg.* . . . *U. S. Mil. Acad.* (1891); *Hist. Report of the Chief Engineer, 1917–1919* (1919); *Evening Star* (Washington, D. C.), Jan. 28, *N. Y. Times,* Jan. 29, 1930.]

C. H. L.

TAYLOR, JAMES BARNETT (Mar. 19, 1804–Dec. 22, 1871), Baptist clergyman, administrator, son of George and Chrisanna (Barnett) Taylor, was born in the village of Barton-upon-Humber, Lincolnshire, England, and baptized in the Church of England. His father, a cabinet maker, brought his wife and infant son to the United States in 1805, and settled in New York. Following an illness, George Taylor joined a Baptist church and with his wife was baptized in 1807. Their only son in his thirteenth year was again baptized, becoming a member of the First Baptist Church, New York.

The family moved to Virginia in 1817, living first in Petersburg and then in Mecklenburg County, where James worked in his father's cabinet shop, meanwhile studying with Dr. Bartholomew Egan, principal of an academy at Christiansville near by. Devout and studious, he began speaking in religious meetings when but sixteen years old. When his family moved to Clarksville, across the Roanoke River, he continued his studies through his own reading. At the age of twenty he was licensed to preach and in 1826 was sent as a missionary to the counties of Dinwiddie, Brunswick, Nottoway, and Lunenburg. After several months he resigned this appointment but continued to live in Dinwiddie, studying, preaching, and writing for the *Columbian Star*, a Baptist weekly. Ordained May 2, 1826, at Sandy Creek, he became pastor of the Second Baptist Church in Richmond, a church group of some eighteen white and about as many colored members that had persisted as an organized band for seven years. On Oct. 30, 1828, he married, in Richmond, Mary, daughter of

Rev. Elisha Scott Williams of Beverly, Mass. They had three daughters and three sons, all of whom lived to maturity; one of the sons was George Boardman Taylor [*q.v.*].

Success came to the young minister in his pastorate and he saw his flock grow in numbers and strength. He did editorial work for the *Religious Herald* and in 1836 was elected moderator of the General Association of the state, which office he held for some twenty years. He also found time to publish *Biography of Elder Lott Cary* (1837) and *Lives of Virginia Baptist Ministers* (1837; revised and enlarged, 1838; augmented and issued in 2 vols., 1860).

In 1839 he became chaplain of the University of Virginia, where he attended lectures in Latin, Greek, and Anglo-Saxon and found time to write *Memoir of Luther Rice* (1840) at the request of the trustees of Columbian College. Upon returning to Richmond in 1840, he became pastor of Third Church, subsequently known as Grace Street Church. He deplored the separation of Northern and Southern Baptists, though in 1845 he attended the convention at Charleston that formed the Southern Baptist Convention. Chosen as corresponding secretary of the Foreign Mission Board of the new body, he at first declined the office, but volunteered to give two days a week to its services and in 1846 relinquished his pastorate to assume the secretaryship and devote the major part of his time to missions. For fourteen years, however, he continued to preach twice a month at Taylorsville, near Richmond. He was hopeful in spirit, modest in his estimate of himself, careful in business arrangements, friendly in his counsel to the missionaries, and zealous in traveling, preaching, and writing to enlist interest and aid for the missionary program of his denomination.

At a meeting of the General Association at his church in 1830, with his close friend, J. B. Jeter [*q.v.*], Taylor helped form the Virginia Baptist Education Society to promote the education of ministers. This movement resulted in the establishment of Richmond College. He sought funds for that institution in its early years and was its persistent friend and a vital force in its upbuilding. He also aided in the establishment of a Baptist school for girls which in 1853 was chartered as Richmond Female Institute. During the Civil War his activities in behalf of missions were necessarily curtailed, and resigning his Taylorsville pastorate he became a colporteur for the Virginia Sunday School and Publication Board laboring in camps and hospitals and later became a Confederate post chaplain. After the war his business sense and able leadership were instrumental in reviving Richmond College. He resigned his mission secretaryship only a short time before his death, which occurred in Richmond in his sixty-eighth year.

[George Boardman Taylor, *Life and Times of James B. Taylor* (1872); George Braxton Taylor, *Virginia Baptist Ministers: Third Ser.* (1912); *Religious Herald* (Richmond), Jan. 4, 1872; *Richmond Dispatch*, Dec. 23, 1871; Taylor's diary and letters in archives of the Foreign Mission Board of the Southern Baptist Convention, Richmond.]   M. H. W.

TAYLOR, JAMES BAYARD [See Taylor, Bayard, 1825–1878].

TAYLOR, JAMES MONROE (Aug. 5, 1848–Dec. 19, 1916), Baptist clergyman, college president, was born in Brooklyn, N. Y., the son of the Rev. Elisha E. L. and Mary Jane (Perkins) Taylor and the descendant of Edward Taylor who emigrated from England to New Jersey at the end of the seventeenth century. After five years schooling in the seminary at Essex, Conn., he entered the University of Rochester and graduated in 1868. In 1871 he was graduated at Rochester Theological Seminary. A year's study in Europe in 1872 had much influence on him. On Sept. 10, 1873, he married Kate Huntington of Rochester. Three sons and a daughter were born of this union. For fourteen years he preached, filling Baptist pastorates at South Norwalk, Conn., and Providence, R. I.; and, in 1886, he was elected president of Vassar College, the third Baptist clergyman to hold this post. The college was in sound condition, though suffering from ineffective administration and a certain complacency of attitude.

He obtained ample powers from the trustees at the start, and with great energy, which fully made up for his own deficiency of experience in higher education, he flung himself into his task. Critical alumnae were reconciled and organized into effective battalions, and provision was made for their election as trustees. Incessant travel and public speaking made the college better known and made friends of the school world. Money was solicited under Taylor's watchword "Endow the college." The will of John G. Vassar, Jr. (died 1889) brought several hundred thousand dollars to the college, and Taylor pleaded for the endowment of professorships. The trustees preferred to purchase land and to erect buildings. He succeeded, however, in raising $100,000 before the panic of 1893, and over half-a-million dollars were raised after the panic of 1903, the total endowment due to Taylor's efforts being about one million dollars. This was a tremendous effort for one man, who at the same time was conducting daily chapel, teaching psychology, ethics, and philosophy, and ad-

ministering the whole official college correspondence and registry with but slight assistance. Moreover, he found time for some writing: *Elements of Psychology* (1892), *A New World and Old Gospel* (1901), and *Practical or Ideal?* (1901), as well as *Before Vassar Opened* (1914) and, with E. H. Haight, *Vassar* (1915). It told heavily upon his health, and twice, in 1895 and 1905, he went to Europe for a year's rest. He was one of the first to object to the current conception of the college president's duties as those of a promoter rather than those of an intellectual leader. During this whole period, the trustees maintained their interest in buildings. Taylor's greatest service to Vassar, however, was the high standard he set for its academic work, a standard never relaxed. The college was freed from special and preparatory students, and became a compact, unified faculty of liberal arts. He gathered about him a strong group of teachers, highly individual and often of views on education opposed to his own, with whom he remained on the friendliest terms. Few presidents have held unwavering support for nearly thirty years, as he did.

His early training had been strongly conservative, but his sympathies were with youth, and he steadily broadened the curriculum, especially in the social sciences, in history, economics, political science, sociology, and religion. He obtained the recognition of art and music as academic subjects, and the teaching of science on strictly experimental bases. He created an intense personal devotion to himself and to his college, which for years distinguished Vassar graduates. His refusal of the presidency of Brown University in 1899 elicited marked evidence of this. He was for four years a member of the Carnegie Foundation, 1910–14, and his advice on educational policy was widely sought. His later years in office were somewhat hampered by physical causes, and in 1914 he resigned. His death followed after only two years. Memorials to him exist at Vassar in a gate, a stained-glass window, a professorship of philosophy, an endowment fund, a library fund, and Taylor Hall of Art. A portrait by William Chase was presented by the alumnae. All these are less significant than the innumerable memories of his idealism and genial humor in the unrecorded history of the college, and the loyalty that he guided to fruition in the college of today.

[MSS. in Vassar College archives; *Vassar*, ante; E. H. Haight, *Life and Letters of James Monroe Taylor* (1919); Elisha Taylor, *Geneal. of Judge John Taylor and His Descendants* (1886); *N. Y. Times*, Dec. 20, 1916.]   H. N. M.

TAYLOR, JAMES WICKES (Nov. 6, 1819–Apr. 28, 1893), consular officer, author, journalist, was born at Starkey, Yates County, N. Y., the eldest of five children of James and Maria (Wickes) Taylor. His father was a lawyer, the son of an Englishman who had served in Burgoyne's army. Taylor was graduated from Hamilton College in 1838 and soon settled in Cincinnati, where he combined the study of law with journalism. He established the *Cincinnati Morning Signal* in 1846 and later edited a newspaper at Sandusky. He was a representative at the second Ohio constitutional convention, 1850–51; secretary of a commission to revise the judicial code of the state, 1851–52; and head of the Ohio state library, 1854–56 (see D. J. Ryan, "The State Library and Its Founder," *Ohio Archaeological and Historical Quarterly,* January 1919). In 1856 he established a law office in Saint Paul, Minnesota Territory. Already the author of *The Victim of Intrigue* (1847), a defense of Senator John Smith [*q.v.*] of Ohio in relation to the Burr conspiracy; a competently done *History of the State of Ohio* (1854), covering the period to 1787; and a *Manual of the Ohio School System* (1857), he took an active part in discussions preceding the first constitutional convention of Minnesota. As secretary of the Minnesota and Pacific Railroad he urged upon the state legislature the passage of a "Five Million Loan" to railroads distressed by the panic of 1857.

Sensing the growing importance of the Canadian Northwest, he made a report to the Minnesota legislature on *Northwest British America and Its Relations to the State of Minnesota* (1860). In 1859 he had been appointed a special agent of the Treasury Department, charged with investigating trade and transportation between the United States and Canada, and in 1860 with I. T. Hatch of New York state he reported on the reciprocity treaty of 1854 (*House Exec. Doc. 96, 36* Cong., 1 Sess.). In 1862 he reported on relations between the United States and Northwest British America (*House Exec. Doc. 146, 37* Cong., 2 Sess.), and in a later study (*House Exec. Doc. 128, 39* Cong., 1 Sess.) proposed a union of the United States and British America. With J. Ross Browne he published *Reports upon the Mineral Resources of the United States* (1867). After leaving the service of the Treasury Department (1869) he became an agent for the Lake Superior and Mississippi Railroad and for the Saint Paul and Pacific Railroad, composing newspaper articles and helping with congressional legislation. The outbreak of discontent in Canada in the Red River Rebellion of

1869–70 brought him an appointment as special agent for the State Department. (For some of Taylor's reports, see *Sen. Exec. Doc. 33,* 41 Cong., 2 Sess.) In 1870 he became American consul at Winnipeg (appointment confirmed, Dec. 9, 1870). Through his discovery of plans for a Fenian attack from the United States upon Manitoba (1871), the authorities were enabled to check the movement immediately. Later, in 1885, when Saskatchewan half-breeds rose against the Dominion government, he prevented assistance to them from Indians in the United States. His valuable service and loose political attachments secured his retention under both Republican and Democratic administrations until his death at Winnipeg from paralysis. Scholarly rather than political in his inclinations, a gentleman of charming personality, he endeared himself not only to Americans but to Canadians, who placed a large portrait of him in the city hall at Winnipeg. His wife, Chloe Sweeting Langford, whom he married in 1845 (Blegen, *post,* p. 156), bore him four daughters, two of whom survived him. He was buried at Utica, N. Y.

[See T. C. Blegen, "James Wickes Taylor: A Biog. Sketch," *Minn. Hist. Bull.,* Nov. 1915, based on extensive colls. of Taylor MSS., with bibliog.; W. W. Folwell, *A Hist. of Minn.,* vol. II (1924), pp. 102 n., 257, vol. III (1926), pp. 377, 379; H. M. Wriston, *Executive Agents in Am. Foreign Relations* (1929), pp. 738–42; obituaries in *Appletons' Ann. Cyc.,* 1893, and *Daily Pioneer Press* (St. Paul), Apr. 29, 1893. Examples of Taylor's consular reports are in *Ann. Report on the Commercial Relations between the U. S. and Foreign Nations . . . 1871* (1872), and *Commercial Relations of the U. S. with Foreign Countries, 1893* (1894).]   F. P. W.

TAYLOR, JOHN (1752–Apr. 12, 1835), frontier Baptist preacher, was the son of Lazarus and Anna (Bradford) Taylor of Fauquier County, Va., and the great-grandson of John Taylor, who with two brothers, Argyle and William, emigrated from England to Virginia in 1650. His maternal grandfather was a native of Scotland; his maternal grandmother, of France. During John's early boyhood his father moved to Frederick County, on the Shenandoah River. Because of the intemperate habits of the father, the burden of supporting the family came to rest chiefly on the son, and as a result he grew up with little education. At about the age of seventeen, he fell under the influence of William Marshall, a Baptist minister, uncle of the future Chief Justice of the United States, and professed conversion. Three years later he was baptized by John Ireland, one of the famous Virginia Baptist preachers. Soon afterward he was licensed to preach and for a number of years, he, with Joseph Redding, another Baptist minister, ranged through the mountains preaching and organizing churches among the scattered settlements on the Shenandoah, Potomac, Monongahela, and Green Brier rivers, occasionally crossing into Kentucky.

In 1782 he was married to Elizabeth, the daughter of Philemon and Nancy (Cave) Kavanaugh, "a young lady of a respectable family, and a member of the Baptist Church" (Sprague, *post,* p. 154). Soon after his marriage he fell heir to the estate of a bachelor uncle in Virginia, amounting to about $3,000. In 1783, he moved with his wife to Kentucky, sojourning for a time on Gilbert's Creek, south of the Kentucky River, and in 1784 settling in Woodford County, where he acquired about 1,500 acres of land, which, with the exception of some 400 acres, he gradually disposed of to friends. Here he lived until 1795, in which year he moved with his family to Boone County, across from the mouth of the Great Miami, where he had acquired 3,000 acres of land in different tracts. In 1802 he transferred his abode some sixty miles down the Ohio to Corn Creek, across from the present site of Madison, Ind. Here again he soon had a large farm under cultivation. Thirteen years later he moved to Big Spring in Woodford County. Altogether, Taylor cleared more than four hundred acres of heavily timbered land in Kentucky besides making other improvements.

Throughout his life he was active in the work of frontier Baptist churches, and is one of the best examples of the farmer-preachers who were so largely responsible for the founding of Baptist churches in Western Virginia, North Carolina, Kentucky, and Tennessee. He was connected with ten different churches, two in Virginia and eight in Kentucky; the story of his pastoral activities he related in *A History of Ten Baptist Churches* (1823), which presents an excellent picture of frontier religion. It was Taylor's custom to visit eight or ten Baptist associations each year, and in these his counsel was always highly valued. In 1820, he published a pamphlet called *Thoughts on Missions,* in which he bitterly attacked the missionary movement just then getting under way in the West. He contended that the missionary system was opposed to the Baptist scheme of church government and that the chief object of the missionary societies was to get money. During the latter years of his life he seems to have repented of his opposition, but his pamphlet was one of the principal influences which started the anti-mission movement among Western Baptists. He was also the author of *History of Clear Creek Church: and Campbellism Exposed* (1830). He was strong of body, bold and fearless, always cheerful, judicious, and zealous. Probably he exercised a larger influence among Baptists in Kentucky during his generation than any other single individual.

[Besides the books mentioned above, see W. B. Sprague, *Annals of the Am. Baptist Pulpit* (1860); W. W. Sweet, *Religion on the Am. Frontier: The Baptists* (1931); J. H. Spencer, *A Hist. of Ky. Baptists* (copr., 1885), vol. I; J. B. Taylor, *Va. Baptist Ministers,* 1 ser. (1860); *Frankfort Argus,* Apr. 22, 1835, which gives date of death.]   W. W. S.

TAYLOR, JOHN (Dec. 19 (?), 1753–Aug. 21, 1824), political writer and agriculturist, generally known as "John Taylor of Caroline," was the son of James and Ann (Pollard) Taylor. The exact place of his birth has not been established, both Orange and Caroline Counties in Virginia claiming the honor, with inconclusive evidence in favor of the latter. His father died when John was three years of age and his mother a few years later, leaving his rearing to Edmund Pendleton [*q.v.*], who was the double first cousin of James Taylor and had married Ann Pollard's sister. The boy received his early education from private tutors and in a private school conducted in King and Queen County by Donald Robertson, also the teacher of President James Madison, whose grandmother, Frances Taylor, was a first cousin of John's father. Here he studied Greek and Latin and acquired the rudiments of both French and Spanish. In 1770 he entered the College of William and Mary, continuing for at least two years, and then turned his efforts to the reading of law in the office of his patron. He received a license to practise in 1774.

With the outbreak of the American Revolution Taylor entered the army. He served first in his native state, then around New York and Philadelphia. He had reached the rank of major when the reduction of the Continental Army in 1779 left more officers than were needed, causing him to resign and return home. Two years later he was appointed lieutenant-colonel in the Virginia militia and ended his military career fighting with Lafayette against the invading Hessians. In 1783 he was married to a cousin, Lucy Penn, daughter of John Penn [*q.v.*], the signer, a prosperous lawyer and planter of North Carolina, who was to contribute generously to his economic establishment. To them were born six sons and two daughters. They made their home at "Hazlewood," one of several plantations purchased by Taylor in Caroline County.

On his return from the army in 1779 he was elected to the Virginia House of Delegates, where he remained, with the exception of the year 1782, until 1785. He returned again for a four-year period in 1796. At three different times he was a member of the United States Senate. In 1792 he was chosen to fill the post vacated by the illness of Richard Henry Lee, and served until 1794. The death of Senator Stevens Thomson Mason in 1803 brought him back for a second period of service and the resignation of James Pleasants, Jr., in 1822 led to his appointment for a third time. Taylor early cast his lot with the rising democratic group led by Thomas Jefferson. In the Virginia House he took part in the final steps toward religious freedom and was prominent in forwarding land legislation and extending the North Carolina boundary line to the advantage of actual settlers. He favored a wider franchise and supported the moves for a more equal system of representation. Though not a member of the Virginia convention which ratified the federal Constitution, he joined with Patrick Henry and George Mason in opposition on the grounds that the rights of the individual and of the states were not sufficiently protected. When the new central government was established and showed signs of making the most of its powers, he quickly saw the dangers in "consolidation" and the desirability of a strict construction of the Constitution. His first political pamphlets, *A Definition of Parties* (1794) and *An Enquiry into the Principles and Tendencies of Certain Public Measures* (1794), were a condemnation of Hamilton's funding and banking measures. These he viewed as "usurpations upon constitutional principles" which, "if suffered to acquire maturity" would "only yield to the dreadful remedy of a civil war." They aimed, he thought, at the creation of an aristocratic "paper" junto and the subversion of democratic government. In 1795 he published *An Argument Respecting the Constitutionality of the Carriage Tax.* He held the Alien and Sedition Acts null and void and in December 1798 introduced into the Virginia legislature the famous resolutions in support of the doctrine of delegated powers and the right of the states to interpose in cases of "deliberate, palpable and dangerous exercise of other powers."

Taylor was a stanch supporter of Jefferson in the presidential election of 1800 and played an important part in the passage of the Twelfth Amendment in order to protect the popular choice of the president. In *A Defence of the Measures of the Administration of Thomas Jefferson* (1805) he upheld even the purchase of Louisiana, but drifted gradually over to the Tertium Quid group and supported Monroe against Madison in 1808. Always consistent, he

opposed the War of 1812 as tending to increase the activity and powers of the Central government and endangering "the pursuit of happiness."

Taylor's greatest influence came from his larger political writings. In 1814 he published *An Inquiry into the Principles and Policy of the Government of the United States*—a volume first conceived in 1794 as an answer to John Adams' *A Defence of the Constitutions of Government of the United States of America.* Of this work it has been said: "Whatever its shortcomings in prolixity of style, it deserves to rank among the two or three really historic contributions to political science which have been produced in the United States" (Beard, *post,* p. 323). In it he denied the existence of "a natural aristocracy" and condemned a permanent debt with taxes and a banking system to support it. He thought the executive too powerful. He would shorten the terms of both the president and the senators and check their patronage. The American government, he explained, was one of divided powers, not classes, and its agents were responsible to the sovereign people alone. The great danger to democracy lay in consolidation and in the creation of an aristocracy of "paper and patronage." In 1820 his *Construction Construed and Constitutions Vindicated* appeared. John Marshall's decisions, especially in the case of *McCulloch* vs. *Maryland,* had aroused him and the Missouri Compromise excited his fears. He sharply denied the validity of appeals from state courts to the United States Supreme Court and insisted that the jurisdiction of the latter, except in specified cases, was confined to appeals from courts established by Congress. The states, he thought, had the right to unlimited taxation, except on imports and exports. Marshall's bank decision was a continuation of the old effort to create private property beyond the reach of the state and to upset the balance created by the Constitution in which neither state nor federal government was supreme or subordinate. The whole question of a federal negative on state action, he later declared, had been discussed and rejected in the Constitutional Convention. To Taylor the Missouri question was also the product of the same self-seeking group who had brought forward the bank and the bounties to manufactories. Slavery was but an excuse for securing a balance of sectional powers in order to "beget new usurpations of internal powers over persons and property" (*Construction Construed,* p. 298). He denied the right of Congress to dictate to Missouri, since the presence or absence of slavery had nothing to do with a republican form of government. A third pamphlet, *Tyranny Unmasked* (1822), was a direct and powerful attack on the protective tariff system. He viewed this as unconstitutional and as creating privilege and diminishing revenue. The home-market argument was false, the idea of a favorable balance of trade foolish. Tariffs interfered with the sound and natural development of the nation's economic life. Government was becoming superior to the governed. Another work was *New Views of the Constitution of the United States* (1823).

As implied in these writings, Taylor's fundamental purpose was to preserve the old agricultural order and the security of the freeholder on which it rested. His practical efforts were aimed in the same direction. A farmer himself, he strove to improve agricultural methods on his own estate and in 1803 published a series of essays in a Georgetown newspaper to explain his methods and his ideas. These were later reprinted (1813) in book form under the title *The Arator*. The central idea in this work was the restoration of lost fertility to the soils by what he called "enclosing." He believed that plants drew on the atmosphere for life and that as a result of plowing under crops and applying manure soils would regain lost fertility. He would exclude all stock from arable and grass lands and produce only those crops which afforded the largest quantity of offal for feeding and plowing under. His favorite crop was corn but he advocated the growing of clover and field peas in rotation, and the employment of deeper plowing for all crops. He rejected tobacco, the overseer system, and the use of unprofitable slaves. He would make the farmer a power capable of protecting his interests against the encroachments of central government.

John Taylor was one of America's greatest disciples and philosophers of agrarian liberalism. He was the champion of local democracy and one of the first and clearest spokesmen of state rights. The laborious style of his writings has probably prevented his receiving recognition equal to that given other champions of these ideas.

[H. H. Simms, *Life of John Taylor* (1932); W. E. Dodd, "John Taylor, of Caroline, Prophet of Secession," in *The John P. Branch Hist. Papers of Randolph-Macon College*, vol. II (1908); Gaillard Hunt, ed., *Disunion Sentiment in Congress in 1794. A Confidential Memorandum . . . by John Taylor of Caroline* (1905), with a useful introduction; J. T. Carpenter, *The South as a Conscious Minority* (1930); C. A. Beard, *Economic Origins of Jeffersonian Democracy* (1915), ch. XI; B. F. Wright, Jr., "The Philosopher of Jeffersonian Democracy," in *Am. Pol. Science Review*, Nov. 1928; A. O. Craven, *Soil Exhaustion as a Factor in the Agricultural Hist. of Va. and Md.*, 1606–

1860 (1925); L. C. Gray, *Hist. of Agriculture in the Southern U. S. to 1860* (2 vols., 1933).]   A. O. C.

TAYLOR, JOHN (Nov. 1, 1808–July 25, 1887), third president of the Utah branch of the Mormon Church, was born in Milnthorpe, Westmoreland County, England, the son of James and Agnes (Taylor) Taylor. He received only the rudiments of an elementary education, being apprenticed at fourteen to learn the trades of cooper and turner. Although his family was nominally Anglican, in his sixteenth year he became interested in Methodism and during the following year was appointed exhorter, or local preacher. In 1832 he followed his parents to Toronto, Canada. The next year he married Leonora Cannon. In Canada he at once became active in the local Methodist organization, but, possessed of somewhat mystical tendencies, he was not entirely satisfied with Methodism, and turned to Irvingism, which, also, in a short time he abandoned. Not long afterward he was introduced to Mormonism by Parley P. Pratt [*q.v.*] and in 1836 was baptized in the Mormon church. Presently he was ordained an elder and put in charge of missionary work in upper Canada.

He made several visits to Kirtland, Ohio, participated in the Mormon migration to Missouri in 1838, and on July 8 of that year was chosen by Joseph Smith [*q.v.*] an apostle "by revelation." He did not assume his official responsibilities until December, however, when he was "ordained to the office" by Brigham Young and Heber C. Kimball [*qq.v.*]. During the conflicts between Mormons and non-Mormons in Missouri and Illinois he played a prominent rôle in defending the Mormon cause and in keeping up morale. At Nauvoo, Ill., he served from 1842 to 1846 as editor for the *Times and Seasons*, the official Mormon periodical, and also owned and published the *Nauvoo Neighbor*, a strong proMormon newspaper. He was city councilman, a regent of "Nauvoo University," and judge advocate of the Nauvoo Legion. When in June 1844 Joseph and Hyrum Smith were imprisoned in the jail at Carthage, Ill., Taylor and Willard Richards, another apostle, accompanied them "as friends." In the attack on the jail by the lynching mob seeking the Prophet, Taylor was seriously wounded, but recovered.

In the controversy over the successorship to Smith, Taylor, like most of the Twelve Apostles, threw in his lot with the Brigham Young faction. He trekked across the plains to Utah, assisted in colonizing there, and was always ready to defend his Church against all critics. He was a member of the territorial legislature from 1857 to 1876 and served as speaker of the lower house for five successive sessions, beginning in 1857. From 1868 to 1870 he was probate judge of Utah County, and in 1877 he was elected territorial superintendent of schools. After Brigham Young's death in 1877, Taylor, who was head of the quorum of Twelve Apostles, directed the affairs of the Church for three years in the capacity of acting president. It was not until October 1880 that he was officially sustained by the semi-annual conference as "President of the Church of Jesus Christ of Latter-day Saints and Prophet, Seer, and Revelator to the Church in all the world" (Jenson, *post*, p. 18).

A man of great spiritual gifts, Taylor had a strong faith in divine revelation. He did not add materially to church dogma or organization, but ably carried on the traditions established by his two predecessors. He was a very effective speaker, and his most noteworthy contribution was his active proselyting. His first extensive missionary work was done in 1840 and 1841 in England; he introduced Mormonism to the Isle of Man, to Ireland, and to Scotland, and managed the migration of many of the new converts from England to the United States. After Brigham Young assumed control over the main body of the Mormons and had managed their exodus from Illinois to the Missouri River, Taylor, with Orson Hyde and Parley P. Pratt, returned to England in 1846 to insure the support of the British converts. He and his colleagues successfully counteracted the claims of Sidney Rigdon [*q.v.*] to be successor to Joseph Smith, and the similar claims of James J. Strang [*q.v.*], thus saving the British mission to the Utah Mormons. After a short period in Utah, Taylor was dispatched to France in 1849 and later to Germany to carry the Mormon gospel to these countries. He arranged for both the German and the French translations of *The Book of Mormon*. During the fifties, when the conflict between the Mormons and non-Mormons in the United States took on national interest, he was put in charge of missionary work in the Eastern states. In 1854 he established a newspaper in New York City called *The Mormon,* designed to answer the attack of anti-Mormon agitators, most notable among whom was James Gordon Bennett [*q.v.*]. In 1857, because of the impending invasion of Utah by federal troops, he gave up his newspaper campaign and returned to Salt Lake City, but in the years that followed continued to answer the accusations of the critics of his faith both in the local and in the Eastern metropolitan press. His replies to the charges of Vice-President Schuyler Colfax [*q.v.*], who had taken a hand in the public clamor, furnish

an excellent picture of the pro-Mormon view of the so-called Mormon "menace."

Taylor accepted the doctrine and practice of plural marriage in Nauvoo. He had seven wives, four of whom outlived him. These women bore him thirty-four children. After the passage of the Edmunds-Tucker act in 1882, Taylor tried to assuage the federal prosecution by maintaining his official residence in the Gardo House in Salt Lake City with his sister as his housekeeper, while his wives and children remained in semi-seclusion in their respective households. In spite of this public gesture of compliance, and in spite of his public admonition to his followers to "be quiet" in the face of federal prosecution, Taylor himself was forced in 1884 to go into voluntary exile to escape arrest. His health became rapidly enfeebled and he died in 1887 at Kaysville, Utah. For nearly three years he had directed the Church while in effect a fugitive from justice. He published a theological work entitled, *An Examination into and an Elucidation of the Great Principles of the Mediation and Atonement of Our Lord and Savior Jesus Christ* (1882), and was the author of numerous pamphlets, editorials, and letters.

[Andrew Jenson, *Latter-day Saint Biog. Encyc.* (1901), I, 14–19; B. H. Roberts, *The Life of John Taylor* (1892) and *A Comprehensive Hist. of the Church of Jesus Christ of Latter-Day Saints: Century I* (1930); *Deseret Evening News,* July 26, 1887.]

K. Y.

TAYLOR, JOHN LOUIS (Mar. 1, 1769–Jan. 29, 1829), jurist, was born in London, England, of Irish parentage. At the age of twelve he came to America, an orphan, with his elder brother James, by whose assistance he was able to pursue classical studies at William and Mary College. Compelled to leave college before graduation, he went to North Carolina, studied law, was licensed to practise in 1788, and settled at Fayetteville. His handsome physique, native talent, genial nature, ingenuity in argument, power of oratory, and Federalism in politics, quickly brought him legal, social, and political distinction. As borough representative of Fayetteville in the House of Commons (1792, 1794–95), he supported measures to encourage trade, prohibit the importation of slaves, permit manumission, and improve the administration of justice. He was a presidential elector in 1792 and an unsuccessful candidate before the General Assembly for solicitor general in 1790 and for attorney general in 1795. His first wife was Julia Rowan, by whom he had a daughter. About 1797 he moved to New Bern and in that year married Jane, the sister of William Gaston [*q.v.*], by whom he had a son and a daughter.

In 1798 he was elected by the General Assembly as a judge of the superior court and began a distinguished judicial career of thirty years. In the absence of a state court of appeals, the superior court judges were required from 1799 to meet twice each year in Raleigh as a court, called the court of conference from 1801 and the supreme court from 1805, for the determination of questions of law and equity arising on the circuits. In pursuance of a law of 1810, the judges selected Taylor in July 1811 as presiding officer with the title of chief justice. From about this time he resided in Raleigh. In 1818 the General Assembly established a distinct supreme court and chose Taylor one of the three judges. At the first term of this court, in January 1819, his associates elected him chief justice—a position which he held until his death in 1829. As the first chief justice, Taylor brought learning, respectability, and prestige to the supreme court. "Preëminently a safe judge" who followed precedent with religious zeal, he made no distinctive contributions to jurisprudence; but broad information, exemplary patience, unfailing courtesy, high feelings, good judgment, and love of justice won esteem for him and respect for the law. His opinions, as found in 1–12 *North Carolina Reports* are marked in many instances by thoroughness of legal investigation and clarity of composition.

Early in his career he began to make notes on cases which came before him and in 1802 issued *Cases Determined in the Superior Courts . . .*, reprinted in the first volume of *North Carolina Reports*. He subsequently published *Carolina Law Repository* (2 vols., 1814–16), and *Cases Adjudged in the Supreme Court of North Carolina from July Term 1816, to January Term, 1818, Inclusive* (1818), known as "North Carolina Term Reports," both reprinted in part in 4 *North Carolina Reports*. Under legislative appointment of 1817 to revise the statute law, Taylor, Henry Potter, and Bartlett Yancey issued *Laws of the State of North Carolina* (2 vols., 1821), known as "Potter's Revisal"; Taylor continued the work through 1825 in *A Revisal of the Laws . . .* (1827), known as "Taylor's Revisal." He also published *A Charge Delivered to the Grand Jury of Edgecombe Superior Court . . .* (1817) and *A Digest of the Statute Law of North Carolina Relative to Wills, Executors and Administrators, the Provision for Widows, and the Distribution of Intestates Estates* (1824). He was grand master of the Masonic fraternity in North Carolina (1802–05, 1814–17), a benefactor of the University of North Carolina, and a trustee (1793–

1818). His death occurred at his home in Raleigh.

[*Laws of N. C.,* 1799–1818; *Jours. of the House of Commons,* 1790–1818; Craven County Marriage Bonds, in N. C. Hist. Commission; *Fayetteville Gazette,* Dec. 11, 1792; *Raleigh Reg. and North-Carolina State Gazette,* July 5, 1811; *Raleigh Reg. and North-Carolina Gazette,* Jan. 8, 1819, Feb. 3, 1829; W. H. Hoyt, *The Papers of Archibald D. Murphey* (1914), vol. I; 16 *N. C. Reports,* 308; 107 *N. C. Reports,* App. following p. 985; W. H. Battle, "Memoir of John Louis Taylor," in *N. C. Univ. Mag.,* Mar. 1860; S. A. Ashe, *Biog. Hist. of N. C.,* vol. V (1906); K. P. Battle, *Hist. of the Univ. of N. C.,* vol. I (1907); Walter Clark, "Hist. of the Superior and Supreme Courts of N. C.," in *The N. C. Booklet,* Oct. 1918.]   A. R. N.

TAYLOR, JOHN W. (Mar. 26, 1784–Sept. 18, 1854), anti-slavery leader, was born at Charlton, N. Y., the son of Judge John Taylor and Chloe (Cox) Taylor, and a descendant of Edward Taylor who settled in Monmouth County, N. J., in 1692. After graduating from Union College, Schenectady, he began the study of law with Samuel Cook. Admitted to the bar in 1807, he formed a partnership with Cook and began to practise at Ballston Spa. On July 10, 1806, he married Jane Hodge, who died in 1838, having borne him three daughters and five sons. After two years in the New York Assembly (1811–12), he represented Saratoga County for twenty consecutive years in the federal House of Representatives (Mar. 4, 1813–Mar. 3, 1833). He favored a national bank and a protective tariff, although he regarded federal appropriations for roads and canals as unconstitutional. During the presidency of the second Adams he was a leader of administration policies and later a member of the Whig party.

The slavery question brought him into national prominence. He seconded the amendment of James Tallmadge [*q.v.*] to the Missouri bill, prohibiting the further introduction of slavery in the proposed state and liberating at the age of twenty-five all children born of slave parents. To the bill organizing Arkansas Territory, he moved a similar amendment. When his motion was lost he submitted a proposal prohibiting the introduction of slavery into the territories north of 36° 30', in support of his restrictive policy delivering some of the first anti-slavery speeches heard in Congress (*Annals of Congress,* 15 Cong., 2 Sess., pp. 1170–93; 16 Cong., 1 Sess., pp. 958–66). He argued that the power of Congress to admit new states implied a power to refuse to admit, and hence a power to prescribe conditions on which it would admit. As precedents he pointed to Ohio, Indiana, and Illinois, which had been compelled to frame constitutions excluding slavery, and to Louisiana, where Congress had insisted on English as the official language and the guarantee of *habeas corpus*, jury trial, and religious liberty. He also held that the provision vesting in Congress power to prohibit the "importation or migration" of slaves after 1808 was applicable in this connection, since the word "migration" meant the passage from one commonwealth to another. As to the expediency of restriction, he contended that slavery was ruinous to the economy of the country. He declared, also, that Congress was obligated to restrict slavery since slavery was incompatible with the "republican form of government" which it was the constitutional duty of the United States to guarantee to every state.

Taylor served two terms as speaker of the House of Representatives (Nov. 15, 1820–Mar. 3, 1821, Dec. 5, 1825–Mar. 3, 1827), in each case being defeated for reëlection. In a letter to his son, he said: "I lost my third election as Speaker through my direct opposition to slavery" (MS., in the possession of Taylor's granddaughter, Mrs. Clarissa Taylor Bass, Freeport, Ill.). While the South never forgave the part he played in the Missouri controversy, the chief opposition came from his own state The anti-Clintonian faction in New York encompassed his defeat in 1821, and the Van Buren Democrats were largely responsible for it in 1827. In November 1832 they thwarted his reëlection to Congress. From 1840 to 1842 he was a member of the New York Senate, from which ill health compelled his retirement. In 1843 he removed to Cleveland, Ohio, where he spent the remainder of his life at his daughter's home.

[Elisha Taylor, *Geneal. of Judge John Taylor and His Descendants* (1886); *Biog. Dir. Am. Cong.* (1928); *Memoirs of John Quincy Adams*, vols. IV–VII (1875); S. B. Dixon, *The True Hist. of the Mo. Compromise and Its Repeal* (1899); D. S. Alexander, *A Pol. Hist. of the State of N. Y.*, vols. I, II (1906); E. F. Grose, *Centennial Hist. of the Village of Ballston Spa* (1907); *N. Y. Tribune*, Sept. 22, 1854.]   J. G. V—D.

TAYLOR, JOSEPH WRIGHT (Mar. 1, 1810–Jan. 18, 1880), philanthropist, physician, merchant, founder of Bryn Mawr College, was born in a farmhouse in Upper Freehold Township, Monmouth County, N. J., the youngest of a family of seven. His father, Edward, descended from Edward Taylor who settled in Monmouth County in 1692, was a country physician, a graduate of the College of New Jersey. The Taylors were Baptists, but Edward joined the Society of Friends after his marriage to Sarah Merritt, whose family had been among the early Quaker settlers of New Jersey. Sarah Taylor "had a concern" (in the Quaker phrase) for the insane, and in 1823 she and her husband

became respectively matron and physician of the Friends' Asylum near Frankford, a suburb of Philadelphia. Joseph was educated at a boarding school near Frankford, and later studied medicine at the University of Pennsylvania, where he received the degree of M.D. at the early age of twenty. That same year, 1830, he sailed for India as surgeon and supercargo on a merchant vessel. Three years after his return he set off to join his brother Abraham, who had successfully established himself ten years earlier in Cincinnati as a tanner and dealer in leather. Joseph became purchasing agent for the firm and traveled widely in Ohio, Kentucky, and Indiana.

After fifteen prosperous years Taylor, an ardent traveler, started on his first European tour, and two years later settled in Burlington, N. J., where he purchased an estate and lived the life of a country gentleman. He was unmarried, but was devoted to his sister Hannah who kept house for him and had several warm friendships with other cultivated women. Descriptions in this period picture him as of medium height, unusually handsome in feature, exquisitely neat in dress, and distinguished in carriage. In 1861 he took another trip to England and the Continent, and in his later life traveled much in the United States. He was able to increase his fortune very materially by judicious investments after retiring from his brother's business.

Taylor was interested in most of the causes supported by the Society of Friends, such as abolition of slavery and promotion of international peace, temperance, and education. His determination to found a woman's college, which appears to have been fixed by the year 1875, probably had its origin in his perception of the real need for such an institution for the education of Quaker girls and his feeling that it was consistent with Quaker principles to provide the same facilities for the higher education of women in the neighborhood of Philadelphia as was provided for the education of men at Haverford College, of which he had been one of the managers since 1854.

His first plan was to open the college at Burlington near his own house in order to direct its growth himself. He was persuaded by his advisers, of whom Francis King, the president of the trustees of the Johns Hopkins Hospital, was the most trusted, that it would be wise to find a location more convenient to Philadelphia. President Gilman of Johns Hopkins, President Seelye of Smith, and other experienced educators were consulted, and two trips were made to New England to visit Mount Holyoke, Smith, and Wellesley. Land was purchased at Bryn Mawr, eleven miles from Philadelphia, in 1878, and the building begun in 1879. Taylor directed the architect to use the administration building at Smith College as the model for the main building, later named Taylor Hall. He superintended the work of construction himself, making almost daily trips to Bryn Mawr. These activities were apparently too strenuous for his health and hastened his death, which resulted from heart disease. He bequeathed practically his entire fortune of about eight hundred thousand dollars, in addition to the land and buildings, to Bryn Mawr College, appointing a board of trustees of eminent Quakers, among them Dr. James E. Rhoads [q.v.], later president of the College. While unquestionably Taylor's purpose in founding Bryn Mawr was in part religious and even sectarian, it is clear from his choice of advisers and careful consideration of the need for educational facilities in the broadest sense that he wished to found a college which would be preëminent in cultivating the intellectual as well as the spiritual interests of the rising generation of women.

[*Memoir of Joseph W. Taylor, M.D.* (privately printed, 1884), written by President Rhoads in consultation with members of the Taylor family; Joseph Parrish, "Memorial Notice of Dr. Joseph W. Taylor," *Trans. Medic. Soc. of N. J.,* 1880; *Addresses at the Inauguration of Bryn Mawr College* (1886); Elisha Taylor, *Geneal. of Judge John Taylor and His Descendants* (1886); *Phila. Inquirer,* Jan. 20, 1880; unprinted letters and diaries in the possession of the Taylor family.]
H. T. M.

TAYLOR, MARSHALL WILLIAM (July 1, 1846–Sept. 11, 1887), Methodist Episcopal clergyman and editor, was born in Lexington, Ky. Both his parents were, or had been, slaves; ultimately both acquired freedom. Marshall, according to one authority, adopted the name of Taylor, that of his father being Samuel Boyd and that of his mother Nancy Ann (Williams, *post,* p. 469). The former was of Scotch-Irish and Indian descent; the latter, of African and Arabian, her mother having been brought from Madagascar when a child. Marshall's opportunities for education were few. He attended schools for free negro children in Lexington and at Louisville, to which place the family moved after his father's death. In the latter city he became a messenger for a law firm. In 1866 he taught school in Breckenridge County, Ky., and two years later presided at an educational convention held at Owensboro, Ky.

At a quarterly conference of the Hardinsburg Circuit, Ky., in 1869 he was licensed as a Methodist Episcopal preacher. He then did missionary work in Arkansas and other parts of the Southwest. In 1872 he was admitted on trial to the Lexington Conference, and that same year was sent to the General Conference as a lay delegate. For five consecutive years he was corresponding secretary of the Annual Conference to which he belonged. He was ordained deacon in February 1874, and elder in March 1876. From 1872 to 1875, in addition to his pastoral work, he issued the *Kentucky Methodist.* He served first as pastor of the Litchfield Circuit and then of the Coke Chapel Circuit at Louisville. In 1875 he was placed in charge of Coke Chapel at Indianapolis, and two years later was sent to the Union Methodist Episcopal Church in Cincinnati. In 1878 he became presiding elder of the Ohio District. He was a fraternal delegate from his Church to a conference of the African Methodist Episcopal Church, in 1880, and the following year a delegate to the Ecumenical Conference in London. Made presiding elder of the Louisville District in 1883, he was the senior ministerial delegate to the General Conference of 1884. At this gathering he was chosen at a caucus of the negro delegates as their nominee for the bishopric of West Africa. His health was poor, however, and, fearing the effect of the African climate, he declined to be a candidate. He was thereupon elected editor of the *Southwestern Christian Advocate,* published in New Orleans, which position he filled until the time of his death.

The acceptance of this editorship proved to be an unfortunate move for Taylor. Desk work was unfavorable to his health and he disliked it. Furthermore, although in private intercourse and in his public addresses he spoke fluently, he could not express himself as easily and forcibly in print. A zealous adherent of his Church, he upheld the action of the Methodist authorities in refusing to admit negroes to the Chattanooga denominational school established for white pupils. In his editorials he urged the colored people to work out their own destiny apart from the whites if necessary and not to strive for educational, social, and religious equality with them. The negro press took exception to his views, which differed widely from those held by many leaders of his race, so that in his later years he lost in popularity. In his own Church he attained a high reputation. He contributed to Methodist periodicals, wrote *The Life . . . of Mrs. Amanda Smith: The Famous Negro Missionary Evangelist* (1886) and published *A Collection of Revival Hymns and Plantation Melodies* (1882). His voice was sonorous and musical and his manners were ingratiating. He married Kate Heston, by whom he had two children.

[W. J. Simmons, *Men of Mark* (1887); G. W. Williams, *Hist. of the Negro Race in America* (1883), II,

469–74; *Minutes of the Annual Conferences of the Methodist Episcopal Church,* 1888; *Christian Recorder, Christian Advocate* (N. Y.), and *Southwestern Christian Advocate,* Sept. 22, 1887; *Indianapolis Jour.,* Sept. 14, 1887.]   H. G. V.

TAYLOR, MOSES (Jan. 11, 1806–May 23, 1882), banker and capitalist, was born in New York City, a son of Jacob B. and Mary (Cooper) Taylor and great-grandson and namesake of the founder of the family in America, who came from England in 1736. Moses' father was a New York business man, a confidential agent of John Jacob Astor. He lived on lower Broadway and the boy attended at least three private schools in the vicinity of his home. At fifteen, however, his school days were over and he became a clerk with the importing house of G. G. & S. Howland on South Street. That clerkship marked the beginning of a business career filling six decades, in which nothing was permitted to interrupt his continuous accumulation of wealth.

By 1832 he had amassed a capital of $15,000 and was in a position to set up in trade for himself. He began by handling the output of Cuban sugar planters and in his hands this business became a profitable enterprise. The great fire of December 1835 destroyed his South Street store and practically all his possessions, but hardly halted his advance to business success. At forty he was a capitalist and before he was fifty, he could well afford to leave the importing trade to become president, in 1855, of the City Bank. The panic of 1857, causing distress to more than one bank president, was for Taylor an ill wind that brought economic good. When the Delaware, Lackawanna & Western Railroad stock had fallen to five dollars a share he was able to buy outright in the open market a controlling interest in the road, which he retained until his death. Within seven years after the purchase the stock was selling at $240 a share.

Taylor was induced by Cyrus W. Field [q.v.] to join him in the first Atlantic Cable venture and he acted as treasurer of the company throughout its period of failure and near-collapse until success was won. After the discouraging break in the first cable the country was involved in civil war, with the Lincoln administration looking to New York for financial backing and leadership. Taylor, who was known as a "hard-money" Democrat but a supporter of the Washington government, acted as chairman of the bankers' committee which took the first federal loan in 1861. After the war he made heavy investments in public utilities, but the Delaware, Lackawanna & Western Railroad, in which he was closely associated with Samuel Sloan [q.v.], and the allied Lackawanna Coal & Iron Com-

pany remained his chief interests. He was noted for his complete mastery of the complicated details of his business and as late as 1870 kept his own set of books at his Fifth Avenue home (Smith, *post,* p. 376). His most distinctive banking policy was the holding of large cash reserves. In 1832 he married Catherine A. Wilson, who with three daughters and two sons inherited his estate, estimated at $40,000,000.

[*N. Y. Tribune,* May 24, 1882; *Merchants' Mag. and Commercial Rev.,* June 1864; *Railway World,* May 27, 1882; *Geneal. Record: St. Nicholas Soc. of the City of N. Y.,* vol. II (1916); George Wilson, *Portrait Gallery of the Chamber of Commerce of the State of N. Y.* (1890); H. M. Field, *Hist. of the Atlantic Telegraph* (1866); M. H. Smith, *Twenty Years among the Bulls and Bears of Wall Street* (1870); J. I. Bogen, *The Anthracite Railroads* (1927); Henry Clews, *Twenty-eight Years in Wall Street* (1886).]   W. B. S.

TAYLOR, NATHANIEL WILLIAM (June 23, 1786–Mar. 10, 1858), theologian and educator, born in New Milford, Conn., was the second son of Nathaniel and Anne (Northrop) Taylor, and grandson of the Rev. Nathanael Taylor for some fifty years the pastor of the church in that town. His first American ancestor was John Taylor who came to Windsor, Conn., probably about 1639. Prepared for college by the Rev. Azel Backus [q.v.] of Bethlehem, Nathaniel entered Yale in 1800, one of his classmates being Bennet Tyler [q.v.]. An affection of the eyes twice interfered with his studies, deferring his graduation until 1807. For a year he served as tutor in the family of Gen. Stephen Van Rensselaer of Albany, then he returned to New Haven to study theology with President Timothy Dwight [q.v.]. He was taken into the family of the president and became his amanuensis. This intimate association stimulated his interest in theological doctrines and profoundly influenced his thought and career. On Oct. 15, 1810, he was married to Rebecca Maria Hine of New Milford, and on Apr. 8, 1812, was ordained and installed minister of the First Church of Christ, New Haven. This pulpit he filled with conspicuous success for ten years. His personal dignity and uncommon beauty, reinforcing an eloquence expressive of weighty and well-ordered thought, made him one of the most powerful preachers of his day. In September 1822, upon the formation of a theological department in the college known as the Yale Divinity School, he was appointed Dwight Professor of Didactic Theology, a professorship established by the eldest son of President Dwight with the understanding that it be filled by Taylor.

The creedal faith of the Congregational and Presbyterian churches in America in those years was a type of thought associated with Augustine, systematized by Calvin, and adapted to the conditions of this country by Jonathan Edwards [*q.v.*]. In order to guard against the idea that man is saved by any merit of his own, Calvinism seemed to exclude any real freedom of choice. Edwards in his treatise on the will in grappling with this difficulty had declared that man has a natural ability to repent but is inhibited by his moral disinclinations; his only freedom is liberty to obey the strongest motive. The Edwardean system of thought, modified by Hopkins, Bellamy, and Dwight, was the orthodox belief commonly held in the New England churches and was largely influential in the West and South when Taylor assumed his duties at Yale. Being of a bold and original mind, endowed with speculative talents of a high order, and having for a motto, oft repeated, "Follow truth if it carries you over Niagara," he broke through the narrow confines of the accepted theology. Moreover, he was a revival preacher deeply concerned with relating religious truth to the facts of human consciousness. His point of divergence was the reality of the freedom of choice. He denied that our consciousness of freedom is an illusion and asserted that the will is not another name for the strongest motive, but is a power to chose between motives. Man, he affirmed, is not born totally depraved, but with certain sinful inclinations, and his "sin consists in sinning." To induce men to turn from their evil ways and choose the highest good, appeal must be made to man's natural desire for happiness, which Taylor unfortunately called "self-love." This self-love will finally become, in a regenerated mind, identical with an unselfish love for God. Such an interpretation of the freedom of the will and the modifications of Calvinism attendant upon it aroused a storm of controversy and divided the churches of New England into "Taylorites and Tylerites" the adherents of Taylor and of his principal opponent, Bennet Tyler. The debate, passing beyond the borders of New England, became the chief theological reason for the disruption of the Presbyterian Church in 1838. Taylor's controversial articles were contributed chiefly to the *Christian Spectator* (later the *Quarterly Christian Spectator*) and to the *Spirit of the Pilgrims*. Other writings of his appeared posthumously and include *Practical Sermons* (1858), *Lectures on the Moral Government of God* (1859), *Essays ... upon Selected Topics in Revealed Theology* (1859).

Taylor continued in his professorship until within a few weeks of his death. He was beloved by his pupils for his intellectual independence, the stimulating power of his thought, and his personal kindness. In 1902 the Nathaniel W. Taylor Lectureship was established in the Yale Divinity School by his daughter.

[W. O. Taylor, *Descendants of John Taylor of Windsor* (4 vols., 1931); Samuel Orcutt, *Hist. of the Towns of New Milford and Bridgewater, Conn.* (1882); F. B. Dexter, *Biog. Sketches Grads. Yale Coll.*, vol. VI (1912); Timothy Dwight, *Memories of Yale Life and Men* (1903); *Semi-Centennial Anniversary of the Divinity School of Yale Coll.* (1872); Leonard Bacon and others, *Memorial of Nathaniel W. Taylor, D.D., Three Sermons* (1858); F. H. Foster, *A Genetic Hist. of the New England Theology* (1907); T. D. Bacon, *Leonard Bacon: A Statesman in the Church* (1931).]

C. A. D—e.

TAYLOR, RAYNOR (*c.* 1747–Aug. 17, 1825), musician, composer, was born in England. Data concerning his early life are meager, and the year of his birth must be conjectured from the fact that he was twelve years old when he attended Handel's funeral as a choir boy of the Chapel Royal in 1759, and from his tombstone at St. Peter's Church, Philadelphia, Pa., which states that he died in his seventy-eighth year. He was educated at the King's Singing School in London and in 1765 became organist of a church at Chelmsford. In 1765 he became music director at Sadler's Wells Theatre in London and achieved some success as a composer of ballads. Some of his time was spent in teaching, and among his pupils was Alexander Reinagle [*q.v.*]. Taylor followed Reinagle to America in 1792, making his first appearance in Baltimore, Md., at a musical entertainment in October. He then settled in Annapolis where he had been appointed organist of St. Anne's Church, but left after a few months to become organist at St. Peter's Church in Philadelphia. He held this position until the closing years of his life. In 1820 he was one of the group that founded the Musical Fund Society in Philadelphia.

Taylor is most interesting for the type of entertainment he offered. His "olios," as he called them, were burlesques and parodies. In January 1793 he presented a "Dramatic proverb being a burletta, in one act, called *The Gray Mare's The Best Horse*"; this consisted of such episodes as "A Breakfast scene a month after marriage," "Mock wife in a violent passion," "A Father's advice to his son in law," "Dame Pliant's obedience to her husband," etc. (*Maryland Gazette*, Jan. 24, 1793). In Philadelphia Taylor gave more of his entertainments, one of them an "olio," "The Poor female ballad singer, a pathetic song; ... Ding, Dong Bell, or the Honeymoon expired; ... Character of smart Dolly, a laughing song; Rustic courtship, or the unsuccessful love of poor Thomas, a crying song with duet," etc. (*Dunlap and Claypoole's American Daily Advertiser,* Jan. 11, 1794). In April 1796 he gave an orchestral concert at Oeller's Hotel in Philadelphia; his own works on the program were "New Overture," "Divertimento" for orchestra, and a violin concerto.

Of Taylor's compositions published before he came to America, three may be found in the *Cathedral Magazine of London:* "Hear my Crying O God" (volume I, pp. 146–160); "Hear, O Lord, and Consider my Complaint" (volume II, pp. 85–96); "I Will Give Thanks unto the Lord" (volume III, pp. 85–96). A number of his works composed in America are still extant. Several songs and the libretto of a melodrama, *The Rose of Arragon* (1822), are in the New York Public Library; a manuscript piece for piano, "The Bells" (included in J. T. Howard, *A Program of Early American Piano Music,* 1931), and printed copies of "The Wounded Sailor" and "The Philadelphia Hymn" are in the Hopkinson collection at Philadelphia; two songs, *The Merry piping lad,* and *The Wand'ring village maid,* are in the Yale library. Taylor also composed music for the ballad-operas, *La Petite Piedmontesse* (1795); *The Iron Chest* (1797), *The Shipwrecked Mariner Preserved* (1797), and, with Alexander Reinagle, *Pizarro, or The Spaniards in Peru* (1800).

[In the Philadelphia city directories for the years 1810 and 1817, Taylor's first name appears as René; on his tombstone, see *Inscriptions in St. Peter's Churchyard, Philadelphia* (1879), p. 375, it appears as Rayner. For further biographical data, see *Grove's Dict. of Music and Musicians, Am. Supp.* (1930); O. G. Sonneck, *Bibliography of Early Secular Music* (1905), *Early Concert-Life in America* (1907); L. C. Madeira, *Annals of Music in Phila.* (1896); J. T. Howard, *Our Am. Music* (1931); *Poulson's Am. Daily Advertiser,* Aug. 18, 1825.]   J. T. H.

TAYLOR, RICHARD (Jan. 27, 1826–Apr. 12, 1879), Confederate soldier, the only son of Zachary [*q.v.*] and Margaret Mackall (Smith) Taylor, was born at "Springfields," the family estate near Louisville, Ky. After spending much of his boyhood at frontier camps, he was tutored by a certain Brooks at Lancaster, Mass. He was sent to Europe, probably in 1841, and studied at Edinburgh and in France. In 1843 he entered Harvard College but soon transferred to Yale, where he graduated in 1845. In July of the following year he visited General Taylor's camp at Matamoras, but rheumatism forced him to seek relief at Arkansas and Virginia springs. After managing his father's Mississippi cotton plantation, 1848–49, he established "Fashion," a sugar plantation in Saint Charles Parish, La. There he collected a valuable library, studied the works of great military masters, and read widely in English and French literature. In February 1851 he was married to Louise Marie Myrthé

Bringier (d. 1875); of their five children, two died of scarlet fever during the Civil War. Originally a Whig, Taylor became a Democrat in the fifties, attended the Charleston convention in 1860, and sought to prevent a disruption of his party. As chairman of the committee on federal relations in the state Senate, where he served from 1856 to 1861, he reported the bill to call a convention which assembled in 1861. He was elected a delegate to that body, voted for secession, and as chairman of the committee on military and naval affairs urged preparation for war. Appointed colonel of the 9th Louisiana Infantry, mustered into service July 6, he hastened to Virginia but arrived too late to participate in the Confederate victory at Bull Run. On Oct. 21, 1861, he was appointed brigadier-general by President Jefferson Davis, and served in the Valley campaign under "Stonewall" Jackson. As part of Jackson's command he joined Lee at Richmond, and, although prostrated by illness during the Seven Days' battles, he directed his troops from an ambulance. In July 1862 Taylor was promoted major-general and assigned command of the District of West Louisiana. Avoiding drawn battles, as his men were greatly outnumbered, he made numerous surprise attacks, captured arms, ammunition, and medical stores, and destroyed Federal gunboats. On Apr. 8–9, 1864, he stopped Nathaniel P. Banks's Red River campaign by decisive battles against great odds at Pleasant Hill and Mansfield (Sabine Crossroads), but was prevented from following up his victory by what he regarded as the stupid policy of the departmental commander, Edmund Kirby-Smith. In spirited letters to his superior officer he asked to be relieved of his command. After brief residence with his family at Natchitoches, he was promoted lieutenant-general on Aug. 15, 1864, and assigned to the Department of East Louisiana, Mississippi, and Alabama; three months later the command of Gen. John Bell Hood's defeated army also devolved upon him. Prompt and vigorous action was insufficient to overcome demoralization, desertion, and fraudulent practice, and on May 4, 1865, he surrendered the last Confederate army east of the Mississippi to Gen. Edward R. S. Canby at Citronelle, Ala.

Taylor's estate had been confiscated during the war, and after its close he divided his time between New Orleans and New York. He visited Washington frequently, labored to secure release of imprisoned Confederates, and exerted some influence upon President Johnson's Louisiana policy, though he failed to persuade Grant to withdraw Federal support from the Kellogg-Packard régime. In May 1873 he sailed for

Europe and was cordially received in England, France, and Germany. In his later years he served as trustee of the Peabody Education Fund for promotion of education in the South. He died of dropsy in 1879 at the home of a New York friend, Col. S. L. M. Barlow. His reminiscences, *Destruction and Reconstruction* (1879), parts of which appeared in the *North American Review,* January–April 1878, reveal literary ability of a high order. His pen portraits of Civil War characters, whether Union or Confederate, are unusually fair; his discussion of the Reconstruction period is less bitter than one might expect.

[In addition to Taylor's reminiscences, see *Official Jour. Senate of La. . . . 1856–61*; *Official Jour. of Proc. Convention of the State of La.* (1861); *War of the Rebellion: Official Records (Army)*; *Lib. of Southern Lit.*, vol. XII (1910), ed. by E. A. Alderman, etc.; *Letters of Zachary Taylor* (1908); *Obit. Record Grads. Yale Coll. . . . 1879* (1879); *Times-Picayune* (New Orleans), Apr. 5, 1925; obituary in *N. Y. Times,* Apr. 13, 1879, and the Richard Taylor Scrapbook, in the possession of his daughter, Mrs. Betty Taylor Stauffer.]

W. H. S—n.

TAYLOR, RICHARD COWLING (Jan. 18, 1789–Oct. 27, 1851), geologist and antiquarian, was born in England at Hinton, Suffolk, or at Banham, Norfolk, the third son of Samuel Taylor, a weathy farmer. His early education at Halesworth, Suffolk, was extensive in higher mathematics and mapping, and about 1805 he was articled to a land surveyor in Gloucestershire, with whom he remained until about 1811. His first instructor, William Smith, the "Father of British Geology," later became his close friend. A Norman ruin on his father's estate interested Taylor in antiquities, and in 1821 he published his first volume, *Index Monasticus, or the Abbeys and Other Monasteries . . . Formerly Established in the Diocese of Norwich and the Ancient Kingdom of East Anglia.* Later (1830) he brought out an index to the new edition of Sir William Dugdale's *Monasticon Anglicanum; A History of the Abbies and Other Monasteries . . . in England and Wales.* These works brought him high commendation from such men as Sir Walter Scott, who expressed his admiration of the book in a letter to Taylor (Taylor, *post,* p. 39). In the meantime his interest in geology had been growing. Between 1811 and 1813 he surveyed in various parts of the country, and at one time had charge of a department of the ordnance for Buckingham and Bedford. In the fall of 1826 he removed to London, where he was engaged on the ordnance survey of England. A year later he published *On the Geology of East Norfolk* (1827), which emphasized facts relating to successive stratification. Among his reports on

mining properties was one on the British Iron Company of South Wales, and his plaster model of its mines, said to be the first ever made, earned the Isis Medal of the Society of Arts.

In July 1830 Taylor sailed with his wife, Emily Errington, whom he had married in 1820, and four daughters for the United States. British geologists and engineers later believed that, had he remained a little longer in England, he would have taken a leading part in railway development. In Pennsylvania he became engaged in a survey of the Blossburg coal region, and in the exploration of the coal and iron veins of the Dauphin & Susquehanna Coal Company. He was able, because of his intimate knowledge of theoretical geology, for the first time to relate the Old Red Sandstone underlying the coal fields of Pennsylvania to its true place, corresponding with its place in the series of European rocks. He later explored many mineral districts containing gold, silver, lead, copper, coal, asphaltum, and other materials, and ranged as far as the copper mines of Cuba, the gold fields of Panama, and the asphaltum of New Brunswick. His chief and monumental work, *Statistics of Coal* (1848), published in Philadelphia, drew extravagant praise from scientific journals of the day all over the world. He himself felt the results to be extremely uncertain because "this species of investigation savours too much of scrutiny into the private concerns of men" (*Statistics of Coal,* p. xi). While some of his conclusions were disproved in later years in the light of subsequent investigations (Lesley, *post,* p. 20), his careful and intricately detailed work in geology placed him in the first ranks of his day. He died in Philadelphia.

[P. M. Taylor, *A Memoir of the Family of Taylor of Norwich* (privately printed, 1886); *Dict. of Nat. Biog.*; Isaac Lea, in *Proc. Acad. Natural Sciences of Phila.*, vol. V (1852); G. P. Merrill, *The First One Hundred Years of Am. Geology* (1924), pp. 211–12, 667; J. P. Lesley, *Hist. Sketch of Geological Explorations in Pa. and Other States* (1876); obituary in *Gentleman's Mag.* (London), Feb. 1852; death notice in *North Am. and U. S. Gazette* (Phila.), Oct. 28, 1851.] H. S. G—n.

TAYLOR, ROBERT LOVE (July 31, 1850–Mar. 31, 1912), governor of Tennessee, United States senator, lecturer, the fourth of the nine children of Nathaniel Green and Emmeline (Haynes) Taylor, was born in Happy Valley, Carter County, Tenn. He apparently absorbed more politics from his mother's brother than from his father, with the result that from early boyhood he and his elder brother, Alfred Alexander Taylor [*q.v.*], consistently took opposite sides on political questions. He was educated at Pennington Seminary in New Jersey and at Buffalo Institute (later Milligan College), Milligan,

Tenn., and later studied law. Immediately following his admission to the bar in 1878, he became a successful candidate for representative in Congress. He served in Congress (1879–81) as a Democrat from the same district that his father had represented as a Whig and that his brother was later to represent as a Republican. He was defeated for reëlection in 1880 and in 1882. Following his retirement from Congress he engaged in the practice of law and became publisher of the *Johnson City Comet,* but met with little financial success in either undertaking. In December 1885 he was appointed federal pension agent at Knoxville (appointment confirmed, Apr. 16, 1886), a position which he held until 1887.

In 1886, as the result of factional strife between the old state-rights group and the new Whig-industrialist group within the Democratic party, the rural element, which had little sympathy with either faction and which had been leaderless since the death of Andrew Johnson [*q.v.*], joined the young men of the party to force the nomination of Taylor, who was recognized to be a rising young leader, as the Democratic candidate for governor. He was accepted by the party leaders only when it became evident that any other course would bring a victory for the Republicans, who had already named his brother, Alfred, as their standard bearer. The result was the picturesque "War of the Roses," in which "Bob" and "Alf" canvassed the entire state in joint debate and through their inimitable skill as entertainers kept the campaign from becoming centered around issues which might arouse strife. "Bob" won the election, but as governor soon faced the opposition of the party leaders, who sought to prevent his renomination. In 1888, however, the same forces which had brought about his success in 1886 staged a determined fight in the party convention, and he again led his party to victory in the election. During his two terms as governor (1887–91) he applied his political philosophy that more could be gained by cooperation and conciliation than by antagonism, and succeeded in securing a more equitable distribution of the burden of taxation, in providing for improvement of the state educational system, in starting a movement for reform of the state prison system, and in encouraging the development of the natural resources of the state.

At the end of his second term, turning to the lecture platform as a means of making a living, he established a reputation through his ability to combine humor and pathos in describing the life and thoughts of the common man in such lectures as "The Fiddle and the Bow," "Visions and Dreams," and "Castles in the Air." When in 1895 his brother joined him in a lyceum lecture tour, the two are said to have taken in $40,-000 in seven months with a joint lecture on "Yankee Doodle" and "Dixie." In the meantime the condition of the Democratic party in Tennessee was once more becoming precarious because of the development of the agrarian movement and the extreme conservatism of the controlling faction. As a result Taylor was again drafted in 1896 as his party's nominee for the governorship and after a strenuous campaign succeeded in defeating his Republican opponent by a small margin. The opposition of the party machine had repeatedly frustrated his ambition to become a United States senator, but in 1906, when he opposed the popular Senator Edward Ward Carmack [*q.v.*] for the Democratic nomination in the first senatorial primary election held in Tennessee, he received a majority of the votes and took the seat in 1907 which he held until his death. In 1910, however, he was again drafted by his party to become a candidate for governor in an attempt to close a break that had occurred in the party ranks. Again the young men in the party were in revolt, and for the first time in his life he was the favorite of the party leaders and organization. But he was now an old man, the people failed to respond to his appeals, and the Republican candidate was elected by a large majority. For a time, between his last term as governor and his first term as senator, he lectured and published *Bob Taylor's Magazine,* which in 1907 became the *Taylor-Trotwood Magazine.* He was married three times, first in 1878 to Sarah L. Baird of Asheville, N. C., second to Mrs. Alice Hill of Tuscaloosa, Ala., and third in 1904 to Mamie L. St. John of Chilhowie, Va. He was survived by five children of his first marriage. In 1912 the *Lectures and Best Literary Productions of Bob Taylor* was published.

Immensely popular with the common people because of his genial personality and his ability to entertain them through lectures which Champ Clark once called "a strange commingling of wit, humor, philosophy, pathos, eloquence, common sense, and good morals," Taylor was unpopular with the party leaders, who could not control him, and who sought to discredit him by branding him as "a shallow fiddler." Yet, because he could not be ignored, he secured his opportunity to play the rôle of conciliator, and thus to make his greatest contribution to the political history of his state. He was preëminently a Democrat to whom party interest was above faction and above the individual. He probably saved his state from the excesses of the agrarian revolt, and he had great influence in the transition from reconstruction prejudice to the recovery of party consolidation in Tennessee.

[*Who's Who in America*, 1912–13; *Biog. Directory of the Am. Congress* (1928); D. M. Robison, *Bob Taylor and the Agrarian Revolt in Tenn.* (1935), the best study of Taylor's career; P. D. Augsburg, *Bob and Alf Taylor* (1925); J. P., A. A., and H. L. Taylor, *Life and Career of Senator Robert Love Taylor* (1913); DeLong Rice, *"Old Limber," or the Tale of the Taylors* (1921); *Notable Men of Tenn.* (1905), ed. by John Allison; *Robert Love Taylor . . . Memorial Addresses Delivered in the Senate and the House of Representatives* (1913); memorial and obituary notices in *Nashville Banner*, Apr. 1, and *Nashville Democrat*, Mar. 31, Apr. 1, 1912.]   W. C. B.

TAYLOR, ROBERT TUNSTALL (Jan. 16, 1867–Feb. 21, 1929), physician, was born in Norfolk, Va. One month later he was brought to Baltimore, Md., where he lived for the remainder of his life. The son of Robertson Taylor, a coffee merchant, and Baynham Baylor (Tunstall) Taylor, he was accorded many cultural and social advantages. After preparatory education in private schools he entered the Johns Hopkins University and received the B.A. degree in 1889. Following in the footsteps of his maternal grandfather, Dr. Robert Tunstall, of Norfolk he began the study of medicine and graduated from the University of Virginia in 1891. He was married to Florence Templeman, of Baltimore, on Oct. 6, 1891, and began the practice of medicine. A newly acquired interest in orthopaedic surgery led him to devote a year to post-graduate work in this specialty at Harvard, 1894–95, and at Columbia, 1895. When he returned to Baltimore he founded the Hospital for the Relief of Crippled and Deformed Children, the first of its kind in the city. Through this institution he helped to bring the problem of the handicapped child to the attention of the public. His efforts led to the growth of this hospital so that, under the name of The James Lawrence Kernan Hospital and Industrial School, it assumed a major rôle in the hospitalization of Baltimore's crippled children. His zeal manifested itself in the organization of public school facilities for the handicapped. He was likewise instrumental in the development of a service for standard pasteurized milk in the city.

Taylor's enthusiastic efforts were in large part responsible for the opening in 1901 at the University of Maryland of the first orthopaedic department in a medical school in Maryland. He was appointed associate professor of orthopaedic surgery for the 1901–02 session and the following year was promoted to the professorship. He remained head of the department until his death. Concurrently he was orthopaedic surgeon to the

St. Joseph's, the Women's, the St. Agnes' hospitals, and consultant to the West Baltimore General Hospital. From time to time he conducted clinics in various communities throughout the state. During the World War he served in the medical corps of the United States Army at Fort Myer, Va., and in the surgeon-general's office in Washington, D. C., as major. Later he became lieutenant-colonel with instruction and examining duties, chief of the orthopaedic service at Fort McHenry, and, later, consultant to the United States Veterans Bureau in Baltimore.

A pioneer in his community in the field of orthopaedics he helped to bring to the attention of the public the existence of a handicapped group of children and to develop a sympathetic interest. Through his teaching he was able to influence the development of orthopaedic surgery wherever his students entered into practice. He wrote two books in the field: *Orthopaedic Surgery for Students and General Practitioners* (1907), and *The Surgery of the Spine and Extremities* (1923). His value as a teacher was enhanced by the skilful technique he displayed in his operative clinics. Articles written by him on surgical tuberculosis, traumatic conditions, such as fractures, infantile paralysis, and new operative procedures, helped to enrich the literature of a new field. The illness that attended the last few years of his life did not deter him from carrying on his work with his characteristic vigor until the day of his death. He was survived by his wife. Richard Lucien Page [*q.v.*] was his great-uncle.

[Personal acquaintance; information from the family; *Who's Who in America*, 1928–29; obituary article, *Bull. of the School of Med., Univ. of Md.*, Apr. 1929; *Baltimore Sun*, Feb. 22, 1929.]   I. W. N.

TAYLOR, SAMUEL HARVEY (Oct. 3, 1807–Jan. 29, 1871), educator, was born at Londonderry, N. H., the son of Captain James Taylor and Persis (Hemphill) Taylor. At fourteen he was largely responsible for the conduct of two extensive farms, and he seemed destined for a life of hard manual labor until a fall weakened his physique and made him decide to follow an intellectual life. Entering Pinkerton Academy in his native town, he prepared himself in two years to enter the sophomore class at Dartmouth, whence he graduated with honors in 1832. For the next five years he studied at the Andover Theological Seminary, from which he graduated in 1837, taught at Phillips Academy, Andover, and at Dartmouth, and occupied his Sundays with preaching. On Dec. 8, 1837, he married Caroline Persis Parker. In the same year he became the sixth principal of Phillips Academy, a position he held for nearly thirty-four years.

His strong personality left its stamp enduringly upon the school. His word was law, his position that of an autocrat to whose will even the trustees deferred. Under his guidance Phillips Academy prospered, its numbers more than doubled, and its standards of scholarship and conduct improved until it reached into the far West and South and even to foreign countries for its students. In the classroom, where at times Taylor taught as many as seven different subjects, his stern and domineering manner made him the terror of shy and sensitive boys, but those who had the strength to stand up under his merciless questioning, his emphasis upon absolute accuracy of memory in the smallest detail, learned the delight and the value of thorough scholarship. Taylor was not an innovator, and the curriculum of Latin, Greek, and mathematics he devised remained unchanged throughout his long administration despite the altered entrance requirements of the colleges. Between 1843 and 1870 he published five textbooks exemplifying his theories: *Guide for Writing Latin* (1843), from the German of J. P. Krebs; *Grammar of the Greek Language* (1844) and *An Elementary Grammar of the Greek Language* (1846), both from the German of Raphael Kühner; *Method of Classical Study* (1861); and *Classical Study; Its Value* (1870). While they were models of accuracy, these showed little breadth of vision or literary appreciation. For many years, 1852–71, he was an editor of *Bibliotheca Sacra*. The spiritual health of his pupils was always a matter of vital import to Taylor. In addition to frequent church services and prayer meetings, he fostered with what to many would seem mistaken zeal the hysterical revivals common in Andover at the time, in which youngsters still in their teens were "converted." On the stormy morning of Jan. 29, 1871, while hastening to meet his Sunday Bible class, he fell dead in the entry of the Academy building. He was survived by his three sons. In both his virtues and his faults he was representative of that Puritan New England where Phillips Academy was founded. His sternness, his accuracy, his dislike of frivolity and hatred of evil, his confidence in religious conversion, his absolute trust in his own infallibility were all qualities of the old, strict Puritan code which has passed away.

[C. M. Fuess, *An Old New England School* (1917), contains a thorough analysis of Taylor's personality and accomplishments. See also D. G. Annis and G. W. Browne, *Vital Records of Londonderry, N. H.* (1914); John Albee, *Three Memorials* (1878); *A Memorial of Samuel Harvey Taylor, Compiled by His Last Class* (1871), from which an address by E. A. Park was reprinted in *Bibliotheca Sacra*, Apr. 1871, and in *Cong. Quart.*, Jan. 1872; death notice in *Boston Transcript*, Jan. 31, 1871.]
S. H. P.

TAYLOR, STEVENSON (Feb. 12, 1848–May 19, 1926), marine engineer, was born in West Houston Street, New York City, the son of Hugh and Alice (MacWhinney) Taylor. He attended public elementary schools and the New York Free Academy, now the College of the City of New York, and as an apprentice entered the employ of Fletcher, Harrison & Company, proprietors of the North River Iron Works, in 1864. After the usual training in shops and drawing room with outside work in the installation of machinery, he became chief draftsman for the firm about the time he reached his majority and continued in charge of the drawing room and work of design until 1883, when the concern became a corporation under the style of W. & A. Fletcher Company and Taylor was made vice-president. Henceforth he was the active head of the business until 1904, when he disposed of his interest and resigned. During this period he was responsible for designing the machinery for such notable side-wheel steamboats as the *Pilgrim* (1883) of the Fall River Line, the first iron steamboat built on Long Island Sound, and her sister ship, the *Puritan*.

In 1904 he was appointed receiver of the United States Shipbuilding Company, and in the same year became vice-president of the Quintard Iron Works. It was while holding this office that he made the designs and took the contract for the steamer *Commonwealth*, for the Fall River Line, which when put into service was the "largest and most magnificent steamship built for service on inland waters" (E. K. Chatterton, *Steamships and Their Story*, 1910, p. 263). In 1916, having severed his connection with the Quintard works the year before, he was chosen president of the American Bureau of Shipping for the inspection and registration of hulls and machinery of ships. Under his wise and capable management the standing of the American bureau was raised until it became the equal of any of the registration societies. After ten years of service here, having attained his seventy-eighth year, he wished to retire, but was persuaded to continue his connection, with the title of chairman. This relation lasted the few remaining months of his life. During the World War he was appointed, Apr. 2, 1917, a lieutenant commander in the United States Naval Reserve Force (later promoted commander) and rendered valuable service as a member of the board charged with the rehabilitation of seized German vessels and subsequently as a member of the board of appraisal of vessels commandeered by the government. For this latter work he was specially fitted by his judicial temperament as well as by his long experience.

Taylor was a very active member of a number of engineering associations. He was a charter member, one of the few honorary members, and twice president (1910–12, 1916–18) of the Society of Naval Architects and Marine Engineers, and for many years was a trustee, and for three years (1913–15) president, of the Engineers Club of New York. During nearly forty years he gave much time and effort to the management of Webb Institute of Naval Architecture, founded by William H. Webb [q.v.] as a school of collegiate grade for the gratuitous instruction of young men as naval architects and marine engineers, and also as a home for aged mechanics in the trades of shipbuilding and marine engineering and their wives or widows. Taylor was one of the original trustees, and upon Webb's death in 1899 succeeded him as president. He undertook the task as a labor of love, with no compensation of a financial character, and it was probably that part of his life work in which he took the most satisfaction.

Taylor was of medium height and build, with hair snow white from an early age and a rosy complexion. He was always one of the most popular men in any organization, had remarkable skill in composing differences, and was an ideal presiding officer. On Sept. 10, 1874, he married Alma L. Partridge, who died in 1918. He died eight years later, at his home in New York, survived by a daughter and two sons.

[*Who's Who in N. Y.*, 1924; *Who's Who in Engineering*, 1925; *Trans. Soc. of Naval Architects and Marine Engineers*, vol. XXXIV (1926); *Trans. Am. Soc. Mech. Engineers*, vol. XLVIII (1926); *N. Y. Times*, May 20, 1926.]
W. M. M.

TAYLOR, WILLIAM (May 2, 1821–May 18, 1902), evangelist, missionary, bishop of the Methodist Episcopal Church, was born in Rockbridge County, Va. His father, Stuart Taylor, came of Revolutionary stock, and his mother, Martha (Hickman), of an old Delaware family. In his tenth year he had a profound religious experience, which was renewed in 1841. As a result he entered the Methodist ministry, being admitted on trial to the Baltimore Conference on Mar. 15, 1843, ordained deacon in 1846, and elder in 1847. For fifty-three years he traveled and toiled as no other man of his denomination, becoming a missionary evangelist to all lands. He was endowed with a physical frame and vitality that were equal to every demand: "I am six feet high, weigh 207 pounds," he wrote on a photograph, Mar. 14, 1881, "and lifted at one raise 760 lbs. in my fifty-ninth year." In addition to bodily strength, he also had a voice of unusual

melody, range, and power, and a commanding personality.

His evangelistic work began in the market house of Georgetown, D. C. In 1848 he was appointed to California under the missionary society of his church and arrived in San Francisco, via Cape Horn, in September 1849, when it was still a city of tents. To the "forty-niners" he preached for seven years. Standing on a pork or whiskey barrel in the Plaza he could be heard by 20,000 people at a time. His work of saving souls carried him into brothels and saloons. He built his own home and his own chapel. From 1856 to 1861 the cities of the United States and Canada, East and West, were his field. In the latter year he sailed for Australia by way of England. After preaching seven months in England and Ireland he visited Asia Minor, Syria, Palestine, Egypt, and Ceylon. For three years he labored in Australia, Tasmania, and New Zealand, where he added thousands to the membership of the Wesleyan Methodist churches. During all this time he derived support for himself and family from books which he published. From Australia in 1863 he sent seeds of the eucalyptus tree to a California horticulturist, and from these seeds came the eucalyptus trees on the Pacific Coast. In 1866 he was in South Africa working with colonists and Kaffirs; the following year, in England and Scotland. In 1869 he was back in Australia. In 1870 he went to India, where he spent seven years preaching to Anglo-Indians and expanding and organizing the work of the Methodist Episcopal Church among them. Here he developed the "Pauline System" of support for missionaries. They were to depend upon contributions from their converts and the communities in which they worked, and if such contributions proved insufficient, they, like Paul, were to labor with their own hands. One of the results of his activities was the organization of the South India Conference. In 1877 and 1878 he was in Peru and Chile, where he organized a system of self-supporting schools, conducted by missionaries; Coquimbo, Chile, became the center of this remarkable school system.

In 1884, having retired from the "itinerant ministry" that he might pursue his evangelistic work independent of ecclesiastical oversight, he went from South America as a lay delegate of the South India Conference to the General Conference in Philadelphia, and was there elected, at the age of sixty-three, missionary bishop for Africa. For twelve years he poured missionaries into this Continent—men and women willing to trust God and the people they served for daily bread, and to receive their salary in full after their arrival in the heavenly Jerusalem (Davies, *post*, p. 106). Africa, however, proved unusually difficult for his self-supporting missionaries, and his great strength began to break under the burdens he carried. In 1896, at the age of seventy-five he was relieved of his responsibilities by the General Conference. He had been married, Oct. 21, 1846, to Isabelle Anne Kimberlin, and three of their sons grew to maturity. His last years were spent quietly in Southern California with his family, from whom he had been separated again and again for years at a time.

In many ways Taylor was the outstanding man in his denomination. His imagination has been compared with that of Cecil Rhodes, and his energies matched his imagination. His firm belief that "God had taken William Taylor into a peculiar partnership" filled him with "the intrepidity and assurance of an apostle" (J. M. Buckley in *Christian Advocate*, June 12, 1902). He was saved from the fevers of fanaticism by a rugged common sense and an abundant humor. His writings include *Seven Years' Street Preaching in San Francisco* (1857); *California Life, Illustrated* (1858); *Model Preacher* (1859); *Infancy and Manhood of Christian Life* (1867); *Christian Adventures in South Africa* (1868); *Reconciliation; or, How to be Saved* (1875); *Four Years' Campaign in India* (1875); *Our South American Cousins* (1878); *Pauline Methods of Missionary Work* (copyrighted 1879); *Election of Grace* (1880); *Letters to a Quaker Friend on Baptism* (1880); *Ten Years of Self-Supporting Missions in India* (1882); *Story of My Life* (1895); *Africa Illustrated* (1895); *Flaming Torch in Darkest Africa* (1898). He died in Palo Alto, Cal.

[Files of the Board of Foreign Missions of the Methodist Episcopal Church; *Christian Advocate*, May 29, June 5, 12, 1902; *Indian Witness*, July 27, Oct. 12, 1921; *Who's Who in America*, 1901–02; *San Francisco Call* and *San Francisco Chronicle*, May 19, 1902; G. F. Arms, *Hist. of the William Taylor Self-Supporting Missions in South America* (copr. 1921); Edward Davies, *The Bishop of Africa* (1885); O. von Barchwitz-Krauser, *Six Years with Bishop Taylor in South America* (1885); J. H. Paul, *The Soul-Digger; or, Life and Times of William Taylor* (copr. 1928).]

O. M. B.

TAYLOR, WILLIAM LADD (Dec. 10, 1854–Dec. 26, 1926), illustrator, was born at Grafton, Mass., the son of William H. and Anna Maria (Darling) Taylor. His education in the public schools of Worcester, Mass., was supplemented by a course in mechanical drawing, and for a time he had employment as a draftsman, but found the work exacting and sought restored health in Colorado. Deciding to become an artist, he studied at the newly established Art Students' League of New York, and in 1881

moved to Boston, "with more ambition than pennies" (Robinson, *post*, p. 167), and established a small studio on School Street. Having won some success as an illustrator, he was soon enabled to go to Paris, where in 1884–85 he registered as a pupil of G. C. R. Boulanger and Jules-Joseph Lefebvre. As an art student and young artist he was remarkable for the seriousness and conscientiousness of his work—characteristics which remained with him. Among his earliest important illustrations were those made for the *Woods and Lakes of Maine* (1884) of Lucius L. Hubbard, whom Taylor accompanied in his adventurous wanderings. By 1888, when he married Mary Alice Fitz, of Norfolk, Va., he had become one of the most popular of American illustrators. He and his wife settled at Wellesley, Mass., where Taylor set up his studio. In it were made almost countless illustrations, notable both for competent documentation and esthetic content.

Taylor became a favorite illustrator of the *Ladies' Home Journal*, called upon year after year for paintings, suitable for reproduction, of historical, literary, and sentimental subjects. Behind these lay careful and elaborate first-hand studies. Taylor never drew from imagination details which he could secure through travel or by other means. Toward his New England themes he accumulated a great collection of costumes and other antiques. His Bible pictures were based on drawings from Near-Eastern bas-reliefs and other similar documents. He avoided the usual run of studio models, and utilized accommodating friends and neighbors who seemed to him typical. His pictures devoted to the nineteenth century in New England, reprinted in his *Our Home and Country* (1908), have been justly acclaimed as "an historical record in pictorial form of a period of enormous importance" (Downes, *post*, p. xvi). Files of the *Ladies' Home Journal* may be valued by collectors very considerably because of Taylor's drawings. Especially important among these are the series, "Those Days in Old Virginia," the illustrations to accompany Longfellow poems, and the Bible Series, most of them reprinted in *Our Home and Country*.

Leading at Wellesley a life uneventful and somewhat apart from that of other professional artists, Taylor worked incessantly until his last year upon many commissions. He belonged to the Boston Art Club, but he was not usually represented at its exhibitions. Many of the originals of his works were shown to interested visitors at the Curtis Publishing Company, Philadelphia. Personally reticent and somewhat austere, he had few of the qualities usually attributed to the artistic temperament. He has been described as "an agreeable and gentlemanly person, common-sensed in his views of affairs, pleasant in conversation and . . . well informed in literature" (Robinson, *post,* p. 172). Though never of robust health, he was devoted to outdoor sports as he was to horses and woodcraft.

[*Who's Who in America,* 1926–27; F. T. Robinson, *Living New England Artists* (1888); W. H. Downes, in Taylor's *Our Home and Country* (1908); *Mentor,* Dec. 1920; *Ladies' Home Jour.,* Mar. 1916, Aug. 1926, p. 28; death notice in *Boston Transcript,* Dec. 27, 1926.]

F. W. C.

TAYLOR, WILLIAM MACKERGO (Oct. 23, 1829–Feb. 8, 1895), Congregational clergyman, was born in Kilmarnock, Scotland, the son of Peter and Isobel (Mackergo) Taylor. His father was a shopkeeper, and the boy grew up in a home where Scotch sagacity, piety, and zest for theological discussion prevailed. Having received his preliminary education in the local academy, he entered the University of Glasgow, from which he graduated in 1849. His training for the ministry he received at the Divinity Hall of the United Presbyterian Church, Edinburgh. Finishing his course there in 1852, he was licensed to preach by the United Presbytery of Ayrshire on Sept. 14, of that year. He was ordained at Kilmaurs, a town about two miles from his birthplace, June 28, 1853, and was pastor there until called, in 1854, to the recently formed United Presbyterian Church of Derby Road, Bootle, a suburb of Liverpool. On Oct. 4, 1853, he had married Jessie, daughter of John and Mitchell (Gregg) Steedman of Kilmarnock. Bootle, situated at the mouth of the Mersey, was the loading place for ships, and Taylor's parishioners were chiefly from the families of those that the activities of a seaport had called thither. For sixteen years he labored among them, building up a substantial church, and gaining in Liverpool and beyond a reputation as a preacher and public speaker of unusual powers.

In the spring of 1871 he came to the United States and for ten Sundays supplied the pulpit of the Church of the Pilgrims, Brooklyn, of which Dr. Richard Salter Storrs, 1821–1900 [*q.v.*], was pastor. So impressed by his preaching were some of his hearers that they proposed building a great tabernacle for him in New York, if he would consider settling there (*Harper's Weekly,* July 18, 1874). In November 1871, however, Dr. Joseph P. Thompson [*q.v.*] relinquished the pastorate of Broadway Tabernacle, New York, and Taylor was immediately invited to be his successor. He accepted the invitation, and on Apr. 9, 1872, was formally in-

stalled. His ministry in this connection continued until 1892, when he was stricken with paralysis. Resigning on Oct. 27, he was made pastor emeritus, and died somewhat more than two years later, survived by six of his nine children.

He was a typical Scotchman of rugged character, conservative theology, analytical mind, and keen discernment. As a preacher he took rank in public esteem along with his noted neighbors, Beecher, Storrs, and John Hall [*qq.v.*]. He was a powerful expositor of the Scriptures and their practical application, a strong advocate of the written sermon, which he himself could make picturesque and glowing. His published works number more than forty, among them being *David King of Israel* (1875); *Elijah the Prophet* (1876); *The Ministry of the Word* (1876), Lyman Beecher Lectures at Yale; *Moses the Lawgiver* (1879, 1894); *The Gospel Miracles in Their Relation to Christ and Christianity* (1880), lectures at Princeton; *John Knox* (1885); *The Parables of Our Saviour Expounded and Illustrated* (1886); *The Scottish Pulpit from the Reformation to the Present Day* (1887), Lyman Beecher Lectures; *The Christian in Society* (1891); *At the End of Twenty Years* (1892); *Contrary Winds and Other Sermons* (1899); *The Limitations of Life and Other Sermons* (1904). From October 1876 to June 1880 he was editor-in-chief of *The Christian at Work.* He took an active part in the missionary activities of the Congregational churches, being a corporate member of the American Board of Commissioners for Foreign Missions (1872–95), and president of the American Missionary Association (1872–95) and of the Congregational Church Building Society (1885–95). He was also a trustee of the University of the City of New York and of Mount Holyoke College, and a manager of the Presbyterian Hospital, New York.

[W. I. Addison, *A Roll of the Grads. of the Univ. of Glasgow* (1898); S. H. Ward, *The Hist. of the Broadway Tabernacle Church* (1901); *The Congregational Year-Book, 1895* (1896); *Outlook* (N. Y.), Feb. 16, 1895; *Congregationalist,* Feb. 14, 1895; *N. Y. Tribune,* Feb. 9, 1895.]

H. E. S.

TAYLOR, WILLIAM ROGERS (Nov. 7, 1811–Apr. 14, 1889), naval officer, was born at Newport, R. I., son of Capt. William Vigneron Taylor [*q.v.*] and Abby (White) Taylor. Through the influence of his father, who spoke of him at sixteen as "a very fair French and Latin scholar" with "some knowledge of rigging and drafting" gained at the Boston Navy Yard (letters, Personnel Files, Navy Department Library), he was made midshipman Apr. 1, 1828. He was in the *Hudson* on the Brazil station,

1829–32. After brief study at the naval school in New York he became passed midshipman (1834), and then joined the *Peacock* on a cruise to the East Indies, 1835–36. When his ship grounded on Mazeira Island, Arabia, Sept. 21, 1835, he commanded a cutter which was sent to Muscat for aid and to convey thither Edmund Roberts [*q.v.*], the United States diplomatic agent (see correspondence, Roberts MSS., vol. IV, Library of Congress). The boat was at sea five days and was pursued for several hours by pirates.

Made lieutenant in 1840, Taylor was on coast survey duty for some time, then on the Brazil station. During the Mexican War he was in the *St. Mary's* at the attack on Tampico and later in command of an 8-inch gun on shore at the siege of Vera Cruz. He was promoted commander in 1855. During this decade his work was largely at Washington in ordnance, in connection with which he attained some reputation, as evidenced by Admiral Du Pont's characterization of him later as "an admirable ordnance officer" (H. A. du Pont, *Rear Admiral Samuel Francis du Pont*, 1926, p. 288). In July 1862 he was made captain and assigned to the steam sloop *Housatonic* on the Charleston blockade. Here he was at various times senior officer, notably on Jan. 31, 1863, when the blockaders were attacked by the Confederate rams *Chicora* and *Palmetto State* (see his report, *Official Records, post,* vol. XIII, pp. 587–88). He was Admiral Dahlgren's fleet captain during the operations against Morris Island, July 10–19, 1863, and afterward until he was invalided home on July 24. In May of the next year he reported to the *Juniata* at Philadelphia and commanded her during the first attack on Fort Fisher, Dec. 24–25, 1864, in which she was hulled six or seven times and lost five killed and eight wounded from the bursting of a Parrott rifle. Apparently at this time he had not fully recovered from his illness of the preceding year, for his fellow captain, Charles Steedman, in a letter of Jan. 6 speaks of his "extremely nervous temperament" and adds, "Poor Taylor has gone home completely broken down physically" (A. L. Mason, *Memoir and Correspondence of Charles Steedman*, 1912, p. 397).

After the war he was made commodore (1866), and rear admiral (1871). He commanded the northern squadron of the Pacific fleet (1869–71), was president of the examining board (1871–72), and had command of the South Atlantic station from May 1872 until his retirement for age Nov. 7, 1873. His death from paralysis occurred at his home in Washington, D. C., and he was buried in the Congressional Cemetery.

He was married Apr. 30, 1840, to Caroline, daughter of Gold S. Silliman of Brooklyn, N. Y. (*Newport Mercury,* May 16, 1840), and was survived by two daughters.

[W. S. W. Ruschenberger, *A Voyage Round the World* (1838); *War of the Rebellion: Official Records* (*Navy*), esp. 1 ser. III, XIII, XIV; L. R. Hamersly, *The Records of Living Officers of the U. S. Navy and Marine Corps* (4th ed., 1890); *Washington Post,* Apr. 16, 1889; *Army and Navy Jour.,* Apr. 20, 1889.]

A. W—t.

TAYLOR, WILLIAM VIGNERON (Apr. 11, 1780–Feb. 11, 1858), naval officer, was born at Newport, R. I., son of James and Mary (Vigneron) Taylor, and a descendant of **Dr.** Norbent F. Vigneron who came to Newport from Artois, France, in 1690. Both his parents belonged to the Society of Friends. From the local schools and from reading in the library of his uncle, William Vigneron, a successful seaman and merchant, he attained a good foundation of learning. At about eighteen he went to sea, and soon rose to mate and captain in the merchant service.

In the War of 1812 he was among the numerous seamen who joined the navy at Newport under Lieut. O. H. Perry [*q.v.*], his warrant as sailing-master being dated Apr. 28, 1813. His actual entry, however, was considerably earlier, for on Feb. 21, 1813, he left Newport for Sackett's Harbor, Lake Ontario, in charge of a detachment of fifty sailors. On Mar. 30 he joined Perry on Lake Erie, where, with Lieut. Daniel Turner, he had special supervision of the rigging, equipping, and arming of Perry's squadron. According to his fellow officer, Usher Parsons (*post,* p. 18), he was "more experienced than any one on the station in the duties of seamanship." In the battle of Lake Erie, Sept. 10, 1813, he was sailing master of the flagship *Lawrence.* Though wounded in the thigh, he kept the deck, and remained in the battered *Lawrence*—which had twenty-two killed and sixty-one wounded of her complement of 103—when Perry shifted his flag to the *Niagara.* The log of the *Lawrence,* largely written by Taylor, is preserved by the Newport Historical Society. With other officers in the action he received the thanks of Congress and a sword, and on Dec. 9, 1814, he was promoted to lieutenant. After the battle he returned to Erie, Sept. 23, in the *Lawrence,* which had been made hospital ship of the squadron and was then sent to Lake Ontario with dispatches. Shortly afterward he returned to Newport. In the protracted controversy between Perry and his second-in-command, Jesse D. Elliott [*q.v.*] over the conduct of the Lake Erie action, Taylor was naturally a strong partisan of Perry, his affidavit before the Rhode Island legislature in June 1818 being characterized by Elliott's biographer as "a prolix narrative . . . from a warm friend of one party and a decided enemy of the other" (*A Biographical Notice of Com. Jesse D. Elliott*, 1835, p. 217). At the close of 1814 he was engaged in fitting out the *Java* under Perry at Baltimore, and he sailed in her to the Mediterranean in 1815. From 1816 to 1823, partly because of recurrent trouble from his wound, he was on leave or nominal duty at Newport.

During the ensuing quiet naval period up to the Mexican War his sea service included a Mediterranean cruise in the *Ontario*, 1824–26; service on the Brazil station, 1829–30; and in the late thirties, command of the sloops *Erie* and *Warren* in the Gulf. He was made captain Sept. 8, 1841, and late in 1847 took the ship-of-the-line *Ohio* around Cape Horn for operations on the Mexican west coast, where he remained until the latter part of 1848, after the close of the Mexican War. Owing to age and declining health, this was his last sea service. He was placed on the reserved list Sept. 13, 1855. His funeral was in Trinity Church, Newport, which he had joined a few years before his death, and his burial was in the Island Cemetery. He was married Dec. 31, 1810, to Abby, daughter of Capt. Thomas White of Newport, and had seven children, three of whom died young; a son, William Rogers Taylor [*q.v.*], became a naval officer; another, Oliver Hazard Perry Taylor, rose to a brevet captaincy in the army and was killed May 17, 1858, in Indian warfare in Washington Territory.

[Usher Parsons, *Brief Sketches of the Officers Who Were in the Battle of Lake Erie* (1862), pub. also in *New England Hist. and Geneal. Reg.*, Jan. 1863; L. M. Mayer, "The Log of the Lawrence," *Bull. of the Newport Hist. Soc.*, Apr. 1923; *Newport Advertiser*, Feb. 17, 1858; Commandants' and Captains' Letters, Navy Dept. Lib.] A. W—t.

TAYLOR, ZACHARY (Nov. 24, 1784–July 9, 1850), soldier and twelfth president of the United States, was born at Montebello, Orange County, Va. His ancestor, James Taylor (d. 1698), migrated from Carlisle, England, and settled on the Mattapony River in the sixteen-thirties. A son, James Taylor, served on Gov. Spotswood's staff, accompanied him on the expedition to the Blue Ridge, and purchased land on the Rapidan River. Zachary Taylor (1707–1768), son of the second James and grandfather of the future president, married Elizabeth Lee, established "Meadow Farm" plantation, and acquired twenty-six slaves. One of their four children, Richard (1744–1829), married Mary

Strother, received a degree at William and Mary, became lieutenant-colonel of a Virginia regiment in the American Revolution, served in the Virginia Assembly, and settled at "Hare Forest" estate. The third of their nine children, Zachary, was born a short time before the family migrated to Jefferson County, Ky., in the spring of 1785. There Richard established a plantation on the Muddy Fork of Beargrass Creek, acted as collector of the port of Louisville under appointment from Washington, served as a delegate in the constitutional convention of 1792, and represented his county in the legislature. Zachary received his only formal education from a tutor, Elisha Ayres of Connecticut, who declared that his pupil displayed qualities of stability, firmness, and studiousness. During the formative years in Kentucky, he assisted his father on the plantation.

Although Taylor saw brief service as a volunteer in 1806, his military career of forty years did not actually begin until two years later with an appointment as first lieutenant in the 7th Infantry. He reported to Gen. James Wilkinson at New Orleans but an outbreak of yellow fever forced him temporarily from the service. He was promoted captain in 1810, and the following year his company was placed under Gen. William Henry Harrison, governor of Indiana Territory, who assigned him command of Fort Knox. His company, numbering not more than fifty men, was soon transferred to Fort Harrison which he successfully defended against 400 Indians, Sept. 4, 1812, and as a result he was brevetted major. The following year he recruited, mustered, and inspected troops in Indiana and Illinois Territories, and assisted in the defense of the frontier from Indiana to Missouri. In August 1814, he ascended the Mississippi to destroy Indian villages at the mouth of Rock River; failing in this he returned to the mouth of the Des Moines and erected Fort Johnson. From December until the close of the War of 1812 he was again in command at Fort Knox as major, but when the army was disbanded on June 15, 1815, he was retained as captain. He declined the service but in 1816 Madison restored his former rank and ordered him to join the 3rd Infantry at Green Bay, Wis. Two years in command at Fort Winnebago were followed by a year's furlough which he spent in Kentucky. On Apr. 20, 1819, he was appointed lieutenant-colonel of the 4th Infantry and ordered to report at New Orleans. Four regimental transfers in as many years left him in the 1st Infantry where he remained for an uneventful decade. In 1822 he built Fort Jesup on the Louisiana frontier; in

1824 he served first as recruiting officer at Louisville and later on a board at Washington, headed by Gen. Winfield Scott, designed to perfect the militia organization. In 1827–28 he was again in the Southwest with headquarters at Baton Rouge, and from 1829 to 1832 in the Northwest at Fort Snelling where he acted as Indian "superintendent."

On April 4, 1832, at the age of forty-seven, Taylor was promoted colonel, given command of the 1st Regiment, and stationed at Fort Crawford (Prairie du Chien). In the Black Hawk War he commanded 400 regulars under Gen. Henry Atkinson [q.v.] and received custody of the captured Black Hawk, whom he sent to Jefferson Barracks in the charge of Jefferson Davis. His regiment was ordered to Fort Jesup in 1837, but while descending the Mississippi he received instructions dated July 31 directing him to take command of the field force in Florida. In December he set out from Fort Gardner with 1100 men, followed the Seminoles into the Everglades, defeated them in a desperate battle at Lake Okeechobee on the 25th, and captured much valuable property. For this achievement he was brevetted brigadier-general and soon thereafter (May 1838) superseded Gen. Thomas S. Jesup in command of the department. Dividing his men into several detachments he gave each a limited district to patrol, and he armed white settlers to defend themselves against assault; as a result of this policy, there were numerous skirmishes but no drawn battles. After he had served two years in Florida without accomplishing his major object, his request to be relieved of the command was reluctantly granted, Apr. 21, 1840. He was then transferred to the Southwest with headquarters at Baton Rouge. A year later he was ordered to Fort Gibson to relieve General Arbuckle, and after a brief visit of inspection he established himself and family at Fort Smith, Ark. Although he looked upon the new assignment as a mark of confidence, he accepted it reluctantly as he had hoped to continue at Baton Rouge for some time to create a sufficient competence to support himself and family in retirement. He received little cooperation from Indian agents, but with few exceptions he kept the southwestern frontier quiet during the next three years.

In May 1844 Taylor was ordered to Fort Jesup and, in anticipation of the annexation of Texas, he was directed a few months later to have his command ready to take the field on the slightest notice. Instructions from Marcy, dated May 28, 1845, ordered him to correspond with Texan authorities and repel invasion of the state after it approved annexation. On June 15 he was directed to prepare to depart for the new frontier, and a month later he left New Orleans for Corpus Christi at the mouth of the Nueces where he soon collected an army of about 4,000 men. He was ordered to advance to the Rio Grande on Jan. 13, 1846, and two months later he established a base at Point Isabel and entrenchments opposite Matamoras. On May 8 he met the Mexicans under Gen. Arista at Palo Alto and defeated a force three times the size of his own army, a victory for his artillery. The following day he was again successful at Resaca de la Palma, using artillery, dragoons, and infantry. Because of lack of preparation and insufficient troops he did not cross the Rio Grande at once, and when he did General Arista had abandoned Matamoras. As soon as Polk received official dispatches of the two engagements, he promoted Taylor major-general by brevet. In the states there was almost universal commendation of the American commander. The administration lacked confidence in him, but as it distrusted Scott also, Taylor was officially designated commander of the Army of the Rio Grande.

By the middle of June thousands of volunteers were arriving at Point Isabel but without adequate supplies or transportation into the interior, and many of them had to be disbanded without seeing service. A month later Taylor established a base at Camargo at the mouth of the San Juan. With Saltillo as a goal he departed in September with 6,000 men divided equally between regulars and volunteers, and on the 21st he attacked Monterey. After three days of skirmishing in which bayonet assaults predominated, the Mexican army, somewhat larger than the American, capitulated, and an eight weeks' armistice was arranged subject to the approval of the respective governments. Although Taylor cited cogent reasons for the lenient terms accorded the Mexicans, he was severely criticized by the administration and five days before the end of the armistice he received orders to terminate it. The situation might have served as a pretext for superseding him had it not been for his growing popularity at home. The publication of his letter of Nov. 5 to General Gaines in the *New York Morning Express*, Jan. 22, 1847, defending the Monterey armistice and attacking the administration for lack of support, increased the tension between President and commander.

Meanwhile, Gen. Scott had been commissioned to lead an expedition against Mexico city and empowered to draw upon Taylor's army for a part of his troops. When Taylor received a communication to that effect he was disgruntled and evaded a meeting with his superior officer (Smith, *post*, I, 356, 358, 362, 540–43). Although he was advised to concentrate his remaining force at Monterey and act entirely on the defensive, he disobeyed orders by attempting to defend a line 400 miles long and thus, according to Polk, invited attack (Polk, *Diary*, II, 452; see also 433, 438, and Smith, I, 373). Advancing southward, he received word that Santa Anna was marching on him with 20,000 troops, while he had a fourth of that number. At Buena Vista, Feb. 22–23, the American army defeated the Mexicans and thus ended the war in the northern provinces. The battle was fought for the most part by volunteers, some of whom fled from the field, but it was to the small number of regular artillery that Taylor ascribed a large measure of responsibility for success. However, the victory "was due primarily to Taylor's prestige, valor and gift of inspiring confidence" (Smith, *post*, I, 395). Reluctantly Taylor remained in Mexico until November 1847, convinced that Polk, Marcy, and Scott had plotted to break him down, though he later absolved the Secretary of War from implication (Taylor to Col. J. P. Taylor, Jan. 19, 1848, in Taylor Papers). Largely unfounded as the charge was, the belief increased that he had been victimized by an administration that was jealous of his growing popularity.

Taylor's Whiggism antedated the Mexican War. He registered disapproval of Andrew Jackson and criticized the army patronage of the thirties. He believed the Whig victory of 1840 most timely, professed a deep interest in the success of Harrison's administration, recommended numerous military appointments, and regretted the breakup of the cabinet in 1841. He confessed in 1847 that he had never voted for president, but had he done so in 1844 he would have cast his ballot for Henry Clay (Fry and Conrad, *post*, p. 324). His victories early in the war convinced Whig politicians of his availability as a candidate in 1848. Popular meetings, some of them spontaneous and others inspired by leaders, assembled in the summer of 1846 to applaud his victories. As early as May of that year Thurlow Weed [*q.v.*] began to labor for his nomination (H. A. Weed, ed., *Autobiography of Thurlow Weed*, 1884, pp. 571–73). Of more significance was the indorsement of John J. Crittenden [*q.v.*], lifelong friend of Clay and universally respected for sound judgment and honest conviction. Taylor himself wrote numerous letters to soldiers, public men, and editors, much to the discomfiture of the politicians. Whether he realized it or not, there was political wisdom in his correspondence. He must have written fifty times that he was not a candidate for the presidency and doubted his qualifications for the office, but if the people spontaneously called him he would accept. He would not be the candidate of a party nor would he reach the office through any agency of his own. If called to the highest office, he would serve the people honestly and faithfully; if not he would be neither mortified nor disappointed. Especially did his letter of May 18, 1847, to the editor of the Cincinnati *Signal* (published in *Niles' National Register*, July 3, 1847, p. 288) agitate newspaper comment as its "no-party" doctrine divided Whig leaders.

Upon vital issues before the country, Taylor expressed himself too freely to please the politicians. In private correspondence with Jefferson Davis (July 27, Aug. 16, 1847, Taylor Papers), and in public letters of Apr. 22 and Sept. 4 to Capt. J. S. Allison (*Niles' National Register*, July 8, 1848, p. 8; Sept. 27, 1848, pp. 200–01), he stated his views on current problems. The national bank was a dead issue, he said, and there would be no surplus revenue from the sale of public lands to distribute. Congress was the proper authority to decide between a protective tariff and direct taxation to defray the cost of the war. Internal improvements would continue regardless of what party controlled Congress or what man was president. The executive office should return to the position of a coordinate branch of the government; the veto power should be used to protect the Constitution but sparingly for other purposes. No more territory should be taken from Mexico than that already held in the northern part. The Wilmot Proviso was "a mere bugbare" agitated to produce excitement, and would soon disappear. Although he did not believe Congress would permit slave states to be admitted from territory acquired from Mexico, he felt that the South should resort to arms if necessary to protect their rights in states where slavery already existed. He had no sympathy for extremists in either section. In the first "Allison" letter, which was widely printed, he explained his political position: "I AM A WHIG, *but not an ultra Whig*. If elected I would not be the mere President of a Party. I would endeavor to act independent of party domination. I should feel bound to administer the government untrammeled by party schemes" (*Niles' National Register*, July 8, 1848, p. 8).

Meanwhile, Henry Clay's silence led politicians to believe that he would be a candidate; his visit to Philadelphia and New York in the summer of 1847 was ominous; and his announcement of a Whig platform in his Lexington speech of Nov. 13 placed him definitely before the country. When discussion of a Whig nominating convention began early in 1847, Taylor expressed opposition, viewing the movement as a plot of the politicians to defeat him. Nevertheless, he finally concluded that he would not dictate to the people how he should be nominated, and if the Whigs named him without pledges he would accept. He would not withdraw from the contest, however, if neither major party nominated him. When the Whigs met in Philadelphia on June 7, 1848, he led the field on the first ballot and was nominated on the fourth over Clay, Scott, and Webster. Since no platform was adopted, reliance had to be placed on the hazy statements of the candidate. On Sept. 4, he wrote a second "Allison" letter which explained the history of his candidacy, his consistency in accepting the Whig nomination, his freedom from party pledges, and the non-partisan character of his administration if elected (*Niles' National Register*, Sept. 27, 1848). His victory over Lewis Cass [*q.v.*] in November was promoted by divisions in the New York Democracy and by the support of Taylor Democrats, largely making good the defection of anti-slavery Whigs to the Free Soil party and Van Buren. He carried exactly half of the states, seven in the North and eight in the South. In his brief inaugural address of Mar. 5, 1849, he advocated efficient military and naval establishments, friendly relations with foreign powers, capacity, fidelity, and honesty as qualifications for office-holding, the encouragement of agriculture, commerce, and manufactures, and congressional conciliation of sectional controversies (Richardson, *post*, V, 4–6). The Washington *Daily Union* (Mar. 6, 1849) observed that the address consisted of noncommittal platitudes, and noted an ultra-Whig spirit of federalism; Whig papers applauded its moderation, simple style, and strict adherence to Whig principles.

Although Taylor did not discuss cabinet making openly until after his election, he had informed Davis that should he be chosen, he would compose it entirely of Whigs. The party leaders had accepted Taylor largely upon the indorsement of Crittenden, and it was generally understood that the latter would accept the premiership. Emphasizing the President's inexperience in civil affairs and his unacquaintance with political leaders and methods, both Democrats and Whigs warned the Kentucky statesman that as he would be held responsible for the

success of the administration, he should consent to head it. But as he had just been elected governor of Kentucky he declined a place in the cabinet, and John M. Clayton [*q.v.*] of Delaware was appointed secretary of state. Of the seven ministers four were from slaveholding states. Taylor expected his cabinet to be "harmonious, honorable, patriotic, talented, & *hard working*" (A. T. Burnley to Crittenden, Jan. 12, 1849, Crittenden Papers). Though it measured up to his specifications in some respects, in others it was decidedly inferior. It was harmonious and industrious, but it contained no man of outstanding ability, a scandal broke during its brief tenure, and worst of all it made no effort to conciliate the legislative branch. Clayton promised that he would "be as independent of Congress as a wood-sawyer" (Clayton to Crittenden, Aug. 23, 1849, Crittenden Papers). Before Taylor had been in office a month many individuals, including the Secretary of State, were urging Crittenden to hasten to Washington to set the Whig household in order, and by the time he faced his first and only Congress, dissension and discord existed among party leaders and rumors of cabinet reorganization were rife. Democratic papers asserted that in making appointments and forming policies, the President had only one vote in the cabinet council and that the ministers constituted a regency. Nonpartisan declarations during the campaign led to charges of proscription by both Democratic and independent papers. Although Taylor may have entertained idealistic notions on the subject of appointments and removals, he had concluded by May 1849 that it was necessary to fill all offices with his own partisans. As the *National Intelligencer* opposed Taylor's nomination and disagreed with many of his political views, a new official organ, *The Republic*, was established with Alexander C. Bullitt and John Sargent as editors. A. T. Burnley of Kentucky, an enthusiastic Taylor partisan during the campaign, owned a third interest in the paper. A prospectus appeared on Apr. 14 pledging it to support the "liberalizing" campaign doctrines. Friction soon developed between the cabinet and the official organ, and as a result there was little intercourse and no cooperation between the two. Outside of the cabinet the President's most intimate advisers were Burnley and Orlando Brown, commissioner of Indian affairs.

By 1849 Taylor's attitude toward the Wilmot Proviso experienced serious modification. In letters to Davis he said in July 1847 that it "amounts to nothing" (Going, *David Wilmot*, pp. 234–35); in April 1848 that nature had excluded slavery from the new Southwest. Soon after his inauguration it was apparent that he would not veto the Proviso should a bill containing it be presented to him. In a public speech at Mercer, Pa., in August 1849, while he was touring Pennsylvania and New York ostensibly to acquaint himself with the material needs of the people but in reality for political effect, he declared that Northern people *"need have no apprehension of the further extension of slavery"* (*Pittsburgh Daily Gazette,* Sept. 3, 1849). Hoping to prevent sectional agitation of the question, he dispatched an emissary, Thomas Butler King, to counsel the Californians to form a state constitution and apply for statehood, and inhabitants of New Mexico were similarly encouraged. In his message to Congress, Dec. 4, 1849, Taylor recommended that both be admitted into the Union if they presented governments republican in form (Richardson, V, 18–19). In special messages to the House and Senate, Jan. 21 and 23, 1850 (*Ibid.,* V, 26–30), he again urged the unconditional admission of California, and suggested statehood for New Mexico in order that the boundary dispute with Texas could be settled by the Supreme Court. Five months later he recommended that the United States maintain possession of the disputed territory until the boundary was established (*Ibid.,* V, 47–48).

Meanwhile, Southern representatives led by Alexander H. Stephens [*q.v.*] organized a filibuster to prevent a vote on the admission of California and to insist that all proposals affecting the Mexican cession be combined in a single measure. In April delegates from a Southern caucus had called upon the President to warn him of the loss of Southern Whig support if he persisted in his plan to admit California and New Mexico as states and continued his hostile attitude toward Texas; and Stephens and Robert Toombs called on him in July, as they had earlier, threatening secession (A. C. Cole, *The Whig Party in the South,* 1913, pp. 166–67). Taylor was obstinate, and when Secretary of War George W. Crawford [*q.v.*] refused to revoke an earlier order recognizing the Rio Grande to its source as the Texan boundary, Taylor himself signed the order to prevent a cabinet rupture. Before the separate measures known as the Compromise of 1850 passed, Taylor had died. On July 4 he attended a ceremony connected with the building of the Washington Monument. He felt the heat, drank much cold water, and afterward ate cherries and drank iced milk. That night he was attacked by cholera morbus and fever, from which he died July 9. He had decided, however, a few days before his death, to reorganize his cabinet. The "Galphin claim" brought the matter to an issue as three members were implicated in what appeared to be a scandal. Crawford had a pecuniary interest in the claim, and upon Attorney General Reverdy Johnson's opinion, William Meredith, secretary of the treasury, paid it without investigating its merits. According to Weed, who says the President sought his counsel, all members were to be superseded, with diplomatic posts for those not involved (*Autobiography of Thurlow Weed,* pp. 589–93).

Although Taylor's administration muddled through foreign relations with only a fair degree of success, Clayton performed more creditably as a diplomat than as a politician. The President was unacquainted with diplomatic procedure, but he followed the trends of foreign affairs closely, and several times his dominating influence either encouraged Clayton's own tactlessness or seriously embarrassed the Secretary of State. His arbitrary attitude in the Poussin affair might have led to serious trouble with France had not negotiations taken a fortunate turn (Bemis, *post,* VI, 18–31); his uncompromising position on claims against Portugal was unwarranted and unfair; his stand in supporting Clayton, over the advice of other cabinet members in demanding the release of alleged filibusters captured by a Spanish vessel on the coast of Mexico, may have been unnecessarily bold. In general Clayton had a free hand in negotiating the treaty of 1850 with Bulwer, the most significant achievement of the administration in foreign affairs.

On June 18, 1810, Taylor was married to Margaret Mackall Smith (1787–1852), descendant of a prominent Maryland family. Of their six children, two died in childhood; the three daughters who survived, Ann Mackall, Sarah Knox, and Mary Elizabeth, married army men: Robert C. Wood, Jefferson Davis, and William Bliss. Their only son, Richard Taylor [*q.v.*], became lieutenant-general in the Confederate army. Taylor owned sundry tracts of land in Jefferson County, Ky., but in 1840 he established his residence at Baton Rouge and purchased a cotton plantation, "Cypress Grove," near Rodney, Miss., forty miles above Natchez. The latter proved a bad investment as the river overflowed and ruined his crops nearly every year in the forties. Taylor was muscular and stocky and in early years possessed an iron constitution that won for him the sobriquet of "Old Rough and Ready" in the Seminole War. He seldom appeared in full military dress, and he preferred the discussion of agricultural prospects to military achievement. Although his experience prior to the Mexican War had been limited to frontier fighting, there is evidence of ability to comprehend larger problems. Dissatisfied with the military establishment of the Jackson period, he submitted to a member of Congress an elaborate and meritorious plan for army reorganization. In 1841, while stationed at Fort Smith, he worked out a practical plan for the defense of the frontier from Missouri to Louisiana. He placed little reliance in volunteers but freely criticized West Point graduates. His letters were legible and fairly well composed considering his slender education, but it was fortunate that he had an intelligent, well-informed and loyal adjutant-general, Major Bliss, whose skilled pen colored official dispatches with the glamor necessary to promote Taylor's reputation. Without political background or experience, his practical wisdom, common sense, honest simplicity, and resolute purpose served him well during his brief public career, but were insufficient to produce the leadership demanded by the crisis of 1850. He looked to George Washington as a model, and admiring contemporaries convinced themselves of many analogies existing between the warrior of the Revolution and the hero of Buena Vista.

[The latest biography is O. O. Howard, *General Taylor* (1892). The principal contemporary accounts, many of which contain letters and military reports, are: C. F. Powell, *Life of Major-General Zachary Taylor* (1846); An Officer of the U. S. A., *Life and Public Services of Gen. Z. Taylor* (1846); Henry Montgomery, *The Life of Major General Zachary Taylor* (1847); J. R. Fry and R. T. Conrad, *A Life of Gen. Zachary Taylor* (1847); *Taylor and his Generals* (1847); John Frost, *Life of Major General Zachary Taylor* (1847, reprinted with slight modifications and varying titles as late as 1887); *The Life and Public Services of Major General Zachary Taylor* (1847); *The Life of Gen. Zachary Taylor, and a History of the War in Mexico* (1847). Of the manuscript sources, the Zachary Taylor, John J. Crittenden, Henry Clay, and John M. Clayton Papers, in the Lib. of Cong., are most pertinent. The Deed and Will Books of Orange County, Va., Jefferson County, Ky., Jefferson County, Miss., and East Baton Rouge Parish, La., contain land transfers, wills, etc. Copies of the family genealogical records are deposited in the courthouse at Orange, Va. *Some Eminent Sons of Orange* (1919), contains a sketch of Taylor by Daniel Grinnan. Valuable published sources are: *Letters of Zachary Taylor from the Battlefields of the Mexican War. Reprinted from the Originals in the Collection of Mr. William K. Bixby, of St. Louis, Mo.* (1908), with introduction by W. H. Samson; Mrs. Chapman Coleman, *The Life of John J. Crittenden . . . Correspondence and Speeches* (2 vols., 1871); J. D. Richardson, *A Compilation of the Messages and Papers of the Presidents* (1897), vol. V; M. M. Quaife, ed., *The Diary of James K. Polk* (4 vols., 1910). There are valuable notes in Mary W. Williams, "John Middleton Clayton," in S. F. Bemis, ed., *The American Secretaries of State and Their Diplomacy,* vol. VI (1928); and J. H. Smith, *The War With Mexico* (2 vols., 1919). See also R. M. Johnston, *Leading American Soldiers* (1907).]

W. H. S—n.

TAZEWELL, HENRY (Nov. 27, 1753–Jan. 24, 1799), lawyer, judge, senator, son of Littleton and Mary (Gray) Tazewell, was born in Brunswick County, Va., of which county his father was the clerk. His grandfather, William Tazewell, had emigrated from England to Northampton County *c.* 1715, but his ancestor Nathaniel Littleton, a descendant of Sir Thomas Littleton, the author of the *Tenures,* had been sheriff of Accomac County in 1636. The line of descent exhibits a procession of lawyers and court officers that imposed almost a hereditary compulsion upon the careers of Henry Tazewell and his son, Littleton Waller Tazewell [*q.v.*]. After a course at William and Mary, which he finished in 1770, Tazewell studied law in the office of his uncle, John Tazewell, later a judge of the general court. In January 1774, he married Dorothy (or Dorothea) Elizabeth Waller, daughter of Benjamin Waller, later presiding judge of the court of admiralty. Tazewell then began the practice of law in his native county of Brunswick, and the following year, after a severe contest, was elected to the General Assembly.

Revolution was in the air; but though Tazewell had raised and been commissioned captain of a troop of cavalry, he was of the element that still hoped for conciliation. As the author of resolutions in this sense, he was the object of a hasty attack by Jefferson in the Assembly of 1775, but met it with a manly independence that won him for life the high regard of that statesman. (For evidences of their later friendship, see A. A. Lipscomb, ed., in *The Writings of Thomas Jefferson,* IX, 1903, pp. 308, 365.) The revolutionary convention of 1776 was unanimous in its declaration of independence; and Tazewell became a member of the important committee named to frame a constitution and bill of rights for the state.

He represented Brunswick in the General Assembly until 1778, when he removed to Williamsburg, and was almost immediately elected to represent that borough in the same body, and continued to do so until his election to the old general court in 1785. The tribute was the more notable in that his practice had been subjected to severe interruptions by the removal of the capital to Richmond and the frequent closing of the courts in Williamsburg as the result of military operations. His state-wide reputation and popularity were established and enhanced by his service on the reorganized general court, created in 1788, the judges of which "rode the circuits" into which the state was divided. The next year he became the chief justice of the general court, and in 1793 was appointed to the court of appeals. Meanwhile he had served as one of the revisors of the law, the revision of 1792 being in principal part the work of his hands. On the simultaneous retirement of James Monroe and John Taylor of Caroline from the United States Senate, each of them requested Tazewell to stand for his place. Choosing Taylor's, he was elected by a large majority for the unexpired term and took his seat on Dec. 29, 1794. Tazewell had been opposed to the ratification by Virginia of the federal Constitution, and his views brought him, on entering the Senate, into opposition to the administration and the Federalist majority. In keeping with the Virginia position, he opposed the ratification of the Jay treaty. But notwithstanding these circumstances, he was, on Feb. 20, 1795, elected president *pro tempore,* and reëlected the following December. Reëlected in 1798 for the full term, he contracted a severe cold in traveling to Philadelphia to resume his duties, and died of pleurisy a few days after arrival in that city. He was buried there in Christ Church yard.

It has been said that Tazewell's posthumous reputation has been overshadowed by that of his distinguished son; but it was rather his being cut off in mid-career that has narrowed for posterity the place that he undoubtedly held among his contemporaries. Never defeated in a political contest, he was probably the most popular Virginian of his day, and this without surrender of strong opinions strongly held. Gifted and genial, he maintained a dignity that impressed without offending, and achieved general recognition of his ability while avoiding all appearance of asserting it. Ambition was cloaked in dedication to the public service. Never has any other Virginian achieved at so early an age so impressive a series of political and judicial honors.

[The most important source is the account (41 closely written pages) in the manuscript "Sketches of his Own Family," written by Gov. L. W. Tazewell in 1823, two copies of which are in the possession of descendants in Norfolk, Va. Printed sources include H. B. Grigsby, *The Va. Convention of 1776* (1855), a brief notice, inaccurate in some respects; *The History of the Va. Federal Convention of 1788* (2 vols., 1890–91), and *Discourse on the Life and Character of the Hon. Littleton Waller Tazewell* (1860). D. G. Tyler, "Henry Tazewell," *Proc. Va. State Bar Asso. . . . 1928,* vol. XL, follows Grigsby. See also R. B. Tunstall, "Henry Tazewell," in A. W. Weddell, ed., *A Memorial Volume of Va. Historical Portraiture* (1930); a thumb-nail sketch in 4 *Call's Va. Reports,* pp. xxiii–xxiv; and, for genealogical data, *Va. Mag. of Hist. and Biography,* Jan. 1910, pp. 20–23.]

R. B. T.

TAZEWELL, LITTLETON WALLER (Dec. 17, 1774–May 6, 1860), lawyer, senator,

governor of Virginia, son of Henry Tazewell [*q.v.*] and Dorothy Elizabeth (Waller) Tazewell, was born in Williamsburg, Va. His mother's death in 1777 and his father's many public employments led to his being placed under the tutelage of his maternal grandfather, Judge Benjamin Waller. To the intimate relation between them, terminated by Judge Waller's death in Tazewell's twelfth year, he attributed "whatever worthy of imitation there may be in any part of my character" ("Sketches of His Own Family," *post*). From his twelfth to his fifteenth year he was under the personal instruction of Chancellor George Wythe, with whom for a time he made his home. In his eighteenth year (1791) he graduated B.A. from William and Mary—a degree then of such difficulty that his was one of very few conferred by the college for many years. After completing his legal studies in the office of John Wickham in Richmond, Tazewell obtained his license in May 1796. Brilliant, handsome, an adept in manly sports, he was already a conspicuous young man.

From 1798 to 1800 he represented James City County in the House of Delegates, and in the latter year was elected to Congress to succeed John Marshall. Remaining but one session (Nov. 26, 1800–Mar. 3, 1801), he removed to Norfolk in 1802 and married Anne Stratton Nivison, daughter of one of its leading lawyers. They had several children. The ravages of war and fire had brought about in Norfolk an approach to pioneer conditions, which combined with the disturbance of its commerce by the country's unsettled foreign relations during the Napoleonic wars to produce a rich field for the lawyer. To the routine of civil and criminal work were added cases involving admiralty and international law. As early as 1805 William Wirt describes Tazewell as at the head of the local bar (J. P. Kennedy, *Memoirs of the Life of William Wirt,* 1856, vol. I, 126). But about the year 1822 Tazewell withdrew from general practice, though he appeared occasionally in noteworthy cases. One of the most famous cases in which he took part, was that of *The Santissima Trinidad* (7 *Wheaton,* 283).

He served in the General Assembly from 1804 to 1806 and again in 1816–17, being elected on the latter occasion without his knowledge and during his absence from the city. In 1807 he was the spokesman of the city in its spirited defiance of the British fleet after the attack on the *Chesapeake* by the *Leopard,* conducting negotiations with Capt. Sir Thomas Hardy, of Trafalgar fame (*Calendar of Virginia State Papers,* vol. IX, 1890, pp. 568 ff.). But in general his part during his professional career was that of a thoughtful and detached observer, with a notable indifference to party lines. By inheritance and principle an anti-Federalist, he nevertheless opposed many important policies of Jefferson's administration, notably the Embargo of 1807 and the Non-Intercourse Act, favoring rather a declaration of war against both Great Britain and France. He opposed the election of Madison, and also the War of 1812, deeming that the time for action had passed; but when war was declared he loyally supported it. Monroe appointed him in 1821 as one of the commissioners under the eleventh article of the treaty of 1819 with Spain.

In 1824 Tazewell was elected to fill the vacancy in the United States Senate caused by the death of John Taylor of Caroline, whom his father had likewise succeeded upon Taylor's resignation from the Senate thirty years before. Relishing debate and excelling in it, he took place with the parliamentary giants of the day and was recognized as one of the leaders of a group opposing President Adams (B. C. Clark, *John Quincy Adams*, 1932, p. 241). As a member (later chairman) of the committee on foreign affairs, he drafted the report against the Panama mission. Later he published in the *Norfolk Herald* a carefully written series of articles subsequently reprinted in England as *A Review of the Negociations between the United States of America and Great Britain, Respecting the Commerce of the Two Countries* (1829). Re-elected in 1829, he became president *pro tempore* on July 9, 1832, but resigned shortly thereafter, alleging the pressure of personal affairs. It is probable that more lay behind. He had supported Jackson for the presidency, and had been offered successively the posts of secretary of war and minister to Great Britain, both of which he had declined. But one whose state-rights views were so instinctive that he habitually referred to Virginia as his "country" could not brook the imperious leadership of the toaster of "Our Federal Union." He opposed nullification, but more strongly still he opposed coercion; and Jackson's proclamation of Dec. 10, 1832, drew from him a weighty reply (*Norfolk and Portsmouth Herald*, Dec. 28, 1832–Jan. 30, 1833; reprinted in 1888 as *A Review of the Proclamation of President Jackson*).

During his senatorial term he had served as a member of the notable constitutional convention of 1829–30, in which he spoke not often, but always impressively. Significant as evidence of contemporary estimation was his membership on the important committee of seven appointed to draft the new constitution. On Jan. 7, 1834, he was elected governor of Virginia. The times were stormy. The movement for abolition was growing; federal encroachments were increasing; and the request of the General Assembly that the governor forward instructions to the Virginia senators on the expunging resolution brought the climax. On Feb. 22, 1836, he declined to forward the resolutions, and on Mar. 30 resigned, without explanation (Letter to Wyndham Robertson, Va. State Library). For nearly twenty-five years longer he enjoyed in Norfolk the retirement he had repeatedly sought. Indisputably its first citizen, he was the recipient of local veneration that passed almost into apotheosis.

Tazewell's fame must rest largely on the estimate of his contemporaries. He can claim the paternity of no enduring policy. Such of his writings as have been collected from newspapers and periodicals, while accurate and substantial, are inescapably the work of a lawyer who could or would not disguise the lawyer's heavy hand. His legal arguments, mostly in local courts, are almost wholly lost. Yet of his contemporary reputation there can be no doubt. John Randolph of Roanoke held him "second to no man that ever breathed" (W. C. Bruce, *John Randolph of Roanoke*, 1922, I, 461). William Wirt placed him, as a lawyer, first in Southern estimation, as Webster was in Northern (J. P. Kennedy, *Memoirs of the Life of William Wirt*, II, 121). John Marshall and Spencer Roane are said to have agreed, perhaps for the only time in their lives, that he was "unsurpased . . . by any competitor of his day" (Grigsby, *post*, p. 113). Hugh Blair Grigsby, in his memorial discourse, has added corroborative testimony of other eminent contemporaries. The stress is on his intellectual powers. The only shadow is itself a tribute to his genius for dialectics: a suggestion that the massive and versatile intellect so loved triumph for its own sake as at times to be unheeding of the ultimate right.

But it is noteworthy that his contemporaries repeatedly indulged in discussions of his self-effacement and doubts as to his career. Coldness, lack of broad human sympathy, perhaps a little of the public suspicion that dogs the path of brilliancy, are all put forward to account for Tazewell's failure to take and hold the place to which they felt him entitled. Undoubtedly there is lack of human appeal, not to speak of the "saving element of common sense," in logical processes so severe as to lead a public man to oppose, as did Tazewell, the celebration of George Washington's centenary because it savored of "man worship" (*Register of Debates in Congress,* 22 Cong., 1 Sess., col. 297). Appearing rather awe-inspiring for a democratic society, he made no effort to alter the impression. Unlike his father, to whom we may believe that the implications of the new republic were thoroughly congenial, Tazewell was an extreme individualist, wholly unaffected by trends of social thought. In him the English ancestors reasserted themselves. In a non-elective legislative body, like the House of Lords, freed from the importunity of constituents, he would have left an impress on the times in which he lived. But no urgency of desire impelled him to the compromises, even had he been capable of them, ordinarily required for repeated elections; and the daily legislative grind would have brought to him a tedium not easily endured. He keenly felt the duty to serve, if called upon; he may have secretly hoped for the call; but he would not invite it. What his friends viewed as a career of negations and abnegations was in fact a life, indifferent to official place, in which duty formed the sole impelling motive.

[Tazewell's own manuscript, "Sketches of His Own Family" (referred to in the sketch of Henry Tazewell), is the best account up to his twenty-second year, where it ends. Considerable manuscript material is in the possession of descendants in Norfolk, some in the Univ. of Va. Lib., and his correspondence as governor is in the Va. State Lib. The principal secondary source is H. B. Grigsby, *Discourse on the Life and Character of the Hon. Littleton Waller Tazewell* (1860), a work displaying both the advantages and the disadvantages of intimate personal knowledge. Its appendices contain valuable contemporary estimates, of which that by Wirt should be compared with a striking and intimate letter from him to Francis W. Gilmer, Mar. 16, 1820, in the Lib. of the Univ. of Va. Brief sketches are Richard Walke, in *Va. Law Register,* Nov. 1898, p. 409; R. A. Brock, *Virginia and Virginians* (2 vols., 1888); L. G. Tyler, in *Hist. of Va.* (6 vols., 1924), vol. II, ch. 7; and R. B. Tunstall, "Littleton Waller Tazewell," in A. W. Weddell, ed., *A Memorial Volume of Va. Hist. Portraiture* (1930).]   R. B. T.

TEALL, FRANCIS AUGUSTUS (Aug. 16, 1822–Nov. 16, 1894), editor, was born at Fort Ann, Washington County, N. Y., the fifth of the eight children of Horace Valentine and Sarah Buyss (Shaw) Teall and a great-grandson of Oliver Teall, a druggist, who emigrated from England to New Haven about 1723. Horace Valentine Teall was a minister of the sect founded by Abner Jones [*q.v.*], but, persuaded by the arguments of William Miller [*q.v.*], confidently awaited the second Advent in the early forties. Francis, meanwhile, attended schools at Rhinebeck and Schenectady, learned the printer's trade, and went to New York in 1841 to seek larger opportunities. There, on one of his first jobs, he worked beside Walt Whitman at the composing-case and was later advanced to the proof-reader's

desk. Toward the close of 1844 he joined the staff of George Hooker Colton's *American Review: A Whig Journal*; years afterward he recalled how, after passing the final proofs of "The Raven" for the February 1845 issue, he had, as a matter of routine, dropped Poe's manuscript into the wastebasket. He was employed on the *New York Recorder* during the editorship of Martin Brewer Anderson [*q.v.*], who remembered him gratefully and in 1875, as president of the University of Rochester, conferred on him the honorary degree of A.M. Teall was married about 1850 to Orcelia Shaw of West Troy, N. Y., by whom he had a daughter and three sons. In 1853 he became editor of the Huntington *Long Islander*. His next position of importance was on the *New York Tribune,* where the astonishingly broad and exact scholarship that he concentrated on proof-reading soon won the admiration of his associates.

When George Ripley and Charles Anderson Dana [*qq.v.*] contracted in 1857 to edit the *American Cyclopædia* for D. Appleton & Company, they engaged Teall to take charge of the proofs. Not only did he read critically every line of both editions of the *Cyclopædia,* but he also contributed a number of articles and performed other editorial duties. In 1882 he published an American edition, much annotated, of William B. Hodgson's *Errors in the Use of English.* Over a period of many years he gathered great stores of material for a treatise on punctuation and for a vast dictionary of proper names, but neither work was ever completed. Among printers and publishers he was held to have raised proof-reading to the rank of a learned profession, and many anecdotes were told to illustrate his omniscience and his passion for accuracy and consistency. On the organization of the staff of the *Century Dictionary* in 1882, William Dwight Whitney and Benjamin Eli Smith [*qq.v.*] inevitably chose him to supervise the proofs. He also wrote the preliminary definitions of most of the common words as far as the letter M, and remained with the *Dictionary* until its completion. After his wife's death in 1887 he made his home with his son in Bloomfield, N. J., where he died. As the result of a broken hip he was an invalid for the last year of his life.

[James Boughton, *Bouton-Boughton Family* (1890); D. P. Worden, *Descendants of Oliver Teall and Allied Families* (1922); *Evening Post* (N. Y.), Nov. 16, 1894; *N. Y. Daily Tribune,* Nov. 17, 1894; *Appletons' Ann. Cyc. . . . 1894* (1895).]   G. H. G.

TEASDALE, SARA (Aug. 8, 1884–Jan. 29, 1933), poet, was born in St. Louis, Mo., the youngest child of John Warren Teasdale and Mary Elizabeth (Willard) Teasdale, both of whom had soldier-ancestors in the Revolutionary War. Being a shy and sensitive child, never strong, she was tutored at home and later attended a private school nearby, from which she was graduated in 1903. She began to write verse in school. In 1905 she made a first visit to Europe and the Near East which enriched her imaginative background. Upon her return in 1907 William Marion Reedy [q.v.] introduced her in *Reedy's Mirror* with "Guenevere," a blank-verse monologue of about seventy lines. Soliloquies by Sappho, Helen, Beatrice, and other far-off heroines soon followed, to be collected in her first book, *Sonnets to Duse and Other Poems* (1907), a further exhibit of her girlish imaginary loves, for she had never seen the Italian actress when she wrote the nine poems in her honor. This book and *Helen of Troy and Other Poems* (1911) offered a mere hint of the lyric talent which was to develop under a richer experience of life and a closer study of her medium. Except for two or three winters in New York from 1911 to 1913, she lived in St. Louis with her parents until her marriage to Ernst B. Filsinger, Dec. 19, 1914. Her husband's business as an exporter soon called him to New York, where for years they lived happily together. Gradually, however, the two were separated; the wife's frail health made her more and more a recluse, and the husband's business required long absences abroad. At last, Sept. 5, 1929, they were divorced.

Meanwhile, Sara Teasdale had published four other books of original poems, in addition to two compilations, *The Answering Voice: One Hundred Love Lyrics by Women* (1917), and *Rainbow Gold* (1922), an anthology of poems for children. In *Rivers to the Sea* (1915) there is evidence of the beginning of a hardening process which was shaping the girl into a woman and her enthusiastic outpourings into poems—poems of a finished and delicate, if narrow, technique. In *Love Songs* (1917) and in the more austere *Flame and Shadow* (1920) she expressed her sensitive reactions to life with the economy of phrase and the simple lyric intensity of a matured art. In *Dark of the Moon* (1926) her technique became still more subtle, her choice of words more exact and distinguished, and her rhythms more delicately harmonized. In all these books she used the simplest lyric forms—usually two or three quatrains of three- or four-footed iambic lines, each quatrain emphasized by a single rhyme. In June 1932 she went to London for research work toward a biographical study of Christina Rossetti, whose "Christmas Carol"— "In the bleak mid-winter Frosty wind made moan"—had first inspired her, as a child, with

a love of poetry. There an attack of pneumonia prostrated her, and at her desire she was taken back to New York. Her recovery, which was slow and incomplete, led to sleeplessness and an overwrought nervous condition. On the morning of Jan. 29, 1933, she was found dead, apparently as the result of an overdose of a sleeping-draft. Her body was cremated. Her last book, *Strange Victory* (1933), which was published after her death, shows her characteristic emphasis upon the inviolateness, the essential aloofness of the human soul amid perishable things and fugitive emotions. All her poems, which bear a record of spiritual experience and growth, are intimately personal and confessional, from the love songs which serve as an "answering voice" for the countless masculine poems of love in English, to the later lyrics which present with impassioned intensity her rather stark philosophy, her courageous outlook upon the mystery of life and death.

[*Who's Who in America,* 1932–33; "Sara Teasdale," pamphlet printed in 1927 by the Macmillan Company; Louis Untermeyer, *American Poetry Since 1900* (1923); Harriet Monroe, *Poets and Their Art* (1926); *New Republic,* and *Commonweal,* Feb. 15, 1933; obituary in *New York Times,* Jan. 30, 1933; information from John Hall Wheelock and from Sara Teasdale's sister.]

H. M.

TECUMSEH (Mar. 1768?–Oct. 5, 1813), Shawnee chief, was the brother, usually said to be the twin brother, of Tenskwatawa [q.v.], the Prophet. His name is more properly spelled Tikamthi or Tecumtha. The place of his birth and the circumstances of his youth are not surely known, although it has been claimed that the remnant of his tribe maintain a valid tradition that he was born at the great springs near Old Chillicothe, now Oldtown, Ohio (Galloway, *post,* p. 108). His mother may have been a Creek but more probably was a Shawnee, and there seems to be no adequate evidence of any admixture of white blood in his veins. His father, Pucksinwa, also a Shawnee chief, was killed at the battle of Point Pleasant in 1774. By the time the boy reached adult life he had attained distinction as a warrior; and, from the testimony of his hereditary enemies, the white settlers, it is clear that he had established a remarkable reputation for mercy and humanity, that he had set his face against the torture of prisoners and other cruel practices of border warfare, and that his word was trusted on both sides of the frontier. Early in 1805 he and his brother, with a group of followers, were living in a Delaware village at the west fork of the White River, now in Indiana. Later in the year they removed to Greenville, Ohio. In 1808 they were forced by the white settlers to take themselves farther into the Indian country, within the present state of Indiana. With the permission of the Potawatomi and the Kickapoo they settled on the Wabash near the mouth of the Tippecanoe at a place afterward known as Prophet's Town. For many years white observers, both American and British, recognized only the importance of the Prophet, and as late as August 1810 William Henry Harrison [q.v.], then governor of Indiana Territory, referred to Tecumseh as "the Prophet's brother" ("Messages," *post,* I, 460, 470).

Nevertheless, it is clear that Tenskwatawa's religious revival was only an episode in the history of religious revivals, whereas Tecumseh developed a philosophy and a program that threatened to stop the westward thrust of American agricultural settlement. His argument was logical and eloquently defended. He maintained, with historical justification, that no sale or cession of Indian land could be valid without the consent of all the tribes assembled, since the Indians owned the land in common and no particular region belonged to any tribe. Before the white man came each tribe roamed wherever it willed, restrained only by the exigencies of the situation or the location of more powerful tribes; century by century the homelands of almost every tribe shifted and changed. Moreover, he pointed out that at the making of the treaty of Greenville in 1795 the United States government had negotiated with all the tribes assembled and had guaranteed to all the tribes together the title to unceded land. It was only later that frontier leaders saw the implications of such a precedent and set to work to mend matters. Harrison wrote that, when he became governor of Indiana Territory, he "at once determined, that the community of interests in the lands amongst the Indian tribes, which seemed to be recognized by the treaty of Greenville, should be objected to" ("Messages," *post,* II, 639; for Tecumseh's theory see *Ibid.,* I, 460, 465–66; McAfee, *post,* p. 9; Drake, *post,* pp. 121, 124, 231–32).

Tecumseh sought to combine the tribes into a confederacy to prevent land cessions and to develop Indian character and stamina against the temptation offered by the white settlers. To this end he visited the various tribes and brought more and more of them within the scope of his plans. Also he was increasingly successful in his efforts to persuade his immediate followers at Tippecanoe, the "Prophet's Town," to stop drinking the white man's rum, to establish themselves in an agricultural life, and to live on what they earned. On Aug. 7, 1811, Harrison, his worst enemy, wrote: "The implicit obedience

and respect which the followers of Tecumseh pay to him is really astonishing and more than any other circumstance bespeaks him one of those uncommon geniuses, which spring up occasionally to produce revolutions and overturn the established order of things. If it were not for the vicinity of the United States, he would, perhaps, be the founder of an Empire that would rival in glory Mexico or Peru. No difficulties deter him" ("Messages," *post,* p. 549). His was a simple program, but it was the beginning of adaptation to civilization. He hoped that the Indians might be unmolested by the white people for a little while and might find a way to escape decadence and destruction.

To support his theory and his program he looked to the aid of British arms and British diplomacy. Hard pressed by the Napoleonic wars, British officials in Canada steered an uneasy course, trying to keep the Indians from actual warfare without running any risk of losing their support in case Great Britain went to war with the United States. Out of such a troubled situation Tecumseh expected to obtain much. From the documents, the orders, and the reports of the period, it is difficult to determine what promises were made, openly and by implication, and what hopes were nourished in his heart. In 1816 Robert Breckinridge McAfee [q.v.] wrote that Tecumseh had believed he could, with British aid, drive the Americans south of the Ohio River, and that "from the *sine qua non* advanced by the British commissioners in the negotiation at Ghent, it would appear, that the British ministry had indulged a delusion not much less extravagant" (McAfee, *post,* pp. 14–15; see Public Record Office report of confidential board, CO, 42:150, and letter of Cochrane to Bathurst, July 14, 1814, WO, 1:141). The existence of a powerful Indian confederation such as the one destroyed at Tippecanoe would have lent point to the British proposals for the international guarantee of an Indian buffer state in the old Northwest. Tecumseh's purpose was to avoid war with the United States "until he should effect a combination strong enough to resist them, or until the expected war with Great Britain should commence" (McAfee, *post,* p. 15). In the years from 1803 to 1811, during which Harrison negotiated with individual tribes one treaty of cession after another, some fifteen in all, Tecumseh constantly took his troubles to the British officials in Canada for advice and sympathy; and he constantly received supplies of arms, ammunition, and clothing from the royal warehouses. After a stormy scene at Vincennes in August 1810 in which he defied Harrison and threatened violence, Tecumseh again visited his British friends in Canada and bore witness to his gratitude for aid from his "Father" the British: "You, Father, have nourished us, and raised us up from Childhood. We are now Men, and think ourselves capable of defending our Country" (Public Record Office, CO, 42:143).

However, he hesitated on the brink of a war unsupported by British arms. A little later he had gone south to tighten the bonds of his confederacy. Tall, straight, and lean, with a light copper complexion, he was a magnificent figure of a man as he traveled from tribe to tribe in the south, making a profound impression and winning many adherents to his cause. He reminded the Indians that "Our fathers, from their tombs, reproach us as slaves and cowards. I hear them now in the wailing winds" (Claiborne, *post*, p. 59); and he foretold, with great effect, the appearance of a comet flaming in the sky. In spite of the delay caused by the able opposition of such leaders as Pushmataha [*q.v.*], he appeared to be on the highroad to the fulfillment of his plans. The imminence of war between the United States and Great Britain gave him further cause to expect success.

The battle of Tippecanoe, into which his brother, the Prophet, allowed himself to be maneuvered in Tecumseh's absence, was disastrous to his hope of a powerful confederacy, of sustained British aid in return for his military support, and of an international guarantee to Indian tenure of territory on which to work out an adjustment to a changing world. When he went south he had cautioned his brother on no account to allow himself to be drawn, unprepared, into a battle (Drake, *post*, pp. 156, 221, 234, Tupper, *post*, p. 191). The drought of the summer of 1811, by ruining the crops and driving away the game, increased the difficulties of the situation, as did the continued glutting of the fur market with no outlet in war-stricken Europe. The confederacy that had been so near realization melted away in his very grasp. The provisions carefully husbanded against a time of need were destroyed. The bravest of his warriors were scattered. At an Indian council in May 1812 he defied any "living creature to say we ever advised anyone, directly or indirectly, to make war on our white brothers . . . Governor Harrison made war on my people in my absence . . . had I been at home, there would have been no blood shed at that time" ("Messages," *post*, II, 52, 51).

With no time to repair his fortunes before the War of 1812 was upon him, he and a few followers entered the British army, in which he received the rank of brigadier-general. He en-

couraged Sir Isaac Brock in his decision to attack Detroit at once and, after the capture of the fort, was active in rallying some of his old warriors to the victorious British cause. He fought with great courage at the River Raisin (Brownstown), Fort Meigs, and Fort Stephenson, trusting that at long last British aid would not fail him; but, when, after Perry's victory on Lake Erie, he apprehended Brig.-Gen. Henry A. Procter's purpose to burn Amherstburg and Detroit and to retreat eastward, he saw the ruin of all his hopes. In a scathing speech he reviewed the course of British friendship, blowing now hot and now cold according to the changing interests of imperial policy: "You always told us, that you would never draw your foot off British ground; but now, father, we see you are drawing back . . . We must compare our father's conduct to a fat animal, that carries its tail upon its back, but when affrighted, he drops it between his legs and runs off . . . You have got the arms and ammunition . . . sent for his red children, if you have an idea of going away, give them to us. . . . Our lives are in the hands of the Great Spirit. We are determined to defend our lands, and if it be his will, we wish to leave our bones upon them" (*Weekly Register, post,* Nov. 6, 1813, p. 175). Reluctantly, distrusting Procter thoroughly, he covered the British retreat as far as Moraviantown, where, at the Battle of the Thames, he fell. He remained a tradition of glory to his own people and a bone of contention to a generation of American politicians intent on making political capital out of his destruction.

[Files of the Office of Indian Affairs, Washington, D. C.; papers in Public Record Office, London; "Governors Messages and Letters. Messages and Letters of Wm. H. Harrison," *Ind. Hist. Colls.* (2 vols., 1922), ed. by Logan Esarey; Moses Dawson, *A Hist. Narrative of the Civil and Mil. Services of Maj.-Gen. Wm. H. Harrison* (1824); R. B. McAfee, *Hist. of the Late War in the Western Country* (1816), reprinted with index (1919); John Richardson, *Richardson's War of 1812* (1902) with notes by A. C. Casselman; J. F. H. Claiborne, *Life and Times of Gen. Sam. Dale* (1860); F. B. Tupper, *Family Records: Containing Memoirs of Maj.-Gen. Sir Isaac Brock* (1835); Benj. Drake, *Life of Tecumseh* (1841); W. A. Galloway, *Old Chillicothe* (1934); James Mooney, "The Ghost Dance Religion," *14th Ann. Report of Bureau of Ethnology*, pt. 2 (1896); *Weekly Register* (Niles), Oct. 9, 23, 1813, Nov. 6, 1813, Apr. 9, 16, 1814.]   K. E. C.

TEDYUSKUNG (*c.* 1700–Apr. 19, 1763), Delaware chief, was born in New Jersey east of Trenton, the son of a well-known Delaware Indian called "Old Captain Harris." His name was spelled in many different ways, of which the more important are Tadeuskund, Tedyuskung, Teedyuskung, and even Detiuscung and Deedjoskon. He was also sometimes referred to as Honest John. About 1730 he migrated with those of his tribe who, defeated by the Iroquois and crowded by the white settlers, settled in the forks of the Delaware River, near Easton, Pa., and ten years later were living in the Wyoming region between the forks of the Susquehanna. Touched by the preaching of the Moravian missionaries, with his wife, Elizabeth, he became a member of the Indian Christian settlement of Gnadenhuetten on the Mahoning River, after some hesitation was baptized by John Christopher Cammerhoff [q.v.], and took the name of Gideon. In 1754 he became a Delaware chief and turned his back on any further attempt to reconcile himself to the clash between European and Indian culture by adopting a religion of submission. Instead he chose war. In spite of the earlier successes of Shikellamy [q.v.] and the support given to the Iroquois pretensions by William Johnson, Conrad Weiser, and George Croghan [qq.v.], he was in a large measure successful in asserting Delaware independence of the Iroquois. He denounced as frauds all the cessions of Delaware lands by the Iroquois; and, in the hope of bringing about some readjustment, he espoused the cause of the English colonists against the French and against the Indian resentment that burst into flame as the news of Braddock's defeat spread through the Indian country. He favored the mission of Christian Frederick Post [q.v.] to the Ohio Indians in 1758 and, with Post, was largely responsible for British success at Fort Duquesne and for the ultimate failure of French arms.

He shared the curse of his people in being unable to resist the temptation of strong drink. At important councils between his tribe and the white government, he was reported as being drunk every night. Conrad Weiser said that "though he is a Drunkard ... yet he is a man that can think well" (*Pennsylvania Archives, post,* I ser., vol. III, p. 68), and another contemporary wrote "but he is really more of a Politician than any of his Opponents, whether in or out of our proprietary Council; and if he could be kept sober, might probably soon become Emperor of all the neighbouring Nations" (Thomson, *post,* p. 183). He seems to have been able to transact the business of each day with a head clear enough to baffle the provincial officials. Nevertheless his weakness must have played its part in the final failure to make good the Delaware protests against undoubted fraud in land cessions. It was also the immediate cause of his death. His house in Wyoming was set on fire, probably by some Iroquois for revenge, and he was burned to death in a drunken stupor.

[John Heckewelder, "An Account of the Hist., Manners, and Customs of the Indian Nations," *Trans. of the ... Am. Philosophical Soc.,* vol. I (1819), and in *Hist. Soc. of Pa. Memoirs,* vol. XII (1876); W. C. Reichel, *Memorials of the Moravian Church,* vol. I (1870), esp. pp. 217–28, 265; "The Jour. of Christian Frederick Post," in Charles Thomson, *An Enquiry into the Causes of the Alienation of the Delaware and Shawanese Indians from the British Interests* (1759, reprinted 1867); esp. app.; Edmund De Schweinitz, *The Life and Times of David Zeisberger* (1870); *Pa. Archives,* esp. 1 ser. vols. II–IV (1853); *Minutes of the Provincial Council of Pa.,* vols. VII–VIII (1851–52); J. S. Walton, *Conrad Weiser* (1900).]

K. E. C.

TELFAIR, EDWARD (c. 1735–Sept. 19, 1807), merchant, member of the Continental Congress, governor of Georgia, was born on the Telfair estate at "Town Head" in Scotland. Having received his formal education in the Kirkcudbright grammar school, he entered a commercial house, and at the age of twenty-three came to Virginia as its agent. About 1766 he settled in Georgia where, two years later, he represented St. Paul's Parish in the Commons House of the Assembly. He identified himself, thereafter, with the city of Savannah, although for a time he lived in Burke County and at "The Grove" near Augusta. In Savannah he formed numerous business partnerships, the firms becoming the principal commercial houses in colonial Georgia, dealing largely in European and East India goods, and also selling some slaves. Telfair engaged also in ship-building and accumulated large land holdings, especially after the Revolution. So successful were his businesses that when he died he left a fortune, which, with the extinction of the family in 1875, was devoted to the establishment of the Telfair Academy of Arts and Sciences and other benefactions in Savannah.

Though prosperous in business and honored by appointment to various commissionerships in the colony, Telfair joined the Liberty Boys, on the rise of discontent in 1774, and became one of the most prominent rebels during the next two years. He was present at the various Tondee Tavern meetings in 1774, was a member of the committee appointed to receive donations for the Boston sufferers, attended the first three provincial congresses, was a member of the original council of safety, and a leader of the mob which broke open the royal powder magazine in Savannah. He was also appointed assistant commander of the up-country militia and was a member of the committtee to arm the state, yet, in June 1776, he was listed in a group described as dangerous to the liberties of America. Whether the petty spite of enemies or a temporary relapse in patriotism was responsilbe (William Telfair, a brother, and Basil Cowper, both business associates, remained loyal to the king), he was soon back in the rebel ranks, with patriotic fervor never again to be questioned. In 1780 and 1781, his name was in the lists attainted for high treason by the restored British authority in Savannah, and from this time forth he remained a bitter enemy of the British. He was a member of the Continental Congress from 1777 to 1783.

At various times from 1781 to 1784 he was justice and assistant justice for Burke County, and in the year 1783 he held the following positions: Indian commissioner to treat with the Creeks and Cherokees, commissioner to adjust the boundary dispute with South Carolina, and representative in the legislature from Burke County. In 1785 he was reëlected to the legislature and the next year he was elected governor. During his one-year term he showed great vigor in dealing with the Indians and with South Carolina in the boundary dispute. In 1788 he was a member of the convention which ratified the federal Constitution, in 1789 he was a member of the legislature from Richmond County, and became the first governor under the new Georgia constitution of 1789. As governor he came into conflict with the United States over the Indian question precipitated by the Treaty of New York, and over the *Chisholm* vs. *Georgia* case (*2 U. S.*, 419), which he pushed forward into such a burning issue that it led to the Eleventh Amendment. He was reckless in his dealings with the state's public lands, illegally signing warrants for as much as 100,000 acres to one person. On May 18, 1774, he was married to Sally, a daughter of William Gibbons [*q.v.*]. They had three sons and three daughters.

[W. J. Northen, ed., *Men of Mark in Ga.*, vol. I (1907); A. D. Candler and C. A. Evans, eds., *Georgia* (1906), vol. III; W. B. Stevens, *Hist. of Ga.*, vol. II (1859); *Biog. Dict. of the Am. Cong., 1774–1927* (1928); U. B. Phillips, *Ga. and State Rights* (1902); A. D. Candler, ed., *Revolutionary Records of the State of Ga.* (1908), vols. I–III; *Colonial Records of the State of Ga.* (1907–11), vols. X, XI, XIX, pt. 2; George White, *Hist. Colls. of Ga.* (3rd ed., 1854); *Am. State Papers, Indian Affairs*, vol. I (1832); E. C. Burnett, ed., *Letters of Members of the Continental Cong.*, vols. III, V, VI (1926–33); *Ga. Hist. Quart.*, Mar., June 1917, *Ga. Gazette*, 1774, 1775, 1783–1791; *Columbian Museum & Savannah Advertiser* and *Republican and Savannah Evening Ledger*, Sept. 22, 1807; *Augusta Chronicle*, Sept. 26, 1807; manuscript letter-book covering most of the year 1786, Lib. of the Ga. Hist. Soc. in Savannah, and other manuscripts relating to the governorship, Dept. of Archives and Hist., Atlanta.]   E. M. C.

TELLER, HENRY MOORE (May 23, 1830–Feb. 23, 1914), lawyer, United States senator, secretary of the interior, the eldest son of John and Charlotte (Moore) Teller, was born on a farm in Allegany County, N. Y. He was a descendant of Wilhelm Teller, who settled in Albany in 1639 and later moved to New York. Henry attended rural schools in the vicinity of his home and the academies at Rushford and Alfred, N. Y. Subsequently he taught school, read law in the office of Martin Grover at Angelica, N. Y., and was admitted to the bar at Binghamton in 1858. Immediately thereafter he moved to Morrison, Ill., where he practised law and engaged in politics. Three years later he went to Colorado and established a law office at Central City.

During the Civil War period he became one of the leading figures of Colorado. He was an unconditional unionist, a major-general of the militia, and took an active part in raising troops and preparing Denver for the defense against threatened Indian attacks. After the war he devoted his energies to his legal practice and business enterprises, serving as attorney for numerous corporations and as president of the Colorado Central Railroad (1872–76), and building the territory's largest hotel.

When Colorado was admitted into the Union in 1876, Teller was elected to the United States Senate as a Republican, serving until Apr. 17, 1882, when he resigned to accept the position of secretary of the interior in the cabinet of President Arthur. He was again elected to the Senate in 1885 and served four terms, the first two as a Republican; the third as an Independent Silver Republican; and the fourth as a Democrat. His most spectacular legislative activities were aimed at the remonetization of silver, and his fight against the repeal of the Sherman Silver Purchase Act in 1893 probably marked their climax. His most notable speeches were those of September 1893 (*Congressional Record*, 53 Cong., 1 Sess., pp. 1348, 1385, 1419) when he attempted to convict the bankers of bringing on the panic, and that of Oct. 26 (*Ibid.*, pp. 2838–50) on the evils of the appreciation of money on the gold standard.

In the field of national politics his bolt from the Republican Convention of 1896 over the silver question was an event of outstanding significance. For a few weeks following, he was a candidate for the Democratic nomination for president, and the agitation back of his campaign stimulated the drift in the convention to Bryan. The Republican bolters organized the Silver Republican party, and during the campaign this group supported the Democratic nominee, an alliance that was repeated in 1900. After the latter campaign Teller announced himself a Democrat. Although traditionally an expansionist, at the outbreak of the war with Spain in 1898 he secured the adoption of the Fourth, or Teller

Resolution (*Congressional Record*, 55 Cong., 2 Sess., p. 3954), which pledged the United States to an independent Cuba. Teller voted against a similar pledge regarding the Philippines, but the Administration's policy of crushing the Aguinaldo government brought forth a devastating attack from him in February 1902 (*Ibid.*, 57 Cong., 1 Sess., pp. 1574, 1640, 1682). He manifested a like opposition to Theodore Roosevelt's policy toward Panama. Teller's later years in the Senate were taken up with perfecting legislation regarding public lands, Indians, reclamation, and the monetary system. When he retired from the Senate in 1909, he retained his place on the National Monetary Commission, on which he served until it was disbanded in 1912.

In personal appearance he was a moderately tall, slender man, almost always dressed in the conventional black frock coat of a senator of the eighties. His most striking feature was a shock of stiff dark hair which he unsuccessfully tried to comb straight back. His beard was full and his upper lip smooth shaven. Rather puritanical in his tastes and outlook, he was cosmopolitan in his friendships. He was not an orator but in the opinion of his contemporaries ranked among the more effective debaters in the Senate. Rather retiring by nature, he was usually willing to let his Colorado colleague assume the burden of debate and floor leadership. His fight over the silver question began as a defense of local interests, but as its relation to the larger struggle between the debtor and creditor classes became clearer to him, he tended more and more to align himself with the weaker groups in society. Certain reforms, unpopular at the time, such as woman's suffrage, always had his support, but after 1890 he was found with considerable regularity supporting discriminating income taxes, the government regulation of large-scale business, and laws for the protection of native interests against those of a distant government.

On June 7, 1862, he married Harriet M. Bruce of Cuba, N. Y., by whom he had three children. He died in Denver.

[*Biog. Dir. Am. Cong.* (1928); *Cong. Record*, 67 Cong., 4 Sess., pp. 3589–3601; T. F. Dawson, *Senator Teller: A Brief Account of His Fifth Election to the U. S. Senate* (1898); Teller MSS., State Museum, Denver, Colo.; Elmer Ellis, "The Public Career of Henry Moore Teller," unpublished MS. in Univ. of Iowa Lib.; W. F. Stone, *Hist. of Colo.*, vol. II (1918); *Who's Who in America*, 1912–13; *Rocky Mountain News* (Denver), Feb. 23, 1914; *N. Y. Times*, Feb. 24, 1914.]　　　　　　　　　　　　　　E. E—s.

TEMPLE, OLIVER PERRY (Jan. 27, 1820–Nov. 2, 1907), lawyer and author, was born near Greeneville, Greene County, Tenn., the son of James and Mary (Craig) Temple, and a de-

scendant of William Temple, a native of England who was living in Goshen, Pa., in 1721. While a student at Greeneville College in 1838 Oliver volunteered as a soldier to aid regulars under Gen. Winfield Scott [*q.v.*] in his work of pacifying the Cherokee Indians then being moved beyond the Mississippi. In 1841 he entered Washington College, Washington County, Tenn., and was graduated with the class of 1844. He at once entered the field of politics, delivering speeches throughout his congressional district in behalf of Henry Clay [*q.v.*], candidate for the presidency. Subsequently he read law in Greeneville under Robert J. McKinney, and in 1846 was admitted to the bar. In July of the following year he was the Whig candidate for Congress against Andrew Johnson [*q.v.*], and in a campaign of three weeks, by dexterous attacks on his opponent's record he cut Johnson's usual majority of about 1500 to 314 votes.

In 1848 Temple removed to Knoxville, where he practised law in partnership with leaders of the East Tennessee bar. He was appointed in 1850 one of the commissioners to negotiate with the Indian tribes of Texas, New Mexico, and Arizona. On Sept. 9, 1851, shortly after his return to Knoxville, he was married to Scotia C. Humes, of that city. He took a leading part in the Southern Commercial Convention held in Knoxville in 1856, as proponent and advocate of resolutions against the reëstablishment of the slave trade. In 1860 he was a delegate to the National Union Convention, held at Baltimore, and aided in the nomination of John Bell [*q.v.*] as candidate for the presidency; subsequently, as a Bell and Everett elector, he canvassed his congressional district. In November of the same year he made the first speech in Tennessee, after Lincoln's election, in behalf of the Union, and in December he planned a meeting of East Tennessee Unionists at Knoxville to consolidate the sentiment of that section against secession. The following year he stumped East Tennessee for the Union cause, and took a leading part in the Greeneville Convention of June 17, 1861, which declared for a separation of East Tennessee from the state of Tennessee. In July 1866, he was appointed one of the chancellors of Tennessee by Gov. W. G. Brownlow [*q.v.*], and continued as such until September 1878. He then returned to the bar but after 1881 devoted his attention to his large estate.

When more than seventy-five years old he turned to authorship. His first production was *The Covenanter, the Cavalier and the Puritan* (1897). This was followed by *East Tennessee and the Civil War* (1899), and *Notable Men of*

Tennessee, published in 1912, after his death. He wrote in a vigorous and interesting, though not graceful style, and drew copiously from his own rich store of reminiscences.

His contribution to the progress of transportation and agriculture in East Tennessee was considerable. He was one of the originators of the Knoxville & Ohio Railroad; a director of the East Tennessee & Georgia Railroad Company, and president of the first macadam turnpike company in his section of the state. Before the Civil War he was a member of the state board of agriculture, and in 1872 he was the prime mover in the organization of the East Tennessee Farmers' Convention. For many years he was active as a trustee of the University of Tennessee, and for a period served as chairman of the board. His work for the institution was directed principally toward the development of the agricultural department. After his death the Farmers' Convention built Temple Hall on the experimental farm of the University, in his honor.

[W. S. Speer, *Sketches of Prominent Tennesseans* (1888); biog. sketch by Temple's daughter, Mary B. Temple, in his *Notable Men of Tennessee* (1912); William Rule, *Standard Hist. of Knoxville, Tenn.* (1900); T. W. Humes, *The Loyal Mountaineers of Tenn.* (1888); W. T. Hale and D. L. Merritt, *A Hist. of Tennessee and Tennesseans* (1913), vols. II, III, VII; *Who's Who in America,* 1906–07; *Nashville Banner,* Jan. 30, 1904; *Journal and Tribune* (Knoxville), Nov. 3, 1907.]

S. C. W.

TEMPLE, WILLIAM GRENVILLE (Mar. 23, 1824–June 28, 1894), naval officer, was born in Rutland, Vt., the son of Robert and Charlotte Eloise (Green) Temple, and a descendant of Robert Temple, who was born in Ireland and emigrated to Boston, Mass., in 1717. Appointed midshipman on Apr. 18, 1840, he made his first cruise in the *Constellation* around the world, 1840–44. Then, after service in the Home Squadron, he studied six months ashore until his promotion to passed midshipman, July 11, 1846. He was wrecked in the *Boston* on Eleuthera Island (Bahamas), Oct. 5 following, and subsequently had charge of the sick men sent to Norfolk in the schooner *Volant.* Returning to the Gulf of Mexico in the steamer *Scourge,* he participated in the chief naval events of 1847 in the Mexican War, including the siege of Vera Cruz; the capture of Alvarado, Mar. 31, where he and two men occupied the town for a day after the *Scourge* had taken it unassisted (thus upsetting Commodore Matthew Calbraith Perry's plan for a grand-scale operation); and the occupation of Túxpan and Tabasco. His "Memoir of the Landing of the United States Troops at Vera Cruz in 1847," dated Mar. 23, 1852, but first published in P. S. P. Conner's *The Home Squadron under*

Commodore Conner in the War with Mexico (1896), shows keen professional interest and ability. His duty in the next decade, save for a Mediterranean cruise in 1852–55 and an assignment as flag lieutenant in the Pacific Squadron in 1859–61, was in coast survey work, ranging from New York harbor to Florida. In the Civil War he first commanded the steamer *Flambeau,* sent in November 1861 to cut off blockade runners at Nassau. His work there was not aggressive enough to satisfy the American consul at Nassau (*War of the Rebellion: Official Records, Navy,* I ser., vol. XI, 1901, p. 532), but Flag Officer Samuel Francis Du Pont [*q.v.*] spoke approvingly of it (R. M. Thompson and Richard Wainwright, *Confidential Correspondence of Gustavus Vasa Fox, Assistant Secretary of the Navy,* vol. I, 1918, p. 102). On Jan. 22, 1862, he was invalided north. After seven months' ordnance duty in New York he commanded the *Pembina* on the Mobile blockade until November 1863, and was then made flag captain of the East Gulf Squadron. A year later he took command of the side-wheeler *Pontoosuc,* which was in the first line of Admiral David Dixon Porter's fleet in both attacks on Fort Fisher, Dec. 23–25, 1864, and Jan. 13–15, 1865. His report of the first attack, revealing the ineffective use of Gen. B. F. Butler's landing forces, was forwarded by Porter with the comment, "Important as a matter of history, and tells the whole story" (*Ibid.,* vol. XI, 1900, p. 287). Porter included him in recommendations for promotion (*Ibid.,* p. 455). After participating in Virginia waters in the closing operations of the war, he was detached May 25, 1865. He was made commander, Mar. 3, 1865; captain, Aug. 28, 1870; commodore, June 5, 1878; and rear admiral, Feb. 22, 1884, just before his voluntary retirement on Feb. 29.

His post-war service included ordnance duty at Portsmouth, N. H. (1866–69); an assignment as escort to King Kalakaua of Hawaii during his visit to the United States, Dec. 11–28, 1874, for which he was made knight commander of the order of Kamehameha I; service as chief of staff in the European Squadron (1871–73), with a subsequent leave of eighteen months in Europe, as captain of the New York navy yard (1875–77), and as member of the retiring board (1879–84). His death from apoplexy occurred in Washington, where he resided after his retirement, and his burial was in the Congressional Cemetery. He was married Oct. 7, 1851, to Catlyna, daughter of Gen. J. G. Totten, but had no children. As suggested by his frequent staff assignments, he was an officer of unusual ability and striking personality. A relative describes him as "the beau ideal of a handsome man, very tall and very large, celebrated for his wit and gifts as a raconteur."

[Temple Prime, *Some Account of the Temple Family* (1894) ; L. H. Hamersly, *Records of Living Officers of the U. S. Navy and Marine Corps* (4th ed., 1890) ; E. L. Temple, *The Vermonter*, vol. XXVIII, no. 12 (1923) ; obituaries in *Army and Navy Jour.*, June 30, and *Evening Star* (Washington, D. C.), June 29, 1894.]
A. W—t.

TEN BROECK, ABRAHAM (May 13, 1734– Jan. 19, 1810), soldier, jurist, was born in Albany, N. Y., the tenth child of Dirck Ten Broeck and his wife, Grietja (Margaret) Cuyler. He was a descendant of Wessel Ten Broeck who came to New Netherland with Peter Minuit in 1626. His marriage on Nov. 1, 1763, to Elizabeth, the daughter of Stephen Van Rensselaer, united him with one of the most influential families in upper New York. His father, in addition to holding municipal offices and serving as commissioner of Indian affairs, was a prominent merchant and dealer in furs. Abraham prepared for a business career under the tutorage of his brother-in-law, Philip Livingston [*q.v.*]. By 1752, however, he was back in Albany and soon relinquished mercantile pursuits, for in 1761 he became a member of the colonial assembly and thereafter remained in public life almost continuously until his death. He was a stanch defender of popular rights, and in 1775, still holding his seat in the colonial assembly, he voted approval of the course of the merchants in signing the Association as recommended by the Continental Congress. An ardent patriot, he was a deputy in the New York Provincial Congress 1775–77 and served on the Committee of Safety. He was a member of the convention which in 1777 framed the first constitution for New York State.

With the outbreak of the Revolution and the passage of the new militia law he helped to draft, Ten Broeck, who had held commissions in the colonial militia, was made brigadier-general, first of the Albany and Tryon County militia, and subsequently of the Albany County militia only. At his headquarters in Albany, a strategic center, he was constantly confronted with the dilemma of obeying orders to reinforce the Continental troops and responding to the appeals of the alarmed inhabitants on the western and northern frontiers that the militia be allowed to guard their own homes. His task was further complicated by the lack of equipment and supplies. Zeal for his country's cause was tempered with a caution and practical-mindedness that won him the respect and confidence of his superior officers. His outstanding military achievement was his participation at the most critical moment

in the battle of Bemis Heights in 1777, which resulted in the forced retreat of General Burgoyne. Ill health following an accident compelled him to resign his commission in 1781.

Ten Broeck had acquired a wide acquaintance with the law from his committee work in the colonial and the provincial assembly, where he had helped to revise old laws and draft new ones relating not only to military affairs but also to questions of currency, taxation, land titles, and other civil matters; his land and other business interests had familiarized him with the application of the laws. He had been a justice in various colonial courts, and with the relinquishment of his military duties in 1781 he returned to the judicial field to act for thirteen years as first judge of the court of common pleas of Albany County. From 1779 to 1783 and from 1796 to 1799 he was mayor of Albany.

As an influential resident of a key city in one of the leading colonies and states, he rendered able service to his state and country during the late colonial, the Revolutionary, and the early national periods. He died at the age of seventy-five years. He and his wife had five children.

[G. E. B. Jackson, *Gen. Abraham Ten Broeck* (1886) ; Emma Ten Broeck Runk, *The Ten Broeck Geneal.* (1897) ; M. K. Van Rensselaer, *The Van Rensselaers of the Manor of Rensselaerswyck* (1888) ; F. B. Heitman, *Hist. Reg. of Officers of the Continental Army* (1914) ; *Jour. of the Votes and Proc. of the Gen. Assembly of the Colony of N. Y. from 1766 to 1776* (1820) ; *Jour. of the Provincial Cong., Provincial Convention . . . of the State of N. Y., 1775–1776–1777* (2 vols., 1842) ; *Pub. Papers of George Clinton . . . Military* (1899–1914) ; *Docs. Relating to the Colonial Hist. of the State of N. Y.*, vol. XV, *State Archives*, vol. I (1887) ; *Calendar of Hist. MSS. Relating to the War of the Revolution in the Office of the Secretary of State, Albany, N. Y.* (2 vols., 1868) ; correspondence in New York State Library, Albany.]   E. L. J—en.

TEN BROECK, RICHARD (May 1812–Aug. 1, 1892), the first American horseman to assert the prowess of his country on the English turf, was born at Albany, N. Y., the son of Richard Ten Broeck. He was, according to his own account, a grandson of Henry Bicker of Philadelphia, an officer of Pennsylvania troops during the Revolution, and of Col. Dirck Ten Broeck of Albany, likewise a Revolutionary officer. In 1823 the boy saw the famous match race between Eclipse and Henry at the Union Course on Long Island. In 1829 he was admitted to the United States Military Academy at West Point, but left the following year and went South. Here he began the long racing career which continued with some interruptions until he retired in 1887.

When about thirty-five years old Ten Broeck became the partner of the veteran William R. Johnson [*q.v.*], "the Napoleon of the Turf," in racing on Southern tracks. In 1853 he purchased an obscure colt by Boston out of Alice Carneal, and in a series of bold matches and interstate stake races which attracted nation-wide attention scored a succession of brilliant victories that made its name, Lexington, one of the greatest in American turf history. Convinced by this horse's unexampled feat of running four miles in 7:19¾ that American racehorses and training methods excelled those of the mother country, Ten Broeck in 1856 went to England with a quartet of representative runners, one of which was Lecomte, the only horse that ever won a heat from Lexington, and another Pryor, that had beaten Lecomte. Undismayed by the fact that Lexington had to be left behind because he had become blind, and that Lecomte was found to be too unsound to race again, Ten Broeck offered on his arrival to run an American horse at four-mile heats for $25,000 a side against any English thoroughbred that could be produced. This challenge excited widespread and anxious interest in England and the warmest national enthusiasm in all sections of the United States. It was not accepted. The American four-milers were only moderately successful when racing under the British system of dash races at shorter distances, yet Ten Broeck's Prioress scored a sensational victory in the Cesarewitch Stakes, outlasting her competitors, while Starke, half-brother to her and to Lecomte, won the Goodwood Cup and the Bentinck Memorial Plate —the latter at four miles and a quarter, the longest race in England. Ten Broeck remained in England about ten years, winning with English and American horses almost $200,000 in purses, stakes, and matches.

His subsequent career in America was not noteworthy. Financial stress and mental infirmity came upon him in old age, and the last years of life drew to a gloomy close in a lonely little home called "The Hermitage," near Menlo Park, in California. Always a man of quick temper, he had fought several duels, parted from two wives, and at the time of his death driven away his only servant. His second wife, whom he married late in life when she was the widow of H. D. Newcomb of Louisville, Ky., applied unsuccessfully in 1888 for an examination as to his sanity, so eccentric had he then become. Yet one who knew him in his prime wrote in the New York *Sun* when he died: "Mr. Ten Broeck was a genial, well beloved companion, an honest, enthusiastic horseman, and the most intrepid gambler that ever backed a racehorse, bucked the tiger, or bluffed on a pair of deuces." An article of his, "Some Personal Reminiscences, Incidents, and Anecdotes," appeared in the *Spirit of the Times* for Dec. 27, 1890.

[Emma Ten Broeck Runk, *The Ten Broeck Geneal.* (1897); C. E. Trevathan, *The Am. Thoroughbred* (1905); "The American Horses in England," a series of articles in *Porter's Spirit of the Times* in 1857; *Spirit of the Times*, Aug. 6, 1892; *Sun* (N. Y.), Aug. 2, 1892; *N. Y. Herald*, Aug. 2, 1892; letter from Maj.-Gen. Wm. D. Connor, Supt. U. S. Mil. Acad.]

G. C. G.

TENÉ-ANGPÓTE [See KICKING BIRD, d. May 3, 1875].

TENNENT, GILBERT (Feb. 5, 1703–July 23, 1764), Presbyterian clergyman, was the eldest of the four sons of William [*q.v.*] and Catharine (Kennedy) Tennent, all of whom were educated by their father and entered the ministry. Of these Gilbert and the second born, William [*q.v.*], were the most distinguished; John died in his middle twenties while pastor of the church at Freehold, N. J.; Charles, the youngest, was pastor of the congregation at Whiteclay Creek, Del., for twenty-four years, and then of the church at Buckingham, Md., until his death. Gilbert was born in County Armagh, Ireland, and was about fourteen years old when the family emigrated to America. From his father he seems to have received a good grounding in the classics, some knowledge of Hebrew, a thorough understanding of the theological problems of the day, and an excellent mental discipline. Yale College conferred the honorary degree of A.M. upon him in 1725.

His early religious experience was a troubled one, but at length he was brought to a sense of saving conversion. Not convinced of his spiritual fitness for the ministry, however, he studied medicine for a year, but at length, May 1725, presented himself to the Philadelphia Presbytery as a candidate for licensure and successfully passed the examination. In December of the same year he was called to the church in Newcastle, Del., but after preaching there for a short time left abruptly. Both the church and the Newcastle Presbytery complained of his action to the Synod, which administered a rebuke. About this time he seems to have assisted his father in the newly established "Log College," but in the fall of 1726 he accepted a call to New Brunswick, N. J., and was ordained there by the Philadelphia Presbytery. The inhabitants of this region, especially the Dutch, had been aroused by the evangelistic labors of the Dutch Reformed pastor, Theodorus Jacobus Frelinghuysen [*q.v.*]; but the English-speaking people were as sheep without a shepherd. Tennent's task was to gather them together and minister to them. Some of the Dutch gave encouragement by contributing to his support. Although Frelinghuysen seems not to have been favorable to his coming, a warm friendship later sprang up between them. Frelinghuysen permitted Tennent the use of the buildings in which the Domine was accustomed to preach, and occasionally the two would address the same congregation, the one in Dutch, and the other in English (*Ecclesiastical Records: State of New York,* vol. IV, 1902, pp. 2557, 2667, 2587, 2588). Undoubtedly Tennent's natural evangelistic tendencies were strengthened by this association. From the beginning of his ministry his appearance, voice, and manner of preaching made a marked impression on his hearers; but he grieved that he could count so few converts. After a serious illness, during which Frelinguysen wrote him an encouraging letter, his zeal increased. His searching examinations into the experiences of professing Christians—which brought him much unpopularity and abuse—convinced him that many of them had not been converted, and he now preached with great vividness on sin, retribution, repentance, and the need of a conscious inner change. As a result many were aroused to a more vital interest in religion, both in the region about New Brunswick and on Staten Island, where he also labored. As time went on, other ministers of his spirit, some of whom had had their zeal kindled by his father in the "Log College," settled in the vicinity. Thus the Tennents and their associates became one of the sources of the Great Awakening, which had its consummation during the visit of George Whitefield [*q.v.*] to America in 1739–40.

Upon his arrival in the Middle Colonies, Whitefield soon formed an intimate relationship with the Tennent group. He visited New Brunswick and preached for Gilbert on Nov. 13, 1739, recording in his journal (*post*) under that date: "Here we were much refreshed with the Company of Mr. Gilbert *Tennent,* an eminent Dissenting Minister. . . . He and his Associates are now the burning and shining Lights of this Part of *America.*" Tennent accompanied him to New York, and Whitefield, hearing him preach there, wrote in his journal, Nov. 14, "never before heard [I] such a searching Sermon. He went to the Bottom indeed, and did not daub with untempered Mortar. . . . Hypocrites must either soon be converted or enraged at his Preaching. He is a Son of Thunder, and I find doth not fear the Faces of Men." In the later summer and fall of 1739 Tennent made an evangelistic tour in South Jersey and westward into Maryland, his labors meeting with notable success. When in November 1740 Whitefield returned from New England, he was accompanied by Daniel Rogers, a tutor at Harvard, who brought·to Tennent a

message from several New England ministers requesting that he come thither and continue the great work which Whitefield had begun. Persuaded by Whitefield to accept, he reached Boston toward the middle of the following month. The effect of his preaching upon the masses was even greater than that of Whitefield. After Whitefield, wrote the Rev. Timothy Cutler [*q.v.*] in disgust, "came one Tennent, a minister impudent and saucy; and told them all they were *damned, damned, damned!* This charmed them; and in the dreadfullest winter I ever saw, people wallowed in the snow night and day for the benefit of his beastly braying" (John Nichols, *Literary Anecdotes of the Eighteenth Century,* 1812, II, 547). The theme of his first sermon was "The Righteousness of the Scribes and Pharisees," and during his stay he was unsparing in his condemnation of religious formalism; he brandished the terrors of God before the eyes of sinners, and he boldly summoned his hearers to repentance and newness of life. Those unfriendly to him ridiculed his personal appearance and unpolished manners; some deplored the uncharitableness of his denunciations; the hardheaded Cutler resented the financial loss to the city, declaring that Whitefield and Tennent "carried more money out of these parts than the poor could be thankful for" (*Ibid.*); but no one could deny the power of his preaching. One of the Boston ministers testified that about 600 persons concerned for their souls had visited him in three months' time; another reported 1,000 or more. Before leaving New England Tennent preached in some twenty other Massachusetts and Connecticut towns, almost always with like effect.

He returned to the Middle Colonies shortly before the meeting of the Synod at Philadelphia in May 1741, at which occurred the famous schism. In the events leading up to this unfortunate occurrence Tennent had played a prominent part. The ecclesiastical procedure of the more conservative majority of his Presbyterian associates, and the sincerity of their religious pretentions as well, had been attacked by him with unseemly virulence. These conservatives had had no deeply emotional religious experiences, and attached little importance thereto; they were insistent that candidates for the ministry should be men of good character, of sound theology, and adequately trained, but they did not seek for evidences of their conversion and call; they placed emphasis on conformity to the standards rather than on essential orthodoxy, and were inclined to enforce strict obedience to the decrees of the Church. In the judgment of Tennent they were

Scribes and Pharisees—hypocrites; and since he felt it his duty to expose them and to awaken the Church from its "carnal security," it was inevitable that he should come into violent conflict with the Synod. In 1737 that body passed an act forbidding members of one Presbytery to preach without formal invitation to a congregation within the bounds of another Presbytery. In the heat of the revival, the evangelical group felt justified in disregarding this rule. In 1738 the Synod passed a resolution to the effect that candidates for the ministry before being taken on trial must either present a diploma from some European or New England college, or a certificate of satisfactory scholarship from a committee of the Synod. Tennent viewed the action as a blow at his father's "Log College," and also as tending to keep devout and capable men out of the ministry. The New Brunswick Presbytery, organized in 1738, of which Tennent was the leading spirit, ignored this requirement in the case of John Rowland, an alumnus of the "Log College." At the meeting of the Synod in 1739, the presbytery was adjudged to be very disorderly" and admonished to avoid such action in the future. Tennent and others of the presbytery then presented an "Apology for Dissenting from Two Acts or New Religious Laws Passed at the Last Session of the Synod." When the Synod met the following year Tennent and Samuel Blair [q.v.] presented formal papers charging many of their brethren with unsoundness in some of the principal doctrines of Christianity and with being strangers to a knowledge of God in their hearts. When asked to name individuals and produce evidence, they admitted that they had not investigated the reports they had received or discussed the matter with those they condemned. Soon afterward Tennent preached his notoriously abusive "Nottingham Sermon," printed under the title, *The Danger of an Unconverted Ministry, Considered in a Sermon on Mark VI. 34, Preached at Nottingham in Pennsylvania, March 8, anno 1739, 40* (1740). This sermon, which vividly portrayed the majority of ministers as plastered hypocrites, having the form of godliness but not its power, was widely circulated and did much to precipitate the schism of 1741. At the Synod of that year a written protest was offered by certain ministers and elders arraigning the Tennent party for disregarding the authority of the Synod and for other disturbing and unwarranted actions, and denying the right of the offenders to sit in that judicatory. The outcome of the matter was that Tennent and the other members of the New Brunswick Presbytery, finding themselves in a minority, withdrew, and a division of the Presbyterian Church occurred which lasted seventeen years. Tennent immediately published *Remarks upon a Protestation Presented to the Synod of Philadelphia, June 1, 1741* (1741). Not long afterward he made an attack upon the Moravians, preaching several sermons against them in New York which were published under the title, *The Necessity of Holding Fast the Truth Represented in Three Sermons ... Relating to Errors Lately Vented by Some Moravians ...* (1743). The fact that in these sermons he seemed to condemn views and practices he had formerly approved called forth from the Rev. John Hancock (1719–1744) of Braintree *The Examiner, or Gilbert against Tennent* (1743), published under the pseudonym Philalethes. To this Tennent replied in *The Examiner, Examined; or, Gilbert Tennent, Harmonious ...* (1743).

In 1743 he removed to Philadelphia to take charge of a newly organized Presbyterian church composed of Whitefield sympathizers. His career here, which lasted until his death, was less spectacular. He labored hard to build up his congregation and to secure funds for a church edifice. In his dress and in his manner of preaching he became more conventional. As time went on he displayed evidences of regret for his earlier contentiousness, working for a reunion of the Presbyterian Church, and publishing in 1749, *Irenicum Ecclesiasticum, or a Humble, Impartial Essay upon the Peace of Jerusalem.* He was, however, a sturdy opponent of Quaker pacifism, issuing in 1748 two sermons entitled: *The Late Association for Defence Encourag'd, or, the Lawfulness of a Defensive War,* and *The Late Association for Defence Farther Encouraged, or, Defensive War Defended; and Its Consistency with True Christianity Represented.* His published discourses on other subjects were numerous. With the establishment of the College of New Jersey he became one of its trustees, and late in 1753 went to England with the Rev. Samuel Davies [q.v.] to solicit funds for the institution. His first wife died about 1740 and in 1741 he married Cornelia (De Peyster), widow of Matthew Clarkson; she died Mar. 19, 1753, and subsequently he married Mrs. Sarah Spofford. Three children survived him. He was buried beneath the middle aisle of the Second Presbyterian Church, Philadelphia, but his body was later removed to the cemetery at Abington, Pa. Among the leaders of the Great Awakening he ranks with Jonathan Edwards and Whitefield.

[Archibald Alexander, *Biog. Sketches of the Founder and Principal Alumni of the Log Coll.* (1851); W. B. Sprague, *Annals Am. Pulpit,* vol. III (1858); Richard Webster, *A Hist. of the Presbyt. Church in America*

(1857); Charles Hodge, *The Constitutional Hist. of the Presbyt. Church in the U. S. A.* (1851); Thomas Murphy, *The Presbytery of the Log Coll.* (1889); C. H. Maxson, *The Great Awakening in the Middle Colonies* (1920); H. L. Osgood, *The Am. Colonies in the Eighteenth Century*, vol. III (1924); *The Gen. Assembly's Missionary Mag.*, May 1805; *A Continuation of the Rev. Mr. Whitefield's Journal from His Embarking after the Embargo* (1740); Samuel Finley, *The Successful Minister of Christ, Distinguished in Glory* (1764); *Jour. of the Presbyt. Hist. Soc.*, passim.]

H. E. S.

TENNENT, JOHN (c. 1700–c. 1760), physician, author, was born in England. He appeared first in the colony of Virginia about 1725, and five years later married Dorothy Paul. A son, John Tennent, living in Caroline County, Va., unsuccessfully petitioned the Virginia Assembly in 1760 for assistance in securing a medical education as a recognition of his father's medical contributions and later served as a surgeon in the Continental Army. The elder Tennent appears to have settled first in Spotsylvania County. He acquired property in Fredericksburg and in Prince William County as well. By 1735 he was in Williamsburg, where a year later William Parks [*q.v.*] published Tennent's *Essay on the Pleurisy.* This little publication contained the author's experience in the therapeutic use of rattlesnake-root and gained for him widespread notoriety. He learned of the plant from "a Nation of *Indians,* called the *Senekkas*," and reasoning "that this Root must be of general Use in Coagulations and Viscidities of the Blood"—a theory he adopted in the treatment of pleurisy and 'peripneumony'—he so employed it; "my Success was so great," he claimed, "that I did not lose above four or five Patients in an Hundred, tho' other Practitioners lost two Thirds" (*A Brief Account of the Case of John Tennent, M.D.*, see Blanton, *post*, p. 125).

In 1737 he returned to London, made himself known to the leading physicians of the town and did his best to popularize the use of his rattlesnake-root. The next year he was back in Virginia, where a controversy had been raging in the *Virginia Gazette* over his plan of treatment. Although tthe House of Burgesses paid him £100 at this time for having made public his discovery, he was not satisfied with his reception. "Meeting with Ingratitude from the Colony where I resided," he wrote, "I came over to settle in *London* in the Year 1739" (*Ibid.*, p. 125). On Nov. 8, 1741, he was married to a Mrs. Hanger, "a Widow Lady from Huntingdon" (*Ibid.*, pp. 124, 127). His subsequent career was not a happy one. *Detection of a Conspiracy . . . The Singular Case of John Tennent,* published by him in London in 1743, is a defense of ques-

tionable conduct. It reveals a man "with hopes of making one Day a Figure in the Medical World," chagrined over the fact that a large portion of the medical profession in Virginia and Great Britain refused to recognize the virtues of his discovery (*Ibid.*, p. 126). He ended by fraternizing with the notorious quack Joshua Ward, stooped to the "foolish step in having kept one Mrs. Carey under the name of Mrs. Tennent," and was finally brought to trial at the Old Bailey for bigamy (*Ibid.*, p. 127). From this predicament he was rescued by no less a person than Sir Hans Sloane. In a letter of thanks written in April 1740, Tennent intimated his intention of going to Jamaica, but nothing is known of his later years.

Besides the broadsides, . . . *Singular Case of John Tennent, M.D.,* and *A Brief Account of the Case of John Tennent, M.D.,* he published anonymously *Every Man His Own Doctor* (2nd edition, 1724), purporting to offer "a Plain and Easy Means for Persons to cure themselves" by medicines grown chiefly in America; *A Reprieve from Death* (London, 1741), containing objections to the use of vinegar and other acids on board His Majesty's ships in the treatment of epidemic fevers of the West Indies; *An Epistle to Dr. Richard Mead, Concerning the Epidemical Diseases of Virginia, Particularly, a Pleurisy, and Peripneumony* (Edinburgh, 1738), elaborating a fantastic theory of disease and expanding the therapeutic uses of snake-root for gout, rheumatism, dropsy, and many nervous disorders; *Physical Enquiries* (1742), discussing the constitutional effects of change of climate and giving his views concerning the irregular practice of medicine; and, finally, *Physical Disquisitions* (London, 1745).

[*A Brief Account of the Case of John Tennent, M.D.*; W. B. Blanton, *Med. in Va. in the Eighteenth Century* (1931); H. A. Kelly, article in H. A. Kelly and W. L. Burrage, *Am. Medic. Biog.* (1920); *William and Mary Quart.*, July 1923; *Jour. of the House of Burgesses, Va.*, 1727–40, 1758–61; *Va. Gazette* for 1736, Nos. 6, 9, 10, 14, 31; *Ibid.* for 1737, Nos. 45, 50, 72; Park's *Va. Gazette*, Aug. 6, 1736.]

W. B. B.

TENNENT, WILLIAM (1673–May 6, 1745), Presbyterian clergyman, founder of the "Log College," was born in Ireland. On July 11, 1695, he graduated from the University of Edinburgh (*A Catalogue of the Graduates . . . of the University of Edinburgh*, 1858, p. 151), and on May 15, 1702, married Catharine, daughter of Rev. Gilbert Kennedy, a prominent Scotch Presbyterian. Tennent was ordained deacon in the Church of Ireland on July 1, 1704, and priest on Sept. 22, 1706. He is said to have been chaplain to an Irish nobleman but never to have had a parish, possibly because of non-conformist tendencies.

In middle life, sometime between 1716 and 1718, with his wife, four sons, and a daughter, he emigrated to Philadelphia, drawn to this particular city, perhaps, because here resided his wife's cousin, James Logan [*q.v.*], a prominent Pennsylvania official. On Sept. 17, 1718, the Synod of Philadelphia acted upon a petition from Tennent requesting that he be admitted to the Presbyterian ministry. In a statement of his reasons for leaving the Established Church he affirmed his belief that the Episcopal form of church government was "anti-scriptural," and expressed his objection to the Church's "conniving at the practice of Arminian doctrines inconsistent with the eternal purpose of God, and an encouragement of vice" (statement printed in Archibald Alexander, *Biographical Sketches of the Founder and Principal Alumni of the Log College,* 1851, p. 15). Admitted to the Presbyterian fellowship, he lived in East Chester, N. Y., from Nov. 22, 1718, to May 1, 1720, and then accepted a call to the church in Bedford, which he served until August 1726 (C. W. Baird, *History of Bedford Church,* 1882, p. 47f.), though apparently in 1721 he preached for a brief period in Bensalem, Bucks County, Pa. In the fall of 1726 he became pastor at Neshaminy, Pa., where he remained until his death. Soon after beginning work there, he took charge, also, of a congregation at Deep Run, to which he ministered until 1738.

Tennent was well educated, a faithful pastor, a teacher of unusual ability, and withal a man of genuine piety and evangelistic zeal. His significance in American church history lies in the fact that he trained for the ministry and imbued with his own spirit a notable group of men who became religious and educational leaders, and that indirectly he gave impetus to the creating of educational institutions. After living on a farm between Neshaminy and Bensalem, said to have been given him by James Logan, he bought in 1735, perhaps through the financial assistance of Logan, 100 acres of land on the road from Philadelphia to New York. Here he lived and in 1736 erected his famous "Log College," though he had earlier been giving instruction to his sons and possibly to others. The Presbyterians insisted upon an educated ministry, and the fact that candidates in that region could be properly fitted for the work only by going to New England or abroad made it difficult to increase the supply. The "Log College" was an attempt to meet this condition. Here Tennent's three younger sons, William [*q.v.*], John, and

Charles, all of whom entered the ministry, continued their training; the eldest, Gilbert [*q.v.*], destined to be one of the chief agencies in the Great Awakening, was ordained about the time of its establishment. Here, too, such men as Samuel Blair and Samuel Finley [*qq.v.*] were trained. Both conducted academies of their own and Finley became president of the College of New Jersey.

The "College" was not without its detractors, however; in fact the title was given it in a spirit of derision. Many thought the training it offered, however good, inadequate, and in 1738 the Philadelphia Synod decreed that all candidates without diplomas from the Old World universities, Harvard, or Yale must be approved by a commission of the Synod. This edict the recently formed Presbytery of New Brunswick, made up largely of "Log College" men, opposed and disregarded. The feeling between the two parties was intensified by the fact that the Tennents were aggressively evangelistic and welcomed Whitefield and his methods. The elder Tennent went to Philadelphia to visit him in 1739, and in November of that year Whitefield spent several days at Neshaminy, writing in his journal (*post*), under date of Nov. 22, a description of the "College" and its founder. He also preached extensively in the bounds of the New Brunswick Presbytery, giving the weight of his approval and support to its members. Thus the spirit and work of Tennent contributed greatly to strengthen the "New Side" cause and helped to bring about the schism of 1741 in the Presbyterian Church.

Tennent continued his teaching until his death in 1746, at which time the "Log College" ceased to exist; but that same year its supporters united with others in organizing the College of New Jersey.

[In addition to sources cited above, see Richard Webster, *A Hist. of the Presbyt. Ch. in America* (1857); E. H. Gillett, *Hist. of the Presbyt. Ch. in the United States of America* (1864), vol. I; W. B. Sprague, *Annals Am. Pulpit,* vol. III (1858); Thomas Murphy, *The Presbytery of the Log College* (copr. 1889); Elias Boudinot, *Memoirs of the Life of the Rev. William Tennent* (1807, many later editions), a biog. of the younger William; D. K. Turner, *Neshaminy Presbyt. Ch.* (1876); *Jour. of the Presbyt. Hist. Soc.,* June 1902, June 1904, June, Sept. 1912, Sept., Dec. 1913, Sept. 1914, Sept. 1915, Sept. 1919, Oct. 1927; C. H. Maxson, *The Great Awakening in the Middle Colonies* (1920); George Whitefield, *A Continuation of the Rev. Mr. Whitefield's Journal, from His Embarking after the Embargo* (1740).]   H. E. S.

TENNENT, WILLIAM (June 3, 1705–Mar. 8, 1777), Presbyterian clergyman, was the second of the four sons of William [*q.v.*] and Catharine (Kennedy) Tennent, being about two years younger than his brother Gilbert [*q.v.*]. He was born in County Armagh, Ireland, and was brought to America as a boy by his parents. He received his classical education in his father's "Log College" at Neshaminy, Pa., and then studied theology under Gilbert, who had become pastor of the church in New Brunswick, N. J.

During his residence there he narrowly escaped being buried alive. Under the strain of intense mental application his health broke and one day, while conversing in Latin with his brother, he became unconscious. Soon every indication of death was present, the body was laid out, and arrangements made for the funeral. In the meantime, fortunately, a physician, a close friend of Tennent, arrived and thought he detected a faint sign of life. Rather against the judgment of Gilbert, who said it was foolish to try to resuscitate one who was "cold and stiff as a stake," the funeral was postponed. Efforts to revive him were unsuccessful, however, and people were assembling for the obsequies when suddenly he gave unmistakable evidence of life. In about a year's time he had entirely recovered, except that memory of his past life was entirely gone and he could not even read or write. Under instruction he was gradually brought back to his former state of mind. During his unconsciousness, he affirmed, he had had the experience of being with a host of happy beings, surrounded by inexpressible glory, engaged in acts of joyous worship. Other extraordinary experiences came to him later, which modern medical science would probably attribute to physical rather than to supernatural causes. The accounts of some of them, as for example that of his "miraculous" escape from being convicted of perjury, will hardly bear critical scrutiny (see H. W. Green, "The Trial of the Rev. William Tennent," *Biblical Repertory and Princeton Review,* July 1868).

As soon as he was sufficiently recovered he was licensed to preach. His brother John died on Apr. 23, 1732, and the following year William was called to succeed him as pastor of the church at Freehold, N. J., and was ordained by the Philadelphia Presbytery on Oct. 25, 1733. Here he ministered until his death nearly forty-four years later. Indifferent to material things, he became somewhat embarrassed financially and a friend, Isaac Noble, a New York merchant, advised him to get a wife "to attend to his temporal affairs, and to comfort his leisure hours by conjugal endearments." He replied that he did not know how to go about it. Accordingly, his friend told him that he had a sister-in-law to whom he would introduce him—Catharine (van Burgh), widow of John Noble. Tennent went

to New York to see her and within a week, Aug. 23, 1738, they were married. The union proved a happy one; of their children, three sons grew to maturity.

In spite of various peculiarities, Tennent had the character and gifts that made him one of the leading Presbyterian ministers of his day. One in whose home he visited described him as "tall —of large frame, but spare, and of a long thin visage," adding, "He wore a white wig" (S. J. Forman, in Sprague, *post,* p. 62). His manners were pleasing and he was capable of a facetiousness that was delightful. Few were better judges of horses or could excel him in horsemanship. He was noted for the ingenuousness of his faith, his firmness of character, independence, and courage. His preaching had more power than grace of form, but students at the College of New Jersey would walk twenty miles to hear him in his own pulpit. Like the other Tennents he was a friend of Whitefield and a promoter of revivals. He probably sympathized in general with his brother Gilbert, but he was free from the disagreeable qualities of the latter and he was a peacemaker rather than a controversialist. Calls came to him from near and far to settle disputes. His keen judgment of men, tact, and skill in dealing with people in doubt or trouble made him eminently successful as a pastor. He took an active interest in John Brainerd's Indian mission. To his many other labors he added teaching, and such men as Alexander MacWhorter [*q.v.*] profited by his instruction. Upon the establishment of the College of New Jersey he became one of its trustees. He died in his seventy-second year and was buried beneath his church.

[Elias Boudinot, *Memoirs of the Life of the Rev. William Tennent* (1807), originally published in *The General Assembly's Missionary Mag.,* Mar. 1806; W. B. Sprague, *Annals Am. Pulpit,* vol. III (1858); Archibald Alexander, *Biog. Sketches of the Founders and Principal Alumni of the Log. Coll.* (copr. 1851); Thomas Murphy, *The Presbytery of the Log Coll.* (copr. 1889); Richard Webster, *A Hist. of the Presbyt. Ch. in America* (1857); *Pa. Mag. of Hist. and Biog.,* Apr. 1883, pp. 113, 114.]   H. E. S.

TENNEY, CHARLES DANIEL (June 29, 1857–Mar. 14, 1930), missionary, educator, and diplomat in China, was born at Boston, Mass. His father, the Rev. Daniel Tenney, was a descendant of Thomas Tenney who emigrated from Yorkshire, England, to Salem, Mass., in 1638, and settled at Rowley, Mass., the following year; his mother, Mary Adams (Parker), claimed descent from Gov. Thomas Dudley [*q.v.*]. Reared in a Congregationalist family, Tenney reached young manhood during a period of foreign missionary fervor in New England. He graduated from Dartmouth College in 1878 (taught for a year in an academy at Atkinson, N. H., and completed the divinity course at Oberlin Theological Seminary in 1882. In the same year he proceeded to his first missionary post, in the province of Shansi, China, under the auspices of the American Board of Commissioners for Foreign Missions. He was accompanied by his wife, Anne Runcie Jerrell of Bridgeton, N. J.; of their marriage on Mar. 29, 1882, three sons and two daughters were born.

Retiring from the mission field, Tenney moved in 1886 to the "treaty port" of Tientsin, then seat of the Viceroy Li Hung-chang. Here he at once established intimate relations with the great Chinese statesman by becoming tutor to his sons, and the same year was instrumental in establishing the Anglo-Chinese School, an institution for Chinese students, of which he remained the principal from 1886 to 1895. Concurrently with his other activities, he was vice-consul and interpreter to the American consulate at Tientsin from Mar. 6, 1894 to June 30, 1896. In 1895 he was selected by the Chinese government as the first president of the newly organized Imperial Chinese University at Tientsin (after 1900 designated Peiyang University). He served in this capacity until 1906.

The Boxer outbreak of 1900 interrupted his educational work. During the siege of Tientsin, Tenney and Herbert C. Hoover, then in charge of the reorganization of the Kaiping coal mines, devoted themselves to the relief of numerous Chinese and their families who had thrown in their lot with the beleaguered whites. Among these was a young American-trained Chinese, T'ang Shao-yi, who was to become one of China's eminent statesmen. Following the relief of Tientsin by an international column, Tenney served as Chinese secretary of the Tientsin provisional government from 1900 to 1902, earning the gratitude of the local Chinese populace for his determined stand against unnecessary harshness of treatment at a moment when the many outrages of the Boxers were still fresh in the minds of the armies of occupation.

The University was occupied by German troops during the Boxer troubles, and in 1902, on his own responsibility as its administrative head, Tenney made a special journey to Germany to obtain an indemnity for the seizure of the plant. He was successful in his mission, and the institution was rebuilt on a new site. From 1902 to 1906 he was also superintendent of high and middle schools in Chihli, making inspection tours throughout the metropolitan province. His labors in this connection resulted in a de-

velopment of the school system which placed Chihli in an advanced position in that respect among the "eighteen provinces." When he retired as president of Peiyang University in 1906, he was appointed director of Chinese government students in America, which position he held until 1908, making his headquarters at Cambridge, Mass., and establishing in various American universities successive groups of Chinese students. In 1907–08 he was lecturer on Chinese history at Harvard.

Following his retirement in 1908 from his lengthy service to China, Tenney accepted the appointment of Chinese secretary to the American Legation at Peking. In 1909 he was designated one of the three American delegates to the joint International Opium Commission convened at Shanghai. In 1912, when Nanking assumed importance as the capital of the revolutionary government, he was assigned by the American government to that post with title of consul; but owing to the illness of his wife, he resigned in 1913 and returned to the United States. The following year (May 1, 1914) he was reappointed Chinese secretary of the American Legation at Peking. In 1919 he was advanced to secretary of legation, class I, and counselor of legation, serving as chargé d'affaires *ad interim* at Peking from September 1919 to July 1920. He returned to the United States on leave in October of the latter year and retired from the diplomatic service, Mar. 1, 1921, to make his home at Palo Alto, Cal. In 1923 he revisited China, and while at Peking in 1924 suffered a severe illness from which he never recovered, remaining an invalid until his death, six years later, at Palo Alto.

Tenney's life left its impress directly upon a multitude of Chinese students. In the rôle of educator, his character, scholarship, thoroughness, and administrative ability made his example of singular importance; and the fact that his influence was exerted not through the usual alien missionary institution but directly under the viceroys Li Hung-chang and later Yüan Shih-k'ai, gave it a unique independence and authority. His publications, which were incidental to his educational work, enjoyed wide popularity in the Chinese school curriculum; they included a series of English lessons (1890), an English grammar (1892), and a geography of Asia (1898). His contribution to American diplomacy during the final decadence of the Manchu imperial house, the revolution, and the World War must be identified with the events of the terms of successive American ministers; in the diplomatic correspondence of the Peking legation between the years 1908 and 1919 it is virtually impossible to distinguish the actual handiwork of Tenney, but it may be accepted as certain that particularly through his wide personal acquaintance among the highest Chinese officials, he exercised a determining influence upon Sino-American relations. The Chinese government bestowed successive decorations upon him, from the order of the Double Dragon, Third Class, No. 1, in 1895, to the *Chiaho* order, Second Class, awarded in 1921, by the republican government.

[Tenney's private papers are in the possession of his family, from whom much of the foregoing information has been obtained; personal memories of surviving associates in China have also been drawn upon. Printed sources include M. J. Tenney, *The Tenney Family* (1904); issues of the *Register of the Department of State*, especially that for 1922; *Who's Who in America*, 1928–29; *N. Y. Times*, Mar. 16, 1930; *China Weekly Review*, Mar. 22, 1930.]   E. M. G.

TENNEY, EDWARD PAYSON (Sept. 29, 1835–July 24, 1916), Congregational clergyman, educator, and author, was born at Concord, N. H., the son of Rev. Asa Peaslee and Mary (Tenney) Tenney. His parents were cousins and descendants of Thomas Tenney of Yorkshire, England, who came to Salem, Mass., in 1638. Edward prepared for college at Pembroke Academy and entered Dartmouth in 1854, remaining one year. In 1858 he graduated from Bangor Theological Seminary, and then made a trip around the Horn to California. Here he remained about a year, doing some editorial work for *The Pacific* of San Francisco, becoming interested in the College of California, and writing the first of a long series of articles championing the cause of frontier education. Returning East, he was ordained a Congregational minister at West Concord, N. H., on Oct. 19, 1859. For some two years he was pastor of a church in the little mining town of Central City, Colo., near Denver. Thereafter he spent a decade on Cape Ann, Massachusetts, in study, meditation, writing and in correcting the astigmatism and inconsistencies in what he called his "hasty" education.

In 1876 a former pupil of his father's, Prof. E. N. Bartlett, then secretary of the two-year-old Colorado College at Colorado Springs, called Tenney's attention to the precarious condition of that institution. Its assets then consisted of a little frame building, twenty-five preparatory, normal, and special students, and the prayers of pioneers impoverished by the panic of 1873. That same year he assumed the presidency, his salary being provided out of his own private income. His love for the Rocky Mountain region, and his belief in the salutary influence of

a college on the frontier were the inspiration of eight years' service in that post. He poured his enthusiasm into a famous booklet, *The New West as Related to the Christian College* (1878), reprinted in 1880 under the title, *Colorado and Homes in the New West*. This work extolled Colorado as a refuge for those desiring new health and Colorado College as an American mainstay and buttress on a polyglot frontier. It secured for the institution the support of the American College and Education Society, and it inspired the local sacrifice necessary to raise the $10,000 which secured the $20,000 offered tentatively by Eastern friends. This money saved the college. During Tenney's administration the strengthened faculty gathered together a library of some 6,000 volumes, and secured the erection of Palmer Hall, the first substantial building on the college campus. His belief in educational institutions as safeguards of American civilization on the Rocky Mountain frontier led him to found academies at Santa Fé, N. Mex., and at Salt Lake City.

Giving up his work in Colorado in 1884, he returned to Massachusetts. During his residence in this state he served churches at Assonet, Burlington, Ayer, Braintree, and Lowell. He devoted much time to writing and his publications include *The Silent House* (1876); *Coronation* (1877); *Agamenticus* (1878); *Constance of Acadia* (1886); *The Triumph of the Cross* (1895); *Dream of My Youth* (1901); *Contrasts in Social Progress* (1907); *Looking Forward into the Past* (1910). He was twice married: first, Dec. 1, 1860, to Sarah J. Holden, who died Nov. 23, 1861; second Dec. 8, 1862, to Ellen Weeks, by whom he had two children.

[M. J. Tenney, *The Tenney Family* (1904); M. D. and E. R. Ormes, *The Book of Colorado Springs* (1933); *The Congregational Year-Book for 1916* (1917); *Who's Who in America*, 1916–17; *Boston Transcript*, July 25, 1916; I. H. Kerr MSS., Colorado Coll.]   A. B. H.

TENNEY, TABITHA GILMAN (Apr. 7, 1762–May 2, 1837), novelist and compiler, was born in Exeter, N. H., the daughter of Samuel Gilman and his second wife, Lydia (Robinson) Giddings (or Giddinge) Gilman. Her father, a descendant of John Gilman who emigrated from England to Hingham, Mass., in 1638, was a member of a family that had provided many public servants for New Hampshire. Her mother was an educated and forceful woman, and Tabitha's upbringing was Puritanical, bookish, and secluded. She acquired familiarity with intellectual and gentlewomanly accomplishments, and a code of behavior in which a virtuous common sense predominated. In 1788 (intention recorded, Sept. 6, 1788) she married Samuel Tenney (1748–1816), who had just resumed a residence in Exeter that had been interrupted by his service as a surgeon in the Continental Army for the duration of the Revolution. Instead of returning to medical practice, however, he devoted his energies to politics, and his wife was able to spend several winters in Washington during his terms as congressman (1800–07). In 1801 she published the two-volume novel, *Female Quixotism: Exhibited in the Romantic Opinions and Extravagant Adventures of Dorcasina Sheldon,* upon which her claim to remembrance chiefly rests. Sometime prior to this, possibly in 1799 (see bookseller's advertisement in *Newburyport Herald,* Newburyport, Mass., May 7, 1799) she edited a volume called *The Pleasing Instructor,* an anthology of selections from poets and classical writers for the education of young women, of which no copy is known to exist. The collection was especially recommended "For Female Academies, Schools, &c.," and, as the author's aim was "to blend instruction with rational amusement," she included only those "pieces which . . . tend either to inform the mind, correct the manners, or to regulate the conduct."

Female Quixotism is a satire on prevailing literary tastes, and a minor declaration of American intellectual independence. It purports to be the biography of a young woman, in other respects charming and lovable, whose mind has become corrupted by a too-constant diet of current novels and romances. Dorcasina Sheldon, like her prototype, the Spanish knight-errant, forms her grandiose conceptions of existence from the literary extravagances of her day, and her tragedy lies in their lack of correspondence to the world of actuality. The analogy to the book's great model is skilfully and not too slavishly handled, the conception is clever and humorous, but the plot falters in execution and is marred by the repetitious narration of absurd and wearisomely similar events in the career of the heroine. Moreover, the book is written as an object lesson to similar misguided females, and, though the moral is a healthy one, it is too much in evidence for a work of art. In the character of the Irish adventurer, who occupies the major portion of volume one, there is excellently portrayed a type of charlatan from whom the United States suffered much in its infancy. The whole is a plea to American girls to accept the responsibilities of normal living and to give over their affectations, their day dreams, and their preoccupation with foreign romantic sentimentality,

and it commemorates an interesting phase in the intellectual fashions of the early Republic.

Tabitha Tenney was left a widow in 1816, and apparently had no children. The last twenty years of her life she spent in Exeter, occupied with fine needlework and acts of charity quite after the fashion she had recommended to her erring heroine. Some proverbial examples of her reputation for goodness have been preserved (Duyckinck, *post*). She died at Exeter after a brief illness.

[The days of birth and death are taken from Arthur Gilman, *The Gilman Family* (1869). See also M. J. Tenney, *The Tenney Family . . . 1638–1904* (1904); C. H. Bell, *Hist. of the Town of Exeter, N. H.* (1888); S. A. Allibone, *A Crit. Dict. of Eng. Lit.* (1871); E. A. and G. L. Duyckinck, *Cyc. of Am. Lit.* (2 vols., 1855); *Newburyport Herald and Country Gazette* (Newburyport, Mass.), May 7–21, 1799; *Exeter News Letter,* May 9, 1837; death notice in *New-Hampshire Statesman and State Jour.* (Concord), May 13, 1837.]
J. H. B—h.

TENNEY, WILLIAM JEWETT (1811– Sept. 20, 1883), editor, was born at Newport, R. I., the second of the six children of Caleb Jewett and Ruth (Channing) Tenney, and the sixth in descent from Thomas Tenney, a Yorkshireman, who arrived at Salem, Mass., in December 1638 and settled the following spring in Rowley. The month and day of his birth are unrecorded, but he was baptized in the First Congregational Church, Bristol, R. I., July 2, 1811. His father, a classmate of Daniel Webster at Dartmouth College, was a Congregational clergyman of some note. Tenney entered Yale College from Wethersfield, Conn., in 1827 and graduated with the class of 1832. His movements during the next twenty years are somewhat obscure. He began the study of medicine and was connected in 1835 with the Retreat for the Insane at Hartford. At one time he was an instructor on a naval vessel. He is supposed to have migrated to western New York and thence to Ohio; it is certain that he studied law and was admitted to practice. In 1839 he married Elizabeth M. Benton, by whom he had three sons and a daughter. The great event of his inner life was his conversion to Catholicism, which seems to have estranged him from his family and from the friends of his earlier years, but the date of his conversion is also unrecorded. About 1840 he went to New York City and turned journalist, being employed on the *New York Journal of Commerce,* the *Evening Post,* Freeman Hunt's *Merchants' Magazine,* and the *Mining Magazine.* In 1853 he joined the staff of D. Appleton & Company as reader and editor and remained with the company until his death thirty years later.

Tenney's chief accomplishment was *Appletons' Annual Cyclopædia,* which he edited from its inception until his death, when Rossiter Johnson took his place. For the years 1861–1901 it provides a unique summary of events and statistics, especially valuable for its accuracy and comprehensiveness. A by-product of the *Cyclopædia* was Tenney's *Military and Naval History of the Rebellion in the United States* (1865). The only other book to which he put his name as author was *A Grammatical Analyzer* (1866); the great bulk of his literary labor was expended on the writings of others. His most notable collaboration of this sort was on Jefferson Davis' *Rise and Fall of the Confederate Government* (1881). The Appletons had contracted for the work in 1875, but by January 1880 less than half of the first volume existed even in rough draft. Tenney was then sent to "Beauvoir" to replace Davis' original collaborator and brought the work to a conclusion in three or four months. For some years he made his home in Brooklyn, where he was at one time a judge of a criminal court, thereby acquiring the title by which he was always known. Later he lived in Elizabeth, N. J., where he was president of the board of education and, during President Buchanan's administration, collector of the port. His first wife having died, he married Sarah, daughter of Orestes Augustus Brownson [*q.v.*], in 1873. She was the author of a novel, *Marian Elwood, or How Girls Live* (1859), and of a biography, *Life of Demetrius Augustine Gallitzin* (1873). She died in 1876 after the birth of their second daughter. In 1883 Tenney's own health declined. He returned from a visit to "Beauvoir" in good spirits and apparently in restored health, but died unexpectedly at his boarding house in Newark, N. J.

[J. N. Arnold, *Vital Record of R. I.,* VIII (1896), 410; M. J. Tenney, *The Tenney Family* (1904); F. C. Jewett, *Hist. and Geneal. of the Jewetts of America* (1908); E. E. Salisbury, *Biog. Memoranda . . . of the Class of 1832 in Yale Coll.* (1880); *Obit. Record Grads. Yale Coll.* (1884); *N. Y. Daily Tribune,* Sept. 22, 1883; *Appletons' Ann. Cyc. . . . 1883* (1884); J. C. Derby, *Fifty Years Among Authors, Books and Publishers* (1884).]
G. H. G.

TENSKWATAWA (Mar. 1768?–1834?), Shawnee prophet, is believed to have been born at the great springs near Old Chillicothe, now Oldtown, Ohio (Galloway, *post,* p. 108), and to have been the twin of his brother Tecumseh [*q.v*]. His mother was sometimes said to be a Creek, and his father, Pucksinwa, was a Shawnee chief who was killed at the battle of Point Pleasant in 1774. About November 1805 he announced himself to be a prophet and assumed the name of Tenskwatawa instead of his original one of

Lalawethika. The white people usually referred to him as the Prophet. He was also sometimes called Elskwatawa. The history of his ministry is typical of the long line of such religious revivalists as Skaniadariio, Smohalla, and Wovoka [*qq.v.*]. He appeared in a time of great peril and was said to have shown indifference to religious ideas in his earlier life and to have been roused only by heavenly visions seen in a death-like trance. When he foretold the eclipse of the sun in 1806 his following increased rapidly. He also attacked witchcraft and in witch burnings rid himself of several of his most menacing enemies. He worked on the emotions of his followers by the practice of mystic rites, and he preached a reactionary doctrine of primitive ways nearer to the "Master of Life," the necessity of giving up alcoholic liquor and of again becoming self-supporting. To that end he sought a return to the use of primitive clothing of skin and furs and of the firestick for making fire; he forbade intermarriage with the whites; and he advocated the ancient custom of common possession of all property. At what time his religious revival merged with Tecumseh's political program it is impossible to say, as it is impossible to measure what part he played in that program. During most of the time even close observers assumed, erroneously, that the greater share of responsibility lay on the Prophet's shoulders.

Of middle height, blind in one eye, but possessing great personal magnetism, he gave a false sense of ability and power. He seems really to have been a vain, boastful man who preferred to have others do his fighting for him. In 1811, left by Tecumseh with the strict injunction to avoid war, he was unable to maintain as favorable a situation as his brother left. Perhaps because he was unduly persuaded by hotheads or because he wished to create a diversion for those discontented with his administration, he allowed himself to be maneuvered by William Henry Harrison [*q.v.*] into the battle of Tippecanoe on Nov. 7, 1811. During the progress of the fighting he is reported to have kept himself apart, in a safe place, busy with incantations and prophecies, and, from time to time, encouraging his warriors to believe that Harrison's army was just on the point of yielding to his magic. When the battle was over, disastrously, his own prestige was gone, as was the great hope of Indian confederation. He took no part in the fighting of the War of 1812. He received a pension from the British government and was in Canada until 1826, when he returned to Ohio. Later he lived near Cape Girardeau, Mo. In 1832 he was living in what is now Wyandotte County, Kan., where George Catlin [*q.v.*] knew him and painted his portrait.

[Consult James Mooney, "The Ghost Dance Religion," *14th Ann. Report of Bureau of Ethnology*, pt. 2 (1896); Benj. Drake, *Life of Tecumseh* (1841); George Catlin, *Letters and Notes on the . . . North American Indians* (1841), vol. II; *Am. State Papers: Indian Affairs*, vol. I (1832); W. A. Galloway, *Old Chillicothe* (1934); see also bibliog. of sketch of Tecumseh.]   K. E. C.

TERESA, MOTHER (*c.* 1766–Sept. 9, 1846), foundress of the Visitation Order in the United States, was born in Ireland and spent her childhood in Kilkenny. Her family name was Lalor; she was christened Alice. The girl's unusual piety seems to have attracted the attention of Bishop Lanigan, a local prelate, and he relied on her to help him in the foundation of a community of Presentation nuns in his diocese. This project did not meet with the approval of the family, however, and when one of Alice's sisters married an American merchant named Doran the girl was persuaded to accompany the couple to America. She intended nevertheless to return to Ireland later to cooperate with Bishop Lanigan in his projected foundation. On the boat she formed a deep friendship with two women, both widows, a Mrs. McDermott and a Mrs. Sharpe, who like her were eager to become nuns. The three friends landed in Philadelphia on Jan. 5, 1795. In accordance with an agreement they had made that they would seek out a priest and would regard him, whoever he should be, as their spiritual director and would follow his guidance implicitly, they went to the Reverend Leonard Neale [*q.v.*], a man of unusual character and ability, afterwards archbishop of Baltimore. Upon his advice they rented a house, and there Alice Lalor lived with her two friends in a sort of unofficial religious community. They busied themselves with good works and performed notable service during the yellow fever epidemic that swept through Philadelphia in 1797–98.

When in 1798 Father Neale was transferred to Washington as president of Georgetown College, he invited the little community to follow him. They arrived in 1799 and for a time lived with some Poor Clares who had been exiled from France. Afterwards they opened a school, and in 1804, when the Poor Clares returned to their native country, they were able to purchase the tiny convent belonging to the latter. From the beginning Alice Lalor and her companions had looked upon themselves as a religious community, but they had lacked any formal ecclesiastical authorization. Though Archbishop John Carroll [*q.v.*] urged Neale, now a bishop, to merge his community with the Sisters of Charity, and others advised them to adopt the Ursuline rule or unite with the Carmelite nuns, who had already been established at Port Tobacco, Md., Neale was anxious that they should become Visitation nuns, and in spite of great practical difficulties, he succeeded in winning the approval of Rome. On Dec. 28, 1816, the sisters were admitted to solemn vows and became fully accredited Visitation nuns. Mother Teresa resigned her post as superior in 1819 and lived as a simple member of the community for twenty-seven years. During that time she saw the foundation of other houses in Mobile, Ala. (1832), in St. Louis, Mo. (1833), and in Baltimore, Md. (1837). When she died in 1846 she was buried with Archbishop Neale in the crypt of the convent which owed its existence to them.

[See G. P. and Rose Hawthorne Lathrop, *A Story of Courage*; *Annals of the Georgetown Convent of the Visitation of the Blessed Virgin Mary* (1895); J. B. Code, *Great Am. Foundresses* (1929); *Cath. Encyc.*, vol. VIII (1910); and obituary in *U. S. Cath. Mag. and Monthly Rev.*, Oct. 1846. There is a short contemporary account of Mother Teresa's life in MS. in the archives of the Visitation Academy of Georgetown.]   P. H. F.

TERHUNE, MARY VIRGINIA HAWES (Dec. 21, 1830–June 3, 1922), author, writer on household management, better known as Marion Harland, was born in Dennisville, Amelia County, Va., the daughter of Samuel Pierce and Judith Anna (Smith) Hawes. Her father, a descendant of early New England settlers, was a man of education who, through reverses in fortune, had become a country storekeeper. Virginia was taught at home by tutors and governesses, learned to use her father's well-chosen library, and at thirteen was sent for a year to Hampden Sidney, Va., a college town where she heard the table talk of scholarly men and had a glimpse of social life. In 1844, when the family moved to Richmond, she began contributing to the weekly newspaper. In 1853 her story, "Kate Harper," appeared in the *Southern Era* under the pseudonym of Marion Harland (*Marion Harland's Autobiography*, 1910, p. 240). Her first novel, *Alone*, which was also her best and most famous, was written when she was sixteen, though it was not revised for publication until 1854. From that time on she contributed fiction to numerous popular women's magazines and wrote a series of novels, over twenty-five in number, of which the most popular were *True as Steel* (1872), *Nemesis* (1860), *His Great Self* (1892), *A Gallant Fight* (1888), *Judith* (1883), *Dr. Dale* (1900), and *The Hidden Path* (1859). Her fiction in general is of a mild, pleasant type, often with a marked moral or religious tone. Many of her stories are set in the South in the days before the Civil War. Her marriage on Sept. 2, 1856, to the Rev. Edward Payson Terhune (Nov. 22, 1830–May 25, 1907), who later became widely known, carried her to the country parsonage of Charlotte Court-House, Va., where she served her novitiate at practical housewifery. Her struggles with the blind culinary guides then available led to the preparation of *Common Sense in the Household: A Manual of Practical Housewifery,* which she with difficulty persuaded Scribners to publish in 1871. The volume ran through numerous editions in a short time and continued to sell for many years. This, the first intelligently prepared cook book, the first attempt to dignify housewifery as a profession, dimmed her reputation as a novelist and doomed her to life work in the field of domestic economy. She was swamped with orders for newspaper and magazine articles, syndicate paragraphs, and editorial work. She conducted departments for children in *Wide Awake* (1882–83) and *St. Nicholas* (1876), and edited *Babyhood* (1884–86); she established a magazine, the *Home-Maker* and edited it for two years (1888–90); she edited a department of the *Chicago Daily Tribune* for six years (1911–17), and she produced in addition numerous books on home management and cooking, as well as several on home life. It was not literature, she knew. "But," she said, "it is Influence."

In her husband's successive city parishes—Newark, N. J. (1859–76), Springfield, Mass. (1879–84), and Brooklyn (1884–95)—she found time for much church and charitable work, and for distinguished literary friendships, without neglecting home or children or relaxing her literary pace. It is said that she systematized her work and never hurried. In 1876, her lungs being threatened, the family went abroad for two years. This trip and another in 1897 resulted in several travel books, *Loiterings in Pleasant Paths* (1880), *Where Ghosts Walk* (1898), and four biographical studies, *Charlotte Brontë at Home* (1899), *William Cowper* (1899), *John Knox* (1900), and *Hannah More* (1900). In 1893 the *Christian Herald* sent her to the Holy Land, her letters to it appearing later under the title, *The Home of the Bible* (1895). Lecture tours preceded and followed this trip. Even in her old age she remained indefatigable. At seventy an accident crippled her wrist. She mastered the typewriter. At eighty-nine she went blind. She mastered the difficult art of dictation, writing through an amanuensis her last novel, *The Carringtons of High Hill* (1919). She collaborated with each of her children who reached maturity: with Christine Terhune Herrick in

The National Cook Book (1896), with Virginia Terhune Van de Water in *Everyday Etiquette* (1905), and with Albert Payson Terhune in *Dr. Dale.* Her autobiography appeared in 1910 under the title of *Marion Harland's Autobiography.* She died in New York of old age. Of her six children, a son and two daughters survived her.

[In addition to *Marion Harland's Autobiog.* (1910), see *Who's Who in America,* 1922–23; Mary H. Wright, *Mary Virginia Hawes Terhune* (1934); Frances E. Willard and Mary A. Livermore, *A Woman of the Century* (1893); obituary in *N. Y. Times,* June 4, 1922.]

M. B. H.

TERRELL, EDWIN HOLLAND (Nov. 21, 1848–July 1, 1910), lawyer, diplomat, was born in Brookville, Ind. His parents were Rev. Williamson Terrell, a Methodist minister, and Martha Terrell, the daughter of James Jarrell of Kentucky. His grandfather, Capt. John Terrell, moved to Kentucky from Virginia in 1787 and won distinction in the early Indian campaigns under Josiah Harmar, Arthur St. Clair [*qq.v.*], and Anthony Wayne. His first American ancestor was William Terrell (or Tyrrell), who came from England to Virginia as a crownlands agent, according to family tradition, about the middle of the seventeenth century. Terrell was valedictorian of his class at Asbury (later De Pauw) University, where he received the degree of A.B. in 1871. Two years later he received the degree of LL.B. from Harvard, and spent the following year in Europe, studying international law and modern languages. He became a member of the firm of Barbour, Jacobs, and Terrell in Indianapolis in 1874. In 1877 he moved permanently to San Antonio, Tex., established a law office, and quickly became closely identified with the political, professional, and business life of the city. He was a delegate to the Republican National Conventions of 1880, 1888, and 1904, and was a member of the Republican state executive committee of Texas from 1894 to 1900.

On Apr. 1, 1889, President Harrison appointed Terrell envoy extraordinary and minister plenipotentiary to Belgium, where he served with distinction throughout the Harrison administration. With Henry Shelton Sanford [*q.v.*] he represented the United States at the Brussels International Slave Trade Conference, 1889–90, and signed the General Act for the repression of the African slave trade. He was also United States delegate to the Brussels customs tariff conference of 1890, and signed the convention concerning the formation of an international union for the publication of customs tariffs, July 5, 1890. The same year he was made a member of the *Commission Technique* to revise the tariff provisions of the Berlin Treaty of 1885 under the General Act of Brussels, and on Jan. 24, 1891, he concluded with Leopold II a treaty of commerce, amity, and navigation between the United States and the Congo Free State. In 1891 he also succeeded in persuading the Belgian government to modify greatly the quarantine restrictions which barred American live stock from the Belgian market. Early in 1892, at the request of Secretary of State James G. Blaine, he returned to Washington and aided in persuading the Senate to consent to the ratification of the slave trade treaty. Returning to Brussels, he served as United States commissioner at the International Monetary Conference of 1892, of which he was elected vice-president, and delivered the response to the address of welcome made by the Belgian prime minister. In 1893 he retired from the diplomatic service. In October of that year he was made a grand officer of the Order of Leopold. Returning to San Antonio, he again took an active part in political, business, and civic affairs. On Aug. 17, 1874, he married Mary Maverick, daughter of Samuel A. Maverick, one of the founders of the Republic of Texas. She died in Brussels in 1891, leaving six children. On Feb. 7, 1895, he married Lois Lasater of Corpus Christi, Tex., daughter of Albert Lasater. They had three children. Terrell died in San Antonio after an illness of two years. He was survived by five children of his first marriage and one child of his second.

[See J. H. Tyrrell, *A Geneal. Hist. of the Tyrrells* (n.d.), and *The Geneal. of Richmond and William Tyrrell or Terrell* (n.d.); E. H. Terrell, *Further Geneal. Notes on the Tyrrell-Terrell Family* (2nd ed., 1909); *Who's Who in America*, 1910–11; *A Twentieth Century Hist. of Southwest Tex.* (1907), vol. I, pp. 339–40; and obituary in *Daily Express* (San Antonio), July 2, 1910. Terrell's diplomatic correspondence is in the archives of the Dept. of State, Washington, D. C.; part of it has been printed in *Papers Relating to the Foreign Relations of the U. S. . . . . 1891* (1892).]   I. L. T.

TERRY, ALFRED HOWE (Nov. 10, 1827–Dec. 16, 1890), soldier, was a descendant of Samuel Terry who settled in Springfield, Mass., in 1650. Born in Hartford, Conn., the eldest son of Alfred and Clarissa (Howe) Terry, he entered the Yale Law School in 1848, but on admission to the bar the following year left without graduating. He was clerk of the superior court of New Haven County, 1854–60. Soon after the outbreak of the Civil War he was commissioned colonel of the 2nd Connecticut Militia, a three months' regiment, and participated in the first battle of Bull Run. On the expiration of his service, he returned to Connecticut, and with Joseph R. Hawley [q.v.] soon raised the 7th Connecticut Volunteers for three years or the duration of the war. Terry was commissioned colonel and Haw-

ley lieutenant-colonel. This regiment took part in the capture of Port Royal, S. C., in November 1861 and subsequently in the bombardment, siege, and capture of Fort Pulaski, Ga., Apr. 10–11, 1862. On Apr. 25 Terry was promoted brigadier-general of volunteers. After the attempted advance on Charleston across James Island had been turned back by the repulse at Secessionville, June 16, he was stationed for some months at Hilton Head, taking part in the action at Pocotaligo Bridge, S. C., Oct. 22. On Oct. 29, 1862, he was placed in command of the forces on Hilton Head.

To supplement the naval operations of Rear Admiral Samuel Francis du Pont [q.v.] off Charleston, in the summer of 1863 the army under Gen. Quincy Adams Gillmore [q.v.], in cooperation with Rear Admiral John A. Dahlgren [q.v.], conducted a siege of Battery Wagner, Morris Island, S. C. Terry's command was sent on a diversion up the Stono River to James Island, whence it soon returned and advanced along Morris Island to reënforce the siege. Later in 1863, Terry was transferred to the Army of the James under Gen. B. F. Butler, and during 1864 was engaged mainly in operations against Richmond and Petersburg. On Aug. 26, 1864, he was brevetted major-general of volunteers.

After the failure of Butler's expedition against Fort Fisher, N. C., in December 1864, Grant assigned the same task to practically the same military forces under Terry, adding only one small brigade and a siege train which was not used. On Jan. 15, 1865, the fort was taken by a series of assaults after severe bombardments by the fleet under Rear Admiral David D. Porter [q.v.]. Terry's report, dated Jan. 25, 1865, is the most detailed and comprehensive description of that action (*War of the Rebellion: Official Records, Army,* 1 ser. XLVI, pt. 1, pp. 394–400). He was advanced as of Jan. 15, 1865, to brigadier-general in the regular army and received the thanks of Congress with particular reference to the capture of Fort Fisher. Following that supreme accomplishment of his military career, he occupied Wilmington, N. C., in cooperation with J. M. Schofield [q.v.] and soon thereafter started with the X Corps to join Gen. William T. Sherman, then coming up from Georgia. A junction was made near Goldsboro, N. C., and for a time Terry and his corps served under Schofield in the Army of the Ohio. On Apr. 20, 1865, he was commissioned major-general of volunteers.

After the war Terry was mustered out of the volunteer service, and in 1866, as a regular officer, assumed command of the Department of

Dakota, with headquarters at St. Paul and later at Fort Snelling, Minn. In 1869 he was transferred to the Department of the South, but in December 1872 was returned to the Northwest, where he continued at the head of the Department of Dakota during the exploration of the Black Hills in 1874 and the Sioux war, taking the field in personal command of the expedition from Fort Abraham Lincoln on the Missouri River in Dakota to the Yellowstone-Big Horn region of Montana in the summer of 1876. The disaster to the force under Gen. George A. Custer [q.v.] at the Little Big Horn, June 25, 1876, led to a controversy as to whether or not Custer had disobeyed or exceeded Terry's order of June 22, but Terry never made any statement on that point, preferring (it is generally believed) to accept responsibility and criticism rather than create an issue (see Hughes, post). His assignments to the Northwest covered the most important period of railroad construction and development in the present North and South Dakota and Montana. On Mar. 3, 1886, he was advanced to the full rank of major-general, and on Apr. 9 was placed in command of the Division of the Missouri, with headquarters at Chicago. He was retired for disability, Apr. 5, 1888.

Terry was a member of several boards and commissions, notably the Indian Commission created by Congress in 1867 to treat with the Plains Indians. He was the ranking officer in the attempted negotiations with Sitting Bull in the fall of 1877, and a member of the board of army officers appointed in 1878 to review the court martial and sentence of General Fitz-John Porter [q.v.]. Terry was a thorough student of the science and art of war. He was about six feet in height, straight, vigorous and active. A conspicuous trait was his ability to cooperate with superiors, equals, or subordinates. He never wrote for publication outside of numerous official reports of a high order. He was one of very few Civil War volunteer officers who reached the highest permanent rank in the regular army; for a considerable time he was the first general officer on the army list not a West Point graduate. After retirement, he returned to New Haven, where he died. He was unmarried. A full length portrait of him hangs in Memorial Hall, Connecticut State Building, Hartford.

[Stephen Terry, *Notes of Terry Families in the U. S. A.* (1887); *Record of Service of Conn. Men . . . during the War of the Rebellion* (1889); Stephen Walkley, *Hist. of the Seventh Conn. Vol. Infantry* (1905); A. D. Osborne, *The Capture of Fort Fisher by Maj. Gen. Alfred H. Terry and What It Accomplished* (New Haven Colony Hist. Soc., 1911); *War of the Rebellion, Official Records (Army)* and *(Navy)* both, for operations along the Atlantic Coast; F. B. Heitman, *Hist.*

Reg. and Dict. U. S. Army (1903), vol. I; *Battles and Leaders of the Civil War* (4 vols., 1887–88). D. D. Porter, *The Naval Hist. of the Civil War* (1886); *Personal Memoirs of U. S. Grant*, vol. II (1886) and *Memoirs of Gen. Wm. T. Sherman* (2 vols., 1875); J. M. Schofield, *Forty-six Years in the Army* (1897); N. A. Miles, *Personal Recollections* (1896); R. P. Hughes (Terry's brother-in-law), "The Campaign against the Sioux in 1876," *Jour. of the Military Service Inst.*, Jan. 1896; *General Orders*, Hdqrs. Army, Washington, Dec. 16, 1890; *Army and Navy Jour.*, Dec. 20, 1890; *Harper's Weekly*, Dec. 27, 1890; *Sun* (N. Y.), Dec. 17, 1890.]   R. B.

TERRY, DAVID SMITH (Mar. 8, 1823–Aug. 14, 1889), soldier, California jurist and political leader, was born in Todd (then part of Christian) County, Ky. His great-grandfather, Capt. Nathaniel Terry (d. 1780), of Halifax County, Va., was a man of considerable prominence. His grandfathers, Nathaniel Terry and David Smith, had been officers in the Revolutionary War, and the latter served under Andrew Jackson in the War of 1812. While he was still a boy, his parents, Joseph R. and Sarah (Smith) Terry, removed to Mississippi, where they separated. Subsequently, Mrs. Terry and her sons settled in Texas. Although only thirteen years of age, Terry served as a volunteer in the war for Texan independence but did not participate in any actual fighting (Potts, post, p. 297). In the Mexican War he served as a lieutenant in a company of Texas Rangers and participated in the battle of Monterey. In December 1849, Terry became a resident of Stockton, Cal., where he engaged actively in the practice of law. In 1852 he married Cornelia Runnels, a niece of Governor Runnels of Mississippi. In 1855 he accepted the nomination of the Know-Nothing party for the office of associate justice of the California supreme court and was elected to that place when the new party, in an astonishing political upset, swept the state. In 1856 he rashly went to San Francisco to aid in organizing resistance to the Vigilantes, who were in extra-legal control there. When Sterling A. Hopkins, one of the agents of the Vigilance Committee, while endeavoring to arrest illegally one Reuben Maloney, also sought to disarm Terry, a scuffle ensued in which Terry seriously wounded Hopkins in the neck with a bowie knife. Terry was immediately taken into custody by the Vigilance Committee, but, when Hopkins recovered, was released after undergoing an imprisonment of several weeks.

Resuming his place on the supreme court, he became chief justice in the October term 1857. In 1859 he affiliated himself with the Gwin or Southern branch of the Democratic party in California but, because of his Know-Nothing record, its convention refused him a renomination to the supreme court. He made, however, before the state convention of the faction, a vigorous speech in which he assailed Senator David Broderick [q.v.], the leader of the other Democratic faction, as a follower of the negro, Frederick Douglass [q.v.], rather than one of Stephen A. Douglas [q.v.]. Incensed by this attack, Broderick denounced Terry, as a "miserable wretch" and as a dishonest man and judge (Potts, p. 309).

When Broderick refused to retract these intemperate and unjustified statements, Terry challenged him to a duel which Broderick accepted, the seconds naming pistols, with which Broderick was an expert shot, as the weapons. The duel was fought on Sept. 13, 1859, and resulted in Broderick's receiving a fatal wound after having fired prematurely. To allay unwarranted rumors as to the conduct of the duel, Congressman Joseph C. McKibben, Broderick's second and political follower, testified that there was "no perceptible difference in the weapons" (San Francisco *Daily Alta California*, Sept. 18, 1859, evidence at coroner's inquest; Wagstaff, *post*, pp. 20, 207–08). Before this tragic affair, Terry filed his resignation as chief justice, and he afterward went through the formality of a trial for murder, being speedily acquitted. In 1863 he joined the Confederate forces and was wounded at Chickamauga and later commanded a regiment and a brigade in Texas. Upon the collapse of the Confederacy, he was for a time in Mexico, but in 1869 returned to California and resumed the practice of the law at Stockton. In 1878 he was elected to the California constitutional convention.

In 1884 Terry became involved, as one of the attorneys for the plaintiff, Sarah Althea Hill, in the notorious William Sharon divorce case. After lengthy proceedings, judgment was rendered for her in the trial court. On Jan. 7, 1886, while an appeal from this judgment was pending, Terry, whose first wife had died Dec. 24, 1884, married his client. The supreme court of California at first approved the decree of the lower court, but later changed its position. In the meantime, the federal court had decreed the documents, on which the plaintiff relied, to be fraudulent and had ordered their surrender and cancellation. Sharon died and the heirs had to revive the suit to have the decree carried out. When Justice Stephen J. Field [q.v.], acting as circuit justice, announced the decision of himself and Judges Sawyer and Sabin, a violent court room scene was precipitated by Mrs. Terry, which resulted in the imprisonment of both herself and her husband for contempt of court. After his release from this imprisonment, Terry threatened physical harm to Field. Because of this, the

Attorney General of the United States had David Neagle assigned to Field as his bodyguard. On Aug. 14, 1889, while Field and Neagle were having breakfast at the railroad eating house at Lathrop, Cal., Terry approached Field and struck him twice and was thereupon shot and killed by Neagle, who was immediately arrested and imprisoned on a charge of murder. From such imprisonment and charge he was freed by the federal courts, the Supreme Court of the United States holding that he was justified in his act, which was performed as a federal officer.

Terry was buried at Stockton and both its bar and the bar of Fresno adopted resolutions laudatory of his character. While he was a man of rash judgment and violent impulses, his honesty was as unquestionable as his courage and his ability as a judge, lawyer, and political leader was not inconsiderable. Much of a derogatory nature that has been written of his career will not bear critical scrutiny. For the duel with Broderick, he cannot, according to the standards of the day, justly be blamed; and for his final offense he paid tragic penalty.

[In this article the Broderick duel is interpreted and the attack on Field described somewhat differently than in the sketches of these men in earlier volumes of this work. It is possible that Broderick's premature firing may have been due to nervousness, and it seems unfair to say that at the time of the attack on Field, Terry was "already known as the assassin of Broderick." It would appear that Terry did not specifically threaten to "shoot" Field, and the tragedy occurred, not in a dining-car, but in a station restaurant.

Sources are: A. E. Wagstaff, *Life of David S. Terry* (1892); H. H. Hagan, "A California Saga," *Commercial Law League Journal*, Nov. 1929; C. S. Potts, "David S. Terry," *Southwest Review*, Apr. 1934; T. H. Hittell, *Hist. of California*, vols. III, IV (1897); H. H. Bancroft, *Hist. of California*, vols. VI (1888), VII (1890); Jeremiah Lynch, *The Life of David C. Broderick* (1911); James O'Meara, *Broderick and Gwin* (1881); *Stephen J. Field Arrested for Conspiracy and Murder of the Hon. David S. Terry* (1889), a violent pro-Terry pamphlet; S. J. Field, *Personal Reminiscences of Early Days in California* (privately printed, 1893); C. B. Swisher, *Stephen J. Field. Craftsman of the Law* (1930); E. G. Waite, in *Overland Monthly*, Oct. 1889, pp. 434–42; *Daily Examiner* (San Francisco), beginning Sept. 4, 1884, and Aug. 15, 1889; 26 *Federal Reporter*, 337; 36 *Federal Reporter*, 337, 419; 128 *U. S. Reports*, 289; 135 *U. S.*, 1; 7 *Pacific Reporter*, 456, 635; 8 *Pacific*, 614, 709; 9 *Pacific*, 187; 16 *Pacific*, 345; 22 *Pacific*, 26, 131.]　　　　H. H. H.

TERRY, ELI (Apr. 13, 1772–Feb. 26, 1852), inventor, pioneer clock manufacturer, the eldest of ten children of Samuel and Huldah (Burnham) Terry, was born at East (later South) Windsor, Conn. He was a descendant of Samuel Terry who emigrated from England to Springfield, Mass., in 1650. Equipped with but a smattering of a common school education, at the age of fourteen he began his clockmaker's apprenticeship. For the succeeding six years (1786–92) he worked for a number of clockmakers in his native state, among them Daniel Burnap of East Windsor and possibly Timothy Cheney of East Hartford. In 1793, a year after making his first clock (still in existence in 1923), he settled in Plymouth, Conn., and set himself up in the business of making and repairing clocks, engraving on metal, and selling spectacles. In his clockmaking he used the simple hand tools of the day and made but one or two hang-up clocks at a time, under orders. Having little difficulty in disposing of his wares, about 1800 he decided to increase his production by using water power to drive his tools, and about three years later he began, with two or three apprentices, to turn out ten to twenty clocks at a time. This enterprise, much ridiculed by Terry's neighbors and fellow clockmakers, was the first clock factory in America. In 1807 he obtained a contract for making four thousand wood clocks at four dollars apiece, sold his original water power factory, bought a large mill with water power in another part of Plymouth, and with Seth Thomas [q.v.] and Silas Hoadley established the firm of Terry, Thomas & Hoadley. The four thousand clocks having been completed in three years and sold at a good profit, Terry sold out to Thomas & Hoadley (1810) and established a business of his own at Plymouth Hollow. He concentrated his attention on one-day shelf clocks with wooden works rather than on uncased grandfather clocks, and in the course of the succeeding four years designed a number of different styles, making as many as several hundred clocks of each pattern. It was not until 1814 that he devised a clock that completely satisfied him—his "perfected wood clock." This shelf clock, which was called the "pillar scroll top case," was made entirely of wood. It immediately took the popular fancy and in the course of the succeeding ten years "drove out all other clocks for a time" (Milham, *post*, p. 352). With the help of his sons Terry gradually increased the production of these clocks to ten or twelve thousand a year, selling them at fifteen dollars each, and by 1825 is said to have accumulated a fortune of about a hundred thousand dollars.

In the course of his life he patented in the neighborhood of ten improvements in clocks, among them one issued on Nov. 17, 1797, for an "equation" clock, which showed both apparent and mean time. In addition to manufacturing the popular shelf clock he made brass clocks of fine quality which were sold to watchmakers as regulators. He built, too, a number of tower clocks which were of novel design. Terry was twice married, first on Mar. 12, 1795, to Eunice Warner of Plymouth (d. Dec. 15, 1839), and second to Mrs. Harriet Ann (Pond) Peck of

Plymouth in October 1840. He was the father of eleven children, nine by his first marriage and two by his second. At the time of his death in Plymouth, in the part of the town known as Terryville, he was survived by the two sons of his second marriage, and two daughters and three sons of his first.

[Stephen Terry, *Notes of Terry Families* (1887); H. R. Stiles, *The Hist. and Genealogies of Ancient Windsor, Conn.*, vol. II (1892); Henry Terry, *Am. Clock Making, Its Early Hist., and Present Extent of the Business* (1870); P. R. Hoopes, *Conn. Clockmakers of the Eighteenth Century* (1930); Francis Atwater, *Hist. of the Town of Plymouth, Conn.* (1895); W. I. Milham, *Time & Timekeepers* (1923); Mrs. N. Hudson Moore, *The Old Clock Book* (1911); J. T., in *Sci. Am. Supp.*, June 15, 1889; death notice in *New Haven Daily Palladium*, Feb. 28, 1852; *Subject-Matter Index of Patents for Inventions Issued by the U. S. Patent Office from 1790 to 1873* (1874), vol. I, compiled by M. D. Leggett; Patent Office records.]
C. W. M.—n.

TERRY, MARSHALL ORLANDO (June 21, 1848–Oct. 11, 1933), physician, was born at Watervliet Center, N. Y., the son of William Henry and Sarah (Burke) Terry. In 1850 the family moved to Ohio, settling first at Plymouth and later in Ashtabula. Here young Terry attended the local high school and academy, after which he entered the Homoeopathic Hospital College of Cleveland, where he received the degree of M.D. in 1872. After a short period of practice in Akron, Ohio, he removed to Utica, N. Y., in 1873. The several succeeding years were largely occupied in postgraduate study of ophthalmology in New York City and abroad. In addition to practising this specialty, he developed a high degree of skill as a general surgeon and also practised internal medicine. He served as head of the surgical staff of the Utica Homoeopathic Hospital from 1895 to 1905 and was an attending surgeon for the Utica General Hospital. In 1880 he was appointed surgeon to the 4th Brigade, New York National Guard, with the grade of major, and in 1895 he was promoted to the position of surgeon-general of the state troops with the grade of brigadier-general. He served throughout the Spanish-American War on active duty under his state commission. Beginning with the supervision of the medical service of the state camp, he was later commissioned to investigate the care of New York troops in federal camps, with special reference to the cause of the high incidence of typhoid fever, at that time epidemic in these camps. His report to the governor, in which he held that the prevalence of flies was a major factor in the spread of the disease, aroused a storm of discussion and criticism, and resulted in the appointment by the government of the so-called Shakespeare board for the thorough investigation of the camp epidemics. He was offered the appointment of division chief surgeon of volunteers by President McKinley, but his duties to the state troops prevented his accepting it. He perfected a litter, a field operating case, and an ambulance, and developed a medical and surgical field chest. He retired from practice in Utica in 1905, and in the same year married Mrs. A. M. McGregor of Mamaroneck, N. Y. He became interested in the development of Fort Myers, Fla., where he became the owner of a large hotel, and was instrumental in the construction of a sea-wall and of a boulevard connecting the city with Puntarassa, eighteen miles distant on the Gulf of Mexico. For many years he maintained a summer home at Mamaroneck and a winter home at Fort Myers. His wife dying in 1912, he subsequently married Mrs. Adabelle R. Merritt of Berkeley, Cal. During his later years he divided his residence between New York City and Coronado, Cal., where he died of pneumonia. He was buried at his boyhood home at Ashtabula, Ohio.

Military medicine was Terry's abiding interest. He joined the Association of Military Surgeons of the United States in 1895, soon after its organization, and maintained an active membership for the remainder of his life. He wrote numerous journal articles on topics relating to military medical service, and during the World War he published for free distribution *The Soldier's Medical Friend: A Gift to the Surgeons of the United States Government and their Allies* (1917). This handbook was largely a collection of reprints of previous journal articles, which he considered would be useful to the military surgeon. He was a member and one-time president of the state association of medical officers and of the state homoeopathic medical society, and a member of the American Institute of Homoeopathy. He had a high conception of his civic duties, and was much interested both in public and in private philanthropies.

[*Who's Who in American Medicine* (1925); *Who's Who in America*, 1932–33; *Military Surgeon*, Nov. 1933; obituary in *N. Y. Herald-Tribune*, Oct. 13, 1933.]

J. M. P—n.

TERRY, MILTON SPENSER (Feb. 22, 1840–July 13, 1914), Methodist clergyman and educator, was born in Coeymans, N. Y., the son of John and Eliza (McLaughlin) Terry. He was christened Milton Seaman but when he became a young man adopted Spenser as his middle name. His father was a Hicksite Quaker, mystical in temperament; his mother was of Scotch descent, practical and energetic. The son inherited the spirituality of the father and the practical common sense of the mother. He was the youngest of eleven children. Books were a luxury in the

Terry home, but the Bible, Milton, and Shakespeare held first place. At fifteen, young Terry could recite whole books of *Paradise Lost* from memory. He was eager for an education in the schools but was hindered by lack of means from completing any course. From 1857 to 1859 he attended the New York Conference Seminary at Charlotteville, N. Y., leaving to teach school and obtain needed funds. He planned a college course, which circumstances made impossible, and finally spent a year (1862–63) in the Yale Divinity School instead. Thereafter he studied day and night by himself, read assiduously, and soon attained a reputation for unusual scholarship. He acquired nine languages, ancient and modern, besides his own.

He had joined the Methodist Episcopal Church at the age of eighteen and been licensed to preach on Jan. 28, 1860. Having been admitted to the New York Conference, he was ordained deacon in 1864, and elder in 1866. During his active ministry, which lasted until 1884, he served churches in Delhi, N. Y., Peekskill, Poughkeepsie, and New York City. From 1879 to 1883 he was presiding elder of the New York district. In 1884 he was made head of the department of Hebrew and Old Testament exegesis and professor of Christian doctrine at the Garrett Biblical Institute, Evanston, Ill.

In 1887 he attended lectures at the University of Berlin under Dillmann, Weiss, Kaftan, and Pfleiderer, and there learned something of the newer approach to the Bible through the higher criticism. With growing knowledge he revised many of the conclusions of his earlier years and then stood courageously and consistently for all he had come to believe valid and true. It was his fortune to bear the brunt of a large part of the opposition these newer views encountered in the Church to which he belonged. He had the courage of his convictions and in the days of heated controversy he always could be depended upon to represent the best scholarship of his day with calmness, clearness, and unfailing courtesy. He survived the years of stress and strain and lived to see most of the issues for which he contended in peaceful possession of the field. Meanwhile, he had become a recognized authority in the theological field. His three major works, *Biblical Hermeneutics* (1883), *Biblical Apocalyptics* (1898), and *Biblical Dogmatics* (1907), established his reputation as a sound and progressive thinker and some of his lesser works, notably *Moses and the Prophets* (1901) and *Primer of Christian Doctrine* (1906), were read more widely and created more commotion in the church than the larger books. Other writings include three volumes in D. D. Whedon's *Commentary on the Old Testament,* as well as *The Sibylline Oracles* (1890), *The Prophecies of Daniel Expounded* (1893), *The Song of Songs Analyzed* (1893), *Rambles in the Old World* (1894), *The New Apologetic* (1897), *The New and Living Way* (1902), *The Mediation of Jesus Christ* (1903), *Baccalaureate Sermons and Addresses* (1914). He also contributed many articles to theological magazines. He was a delegate to three General Conferences of the Methodist Episcopal Church (1880, 1896, 1904), and to two Methodist Ecumenical Conferences (1891, 1911).

On May 15, 1864, he was married to Frances O. Atchinson of Hamden, N. Y. While sojourning in California with his wife in 1914, he preached one Sunday night on Jacob's vision of the ladder reaching to heaven and of the angels ascending and descending upon it and, returning to his home in Los Angeles, he died on Monday morning with little warning or pain.

[Stephen Terry, *Notes of Terry Families* (1887); memoir by Terry's daughter in his *Baccalaureate Sermons and Addresses* (1914); *Garrett Biblical Institute Bull.,* Terry Memorial Number, Nov. 1914; *Who's Who in America,* 1914–15; *Los Angeles Times,* July 14, 1914; information regarding baptismal name and name of mother from Terry's daughter, Miss Minnie Terry.]

D. A. H.

TESTUT, CHARLES (c. 1818–July 1, 1892), journalist, poet, and physician, was born in France. He was in New York in November 1839 and assisted at the birth of a new French newspaper, *L'Indicateur.* After it died, almost stillborn, he moved to Pointe-à-Pitre on the island of Guadeloupe. Testut lost his small fortune of 85,000 francs when the terrible earthquake of 1843 completely destroyed that city; but he escaped with his wife and daughter to a ship in the harbor, and it eventually landed him in New Orleans, La., bare of all possessions except a broken trunk, an old mattress, and fifteen cents in cash. During the next few years he supported his family by writing for the Creole newspapers until he had saved enough money to buy a weekly of his own, *Le Chronique.* He immediately augmented it by a "literary supplement" which contained serialized romances based on Louisiana history. Many of these he wrote himself, and he later collected them in two volumes under the title *Las Veillées Louisianaises* (1849). In 1850 he went to Mobile and launched a bilingual paper called the *Alabama Courrier,* but it soon failed and he returned to New Orleans. For the rest of his life he was ridden by an irresistible urge to found newspapers; they multiplied like mushrooms and died like flies. Among the ones he or-

ganized were *La Semaine de la Nouvelle Orléans* in 1852, *L'Equité* in 1871, *La Lanterne* in 1873, *La Semaine Littéraire* in 1876, and *Le Journal des Famille* about 1888 (changed in 1890 to *Le Journal du Peuple*).

He wrote poetry as well as prose, and in 1849 published his first book of verses, *Les Échos.* This was followed two years later by a second volume of poetry, *Fleurs d'Été.* In 1850 he brought out a collection of short criticisms of the local writers, under the title *Portraits Littéraires,* and in 1852–53 a series in parts of Creolized dime novels called *Les Mysteres de la Nouvelle-Orléans.* These were full of counterfeiters, seducers, and noble heroes. They first appeared as "literary supplements" to *La Semaine.* His most interesting novel was *Le Vieux Salomon,* which he wrote in eighty-nine consecutive evenings while on a visit to New York in 1858. It resembled *Uncle Tom's Cabin,* and told the story of a wise old African of Guadeloupe who helped two young slaves to get married. Unfortunately after the ceremony their master lost his fortune and the young couple were sold and shipped to New Orleans. Their new master tried to seduce the wife and treated the husband with the greatest brutality. Knowing the feeling of the South towards this sort of abolition propaganda, Testut did not dare publish it until 1872, when he serialized it in *L'Equité* before bringing it out in book form. Even then, however, it created a great deal of animosity, a feeling he fanned by openly advocating the cause of the former slaves in his editorials. With a consummate aptitude for antagonizing his friends and subscribers, he wrote a series of slurring attacks against Pope Pius IX, which enraged all the Catholics in New Orleans, and published a defense of Free Masonry which certainly did nothing to placate them. Finally a number of editorials affirming his implicit belief in spiritism deprived him of his remaining readers and *L'Equité* died of starvation. With a temperament such as Testut's he could never make money. Inevitably he became a penniless old man and during his latter years was kept alive by a group of generous women who took turns in bringing him food each day. When he died in July 1892, they paid for his funeral.

[E. L. Tinker, *Les Écrits de Langue Française en Louisiane aux XIXe Siècle* (1932); Ruby Van A. Caulfeild, *The French Lit. of La.* (1929); letter by Testut, in *Le Courrier* (New Orleans), Mar. 14, 1843; *L'Abeille de la Nouvelle Orléans,* July 2 (obituary), 3, 1892.]

E. L. T.

TEUSLER, RUDOLF BOLLING (Feb. 25, 1876–Aug. 10, 1934), surgeon, founder of St. Luke's Hospital, Tokyo, was born in Rome, Ga., the son of Rudolf and Mary Jefferson (Bolling)

Teusler; his father was of German descent. Part of his childhood was spent in Wytheville, Va., but in 1884 Richmond became his home. His preliminary education was received in Gordonsville Academy and in private schools. At the early age of seventeen he entered the Medical College of Virginia, where he was graduated in 1894. After visiting hospitals in Baltimore, Montreal, and Quebec, he began practice in Richmond, and almost immediately joined the faculty of the Medical College of Virginia as assistant professor of pathology and bacteriology. Beginning in 1894, he also served in the city dispensary of Richmond and as assistant surgeon and later as surgeon in the 1st Regiment of Virginia Volunteers, Infantry. On July 21, 1898, he married Mary Stuart Woodward, by whom he had four children.

In 1900 he went to Tokyo, Japan, under the Domestic and Foreign Missionary Society of the Protestant Episcopal Church and there, in the service of that Society, entered upon the career which brought him distinction and which was ended only by his death. On his arrival he discovered the hospital building and equipment placed at his disposal to be hopelessly inadequate. He thereupon closed the establishment and gave himself to the study of the language and to making contacts with Japanese. Later, having formulated plans which seemed to him adapted to the situation, he opened a small hospital which, under the name of St. Luke's, was to achieve a place in Japan of unique importance. He combined single-hearted unselfishness with indomitable perseverance, resourcefulness, personal charm, rare gifts as an organizer, and marked skill as a surgeon. For years he served as physician to the foreign embassies in Tokyo and devoted the large income which came to him from these appointments and from other private practice to the enlargement and work of the hospital. He was a pioneer in Japan in public health methods, the professional training of nurses, preventive medicine, and child welfare. He also supervised the Hospital of St. Barnabas in Osaka. From 1918 to 1921 he interrupted his life in Tokyo to serve in Siberia with the Allied Forces as commissioner of the Red Cross. The fire following the earthquake which devastated so much of Tokyo in 1923 destroyed St. Luke's, but the staff of physicians and nurses displayed great heroism in ministering to the sufferers from the disaster. A few months later a second, improvised hospital was also destroyed by fire. Undaunted, Teusler seized the opportunity to realize a project for a greatly enlarged building. This had been proposed as early as 1912 and part of the necessary

money had already been collected. Large additional funds were now obtained, mainly from the United States, and in the heart of Tokyo a model plant was erected, which included what was said to be the largest X-ray equipment in the Far East and provision for a college for nurses, the first of its kind in Japan. The Japanese government gave official recognition and assistance, the Emperor served as patron and made a substantial contribution, help came from private Japanese sources, and in June 1933, only a little over a year before Teusler's death, the new building of St. Luke's International Medical Centre was formally dedicated. In recognition of his services Teusler was, at different times, decorated with the Russian Order of Saint Vladimir, the Czechoslovakian War Medal, and the (Japanese) Order of the Rising Sun.

[Who's Who in America, 1934–35; Spirit of Missions, Aug. 1933, Sept. 1934; files of the department of foreign missions of the National Council of the Protestant Episcopal Church; Japan Chronicle (Kobe), Aug. 16, 1934.]   K. S. L.

TEVIS, LLOYD (Mar. 20, 1824–July 24, 1899), capitalist, was born in Shelbyville, Ky., and was the son of Samuel and Sarah (Greathouse) Tevis. His father was a prominent attorney in his county, and for a time circuit court clerk. Finishing his formal education at eighteen, Tevis read law under his father, and for nearly two years assisted him in his clerk's office. After a further brief period of law study and work at a neighboring county seat, he took a position as salesman with a wholesale dry goods company in Louisville, Ky. He rose rapidly to a high place in the counting room, and when the firm failed he was appointed assignee. He displayed such ability in this position that he was offered a place in the Bank of Kentucky—all this before he was twenty-five. He left the bank shortly to enter the office of an insurance company in St. Louis. In the spring of 1849 he joined the gold rush to California, crossed the plains in a covered wagon, and tried his luck for nine months in the diggings. But having little success there, and being in any case more disposed towards a commercial and financial career, he went to Sacramento and as a beginning found a place in the county recorder's office. Saving a portion of his salary, he made within a few months his first investment in land, buying a lot for $250. In October 1850 he and a recent acquaintance, James Ben Ali Haggin [q.v.], set up a law office together in Sacramento. This noted partnership, which endured until Tevis' death, forty-nine years later, became, as years went on, more and more a partnership for business and finance rather than law. The association between the two men was cemented by the fact that they married sisters, daughters of Col. Lewis Sanders, a prominent ex-Kentuckian, Tevis' wife being Susan G. Sanders, whom he married on Apr. 20, 1854.

By 1853 Haggin & Tevis found their interests too large to be handled in Sacramento, and so removed to San Francisco. There Tevis became identified with some of California's greatest business undertakings. He was one of the principal owners of the California Steam Navigation Company and one of the early projectors of telegraph lines throughout California. He conducted the negotiations by which the State Telegraph Company was taken over by the Western Union, and it is said that his profits and commissions on the deal amounted to $200,000. He was the leading projector of the California dry dock and the California market in San Francisco; one of the promoters of the Southern Pacific Railroad and its president, 1869–70; president and principal owner of the Pacific Ice Company, and one of the early manufacturers in California of illuminating gas. In 1868, while the Central Pacific Railroad was being built, Tevis led the way in organizing the Pacific Express Company to take over the express business on the line and threaten the East-and-West supremacy of Wells, Fargo & Company, then operating the Overland Mail stage line, which was soon to be rendered obsolete by the railroad. Wells, Fargo stock declined greatly in price, and Tevis and his associates bought quantities of it. Wells, Fargo & Company was finally forced to buy the Pacific Express Company in 1869 at an enormous figure, the Tevis faction becoming the controlling element in the older company. Joint operation was begun in 1870, and Tevis served as president from 1872 to 1892. He was a large stockholder in the Spring Valley Water Company, the Risdon Iron Works, and the Sutro Tunnel at Virginia City, Nev. He owned at one time 1,300 miles of stage-coach line in California, as well as street-car lines in San Francisco, thousands of acres of ranch lands, and enormous herds of cattle and sheep. He was one of the pioneers in reclaiming tule or swamp lands in central California. He was owner or part owner of gold and silver mines in California, Nevada, Utah, Idaho, and South Dakota. These included the Homestake mine in the Black Hills and the Ontario in Utah, in both of which he had George Hearst [q.v.] for a partner. Tevis, Haggin, Hearst, and Marcus Daly [q.v.] owned the great Anaconda copper properties in Montana. The Hearst share was sold to an English syndicate in 1897, and two years later (May 1899) the others sold their holdings to a syndicate headed by John D. Rockefeller. Tevis is said to have received $8,000,000 for his share. He died in San Francisco, survived by his wife, three sons, and two daughters.

[See article on Old Sacramento in *Morning Call* (San Francisco), Nov. 12, 1882; Alonzo Phelps, *Contemporary Biog. of California's Representative Men*, vol. I (1881); *California . . . Fifty Years of Progress* (1900), p. 210; G. T. Marye, *From '49 to '83 in Cal. and Nev.* (1923); and obituaries in *San Francisco Chronicle*, *San Francisco Call*, and *Examiner* (San Francisco), July 25, 1899. For Tevis' testimony concerning the sales of the Pacific Express Company, see *Sen. Exec. Doc. 51*, 50 Cong., 1 Sess., pt. VII, pp. 3114–39. Information about Tevis' parents was supplied by Mrs. Jouett T. Cannon, secretary of the Ky. State Hist. Soc., and by Ludie J. Kinkead, curator of the Filson Club, Louisville, Ky.]   A. F. H.

THACHER, EDWIN (Oct. 12, 1839–Sept. 21, 1920), civil engineer, was born at De Kalb, St. Lawrence County, N. Y., the youngest of four children and the only son of Dr. Seymour and Elizabeth (Smith) Thacher. Both his parents were of New England stock and his father was for almost a half century one of the leading physicians of St. Lawrence County. During Edwin's childhood the family moved to Hermon, in the same county, where they made their home. Thacher entered Rensselaer Polytechnic Institute at Troy, N. Y., in September 1860, and was graduated with high honors as a civil engineer in 1863. After a brief experience with the Cedar Rapids & Missouri River Railroad he was drawn into Civil War service and from 1864 until the end of the conflict acted as assistant engineer of the United States military railroads, being attached to the Department of the Cumberland with headquarters at Nashville, Tenn. In 1866 he accepted a position at Louisville, Ky., in connection with the construction of the Cincinnati branch of the Louisville, Cincinnati & Lexington Railroad.

Two years later he changed from general railroad work to the important related field of bridge construction, becoming in 1868 assistant engineer of the Louisville Bridge Company, then building the Fourteenth Street Bridge over the Ohio River at Louisville. This change marked the turning point in his career, for his later work was entirely of a structural type and it was in the structural field that his reputation was achieved. He remained with the Fourteenth Street Bridge until it was completed and opened for traffic; then resigned, and in August 1870 became assisting and computing engineer of the Louisville Bridge & Iron Company. After nine years in this connection, he became computing engineer for the famous old Keystone Bridge Company of Pittsburgh, Pa., one of the elements in the early career of the great American steel master, Andrew Carnegie. Thacher was made chief engineer about 1883, but in 1887 resigned to become chief engineer, and later receiver, for the Decatur Bridge & Construction Company at Decatur, Ala. Late in 1889 he severed this connection and began his career as a consulting engineer in Louisville, Ky. In 1894 he moved to Detroit, Mich., to become a partner in the firm of Keepers & Thacher and in 1901 became associated with William Mueser in the Concrete Steel Engineering Company, New York City. This last association continued until his retirement in 1912.

Thacher's particular interest in the calculations of structural design was reflected in his invention of the Thacher cylindrical slide rule, which he patented in 1881, and in the many tables for such work which he prepared. His most important contribution to his profession, however, was his pioneer work in the introduction of reinforced concrete construction in the United States. As early as 1889 he became interested in concrete-steel construction and in 1899 his firm built the concrete-steel arch over the Kansas River at Topeka. This was the most famous of his arches of this type, and, while completely eclipsed by modern works, was a notable bridge in its day. Another of his contributions was the "Thacher bar," one of the first of the so-called deformed bars used in reinforced concrete construction—later a standard type of reinforcing. He was a frequent contributor to the *Transactions* of the American Society of Civil Engineers, of which he was elected a member in 1869. On Apr. 22, 1872, he was married at Indianapolis, Ind., to Anna Elbertine Bartholomew, who died in 1905. He died fifteen years later at his home in New York City, survived by his only child, a daughter.

[*"Memoir of Edwin Thacher," Trans. Am. Soc. Civil Engineers, vol. LXXXIV (1921); Who's Who in America, 1920–21; H. B. Nason, Biog. Record of the Officers and Grads. of the Rensselaer Polytechnic Inst. (1887); N. Y. Times, Sept. 23, 1920.] J.K.F.*

THACHER, GEORGE (Apr. 12, 1754–Apr. 6, 1824), congressman and jurist, was born in Yarmouth, Mass., tenth of the eleven children of Lieut. Peter and Anner (Lewis) Thacher, and a descendant of Ant[h]ony Thacher who came to New England in 1635. He was prepared for college under the direction of Timothy Hilliard, the minister at Barnstable. He graduated from Harvard in 1776, and, except for one cruise on a privateer during the Revolution, he spent the three years thereafter studying law with that famous Cape Cod instructor, Shearjashub Bourne (letter, Apr. 12, 1794, Massachusetts Historical Society). The confused land titles and rapidly growing settlements in Maine offered at that time special inducements to young lawyers, and thither he removed, settling finally in 1782 at Biddeford, where he succeeded to the practice of James Sullivan. After his election by the Massachusetts legislature in 1787 as delegate to the Continental Congress he was elected by the District of Maine as a Federalist to every Congress from 1789 until his retirement in 1801, when he accepted an appointment as associate judge of the supreme judicial court of Massachusetts. He held this office until his resignation in January 1824.

As a member of Congress he was faithful in attendance, although his long absences from home irked him. Not a partisan by nature—he once wrote, "Parties are not necessary to the existence or support of political liberty" (*Ibid.*, May 11, 1796)—he was not especially active in Congress, although on occasion he spoke his mind in no uncertain terms. He did not believe a bill of rights necessary. He favored assumption of state debts, and was reconciled to the Potomac Bill. He opposed attempts to prevent Quaker anti-slavery petitions being read in Congress (*Annals of Congress*, 5 Cong., 2 Sess., p. 658), and he again defended the right of petition when he urged the reference of the petitions of certain free blacks (*Ibid.*, 6 Cong., 1 Sess., p. 232). When the Mississippi Territory Bill came up in Congress, Mar. 23, 1798, he moved to strike out the words "excepting that slavery shall not be forbidden." He defended Matthew Lyon [*q.v.*] in the Griswold-Lyon fight, but objected to the expulsion of either. Though an ardent champion of the rights of Americans and strongly anti-French, he believed that peace should be preserved. With less than his usual judgment, he advocated making the Sedition Act permanent (*Ibid.*, 5 Cong., 3 Sess., p. 2902).

The political support which he gained in his district because of his intellectual power, his integrity, and his natural gift for friendship was sometimes challenged by current reports of his irreligion. A deist, he advocated cheerfulness in religion; he did not believe in the existence of a soul apart from the body; he was a "mortal enemy to the Devil and all such Notions." "Religion," he wrote, "heretofore destroyed the pleasures of Life and made the world a state of misery" (letters, Feb. 22, 1789, and May 16, 1790, Massachusetts Historical Society Collections). He was a follower of Joseph Priestley [*q.v.*], whom he met while in Congress. He was sympathetic to Unitarian beliefs and was one of the founders of the Second Church in Biddeford. He was a great reader both in the classics and in contemporary books on religion, history, and education. In temperament he was more judge than politician. Of his judicial duties, in which his talent for weighing questions came to the fore, he wrote, "This Judge business is more agreeable than I had apprehended" (*Ibid.*, June 17, 1801). When Maine was separated from Massachusetts in 1820, he moved, somewhat unwillingly, to Newburyport in order that he might continue in office, but on his retirement he returned to Biddeford, where he died shortly after. He married on July 21, 1784, Sarah, the daughter of Samuel Phillips Savage of Weston, Mass. He was survived by his wife and nine of their ten children.

[See J. R. Totten, "Thacher-Thatcher Geneal.," *N. Y. Geneal. and Biog. Record*, Apr. 1910–Apr. 1913; D. W. Allen, *Geneal. and Biog. Sketches of the Descendants of Thomas and Anthony Thacher* (1872), which is not entirely accurate; Lawrence Park, *Maj. Thomas Savage of Boston and his Descendants* (1914); *Biog. Dir. Am. Cong., 1774–1927* (1928); William Willis, *A Hist. of the Law, the Courts and the Lawyers of Me.* (1863); *George Folsom, Hist. of Saco and Biddeford* (1830); death notice in *Eastern Argus* (Portland, Me.), Apr. 13, 1824. One coll. of Thacher's papers, mostly letters to his wife, is in the possession of the Mass. Hist. Soc.; another, composed of letters to him—some of which are printed in *Hist. Mag., and Notes and Queries*, Nov., Dec. 1869 —is in the Boston Pub. Lib.; a third, less important, is in the Me. Hist. Soc. Until about 1815 he spelled his name Thatcher.]   R. E. M.

THACHER, JAMES (Feb. 14, 1754–May 23, 1844), physician, patriot, historian, was born in Barnstable, Mass., the third son of John and Content (Norton) Thacher. The Thacher (often spelt Thatcher) family were of English stock, and James was a descendant of Ant [h] ony Thacher who came to America in 1635. They were honest, hardworking people of more than average distinction. Thacher's father was a poor farmer and consequently could give his son scant education. Without academic training the boy was apprenticed at the age of sixteen to Abner Hersey, the leading physician in Barnstable, an eccentric, hard-headed, morose man, greatly respected for his medical skill. Five years of work with Hersey, without leisure for social intercourse, gave young Thacher a sound knowledge of practical medicine. He was about to begin to practise for himself at the age of twenty-one when the events in Boston of the summer of 1775 stirred the young Whig, and in July, after examination by the medical board of the Provincial Congress sitting in Watertown, he was appointed surgeon's mate to the military hospital in Cambridge.

His medical ability, in spite of his lack of training, was soon appreciated. In February 1776 he was promoted to serve as assistant to David Townsend, in Asa Whitcomb's regiment at Prospect Hill and in Boston just after the evacuation by the British. He also went with Townsend to Ticonderoga, taking part in the retreat, which he vividly describes. A long service in the General Hospital at Albany was followed by another period in the field, first with the 1st Virginia Regiment, November 1778 to June 1779, and later with his old friend Townsend in a Massachusetts regiment under Col. Henry Jackson. During this latter period he took part in the ill-fated Penobscot expedition, spent a miserable winter in New Jersey, and witnessed the execution of Major John André, of which he wrote an excellent account in his diary, and in the *New England Magazine,* May 1834. The year 1781 found Thacher acting as surgeon to a select corps of light infantry, under Col. Alexander Scammell [*q.v.*]; he was present at the siege of Yorktown and the surrender of Lord Cornwallis. He retired from the army on July 1, 1783. His diary, *A Military Journal during the American Revolutionary War,* carefully kept from 1775 to 1783, was published in 1823, with a second edition in 1827, and was reprinted as *Military Journal* in 1854 and 1862 and as *The American Revolution* at least six times from 1856 to 1862. It gives a good picture of the spirit of the army, especially under the adverse circumstances of hunger, fatigue, and cold, and provides detailed descriptions of men and events almost unequaled by any of his contemporaries. He was a keen observer of the habits of his fellow-soldiers and, for a young country boy untrained in narration, his *Journal* must be considered a remarkable historical document. Unfortunately, Thacher failed to give many details of his hospital experiences, except in regard to smallpox inoculation, which he carried out on a large scale.

He began the practice of medicine and surgery in Plymouth in March 1784, well qualified, for his time, by his long experience in the army, and he soon established himself as the leading physician of the county. Students came to him for their apprenticeship and rumors that "dissecting material for his demonstrations was obtained from a neighboring church-yard" interrupted instruction for a time (Brewster, *post,* p. 573). Medical writing was begun under difficult circumstances and books soon began to appear, so that Thacher's name came to be known in the thirteen states and even in Europe. His reputation as a man of exceptional worth was well deserved, for to Thacher we owe not only an account of the Revolution, as noted above, but also the first American medical biography. This book, the product of his later years, when deafness was a serious handicap to his practice, has preserved for posterity the names of many physicians that otherwise might have been lost. The *American Medical Biography* (1828), a substantial volume in two parts, is the chief source-book of the period; nearly always accurate, reasonably judicious, and strictly impartial, Thacher did not hesitate to draw exact pictures of his contemporaries, few of which we would care to change a hundred years later. Other works by Thacher are *The American New Dispensatory* (1810, fourth edition, 1821), a sound application of American pharmacopœial principles; *Observations on Hydrophobia* (1812), a good summary of the disease, showing Thacher's extensive reading in spite of his isolation; *American Modern Practice* (1817; second edition, 1826), an early textbook of medicine in this country; *The American Orchardist* (1822, second edition, 1825); *A Practical Treatise on the Management of Bees* (1829), useful compilations for farmers; *An Essay on Demonology, Ghosts, and Apparitions* (1831), dealing with Salem witchcraft; and *History of the Town of Plymouth* (1832; second edition 1835).

Thacher's place as an historian of the Revolution is secure. His *Military Journal* was highly praised by John Adams (see preface to the second edition), and many writers have paid tribute to his portraits of Washington, Lafayette, Steuben, and other generals as they appeared in the field. As a practitioner he was sufficient for his time and place; his influence, through his numerous books, was wide-spread, for his *Dispensatory* and his *Practice* received immediate recognition in the United States and soon replaced the English textbooks used previously. He trained many students in medicine and for forty years was without a medical rival in Plymouth. He was married to Susannah Hayward of Bridgewater, Mass., on Apr. 28, 1785. Two of their six children survived him at his death. He was a member of the American Academy of Arts and Sciences, the Massachusetts Medical Society, the Pilgrim Society of Plymouth, and the French Society of Universal Statistics. For many years he was an active member in the First Church of Plymouth. His interest in the town was evidenced by his importation of many rare fruit trees and shrubs. Harvard College granted him an honorory M.D. degree in 1810. Small of stature, light and agile in movements, Thacher was fond of social intercourse, yet regularly studious. His patriotic spirit and sterling integrity endeared him to many; his well-disciplined mind and productive

antiquarianism led to literary endeavors of enduring worth.

[Letters, manuscript biography by his daughter, portrait, and other material, in the Boston Medical Library; J. R. Totten, data on the Thacher-Thatcher family, *N. Y. Geneal. and Biog. Record*, Apr. 1910–Oct. 1913, particularly Jan. 1912, and Oct. 1913; D. W. Allen, *Geneal. and Biog. Sketches of the Descendants of Thomas and Anthony Thacher* (1872); S. W. Williams, *Am. Medic. Biog.* (1845); article by N. S. Davis in S. D. Gross, *Lives of Eminent Am. Physicians and Surgeons* (1861); J. B. Brewster, *Boston Medic. and Surgical Jour.*, June 11, 18, 1891, and J. A. Spalding, *Ibid.* June 19, 1919; *Medic. Communications, Mass. Medic. Soc.*, vol. VII (1848), vol. XV (1892); *Quincy Patriot*, June 1, 1844.]   H. R. V.

THACHER, JOHN BOYD (Sept. 11, 1847–Feb. 25, 1909), author, bibliophile, public servant, was born at Ballston Spa, N. Y., the son of George Hornell Thacher and his wife, Ursula Jane, the daughter of David Boyd. He was a direct descendant of Peter Thacher, 1651–1727 [*q.v.*]. His early education was acquired under private tutors. He entered Williams College in 1865 and was graduated, *cum laude*, in 1869. He at once began at the bottom in the Thacher Car Wheel Works, at Albany, N. Y., learned the trade of a molder, attended business school in the evenings, and when thoroughly acquainted with the business was taken into the firm, a connection he maintained until his death. On Sept. 11, 1872, he was married to Emma, the daughter of George Curtis Treadwell, of Albany, who survived him. There were no children.

In his own city and state, he was best known through his political activities and his many public services. Following a dozen years of strenuous attention to his business, he became, in 1882, a member of the Albany Board of Health, which he had helped to organize. He served as state senator from 1884 to 1885. As mayor of Albany, 1886–88, 1896–98, he gave the city two clean, vigorous, business administrations. He was named by President Harrison a member of the World's Columbian Exposition Commission, and became chairman of the committee of awards. Governor Hill made him a member of the analogous New York State Commission. In 1896, Thacher, always a Democrat, was nominated by that party for the governorship of New York, but he roused the indignant wrath of most of his political colleagues by declining to run on a free-silver platform with which he was distinctly out of sympathy.

Thacher was a singularly active and versatile man, indefatigable in advancing the interests and welfare of the capital district. As senator he vigorously sponsored laws for prison and housing reforms; he was influential in financing a new capitol building; and against party advice and public criticism he carried through to adoption by the New York legislature and the federal Congress a measure restoring Ex-President Grant to the retired list of generals. During his first term as mayor, Albany celebrated her bicentennial anniversary, an affair which permitted Thacher to exploit all his zeal and enthusiasm as well as his interest in scholarship and historical research. The management of a successful winter carnival in February 1888, the procurement of a public market square, a much-needed public hall, and a new union station, were typical of his municipal achievements. A lasting memorial to his constant and generous thought for his community is the John Boyd Thacher Park, a scenic mountain and forest tract of 400 acres, which Mrs. Thacher, in fulfillment of her husband's plan and purpose, gave to the people of the state of New York in 1914.

Thacher's private life, as author and bibliophile, was equally fruitful and distinguished. A foremost and discriminating book collector, he assembled one of the two dozen existing complete sets of the signatures of the signers of the Declaration of Independence. His nearly nine hundred *incunabula* are a notable enrichment of the Library of Congress. He was long prominent as a Free Mason and gave an exceptional Masonic library to the Albany lodge. He left important collections on the French revolution and on Columbus and his voyages. As a writer, he made worthy contributions to early American history: *Christopher Columbus* (three volumes, 1903–04), *The Continent of America* (1896), and *The Cabotian Discovery* (1897). To a vivid, magnetic personality, there were joined in Thacher many lovable traits. He was simple and unaffected in behavior, quick in sympathy and unostentatious benevolence, a liberal patron of arts and letters, a genial, many-sided, and accomplished scholar.

[*Who's Who in America,* 1908–09; biographical sketch by F. W. Ashley and a bibliography of works in *Lib. of Cong. Cat. of the John Boyd Thacher Coll. of Incunabula* (1915); J. R. Totten, genealogical data on the Thacher-Thatcher family, *N. Y. Geneal. and Biog. Record,* Apr. 1910–July 1918; W. P. Boyd, *Hist. of the Boyd Family* (1912), p. 440; J. H. Manning, ed., *N. Y. State Men,* vol. VI (1912–15); *Albany Evening Jour.,* Feb. 25, 1909.]   J. I. W.

THACHER, PETER (July 18, 1651–Dec. 17, 1727), theologian, clergyman, was born in Salem, Mass. He was the youngest son of the Rev. Thomas Thacher, who came to America in 1635, and Eliza (Partridge) Thacher. A direct descendant of the first Peter Thacher to take the cloth in Sarum, England, during the time of the Puritan ascendancy, he inherited a tendency to the ministry. In 1671 he graduated from Harvard College, where his social position had been unusually advantageous owing to the friendship between his father and President Chauncy. After his graduation he became a tutor in the college, numbering Cotton Mather among his charges. On June 15, 1674, he was appointed a fellow. He appears to have extended his interests beyond theology, for contemporaries refer to his skill in medicine and civil law. During a visit to England in 1676 he manifested great interest in medical practice.

Upon his return he accepted a call to Barnstable, where he preached until invited to the Milton parish. He records in his journal how he was escorted out of Barnstable in September 1680 by fifty-seven horsemen, to make the journey to Milton; after nine months' trial he accepted the post and was installed on June 1, 1681. Here he continued until his death. His journal (printed in Teele, *post,* pp. 641–57), which was begun in Barnstable in 1679 and kept for the better part of three years, attests to his scholarship. He began each day by reading three chapters in the Greek version of the New Testament. On Nov. 21, 1677, he married Theodora, daughter of the Rev. John Oxenbridge, and by her had nine children. She died on Nov. 18, 1697, and on Dec. 25, 1699, he married Susannah, widow of the Rev. John Bailey (or Bayley). She bore him one son, and died in 1724. A few months before his own death he married a second cousin, Elizabeth (Thacher) Gee, widow of Joshua Gee, of Boston. That Thacher was prosperous is indicated by the disposal, in his will, of an unusually large number of slaves. His Milton home was built in an Indian cornfield, which later came to be known as "Thacher's Plain." He acquired enough knowledge of the Indian language to propagate the gospel among the natives in Milton and Ponkapoag. A further example of his missionary work is found in a *Letter,* published in 1721 in the form of a broadside (Harvard College Library), to procure funds for the erection of a church in Providence. Owing to his widespread activity he was proposed, in the draft of the college charter for 1723, as vice-president of Harvard under John Leverett, but failing health forced him to decline. After forty-six years of service as pastor of the Milton church, he died on Dec. 17, 1727.

In theological teaching, he followed the Calvinistic doctrine with slight modification. Among his sermons, *Unbelief Detected and Condemned* (1708) and *The Alsufficient Physician* (1711) best characterize the orthodoxy of his theological belief. To *A Sermon Occasioned by the Late Great Earthquake* (1728), by John Danforth, verses in memory of his brother, the Rev. Samuel Danforth, and Thacher are appended, characterizing them as

"Careful that Christ's Sheep should never feed
  On Arian, Popish, or Arminian Weed" (reprinted in Emery, *post*, I, 187–91).

Another pamphlet, entitled *An Essay Preached by Several Ministers of the Gospel . . . Concerning the Singing of Psalms* (1723), written by Thacher in collaboration with the Danforths, justifies psalm-singing in church, an important issue in Thacher's time. The authors defend the practice, but stipulate that "Irregular, Jarring, Disorderly Singing becomes not the House and Worship of God" (reprint in Emery, I, 272). Such scattered sermons as were published are scarcely representative testimony to the work of a preacher, who, although he lacked the luster of the succeeding Thachers, labored well in the Milton parish for nearly half a century.

[D. W. Allen, *Geneal. and Biog. Sketches of the Descendants of Thomas and Anthony Thacher* (1872); A. K. Teele, ed., *The Hist. of Milton, Mass., 1640 to 1887* (n.d.); *Register of Marriages in Milton, Mass., from the Diary of Rev. Peter Thacher, 1686–1727* (1883); "Harvard College Records," *Pubs. of the Colonial Soc. of Mass.,* vols. XV, XVI (1925); J. L. Sibley, *Biog. Sketches of Grads. of Harvard Univ.,* vol. II (1881), which quotes liberally from Cotton Mather, *The Comfortable Chambers Opened* (1727), a sermon delivered at Thacher's funeral; S. H. Emery, *The Ministry of Taunton* (2 vols., 1853); W. B. Sprague, *Annals of the Am. Pulpit,* vol. I (1857), pp. 196–97.]

                                        E. H. D.

THACHER, PETER (Mar. 21, 1752–Dec. 16, 1802), Congregational clergyman, was the eldest son of Oxenbridge Thacher, Jr., and Sarah (Kent) Thacher, and a great-grandson of the Rev. Peter Thacher, 1651–1727 [*q.v.*]. His father, who had given up the ministry to become a lawyer, represented Boston in the General Court and in 1764 defended Colonial rights in a publication entitled *The Sentiments of a British American* (Corey, *post,* p. 655). Peter was born in Milton, Mass., whither his parents had gone to escape the smallpox epidemic then raging in Boston. He received his early education in Master Lovell's school, and entered Harvard in 1766, where he was graduated with highest honors in 1769. For a few months after his graduation he was master of the Chelsea grammar school, at a salary of six pounds a quarter, but having preached for some months at the Congregational Church in Malden, Mass., he was ordained and installed as its pastor on Sept. 19, 1770. A few weeks later, Oct. 8, he married Elizabeth (Hawkes), widow of Zachariah Poole, by whom he had ten children. It is said of him that "his voice was peculiarly melodious,

and in his public devotions his fluency and fervor were so impressive, that he seldom failed to produce general admiration and applause" (Allen, *post,* p. 19). The theology of his early years seldom departed from Calvinism. He was among the few to be praised by George Whitefield, who referred to him in prayer as the "young Elijah" (Eliot, *post,* p. 280). As the years advanced, he became less rigid and more charitable to other denominations and beliefs, with the exception, perhaps, of the Episcopalians. He was one of those who opposed the coming of bishops to America, although he based his objections more on civil than ecclesiastical grounds.

Throughout the Revolution he was a zealous, outspoken champion of the cause of freedom. At the outbreak of hostilities he enlisted for military duty, but his services as an orator and adviser were in such great demand that he stayed behind. On Mar. 5, 1776, he gave an address in the Old South Church in Boston which awakened such enthusiasm that he was called to repeat it in Watertown in the afternoon. It was subsequently published under the title *An Oration Delivered at Watertown . . . to Commemorate the Bloody Massacre at Boston: Perpetrated March 5, 1770* (1776). Its spirit is indicated by the following extract: "The legislature of Great Britain is totally corrupt; her administration is arbitrary and tyrannical; the people have lost their spirit of resentment; and like the most contemptible of animals, *bow their shoulders to bear and become servants unto tribute.*" As a result of this address, the Provincial Congress declared that Thacher should have "beating orders," or a certificate which endowed him with recruiting powers, for the sea-coast defense of Massachusetts. He was also made chaplain to the General Court, a post which he held until his death. He has been credited (Corey, *post,* p. 765) with the authorship of the Malden resolutions to its General Court representative, which promised that if the Continental Congress declared America "to be a free & Independent Republick, your constituance will Support & Defend the measure to the last Drop of their Blood & the last Farthing of Their Treasure." That he penned these words, however, has not been definitely established. When a convention met in 1780 to form the Massachusetts constitution, Thacher was the Malden delegate. He was opposed to Massachusetts having a governor and later to his being given the title of "Excellency."

At his own request, he was dismissed from the Malden pulpit on Dec. 8, 1784, and on Jan.

12 of the following year was installed as pastor of the Brattle Street Church in Boston. The University of Edinburgh conferred the degree of D.D. upon him. In 1787 the Society for the Propagation of the Gospel among the Indians at Boston was incorporated by the Massachusetts General Court, and four years later Thacher became its secretary. He also served as secretary of the Society for Promoting Christian Knowledge. He was a trustee of the Humane Society, a member of the Charitable Fire Society and of the American Academy of Arts and Sciences, and a proprietor of the Town Library in Boston. In 1790 a group of five men under the informal direction of Jeremy Belknap [q.v.] met to form an historical society for Massachusetts. Thacher was one of this group, and when the Massachusetts Historical Society was formally instituted in 1791, he was influential in its origin and design, serving on its Select Committee until his death in 1802. In that year pulmonary tuberculosis forced him to seek a milder climate, and at his physician's order he sailed to Savannah, where, six weeks after leaving Boston, he died.

Between 1776 and 1800 he published twenty-two sermons, which included funeral eulogies for Governors James Bowdoin and Increase Sumner (1791, 1799), John Hancock (1793), and Washington (1800). His *Observations upon the Present State of the Clergy of New England* (1783), while ostensibly composed to deprecate the delayed payment of New England ministers, also gives renewed expression to his hatred of tyranny.

[For a list of Thacher's sermons, see William Emerson, *A Sermon on the Decease of the Rev. Peter Thacher, D.D.* (1803). Other sources include *A Report of the Record Commissioners . . . Containing the Boston Town Records, 1770–1777* (1887); A. M. Baldwin, *The New England Clergy and the Am. Revolution* (1928); *Proc. Mass. Hist. Soc.,* vol. I (1879); John Eliot, in *Mass. Hist. Soc. Colls.,* 1 ser., vol. VIII (1802); *New England Hist. and Geaneal. Reg.,* Apr. 1854; D. W. Allen, *Geneal. and Biog. Sketches of the Descendants of Thomas and Anthony Thacher* (1872); D. P. Corey, *The Hist. of Malden* (1889); W. B. Sprague, *Annals of the Am. Pulpit,* vol. I (1857); S. K. Lothrop, *A Hist. of the Church in Brattle Street* (1851).]   E. H. D.

THACHER, SAMUEL COOPER (Dec. 14, 1785–Jan. 2, 1818), theologian, author, was born in Boston, the sixth son of Peter Thacher, 1752–1802 [q.v.], and Elizabeth (Hawkes), widow of Zachariah Poole. From the Public Latin School he went to Harvard in 1800, and was graduated with highest honors in 1804. The most important influence in his early life was the friendship and tutelage of William Ellery Channing [q.v.]. After his graduation, he began to teach. In 1805 he was the acting headmaster of the

Latin School and would probably have continued happily in that position had not the illness of his close friend, the Rev. Joseph Stevens Buckminster [q.v.] of the Brattle Street Church, Boston, intervened. Buckminster, who suffered from epilepsy, was ordered abroad by his physicians, and as he needed a companion-nurse, Thacher volunteered to accompany him. The two spent the greater part of 1806 in Europe. Thacher's letters during this trip are of general interest. Paris he found "the centre of . . . everything but goodness"; at St. Cloud he had a sight of Napoleon. Traveling in desultory fashion, he visited many libraries and universities on the Continent.

In 1808 he became librarian of Harvard College. John T. Kirkland [q.v.], pastor of the New South Church in Boston, was called to the presidency of the College in 1810, and although Thacher had not been prominent as a theologian, his interest in theology and his wide knowledge of the subject brought about his nomination to the vacant pastorate. On May 15, 1811, he was formally installed. In his sermon on this occasion he voiced professedly Unitarian sentiments, expressing "a belief of the principles of natural religion, and a general acceptance of the truths of Christianity." Subsequently he developed the system of the single personality of God, and some of his discourses, notably *An Apology for Rational and Evangelical Christianity* (1815) and *The Unity of God* (Liverpool 1816, Boston 1817), are among the ablest sermonic defenses of Unitarianism which up to that time had appeared in America. He had inherited tubercular tendencies, and from 1814 until his death, his work was constantly impeded by ill health. At the request of his parishioners he went to England to consult the King's physician in 1815, never to return. After a brief rally he had a series of hemorrhages and the physician dispatched him immediately to Capetown. Here he found that some of his speculations on the dignity of the human race had never received so severe a rebuke as when he looked in the face of a Hottentot (*Sermons,* "Memoir," pp. li–lii). Here, also, he failed to make a recovery. On June 25, 1817, he returned to London, after a stormy voyage of three and one-half months which robbed him of the little strength he had left. He was sent immediately to France, and on Jan. 2, 1818, died at Moulins.

He was a member of the Anthology Club, and made frequent contributions to the *Monthly Anthology,* which he edited from November 1805 to May 1806. With William E. Channing, Charles Lowell, and Joseph Tuckerman, he helped to found, in 1813, *The Christian Disciple* (later *The Christian Examiner*). He wrote a memoir of Joseph S. Buckminster, prefixed to the first collection of Buckminster's sermons (1814), and one of William Emerson (*Collections of the Massachusetts Historical Society*, 2 ser., vol. I, 1814). Among his other publications may be mentioned *On the Evidence Necessary to Establish the Doctrine of the Trinity* (1828), the substance of which, under a somewhat different title, was first appended to James Yates's *A Vindication of Unitarianism* (1816). A collection of Thacher's discourses, *Sermons ... with a Memoir by F. W. P. Greenwood*, appeared in 1824.

[In addition to the memoir of Thacher mentioned above and his writings, see D. W. Allen, *Geneal. and Biog. Sketches of the Descendants of Thomas and Anthony Thacher* (1872); G. W. Cooke, *Unitarianism in America* (1902); W. B. Sprague, *Annals of the Am. Unitarian Pulpit* (1865); S. A. Eliot, *Heralds of a Liberal Faith* (1910), vol. II.]   E. H. D.

THACHER, THOMAS ANTHONY (Jan. 11, 1815–Apr. 7, 1886), classicist, college administrator, was born in Hartford, Conn., the son of Peter and Anne (Parks) Thacher. His first American ancestor on his father's side was Thomas Thacher who emigrated from England to Massachusetts in 1635, and later became minister of the Old South Church in Boston; on his mother's side he was descended from the Rev. Thomas Buckingham of Saybrook, one of the founders of the Collegiate School of Connecticut, since known as Yale College. He had his preparatory training at the Hopkins Grammar School, Hartford, and graduated from Yale with the class of 1835. For a short time he held a temporary teaching position in New Canaan, Conn., and then went to a school in Georgia, which was later to become Oglethorpe University. In all he spent three years teaching in two academies in Georgia, returning to Yale College on Dec. 1, 1838, to take the position of tutor. He was appointed assistant professor of Latin and Greek in 1842 and one year later the title was restricted to Latin and he was given a year's leave of absence for study in Europe. This year was eventually extended to two years and from 1843 to 1845 he studied in Germany and Italy. While in Berlin he instructed the Crown Prince of Prussia, and his cousin, Prince Frederick Charles. Six years after his return to Yale he was made professor of Latin. He was long a trustee of Hopkins Grammar School in New Haven and for several years a member of the state board of education. He was on the committee for building the Yale Art School, serving with President Noah Porter and Professor Daniel C. Gilman [*qq.v.*]. On Sept. 16, 1846, he married Elizabeth Day, the daughter of President Jeremiah Day [*q.v.*] of Yale. She died on May 18, 1858, leaving five sons, and on Aug. 1, 1860, he married her cousin Elizabeth Baldwin Sherman, who with three sons and one daughter survived him. Both wives were granddaughters of Roger Sherman [*q.v.*].

Thacher was identified with Yale College more closely than any of his contemporaries. President Timothy Dwight (*post*, p. 352) said of him, "His influence with the Faculty and the Corporation equalled or even surpassed that of any other College officer." This extraordinary position was due not primarily to his scholarship, although he had the reputation of being a sound and thorough scholar, but to his keen interest and constant activity in the management of college affairs both faculty and undergraduate. Before the day of deans, Thacher did much of the work which a dean would perform today. He was known as one of the best disciplinarians that the college ever had and yet he retained the devotion and affection of undergraduates to an extraordinary degree. As an undergraduate he had been "exuberant in spirit," and one who was a student under him in Yale writes of "Tutor Thacher, the florid and fiery, of perpetual youth and enthusiasm." He and Prof. Theodore Dwight Woolsey [*q.v.*] were the first advocates at Yale of graduate instruction in non-technical fields and he himself was one of the first classicists to go abroad for the advancement of his scholarship. This scholarship was never very productive. He edited Cicero's *De Officiis* in 1850, and largely as a result of his work with Karl Zumpt in Berlin he published in 1871 *A Latin Grammar for the Use of Schools,* a translation of the work of Johan Nikolai Madvig. Aside from these productions, a few slight essays and book reviews in the *New Englander* comprise his professional output. A teacher always, rather than an investigator, he seems even to have had a slightly suspicious attitude toward those who gave too much time to research. Even in his teaching he was possibly too much of a disciplinarian and was sometimes thought to stick too rigorously to the grammar. To his work as administrator, Thacher brought exceptional qualifications and in this line lay his great achievements. As a teacher he contributed his share to the department's prestige while, with his strong convictions and fearless courage, his energy in raising and administering funds, his interest in people, his wide acquaintance with Yale alumni, and his devout and conscientious character, he played a larger rôle in the building of modern Yale than that of any one of his contemporaries.

[D. W. Allen, *Geneal. and Biog. Sketches of the Descendants of Thomas and Anthony Thacher* (1872); T. T. Sherman, *Sherman Geneal.* (1920); *Obit. Record, Grads. of Yale Coll.*, 1886; *Biog. and Hist. Record of the Class of 1835 in Yale Coll.* (1881); W. L. Kingsley, *Yale Coll.: A Sketch of Its Hist.* (1879); Timothy Dwight, *Memories of Yale Life and Men* (1903); J. L. Chamberlain, *Universities and Their Sons, Yale Univ.* (1900); Noah Porter, in *New Englander and Yale Review*, May 1886; *New Haven Evening Register*, Apr. 7, 1886; files in the secretary's office, Yale Univ.]   C. W. M—l.

THATCHER, BENJAMIN BUSSEY (Oct. 8, 1809–July 14, 1840), author, editor, and lawyer, was born at Warren, Knox County, Me. He was the son of Sarah (Brown) and Samuel Thatcher and a first cousin of Henry Knox Thatcher [*q.v.*]. His father, a graduate of Harvard and a descendant of Samuel Thatcher who was admitted freeman at Watertown, Mass., in May 1642, served as representative to the General Court of Massachusetts, as congressman, and as sheriff of Lincoln County, Me. Benjamin attended Warren Academy, of which his father was a founder, and in 1826 was graduated from Bowdoin College. After studying law in Boston, he was admitted to the bar, and nominally practised law until his death. His deepest interest was in writing, however, and perhaps his greatest mistake in life was "an overestimate of literature as a profession and source of reputation" (Cleaveland and Packard, *post*, p. 357). He became a prolific author, contributing critical articles and verse to the leading magazines, especially the *North American Review* and the *Essayist*. In 1833 he edited the *Colonizationist and Journal of Freedom*, the organ of the Young Men's Colonization Society, of which he was corresponding secretary. Upon the lecture platform he constantly urged that African colonization should be supported "as offering the most effectual and unexceptionable proposal for promoting the welfare . . . of our fellow-men now held in bondage" (*Colonizationist*, April 1833, p. 11). To further this project he wrote a *Memoir of Phillis Wheatley* (1834), and a *Memoir of S. Osgood Wright* (1834), the Liberian missionary. He strove continually to restrain the more extreme reformers in his society, and to prevent the colonizationists from being identified with William Lloyd Garrison [*q.v.*] and the abolitionists. In 1834 he abandoned the *Colonizationist* in the belief that a magazine was not an effective vehicle for his cause. Despite the failure of the American Colonization Society, his faith in the Liberian venture never wavered, and he increasingly devoted

more time and energy to the work of the local Massachusetts organization (*Colonizationist*, April 1834, pp. 357, 384). In 1836 he was forced to go abroad to recover his health. In England he contributed an article on "Atlantic Steam Navigation" to the *Quarterly Review* of June 1838—sufficient evidence of his reputation as an author—and on his return to America published in the reviews sketches of his travels, with intimate vignettes of eminent people whom he had visited. His health, never robust, became increasingly poor, and in 1840 he died, it is said, from overwork (Cleaveland and Packard, *post*, p. 357).

Thatcher was prominent in philanthropic work in Boston, and wrote occasional verse to aid charity. His "Prayer for the Blind," printed on a piece of satin (5″ x 8″), was widely sold for the benefit of the Institution for the Blind. He numbered most of the prominent authors of America among his friends. He was best known for his *Indian Biography* (2 vols., 1832), which received flattering comment in the journals (*North American Review*, April 1833, p. 472) and was the first work of its kind to seek accuracy of portrayal. In general, his writings were ephemeral, and have little interest for the present-day reader. Among his more important works are seven articles in the *North American Review*, the first of which appeared in April 1832; *Indian Traits* (2 vols., 1833), in Harper's Family Library; *Traits of the Tea Party* (1835); and *The Boston Book* (1837), a local literary anthology. He is said to have left an unpublished manuscript of his travels. His portrait, painted in England, now hangs in the Bowdoin Gallery.

[G. T. Little, *Geneal. and Family Hist. of the State of Me.* (1909), vol. III, pp. 1491–93; Nehemiah Cleaveland and A. S. Packard, *Hist. of Bowdoin Coll.* (1882); R. W. Griswold, *The Biog. Ann.* (1841); *Colonizationist and Jour. of Freedom*, Apr. 1833–Apr. 1834; obituaries in *Boston Daily Advertiser* and *Daily Atlas* (Boston), July 15, 1840.]   C. B—h.

THATCHER, GEORGE [See THACHER GEORGE, 1754–1824].

THATCHER, HENRY KNOX (May 26, 1806–Apr. 5, 1880), naval officer, was born at Thomaston, Me., at "Montpelier," the seat of his grandfather, Gen. Henry Knox [*q.v.*]. Descended from Deacon Samuel Thatcher, born in England, who was admitted freeman in Watertown, Mass., in 1642, he was the second of eight children of Ebenezer and Lucy Flucker (Knox) Thatcher and a first cousin of Benjamin B. Thatcher [*q.v.*]. His father was a lawyer and a graduate of Harvard. After attending the Boston schools, Henry was admitted, on July 1, 1822, as a cadet at the United States Military

Academy, West Point, where he remained less than a year. Preferring the navy, he was appointed midshipman, Mar. 4, 1823, and in September was ordered to the Washington navy yard to join the "mosquito fleet" of Commodore David Porter [q.v.], which was preparing to operate against the West India pirates. From 1824 to 1827 he was attached to the *United States* of the Pacific squadron, the flagship of Commodore Isaac Hull [q.v.].

Promoted passed midshipman on Mar. 23, 1829, while serving on board the *Independence,* stationed at the Boston navy yard, he made a cruise in the West Indies in 1831 as acting master of the *Erie* and in 1834 made a second cruise there as lieutenant of the *Falmouth,* a rank to which he had been promoted on Feb. 28, 1833. In 1839–41 he was attached to the *Brandywine* of the Mediterranean Squadron, and in 1847–50 to the *Jamestown* of the African Squadron. His shore assignments during this period were to the receiving ship *Ohio* and to duty as inspector at the Boston navy yard. In 1851–52 he commanded the storeship *Relief* of the Brazil Squadron and in 1854–55 he served as executive officer of the Naval Asylum, Philadelphia. When in the last-named year he was made commander, he was advanced eighty-seven numbers by reason of the Naval Efficiency Act of 1855. In 1857–59 he commanded the *Decatur* in the Pacific.

The outbreak of the Civil War found him serving as the executive officer of the Boston navy yard, from which office he was detached in November 1861 to take command of the corvette *Constellation,* fitting out at Portsmouth, N. H., for special duty in the Mediterranean. After his promotion as of July 16, 1862, to commodore, desiring active war service, he hastened home and on Aug. 26, 1863 was assigned to the *Colorado* of the North Atlantic blockading squadron. From December 1864 to January 1865 he commanded the first division of Admiral David D. Porter's fleet and for his attack on Fort Fisher, N. C., was highly commended by the admiral for his share in the Union victory. Appointed acting rear-admiral, he was ordered on Jan. 24, 1865 to take command of the West Gulf blockading squadron in succession to Admiral Farragut. Cooperating with the army in the reduction of Mobile, Thatcher on the surrender of that city pursued the Confederate fleet up the Tombigbee River and received its surrender, an operation for which he was congratulated by the Navy Department. Later his naval force took possession of Sabine Pass and the defenses of Galveston. On the consolidation of the two squadrons in the Gulf of Mexico, Thatcher commanded the combined fleet

known as the Gulf Squadron, with the *Estrella* as his flagship. From 1866 to 1868 he commanded the North Pacific Squadron, with the *Pensacola* as his flagship. Promoted rear-admiral from July 25, 1866, he was retired in that grade on May 26, 1868. In 1869–70 he was port admiral at Portsmouth, N. H.

Thatcher resided at Winchester, Mass., maintaining a summer home at Nahant. On Dec. 26, 1831 he had married Susan C. Croswell of Plymouth, Mass. He died of a disease of the kidneys at Boston, leaving an adopted daughter, the child of a sister, but no children of his own. In 1918 a torpedo-boat destroyer was named for him.

[Bureau of Navigation, Record of Officers, 1818–88; Navy Registers, 1824–68; G. H. Preble, *Henry Knox Thatcher* (1882), repr. from *New Eng. Hist. and Geneal. Reg.,* Jan. 1882; Henry Bond, *Geneals. of the Families and Descendants of the Early Settlers of Watertown, Mass.* (1860); Cyrus Eaton, *Hist. of Thomaston, . . . Me.* (1865), vols. I, II; *Boston Transcript,* Apr. 6, 1880; *Army and Navy Jour.,* Apr. 10, 1880; *Ann. Report of the Secretary of the Navy,* 1865; *Official Records of the Union and Confed. Navies in the War of the Rebellion,* vols. X, XI, XV, XX–XXII; J. T. Headley, *Farragut and Our Naval Commanders* (1866), pp. 426–34.]   C.O.P.

THATCHER, MAHLON DANIEL (Dec. 6, 1839–Feb. 22, 1916), a pioneer merchant, banker, and financier of Colorado, was the second and most widely known of three brothers who were all significant in the early history of that state. Like his brothers, he was born at New Buffalo, Perry County, Pa., a son of Henry and Lydia Ann (Albert) Thatcher. Their father had moved West from New Jersey to the Susquehanna, where he was successively a canal blacksmith, a school-teacher, and a storekeeper; their mother was the daughter of a Pennsylvania farmer of remote Swiss ancestry who had been also a justice of peace and a maker of "grandfather" clocks. The family migrated further westward gradually, following the developing railroads, and the boys received their education in the schools and academies of a succession of Western Pennsylvania towns. The eldest brother, John Albert Thatcher (Aug. 25, 1836–Aug. 14, 1913), set out for Missouri at the age of twenty-one, and in 1862, with a partner and a stock of merchandise, drove across the plains from Nebraska City, Neb., to Denver, Colo. The following year he opened the first general store in Pueblo, then a village of frame and adobe buildings, eight days by wagon south of Denver and hundreds of miles from the nearest railroad. Mahlon joined him here in 1865; for some time he had been a partner in his father's store at Martinsburg, Pa., and when he started West he invested $2,900, the proceeds of the sale of his interest in that business, in a stock of goods bought in Philadelphia, New

York, and Boston. A year later Frank G. Bloom, another clerk from Henry Thatcher's store, settled in Trinidad, Col., where he became a lieutenant of the Thatchers and married their sister, Sarah.

Under the style of "Thatcher Brothers, Merchants," the brothers built up a lasting reputation for honesty and reliability. Gradually, the safe in their store at Pueblo became a repository for funds of cattlemen and miners. In 1871, as "Thatcher Brothers, Bankers," they transferred the banking part of their growing business to a new brick building. Mahlon Thatcher now made a trip to Washington and obtained a charter (1871) for the First National Bank of Pueblo, providing a capital of $50,000. This bank became his chief interest, and he was president from 1889 until his death. John, meanwhile, conducted the outdoor part of their joint activities, especially the cattle and horse ventures in which they were involved. Talking and trading horses with ranchers and miners, he gathered the gossip about men's business and credit. He was known personally to more people than his brother and was popular, while Mahlon was taciturn and less approachable. The reputation of both was that of shrewd dealers, but of established honesty; they kept out of politics and out of lawsuits. They were equal partners in all their principal ventures, including the bank.

Despite the loss and suffering of the critical winter of 1878–79 and the panic of 1893 which paralyzed most western communities, the Thatchers accumulated large fortunes. Their cattle and horse enterprises came to include immense ranches in New Mexico, Colorado, South Dakota, and Canada. In 1911, on the death of David H. Moffat [q.v.], Mahlon took over control of the First National Bank of Denver, the largest bank of the state; he also operated an important trust company in Denver, controlled two Pueblo banks besides the parent institution, and banks in at least six other Colorado cities. His holdings spread ultimately to nearly forty banks. He was heavily interested in electric power in California, beet-sugar manufacturing on a large scale, cement, firebrick, smelting, and sometimes in mining. He built a huge house, "Hill Crest," set beside his brother's "Rosemount" on the highest hill in Pueblo. At his death in 1916 he was perhaps the most important banker in the mountain states and a national financial figure. On Aug. 1, 1876, he had married Luna Ada Jordan of Pueblo, who bore him six children; a son and three daughters survived him. John's death had come three years before. Their sons succeeded them in the chief institutions.

Mahlon and John Thatcher were conspicuous leaders in the period of the "empire builders" in the mountain states. Their wealth became greater and was more stable than in the case of most such leaders, their influence was more permanent in finance, but their public and civic activities were less notable. The youngest brother, however, Henry Calvin Thatcher (Apr. 21, 1842–Mar. 20, 1884), who in 1866 opened a law office in Pueblo, was an important member of the state constitutional convention of 1876 and in that year was elected on the Republican ticket one of the three judges of the first state supreme court. He drew by lot the shortest of the terms and by virtue of this fact became chief justice, in which office he served three years.

[H. H. Hain, *Hist. of Perry County, Pa.* (1922); W. F. Stone, *Hist. of Colorado,* vols. II, III (1918); Frank Hall, *Hist. of the State of Colorado,* vol. IV (1895); *Hist. of Colorado* (1927), vol. V, "Biographical"; *Who's Who in America,* 1914–15; and for H. C. Thatcher, *7 Colorado Reports,* xvii, and *Denver Republican,* Mar. 21, 1884; obituaries of John and Mahlon, respectively, in *Rocky Mountain News* (Denver), Aug. 15, 1913, and Feb. 23, 1916; *Denver Post,* Aug. 15, 1913, Feb. 23, 1916; *Denver Tribune,* Mar. 21, 1884, and *Pueblo Chieftain,* Aug. 15, 1913, Feb. 23, 1916.]

J. G. R—s.

THATCHER, ROSCOE WILFRED (Oct. 5, 1872–Dec. 6, 1933), agricultural chemist, experiment station director, and college president, was born on a farm at Chatham Center, Ohio, the son of Charles Phelps and Lida Elizabeth (Parkard) Thatcher. His parents moved to Nebraska in 1885 and settled on a prairie farm near Gibbon. In 1892 he entered the University of Nebraska, where he worked his way through the preparatory and collegiate departments. After receiving the degree of B.S. in chemistry in 1898, he taught in a high school for a year, spent two years as assistant chemist at the Nebraska agricultural experiment station, and then accepted a similar position at the Washington State Agricultural Experiment Station, where he later served as chief chemist (1903–07) and as director (1907–13). During the latter period he was also professor of agricultural chemistry at the State College of Washington. During his connection with the Washington station he published in its bulletins a number of important papers upon the chemistry of forage crops, insecticides, soils, fertilizers, and upon the composition and milling properties of Washington wheats. From 1913 to 1917 he served as professor of plant chemistry in the University of Minnesota. In 1917 he was appointed dean of the School of Agriculture and director of the Minnesota experiment station. During this period he reorganized and greatly strengthened the department of agricultural chemistry at the University; at the same time he conducted researches upon forage and cereal crops, insecticides, apples, and dairy products. In 1921 he became director of the New York agricultural experiment station at Geneva, and in 1923 director of the Geneva and Cornell agricultural stations, which were united at that time. In 1924–25 he served as a member of the conference on agricultural legislation called by President Calvin Coolidge. His broad interests in agronomy, organization of agricultural research, and agricultural education induced him to accept in 1927 the presidency of the Massachusetts Agricultural College at Amherst, which in 1931 became the Massachusetts State College. He discharged the administrative duties of this position with great ability. He instituted a new system of freshman dormitories, made important revisions in the curriculum of studies, enlarged opportunities for staff members to do post-graduate study, and entered upon a five-year building program of remodeling and construction which he did not live to carry through to completion. His health, which on previous occasions had shown signs of breaking, had become seriously impaired, and after a temporary leave of absence he was finally obliged in 1932 to resign the presidency of the college. Following a period of rest he resumed his connection with the college in April 1933 as research professor of agricultural chemistry. He began a study of the rôle of the lesser known chemical elements in plant growth, but his work was cut short by an attack of cerebral hemorrhage from which he died in his laboratory on Dec. 6, 1933. He was survived by his wife, Nellie Elizabeth Fulmer of Gibbon, Neb., whom he had married on Aug. 25, 1896, and one daughter.

Thatcher's wide experience in all branches of agricultural chemistry together with his rare gifts as an administrator and organizer made him a leader in the fields of agricultural research and education. He was the author of many bulletins, addresses, and reports. In 1921 he published his *Chemistry of Plant Life*. He was president of the American Society of Agronomy in 1912, of whose *Journal* he was assistant editor from 1913 to 1919, and editor from 1920 to 1927. He was president of the American Society for the Promotion of Agricultural Science in 1919. His reports as chairman of the committee on experiment station organization and policy (1921–23), and as a member of the committee on publication of research for the Association of Land Grant Colleges were most valuable. He was a fellow of the American Association for the Advancement of Science and a member of the American Chemical Society, serving the latter

as chairman of the committee in charge of the Frasch bequest for agricultural research.

[*Who's Who in America*, 1932–33; *Bull. Mass. Agricultural Experiment Station*, Mar. 1934; *Experiment Station Record*, Mar. 1934; *Jour. Am. Soc. of Agronomy*, Dec. 1933; *School and Society*, Dec. 16, 1933; *Mass. Collegian*, Dec. 7, 1933; obituary in *Evening Star* (Washington, D. C.), Dec. 7, 1933.]   C. A. B.

THAW, WILLIAM (Oct. 12, 1818–Aug. 17, 1889), capitalist, philanthropist, was born in Pittsburgh, Pa. His parents, John and Elizabeth (Thomas) Thaw, were natives of Philadelphia and his father was of Scotch-English and Quaker ancestry. John Thaw had removed to Pittsburgh in 1804 to take a position as chief clerk in the Pittsburgh branch of the Bank of Pennsylvania at Philadelphia. William attended the local schools and the Western University of Pennsylvania (now the University of Pittsburgh). At sixteen he traveled through the Ohio Valley on horseback making collections for the Bank of the United States, and thereafter the improvement of transportation facilities was a dominant interest in his career. In 1835 he was employed in the forwarding and commission house of McKee, Clarke & Company and in 1840 he went into partnership with Thomas S. Clarke, his brother-in-law.

The firm of Clarke & Thaw took over the Pennsylvania & Ohio Canal Line and did a large business in receiving and forwarding merchandise by river and canal. Between 1840 and 1859 Thaw had interests in over 150 steamboats operating on various lines, the most famous of which was the Pittsburgh & Cincinnati Packet Line. Realizing the futility of attempting to compete with transportation by rail, he and his partner disposed of the canal line in 1855. The following year he joined the firm of Leech & Company, freight agents of the Pennsylvania Railroad Company, and in 1857 he and Clarke formed the firm of Clarke & Company to take charge of the freight business west of Pittsburgh. He had a large share in promoting the rapid extension of the railroad to St. Louis, which proved a definite advantage to Northern interests during the Civil War. Having helped to devise the first system of through freight transportation over different lines, he took charge in 1864 of the resultant Union Line, later the Star Union Line, and managed it until 1873, when he turned his attention to the internal and financial affairs of the Pennsylvania Railroad Company, of which he served as director from 1881 to 1889. In 1871 he was elected vice-president of the Pennsylvania Company, a corporation chartered in 1870 to manage the lines controlled by the Pennsylvania Railroad Company north and west of Pittsburgh, and of the Pittsburgh, Cincinnati & St. Louis Railway Company; in 1884 he was made a vice-president of the Chicago, St. Louis & Pittsburgh Railroad Company. He also served as director of the Atlantic & Pacific Ship-Railway Company and of the International Navigation Company, in connection with which he furthered the establishment of the Red Star Line. His fortune, estimated at between eight and twelve million dollars, was invested largely in railroad holdings and transportation companies and in coal lands in Westmoreland and Fayette counties, Pennsylvania.

Thaw's wide interests and philanthropic activities made him a force in his community. He avoided publicity and ostentation, but he gave largely to charity organizations, churches, and individuals, and to schools in various parts of the country. One of his chief concerns was to make Pittsburgh an educational center; to further this end he devoted time and money to the Western University of Pennsylvania. Motivated by a desire to advance the frontiers of knowledge, he substantially supported Samuel Pierpont Langley [q.v.] in his work at the Allegheny Observatory, his scientific expedition to California in 1881, and his study of the laws governing flight. He also gave financial aid to John A. Brashear [q.v.]. In 1841 he married Eliza Burd Blair of Washington, Pa., who died in 1863, and in 1867 he married Mary Sibbet Copley of Pittsburgh. He was over the average in height and had an unusual combination of mental and physical powers and great force of character. Survived by ten children—five by each marriage—he died in Paris, France, of a heart attack.

[Thaw Papers in the Hist. Soc. of Western Pa.; *In Memoriam William Thaw* (1891); *William Thaw, a Biog. Sketch* (1911); *Encyc. of Contemporary Biog. of Pa.*, vol. I (1889); George Reed, *Century Cyc. of Hist. and Biog. of Pa.* (1904), vol. I; H. W. Schotter, *The Growth and Development of the Pa. Railroad Company* (1927); *The Pa. Company: Charter with Supplements* (printed for the officials), vol. I (1875); *Pittsburgh Chronicle Telegraph*, Aug. 17, *Pittsburgh Post*, Aug. 19, *Pittsburgh Commercial Gazette*, Aug. 19, 31, *Presbyterian Banner*, Aug. 21, and *Harper's Weekly*, Sept. 7, 1889; *Pittsburgh Leader*, Dec. 12, 1886; *Mag. of Western Hist.*, Oct. 1885; *Gazette Times* (Pittsburgh), Oct. 21, 28, 1917.]   S. J. B.

THAXTER, CELIA LAIGHTON (June 29, 1835–Aug. 26, 1894), poet, was born in Portsmouth, N. H., the daughter of Thomas B. and Eliza (Rymes) Laighton. Her father, a descendant of one of the oldest Portsmouth families, was a successful dealer in lumber and West India goods, editor of the *New-Hampshire Gazette,* and a member of the state legislature. Disappointed in his expectation of being elected to the governorship, he had himself appointed keeper of the lighthouse at the Isles of Shoals,

and in October 1839 removed with his wife and children to the keeper's cottage on White Island, determined never again to set foot on the mainland. Except for the decayed fishing village of Gosport on Star Island, the Shoals were practically uninhabited when the Laightons came. Celia and her two younger brothers had no playmates but sky and ocean. Their education, however, was carried on by their parents with the assistance of chance visitors such as John Weiss and Levi Lincoln Thaxter. The latter spent an entire winter at the lighthouse as tutor to the lonely children. The long seclusion of the family was broken in 1848 when Laighton opened a summer hotel on Appledore Island, the first of its kind on the Atlantic coast. It soon attracted many visitors, including among the earliest Lowell and Henry David Thoreau, and became noted as the summer haunt of artists and men of letters. The poet Whittier and the painters William Morris Hunt [qq.v.] and Childe Hassam, among many others, were constant visitors and close friends of the Laightons.

Meanwhile Thaxter had spent a second winter at the Shoals and had fallen in love with his pupil. With her parents' consent Celia was married at Appledore on Sept. 30, 1851. For some time she continued to live with her family, while her husband occupied himself with the pastoral care of the fisher-folk on Star Island and the study of Browning's poetry, his lifelong passion. Three sons were born in the course of seven years, the eldest a mental defective who required his mother's care for the remainder of her life. The youngest son, Roland Thaxter [q.v.], became a professor of botany at Harvard. About 1860 the Thaxters removed to Newtonville, Mass. In her inland surroundings Mrs. Thaxter pined for the sea; a poem expressing her homesickness reached Lowell's hands through the mediation of a friend and without the author's knowledge appeared in the *Atlantic Monthly* for March 1861 with the title "Land-Locked." Thereafter Mrs. Thaxter was a frequent contributor of poems, sketches, and children's stories to various magazines. Her first volume, *Poems* (1872), was followed by the notable prose sketches called *Among the Isles of Shoals* (1873), which had appeared serially in the *Atlantic.* Later, among others, came *Drift-Weed* (1879), *Poems for Children* (1884), *Idyls and Pastorals* (1886), and *An Island Garden* (1894), with illustrations by Childe Hassam.

The death of her father in 1866 brought Mrs. Thaxter back to Appledore to care for her mother, who survived until 1877. Her two brothers continued to manage the hotel, and Mrs. Thaxter spent at least a part of each year in a nearby cottage. Her garden was famous for its splendor of poppies, and her living-room became a salon where the finer spirits of the summer colony delighted to gather. Her spontaneous appreciation of poetry and painting, her deep passion for music, and her childlike joy in nature endeared her to many friends. In 1880 the Thaxters moved to Kittery Point, Me., and in the autumn of the same year Mrs. Thaxter visited Europe, met Robert Browning, and indulged herself in a long rapture of picture-galleries and concerts. At home once more she settled into the quiet routine of a literary life, spending the summers at the Shoals and the winters in Boston or Portsmouth. Her husband died in 1884 and was honored by an epitaph from his favorite poet. Ten years later Mrs. Thaxter died suddenly at Appledore and was buried there. In 1895 a selection from her letters, *Letters of Celia Thaxter,* was edited by her friends Annie Adams Fields [*q.v.*] and Rose Lamb, who also prepared the final edition of her *Poems* (1896).

[The date of birth is from the Laighton family Bible; the date of marriage from the town records of Kittery, Me. See *Rymes Geneal.: Samuel Rymes of Portsmouth, N. H., and His Descendants* (1897) ; Oscar Laighton, *Ninety Years at the Isles of Shoals* (1930) ; Annie Fields, *Authors and Friends* (1896) ; Aubertine W. Moore, "The Story of the Isles of Shoals," *New England Mag.,* July 1898; John Albee, *Ibid.,* Apr. 1901; Celia Thaxter, *The Heavenly Guest* (1935), which contains recollections by various friends; *Appletons' Ann. Cyc.,* 1894; obituary in *N. Y. Times,* Aug. 28, 1894.] G. F. W.

THAXTER, ROLAND (Aug. 28, 1858–Apr. 22, 1932), botanist, was born in Newtonville, Mass., the youngest son of Levi Lincoln Thaxter, lawyer, scholar, authority on the work of Robert Browning, and Celia (Laighton) Thaxter [*q.v.*], and a descendant of Thomas Thaxter of Hingham, Mass. He attended the Boston Latin School, the private school of Joshua Kendall in Cambridge, and was graduated from Harvard in 1882 with A.B. degree, *magna cum laude*. Although interested chiefly in botany and entomology, he started work at the Harvard Medical School in 1883, but after one year, through receiving the Harris fellowship, he was enabled to enter the Graduate School of Arts and Sciences, where he concentrated on cryptogamic botany under William G. Farlow [*q.v.*], published the first of his famous mycologic papers, and received in 1888 the degrees of M.A. and Ph.D. On June 8, 1887, he was married to Mabel Gray Freeman of Springfield, Mass. With their four children, they made up an unusually congenial family; it was the great sorrow of Thaxter's life that his eldest son died in the flower of his youth.

Thaxter's first position, as mycologist at the

Connecticut Agricultural Experiment Station, led him into the practical field of mycology in relation to agriculture and, although he was primarily interested in pure research, his contributions to plant pathology were numerous and valuable. In 1891, he returned to Harvard as assistant professor of cryptogamic botany under Professor Farlow; in 1896 he assumed the full responsibilities of teaching and research in this field; in 1901 he was made full professor; and in 1919, at his own request, he was retired from active academic work, became professor emeritus, and devoted himself to his own research and to the administration as honorary curator of the Farlow Herbarium and Library. During his forty years of teaching, nearly one thousand students passed through his courses or worked under his guidance toward higher degrees. A thorough and exacting teacher, his training left a lasting impression even upon men who went no further in scientific fields. By transmitting his knowledge, ideals, and methods to a large number of younger men, he developed, in a sense, a school which has contributed notably to the progress of botany.

It is for his research, however, that he is renowned. His greatest work is his *Contribution Towards a Monograph of the Laboulbeniaceae,* which appeared as *Memoirs of the American Academy of Arts and Sciences* (5 volumes, 1896–1931), and stands out as one of the greatest single pieces of work in the whole field of mycology. Had he never published another paper this monograph would have gained him preeminence. Yet in addition, in more than eighty papers, shorter but of similar excellence, he added notably to our knowledge of the structure, development, and relationship of each of the major groups of fungi. He traveled widely in the course of his investigations, studying fungi intensively in many tropical as well as temperate regions, and as a result his familiarity with the fungi, not only as laboratory specimens but also as living organisms in their habitats, was phenomenal. Without question he had the widest and yet most intimately detailed knowledge of the fungi of any mycologist of his time.

He was a fellow of the American Academy of Arts and Sciences, the American Philosophical Society, the National Academy of Sciences, Phi Beta Kappa, the American Association for the Advancement of Science, and other learned or technical societies. He served as president of the New England Botanical Club, the American Mycological Society, and the Botanical Society of America. He was an honorary member of the Russian Mycological Society, the Linnean Societies of London and of Lyons, the Royal Botanical Society of Belgium, the Royal Academies of Sweden and of Denmark, the Botanical Society of Edinburgh, and the Academy of Science of the Institute of France. He was the only American botanist of his time on whom honorary membership was conferred by the British Mycological Society and the Deutsche Botanische Gesellschaft. From 1907 until his death he was the American editor of the *Annals of Botany*. In recognition of his earlier work on the *laboulbeniales* he was awarded the *Prix Desmazières* by the French Academy.

Tall, well built, of great dignity, poise, and self-restraint, austere, devoted to his work, yet with a dry sense of humor and a reserved kindliness, he had a keen appreciation of beauty, was an accomplished musician, a scholarly and discriminating reader, an unequaled draughtsman of exquisite, accurate botanical illustrations. His death was a severe loss to botany.

[*Who's Who in America*, 1932–33; J. M. and Jaques Cattell, ed., *Am. Men of Sci.* (4th ed., 1927); W. H. Weston, biographical notes in *Mycologia*, Mar.–Apr. 1933, in *Phytopathology*, July 1933, and in the *Berichte der Deutsche Botanische Gesellschaft* (in press); G. P. Clinton, in *Proc. Am. Acad. Arts and Sciences*, vol. LXVIII (1933); *Class of 1882, Harvard Coll., 7th Report of the Secretary*. The human and delightful narrative of Thaxter's uncle, Oscar Laighton, *Ninety Years at the Isles of Shoals* (1930), yields revealing glimpses of Thaxter's parents. See also death notice in *Boston Evening Transcript*, Apr. 23, 1932.]

W. H. W., Jr.

THAYER, ABBOTT HANDERSON (Aug. 12, 1849–May 29, 1921), painter, was born in Boston, Mass., the son of Dr. William Henry and Ellen (Handerson) Thayer. The American progenitor of the family was Thomas Thayer, an early settler of Braintree, Mass. Dr. Thayer was a Harvard graduate, an army surgeon during the Civil War, a lecturer at Vermont Medical College, and a practitioner at Keene, N. H., and later in Brooklyn, N. Y. Abbott Thayer lived in the country near Keene until he was about eighteen years old, with a three-year period (1863–66) at the Chauncy-Hall School in Dorchester, Mass., established by his paternal grandfather, Gideon French Thayer [*q.v.*]. From an early age he drew and painted birds, dogs, and horses, and the animals of the menageries he frequented. He is said, in fact, to have made something of a profession of canine and equine portraiture, charging from ten to fifty dollars apiece before his school days were over. After some informal art instruction in Dorchester, he attended the classes of H. D. Morse in Boston, of J. B. Whittaker in Brooklyn, and of L. E. Wilmarth in New York. By 1869 he had opened a studio in Brooklyn. On June 5, 1875, he married Kate Bloede of Brooklyn, and left for Paris with the intention of specializing in animal painting. After a short period at the École des Beaux-Arts in the Lehmann studio, however, he entered the atelier of Jean Léon Gérôme, and gradually turned his attention to portraits and figure painting, with occasional landscapes. Returning to America in 1879, he opened a studio in New York, was chosen president of the young Society of American Artists, and for the next ten years or more lived in the Hudson River towns, going to New Hampshire for the summer vacations. Two daughters and a son were born to the Thayers, and they with Mrs. Thayer became admirable models. Thayer was elected an Academician in 1901, and in 1909 became a member of the American Academy of Arts and Letters. He won numerous important prizes—among them gold medals at the Pennsylvania Academy of the Fine Arts (1891), at Paris (1900), at the Pan-American Exposition, Buffalo (1901), and at the Carnegie Institute, Pittsburgh (1920); the Elkins Prize, Pennsylvania Academy (1895), the Thomas B. Clarke Prize, National Academy (1898), and the Saltus Medal, National Academy (1915). When mental illness blighted the career of his wife, Thayer's whole outward life changed. After her death he married, on Sept. 3, 1891, her close friend Emeline B. Beach of Peekskill, N. Y. About 1901 he moved to New Hampshire, where he lived at the foot of Mount Monadnock and became more and more hermit-like in his habits, his communion with nature for long hours expressing itself in his growing interest in the coloration of animals. During his later career he made three trips to Europe. He died at Monadnock, his ashes being cast from the top of the mountain he had loved and painted so grandly. Memorial exhibitions of his works were held at the Metropolitan Museum, New York, at the Corcoran Art Gallery, Washington, and the Carnegie Institute, Pittsburgh, and of his coloration models at the Brooklyn Museum.

Thayer's paintings are varied in subject and in technique, with the ideal figures and landscapes supplying the masterpieces. "Caritas" in the Boston Museum of Fine Arts, "Virgin Enthroned" and "Angel," Gellatly Collection, and "Virgin" in the Freer Collection, Washington, represent the first group; "Winter Sunrise, Monadnock," Metropolitan Museum, dominates the second. The boy's head from the "Virgin Enthroned" is probably unsurpassed. The serene magnificence of "Figure—Half Draped" in the Gellatly Collection, from the New York studio days and long forgotten; "Roses," in the Worcester Museum; the "Lady in Green Velvet," in the Addison Gallery, Andover, Mass.; the promising mural, "Florence Protecting the Arts," at Bowdoin College; "Capri," in the Freer Collection, and the Stevenson memorial in the Albright Art Gallery, Buffalo, also demand listing. Worthy of note, too, are the earliest "Winged Figure" at Smith College, the startling sincerity of the "Self-Portrait" at the Corcoran Gallery, the "Baby Asleep," Thayer's own favorite "Boy and Angel," the "Mary," where a light blue strip in the background is inexplicable but absolutely right, and the "Seated Angel" of the Freer Collection, with its haunting dedication to Kate Bloede Thayer.

Like Thomas Dewing, Thayer idealized women; like Winslow Homer [q.v.] he realized his figures on canvas directly and sincerely. Unlike many of his contemporaries, however, he was free from the control of French technique. Originality was the very basis of his style. With an almost mystic consciousness of his mission he felt compelled to make visible the beauty of spirit he saw in the person, in the natural object—such qualities as dominating purity or love of truth that demanded a painter's interpretation. To gain monumentality he exaggerated light and shadow, and placed his colors in large, simple masses. His color range was limited—dark green, wine, pure blue, and purple, usually resolved into white. The whites—sometimes luminous, sometimes flat, but always suggestive— are as essentially part of Thayer's vision as the wings of his humane angels. The sense of outside guidance under which he worked may also explain the lack of finish so often met with in his pictures. He painted until he said as well as he could what he had to say; then he stopped. (His article, " 'Restoration'; the Doom of Pictures and Sculpture," in *International Studio,* March 1920, is a vigorous expression of his objection to any modification by others of work which has left an artist's hands as finished.) Yet "Passenger Pigeons" illustrates the perfection of finish he could achieve when he cared to, and the sculpturesque rather than fabricated drapery of his figures, with its value relation to the head the essence of its perfection, indicates how far he was willing to go to express rather than to exploit. His letters, with their molten, illuminating metaphors, make clear that his personality was not that of the eccentric, much less that of the poseur, but that of one whose utter sincerity knew only originality.

Thayer's experiments in the protective coloration of animals dominated a large part of his later career. The essential theory of "Thayer's Law," as it came to be known, was that "animals are painted by nature darkest on those parts which tend to be most lighted by the sky's light, and vice versa" (*Annual Report . . . of the Smithsonian Institution . . . 1897,* 1898, p. 477), the upper colors, when seen from below, tending to disappear in the blue of the sky, the lower in the brown of the earth. In addition to writing articles on the subject which appeared in *Popular Science Monthly,* December 1909 and July 1911, and in the *Scientific Monthly,* December 1918, Thayer made many illustrations for *Concealing-Coloration in the Animal Kingdom* (1909), an exposition of his theories written by his son, Gerald H. Thayer. The interested public varied in its reception of the theory, to Thayer absolutely irrefutable. On one side was such a voluble critic as Theodore Roosevelt, who, with more vigor than acumen, denied the validity of the whole point of view. On the other side were an increasing number of naturalists who realized the fundamental significance of the discoveries, but thought Thayer went too far in his belief that the new theories largely replaced those of mimicry and of warning colors. The application of Thayer's law to camouflage devices in the World War is a matter still controverted, but there is little doubt that England, France, and Germany studied *Concealing-Coloration* in an effort to devise ways of concealing arms and movements, and that his theories had a general influence upon the designs used. Another aspect of his interest in the study of animals is seen in the Thayer Fund, raised through a period of years to protect seabirds of the Atlantic coast. These efforts at protection led to the passing of Audubon laws by eleven states, and were influential in the organization of the National Association of Audubon Societies. More poetically, one likes to speculate on the lover of sea-gulls who was fond of providing his figures with wings.

To those who knew and loved the man, he was primarily a great soul; Dewing and George De Forest Brush among the painters, George Grey Barnard and Daniel Chester French among the sculptors, and a whole company of young people, among them Rockwell Kent, William James, Louis Agassiz Fuertes [q.v.] and Richard S. Meryman, testify to one effect. French wrote Mrs. Thayer at the death of his friend, "A soul the like of which I believe does not exist on earth has flown . . ." A country minister found the man who hated both clergymen and undertakers strangely Christlike. Thayer continually expressed himself with unconscious kindliness, generosity, and humor, and he was a man who attracted worshippers. He loved the primitive, he adored Stevenson and the old sagas, he cared nothing for outward comforts, he knew all weathers. He collected bird feathers and anything which seemed to him beautiful. He was of slight build, of nervous temperament, penetrating in his glance, with a voice of fine timbre. He was marked above all by an earnestness, a passion for beauty which could reveal the strength of womanhood, the hush of the angelic, or the mysterious assurance of a mountain mass lit by the rising sun. He was always the crusader—always intense, always awkward, always followed. In a day when sentiment is taboo in painting, the sincerity of the man disarms the critic.

[The chief center for the study of Thayer's work is Washington, D. C., where he is admirably represented in the Freer Coll., the Nat. Gallery of Art, to which the Gellatly Coll. was bequeathed, and the Corcoran Gallery of Art. For biog. and crit. material see *Who's Who in America*, 1920–21; Nathaniel Pousette-Dart, *Abbott H. Thayer* (1932), with bibliog.; E. H. Blashfield, *Commemorative Tribute to Abbott Handerson Thayer* (1922); cats. of the memorial exhibitions at the Metropolitan Museum of Art, N. Y., the Corcoran Gallery (1922), and the Brooklyn Museum (1922), and of the exhibition at the Carnegie Institute (1919); Royal Cortissoz, *Am. Artists* (1923), Samuel Isham, *The Hist. of Am. Painting* (1927 ed.); Suzanne La Follette, *Art in America* (1929); Catherine B. Ely, in *Art in America*, Feb. 1924; Maria O. Dewing, in *Internat. Studio*, Aug. 1921; Homer Saint-Gaudens, *Ibid.*, Jan. 1908; memorial issue, *Arts*, June–July 1921; and obituary in *N. Y. Times*, May 30, 1921. Other information has been supplied by R. S. Meryman. The line of Thayer's descent is shown in Bezaleel Thayer, *Memorial of the Thayer Name* (1874). A number of his letters are in the possession of Royal Cortissoz, New York. For comment on Thayer's theories of coloration and his work for bird protection, see *Nature*, May 12, 1921, and *Bird-Lore*, July 1921.]

W. S. R.

THAYER, ALEXANDER WHEELOCK (Oct. 22, 1817–July 15, 1897), biographer of Beethoven, United States consul at Trieste, was born at South Natick, Mass., the son of Dr. Alexander and Susanna (Bigelow) Thayer, and a descendant of Thomas Thayer who was in Braintree, Mass., by 1647. The younger Alexander attended Phillips Academy at Andover, Mass., and entered Harvard College, from which he graduated in 1843. He then studied at the Harvard Law School, and received the degree of bachelor of laws in 1848. For several years he was employed in the college library at Harvard. In 1849 he went abroad and spent more than two years in Europe, studying the German language and corresponding with American newspapers. He also commenced gathering data for a life of Ludwig van Beethoven, a project which he had conceived while a student at Harvard, and which became the principal undertaking of his life. At first he intended merely to make an English translation of Anton Felix Schindler's biography of Beethoven, but as he came into possession of fresh material he decided to continue original researches and write an entirely new work.

In 1852 he returned to New York, and for a time was on the staff of the *New York Tribune*. He also became one of the contributors to *Dwight's Journal of Music,* published in Boston. His duties in New York proved so detrimental to his health that he returned to Germany in 1854, and sought Beethoven data in the Royal Library at Berlin. Because of continued ill health and straitened finances he came back to America in 1856 and was employed in cataloguing the extensive music library of Lowell Mason [*q.v.*]. Two years later, chiefly through Mason's financial assistance, he was able to return to Europe. In Breslau he examined the Lansberger collection of Beethoven autographs; he consulted the archives of libraries at Prague, Vienna, and Bonn; he journeyed to Paris on a fruitless search for documents on the history of Bonn (Beethoven's birthplace); and in London he secured the reminiscences of Charles Neate, George Hogarth, and Philip Potter, Englishmen who had known Beethoven personally. On subsequent occasions he consulted Anselm Hüttenbrenner, Caroline van Beethoven, Ignaz Moscheles, Gerhard von Bruening, and other relatives or associates of Beethoven.

Thayer completed the first volume of his work in 1856. To Hermann Deiters, whom he had met in Bonn, he entrusted the editing and translation of the manuscript into German, and the first volume, published by Weber of Berlin, did not appear until 1866, the second was issued in 1872, and the third in 1879. The three volumes covered all but the last ten years of Beethoven's life. Thayer never finished the last volume; a malady which caused severe headaches prevented his final writing of the notes he had arranged in chronological order. After his death in Trieste, Deiters undertook to revise the first three volumes and complete the work. He died before the task was finished, and Hugo Riemann completed it, the biography appearing in five volumes between the years 1901 and 1911. In the meantime, Henry E. Krehbiel [*q.v.*], the American music critic, had been preparing an English version in three volumes, based on Thayer's original manuscript in English. The World War prevented the original plans for the publication of Krehbiel's work, and it was not issued until, subsidized by the Beethoven Association, it appeared under the title *The Life of Ludwig van Beethoven* in 1921.

In order to support himself, Thayer had entered the diplomatic service. According to several accounts, including a report of the United States consul at Trieste in 1897, he took a small post in the legation at Vienna in 1862, but the

Department of State has no record of this appointment. On Nov. 1, 1864, President Lincoln, on recommendation of Senator Charles Sumner, appointed Thayer consul at Trieste, and he retained this position until Oct. 1, 1882. As a consul he succeeded in modifying and improving commercial relations between the merchants of Trieste and those in American ports, and for this service was decorated by the Emperor of Austria with the Iron Cross, third class.

Thayer's biography of Beethoven has become the standard work on the subject. It is fair in its judgments, and makes no attempt to idealize its subject or to present a critical estimate of Beethoven's music; it deals with the composer as a man, and relates the facts of his life. Thayer also edited *Signor Masoni: and Other Papers of the Late I. Brown* (Berlin, 1862), and was the author of *Ein kritischer Beitrag zur Beethoven-Literatur* (Berlin, 1877); and *The Hebrews and the Red Sea* (Andover, Mass., 1883). He never married.

[For sources see Bezaleel Thayer, *Memorial of the Thayer Name* (1874); G. B. Howe, *Geneal. of the Bigelow Family of America* (1890); H. E. Krehbiel, "Alexander Thayer and His Life of Beethoven," *Musical Quart.*, Oct. 1917; *Musical Courier*, July 21, 1897; *Grove's Dict. of Music and Musicians* (3rd ed., 1928), vol. V; *New England Hist. and Geneal. Reg.*, Jan. 1883, p. 84; *N. Y. Tribune*, July 20, 1897. The Dept. of State has in its archives a report from the consul at Trieste, following Thayer's death in 1897, which contains biog. material.]   J. T. H.

THAYER, AMOS MADDEN (Oct. 10, 1841– Apr. 24, 1905), jurist, teacher of law, was a descendant of Thomas Thayer who emigrated from Braintree, Essex, England, to Braintree, Mass., before 1647. The son of Ichabod Thayer, a farmer, and Fidelia (La Due) Thayer, he was born at Mina, Chautauqua County, N. Y. After attending Westfield Academy he entered Hamilton College, graduating in 1862. From August of that year until August 1865 he was in the Federal military service, first as a second lieutenant of the 112th New York Volunteers and eventually as chief signal officer of the Department of the Susquehanna, with the brevet rank of major.

In 1866 he moved to St. Louis, Mo., where, after studying law for two years in the office of a maternal uncle, he was admitted to the bar. In 1876, as a Democrat, he was elected judge of the circuit court of St. Louis and in 1882 was re-elected, but resigned in 1887 to accept appointment by President Cleveland as federal judge for the eastern district of Missouri. In 1894 he was elevated to the position of federal circuit judge for the eighth circuit. Meanwhile, in 1890, upon the urging of William Gardiner Hammond [*q.v.*], he had become a teacher at the Law

School of Washington University, St. Louis. From this time until his death he helped in the important work of changing typical American legal education from an apprentice system into a university process.

As a federal judge, Thayer made a deep and favorable impression on the lawyers of his generation by reason of his patience, impartiality, thorough study of facts, and especially his ability to adjust the doctrine of *stare decisis* to the changing needs of society. His written opinions, generally short and concise, can be found in volumes 30 to 134 of the *Federal Reporter*. The two most notable are those in *Hopkins* vs. *Oxley Stave Company* (83 *Fed. Rep.*, 912) and *United States* vs. *Northern Securities Company* (120 *Fed. Rep.*, 721), both involving the law of conspiracy. In the first of these cases (1897) the common law of conspiracy was made effective by injunction against members of a labor union. In the latter case (1903) the statutory law of conspiracy in interstate commerce was made effective by injunction against an impressive group of railroad corporations and prominent financiers. Thayer's opinion was afterwards affirmed by the United States Supreme Court (193 *U.S.*, 197). Thayer published for the use of law students *Jurisdiction of the Federal Courts* (1895) and *A Synopsis of the Law of Contract* (1897). His address before the American Bar Association on the Louisiana Purchase (*Report*, 1904) presented the orthodox constitutional justification for the federal policy adopted in developing the vast territory ceded to the United States by France in 1803.

In 1880 Thayer married Sidney Hunton Brother, who with one daughter survived him.

[Bezaleel Thayer, *Memorial of the Thayer Name* (1874); Adin Ballou, *Hist. of the Town of Milford, Mass.* (1882), p. 1057; Wm. Hyde and H. L. Conard, *Encyc. of the Hist. of St. Louis* (1899), IV, 2250; *Who's Who in America*, 1903–05; *In Memoriam: Amos Madden Thayer*, 1841–1905 (1905), proceedings of the federal courts in St. Louis, May 13, 1905; *Report of the . . . Am. Bar Asso.*, 1905; *St. Louis Globe-Democrat*, Apr. 25, 1905.]   T. W.

THAYER, ELI (June 11, 1819–Apr. 15, 1899), educator, originator of the Emigrant Aid Company, congressman, was born in Mendon, Mass., the eldest child of Cushman and Miranda (Pond) Thayer, and a descendant of Thomas Thayer, an early settler of Braintree, Mass. Cushman Thayer was a farmer and later kept a store. Eli was educated somewhat irregularly, with interludes for school teaching and working in his father's store; but by the autumn of 1840, having finished his preparation at the Worcester Manual Labor High School (later Worcester Academy), he was able to enter Brown University. Here, delayed again by teaching, he graduated as salutatorian of his class in 1845. A position awaited him at his old school in Worcester, and from 1847 to 1849 he was principal. On Aug. 6, 1845, he married Caroline M. Capron, by whom he had five daughters and two sons.

On Goat Hill, in an undeveloped part of Worcester, where he had been purchasing land since 1845, Thayer erected between 1848 and 1852 a large "castle," completely machicolated and with four-story round towers at its ends. This was the site of the Oread Collegiate Institute, a school for young women which Thayer established, and the residence of Thayer and his family for the greater part of fifty years. One of the pioneers in the history of education for women, he made provision in the institution for collegiate instruction. Three departments were established, primary, academic, and collegiate, the last offering a four-year course closely modeled on that of Brown and leading to the diploma of *Oreas Erudita.* Thayer himself retained the active headship—including the instruction in Latin and mathematics—for only a few years, and thereafter the Institute, which under his own guidance had flourished, soon lost much of its college emphasis and became a young ladies' seminary more close to the usual type.

Entering public life, Thayer held one or two municipal offices, and in 1852 was elected to the General Court as a Free Soiler, serving in 1853–54. There his chief effort was directed to securing a charter of a bank of mutual redemption. Its purpose was to redeem the bills of New England banks—its stockholders being such banks as cared to subscribe—and thus to enable country bankers to escape the tyranny of the Suffolk Bank in Boston. The charter was granted in 1855, though the institution did not begin operation till sometime later. Meantime, Thayer embarked on the great enterprise of his life, that of promoting organized emigration. In the spring of 1854, while the Kansas–Nebraska bill was pending, he interested a number of influential people in the cause of making Kansas free by colonization, and within six weeks (Apr. 26, 1854) obtained a charter for the Massachusetts Emigrant Aid Company. The charter was thought to be defective and was given up, and a voluntary organization took its place, under the name New England Emigrant Aid Company, chartered Feb. 16, 1855. Thayer always believed in the scheme as an investment, though many of his associates did not. Throughout various changes of organization and until its work was largely done (1856), he remained by far its most energetic promoter and for a period was paid a commission for the sums obtained through his efforts. His early enlistment of Horace Greeley and the *New York Tribune* in support of the movement gave it great aid. For over two years Thayer spent most of his time traveling in New England and New York on the business of the company.

In 1856 he was suddenly drafted as Republican candidate for Congress in the Worcester district, and served two terms, 1857–61. His position in Congress was unusual. So great was his enthusiasm for company colonization of new lands that he came to regard the method as almost a panacea. It was his belief that free men, backed by investors and preceded by efficient agents to form "receiving stations," would suffice to create free and prosperous communities, and that the question of slavery—or, in the case of Utah, polygamy—would soon disappear. Even the border states, he thought, might be brought to freedom by this means, and in 1857–59 he worked hard in connection with the founding of Ceredo in western Virginia. Filibustering in Central America, he was convinced, could be stopped by the same means. All his very witty and genially satirical congressional speeches were directed to this theme, the implications of which formed a sort of popular-sovereignty doctrine which made him totally uninterested in congressional action about slavery in the territories. This most unorthodox Republicanism was anathema to many of Thayer's constituents, and when in 1859 he swung a decisive though small group in the House to vote for the admission of Oregon, his political fate was sealed. As a delegate at the Chicago Convention his support of Lincoln rather than of Seward was a further count against him. In 1860 he was forced to run as an independent and was defeated. A painful episode of these years was Thayer's contact with John Brown, who visited him at the Oread, asked for arms to defend the free settlers of Kansas, and received all Thayer had. These arms were used at Harpers Ferry, and Thayer was always very bitter about the deception that had been practised on him (*Boston Herald,* Aug. 22, 1887).

Thayer's subsequent life was not a happy one. He served as a treasury agent in 1861–62, obtained some support at Washington for a plan of military colonization of Florida, and in 1864–70 was land agent in New York for Western railroad interests. Returning to Worcester, he was a candidate for Congress on the Democratic ticket in 1874 and 1878. In 1887 he entered on a period of vigorous newspaper controversy with the Garrisonian abolitionists, whom he condemned whole-heartedly as disunionists and as having added nothing but disloyalty to the national struggle against slavery. He felt that his efforts in securing Kansas for freedom were not properly recognized. His speeches in Congress appear in *Six Speeches, with a Sketch of the Life of Hon. Eli Thayer* (1860). He was the author of *The New England Emigrant Aid Company, and Its Influence, through the Kansas Contest, upon National History* (1887), also printed in *Collections of the Worcester Society of Antiquity* (vol. VII, 1888), and of *A History of the Kansas Crusade, Its Friends and Its Foes* (1889), in which he expressed his feelings regarding the part he played in that movement.

[A manuscript life of Thayer by his friend F. P. Rice, with a collection of clippings, is in the Harvard Coll. Lib.; Thayer Papers and clippings are at Brown University, and other clippings, in the American Antiquarian Society; the Kans. State Hist. Soc. has much material on the Emigrant Aid Company. Other sources include: Bezaleel Thayer, *Memorial of the Thayer Name* (1874); G. O. Ward, *The Worcester Acad.* (1918) and sketch of Thayer in *Worcester Acad. Bull.*, June 1917; M. E. B. Wright, *Hist. of the Oread Collegiate Institute . . . 1849–1881* (1905); F. P. Rice, *The Worcester of Eighteen Hundred and Ninety-eight* (1899); R. V. Harlow, in *Am. Hist. Rev.*, Oct. 1935; S. A. Johnson, in *New England Quart.*, Jan. 1930; *Boston Transcript*, Apr. 15, 1899; *Worcester Evening Gazette*, Apr. 15, 1899; *Worcester Sunday Telegram*, Apr. 16, 1899.]   H. D. J.

THAYER, EZRA RIPLEY (Feb. 21, 1866–Sept. 14, 1915), professor of law, was the brother of William Sydney Thayer [*q.v.*], and the son of James Bradley Thayer [*q.v.*], a distinguished legal scholar and professor in the Harvard Law School. His mother, Sophia Bradford (Ripley) Thayer, was the daughter of Rev. Samuel Ripley and a cousin of Ralph Waldo Emerson. Thayer was born in Milton, Mass., but in 1874, when his father turned from practice to teaching law, the family moved to Cambridge. Very early the son's marked ability was evident. He led his class in the Cambridge High School, where he began his preparation for college; and after a year in Athens studying Greek under Prof. W. W. Goodwin [*q.v.*] and further preparation at Hopkinson's School in Boston, entered Harvard in 1884 and was graduated in 1888. Here, also, though taking part in athletic sports and in college societies, he led his class, as he did in the Harvard Law School, from which he was graduated in 1891.

He then spent a year in Washington as secretary to Justice Horace Gray [*q.v.*] of the United States Supreme Court and upon returning to Boston entered the office of the firm of which Louis D. Brandeis, afterwards a justice of the same high court, was a member. Thayer became a partner of the firm in 1896, under its later name of Brandeis, Dunbar & Nutter. In 1900 he gave up that association to become a member of Storey, Thorndike, Palmer & Thayer.

He was highly successful as a practitioner, and also gave his time freely to work of the Boston, Massachusetts, and American bar associations. He was a member of the committee of the last-named body which drafted the national code of legal ethics, and he had a large share in this work.

His distinction as a student had led, immediately after his graduation, to an offer of an assistant professorship in the Harvard Law School, but he declined the offer and when tendered full professorship in 1902, on his father's death, again refused to exchange the life of a practitioner for that of a teacher and scholar. In 1910, however, on the death of Dean James Barr Ames [*q.v.*], when urged to take the direction of the Law School, he consented, though with some hesitation, to do so. After the new work was once undertaken, he threw himself into it with characteristic conscientious thoroughness, cutting off all connection with practice. From similar motives, when offered an appointment in 1913 to the supreme judicial court of Massachusetts, he declined because he felt that having undertaken to give himself to the Law School he was bound to persist in his work there. As an administrator and director of the policy of the school, Thayer achieved immediate success. Equal success in his new work as a teacher and scholar was evidently sure to follow after a brief novitiate. Undoubtedly overwork caused by conscientious devotion to the task he had undertaken led to his suicide, by drowning, in 1915. In person, Thayer was handsome and attractive, with great social gifts. He continued to the end of his life the love of Greek and the reading of Greek authors as well as of English classics. This gave an intellectual charm without pedantry to his conversation. On June 23, 1898, he married Ethel Randolph Clark of Pomfret, Conn., who with three children survived him.

[*The Centennial Hist. of the Harvard Law School* (1918); *Harvard Law Review*, Nov. 1915; *Harvard Grads. Mag.*, Dec. 1915; *Harvard Coll. Class of 1888, Secretary's Report*, no. 8 (1920); *Ezra Ripley Thayer; An Estimate of His Work as Dean of the Harvard Law School; a Sketch of His Life, and Reprints of Certain of His Writings* (Harvard Law School Asso., 1016); *Proc. at the Meeting of the Bar in the Supreme Judicial Court of Mass., in Memory of Ezra Ripley Thayer, July 7, 1916* (1916); *Who's Who in America*, 1914–15; *Boston Transcript*, Sept. 16, 1915.]   S. W.

THAYER, GIDEON FRENCH (Sept. 21, 1793–Mar. 27, 1864), educator, was born in Watertown, Mass., the son of Zephion and Susannah (Bond) Thayer. He was a descendant of Thomas Thayer who was in Braintree, Mass., as early as 1647. In his early boyhood his parents removed to Brookline, Mass., where he had his first schooling. Within a few years both parents died, and Gideon was adopted by Gideon French, a tallow merchant of Boston, whose name he bore. A period of schooling in Boston was followed by his apprenticeship, at fourteen, to a retail shoe-merchant, with whom he remained for six years. Throughout this time he studied privately to prepare himself for teaching. In 1814 he was appointed usher in the South Writing School of Boston, where he acquired a reputation for his instruction in penmanship. To augment his salary he conducted an evening school for apprentices. A severe hemorrhage of the lungs in 1818 forced him to withdraw from teaching, and at the expense of sympathetic friends he was sent to New Orleans. Returning two years later, he took up his residence in Milton, Mass. He married, Aug. 27, 1821, Nancy Pierce, daughter of Rufus and Elizabeth Pierce of Milton, by whom he had three sons and a daughter. In 1820 he established a private school in Boston, where two innovations which proved popular with his students were the installation of gymnastic apparatus and his practice of taking the boys to the Boston Common for exercises and games during periods of recess. In lectures to schoolmasters he stressed the importance of a well-balanced program of mental, moral, and physical instruction. The school succeeded so well that he was able in 1828 to secure sufficient credit for the purchase of a site and the erection of a school-building on Chauncy Place (later Chauncy Street). This was the famous Chauncy-Hall School. Among his first pupils was Francis Parkman [q.v.], the historian. A noteworthy feature of the school was its departmental plan of instruction, with competent teachers in charge of the various courses of study. William Russell [q.v.] was the instructor in elocution. Singing by note was introduced in the school, as a general exercise, some years before it appeared in the public schools. Thayer was invited frequently to lecture on the work of the school, and to give addresses on educational topics before various teachers' associations. One of his lectures, delivered in 1840 before the American Institute of Instruction, entitled "On Courtesy, and its Connexion with School Instruction" (*Common School Journal*, Dec. 15, 1840), was reprinted in pamphlet form by Horace Mann and distributed to all the schools in Massachusetts; over fifty thousand copies were also printed and circulated by Henry Barnard [qq.v.], in whose journal Thayer was publishing a series of articles, later separately printed as *Letters to a Young Teacher* (1858).

In 1831 he removed from Milton to Quincy, Mass. There he was influential in establishing the first high school (1852) and in organizing a lyceum for the encouragement of cultural interests in the community. He was one of the organizers of the American Institute of Instruction, serving as its first recording secretary (1830–31) and as president (1849–52). His name also appears among the founders of the American Association for the Advancement of Education, the Massachusetts State Teachers' Association, and the Norfolk County Teachers' Association. In 1848 he was one of the editors of the *Massachusetts Teacher*; and from July 1851 to April 1852 he edited the *Quincy Patriot*, a weekly journal devoted to the arts and sciences, a venture in which he lost a considerable sum of money. He was one of the organizers of the Boston public library, a member of the Boston Common Council (1839, 1844–48), and president of the Boston Dispensary (1840–46). He withdrew from the Chauncy-Hall School in December 1855, leaving it in the charge of Thomas Cushing, who had been his partner since 1840. On Jan. 1, 1856, he became president of the Quincy Fire and Marine Insurance Company (later the Prescott Insurance Company). He resigned in 1860 because of ill health and retired to Keene, N. H., where he died. One of his grandsons was Abbott Handerson Thayer [q.v.] the artist.

[Bezaleel Thayer, *Memorial of the Thayer Name* (1874); Thomas Cushing, *Hist. Sketch of Chauncy-Hall School* (1895), and "Memoir of Gideon F. Thayer," *New Eng. Hist. and Geneal. Reg.*, Apr. 1865; *Am. Jour. of Educ.*, Mar. 1858, June 1865; obituary in *Boston Transcript*, Mar. 28, 1864.]   R. F. S.

THAYER, JAMES BRADLEY (Jan. 15, 1831–Feb. 14, 1902), professor of law, was born in Haverhill, Mass., the second son of Abijah Wyman and Susan (Bradley) Thayer, and a descendant of Thomas Thayer who was an early settler of Braintree. During his boyhood the family moved to Northampton. Since his father did not greatly prosper, young Thayer, besides going to school, worked in various ways—doing chores, setting type in a printing office, and helping in a physician's office. With the aid of friends he entered Harvard College in 1848, and was graduated with distinction in 1852, being the class orator on Commencement day. After a brief period of teaching, he entered the Harvard Law School in 1854, having made up his mind "after infinite distraction, to study law rather than divinity, toward which I had had a strong inclination" (Thayer, quoted by Hall, *post*, p. 350).

In December 1856 he was admitted to the Boston bar and on Apr. 24, 1861, married Sophia Bradford Ripley. For the next thirteen years he made his home in Milton. In 1865 he became a partner of Peleg W. Chandler [q.v.] and George

O. Shattuck, leading Boston lawyers of the time. During the following years he contributed to Bouvier's *Dictionary of Law* and to the *American Law Review,* and in 1870 was chosen editor of the twelfth edition (1873) of Kent's *Commentaries.* He secured for the last-named work the aid of Oliver Wendell Holmes, Jr., and eventually Thayer's part in the undertaking was limited to some revision. He kept up his interest in Greek and Latin, and published elaborate reviews of a number of Greek and Latin translations. Somewhat later he also printed privately *Letters of Chauncey Wright* (1878); *A Western Journey with Mr. Emerson* (1884), recounting the events of a trip to California of a small party in which Thayer was included; and *Rev. Samuel Ripley of Waltham* (1897), a short biography of his father-in-law. In all his writings his mastery of a style exact, flexible, and distinguished is noticeable.

In 1874, having previously refused a Harvard professorship of English, he accepted the professorship in the Harvard Law School which he held for the remainder of his life. This period witnessed great changes in the school resulting from Dean Langdell's introduction of the case system of study and teaching. Langdell, Thayer, John C. Gray, and James Barr Ames [*qq.v.*], together laid the foundation for the future success of the method, and of the school. Aside from this contribution, Thayer's reputation rests on his work in constitutional law and in the law of evidence. On both subjects he became recognized as the leading scholar in the United States. He set himself first to find the causes of the disorderly and unreasoned condition of the law of evidence, as a preliminary step to rationalizing and restating the subject. In *A Preliminary Treatise on Evidence at the Comman Law* (1898), a portion of which, in substance, had been issued in 1896, under the title, "Development of Trial by Jury," he was the first to show the various steps in the early development of the English trial by jury, and the dependency of the rules of evidence on this development. The elaborate treatise on the modern law of evidence, to which the *Preliminary Treatise* was intended as an introduction, was never written, although materials for it were assiduously collected for more than twenty years. It was left for Thayer's pupil, J. H. Wigmore, to erect the superstructure (Wigmore, *A Treatise on the System of Evidence in Trials at Common Law,* 4 vols., 1904–05).

In regard to constitutional law, to which Thayer also devoted himself, he early adopted and always upheld the view that no legislative act should be held unconstitutional unless it was so beyond a reasonable doubt; and further, that the function of a constitution is to lay down in general terms broad fundamental principles. As early as 1859 he wrote a vigorous criticism of a provision in the Kansas constitution prohibiting the manufacture and sale of intoxicants. Constitutions, he said, "were not made to be codes of laws, or to embody the opinion of a momentary majority" (quoted by Hall, p. 366). During his professorship, besides the *Preliminary Treatise on Evidence,* he published *Select Cases on Evidence at the Common Law* (1892, 1900); *Cases on Constitutional Law* (2 vols., 1895), and *John Marshall* (1901), a brief biography. After his death his son edited a volume of his shorter papers under the title *Legal Essays* (1908).

As a citizen and neighbor Thayer neglected no duties. He urged reforms of the tariff and of the methods of granting corporate franchises. The treatment of the Indians by the national government engaged his interest, and with others he was instrumental in securing the passage of the Dawes Bill of 1887 to provide for allotment of lands to the Indians in severalty. Before enactment of the law, and afterwards to insure its proper administration, he wrote articles and delivered addresses (see especially the *Atlantic Monthly,* March 1888, October and November 1891). On questions of local as well as of national politics, his tongue and pen were always at the service of what he deemed a righteous cause. His early inclination towards divinity furnishes a correct indication of his subsequent devotion to the Unitarian church. In 1900 President McKinley offered him a position on the Philippine Commission, but his age compelled him to decline.

Thayer was of distinguished appearance and fine manners, receiving a ready welcome in any society in which he found himself. He died at his home in Cambridge, after an illness of a single day, survived by his widow, two daughters, and two sons, Dr. William Sydney Thayer and Ezra Ripley Thayer [*qq.v.*].

[J. P. Hall in W. D. Lewis, *Great Am. Lawyers,* vol. VIII (1909); *Harvard Law Review,* Apr. 1902; *Proc. Mass. Hist. Soc.,* 2 ser., XVI (1903); *Pubs. Col. Soc. of Mass.,* vol. VII (1905); *The Centennial Hist. of the Harvard Law School* (1918); Grace W. Edes, *Annals of the Harvard Class of 1852* (1922); *Am. Law Review,* Mar.–Apr. 1902; Bezaleel Thayer, *Memorial of the Thayer Name* (1874); *Who's Who in America,* 1901–02; *Boston Transcript,* Feb. 15, 1902.]   S. W.

THAYER, JOHN (May 15, 1758–Feb. 17, 1815), Roman Catholic missionary, fourth son of Cornelius and Sarah (Plaisted) Thayer, was born in Boston, Mass. He was a descendant of Richard Thayer, an early settler of Braintree. Despite an irregular education, he received an honorary degree of A.B. from Yale College in 1779. Licensed but not ordained a Congregational minister, Thayer preached from various pulpits and served as chaplain at Castle William under John Hancock (1780–81) until he went to Paris, where Benjamin Franklin brusquely declined his services as a personal chaplain. As a result of theological controversies with priests in France and in Rome, and a reputed miracle of which he had first-hand knowledge, he entered the Roman Catholic Church (May 25, 1783), and studied theology at the College of Navarre and at Saint-Sulpice in Paris. Ordained, June 2, 1787, by the archbishop of Paris, he was lionized by ecclesiastics as the first converted American divine, who had grand plans for the conversion of his fellow Puritans. In the year of his ordination there appeared *The Conversion of John Thayer . . . Written by Himself*. After two years in the London mission, Thayer set forth for Boston, where his arrival (Jan. 4, 1790) and early activities attracted numerous notices in the New England press. On the whole "John Turncoat," as he was called, was not badly received by native Americans, although the rather tolerant Ezra Stiles confided a harsh estimate of his guest to his *Literary Diary*: "Commenced his Life in Impudence, Ingratitude, Lying & Hypocrisy, irregularly took up preach^g among the Congregationalists, went to France & Italy, became a Proselyte to the Romish Church, & is returned to convert America to that Chh . . . of haughty insolent & insidious Talents" (*The Literary Diary of Ezra Stiles*, 1901, vol. III, p. 416).

In Boston, his tactless zeal, his uncompromising Puritan spirit, his uneasiness under ecclesiastical restraint, and his egotism prevented any degree of success. Soon in conflict with Abbé Louis de Rousselet, who was supported by the French members of the congregation, he was placed in temporary control (1791) by Bishop John Carroll [*q.v.*]. About this time he engaged in embittered disputations with two ministers, George Leslie and John Gardner, which were later reprinted (Boston, 1793; Dublin, 1809). When in 1792 he was succeeded by Dr. Francis Anthony Matignon [*q.v.*], he continued as a roving missionary who held Catholic services for the first time in the chief New England towns. For this courageous work he had real talents; his friend William Bentley described him as "a real Dreadnought in adventures" (*The Diary of William Bentley*, vol. IV, 1914,

p. 363). In 1793 he was in Alexandria, Va., where he held services and prepared to build a church. When his pronounced anti-slavery views as well as his excessive zeal destroyed his popularity, he sought an assignment to assist William O'Brien, O.P., of St. Peter's Church, New York, but it was denied (1796). Thayer once more visited Hartford and other New England towns, and Quebec. One of his noteworthy sermons was *A Discourse, Delivered . . . on the 9th of May 1798, a Day Recommended by the President for Humiliation and Prayer Throughout the United States* (1798). A year later he was assigned to assist Stephen Theodore Badin [*q.v.*], whose missionary field covered Kentucky. Despite conflicts over slavery, Thayer throve on the frontier until in 1803, somewhat to his ordinary's relief, he retired under a cloud to Limerick, Ireland.

Apparently he was happy in Ireland. Aside from brief excursions to England and the continent (as to La Trappe in France, 1807), he remained a missionary in Limerick, where he was considered "a priest of edifying piety and ascetic life," until his death. Thayer was not idle. He did his share in giving an impulse to emigration from the south of Ireland to America and urged Irish priests to volunteer for the missions. Determined to establish a convent in Boston, he collected several thousand dollars, vainly applied to Dublin and London convents for volunteers, and finally trained his own postulants. After his death his legacy enabled several postulants to go in 1817 to Three Rivers, Quebec, and on the completion of their novitiate to establish (1819) a house in Boston, the nucleus of the famous Ursuline Convent in Charlestown which was burned by a nativist mob in 1834.

[In addition to Thayer's *The Conversion of John Thayer* (1787), see Percival Merritt, "Sketches of the Three Earliest Roman Cath. Priests in Boston," *Pubs. Colonial Soc. Mass.*, vol. XXV (1924), in which fugitive notices in newspapers, letters, and memoirs have been brought together in critical and documented form. See also *U. S. Cath. Hist. Mag.*, vol. II, no. 7 (1889); T. E. Bridgett, *A New England Convert* (1887); James Fitton, *Sketches of the Establishment of the Church in New England* (1872); *Am. Mag.*, Sept. 1788, p. 738; Peter Guilday, *Life and Times of John Carroll* (1922); J. J. Dillon, *The Hist. Story of St. Mary's, Albany* (1933); R. H. Clarke, in *Am. Cath. Quart. Rev.*, Jan. 1904; and Bezaleel Thayer, *Memorial of the Thayer Name* (1874).]   R. J. P.

THAYER, JOHN MILTON (Jan. 24, 1820–Mar. 19, 1906), lawyer, soldier, politician, was born at Bellingham, Mass., the youngest of nine children of Capt. Elias Thayer and his wife, Mrs. Ruthe T. Staples, and a descendant of Thomas Thayer who settled at Braintree before 1647. He was reared upon a farm and educated in a district school. After some experience as a rural teacher he attended Brown University from which he was graduated with honor in 1841. He then read law in Worcester, was admitted to the Worcester County bar, and practised until about 1854. During this time he became a lieutenant of the Worcester Light Infantry, and, for a while, was editor of the *Worcester Magazine and Historical Journal*. In the spring of 1854 he made an exploratory expedition to Nebraska and in the autumn moved with his family to Omaha where he acquired land and engaged in farming. In the following year he was admitted to the bar in Nebraska. Indian troubles arose and he was commissioned the first brigadier-general of the territorial militia. He led expeditions against the Pawnee Indians in 1855 and 1859, and at the outbreak of the Civil War was commissioned colonel of the 1st Nebraska Volunteers. He served with distinction with the army of the West throughout the war and returned home at its conclusion, having been brevetted major-general of volunteers.

His political career began in the territorial council of 1860. He was a member of the constitutional conventions of 1860 and 1866 and was elected one of the first United States senators from Nebraska on the Republican ticket. He served from 1867 to 1871. In the reconstruction contests he was an ardent and active radical. He served on various committees: Military Affairs, Indian Affairs, Patents and Patent Office, and Enrollment of Bills. He was an ardent supporter of President Grant's administration. His best work in Congress was relative to Indian affairs. Of this subject he had first-hand knowledge and offered realistic solutions in contrast to the idealism of his fellow radicals from the Northeast. President Grant appointed him governor of Wyoming Territory, 1875–79. On his return to Nebraska he became especially active in the G.A.R. and acted in the capacity of state commander—a position yielding much publicity. He was elected governor on the Republican ticket in 1886 and reëlected two years later. Although not a candidate for reëlection in 1890 he brought suit against Gov. James E. Boyd on the grounds that the latter was not a citizen of the United States and secured a decision from the Nebraska Supreme Court that left him in the governorship until this decision was reversed by the United States Supreme Court in 1892 (143 *U. S.*, 135). Thayer's career as governor was not distinctive. His imposing personal appearance, his military experiences, and his willingness to conform to the demands of his party were his primary assets. In the con-

tests between the anti-monopolists and the railroads he occupied a neutral position.

At the expiration of his governorship, he retired to live in Lincoln. The federal government voted him a liberal pension. His wife, Mary Torrey Allen, to whom he had been married in Sterling, Mass., on Dec. 27, 1842, and four of his six children preceded Thayer in death.

[*Who's Who in America*, 1906–07; *Biog. Directory of the Am. Cong.*, *1774–1927* (1928); *Vital Records of Bellingham, Mass.* (1904); G. F.. Partridge, *Hist. of the Town of Bellingham* (1919); H. L. Adams, *Worcester Light Infantry* (1924); J. S. Morton, *Illustrated Hist. of Nebr.*, vols. I (1905), III (1913); T. W. Tipton, *Forty Years of Nebr.*, *Proc. and Colls.*, *Nebr. State Hist. Soc.*, 2 ser., vol. IV (1902); *Congressional Globe*, 40 and 41 Cong., 1867–1869; *War of the Rebellion: Official Records* (see Index); R. D. Rowley, "Judicial Career of Samuel Maxwell," Masters thesis, Univ. of Nebr., 1928; for date of marriage, *Mass. Spy* (Worcester), Jan. 11, 1843; *Nebr. State Jour.* (Lincoln), Mar. 20, 1906.]   J. L. S.

THAYER, JOSEPH HENRY (Nov. 7, 1828– Nov. 26, 1901), Congregational clergyman and New Testament scholar, was born in Boston, Mass., the son of Joseph Helyer and Martha Stevens (Greenough) Thayer. He was a descendant of Richard Thayer an early settler of Braintree, Mass. The foundation of his scholarly career was laid by a thorough classical education at the Boston Latin School and at Harvard College, from which he was graduated in 1850. After tutoring and travel in Europe he entered Andover Theological Seminary and completed the course there in 1857. He was resident licentiate at Andover the following year and in 1858–59, acting pastor of a church in Quincy, Mass. On Dec. 29, 1859 he was ordained pastor of the Crombie Street Church in Salem. For a brief period (1862–63) he served as chaplain of the 40th Massachusetts Volunteers. In 1864 he began a long career as teacher of the New Testament, serving as professor of sacred literature at Andover Theological Seminary (1864–82), as lecturer in the Harvard Divinity School (1883–84), and as Bussey Professor of New Testament Criticism and Interpretation (1884–1901). On Nov. 30, 1859 he married Martha Caldwell Davis, by whom he had five children. One of his daughters became the wife of Caspar René Gregory [*q.v.*], and another, the wife of Theodore W. Richards [*q.v.*].

Thayer's main interest was in the Greek language of the New Testament, though he read widely in the whole New Testament field and held positive views on theological problems that were controversial in his time. He accepted the newer methods of Biblical criticism that were causing much alarm and through his teaching and writing commended them by his own genuine religious piety and by his evident sincerity in striving for truth and accuracy. As a teacher his work was marked by conscientiousness and enthusiasm; as a scholar, by industry, accuracy, and self-effacing modesty.

Only two small books were published as exclusively his own, *The Change of Attitude Towards the Bible* (1891) and *Books and Their Use* (1893). He wrote many articles and reviews and was content to put his time and learning into editing and translating the works of others. His *Greek-English Lexicon of the New Testament, being Grimm's Wilke's Clavis Novi Testamenti, Revised and Enlarged* (1887) is an example. Though nominally a translation it was richly supplemented, having received for some twenty years the full benefit of the accuracy and learning of Thayer's mind. When published it represented the full fruition of international scholarship to that date, and a new standard in New Testament lexicography. His hope that his work might be lasting rather than ephemeral is well fulfilled in this achievement. Earlier, 1869 and 1873, he had published translations from the German of the New Testament grammars of B. Winer and Alexander Buttmann.

While the revision of the English New Testament published in 1881 was being made Thayer served as a member and secretary of the American Committee. Here again his own learning was merged with that of others, but he more than anyone else bore the burden of recording the work of the committee and later of preparing and carrying through the press the American edition published in 1901. In his presidential address before the Society of Biblical Literature and Exegesis in 1895 he proposed an American school for Oriental study and research in Palestine. The idea met hearty approval from other scholars and was realized by the founding of the American School of Oriental Research in Jerusalem. At the time of his death he was recognized as the dean of New Testament scholars in America.

[C. J. H. Ropes, in *The Biblical World*, Apr. 1902, and in *Am. Jour. of Theology*, Apr. 1902; C. H. Toy, in *Proc. of the Am. Acad. of Arts and Sciences*, Aug. 1902; *Congregationalist and Christian World*, Dec. 7, 1901, portr.; *Harvard Grads. Mag.*, Mar. 1902, portr.; *Who's Who in America*, 1901–02; Bezaleel Thayer, *Memorial of the Thayer Name* (1874); *Boston Transcript*, Nov. 27, 1901.]   H. J. C.

THAYER, NATHANIEL (Sept. 11, 1808– Mar. 7, 1883), financier, philanthropist, was was born in Lancaster, Mass., seventh of the eight children of the Rev. Nathaniel and Sarah (Toppan) Thayer. His father, minister of the only church then existing in Lancaster, was of a

branch of the Thayer family that traced its New England ancestry to Richard Thayer, an early settler of Braintree, Mass. In the intervening generations the family developed a tendency towards the ministry, several of Dr. Thayer's relatives having been like him Congregational clergymen and graduates of Harvard, while a collateral branch produced Father John Thayer [*q.v.*], who was converted in France in 1783, and had the distinction of being the first priest of a regularly organized Roman Catholic church in Boston.

Nathaniel Thayer, Jr., was educated in the academy of his native town, but he chose commerce instead of the ministry as a career. In 1829, when he was but twenty-one years old, he was listed in the Boston directory as already a partner in a firm engaged in the West India trade, an apprenticeship as a clerk in other establishments having preceded his attainment of a partnership at such an early age. About 1840 he became associated with the banking house established by his brother, under the firm name of John E. Thayer & Brother, and on the death of John in 1857 Nathaniel became the senior member and principal director of the business. The organization of which the Thayer brothers laid the foundation became prominent in American business, and it amassed for Nathaniel one of the largest fortunes acquired by any New Englander of his day. Its operations were principally connected with the building of railroads and the organizing of manufacturing and other corporations of large capital. Thayer's fortune, though considerable even in his early career, became notable during the expansion following the Civil War. By the late sixties his benefactions for charitable and educational purposes had made him conspicuous. In 1866 he was chosen an overseer of Harvard College, and in 1868 became one of the board of fellows. Membership in this small and select administrative body is usually restricted to graduates, but, though Thayer could not qualify in this respect, he had an hereditary interest in Harvard that made him a desirable official. Until his resignation in 1875 he was the dominant factor in the financial management of the College. His largest individual gifts were made to it, although he gave away much more than their total in smaller donations to churches, hospitals, libraries, and persons in need. In behalf of Harvard's department of zoölogy he assumed the expense of the Agassiz expedition to Brazil in 1865; he built a dining hall for the students, an herbarium for the department of botany, and a dormitory called Thayer Hall in memory of his brother. These undertakings, with many smaller gifts, involved an outlay of at least $250,000, and made him one of the institution's most munificent patrons up to that time.

Although he never held public office, he exerted considerable personal influence on the community in which he lived in addition to that resulting from his business activities and philanthropies. On June 10, 1846, he married Cornelia Paterson, daughter of Stephen Van Rensselaer of Albany, N. Y., and grand-daughter of Stephen Van Rensselaer [q.v.], the eighth patroon. With six of their seven children she survived her husband. He died in Boston and was buried in Mount Auburn Cemetery.

[H. S. Nourse, *The Birth, Marriage, and Death Reg. . . . of Lancaster, Mass.* (1890); *New England Hist. and Geneal. Reg.*, Jan.–Oct. 1883; G. E. Ellis, *Memoir of Nathaniel Thayer, A.M.*, reprinted from *Proc. Mass. Hist. Soc.*, 2 ser. II (1886); S. E. Morison, *The Development of Harvard Univ. Since the Inauguration of President Eliot, 1869–1929* (1930); *Boston Transcript*, Mar. 7, 1883; *Boston Post*, Mar. 8, 1883.]   S. G.

THAYER, SYLVANUS (June 9, 1785–Sept. 7, 1872), military engineer, educator, the son of Nathaniel and Dorcas (Faxon) Thayer, was born at Braintree, Mass., where his ancestor, Richard Thayer, had settled in the second quarter of the seventeenth century. He pursued a classical course at Dartmouth College, from 1803 until the early part of 1807, when he entered the United States Military Academy; here he was graduated in 1808, and commissioned second lieutenant in the corps of engineers. For the next few years he was engaged as an assistant in the design and construction of fortifications on the coast of New England and New York. During the War of 1812 he saw service on the Canadian frontier and at Norfolk, Va., and received the brevet of major. In 1815 he was sent by the government to Europe to study military schools, armies, and fortifications, and after nearly two years abroad returned to the United States thoroughly equipped for what was to be his next assignment to duty.

On July 28, 1817, at the age of thirty-two, he was appointed superintendent of the United States Military Academy at West Point, which position he held until relieved at his own request, July 1, 1833. During his first years there he was fortunate in having the enthusiastic support of John C. Calhoun [q.v.], then secretary of war. When Thayer took command, he found the Military Academy in a chaotic condition, without system or regularity in its administration. He at once held examinations, dismissed the incompetent, and made the idle work. He promptly organized the cadets into companies officered

by members of their own body and appointed an officer of the army as commandant of cadets responsible for their tactical instruction and soldierly discipline. He classified them according to their proficiency in studies, divided classes into small sections for more thorough instruction, required weekly class reports showing progress, and greatly improved the curriculum according to a well digested program. He also established the system of summer encampments. The diploma now became evidence of the completion of the full course of studies, and a high standard of honor and efficiency was maintained. Commendation, official and unofficial, of Thayer's superintendency came from all quarters. As early as 1826 General Scott recommended him for the brevet of colonel "for the highest development and effect" given the Military Academy, to which, "for more than eight years he has devoted his great attainments and most unwearied zeal and application to its duties." Scott added: "It is believed that he has at length given the school an excellence equal to the most celebrated in the world" (Cullum, *Biographical Sketch, post*, pp. 22–23). The Academy, hardly more than a secondary school when Thayer took charge, claimed before he left a number of able and distinguished professors and was offering instruction of college grade in several fields. Thayer was truly the "Father of the Military Academy," as he was affectionately known to its graduates, and probably had a greater influence on their character and through them on the United States Army than any other of its distinguished sons.

After his relief from the superintendency and until his retirement, June 1, 1863, he was engineer in charge of the construction of fortifications at the entrance of Boston Harbor and of the improvement of harbors on the New England coast. He was also a member of various special engineer, artillery, and ordnance boards. From 1858 to 1863 he was on leave of absence because of broken health. On June 1, 1863, he was retired from the Army, having been brevetted brigadier-general the year before "for long and faithful service."

Thayer's interest in education did not end with his superintendency of West Point. After his retirement he established (1867) and endowed the Thayer School of Engineering of Dartmouth College, drawing up the entrance requirements, planning the curriculum, and appointing the first director—a graduate of West Point. He also provided a fund for a public library in Braintree, Mass., and in his will provided for another scientific academy to be located in Braintree or

Quincy. Because of unfortunate investments, however, some of his plans could not be carried out. He was a member of the American Academy of Arts and Sciences and the American Philosophical Society of Philadelphia, and received several honorary degrees. After his retirement he made his home at Braintree, Mass., where he died. He never married.

[G. W. Cullum, *Biog. Sketch of Brig.-Gen. Sylvanus Thayer* (1883), address delivered at the unveiling of a statue of Thayer at West Point, June 11, 1883; G. W. Cullum, *Biog, Reg. Officers and Grads. U. S. Mil. Acad.* (3rd ed., 1891), vol. I; Bezaleel Thayer, *Memorial of the Thayer Name* (1874); L. B. Richardson, *Hist. of Dartmouth Coll.* (1932), vol. II; *Army and Navy Jour.*, Sept. 14, 1872; *Boston Transcript*, Sept. 7, 1872.]
G. J. F.

THAYER, THOMAS BALDWIN (Sept. 10, 1812–Feb. 12, 1886), Universalist clergyman, editor, author, was born in Boston, Mass., the son of Benjamin and Catherine (Davis) Thayer and a descendant of Richard Thayer, an early settler of Braintree. Thomas received his early education in the public schools of Boston and at the Boston Latin School. He was tutored in the studies of the freshman year at Harvard, by F. R. Leverett, master of the Latin School from 1828 to 1831, and then taught in Hawes Grammar School and later in a preparatory school for boys established by Leverett. While teaching he supplied Universalist churches, and in December 1832 was ordained by the Boston Association of Universalists. The following year he became pastor of the First Universalist Society in Lowell, Mass.

He seems to have entered the ministry with the fervor and zeal of a missionary. Theological disputations were the fashion and were carried on uncompromisingly. Thayer quickly took a leading position in the warfare against the doctrine of eternal punishment. He fought with his pen with even greater vigor than with his voice. Assisted by the Rev. Abel C. Thomas, he established and edited (1841–42) *The Star of Bethlehem*, a journal devoted to Universalist propaganda. During the same period he and Thomas wrote and published the *Lowell Tracts*, five of which are credited to Thayer—"What is Universalism?", "Scripture Doctrine of the Devil," and "Truth and Reason Against Creeds" being the best known. He also assisted Thomas in publishing the *Lowell Offering*, the articles in which were written by the mill girls of Lowell. In 1845 he accepted a call to Brooklyn, N. Y. He now became less militant, partly because his spare time was devoted to editing *The Golden Rule and Odd Fellows' Family Companion*, a fraternal publication. In 1851 he returned to his first charge in Lowell, and in March 1853 he

married Mrs. Sarah Athena Peck, daughter of Samuel H. Harris of Methuen, Mass., by whom he had a daughter. In 1859 he left Lowell to become pastor of the Shawmut Avenue Universalist Church in Boston, with which he remained until he retired from the active ministry in 1867.

His earliest polemic was *Christianity against Infidelity* (1836) which was reissued in considerably enlarged form in 1849. One of his most successful and influential works was *The Bible Class Assistant, or Scriptural Guide for Sunday Schools* (1840). It was a pioneer work in the direction of more sensible and illuminative methods of Biblical instruction, and passed through many editions. In 1855 he copyrighted *The Origin and History of the Doctrine of Endless Punishment*, and in 1862, *Theology of Universalism*. He was a frequent and forceful contributor to the *Universalist Quarterly*, of which he became editor in 1864. With the exception of a few months' absence on a tour of Europe and the Far East he conducted this journal until his last illness. In it are found his most lasting contributions to the literature of Universalism. He was also the author of much verse which, however, is not available in collected form. Thayer was an overseer of Harvard from 1858 to 1864 and again from 1865 to 1871. He died in Roxbury (part of Boston), Mass.

[Bezaleel Thayer, *Memorial of the Thayer Name* (1874); G. H. Emerson, in *Universalist Quart.*, July 1886; *Autobiog. of Rev. Abel C. Thomas* (1852); J. G. Adams, *Fifty Notable Years* (1882); Richard Eddy, *Universalism in America* (2 vols., 1884–86); *Universalist Reg.*, 1887; *Christian Leader*, Feb. 18, 1886; *Boston Daily Advertiser*, Feb. 13, 1886.]
C. G.

THAYER, WHITNEY EUGENE (Dec. 11, 1838–June 27, 1889), organist, composer, was born in Mendon, Mass., the son of Perry and Charlotte (Taft) Thayer, and a descendant of Thomas Thayer, an early settler of Braintree, Mass. He began the study of music at an early age, but he did not consider it seriously as a profession until he came under the influence of John Knowles Paine [q.v.], and was chosen with Paine, Benjamin J. Lang [q.v.], and others to play at the dedication of the organ in Boston Music Hall on Nov. 2, 1863. In 1865 he went abroad to study organ and counterpoint with Haupt and composition with Wieprecht. The following year he made a concert tour of Europe and a trip to England where he played at Westminster Abbey and at St. Paul's in London. When he returned to Boston, he immediately became active as an organist and teacher, and, until he went to New York in 1881, he occupied the organ-lofts successively of the Arlington Street, Hollis Street, Old First Unitarian, and New

England Churches in Boston, and the Harvard Church in Brookline. He was also active as a recitalist on the organ, and in 1868 inaugurated a long series of concerts in Boston, the first free organ concerts to be given in the country. He gave many others, in America and abroad. When Ole Bull, the violinist, made his American tour, Thayer was his official pianist. In 1875 he opened a private organ studio in Boston, said to be the first of its kind in the United States. From 1881 to 1886 he was organist of the Fifth Avenue Presbyterian Church in New York City, and then played for a season at Holy Trinity Episcopal Church in Harlem, after which he retired to devote the remaining twelve years of his life to teaching and composition.

As a teacher Thayer exerted a strong influence. He was one of the early teachers of George W. Chadwick, and his many pupils numbered such musicians as Edward Fisher, Walter C. Gale, Gerrit Smith, J. Warren Andrews, and Sumner Salter. Throughout his life he sought to bring about an improvement in church music and to raise the standards of taste. In addition to his many lectures, he preached his doctrines in the pages of the two magazines he edited at various times while in Boston, probably between 1870 and 1881,—the *Organist's Journal and Review,* and the *Choir Journal and Review.* He also conducted the Boston Choral Union and the New England Church-Music Association. His talents were recognized in his own time by the award of a Doctor of Music degree from Oxford University, for the composition of his "Festival Cantata" for soli, eight-part chorus and orchestra. Among his other compositions were a Mass in E flat, a Fugue for the organ, five organ sonatas, variations for two performers on the organ on the Russian national hymn, many shorter pieces for the organ, and solo and part songs. His most ambitious educational publication was *The Art of Organ Playing Complete in Five Parts* (1874), and his *Vest Pocket Harmony Book* (1883).

On Oct. 8, 1862, Thayer was married to Elizabeth Davis Eaton, of Worcester, Mass. She and three of their five children survived him when he died, by his own hand, at Burlington, Vt. For some time before his death he had been mentally unsound. The family home "Mt. Ida" at Newton provided a place of happy diversion for Thayer, and it was there that he indulged especially his great interest in philosophical speculation and in astronomy.

[In view of his contemporary prominence Thayer is surprisingly neglected by writers on American music. He is omitted from the standard books on the subject by Ritter, Hughes, and Howard, and L. C. Elson, in *The Hist. of Am. Music* (rev. ed., 1925), gives him only casual and perfunctory mention. See, however, *Grove's Dict. of Music and Musicians, Am. Supp.* (1930), an article by his daughter, Louise Friedel Thayer, in *Am. Organist,* Aug. 1933, and two articles by Sumner Salter in the *Musician,* Dec. 1912, and by J. W. Andrews, in the *Am. Organist,* Mar. 1932. For names of his parents see *Vital Records of Mendon, Mass.* (1920); for ancestry, L. T. Ojeda, *Catálogo Biográfico de la Casa de Thaye de Braintree* (1904), p. 51; and, for obituary, the *N. Y. Times,* June 28, 1889.]   J. T. H.

THAYER, WILLIAM MAKEPEACE (Feb. 23, 1820–Apr. 7, 1898), clergyman, editor, and writer, was born and died in Franklin, Mass. His father, Davis Thayer, merchant and early manufacturer of straw hats, was a descendant of Thomas Thayer, freeman of Braintree, Essex, England, who received title of lands at Braintree, Mass., soon after its first settlement. His mother, Betsey (McKepiece) Thayer, of limited education and unsatisfied literary longings, aroused in him a desire for education and a professional life. He began attending the district school when he was four. Before he was fifteen he was studying at the Franklin academy. In 1843 he received the A.B. degree from Brown University. He taught school in Attleboro, South Braintree, and Franklin, Mass., and studied theology with the Rev. Jacob Ide of West Medway, Mass. In 1844 he was licensed to preach by the Mendon conference of orthodox churches, but he did not at once give up teaching, which he considered a useful preparation for preaching. On Oct. 19, 1845, he married Rebecca W. Richards, the daughter of Calvin Richards of Dover, Mass., by whom he had five children. He began preaching at Edgartown, Martha's Vineyard, Mass. In 1849 he accepted the pastorate of the Congregational Church at Ashland, Mass., which he held until 1857 when he was forced to give up preaching because of throat trouble. He continued to the end of his life to preach occasionally in neighboring churches.

In 1858 he extended his educational and religious work beyond the bounds of school room and church. From 1858 to 1862 he was editor of *The Home Monthly* to which he and many of his ministerial friends were prolific contributors. He was editor successively of the *Nation,* 1864–68, and *Mother's Assistant,* 1868–72. He was twice a member of the Massachusetts General Court, in 1857–58 and in 1863–64. He was also secretary of the Massachusetts State Temperance Alliance from 1860 to 1876. He never ceased writing from his early school days until his death. While still at the academy he began publishing his compositions in local temperance and religious papers. He frequently wrote funeral hymns and occasional verse. In 1853 he published *The Gem and Casket,* and the following year *Life at the Fireside.* In *The Poor Boy and Merchant Prince . . . the Life of . . . Amos Lawrence* (1857) and *The Poor Girl and the True Woman . . . Life of Mary Lyon* (1857), he hit upon a form of biography that proved a popular way to point morals and to preach the gospel of virtue and success. Among his early biographies were *The Bobbin Boy* (1860), *The Pioneer Boy and How he Became President* (1863); among the later ones was *A Youth's History of the Rebellion* (4 vols., 1864–65), which gave a partisan and contemporary account of the Civil War. In the last decade of his life he published *Success and its Achievers* (1891), later published as volume III of *Ethics of Success* (3 vols., 1893–94), a series of school readers, *Turning Points in Successful Careers* (1895), *Men Who Win* (1896) and *Women Who Win* (1896). After his death the *Unfinished Autobiography of William M. Thayer* was privately printed by his son (n.d.). He traveled through the West once, to describe which he wrote *Marvels of the New West* (1887), but otherwise his experiences and associations were confined to his native state. He limited his reading to books he considered inspirational and ruled out novels as not contributing to intellectual strength. From his reading he compiled many notebooks of facts and incidents and others of his random thoughts, from which he later drew for illustrative material in his writing. His work was didactic and depended for its interest largely upon anecdote and incident.

[*Autobiography, ante;* Bezaleel Thayer, *Memorial of the Thayer Name* (1874), pp. 184, 222, 332, 432; *Hist. Cat. of Brown University* (1895); *N. Y. Tribune,* Apr. 8, 1898.]   V.L.S.

THAYER, WILLIAM ROSCOE (Jan. 16, 1859–Sept. 7, 1923), biographer, historian, was born in Boston, Mass., the son of Frederick William and Maria (Phelps) Thayer. He was descended on both sides from a straight English and New England ancestry; his paternal ancestor, Thomas Thayer, was an early settler of Braintree, Mass. Frederick William Thayer, a prosperous shipping merchant, had business connections in England and there became so much interested in the work of the Liverpool banker-historian of Italy, William Roscoe, that he gave his name to his own son. Thus from earliest childhood the thoughts of the boy were turned toward the history of the country which next to his own was to be the ruling interest of his mature life.

He attended St. Paul's school at Concord,

N. H., for three years, and was then taken to Europe, where he remained two and a half years, most of the time under the care of an exceptionally gifted private tutor. Entering Harvard College in 1877, he was graduated in due course. Meanwhile a change in the family fortunes had made it necessary for him to seek gainful occupation. From the very beginning of his conscious life he had shown more than ordinary capacity for writing in both prose and verse, and he at once accepted a very humble position as "space writer" for the *Boston Sunday Budget.* This experience led to an engagement on the *Philadelphia Evening Bulletin,* where he served an apprenticeship of four years, writing literary, musical, and dramatic criticism and editorials upon all subjects except politics.

In the autumn of 1885 a modest inheritance from his mother made it possible for him to give up the unsatisfying routine of journalism and return to his studies and literary ventures. As a preliminary he spent a year in the Harvard Graduate School, receiving his master's degree in 1886. After another year in Europe he settled in Cambridge and accepted an appointment as instructor in English at Harvard (1888–89), hoping that by performing the "chore-work" of theme correcting "I might eventually have an opportunity of testing my ability in a more congenial course" (*Letters, post,* p. 63). In this hope he was disappointed. The appointment was not renewed, and alluring offers from other places did not attract him.

His marriage, Nov. 24, 1893, to Elizabeth Hastings Ware of Cambridge, member of a notable family of scholars and divines, strengthened Thayer's purpose to go on with the historical study and writing for which he had long been steadily preparing. His devotion to the University continued unabated. He was chosen as editor of the new *Harvard Graduates' Magazine* and continued in that capacity for twenty-three years (1892–1915). He was twice elected to the board of overseers (1913–19 and 1920–23). The Harvard Union owed its origin to him, and it was largely through his persistent advocacy that it was founded and began its beneficent service.

Thayer's interest in Italian history began early to center about the period of the *Risorgimento,* the struggle for unity and independence. The first fruit of this interest was *The Dawn of Italian Independence* (2 vols., 1893), a survey of the preparatory stages. For the central figure of his work he chose Cavour as the chief constructive agent about whom he might group the other elements, both radical and reactionary, that contributed to the final result. With his ardent love of liberty and hatred of tyranny there could be no question of "impartiality" in his treatment of the subject, yet he was equally far from blind admiration of his hero. His two volumes, *The Life and Times of Cavour,* published in 1911, at once placed him in the front rank of biographical historians. The appreciation of the Italian government was shown by his nomination to membership in the Order of the Crown of Italy and in the Order of Saints Maurizio & Lazzaro with the title of *Commendatore,* the highest civic honor in the gift of that country. In 1905 he had published *A Short History of Venice.*

Work on the Cavour was interrupted for four years by a serious nervous disorder which he faced with unflinching courage and overcame at last by persistent occupation within the limits of his strength. Upon its completion he turned with renewed energy to a new field of study in preparation for *The Life and Letters of John Hay* (2 vols., 1915). Four years later he published *Theodore Roosevelt; an Intimate Biography* (1919), and in 1920, *The Art of Biography.* In 1918–19 he was president of the American Historical Association. Meanwhile, his affection for Italy had developed in him an equal detestation of Bismarckian Germany. The events of 1914 roused him to intense hostility and he gave himself wholeheartedly to the task of stirring American opinion to the point of war. His pamphlets, *Germany vs. Civilization* (1916) and *The Collapse of Superman* (1918), and his letters to men of political importance indicate his point of view during this period. He died in Cambridge, at the age of sixty-four, survived by his wife and one daughter.

[*The Letters of William Roscoe Thayer* (1926), ed. by C. D. Hazen; *Who's Who in America,* 1922–23; J. F. Rhodes, *Commemorative Tribute to William Roscoe Thayer* (1924); Bezaleel Thayer, *Memorial of the Thayer Name* (1874); Owen Wister, "William Roscoe Thayer," *Harvard Grads. Mag.,* Dec. 1923; *Twenty-fifth Anniv. Report . . . Class of 1881 of Harvard Coll.* (1906); *Harvard Coll. Class of 1881, Fiftieth Anniv.* (1931); *Boston Transcript,* Sept. 8, 1923; personal acquaintance.]   E. E—n.

THAYER, WILLIAM SYDNEY (June 23, 1864–Dec. 10, 1932), physician, was born in Milton, Mass., the eldest son of Sophia Bradford (Ripley) and James Bradley Thayer [*q.v.*], and the descendant of Thomas Thayer who emigrated from Braintree, England, to Braintree, Mass., before 1647. His brother was Ezra Ripley Thayer [*q.v.*]. He graduated from Harvard College in 1885 and in 1889 from the Harvard Medical School. After serving as interne in the Massachusetts General Hospital, he studied under Paul Ehrlich and others in Berlin and Vienna. On his return to America, he practised for a short time in Boston and in November 1890 became a member of the house staff of William Osler [*q.v.*] in the Johns Hopkins Hospital and was resident physician there for seven years. He became professor of clinical medicine in the Johns Hopkins Medical School and, later, professor of medicine and physician-in-chief to the hospital. In 1921 he was made professor emeritus of medicine. Throughout his career he was prominent in medical research, teaching, organization, and practice. He investigated the blood in leukaemia, typhoid fever, and malaria, and he made numerous contributions to knowledge of the circulatory system, including publications upon the third heart sound, heart murmurs, bacterial endocarditis, heart block, angina pectoris, and arteriosclerosis. He published several volumes, including: *Lectures on the Malarial Fevers* (1897), *America—1917 and Other Verse* (1926), and *Osler and Other Papers* (1931). He inspired younger men to engage in research work, and many men were grateful to have been his pupils. As a teacher he laid great stress upon the accuracy of physical examinations and set an example of painstaking work himself. Skilled, too, in the use of the methods of the clinical laboratory, he drilled his students rigorously in their application to the study of patients. He insisted upon the keeping of most careful clinical records from the time of admission until the discharge of each patient; such records became very valuable later for statistical analyses. With William George MacCallum he held regular clinical-pathological conferences with regard to fatal cases, at which the clinical studies made during life were compared with the findings at autopsy. His students were urged, too, to make use of the library and were taught the importance and the technique of studies of the bibliography of the maladies that came under observation. A linguist himself, he encouraged his students to learn to read and to speak two or three foreign languages. As a consulting practitioner in medicine, he was much sought after because of his vast experience, his soundness of judgment, and his powers of inspiring confidence. A brilliant diagnostician, he was also a competent therapist, emphasizing always the adoption of the simpler methods of physical and mental treatment.

In 1917 he and his friend Frank Billings of Chicago were made members of the American Red Cross Mission to Russia, for which in 1918 he received the distinction badge of the Red Cross of Russia. While he was absent, in August 1917, his wife, Susan Chisolm (Read) Thayer, to whom he had been married on Sept. 3, 1901, died in Baltimore after a long invalidism. She left no children. He served successively as major, colonel, and brigadier-general of the medical corps in the World War and, during 1918–19, acted as chief consultant of the American Expeditionary Force in France. For these services he received the Distinguished Service Medal of the United States in 1919 and a commandership of the Legion of Honor in France in 1928. He was made fellow of many foreign medical academies and honorary member of a large number of scientific associations in this country and abroad. He was president of the American Medical Association, 1928–29. He served as a trustee of the Carnegie Institution of Washington and for two terms as a member of the board of overseers of Harvard University. Numerous honorary degrees were conferred upon him. He accepted invitations to deliver the Bright Lecture in London in 1927, the Gibson Lectures at Edinburgh in 1930, and the Frank Billings Lecture in Chicago in 1932. In May 1927 the "William Sydney Thayer and Susan Read Thayer Lectureship in Clinical Medicine," providing for one or more lectures annually at the Johns Hopkins, was endowed by a group of their friends. Physically he was of average height, slender in later life, and healthy until some three years before his death, when he began to suffer from anginal attacks. He died suddenly from a heart attack while visiting in Washington.

[L. F. Barker, "Wm. Sydney Thayer," *Science,* Dec. 30, 1932; *Harvard College Class of 1885 Secretary's Report,* no. 2–9 (1889–1925); *Who's Who in America,* 1932–33; Bezaleel Thayer, *Memorial of the Thayer Name* (1874), esp. pp. 184, 587, 590, 621; *N. Y. Times,* Dec. 12, 1932.]   L. F. B.

THÉBAUD, AUGUSTUS J. (Nov. 20, 1807– Dec. 17, 1885), Roman Catholic priest and educator, was born of an aristocratic family of wealth in Nantes, France, which was then still under the shadow of Carrier's terrorism. Its ruined churches depressed the spiritual and precocious child, who read tolerably well at four years of age and who progressed so rapidly under tutors in private schools that he was well advanced when he entered the local *petit séminaire* which accommodated candidates for the priesthood and young aristocrats who held aloof from Napoleonic foundations. Thereafter he studied theology in the Grand Seminary of Nantes, and on ordination to the priesthood he was named *vicaire* of St. Clement's Church in his native town. In 1835 he entered the Jesuit novitiate at Rome, completed a course of higher studies in the Roman College, and studied science at the Sorbonne in Paris (1836–38). In the meantime he took

his final vows in the Society on Dec. 3, 1837. Acquainted with the shortage of priests in America through the appeals of visiting prelates from the United States and the reports in the *Annals of the Propagation of the Faith,* Thébaud petitioned successfully to be sent on the American missions and arrived in New York, Dec. 18, 1838. His first assignment was at St. Mary's College, Marion County, Ky., where he taught chemistry and in 1846 presided as rector. When the Jesuits withdrew from the institution because of an apparent lack of episcopal appreciation (1846), and assumed control of St. John's College, Fordham, N. Y., on the invitation of Bishop John J. Hughes [*q.v.*], Thébaud went to St. John's, and served as rector and director of the diocesan seminary until he became pastor of St. Joseph's Church in Troy (1852–60). A tolerant man of tactful approach, he moderated nativist antagonism and established friendly relations with Episcopalian leaders and the Presbyterian employers of Irish labor. He was loved by the Irish for his dispatch of Jesuits to care for the stricken immigrants at Grosse Isle, Canada, in 1847. In accordance with the policy of his society, he was transferred frequently. He was rector and professor in Fordham (1860–63, 1874–75), pastor at Troy, N. Y. (1863–69, 1873–74), professor and preacher at a Jesuit institution and at St. Mary's Church in Montreal, pastor at Hudson City, N. J. (1870–73), and teacher and pastor at St. Francis Xavier's College and Church in New York City (1875–85). He died at Fordham and was buried in the college cemetery.

As a missionary, lecturer, distinguished preacher, and an associate of prelates, Thébaud became widely acquainted with the country, and undertook a serious study of immigration and social problems. He was a faithful observer, and his books and numerous essays on current religious, historical, and educational problems, published in Catholic magazines, have historical value. Two of his most valuable articles are those on "Superior Instruction in our Colleges" (*American Catholic Quarterly Review,* Oct. 1882) and "Freedom of Worship in the United States" (*Ibid.,* Apr. 1885). His books include *Gentilism* (1876), *The Church and the Gentile World at the First Promulgation of the Gospel* (2 vols., 1878), *The Church and the Moral World* (1881), and *The Irish Race in the Past and Present* (1873). In addition to *Louisa Kirkbride* (1879), an ephemeral novel of New York life, he left two valuable manuscript memoirs which were edited by C. G. Herbermann as *Forty Years in the United States of America* (1904), with a biographical sketch by T. J. Campbell, S. J., and *Three-Quarters of a Century* (2 vols., 1912–13).

[For biog. materials see Thébaud's own writings; Woodstock Letters; J. T. Smith, *The Cath. Church in N. Y.* (1905); B. J. Webb, *The Centenary of Catholicity in Ky.* (1884); rev. of *Gentilism*, in *Month and Cath. Rev.* (London), Apr. 1876; "Father Thébaud and His Critics," *Ibid.,* June, July 1876; obituaries in *Sun* (N. Y.), Dec. 18, *N. Y. Times,* Dec. 20, and *N. Y. Freeman's Jour.,* Dec. 26, 1885.]   R. J. P.

THEOBALD, SAMUEL (Nov. 12, 1846–Dec. 20, 1930), ophthalmologist, was born in Baltimore, Md., the son of Dr. Elisha Warfield Theobald and Sarah Frances (Smith) Theobald. His mother was a daughter of Dr. Nathan Ryno Smith [*q.v.*], and after the death of his father when he was five Theobald lived with his grandfather. He was educated at the preparatory school of George Carey, studied in his grandfather's office, and at the same time pursued his medical course at the University of Maryland, from which he received the degree of M.D. in 1867. On Apr. 30, 1867, at Bristol, R. I., he married Caroline Dexter de Wolf, by whom he had two daughters and one son. In 1870, after working with his grandfather for several years, he went abroad for eighteen months to specialize in ophthalmology and otology. In Vienna he studied the eye with Ferdinand von Arlt, Eduard Jaeger, and the ear with Leopold Maximilian Politzer; later he worked with William Bowman, George Critchett, and Jonathan Hutchinson at the Royal London Ophthalmic Hospital. In 1871 he returned to Baltimore to practise his specialties. He was the leading spirit in establishing the Baltimore Eye and Ear Dispensary in 1874, and in 1882, together with some colleagues, he founded the Baltimore Eye, Ear, and Throat Charity Hospital, with which he kept up an active association until within a few years of his death. From 1889 to 1925 he was ophthalmic surgeon to the Johns Hopkins Hospital; from 1896 until 1912, clinical professor of ophthalmology and otology in the Johns Hopkins School of Medicine; from 1912 to 1925, clinical professor of ophthalmology; from 1925 until his death, professor emeritus of ophthalmology.

In spite of a very large private and hospital practice, he was a prolific and forceful writer. A collection of one hundred and eighteen reprints of his articles covers a wide range of subjects of ophthalmological and otological interest. Those on the eye include descriptions of instruments that he devised, surgical procedures, clinical discussions, case reports, discussions of the relation of diseases of the eye to general disease, studies in the prevention of blindness, and reports upon new medicines and apparatus. His genius is

memorialized by his method of treating closure of the tear ducts and by his invention of lachrymal probes, which he described in 1877. He introduced boric acid to ophthalmologists ("Boric Acid; A New Remedy in Eye Diseases," *Medical Record,* Feb. 7, 1880), and in 1884, shortly after the discovery of the anesthetic properties of cocain, he wrote concerning his clinical experience with this drug. In 1892 he described the use of the electro-magnet for removing metallic particles from the eye. In 1906 he published his *Prevalent Diseases of the Eye,* an eminently practical volume of over five hundred pages. In addition to his articles on ophthalmological subjects, he wrote several papers upon the ear. He was keenly interested in the activities of medical societies, and served as president of the Medical and Chirurgical Faculty of Maryland (1900) and as president of the American Ophthalmological Society (1910). Throughout his career he took time for the courtesies of life, and he possessed to a rare degree the gift of friendship. Slightly but strongly built, he was exceedingly good to look upon. He was a skilful surgeon and a painstaking ophthalmologist, who held the esteem of the entire medical profession and whose patients became his friends and ardent admirers.

[See *Who's Who in America,* 1930–31; Harry Friedenwald, in *Archives of Ophthalmology,* Mar. 1931, and *Trans. Am. Ophthalmological Soc.,* vol. XXIX (1931); W. H. Wilmer, in *Bull. School of Medicine, Univ. of Md.,* May 1931, and *Am. Jour. of Ophthalmology,* Apr. 1931; obituary in *N. Y. Times,* Dec. 21, 1930. Information has been supplied by Theobald's daughter, Mrs. J. W. Williams, and by Dr. J. M. H. Rowland. A large collection of reprints of articles by Theobald is in the possession of the lib. of the Medical and Chirurgical Faculty, Baltimore, Md.]   W. H. W.

THEUS, JEREMIAH (*c.* 1719–May 18, 1774), portrait painter, was born, it is believed, in Switzerland. About 1739 his parents with their three sons joined the colony of Swiss and German immigrants then lately settled in Orangeburg County, S. C. (Salley, *post,* p. 81). One son, the Rev. Christian (or Christianus) Theus, became a celebrated and effective preacher in South Carolina. What training in art Jeremiah may have had is unknown. By 1740 he was painting in Charleston, for he advertised, Aug. 30, 1740, in the *South Carolina Gazette:* "Jeremiah Theus, Limner, gives notice that he is removed into Market Square, near Mr. John Laurens, Sadler, where all Gentlemen and Ladies may have their pictures drawn, likewise Landscapes of all sizes, Crests and Coats of Arms for Coaches and Chaises. Likewise for the convenience of those who live in the country he is willing to wait on them at their respective Plantations." Four years later, Nov. 5, 1744, he inserted a notice in the *Gazette* "to all young Gentlemen and Ladies inclinable to be taught the Art of *Drawing*" that he would open an evening school at his house in Friend Street, where "every Branch of that Art" would be taught "with the greatest Exactness" (*South Carolina Historical and Genealogical Magazine,* October 1930, p. 315). Thus began a career during which Theus made likenesses of many men and women of the southern colonies.

In connection with an exhibition of colonial portraits at the Copley Gallery, Boston, about forty canvases by Theus were listed (*Boston Evening Transcript,* June 1, 1917), some of them previously mistaken for works by John Singleton Copley [*q.v.*]. Several portraits were of the South Carolina Huguenot connection, with whom Theus was evidently intimate: Samuel Prioleau and his wife, Mr. and Mrs. Gabriel Manigault, Peter Porcher, Mrs. Thomas Cordes, and others (A. H. Hirsch, *The Huguenots of Colonial South Carolina,* 1928, p. 163). Among his portraits of Jewish sitters were those of Mr. and Mrs. Manuel Josephson (Hannah R. London, *Portraits of Jews by Gilbert Stuart and Other Early American Artists,* 1927). A not inept characterization of Theus' artistry is that of Dunlap (*post,* vol. I, p. 31), who says that, though the faces were painted with great care, "he had not the art to give grace and picturesque effect to the stiff brocades, enormous ruffles, and *outre* stays and stomachers of our grandmothers; or the wigs, velvet coats, and waistcoats . . . of our grandfathers. His pictures were as stiff and formal as the originals, when dressed for the purpose and sitting for them." The characteristic concealment of the sitter's hands may indicate a weakness in his powers, but his drawing was accurate, his coloring good, and the likenesses unmistakably true (Wilson, *post,* p. 142).

Theus married, Jan. 13, 1741/42, Elizabeth Catherine Schaumlöffel, who died Nov. 8, 1754, leaving three sons and two daughters. Late in life he married Mrs. Eva Rosanna Hilt, who bore him two sons and two daughters. He accumulated a sizable fortune, his estate including a house at Broad and Mazyck streets (destroyed by fire in 1861), and a pew in the south gallery of St. Michael's Church, Charleston. Doubtless many of his portraits, unlisted, the artist's name unknown to the owners, still hang in plantation houses.

[According to J. H. Morgan, *Early Am. Painters* (1921), p. 9, Theus sometimes signed his name Theüs. See also Robert Wilson, in *Year Book, 1899, City of Charleston, S. C.,* App., p. 137; A. S. Salley, Jr., *The Hist. of Orangeburg County, S. C.* (1898); William Dunlap, *A Hist. of the Rise and Progress of the Arts of Design in the U. S.* (3 vols., 1918), ed. by F. W. Bayley, and C. E. Goodspeed.]   F. W. C.

THIERRY, CAMILLE (October 1814–April 1875), Louisiana poet, was born in New Orleans, the son of a Frenchman from Bordeaux and his octoroon mistress. Camille at first had private tutors but when he was older went to day school. He was preparing to go to a college in Paris when his father died, leaving him a small fortune. What decided him to change his mind no one knows, but he remained in New Orleans and went into business. Being entirely unfitted for its drudgery, however, he soon gave it up. Once free from its restraint he made frequent trips to Paris, where he lived in a spectacularly dissipated fashion and wasted his patrimony. In 1855, convinced by these visits that he could no longer bear the intellectual and social isolation imposed upon him in New Orleans because of his color, he placed all his affairs in the hands of his agents, Lafitte, Dufilho & Company, and went to Paris to live. There he frequented literary circles and continued his tempestuous career for some years until, suddenly tiring of it, he withdrew to Bordeaux, where he lived the life of an anchorite. He had written a good deal of French verse, and as early as 1843 his "Idées" was published in *L'Album Littéraire* of New Orleans. When Armand Lanusse in 1845 was preparing his anthology of French verse written by Louisiana men of color, he included in *Les Cenelles,* as he called it, fourteen of Thierry's poems, twice as many as those of anyone's else, which goes to show that Thierry was regarded as one of the leading poets of his race. His verses were especially admired for their quality of freshness and gentleness, although a note of bitterness born of racial discrimination crept into his later poetry, which clearly showed the inspiration of Charles-Hubert Millevoye and Lamartine.

In 1873 his Louisiana agents became bankrupt, and Thierry lost both the rents they had collected and the capital he had invested in their firm. Leaving his retreat in Bordeaux, he sailed for New Orleans to attempt to straighten out his affairs. But he was more a poet than a business man, and so he was persuaded to transfer all title in his real estate to his agents, who had reembarked in business, upon their promise to pay him an annuity of fifty dollars a month for the rest of his life. He returned to Bordeaux and, collecting all his fugitive poems, published them there at his own expense in a small volume called *Les Vagabondes,* which appeared in 1874. Shortly after this Lafitte, Dufilho & Company failed again, Thierry's annuity was discontinued, and he was left practically penniless. This shock was too much for him, and in April 1875 he died in Bordeaux. His verses were so popular that for years after his death they were reprinted from time to time in the Creole press of Louisiana.

[E. L. Tinker, *Les Écrits de Langue Française en Louisiane aux XIXe Siècle* (1932), and *Les Cenelles: Afro-French Poetry in Louisiana* (1930), reprinted from the *Colophon*, pt. III; R. L. Desdunes, *Nos Hommes et Notre Histoire* (1911); Armand Mercier, in *Comptes Rendus de l'Athénée Louisianais*, Jan. 1, 1878, p. 135; Ruby Van A. Caulfeild, *The French Lit. of La.* (1929).]   E. L. T.

THOBURN, ISABELLA (Mar. 29, 1840–Sept. 1, 1901), missionary and educator, was born at St. Clairsville, Ohio, the daughter of Matthew and Jane Lyle (Crawford) Thoburn, and a sister of James M. Thoburn [*q.v.*]. She attended the public schools, and in her fifteenth year entered the Female Seminary of Wheeling, Va. (now W. Va.). After a period of teaching she returned to the Wheeling institution, now become a college, for further study, and subsequently spent a year in the Cincinnati Academy of Design. During the Civil War she gave herself freely to organizing relief groups and sewing circles, collecting supplies, feeding passing troops, and nursing the wounded in the hospitals. Teaching in Wheeling, W. Va., Newcastle, Pa., and West Farmington, Ohio, prepared her further for what was to be her life career.

In 1869 her brother James, then in India, convinced that because of their home responsibilities the wives of missionaries could not be depended upon to meet the demands of women's work, wrote a letter to his sister which he closed with these words: "The women of India need you. How would you like to come and take charge of … a school, if we decide to make the attempt?" By return steamer Isabella replied that she would "come just as soon as a way was opened" (Thoburn, *post*, p. 34). That same year the Woman's Foreign Missionary Society of the Methodist Episcopal Church was founded in Boston, Mass., and under its auspices, on Nov. 3, accompanied by Dr. Clara A. Swain [*q.v.*], she sailed for India, arriving in Bombay on Jan. 7, 1870. The city of Lucknow in Oudh became the center of her activities. Into the education of the girls and young women of India she threw herself with zeal and courage. On Apr. 18, in Aminabad bazaar, she began a school with six girls and herself the only teacher, while a Christian youth guarded the group with a stout bamboo. From a day school it developed into a boarding school, then into a high school, and finally into a college for women—now the Isabella Thoburn College, the women's college of Lucknow University. Buying the beautiful estate of the Ruby Garden

(Lal Bagh) with its seven acres from a Mohammedan nobleman of the old kingdom of Oudh, she erected her buildings. The college that came into being was for Indian and Eurasian, Hindu, Mohammedan, and Christian alike; no religious or racial prejudice was to mar its peace and fellowship.

She was in America in 1880–81, and again from 1886 to 1891. During this latter period she was closely associated with the new Deaconess movement in the Methodist Episcopal Church, and herself became a graduate deaconess. She assisted Lucy Rider Meyer in the Chicago Training School, and was the founder in Cincinnati, Ohio, of the Elizabeth Gamble Deaconess Home and Training School, and of the Christ Hospital. Returning to India, she continued her educational activities. In 1899 she came back to the United States, accompanied by Lilavati Singh, one of her graduates and teachers, seeking funds. The two Christian women made a deep impression upon the Ecumenical Conference held in New York in 1900. That same year she returned to India and on Sept. 1, 1901, died of Asiatic cholera in Lucknow. The Isabella Thoburn College and the Lal Bagh High School remain her perpetual memorials. She also founded the Girls' High School in Cawnpore (1874), and helped in establishing the Wellesley School for girls in Naini Tal (1891). For years she edited the *Rafiq-i-Niswan* (*The Woman's Friend*), a paper that went into non-Christian *zenanas* and Christian homes. She also wrote and published in 1899 a life of Phoebe Rowe, one of her teachers and friends.

[Files of the *Indian Witness*, *Heathen Woman's Friend*, and *Woman's Missionary Friend*; W. F. Oldham, "Isabella Thoburn," in *Effective Workers in Needy Fields* (1902); J. M. Thoburn, *Life of Isabella Thoburn* (1903); B. T. Badley, *Visions and Victories in Hindustan* (2 vols., 1932); *Christian Advocate*, Oct. 17, 1901; *Northwestern Christian Advocate*, Sept. 11, 1901.]   O. M. B.

THOBURN, JAMES MILLS (Mar. 7, 1836–Nov. 28, 1922), missionary bishop of the Methodist Episcopal Church, was born in St. Clairsville, Ohio. He was the seventh child of Matthew Thoburn (originally Thorburn) and Jane Lyle (Crawford), Irish immigrants (1825) from counties Down and Antrim. On their way to Ohio the four-story brick building of Allegheny College at Meadville captured their imagination, and to this college in later years they sent all five of their sons. James entered in 1851; for two years he taught school at Loydsville, Ohio; then returned to graduate in 1857. While he was teaching, religious difficulties by which he had been disturbed became clarified, and he entered the ministry of the Methodist Episcopal Church, being admitted on trial to the Pittsburgh Conference in 1858.

Feeling called to missionary service, he was sent to India in 1859 by the Missionary Society of his Church, after ordination under the auspices of the New England Conference. His first appointment was Naini Tal, a hill station in the Himalayas (Kumaon Division, United Provinces). Preaching each Sunday to British troops in a formal "parade-service," he made a discovery: "I found," he said, "I could give the people God's message a great deal more effectively in thirty minutes than in sixty" (*My Missionary Apprenticeship*, p. 72). In time he became known as the best preacher of his church in India. On Dec. 16, 1861, he married Sarah Minerva (Rockwell), widow of J. R. Downey; she died on Oct. 30, 1862, leaving him a son. Thoburn returned to America with his motherless child in October 1863, and was tempted strongly to remain and organize a school for preparing missionaries, but the frank questioning of his sister Isabella [*q.v.*] as to the nature of his "call" sent him back to India in 1865. The North India Conference appointed him to Pauri (Garhwal), a remote station in the Himalayas, where for over two years he had few returns for his labors but much time to brood over big ideas. He was sent next to the thickly populated plains of the upper Ganges Valley, serving at Moradabad (1868), Sambhal (1869), Rae Bareilly (1870), and Lucknow (1871–73). During these years he matured rapidly and became intimately associated with the problems occasioned by the influx of converts from the depressed classes, the opening of work among Indian women by unmarried women missionaries from America, and the expansion of religious activities throughout India in consequence of the evangelistic meetings of William Taylor [*q.v.*].

On Taylor's insistence Thoburn left Lucknow in 1874 to shepherd, without salary from the Missionary Society, the little group of Taylor's converts in Calcutta, and until 1888 he was associated with missionary enterprise in that city. On one of the busiest streets he built, and later rebuilt, a church, which was filled twice every Sunday. "It is the strangest church I ever saw," one person remarked. "It seemed to me that all the bad people in Calcutta were there" (*My Missionary Apprenticeship*, p. 319). Sailors, soldiers, Europeans, and Asiatics were in the congregation. In religious work among Europeans and Anglo-Indians, Thoburn became the outstanding figure in India. All the time, however, he was dreaming of farther India, and in 1879

he began work in Rangoon; in 1884–85 with William F. Oldham he was in Singapore founding a church; in 1885 he was appointed general evangelist. The General Conference of 1888 elected him missionary bishop for India (later Southern Asia), and until his retirement in 1908 he performed the duties of this office with notable skill and power, being the acknowledged missionary leader in his denomination. In America he won innumerable friends for his far-flung missions; on the field his "singular blend of the mystical enthusiast and the clear-seeing practically-minded man" (Oldham, *post*, p. 17) gave him great effectiveness. The years of his administration witnessed a remarkable growth both in number of converts and in extent of territory occupied. Soon the Methodists were in almost every great city of India, in Baluchistan, in Java, in Sumatra, and in British Borneo. When the Philippines were opened in 1898 Thoburn was first on the field. After his retirement he settled in Meadville, Pa. Allegheny College honored him by a jubilee celebration in 1909, which brought fitting recognition to his career. When he died he was buried in the college plot. His second wife, whom he married in Philadelphia, Nov. 11, 1880, was Dr. Anna Jones of Kingston, Ohio. At the time of their marriage she was preparing for medical missionary work, and in 1882 she joined her husband in India; she died in 1902. Of Thoburn's five children three grew to maturity.

In spite of his numerous activities, Thoburn was continually busy with his pen. In 1871, with James H. Messmore, he started a small paper to which he contributed and which developed into the *Indian Witness*, official organ of the Methodist Episcopal Church in India. He was also the author of a number of books, among which may be mentioned: *My Missionary Apprenticeship* (1887); *Missionary Addresses before Theological Schools* (1887); *India and Malaysia* (1892); *The Deaconess and Her Vocation* (1893); *Light in the East* (1894); *The Christless Nations* (1895), Graves Lectures at Syracuse University; *The Church of Pentecost* (1901); *Life of Isabella Thoburn* (1903); *The Christian Conquest of India* (1906); *India and Southern Asia* (1907). To the *Western Christian Advocate* he contributed "Wayside Notes: An Autobiography," published between Jan. 4 and Dec. 27, 1911, and to the *Northwestern Christian Advocate*, "How Christ Came to India," published between Jan. 3 and Apr. 24, 1912.

[Files of the Board of Foreign Missions of the Methodist Episcopal Church; files of *Indian Witness*; *Christian Advocate*, Apr. 22, 1909; *Western Christian Advocate*, Apr. 21, 1909; *Northwestern Christian Advo-*

cate, Dec. 6, 1922; *World Wide Missions*, Dec. 1904; W. F. Oldham, *Thoburn—Called of God* (1918); B. T. Badley, *Visions and Victories in Hindustan* (2 vols., 1932); W. H. Crawford, *Thoburn and India* (1909); *Who's Who in America*, 1908–09; *N. Y. Times*, Nov. 29, 1922.]
O. M. B.

THOMAS, ALLEN (Dec. 14, 1830–Dec. 3, 1907), Confederate soldier, diplomat, was born in Howard County, Md., the son of Allen and Eliza Bradford (Dall) Thomas. He was a descendant of Tristram Thomas, born in England, who settled in Talbot County, Md., in 1666. Tristram's father, Christopher, had been in Maryland in 1637–38, but returned to England and came back to Maryland in 1664. The elder Allen Thomas, a physician and farmer, was a leading man in the neighborhood, a member of the legislature for several terms, and once a presidential elector. The son entered Princeton as a sophomore in 1847 and graduated in 1850. He studied law under John S. Tyson in Ellicott City, Md., was admitted to the bar, and practised for several years in Howard County, but following his marriage, Jan. 8, 1857, to Anne Octavie Marie, daughter of Michel Doradu Bringier of New Orleans, he removed to Louisiana and became a planter, retaining, however, his family estate, "Dalton," in Maryland. His wife, through her sister's marriages, was a sister-in-law of Duncan F. Kenner, Richard Taylor [qq.v.], and Horr Browse Trist, brother of Nicholas P. Trist [q.v.]. Thomas had four sons.

At the beginning of the Civil War he organized a battalion of infantry, of which he was appointed major. It was later expanded into the 28th Louisiana Regiment (some official records call it the 29th). Thomas was elected its colonel and was appointed in October 1862 with rank antedated to May 3. He served during the Vicksburg campaign, notably at the battle of Chickasaw Bluffs, and during the subsequent siege, commanding his regiment and at times a brigade. After the surrender of Vicksburg he was paroled and carried the report of Gen. John C. Pemberton [q.v.] to President Davis. Subsequently, he was put in charge of collecting other paroled prisoners and reorganizing them west of the Mississippi. Appointed brigadier-general, Feb. 4, 1864, to the place vacated by Gen. Henry W. Allen [q.v.], who had resigned upon his election as governor of Louisiana, Thomas was assigned to the command of a brigade of troops from that state, then stationed at Alexandria, La. He served with it until Polignac's departure for France, when he succeeded to the command of the division. He surrendered and was paroled at Natchitoches, La., on June 8, 1865.

Again he became a planter at New Hope on the Mississippi River. He was a presidential elector in 1872 and in 1880, voting for Greeley and Hancock; in 1876 he declined nomination for Congress. He was a member of the board of supervisors of Louisiana State University in 1882, and from 1882 to 1884 was professor of agriculture in that institution. Following a term of service as coiner of the mint in New Orleans during Cleveland's first administration, he removed in 1889 to Florida, which remained his home till near the end of his life. In January 1894 he was commissioned consul at La Guayra, and in July of the next year took over the legation at Caracas as envoy extraordinary and minister plenipotentiary to Venezuela. His tenure of office covered the period of controversy over the boundary of British Guiana. There is nothing in his dispatches to the state department, however, to suggest that he was consulted as to American policy toward Great Britain, or that he had any influence upon President Cleveland's vigorous action in defense of Venezuela's rights. Resigning after the change of administration, he left the legation in June 1897 and returned to Florida. Some ten years later he removed to a plantation which he had bought at Waveland, Miss., and there he died. He was buried in the Bringier family vault at Donaldsonville, La.

[R. H. Spencer, *Thomas Family of Talbot County, Md.* (1914); C. A. Evans, *Confederate Mil. Hist.* (1899); A. B. Booth, *Records of La. Confederate Soldiers and La. Confederate Commands* (1920); *War of the Rebellion: Official Records* (Army); S. C. Arthur and G. C. H. de Kerniou, *Old Families of La.* (1931); *New Orleans Picayune* and *New Orleans Times-Democrat*, Dec. 4, 1907, valuable for facts but inaccurate as to several dates; *Princeton Alumni Weekly*, Jan. 22, 1908; papers in U. S. State Dept. archives.] T. M. S.

THOMAS, AMOS RUSSELL (Oct. 3, 1826–Oct. 31, 1895), homoeopathic physician, teacher of anatomy, was born at Watertown, N. Y., the son of Azariah and Sarah (Avery) Thomas. He was a descendant of Evan Thomas who emigrated from Wales to Massachusetts in 1640. He spent his early life on a farm, where much of his spare time was occupied by reading. He was educated in the common schools and in the Jefferson County Institute, and in 1846 he began teaching in the schools of western New York. On Sept. 26, 1847, he married Elizabeth M. Bacon of Watertown, by whom he had a son and a daughter. In 1850 he entered business in Ogdensburg, N. Y., but found it distasteful and soon abandoned it. Meanwhile his study of an Indian skull so aroused his interest in anatomy that he arranged to study medicine, and in 1852 under the preceptorship of Dr. S. Potter of Syracuse, N. Y., he entered the Syracuse Medical College, from which he graduated in February 1854. He then moved to Philadelphia and entered Penn Medical University, where he was later professor of anatomy (1856–66). For some years he was lecturer on artistic anatomy in the Philadelphia Academy of the Fine Arts (1856–70) and in the Philadelphia School of Design for Women (1863–71). During the Civil War he served as a surgeon and was assigned a post in charge of a ward at the Armory Square Hospital, Washington, D.C. On being mustered out, he returned to Philadelphia. He had become interested in homoeopathy, and in 1867 he accepted the position of professor of anatomy in the Hahnemann Medical College of Philadelphia, which he held until his death. From 1874 until 1895 he served with great interest and enthusiasm as dean of the college and it was largely through his efforts that funds were raised for a new college building.

His publications include *A Practical Guide for Making Post-Mortem Examinations and for the Study of Morbid Anatomy, with Directions for Embalming the Dead and for the Preservation of Specimens of Morbid Anatomy* (1873); *The Diseases of the Pancreas, and their Homoeopathic Treatment* (1882), with several collaborators; *A New Preparation of the Nervous System* (1889), which contains a description of a unique dissection of the entire nervous system in the museum of Hahnemann Medical College; *History of Anatomy* (1893); and *Genealogical Records and Sketches of the Descendants of William Thomas of Hardwick, Mass.* (1891). In addition to these, he was the author of numerous papers on general medicine published in various homoeopathic journals, and in the transactions of the American Institute of Homoeopathy and of the Homoeopathic Medical Society of Pennsylvania. He was editor of the *American Journal of Homoeopathic Materia Medica* (1871–76) and co-editor of the *Hahnemannian Monthly* (1877–78). In 1887 he was president of the Homoeopathic Medical Society of Pennsylvania. He was a member of a number of scientific, historical, and art associations. He died in Philadelphia, survived by his son.

[A. R. Thomas, *Geneal. Records . . . of the Descendants of William Thomas of Hardwick, Mass.* (1891); L. B. Thomas, *The Thomas Book* (copr. 1896); T. L. Bradford, *Hist. of the Homoeopathic Medic. Coll. of Pa., the Hahnemann Medic. Coll. and Hospital of Pa.* (1898), and "Biogs. of Homoeopathic Physicians," vol. XXXI, in the lib. of the Hahnemann Medic. Coll.; H. A. Kelly and W. L. Burrage, *Am. Medic. Biogs.* (1920); *Hahnemannian Monthly*, Oct. 1892, Dec. 1895; *Pacific Coast Jour. of Homoeopathy*, Jan. 1896; obituary in *Pub. Ledger* (Phila.), Nov. 1, 1895.]

C. B—t.

THOMAS, AUGUSTUS (Jan. 8, 1857–Aug. 12, 1934), dramatist, was born in St. Louis, Mo., the son of Elihu Baldwin and Imogene (Garrett-

son) Thomas. Between grade and high school in St. Louis he served as a page boy, first at the Missouri state capitol (1868) and then in the House of Representatives at Washington (1870–71). While in Washington he was caught by Gen. Benjamin Franklin Butler [*q.v.*] making a caricature of that statesman. Butler (who had a huge cranium) took his hat and jammed it down over the boy's head to the shoulders, remarking, "When you can fill that hat, young man, you make caricatures of General Butler" (*The Print of My Remembrance*, 1922, p. 50). Young Thomas followed most of the debates, and laid the foundation of a lasting interest in public affairs and public speaking. Beginning at fourteen he worked in the St. Louis railroad yards, with evening study and practice in drawing, acting, and playwriting. For a time he was a reporter on the *St. Louis Post-Dispatch* (1885). In 1887 he worked in Kansas City as a newspaper man, and the next year returned to St. Louis, where he was staff artist on a newspaper. But in the meantime, between jobs, he had made a stage version of Mrs. Frances Hodgson Burnett's story, "Editha's Burglar," and with this and an improvised vaudeville program he and several other stage-struck young people, including Della Fox, had attempted to tour the Middle West. They made two trips, in fact, but secured more adventure than cash. The experience fixed Thomas in his determination to become a playwright, however, and with several play scripts in his bag he set out for New York in 1888. Failing to sell the plays, he took a job as business assistant to Julia Marlowe, and then as "press agent" to the so-called thought reader, Washington Irving Bishop. A year later he sold *The Burglar* to Maurice Barrymore [*q.v.*], and in 1891 attracted wide attention with *Alabama*, produced by the Palmer stock company.

After this success his road was easy. Among his better known plays produced in the nineties were *In Mizzoura* (1893), *Colonel Carter of Cartersville* (1892), *The Capitol* (1895), *Colonel George of Mount Vernon* (1895), *Chimmie Fadden* (1896), *The Hoosier Doctor* (1897), and most successful of all, *Arizona* (1899). Nearly all these plays, it will be noted, belonged to the local-color school. After the turn of the century Thomas inclined to farce comedy for a time, and in rapid succession wrote *The Earl of Pawtucket* (1903), *The Other Girl* (1903), *Mrs. Leffingwell's Boots* (1905), and *De Lancey* (1905). In 1907 he produced *The Witching Hour*, which was based on his experiences with Bishop many years before, and which was in a much more serious vein than his previous work.

This drama proved extremely popular. Thomas followed it with two others in the same general vein, *The Harvest Moon* (1909), and *As a Man Thinks* (1911). The last remains probably his best play, both in technique and substance. He wrote a dozen or fifteen more plays, the best known being *The Copperhead* (1918), but never again reached the level of popularity or achievement which marked his work in the late nineties and the first decade of the new century. In all, he wrote or adapted nearly seventy plays.

He was president of the National Institute of Arts and Letters (1914–15), a member of the American Academy of Arts and Letters, and a recipient of its medal for drama (1913). From 1922 through 1925 he acted as executive chairman of the Producing Managers' Association, and during that time made a vain effort to found a national theatre. He took a life-long interest in public speaking and debate, and was in constant demand as an after-dinner speaker because of his wit, and as a speaker for the Democratic party. It was frequently noted that his curtain speeches at the first nights of his plays seemed sometimes to have more style and substance than the plays. This was perhaps because he was reared in the old-fashioned theatre of melodrama and sheer entertainment, and was quite unaffected by the "new drama" which came in during the nineties. (He makes no reference to it whatever in his autobiography, *The Print of My Remembrance,* 1922). His descriptions of securing local color for his "State" plays, like *Arizona* and *Colorado,* disclose painstaking trips to the chosen scenes, but no stirring of dramatic interest in what lay below the surface. It was only his reflections on the telepathic feats of Bishop that prompted him, in *The Witching Hour* and *As a Man Thinks,* to probe below surfaces. Technically, his plays were well put together, and because of their theatrical expertness and local color were important in their day in helping to free the American stage from bondage to Europe and in solidifying the dramatist's craft in America. As president of the American Dramatists' Association from 1906 to 1911, also, Thomas was able by his shrewdness and force of character to exert a great influence. But, in spite of his successes, his plays (with the possible exception of *As a Man Thinks*) did little to further the development of playwriting or to inspire younger writers to tackle more significant and less "theatrical" themes. Considering his wide acquaintance with the American scene and with the leading men of the day, his interest in political questions, his keen mind and sharp wit, it is curious that he was so little affected by the new drama which was being born around him, and apparently made so little effort to put his best powers into his plays.

Thomas was a moderately tall, sturdy man, both democratic and dignified, with a square, smooth-shaven face, a generous mouth set in parentheses, and a pugnacious chin. He had a rather slow, clear-cut speech in public, and a masterly technique for making his incisive wit and epigram tell to the full. After coming to New York, he lived most of his life in New Rochelle, near his intimate friend, Frederic Remington [*q.v.*], but passed a few years early in the twentieth century in Paris, and the last two years of his life near Nyack, where he died. He was survived by his wife—Lisle Colby of St. Louis, sister of Bainbridge Colby, whom he had married on Aug. 16, 1890,—a daughter, and a son.

[In addition to *The Print of My Remembrance,* see *Who's Who in America,* 1934–35; A. H. Quinn, *A Hist. of the Am. Drama from the Civil War to the Present Day* (2 vols., 1927); Burns Mantle, *Am. Playwrights of Today* (1929); W. D. Howells, in *North Am. Rev.,* Mar. 1901; preface to *The Witching Hour,* and other plays by Thomas, Samuel French edition; Locke Theatre Coll. in N. Y. Pub. Lib., and Theatre Coll. in Harvard Univ. Lib.; obituaries in *N. Y. Times, N. Y. Herald Tribune,* and *St. Louis Post-Dispatch,* Aug. 13, 1934.]
W. P. E.

THOMAS, CALVIN (Oct. 28, 1854–Nov. 4, 1919), German scholar, was born in a log cabin at Lapeer, Mich., the son of Stephen Van Rensselaer Thomas and Caroline Louisa (Lord) Thomas, who had not long before emigrated from the state of New York. Stephen Thomas was a sturdy and enterprising young farmer who fought under Burnside and Stoneman in the Civil War, and won a captaincy in the 10th Michigan Cavalry. Later he became a lawyer and attained some prominence in politics. The bracing life of early farming days offered the son a wholesome opportunity for all-round development. At eleven years he had not only become something of a naturalist and hunter, but had won great renown as a young spelling prodigy. Ready for college at fourteen, two years before he could be admitted, he entered the University of Michigan in 1870 as the youngest of his class, specializing in Latin and Greek, and graduating in 1874 as valedictorian. After three years of teaching at the high school in Grand Rapids, he went in 1877 to Leipzig for further study of the classics. Before the year was out, however, he was called back to his university to teach Greek; but, owing to certain exigencies, he was almost at once given full-time work in German and was made professor in 1886.

From this point on, his career as teacher and scholar was one of steady progress. During the next ten or fifteen years he contributed upward of one hundred articles and reviews to various journals, especially to the *Nation*. But he soon began to concentrate on the subject of Goethe. In 1888 he published *Goethe's Torquato Tasso* and within the next ten years made a notable contribution to scholarship in his brilliantly edited *Goethe's Faust* (2 vols., 1892–97), one of the greatest literary commentaries in the English language. His other publications include his widely used *A Practical German Grammar* (1896), *The Life and Works of Friedrich Schiller* (1901), *An Anthology of German Literature* (1907), and *A History of German Literature* (1909). Finally came the work upon which he bestowed some of his most loving care and labor, his *Goethe* (1917). A complete enumeration of his edited texts, reviews, and addresses would make a list many times as long. Thirteen of his papers were published by his colleagues in 1924 under the title *Scholarship, and Other Essays*. As consulting editor (1909) of the *New Standard Dictionary,* he wrote each of the twenty-six articles on the history of the letters of the alphabet and their phonetic values. For a time he was an enthusiastic spelling reformer and a member of the Simplified Spelling Board. He was also one of the founders of the Modern Language Association of America and its president for 1896–97. In 1896 he was called to Columbia University as Gebhard Professor of Germanic Languages and Literatures, where the wide range of his scholarship, his tolerance and wisdom, no less than the warm glow of his sympathy and sense of humor, endeared him to his students and colleagues alike. He was married first, on Mar. 25, 1880, to Mary J. Sutton of Lapeer, who died in the same year, and again, on June 16, 1884, to Mary Eleanor Allen of Grand Rapids, by whom he had two sons.

[*Who's Who in America,* 1918–19; B. A. Hinsdale, *Hist. of the Univ. of Mich.* (1906), ed. by I. N. Demmon; W. A. Braun, biog. introduction to *Scholarship, and Other Essays* (1924); obituary in *N. Y. Times,* Nov. 5, 1919; Thomas' unpublished autobiog. notes.]
W. A. B.

THOMAS, CHARLES SPALDING (Dec. 6, 1849–June 24, 1934), senator, lawyer, was born on a plantation near Darien, Ga., the son of William Brownell and Caroline Baldwin (Wheeler) Thomas, Connecticut Yankees who had moved into the South. His father died during his early boyhood. Charles was sent to a private school where discipline was strict but instruction good, and during the final months of the Civil War he served in the Confederate army. After Appomattox his mother returned to Connecticut and later moved to Michigan, where after her death

Charles attended the University of Michigan, graduating in law in 1871. Since Georgia offered no prospects for the future, he migrated to Denver, Col., in the same year.

Denver in 1871 was a small city with limited opportunities, but Thomas quickly won success as a criminal lawyer. In 1875 and 1876 he was city attorney; in 1873–74 and again from 1879 to 1890 he was a partner of Thomas M. Patterson [*q.v.*]. Following the rush of 1879 to Leadville, he built up a solid reputation as one of the leading mining lawyers of the state. His most famous case, the Del Monte-Last Chance case (171 *U. S.,* 55), resulted in the settlement of several difficult and important points in the interpretation of mining law. In 1885 he returned to Denver to be associated with several partners until he retired from active practice in 1927. He was noted as one of the keenest and most fearless attorneys in Colorado.

Thomas entered early upon a political career that witnessed many vicissitudes. He was too frank and critical to be a conventional party man. In 1882 he was state chairman of the Democratic party and from 1884 to 1896, a member of the Democratic National Committee. He was an unsuccessful candidate for the House of Representatives in 1884, but his greatest political ambition was to be elected United States senator. A candidate for that office in 1889, he was defeated by Edward O. Wolcott [*q.v.*]. In 1894 he ran for the governorship without hope of election; in January 1895 he was again a candidate for the senatorship, but received only three votes in the joint session of the legislature. In 1898 he was elected governor by the silver fusionists, and when his term was drawing to a close (1900–01) he once more entered the senatorial race, but withdrew when he found that the majority of the Democrats were pledged to Thomas M. Patterson. At last, in 1913, he realized his ambition when he entered the Senate to complete the term of Charles J. Hughes. He was elected for a full term in 1914, but in 1920, persuaded by friends to run as an independent candidate, he went down to overwhelming defeat.

Thomas was in Washington, as he had been in Colorado, a non-conformist. He opposed the Treaty of Versailles, the League of Nations, the soldiers' bonus, and the demands of the railroad brotherhood and profiteering capitalists. He was an ardent bimetallist, even after his party had abandoned the cause. He served as special counsel for the Korean Commission while the United States watched in apathy the actions of Japan. A lawyer, he denounced the conservatism and venality of the bar; a politician, he poured out his scorn upon time-serving congressmen and party leaders. He opposed the "New Deal" of President Franklin D. Roosevelt. One of his last acts, at eighty-four, was to defy the presidential proclamation against the hoarding of gold (*New York Times,* May 4, 5, 1933).

Thomas was married, Dec. 29, 1873, to Emma Fletcher of Kalamazoo, Mich., by whom he had five children. He died in Denver after writing "A Salute to Death" in which he explained his refusal to give allegiance "to any man-made religion either revealed or otherwise."

[The brief sketch in vol. V, "Biographical," accompanying J. H. Baker and L. R. Hafen, *Hist. of Col.* (1927), is reasonably accurate; the account of Thomas' legal work in the *Rocky Mountain Law Review,* Apr. 1931, has merit; the privately printed *Closing Events in the Last Years of the Career of Charles S. Thomas* (Denver, 1934), contains reprints of newspaper biographies and other pertinent material. See also *Who's Who in America,* 1932–33; *Portr. and Biog. Record of the State of Col.* (1899); W. N. Byers, *Encyc. of Biog. of Col.* (1901); *Biog. Dir. Am. Cong.* (1928); *Rocky Mountain News* (Denver), June 25, 1934.] J. F. W.

THOMAS, CHRISTIAN FRIEDRICH THEODORE (Oct. 11, 1835–Jan. 4, 1905), musician, conductor, was born at Esens, Germany, the eldest child of Johann August Thomas, the *Stadtpfeifer,* or chief town musician of Esens, and his wife Sophia, the daughter of a physician at Göttingen. The boy showed his talent for music when he was only two years old. His father gave him a few violin lessons, and according to the *Memoirs* of Mrs. Thomas (*post*) he seemed to be recalling something he had known before whenever he was taught anything in music. In 1845 the household emigrated to New York, for the meager income of the *Stadtpfeifer* was not enough to support the growing family. In New York, matters were not much better and it was necessary for Theodore to play his violin for dances, weddings, in theatres, and sometimes in saloons, where he passed his hat for the coins of the generous.

In 1850 Thomas took a concert trip through the South, unaided and alone. When he came to a town he would tack up a few posters announcing a concert by "Master T. T.," the remarkable prodigy. Then he would stand at the door and sell tickets until he decided that all who were coming had arrived. At this point he would rush backstage to change his clothes, and then appear before the audience with his violin. When Louis Antoine Jullien came to America in 1853, Thomas was chosen as one of the first violins of the orchestra. He was disgusted with Jullien's antics and showmanship, but he gained his first idea of the symphony from this conductor. In 1854 he was elected a member of the Philharmonic Society of New York, and in the following

year he joined William Mason, 1829–1908 [*q.v.*], in the series of Mason-Thomas chamber music concerts which were given at Dodworth's Hall, next to Grace Church, Broadway, for a number of years. During the season 1857–58 he appeared in New York and on tour as a violin soloist with several famous artists, among them Carl Formes and Sigismund Thalberg. In 1858 he became a member of the orchestra for the opera at the Academy of Music.

In December 1860 Carl Anschütz, conductor of the opera at the Academy, was suddenly unable to appear one evening, and Thomas was called to take his place. He conducted Halévy's *Jewess,* a score he had never seen before, so well that the retirement of Anschütz became permanent and Thomas was made conductor. Conducting was a revelation to him; he found that he could play on an orchestra as he could on a great instrument, and from that time his mission in life became the development of a taste for orchestral and symphonic music throughout the United States. He continued as an operatic conductor in New York, at the same time giving chamber music concerts, as well as recitals with Carl Wolfsohn, in Philadelphia. In 1862 he organized an orchestra of his own, which gave its first concert in Irving Hall, New York, on May 13. Thomas soon realized that only a permanent orchestra could achieve the results he wanted. In 1862 he was made alternate conductor with Theodore Eisfeld of the Brooklyn Philharmonic Society, and four years later he became its sole conductor. During 1863 he continued his own orchestral concerts at Irving Hall, and on Dec. 3, 1864, he began his symphony *soirées.* In 1865 he was appointed musical director of the New York Institution for the Blind. In the following year he commenced his famous summer concerts at Terrace Garden, and two years later he moved them to the Central Park Garden. By 1867 Thomas was able to guarantee his men a full season's engagement, and his orchestra was permanent in the sense that its members were not engaged in other pursuits. His concerts in New York were not well enough attended to support the orchestra, so in 1869 Thomas took his men for a tour, discontinuing the New York concerts until a committee of prominent citizens asked that they be resumed. They were accordingly continued from 1872 to 1878.

In 1873 Thomas was invited to organize and conduct the music festivals in Cincinnati, which came to be biennial, and in 1876 he conducted the Philadelphia Centennial concerts. The latter led to financial disaster; they were poorly attended, and finally the sheriff put a stop to them and sold

Thomas' music library at auction. Although he could have evaded his debts by voluntary bankruptcy, Thomas paid every cent he owed during the following twelve years. By this time Thomas had received several offers to conduct the New York Philharmonic, but he had previously declined them because acceptance would have compelled him to abandon his own orchestra. In 1877, however, the directors renewed the offer and agreed to let him continue his own concerts. He arranged that the programs of his own orchestra would be lighter in character than those of the Philharmonic, to avoid competition.

In 1878 Thomas left New York to assume the directorate of the College of Music in Cincinnati. He immediately clashed with the backers of the school when he concluded that they intended the institution to be a commercial enterprise, rather than one which would fulfil his own ideals as an educational center. He accordingly returned to New York in the spring of 1880 and again became the conductor of the Philharmonic Society. The orchestra at this time was distressed financially, and its playing was mediocre. In his first season as its conductor, Thomas brought it to artistic heights far beyond any of its former achievements, and the attendance accordingly increased. The players were engaged on a co-operative basis, and they made more money. From this period Thomas became something of a storm center. The Symphony Society of New York was organized in 1878, and Leopold Damrosch [q.v.] was appointed its conductor. Musical New York was soon divided into Thomas and Damrosch factions, and, while the two conductors might have remained at peace had they been allowed to arrange matters themselves, their followers urged them to bitter rivalry.

In 1885 Thomas was induced to accept the directorship of the American Opera Company (first performance in January 1886), thinking that its wealthy sponsors would continue to back it even though its first seasons showed a deficit. He accordingly employed all his resources to present opera as finely as it could be given, and it was generally agreed that he had done so; but after the first season, and a resulting loss, the sponsors left the company to founder, and Thomas, merely a salaried employee, was blamed for the unpaid debts of the company. This tragedy was followed by several years in New York, and on tour with his own orchestra, before it disbanded in 1888, journeying to small cities which had never heard an orchestra before, and where later there were permanent orchestras for which Thomas originally planted the seeds. In 1891 he received an offer to go to

Chicago, to conduct an orchestra whose existence would be guaranteed by a group of public-spirited citizens. He was not eager to leave New York, but he saw an opportunity to realize his ideals. He accordingly accepted, and conducted the Chicago Symphony Orchestra for the next fourteen years, until his death in Chicago in 1905.

In 1893 Thomas acted as music director for the World's Fair in Chicago. He planned an all-summer series of programs, designed to show the world what America had accomplished musically, and to show America the music of the world. The plans for the festival offered one of the most comprehensive schemes that had ever been presented in the country. Thomas arranged for an orchestra of over a hundred players, and for an exposition chorus. He invited the leading soloists of the world to appear in the concert hall, and asked the foremost orchestras of the world to give concerts. He again became the storm center in a controversy between artistic ideals and commercial interests. The exhibitors of musical instruments made a rule that no instruments not exhibited at the Fair should be used in the concert hall. Paderewski had already been engaged as a soloist, and since Steinway & Sons had not rented exhibit space the exhibitors sought to prevent Paderewski from using his own Steinway piano. Thomas insisted that there be no interference with Paderewski, and the exhibitors accused the conductor of being in the pay of instrument manufacturers. Even though the charges were disproved and attempts to force Thomas' resignation were fruitless, he incurred the enmity of those who controlled the exposition. Finally the panic of 1893 necessitated curtailment of expenditures for music, so Thomas resigned, and though he was asked to resume his duties at the Fair when matters improved he declined the invitation.

Thomas was an able conductor, yet it was as a musical missionary that he accomplished his greatest work, by taking his orchestra through the country and cultivating a taste for the best in music. As a program maker he was shrewd. Rather than conceiving a program as a single unit, he concerned himself with series of programs, planned to elevate the public taste progressively and gradually. At first he would select lighter pieces to play between heavier selections—melodious compositions chosen for their relation to the more substantial works with which they were paired. Thomas knew that if he could enable his hearers to recognize the themes of a symphony, they would grow eventually to like it. Consequently, when he played a movement of a symphony, he would follow it with a waltz or light overture in which the themes had some relation to those of the symphony. Eventually he found his audiences prepared to listen to an entire symphony, without the interruption of other pieces between its movements.

Thomas was married twice—in 1864 to Minna L. Rhodes, who died Apr. 4, 1889. She bore him three sons and two daughters. His second wife was Rose Fay, whom he married May 7, 1890, and who survived him without issue.

[C. E. Russell, *The American Orchestra and Theodore Thomas* (1927), is excellent in its appreciation of the importance of Thomas in the growth of American culture, and in its understanding of him as an epic figure. His second wife, Rose Fay Thomas, published in 1911 her valuable *Memoirs of Theodore Thomas*. G. P. Upton edited *Theodore Thomas, A Musical Autobiography* (2 vols., 1905); the biographical material, written by Thomas himself, is meager and reticent, but the second volume is invaluable because it contains all of his programs. For an obituary, see *Chicago Daily Tribune*, Jan. 5, 1905.]   J. T. H.

THOMAS, CYRUS (July 27, 1825–June 26, 1910), ethnologist, entomologist, was born at Kingsport, Tenn. His father, Stephen Thomas, was of German descent, and his mother, Maria (Rogan) Thomas, was of Irish parentage. Cyrus received a village school education and attended the academy at Jonesboro, Tenn. In his formative period, filled with ambition and in perfect health, he studied medicine, law, theology, and natural history, and occupied several teaching and official positions before he found his major pursuit in anthropology. Of his earlier studies entomology was his chief interest, especially on the economic side, and he wrote in this period thirty-eight valuable scientific papers among which was his *Noxious and Beneficial Insects of the State of Illinois, Sixth to Eleventh Reports of the State Entomologist, 1877–1882*. In 1882 the Bureau of American Ethnology called for his services. He had already done some work on the mounds (see *Ancient Mounds of Dakota, Geological Survey of the Territories for 1873*), and for the Bureau he pursued the study of the mound areas of the United States for several field seasons, directing a large force in plotting and excavating the mounds, the collections being placed in the National Museum. A review of this work was published as the twelfth annual report of the Bureau in 1894 under the title *Report on Mound Explorations*. A number of his papers on the aspects of the mound question appeared in various bulletins and journals. He did much to controvert the general belief that the mound builders were a mysterious ancient race by proving that the remains are those of American Indians.

In the interim of seasonal field expeditions he pursued the study of the Maya culture, begin-

ning as early as 1881 when he published several papers. The more important of these are *A Study of the Manuscript Troano, Contributions to North American Ethnology,* volume IV (1882); *Notes on Certain Maya and Mexican Manuscripts, Third Annual Report of the Bureau of American Ethnology* (1884); *Aids to the Study of the Maya Codices, Sixth Annual Report* (1888); and *The Maya Year, Bulletin No. 18, Bureau of American Ethnology* (1894). Papers by him on *Mayan Calendar Systems, Numeral Systems of Mexico* and *Central America* are to be found in the nineteenth and twenty-second Bureau reports, published in 1900 and 1904. His work on the Maya subject has emerged from the fray of controversy and he is acclaimed as a pioneer in this difficult field. He also found time to produce works of a more general character: *The Indians of North America in Historic Times* (1903), second volume of the History of North America Series and, with William J. McGee [*q.v.*], *Prehistoric North America* (1905), the nineteenth volume of the Series.

Thomas was possessed of tireless energy and an individuality that brushed aside all obstacles to his mental growth. His first wife was Dorothy Adeline Logan, the sister of John A. Logan [*q.v.*], to whom he was married on June 13, 1853. After her death he was married to Viola L. Davis on Apr. 20, 1865. They had six children. Thomas held many positions of trust. He was clerk of Jackson County, Ill., 1850–53, and later in charge of the schools of DeSoto, Ill. From 1865 to 1869 he was minister of the Evangelical Lutheran Church in that town. He was principal founder of the Illinois Natural History Society in 1858, professor of natural sciences in an Illinois normal school, 1873–75, state entomologist of Illinois, 1874–76, and member of the United States Entomological Commission, 1876–77. He was member of many scientific societies. At his death he was survived by three daughters.

[*Who's Who in America*, 1910–11; Cyrus Thomas, *Geneal. Descendants of Gabriel Thomas, John Thomas, etc.* (1905); *Am. Anthropologist*, Apr.–June 1910; personal recollections of the author.]   W. H.

THOMAS, DAVID (June 11, 1762–Nov. 27, 1831), Revolutionary soldier, member of Congress, New York politician, was probably descended from John Thomas who came to Massachusetts from London about 1635 and settled at Marshfield. He was born in Pelham, Mass., the son of David Thomas and Elizabeth (Harper), his second wife. After participation in 1777 in expeditions of Massachusetts troops for the relief of Rhode Island, the boy was apprenticed to a shoemaker in Worcester, but in 1781 reëntered the army, serving with the 3rd and 5th Massachusetts regiments and ultimately reaching the rank of sergeant.

Shortly after the war he went to Salem, N. Y., where his father's sister had her home. Here, in 1784, he married Jeannette Turner, his aunt's daughter, and entered vigorously into the life of the community. For some years he kept a tavern in partnership with his brother-in-law. In 1793 he was elected to the Assembly and immediately evinced Republican orthodoxy by moving for the election of the Assembly from single-member districts, a principle embodied fifty-two years later in the constitution of 1846. He was again elected to the Assembly in 1798 and in 1799. Meanwhile, he was active in the state militia and in 1805 attained the rank of major-general, in command of the 3rd Division.

In 1800 he was elected to Congress from the seventh New York district. He served four terms, maintaining fairly consistent regularity as a supporter of the Jefferson administration. On Mar. 29, 1806, he moved a resolution for an amendment to the federal Constitution providing for the choice of presidential electors by districts within the states. On Feb. 17, 1808, he resigned his seat to accept the office of treasurer of the state of New York. This position he held until Feb. 10, 1810, when Federalist control of the legislature turned him out, but he was elected to the same position by a new legislature in 1812. He achieved a wide acquaintance among the figures in New York's political life and developed a reputation for great sagacity in political diagnosis and manipulation. He also became prominently identified with the cause of DeWitt Clinton [q.v.]. Under these circumstances, his acceptance in 1811 of the position of agent for the Bank of America in its application for a charter exposed him to savage attack. During the summer of that year he traveled over the state in the campaign to get legislators committed to the cause of the Bank before the beginning of the session of 1812. He was subsequently indicted for attempted bribery of a state senator, and was tried, Sept. 17–18, 1812 (*New York Gazette & General Advertiser*, Sept. 25, 1812). The trial aroused intense popular interest, since the affair was regarded as a political prosecution. Though he was acquitted, his canvass for reëlection to the treasurership in February 1813 resulted in defeat. This experience seems to have led to his determination, in the prime of life, to retire not only from politics but also from residence in the state.

His first wife had died in 1795, leaving one daughter, and on Jan. 15, 1800, he had married Mary Hogeboom of Claverack, N. Y. They separated, Thomas arranging for her to live with her sister in Troy, N. Y., while he went to his sister in Providence, R. I., where he spent his remaining years.

[*Biog. Dir. Am. Cong.* (1928) ; W. H. Hill, *Hist. of Washington County, N. Y.: The Gibson Papers* (1932) ; J. D. Hammond, *The Hist. of Political Parties in the State of N. Y.* (1842), I, 115, 263, 300–17 ; D. S. Alexander, *A Political Hist. of the State of N. Y.,* I (1906), 190–94 ; *Military Minutes of the Council of Appointment of N. Y.,* vol. I (1901) ; *Providence Patriot,* Nov. 30, 1831.]
           C. W. S.

THOMAS, DAVID (Nov. 3, 1794–June 20, 1882), iron manufacturer, was born at Tyllwyd, in the parish of Cadoxtan, Glamorganshire, Wales, the only son of David and Jane Thomas, who gained a poor livelihood at farming. Both parents were deeply religious, belonging to the "Independent" community at Maesyrhaf Chapel, and they gave David strict training. He attended school first at Alltwen, but his progress was so rapid that he was sent to a more advanced school at Neath at the age of nine. Beginning in 1812, he was employed at the Neath Abbey iron works, where he acquired a thorough knowledge of blast furnaces as well as technical training in building mining machinery and Cornish pumping engines. After five years here he was made general superintendent of the Yniscedwyn Iron Works, which three years later was acquired by George Crane.

This plant was erected on the only bed of anthracite coal in Great Britain, but no method had yet been devised to use this fuel in the smelting of iron ore. For years both Crane and Thomas tried to utilize the anthracite without success, two expensive experiments terminating in absolute failure. In 1836, however, their opportunity came when they read about the hot-blast invention of James Beaumont Neilson (see sketch of Neilson in *Dictionary of National Biography*). As a result Thomas went to Scotland, where the hot-blast method was already being employed, and returned with permission to use this patented process. Work was started immediately on the construction of a furnace and it was blown in February 1837 with such successful results that world-wide attention was at once focused upon the plant. Within a short time the Lehigh Coal & Navigation Company of Pennsylvania reached an agreement with Crane and Thomas by which the latter signed a generous contract to construct and operate similar furnaces on the Lehigh River, the plant to be called the Lehigh Crane Iron Company. Thomas was hesitant about going to the United States, but his ambitious wife urged him to accept the position. In May 1839, after he had spent four months in purchasing machinery, he set sail with his family from Swansea to Liverpool and thence to New York. They arrived in Allentown, Pa., July 9, 1839.

Construction of the blast furnace was begun almost immediately and was carried to completion in the face of great odds. It was necessary to have the blowing cylinders built in the United States, and none of the few foundries in existence had ever made machinery of such large size. Thomas suffered a severe illness in the autumn of 1839 which prevented him for a time from overseeing the actual construction. He found it hard to secure experienced labor, and the ores and fuels with which he was supplied were of unknown and varying constituents. Nevertheless, his indomitable energy, activity, courage, and tenacity enabled him to overcome all these difficulties and on July 4, 1840, the first furnace of the Lehigh Crane Iron Company produced four tons of good foundry anthracite iron. Small amounts of anthracite iron had been manufactured a year or two earlier, but Thomas' Catasauqua furnace was the first of all the early anthracite-iron manufacturing establishments to be permanently successful from both the engineering and the commercial standpoint. For this reason and because he subsequently became identified with the manufacture of anthracite pig-iron on a more extensive scale than any of his contemporaries, he has been justly called "the father of the American anthracite-iron industry."

While Thomas did not develop any new basic principles in the smelting of iron ore, he was directly responsible for many improvements, among which were the erection of higher and larger furnaces and better and more powerful blast machinery, and the use of steam instead of air for making the blast. In 1854, he and several others organized the Thomas Iron Company at Hokendauqua, Pa. Although he did not take an active part in the management of this enterprise for several years, because he maintained his connection with the Lehigh Crane Company, he took an active interest in its affairs even to the extent of indorsing and filing a personal bond guaranteeing the money borrowed by the Company during the financial panic of 1857. He was principally interested in other manufactories, including the Lehigh Fire-Brick Company and the Catasauqua Manufacturing Company, and for a great part of his declining years was president of the latter concern. He took much interest in the political, financial, religious, and charitable affairs of Catasauqua, where he lived until his death. He was president of the Catasauqua & Fogelsville Railroad and a director of the Lehigh Valley Railroad Company. He was elected first president of the American Institute of Mining Engineers because it was felt that he was "the man whose name would do more than any other name to unite in support of our new enterprise the enthusiasm of science with the experience of practice" (*Transactions, post,* XI, 15). Thomas' wife was Elizabeth, daughter of John Hopkins, a native of Gilvendre, South Wales. Five children were born of this union; the three sons all became connected with the iron industry.

[*Trans. Am. Inst. Mining Engineers,* vols. I (1874), III (1875), XI (1883); William Firmstone, "Sketch of Early Anthracite Furnaces," *Ibid.,* III (1880); Samuel Thomas, "Reminiscences of the Early Anthracite-Iron Industry," *Ibid.,* vol. XXIX (1900); *Iron Age,* June 22, 29, 1882; *Hist. of the Lehigh Valley Railroad Company* (1872); *The Thomas Iron Company, 1854–1904* (1904); C. R. Roberts and others, *Hist. of Lehigh County, Pa.* (1914), vols. I, III; J. M. Swank, *Hist. of the Manufacture of Iron in All Ages* (2nd ed., 1892); *Bull. Am. Iron and Steel Asso.,* June 28, 1882; *Public Ledger* (Phila.), June 22, 1882.] H.S.P.

THOMAS, EDITH MATILDA (Aug. 12, 1854–Sept. 13, 1925), poet, was born at Chatham, Ohio, the daughter of Frederick J. and Jane Louisa (Sturges) Thomas. Her father's family, originally Welsh, had moved to Ohio from New York; her mother was a native of Connecticut. Her father, a school-teacher and farmer, moved from Chatham to Kenton soon after 1854, and thence to Bowling Green, Ohio, where he died in 1861. Soon after her father's death Edith was taken by her mother to Geneva, Ohio, and in 1872 she was graduated from a normal school there. She then spent a short, dissatisfied period at Oberlin College, following which she taught school for several months. Unhappy in this work, she learned, and for a short while practised, the trade of typesetting. At the normal school she had succeeded in having a class in Greek organized, and her eager study of the language and its literature stimulated her in a way that was profoundly to influence her poetry, which as a student she had begun submitting to Geneva and Cleveland newspapers. She also became a disciple of Keats, perceiving in his poetry that sensuous yet spiritual love of beauty which she herself felt. Her desire to give herself to poetry had been whetted by an uncle, James Thomas, a romantic adventurer, who had made her gifts of books and who in 1881 took her to New York. There he presented her to Anne Charlotte Lynch Botta, who in turn sent her to Helen Hunt Jackson [*qq.v.*]. The latter read her poetry, thought it excellent, and secured publication of some of it in the *Century.*

After her mother's death (1887), Edith Thomas moved to New York. Her first book, *A New Year's Masque and Other Poems,* had been published in 1885, and her verse had begun to appear in the pages of *Scribner's,* the *Atlantic Monthly, Harper's,* the *Nation,* the *Critic,* the *Independent,* the *Outlook,* and several metropolitan newspapers. Sponsored by Richard Watson Gilder [*q.v.*] and others, she won the friendship of some of the most prominent writers of the day. For a decade after her removal to New York she made her home with Dr. and Mrs. Samuel Elliott, at whose house she met such men as Charles Anderson Dana, Parke Godwin, and Edwin Booth [*qq.v.*]. For a while she helped prepare the *Century Dictionary.* In 1908 she became a reader for *Harper's Magazine,* under Henry Mills Alden [*q.v.*], and continued in this work until her death. She wrote several books of a pedestrian sort, among them a series of books for children, called the Children of the Seasons Series (1888). She also wrote one book of prose, nature-sketches, *The Round Year* (1886). Representative volumes of her verse are *Lyrics and Sonnets* (1887), *The Inverted Torch* (1890), *In Sunshine Land* (1895), *The Dancers, and Other Legends and Lyrics* (1903), and *The Flower from the Ashes* (1915).

She was a frail little woman who preferred a nunlike seclusion. She made many friends, but only those who came to recognize the quiet, reserved manner as one which concealed a consuming passion for poetry really appreciated her personality, her work, or her refined intelligence. Her muse was remote, unimpassioned, classical; she was "more Greek than American" (F. L. Pattee, *A History of American Literature since 1870,* 1915, p. 341). Her verse is characterized by painstaking craftsmanship, genuine lyric feeling, and an excellent sense of rhythm, but it made little appeal to the public because of its pervading spirituality, and has had little influence upon later writers.

[See *Who's Who in America,* 1920–21; Jessie B. Rittenhouse, in *Selected Poems of Edith M. Thomas* (1926); R. H. Stoddard, in *Book Buyer,* Mar. 1888, pp. 56–57; *N. Y. Times,* Sept. 15 (obituary), 16, 1925; for critical analyses of Edith Thomas' poetry, see *Atlantic Monthly,* Mar. 1885, pp. 418–21, Dec. 1890, pp. 844–45, and *Dial* (Chicago), Nov. 1886, pp. 158–60, Feb. 1888, pp. 249–50.]   H. S., Jr.

THOMAS, FRANCIS (Feb. 3, 1799–Jan. 22, 1876), congressman from Maryland and governor, was born at "Montevue" near Petersville, Frederick County, Md., the seventh child of John and Eleanor (McGill) Thomas, and the descendant of Hugh Thomas who emigrated from Wales to Pennsylvania about 1702. He matriculated at St. John's College, Annapolis, but turned directly to the study of law, when

classes closed temporarily at that institution. Opening an office in Frederick after admission to the bar in 1820, he soon became one of the leading lawyers in western Maryland. His record before 1841 was a succession of triumphs. In 1822, as a stripling of twenty-three and a Democrat, he won election to the state assembly from a Federalist section on the issue of legislative reapportionment. He appeared as a successful candidate for the same position in 1827 and 1829, and even won the speakership of the house in his last term. The manner in which he handled the house led to his being made congressional candidate the next year. For ten years, 1831–41, he sat in Congress, where his eloquence and parliamentary skill made him an active participant in most of the important legislation. As chairman of the judiciary commitee, he became a defender and friend of Jackson. For a brief period, 1839–40, he was president of the Chesapeake and Ohio Canal Company and also found time to lead a revolt for popular election of state senators in Maryland. Though temporarily unsuccessful, this ultimately brought reorganization of the legislative department. It was during his congressional campaign of 1840 that he became involved in a duel with William Price. His nomination and election for governor in 1841 ushered in the most tempestuous period of his life. His marriage to Sally Campbell McDowell, the daughter of Gov. James McDowell [*q.v.*] of Virginia on June 8, 1841, had united the forty-two-year old bachelor to a twenty-year old girl. Discord manifested itself in a few weeks. They were divorced after an unusually unsavory scandal during which he issued a pamphlet, *Statement of Francis Thomas* (1845), setting forth, entirely without reserve, the details of the courtship, marriage, and estrangement. Ten years later his wife married John Miller, 1819–1895 [*q.v.*], a Presbyterian clergyman. The quarrel and divorce involved Thomas in a libel suit and led him to wild charges against John Carroll Le Grand, whom he had just appointed judge. Ultimately, it cost him his possible opportunity of being president because of the bitterness of his father-in-law in the convention of 1844.

He did not allow his domestic difficulties to interfere with his duties as governor. His chief contribution was to save the state from repudiation, although it was heavily involved in debt for internal improvements. After his governorship he led the life of a recluse until the Civil War, emerging only to fight, in the constitutional convention of 1850–51, the system of representation whereby the small slave-holding counties held power over the populous western counties, and to run unsuccessfully in 1853 as an independent candidate for Congress. At the outbreak of the Civil War he enlisted a volunteer regiment of 3,000, though he left the command to younger men, and inspired union sentiment in western Maryland with his eloquence. In 1861 he returned to Congress as a Unionist and served until 1869. During Reconstruction he whole-heartedly supported the extreme Radicals. Upon his retirement from Congress, he was appointed in 1870 internal revenue collector for Maryland. He resigned to accept the post of minister to Peru, where he served from 1872 to 1875. The remaining year of his life he occupied with law practice and with sheep-raising on a large tract of land near Frankville. He was killed by an engine of the Baltimore and Ohio railroad.

[M. P. Andrews, *Tercentenary Hist. of Md.* (1925), vol. I; E. S. Riley, *A Hist. of the General Assembly of Md.* (1905); C. W. Sams and E. S. Riley, *The Bench and Bar of Md.* (1904); J. W. Thomas and T. J. C. Williams, *Hist. of Allegany County, Md.* (1923), vol. I; T. J. C. Williams, *Hist. of Frederick County* (1910), vol. I; L. E. Blauch, "Education and the Md. Constit. Convention, 1850–51," *Md. Hist. Mag.*, June 1930; *N. Y. Herald*, Apr. 8, 1845; *Inquirer and National Gazette* (Philadelphia), Nov. 13, 1845; *Baltimore Amer. and Commercial Advertiser* and *Sun* (Baltimore), Jan. 24, 1876.]   E. L.

THOMAS, FREDERICK WILLIAM (Oct. 25, 1806–Aug. 27, 1866), journalist and novelist, was the son of Ebenezer Smith and Ann (Fonerden) Thomas, and a descendant of Evan Thomas, a Welshman who emigrated to Massachusetts in 1640. Ebenezer Thomas, born in Massachusetts, learned the printing trade in the shop of his distinguished uncle Isaiah [*q.v.*] and as a young man went to Charleston, S. C., where he became a bookseller. He also had business interests in Providence, R. I., and there Frederick William, eldest of eight children, was born. After two years (1807–09) on a farm near Baltimore, Md., the family returned to Charleston, where E. S. Thomas was for some years editor of the *City Gazette*. Injured by a fall as a child and later permanently lamed by another injury, Frederick was sent to live with relatives in Baltimore, where his family joined him in 1816. He was admitted to the bar in 1828 and began the practice of law in Baltimore, but in 1831 he followed his father to Cincinnati, assisted him there in the editing of the *Commercial Daily Advertiser*, and resumed the practice of law. For the next ten years, a citizen of Cincinnati, he combined literary and journalistic work—including six months as editor of the *Democratic Intelligencer*—with extensive travel, chiefly in the Middle West. For some years

after 1841 he held a clerkship in the Treasury Department in Washington, for which he also collected a library. In 1847–48 he was professor of rhetoric and English literature in the University of Alabama; in 1850, after some journalistic work in Kentucky, he entered the ministry of the Methodist Episcopal Church in Cincinnati, and achieved some success as preacher and lecturer. After practising law for a time in Cambridge, Md., he became in 1860 literary editor of the *Richmond Enquirer* and was later a member of the staff of the Columbia *South Carolinian*. His death, caused by typhoid fever and complications, occurred in Washington, D. C.

In 1833 he published a descriptive poem of considerable length called *The Emigrant*. A song entitled, " 'Tis said that absence conquers love," which was set to music and enjoyed a wide popularity, appeared in a Cincinnati paper in the same year, and in 1840 another song, "Oh blame her not, her love was deep," was printed in Baltimore. His first novel, *Clinton Bradshaw; or the Adventures of a Lawyer* (2 vols., 1835), was published anonymously in Philadelphia. This was followed in 1836 by *East and West*, credited to the author of *Clinton Bradshaw*, and in 1840 by *Howard Pinckney: a Novel* (2 vols.). His other books were *The Beechen Tree, a Tale Told in Rhyme* (1844); *Sketches of Character, and Tales Founded on Fact* (1849), a volume of essays; *An Autobiography of William Russell* (1852), a novel; and *John Randolph, of Roanoke* (1853).

Thomas is remembered as a loyal friend and correspondent of Edgar Allan Poe [*q.v.*], whom he first met in Philadelphia in 1840. He is described by a contemporary as five feet nine inches tall and compactly built, his hair black and wavy, "worn long and negligently about his temples" (*Southern Literary Messenger, post*, p. 301). Because of his childhood injury he could not walk without a cane. His literary work was in the mode of the time and won some critical approval, his fiction being regarded as imitative of Bulwer-Lytton.

[The dates of birth and death are from the Thomas family Bible, which, with a portrait and some correspondence, is in the lib. of the Am. Antiquarian Soc. See also E. S. Thomas, *Reminiscences of the Last Sixty-Five Years* (1840), vol. II, pp. 46–47; F. W. Thomas' letter, Aug. 3, 1841, in J. A. Harrison, *The Complete Works of Edgar Allan Poe* (1902), vol. XVII, pp. 95–100; W. T. Coggeshall, *The Poets and Poetry of the West* (1860), p. 185; *Southern Literary Messenger*, May 1838, pp. 297–301; memoir in 1872 ed. of *The Emigrant;* R. L. Rusk, *The Lit. of the Middle Western Frontier* (1925), vol. I, pp. 296–97; and death notice in *Daily Nat. Intelligencer* (Washington, D. C.), Aug. 30, 1866.]   J. C. F—h.

THOMAS, GEORGE (*c.* 1695–Dec. 31, 1774), colonial governor of Pennsylvania and Delaware, son of Col. George Thomas and Sarah (Winthrop) Thomas, was born and educated in Antigua in the British West Indies. He was a member of the Assembly of Antigua, 1716–17 and 1721–28, being speaker in 1727–28, and a member of the council of the Leeward Islands from 1728 to 1738. In 1737 he was in England and appeared before the Board of Trade and Plantations to give information on the problem of suppressing the contraband trade in the West Indies. In the summer of that year he was appointed deputy governor of Pennsylvania and the Lower Counties on the Delaware, but because of the opposition of Lord Baltimore, who claimed proprietary rights in the Lower Counties, the appointment was not confirmed by the Crown until the following February. He arrived in Philadelphia on June 1, 1738.

Thomas' administration as governor of Delaware was uneventful, but in Pennsylvania he soon became involved in a bitter quarrel with the Assembly over financial and military affairs. In 1738–39 he refused to approve a bill for the emission of paper currency until provision had been made for the payment of the proprietary rents at the old rate of exchange. In this connection he wrote a communication to the Board of Trade a copy of which was obtained surreptitiously by Richard Partridge [*q.v.*], the colonial agent, and sent to Philadelphia, where it was printed by Benjamin Franklin. (*A Letter to the Lords of Trade,* 1740). Shortly after this dispute was settled, war broke out between Great Britain and Spain. Thomas urged the Assembly to provide funds for local defense and the support of the Pennsylvania troops who were to participate in the expedition against the Spanish West Indies. They replied that war was contrary to Quaker principles, that the colony was not really in danger, and that troops could be raised without a vote of the Assembly. This episode gave rise to a series of recriminations, in the course of which the Assembly withheld the Governor's salary and he refused to sign their bills. The controversy was intensified after France entered the war in 1744, but Thomas finally admitted defeat, and his relations with the Assembly were friendly during the latter part of his administration. He was more successful in dealing with the Indians. Conferences were held with the Shawnees and the Delawares and important treaties were concluded with the Iroquois Confederacy at Philadelphia in 1742 and at Lancaster in 1744. Delegates were sent to the conference at Albany in 1745.

He relied to a large extent on the advice of Conrad Weiser [*q.v.*] and accepted the policy of recognizing the suzerainty of the Six Nations over the Indians of Pennsylvania. This caused some friction with the local tribes, but the neutrality of the Iroquois was secured and as a result the back country was rapidly settled. Thomas also acted as a mediator in a quarrel between the Iroquois and the governments of Maryland and Virginia.

In 1747, his health failed and he sailed for England about the first of June (*Pennsylvania Gazette,* June 4, 1747). He was governor of the Leeward Islands from Jan. 25, 1753 until Dec. 18, 1766. In 1765, after the Stamp Act went into effect, he wrote to England that the stamps had been seized and the distributor forced to resign at St. Kitts, but Antigua remained quiet and loyal. He sailed for England in June 1766 and was created a baronet on Sept. 6 of that year. After his retirement he settled in England and acquired the manors of Yapton and Ratton in the county of Sussex. He died in London in his eightieth year and was buried in the parish church at Willingdon, Sussex. Thomas was married, Apr. 18, 1717, to Elizabeth King (*c.* 1700–Sept. 24, 1763), daughter of Capt. John King of Antigua. They had two sons and three daughters.

[V. L. Oliver, *The Hist. of the Island of Antigua* (3 vols., 1894–99); *Jour. of the Commissioners for Trade and Plantations, 1734/5–1741* (1930), *1741/2–1749* (1931), *1749/50–1753* (1932); *Acts of the Privy Council of England, Colonial Series,* vol. IV (1911); *Minutes of the Provincial Council of Pa.,* vols. IV–VI (1851–52); *Votes and Proceedings of the Assembly of Pa.,* vols. III–IV (1754, 1774); G. P. Donehoo, *Pennsylvania, a Hist.,* vol. I (1926); W. T. Root, *The Relations of Pa. with the British Government, 1696–1765* (1912); obituary in *Gentleman's Magazine* (London), Jan. 1775; character sketch, *Ibid.,* Sept. 1775.]

W. R. S.

THOMAS, GEORGE CLIFFORD (Oct. 28, 1839–Apr. 21, 1909), banker, philanthropist, and collector, was born in Philadelphia, Pa., the son of John W. and Sophia Kezia (Atkinson) Thomas. On his father's side he was the grandson of John Thomas who emigrated from Wales prior to 1802; his mother's ancestors came to Maryland with Lord Baltimore. After graduating from the Episcopal Academy, he worked six years as a clerk for his father, a dry-goods merchant with banking connections. In 1863 his financial aptitude attracted the attention of Jay Cooke [*q.v.*], whose banking house Thomas entered, and there proved himself a quick pupil, working hard to promote the flotation of government war loans. When Cooke rearranged his partnerships, Jan. 1, 1866, he included Thomas with a share of 5% and assurance of $3000 annually, although the young man brought no property into the firm and was then possessed of not more than $3000, his savings from his salary as clerk. The next year, Nov. 26, Thomas married Ada Elizabeth, daughter of J. Barlow Moorhead, a brother of Cooke's partner, William G. Moorhead, and a prominent Pennsylvania iron master.

Thomas rapidly became Cooke's right-hand man in Philadelphia, but the latter's failure in 1873 unfortunately absorbed all of Thomas' small fortune. By December following, however, he was forming a new banking and brokerage connection, known first as Joseph M. Shoemaker & Company, and later as Thomas & Shoemaker. The steady success of this house attracted the interest of another prominent financier, Anthony J. Drexel [*q.v.*], and on Jan. 1, 1883, Thomas was admitted to partnership in the local firm of Drexel & Company, in the New York firm of Drexel, Morgan & Company, and in the Paris firm of Morgan, Harjes & Company. Again, he became a strong asset to the houses with which he was connected, and from Dec. 31, 1894 he served for ten years as the senior resident partner in the Philadelphia firm. Through these connections with the leading American bankers he contributed to the directive genius which placed the control of United States transportation in banking hands.

While Thomas' business career differed little from that of other successful financiers of his generation, he won some claim to notice through his avocations—church work, philanthropy, and the collection of rare objects. As early as 1868 he began employing his talent for organization in building up the Protestant Episcopal Church. For many years he was superintendent of the Sunday School connected with the Church of the Holy Apostles, and he gave much time and thought to the training of teachers and the advancement of religious education. He set up the machinery for the annual financing of the Church's missions and schools, serving as treasurer of the Board of Missions. As wealth grew he and his wife became known, not alone for the generosity of their public benefactions, but particularly for the private aid which they bestowed. Donations for parish chapels, parish houses, a gymnasium, and a nurses' home on the one hand, were matched by quiet help to students and hard-pressed families on the other. In his later years he became known to agents abroad and at home as a discriminating purchaser willing to pay the large prices exacted for rare things. His collections included Shakespeare folios; many autographs, including those

of the signers of the Declaration of Independence; and William Penn's original "Charter of Liberties to the people of the State of Pennsylvania." In the room where these treasures were kept, he installed a pipe organ, whereon he played with skill for his own relaxation. He died in Philadelphia, survived by his widow, two sons, and a daughter.

[L. B. Thomas, *The Thomas Book* (copr. 1896); J. W. Jordan, *Encyc. of Pa. Biog.*, vols. X (1918), XVI (1927); E. P. Oberholtzer, *Phila., a Hist. of the City and Its People* (n.d.), vol. IV, and *Jay Cooke; Financier of the Civil War* (1907), vol. II; *In the Matter of Jay Cooke & Company, Bankrupts, in the District Court of the U. S. for the Eastern District of Pa.* (1875); *Spirit of Missions*, May, June 1909; *Cat. of the More Important Books, Autographs, and MSS. in the Lib. of George C. Thomas* (1907); *Autograph Letters and Autographs of the Signers of the Declaration of Independence in the Possession of George C. Thomas* (1908); *Phila. Inquirer* and *North Am. Press* (Phila.), Apr. 22, 1909; information from Drexel & Company.]
J. P. N.

THOMAS, GEORGE HENRY (July 31, 1816–Mar. 28, 1870), soldier, was born in Southampton County, in southeastern Virginia, the son of John and Elizabeth (Rochelle) Thomas. The family, on his father's side, was Welsh and English; on his mother's, French Huguenot. He received his early education in the local Southampton Academy and began the study of law, serving meanwhile as deputy to his uncle, James Rochelle, clerk of the county court. Through the influence of this uncle he received an appointment to the United States Military Academy, entered in 1836, and was graduated in 1840, number twelve in a class of forty-two members. Among his classmates were William T. Sherman and Richard S. Ewell [*qq.v.*]. He received his commission as second lieutenant in the 3rd Artillery, then on field service in the Florida War. He remained in Florida for two years, and received the brevet rank of first lieutenant for gallantry in action against the Indians; then he served in several Southern garrisons, receiving his promotion to the substantive grade of first lieutenant in 1844. The following year he was assigned to Bragg's light battery with Taylor's force in Texas, and served throughout Taylor's Mexican campaign. He was brevetted captain and major for gallantry at Monterey and Buena Vista. He again served in Indian troubles in Florida, and then was an instructor in artillery and cavalry at West Point, 1851–54, being promoted, meanwhile, to the rank of captain.

Upon relief at the Academy he went with a detachment of his regiment via Panama to California, and to Fort Yuma, where he served for a year. He then accepted a commission as major in the newly raised 2nd (later designated as the 5th) Cavalry, and joined at Jefferson Barracks,

Mo. In this regiment, Albert S. Johnston was colonel, Robert E. Lee lieutenant-colonel, and William J. Hardee the other major; in it served many other officers who later became famous, including the Federal general George Stoneman, and the Confederate generals John B. Hood, Fitzhugh Lee, and Earl VanDorn [*qq.v.*]. He served with the new regiment in Texas, and on garrison and exploration duty. On one of his exploring expeditions he was wounded in the face by an Indian arrow. On Nov. 1, 1860, he was granted a twelve months' leave of absence and was in the East at the outbreak of the Civil War.

In spite of his Southern birth, Thomas decided to remain with the Union army, and on Apr. 14 he joined his regiment at Carlisle, Pa. In April he became a lieutenant-colonel, and in May a colonel. He commanded a brigade in the opening operations in the Shenandoah Valley. On Aug. 17, 1861, he was made brigadier-general of volunteers and assigned to duty in Kentucky, organizing new troops. In November 1861, he assumed command of the 1st Division, Army of the Ohio, and won the small but decisive action of Mill Springs on Jan. 19, 1862. His command was then withdrawn to Louisville and took part in Buell's advance to Nashville and to Pittsburg Landing. Here, on Apr. 25, 1862, he was promoted major-general of volunteers, and commanded the right wing of Halleck's army in the advance to and capture of Corinth. He remained in command of the garrison at that place until June 22, when, with his own division, he was reassigned to Buell's army with which he served during the campaign against Bragg in Kentucky. Buell's retreat to Louisville caused dissatisfaction in Washington, and on Sept. 29 Thomas received orders to supersede him. Thomas declined the command, pointing out that Buell had already issued orders for the offensive, and served as Buell's second in command in the Perryville operations in October.

On Oct. 30 General Rosecrans replaced Buell. Thomas, although he had declined to supersede Buell himself, protested against serving under Rosecrans, a former junior; but the president antedated Rosecrans' commission to make him senior, and Thomas promptly acquiesced and served under him loyally. The command was several times reorganized, and was finally designated the Army of the Cumberland; Thomas' own command became the XIV Army Corps, one of three corps in the army. This corps he commanded at Stones River (Dec. 31–Jan. 3), and in the Tullahoma campaign in June and July

1863, which pushed Bragg out of Tennessee. Early in September, Rosecrans crossed the Tennessee River and maneuvered Bragg out of Chattanooga as he had out of the Tullahoma lines. In this process his army became widely extended, and Bragg, having been reënforced by Longstreet's corps from Virginia, made an effort to cut him off from Chattanooga. He succeeded in concentrating in time, and took position on Chickamauga Creek. Of this line, Thomas' corps formed the left, or northern flank.

The battle of Chickamauga began on Sept. 19, but the heaviest fighting came the next day. Bragg's attack came first upon Thomas' position, which was reënforced progressively by parts of other corps. Toward noon, a gap opened on Thomas' right through an erroneous movement by a division not at the time engaged, and Longstreet penetrated the lines. Thomas' right was violently bent back, and all the troops south of that point were driven in disorder across Missionary Ridge, where they took the road to Chattanooga. Rosecrans, whose headquarters were behind the right wing, was carried to the rear by what seemed the rout of his whole force. Thomas, however, was still in the field with over half the army. His line was bent into horseshoe shape, but not broken; and here he stood all day, earning his title, "the Rock of Chickamauga." After dark, he drew off to Rockville, five miles to the north, and he retired unmolested to Chattanooga. For this service he was promoted brigadier-general in the regular army on Oct. 27, 1863.

The situation at Chattanooga was critical. The army was in a state of siege, its supply being so reduced as to place it in a starving condition. All the energy of the North was turned toward its relief, active operations elsewhere being suspended. Grant was given supreme command in the West, and directed upon Chattanooga his own old Army of the Tennessee, now under Sherman; Hooker was sent by rail from Washington with two corps of the Army of the Potomac; Rosecrans was relieved from command of the Army of the Cumberland, and Thomas put in his place. Grant's first telegram to him directed that Chattanooga be held "at all hazards." Thomas replied, "We will hold the town till we starve"—which seemed not a mere rhetorical expression, for the men, to use their own language, were on "half rations of hard bread and beef dried on the hoof" (see Van Horne, *post*, p. 156). By the use of Hooker's command, a new and direct line of supply was opened; and when Sherman finally assumed his position on Nov. 23, after having been delayed by bad weather, Grant was ready to undertake a general offensive. As a first move, Thomas made a reconnaissance in force on Nov. 23, which cleared up the question of Bragg's strength and position, and secured favorable ground for the decisive action, but which also served to put Bragg on his guard. On the following two days was fought the battle that forced Bragg back from Chattanooga. Thomas' right, under Hooker, seized Lookout Mountain; the rest of his army carried Missionary Ridge.

Operations during the winter were of minor character, but in May 1864 Sherman's Atlanta campaign began. In this campaign, Thomas' Army of the Cumberland constituted over half of Sherman's entire force. It was constantly engaged, was in every offensive move, and bore the brunt of the only serious Confederate counter-stroke—Hood's attack at Peachtree Creek, Ga., on July 20. Troops of this Army received the surrender of Atlanta and were first to enter the city. Thomas now suggested that his army be detached from Sherman's command, and sent on a march to the sea. When it was decided that Sherman's main force should make this movement, it became necessary to form a new army to oppose Hood in the west; Thomas was designated to command it, and was ordered to Nashville in October. The nucleus of his force, 35,000 men, was furnished from Sherman's army, but it was necessary to collect another 35,000 by drawing in detachments, even from beyond the Mississippi, and by bringing new troops from the north. Hood began his advance northward late in November. Thomas kept his entire field force, under Schofield, in front of Hood, delaying him. This force, having held out so long as almost to be cut off, finally took position at Franklin, vigorously checked Hood there on Nov. 30, and then withdrew into Nashville. General Grant insisted strongly upon an immediate offensive by Thomas' whole force, but the latter insisted that he was not yet strong enough to gain a decisive victory, and that nothing less should be considered. On this point he remained firm, although his fitness for independent command and even his loyalty, were seriously questioned. It is a moot question whether Thomas did not seriously jeopardize the success of the campaign as a whole by his insistence. On Dec. 9 Grant directed that he be relieved, and Schofield put in his place; but meanwhile Thomas reported himself ready to move, and the order was suspended. A violent storm, with snow and ice, caused another delay. Grant then dispatched General Logan with orders to supersede Thomas; and he himself started from the James

River for Nashville on Dec. 15. But before either arrived, Thomas had moved. In a two days' battle, Dec. 15–16, he fully vindicated his plan of action, and administered so severe a defeat to Hood that his army played no further important part in the war. He was promoted to the rank of a major-general in the regular army and on Mar. 3, 1865, received the thanks of Congress.

He remained in command in this region for the rest of the war, and for some years after. In 1868 President Johnson sent his name to the Senate for promotion to the brevet ranks of lieutenant-general and general, but, believing that the purpose of these promotions was to use him as an instrument for displacing General Grant in command of the army, he declined, saying that the honor was too great for his services since the war, and came too late to be acceptable for war service. In the same year he was strongly urged to become a candidate for the presidency, but he refused to allow his name to be used. In June 1869, he assumed command of the Military Division of the Pacific, at San Francisco, Cal., where he died of apoplexy, leaving a widow but no children. He was buried at Troy, N. Y., the home of his wife, Frances Lucretia Kellogg, to whom he had been married on Nov. 17, 1852.

Thomas was a man of fine presence—six feet in height and weighing about 200 pounds. He was studious in his habits, deliberate but decided in action, and fastidious to the point of exasperation. He is said to have remarked to a less tidy officer, "The fate of an army may depend on a buckle" (B. A. Liddell Hart, *Sherman,* 1930, p. 257). He was respected by his superiors and beloved by his subordinates; at the same time, his deliberateness was often looked upon as sluggishness, and his Southern birth sometimes led to suspicion of lukewarmness. Even his various nicknames are indicative of his dominant traits of character: as a cadet, he was called "Old Tom"; as an instructor, "Slow Trot"; and in the Army of the Cumberland, "Pap Thomas." His military reputation, however, may rest upon the judgments of two superiors. Sherman, although sometimes impatient at Thomas' deliberateness, remarked on one occasion, "I wish Old Thom was here! he's my off-wheel horse" (W. F. G. Shanks, *Personal Recollections of Distinguished Generals,* 1866, p. 58). And Grant writes (*Personal Memoirs,* volume II, 1886, p. 525), that although Thomas could hardly have conducted the offensive operations of the Atlanta campaign as Sherman did, he could have handled Johnston's problem in that campaign to perfection; that his dispositions were always good, and that he could not be driven from a point he was given to hold.

[Letters filed with the manuscript "Reports of General Officers," Old Records Division, Adjutant-General's Office, War Dept.; G. W. Cullum, *Biog. Reg. . . . Officers and Grads., U. S. Mil. Acad.* (1891); T. B. Van Horne, *The Life of Major-General George H. Thomas* (1882); Henry Coppée, *General Thomas* (1893); R. W. Johnson, *Memoir of Maj.-Gen. George H. Thomas* (1881); Timothy Hopkins, *The Kelloggs in The Old World and The New* (1903), vol. I; *Morning Bull.* (San Francisco, Cal.), Mar. 29, 1870; *N. Y. Tribune,* Mar. 30, 1870.]   O. L. S., Jr.

THOMAS, ISAIAH (Jan. 19, 1749 o.s.–Apr. 4, 1831), printer, historian of the press, founder of the American Antiquarian Society, was born at Boston, Mass., the son of Moses and Fidelity (Grant) Thomas and great-great-grandson of Evan Thomas who came to Boston from Wales in 1640. Isaiah's grandfather, Peter Thomas, was a local merchant of some ability and means, but his father was an unsuccessful dabbler in many occupations. He died in 1752, leaving a penniless widow and five children who, with the aid of friends and a small shop, managed to escape poverty. With but six weeks of indifferent schooling Isaiah began at the age of six hi education before the type cases of a printi fice. In 1756 he was apprenticed to Zecl Fowle of Boston, an ignorant and shiftless and peddler of ballads and chapbooks, by he was misused. Having learned much trade from one of Fowle's short-time p Samuel Draper, and from another local Gamaliel Rogers, Thomas took over, wr in his early teens, the management of shop. By the age of seventeen he was co an excellent printer. He read much, wr English with a dash of satire, and atten casional verses to fill out a column. T some, always neatly dressed, he ma friends in the trade and among the me stance of the town.

In 1766 Thomas had a "serious fra his master and left Boston secretly fo whence he hoped to reach London i perfect his knowledge of printing. He mediate employment with the *Halif* but soon got into trouble because of tion to the Stamp Act, returned via l N. H., to Fowle's shop in Boston, a final release from his unexpired ap He then started south with the hope England by way of the West Indies ous adventures he found himself in S. C., where he worked for a time *Carolina and American General* failed to reach England or to establ

of his own and finally, in the spring of 1770, returned to Boston. He became Fowle's partner in July, established the *Massachusetts Spy,* which was destined to live until 1904, soon bought out his partner, and made his paper famous for its support of the liberties of the people. He was in constant conflict with the royal government and every effort was made to suppress his fearless and dangerously successful Whig newspaper.

The British occupation of Boston in 1775 finally drove him from the city. Escaping with his press and type on the night of Apr. 16, Thomas sent his equipment before him to Worcester while he, two nights later, joined Paul Revere and others in alarming the countryside. As a minute-man he took part in the skirmishes at Lexington and Concord and on the 20th arrived in Worcester; here he reëstablished his newspaper and did the official printing for the patriots of the colony. In the spring of 1776 Thomas leased his paper and moved to Salem, where he made an unsuccessful attempt to carry on the printing business; he returned to Worcester in the spring of 1778 and resumed publication of the *Spy.* These were trying days for the young printer but by the end of _____ ___ ___ was on a firmer footing and

ay.
en-
ven
his
ners
ores.
ield,
nore,
igers
1774–
Royal
cester
;achu-
s first
ts Cal-
ie title
ngland
to bear

able for
pularity
Iis more
io Bible,
d States,
is scores
exander's
published
:, the first
n Perry's,
irteen edi-

tions and 300,000 copies of Perry's spelling book. He was the first American publisher to do extensive printing from musical type. Blackstone's *Commentaries* came from his press as well as many other works in law, medicine, and agriculture. He reprinted the best English literature of his day and issued the first edition of *The Power of Sympathy* (1789), attributed to William Hill Brown and earlier to Sarah Wentworth Apthorp Morton [*q.v.*], the first novel by a native American.

He is still famous for his more than a hundred children's books of which he published tens of thousands of copies. Of these his first American edition of *Mother Goose's Melody* (1786), is the most famous but he also printed inexpensive but attractively illustrated editions of the *New England Primer, The History of Little Goody Twoshoes, The Pilgrim's Progress,* and *Travels of Robinson Crusoe.* He may be regarded as the greatest early publisher of juveniles in the country. Franklin called him "the Baskerville of America," and an examination of the products of his busy presses bears out this high praise from the only other American printer of his day who had anything like his success as a publisher.

By 1802 Thomas had become rich and so was able to retire in favor of his son and devote the rest of his life to scholarship. His personal library, perhaps the best in the country in the field of American history, furnished the source materials for *The History of Printing in America* (2 vols., 1810), which is still (1935) the recognized authority on the subject. Realizing the need for a national society for the preservation and study of the materials of American history, Thomas founded and, on Oct. 24, 1812, incorporated the American Antiquarian Society of which he became the first president. His gifts to the society, including books, manuscripts, building, land, and endowment, amounted to $50,000. Thomas was the first printer and the first postmaster of Worcester (1775–1801), the first in Massachusetts known to have read the Declaration of Independence to a public gathering (July 24, 1776), the first master of the first Masonic lodge in Worcester and later master of the Grand Lodge of Massachusetts. He received the honorary degree of A.M. from Dartmouth in 1814 and that of LL.D. from Allegheny College in 1818. He was apparently a member of every learned society in America. His personal friends included Washington, Franklin, the Adamses, Jefferson, Hancock, and many of the other leaders of his time.

One of his old friends, Gov. Levi Lincoln of Worcester, has left this picture of Thomas in his later years: "With a strong and vigorous mind and a cultivated intellect, enterprise, energy and industry, in early life, gave him wealth, and possessed of this, he lived in courtly style, and with beneficent liberality. . . . In his person, he was tall and slender, stooping somewhat in his gait. His address was courteous, his conversation frank, but something conventional, and his attention to appearance and dress singularly precise and studied. He was a public spirited citizen, generous in his contributions to all worthy objects, and a most efficient co-operator with others in promoting the growth, improvement and prosperity of the place." Thomas was married three times: first, Dec. 25, 1769, in Charlestown, S. C., to Mary, daughter of Joseph and Anne Dill of Bermuda, from whom he was divorced in 1777; second, May 26, 1779, in Boston, to Mary Fowle (d. Nov. 16, 1818), daughter of William and Rebecca (Bass) Thomas and widow of Isaac Fowle; third, Aug. 10, 1819, in Boston, to Rebecca Armstrong (1757–1828), daughter of John and Christian (Bass) Armstrong, a cousin of his second wife. Two children by his first wife survived, Mary Anne and Isaiah.

[Thomas' original diaries, business papers, and correspondence, a virtually complete collection of works from his press, including newspapers, periodicals, books, pamphlets, and broadsides, at Am. Antiquarian Soc., Worcester, Mass.; C. L. Nichols, ed., "Extracts from the Diaries and Accounts of Isaiah Thomas from the Year 1782 to 1804 and His Diary for 1808," in *Proc. Am. Antiquarian Soc.,* n.s., vol. XXVI (1916); B. T. Hall, ed., "The Diary of Isaiah Thomas, 1805–1828," in *Trans. and Colls. Am. Antiquarian Soc.,* vols. IX, X (1909); Isaiah Thomas, *History of Printing in America* (2nd ed., enlarged, in *Trans. and Colls. Am. Antiquarian Soc.,* vol. V (1874)); same as separate (1874, 2 vols.); B. F. Thomas, "Memoir of Isaiah Thomas," in *Trans. and Coll. Am. Antiquarian Soc.,* vol. V (1874), pp. xvii–lxxxvii; Levi Lincoln, *Reminiscences of the Original Associates of the Worcester Fire Society* (1862), pp. 32–33; C. L. Nichols, *Isaiah Thomas, Printer, Writer & Collector* (1912), with bibliography of imprints; C. L. Nichols, *Bibliography of Worcester, 1775–1848* (2nd ed., 1918); C. L. Nichols, "The Portraits of Isaiah Thomas with Some Notes upon his Descendants," in *Proc. Am. Antiquarian Soc.,* n.s., vol. XXX (1921), pp. 251–77; J. T. Buckingham, *Personal Memoirs* (2 vols., 1852); Annie Russell Marble, *From 'Prentice to Patron: The Life Story of Isaiah Thomas* (1935); L. N. Richardson, *A Hist. of Early Am. Magazines* (1931).]   R. W. G. V.

THOMAS, JESSE BURGESS (1777–May 3, 1853), United States senator, territorial judge, was born in Shepherdstown, Va. (now W. Va.), the son of Jesse and Sabina (Symmes) Thomas. Through his mother he claimed descent from Lord Baltimore. In 1799 he was studying law with his brother at Washington, Mason County, Ky., where he also served as county clerk until 1803. An early marriage ending with the death of his wife in that year led him to leave Kentucky, and he began practising law in Lawrenceburg,

Indiana Territory. He was soon elected (1805) to the lower branch of the territorial legislature, where he served as speaker for three years. In 1805 he was appointed captain of militia in Dearborn County by Gov. William H. Harrison. On Dec. 2, 1806 he married Rebecca (Mackenzie) Hamtranck, widow of Col. Hamtranck and mother of John Francis Hamtranck [*q.v.*].

In 1808 Thomas was elected as delegate to Congress to fill a vacancy, thanks largely to the support of Illinoisans who desired division of Indiana Territory. He kept his preëlection promise to work for this end, and was successful before the end of the session in March 1809 (*Annals of Congress*, 10 Cong., 2 Sess., pp. 339, 1095). Realizing that "the service he had rendered the Illinoisans was fatal to his further political aspirations in Indiana" (Snyder, "Forgotten Statesmen," *post*, p. 515), he shrewdly obtained from President Madison appointment to one of the three federal judgeships in the newly created territory of Illinois. Removing thither, he served continuously as federal judge until 1818, winning a reputation for ability and fairness.

As a delegate from St. Clair County, Thomas was chosen president of the first constitutional convention of Illinois in 1818 (R. V. Carpenter, in "The Illinois Constitution Convention of 1818," *Journal of the Illinois State Historical Society*, October 1913). He was one of the first United States senators from the state of Illinois, serving until March 1829. His most important senatorial action occurred in 1820 during the debate over slavery and the admission of Missouri into the Union. Although not a slaveholder himself, he believed in the institution and favored its establishment in Illinois. During the congressional deadlock relative to the admission of Missouri and Maine, however, he introduced an amendment prohibiting slavery north of the line 36° 30' except for the section included in the proposed state of Missouri. This amendment was embodied in the famous "Missouri Compromise" (*Annals of Congress*, 16 Cong., 1 Sess., p. 427). Thomas' support of his friend William H. Crawford [*q.v.*] for the presidency in 1824 led to alienation from his party, which was largely composed of Jackson followers. He therefore refused to stand for reëlection at the expiration of his term and left Illinois for Mount Vernon, Ohio, where his wife had considerable property. In 1832 he saw service in the Black Hawk War. His last participation in politics was the nomination of his friend William H. Harrison [*q.v.*] for the presidency in 1840.

Always interested in business (in 1817 he had set up the first wool-carding machine in Illinois), he now turned his attention to the management of his wife's property with such success that he accumulated a moderate fortune. He assisted in organizing St. Paul's Episcopal Church, at Mount Vernon, of which he was a member. After the death of his wife in 1851 his mind became deranged and he committed suicide on the night of May 3, 1853, dying childless. Jesse Burgess Thomas, 1832–1915 [*q.v.*], a Baptist minister, was his grand-nephew.

Thomas was better as a politician than as a judge or lawyer. Despite nine years on the federal bench, his knowledge of the law was superficial and his primary interest was politics. His "quickness of perception, clear intellect, sound judgment, and knowledge of human nature, constituting strong common sense" (Snyder, *op. cit.*, p. 516) were invaluable to him as a politician. He was considered "tricky" by some contemporaries, yet won a reputation for fairness and justice for which there must have been considerable basis.

[N. N. Hill, *Hist. of Knox County, Ohio* (1881); J. M. Palmer, *The Bench and Bar of Ill., Hist. and Reminiscent* (1899); Charles Robson, *The Biog. Encyc. of Ill. of the Nineteenth Century* (1875); J. F. Snyder, *Adam W. Snyder, and His Period in Illinois Hist., 1817–1842* (1903) and "Forgotten Statesmen of Illinois," *Trans. Ill. State Hist. Soc. for the Year 1904* (1904); L. B. Thomas, *The Thomas Book* (copr. 1896); *Biog. Dir. Am. Cong.* (1928); *Commercial Register* (Sandusky), May 6, 1853.]   E. B. E.

THOMAS, JESSE BURGESS (July 29, 1832–June 6, 1915), Baptist clergyman, son of Jesse Burgess and Adeline Clarissa (Smith) Thomas, was descended from English ancestors who settled in Maryland in the middle of the seventeenth century. Several of the family were distinguished members of the legal profession; his father was a judge of the supreme court of Illinois; his great-uncle, another Jesse Burgess Thomas [*q.v.*], had been a federal judge in Illinois Territory and one of the state's first senators. Young Jesse graduated from Kenyon College in 1850, studied law, and was admitted to the bar in 1852. Later, feeling an obligation to prepare for the ministry, he entered Rochester Theological Seminary, but withdrew after a year to engage in mercantile business, and soon returned to the law. After five years more of practice, however, he decided definitely for the ministry and in 1862 was ordained at Waukegan, Ill., becoming pastor of the local Baptist church. His gifts of eloquence and leadership recommended him to the Pierrepont Street Baptist Church, Brooklyn, N. Y., where he served four years, a period followed by a few months in the First Baptist Church, San Francisco, and a longer term as pastor of the Michigan Avenue Baptist Church, Chicago. In 1874, the Pierrepont Street and First Baptist churches of Brooklyn having merged, he was called to be pastor of the united congregation. Here he remained for fourteen years.

A natural orator, logical in thought, incisive in utterance, picturesque in style, kindly of heart, and of winsome personality, he was one of several Brooklyn ministers—including Henry Ward Beecher, Richard S. Storrs, and T. De Witt Tallmage [qq.v.]—who were nationally renowned as preachers. In theology he was conservative; when it seemed as if the higher criticism and the arguments of the scientists threatened his cherished beliefs, he spoke strongly of his convictions in the pulpit and on the lecture platform, and wrote books to express his opinions more amply.

In 1888 Thomas left the pastorate to become professor of church history in the Newton Theological Institution, Newton Center, Mass. After seventeen years of teaching he became professor emeritus, serving as minister-at-large. He was also nominally pastor emeritus of his old church in Brooklyn, in which city he died.

His publications included *The Old Bible and the New Science* (1877); "Significance of the Historic Element in Scripture," in Joseph Cook's *Christ and Modern Thought* (1881); *The Mould of Doctrine* (copyright 1882); *Some Parables of Nature* (1911); and *The Church and the Kingdom, a New Testament Study* (1914). He was married, May 30, 1855, to Abbie Anne Eastman of Ottawa County, Mich., and had five sons and three daughters; four of his children died young.

[Wm. Cathcart, *The Baptist Encyc.* (1881); *Who's Who in America*, 1914–15; L. B. Thomas, *The Thomas Book* (copr. 1896); *Watchman-Examiner*, June 17, 1915; *Standard*, June 26, 1915; *Brooklyn Daily Eagle*, June 7, 1915; *Sun* (N. Y.), June 8, 1915.] H. K. R.

THOMAS, JOHN (Nov. 9, 1724–June 2, 1776), Revolutionary soldier, great-grandson of John Thomas who came to Massachusetts in 1635 as a fourteen-year-old orphan, was born in Marshfield, Mass., the son of John and Lydia (Waterman) Thomas. After studying medicine in the office of Dr. Simon Tufts of Medford, he practised for a short time at Green Harbor, then went to Kingston, Mass., where he resided for the rest of his life except when absent on military duty. On Mar. 1, 1746, he was authorized by Governor Shirley to practise "Chirurgery and Medicine" in the army and in the following year he served under General Waldo in Nova Scotia. In February 1755 he was commissioned lieutenant and surgeon's mate and empowered to enlist volunteers in the province; later the same year he

participated in Winslow's descent upon Acadia; and in 1759–60 he served in Nova Scotia and in the expedition dispatched to Canada under Amherst. During the next fifteen years he was principally occupied in practising his profession at Kingston. In 1770 Governor Hutchinson appointed him a justice of the peace.

At the outbreak of the Revolution he was chosen (Feb. 9, 1775) by the Provincial Congress of Massachusetts one of five general officers, on May 19 was commissioned lieutenant-general of the state troops, and on June 22, elected brigadier-general by the Continental Congress. Learning that his Continental commission was antedated by those of William Heath and Seth Pomeroy [qq.v.] who had previously served under his command in the Massachusetts forces, he decided to resign, but Washington, who held him in high esteem, appealed to him in an earnest and eloquent letter (W. C. Ford, *The Writings of George Washington*, vol. III, 1889, pp. 39–43) to subordinate personal considerations to the common interest, and Thomas consented to remain. During the winter of 1775–76, he was in command at Roxbury, the most important post in the American siege lines. Washington directed him to occupy Dorchester Heights, overlooking both the harbor and town of Boston, and on the night of Mar. 4, accompanied by about 3,000 picked men, several pieces of artillery, and 360 ox teams laden with entrenching materials, he seized and fortified this strategic site. Howe planned an attack, but a violent storm delayed the movement and enabled Thomas to render his position impregnable. As a result the British were obliged to evacuate Boston.

In the meantime disaster had overtaken the American arms in Canada. In a futile assault upon Quebec on the night of Dec. 31, 1775, Montgomery had been killed and Arnold had been wounded; sickness and desertion were decimating the Patriot ranks. Chosen by the Continental Congress to take charge of this discouraging situation, Thomas was promoted to the rank of major-general on Mar. 6, 1776, and ordered north. Arriving before Quebec on May 1, he found that of a force of some 1,900 men, only about 1,000 were fit for duty; there were only 150 pounds of powder and less than a week's provisions; a large British fleet laden with supplies and reënforcements was approaching Quebec. Thomas summoned a council of war at which it was unanimously decided to retreat, and the army accordingly fell back to Sorel. Shortly thereafter Thomas died of smallpox and was buried near the fort at Chambly.

He had married in 1761 Hannah Thomas of

Taunton, daughter of Nathaniel Thomas, who although bearing the same name as her husband was not related to him. They had two sons and a daughter. John Thomas was a man of commanding presence, six feet tall and well proportioned. Washington commended him (Ford, *op. cit.*, III, 16) as "an able good Officer."

[Milton Halsey Thomas, Esq., Columbia Univ. Library, has compiled a manuscript bibliography of material relating to General Thomas. The General's diaries (1748–60), orderly books, commissions, many of his letters and personal belongings, and a portrait by Blythe are in the possession of the Mass. Hist. Soc. His diary of the expedition to Acadia is published in *New Eng. Hist. and Geneal. Reg.*, Oct. 1879. Arthur Lord has contributed biographical sketches to *Proc. Mass. Hist. Soc.*, 2 ser. XVIII (1905), and *Bostonian Soc. Pubs.*, vol. XII (1915). A sketch by Milton Halsey Thomas appeared in the *Boston Sunday Globe*, May 31, 1925. See also *Vital Records of Kingston, Mass.* (1911); M. A. Thomas, *Memorials of Marshfield* (1854); Peter Force, *Am. Archives*, 4 and 5 ser. (9 vols., 1837–53); Jared Sparks, *Corresp. of the Am. Revolution* (4 vols., 1853); J. H. Smith, *Our Struggle for the Fourteenth Colony* (2 vols., 1907); Charles Coffin, *The Life and Services of Major General John Thomas* (1844).]
E. E. C.

THOMAS, JOHN JACOBS (Jan. 8, 1810–Feb. 22, 1895), pomologist, author, editor, was born at Ledyard, Cayuga County, N. Y., the son of David and Hannah (Jacobs) Thomas, and a descendant of David Thomas who is said to have emigrated from Wales with William Penn in 1699. His father, a Quaker, was a self-taught engineer active in the construction of the Welland Canal and of the Erie Canal from Rochester to Buffalo; he was also the author of *Travels through the Western Country in the Summer of 1816* (1819), and a pioneer fruit-grower and nurseryman of central New York. John Jacobs Thomas early demonstrated unusual ability in a wide range of rural activities. For some thirty years he conducted nurseries successively at Palmyra, Macedon, and Union Springs, N. Y., and it is recorded that each tree he sold was allowed to bear fruit first to be sure that it was true to name. Although he had only the education afforded by the neighborhood district school, he early acquired a clear style of expression. He was assistant editor of the *Genesee Farmer* from 1838, an editor of the *New Genesee Farmer and Gardeners' Journal*, 1840–41, and associate editor of the *Country Gentleman* from its foundation in 1853 until shortly before his death in 1894, his editorials in the *Cultivator* and the *Country Gentleman* constituting the most varied and extensive series of discussions of rural topics written by an American during that period. His *Farm Implements and Machinery* (1854) and a series of nine volumes entitled *Rural Affairs* (1869–81), of which he was editor, covered a wide range of topics of interest to practical farm-

ers. He developed skill as an artist, and illustrated his published articles and books with cuts from his own drawings. He invented several tools and implements, one of which, the smoothing harrow, came into extensive use throughout the eastern and northern states. He was active in the formation of the American Pomological Congress (later the American Pomological Society), and served as the first president of the large and influential Western New York Horticultural Society, organized in 1855.

In 1846 he published *The Fruit Culturist*, a paper-covered volume of some two hundred pages devoted primarily to practical instruction in the nursery propagation and commercial growing of temperate climate fruits. In 1849 this was expanded into *The American Fruit Culturist*, in which the content was trebled and the information condensed, systematized, and generously illustrated. Although it was preceded by the publications of many other able pomologists, it marks the beginning of systematic pomology in America. The most comprehensive of the earlier fruit books—*The Fruits and Fruit Trees of America* (1845), by Andrew Jackson Downing [*q.v.*]—was essentially encyclopedic in character, with little attempt at systematization of varietal description and no effort to classify varieties in such way as to facilitate the identification of unknown sorts. Thomas gave careful attention to the selection and use of terms in his descriptions of varieties, and covered not only the characteristics of the fruits themselves but habit of growth, characteristics of bark, bud, leaf, and flower, productiveness, hardiness, etc., as well. For each of the major fruits he developed a "Synopsis of Arrangement" which, though artificial in character, constituted a convenient guide to the identification of the varieties included in the book. Adopted by agricultural colleges as a standard text in horticultural courses, the book was important in the advancement of technical pomology and in the training of pomologists, as well as in the development of amateur and commercial fruit growing. It went through many editions during Thomas' life, and after his death was revised and enlarged (1897) by W. H. S. Wood.

Thomas married Mary Slocum Howland, Aug. 23, 1838, at North Street Brick Meeting House, near Union Springs, N. Y. He died in Union Springs, where he had lived for nearly forty years, survived by his wife and four of their seven children. He was a man of singular gentleness and sweetness of character, with a kindly, humorous, somewhat square face and alert eyes. Because of a lameness in one foot he went on crutches. For many years his study was near his garden and his orchard, to which he made frequent daily visits and where he conducted numerous experiments.

[Sources include W. T. Lyle, *The Thomas Family* (1908); L. H. Bailey, *Standard Cyc. of Horticulture*, vol. III (1915), pp. 1599–1600; W. H. S. Wood, in J. J. Thomas' *Am. Fruit Culturist* (1897 ed.), pp. v–vi; *Cultivator and Country Gentleman*, Feb. 28 (reprint of obituary in *Union Springs Advertiser*), Mar. 7, 1895; correspondence with David Fairchild, Paul H. Fairchild, and Mrs. Emily Thomas. For David Thomas, see U. P. Hedrick, *Peaches of N. Y.* (1917), pp. 55–56, n.]   W. A. T.

THOMAS, JOHN WILSON (Aug. 24, 1830–Feb. 12, 1906), railway executive, was descended from a pioneer family which had settled on a farm on the Cumberland River near Nashville, Tenn., during the latter part of the eighteenth century. James Thomas, his father, after marrying Ellen Meneese, left the farm to enter the saddlery business in Nashville, and there John was born and grew to manhood. After attending preparatory schools in Nashville and at Georgetown, Ky., he entered Union University, Murfreesboro, Tenn., where he graduated in 1851 with the highest honors in his class. He served as instructor in that institution from 1851 until ill health forced his resignation in 1854, and then operated a hotel at Murfreesboro until 1858, when he became local agent for the Nashville & Chattanooga Railroad. In this position he played an important part in the transportation of Confederate troops during the early months of the Civil War, and in 1863 he was made custodian of the rolling stock and records of the road. In order to save this property from the Federal forces he took all movable materials to Augusta, Ga., and later to Wilmington, N. C.

After the close of the war his promotion was rapid. He became auditor and paymaster in 1865, division superintendent in 1868, general superintendent of the enlarged system which became the Nashville, Chattanooga & St. Louis Railway in 1872, general manager in 1883, and president in 1884, which position he held until his death. In his work as an executive he quickly gained a reputation for honesty and integrity which won the respect of his business associates, while his spirit of sympathy and good will toward the employees of his company made him one of the most popular and most beloved railroad executives of his time. These qualities, combined with his energy and efficiency, enabled him to place his road in a leading position in Southern transportation development.

His most important service to his state, aside from his railroad activity, was rendered as president of the Tennessee Centennial and International Exposition which was held in Nashville in 1897. Serving without salary, he directed the organization, managed the finances, and acted as host with such success that the Exposition closed free from indebtedness. He was an active worker in church circles, and among his outstanding contributions in that field were the organization and financing of the Monteagle Sunday School Assembly as an intellectual and recreational center in the Cumberland Mountains. Records show that during the later years of his life he was the most liberal man in Nashville in his support of charitable organizations; but while his gifts were large they were always made unostentatiously, and it is believed that at the time of his death he was a comparatively poor man.

He was twice married; first, in 1852, to Elizabeth Thomas of Murfreesboro, who died in 1886; and second, May 14, 1891, to Evalina DeBow of Nashville. A son and a daughter were born of the first marriage; the son survived his father, who died in Nashville in his seventy-sixth year.

[*Nashville American*, Feb. 13, 1906; *Nashville Banner*, Feb. 12, 1906; Herman Justi, *Official Hist. of the Tenn. Centennial Exposition* (1898); *John W. Thomas: A Memorial* (1906), a collection of addresses delivered at the various mass meetings held in his honor after his death.]   W. C. B.

THOMAS, JOSEPH (Sept. 23, 1811–Dec. 24, 1891), lexicographer, educator, and physician, was born at Ledyard, Cayuga County, N. Y., the son of David and Hannah (Jacobs) Thomas, and a brother of John Jacobs Thomas [*q.v.*]. After attending Rensselaer Polytechnic Institute at Troy, N. Y., where he received the degree of A.B. in 1830, he entered the senior class at Yale College (1832) to pursue a classical course but left almost immediately because of illness. In 1833–34 he taught Latin and Greek at Haverford College. He then entered the School of Medicine of the University of Pennsylvania, and took the degree of M.D. in 1837 with a thesis on the pulse. Although he lived in Philadelphia during the remainder of his life, and took further courses at the same institution in subsequent years, he seems not to have practised medicine for long, turning instead to his earlier training in classical languages and in literature as the means for a career. He returned to Haverford College as professor of elocution in 1852–53, but again remained for only one year. Between 1854 and 1871 he was associated with J. B. Lippincott and Company of Philadelphia as compiler and editor of a series of reference books: *A New and Complete Gazetteer of the United States* (1854); *Lippincott's Pronouncing Gazetteer: a Complete Geographical Dictionary of the World* (1855), both with Thomas Baldwin; *A Comprehensive Medical Dictionary* (1864); and a *Universal Pronounc-*

ing Dictionary of Biography and Mythology (2 vols., 1870). In 1852 he also prepared *The First Book of Etymology,* based on that of James Lynd, an elementary text for use in schools. In order to improve his knowledge of the pronunciation of Oriental proper and place names, he took a rapid tour of Egypt and Palestine in 1852–53. The record of this trip, *Travels in Egypt and Palestine* (1853), displays considerable antiquarian knowledge. In 1857 he made a similar trip to India to study Sanskrit and remained for fourteen months.

About 1866, through his friendship with Edward Parrish [*q.v.*], he became identified with the founding of Swarthmore College and with other activities of the Society of Friends, although he himself was not at that time a member. During 1865 and 1866 he delivered numerous lectures in Philadelphia, most of them under the auspices of the Friends' Social Lyceum, on ancient philosophy and philosophers, and on topics dealing with travel, education, and literature. At the laying of the cornerstone of Swarthmore College on May 10, 1866, he made an address in which he stressed the advantages of a liberal education for leadership in a democracy, and of higher education for women. During 1874–75 he gave the first series of lectures on English literature at Swarthmore, and was professor of English there until 1887, when he retired. His attainments as a scholar led to his election to membership in the American Philosophical Society. He died, unmarried, in Philadelphia.

His knowledge of Latin, Greek, and many other foreign languages made it possible for him to become one of the authorities of his day on etymology and the principles of pronunciation, and he did much to clarify the confusion of usage in works of reference. He emphasized the historical derivation of word meanings, and the use of phonetic re-spelling and native pronunciation of foreign place and proper names, made increasingly important in gazetteers and dictionaries by the decline of classical and linguistic training in the schools. As an authority he was invited to contribute the pronouncing vocabularies of biographical and geographical names to the 1867 edition of Webster's *An American Dictionary of the English Language,* unabridged. His contributions to education were not as specific or as original as those to lexicography, but were none the less consistent and courageous. His advocacy of modernized liberal studies for men and women alike was radical doctrine for his day, and his courses in English literature were in accord with the best practices of the present. He was a man of commanding presence, admired and respected by those who knew him.

[W. T. Lyle, *The Thomas Family* (1908); H. B. Nason, *Biog. Records ... of the Rensselaer Polytechnic Institute* (1887); E. H. Magill, *Sixty-five Years in the Life of a Teacher* (1907), pp. 159–62; H. A. Kelly and W. L. Burrage, *Am. Medic. Biogs.* (1920); manuscript diary of Edward Parrish in the possession of a descendant; minutes of the board of managers of Swarthmore Coll.; W. I. Hull, "A Hist. of Swarthmore Coll.," in MS.; alumni records, Univ. of Pa.; prefaces to Thomas' reference works; obituary in *Pub. Ledger* (Phila.), Dec. 25, 1891.]   R. E. S.

THOMAS, LORENZO (October 1804–Mar. 2, 1875), soldier, was born in New Castle, Del., the son of Evan and Elizabeth (Sherer) Thomas. There was a military tradition in the Thomas family and in 1819 Lorenzo entered the United States Military Academy. At his graduation in 1823 he stood seventeenth in his class and was made a second lieutenant in the 4th Infantry. Subsequently he rose to the rank of major (1848) in this regiment. Except for service as quartermaster in the Seminole War (1836–37), his early duties were mostly of a routine nature. He was appointed assistant adjutant-general at Washington in 1838, with the rank of brevet major, and remained there almost continuously until 1846, when he joined the volunteer division of Maj.-Gen. William O. Butler [*q.v.*] as chief of staff during the Mexican War. "For gallant and meritorious conduct" at Monterey he was brevetted lieutenant-colonel, Sept. 23, 1846. At the close of the war he returned to his duties as assistant adjutant-general at Washington and continued in that capacity until designated as chief of staff to Lieut.-Gen. Winfield Scott in 1853. Upon the resignation of Col. Samuel Cooper [*q.v.*], the adjutant-general of the army, Thomas was promoted to a colonelcy and put in charge of that office, Mar. 7, 1861. Five months later he was made adjutant-general and given the rank of brigadier-general.

Like other bureaus of the War Department, when the Civil War came, the office over which Thomas presided proved hopelessly inadequate in equipment and personnel and gradually had to be expanded. Meanwhile, he was subjected to sharp criticism from some of the zealous war governors because he seemed too slow in furnishing state quotas and other necessary information. There apparently was considerable laxity and inefficiency in his bureau and many persons surmised that he was "lukewarm" regarding the war, but there was no sound basis for this suspicion. In what was probably an effort to be rid of him, Secretary Stanton ordered him to the Mississippi Valley in March 1863 to organize negro regiments. This work, together with arranging for the exchange of prisoners and the consolidation of depleted regiments, kept him occupied until the end of the war. He was brevetted major-general on Mar. 13, 1865. The next year Stanton sent him on an inspection tour of the provost marshal general's office and in 1867 on an extended inspection tour of the national cemeteries.

While he was engaged in the latter work the difficulties between President Johnson and Stanton came to a head, and the President, desiring to have a "rightminded" man in the adjutant general's office, directed Thomas on Feb. 13, 1868, to resume full charge of the bureau. On Feb. 21, Johnson dismissed Stanton, appointed Thomas secretary *ad interim,* and requested him to take possession of the department. The selection was unfortunate, for the Adjutant-General proved to be a vain and garrulous person. When he publicly boasted that he would oust the Secretary by force if necessary, Stanton ordered his arrest for violation of the Tenure of Office Act. Although immediately admitted to bail and discharged within a week, the General failed to displace the recalcitrant Secretary, the contest between them degenerating into opera bouffe. Thomas' testimony and his naïveté in the impeachment trial of the President effectively dispelled the charge that he and Johnson had conspired forcibly to eject Stanton and helped to win for the President an acquittal. After the adjournment Thomas resumed his inspection duties, but was retired from active service on Feb. 22, 1869. He died in Washington six years later.

[G. W. Cullum, *Biog. Reg. Officers and Grads. U. S. Mil. Acad.* (3rd ed., 1891); F. B. Heitman, *Hist. Reg. and Dict. U. S. Army* (1903), vol. I; *War of the Rebellion: Official Records (Army)*; *Diary of Gideon Welles* (1911), vol. III; *Trial of Andrew Johnson* (1868), vol. I; G. C. Gorham, *Life and Public Services of Edwin M. Stanton* (1899), vol. II; Frank Leslie's *Illustrated Newspaper,* Nov. 25, 1865; *Army and Navy Journal,* Mar. 6, 1875; *National Republican* (Washington), Mar. 3, 1875; bibliog. of article on Edwin M. Stanton.]
A. H. M.

THOMAS, PHILIP EVAN (Nov. 11, 1776– Sept. 1, 1861), railroad pioneer, was born at "Mount Radnor," Montgomery County, Md., the third son of Evan and Rachel (Hopkins) Thomas. When he went to Baltimore to work, the town had a population of only 15,000. In 1800 he began business for himself as a hardware merchant. On Apr. 20, 1801, he was married to Elizabeth George of Kent County, Md. He was already prominent as president of the Mechanics' Bank when the means by which Baltimore might retain its important trade with the "Ohio country" came under anxious discussion. The National Road had been Baltimore's link with the extending settlements in the Ohio and Missis-

sippi valleys, and had contributed to make the city the third in the Union by 1827. But the Erie Canal had been opened in 1825, and the "Pennsylvania system of public works," connecting Philadelphia with Pittsburgh, had been begun the following year. The speed and cheapness of transportation which these offered threatened to draw off western trade to New York and Philadelphia. Maryland and Virginia joined in reviving the project of the Chesapeake and Ohio Canal, designed to run from Georgetown to the Youghiogheny. Thomas was made a Maryland commissioner in this undertaking, but withdrew after a year, convinced that the canal could do nothing commercially for Baltimore. Interested by an account of the newly completed Darlington and Stockton Railroad in England, he immediately began to investigate the railroad as a means of solving the transportation problem, and in February 1827, with George Brown, 1787–1859 [*q.v.*], he called a meeting of business men at which he explained the superiority of railroads over canals. The call of a second meeting the same month declared it would "take under consideration the best means of restoring to . . . Baltimore that portion of the western trade which has recently been diverted from it by the introduction of steam navigation and by other causes" (Hungerford, *post,* vol. I, p. 19). Within a week Thomas, as chairman of a subcommittee on definite plans, reported in favor of a "double railroad" to the Ohio. Progress thereafter was rapid. The Maryland act to charter the Baltimore and Ohio Railroad was approved Feb. 28, 1827, and the actual incorporation took place Apr. 24. Except for the Mohawk and Hudson Railroad, chartered two months earlier, the Baltimore and Ohio thus became the first railroad chartered in the United States to carry passengers. Thomas was made president and a director. Charles Carroll [*q.v.*] of Carrollton laid the first stone, July 4, 1828. Thomas was unfaltering in overcoming the many difficulties which presented themselves once the first enthusiasm had died down—the delays in payment of Baltimore's subscription, the hostility of the Chesapeake and Ohio directors, the discord over the route of the road, the unexpected costs of excavation in the first westward miles, the designing of a locomotive which would go around curves, the refusal of Congress to remit the import duty on scrap iron for the tracks. When he resigned the presidency in 1836, the road had reached Harpers Ferry and the chief mechanical problems had been solved.

Like his father and his first ancestor in America, Philip Thomas, who came to Maryland from Wales about 1651, Thomas was a Quaker. He took active part in protecting the Indians of New York against the taking of their reservations by land speculators, and for this the Senecas made him "Chief Sagouan" (Bountiful Giver) and constituted him their representative in Washington. He was president of the Mechanical Fire Company, the first president of the Maryland Bible Society, and advanced $25,000 that the state might begin the erection of the Washington monument in Baltimore. He was a stout man, clean-shaven, with high forehead, prominent nose, and a pleasant expression. He died in Yonkers, N. Y., while on a visit to his daughter some years after his retirement from business. He was survived by five daughters and two sons.

[L. B. Thomas, *The Thomas Book* (copr. 1896); P. E. Thomas, *Proc. of Sundry Citizens of Baltimore ... for Intercourse between that City and the Western States* (Baltimore, 1827); G. W. Howard, *The Monumental City* (1873–76), pt. 2; Edward Hungerford, *The Story of the Baltimore and Ohio Railroad, 1827–1927* (1928), vol. I; obituaries in *Sun* (Baltimore), Sept. 2, and *Baltimore American and Commercial Advertiser*, Sept. 3, 1861. The mural painting, "Builders of the Baltimore and Ohio," Baltimore and Ohio Building, Baltimore, shows Thomas at the extreme left.]
B. M.

THOMAS, PHILIP FRANCIS (Sept. 12, 1810–Oct. 2, 1890), secretary of the treasury, congressman from Maryland, and governor, was born in Easton, Talbot County, Md., and figured in Maryland politics for more than half a century. He was the son of Maria (Francis) and Tristram Thomas, a prominent physician, and a descendant of Tristram Thomas who settled in Talbot County in 1666. After attending the Easton academy he studied at Dickinson College for two years, until his college course was abruptly terminated by a youthful prank. He then returned home to read law in the office of William Hayward and was admitted to the bar in 1831. Defying the political affiliations of his family and neighbors in this Whig stronghold, he declared himself, unsuccessfully, as Democratic candidate for the state legislature in 1834. Undaunted by defeat, he offered himself again in 1836, when he advocated reapportionment of representation in the state Assembly, a most unpopular measure on the Eastern Shore, and yet again in 1837. In 1838, however, he piled up a majority greater than that accorded the governor. In 1838 he was named congressional candidate and defeated his veteran opponent, James Alfred Pearce [*q.v.*]. For personal reasons he declined a renomination and resumed his law practice. He accepted, however, appointment as judge of the Eastern Shore land office court.

His prominence in the Assembly, to which he returned in 1843 and 1845, won him the Democratic nomination for governor in 1847 and suc-

cess at the polls. In his inaugural address he undertook a campaign to replace the seventy-year-old constitution by one more modern. It was at this time that the directors of the Baltimore and Ohio Railroad offered him the presidency of the road, even urging him to name his own salary. He declined the portfolio of the navy offered by Pierce because of the inadequacy of the salary but soon accepted the post of collector of the port at Baltimore. When a change in administration lost him that position, he practised law for a time in St. Louis, Mo. President Buchanan offered him, first, the governorship of Utah Territory, then the secretaryship of the treasury, and, finally, the humble post of commissioner of patents, which he accepted. Within a few months he resigned in order to enter the cabinet finally as secretary of the treasury, but he felt obliged to retire within a month, with the southern members of the cabinet. Though he took no part in the Civil War, it is known that his sympathies were with the Confederacy and that his only son joined the southern army. This attitude cost him a seat in the federal Senate, for, when the conservatives obtained control of the Maryland legislature, to which he had returned in 1867, and chose him senator, he was denied his seat on the charge of disloyalty. The vote of a Democrat against Johnson's impeachment seemed so necessary that Thomas urged immediate choice of a democratic candidate who could not be challenged. However, his loyalty was not questioned when he was elected to the House of Representatives in 1874. After a single term in Congress, he returned once more in 1878 to the Maryland Assembly in the hope of being elected to the federal Senate but was defeated in caucus. He made his final unsuccessful attempt at the coveted senatorship by allowing himself to be returned to the assembly of 1884. On Feb. 5, 1835, he was married to Sarah Maria Kerr. After her death in 1870 he was married, Jan. 29, 1876, to Clintonia (Wright) May. Of his thirteen children, three daughters survived him.

[M. P. Andrews, *Tercentenary Hist. of Md.* (1925), vol. IV; H. E. Buchholz, *Governors of Md.* (1908); Oswald Tilghman, *Hist. of Talbot County, Md.* (1915); E. S. Riley, *A Hist. of the General Assembly of Md.* (1905); R. H. Spencer, *Thomas Family of Talbot County, Md.* (1914); *Baltimore American* and *Sun* (Baltimore), Oct. 3, 1890.]
E. L.

THOMAS, RICHARD HENRY (Jan. 26, 1854–Oct. 3, 1904), religious leader, physician, and author, was born in Baltimore, Md., son of Dr. Richard Henry and Phebe (Clapp) Thomas, and a descendant of Philip Thomas who emigrated from Wales and settled on Chesapeake Bay in 1651. His parents were members of the

Society of Friends. He was a sickly child, though mentally keen, sensitive, and imaginative. He entered the sophomore class in Haverford College in 1869 and received the degree of B.A. in 1872. After three years at the University of Maryland, where he received the degree of M.D. in 1875, he studied in London (1876), at the Johns Hopkins University (1876–77) as a special student in biology, and in Vienna (1880–81). He was professor of the diseases of throat and chest in the Woman's Medical College of Baltimore from 1882 to 1893, and at two different periods was dean of the faculty. He prepared many medical papers for this institution, and was a beloved and effective teacher. Early in life he showed a profound interest in religion, and before he finished his medical studies he had begun to be a public interpreter of the Quaker faith and ideals. Recorded a minister of the Society of Friends in 1883, he became one of the foremost ministers in that Society in his generation, and a leading interpreter of its principles both in America and England. On Mar. 28, 1878, he married in London Anna Lloyd Braithwaite, daughter of J. Bevan Braithwaite, who was one of the most distinguished English Quakers. One daughter was born of this union. Traveling extensively with his father-in-law in England, Europe, and America, Thomas concentrated his interest on the interpretation of Christianity to meet the challenges of modern science and criticism. His preaching came to many in England and America as a solvent of doubt, and he helped many of the youth of his generation to adjust their religious faith to the new discoveries of the age. He was a clear and effective advocate of methods of peace as a solution for international controversies. For several years he was president of the Peace Association of Friends in America.

He possessed a poetical gift and wrote poetry throughout his life, much of which was published in contemporary periodicals. His writings include one volume of collected poems, *Echoes and Pictures* (London, 1895); a novel, *Penelve* (1898); and *The History of the Society of Friends in America* (1894), with his brother, Allen C. Thomas, in which he interpreted the original Quaker message and treated the history of the two American "separations." He wrote a striking paraphrase translation of the medieval hymn, "Veni Sancte Spiritus," which was praised by the poet Whittier. He was joint editor and founder of the *Interchange,* a periodical. Two of his most important essays were printed in the third volume of *Present Day Papers* (5 vols., 1898–1902) under the title "Fides et Spes Medici." He died in Baltimore. His reminis-

cences were printed after his death in *Richard H. Thomas, M.D., Life and Letters* (1905), edited by his wife. His greatest single characteristic was his religious influence on other lives, made very evident in the numerous letters written to him.

[In addition to Thomas' reminiscences, see L. B. Thomas, *The Thomas Book* (copr. 1896); *Who's Who in America,* 1903–05; *Biog. Cat.* . . . *Matriculates of Haverford Coll.* (1922); death notice in *Sun* (Baltimore), Oct. 4, 1904.]   R. M. J.

THOMAS, ROBERT BAILEY (Apr. 24, 1766–May 19, 1846), founder, editor, and publisher of the *Farmer's Almanack,* was born at Grafton, Mass., the son of William and Azubah (Goodale) Thomas. Both his father and his grandfather were men of some education; the grandfather, William Thomas, emigrated from Wales about 1718 and about 1720 settled in Marblehead. Young Thomas grew up in Sterling (later West Boylston), Mass., where his father was a farmer and a schoolmaster. Although it was intended that he should go to Harvard, he preferred self-education, which consisted of reading all the books in his father's library. Among these was James Ferguson's *Astronomy Explained* (1756), which first gave him the idea of "calculating an Almanack." But at sixteen he realized that he lacked the necessary mathematical background for astronomical computations, so he temporarily followed in his father's footsteps and became a school-teacher. He left this occupation almost immediately to become an apprentice bookbinder, and at twenty-four took the first step toward his goal. He had been studying mathematics and astronomy; now he hired a printer, N. Coverly, to print a thousand copies of a spelling book—William Perry's *The Only Sure Guide to the English Tongue; or, New Pronouncing Spelling Books* (1790),—bound them himself, and sold them to the country schools. With the profits he paid his tuition in and attended a mathematics school in Boston run by Osgood Carleton, an almanac-maker. In 1792, when Carleton retired, he stepped into the breach with an almanac of his own—shrewdly titled *The Farmer's Almanac . . . for the Year of Our Lord 1793* (1792). It was afterwards called *The Farmer's Almanack,* and later *The Old Farmer's Almanack.*

This was a success from the start, mainly because Thomas knew his audience, an intelligent group of well-to-do farmers. His realization of the intelligence of his readers led him into an unprecedented and heretical departure from the science of almanac-making—the omission of the *Homo Signorum* (Man of the Zodiac). He considered astrology quackery, and thought the stars followed their courses with no influence on the life of man. Consequently, he omitted the conventionalized figure of the naked man surrounded by the zodiacal signs, which were connected by arrows to the organs of the body each had under its especial care. The zodiacal signs themselves he did not omit. With characteristic shrewdness, however, he translated them into the terms of the farmer's daily life. Gemini, the Twins, were no longer Castor and Pollux, but two farmers walking through a field of wheat. In Thomas' *Almanack* all questions of the day were touched upon: slavery, the Indian wars, witchcraft, the morality of the theatre, and the condition of the post roads. These discussions were larded with agricultural advice, poetry, and philosophical comment, homely epigrams and pointed wit, some culled from the classics but more being of Thomas' own production. Among maps of the traveled roads between Quebec and Savannah, too, there might appear stanzas of doggerel exuding the patriotic zeal of the new Union, or an imposing list of the "First-line ships of the American Navy," thrillingly set down in order of their complement of guns, for in those feverish days patriotic material never failed to arouse·interest.

On Nov. 17, 1803, Thomas married Hannah Beaman of Princeton, N. J. By this time the *Almanack* was ten years along the road of success. It was sold in Boston, Salem, New York, and Philadelphia, but the bulk of the sales was in the backwoods reached by itinerant pack pedlars, whose books formed the literary "circulating" libraries of the day. Thomas' accounts show that in the decade 1820–30 more than 200,-000 copies were sold by these men to outlying readers. In 1837, by popular demand, Thomas ran a woodcut of himself—a Pickwickian, round-faced character, as healthy and hearty as the *Almanack* itself. A memoir of his life appeared in the *Almanack* in the years 1833–37 and 1839. In the spring of 1846, putting aside a proof sheet of his *Almanack* for 1847, and remarking that his eyes were dim "from reading such a quantity of fine print," Thomas went to his room, lay down, and in a little while quietly died. He had no children. In his will he entrusted further publication of the *Almanack* to two nephews, in whose hands it stayed until 1904.

[The date of death is from *Vital Records of West Boylston, Mass.* (1911). See also G. L. Kittredge, *The Old Farmer and His Almanack* (1920) and H. M. Robinson, "The Almanac," *Bookman*, June–July 1932.]

H. M. R.

THOMAS, SETH (Aug. 19, 1785–Jan. 29, 1859), pioneer clock manufacturer, was born at Wolcott, Conn., the son of James and Martha (Barnes) Thomas. His father was an immigrant from Scotland. Thomas had a very meager education consisting of intermittent attendance at the district school, and at an early age began his apprenticeship as a carpenter and joiner. Upon completing this he worked for a number of years building houses and barns, generally in the country and towns near his home, although occasionally he went as far afield for work as New Haven, where he spent some time in the construction of Long Wharf. About the time this work was completed, Eli Terry [*q.v.*] at Plymouth, Conn., was ready to begin his unusual venture of making clocks at a wholesale rate. He needed both craftsmen and financial help, and suggested to Thomas—who, though he had very little money, was a skilful wood-worker—that he join him and Silas Hoadley in the undertaking. Between 1807 and 1810 the firm of Terry, Thomas & Hoadley was busily engaged in making four thousand clocks. In the first year they made and fitted up the necessary machinery to be operated by water power; in the second year they made one thousand clocks, and in the third year, three thousand. These were all "hang-up" or "wag-on-the-wall" clocks, usually without cases, the purchasers depending upon local cabinetmakers to make the grandfather cases if they were desired. In this undertaking Thomas did the joiner work, and fitted the wheels and different clock parts together. Upon the completion of this job in 1810, Thomas & Hoadley purchased Terry's interest in the firm and for two years continued making clocks in partnership.

In 1812 Thomas sold out to Hoadley and began a clock factory of his own in Plymouth Hollow. While he was not an inventive genius, he was an excellent mechanic and a keen business man, and from the beginning of this undertaking he was successful. Two years after he began operations he boldly paid Terry one thousand dollars (an unheard-of price at the time) for the manufacturing rights of the latter's popular shelf clock, and was soon making and selling as many clocks as Terry. As his business developed Thomas built a mill for rolling brass and making wire at Plymouth Hollow, and operated it in conjunction with the clock factory. Finally, in 1853, he established the business on a firm foundation by organizing the Seth Thomas Clock Company, with a capital of seventy-five thousand dollars. Thomas was twice married: first, on Apr. 20, 1808, to Philena (or Philinda) Tuttle (d. Mar. 12, 1810) of Plymouth, and second, on Apr. 14, 1811, to Laura Andrews of Plymouth, who with three sons and three daughters survived him.

His son Seth (1816–1888) carried on the business and enlarged it. Shortly after Thomas' death at Plymouth the town was divided by act of the legislature, and the western portion, which contained the Thomas factory, was made into a new town, named Thomaston in his honor.

[Samuel Orcutt, *Hist. of the Town of Wolcott (Conn.) from 1731 to 1874* (1874); Francis Atwater, *Hist. of the Town of Plymouth, Conn.* (1895); W. I. Milham, *Time & Timekeepers* (1923); Mrs. N. H. Moore, *The Old Clock Book* (1911); Henry Terry, *Am. Clock Making, Its Early Hist., and Present Extent of the Business* (1870); death notice in *Columbian Weekly Reg.* (New Haven), Feb. 5, 1859.]   C. W. M—n.

THOMAS, THEODORE [See THOMAS, CHRISTIAN FRIEDRICH THEODORE, 1835–1905].

THOMAS, THEODORE GAILLARD (Nov. 21, 1831–Feb. 28, 1903), obstetrician and gynecologist, was born on Edisto Island, near Charleston, S. C. His father, the Rev. Edward Thomas, a priest in the Episcopal Church, was a descendant of Samuel Thomas, an Anglican clergyman, who came to America about 1700; his mother, Jane Marshall (Gaillard), was the daughter of Judge Theodore Gaillard, descendant of a Huguenot refugee who fled from France and settled in Charleston after the revocation of the Edict of Nantes. Thomas entered the College of Charleston at the age of fourteen. In 1852 he graduated from the Medical College of South Carolina, and in this same year left New York, sailing on a coasting vessel as a common sailor. After serving as an interne at Bellevue Hospital, he spent six months at the immigrant's hospital on Ward's Island. His training here was supplemented by a year in Paris and several months at the Rotunda Hospital, Dublin. He returned to the United States in 1855 to begin the practice of his profession in New York, and was soon taken into partnership by Dr. John T. Metcalfe. With Dr. William Donaghe he started a "quiz class" which proved so successful that he was soon appointed adjunct to the clinic of obstetrics in the medical department of the University of the City of New York. In 1855 he was made professor of obstetrics, but resigned this post in 1863 to accept an appointment at the College of Physicians and Surgeons, where he succeeded to the chair of obstetrics in 1865. In 1879 he was transferred to the chair of gynecology and in 1881 became professor of clinical gynecology in which capacity he continued to teach until his retirement as professor emeritus in 1890. From 1872 to 1887 he was also attending surgeon to the Woman's Hospital. After 1879 he devoted himself entirely to gynecology, serving on the staffs of several hospitals and attending to private practice as late as 1900.

His contributions to his profession were varied. He was one of the first to distinguish the cervix and body of the uterus as different organs. He played a principal part in disproving the inflammatory nature of chronic metritis, as well as in putting a stop to the wide-spread custom of alarming patients about ulcers. He was the inventor of many surgical instruments and the originator of many new methods in surgery, most notably, perhaps, the operation of laparoelytrotomy. He was the first to remove a small ovarian tumor by cutting through the vagina. As early as 1867 he suggested and used an incubator. Although a careful operator, he was rapid and deft and not afraid of progress. He was willing to try antiseptic surgery in its pioneer days. With the orator's rich voice and an impressive style, he had few peers as a clinical lecturer, enlivening his discourses with a variety of phrase and illustration. His writings were fluent but exact. The chapters on chronic cervical and chronic corporeal endometritis in his *Practical Treatise on the Diseases of Women* (1868) made that textbook famous. It was translated into twelve languages and went through many editions, a classic of its kind. He wrote numerous medical articles and was the author of *A Contribution to the History of the Huguenots of South Carolina* (1887), which includes notes about his own ancestors. He was a member of many medical societies, was founder and president of the New York Obstetrical Society, and third president (1879) of the American Gynecological Society.

Thomas was married twice: first to a cousin, Mary Gaillard, and second, in 1862, to Mary Theodosia Willard, daughter of John Hart Willard and grand-daughter of Emma (Hart) Willard [q.v.]. He had four sons and one daughter. His sister, Jane, became the wife of Dr. Edwin Samuel Gaillard [q.v.]. Thomas was a man of great culture, a born leader, and one who brought confidence and cheer into the sick room. He was kind, generous, and hospitable, and his friendship and advice were sought by many. He was a handsome, well-groomed man, of robust build and medium height. Physically alert, he was known to be an excellent horseman. He died suddenly of rupture of the aorta at Thomasville, Ga.

[*Yearbook of the Medic. Asso. of the Greater City of N. Y.* (1903); *Trans. Am. Gynecol. Soc.*, vol. XXVIII (1903); *Addresses at the Dinner given to Dr. T. Gaillard Thomas on His Seventieth Birthday* (1901); William Gaillard, *Hist. and Pedigrees of the House of Gaillard* (1872); L. B. Thomas, *The Thomas Book* (copr. 1896); *S. C. Hist. and Geneal. Mag.*, Apr. 1903; *Who's Who in America*, 1901–02; H. A. Kelly and W. L. Burrage, *Am. Medic. Biogs.* (1920); John Shrady, *The Coll. of Phys. and Surgeons, N. Y., A Hist.* (n.d.), vol. II; *Am. Jour. Obstetrics,* Apr. 1903; *N. Y. Jour. of Gynecol. and Obstetrics,* Dec. 1891; *N. Y. Times,* Mar. 4, 1903.]   G. L. A.

THOMAS, WILLIAM WIDGERY (Aug. 26, 1839–Apr. 25, 1927), lawyer, politician, diplomat, was born in Portland, Me., the son of William Widgery and Elizabeth White (Goddard) Thomas. After his graduation from Bowdoin College in 1860, he studied law until he was appointed a carrier of diplomatic dispatches in 1862. He then served successively as vice-consul-general at Constantinople, acting consul-general at Galatz, Moldavia, and consul at Gothenburg, Sweden. In 1865 he resigned and in the following year completed his legal studies at Harvard, whereupon he established his residence at Portland and became active in politics. He served as commissioner of public lands for Maine (1869), as a member of the commission of immigration (1870–73), as a member of the Maine House of Representatives (1873–75), and as a member of the upper house of the state legislature (1879).

During his residence at Gothenburg, Thomas had acquired a deep attachment for Sweden and a great admiration for its people (he learned to speak fluent Swedish and translated into English Viktor Rydberg's masterpiece *The Last Athenian,* 1869), and in 1870 he played an important part in the establishment of the Swedish settlement in Aroostook County, Me. As a member of the commission of immigration appointed to find means of attracting settlers to increase the declining population of Maine, he went to Gothenburg in May 1870, embarked on an extensive advertising campaign in the newspapers, commissioned agents armed with circulars to visit the northern provinces, and himself visited many parishes. On July 23, 1870, with Thomas as their leader, a party of some fifty immigrants arrived at a spot in the woods destined to be known as New Sweden. The advertising campaign in Sweden continued, and from time to time new immigrants came, until at the end of a decade Maine's Swedish colony boasted a population of almost eight hundred. In 1883, as a reward for his services to the Republican party, he received the appointment of minister to Sweden and Norway, and served under four presidents (1883–85, 1889–94, 1897–1905). He was married on Oct. 11, 1887, to Dagmar Törnebladh (d. 1912), a Swedish noblewoman. In 1892 he published a bulky volume, *Sweden and the Swedes* (which was also published in Sweden), a description of the country and the customs of the people, with some account of his experiences as a diplomat. After his retirement as a diplomat

he lived in Portland. His ability to deliver speeches in Swedish made him a valuable stump speaker in states like Minnesota and Illinois, and he continued to hold a position of prominence in Maine. The genial founder of the Swedish colony was always a welcome visitor there, and was present on a number of ceremonial occasions. He was married a second time, on June 2, 1915, to Mrs. Aina Törnebladh. He had two children by his first marriage, and one adopted son.

[See *Who's Who in America,* 1926–27; *Biog. Rev. . . . of Cumberland County, Me.* (1896); Sidney Perham, *Address of Gov. Perham to the Legislature of the State of Me.,* Jan. *1871* (1871); W. W. Thomas, *Reports of the Board and Commissioner of Immigration, 1870* (1871); E. H. Elwell, *Aroostook: with some Account . . . of the Colony of Swedes, Settled in the Town of New Sweden* (1878); *Celebration of the Decennial Anniversary of the Founding of New Sweden, Me.* (1881); *The Story of New Sweden* (Portland, 1896); and obituary in *Portland Press Herald,* Apr. 26, 1927. Advertisements and news items about the Swedish colony appeared in *Amerika* (Gothenburg), June 30, 1870, June 14, 1871; *Oresunds-Posten* (Oresund), Mar. 20, Apr. 14, 1871; *Hemlandet* (Chicago), Mar. 11, 1873; *Nya Verlden* (Gothenburg), Apr. 3, 1873. In the papers of John Lind at Minneapolis are two letters from Thomas, Dec. 17 and 26, 1888, with reference to his diplomatic appointment.]   G. M. S.

THOMES, WILLIAM HENRY (May 5, 1824–Mar. 6, 1895), author, was born in Portland, Me., the child of Job and Mary (Lewis) Thomes. The family shortly afterwards moved to Boston, and there both parents died. The orphan, reared by a guardian, did not take well to schooling, and in October 1842 shipped on the *Admittance* in the California hide-trade. His experiences are related with essential accuracy in his *On Land and Sea* (1883), and are comparable to Richard Henry Dana's as described in *Two Years before the Mast.* The ship arrived in Monterey, Mar. 4, 1843, and after numerous voyages up and down the coast sailed from San Diego, Jan. 25, 1846. Shortly before this, however, Thomes had deserted or, according to a less likely story, had arranged by a ruse to be left behind. The chief authority for his life in the next year is his *Lewey and I* (1884), which even he admitted to be largely fiction. It is probable, however, that he was knocked about considerably, saw some military service during the conquest of California, and left California in December 1846. By way of Mazatlán and England Thomes returned to Boston. There he served as printer and reporter on the *Boston Daily Times* for about a year, and also married. His wife seems to have been the daughter of Capt. Peter Peterson, his old master on the *Admittance* (Bancroft, *post*). But he got the gold-fever, and joined the Boston and California Joint Stock Mining and Trading Company, which sailed on the *Edward Everett* in

January 1849 and arrived in San Francisco on July 6. Although not an officer, Thomes had risen to be of some importance in the company, and was assigned to remain with the ship. After the break-up of the company in August, he mined at Bidwell's Bar, with some success for a while; but finally, broken in health and almost penniless, he returned to San Francisco. There he served as caretaker of a ship. In 1851 he sailed for the Hawaiian Islands, and after some months' residence there, visited Guam, the Philippines, China, and finally the gold mines of Victoria. Of his activities during these three years little can be determined. He made some money, probably by keeping a store at Ballarat, and returned to the United States by way of the Cape of Good Hope early in 1855.

After a short time in New Orleans he returned to Boston, and for several years was a reporter for the *Boston Herald*. He was also married again, to Frances Ullen. About 1860 he became a member of Elliott and Thomes, publishers of the *American Union,* a weekly magazine. For this he wrote *The Gold Hunters' Adventures; or, Life in Australia* (1864), a long tale of lurid adventure. Its success encouraged him to its sequel, *The Bushrangers* (1866), and his profession was established. His other books were *The Gold Hunters in Europe* (1868), *The Whaleman's Adventures* (1872), *Life in the East Indies* (1873), *A Slaver's Adventures* (1872), *Running the Blockade* (1875), *The Belle of Australia* (1883), *The Ocean Rovers* (1896), and *Daring Deeds* (n.d.). With the exception of *On Land and Sea,* which contains vivid and accurate descriptions of early California, his books are of no literary or historical importance; they are little removed, indeed, from the dime-novel. Partial figures, however, indicate a sale of over half a million copies by 1895.

In later life Thomes was a member successively of Elliott, Thomes and Talbot, and Thomes and Talbot. Publications of these firms included the *Flag of our Union,* and *Ballou's Monthly.* Thomes lost heavily in the fire of 1872 but otherwise was highly successful in business. His activities included politics, Masonry, and collecting. In 1888 he organized, and became president of, the Society of California Pioneers of New England, and in 1890 he was the leader of its elaborate excursion to California. He died suddenly of heart-failure.

[In addition to Thomes's autobiographical books, see his "The Reminiscences of a Gold Hunter," *Ballou's Monthly Mag.,* Sept. 1882, reprinted in *Alta California* (San Francisco), Oct. 22, 29, 1882; O. T. Howe, *Argonauts of '49* (1923); Nicholas Ball, *The Pioneers of '49* (1891); H. H. Bancroft, *Hist. of Cal.,* vol. V (1886), Pioneer Register and Index; obituary in *Boston Evening Transcript,* Mar. 7, 1895. A manuscript statement by Thomes is in the Bancroft Lib., Berkeley, Cal. The names of Thomes's parents and information about his second marriage were supplied by Clarence H. Carter, of Boston.]   G. R. S., Jr.

THOMPSON, ALFRED WORDSWORTH (May 26, 1840–Aug. 28, 1896), landscape, figure, and historical painter, was born in Baltimore, Md. His parents are said to have been of Maryland and Virginia stock, their ancestors early settlers on the tributaries of Chesapeake Bay. Thompson was educated in Baltimore, and, though he began the study of law in his father's office, he turned to art before coming of age. At the time of John Brown's raid he went to Harpers Ferry, and made drawings of the places of interest and a likeness of Brown, whom he visited in prison. He opened a studio in Mulberry Street, Baltimore, just before the Civil War began. Many of the war pictures which appeared in *Harper's Weekly* and the *Illustrated London News* during the first year of the war were his. In 1861 he went to Paris, where he was a pupil successively of C. G. Gleyre, Émile Lambinet, A. Pasini, Adolphe Yvon, and finally of Antoine Barye, the sculptor, under whose tutelage he studied the anatomy of the horse. In 1864–65 he worked at the École des Beaux-Arts, and in the same year he sent to the Salon his first picture, "Moorlands of Au Fargis." To make a painting of the great Gauli glacier he climbed in the company of three mountaineers to a desolate place ten thousand feet above sea-level, surrounded by snow and ice. Later he made some extensive tours on foot through the Eifelwald in Germany, along the banks of the Rhine and the Danube, and through the rugged regions of the Tyrol and Bohemia. One of his trips was a six months' walk from Heidelberg to Calabria in the south of Italy. He walked through Sicily and climbed to the summit of Mount Etna. At a later period he made several visits to Corsica and Sardinia on mule-back.

In 1868 he returned to America and opened a studio in New York, where he soon received a gratifying measure of recognition. He was one of the first members of the Society of American Artists. After his election as an Academician in 1875, he regularly sent pictures to the annual exhibitions of the National Academy. To the Centennial Exhibition, Philadelphia, 1876, he sent "On the Sands, East Hampton" and "Virginia in the Olden Time," and to the Paris Exposition of 1878 his "School-house on the Hill." Among the best known of his works are "Annapolis in 1776," in the Albright Art Gallery, Buffalo, N. Y.; "The Parting Guests," owned by the New York Historical Society; "Old

Bruton Church, Virginia, in the Time of Lord Dunmore," in the Metropolitan Museum, New York; and "Washington Reviewing the Troops, 1777." In his later years he made occasional voyages to France, and traveled in Spain, Morocco, and Asia Minor, his zeal for fresh subjects leading him to wander in many lands. In the early part of his career the scenery of Italy engaged his attention; later he turned to the delineation of American landscape and life; and finally he ventured into the realm of history. He painted a few scenes from the Revolutionary period, or the one just preceding it, "with a smoothness and skill of handling recalling that if he worked under Gleyre, he was also a pupil of Pasini" (Samuel Isham, *The History of American Painting*, 1905, p. 349). He died at Summit, N. J., aged fifty-six. He was survived by his widow, whose name is said to have been Pompella or Pumpelly.

[*Boston Globe*, May 7, 1873; G. W. Sheldon, *Am. Painters* (1879); S. G. W. Benjamin, *Our Am. Artists* (1879); Clara E. Clement and Laurence Hutton, *Artists of the Nineteenth Century* (1879), vol. II; Edward King, in *Monthly Illustrator*, May 1895; *Cat. of Am. Paintings Belonging to William T. Evans* (1900); *Illustrated Cat.: Paintings in the Metropolitan Museum of Art, N. Y.* (1905); *Reports . . . U. S. Commissioner . . . Paris Universal Exposition, 1878* (1880), vol. I, p. 389; obituaries in *N. Y. Tribune*, Aug. 29, and *Sun* (Baltimore), Aug. 31, 1896.] W. H. D.

THOMPSON, ARTHUR WEBSTER (May 8, 1875–Nov. 9, 1930), railroad and utilities executive, was born at Erie, Pa., the son of Sheldon Elisha and Barbara LaVerne (Webster) Thompson. He grew up in Meadville, Pa., and after preparing in the local schools entered Allegheny College, where he was graduated with the degree of civil engineer in 1897. His father had been in the employ of the Santa Fé railroad and while Arthur was still an undergraduate he spent one summer as a rodman on location work for the Bessemer & Southwestern road, and another in the locomotive shops of the Erie Railroad at Meadville. For a brief period after his graduation he worked as instrument man on the Pittsburgh & Lake Erie, but within a short time, Aug. 7, 1899, he went to the Baltimore & Ohio as chief of a party of surveys.

With the Baltimore & Ohio he spent most of his extremely active life. In a space of a little less than twenty years he headed its most important and diverse departments—engineering, operation, traffic, and commercial development. At the age of twenty-eight, he was superintendent of one of the most important divisions of the road; at thirty-five, he was its general manager; and a year later he became its vice-president in charge of operation. At the beginning of the

World War he was senior vice-president, in full charge of operating, traffic, engineering, and commercial development. The final weeks of the war brought governmental control of the entire railroad system of the United States. In the new order of things, Thompson was made federal manager in charge of a large group of roads, of which Baltimore & Ohio was the most important. He established headquarters at Pittsburgh and kept traffic moving steadily against almost insuperable odds and difficulties.

His work at Pittsburgh brought him to the personal attention of numerous capitalists and industrial leaders, with the result that on Feb. 1, 1919, he abandoned steam railroading and became the president of the Philadelphia Company, which owned and operated the street railroads and the lighting systems and other utilities of Pittsburgh. His record here maintained the high level that he had set at Baltimore; hardly a half dozen years had passed before, in 1926, he was made president of one of the outstanding utilities of the country—the United Gas Improvement Company of Philadelphia. This post he resigned, shortly before the time of his death. Personally he did not approve the "high financing" of the period.

He was a man of keen wit, great kindliness, and a charm that made almost everyone associated with him his friend. His homes were veritable treasure houses of the many things that interested him, and he gathered about him men of every thought and shade of opinion. Intensely democratic, he was nevertheless a good disciplinarian, and an excellent executive. He was married, June 29, 1905, to Marion Dinwiddie Gordon, daughter of Judge Robert H. Gordon, of Cumberland, Md., who with two sons survived him. He died in Pittsburgh.

[T. W. Morris, "Biog. Sketch of Arthur W. Thompson" and P. H. Utech, "Reminiscences of Arthur Webster Thompson," MSS. in possession of author; W. H. and M. R. Webster, *Hist. and Geneal. of the Gov. John Webster Family of Conn.* (1915); E. A. Smith, *Allegheny—A Century of Education* (1916); *Railway Rev. and Outlook*, Aug. 1919; *Who's Who in America*, 1930–31; *Public Ledger* (Phila.), Nov. 10, 1930.] E. H.

THOMPSON, BENJAMIN (Mar. 26, 1753–Aug. 21, 1814), better remembered by his title, Count Rumford, physicist, organizer, and philanthropist, the only child of Benjamin and Ruth (Simonds) Thompson, was born in Woburn, Mass., where his ancestor, James Thompson, had settled in 1642. His paternal grandfather, in whose house he was born, was Capt. Ebenezer Thompson; his maternal grandfather had performed distinguished service in the French and Indian Wars. His father died in November

1754, and his mother in 1756 married Josiah Pierce, Jr., of Woburn. A small inheritance from his grandfather was used toward the support and education of the boy. He attended school in Woburn, Byfield, and Medford. His writing was clear and spelling accurate, and he early showed an aptitude for drafting and mathematical studies. His guardians, realizing that he was not likely to develop into a thriving farmer, apprenticed him on Oct. 14, 1766, to John Appleton of Salem, a warehouseman and dealer in British goods, with whom he remained for about three years. He seems to have performed his duties satisfactorily but to have been more interested in tools, mechanical devices, and other scientific matters. He studied algebra, geometry, astronomy, and higher mathematics with the Rev. Thomas Barnard of Salem, and carried on experiments and scientific discussions and correspondence with his lifelong friend, Loammi Baldwin, 1744–1807 [q.v.], of Woburn. In October 1769 he commenced the study of the French language at Boston and began to keep a boyish notebook which still survives and shows the breadth of his early interests.

In 1771 he commenced the study of medicine with Dr. John Hay of Woburn, and while continuing with him, contrived to attend the lectures of Professor John Winthrop at Harvard. He taught school for a short time, first probably at Bradford, Mass., and later at Concord, N. H., where he met and, about November 1772, married, the wealthy widow of Col. Benjamin Rolfe, Sarah (Walker) Rolfe (Oct. 6, 1739–Jan. 19, 1792), daughter of the Rev. Timothy Walker. On their wedding tour the couple visited Portsmouth, where Thompson's fine appearance on horseback, his courtly manner, and his new family connections so impressed Governor Wentworth that he at once commissioned him to a majorship which happened to be vacant in the 2nd Provincial Regiment of New Hampshire. The appointment aroused the jealousy and resentment of experienced junior officers who were qualified for promotion. Throughout his life Thompson seems to have neglected no opportunity for his own advancement. He knew how to ingratiate himself with men of powerful position, and incurred the enmity of those of lesser rank.

For two years after his marriage, Thompson devoted himself chiefly to farming his wife's land and to conducting experiments with gunpowder. Their only child, Sarah, was born Oct. 18, 1774, in the Rolfe mansion; her parents separated in May of the following year and never saw one another again. Thompson's indebted-

ness to Governor Wentworth committed him in a manner to the British or Loyalist side in the Revolutionary War, though he seems at first to have had no strong inclination toward one side or the other. In the summer of 1774 he was summoned before a committee of the people of Concord to answer to the charge of "being unfriendly to the cause of Liberty," but was discharged for lack of evidence. He was publicly threatened at Concord and sought refuge at Woburn, where he was again tried on a similar charge with similar result. He mingled with the patriots of Medford, Cambridge, and Charlestown, and applied for a commission in Washington's army but was refused, probably because of the disapproval of the officers from New Hampshire. He then definitely chose the British side. Leaving Woburn on Oct. 13, 1775, he embarked on the British frigate *Scarborough* at Newport. The vessel proceeded to Boston and lay in the harbor until after the town had been evacuated by the British forces in March 1776, then proceeded to England with dispatches. On reaching London, Thompson quickly secured the favor of Lord George Germain, secretary of state for the colonies, was given a position in the Colonial Office, and was soon appointed to a sinecure, the secretaryship of the Province of Georgia. He continued his experiments on gunpowder, sent a paper on cohesion to the Royal Society, became acquainted with its president, Sir Joseph Banks, and in 1779 was elected a fellow of that body. In September 1780 he was made under-secretary of state for the Northern Department, and later, probably in 1781, was commissioned lieutenant-colonel in the British army for service in America. In March 1782 he was engaged in action near Charlestown, S. C.; he then served on Long Island until April 1783, where he commanded a regiment and built a fort for winter quarters near Huntington. In August of that year, after his return to England, he was made colonel of the King's American Dragoons.

Having retired from active service on half pay, with the King's permission to leave England, he set out in September 1783 for a tour of the Continent. At Strasbourg he met Prince Maximilian des Deux Ponts, field-marshal of France, who gave him a letter of introduction to his uncle, the Elector of Bavaria. The latter, impressed with Thompson's abilities, invited him to enter his services in a half military, half civil capacity, and Thompson returned to England to secure the permission of the King. The King approved and on Feb. 23, 1784, conferred on him the honor of knighthood (the original parchment is in the possession of the American Academy of Arts and Sciences). Sir Benjamin returned at once to Munich, where he was made colonel of cavalry and general aide-de-camp and in 1788 major-general, privy councilor of state, and head of the war department. On request of the Elector, the King of Poland conferred on him the Order of Saint Stanislaus. He was elected to the academies of Berlin, Munich, and Mannheim. In 1791 the Elector of Bavaria, being at the time Vicar of the Empire, made him a count of the Holy Roman Empire, with the Order of the White Eagle; Thompson chose the title Count Rumford after the old name of Concord, N. H. He improved the living conditions of the soldiers of the Bavarian army, their homes, food, clothing, and the use of their leisure, abolished beggary in Munich, established workhouses, and devised methods and equipment for the preparation of wholesome food cheaply on a large scale. In 1790 he converted a large tract of waste land on the outskirts of Munich into the Englisches Garten, where, in 1795, upon his return to England, the citizens erected a monument in recognition of his services. He continued his scientific experiments—on gunpowder, on the transmission of heat, on the absorption of moisture by various substances. He concluded that the large part of the heat of a hot body cooling in air is lost by radiation, and showed by his experiments on the boring of cannon and the friction of metal surfaces that heat is a mode of motion.

In the fall of 1795 he returned to England in order to renew his friendships with men of science, to read papers before the Royal Society, and to publish the first volume (1796) of his *Essays, Political, Economical, and Philosophical* (3rd ed., 2 vols., 1798; 5th ed., 3 vols., 1880; vol. IV added, 1802). He visited Ireland for two months in the spring of 1796, installing important improvements in the workhouses and hospitals of Dublin, and in a church, a steam-heating system. He was elected honorary member of the Royal Irish Academy of Dublin and of the Society for the Encouragement of Arts and Manufactures. His improvements in heating and cooking equipment aroused much interest in England. He installed non-smoking and more efficient fireplaces in more than 150 houses of London, among them those of Lord Palmerston, Sir Joseph Banks, and the Marquis of Salisbury. Rumford Roasters came into extensive use in Great Britain and the United States. He presented £1000 at this time to the Royal Society for the establishing of a Rumford prize and medal for "the most important discovery, or useful improvement—in any part of Europe during the preceding two years, on Heat or on Light," and

$5,000 to the American Academy of Arts and Sciences (of which he had been elected a foreign honorary member May 29, 1789), for the most important discovery in the same fields "in any part of the Continent of America, or in any of the American Islands." His letters offering these funds were both dated July 12, 1796. The first award of the Royal Society's Rumford Medal was made in 1802 to Count Rumford himself.

He had previously sent for his daughter, Sarah, to whom he seems to have sent money regularly; she joined him in London, and in midsummer, 1796, accompanied him to Munich. Here, as head of the council of regency, he was able to prevent the French and Austrian armies from entering the neutral city. He did important service in feeding and sheltering the large Bavarian force which was quartered there. The Elector made him head of the department of general police of Bavaria, and later sent him to London as minister plenipotentiary of Bavaria to Great Britain. On arriving there in September 1798, he was informed that being a British subject he would not be accepted as the minister of another nation. Disappointed and relieved of his diplomatic and political duties, he remained for a time in London devoting himself to humanitarian and scientific activities. His daughter returned to America late in the summer of 1799. He had some intention of joining her there and was offered through Rufus King, the American minister, both the inspectorship of artillery in the United States Army and the superintendency of the Military Academy, but was kept in London by the affairs of the Royal Institution. This organization, incorporated in January 1800 under the patronage of the King, was the direct outcome of Rumford's published *Proposals for Forming by Subscription in the Metropolis of the British Empire, a Public Institution for Diffusing the Knowledge and Facilitating the General Introduction of Useful Mechanical Inventions and Improvements, and for Teaching, by Courses of Philosophical Lectures and Experiments, the Application of Science to the Common Purposes of Life* (1799). He personally supervised the construction of the Royal Institution's building on Albemarle Street, lived there himself, and secured for the Institution the services of Humphry Davy.

His life in London was not altogether happy. He was not able to carry out his plans arbitrarily and without resistance as he had done in Bavaria, and he quarreled with the managers of the Royal Institution. In October 1801 he visited Munich, where he helped plan the organization of the Bavarian Academy of Arts and Sciences, and in the same month visited Paris for the first time. Here he was cordially received, found his work well known, and met Madame Lavoisier, widow of the chemist. In May 1802 he left England, never to return. He visited various places in Europe, especially Munich and Paris, and on Oct. 24, 1805, married Madame Lavoisier (Marie Anne Pierrette, *née* Paulze). Their life together was not happy; Thompson loved flowers and tranquility, while his wife loved neither of these but wanted dinner parties and entertainments to such an extent that he found it difficult to entertain his own friends in the quiet way he enjoyed. They separated amicably on June 30, 1809, and the terms of the marriage contract were respected as regarded their joint property. Thompson then sent to America for his daughter, and in the late autumn of 1811 she came to live with him at Auteuil, near Paris, in a house which he had rented. Here he spent much time in walking and in cultivating a flower garden. He had been elected a foreign associate of the Institute of France in 1803, attended its meetings, and from that time onward read many papers and demonstrated experiments before the Institute. He also transmitted papers to the Royal Society of London and published in its *Philosophical Transactions*. Some of these studies appeared in his *Philosophical Papers* (1802), projected as a two-volume work, of which only one volume was issued. He studied the traction of broad and of narrow wheels, favored the former, and rode about Paris in the only carriage in the city which was equipped with broad-rim wheels. He developed his calorimeter and photometer, made improvements in lamps and illumination, and described the drip coffee pot in a fascinating essay, *Of the Excellent Qualities of Coffee, and the Art of Making It in the Highest Perfection* (1812). By temperament he was not adapted to genial companionship, and he had few friends among the French men of science. He lived a lonely life and died at Auteuil during a temporary absence of his daughter. A natural son, born the year of Thompson's death, became an officer in the French army; a natural daughter had died some time before, in childhood. Thompson's will, executed Sept. 28, 1812, made a bequest to Harvard College for the establishment of a professorship, "in order to teach by regular courses of academical and public Lectures, accompanied with proper experiments, the utility of the physical and mathematical sciences for the improvement of the useful arts, and for the extension of the industry, prosperity, happiness, and well-being of Society." His daughter returned to America, and died Dec. 2, 1852, in the chamber

in which she was born. The American Academy of Arts and Sciences and Harvard College at present share the expense of caring for his grave at Auteuil.

[G. E. Ellis, *Memoir of Sir Benjamin Thompson, Count Rumford, with Notices of His Daughter* (1871), published by the Am. Acad. of Arts and Sci. in connection with *The Complete Works of Count Rumford* (4 vols., 1870–75); T. E. James, "Rumford and the Royal Institution: A Retrospect," *Nature*, Sept. 19, 1931; H. B. Jones, *The Royal Institution: Its Founder and Its First Professors* (1871); F. K. Möhl, *Die vorläufer der heutigen Organisation der öffentl. Armenpflege in München, insbesondere: Das Armeninstitut des Grafen Rumford* (Erlangen, 1903); R. W. Hale, "Benjamin Thompson: Count Rumford: His Romantic Career in Statesmanship and Science," *Technology Review*, Nov. 1931; J. A. Thompson, *Count Rumford of Mass.* (1935); Leander Thompson, *Memorial of James Thompson* (1887); Allen French, *Gen. Gage's Informers* (1932); L. D. Einstein, *Divided Loyalties: Americans in England during the War of Independence* (1933); W. F. Rae, in *Dict. Nat. Biog.*; *Gentleman's Mag.*, Sept., Oct. 1814; *Times* (London), Aug. 29, 1814.]   T. L. D.

THOMPSON, CEPHAS GIOVANNI (Aug. 3, 1809–Jan. 5, 1888), painter, was born at Middleboro, Mass., a son of Cephas and Olive (Leonard) Thompson, and a descendant of John Thomson, a Welshman who emigrated to New England before 1623. He was a brother of Marietta and Jerome B. Thompson [*q.v.*], both of whom attained celebrity as artists. The elder Cephas Thompson (1775–1856) was a self-taught portraitist whose permanent home was at Middleboro, but who was accustomed winters to make painting tours of the cities from New York to New Orleans. Among his famous sitters were John Marshall, Stephen Decatur, and David Ramsay. Taught and encouraged by his father, Cephas Giovanni at eighteen set up for himself at Plymouth. He later drew from the antique at the Boston Athenaeum, and he made many portraits at Providence. In 1837 he took a studio at New York. There, a handsome little man, with engaging smile and good manners, he became a favorite in the literary and artistic coterie of which William Cullen Bryant, Fitz-Greene Halleck, and Henry T. Tuckerman [*qq.v.*] were prominent figures. He married in December 1843 Mary Gouverneur Ogden, daughter of Samuel Gouverneur Ogden, a prominent New York merchant. They had two sons and a daughter. They lived during brief periods at New York, Boston, and New Bedford, and in 1852 went to Rome, where for seven years Thompson painted portraits and copied old masters. His intimacy at this time with the Hawthorne family, also resident at Rome, is of familiar record. Nathaniel Hawthorne accorded him high praise as "earnest, faithful and religious in his worship of art" (Arvin, *post*, p. 265), and it was Julian

Hawthorne's opinion that no other artist in Rome "could paint as well as Mr. Thompson," whose color, even though "he had never learned how to draw correctly ... redeemed all and made his pictures permanently valuable" (Hawthorne, *post*, p. 262–63). This judgment has not been confirmed; Thompson's works have little value, though many of them are of historic importance as portraits of celebrities.

He returned in 1859 to New York, where for many years he painted portraits, some of them quite elaborate family groups (Tuckerman, *post*, p. 491). In 1861 he was elected an associate of the National Academy of Design. He kept up his friendships with authors and through his sister-in-law, Anna Cora Ogden Mowatt [*q.v.*], he had a large acquaintance with actors. Several of his portraits were acquired by the New York Historical Society; his likeness of Chancellor James M. Matthews, by the University of the City of New York (later New York University). In 1887 the aged artist was appointed United States inspector of life preservers at New York, a post which he filled faithfully almost to the day of his death. He died at his home, 8 East Eighty-fifth St. A follower of Swedenborg, he was buried from the Church of the New Jerusalem.

[C. H. Thompson, *A Geneal. of Descendants of John Thomson, of Plymouth, Mass.* (1890); W. O. Wheeler, *The Ogden Family in America* (1907); Thomas Weston, *Hist. of the Town of Middleboro, Mass.* (1906); Clara E. Clement and Laurence Hutton, *Artists of the Nineteenth Century* (1884); H. T. Tuckerman, *Book of the Artists* (1867); Julian Hawthorne, *Hawthorne and His Circle* (1903); Rose Hawthorne Lathrop, *Memories of Hawthorne* (1923); *The Heart of Hawthorne's Journals* (1929), ed. by Newton Arvin; death notice in *N. Y. Times*, obituary in *N. Y. Tribune*, Jan. 7, 1888.]

F. W. C.

THOMPSON, CHARLES OLIVER (Sept. 25, 1836–Mar. 17, 1885), engineer, educator, was born at East Windsor Hill, Conn., where his father, Rev. William Thompson, was a professor in the Theological Institute of Connecticut. He was a descendant of Anthony Thompson, who came to Boston in 1637 and later was one of the founders of New Haven, Conn. Charles's mother was Eliza Butler, whose ancestors were among the pioneer settlers who established Hartford, Conn. Young Thompson entered Dartmouth College in 1854 and four years later, having taken high rank, was graduated with the degree of A.B. For six years he had a varied experience in teaching and engineering practice. Until 1864 he was principal of the Peacham Academy at Peacham, Vt., but used his vacation periods in the practice of surveying and civil engineering.

From 1864 to 1868 he was principal of the Cotting High School at Arlington, Mass. Here he established a reputation which led to his being called to Worcester in February 1868 as principal of the new Worcester County Free Institute of Industrial Science (later Worcester Polytechnic Institute). He spent the summer of 1868 abroad, studying European technical schools. Upon his return in November, he put into effect at Worcester what were then considered rather radical innovations in American technical education. "In all the great schools that began before 1868," he said in after years, "there were collections of apparatus and models, drawing-rooms and laboratories for the proper teaching of practical science, but there was no workshop worthy of the name. The mechanical arts were the last to be recognized in schools of engineering. The first school to embody in the course a thoroughly equipped and genuine workshop was the Free Institute at Worcester, Mass., in 1868" (*Transactions American Institute of Mining Engineers, post,* p. 193). Thompson was thus a pioneer in the introduction of shop practice in engineering teaching. He even planned to have the articles made by the students in the shops compete in the open market with those produced by commercial manufacturers. He thus sought a solution of the still important problem of the relation of engineering education to engineering industry by bringing industry into the technical school. His scheme has since been largely abandoned in advanced engineering schools, in favor of sending students to industrial works to secure this training; but to Thompson belongs the credit of being the first to emphasize this important feature in engineering education.

The great success of the Free Institute led to its director receiving many offers from other institutions. These he refused until, in 1882, he had the opportunity to become the first president of Rose Polytechnic Institute at Terre Haute, Ind., Chauncey Rose [*q.v.*], the founder of this school, having decided after making a careful survey of the field that Dr. Thompson was the person best fitted to establish the institution. It was opened on Mar. 7, 1883, but Thompson was destined to do no more than organize it and start it on its career, for he died at Terre Haute almost exactly two years later.

He published several papers on teaching and manual training, which include *Hints Toward a Profession of Teaching* (1867); *The Modern Polytechnic School* (1883); *Manual Training in the Public Schools* (n.d.); and "A Review of the Reports of the British Royal Commissioners on Technical Instruction" (*Circulars of Information of the Bureau of Education,* no. 3, 1885). He was a member of a number of societies, including the American Association for the Advancement of Science and the American Institute of Mining Engineers. On May 14, 1862, he married Maria, daughter of Dr. Horace and Elizabeth (Dickinson) Goodrich of Ware, Mass., who with their two sons and a daughter survived him.

[*Memorials of the Families of Mr. James Thompson and of Dea. Augustus Thompson of Goshen, Conn.* (1854); L. W. Case, *The Goodrich Family* (1889); *Proc. of the Am. Antiquarian Soc.*, n.s., vol. III (1885); *Trans. Am. Inst. Mining Engineers*, vol. XIV (1886); *Indianapolis Jour.*, Mar. 18, 1885.]   J.K.F.

THOMPSON, DANIEL PIERCE (Oct. 1, 1795–June 6, 1868), author, lawyer, was born at Charlestown, Mass., the son of Daniel and Rebecca (Parker) Thompson. On his father's side he was descended from James Thompson, who settled in Massachusetts before 1632; on his mother's he was apparently descended from Ezekiel Cheever [*q.v.*], seventeenth-century educator (Flitcroft, *post*, p. 317). In 1800 his father, being unsuccessful in business, moved to a small farm at Berlin, Vt. Thus Daniel grew up in a frontier settlement in which there was neither a library nor an adequate school. At sixteen, however, he chanced upon a volume of English poetry, and this book opened a new world to him. He worked hard on the farm, studied and later taught in the district schools, saved money, and finally, after a winter's residence at the Randolph-Danville Academy at Danville, Vt., entered Middlebury College with advanced standing. While in college he contributed a number of poems and essays to periodicals. After his graduation in 1820, he went to Virginia (probably Culpeper County), where he remained for three or four years as a tutor in a wealthy family. During this period he studied law, obtained an interview with Thomas Jefferson ("A Talk with Jefferson," *Harper's New Monthly Magazine*, May 1863), and was admitted to the bar.

Returning to Montpelier in 1823 or 1824, Thompson began the practice of law, and soon became prominent in the political and cultural life of Vermont. He served as judge of probate for Washington County (1837–40; 1841–42), clerk of the county court (1844–46), and secretary of state for Vermont (1853–55). He compiled *The Laws of Vermont . . . Including the Year 1834* (1835), was one of the founders of the Vermont Historical Society, and during 1846 served as secretary of the state education society. He took part in the anti-Masonic controversy to the extent of publishing, in the guise of "A Member of the Vermont Bar," *The Adventures of Timothy Peacock, Esquire* (1835), a satirical novel concerned with "the amusing adventures of

a Masonic Quixot." In the same year he wrote for the *New England Galaxy* a story called "May Martin, or the Money Diggers," which won a prize of fifty dollars, and thus encouraged him to continue with the writing of fiction as an avocation. Originally a Jeffersonian Democrat, Thompson later became active in the Liberty party, editing from 1849 to 1856 the *Green Mountain Freeman*, a weekly paper identified with the anti-slavery movement. In 1856 he joined the Republicans because they were making opposition to the extension of slavery the chief issue in their presidential campaign. He was well known as a lyceum lecturer. On Aug. 31, 1831, he was married to Eunice Knight Robinson, by whom he had six children.

Thompson's claim to recognition is based mainly on his achievement as a historical novelist in the school of Cooper. Through his fiction he probably did more than any other person to popularize the early history of Vermont. Local tradition represents him as wandering through the country with his fishing rod, stopping at intervals to chat with some old settler by the roadside. He would spend hours listening to stories about Ethan Allen, Seth Warner, and Colonel Stark; and he kept careful notes of all he heard. Influenced by Scott and Cooper, he blended history with romance in a half dozen novels of adventure, of which the best known is *The Green Mountain Boys* (1839). This book deals with the land-grant controversy between New York and New Hampshire, and with such incidents of the Revolution as Ethan Allen's capture of Fort Ticonderoga and the battle of Hubbardton. Its popularity is evidenced by the sale of fifty editions before 1860 and sixty editions by 1900. A sequel, *The Rangers*, appeared in 1851. Another novel, *Locke Amsden* (1847), deserves mention for its truthful record of frontier life, its autobiographical significance, and its interest to the student of American education. Among his other publications are *Gaut Gurley* (1857), *The Doomed Chief* (1860), *History of the Town of Montpelier* (1860), and *Centeola* (1864). An old-fashioned Yankee with a keen sense of humor, Thompson possessed genuine narrative ability, but fell far short of Cooper in imaginative power.

[See Leander Thompson, *Memorial of James Thompson* (1887); E. A. and G. L. Duyckinck, *Cyc. of Am. Lit.* (2 vols., 1855), which contains a brief autobiog. memoir; *Biog. Encyc. of Vt.* (1885), pp. 256–60; D. F. Wheaton, in *Vt. Hist. Gazetteer*, vol. IV (1882), pp. 69–72; obituary in *Burlington Times*, June 9, 1868. The dates of Thompson's public offices are from J. M. Comstock, *A List. of the Principal Civil Officers of Vt.* (1918). The only full biog. is J. E. Flitcroft, *The Novelist of Vt.* (1929), which contains Thompson's unfinished novel, "The Honest Lawyer."]   J.E.F.

THOMPSON, DAVID (Apr. 30, 1770–Feb. 10, 1857), explorer, geographer, fur-trader, was born in London, England, the son of David and Ann Thompson. His family was of obscure Welsh lineage and, before moving to London, used the name ApThomas. When David was three years of age his father died, leaving the mother and several children in abject poverty. The Grey Coat School, then a charity school for boys, admitted the lad when he was seven years of age and he spent the next seven years under strict religious discipline and tutelage. When he was fourteen he was apprenticed to the Hudson's Bay Company for seven years of service in the fur-trade in North America, and was landed at Fort Churchill on the inhospitable west shore of Hudson Bay to begin his career. As far as it is known, he never returned to England.

He received his first training under Samuel Hearne, the explorer, and Philip Turnor, surveyor for the Company, who guided the young man in his passionate study of mathematics and instructed him in the use of the sextant, compass, and astronomical instruments. His field service began in 1789, and for twenty-five years, first with the Hudson's Bay Company and later with the North West Company, he kept daily journals and field notes of his travels, which took him more than 50,000 miles and covered almost every lake and stream in western Canada. Thompson's work was practically unrecognized until about 1900, and only after the publication of some of his documents in 1916 under the title *David Thompson's Narrative of his Explorations in Western America*, volume XII of the *Champlain Society Publications* was he generally recognized as one of the greatest land geographers of the English race. Because of Thompson's groundwork on the Peace River district, Fraser named the largest tributary of the Fraser River for him. Thompson discovered a new route to Lake Athabasca; located by survey the Mandan Indian villages on the Missouri River in the winter of 1797–98; marked the crossing of the forty-ninth parallel by the Red River, and during conditions of almost impossible travel in the spring of 1798, surveyed the most northerly source of the Mississippi, and the course of the St. Louis River to Lake Superior. In 1807 he crossed the Canadian Rockies and discovered the source of the Columbia River. In 1808–10, he penetrated the Kootenai, Pend Oreille, and Clark Fork (Flathead) country of Washington, Idaho, and Montana. In 1811 he surveyed the Columbia River from source to mouth; he placed on the map main routes of travel within 1,200,000 square miles of Canadian territory and 500,000 square miles of the United States. The trading posts he established on the Kootenai, Pend Oreille, and Spokane rivers in the United States antedated the establishment of Astoria by John Jacob Astor, 1763–1848 [q.v.], by several years.

After his retirement from field service in 1812, he devoted two years to drawing a large map, five and a half by ten and a half feet, of the northern part of the United States and Canada, using his own surveys and those of other explorers including Lewis and Clark. It is still preserved in the archives of Ontario, and is remarkable for its accuracy, detail, and extent. From 1816 to 1826 he was in charge of the British commission for establishing and marking the boundary between Canada and the United States from its crossing of the St. Lawrence River west to the angle of Lake of the Woods. After ten more years of public and private surveying, he retired to live in Williamstown, county of Glengarry, and then in Longueuil.

In June 1799 he was married to Charlotte Small, the half-breed daughter of Patrick Small, who bore him seven sons and six daughters. Financial reverses reduced him to extreme poverty in his old age and he was forced finally to sell the precious instruments that had served him so well. He was buried in the Mt. Royal Cemetery in Montreal. Washington Irving is said to have offered to buy Thompson's journals but the old man refused to sell, and probably thus denied to the world a sequel to Irving's *Astoria*.

[Journals and note-books in the archives of Ontario; J. B. Tyrrell, ed., *Jour. of Samuel Hearne and Philip Turnor, Champlain Soc. Pubs.*, Toronto, vol. XXI (1934); C. N. Cochrane, *David Thompson the Explorer*, Canadian Men of Action Series, No. II (1924); T. C. Elliott, "The Discovery of the Source of the Columbia River," *Oregon Hist. Soc. Quart.*, Mar., June 1925; L. J. Burpee, "Some Letters of David Thompson," *Canadian Hist. Rev.*, June 1923, and also *Canadian Mag.*, Jan. 1926; S. F. Bemis, "David Thompson, Explorer," *Sunset*, Mar. 1923; F. W. Howay, in *Queen's Quart.*, Aug. 1933.] T.C.E.

THOMPSON, DAVID P. (Nov. 8, 1834–Dec. 13, 1901), contractor, banker, public official, was born at Cadiz, Ohio. His father, a mill-owner, was of Irish descent; his mother, of Scotch. David's schooling was such as was afforded by the village and he was early apprenticed as a blacksmith. He earned his way to Oregon with the immigrant train of 1853 by driving a flock of sheep, arriving at Oregon City with his capital reduced to twenty-five cents. Here he worked as a wood cutter, blacksmith, and surveyor's assistant, becoming in a few years a United States deputy surveyor for Oregon and Washington. He ran the base line of Oregon across the Cascades to the Blue Mountains, and the Columbia Guide Meridian north to the Big

Bend of that river. In 1869 he surveyed the Dalles-California military wagon road and in 1872 surveyed and alloted lands to the Indians of the Grande Ronde Reservation.

In the meantime he engaged in numerous business and construction enterprises. He built the first railroad in Oregon—a horse railroad around the Willamette Falls, between Oregon City and Canemah. The road yielded dividends of $48,000. From 1866 to 1868 he was president and manager of the Oregon City Woolen Manufacturing Company. He was a member of the Willamette Falls Canal and Locks Company, which built, and opened on Jan. 1, 1873, the canal around the Willamette Falls, and he served as president of the Oregon Construction Company, which built most of the lines of the Oregon Railway & Navigation Company, of which he was a vice-president and director. He secured profitable contracts (1872–78) to carry mail through the Pacific Northwest. In 1880 he organized the Portland Savings Bank, of which he became president; he was also president of the Commercial National Bank of Portland and a director in many other financial institutions.

During these years he was one of the leaders of the Republican party in his state and for the most of the time a public official. He served as state senator (1868–72); as governor of Idaho Territory (1875–76); as representative in the Oregon legislature (1878–79, 1889–90); as mayor of Portland (1879, 1881). In 1890 he was the Republican candidate for governor but was defeated by Sylvester Pennoyer [q.v.]. From November 1892 to April 1893 he was minister to Turkey, succeeding in that position another resident of Oregon, Solomon Hirsch. For ten years he served as regent of the University of Oregon. Unlike most bankers he campaigned for free silver (1895–96) and served as chairman of a bimetallic conference held at Salt Lake City in May 1895. He was married in 1861 to Mary R. Meldrum of Salem, Ore., by whom he had three children.

[*Morning Oregonian* (Portland), Oct. 5, 1888, Dec. 14, 1901; H. H. Bancroft, *Hist. of Washington, Idaho, and Montana* (1890); H. W. Scott, *Hist. of the Oregon Country* (1924), vols. II, III; *Oregon Native Son and Hist. Mag.*, May 1899; *Papers Relating to the Foreign Relations of the U. S. . . . 1893* (1894); *Who's Who in America*, 1899–1900.] R. C. C.

THOMPSON, DENMAN (Oct. 15, 1833– Apr. 14, 1911), actor and playwright, was born in a log cabin near Girard, Pa., the son of Capt. Rufus Thompson and Anna Hathaway (Baxter), daughter of Dr. Henry Baxter of Swanzey, N. H. He was named Henry Denman, but later used only his middle name. His parents had moved to Pennsylvania from Swanzey, where his paternal forebears had been established for some four generations, and during the boy's teens they returned to that place. In 1850 Denman went to Boston, where he worked first as a chore boy with a circus and later got a job as a super with Charlotte Cushman. During the next few years he drifted to various cities, nearly always in some minor capacity in a theatrical troupe. It was not until the middle of the decade, when he became a member of the Royal Lyceum Company in Toronto, that he secured any worthwhile training. With this company he remained for several seasons, playing a variety of parts, including Uncle Tom in *Uncle Tom's Cabin*. In 1862 he went to England, hoping to play Salem Scudder in the London production of *The Octoroon,* but he failed to secure the rôle and returned to Toronto, where he remained until 1868.

During the next seven years he led the wandering life of a minor actor; he had found no place in the theatre which brought him distinction. In 1875, however, he evolved a brief sketch, in two scenes, based on his boyhood observation of rural Yankee types (and, it must be confessed, also on innumerable other Yankee sketches), in which he played the part of an old New Hampshire farmer on a trip to Boston. This sketch was first tried in Pittsburgh, in February 1875, and met success. In Chicago, J. M. Hill suggested that he expand it into a full-length play. Hill became his manager, and at Haverley's, Chicago, in 1877, a three act comedy was presented called *Joshua Whitcomb,* after the name of the old farmer. For the next nine years it was acted under that title, undergoing numerous changes, and being worked over by at least one collaborator—George W. Ryer. In September 1878 it was acted at the Lyceum Theatre, New York, and it later ran for two seasons at the Fourteenth Street Theatre. On Apr. 5, 1886, at the Boston Theatre, an augmented version, in four acts, now called *The Old Homestead,* was presented, and it was this play which Thompson continued to act almost to the end of his life, carrying it all over the country and making it one of the best known dramas on the American stage. Conservative estimates set its earnings at $3,000,000. Thompson became completely identified with this play, and never again acted any other character. His kindly old face as Josh Whitcomb was as familiar to Americans in the nineties as the Statue of Liberty. Asked why he played no new parts, he replied, "My ambition's satisfied, and bein' so, it's gone." Although it was a crude and sentimental affair, *The Old Homestead* had a homely flavor of veracity in its leading character, and plenty of broad comedy. The more sophisticated laughed at rather than with the play, but with Thompson acting it its appeal to the masses was enormous.

On July 7, 1860, Thompson married Maria Ballou, who died in 1904. They had three children. After his success, he remodeled an old house in West Swanzey, N. H., where he made his home thenceforth, and where he died. His last appearance in New York was at the City Theatre, in September 1910. Thompson was the author of one or two other plays and sketches, notably *The Sunshine of Paradise Alley* (with George W. Ryer) in 1896, but it is entirely on *The Old Homestead* and especially on his impersonation of the old Yankee farmer, Joshua Whitcomb, that his reputation rests. Asked in later years what he thought of Ibsen, he replied, "Funny, but I never saw an Ibsen play nor a baseball game; them's two things I've escaped" (*Current Literature*, June 1911, p. 650). In person, he was of medium size, inclined to stoutness in later years, with a round, genial face framed in white hair; he looked at all times far more the shrewd but kindly Yankee farmer than the actor.

[J. J. Brady, *The Life of Denman Thompson* (1888); *Who's Who in America*, 1910–11; E. S. Stearns, *Geneal. and Family Hist. of the State of N. H.* (1908), vol. III; Benj. Read, *The Hist. of Swanzey, N. H.* (1892); W. W. Walsh, "Reminiscences of Denman Thompson," *New Eng. Mag.*, Sept. 1910; *Theatre*, May 1911; *Current Literature*, June 1911; *Boston Transcript*, Apr. 14, 1911; *Concord Evening Monitor* (Concord, N. H.), Apr. 14, 1911; *N. Y. Times*, Apr. 15, 1911; theatre collections, N. Y. Pub. Lib. and Harvard College Lib.]   W. P. E.

THOMPSON, EGBERT (June 6, 1822–Jan. 5, 1881), naval officer, was born in New York City, the son of Egbert and Catherine (Dibble) Thompson, a nephew of Smith Thompson [*q.v.*], and a descendant of Anthony Thompson, who came to Boston in 1637. Egbert was appointed midshipman Mar. 13, 1837. After a year's cruise in the *Independence,* he experienced unusual and trying duty, first in the Wilkes Exploring Expedition, 1838–42, in the Antarctic and South Seas, and next in the brig *Somers,* commanded by Capt. Alexander S. Mackenzie [*q.v.*], at the time of the alleged mutiny led by Midshipman Philip Spencer, which resulted in Spencer's execution. Thompson's testimony at Mackenzie's court martial (*Proceedings, post,* pp. 185–88) revealed that he had once had an altercation and scuffle with Spencer, and though small of stature had bested him; also that, while not implicated in Spencer's intrigues, he had been the only officer to bid him farewell at his death, and had been moved to tears. He was executive of the

schooner *Bonita* during the Mexican War, participating in the capture of Tabasco, Tampico, Vera Cruz, and Tuxpan. Subsequently, he was in the *Michigan* on the Great Lakes, 1847–50; in the *Decatur,* Home Squadron, 1851–52; and in the *St. Louis,* African Squadron, 1855–58.

During the Civil War, he served on the *Powhatan* in the Gulf and in January 1862 joined Foote's Mississippi flotilla at Cairo. Commanding the gunboat *Pittsburg,* he participated in the attack on Fort Donelson, Feb. 13, in which his vessel was struck forty times and narrowly escaped sinking. Before dawn on Apr. 7 following (two nights after Commander Walke's similar exploit in the *Carondelet*), he ran the heavy batteries at Island No. 10, Mississippi River, to aid Polk's army below. In operations that same morning to support Polk's crossing of the river, Thompson, according to Walke (*post,* p. 152), executed the latter's orders very tardily, and "at a distance astern throwing shell in a dangerous proximity over our bow." Walke's criticism is weakened by his general tendency to monopolize credit, but it undoubtedly worked against Thompson's subsequent advancement. The Navy Department, upon Foote's report, included both vessels in its official thanks for hazardous service. After joining in the action of May 10 against the Confederate river flotilla, and in the capture of Fort Pillow on June 6, the *Pittsburg* remained at the latter point, and on June 16 returned to Cairo for overhaul. Thompson's later river service was uneventful. He went ashore in October, and in 1863–64 was at the Philadelphia naval rendezvous. He was made commander, dating from July 16, 1862, but only after an appeal from the advisory board's adverse report, in which he declared himself the only instance of an officer "commended for a daring and heroic act" and then passed over. From October 1864 until the close of the war he commanded the *Commodore McDonough* and later the *Cimarron* on blockade duty, being senior officer at Stono Inlet and for a time in May at Charleston.

Made captain in 1867, he commanded the *Dacotah,* Pacific Squadron, 1866–67, and then, as stated in an obviously inspired article in the *Chicago Tribune* (quoted in Walke, *post,* p. 79), "was sent . . . with his scars and his ironclads to rust away" at the Mound City (Ill.) Naval Station. His last command was the *Canandaigua,* 1871–72. He was retired for physical disability Jan. 5, 1874, and lived subsequently in Washington, occupied till his death in vain efforts to secure restoration. He was survived by his wife, Emily B. Thompson, and a daughter, Kate, wife of Capt. Edward Lloyd, U.S.A.

[W. B. Thompson, *Thompson Lineage* (1911) ; *Proc. of the Naval Court Martial in the Case of Alexander Slidell Mackenzie* (1844) ; Henry Walke, *Naval Scenes and Reminiscences* (1877) ; *War of the Rebellion: Official Records* (*Navy*) ; *Petition of Lieut. Egbert Thompson. U.S.N. against the Action of the Late Advisory Board* (1862) ; L. R. Hamersly, *The Records of Living Officers of the U. S. Navy and Marine Corps* (3rd ed., 1878) ; *Army and Navy Journal,* Jan. 8, 1881, and Jan. 13, 1894 (death of his wife).]   A. W.—t.

THOMPSON, HUGH MILLER (June 5, 1830–Nov. 18, 1902), bishop of the Protestant Episcopal Church, was born at Londonderry, Ireland, the eldest son of John T. and Annie (Millar) Thompson. At the age of six he was brought to the United States and attended the public school at Caldwell, N. J., and later an academy at Cleveland, Ohio. Deciding to enter the ministry of the Protestant Episcopal Church, in 1849 he walked from Cleveland to Nashotah, Wis., and enrolled as a student at Nashotah House. On June 6, 1852, he was ordered deacon by Jackson Kemper, bishop of Wisconsin, and was ordained priest by the same bishop at Portage, Wis., on Aug. 31, 1856. His early ministry was spent as a missionary in Wisconsin and Illinois. He served successively at Grace Church, Madison, Wis., and the Church of the Nativity, Maysville, Ky.; at Portage, Baraboo, Elkhorn, Kenosha, and Milwaukee, Wis.; and at Galena, Ill. For one year he was rector of St. James's, Chicago, and in 1872 he became rector of Christ Church, New York, where he attracted large congregations. For several years he was rector of Trinity Church, New Orleans. He combined his rectorship at Kenosha with the chair of ecclesiastical history at Nashotah House, and founded Kemper Hall, a school for girls. In 1853 he married Caroline Berry, by whom he had a son and a daughter; his wife died in 1857 and on Oct. 25, 1859, he married Anna Weatherburn Hinsdale, by whom, also, he had a son and a daughter.

Late in 1882 he was elected bishop coadjutor of Mississippi and was consecrated in New Orleans on Feb. 24, 1883. Four years later, on the death of William Mercer Green, senior bishop, Thompson became diocesan bishop and served until 1902. He had an unusual combination of gifts; he was an excellent teacher, and had a natural aptitude for metaphysics, large attainments as a scholar, and popular gifts as a preacher. Doctrinally he was a high churchman with a strong antipathy to the Anglo-Catholic movement and extreme ritualism. He used his pen with good effect in church journalism. From 1860 until its consolidation with the *Churchman* in 1871, he was editor of the *American Churchman,* published in Chicago, and subsequently he edited the *Church Journal,* published in New York. He had the knack of making the commonplace interesting, and his comments on current events were shrewd and shot through with sound common sense. Many of his editorials were widely copied and in 1872 selections from them were published under the title of *"Copy": Essays from an Editor's Drawer.* The volume passed through many editions and had a wide circulation in England. In 1897 he published *More "Copy"; a Second Series of Essays from an Editor's Drawer.* Among his other writings were *Unity and Its Restoration* (1860) ; *First Principles* (1869) ; *Absolution* (1872) ; *The World and the Logos* (1886), Bedell Lectures; *The World and the Kingdom* (1888), Paddock Lectures; *The World and the Man* (1890), Baldwin Lectures; *The World and the Wrestlers: Personality and Responsibility* (1895), Bohlen Lectures. Bishop Thompson died at Jackson, Miss., at the age of seventy-two.

[*Jours. of the Diocese of Miss.,* 1883–1903 ; *Who's Who in America,* 1901–02 ; *Churchman* and *Living Church,* Nov. 22, 1902 ; *Weekly Clarion-Ledger* (Jackson, Miss.), Nov. 20, 27, 1902.]   E. C. C.

THOMPSON, HUGH SMITH (Jan. 24, 1836–Nov. 20, 1904), educator, governor of South Carolina, was born at Charleston, S. C., the son of Agnes (Smith) and Henry Tazewell Thompson. Waddy Thompson [*q.v.*] was his uncle. His youth was passed in poverty on his father's farm in Greenville District. He entered the Citadel Academy at Charleston in 1852, where he graduated, four years later. On Apr. 6, 1858, he married Elizabeth Anderson, the daughter of Thomas Boston Clarkson, and taught at the Arsenal Academy in Columbia. In 1861 he returned to the Citadel, where until 1865 he taught French and belles-lettres and served in the Confederate Army as captain of a company of cadets of that academy in the defense of the Charleston harbor and the coastal region of South Carolina. Immediately after the war he became principal of the Columbia Male Academy, a position he held until 1880. His unusual ability as a teacher and disciplinarian raised this school to a position of preëminence among the educational institutions of South Carolina. His success as an educator, coupled with his engaging personal qualities, facilitated his entrance into public life. His handsome physique, mellow voice, and ease of speech made him a popular orator. In 1876 he became the Democratic candidate for state superintendent of education and in the canvass of that year aided Wade Hampton [*q.v.*] in winning the election for his party. He was state superintendent of education from May 1877 until December 1882. His conduct of this office was brilliantly constructive. The plans for universal education drawn up by his Radical predecessors were put into operation by him. He reformed the educational administration, spent wisely the funds he had at his disposal for the benefit of both whites and blacks, and in a series of moving addresses and reports largely removed from the public mind the prejudices against universal public education. In 1880 he established summer teachers' institutes, and the following year directed the foundation of a state teachers' association.

In 1882 the Democrats nominated him for governor. Being easily elected for two terms, he served in that office from December 1882 until his resignation three and one half years later. His conduct of the governorship was efficient but unsensational. He promoted tax reform, rigid economy, and education. In June 1886 President Cleveland appointed him assistant secretary of the treasury. In the summer of 1887 he resolutely anticipated and averted a seasonal monetary stringency by releasing an unusually large treasury surplus to purchase federal bonds in the market over and above the annual sinking fund requirements. From 1889 to 1892 he was a member of the civil service commission on the appointment of President Harrison. In this capacity he cooperated with his fellow-commissioner, Theodore Roosevelt, in carrying out the intentions of the Pendleton act. During the last twelve years of his life he was comptroller of the New York Life Insurance Company. He died in New York City and was buried in Trinity Church Yard, Columbia, S. C., leaving behind him the memory of one who had discharged with efficiency as many important public trusts as have been held by any South Carolinian since the Civil War.

[H. T. Thompson, *Establishment of the Public School System of S. C.* (1927); *Cyc. of Eminent and Representative Men of the Carolinas* (1892), vol. I; A. D. Mayo, in *A Report of the Commissioner U. S. Bureau of Education . . . 1904*, vol. I (1906), pp. 1031–39; *Confederate Veteran Camp of N. Y. Memorial on the Death of Comrade Hugh Smith Thompson* (1905?); *News and Courier* (Charleston, S. C.), and *N. Y. Times*, Nov. 21, 1904; information from his son Waddy Thompson, Atlanta, Ga.]   F. B. S.

THOMPSON, JACOB (May 15, 1810–Mar. 24, 1885), congressman from Mississippi, secretary of the interior, secret agent of the Confederate government, was born at Leasburg, Caswell County, N. C., of English and Dutch stock. Nicholas Thompson, his father, went to North Carolina from Virginia as a humble tanner but by his own diligence as well as by his marriage

to Lucretia Van Hook had acquired wealth. As a thank offering for his success, Nicholas decided to make a minister of his studious, quiet and rather ugly third son, Jacob, who could not summon courage to oppose his stern father until he was a student in the University of North Carolina. From that institution he graduated in 1831, and there he remained for eighteen months as a tutor. He read law in Greensboro and was admitted to the bar in 1835. Possibly because he had disagreed with his father, he chose to begin his career in a distant region and with his next elder brother, James Young Thompson, a physician, settled at the booming town of Pontotoc in north Mississippi. Later he removed to Oxford, Miss., where he married Catherine, the daughter of Paton Jones, a wealthy planter. They had one son. Both brothers prospered, and Jacob soon entered politics. In 1837 he was one of the leaders in the fight of the new counties of his section for immediate representation in the state legislature. The same year he was defeated for the attorney-generalship of the state, but he was soon elected to Congress, where he attained some prominence and was for a time chairman of the committees on public lands and Indian affairs. After six terms, Mar. 4, 1839–Mar. 3, 1851, he was defeated by a temporarily powerful combination of Whigs and Union Democrats. In the spring of 1845 an executive appointment to the Senate was sent him by Gov. A. G. Brown, but Robert J. Walker, to whom the commission was intrusted, did not deliver it and thereby caused a small political tempest in Mississippi. After playing an important part in the Democratic conventions of 1852 and 1856, he was appointed secretary of the interior in 1857. He reorganized this department to increase its efficiency and seems to have had considerable influence over President Buchanan. He resigned because of his state-rights views, when the *Star of the West* was sent to Fort Sumter.

Serving with the Confederate forces until the fall of Vicksburg, he became chief inspector of the army under Pemberton. In the autumn of 1863 he was elected to the legislature of Mississippi. In 1864 he and C. C. Clay [*q.v.*] were sent to Canada as secret agents of the Confederacy. From that base he cooperated with the "Sons of Liberty" of Ohio, Indiana, and Illinois until convinced that this organization would not take up arms against the Union. After that he sought to free thousands of Confederate soldiers imprisoned near the Great Lakes and to encourage the hoarding and export of gold from the North so as to damage its financial strength. He even abetted plans for burning several northern cities, including New York (*Official Records, post,* ser. 1, vol. XLIII, pp. 930–36). An attack against Saint Albans, Vt., by revengeful, escaped Confederate prisoners focused the fear and hatred of northern patriots on him. He, however, disclaimed any share in that episode. Being thus in the limelight when Lincoln was assassinated, it was natural that he should have been charged with complicity in that crime. A large reward was offered for his capture. With his wife, who joined him in Canada, he lived there and in Europe for several years. Certainly not earlier than the summer of 1868 he returned to Oxford. Soon after this he settled permanently in Memphis. In 1876 he was for a short time brought out of private life when, as a political move to divert attention from the Belknap scandals, he was sued for a large sum stolen from the Indian funds of the department of the interior during his administration. Though the money had indeed been stolen, he had at the time been judged innocent by a congressional committee, and, as soon as the election of 1876 was over, the case was dismissed at the cost of the government. He died in Memphis.

[Letters and papers in Lib. of Univ. of N. C., and in Lib. of Cong.; J. F. H. Claiborne, *Miss. as a Province, Territory and State,* vol. I (1880), the fullest account, based on notes furnished by Thompson for that purpose; P. G. Auchampaugh, *James Buchanan and His Cabinet* (1926); *War of the Rebellion: Official Records (Army),* ser. 1, XLIII, part 2, ser. 2, VIII; D. Z. Oldham, *Life of Jacob Thompson,* MS., a thesis in the lib. of the Univ. of Miss.; J. F. Bivins, "Life and Character of Jacob Thompson," *Pubs. of the Hist. Soc. of Trinity College,* ser. 2 (1898); letter in J. F. H. Claiborne, *Life and Correspondence of John A. Quitman* (1860), II, pp. 62–65.]

C. S. S.

THOMPSON, JAMES MAURICE (Sept. 9, 1844–Feb. 15, 1901), Indiana poet and author, better known as Maurice Thompson, was by traditions and temperament a Southerner. His paternal ancestors, a family of Scotch-Irish extraction, had been pioneers in the South since the seventeenth century. His father, the Rev. Matthew Grigg Thompson (married Diantha Jaeger), was a Baptist minister who was living at Fairfield, Ind., at the time of Maurice's birth, but who shortly moved to Missouri, to Kentucky, and finally, about 1854, to a plantation in the Coosawattee valley of north Georgia. Here the son's education, directed by a mother of unusual gifts and by such tutors as a schoolless region afforded, was almost evenly divided between the study of books and the study of nature, both of which remained lifelong passions ("The School in the Woods," *St. Nicholas,* October 1879). At seventeen Thompson entered the Confederate army, and served for three years with loyalty and distinction. After the war, which left the family

destitute, he studied both civil engineering and law in Calhoun, Ga., until the rigors of Reconstruction drove him to try his fortune in the North. In 1868, quite penniless, he drew up at Crawfordsville, Ind., to work as civil engineer on a railroad there building. In the same year he married Alice Lee, daughter of John Lee, his employer, and settled permanently at Crawfordsville. Civil engineering he soon relinquished (1871) in favor of law, and for thirteen years he was a practising lawyer whose avocation was literature. In 1884 he turned to literary work alone. He was a state legislator in 1879, and for two terms (1885–88) creditably filled the position of state geologist.

In the South he had contributed verse and prose to *Scott's Monthly Magazine* (Atlanta, Ga.) and other literary publications (J. W. Davidson, *The Living Writers of the South,* 1869, pp. 558–67); in 1871 the *New York Tribune* and in April 1873 the *Atlantic Monthly* introduced him to the East. His reputation was speedily increased by a series of magazine articles on archery, a sport which he and his brother, Will Henry Thompson (1848–1918), were the principal agents in reviving (R. P. Elmer, *Archery,* 1926, pp. 112–14), and soon his stories, poems, and sketches, published in all the leading periodicals, contributed to a reputation for letters that grew to be the most commanding of his generation in the Middle West. For the last twelve years of his life he was non-resident literary editor of the *Independent.* After his first book, dialect sketches called *Hoosier Mosaics* (1875), he published several books on archery, a number of books for juvenile readers, three collections of nature sketches—*By-Ways and Bird Notes* (1885), *Sylvan Secrets, in Bird-Songs and Books* (1887), and *My Winter Garden* (1900) —, a number of books of fiction, and two of poems, *Songs of Fair Weather* (1883) and *Poems* (1892). It is on the poems that his most enduring fame will probably rest. As critic, he was notably the militant and uncompromising opponent of the rising tide of realism. (See his papers in the *Critic* and the *Independent,* and *The Ethics of Literary Art,* 1893). His strong romantic bias found expression in his own fiction. In addition to three or four unimportant novelettes, he wrote *A Tallahassee Girl* (1881), *His Second Campaign* (1883), *At Love's Extremes* (1885), all sentimental novels of Southern life and character; *The King of Honey Island* (copyright 1892), an historical romance of the same region, and *A Banker of Bankersville* (copyright 1886), a study of Indiana village life. No signal success attended any of these performances until *Alice of Old Vincennes* (copyright 1900), an historical romance of the George Rogers Clark expedition of 1779, brought him at the very end of his career nation-wide popularity. Retiring by nature, he shrank from any kind of publicity, refusing repeated offers of editorial position and lectureships. Though lithe and athletic, he was not robust of constitution, and regularly spent the winters in the South. He died of pneumonia at his home, Sherwood Place, Crawfordsville. He was survived by his wife, two daughters, and a son.

[Scattered autobiog. material is to be found in Thompson's accounts of his hunting and exploring experiences. See also *Who's Who in America*, 1899–1900; W. M. Baskervill, *Southern Writers*, vol. I (1897), pp. 89–136; Meredith Nicholson, *The Hoosiers* (1900); Mary H. Krout, in *Independent*, Feb. 21, 1901, which also has a poem by James Whitcomb Riley and an editorial; obituaries in *N. Y. Times*, *Indianapolis Sentinel*, Feb. 16, and *Indianapolis News*, Feb. 15, 16, 1901. Information on the family was supplied by Thompson's daughter, Mrs. Albert Blair Ballard of Tampa, Fla. A thesis on Thompson was prepared by George A. Schumacher at the Univ. of Va., 1934.]   F. H. R.

THOMPSON, JEREMIAH (Dec. 9, 1784–Nov. 10, 1835), merchant and ship-owner, was born of Quaker parentage at Rawdon, Yorkshire, a cloth-manufacturing village midway between Leeds and Bradford. His father, William Thompson, was the eldest of seven brothers engaged in the manufacture of woolen cloths. In 1798, shortly after the opening of the Leeds and Liverpool canal across the Pennine range, the youngest of these brothers, Francis Thompson, came to New York to represent the family business, and in 1801 Jeremiah followed, presumably to assist him. In the course of his business activities in New York, Francis entered into an informal association with Isaac Wright, a Quaker merchant of New York (whose daughter he married), and with Benjamin Marshall [*q.v.*]. In 1807 Francis and Isaac Wright became joint owners of the fast-sailing transatlantic ship, *Pacific*. In 1807 William Thompson had manufactured the first cloth made from Australian wool at the family mill at Rawdon. The product was highly esteemed, and it is probable that the employment of this wool in later years was a powerful influence in promoting the cloth trade of the Thompsons in New York.

Jeremiah seems to have begun business on his own account in 1815, when his name first appears in the New York directory. At that time he also became a joint owner with Francis Thompson, Benjamin Marshall, Isaac Wright, and his son William Wright, in the *Pacific*. The *Pacific* was employed in regular trade with Liverpool and in 1816 her owners placed the *Amity*, and in the spring of 1817 the *Courier*, in the same service. In October 1817 these five men announced the organization of a line of American packets to make regular sailings from New York and Liverpool on a fixed day in each month. This idea of regular monthly sailings, with strict adherence to the advertised day of departure, is attributed to Jeremiah Thompson. The Liverpool line began service in January 1818, with the *Pacific, Amity, Courier,* and a fourth and new ship, the *James Monroe*. For some years it continued operations with difficulty, in the face of business depression; but in 1822, the practice of regular sailings was copied by other firms, and the "Old Line of packets," as it was termed, doubled its fleet to provide regular sailings twice a month.

During the next few years Thompson's commercial and shipping business greatly expanded. He participated in the formation of packet lines from New York to Belfast and to Greenock, and from Philadelphia to Liverpool. In 1827, he was designated the largest ship-owner in the United States and the most extensive cotton dealer in the world, with an annual purchase in the United States of about 150,000 bales. At the end of September 1827, however, the Liverpool house to which he consigned his cotton refused to accept his bills, with the result that he and his brother William (his partner in England) were compelled to suspend payments. He became insolvent in 1828, and all his interests in shipping were sold. Francis Thompson seems also to have failed at about the same time.

The absence of a bankruptcy law in New York State at that time appears to have made it impossible for Thompson ever to secure a release from his debts and to regain an independent position in business; yet it may be conjectured that he had a share in the formation in 1828 of a short-lived Union line of packets for steerage passengers only, and in 1831 of an emigrant packet office, both of which conducted their business at 273 Pearl Street, his own business address. This emigrant agency, which was headed by his cousin Samuel Thompson (previously Francis Thompson's partner), led in the later years to the formation of the Black Star line of packets and of the Guion line of steamships, and also had brief connections with the Cunard line. Thompson died in New York City; he never married. The preëminence of New York among the Atlantic seaports was ascribed by Matthew F. Maury [*q.v.*] in 1839 largely to Thompson's establishment there of shipping service on a regular schedule.

[Records of the New York meeting, Society of Friends; *Boston Commercial Gazette*, Nov. 19, 1827; *New-England Palladium*, Nov. 30, 1827; *New York Commercial Advertiser*, Dec. 1, 1827, Nov. 11, 1835; J. A. Scoville, *The Old Merchants of N. Y. City*, vol.

IV (1866), vol. V (1870); C. P. Wright, "The Packet Ships of N. Y." (unpublished thesis, Harvard Univ. Lib.); *N. Y. Daily Advertiser*, Nov. 12, 1835; *Herald* (N. Y.), Nov. 13, 1835; M. F. Maury, "Direct Trade with the South," in *Southern Lit. Messenger*, Jan. 1839.]

C. P. W.

THOMPSON, JEROME B. (Jan. 30, 1814–May 1, 1886), painter, was one of three artist children of Cephas Thompson, portrait painter, of Middleboro, Mass., and Olive (Leonard) Thompson. His father, who thought that one artist in the next generation would be enough, gave his instruction only to Cephas Giovanni [*q.v.*]. Encouraged, however, by his sister Marietta, who had learned to paint miniatures, Jerome painted in the attic at Middleboro a likeness of a cousin, a divinity student. When he discovered this, his father in anger smashed both canvas and easel, whereupon Jerome left home with his sister and set up for himself in Barnstable as sign and ornamental painter. An interesting anecdote is also recorded of the young painter's facility in making a likeness in five minutes on a wager (Thompson, *post*, p. 141). One of his early sitters was Daniel Webster, who had a house at Marshfield. Having saved a little money from his sign-painting and portraiture, Thompson went with his sister to New York, where both met with considerable success, she as a miniaturist, he as a depictor of rustic scenes, usually combining landscape and figures. He first appeared in New York directories in 1835. He was married twice: on Mar. 23, 1839, to Maria Louisa Colden, and on Apr. 19, 1876, to Marie May Tupper, an artist. He had one son. In 1852 he went to England, where he studied the pictures of Turner and Hogarth and painted portraits of several of the nobility. Upon his return he conducted a farm at Mineola, L. I., gaining distinction as a gardener as well as artist. He was a deeply religious and moral man, keeping regularly a "Book of Advice" for his own edification.

He made many sketches and studies in the Massachusetts Berkshires and Vermont, and in the far West. Some of his paintings of historic, literary, and sentimental subjects were used as "copy" for lithographic and chromolithographic reproduction, as were his "The Old Oaken Bucket," "Home, Sweet Home," "Scenes of My Childhood," "Coming through the Rye," and "Woodman, Spare that Tree." A long and somewhat amusing criticism of his picture, "The Hay Maker," was contributed by "Amateur" to *A Critical Guide to the Exhibition at the National Academy of Design* (1859). After his death, which occurred at "Mount Jerome," his country place at Glen Gardner, N. J., the National Academy of Design, of which he had been elected an

associate in 1851, paid him a glowing tribute as "a most excellent and worthy man, deservedly honored in his life and sincerely mourned in his death" (*Ibid.*, p. 142). It is conceivable that there may at some time be a rediscovery of the merits of Jerome Thompson as a painter; at this writing (1935) he is well-nigh forgotten except by collectors of old lithographs.

[C. H. Thompson, *A Geneal. of Descendants of John Thomson, of Plymouth, Mass.* (1890); Thomas Weston, *Hist. of the Town of Middleboro, Mass.* (1906); Clara E. Clement and Laurence Hutton, *Artists of the Nineteenth Century* (1884); death notice in *N. Y. Times*, May 3, 1886.]

F. W. C.

THOMPSON, JOHN [See THOMSON, JOHN, 1776–1799].

THOMPSON, JOHN (Nov. 2, 1802–Apr. 19, 1891), New York publisher and banker, was born in the town of Partridgefield (now Peru), Berkshire County, Mass. He was a son of Amherst and Sarah (Clarke) Thompson, and a descendant of James Thompson who emigrated to Salem, Mass., in 1630, later moved to Charlestown, and in 1642 settled in Woburn. John's boyhood was spent on a mountain farm, and his early education was obtained in neighboring schools and at Harley Academy. For a time he taught a select school at Albany, N. Y., and then associated himself with the firm of Yates & McIntyre, which was engaged in promoting a lottery for the benefit of Union College.

Thompson seems to have been fairly successful in selling lottery tickets, but in 1833 he appeared in New York City, where he opened a brokerage office in Wall Street on a capital of $2,000. His contact with the financial world revealed to him an opportunity which he was quick to improve. The fact that an increasing number of state banks were circulating currency in every part of the country made it next to impossible for bankers or merchants in the East either to detect counterfeits or to know the actual value at a given time of any form of bank paper issued in the West or South. Thompson believed that reliable information on these matters would be welcomed by the business community, even if the cost of acquiring it should be relatively high. Accordingly, in 1842 he began the periodical publication of *Thompson's Bank Note and Commercial Reporter*, which not only pointed out differences between the actual and the spurious issues of particular banks, but gave quotations of discount rates on currency and a record of actual rates of exchange throughout the country. It thus presented facts not otherwise obtainable by the individual except at great expense, and it attained a large weekly circulation.

In the course of the Civil War Thompson, through his publication, attracted the attention of Secretary Chase and readily obtained a hearing on legal-tender and national bank policies. In 1863 soon after the establishment of the system of national banks, he received the charter for the First National Bank in New York City. He and his sons, Samuel and Frederick, originally owned the entire capital stock of $300,000. Most of the city's banks, operating under state charters, were distrustful of Secretary Chase's policies and looked with disfavor on his national banking system. Consequently, for some time Thompson's institution could not get clearinghouse privileges and was chiefly engaged in the marketing of United States bonds. In 1873, the year that Jay Cooke [q.v.] failed, George F. Baker and Harris C. Fahnestock [q.v.] bought a controlling interest in the First National on condition that Thompson retain the presidency (article on George F. Baker, *New York Times*, May 3, 1931). Four years later, at the age of seventy-five, he withdrew and with his two sons founded the Chase National Bank, of which for a short time, after the death of his son Samuel in 1884, he was president. In his latter years he became erratic on questions of money and finance. The Chase Bank admitted in 1887 that its venerable founder was "a strong advocate of silver," and two years later he was joint author with Thurlow Weed and Pierrepont Edwards of *The Silver Dollar of the United States and Its Relation to Bi-Metallism* (1889), but he did not live to see the "sixteen-to-one" agitation of the next decade. In 1829 he had married Electa Ferris, who with a son and a daughter survived him.

[Leander Thompson, *Memorial of James Thompson . . . and of Eight Generations of His Descendants* (1887); *Vital Records of Peru, Mass., to the Year 1850* (1902); B. J. Lossing, *Hist. of N. Y. City* (1884), pp. 733–35; E. P. Oberholtzer, *Jay Cooke* (1907), I, 344; W. T. Hardenbrook, *Financial N. Y.*, pt. 3 (1897), p. 267; *N. Y. Herald*, *N. Y. Times*, and *N. Y. Tribune*, Apr. 20, 1891.]　　　　　　　　W. B. S.

THOMPSON, JOHN BODINE (Oct. 14, 1830–Sept. 4, 1907), educator and clergyman, was born at Readington, N. J., the son of Joseph and Ann (Post) Thompson. He was the great-grandson of John Thomson, a Scotch emigrant who settled in Hunterdon County, N. J., married Juda Bodin (Judith Bodine), a descendant of the early Huguenot settlers, and about 1777 joined a group that undertook settlement in the Shamokin country of Pennsylvania. When he was killed in an Indian attack of 1778, his widow accomplished the feat of walking back to New Jersey, wheeling their only son and the family Bible in a small cart. There she reared the boy, also called John, to a place of influence and responsibility. He changed the spelling of the

family name. Her grandson, Joseph, was one of the leading citizens of central New Jersey, a teacher, surveyor, farmer, and for over thirty years county judge of either Hunterdon or Somerset county courts. John Bodine Thompson was his eldest son. When a mere boy he taught in a rural school and in 1851 was graduated from Rutgers College. He was active in the mid-century movement to improve the educational system of New Jersey, led by Richard S. Field [q.v.]. As agent of the New Jersey Teachers' Association from 1856 to 1859, he traveled up and down the state, delivering addresses and organizing teachers' institutes and urging the establishment of high schools and normal schools. He also advocated school libraries and the social use of school houses and libraries by the community, and he was among the first to urge summer schools.

Meanwhile he had entered the Theological Seminary of the Reformed Church in America at New Brunswick, was graduated in 1858, and was licensed to preach. On Apr. 5, 1859, he was married to Hannah Garrigues Reeve. They had two sons. He held pastorates at Metuchen, N. J., 1859–66, and at Tarrytown, 1866–69, Saugerties, 1869–71, Peekskill, 1873–74, and Catskill, 1874–84, in New York. During a long vacation, 1871–73, he went to Europe, where he supplied the pulpit of the American Protestant Church at Florence and studied at Tübingen University, still at the height of its fame as a seat of liberal theology. In company with Alessandro Gavazzi, the leader of the Free Italian Church and in his time one of the greatest of the Italian orators, he returned to the United States and was helpful in obtaining contributions for that movement. Religiously he was a liberal, philosophically a Hegelian, and he believed that the doctrine of the Trinity ought to be formulated in more philosophical terms. A large and dynamic man, he was an inspiration to those with whom he came in contact, and especially to young men and women in the formative years. Many of these later regarded his influence as the intellectual and moral background of their lives. From 1884 to 1888 he was minister of the First Presbyterian Church at Berkeley, Cal., where he became close friend of Joseph LeConte [q.v.]. He was also professor in the Presbyterian Theological School at San Francisco. He published voluminously, addresses such as *The Evolution of the American College* (1894), bits of family description as *John Thomson and Family* (1889, also in J. F. Meginness, *Otzinachson: A History of the . . . Susquehanna*, 1889, vol. I), and such other contributions as the chapter on "The Middle of the

Century" in David Murray's *History of Education in New Jersey* (1899). He was chairman of the committee responsible for *Reformed Church . . . Hymns* (1869). He died in Trenton, N. J.

[E. T. Corwin, *A Manual of the Reformed Church in America* (4th ed., 1902); *The Acts and Proc. of the . . . General Synod of the Reformed Church in America . . . 1908* (n.d.); J. P. Snell, *Hist. of Hunterdon and Somerset, N. J.* (1881), pp. 491–93; M. C. Stuart, *Zes Maanden in Amerika* (1875), vol. II, pp. 66–74; *Cat. of the Officers and Alumni of Rutgers College* (1909); *Marriage Records of Hunterdon County, N. J.*, vol. I (1918); *Daily True American* (Trenton, N. J.), Sept. 6, 1907; information from his nephew, James Westfall Thompson, Berkeley, Cal.]   K. E. C.

THOMPSON, JOHN REUBEN (Oct. 23, 1823–Apr. 30, 1873), editor and poet, was born in Richmond, Va., the son of John Thompson of New Hampshire and Sarah (Dyckman) Thompson of New York. He attended schools in Richmond and in Easthaven, Conn. He was a student at the University of Virginia from 1840 to 1842, read law in the office of James A. Seddon [*q.v.*], and returned to the law class of the university, where he received the degree of Bachelor of Laws in 1845. For two years he practised law in Richmond. His father, then a prosperous merchant, purchased for him *The Southern Literary Messenger,* the editorship of which Poe had surrendered just ten years before. Thompson was owner and editor from 1847 to 1853, when he disposed of the ownership to his printers and continued as editor until he was succeeded in 1860 by George W. Bagby. The period of Thompson's editorship was that of the magazine's greatest influence and reputation. The acknowledged representative of the South, it printed especially the work of its leading writers. In 1854, with John Esten Cooke acting for him on the *Messenger,* Thompson sailed for his first visit to Europe. His travel sketches were printed in 1856 by Derby & Jackson, with the title, *Across the Atlantic,* but the whole edition was destroyed in a New York fire, except for one volume, now at his own university. Thompson left the *Messenger* in 1860 to become—for only a few months—editor of a weekly publication of Augusta, Ga., the *Southern Field and Fireside.* When Virginia seceded, his pen became one of the readiest in the Confederacy. In addition to his duties as assistant secretary of the Commonwealth of Virginia, he helped edit, while they were printed, the *Richmond Record* and *The Southern Illustrated News,* and he contributed to the *Index,* spokesman of the Confederacy in England. When his health failed, he resigned his office and in July 1864 ran the blockade to England, where he was the chief writer on the *Index* until the fall of the Confederacy. In England his influence

was especially favorable to the South because of his wide friendship among celebrated writers. He had known Bulwer-Lytton, Thackeray and the Brownings on his earlier visit to Europe and among the many friends of the later period were Tennyson and Carlyle. After the defeat of the South, he maintained himself for a time in England by newspaper work and by preparing for *Blackwood's Edinburgh Magazine* from the notebooks of Major Heros von Borcke the "Memoirs of the Confederate War for Independence" (Sept. 1865–June 1866 and published in two volumes in 1866). In September 1866 he returned to America. He was American correspondent for the London *Standard* and lectured, besides writing for other papers. In April 1867 he left Virginia for New York and, after one or two temporary engagements, was appointed by William Cullen Bryant to the literary editorship of the New York *Evening Post.* He held that position until the development of tuberculosis forced him to seek rest in Colorado in 1873. He died in New York and was buried in Hollywood Cemetery in Richmond.

His importance is chiefly as an influence upon his own times and as the author of a considerable body of verse, most of it "occasional," that was accepted by his contemporaries as perfectly expressing the Southern sentiment of the decades following the Civil War. He was looked upon as the poet consecrated to the traditions of Virginia. Five or six of his poems are memorable for their own worth. Among those that have been best known are "Music in Camp," "The Burial of Latané," "Lee to the Rear," "Ashby," and "The Window-Panes at Brandon." His collected *Poems* were first published in 1920, edited by John S. Patton, with an excellent biographical sketch. Of his lectures, which were popular in his lifetime, *The Genius and Character of Edgar Allan Poe* was privately printed in Richmond in 1929.

[Some letters in Lib. of Cong.; sketch by W. G. McCabe, in *Lib. of Southern Literature,* vol. XII (1910); biog. introduction in *Poems of John R. Thompson, ante*; J. R. Miller, Jr., "John R. Thompson: His Place in Southern Life and Literature," manuscript dissertation, 1930, Univ. of Va. Library; E. A. and G. L. Duyckinck, *The Cyc. of Am. Lit.* (1875), vol. II; manuscript minutes of the Faculty, Univ. of Va., 1845; *Evening Post* (N. Y.), May 1, 3, 1873.]   J. S. W.

THOMPSON, JOSEPH PARRISH (Aug. 7, 1819–Sept. 20, 1879), Congregational clergyman, editor, author, was born in Philadelphia, Pa., the son of Isaac and Mary Anne (Hanson) Thompson, and a descendant of John Thompson who emigrated from London to Stratford, Conn., in 1635. His father was a druggist. Thompson graduated from Yale College in 1838, studied for the ministry at Andover and New Haven, and, as a favorite pupil of Nathaniel W. Taylor [q.v.], was drawn early into an influential circle of clergymen. In consequence he was ordained, Oct. 28, 1840, as pastor of the Chapel Street Church (later the Church of the Redeemer) at New Haven and was called thence in 1845 to the Broadway Tabernacle, New York, one of the strategic outposts of New England Congregationalism. To this large and discriminating congregation he ministered successfully for a quarter-century. He was one of the conspicuous leaders of the home missionary movement in his denomination, was the instigator of the Albany Congregationalist Conference of 1852, and worked unceasingly to arouse public opinion in behalf of the negro slaves. He made two visits to Europe, Palestine, and Egypt, and acquired some esteem as an Egyptologist. While still in New Haven he had helped Leonard Bacon [q.v.] to found the *New Englander,* and he wrote frequently for it and for *Bibliotheca Sacra.* With Bacon, Richard Salter Storrs, and Joshua Leavitt [qq.v.] he was a member of the editorial board of the *Independent* from its organization at the close of 1848, but as the result of differences with the proprietor, Henry Chandler Bowen [q.v.], he resigned in 1862. During this period he published some fifteen books, besides numerous pamphlets, sermons, lectures, and contributions to periodicals and reference works. He wrote well, and evidently with ease. Among his books were memoirs of the younger Timothy Dwight (1844), David Hale (1850), David Tappan Stoddard (1858), and Bryant Gray (1864); *Egypt Past and Present* (1856); *Love and Penalty, or Eternal Punishment consistent with the Fatherhood of God* (1860); *Man in Genesis and in Geology* (1869); *The Theology of Christ from His Own Words* (1870); and *Home Worship* (1871). He had no new ideas and was a thorough scholar in no department of knowledge, but he readily assimilated ideas and information from all sides and presented them in an intelligible form, he served no cause or institution perfunctorily, and his capacity for work was awe-inspiring. He was married twice: on May 5, 1841, to Lucy Olivia Bartlett of Portsmouth, N. H., who bore him five children and died in 1852; and on Oct. 25, 1853, to Elizabeth Coit Gilman of New York, a sister of Daniel Coit Gilman [q.v.]. By her he had one son, William Gilman Thompson [q.v.]. Two of his sons fought in the Civil War; the elder, John Hanson, died in the service and was commemorated by his father in *The Sergeant's Memorial* (1863). Thompson himself

was a delegate of the Sanitary Commission with Sherman's army.

In 1871 his health broke down, and with scant hope of future usefulness ahead of him he resigned his charge. William Mackergo Taylor [q.v.] became his successor. His congregation and some personal friends presented him with $70,000. He removed to Germany and established himself in Berlin, where he worked desultorily on a monograph on the Hebrews in ancient Egypt. As his health improved he appeared in society, preached frequently, and soon became an active publicist, devoting himself to the complicated ecclesiastical problems of the Reich, and to strengthening comity between the United States and Germany. He lectured in England, Scotland, Germany, Switzerland, France, and Italy; published several volumes, including *Church and State in the United States* (1873), *The United States as a Nation* (1877), and *The Workman: His False Friends and His True Friends* (1879); interested himself in international law; attended conventions of all kinds and delivered numerous occasional addresses. He spoke German and French readily. He kept alert mentally to the last, in spite of pain, headaches, partial paralysis, and the humiliation of an attempt to blackmail him. He died of an apoplectic stroke and was buried in the graveyard of the Jerusalem Church in Berlin. His brother-in-law edited a posthumous volume of *American Comments on European Questions* (1884).

[Arthur Gilman, *The Gilman Family* (1869); *Biog. Record of the class of 1838 in Yale Coll.* (1879) and *Supplement* (1889); *Obit. Record Grads. Yale Coll. . . . June 1880* (1880); *Broadway Tabernacle Church: Its Hist. and Work* (1871); Susan H. Ward, *The Hist. of the Broadway Tabernacle Church* (1901); obituary in *N. Y. Daily Tribune,* Sept. 22, 1879; obituary and editorial in *Phila. Press,* Sept. 22, 1879; *Independent,* Sept. 25, 1879 (editorial); Leonard Bacon, *Ibid.,* Oct. 2, 1879; G. W. Gilman, *Ibid.,* Oct. 16, 1879; W. H. Ward, *Ibid.,* Dec. 10, 1908.]   G. H. G.

THOMPSON, JOSIAH VAN KIRK (Feb. 15, 1854–Sept. 27, 1933), coal operator, banker, was the son of a Scotch-Irish father and a German-Dutch mother, Jasper Markle and Eliza (Caruthers) Thompson. Born on a farm near Uniontown, Fayette County, Pa., he was educated in the local schools and at Washington and Jefferson College, Washington, Pa., from which he graduated in 1871. In November of the same year he began to work in the First National Bank of Uniontown, an institution that Jasper Thompson had been instrumental in organizing and the presidency of which he held. The son advanced rapidly to the positions of teller and cashier, and in 1889, at the death of the elder Thompson, he became president. He served in this capacity for the next twenty-five years, at the same time carrying on another activity that his father had started in a small way—speculation in coal lands. He reputedly bought lands at from $30 to $100 an acre and sold them at from $170 to $2,850 an acre. Most of the coal under Greene and Fayette counties passed through his hands, as well as that under several thousand acres in the other counties of southwestern Pennsylvania and in West Virginia. At the peak of his career, with a fortune that was conservatively estimated at seventy million dollars, he was believed to control more than half of the coking coal in Pennsylvania and was known as the largest individual owner of coal lands in the country.

His bank was believed to be as prosperous as he was. It paid regular semi-annual dividends of eleven per cent. in addition to special ones. After 1903 it was housed in an eleven-story "skyscraper," the only such building in a town the size of Uniontown (7,500) in the country. It paid no interest on deposits, and carried a surplus of more than a thousand dollars for every hundred dollars of capital stock. When, however, Thompson refused to sell coal to the large steel interests except on his own terms, his troubles began. Early in 1914 he found himself blocked both in making sales and in getting extensions of credit. His bank was involved, because a large part of its supposed surplus was out in direct and indirect loans to him, and on Jan. 18, 1915, it was forced to keep its doors closed. After fruitless efforts to reëstablish himself, Thompson sold out in 1919 to the Piedmont Coal Company for a reported sum of five and a half million dollars, retaining only his home. For the rest of his life he continued to hope to "put through a deal," but only became more involved. Between 1926 and 1930 he faced charges of embezzlement for mismanagement of the estates of Emma Messmore and John A. Niccolls, and in December 1930, served a few days in jail for contempt of court, being released because of ill health.

Previous to the failure of the bank, Thompson was a dominating influence in Uniontown, and took an active interest in the town's welfare. Friendly, cheerful, and a tireless worker, he inspired a faith that was akin to religion. A number of his fellow townsmen became wealthy through opportunities he opened to them, and none lost a penny through deposit in his bank. His home, "Oak Hill," was lavishly furnished and housed a large library. He served as a trustee of Washington and Jefferson College from 1889 until his death, and in 1901 he contributed $100,100 to its endowment. From 1900 to 1915 he was president of the Presbyterian Banner

Publishing Company. On Dec. 11, 1879, he married Mary Anderson, who died in 1896, and on Aug. 11, 1903, he married Mrs. Blanche A. Gardner Hawes, who divorced him in 1912. On Dec. 14, 1929, he married Mrs. Rose Maloney of Pittsburgh. By his first wife he had two sons. He died in Uniontown.

[J. W. Jordan and James Hadden, *Geneal. and Personal Hist. of Fayette and Greene Counties, Pa.* (1912); scrapbooks on Uniontown kept by James Hadden, in Carnegie Lib., Pittsburgh; *N. Y. Times*, Jan. 19, 22, 1915, June 14, 1919, May 5, 1927, Apr. 14, 1929, Dec. 18, 1930, Sept. 28, 1933; *Pittsburgh Post-Gazette*, Sept. 1933; *Who's Who in America*, 1918–19.] M. S.

THOMPSON, LAUNT (Feb. 8, 1833–Sept. 26, 1894), sculptor, was born at Abbeyleix, Queens County, Ireland, and came with his widowed mother to the United States in 1847. They made a home in Albany, N. Y., where he soon found a place in the office of Dr. James H. Armsby. In 1848 Erastus Dow Palmer [*q.v.*], who had made a portrait bust of Dr. Armsby, accepted Launt as a studio boy, doubtless because of the striking talent shown in his drawings of bones and muscles, made at the doctor's office. During the nine years he spent as assistant to Palmer, a kindly, conscientious master, Thompson developed into a capable young sculptor, expert in all studio processes, especially clay modeling and marble carving. In 1857, thus equipped, he set up a studio for himself in New York City, where he promptly met recognition, at first for ideal medallion heads in Palmer's vein and soon afterward for more original productions not only in relief but also in portrait busts and statues. He was made an associate of the National Academy of Design in 1859, and a full member in 1862. Three years later Thomas Bailey Aldrich described for young readers (*Our Young Folks*, Dec. 1865) his visit to Thompson in the famous Tenth Street studio building, where the sculptor was at work on the plaster cast of a colossal statue of Napoleon I, almost ready for the bronze. On the walls were many medallions, portrait or ideal, the subjects of the latter including Elaine and other heroines from the *Idyls of the King*. "Morning Glory," the profile of a child with a flowery fillet, became a popular work. There are three life-size busts, representing the "Rocky Mountain Trapper," Edwin Booth as Hamlet, and the poet William Cullen Bryant. Thompson's carefully studied head of Bryant, of which there is a copy in the Metropolitan Museum, New York, has remained for sculptors the authentic source portrait of the poet.

The "Trapper" and the Napoleon I were

shown in 1867 at the Paris Exposition, after which the sculptor spent some months in Rome, Italy. The Napoleon has been praised as an example of "dignified monumental art," "self-contained in every line" (Taft, *post,* p. 235), and irreproachable in modeling. Equally sculptural in conception, though less pleasing in detail, is Thompson's bronze statue of Abraham Pierson, the younger, erected on the campus of Yale University in 1874. In September 1869 Thompson married at Schenectady, N. Y., Maria L. Potter, daughter of Bishop Alonzo Potter [*q.v.*]. Six years later he went to Italy for a prolonged stay, from which he returned to New York in 1881. During his Albany years the Palmers must have felt a true esteem for the young sculptor, for they gave his name to their son, Walter Launt Palmer [*q.v.*]. Thompson learned many things from his generous elder, but not the secret of orderly living. He was endowed, it has been said (*Ibid.,* p. 236), "with an intuitive grasp of the sculptural side of things, and with an artistic conscience, which seems the more remarkable when contrasted with his erratic life." His influence on early monumental art in America was undoubtedly good. He died at Middletown, N. Y.

In the grounds of the Old Soldiers' Home, Washington, D. C., is his bronze figure of Gen. Winfield Scott, founder of the home. His "bewhiskered standing figure" of Admiral Samuel Francis Du Pont was for some time at the center of Du Pont Circle, Washington, but was removed in 1921 to Delaware. Other statues by Thompson are the Gen. John Sedgwick, West Point, N. Y. (1869); the Charles Morgan, Clinton, Conn. (1871); and the bronze equestrian figure of Gen. Ambrose E. Burnside, Providence, R. I. (1887), the last important work from his studio. Among his excellent portrait busts are those of James Gordon Bennett, Robert B. Minturn, Stephen H. Tyng, Capt. Charles H. Marshall, Charles L. Elliott, and S. F. B. Morse.

[Lorado Taft, *The Hist. of Am. Sculpture* (1903); H. T. Tuckerman, *Book of the Artists* (1867); Charles Moore, *Washington Past and Present* (1929), p. 242; *Rand-McNally Guide to Washington* (1925); obituary in *N. Y. Tribune,* Sept. 27, 1894.]   A—e.A.

THOMPSON, MARTIN E. (*c.* 1786–July 24, 1877), architect, first appears in the New York directory in 1816 as a carpenter. He may have been a pupil of Josiah R. Brady, the architect, for among the drawings in the New York Historical Society is one of the Merchants' Exchange, credited in the handwriting of a contemporary to J. R. Brady and M. E. Thompson. In any case, he was commissioned in 1822–23 to design the second Bank of the United States on Wall Street, later the United States Assay Office

(1854–1915), its lovely façade now serving as the south front of the American wing of the Metropolitan Museum of Art. In 1824 he was called on for a design for the Merchants' Exchange, completed in July 1827 and burned in the great fire of 1835. In beauty and richness the building had no peers in the city. It was dignified, simple, and commodious, and the Exchange Room, 85 by 55 feet, with rounded ends and a screen of columns, was well proportioned and impressive. It is shown in one of the Pendleton lithographs of New York. By 1827 Thompson had formed a partnership with Ithiel Town [*q.v.*]. Their office at 32 Merchants' Exchange soon became an artistic center, and was opened as an "Architectural Room" to those who wished to consult Town's magnificent library of architectural books and engravings (*The Picture of New-York, post,* p. 376). The effect on Thompson was to convert him at once to the Greek Revival. In their combined work—especially in the Church of the Ascension (1828) on Canal Street, and in the brick tower and spire of St. Mark's in the Bowery (still standing, 1935)— Town may have had a great part, though Minard Lafever in *The Young Builder's General Instructor* (Newark, 1829) gives Thompson the credit for the Church of the Ascension, and a Mr. Morris in the *New York Mirror,* Mar. 1, 1828, in praising the St. Mark's steeple for its beauty and its omission of such "pretty things" as the common brazen weathercock, mentions only Thompson's name. In 1826 Thompson was one of the thirty founders of the National Academy of Design. Both he and Town exhibited there regularly until about 1833. Their partnership seems to have ended in 1828, for in 1829 Thompson exhibited several designs alone. He was the designer of the Columbia Grammar School (begun 1829), the façades of the houses on the Murray Street lots of Columbia University, and the noted house of Robert Ray, 17 Broadway, burned in the great fire of 1845 (*New York Mirror,* July 26, 1845). In 1839 he received the second premium in the competition for the Ohio capitol at Columbus (diary of Alexander Jackson Davis, Metropolitan Museum of Art, New York). He made several plans for the enlargement of the City Hall. From May 1847 to January 1850 he served as street commissioner of New York City. He lived on East Eleventh Street, 1844–53, and on West Twelfth, 1853–64. After the death of his wife, Mary (who was born in New York City and died there, Feb. 9, 1864, at the age of seventy-five), he seems to have left New York and retired to Glen Cove, L. I., where he died. Besides being one of the founders of the National Academy of Design he was a member of the General Society of Mechanics and Tradesmen from 1822 on.

As a designer Thompson ranks high. The second Bank of the United States is gracious, restrained, delicate, rather in the English tradition, as was the Ray house. The Merchants' Exchange was more original, more daring, more powerful; the recessed portico was a new note, its cupola was unusually effective, and its large Exchange Room both delicate and monumental. The St. Mark's spire is markedly original in conception in its avoidance of the orders, the Columbia Grammar School was well massed, and the plans for the City Hall extensions reveal great planning ability. The Columbia houses are simple and straightforward, and give stylistic support to the assumption that Thompson was probably the architect of many of those dignified houses built in the northern part of Greenwich Village in the forties and fifties.

[*The Picture of New-York, and Stranger's Guide to the Commercial Metropolis of the U. S.* (N. Y., 1828), pub. by A. T. Goodrich; *Proc. and Docs. of the Board of Assistant Aldermen,* vols. XXXIV–XXXVII (N. Y., 1851); Thomas Earle and C. T. Congdon, *Annals of the General Soc. of Mechanics and Tradesmen . . . 1785 to 1880* (1882); I. N. P. Stokes, *The Iconography of Manhattan Island,* vols. III–VI (1918–28); *Memorial of St. Mark's Church in the Bowery, N. Y.* (1899); death notice in *N. Y. Tribune,* July 25, 1877; vital statistics of N. Y. City; cats. of exhibitions, Nat. Acad. of Design; drawings, estimates, etc., in the "Columbiana" Coll., Columbia Univ. Lib.; minutes of the board of trustees, Columbia Univ., 1826–30; MSS. in Columbia Univ. Lib.; City Hall plans, McComb Papers, N. Y. Hist. Soc.; information from Mrs. Charles Curran, librarian of the Nat. Acad. of Design.] T.F.H.

THOMPSON, MAURICE [See THOMPSON, JAMES MAURICE, 1844–1901].

THOMPSON, RICHARD WIGGINTON (June 9, 1809–Feb. 9, 1900), lawyer, politician, author, was born in Culpeper County, Va., the son of William Mills Thompson, a merchant and lawyer, and Catherine Wigginton (Broadus) Thompson. His great-grandfather, the Rev. John Thompson, born near Belfast, Ireland, emigrated to Virginia in 1739. His mother was the daughter of Maj. William Broadus, an officer of the Revolution. Thompson received a "good English and classical education." When twenty-two years old he left Virginia and after a short residence in Louisville, Ky., settled in Lawrence County, Ind., where he taught school, worked in a store, and studied law at night. Coincident with his migration he sloughed off most of the political and cultural viewpoints that had been the heritage of his Virginia birth and took on those predominant in his adopted community. In 1834 he was admitted to the bar and began the practice of law at Bedford. For four terms,

1834 to 1838, he was a member of the Indiana legislature; and in 1840 and again in 1846 he was elected to the Senate. In 1843 he moved to Terre Haute. On May 5, 1836, he married Harriet Eliza Gardiner (d. Mar. 25, 1888), who bore him eight children. On several occasions Thompson was a presidential elector, first on the Whig and later on the Republican ticket. Presidents Taylor, Fillmore, and Lincoln made him proffers of offices, but he declined. He was active in the secession controversies and during the Civil War served as provost marshal for the Terre Haute district. He was a delegate to Republican National Conventions in 1868, 1876, and 1892, and in the last named nominated Benjamin Harrison for the presidency. In 1877 he was appointed secretary of the navy in the Hayes administration (appointment confirmed, Mar. 10, 1877). It has been affirmed that this was the only major appointment made by Hayes that was "dictated entirely by political considerations and it was the only bad one" (Eckenrode, *post,* p. 242). While holding this post he took the chairmanship of the American Committee of the Panama Canal Company at a salary of $25,000 yearly, thinking this no bar to his retaining his post in the cabinet, whereupon Hayes notified him "that his resignation (unoffered) had been accepted" (*Ibid.,* p. 303). Extremely partisan in politics, intolerant in religion, a lobbyist for railroads, Thompson was throughout his active life a figure about whom angry controversy swirled. Few of his contemporaries among public men were so frequently attacked on ethical grounds. Apart from politics and law the major interests of Thompson's life were speech-making and writing, and to these he devoted himself tirelessly whenever opportunity offered. His published writings include two volumes of historical essays, *Recollections of Sixteen Presidents* (1894), of considerable literary and historical merit; *The History of Protective Tariff Laws* (1888), a work of special pleading; and two volumes of polemics against the Catholic Church, *The Papacy and the Civil Power* (1876) and *The Footprints of the Jesuits* (1894), written, it has been said, while Thompson was "manifestly inspired by an undue fear of the Pope's protruding his official sway into American political life" (Bowers, *post,* p. 273).

In his personal relations Thompson was "a man of benevolence and unassuming manners," and throughout his life had hosts of friends, among them many who were at times his outspoken critics. In his old age the people of his state applied to him the affectionate designation of "the Grand Old Man." He loved children and never let pass an opportunity to be in their company. In his habits he was temperate, except in respect to smoking; for fifty years prior to his death he smoked an average of twenty cigars a day. He died in Terre Haute, Ind.

[See *Who's Who in America*, 1899–1900; *Richard W. Thompson Memorial* (copr. 1906); *Biog. Dir. Am. Cong.* (1928); Charles Lanman, *Dict. of the U. S. Cong.* (1869); *A Biog. Hist. of Eminent and Self-Made Men . . . of Ind.* (2 vols., 1880); G. W. Taylor, ed., *Biog. Sketches . . . of the Bench and Bar of Ind.* (1895), which contains a rather florid eulogy; Logan Esarey, *A Hist. of Ind.*, vol. II (1918); Charles Roll, *Ind., One Hundred and Fifty Years of Am. Development* (1931), vol. V, pp. 461–62; Francis Curtis, *The Republican Party . . . 1854–1904* (2 vols., 1904); H. J. Eckenrode, *Rutherford B. Hayes* (1930); C. G. Bowers, in *Green Bag*, June 1900; obituaries in *Sun* (N. Y.), Feb. 10, and *Sunday Sentinel* (Indianapolis), Feb. 11, 1900. Other sources include family information supplied by Thompson's daughter, Mrs. D. W. Henry, of Terre Haute, Ind.; correspondence with Ind. Hist. Soc.; and a letter written by Thompson in 1894, published in the *Culpeper Exponent*, Jan. 5, 1922, which deals with his ancestry and his early life in Va.] W.E.S—a.

THOMPSON, ROBERT ELLIS (Apr. 5, 1844–Oct. 19, 1924), educator, economist, was born of Scotch-Irish parents, Samuel and Catherine (Ellis) Thompson, near Lurgan, County Down, Ireland. As a child he attended the local country school and the Donaghloney Presbyterian Church. His father, driven by economic distress in Ireland, sold his freehold farm and came to Philadelphia in 1857. The boy attended successively the Hancock, Harrison Grammar, and Central High schools, completed his preparation for college at Faires' Classical Institute, and graduated from the University of Pennsylvania (A.B., 1865) with the highest honors. He had long planned to enter the ministry, and after graduating from the Reformed Presbyterian Seminary, Philadelphia, in 1867, was licensed to preach, and seven years later was ordained. After supplying vacant churches as far west as Illinois in 1867–68, he returned to the University as instructor in Latin and mathematics, and after three years was invited to give the newly established course in social science, being appointed professor in 1874. He became the first dean (1881–83) of the Wharton School of Finance and Economy, and continued to teach political economy after he was given (1883) the Welsh Professorship of History and English Literature. He had served in 1872–74 as librarian, was chaplain in 1889–91, and lectured widely on ethics and the social sciences in university extension courses.

Meanwhile, as an editor of the *Penn Monthly*, 1870–81, he was intimately associated with the Philadelphia protectionist group, including Henry C. Carey [*q.v.*], who became Thompson's economic mentor. On relinquishing this post he became an editor (1880–91) of the *American*, a weekly similarly devoted to economics, politics, and literature. He was on the staff of the *Irish World* from 1884 and of the *Sunday School Times* from 1892 to the end of his career. He was an editorial contributor to *Stoddart's Encyclopædia Americana* (4 vols., 1883–86), published as a supplement to the ninth edition of the *Encyclopædia Britannica*. The varied and voluminous reading and ready writing thus done added to his influence, his wealth of illustration, and his literary facility. His first book, *Social Science and National Economy* (1875), which he used as a text with his classes, enjoyed popularity elsewhere. Written with the encouragement of Joseph Wharton [*q.v.*], it was a talented exposition and vigorous defense of the position of the nationalist school of political economy, founded primarily upon the teachings of Carey but marked by Thompson's own personality. With him the nation became, and remained to the end of his life, not only an economic, political, and cultural entity, but an ordinance of God. His own nature fitted in with the buoyant views of the school; he attacked the Ricardian theory of rent and the Malthusian principle of population with more than academic ardor. His method was always in the main inductive, the result gaining much from aptness and concreteness of observation. After a pamphlet on *Hard Times and What to Learn from Them* (1877), came his *Elements of Political Economy* (1881), a revision of his earlier work. An active advocate of a high tariff policy in the Blaine-Cleveland campaign of 1884, he was invited the next year to give lectures at Harvard which were subsequently published under the title *Protection to Home Industry* (1886), an arsenal of persuasive argument. He gave similar lectures at other institutions.

Suddenly, in 1892, his connection of twenty-four years with the University of Pennsylvania was severed. He considered himself forced out. It is probable that his differences with Provost William Pepper [*q.v.*] were occasioned by conflict with younger members of the Wharton School faculty recently returned from German universities. He declined the presidency of Lake Forest College, and discouraged a movement to make him professor of Christian sociology in Princeton Theological Seminary—a consequence of his Stone lectures delivered there and published as *De Civitate Dei—The Divine Order of Human Society* (1891), in which, as in other of his writings on social ethics, he espoused national will to social improvement as against the controlling influence of economic materialism.

Thompson represents as well as anyone the unsuccessful struggle of national economic optimists against the rising tide of reformers, mainly socialists, who thought in international terms and preached class cleavage instead of a harmony of economic interests. In Thompson the moralist frequently threatened to hamper the economist.

In 1894 the second half of his career opened with his election to the presidency of the Central High School of Philadelphia. His early misgivings as to his executive capacity were banished by his brilliant success in greatly enlarging the school and enriching its instruction and influence. His cordial and intimate contacts with pupils and faculty produced an enthusiastic loyalty to him which was manifested on many occasions. He retired from the headship of the Central High School in 1920 in accordance with the new Retirement Act, after a vigorous protest by himself and many alumni and faculty members had failed, but he continued for a time his teaching of ethics and economics. He died in Philadelphia after a lingering illness. Thompson was twice married: in 1874, to Mary E. Neely who died July 8, 1894, and on Aug. 18, 1910, to her sister, Catherine Neely, who with two daughters and a son of his first marriage survived him. He was a large, heavy man, with bald head, drooping eyelids, and an engaging smile. His salient characteristics were conviction, spiritual, mental, and physical vigor, and personal magnetism. To the end of his life he wrote with a quill pen in very large characters, expressive of his positive temperament.

[Richard Montgomery, *Robert Ellis Thompson, a Memoir* (1934); *Who's Who in America*, 1924–25; L. R. Harley, *Confessions of a Schoolmaster and Other Essays* (1914); J. H. Bossard, "A History of Sociology at the University of Pennsylvania," in *Gen. Mag. and Hist. Chronicle* (Univ. of Pa.), April–July 1931; F. S. Edmonds, *Hist. of the Central High School of Phila.* (1902); *Public Ledger* (Phila.), Oct. 20, 1924.]
B. M.

THOMPSON, SAMUEL RANKIN (Apr. 17, 1833–Oct. 28, 1896), educator and scientist, was born at South Shenango, Crawford County, Pa. He was the son of William and Mary (Latta) Thompson, of Scotch and Irish descent. His early life was spent on his father's farm. In 1848, after three months at an academy in Greenville, he began teaching in Clarion County, Pa. From 1848 to 1856 he taught school in the winters and worked on the farm in the summers, with the exception of a year (perhaps 1854–55) in Nebraska, where he worked in a sawmill at Rockbluff. In his spare time he prepared himself for college entirely by home study; he often plowed with book tied to the plowhandle. He entered Westminster College at New Wilmington,

Pa., in 1856, and by alternate teaching and studying he finished with the class of 1860. At commencement time, however, he was serving as superintendent of schools for his home county, so it was not until 1863 that he could return to receive the degree of A.B. He received the degree of A.M. in 1881 from Westminster. He was superintendent of schools for Crawford County, Pa., 1860–65; professor of natural sciences and vice-principal of the state normal school, in Edinboro, Pa., 1865–67; and organizer and principal of the Pottsville, Pa., high school, 1868. He left Pottsville to organize a state normal school at Marshall College, Huntington, W. Va., which he conducted until 1871. In September 1871 he was elected professor of theoretical and practical agriculture at the University of Nebraska and began his work there in September 1872. He was the first dean of the College of Agriculture, which opened for the year 1872–73, and served in that position until December 1875. He was principal at the Nebraska State Normal School, Peru, 1876–77; superintendent of public instruction for Nebraska, 1878–81; superintendent of public schools, Lincoln, Nebr., for six months in 1882; and professor of agriculture at the University of Nebraska once more, with the added chair of didactics, 1882–84. In 1884 he returned to Westminster College as professor of physics and remained there until his death. At Rockbluff, Nebr., in 1859, he married Lucy Gilmour. They had one daughter, who died while a student in college, and whose memorial is the Mary Thompson Science Hall at Westminster College.

Thompson was an ambitious, talented, hardworking, and scholarly man, an influential pioneer in educational organization in three states. In Nebraska he organized the state weather service, started farmers' institutes, incorporated into the public school system some excellent features, and secured important school legislation. He was six feet, three inches tall, slender, of pleasant address and scholarly bearing, and his alert face with its bright blue eyes suggested his eager mind. In later life his white hair and full white beard gave him a prematurely venerable appearance. Restless, roving, and adventurous, he wrote little, preferring to teach, to travel, to plan, and to perform. The historical sketch of Westminster College in *A History of Higher Education in Pennsylvania* (1902), edited by C. H. Haskins and W. I. Hull, is from his pen. A report he wrote as dean of the University of Nebraska College of Agriculture, printed in the chancellor's report for 1874, reveals some of his ideas and ideals.

[R. P. Crawford, *These Fifty Years: a Hist. of the Coll. of Agriculture of the Univ of Nebr.* (1925); *Ann. Report: Nebr. State Board of Agriculture . . . 1896* (1897); *Pa. School Jour.*, Dec. 1896, pp. 292–93.]

J. I. W.

THOMPSON, SEYMOUR DWIGHT (Sept. 18, 1842–Aug. 11, 1904), jurist, was born in Will County, Ill., of English and Scotch-Irish ancestry, the son of Seymour and Betsy (McKee) Thompson. His father, a Presbyterian clergyman, had been compelled by the loss of his voice to give up the ministry and was endeavoring as a farmer to support a large family. In 1855 the Thompsons moved to a farm in Fayette County, Iowa, where in 1858 the father and a younger son were burned to death in a prairie fire. The survivors returned to relatives in Illinois. Seymour now undertook to support himself and to prepare for college. Without a permanent home, he managed to secure a fair education by attending Clark Seminary at Aurora, and Rock River Seminary at Mount Morris, working meanwhile as farm laborer, peddler, and grammar school teacher.

Ready for college when the Civil War began, he went back to Iowa and enlisted, May 21, 1861, in the 3rd Regiment of that state. He was made a first sergeant, Sept. 4, 1862, and in 1866 was mustered out of military service at Memphis, Tenn., with the rank of captain. He took part in the battle of Shiloh and the siege of Vicksburg, and witnessed the riotous burning by Union soldiers of Holly Springs, Miss. In 1864 he published *Recollections with the 3rd Iowa Regiment* an unromantic presentation of actual warfare. After the war he remained in Memphis for five years, making his living as a policeman, as a balloonist, as a court clerk, and, after he was admitted to the bar in 1869, as a self-educated lawyer. In 1872 he moved to St. Louis, where he soon attracted the attention of John Forrest Dillon [*q.v.*], then United States circuit judge. Dillon appointed Thompson to a fairly lucrative position as master in chancery, and in 1874 founded the *Central Law Journal* with himself as editor and Thompson as associate editor. In 1875 Thompson became editor of the publication and served in that position until 1878. From 1883 until his death, he was principal editor of the *American Law Review*. From 1880 to 1892 he was a judge of the St. Louis court of appeals, and from 1892 to 1898 practised law in St. Louis, although chiefly engaged in authorship. Thereafter until his death he maintained a law office in New York City for consulting work and also a residence in the suburbs, though he still claimed St. Louis as his legal domicile.

Thompson was a successful practitioner and a sound judge, but his distinction rests chiefly on his many widely read treatises, which, although designed primarily for the busy lawyer, were more than mere compilations of statutes and court decisions, since they contained vigorous and constructive criticism of law as announced by judges or established by statute. His more important works were *A Treatise on Homestead and Exemption Laws* (1878), *The Law of Negligence in Relations Not Resting in Contract* (2 vols., 1880), *A Treatise on the Law of Trials* (2 vols., 1889), and *Commentaries on the Law of Private Corporations* (7 vols., 1895–99). This last work was the most extensive legal treatise on a single topic ever published in the English language up to the time of Thompson's death (Lawson, *post*, p. 174). Several of Thompson's works have appeared in amplified posthumous editions. He was a hard and rapid worker in the tasks of authorship but generally had earnest pupils as assistants. In January 1865 he married Lucy A. Jennison, who with three sons and two daughters survived him. He died in East Orange, N. J.

[Thompson's judicial opinions appear in 9–53 *Mo. Appellate Reports*. For biog. data, see A. J. D. Stewart, *The Hist. of the Bench and Bar of Mo.* (1898); *Am. Law Rev.*, Sept.–Oct. 1904; *Central Law Jour.*, Sept. 16, 1904; J. D. Lawson, in *Proc. . . . Mo. Bar Asso. . . . 1904* (1905); *Report . . . Am. Bar Asso.*, 1904; *Chicago Legal News*, Oct. 20, 1904; *N. Y. Times*, Aug. 13, 1904; information from a son and a daughter.]

T. W.

THOMPSON, SMITH (Jan. 17, 1768–Dec. 18, 1843), jurist, was born in the town of Amenia (Stanford), Dutchess County, N. Y., the son of Ezra and Rachel (Smith) Thompson. His father was a descendant of Anthony Thompson who arrived in Boston in 1637 and subsequently settled at Milford in the New Haven colony. Smith Thompson graduated from the College of New Jersey (Princeton) in 1788, and studied law in Poughkeepsie under James Kent [*q.v.*], supporting himself meanwhile by teaching school. He was admitted to the bar in 1792 and practised for a time in Troy, but returned to Poughkeepsie in 1793 when Kent went to New York City. In 1794 he married Sarah, daughter of Gilbert Livingston of Poughkeepsie, a member of the powerful Livingston family, and thereafter he was affiliated with the Jeffersonian Republicans of the anti-Burr faction in New York. He was elected to the state legislature in 1800 and represented Dutchess County in the constitutional convention of 1801. The same year he was appointed district attorney for the middle district but his appointment as associate justice of the supreme court of New York on Jan.

8, 1802, prevented his serving. In 1807 the Council of Appointment offered him the mayoralty of New York City, but he declined it, remaining on the bench. On Feb. 25, 1814, he was made chief justice in place of Kent, who became chancellor.

In November 1818 Thompson was appointed secretary of the navy by Monroe. He assumed his duties Jan. 1, 1819, and served until Aug. 31, 1823, when he resigned to accept appointment to the associate justiceship on the Supreme Court left vacant by the death of Henry Brockholst Livingston [q.v.], a position for which both Kent and Van Buren were strongly urged. Thompson debated accepting the appointment for some time because of his poor health, the low salary, and his lack of judicial experience in fields outside the common law, but mainly because he thought the Republicans might nominate him for the presidency in 1824. Finally convinced that he had no chance for the nomination against John Quincy Adams and William H. Crawford, he accepted the judicial appointment and remained on the Court until his death. His judicial duties did not quiet his political ambitions, however. In 1828 he allowed himself to be nominated for the governorship of New York by a badly divided National Republican party and ran against Martin Van Buren [q.v.] in one of the bitterest and most spectacular campaigns the state had seen. He was sharply criticized by his Jacksonian opponents for running for political office without resigning from the Court, and was defeated by a vote of 136,794 to 106,444.

On the Supreme Court Thompson joined the group which had already begun to pull away from the strong nationalism of Marshall. The death of his daughter prevented his taking his seat in February 1824 until after the arguments in *Gibbons* vs. *Ogden* (9 *Wheaton,* 1) had been heard, and he did not participate in the decision. Had he done so he would probably have disagreed with Marshall, since in 1812 he had rendered a decision in the New York court of errors upholding the power of the state to create the steamboat monopoly (*Livingston* vs. *Van Ingen,* 9 *Johnson,* 507, at p. 563). He dissented in *Brown* vs. *Maryland* (12 *Wheaton,* 419), in 1827, in which the Court held void a state license tax on imports in the original package, and in the same year he helped overrule Marshall in *Ogden* vs. *Saunders* (12 *Wheaton,* 214), writing a strong concurring opinion upholding the validity of a state bankruptcy law. He dissented in 1830 from Marshall's decision in *Craig* vs. *Missouri* (4 *Peters,* 410), holding certain state certificates void as bills of credit, and wrote a concurring

opinion in the later case (1837) of *Briscoe* vs. *Bank of Kentucky* (11 *Peters,* 257), upholding the note issue of a state-owned bank. He concurred in a separate opinion in *Mayor of New York* vs. *Miln* (11 *Peters,* 102), 1837, holding valid certain state regulations affecting foreign and interstate commerce, and although personally a bitter opponent of slavery, in 1842 he expressed his agreement with *Prigg* vs. *Pennsylvania* (16 *Peters,* 539), upholding the federal Fugitive Slave Act. He dissented with Story in *Charles River Bridge* vs. *Warren Bridge* (11 *Peters,* 420), 1837, and also dissented in *Cherokee Nation* vs. *Georgia* (5 *Peters,* 1), 1831. The most notable case in which Thompson spoke for the Court was that of *Kendall* vs. *United States* (12 *Peters,* 524), 1838, upholding the right of the federal courts to require a cabinet officer by *mandamus* to perform a ministerial duty. Thompson's oral opinion in this case contained a paragraph vigorously rejecting the theory attributed to Jackson that the president under his power to see that the laws are faithfully executed may enforce his own interpretation of the Constitution by extending protection to his subordinates when they violate the acts of Congress or the mandates of the courts. This paragraph was expunged at the request of Attorney-General Benjamin F. Butler [q.v.], who denied that such a theory had been urged in argument. It is significant as a judicial repudiation of a theory of executive independence generally supposed to have been held by Jackson and Lincoln (see Warren, *post,* II, 317 ff.). Thompson wrote the opinion of the Court in eighty-five cases, few of which related to constitutional matters. He wrote eleven dissenting opinions and five concurring opinions.

In 1836, after the death of his first wife, Thompson married her cousin Eliza, daughter of Henry Livingston. Two sons and two daughters were born of the first marriage and one son and two daughters, of the second. Egbert Thompson [q.v.] was his nephew. In 1813 he was made one of the regents of the University of the State of New York. He was a strong Presbyterian and a vice-president of the American Bible Society. He was small in stature, reserved in manner and speech, but kind and affable upon close acquaintance. He died in Poughkeepsie in his seventy-sixth year.

[Thompson's opinions in the Supreme Court appear in 9 *Wheaton* to 16 *Peters,* inclusive. Biog. material appears in *Law Reporter,* Jan. 1844; A. B. Street, *The Council of Revision of the State of N. Y.* (1859); Charles Warren, *The Supreme Court in U. S. Hist.* (1922), vol. II, *passim*; H. L. Carson, *The Supreme Court of the U. S.* (1891); D. S. Alexander, *A Political Hist. of the State of N. Y.,* vol. I (1906); Alden Chester, *Courts and Lawyers of N. Y.* (1925); W. B.

Thompson, *Thompson Lineage* (1911); *N. Y. Herald,*
Dec. 20, 1843, and *N. Y. Tribune,* Dec. 20, 1843, which
gives incorrect date for death.]   R. E. C.

THOMPSON, THOMAS LARKIN (May
31, 1838–Feb. 1, 1898), editor, congressman, diplomat, son of Robert Augustine and
Mary (Slaughter) Thompson, was born in
Charleston, Va. (now W. Va.). His father and
grandfather, Philip Rootes Thompson, were both
members of Congress. His great-grandfather,
John Thompson, was an Irish Presbyterian minister who came to America in the eighteenth century. At twelve the boy went to work in the office of the *West Virginian* at Charleston. In
1853–54 he attended Buffalo Academy in Putnam
County. The next year he went to San Francisco,
where he worked on the *San Francisco Herald*
until 1858, except for an interlude in 1855–56
when, at the age of seventeen, he established the
*Petaluma Weekly Journal and Sonoma County
Advertiser* at Petaluma, Cal. The two years following he worked in the San Francisco post office. In 1859 he married Marion Satterlee,
daughter of Judge William Satterlee of San
Francisco; of this union one son and four daughters were born. Thompson published the *Sonoma
Democrat* (Santa Rosa, Cal.) from 1860 to 1868,
and the *Solano Democrat* (weekly) and the *Vallejo Daily Independent* at Vallejo, Cal., for the
ensuing five years. In 1871 he again purchased
the *Sonoma Democrat* and in 1873 settled permanently in Santa Rosa. He was a delegate to the
Democratic national conventions of 1880 and
1892. From 1882 to 1886 he was secretary of
state of California. He was elected in 1886 to the
Fiftieth Congress, where he served on the rivers
and harbors and invalid pensions committees.

In 1893 Thompson was appointed by President
Cleveland envoy extraordinary and minister plenipotentiary to Brazil. On his arrival at Rio de
Janeiro, Aug. 25, a diplomatic situation of the
most difficult kind confronted him. The capital
of the four-year-old republic was seething with
revolutionary ferment, which burst into actual
civil war when the Brazilian navy revolted on
Sept. 6 and threatened to bombard the city.
American property and lives were jeopardized,
and South Americans and Europeans jealously
watched for evidence of interference in the internal politics of Brazil by the United States.
Thompson determined to protect American interests and to preserve as impartial an attitude
as possible. During the six months that elapsed
before the surrender of the revolutionists the
United States minister, working in harmony
with other members of the diplomatic corps,
maintained a friendly attitude toward the na-

tional government without allowing himself to
become committed to its support. He refused to
become involved in the revolutionary movement
even to the extent of announcing American neutrality, which would have given the revolting
party the status of belligerents. At the same time,
through his cooperation with United States
naval officers, American commerce was protected
and continued with practically no interruption
throughout the whole period. Disastrous shell-
ing of the capital was also prevented. A less
rigidly maintained position on the part of the
minister might have resulted in a different outcome of the conflict, but the announced intention
of the revolutionists to establish a monarchy precluded either popular or official sympathy in the
United States. As it was, many of the leading
American newspapers of the day wrongly accused
Thompson of favoring the revolutionists. Many
evidences of good will for the United States in
Brazil followed the termination of the naval
revolt; in connection with the presidential inauguration ceremonies on Nov. 15, 1894, the
cornerstone of a monument to the memory of
James Monroe and the Monroe Doctrine was laid
in Rio de Janeiro. Thompson resigned in 1897,
but before his return home he had negotiated and
signed an extradition treaty for the United States
with Brazil (ratified 1903). For many years he
had been suffering from an ear infection, and following his return to his home in Santa Rosa,
Cal., his health failed rapidly. On Feb. 1, 1898,
while temporarily deranged, he took his own life.
His wife and all five of his children survived
him.

[R. T. Green, *Geneal. and Hist. Notes on Culpeper
County, Va.* (1900); J. P. Munro-Fraser, *Hist. of Sonoma County* (1880); W. J. Davis, *Hist. of Political
Conventions in Cal.* (1893); *Biog. Dir. Am. Cong.*
(1928); *Papers Relating to the Foreign Relations of
the U. S.,* 1893, 1894, 1895, 1897; L. F. Hill, *Diplomatic Relations between the U. S. and Brazil* (1932);
San Francisco Chronicle, Feb. 2, 1898; *Examiner* (San
Francisco), Feb. 2, 1898.]   I. L. T.

THOMPSON, WADDY (Sept. 8, 1798–Nov.
23, 1868), congressman from South Carolina,
diplomat, was born in Pickensville, south of the
present town of Easley, S. C., the son of Waddy
Thompson, a distinguished lawyer and a successful local politician, and Eliza (Blackburn)
Thompson, both natives of Virginia. He was the
uncle of Hugh Smith Thompson [*q.v.*]. Young
Waddy was graduated from South Carolina College, now the University of South Carolina, in
1814. He afterward studied law in the private
offices of two South Carolina lawyers and was
admitted to the bar in 1819. After practising for
five years in Edgefield, where he married Em-
mala Butler, the daughter of William Butler,

1759–1821 [*q.v.*] and the sister of Andrew and Pierce M. Butler [*qq.v.*], he removed to Greenville. In 1826 the Greenville District elected him to the state legislature and he served in that body until 1830, when he retired because he was not in accord with the Union sentiment of his constituency. He was then chosen by the legislature as solicitor for the Western District. Opposed to the tariffs of 1824 and 1828, he became an ardent Nullifier and was made a brigadier-general in the forces organized to defend his state against Federal interference, an office that he held until 1842. In 1835 he was the successful Whig candidate to fill the vacancy in Congress caused by the death of Warren R. Davis, and he continued to represent the Greenville District in that capacity until 1841 despite the vigorous opposition of John C. Calhoun, who had gone over to the Democratic party and wished to carry the state with him. Although no candidate announced against Thompson for the campaign of 1840, he decided to retire from the political arena.

Early in 1842, however, the Whig administration appointed him as minister to Mexico. His appointment to the post might have appeared unwise, for his career in Congress had been conspicuous for his hostility to John Quincy Adams with respect to anti-slavery petitions, and for his advocacy first of the recognition and then of the annexation of Texas. Nevertheless, his mission met with a considerable degree of success. He obtained the release of some three hundred prisoners, citizens of the United States in the main, who had been captured during the desultory war between Mexico and Texas; made some progress in the settlement of claims; persuaded the Mexican government not to exclude American immigrants from California; obtained minor commercial concessions; and at one time set in motion negotiations that appeared to promise the peaceful acquisition of California. He won the respect and friendship of the Mexicans and returned to the United States in 1844 an ardent friend of Mexico. Two years later he published his *Recollections* (1846) of his mission, a calm, judicious volume still cited by historians.

Returning to Greenville he resumed his legal practice and accumulated a small fortune in South Carolina and Florida real estate. After the death of his first wife, he married in 1851 Cornelia Jones of Wilmington, N. C., who with their one son survived him. Soon after 1852 he built on the top of Paris Mountain, really a hill about 2,000 feet above sea level, a luxurious house equipped with almost every known convenience and filled with books, paintings, and curios. He might have reëntered politics, if he

had not been too honest to trim his sails to the popular breeze. Disapproving the war with Mexico and doubting the expediency of secession, he preferred to retire to private life. As the result of the Civil War, he lost his fortune. Early in 1867 he removed to Madison, Fla., where he still owned a plantation. His death occurred during a visit to Tallahassee.

[Much of Thompson's personal correspondence was destroyed by fire in 1901; the remainder appears to be in the hands of Waddy Thompson, Atlanta, Ga.; his diplomatic correspondence may be found in the state department archives and his speeches in the *Congressional Globe*; a few letters are in the Lib. of Cong.; see also H. T. Thompson, *Waddy Thompson, Jr.* (rev. ed., 1929); G. L. Rives, *The U. S. and Mexico* (2 vols., 1913); J. M. Callahan, *Am. Foreign Policy in Mexican Relations* (1932); *Charleston Daily Courier*, Nov. 27, 1868.]
J.F.R.

THOMPSON, WILEY (Sept. 23, 1781–Dec. 28, 1835), congressman from Georgia, Indian agent, was born in Amelia County, Va., the son of Isham and Elizabeth (Williams) Thompson. His father, a soldier of the Revolution, removed to Wilkes, now Elbert County, Ga. Educated in the county school, there, Wiley soon rose to local prominence and was appointed by the legislature to be commissioner of the Elbert County academy in 1808. He served in the War of 1812, was elected in 1817 major-general of the 4th Division of Georgia militia, and resigned in 1824. In 1819 he served on a commission to determine the boundary line between Georgia and East Florida (Gov. William Rabun to Secretary of War, Feb. 19, 1819, Georgia Department of Archives and History, Atlanta). He was a member of the state Senate from 1817 to 1819, when he resigned. He served in the federal House of Representatives from 1821 to 1833. As chairman of the committee of military affairs he obtained payment of Georgia militia claims of 1793 and 1824. A bitter opponent of protection, he expressed the view that the South would "be driven to the necessity of resistance" and, while he loved the Union, that "he 'would go with him who goes the farthest' in an effort to stave off oppression" (*Register of Debates*, 21 Cong., 2 Sess., col. 573; 22 Cong., 1 Sess., col. 3733).

In close accord with Jackson on Indian removal, he was appointed as agent of the Seminole Indians in Florida. Instructed to superintend the removal of the Indians on the Apalachicola and Chattahoochee rivers under the treaties of Payne's Landing of 1832, and Fort Gibson of 1833, he won the friendship of some of the chiefs and in 1834 led John Blount and Davy Elliott, with their bands, to New Orleans, where he paid them $8,000 of their allowance in cash. This action was approved by Elbert Herring, then commissioner of Indian affairs. In council after his return, he found some of the chiefs unwilling to emigrate. He made clear Jackson's determination that they go, but Osceola [q.v.] led a group that threatened resistance. Thompson then ordered the sale of liquor and ammunition to the Indians and the purchase of their slaves stopped, and he asked for troops to aid in removal. Jackson approved the order forbidding trade and ordered Gen. Duncan L. Clinch with troops to Florida. On July 8, 1834, Thompson was appointed "superintendent of emigration" and was to continue also as Seminole agent. In a council of 1835 he agreed that the Seminole should be transported by water in one body, rather than overland in three annual parties, as the earlier treaties had provided. When Osceola was still hostile and interrupted the council, Thompson harshly rebuked him and removed him and four other disgruntled chiefs, an action that General Clinch termed as judicious handling of the difficulty. Jackson, however, forbade the removal of chiefs, believing it would arouse hostility, and the press condemned Thompson's action as high-handed and tyrannical. Osceola, still obdurate, later visited Fort King and used abusive language toward Thompson and the United States government because of the forced removal and the seizure of his young wife as a slave. Thompson warned him and then put him in chains but finally released Osceola, who pretended to be penitent and returned a few days later with seventy-nine recalcitrants who appeared to agree to emigrate. However, with a band of sixty warriors Osceola lay in wait for two days near Fort King. As Thompson and Lieut. Constantine Smith were walking, the band attacked and shot Thompson dead, and then scalped him. He was buried at Fort King but later his wife, formerly Mrs. Ellington, had his body removed to Elberton, Ga., where it was buried on his estate.

[Biog. Dir. Am. Cong. (1928); J. T. Sprague, The Origin, Progress, and Conclusion of the Fla. War (1848); C. M. Brevard, "A Hist. of Fla.," Fla. State Hist. Soc. Pubs., no. 4, vol. I (1924); Army and Navy Chronicle, Jan. 21, Feb. 18, Mar. 31, Apr. 7, 1836; Niles' Weekly Register, Jan. 30, 1836, Nov. 4, 1837; Hist. Colls. of the Ga. Chapters, D.A.R., "Records of Elbert County," vol. III (1930); Daily Savannah Republican, Jan. 9, 11, 20, 1836.]   F. M. G.

THOMPSON, WILL LAMARTINE (Nov. 7, 1847–Sept. 20, 1909), writer of sacred and secular songs, was born in Beaver County, Pa., one of seven children of Josiah and Sarah (Jackman) Thompson. His grandfather, William Thompson, had emigrated to Pennsylvania from Ireland. His father was a merchant and a banker, and served for two terms in the state legislature of Ohio. His father's family were all musical, and, after attending the public schools of East Liverpool, Ohio, and Mount Union College, Alliance, Ohio, Thompson began the serious study of music in 1870 at the Boston Music School. Later he studied at the Boston Conservatory of Music and then went to Leipzig, Germany. One of his earliest compositions was a *Schottische* which he named for his home town, "Liverpool"; another was a song, "Gathering Shells from the Seashore," written in 1872. When his price of one hundred dollars for this and three other compositions was refused by a Cleveland publisher, he undertook the management of the sales for himself, the song having been published in New York. It was introduced upon the stage by the Carncross and Dixey Minstrel Company of Philadelphia, and its popularity became so great that the presses were kept running day and night for several months to meet the demand. Thompson's financial returns from it ran above one thousand dollars during the first year. About 1875 he organized a music publishing business and store at East Liverpool, Ohio.

Some of his other popular secular songs are "Drifting with the Tide," "My Home on the Old Ohio," and "The Old Tramp," which during the financial troubles of 1876–77 was on everyone's lips—"I'm only a poor old wanderer, I've no place to call my home." His humorous mode is illustrated by "My First Music Lesson" and "My Sweetheart and I Went Fishing"; among his other compositions are the "Protective Tariff March," "God Save Our Union," a patriotic song, and "Come Where the Lilies Bloom." It is perhaps by his sacred songs that he will be longest remembered, for these have been introduced into many hymn books. The best known is "Softly and Tenderly Jesus Is Calling," which has been translated into many languages. "There's a Great Day Coming" (1903), "Golden Years Are Passing By" (1879), "Jesus Is All the World to Me," "Lead Me Gently Home," and "The Sinner and the Song" are his, both words and music, and he wrote the music for "Break the News Gently to Mother" (1878), the words of which were by Allie E. Wardwell of East Liverpool.

Thompson made his home at East Liverpool, where he established a music store. He later became president of the Thompson Music Company, Chicago. He married Elizabeth Johnston at Wellsville, Ohio, on Apr. 23, 1891. He died in New York at the end of a summer spent abroad with his wife and son. Among the books he published are *Enduring Hymns* (n.d.), *The New Century Hymnal* (copyright 1904), and *The Young People's Choir* (n.d.).

[H. B. Barth, *Hist. of Columbiana County, Ohio* (1926), vol. II, pp. 453–55; *Hist. of the Upper Ohio Valley* (1891), vol. II, pp. 362–65; *Who's Who in America,* 1908–09; C. B. Galbreath, in *Ohio Archaeological and Hist. Quart.,* July 1905; *Musical Million,* Oct. 1909; *Classmate,* Dec. 13, 1913; J. H. Hall, *Biog. of Gospel Song and Hymn Writers* (copr. 1914); C. H. Gabriel, *Gospel Songs and their Writers* (1915), which gives incorrect dates of birth and death; obituary in *Ohio State Jour.* (Columbus), Sept. 21, 1909.]

F. J. M—f.

THOMPSON, WILLIAM (1736–Sept. 3, 1781), Revolutionary soldier, was born in Ireland. Emigrating to America, he settled on a farm near Carlisle, Pa., where he became a surveyor and justice of the peace. During the French and Indian war, he was commissioned captain of a troop of horse and participated in the expedition led by John Armstrong, 1717–1795 [*q.v.*], against Kittanning. He took part in the work of settling the western boundary of Pennsylvania and in locating lands granted by the king to officers serving in the war.

On July 12, 1774, at a meeting of the freeholders from several townships of Cumberland County, called to denounce the closing of the port of Boston, he was elected member of a committee of correspondence; and later, in May 1775, he served upon the provincial committee of safety. When the news of the battle of Bunker Hill reached Pennsylvania, he was placed in command of a battalion of riflemen raised in the southeastern counties, designated at first as the 2nd Pennsylvania Regiment but later as the 1st Continental Infantry. Marching promptly to Boston, it won credit as the first body of men to reach that point from the South. It constituted a crack corps, the privates being unusually "stout and hardy; many of them exceeding six feet and remarkable for the accuracy of their aim." They were dressed in "white frocks, or rifle shirts, and round hats" (James Thacher, *A Military Journal during the American Revolutionary War,* 1823, pp. 37–38). During the siege they were posted on Prospect Hill. On Nov. 9, 1775, they repulsed an attack upon Lechmere Point, for which Thompson was thanked by Washington in general orders (J. C. Fitzpatrick, *The Writings of George Washington,* vol. IV, 1931, p. 79). On Mar. 1, 1776, he was promoted to the rank of brigadier-general and was presently ordered to Canada in charge of a detachment of about 2,000 men, comprising the regiments of Poor, Paterson, Greaton, and Bond. General Sullivan, commanding the American forces on the St. Lawrence, directed him to attack Three Rivers. On the night of June 7, he crossed the stream a few miles above the town, hoping to surprise the foe at dawn, but owing to the treach-

ery of a guide, his men got lost in a swamp and were repulsed while he was made prisoner.

On Oct. 25, 1780, he was exchanged for Baron Riedesel. Prior to this, however, he was placed on parole and returned to Pennsylvania. Here he became involved in a controversy with Thomas McKean [*q.v.*], then serving as a member of Congress, whom he accused of hindering his exchange. He submitted a memorial to Congress in which he referred to McKean in such opprobrious terms that, on Nov. 23, 1778, that body voted that he was "guilty of an insult to the honor and dignity of this house, and of a breach of privilege" (W. C. Ford, *Journals of Continental Congress,* vol. XII, 1908, p. 1151). He was summoned before Congress and tendered an apology. McKean sued him for libel and was awarded £5,700 damages, which he released, since he only desired to see the law and the facts settled (see Peeling, *post*). Thompson died and was buried in Carlisle. His energy, fearlessness, and pugnacity admirably qualified him to occupy high command in an army whose plight was often desperate.

[The Pennsylvania Historical Society possesses manuscript letters of Thompson. Consult also J. H. Peeling, "Life of Thomas McKean," Ph.D. thesis, n.s., Univ. of Chicago; J. T. Scharf and Thompson Westcott, *Hist. of Philadelphia* (1884), vol. I; *Pa. Mag. of Hist. and Biog.,* Apr. 1883, July 1911; *Centennial Memorial of the Presbytery of Carlisle* (2 vols., 1889); J. H. Smith, *Our Struggle for the Fourteenth Colony* (1907), vol. II; E. C. Burnett, ed., *Letters of Members of the Continental Cong.,* vols. I–IV (1921–28); S. W. Parkinson, *Memories of Carlisle's Old Graveyard* (1930); *Pa. Gazette and Weekly Advertiser,* Sept. 12, 1781.]

E. E. C.

THOMPSON, WILLIAM BOYCE (May 13, 1869–June 27, 1930), miner, financier, philanthropist, was born at Virginia City, then a Montana mining camp of ebbing fortunes. He was the elder son of William Thompson, a native of Canada who had lived in the United States since 1853, and of Anne (Boyce), a Missourian of Virginian ancestry. His father, a carpenter by trade, arrived in Virginia City at the height of the gold excitement of 1863; during the territory's pioneer stage he did considerable building and also operated lumber mills. In 1880 he moved his family to Butte, Mont. Stimulated mentally by the principal of the Butte high school, a young Englishman from Balliol College, Oxford, William elected at eighteen to go East to Phillips Exeter Academy in New Hampshire because Daniel Webster had studied there. His father was beginning to develop gold, silver, and copper mining claims in Montana, and in 1889, without graduating, the son went from Exeter to the School of Mines of Columbia University. After one year, however, he returned to

Montana as superintendent of an unsuccessful silver mine. For a time he was secretary of a lumber company of his father's, for a time a coal dealer in Helena. In 1897 he returned to Butte, where he dealt in real estate, mines, and insurance, and recovered a considerable amount of copper from the Butte ore dumps. He was among the first to see the possibilities of working low-grade ores with improved machinery on a large scale, thus utilizing claims that had been abandoned as unprofitable. When, after years of experimentation, he believed he had the technical key to successful mass production he interested capital in his projects.

After a brief attempt to sell mining stocks in New York City (1899), he spent five years developing a copper mine in Arizona. Returning to New York in 1904, he opened a broker's office, operating on the Curb; he was one of the few men dealing in copper stocks in Wall Street who knew at first hand the actual conditions of existing and prospective mining properties. The Nipissing silvermine, which he launched in 1906, laid the foundation of his great fortune. Into Inspiration Copper Company in Gila County, Ariz., he put $17,000,000 before a dollar was taken out, but the first year the mine was operated it showed a net profit of $20,000,000. He became interested in mining properties in all parts of the world and his investments yielded large returns. He was active in politics as a Republican, and was a director of the Federal Reserve Bank of New York for six years (1914-19). Becoming intensely interested in Robert Kennedy Duncan [q.v.] and his scheme of industrial fellowships, he provided thirty-six temporary fellowships in the Mellon Institute, Pittsburgh.

At the beginning of the World War, Thompson bought a considerable interest in Bethlehem Steel and during the conflict entered many other fields which gave him bountiful returns. He was a leader in securing funds for Herbert Hoover's Belgian relief work, and was instrumental in promoting the passage of the first "daylight saving" law. In 1917, having offered to pay the expenses of the American Red Cross mission to Russia, he was sent with that expedition as business manager and after the withdrawal of Dr. Franklin Billings, became its leader. He labored, though vainly, to secure aid from the United States for the Kerensky régime and contributed a million dollars to finance a propaganda campaign designed to keep the Russian army fighting on the Eastern front. After the overthrow of Kerensky, he urged recognition and aid of the new Soviet government by the Allies.

Upon his return to the United States, he be-

came a promoter of Theodore Roosevelt, whom he had opposed in 1912 and 1916, as a candidate for the presidential nomination; after Roosevelt's death in January 1919, Thompson headed the Roosevelt Memorial Association (1919-24). At the Republican National Convention of 1920 he supported Leonard Wood, then Will Hays, but as chairman of the party's ways and means committee raised Harding's campaign fund. His reward for this service was appointment as a United States commissioner to attend the celebration of the centenary of Peru's independence, and as a member of an advisory council connected with the Washington Conference on the Limitation of Armament (1921-22).

Thompson's lifelong interest in vegetable growth was manifested in his personal direction of the planting of his extensive estate "Alder," at Yonkers, N. Y., and of his estate near Superior, Ariz. In 1919 he organized the Farm and Research Corporation for the investigation of plant life. In 1923, after some revision of the plans, the title of this foundation was changed to Boyce Thompson Institute for Plant Research; a liberal endowment was provided; suitable buildings were erected at Yonkers and dedicated in 1924; and before Thompson's death the Institute had already made important advances in botanical experimentation. He also established the Boyce Thompson Southwestern Arboretum in Arizona and gave large sums of money to Phillips Exeter Academy. The bulk of his large estate was left to his wife, Gertrude (Hickman) Thompson, whom he had married on Feb. 6, 1895, and to their daughter.

[Hermann Hagedorn, *The Magnate: William Boyce Thompson and His Time* (1935); *Who's Who in America*, 1930-31; *Inspiration Consolidated Copper Company: Reports*, 1915, 1916; Bessie Beatty, "Gold and Fool's Gold," *Asia* (N. Y.), Aug. 1918; *The Roosevelt Memorial Asso. . . . Report*, 1919-21, 1921-22, 1923, 1924; J. M. Coulter, "Boyce Thompson Institute for Plant Research," *Scientific Monthly*, Aug. 1926; *Contributions from Boyce Thompson Institute for Plant Research, Inc.*, vol. I (1929), containing addresses at the opening of the Institute; *N. Y. Times*, June 28, July 4, 1930; memorandum from William Crocker, Esq., director of the Boyce Thompson Institute for Plant Research, Apr. 3, 1933.]   W. B. S.

THOMPSON, WILLIAM GILMAN (Dec. 25, 1856-Oct. 27, 1927), physician and pioneer in industrial hygiene, was born in New York City, the son of Joseph Parrish Thompson [q.v.], and his second wife, Elizabeth Coit Gilman. Daniel Coit Gilman [q.v.] was his uncle. He received his early education in private schools and the Hopkins Grammar School, New Haven, Conn., with one year of study in Karlsruhe, Germany. He was graduated from Yale with the Ph.B. degree in 1877 and proceeded to the College of

Physicians and Surgeons in New York City. His work here was interrupted by the death of his father in Europe. He crossed the sea at once and spent a year studying at the medical departments of King's College, London, and the University of Berlin. He returned to the United States and received the M.D. degree from Columbia in 1881. In 1885 he won the Joseph Mather Smith prize for his essay, "Structure of the Heart Valves," and the Harsen prize for his essay, "Photography of the Living Heart in Motion." He served for eighteen months as interne of the New York Hospital, and then was appointed visiting physician to the Bloomingdale Asylum at White Plains, N. Y., and at the New York Cancer Hospital. In 1887 he became visiting physician of the New York Hospital and the Presbyterian, serving the former for seven years and the latter for twenty-five. He was made "quiz master" at the College of Physicians and Surgeons in 1884–85, and in 1887 became professor of physiology at the University of the City of New York. He held this chair until 1898. From 1898 until 1916 he served as professor of medicine at Cornell University Medical College in New York City and was then made professor emeritus.

He introduced important changes in the methods of teaching physiology, and was one of the first physicians in America to develop clinical research along with laboratory investigation. When the Loomis Laboratory, the first institute of experimental medicine in America, was opened in 1888, he was made director. He knew the value of clinical research and spent much of his life in the study of disease at the bedside. On his retirement from Cornell, he plunged into the work for which he has become best known—re-education in connection with war and industrial diseases. For many years he was chairman of the Industrial Hygiene Division of the New York Labor Department, organized to carry out a scientific study of hygienic conditions in industries. During the World War he organized a functional reëducational clinic, and from that developed the Reconstruction Hospital, of which he was the founder. Under his direction chronic patients and incurables were taught to do constructive and interesting work.

A dynamic man of untiring energy, he devoted his life to his work and left little time for hobbies. He was forceful and progressive, remarkable for his affability in spite of the fact that among his associates he had few intimate friends. He held offices in the New York Botanical Society and the Garden Club, and was a member of many medical societies in New York. He was considered an authority on foods, and his *Practical Dietetics* (1895) went through many editions. He wrote numerous medical articles which were published in medical journals, newspapers, and textbooks (for bibliography, see Shrady, *post*). He was co-editor, with A. L. Loomis, of *System of Practical Medicine by American Authors* (4 volumes, 1897–98), and author of *Training-Schools for Nurses* (1883), *Text-book of Practical Medicine* (1900), and *Occupational Diseases* (1914). He was married on Aug. 11, 1887, to Harriet Howard Pomeroy, daughter of John Norton Pomeroy [*q.v.*], whom he survived by a few months. He died of heart disease.

[*Who's Who in America*, 1926–27; Ledyard Bill, *Hist. of the Bill Family* (1867); F. W. Chapman, *Coit Family* (1874); John Shrady, ed., *The Coll. of Physicians and Surgeons, A Hist.* (1903–04?), vol. I; J. J. Moorhead, Address at the Unveiling of a Memorial Tablet to Dr. Thompson at the Reconstruction Hospital, May 16, 1933; *N. Y. Times*, Oct. 28, 31, 1927.]

G. L. A.

THOMPSON, WILLIAM OXLEY (Nov. 5, 1855–Dec. 9, 1933), Presbyterian clergyman, university president, the eldest of ten children of David Glenn Thompson and Agnes Miranda (Oxley) Thompson, was born in Cambridge, Ohio, and spent his early years there, in New Concord, and in Zanesville. His paternal grandfather was a native of the North of Ireland; his father was a shoemaker and farmer who served in the Civil War. William's elementary education was interrupted by the war and limited by the short term of the rural schools; when not studying he worked as a farm hand at eight dollars per month. In 1870 he entered Muskingum College but was able to attend only at intervals, between periods of laboring on the farm and teaching school. It took him eight years to complete the course, but he graduated first in his class in 1878. He subsequently taught for a time in the academy at Indiana, Pa.

In early life Thompson had determined to be a missionary, and accordingly he entered the Western Theological Seminary (Presbyterian), Allegheny, Pa., from which he graduated in 1882, again with honors. In the same year he married Rebecca Jane Allison and accepted an appointment to a Presbyterian mission church in Odebolt, Iowa, being ordained at Fort Dodge on July 13, 1882. In Odebolt, a town of some six hundred, his genius as a leader of religious and community activities manifested itself, his interests extending into every community within the traveling range of his team. In 1885 he removed to Longmont, Colo., where for six years he served as pastor of the local Presbyterian church and president of the newly established Synodical

College. In 1886 his wife died, leaving one daughter, and in October 1887 he married Helen Starr Brown of Longmont, who bore him two sons. After her death in 1890 he sought a return to Ohio, and in 1891 was elected president of Miami University at Oxford. On June 28, 1894, he married Estelle Godfrey Clark, a member of the faculty of Oxford College for Women.

His success at Miami was such that in 1899 he was called to the presidency of Ohio State University, where he served until his retirement, as president emeritus, in 1925. During his administration the University grew from a local college of some 1,200 students to an institution comprising all the higher educational activities —undergraduate and graduate—of a modern state university, with an enrollment of some 12,-000. He was an acknowledged leader in the field of education: he was president of the Association of American Agricultural Colleges and Experiment Stations, 1903–04; president of the Ohio Education Association, 1905–06; president of the National Association of State Universities, 1910–11.

Meanwhile, his interest in religious activities continued. His devotions at the college chapel exercises made lasting impressions upon his students. He conducted weekly convocation at the Ohio State University for many years after the number of students made it impossible to hold a general chapel exercise. He was a dominant figure in various religious bodies, special minister to numberless congregations in the Middle West, baccalaureate speaker in colleges and high schools, president of the Ohio Sunday School Association 1897–1902, moderator of the General Assembly of the Presbyterian Church in the United States of America in 1927. He also participated in civic life with enthusiasm. In Oxford he served on the village council; in Columbus, on the Board of Education. He was chairman of the United States agricultural commission sent to Europe to make observations on the food supply in England, France, and Italy in 1918, and chairman of the United States Anthracite Coal Commission in 1920. He was president of the Midland Mutual Life Insurance Company of Columbus, Ohio, from 1905 to 1925.

Thompson was a natural leader, endowed with an admirable physique, boundless energy, and a pleasing voice. He possessed great dignity without imperiousness; his eloquence was uncontrolled by rhetorical rules. He was simple in his habits, frank in conversation and debate, sympathetic toward misfortune. His friends among the simple and poor were as dear to him as those

in positions of influence. Upon his death he was acclaimed as Ohio's first citizen.

[J. J. Burns, *Educ. Hist. of Ohio* (1905); *Ohio Archæol. and Hist. Quart.*, Jan. 1934; *Who's Who in America*, 1932–33; T. C. Mendenhall, *Hist. of the Ohio State Univ.*, vols. I–III (1920–26); *Alumni Cat., Miami Univ. . . . 1809–1909* (n.d.); *Columbus Evening Dispatch*, Dec. 9, 1933; *Ohio State Journal* (Columbus), Dec. 11, 13, 1933; *Ohio State Univ. Mo.*, Dec. 1933.]
H. C. M.

THOMPSON, WILLIAM TAPPAN (Aug. 31, 1812–Mar. 24, 1882), editor and humorist, was born in Ravenna, Ohio. His father, David Thompson, was a settler from Virginia; his mother, Catherine (Kerney) Thompson, had been born in Ireland. He presumably attended school in the small schoolhouse he mentions as existing in Ravenna in 1816; but he was orphaned in his early teens and thrown on his own resources in Philadelphia, where acquaintances of his father befriended him. After working in the office of the *Daily Chronicle*, Philadelphia, he was appointed assistant (1830) to James Diament Westcott, secretary of the territory of Florida, under whom he studied law for several years. By 1835, however, he had turned again to journalism, this time in Augusta, Ga., where he was associated with Augustus Baldwin Longstreet [q.v.] in issuing the *States Rights Sentinel*. For a few months in 1836 he served with an Augusta militia unit in the campaign against the Seminoles in Florida. On June 12, 1837, he was married to Carolina A. Carrié of Augusta. In the spring of 1838 he founded in Augusta a literary journal, the *Mirror*, which in 1842 he merged with the *Macon Family Companion* under the composite title of the *Family Companion and Ladies' Mirror*. Though the new periodical was discontinued in 1843 for lack of patronage, the humorous letters of "Major Jones" which Thompson began in one of its last issues attracted immediate attention, and a small collection of them was published locally as *Major Jones's Courtship* (1843), afterwards enlarged and republished in Philadelphia. Later appeared *Major Jones's Chronicles of Pineville* (1843) and *Major Jones's Sketches of Travel* (1848). From 1843 to 1845 Thompson controlled the *Miscellany*, a weekly published in Madison, Ga., but left in the latter year to assist the poet, Park Benjamin [q.v.], with the *Western Continent*, a weekly in Baltimore, Md. Benjamin withdrew from the partnership after a few months, and Thompson continued the publication alone until 1850. At this time he returned to Georgia and founded the *Savannah Morning News*, which he edited until the time of his death and of which he made one of the strongest newspapers of the state. During the sectional struggle preceding the Civil War he stoutly defended the institution of slavery. He not only wrote editorials in support of the Southern cause, but launched a volume of fictional propaganda, *The Slaveholder Abroad* (1860), full of excerpts from British newspapers designed to show that free England engendered more crime and true slavery than the South. During the Civil War he labored to maintain the morale of his fellow citizens, and in 1864 served as a volunteer soldier. He took an active part in local, state, and national politics. In 1868 he was a delegate to the National Democratic Convention and in 1877 a member of the convention which shaped a new constitution for Georgia. He died in Savannah, survived by his wife and several children. His writings include an unpublished farce, "The Live Indian"; a body of sketches, *John's Alive* (1838), published after his death; and a dramatization of *The Vicar of Wakefield*. He also edited W. A. Hotchkiss' *A Codification of the Statute Laws of Georgia* (1845).

Thompson was a dignified and somewhat retiring man, but an excellent raconteur, a ready conversationalist, a kindly friend. He was independent in his judgments and uncompromising in support of what he considered right. As an editor he was handicapped by sectional prejudices, but he succeeded in keeping the *Morning News* free of petty journalistic squabbling and steadfastly honest in reporting facts. His humorous volumes dealing with Major Jones not only entertained two or three generations of American readers but retain some permanent value as a record of provincial society.

[See L. L. Knight, *Standard Hist. of Ga. and Georgians* (1917), vol. III, p. 1762, vol. VI, p. 3277; J. D. Wade, *Augustus Baldwin Longstreet* (1924); Jennette Tandy, *Crackerbox Philosophers in Am. Humor and Satire* (1925); W. M. Clemens, *Famous Funny Fellows* (1882); autobiog. articles in Thompson's *John's Alive* (1883); obituary in *Savannah Morning News*, Mar. 25, 27, 1882. Information has also been supplied by Thompson's granddaughter, Mrs. T. Fletcher Smith, of Quitman, Ga.; Ruth Blair, State Historian of Ga., Atlanta; and William Harden of the Ga. Hist. Soc., Savannah.]   J. H. N.

THOMPSON, ZADOCK (May 23, 1796–Jan. 19, 1856), historian, naturalist, mathematician, was born at Bridgewater, Vt., the second son of Capt. Barnabas Thompson, a farmer, who was one of the earliest settlers in Windsor County, and Sarah (Fuller) Thompson. He was a descendant of John Thomson who was brought from Wales to Plymouth about 1622. His education came slowly—he was twenty-seven when he graduated from college—for he had to work his way almost from the beginning. He did farm work (as little of it as possible, disliking it intensely), wrote and peddled his own almanacs

and gazetteers, and taught school. He graduated from the University of Vermont in 1823, and the next year, Sept. 4, 1824, married Phebe Boyce, by whom he had two daughters. Appointed tutor at the University of Vermont in 1825, he taught and wrote extensively in Burlington until 1833, edited a magazine, the *Iris,* and the *Green Mountain Repository,* and conducted astronomical observations for his own gazetteers and for *Walton's Vermont Register and Farmer's Almanack*. Between 1833 and 1837 he filled teaching positions in Canada, first in Hatley and then in Sherbrooke. His *History of the State of Vermont, from Its Earliest Settlement to the Close of the Year 1832* (1833) had appeared just before he left Vermont, and in 1835 he published a *Geography and History of Lower Canada,* which went through several editions. In the same year he was ordained deacon in the Protestant Episcopal Church.

Returning to Burlington, Thompson taught in a boys' school at Rock Point and began the preparation of his most important work, *History of Vermont, Natural, Civil and Statistical* (1842). After more than ninety years it is still an indispensable book of reference on a wide variety of Vermont topics, including the involved and dramatic story of Vermont during its turbulent days of conflict, independence, and final statehood. The wealth of information it contains affords impressive evidence of Thompson's versatility, thoroughness, scientific conservatism, and perspicacity. Relatively few additions or corrections have been found necessary. The section on natural history contains a very adequate list of rocks, fossils, and minerals, including the commercial rock products of the state. Thompson himself had built up a private cabinet of over three thousand specimens, widely known and visited. He described with much detail and accuracy, chiefly because he examined most of them personally, over a hundred and fifty species of birds, forty-eight fishes, thirty-five Amphibia and reptiles, fifty mammals, and over four hundred species of plants. He tells of the fossil elephant unearthed at Mount Holly, the fossil whale from Charlotte, and in the Appendix, published in 1853 and bound with the third edition of the work, he carefully describes the catamount (one of the last in the East) caught in Manchester in 1850 and the seal taken on the ice of Lake Champlain in the next year. The book abounds in excellent illustrations.

Thompson was appointed assistant state geologist in 1845, professor of chemistry and natural history in the University of Vermont in 1851 and state naturalist of Vermont in 1853. In 1851 by.

the assistance of friends he was enabled to make a trip abroad, and in the following year published the journal of his travels. Various books besides those named above came from his busy pen, but there remains to mention his only lucrative venture in publication, a school book called *The Youth's Assistant in Practical Arithmetick* (1825). This was popular, at least with school trustees, since it ran into fourteen editions and printings. Thompson lived most frugally in a tiny frame house facing the University, and died of "ossification of the heart." A tall, lean Yankee, kindly and mild-mannered, beloved and trusted by a very wide circle of friends, he enjoyed an enviable position in the community, and holds a high place among the early naturalists and historians of the United States. Hampered by illness and poverty, he nevertheless left behind him a remarkable record as a doggedly determined worker, a keen and careful observer in many fields, a clear and prolific writer, a notable contributor to and recorder of the history of his state.

[See C. H. Thompson, *A Geneal. of Descendants of John Thomson, of Plymouth, Mass.* (1890); Augustus Young, *Preliminary Report on the Natural Hist. of the State of Vt.* (1856); *Hist. Mag.,* Oct. 1858, p. 301, reprinted from *Walton's Vermont Register for 1857,* and Feb. 1859, pp. 48–49; G. H. Perkins, *Report of the State Geologist on . . . Certain Areas of Vt. . . . 1901-1902* (1902); W. H. Crockett, *Vermonters: a Book of Biogs.* (1931); M. D. Gilman, *The Bibliog. of Vt.* (1897); and obituary in *Burlington Sentinel,* Jan. 24, 1856. First editions and MSS. of Thompson's writings are in the lib. of the Univ. of Vt.] H.F.P—s.

THOMSON, CHARLES (Nov. 29, 1729–Aug. 16, 1824), secretary of the Continental Congress, was born in County Derry, Ireland, and came to America when he was ten years of age, one of six orphaned children set ashore at New Castle, Del. The mother had died in Ireland; the father, John Thomson, died on shipboard within sight of the American shores. Charles was ere long enabled to enter the academy of Dr. Francis Alison [*q.v.*] at New London, Chester County, Pa., and after leaving the academy conducted a private school for a few years. In 1750, through his acquaintance with Benjamin Franklin, he received an appointment as tutor in the Philadelphia academy, and subsequently (1757-60) he was master of the Latin school in what ultimately became the William Penn Charter School. In 1760 he turned from teaching to the mercantile trade, in which he appears to have prospered.

Meanwhile, because of his reputation for fairness and integrity, he was chosen by the Indians to keep their record of proceedings at the treaty of Easton (1757), and in the following year he was adopted into the Delaware tribe, with a name meaning "man who tells the truth." An outcome of these relations with the Indians was *An Enquiry into the Causes of the Alienation of the Delaware and Shawanese Indians from the British Interest,* published in London in 1759.

Having long taken an active part in Pennsylvania politics, during the decade preceding the Revolution Thomson was in the forefront of all the colonial controversies with Great Britain, and in all of them the politician in him seems to have dominated the merchant. By the time, therefore, that the crucial days of May 1774 arrived, he had become an adept in politics according to the most approved Pennsylvanian standards, as is evinced by his own account of the neat maneuver by which Pennsylvania was brought into substantial accord with the Massachusetts proposals and the way was prepared for the assembling of the Continental Congress (*Collections of the New York Historical Society: Publication Fund Series,* vol. XI, 1879, pp. 274-86).

Thanks to Joseph Galloway, leader of the Pennsylvania conservatives, Thomson was prevented from being chosen a delegate to the Congress, but he was the very man in Philadelphia with whom John Adams, busily probing the minds of all and sundry on the vital questions involved, would wish to have, as he did have, "much conversation." "This Charles Thomson," Adams wrote, "is the Sam Adams of Philadelphia, the life of the cause of liberty, they say" (C. F. Adams, *The Works of John Adams,* vol. II, 1850, p. 358). Galloway was surprised as well as chagrined when this Charles Thomson, whom he characterized as "one of the most violent of the Sons of Liberty (so called) in America" (*Pennsylvania Magazine,* October 1902, p. 310), was chosen by Congress to be its secretary. Following the adjournment of Congress at the end of October, Thomson was characteristically conspicuous in the Pennsylvanian political scene, and on the reassembling of Congress in May 1775 he was again chosen secretary.

It is as secretary of the Continental Congress that Thomson is best known. For nearly fifteen years he sat at the secretarial table, listening to the debates, minuting the birth-records of a nation. As year succeeded year, delegates came and delegates went, but Charles Thomson, the "perpetual secretary," remained. The great drama of the American Revolution as enacted on the stage of the Continental Congress he beheld from its beginning to its consummation as did no other man. Although Congress from time to time prescribed some of the duties of the secretary, occasionally laid new tasks upon him, and even now and then sought to "regulate" the secretarial functions, the office was from the first to the last conducted much as Thomson was pleased to conduct it.

As the chief surviving link between the old government and the new he was chosen to notify General Washington of his election to the presidency; yet, to his great mortification, he was given no part in the inaugural ceremonies. His hope that he might be continued in a similar or appropriate office under the new dispensation was likewise doomed to disappointment. Accordingly, on July 23, 1789, he transmitted to President Washington his resignation of the office of secretary of the Continental Congress and of the custodianship of its records. Retiring to his estate at "Harriton," near Philadelphia, he devoted the next twenty years to making translations of the Septuagint and the New Testament, translations that have been pronounced both scholarly and felicitous. They appeared in 1808 in four volumes under the title *The Holy Bible, Containing the Old and New Covenant, Commonly Called the Old and New Testament.* He also published *A Synopsis of the Four Evangelists* (1815).

Thomson was twice married. His first wife, Ruth Mather, daughter of John Mather of Chester, Pa., died about 1770. His second marriage, which took place on Sept. 1, 1774, four days before he was elected secretary of Congress, was to Hannah Harrison, daughter of Richard Harrison of Maryland. She died Sept. 6, 1807.

[For sources see L. R. Harley, *The Life of Charles Thomson* (1900), with bibliography; J. F. Watson, "Biographical Memoir," in *Hist. Soc. of Pa. Colls.*, vol. I (1853); J. F. Watson, *Annals of Phila.* (1830); *Pa. Mag. of Hist. and Biog.*, Oct. 1891, pp. 327–35, Jan. 1892, p. 499, July 1909, pp. 336–39; *Pa. Archives*, 1 ser., vol. III (1853); *N. Y. Hist. Soc. Colls. . . . for 1878* (1879); C. J. Stillé, *The Life and Times of John Dickinson* (1891); W. B. Reed, *Life and Correspondence of Joseph Reed* (1847); C. H. Lincoln, *The Revolutionary Movement in Pa., 1760–1776* (1901); A. M. Schlesinger, *The Colonial Merchants and the American Revolution, 1763–1776* (1918); A. H. Smyth, *The Writings of Benjamin Franklin* (10 vols, 1905–07); E. C. Burnett, *Letters of Members of the Continental Cong.*, vols. I–VII (1921–34). The Lib. of Cong. has, besides official papers, two vols. of private papers, a small body of miscellaneous papers, and a part of the translation of the New Testament; the Hist. Soc. of Pa. has a letter-book of Thomson (1784), and a few other Thomson manuscripts; the Lib. Company of Phila., Ridgway Branch, has some letters, chiefly to John Mifflin.]

E. C. B.

THOMSON, EDWARD (Oct. 12, 1810–Mar. 22, 1870), first president of Ohio Wesleyan University, editor, bishop of the Methodist Episcopal Church, was born in Portsea, a suburb of Portsmouth, England, the fourth of thirteen children. His father, Benjamin Thomson, was a dry-goods merchant; his mother, Eliza Moore, a woman of education and attainments. In 1817, because of

financial reverses, the father sought a new business location, first going to southern France and thence to America (1818), finally settling in Wooster, Wayne County, Ohio, where he opened a drug store. Here young Thomson received his early education and manifested such an interest in books that he neglected play. In 1828 he entered Jefferson Medical College in Philadelphia, and after a year's study passed the examinations which admitted him to medical practice. He opened an office at Jeromeville, Ohio, a small village near Wooster. While he was engaged in practice his interest in religion was awakened by the preaching of Russell Bigelow, an eloquent Methodist circuit rider, whom he heard at a camp-meeting, where he had been called to make a professional visit. This interest grew until in December 1831 he united with the Methodist Episcopal Church and the next year, July 1, was licensed to preach. In the fall of 1832 he was admitted on trial to the Ohio Conference and assigned as junior preacher on the Norwalk circuit.

His rise to a place of influence in the Methodist Episcopal Church was rapid. He served at Sandusky and Cincinnati, and at the latter place took a full course of lectures at the Cincinnati Medical College, from which he received the degree of M.D. In 1836 he was appointed to Detroit, and on July 4, 1837, married Maria Louisa, daughter of the Hon. Mordecai Bartley [q.v.]. In 1838 Thomson was appointed principal of Norwalk Seminary, and four years later was chosen president of Ohio Wesleyan University, then in process of establishment. From 1844 until he took up his duties as president in 1846 he edited the *Ladies' Repository* at Cincinnati. His presidency covered the formative years of the institution's life and at the time of his retirement in 1860 the college was well established, with four buildings and a student body of about five hundred.

Thomson was a strong anti-slavery man, and this fact together with his recognized literary abilities led to his selection in 1860 as editor of the *Christian Advocate and Journal* in New York, the chief Methodist organ in the United States. This important post he filled admirably during the years of the Civil War, conducting the paper on a high patriotic plane. He represented the North Ohio Conference in the General Conference from 1840 until in 1864 he was elected bishop. He was sent immediately to visit Methodist missions in the Orient, and later published a two-volume work entitled *Our Oriental Missions* (1870). His other published works include: *Essays, Educational and Religious* (1855, 1856, 1857); and *Evidences of Revealed Religion*

(1872). He died at Wheeling, W. Va., while on his way to preside over the Eastern conferences. His first wife died in 1863, and on May 9, 1866, he married Annie E. Howe, who with a son and daughter by his first wife and a son by the second survived him.

[Thomson's *Our Oriental Missions* contains biog. sketch; see also Edward Thomson, Jr., *Life of Edward Thomson, D.D., LL.D.* (1885); E. T. Nelson, *Fifty Years of Hist. of the Ohio Wesleyan Univ., 1844–1894* (1895); *The Biog. Cyc. and Portrait Gallery ... of the State of Ohio* (n.d.), vol. VI; T. L. Flood and J. W. Hamilton, *Lives of Methodist Bishops* (1882); *The Biog. Encyc. of Ohio* (1876); *Christian Advocate* (N. Y.), Apr. 7, 1870; *Cincinnati Commercial*, Mar. 23, 1870; MSS. in library of Ohio Wesleyan Univ.]

W. W. S.

THOMSON, EDWARD WILLIAM (Feb. 12, 1849–Mar. 5, 1924), editor, author, poet, was born in Toronto, Canada. He was the son of William and Margaret Hamilton (Foley) Thomson, and a member of one of the Loyalist families which removed from the United States to Canada after the Revolution. He was educated in the public schools and at Trinity College School, Weston, Ontario. Before he was sixteen, influenced by his hatred of slavery and his boyish admiration for the character of Abraham Lincoln, he left home to enlist in the Union army during the Civil War. He served in both the 3rd and the 5th Pennsylvania Cavalry during the Virginia campaigns of 1864 and 1865. On his return to Canada he enlisted in the Queen's Own Rifles, and saw service with them during the Fenian raids of 1866. For a number of years (1868–79) he was a civil engineer, and was employed in the construction of the Carillon Canal, around the rapids of the Ottawa River. He discovered, however, a taste for writing and a bent for journalism, and joined the staff of the Toronto *Globe,* one of the most influential of Canadian newspapers. He served the *Globe* as chief editorial writer from 1879 to 1891. In the latter year he moved to Boston, Mass., where he was for twelve years one of the editors of the *Youth's Companion.* After leaving the *Companion,* he was Canadian correspondent of the *Boston Evening Transcript,* resident in Ottawa, but traveling much about the country in the preparation of his articles. During these years he practised independent journalism as well, contributing numerous articles to magazines and newspapers in the United States and Canada. Always a political liberal of the old school, he took a deep interest in Canadian politics. He was the friend of many public men of the Liberal party, and was especially intimate with Sir Wilfred Laurier, long the premier of the Dominion.

Thomson's first work in fiction was *Old Man*

Savarin and Other Stories, published in 1895; this was followed by *Walter Gibbs, the Young Boss* (1896) and *Smoky Days* (1901). More important in a literary way were his contributions to poetry, which were limited in quantity but of no little excellence. They included *Between Earth and Sky* (1897) and *The Many Mansioned House and Other Poems* (1909), published in the United States and England as *When Lincoln Died, and Other Poems* (1909). His verses show considerable imaginative and emotional power. Those that deal with the Civil War reflect his early admiration for Lincoln, which only strengthened with the years; it was always a sentimental satisfaction to him that his birthday was the same as Lincoln's. He also made a metrical version of M. S. Henry's translation of the medieval French romance, *Aucassin and Nicolette,* delicately rendered in a verse form as nearly as possible that of the original poem (1896). He was a fellow of the Royal Society of Canada, and of the Royal Society of Literature of the United Kingdom. He was married in March 1873 to Adelaide (d. 1921), daughter of Alexander St. Denis. He died in Boston, Mass., survived by his only child, a son.

[*Who's Who in America,* 1918–19; W. S. Wallace, *The Dict. of Canadian Biog.* (1926); H. J. Morgan, *The Canadian Men and Women of the Time* (2nd ed., 1912); Archibald MacMurchy, *Handbook of Canadian Lit.* (*English*) (1906); obituary in *Boston Transcript,* Mar. 7, 1924; personal acquaintance, and private information.]

H. S. C—n.

THOMSON, FRANK (July 5, 1841–June 5, 1899), president of the Pennsylvania Railroad, was born at Chambersburg, Franklin County, Pa., the son of Alexander and Jane (Graham) Thomson. His grandfather, Alexander Thomson, emigrated from Scotland in 1771 and established himself in the Cumberland Valley. His son, Frank's father, became a lawyer and took a prominent part in the political life of his day. He represented his district in Congress, 1824–26, and in 1828 was chosen judge of the Sixteenth Judicial District of Pennsylvania. He was also professor of jurisprudence in the law school of Marshall College, the school at that time being located at Chambersburg.

Frank Thomson entered Chambersburg Academy at an early age, but left at seventeen, putting an end to his formal schooling. He chose railroading as his career at the suggestion of Thomas A. Scott [*q.v.*], who was at that time general superintendent of the Pennsylvania Railroad Company. His first appointment was that of machinist's apprentice in the Altoona shops. The Pennsylvania, through the purchase of the state works, had acquired a variety of equipment which had been in service on the Philadelphia & Columbia and the Portage railroads, and there was need of a plan, adapted to the condtions of a modern standardized railroad, that would unify the construction and repair of locomotives. To this problem Thomson gave his principal attention during the early part of his service. He was also occupied with appliances for the burning of coal, both anthracite and bituminous, on locomotives, with car lighting, improvements in braking devices, and similar mechanical problems concerned with improved efficiency in transportation. The Pennsylvania road, under the influence of Scott and others, was taking a progressive attitude toward the introduction of better appliances in all processes of transportation and the Altoona shops provided Thomson with a schooling in applied mechanics which for that period was unequaled.

When, at the outbreak of the Civil War, Vice-President Scott was called to Washington and made assistant secretary of war in charge of military transportation, he took Thomson, then twenty years of age, as one of his assistants. For three years he was engaged in restoring and keeping open service interrupted by the enemy, and in building new lines of railroad and telegraph for the rapid transfer of troops. In the year 1864 he returned to the Pennsylvania as superintendent of the eastern division of the Philadelphia & Erie, which had recently come under Pennsylvania control. For a short period he managed the Oil Creek Railroad during the oil excitement in 1866. In 1873 he became superintendent of motive power and in 1874 was made general manager of the entire system east of Pittsburgh and Erie. In 1882 he was made second vice-president, in 1888 first vice-president, and on Feb. 3, 1897, he became president.

In his capacity as superintendent of motive power and rolling stock, he devoted his attention to the work of practical railroad construction and also laid the foundations of the system that has since produced the standard Pennsylvania engines. Later, as general manager east of Pittsburgh, he introduced many advanced methods of roadway maintenance, particularly methods for the establishment of solid roadway and standard track and systems of track inspection. He introduced superior standards of equipment, planned picturesque stations and ornamental grounds, and was largely instrumental in the establishment of block-signal systems and other operating improvements. He was also responsible for introducing the high grade of discipline which has since prevailed. In his capacity as second and first vice-president, as a direct representative of

the president, he was in position to make effective the reforms that he had earlier instituted.

Although his entire business life was passed in the service of the Pennsylvania Railroad, his career as president which followed closely on the panic of 1893 and was uneventful, lasted only two years and four months. He was married on June 5, 1866, to Mary Elizabeth, daughter of Benjamin Clarke. Thomson died in Merion, Pa., survived by three children.

[J. E. Watkins, "Hist. of the Pa. Railroad Company, 1846–96," incomplete MS. in possession of the Pa. Railroad Company, Phila.; W. B. Wilson, *Hist. of the Pa. Railroad* (1899), vol. II; H. W. Schotter, *The Growth and Development of the Pa. Railroad Company* (1927); *A Biog. Album of Prominent Pennsylvanians*, vol. III (1890); Ernest Spofford, *Encyc. of Pa. Biog.*, vol. XVII (1928); *Public Ledger* (Phila.), June 6, 1899.]
F. H. D.

THOMSON, JOHN (Nov. 3, 1776–Jan. 25, 1799), orator and political writer, who gained a measure of distinction in his fragment of life by his spirited and talented espousal of Jeffersonian thought in politics, was the son of a prominent physician of Petersburg, Va., Dr. John Thomson, and his wife Anne. The early death of his father in 1785 left the boy under the guardianship of his mother, but with a comfortable patrimony. When he was about fourteen he entered the College of William and Mary and shared in college oratorical contests. On leaving college in 1792 he studied law in Petersburg with the help of the library and the advice of his loyal and admiring friend, George Hay, the son-in-law of James Monroe [q.v.]. Thomson learned with phenomenal speed and retentiveness and began to practise law when he was still in his teens. With rather melancholy and thoughtful countenance, grace of manner, and kindly consideration for others, the young attorney soon became popular in Petersburg and the surrounding county of Dinwiddie and gained an unusual practice for so young an advocate. Six feet tall, loosely put together, blue-eyed, he might well have come from the same physical stock as Jefferson; certainly the two were akin in political faith. Thomson voiced his opinions in the press under the popular classical signatures of Cassius, Gracchus, and Curtius, and his writings were widely copied by Republican papers. His style has been caustically criticized by Henry Adams as "stilted and artificial" (*Gallatin, post*, p. 46), but even this critic recognized his unusual promise and conceded that he echoed party feeling.

In August 1795 he attacked Jay's treaty in a speech of biting invective before a meeting of the inhabitants of Petersburg. He revealed in his caustic criticisms, not only the temper of the Virginia Republicans toward the treaty, but remarkable knowledge of the history of his country for one less than twenty years old. This speech gave him prestige among party leaders. Three years later when John Marshall had voiced his views on the Alien and Sedition Acts in his so-called "Answers" (*Times and Virginia Advertiser,* Oct. 11, 1798), Thomson joined the general press attack on him in a series of five letters under the signature Curtius.

Thomson was the leader in a coterie of talented young Republicans in southside Virginia which included his dissipated, ill-fated, but well-loved brother William and John Randolph of Roanoke. Randolph and John Thomson esteemed each other with deep friendly affection and mutual intellectual admiration. Thomson called Randolph "a brilliant and noble young man" (Garland, *post,* I, 73) and Randolph declared that Thomson had held the first place in his heart and the first rank in the intellectual order. Thomson's untimely death as the result of pleurisy caused keen regret in the ranks of his party. Albert Gallatin, who knew him only from his writings and influence, esteemed him as "one of the brightest geniuses of Virginia and the United States" (quoted by Adams in *Gallatin,* p. 227), and keenly regretted his loss as a severe blow to the Republican interest. A partial collection of Thomson's writings was published in *Letters of Curtius . . . to Which is Added a Speech . . . on the British Treaty* (Richmond, 1804). It contains a short sketch of his life, probably by George Hay.

[Printed sources include: Henry Adams, *The Life of Albert Gallatin* (1879), and *John Randolph* (1883); A. J. Beveridge, *The Life of John Marshall* (1919), II, 126–29, 395–96; Powhatan Bouldin, *Home Reminiscences of John Randolph of Roanoke* (1878); W. C. Bruce, *John Randolph of Roanoke* (1922); H. A. Garland, *The Life of John Randolph of Roanoke* (2 vols., 1850); *William and Mary Coll. Quart.,* July 1895, p. 106, Apr. 1919, p. 237. The wills and inventories of the estates of Dr. John Thomson and his son John are in Will Book No. 1 in the Court House at Petersburg, Va.; a manuscript sketch by C. T. Lassiter, "John Thomson of Petersburg and the Genesis of Republican Institutions in the United States," in private hands, contains data not otherwise available.]   M. H. W.

THOMSON, JOHN (Oct. 25, 1853–June 1, 1926), inventor, manufacturer, oldest son of Alexander Thomson, a farmer, and Elizabeth (Hay) Thomson, was born in Fochabers, Morayshire, Scotland. In 1854 the family emigrated to the United States and settled on a farm at Marion, Wayne County, N. Y. Here Thomson spent his youth and obtained a common-school education. At the age of sixteen he left home and went to Rochester, N. Y., where he found employment in a jewelry store and devoted his spare time to the study of mechanical, civil, and electrical engineering. These studies in combination with the intricate and delicate work of watch and clock repair developed his natural bent for mechanics as well as his inventive talent, and in 1877 he obtained his first patents, all for improvements in watches, including two escapements, a regulator, and a stem-winding device. About 1880 he moved to Brooklyn, where he continued his inventive work and by 1884 had obtained several patents on mechanical movements such as a ratchet and pawl and a differential screw.

He had meanwhile begun to give particular attention to improvements in water meters and printing presses. The first of his patented improvements of the former, devised between 1883 and 1885, he assigned to a manufacturer in Brooklyn, while the first of his inventions in the latter field—an intermitting circular feed motion, perfected in 1887—he assigned to the Colt Patent Fire Arms Manufacturing Company, Hartford, Conn. He now went to Hartford and in the next three years, as an employee of the Colt company, made additional improvements which resulted in the production of the Thomson Printing Press. In the meantime, he also obtained ten patents for improvements in water meters, including his basic patent of the disk water meter, Dec. 20, 1887.

Leaving the Colt company about 1890, he organized in Brooklyn the John Thomson Press Company and the Thomson Meter Company, both of which organizations he directed until shortly before his death. The Thomson Press became standard equipment in some 15,000 job-printing plants throughout the country while some 20,000,000 Thomson disk-type water meters were put into service in the United States and abroad. Besides looking after his manufacturing interests Thomson was a registered patent attorney and was retained in a number of important patent cases. He was awarded in all some 350 patents—for his improvements in printing presses and water meters, and also for a number of improvements in electric furnaces, for a process for refining metallic zinc, and for the manufacture of zinc oxide. To exploit the last two inventions he organized the Electric Zinc Company of London, England. Because of his wide experience and practical knowledge in the electrical field, he was at one time chief engineer of the Primary Electrical Subway Commission of New York, which undertook the construction of the first underground conduit for telegraph and telephone wires in that city. He was an active member of a number of clubs and technical societies both in New York and London, and was president of the Engineers' Club of New York,

1898–1901. In 1887 he married Alice Elizabeth McKee of Canandaigua, N. Y., who with two sons and a daughter survived him. He died in Brooklyn.

[*Inland Printer,* July 1926; *Brooklyn Daily Eagle, N. Y. Times, N. Y. Herald Tribune,* June 2, 1926; correspondence with family; Patent Office records.]

C. W. M—n.

THOMSON, JOHN EDGAR (Feb. 10, 1808– May 27, 1874), third president of the Pennsylvania Railroad, was born in Springfield Township, Delaware County, Pa., son of John and Sarah (Levis) Thomson and descended from Quaker forebears said to have come from England with William Penn. His father, a civil engineer, was connected with the construction of important public works of the time, among them the Delaware & Chesapeake Canal. He has been credited with planning for Thomas Leiper [*q.v.*] what was probably the first experimental railroad in the United States. John Edgar had little formal schooling, but from early years he was the constant companion of his father and through parental instruction gained a sound foundation of engineering training which he diligently perfected by reading, observation, and experience. Through his father's influence he became a member of the state's engineer corps which was at the time making preliminary surveys for a rail line from Philadelphia to Columbia. He was soon made assistant engineer, and in 1830, when the line of the Camden & Amboy Railroad was located across the state of New Jersey, Thomson was placed in charge of an engineering division.

The caliber of the man is shown by the fact that as soon as these duties were completed, he made a trip to Europe to study the new form of transportation which George Stephenson's genius was making possible and to familiarize himself with European and especially English civil and mechanical engineering practice. Returning in 1832, he was appointed chief engineer of the Georgia Railroad which was just being chartered to build a line from Augusta to Atlanta. He remained with this company for fifteen years, meanwhile becoming widely recognized as an authority on engineering practice.

The Pennsylvania Railroad was incorporated in 1847 to build a line from Harrisburg to Pittsburgh that would do away with the inefficient Allegheny Portage Railroad and the slow-serving canals, and place the railroad system of the state on a par with the Baltimore & Ohio to the south and the New York Central to the north in the struggle for western business. It was a critical time in the commercial development of Penn-

sylvania, and the directors of the company appointed Thomson as their chief engineer to handle this vital competitive problem. With characteristic energy he set himself to find the most favorable location for the project. When the Portage Railroad was built engineers had declared a road without inclined planes to be impossible of operation in that mountainous territory. The location of the Horseshoe Curve and the construction of a road with practicable grades was Thomson's answer to this pessimistic prophecy and constituted the high point in his career as a railroad engineer. The last link in the through line between Philadelphia and Pittsburgh was completed early in 1854 by the elimination of the Portage Railroad and the completed road was formally opened for traffic in February of that year.

Meanwhile, in 1852, Thomson had been made president, and thus placed in position to use his growing influence in securing the funds necessary to the completion of the western extension. The connecting roads east of the mountains from Lancaster to Philadelphia belonged to the system of state works begun a quarter century earlier. These the state had several times attempted to dispose of, but without success. Finally, in 1857, the entire system of state works, consisting of 278 miles of canals and 117 miles of railroad, together with real estate and rail equipment, was put up at auction. Thomson offered $7,500,000, and the property came into the possession of the Pennsylvania.

A through connection with the headwaters of the Ohio was not the limit of Thomson's ambitions, however. He saw clearly that the railroad of the future would be the one that could pick up freight at point of origin and deliver it in its own cars on its own rails at final destination. He had advocated for years before he became president the extension of the road west of Pittsburgh. His policy had resulted by 1856 in the consolidation of various western lines into the Pittsburgh, Fort Wayne & Chicago Railway. This company was formally leased to the Pennsylvania in 1869 and in 1870–71 the Pennsylvania Company, one of the first of the holding companies, was created to take over the properties west of Pittsburgh which were developing into large northwest and southwest systems.

The growth of traffic from the West made the necessity of a terminal in New York Harbor imperative, a project long contemplated. Thomson's negotiations resulted in a long-time lease, in 1871, of the properties of the United Companies of New Jersey, comprising 456 miles of railroad and 65 miles of canal. In 1869 an independent line from Baltimore to Washington was decided upon and by 1873, through the acquisition of a one-sixth interest in the Southern Railway Security Company, a connection which gave access to all points in the Southern states had been effected. Thomson took great interest in the establishment of Philadelphia as a transatlantic port and was instrumental in the creation of the American Steamship Company in 1870 under the patronage of the Pennsylvania Railroad.

Up to the time of his death, Thomson was thus almost continuously engaged in important construction projects that were to render the Pennsylvania Railroad safe from competitive attack. Furthermore, from the sixties on, the Pennsylvania was a leader in insisting upon high standards of operating practice and a pioneer in the introduction of improved equipment and devices of various kinds. Thomson's career was coincident with the pioneer and construction stage of railway development in the United States. He was associated with the movement in its beginnings and lived to see the Atlantic and Pacific connected by rail, while his keen vision as to the future place of railroads in the industrial life of the country was in process of rapid realization during his service as chief engineer and president of the Pennsylvania. His ability as a financier was shown in his handling of the affairs of three different railroads under panic conditions —the Georgia Railroad in 1837, the Pittsburgh, Fort Wayne & Chicago in 1857, and the Pennsylvania in 1873. The dividend record of the Pennsylvania Railroad was unbroken from the establishment of the through line between Philadelphia and Pittsburgh to the close of his career. Although he was taciturn and abrupt in manner, and inclined to action on his own initiative without consultation with others, his judgment was greatly respected and his services were sought in various capacities outside of the railroad business. He aided the cause of many civic projects in Philadelphia. He was a member of the Park Commission and rendered valuable service in the extension of Fairmount Park. One of the early steel companies organized by Andrew Carnegie [q.v.] was known as the J. Edgar Thomson Steel Company.

Thomson was married late in life to Lavinia Frances Smith; they had no children of their own, but adopted a daughter. He died in Philadelphia in his sixty-seventh year. By his will he left his estate in trust, the income to be employed to educate and maintain the daughters of railroad men killed in the discharge of their duties. This foundation, known as St. John's Orphanage, is still serving its purpose in Philadelphia.

[J. E. Watkins, "Hist. of the Pennsylvania Railroad Company, 1846–96" (1898), incomplete and not printed, in possession of Pa. R.R. Co., Phila.; W. B. Sipes, *The Pa. Railroad* (1875); W. B. Wilson, *Hist. of the Pa. Railroad Company* (2 vols., 1899); H. W. Schotter, *The Growth and Development of the Pa. Railroad Company* (1927); *Ann. Reports . . . Pa. Railroad*, 1847–74; *Mag. of Western Hist.*, Aug. 1888; *Penn Monthly*, July 1874; *Press* and *Public Ledger* (both of Phila.), May 29, 1874.]

F.H.D.

THOMSON, MORTIMER NEAL (Sept. 2, 1831–June 25, 1875), humorist, known as "Q.K. Philander Doesticks, P.B.," was born in Riga, Monroe County, N. Y., the elder of two sons of Edwin and Sophia Thomson. The Thomsons were prominent old settlers there, the grandfather, Joseph Thomson, having held minor public offices. In 1841 the family moved to Ann Arbor, Mich., where the father set up in the practice of law. Thomson matriculated at the University of Michigan in the fall of 1849, but was expelled during the winter because of membership in a secret society. Subsequently he tramped—playing at times, it is thought, with various strolling stock companies—to New York City, where he became a clerk in a jewelry store and rapidly explored the gayeties of Gotham. His first humorous letter, "Doesticks on a Bender," a hilarious sketch of a trip to Niagara, won immediate popularity and was copied widely by the newspapers of the country. In rapid succession (Sept. 22, 1854–May 30, 1855) there followed a series of twenty-nine humorous letters, most of them appearing in the *Detroit Daily Advertiser,* others in the *New York Tribune* and the *Spirit of the Times* (New York). These letters, collected and published as *Doesticks: What He Says* (1855), made "Doesticks" a national figure. In 1855 Thomson joined the staff of the *New York Tribune,* writing police-court sketches (later published as *The History and Records of the Elephant Club,* 1856) in a way they had never before been done, and a series of feature articles on fortune tellers (*The Witches of New York,* 1859). With Thomas Nast [q.v.] he covered such special assignments as the famous Heenan-Morrissey prize fight, Oct. 20, 1858, and reported dramatically and with devastating effect the great auction sale of slaves held in Savannah in 1859. When William Allen Butler's famous poem, "Nothing to Wear," aroused New York, Thomson was offered one dollar a line for a parody. In less than a week he had produced a poem of eight hundred lines, a satire on snobbery called *Nothing to Say* (1857), which was probably more popular than the original. The popularity of "Doesticks" had already been considerably enhanced by the tremendous sale of an earlier piece of parody in verse, *Plu-ri-bus-tah,* *a Song That's-by-No-Author,* which had appeared in May 1856. With this book-length mock-heroic, precipitated by the wave of interest in Longfellow's *Hiawatha,* he achieved a national hit, taking telling hits at American follies, especially American love of money. Although it was probably begun as parody, it soon achieved independent position on its own merits as social satire.

In addition to regular staff duty on the *Tribune,* Thomson ventured in 1858 to edit the *New York Picayune,* the best comic weekly of the day. Later he became dramatic critic for the *Tribune* and wrote a play, *The Lady of the Lake* (1860), a travesty of Scott's poem. During the Civil War he served as staff reporter for the *Tribune,* as well as chaplain to a regiment. He was twice married. His first wife, Anna H. Van Cleve, an old friend, whom he married on Oct. 24, 1857, died in childbirth late in 1858, leaving a son. In July 1861, while home on leave, he married again, this time Grace Eldridge, daughter of Sara Payson Willis Parton [*q.v.*]. Again his happiness was short-lived, for his second wife died twenty days after the birth of their daughter. After the war Thomson continued the humorous lectures he had begun in 1859. For a short time he was an associate editor of the *Minneapolis Tribune,* but in 1873 he returned to New York to become an editor of *Frank Leslie's Illustrated Weekly.* In this position he continued until his death. The Ring Lardner of his day, he brought to American humor terse, vigorous, quick-moving phrases and vivid slang, and became the most popular American humorist writing in the period before that of Charles Farrar Browne [*q.v.*].

[Thomson's name is sometimes spelled Thompson. See Fletcher D. Slater, "The Life and Letters of Mortimer Thomson," 1931, unpublished thesis in the lib. of Northwestern Univ.; obituaries in *N. Y. Times, N. Y. Tribune,* and *N. Y. Herald,* June 26, 1875.]

F. J. M—e.

THOMSON, SAMUEL (Feb. 9, 1769–Oct. 4, 1843), botanic physician, originator of the Thomsonian system of medical treatment, was born in Alstead, N. H., the son of John and Hannah (Cobb) Thomson. His father was a struggling pioneer farmer, who put his son to work on the farm when he was five, though he had been lame from birth. At ten the boy had one month's schooling. He took a great dislike to farm work, and from his earliest years spent most of his time in the fields and woods. Here he became interested in herbs and their medical uses. One especially impressed him because of its peculiar effect in producing vomiting and profuse perspiration. It was *lobelia inflata,* and later he was to use it extensively in his career of healing,

claiming its medical properties as his own discovery. At the age of twenty-one he assumed charge of the family farm, and on July 7, 1790, married Susan Allen, who bore him eight children. Soon after his marriage his wife became ill, and when the regular physicians failed to perform a cure he employed two root doctors, under whose ministrations she rapidly recovered. His confidence in the curative properties of herbs thus strengthened, he began to use them, first in his own family and then among the neighbors. Calls for his services increased and at length, formulating a system, he devoted himself wholly to medical practice, his activities extending over all eastern New England. He soon incurred the enmity of the regular school physicians, who persecuted him for the rest of his life. He became involved in many law suits, was charged with murder on at least one occasion (see *Commonwealth* vs. *Thompson,* 6 *Tyng* 134) and was once confined for six weeks in a loathsome prison. The trials in which he was involved created a considerable sensation in their day.

His theory of disease was based on the assumption that all ills are produced by cold and that any treatment which increases inward heat will hasten recovery. Although he used many other vegetable remedies, his method in general consisted in prescribing *lobelia* followed by Cayenne pepper. Usually the vapor bath was also employed. So great was his success that he decided to obtain a patent for his process. One was granted on Mar. 3, 1813, and a revised patent on Jan. 28, 1823. He also conceived the idea of selling rights to practise his system, and societies were formed in all parts of the country, including the Middle West. Most of the agents whom he employed proved dishonest, and his life was made miserable by their misdeeds. He published *A Brief Sketch of the Causes and Treatment of Disease* (1821); *A Narrative of the Life and Medical Discoveries of Samuel Thomson* (1822); *New Guide to Health: or Botanic Family Physician* (1822); and *Learned Quackery Exposed* (1824). Having had no educational advantages, in writing his books he wisely accepted aid from others. A number of short-lived journals, exponents of his system, were issued, among them the *Botanic Sentinel* (later called *Philadelphia Botanic Sentinel and Thomsonian Sentinel*), 1835–40, and the *Thomsonian Recorder,* started in Columbus, Ohio, in 1832, which was later (1837) called the *Botanic-Medical Recorder* and lasted until 1852.

Although most of the regular school of physicians were jealous of Thomson's success, he was treated with much kindness by such practitioners as Benjamin Rush of Philadelphia, Benjamin Waterhouse of Harvard, and William Tully [*qq.v.*] of Yale. Without question he was sincere, and he exhibited great courage in withstanding the persecutions of his opponents. The significance of his work lies not in any contribution to medical science but in the strong influence that he created against the prevailing practice of his day, in which bleeding, calomel, and opium were the ruling remedies. His residence in his later years was Boston, Mass., where, at his home on Salem Street, he died.

[In addition to Thomson's own writings, see Samuel Robinson, *A Course of Fifteen Lectures Demonstrating Thomson's New Method of Medical Practice* (Columbus, Ohio, 1830); J. W. Comfort, *The Practice of Medicine on Thomsonian Principles* (1843); *Bull. of the Lloyd Lib. of Botany, Pharmacy and Materia Medica,* no. 11, Reproduction Series, no. 7 (1909); Alexander Wilder, *Hist. of Medicine . . . in the Nineteenth Century* (1901); J. M. Ball, in *Annals of Medic. Hist.,* June 1925; F. R. Packard, *Hist. of Medicine in the U. S.* (2 vols., 1931); H. A. Kelly and W. L. Burrage, *Am. Medic. Biogs.* (1920); obituary in *Boston Daily Advertiser,* Oct. 5, 1843.]   A. N. A.

THOMSON, WILLIAM (Jan. 16, 1727–Nov. 2, 1796), Revolutionary soldier, known as "Old Danger," is said to have been born in Pennsylvania, and to have moved with his Scotch-Irish parents, Moses and Jane Thomson, during the 1730's to settle in Amelia Township, S. C. He had the usual frontier education and became an expert rifleman. Beginning life by planting with his father, William Thomson was a trader to the Cherokee Indians probably until the outbreak of the Cherokee War, when, as major commandant of the Rangers, he rendered important services for which the Assembly voted him a gratuity. After the war, having received a number of land grants, he planted indigo, and was active in local affairs as justice of the peace, enquirer and collector of taxes, commissioner for building the parish church, representative in the Assembly, and colonel of the Orangeburg militia. In the disturbances between the Regulators and Scovilites, he was one of the leaders who averted bloodshed, and when courthouses were finally built in the backcountry, he became the first sheriff of Orangeburg. In 1772, he was also a commissioner for adjusting the boundary with North Carolina.

At the opening of the Revolution, he was placed on the General Committee and became a member of the first Provincial Congress. When William H. Drayton [*q.v.*] carried the Continental Association into the backcountry, Thomson as lieutenant-colonel-commandant supported him with the militia, and was one of the witnesses to Drayton's treaty with the Loyalists on Sept. 16, 1775. Under Col. Richard Richardson,

he served in the "Snow Campaign" of that year against the Loyalists, and was in command of the party that captured Robert Fletchall. His dispersal of Patrick Cunningham's followers at the great Cane Brake was supposed at the time to have shattered the king's party in South Carolina. His greatest service was rendered at the battle of Fort Moultrie in June 1776, when with 700 Rangers he blocked the British attempt to land on the east end of Sullivan's Island. For this he received the thanks of Congress. When the Rangers became the third regiment of South Carolina continentals, he was promoted to the rank of colonel, and served under Robert Howe [*q.v.*] in the defense of Savannah. In 1778 he resigned from the continental service and commanded the Orangeburg militia. He was also elected to the state Senate and served there intermittently until the close of his life.

Upon the surrender of Charlestown, he was paroled, and his plantation became a fortified British post. Accused of having broken his parole, he was imprisoned in a dungeon for several months in Charlestown. Upon his exchange in June 1781, he joined Greene and is said to have served in an advisory capacity without a command. After the war, he returned to his devastated plantation and resumed planting, but is said to have been overgenerous to friends who involved him in financial losses. In March 1783, he secured an act establishing upon his plantation the market town of Belleville, which, however, never developed. In the South Carolina convention of 1788, he voted for ratification of the federal Constitution. In the state constitutional convention of 1790, he opposed a movement to return to Charleston as the state capital. In 1795, he was defeated for Congress by Wade Hampton, and the following year he died at Sweet Springs, Va., where he had gone for his health. Amiable, energetic, and without brilliance, he contributed to the Revolutionary party the stabilizing influence of his solid dependability and common sense. On Aug. 14, 1755, Thomson was married to Eugenia Russell. They had twelve children, four sons and eight daughters.

[Thomson's Order Book and other documentary material are in A. S. Salley, *Hist. of Orangeburg County* (1898). His correspondence is in R. W. Gibbes, *Doc. Hist. of the Am. Revolution* (1855); "Journal of the Council of Safety . . ." in *Colls. of the S. C. Hist. Soc.,* vol. II (1858); "Papers of the First Council of Safety . . ." in *S. C. Hist. and Geneal. Mag.,* Jan. 1900–Oct. 1902. Sketches are in *Ibid.,* Apr. 1902, and in Joseph Johnson, *Traditions and Reminiscences Chiefly of the Am. Revolution in the South* (1851). See also John Drayton, *Memoirs of the Am. Revolution* (2 vols., 1821), Wm. Moultrie, *Memoirs of the Am. Revolution* (2 vols., 1802), and Edward McCrady, *The Hist. of S. C. in the Revolution* (1902).]   A. K. G.

THOMSON, WILLIAM McCLURE (Dec. 31, 1806–Apr. 8, 1894), missionary in Syria, was born at Spring Dale, Ohio, near Cincinnati, son of the Rev. John Thomson. He graduated at Miami University in 1828, studied for two years, 1829–31, in Princeton Theological Seminary, and on Oct. 12, 1831, was ordained by the Presbytery of Cincinnati. In October 1832, having married Eliza Nelson Hanna on June 6, he sailed for Syria under appointment of the American Board of Commissioners for Foreign Missions. The Syria mission was then but ten years old. Reaching Beirut in February 1833, Thomson lived there until April 1834, when he moved to Jerusalem. In May, while he was traveling to Jaffa, the peasants rebelled against the rule of Mohammed Ali Pasha of Egypt, who had seized Palestine, and Thomson was imprisoned as a spy. His wife's experiences during the violent warfare around Jerusalem resulted in her death in July, soon after her husband's release. He returned to Beirut in October 1834, with his infant son, William Hanna Thomson, who later became a distinguished physician of New York. In Beirut he preached and taught, opening a boys' boarding-school in 1835, the first in the Turkish Empire, and on Aug. 3 of that year he married Mrs. Maria Abbot, widow of a British consul in Syria. He also traveled much in the country, seeking new missionary fields. In 1843 he moved to a station which he had helped to establish at Abeih in the Lebanon. Here in 1845 there was savage fighting between the Druses and the Maronite Christians, and at risk of his life, Thomson obtained opportunity for the Maronites to escape to Beirut. Thither he, too, went in 1846. In this early period of the Syria mission he was a great source of courage, wisdom, and organizing ability. His kindliness and ability to enter into the life of the natives won the confidence of the conflicting elements of the Syrian population and brought him commanding influence.

On his return to Syria in 1850 after a furlough at home, he went to live at Sidon in order to manage a station at Hasbeiyeh, where he had been a pioneer; in these places he worked until 1857. During another visit to America he published *The Land and the Book* (2 vols., 1858). In 1859 he settled at Beirut, where he lived for the remainder of his service. After the destructive war between the Druses and Maronites in 1860 he was adviser to Lord Dufferin, representative of the allied powers in the reorganization of the government of the Lebanon. In 1870 the Syria mission was transferred to the Presbyterian Board of Foreign Missions, under which Thomson served until 1876. Thereafter, he lived for some time in New York, preparing the second edition of *The Land and the Book* (3 vols., 1880–85). In 1890 he removed to Denver, where he died, survived by his son and two daughters.

Thomson's *The Land and the Book* is a description of Palestine and southern Syria in the form of journals of travel, with constant reference to the Bible. The first edition had an extraordinary circulation. It was republished in England and more copies were sold than of any previous American book except *Uncle Tom's Cabin*. The second edition, more than twice the size of the first and much improved, at once attained great popularity. Thomson had traveled widely and repeatedly in Palestine and Syria, and had studied the topography and the ancient buildings and sites, using the best archeological helps available. His appreciation of natural beauty and power of description were unusual; he knew the life of the people in all its aspects, and spoke their languages; he was minutely familiar with the Bible, and well read in the writers on Palestine, ancient and modern. These qualifications, with an easy graceful style, produced a book of unique appeal. It fulfilled in high degree its purpose of elucidating the Bible and greatly increased knowledge of Palestine in the English-speaking countries. Furthermore, it preserved faithful descriptions of Palestinian life while it was as yet little affected by western civilization.

[*Biog. Cat. of Princeton Theological Sem.* (1933); records of Miami Univ.; reports of Am. Board of Commissioners for Foreign Missions, 1833–70; reports of Presbyt. Board of Foreign Missions, 1870–90; *Missionary Herald*, Mar. 1842, Feb., June, Oct. 1843, June, Nov., Dec. 1844, Apr., June, Oct., Dec. 1845; H. H. Jessup, *Fifty-Three Years in Syria* (1910); J. S. Dennis, in *Church at Home and Abroad*, June 1894.]

R. H. N.

THORBURN, GRANT (Feb. 18, 1773–Jan. 21, 1863), seedsman, author, the son of James and Elizabeth (Fairley) Thorburn, was born near Dalkeith, Scotland, amid scenes made famous by Sir Walter Scott in *The Heart of Midlothian*. His mother died when he was two and a half years of age, and he says that it was the carelessness of a nurse that caused him to be dwarfed in stature, and to have short, feeble legs. His father was a maker of nails by hand, and, notwithstanding his handicap, Grant learned the trade and became expert at it, claiming on one day to have made 3,222 nails between 6 A.M. and 9 P.M. In 1792 he took part in a radical agitation for parliamentary reform, and was imprisoned on a charge of high treason, but was later released with a warning. To escape the odium which he believed he had incurred, he set sail for New York City, and landed in June 1794. He immediately found work as a nailer; met very soon a charming girl, Rebecca Sickles, and was married to her in June 1797. With his wife as shopkeeper he set up a small business in notions in his home and continued his nail-making. Rebecca died in 1800, leaving her husband with a young child. "Thinking it more creditable and wise to marry a wife than to hire a housekeeper," wrote Thorburn later, "I again entered into that state in 1801" (*Lawrie Todd, post*, p. 60). This wife, Hannah Wortemby, lived until 1852.

The invention of the nail-cutting machine deprived Thorburn of an occupation, and he started a small grocery business in his home. Having painted some flower pots one day to encourage their sale, it occurred to him that some growing plants in them might also be attractive to customers. He became interested in plants (which he had never noticed before), and after buying a number of them from a gardener, he began to have inquiries for the seed. It was thus that Thorburn, about 1803, became the first seedsman of any consequence in America, and came to found a business that functioned for more than a century. An English seed catalogue fell into his hands, and after studying it he issued one of his own in 1812, *The Gentleman and Gardener's Kalendar for the Middle States of North America*, the first in American history. He continued issuing these catalogues and manuals at intervals throughout his career. In 1808 he purchased a farm in New Jersey to grow his own seed, but it failed after he had sunk all his earnings into the venture, and he spent a time in debtors' prison. In 1816 he made a fresh start as a seedsman, and was soon on his feet again, prospering from that time on.

Thorburn now indulged his liking for mingling with prominent and intellectual people of all casts of thought, and jeopardized his standing with his church by cultivating an acquaintance with Thomas Paine. He also took to writing. A popular novel of the time, *Lawrie Todd* (1830), by John Galt, was said to have been founded on his life-story, and he assumed Lawrie Todd as a pen name. He wrote many articles and sketches for newspapers and magazines, displaying in them a mixture of naïveté, keen observation, and whimsical or bitter humor. Some of these were published collectively under the title *Sketches from the Note-book of Lawrie Todd* (1847). His principal works were *Forty Years' Residence in America* (1834); *Fifty Years' Reminiscences of New-York* (1845); *Men and Manners in Great Britain* (1834); *The History of Cardens and Carver* (1847); *Laurie*

Todd's Notes on Virginia; with a Chapter on Puritans, Witches and Friends (1848); and an autobiography, *Lawrie Todd, Life and Writings of Grant Thorburn* (1852). He spent the last eight years of his life in New Haven, Conn., where he died. On June 12, 1853, at the age of eighty, he was married to his third wife, Maria ——. His business was carried on by his sons and grandsons.

[Manuscript genealogical notes of the Thorburn family; Thorburn's autobiography, with a supplement, *Grant Thorburn in his Golden Age* (1863); J. A. Scoville, *Old Merchants of N. Y. City* (1863); *N. Y. Herald*, Jan. 25, 1863.]

A.F.H.

THOREAU, HENRY DAVID (July 12, 1817–May 6, 1862), essayist, poet, transcendentalist, was born in the town of Concord, Mass., of a varied ancestry which, on his mother's side, ran back to the Loyalist Jones family of Weston, Mass., and to the Scotch Dunbars of New Hampshire. It was these Dunbars that Henry Thoreau most resembled, having a romantic imagination like that of his grandfather Asa Dunbar, a love of nature and an unconventionality like that of his mother, and an inventiveness and whimsical humor like that of his favorite uncle Charles Dunbar. On his father's side the family derived directly from the Isle of Jersey and remotely from the city of Tours, from which place-name the family name seems to have originated. Henry's father, John Thoreau, was a grandson of Pierre Thoreau of St. Helier, Jersey, and eldest son of John Thoreau, Jersey sailor and adventurer, who in 1772 settled in Boston and began a successful mercantile career, retiring in 1800 to Concord. There his son John, the father of the author, became storekeeper and pencil manufacturer and "remembered more about the worthies (and unworthies) of Concord village . . . than anyone else" (Thoreau's "Journal" for Feb. 3, 1859, *Writings*, Walden ed., XVII, 437). John Thoreau on May 11, 1812, married Cynthia Dunbar, a native of Keene, N. H., and a woman of rare independence of spirit, vivacity, and with a deep love for the out-of-doors unusual at that time. Thoreau was born at the home of his maternal grandmother Mrs. Jonas Minott, widow of Asa Dunbar, on the Virginia Road northeast of the village, and, except for short periods in early childhood in Boston and Chelmsford, Mass., resided in Concord during his entire life, enlarging the town in his imagination until it became a microcosm holding within its borders the phenomena of the world.

His mother and his uncle Charles Dunbar introduced him to the countryside when he was very young, and he took a normal boyish delight in hunting, fishing, and country sports. At college and later as tutor he longed for his native fields and wrote homesick letters about them. In company with his brother he became, after college, a naturalist without rod and gun. His early maturity was made notable by daily exploration of familiar haunts, where he contemplated nature with a wise passiveness that owed something to Wordsworth and something to the Oriental mystics, who were ever attractive to him. The ecstasy of pantheism characterized his journalizing about nature during his first fifteen years out of college. Later in life his nature observation, perhaps under the influence of his friends Louis Agassiz and Thaddeus W. Harris [*qq.v.*] and perhaps as a result of his own middle age, became more objective and scientific. His interest in nature is too early and too nearly a passion to be treated lightly even in thinking of him as more than a naturalist.

He was named David Henry for his uncle David Thoreau who died in Concord in August 1817. After retaining the original order of names until his graduation from college, Thoreau reversed them, assigning no reason for the change. He prepared for college at Concord Academy and entered Harvard in August 1833. At college he submitted himself to the restricted curriculum of the day, entered little into the undergraduate life, went to chapel in a green coat "because the rules required black," and found solace in resorting to the alcove of the college library in which were the writings of the English poets, particularly those of the seventeenth century. In 1834 he began keeping a journal, a practice continued until the end of his life; and in 1835, between terms, he taught school at Canton, Mass., and boarded at the home of Orestes A. Brownson [*q.v.*], who taught him to read German. During his college course he was granted a scholarship in the form of the income from a Chelsea (Mass.) estate and with some difficulty collected the rents himself, as Emerson had done fifteen years earlier. Thoreau felt particularly the influence of two teachers: Edward T. Channing, who taught him to write English sentences, and Jones Very [*q.v.*], who taught him Greek and introduced him to the poetry of the English mystics. He emerged from Harvard in August 1837 far from the top of his class but perhaps the best-read member of the group.

College having prepared him for no occupation, he turned school teacher and for a fortnight in September 1837 taught the town school of Concord, where he sought discipline through moral suasion much as Bronson Alcott had done in Boston a few years before. A member of the school committee so objected to the absence of the ferule that the next day Thoreau, to make whipping absurd, whipped half a dozen surprised pupils and that night resigned his school. During the rest of that year he helped his father in what had become the family industry of pencil making. Early in 1838 he wrote to his brother John, then teaching in Staunton, Mass., proposing that they migrate westward and try teaching in Kentucky. Later they decided to open a private school in their father's house, John in charge and Henry teaching Latin, Greek, French, and mathematics. The next year they moved the school to the old Academy building, and the brothers continued teaching until the spring of 1841, introducing "field trips" for nature instruction, an innovation in American education. John perhaps caught the imagination of more pupils, but Henry's nature lore and thoroughness remained long in the memories of those whom he taught.

It was while they were teaching, during the first half of September 1839, that the Thoreau brothers made their thirteen-day vacation voyage down the Concord River and up the Merrimack as far as Concord, N. H., a pastoral journey not memorable in itself, but immortalized by Henry in his first book. On Apr. 11, 1838, Thoreau delivered the first of his almost annual lectures to the Concord Lyceum, the first one being on the subject of "Society." Later in the year, in December, he wrote his essay "Sound and Silence" and followed it in July 1840 with his rhapsody on courage, refused for the *Dial* by Margaret Fuller but printed in 1902 under the title *The Service*.

Early in 1841, in the full tide of success, the Thoreau brothers announced their school would close because of John's ill health. Henry went to live in the Emerson home, where during a two-year intimacy their long friendship began, a friendship cemented early by keen bereavements, Thoreau's brother dying on Jan. 11, 1841, and Emerson's son Waldo sixteen days later. Their sorrow drew them together and the next few years marked the height of their friendship. It was about this time that Thoreau was disappointed in his brief love affair with Ellen Sewall, and his friendship for her brother Edmund was broken off when the boy went with his parents to live in Scituate, Mass. Years later Thoreau put into the first chapter of his *Walden* a reference to his loss of "a hound, a bay horse, and a turtle-dove"; Edmund Sewall, John Thoreau, and Ellen Sewall. But the residence in the Emerson home brought gains also, for Thoreau began meeting with the group now known as the Transcendental Club and became acquainted with F. H. Hedge, A. Bronson Alcott, James Freeman

Clarke, George Ripley, Margaret Fuller, and Elizabeth Palmer Peabody [*qq.v.*]. In the Emerson household he turned his facile hand to all things from gardening and fence-mending to writing essays and poems, and during Emerson's absence edited the April 1843 number of the *Dial*. In May 1843 he became tutor in the home of his Concord patron's brother, William Emerson. The year on Staten Island constituted Thoreau's longest residence outside of Concord. He published "A Walk to Wachusett," a record of a July 1842 expedition, in the *Boston Miscellany* (January 1843) and while tutoring he translated "The Seven Against Thebes" but did not seek to publish it. In New York he made his acquaintance with the sea and with William Henry Channing, Lucretia Mott, Henry James, Sr., and Horace Greeley [*qq.v.*], and sought out publishers in a generally unsuccessful effort to sell articles to the magazines.

As early as Dec. 24, 1841, Thoreau, in his journal, had expressed a desire to "go soon and live away by the pond." It is not surprising, therefore, to find him upon his return to Concord early in 1844 again turning his thoughts toward this project. His friend Stearns Wheeler had lived in a hut at nearby Sandy Pond in 1841–42 and Thoreau had visited him and lived there perhaps as long as six weeks at one time; moreover, Ellery Channing had written to him on Mar. 5, 1845: "I see nothing for you in this earth but that field which I once christened 'Briars'; go out upon that, build yourself a hut, and there begin the grand process of devouring yourself alive. I see no alternative, no other hope for you. . . . Concord is just as good a place as any other" (*Writings*, Walden ed., VI, 121). Thoreau had some private business to transact, chiefly the writing of his book, *A Week on the Concord and Merrimack Rivers*; in the same month in which Channing had told him to build a hut he began a small house on Emerson's land on the northwest shore of Walden Pond. As Henry S. Salt has said: "Walden was, in fact, to Thoreau what Brook Farm was to others of the transcendentalists—a retreat suitable for philosophic meditation, and the practice of a simpler, hardier, and healthier life" (*Life of Thoreau*, 1896, p. 65).

Thoreau took up residence at the Pond July 4, 1845, and remained there until Sept. 6, 1847. During the summer of 1845 he was arrested for non-payment of poll tax, as Alcott had been in 1843. Both were protesting against slavery as it became a political issue in the Mexican War, and both chose "civil disobedience" as the most effective form of protest. Thoreau spent but one night in jail, the tax, much to his disgust, being paid by one of his aunts. Thoreau told the story of his jailing in his essay "Resistance to Civil Government" (later called "Civil Disobedience" and "On the Duty of Civil Disobedience") in Elizabeth Peabody's short-lived periodical *Æsthetic Papers* (1849), and retold it at the close of the chapter "The Village" in *Walden*. It may well be that the jailing episode, bringing into high relief Thoreau's extension of Jefferson's definition of good government to its ultimate conclusion—anarchy as far as any existing government was concerned—is the most significant incident of his twenty-six months at Walden Pond, for much of the life there has been misunderstood and exaggerated. Viewed as an experiment, these years with their dependence upon the home pantry and the Emerson dinner table become meaningful. Thoreau tried his theories, he gained two years of youthful leisure, he wrote a book, he declared himself on the matter of an individual's duties to his government, and he returned to the village mature and certain of himself. He did not, in spite of his own satisfaction with the experiment, urge his scheme on others as the ideal way of life. He had, however, settled one matter so thoroughly to his satisfaction that he was willing ever after to preach the doctrine of simplification without specifying that the simplifying should be in the Walden mode or in any particular mode except one which each individual should fit to his own life.

On Sept. 6, 1847, Thoreau moved back to his father's house in the village. He brought with him the first draft of his book, *A Week on the Concord and Merrimack Rivers*, a series of comments upon life and literature gleaned from his journals of ten years and strung on the thread of narrative telling the story of the boat trip of the two brothers in September eight years before. He brought back new journals to be reaped in the preparation of *Walden* six years later. "He was a student when he came to Walden; when he returned to Concord he was a teacher" (Salt, *Life*, 1896, p. 84). He began, in the early autumn of 1847, his second residence in the home of Emerson, where he lived for a year while Emerson was in Europe. The *Week* had found no publisher, though Emerson had, on Aug. 6, 1847, solicited the aid of W. H. Furness in getting it published in Philadelphia, saying that "Thoreau is mainly bent on having it printed in a cheap form for a large circulation" (H. H. Furness, ed., *Records of a Lifelong Friendship . . . Ralph Waldo Emerson and William Henry Furness*, 1910, p. 61). Thoreau, after adding to the book (the section on friendship, according to

Alcott's diary, having been written as late as January 1848), finally published his first book at his own risk in the spring of 1849. Slightly over 200 copies were sold, and in 1853 three-quarters of the original thousand copies came back to the author. He salved his wounded spirit by commenting on the lack of sale, "It affects my privacy less, and leaves me freer" ("Journal," Oct. 28, 1853, *Writings,* XI, 460). The six years between the return from Walden Pond and the receipt of the unsold books had also contributed to Thoreau's freedom. Early in 1849 he returned to his father's "yellow house reformed" on Main Street and lived there during the remainder of his life.

One will not well understand Thoreau unless he places him in the midst of the Thoreau family, for that family life was as delightful and as intimate as that of their neighbors the Alcotts. None of the Thoreau children married or left home. Mrs. Thoreau shared with Mrs. Alcott the rare ability to create a rich home life out of simple materials. The family business of pencil making was a home industry, practised in a lean-to of the house, participated in by all, and managed after the father's death Feb. 3, 1859, by Sophia and Henry and made more profitable by the latter's inventiveness. Henry made himself useful in many other ways and became the "handy man" of Concord but was more dependent upon the *esprit de corps* of home life than the family was dependent upon him, more dependent than he or his first biographer, Emerson, would willingly admit. He was happy only when he was fulfilling his early wish expressed in a letter from Staten Island to his mother in 1843: "Methinks I should be content to sit at the back door in Concord, under the poplar tree, henceforth forever" (*Writings,* VI, 99).

Between the publication of the *Week* (1849) and that of *Walden, or Life in the Woods* (1854) Thoreau's friendships multiplied and the poet Ellery Channing replaced Emerson in the center of his acquaintance. In 1849 he came to know Harrison G. O. Blake of Worcester, Mass., with whom he maintained a long correspondence and to whom his sister bequeathed his manuscripts and journals. He toured Cape Cod on foot late in 1849, spent a week in Canada in 1850, went in 1853 on his second journey into Maine. Four of his posthumous books derive in part at least from these expeditions: *Excursions* (1863), *The Maine Woods* (1864), *Cape Cod* (1865), and *A Yankee in Canada* (1866). In the midst of these happy journeyings he made one sad trip as emissary from Concord to Fire Island beach near New York, where July 19, 1850, Margaret Fuller

Ossoli with her husband and son had been drowned in a shipwreck—a melancholy rummaging among the flotsam on the beach.

For five years after the return from the pond Thoreau lived ecstatically. He found keen delight in his daily walks about Concord and in the rarer, more ambitious trips into farther fields. It is the period of his friendship with the Emerson children, the berrying parties, the period of the formation of friendships, the years when one book was on the market (a drug there, to be sure) and when the next was in process of composition. He thought of himself as a poet and late in the period feared that his observation "is from year to year becoming more distinct and scientific" ("Journal," Aug. 19, 1851, *Writings,* VIII, 406). One turns from these five free years to 1852, the year which has been called "the noon of his life" (Odell Shepard, ed., *The Heart of Thoreau's Journals,* 1927, p. 106), when his most fruitful journalizing was done. He became interested in more individuals while his opinions of society became steadily more critical. He discovered a kindred youthful spirit in Emerson's seventy-seven year old aunt, Mary Moody Emerson, and a lively companion in Ellery Channing. He had become involved in the slavery question a second time on Oct. 1, 1851, when he put a fugitive slave on the train for Canada. His growing distrust of society would seem to coincide with his increasing interest in a slavery issue that was rapidly reaching a crisis and in an industrialism that had begun in New England to reproduce the evils of the factory system of old England. The problem of labor is generously discussed in the 1853 journal in entries which were brought together in the posthumously published "Life Without Principle" (*Atlantic Monthly,* October 1863). Though he was suspicious of reformers, Thoreau's excitement over slavery grew to white heat during the notorious Anthony Burns extradition in 1854, while he filled his journal with a denunciation of government which later in the year he delivered as a speech, "Slavery in Massachusetts," at an anti-slavery rally in neighboring Framingham (*Writings,* IV, 387–408). These concerns of 1853 have a place in his book *Walden,* finished during that year and published Aug. 9, 1854.

Walden confused the critics, for the book exhibited many of the paradoxes of its author. Seemingly parochial in its comments on the social condition of Concord, it has universal social criticism in it. With a reputation for being harmless natural history, it strikes blows at all the superficialities of society and government. Those qualities are also the qualities of Thoreau, who was at once as harmless and as devastating as the book, and as disarming to the commentators and critics.

After the publication of *Walden* Thoreau's life is anticlimactic. He became the scientific observer rather than the nature poet, working indefatigably upon his Concord herbarium, his weather records, and his ethnological study of the Indian. He became a lyceum lecturer with indifferent success outside of Concord. He began to finish life, making a last trip to Cape Cod in 1855, a last journey to Maine in 1857. Ill health in the form of tuberculosis began to close in upon him. In October 1854 he became acquainted with his one foreign friend, the donor of his extensive Oriental library, Thomas Cholmondeley. At Christmas 1854 he made his first visit to his Quaker correspondent Daniel Ricketson [*q.v.*] of New Bedford, and formed a lasting friendship which was recorded by the latter's children, Anna and Walton, in *Daniel Ricketson and His Friends* (1902). The third of the new friends was John Brown of Osawatomie [*q.v.*], whom he met in the home of Emerson in March 1857. To these new friends, Emerson added two names of late acquaintances who made a profound impression on Thoreau: Joe Polis, his Indian guide in Maine, and Walt Whitman, whom he met in New York in November 1856.

Thoreau's life burned out in a great enthusiasm, a defense of John Brown, who had been arrested at Harpers Ferry on Oct. 16, 1859. Thoreau was the first American to make public utterance in defense of Brown. He spoke in Concord Vestry on Sunday night, Oct. 30, against the protests of his townsmen, having to ring the bell with his own hands and to open the door with the key which the fearful vestrymen had dared neither to give him nor refuse him and so had left it where he could find it. In "A Plea for Captain John Brown" (*Writings,* IV, 409–40; first printed in James Redpath, *Echoes of Harper's Ferry,* 1860), Thoreau rose to new heights of incisiveness in avowing his approval of Brown's action, and eulogized the man so magnificently that he was heard, as Emerson wrote, "by all respectfully, and by many with a sympathy that surprised themselves" (*Atlantic Monthly,* Aug. 1862, p. 242). On Nov. 1 he read the same lecture in Boston, and the *Liberator* (Nov. 4, 1859) commented on his enthusiasm. He spoke again a month later at the Concord service in commemoration of Brown's death. Thoreau regarded the John Brown affair as a touchstone which brought out the true nature of the American government. It became also the touchstone of his own nature, for his misanthropic reputation sloughed off

when he rose to defend a martyr, and his antisocial position among his neighbors gave way to a respect among many for one in the van of social justice.

In November 1860 he caught cold which led to a bronchial infection aggravated by his insistence on keeping a lecture engagement. After that, tuberculosis made rapid progress. In the spring of 1861 he made a fruitless journey, accompanied by Horace Mann, Jr., to Minnesota in search of health. He observed in semi-invalid fashion the vast new region of the Great Lakes and the Mississippi and went 300 miles beyond St. Paul to witness a gathering of the Sioux at Redwood. But the zest was gone. He returned to Concord weaker than when he had left, made one brief visit to New Bedford in August 1861, and then went to his room. The months of illness became so normal to him that he said he enjoyed the experiences of the sickroom as he had previously enjoyed those of the world of nature. He feverishly edited manuscripts which he left for his sister Sophia to publish. He weakened until the effort of holding the pages was too great for him; and then, at nine in the morning of May 6, 1862, he uttered the words of his beloved wilderness, "moose" and "Indian," and died. His funeral was held May 8, 1862, from the first parish church with a eulogy by Emerson (printed in enlarged form in the *Atlantic Monthly,* August 1862, and as a preface to Thoreau's *Excursions* in 1863) and with burial in the New Burying Ground in Concord. Some years later the body was moved to a new family lot in Sleepy Hollow Cemetery, on the ridge near the places where his friends Hawthorne, Emerson, Alcott, and Channing were to be buried.

Thoreau published but two books and a few magazine articles during his lifetime. From the huge mass of manuscript left at his death his sister published the volumes already mentioned. In 1865 Emerson presented a stoical Thoreau in his editing of *Letters to Various Persons,* enlarged in 1894 as *Familiar Letters of Henry David Thoreau.* His friend H. G. O. Blake edited selections from the journal as *Early Spring in Massachusetts* (1881), *Summer* (1884), *Winter* (1888), *Autumn* (1892). His poems, edited by H. S. Salt and F. B. Sanborn, were published as *Poems of Nature* (1895). The Riverside edition of his works (11 vols., 1894) was superseded by the Walden edition of *The Writings of Henry David Thoreau* (20 vols., 1906), fourteen volumes of which contain virtually all of the extant journal with the exception of two years between April 1843 and July 1845 and a few unimportant nature records. In 1902 his early essay on bravery was published under the title of *The Service*; and in 1905 the Bibliophile Society published his 1843 essay *Sir Walter Raleigh* and a two-volume record of his travels called *First and Last Journeys of Thoreau*. The same society published an enlarged and garbled *Walden* (1909) containing 12,000 rejected words not included in the original edition and badly edited by F. B. Sanborn. There have been some slight additions to the Thoreau canon since 1909, but nothing of great consequence except possibly the themes he wrote in college which, with changes, were included in Sanborn's biography of 1917. Some manuscript, including his notes for a history of the American Indian, remains unpublished, but it does not contain any considerable addition to Thoreau literature.

Thoreau's powerful influence upon later literature, both English and American, is more due to his style than even his admirers have realized. It is a nervous style, usually staccato, though often expanding in poetic passages of complex rhythm, the style of an exhorter who does not "pull his punches," and directly in the tradition of the most characteristic American writing, journalistic and otherwise. It has the pith and force of a man who, more concerned with incisive thought than with sustained argument, cares more for his sentences than for his essays as a whole. Even his descriptions depend more upon a single vivid image than upon a continuity of phrase. At his finest he is one of the best writers, if not the best, of American prose, but just as he wrote often from notes of uneven pitch, so he must be read in excerpts in order to be most impressive.

Of his books, only *Walden* is really organized; the rest are either journals padded with reflections or left as lean and specific narrative, or fragmentary essays made from crystallizations of his thought. *A Week on the Concord and Merrimack Rivers*, which has usually shared the reputation of *Walden,* is memorable now chiefly for the nature studies which were to give him his first eminence in literature. *The Maine Woods* is the same kind of book minus both the literary criticism of the *Week* and the social purpose of *Walden*. His observations of nature, which were lifelong, are characterized, not so much by their accuracy, in which others have exceeded him, as by a characteristic tension that gives them at their best an almost unequaled force and is felt in his style. Thoreau was teetering always between the transcendental and the scientific view of nature. From the first came his deep perceptions of spirit manifest in form which gives to simple, almost trivial, observations upon a flower,

a cloud, a tree, a bird, a significant and often a passionate expression. To the latter is due the careful thoroughness of his study, as of one who looks and looks again at the same thing. If he saw sometimes too much with the inner eye, the accuracy of his words never fails. As he grew older the transcendental seems to have been overborne in him by the very mass of his observations collected in his tireless rambles, until in his later journals the poet is almost lost in the sense of duty of a routine naturalist. Curiously enough, although he is supposed to be the fountain head of American nature writing, Thoreau actually stands apart from the American tradition in that he was unsentimental, and unromantic except in the expansiveness of his transcendentalism. He had a passion for nature which became articulate, and this is very American, but the Concord swamps and fields and the Maine woods were never merely picturesque to him, or sentimentally "wild" and emotionalized in that vein, as with Audubon, Burroughs, Muir, and with the nature fakers.

Walden, though uneven, is his one real book, and for that reason his greatest achievement, although most of its chapters can be duplicated, and some of them excelled, in his other writings. But it was not the nature writing of *Walden* which made it a textbook of the British Labor party, and read throughout the world. Thoreau's sojourn at Walden Pond was an experiment. He bought lime in the village to plaster the cabin he built there, but before he used it gathered a bushel of clamshells on the shores of nearby Fair Haven Bay and burnt them to a double handful of lime. His bean and potato planting, his baking in the ashes, his hunting and fishing, were likewise experiments, all intended to prove that certain transcendental doctrines of simplicity could be practised if need be, and, even more important, that a civilized man could make himself independent of the commercialism and the industrialism of New England. Thoreau has often been called anarchistic or anti-social. It would be more accurate to describe him as one who, urging conscience above government and being determined to rely upon himself before relying upon others, proposed to obey a set of laws which he regarded as more fundamental than those enforced by his particular state. Some of these he deduced from the tested experience of the ages— some were local to his own prejudices. Inevitably this brought him into conflict with both the ideals and the practice of his neighbors. The greed of many, the low and unsatisfactory nature of the values that nearly all sought in experience, inspired an attack which was nothing new in philosophy but which gained freshness and force when made by a man who found his greatest happiness in walking over the land they bought and sold. His perception of the lacks and dangers of the recent industrialism of New England was, however, both new and cogent. Like Carlyle, he saw politics as economics and current economics as spiritual diminution. But he was concrete where Carlyle was cloudy, specific where Carlyle was rhetorical, and a cool-headed Yankee where Carlyle lost his poise in universals and in the admiration of the dubiously great. Size never impressed Thoreau. A Yankee again, he argued for the practicality of the supposedly impractical. Only the grosser wrongs, like slavery, or an occasional esotericism from the Orient, drove him toward rhetoric. Thus *Walden* is a complete report of an experiment in thinking and living, with the definite design or arguing for true values against false and with abundant illustrations drawn from nature of the true; it is an attempt to demonstrate that civilized man can escape the evils of competition, and to show that a nature lover has his own passions worth describing for a world delivered over unto artifice. Its extraordinary influence is due to this organic purpose, excellently expressed, and to its highly important themes, of which, ironically, that furthest from his philosophic purpose though nearest to his heart, joy in nature, gave the book its position as a classic for youth.

The philosophy of his famous essay on civil disobedience is all implicit in the later *Walden*. This is the classic of individualism in its inevitable conflict with government, but, again, implies a state based upon laws in conformity with Thoreau's conception of what is noblest and most worthily human. It is a mistake, however, to define Thoreau as a social philosopher. He was, essentially, a man of letters, an essayist in the best sense, with a touch of the prophet. He was not a reformer, for he distrusted group action, but rather belongs with Walt Whitman as one who, having put his own definition upon morality, exhorted to the moral life. Both men are at the heart of the persistent American tradition of perfectibility, although Thoreau is on the pessimistic, Whitman on the optimistic side.

Thoreau was not a scientist in any true sense (though a good naturalist), not an important philosopher, but an admirable critic of everything except literature, where, in spite of some fine sayings, he was limited by the narrow range of his emotions. It was his own literary skill, however, that made him the best interpreter of the American environment of woods, swamps, meadows, fauna and flora, and weather, to the domesticated Europeans who were his fellow Americans. It was to know the soil, as the English know theirs, that he waded marshes and sought the wisdom of the Indians in the Maine woods. He would seem to be assured of permanence in English literature, partly for his style, though certainly not for any power over form beyond the sentence or, rarely, the paragraph, but still more as a germinal influence completely articulate for ideas which keep recurring in every culture and always search out their best translator into words. He is one of those writers whose particular job is to relate the best of man to the possibilities of his environment. And here he is a landmark in the vital thread of American literature—the conflict between ideals of living and methods of making a living. The environment he described was conditioned by Concord; but few writers in English have been so often clear, lofty, eloquent within such narrow limits of experience. It was a natural, though not inevitable, contribution of rural New England to world literature.

[F. H. Allen, *A Bibliography of Henry David Thoreau* (1908), is definitive up to that year; it may be supplemented by the bibliography in *The Cambridge Hist. of Am. Literature*, vol. II (1918), and R. W. Adams, *A Thoreau Checklist, 1908–1930* (1930). There are numerous full-length biographies. W. E. Channing, *Thoreau, the Poet-Naturalist* (1873; new ed. 1902), gives a personal appraisal. F. B. Sanborn, *Henry D. Thoreau* (1882), enlarged into *The Life of Henry David Thoreau* (1917), is rich in family history and Concord lore but opinionated. Henry S. Salt, *The Life of Henry David Thoreau* (1890), revised as *Life of Henry David Thoreau* (1896), remains the most accurate and complete biography, not superseded by Léon Bazalgette, *Henry Thoreau, Bachelor of Nature* (1924), J. B. Atkinson, *Henry Thoreau, the Cosmic Yankee* (1917), and Mark Van Doren, *Henry David Thoreau; a Critical Study* (1916). F. B. Sanborn, *The Personality of Thoreau* (1901), and Edward Waldo Emerson, *Henry Thoreau as Remembered by a Young Friend* (1917), are particularly valuable studies which emphasize the kindly humanness of their subject. Thoreau has been the subject of a myriad of shorter studies among which, outside the histories of American literature, the reader will find the following valuable: Norman Foerster, "Thoreau," in *Nature in American Literature* (1923); J. R. Lowell, "Thoreau" in *My Study Windows* (1871); H. S. Canby, "Henry David Thoreau," in *Classic Americans* (1931), a study of Thoreau's social thinking.]

R. W. A.
H. S. C—y.

THORNDIKE, ASHLEY HORACE (Dec. 26, 1871–Apr. 17, 1933), scholar, was born in Houlton, Me., the son of the Rev. Edward Robert and Abby Brewster (Ladd) Thorndike. He prepared for college at the Roxbury Latin School, Boston, and in 1893 graduated A.B. from Wesleyan University, where he came under the influence of the distinguished literary scholar, Caleb T. Winchester [*q.v.*]. During the next two years he was principal of the Smith Academy in Hatfield, Mass., where he met Annette Marian Lowell, who became his wife on June 21, 1899. They had four children. In 1895 he went to Harvard University for graduate study, took the A.M. degree in 1896, and the Ph.D. in 1898, at the same time acting as instructor in English in Boston University. For four years, 1898–1902, he was instructor and associate professor in Western Reserve University, and for the next four, professor in Northwestern University. In 1906 he was called to Columbia University, where he taught till his death. Among his colleagues there were his two brothers, Edward L. Thorndike, psychologist, and Lynn Thorndike, historian. He received many honors and distinctions. He was president of the Modern Language Association in 1926–27, and of the Shakespeare Association of America from 1923 till his death; was vice-president of the National Institute of Arts and Letters; and in 1927 gave the annual Shakespeare lecture of the British Academy, published as *Shakespeare in America* (1927).

These facts, while they suggest correctly enough a highly successful academic career, give little indication of either the quality of Thorndike's mind or the range of his influence. Something of these may be gathered from his writings. His doctoral dissertation, *The Influence of Beaumont and Fletcher on Shakspere* (1901), was a work of marked originality which has affected the whole course of Shakespearean criticism in the last thirty years. Barrett Wendell [*q.v.*] had been emphasizing for some years the typical and contemporary elements in Shakespeare's work, and it was probably a suggestion from him that led Thorndike to the specific investigations in which he showed Shakespeare as taking up and developing the methods and devices of his contemporaries rather than originating them. His volume on *Tragedy* followed in 1908, giving evidence of a finely balanced literary judgment. From 1913 to 1915 he edited in collaboration with William A. Neilson The Tudor Shakespeare, with a fortieth volume on *The Facts about Shakespeare* (1913). *Shakespeare's Theatre* (1916) is a compendious account of the scholarship on a subject that had been growing rapidly and to which he made substantial contributions. In his *English Comedy* (1929) he produced a companion study to his *Tragedy* of twenty years before. Though it is as a student of the Elizabethan drama that Thorndike is most widely known, his literary interests were very extensive. He acted for many years as literary adviser to a large publishing house; and from the reading of hundreds of manuscripts he obtained an insight into the intellectual currents of his own time, such as could not have been obtained from published books alone, and exercised an influence, as great

as it was unobtrusive, on literary production. *Literature in a Changing Age* (1920) and *The Outlook for Literature* (1931) deal penetratingly with the place of books in modern culture. In the writing and editing of textbooks for the teaching of English at all stages, he was prolific. These run from his *Elements of Rhetoric and Composition* (1905) through *Everyday English* (2 vols., 1912–13, with F. T. Baker), *The Minor Elizabethan Drama* (2 vols, 1910) for Everyman's Library, an edition of *The Maid's Tragedy* (1906) in the Belles-Lettres Series, *A History of English Literature* (1920 with W. A. Neilson), to those of more general interest as his revision, with John W. Cunliffe, of *The Warner Library of the World's Best Literature* (30 vols., 1917).

Alongside of this activity in the production of books went his life as a busy university teacher. For over a quarter of a century, he was the guide and adviser of a great stream of young men and women engaged in the graduate study of English, and these students carried on his influence in scores of colleges throughout the United States. The characteristic of the training he gave them, as of his own writing, was the combination of a profound respect for facts with a lively interest in their significance. He did not allow the weight of his erudition to crush his interest in general truths, and he retained, as too few scholars do, a sense of the emotional values of the literary documents with which he dealt. Many people depended on him for aid and counsel, for his judgments were sound and his sympathies ready. Externally, he was a man of large physique with a mass of hair which early turned white, and a deliberate manner which masked the quickness of his mind, as his humor and appearance of ironic detachment masked his warmth of feeling.

[Family and personal sources; *Who's Who in America,* 1932–33; *Columbia Univ. Quart.,* June 1933; *N. Y. Times,* Apr. 18–20, 1933.]   W. A. N.

THORNDIKE, ISRAEL (Apr. 30, 1755–May 8, 1832), sailor, merchant, was born in Beverly, Mass., the son of Andrew and Anna (Morgan) Thorndike. He was descended from John Thorndike, one of the original settlers of Ipswich, but does not seem to have been born to much in the way of material possessions, for his lack of education is noted by his contemporaries. He must have gone to sea as a youth, as, on Oct. 30, 1776, he was commissioned commander of the schooner *Warren,* was later first lieutenant of the brig *Tyrannicide,* and commander of the ship *Resource,* all privateers (see *Massachusetts Soldiers and Sailors of the Revolutionary War,* vol.

XV, 1907, p. 691). As the harbor of Salem and Beverly was not controlled by the British during the Revolution, he was able to make valuable captures with these and other ships, and at the close of hostilities to keep vessels in operation at a time when American shipping was practically reduced to the Salem-Beverly fleet. He became an active partner of the shipping firm of Brown and Thorndike, which his brother-in-law, Moses Brown, had established in 1777, and which he conducted alone after Brown's retirement in 1800. This firm took a very conspicuous part in the trade with China and the Orient that originated in Salem and was later expanded from Boston. Before he was thirty-five years of age his part in the Revolution, his financial prominence, and his personal influence made him one of the leading men in the state.

From 1788 to 1814 he was thirteen times elected to the state legislature, seven times to the lower, and six times to the upper branch; he was member of the constitutional conventions of 1788 and 1820; and a presidential elector in 1812 and 1816. In 1810 he changed his residence from Beverly to Boston, where he was already so well known that he was elected to the state Senate from his new constituency in 1812. He continued his extensive business with the Orient, invested largely in manufacturing and other business enterprises, and his mansion became a political and social center. One of his dinner-parties in 1812 was renowned because the famous "Gerrymander" drawing that gave a new word to the English language was exhibited at his home soon after its origin (*New-England Historical and Genealogical Register*, Oct. 1873, Oct. 1892). He contributed freely for public purposes sums then considered large, and in 1818 purchased the library of Professor Ebeling of Hamburg, Germany, a valuable collection of Americana, and presented it to Harvard College. As this was his largest public gift, although he left an estate of $1,500,000, and the outlay was only $6,500, he cannot be considered a pioneer in philanthropy, but he was a sturdy patriot in the Revolution, and he influenced the economic development and politics of Massachusetts for the first half-century of independence.

His oratory was more conspicuous for its substance than its form, but his mastery of fact was often made use of by legislative colleagues of more eloquence for whom he collected material. On Oct. 31, 1784, he was married to Anna Dodge, of Salem, who died in 1817. They had twelve children, three dying in infancy. He died and was buried in Boston, but his body was transferred to Mount Auburn Cemetery in 1896.

[*Memorial Biog. of the N.-E. Hist. and Geneal. Soc.*, vol. VI (1905); Josiah Quincy, *The Hist. of Harvard Univ.* (1840), vol. II; E. M. Stone, *Hist. of Beverly* (1843); Thomas Bridgman, *The Pilgrims of Boston* (1856); obituary articles in *N.-E. Mag.*, June 1832, and *Boston Daily Advertiser and Patriot*, May 10, 23, 1832.]   S. G.

THORNE, CHARLES ROBERT (*c.* 1814– Dec. 13, 1893), actor and manager, was born in New York City of a merchant family. His father may have been Thomas W. Thorne. If the date which is generally given for his birth is correct, his precocity was remarkable, for on Apr. 23, 1829, billed as "a young gentleman in this city," he made his "first appearance on any stage" as Octavian at the Park Theatre, New York (Odell, *post*, vol. III, p. 395). On Apr. 28 he played the difficult rôle of Pierre in Otway's *Venice Preserved*, and on Apr. 30 had a benefit. In December 1830 he acted Pythias to Thomas Hamblin's Damon at the Bowery, and later played the title rôle in *Pizarro*. The same year he married Maria Ann Mestayer, who was of a well-known theatrical and circus family. This is enough, even in those days of juvenile prodigies, to cause some wonder; however, it should be noted that one of his sons was later to exhibit a similar precocity. On May 4, 1831, Thorne appears as "proprietor" of the Chatham Theatre. The *New York Mirror* of June 11, 1831, praises his Pizarro as displaying "force and expression," though wanting "study, practice, and observation." November 1831 found him and his wife at the new theatre on Richmond Hill. During the next few years, like most other actors save those at the Park, Thorne drifted from one house to another and took part in an unbelievable number of plays. In February 1835 he was back at the Bowery, playing Glaucus in *The Last Days of Pompeii*, which ran from Feb. 9 to Mar. 7, a New York record at that time. In June 1836 he was at the Franklin on Chatham Square; in November he supported James Henry Hackett [*q.v.*] at the Bowery in *Horse-Shoe Robinson* and later the elder James Wallack in *Sardanapalus*. On Nov. 27, 1837, he played Wellborn to the elder Booth's Sir Giles Overreach in *A New Way to Pay Old Debts* at the Olmypic. On Dec. 18, 1837, he was again at the Bowery, where on Jan. 2, 1838, he rode the "fiery, untamed steed" in *Mazeppa*. In the late summer of 1838 he managed the little Olympic and in February 1840 took over the Chatham, where he enjoyed success for two years but failed the third. His failure has been attributed (Odell, *post*, vol. IV, p. 647) to lack of any sustained policy; his seasons were hodge-podges.

From this time on his New York appearances grew fewer, and the intervening gaps represent tours made by Thorne and his wife, or attempts at management in other cities. He acted, Feb. 19, 1844, in *Thérèse* and *The Swiss Cottage* at the Bowery Amphitheatre; on Dec. 4, 1848, he and his wife acted *Don Cæsar de Bazan* at Chanfrau's National; at the ill-fated Astor Place opera house, Feb. 22, 1851, he and Chanfrau had a benefit (in the midst of opera); and from Aug. 30, 1852, till Sept. 14, he attempted to manage that house, without success. Beginning Aug. 1, 1853, he attempted to manage a season at the St. Charles. Finally, in 1874, he rented old Niblo's from A. T. Stewart for three years at $35,000 a year, and attempted to create "an American Drury Lane." In 1847, between New York engagements, he and his wife managed the old Boston Theatre on Federal Street, and for a brief time the Howard Athenaeum. In 1849 they went to California; again in 1853 they toured to San Francisco, and thence to the Orient and around the world, being absent many years on an adventurous if not very profitable tour. In 1880 they celebrated their golden wedding. In 1883 a letter from Thorne to Albert Marshman Palmer, asks for a benefit; "No doubt," he writes, "I will be Edwin's [his son's] next care after he pays his debts." Ten years later he died in San Francisco.

Thorne was chiefly notable as one of the early American-born actors and managers, who had courage to adopt the stage as a career. He was good-looking and graceful, and his rather round, healthy face was expressive. But his training was haphazard, gained chiefly in the cheaper Bowery theatres where romantic and melodramatic rant was most appreciated, and his artistic intelligence as a manager does not seem to have been conspicuous. He contributed little to the development of a native drama or style of acting. He and his first wife (d. 1881) had five children, among them Charles Robert [*q.v.*]. In 1883 he married the widow of James Stark, an actor.

[E. D. Barbour, *Geneal. Record of John Thorne* (1913); G. C. D. Odell, *Annals of the N. Y. Stage,* vols. III–VI (1928–31); *Music and Drama,* Oct. 21, 1882; theatre colls. in Harvard Coll. lib. and N. Y. Pub. Lib.; obituary notice in *San Francisco Chronicle,* Dec. 16, 1893.]   W. P. E.

THORNE, CHARLES ROBERT (1840–Feb. 10, 1883), actor, was born in New York City, son of Charles Robert Thorne [*q.v.*] and Maria (Mestayer) Thorne. In 1847 he went to school in Boston, where his parents were playing. He was a student at St. John's (later Fordham) College, 1854–57, and is said to have been a "clerk" with his grandfather Thorne on Wall Street. In 1854, according to his own statement, he acted with his father in San Francisco, and

soon afterwards went to Australia with his parents. It is certain that a C. Thorne was at the Bowery, New York, in September 1857, and "C. R. Thorne, Jr.," was a full-fledged member of Joseph Jefferson's company at Laura Keene's Theatre, New York, May 16, 1860, and played Captain de Boots in *Our American Cousin,* July 23, 1860. In September 1860 he supported Mr. and Mrs. Barney Williams in New York, and then (like many other American actors when the Civil War began) he left the East. He played at McGuire's in San Francisco, quarreled with Edwin Forrest, and set out to find his father and mother in China. The year 1866 found him as leading man at the Boston Theatre, where he remained three years. Touring followed, and in 1871 he joined the Union Square Theatre company in New York, one of the best in the country, where for many years he enjoyed a great measure of popular success. Here he received good training, especially by Dion Boucicault [*q.v.*] in *Led Astray,* and a large salary. Physically, he was of a ruddy but athletic type, looking a bit like a young hunting squire, and as the heroes of the domestic melodramas characteristic of the period he cut a great dash. He had a sonorous voice, which he made much use of. As one critic said after his appearance in 1880 as Sardou's *Daniel Rochat,* his style did not "lend itself to expressions of subtlety." But he could suggest suppressed power, and audiences found him "sympathetic" and good to look at. In 1874 with Stuart Robson [*q.v.*], he played *Led Astray* in London. In 1878 he acted in Bronson Howard's *The Banker's Daughter.* His last days were unfortunate. Late in 1882 he left the Union Square to be made a star in *The Corsican Brothers,* by John Stetson, the famous and eccentric Boston manager. The play opened at Booth's Theatre, New York, early in 1883 to a crowded and expectant house, but Thorne disappointed the audience by his acting, and the production was violently criticized. It quickly developed, however, that Thorne was not well. His illness accentuated by disappointment and the flaming success of young Richard Mansfield [*q.v.*] in *A Parisian Romance* at the Union Square where he had so long been regnant, he broke down completely and soon afterwards died. His funeral, at which the "cloud-capped towers" passage from *The Tempest* and a telegram from Robert Green Ingersoll [*q.v.*] were read for all ceremony, raised a teapot tempest difficult now to understand, and poor Thorne was widely branded "atheist."

Thorne's first wife was a Miss Calder of Boston, whom he married early in 1859. After his wife secured a divorce in Indiana, Thorne married Mary (Smith) Brown of Philadelphia. He was survived by his wife and a daughter of his first marriage. Of him one critic said, "His instincts are mock-heroic, bully-boy instincts, but he knows better." He never knew quite enough, however, or had the ambition to overcome these instincts thoroughly; he was too handsome and easy-going, perhaps. Another critic remarked, after the funeral, "Thorne didn't know enough to be an atheist"—which was another way of saying that he lacked the mental equipment required of the best actors.

[The date of Thorne's birth is given variously as Mar. 10 and June 11, 1840. See E. D. Barbour, *Geneal. Record of John Thorne* (1913); G. C. D. Odell, *Annals of the N. Y. Stage,* vol. VII (1931); records of Fordham Coll.; *N. Y. Times, N. Y. Daily Tribune,* Feb. 11, 13, 1883; theatre colls. in lib. of Harvard Univ. and N. Y. Pub. Lib. The quotations are from newspaper clippings in the Harvard coll.]   W. P. E.

THORNTON, HENRY WORTH (Nov. 6, 1871–Mar. 14, 1933), railroad manager, son of Henry Clay and Millamenta Comegys (Worth) Thornton, was born in Logansport, Ind. He prepared for college at St. Paul's School, Concord, N. H., and was graduated from the University of Pennsylvania in 1894, with the degree of B.S. He began his railroad service in that year as a draftsman in the office of the chief engineer of the Southwest system of the Pennsylvania Railroad and advanced rapidly in that department to the position of engineer of maintenance of way. In 1901 he became a division superintendent and in 1911, after several promotions, was appointed general superintendent of the Long Island Railroad. His work was of such character that it attracted the attention of Samuel Rea [*q.v.*], then president of the Pennsylvania Railroad, and in 1914, when asked by Lord Claude Hamilton, chairman of the board of the Great Eastern Railway of England, to suggest a man for the general managership of that property, Rea recommended Thornton, who was elected to the position a few months before the outbreak of the World War.

When Great Britain entered the war and the Great Eastern was called upon to perform an important part in the transportation of troops and military supplies, Thornton's ability and resourcefulness in adapting the service of his railway to meet the emergency, his tact in relations with railway and governmental officers and the public, and his exceptional powers in inspiring the confidence and loyalty of the workers, quickly overcame the initial prejudice against him as an alien. He was made a member of the national committee of general managers appointed to administer the British railways for the government. In 1916 he was appointed deputy director of inland water transportation, with rank of colonel in the Royal Engineers. In 1917 he became assistant director general of railway movements in France, representing the director and army council in negotiations with the French, Italian, and American governments. Later in that year he became deputy director general of railway movements, with rank of brigadier-general, and in 1918 he was made inspector general of transportation and advanced to the rank of major-general. His military service completed, he returned to the management of the Great Eastern Railway and on several occasions served also on the National Wage Board in arbitration proceedings, as well as on a committee to investigate the operations and finances of the Metropolitan Water Board of the City of London. In 1919 he was gazetted Knight Commander of the Order of the British Empire. He was honored also by decorations from the United States, France, and Belgium.

Thornton became a naturalized British subject in 1919, evidently intending to remain in England, but when steps were taken in 1922 to consolidate all of the English railways into four systems there was some uncertainty as to his position. It was then that the Canadian National Railways, just created in Canada by the amalgamation of a large number of separate railways, sought his services, and in October 1922 he became chairman of the board and president of that large system. The properties brought together as a nationalized system to compete with the strong and well organized Canadian Pacific Railway were typically weak and had little in common. The task of welding them into a coherent and unified whole was one of major proportions. Many of the separate units were bankrupt and in poor physical condition when acquired, and the morale of employees was distinctly low. During his ten years as chief executive Thornton succeeded in welding the properties together, creating an efficient operating organization, and establishing a high degree of *esprit de corps*. While he was unable to satisfy all shades of political opinion or to make the system earn enough in net income to pay interest charges on all of the government obligations incurred in the acquisition of the properties, he raised the net revenue (exclusive of the interest charges) from $2,000,000 in 1922 to almost $60,000,000 in 1928, and brought the quality of public service to a high standard.

With the depression in 1929, however, the Canadian National deficits increased and political opposition became intensified. The government then in power was not of the same political faith as that which had called Thornton from England in 1922. Criticism was focussed upon him personally and fault was found with his policies, especially those which called for expenditures which in his far-sighted view he believed would be ultimately justified by improved service. Despite constantly increasing criticism and political pressure he held to his task, but in July 1932 finally resigned when the opposition became so strong as to impair his usefulness. After his retirement he returned to New York. The strain had told upon his health, and he died of pneumonia following an operation at the age of sixty-one.

On June 20, 1901, Thornton married Virginia Dike Blair of New Castle, Pa. A son and a daughter were born to this marriage, which was ended by divorce in 1926. In September of that year he married Martha Watriss of New York City. In his youth Thornton was an athlete and a member of the football team of his college. Of imposing stature, he was a commanding figure, and he carried himself as a leader of men. One of his outstanding characteristics was his liberal attitude in relations with organized labor, especially in the creation of cooperative committees of shopmen. His death occurred a few days before the scheduled date for a dinner to be given him in New York City by organized labor as a testimonial of confidence and respect.

[*Who's Who in America*, 1930–31; *Travel*, May 1914; *Forum*, Dec. 1922; *Current Opinion*, Jan. 1923; *Canadian Mag.*, Apr. 1924; *Outlook*, June 4, 1924; *Collier's*, Apr. 4, 1925; *Sat. Eve. Post*, July 6, 1929; *Canadian Forum*, Sept. 1932; *Ann. Reports of the Canadian National Railway System*, 1922–32; *N. Y. Times*, July 28, Aug. 31, Sept. 11, 12, 14, 1926, Mar. 15, 1933.]
W. J. C.

THORNTON, JESSY QUINN (Aug. 24, 1810–Feb. 5, 1888), Oregon pioneer, was born near Point Pleasant, Va. (now W. Va.), a descendant of an English immigrant who came to Virginia in 1633. His parents moved to Champaign County, Ohio, when he was an infant. He received a good education. Choosing the law for a profession, he spent nearly three years in London as a student, and on his return continued his preparation in the office of John H. Peyton of Staunton, Va. After his admission to the bar in 1833 he attended law lectures at the University of Virginia. In 1835 he opened a law office in Palmyra, Mo., and in the following year edited a newspaper in that town. On Feb. 8, 1838, at Hannibal, Mo., he married Mrs. Nancy M. Logue, and three years later moved to Quincy, Ill. Their health failing, in 1846 he and his wife set out for Oregon, overtaking on the way the California-bound ox-train of Col. William Henry

Russell [*q.v.*] and arriving in the Salem neighborhood in November.

Thornton at once came into public notice, and on Feb. 9, 1847, Gov. George Abernethy [*q.v.*] appointed him judge of the supreme court of the provisional government. In October he was delegated to proceed at once to the national capital and press the demand of the people for the organization of a territory. Making the trip by water, he arrived in Washington in May 1848, and was soon joined by Joseph L. Meek [*q.v.*], who, with similar instructions, had traveled by land. With the support of President Polk, Thornton worked tirelessly against a hostile, or indifferent, majority in Congress, and was successful in obtaining the passage of an act establishing the territorial government of Oregon on Aug. 14, the last day of the session. A disagreement with the President lost for him, however, a reappointment as judge. While in Washington he wrote *Oregon and California in 1848*, which was published early the following year, in two volumes, in New York; a second edition appeared in 1855.

Returning to Oregon, he was appointed Indian sub-agent for the region north of the Columbia, but soon gave up the post. He then resumed the practice of law and became active in politics. In 1864–65 he represented Benton County in the legislature. For some years he lived in Oregon City, later in Albany and Portland, and from 1871 in Salem. His later years were spent in poverty. He died in Salem, and was buried there in the Methodist churchyard. He was survived by his wife.

Thornton was one of the leading figures in early Oregon, and his work was important and useful. Into the act establishing the territory he succeeded in incorporating a provision doubling the amount of land ordinarily set aside for school purposes, and thus made possible the rapid expansion of educational facilities in the young community. He was a voluminous writer. For the meeting of the Oregon Pioneer Association of 1874 he expanded the sketch of the provisional government given in his book, and for the meeting of 1878 he prepared an account of the emigration of 1846. Both articles are printed in *Transactions* of the Association. He was also the author of a series of political articles in the *New York Tribune* under the pen-name of Achilles de Harley, and he wrote many letters for the local press. Much of his writing is bitterly critical of some of his contemporaries, and though late in life he made partial amends for this censoriousness, he set in motion controversies that continued long after his death.

[H. H. Bancroft, *Hist. of Ore.*, vol. I (1886); H. W. Scott, *Hist. of the Ore. Country* (6 vols., 1924); C. H. Carey, *Hist. of Ore.* (1922); Portland *Morning Oregonian*, Feb. 7, 1888; information from J. Neilson Barry, Portland, Ore.]   W. J. G.

THORNTON, JOHN WINGATE (Aug. 12, 1818–June 6, 1878), historian, was born at Saco, Me., the son of James Brown and Eliza (Gookin) Thornton. His father, a descendant of Thomas Thornton who emigrated to New England in 1663, was a shipping merchant with a lively interest in water power and the promotion of railroads; his mother contributed poems to the *Southern Literary Messenger* and the *Christian Mirror*. After graduating from the Harvard law school in 1840, Thornton practised law in Boston, living first at Brookline, later at Winthrop, in the winters and at Oak Hill, Scarboro, Me., in the summers. He was a typical antiquarian, a founder of the New England Historic Genealogical Society in 1844 and of the Prince Society in 1858. Author of many books and pamphlets, he corresponded with the leading antiquaries of his time, maintaining traditions of old-fashioned politeness. In his fervid and didactic family letters he referred to his wife as "my lady." In his quaintly formal journal covering May 1850 to July 1851, he noted "what would be of permanent interest, of pleasure, or use in retrospect"; he thanked God for the abolition of the slave trade; he animadverted on things literary, political, and legal. His catholicity of mind admitted in 1850 that everything might be possible in physical science "except aerial navigation." In the winter he haunted bookstores, collecting rare Americana, documents, and letters written by famous people. His office at 20 Court St. was a gathering place where men like the historian, John S. Barry, came for consultation with him during the preparation of books and papers.

His separate publications were *A Genealogical Memoir of the Gilbert Family* (1850); *Lives of Isaac Heath and John Bowles, Elders of the Church, and Principal Founders of the Grammar School in Roxbury, and Rev. John Eliot, Jr., Preacher to the Indians, and First Pastor of the Church in Newton* (1850); *Mementos of the Swett Family* (1851); *The Landing at Cape Anne* (1854), one of his most valuable works; *Ancient Pemaquid* (1857); *Peter Oliver's 'Puritan Commonwealth' Reviewed* (1857); *The First Records of Anglo-American Colonization* (1859); *The Pulpit of the American Revolution; or the Political Sermons of the Period of 1776* (1860); *Colonial Schemes of Popham and Gorges* (1863); *D'Amerie, Emery, Amory* (1869); and *The Historical Relation of New England to the English Commonwealth* (1874).

In addition, he wrote many fugitive papers, some of them so controversial in tone that they distressed his friends. His part in the rediscovery of the manuscript of Governor William Bradford's history, "Of Plimoth Plantation," then in the Fulham Library, bringing in the names of Barry, Drake, Charles Deane [*q.v.*], and Nathaniel Bradstreet Shurtleff [*q.v.*], makes good reading (*Proceedings of the Massachusetts Historical Society*, Nov. 1881, pp. 118–20). While abroad in 1872 he ferreted out and obtained for the Maine Historical Society the invaulable Trelawny papers relating to the fishing station at Richmond Island.

He was of a "manly and generous nature," amiable, loyal to his obligations, deeply religious, with a mind "evenly poised and well regulated" (Amory, *post*, p. 273). He had an open, friendly countenance, curly hair, and a generous beard. He loved flowers and the open sea, and his letters show with what eagerness he looked forward to his summers at Oak Hill. He married at Roxbury, Mass., May 31, 1848, Elizabeth Wallace Bowles, daughter of Stephen Jones Bowles. Their son, Henry Thornton Thornton, to whom the father was passionately attached, died at the age of ten; a daughter Elizabeth died at Lexington, Mass., in 1931. Two other daughters, Elizabeth and Agnes, did not survive infancy. Thornton died at Oak Hill in Scarboro, Me.

[See J. W. Thornton, *Thornton Family* (1850); T. C. Amory, in *New England Hist. and Geneal. Reg.*, July 1879, reprinted as *Memoir of John Wingate Thornton, with a List of his Publications* (1879); and obituary in *Boston Transcript*, June 8, 1878. Thornton's journal, 1850–51, and family letters and pictures, 1866–76, are in the Boston Athenaeum; four bound vols., of correspondence, pamphlets, notes, portraits, and clippings, and two bundles are in the possession of the New England Hist. Geneal. Soc., Boston.]   C. K. B.

THORNTON, MATTHEW (*c.* 1714–June 24, 1803), physician and Revolutionary patriot, was born in Ireland. There is some uncertainty as to the date of his birth. He was of Scotch-Irish extraction and his parents, James and Elizabeth (Jenkins) Thornton, emigrated to America about 1718, settling first in Maine and later in the neighborhood of Worcester, Mass., where Matthew received his early education and began to study medicine. He completed his studies in 1740 and began to practise in Londonderry, N. H., where there was a vigorous Scotch-Irish colony whose members and descendants played such a prominent part in New Hampshire history. He resided here until 1779, was married to Hannah Jack about 1760, was successful in his profession, took an active part in the affairs of this somewhat contentious community, and brought up a family of five children. In 1745 he took part in the Louisbourg expedition and his name appears as "under-surgeon" in the roster of the New Hampshire contingent. For some time he held a commission as colonel of militia under the royal government.

In 1758 his name appears in the records as member of the legislature from Londonderry and for the next thirty years he was an outstanding figure in provincial and state politics. From Jan. 17, 1760, when he waited on Gov. Benning Wentworth with a legislative address expressive of gratitude for recent victories and "fresh zeal for his Majesty's service," until June 8, 1775, when he delivered to that governor's successor a denunciation of the "unconstitutional and tyrannical Acts of the British Parliament," Thornton's career was a chronicle of revolutionary progress in that part of New England. Prominent in the agitation against the Stamp Act he advanced steadily in the confidence of the revolutionary party and when the break came was elected president of the provincial congress of 1775 and chairman of the committee of safety that organized resistance and exercised general powers of government in the first stages of the war. His address to the people under the date June 2, 1775, is a model plea for order, self-restraint, and vigorous cooperation in the emergency.

During the war, while governmental organization was in more or less confusion, he held a variety of important places, speaker of the house, member of the council, and president of the constitutional convention. In 1776 he was chosen an associate justice of the superior court, holding office until 1782. It was a period when "separation of powers" had not been fully achieved and when legal training was not a prerequisite to service on the bench. In 1776 he was elected to the Continental Congress and although he did not take his place until November, he was in time to acquire immortality by affixing his signature to the Declaration of Independence. He served about one year as delegate and returned to resume service in state affairs. In 1780 he established his home in Merrimack County. He had given up professional work but continued to be active in political affairs for some years, serving in the newly organized state Senate, 1784–86. His last years were spent on his Merrimack farm where he enjoyed the standing of a rural Nestor who had well served the councils of the state in the critical quarter-century, 1763–89. He died in Newburyport, Mass., while visiting his daughter, but his body was interred near his home in Merrimack. Thornton, N. H., was named in his honor.

[Thornton's private papers and a manuscript biographical sketch by a contemporary, William Plumer, are in the archives of the N. H. Historical Society at Concord. See also C. T. Adams, *The Family of James Thornton* (1905); E. L. Parker, *Hist. of Londonderry* (1851); C. H. Woodbury, "Matthew Thornton," *Proc. N. H. Hist. Soc.*, vol. III (1902); *N. H. State Papers*, vols. XVIII (1890), XX–XXII (1891–93); *Provincial Papers*, vols. VI (1872), VII (1873); *N. H. Hist. Soc. Colls.*, vol. VII (1863); John Sanderson, *Signers to the Declaration of Independence*, vol. V (1823); W. H. Bailey, "Matthew Thornton," *Granite Monthly*, Mar. 1892.]

W. A. R.

THORNTON, WILLIAM (May 20, 1759–Mar. 28, 1828), architect, inventor, and public official, was born on the little island of Jost van Dyke in the community of the Society of Friends centering at Tortola in the Virgin Islands. His father is believed to have been also named William; his mother was Dorcas Downing Zeageus (or Zeagurs). He was sent to England at the age of five, and from 1781 to 1784 attended the University of Edinburgh, where he studied medicine; his degree of M.D., however, he received from Aberdeen University on Nov. 23, 1784 (diploma in Thornton Papers, Library of Congress). After a period in Paris he returned to Tortola (1786) and then came to the United States, being in New York in 1787, and becoming an American citizen in Delaware, Jan. 7, 1788. He soon made Philadelphia his headquarters. He did not practise medicine, and seems to have had some small means and to have been well received. In 1789 he achieved his first public distinction. The Library Company of Philadelphia offered as a prize a share in the Company for the best design for its new building on Fifth Street. Thornton writes in an autobiographic fragment, "When I travelled I never thought of architecture. But I got some books and worked a few days, then gave a plan in the ancient Ionic order, which carried the day." The building, one of the finest in the country in its time, stood until 1880. From 1778, if not earlier, to 1790 Thornton was associated with John Fitch [*q.v.*] in his experiments with steamboats operated by paddles. Fitch had demonstrated his first boat on the Delaware in 1787; his second, in which Thornton had a share, made a trip of twenty miles in 1788. For his third, the *Thornton*, it would appear that Thornton advanced much of the cost and made fruitful suggestions. It made a speed of eight miles an hour, and is said to have been run regularly on the Delaware as a packet boat and to have covered some thousand miles before it was retired in the winter of 1790. After Fulton's success Thornton published in 1814 his *Short Account of the Origin of Steam Boats,* vindicating Fitch's and his own contributions.

On Oct. 13, 1790, Thornton married Anna

Maria Brodeau, then sixteen years of age, and took her to Tortola for two years. While there he learned of the competition for the public buildings in the new federal city of Washington, and wrote the commissioners in July that he would bring his plans to the United States. Delayed by illness, he arrived at the beginning of November, to find that no decision had yet been reached as to the design of the Capitol. Of those first received that of Étienne Sulpice Hallet [q.v.], a French professional, had been most favored, and he had been retained to prepare further studies, while certain other competitors were invited to revise their designs according to new data. It was obvious at once to Thornton that the design brought with him from the West Indies (the drawings are preserved by the Library of Congress and the American Institute of Architects) would not be acceptable, and he undertook a new one. In its preparation he was much influenced by a glimpse of one of Hallet's designs submitted the previous October. The new design was still unfinished on Jan. 31 when it was recommended by President Washington in terms which assured its adoption. This followed early in March. Thornton received as premium a lot in the new city (No. 15 in Square 634) and five hundred dollars. The drawings of this design appear to have been destroyed by Thornton at a later period, but from the manuscript description which accompanied them, and other evidence, it is possible to reconstruct its essential provisions.

Since Thornton was not an architect by profession, nor a builder, there was no idea of employing him to supervise the erection of the Capitol, and Hallet was retained for the task. He and the contractors in Washington at once raised numerous structural and practical objections to the design, some of which, aimed at defects and inconsistencies arising from Thornton's lack of experience, appear to have been justified. At a conference with the President and with Jefferson, the secretary of state, held in July 1793, a revised plan prepared by Hallet—"considered," Jefferson wrote (*Documentary History of the . . . United States Capitol, post,* pp. 26–27), "as Dr. Thornton's plan rendered into practicable form"—was adopted, subject to certain modifications left for future decision. The foundations were begun in accordance with this plan, but in the modifications undertaken differences of opinion arose which resulted in Hallet's dismissal, June 28, 1794. James Hoban [q.v.], architect of the President's House, remained in charge of the erection of the Capitol. On Sept. 12, 1794, Thornton was appointed one of the commissioners of the city, and shortly removed his residence

there from Philadelphia. He considered that he had a mandate to restore the form of the Capitol to conformity with his designs. The progress made rendered this not entirely practicable, and he prepared revised designs determined, in considerable measure, by the work already performed, but returning to some of the principal features of his design which had been abandoned. A complete reconciliation of the two designs was not feasible, and many problems regarding the central portion of the structure remained unsolved. A further confusion had been threatened by the proposition of George Hadfield [q.v.], who was appointed superintendent in 1795, to substitute an attic for Thornton's basement, but Thornton was successful in constraining Hadfield to follow his directions. The north wing had been constructed in accordance with Thornton's ideas by the time Congress removed to Washington in 1800, and the exterior of the south wing, constructed later, necessarily conformed with it. Thornton's idea of a great central rotunda was also adhered to by later architects of the building. In May 1802 the board of commissioners of the city was abolished by Congress, and Thornton had henceforth no official connection with the work on the Capitol. This, however, did not prevent him from continuing to concern himself with it. The elder Benjamin Henry Latrobe [q.v.], whom Jefferson appointed in 1803 to the new post of surveyor of the public buildings, was, like Hadfield, keenly alive to certain difficulties in the design, and proposed changes which Thornton was quick to oppose. He addressed a printed letter "To the Members of the House of Representatives of the United States," Jan. 1, 1805, and a pamphlet war ensued, from which Latrobe, supported by President Jefferson, emerged embittered but victorious, remaining in charge of the work until after the outbreak of the War of 1812.

Thornton's designs in architecture were not limited to those already mentioned. For George Washington he supervised the erection, in 1798–99, of two houses on North Capitol Street between B and C Streets. For John Tayloe he built in 1798–1800 a fine house, the Octagon, still standing (1935), now the headquarters of the American Institute of Architects. It was distinguished by the circular rooms at the corner, in one of which, while the house was occupied by Madison after the burning of the White House in 1814, the Treaty of Ghent was signed. In 1800 Thornton made for Lawrence Lewis, who had married Washington's adopted daughter, Eleanor Custis, a design for Woodlawn, which appears to have been followed in this fine mansion in Fairfax County, Va. The same year he appears to have given Bishop John Carroll [*q.v.*] a plan for the cathedral in Baltimore, but Latrobe's design was followed. Homewood in Baltimore, a Carroll house, may possibly follow a design of Thornton's. Beginning about 1812 Tudor Place in Georgetown was erected from his designs. Mrs. Thornton says in her diary that her husband was the architect of Brentwood in the District of Columbia, and that he gave a plan for the house of Mr. Dobson in Stokes County, N. C., in 1805. The Octagon, Tudor Place, and Brentwood show a plastic and spatial variety and mastery rarely found in America before their time. In 1817 Jefferson outlined to Thornton his plan for the University of Virginia and requested suggestions for the fronts of the pavilions, as "models of taste & good architecture, & of a variety of appearance" (letter quoted in Fiske Kimball, *Thomas Jefferson, Architect*, 1916, p. 75). Thornton supplied two sketches, from one of which Pavilion VII was built (*Ibid.*, pp. 75–76, 187, fig. 212).

At the close of Thornton's service as a commissioner in May 1802, Jefferson appointed him clerk in the State Department, in charge of patents—the first functionary specially assigned to this matter. He is credited (*Daily National Intelligencer*, Sept. 7, 1814) with having saved the Patent Office from destruction on the capture of Washington in 1814. As superintendent of patents he continued in charge of the Patent Office until his death, Mar. 28, 1828 (G. W. Evans, "The Birth and Growth of the Patent Office," *Records of the Columbia Historical Society*, vol. XXII, 1919, 105–24). His own wide curiosity and inventiveness admirably fitted him for this position. A memorandum in his papers lists eight patents of his own between 1802 and 1827, dealing with improvements in boilers, stills, firearms, and other devices.

Thornton's interests and activities were astonishingly varied. He drew and painted with facility. Miniatures by him and his copy of Stuart's profile portrait of Washington survive, as do the manuscripts of three unpublished novels (Thornton Papers, Library of Congress). The Magellanic gold medal of the American Philosophical Society was awarded to him in February 1793 for his *Cadmus: or, a Treatise on the Elements of Written Language*, published the same year. Appended was an "Essay on the mode of teaching the Surd or Deaf, and consequently Dumb to speak." This last Dr. Alexander Graham Bell [*q.v.*] calls the first work upon the education of the deaf actually written and published in America, and says its suggestions "certainly have not received that attention from practical teachers of the deaf that their importance deserves" (*Association Review*, Apr. 1900, pp. 113–15). Thornton's Quaker antecedents and humanitarianism also led him, as early as 1788, to strive for the freeing of slaves through African colonization. In 1791, when at Tortola, he was endeavoring to send blacks to Sierra Leone at the time of the second negro settlement there under the presidency of Henry Thornton, and his pamphlet *Political Economy: Founded in Justice and Humanity*, published in 1804, advocated the abolition of slavery. In later years he was active in the American Colonization Society. Thornton was concerned also in the effort to found a national university in Washington. Following Washington's gift of stock in the Potomac Company to further the enterprise, announced in 1795, the Commissioners set aside a site, and memorialized Congress to authorize the acceptance of contributions. In later years Thornton's sympathies were enlisted by the liberation of South America. In 1815 he published a tract, *Outlines of a Constitution for United North & South Columbia*, a grandiose dream of union, proposing a capital city near Panama, "where a canal may be made from sea to sea, by locks" (p. 8). To his many other vocations Thornton added those of soldier and magistrate. He became a lieutenant and captain of militia, a justice of the peace, and a commissioner in bankruptcy. His business enterprises, from the raising of merino sheep and the breeding of race horses to steamboats and gold mines—he issued a sanguine prospectus of the North Carolina Gold Mine Company in 1806—were uniformly unsuccessful, but his straitened means never prevented him from mingling in the best society, in which he was a general favorite. He assiduously cultivated the acquaintance of persons of distinction, and enjoyed the friendship of the Earl of Buchan, of Franklin, Rittenhouse, Washington, Jefferson, Volney, Trumbull, John Randolph, and particularly of the Madisons.

The best personal characterization of Thornton is the one published just after his death by William Dunlap [*q.v.*]: "He was a scholar and a gentleman—full of talent and eccentricity—a Quaker by profession, a painter, a poet, and a horse-racer—well acquainted with the mechanic arts. . . . He was a 'man of infinite humour'—humane and generous, yet fond of field sports—his company was a complete antidote to dullness" (*History of the Rise and Progress of the Arts of Design in the United States*, vol. II, 1918 ed., p. 8). He died in Washington and was buried in the Congressional Cemetery.

[Many papers of Thornton and his wife, including a number of studies for the Capitol and other buildings, particularly Tudor Place, are in the Lib. of Cong.; certain drawings for private buildings were in the possession of the late Glenn Brown, Esq., of Washington, D. C.; other papers are at the office of public buildings and grounds, and in the office of the superintendent of the Capitol. Many of the personal papers in the Lib. of Cong. were published by A. C. Clark, in *Records of the Columbia Hist. Soc.*, vol. XVIII (1915), and a memorial to Thornton published by the Columbian Institute after his death is quoted. For contemporary allusions see J. P. B. de Warville, *Nouveau Voyage dans les États-Unis de l'Amérique Septentrionale, fait en 1788* (3 vols., 1791); *Autobiog., Reminiscences and Letters of John Trumbull* (1841); and *Letters of Horatio Greenough to His Brother, Henry Greenough* (1887). See also Glenn Brown, in *Architectural Records*, July–Sept. 1896, pp. 53–70, *Hist. of the U. S. Capitol*, vol. I (1900), pp. 81–88, with portrait, and *The Octagon* (1917?), pp. 16–25, the biog. sketches to be used with a certain caution; *Documentary Hist. of the . . . U. S. Capitol* (1904); W. M. Watson, *In Memoriam: Benjamin Ogle Tayloe* (1872), pp. 97–101; W. B. Bryan, *A Hist. of the Nat. Capital* (2 vols., 1914–16); Gaillard Hunt, "William Thornton and Negro Colonization," *Proc. Am. Antiquarian Soc.*, Apr. 1920; death notice in *Daily Nat. Intelligencer* (Washington), Mar. 29, 1828. The degree of Thornton's responsibility for the design of the Capitol has been reconsidered, with many additional docs., by Fiske Kimball and Wells Bennett, in *Art Studies: Medieval, Renaissance and Modern*, vol. I (1923). For the Octagon, see Brown, *The Octagon*; for Woodlawn and Tudor Place, W. R. Ware, *The Georgian Period* (3 vols., 1899–1902); for Brentwood, H. F. Cunningham and J. A. Younger, *Measured Drawings of Georgian Architecture in the District of Columbia, 1750–1820* (1914). The Gilbert Stuart paintings of Thornton and his wife in the T. B. Clarke coll., have been frequently reproduced.]

F. K.

THORNWELL, JAMES HENLEY (Dec. 9, 1812–Aug. 1, 1862), Presbyterian clergyman, president of the South Carolina College, was born in Marlboro District, S. C., the son of James and Martha (Terrel) Thornwell. His father, an overseer on the plantation of Christopher B. Pegues, died in 1820, leaving the family in straitened circumstances, but James Henley managed to enter the old-field school at Level Green, where his diligent study won him the patronage of two prominent citizens of the nearby town of Cheraw, who assumed the burden of his education. After two years at the Cheraw Academy, in December 1829 he entered the junior class of the South Carolina College, then passing through a turbulent period of opposition to the religious liberalism of the president, Thomas Cooper [*q.v.*]. In 1831 Thornwell graduated at the head of his class. While teaching at Sumterville in 1832 he experienced an emotional conversion, joined the Presbyterian Church, resolved to be a minister, and two years later entered the Andover (Mass.) Theological Seminary. Finding the theology of this institution too liberal for his conservative views, he soon withdrew and after a few months at Harvard returned to South Carolina in October 1834, repelled alike by the New England climate and mental attitude.

Licensed to preach by the Harmony Presbytery of the Synod of South Carolina, Nov. 28, 1834, he served as pastor of several churches in Lancaster District, and on Dec. 3, 1835, married Nancy White, the daughter of Col. James H. Witherspoon, a prominent citizen of Lancaster and former lieutenant governor of the state. In 1837 Thornwell's orthodoxy, learning, and effective preaching resulted in his election to the professorship of metaphysics in the South Carolina College by the faction which four years before had ousted Cooper from the control of that institution. Resigning in 1840 to become pastor of the Columbia Presbyterian Church, he returned the following year as chaplain and professor of sacred literature, holding these positions, with the exception of a short interval as pastor of the Glebe Presbyterian Church in Charleston, until 1851, when he was elected to the presidency of the college. In this connection his work was notably successful. His *Letter to Governor Manning on Public Education in South Carolina* (1853) quieted the strong party in the state that was advocating sectarian education at the expense of secular instruction, and his orthodox preaching and teaching, together with his persuasive personality, did much to remove what was left of the "blatant infidelity" that Cooper had implanted. He never found the atmosphere of the college wholly congenial, however, feeling that he should devote his entire time to religious activities. Accordingly, he resigned in 1855 to become professor of didactic and polemic theology at the Presbyterian Theological Seminary at Columbia, a position which he held until his death seven years later.

Thornwell's activities as an educator were overshadowed by his achievements as a preacher and controversialist. Although unprepossessing in appearance and inclined to pedantry, he combined rigorous logic and emotional fervor in an effective manner. In 1847 he founded at Columbia the *Southern Presbyterian Review*, a powerful exponent of his views. Between 1837 and 1860 he attended ten of the annual assemblies of his denomination, serving as moderator in 1847. In these he opposed the participation of the church in such secular affairs as the slavery controversy and temperance reform. When the assembly of 1861 adopted resolutions indorsing the Federal government he induced the Synod of South Carolina to indorse political secession and was a leading spirit in the organization of the Presbyterian Church in the Confederate States of America. He was the author of an "Address to All the Churches of Jesus Christ throughout the Earth," a brilliant exposition of the view-point of the Southern Presbyterian separatists.

A political moderate before 1860, he championed the formation of the Southern Confederacy after the election of Lincoln. His article on "The State of the Country" (*Southern Presbyterian Review,* January 1861) was published as a pamphlet and won wide acclaim as a cogent defense of the Southern point of view, and in a widely circulated address to the Southern soldiers, *Our Danger and Our Duty* (1862), he drew a dire picture of the fate he felt would overtake the South if the North were victorious. His premature death, due to consumption, aggravated by overwork and the excitement of war, prevented the execution of a comprehensive treatise on theology which he contemplated preparing. Most of his addresses and sermons are preserved in *The Collected Writings of J. H. Thornwell* (4 vols., 1871–73), edited by J. B. Adger and J. L. Girardeau.

[B. M. Palmer, *The Life and Letters of J. H. Thornwell* (1875); T. H. Law and others, *Centennial Addresses . . . Commemorating the Birth of J. H. Thornwell* (1913); H. A. White, *Southern Presbyterian Leaders* (1911); Maximilian La Borde, *Hist. of the S. C. Coll.* (1874); E. L. Green, *A Hist. of the Univ. of S. C.* (1916); Alfred Nevin, *Encyc. of the Presbt. Church in the U. S. A.* (1884); *Southern Presbyterian Rev.,* Oct. 1862; *Charleston Daily Courier,* Aug. 2, 1862.]
F. B. S.

THORP, JOHN (1784–Nov. 15, 1848), machinist, inventor, was the son of Reuben and Hannah (Bucklin) Thorp, and was born presumably in Rehoboth, Mass., where his father was engaged at his trade of coach-builder. Practically nothing is known of Thorp's life until he was twenty-eight years old, when he obtained his first patent (Mar. 28, 1812; renewed, Jan. 28, 1843) for a hand- and water-loom. Presumably he had learned the machinist's trade and had worked in the textile mills in Rhode Island; certainly he had developed a marked inventive ability. His loom had an ingenious shedding motion, an automatic take-up, a novel picking motion, and a clever protective device. To acquire the funds to engage in further invention Thorp worked at his trade in various establishments in New England, and while in Taunton, Mass., acquired his second patent (Oct. 14, 1816) for a power loom. This was issued jointly to him and Silas Shepard, a textile manufacturer, who probably retained Thorp during the period of development of the invention. For the next twelve years nothing is known of him. He probably was prosperous, for his two inventions yielded him, if not financial independence, at least a reputation as a skilled machinist, and therefore the highest pay of all artisans of his day, namely $1.50 to $1.75 a day.

On Nov. 25 and Dec. 31, 1828, Thorp, then living in Providence, R. I., and engaged in his own machinist business, received three patents for improvements in spinning and twisting cotton, now called "ring spinning." These are the basic patents of the continuous method of spinning now (1935) employed for more than one hundred million of the one hundred and sixty million cotton spindles in the world, and increasingly employed for the spinning of other textile raw materials. The inventions involved fundamentally the use of a ring and traveler, or hook, and were wholly novel in the art of both hand and machine spinning with respect to the control of the wind and twist of the thread. It is believed, too, that they are the only spinning inventions, with one exception, of the era of transition from hand to machine cotton manufacture that were not adaptations of earlier hand methods or derived directly therefrom. Thorp may have had an agreement with the Fletcher brothers of North Providence, R. I., to help meet the cost of developing these inventions, for they immediately adopted them in their braid manufacturing business and early in 1829 issued jointly with Thorp a warning against the purchase or use of the inventions without their consent (advertisement in *Manufacturers' and Farmers' Journal,* Mar. 9, 1829). Thorp was also granted a patent for a netting machine (Nov. 20, 1828), the principle of which is still in use. During 1829 Thorp and the Fletchers made and sold his ring-spinning equipment to other manufacturers, and Thorp obtained four more patents, including one for a narrow fabric loom (patented Dec. 22, 1829) which was probably the first gang loom operated by power. His arrangement with the Fletchers continued only about a year, after which he worked independently. Sometime in the thirties he established himself as a machine builder in Providence, and later in North Wrentham, Mass. He apparently continued in this until his death. On Sept. 27, 1844, he secured a patent for improvements on his original ring-spinning invention. Thorp received very little financial reward for his great inventions and no honor until 1928, when a memorial tablet was placed in the old Slater Cotton Mill at Pawtucket, R. I., by the National Association of Cotton Manufacturers. He married Eliza A. Williams of Providence on Aug. 18, 1817, and died without issue, outliving his wife. His place of burial is unknown.

[For a biog. sketch of Thorp which includes a discussion of the place and date of his birth, see C. H.

Clark, in *Trans. Nat. Assoc. of Cotton Manufacturers* (1928), pp. 72–94. See also *Textile World*, Apr. 14, May 5, 1928; *Textile American*, Apr. 1928; *Fibre and Fabric*, Apr. 28, 1928; *Evening Bulletin* (Providence, R. I.), Apr. 26, 1928.]   C. W. M—n.

THORPE, THOMAS BANGS (Mar. 1, 1815–Sept. 20, 1878), author, artist, humorist, was born in Westfield, Mass., the son of the Rev. Thomas Thorpe. At the age of sixteen he painted a picture illustrating Washington Irving's "Bold Dragoon" which, after exhibition at the New York Academy of Fine Arts, was hung in Irving's home in Tarrytown. In 1833 Thorpe matriculated at Wesleyan University, Middletown, Conn., but because of delicate health left in his junior year for Louisiana, where he remained until 1853. The years in Louisiana marked the period of his greatest productivity. At once at home in the South, he soon won the genuine love and admiration not only of rough backwoodsmen but also of Southern statesmen. In his Baton Rouge studio he divided his time between brush and pencil. Sketches and vivid paintings of life on the prairies, portraits of such famous personages as Jenny Lind, Joseph Walker, and Zachary Taylor, filled his studio. His masterpiece, the full-length portrait of President Taylor, was purchased by the state legislature and the House of Representatives.

The same talent for careful observation and accurate portrayal that made him a fine painter of scenery rendered him a descriptive writer of power and distinction in American literature. R. W. Griswold's evaluation of Thorpe in his *Prose Writers of America* (1847) is excellent: "He has a genuine relish for the sports and pastimes of southern frontier life, and describes them with remarkable freshness and skill of light and shade. No one enters more heartily into all the whims and grotesque humours of the backwoodsman, or brings him more actually or clearly before us" (p. 546). The first of Thorpe's realistic sketches to achieve international acclaim, *Tom Owen, The Bee-Hunter* (later used by Thorpe as a pseudonym) was translated into French, Italian, and German, and was published and praised in the best English periodicals. Decidedly the most humorous and critically the most important of all Thorpe's stories was the "Big Bear of Arkansas" which first appeared in the New York *Spirit of the Times*, Mar. 27, 1841. In this tall tale Thorpe achieved the first great piece of genuinely "Western" humor; in addition to telling a good story he sustained a continuous and racy exaggeration that marked a new phase in American humor. Representative of his local color descriptive work are "The Prairies of Louisiana," "Wild Turkey Hunting," "Water-

craft of the Backwoods," etc. Many of these were later collected under the titles *Mysteries of the Backwoods* (1846), and *The Hive of the Bee-Hunter* (1854).

Thorpe had a great fondness for politics: he held minor offices and frequently "stumped" for his friends, particularly for Taylor. His speeches and writing show a thorough knowledge of statesmen and politics of his day. He conducted a number of Whig newspapers in Louisiana either alone or with associates: in 1843, the Concordia *Intelligencer*; in 1845, the New Orleans *Commercial Times*; in 1846, the New Orleans *Daily Tropic*; in 1847, the Baton Rouge *Conservative*; in 1850, the Batesville *Eagle*. He was with General Taylor at Matamoras in 1846 and his books, *Our Army on the Rio Grande* (1846), *Our Army at Monterey* (1847), and *The Taylor Anecdote Book* (1848), grew out of these experiences. In 1853 he returned to New York City where he contributed frequently to many prominent periodicals. In 1860 he was co-proprietor and co-editor of the New York *Spirit of the Times*. During the Civil War he served as staff officer to Gen. B. F. Butler with rank of colonel of volunteers (1862), and was surveyor of the port of New Orleans. After the war he was city surveyor in New York, and chief of the warehouse department of the New York Custom House from 1869 until his death.

Thorpe's other published works are: *The Master's House* (1854); *Lynde Weiss, An Autobiography* (1852); *A Voice to America* (1855); *Reminiscences of Charles L. Elliott* (1868). His stories appeared in two anthologies to which they gave titles, *The Big Bear of Arkansas* (1845), collected and edited by William T. Porter [*q.v.*], and *Colonel Thorpe's Scenes in Arkansaw* (1858). Thorpe was married but little is known of his wife.

[R. W. Griswold, *Prose Writers of America* (1847); New York *Spirit of the Times*, 1840–60, especially for July 27, 1850, and Sept. 28, 1878; *Alumni Record of Wesleyan University* (6th ed., 1931); A. N. DeMenil, *Literature of the La. Territory* (1904); *N. Y. Times*, Sept. 21, 1878.]   F. J. M—e.

THRASHER, JOHN SIDNEY (1817–Nov. 10, 1879), editor, author, adventurer, was born at Portland, Me. After receiving a good education in the United States, he moved with his parents in 1832 or 1833 to Cuba, where he was destined to win notoriety. In this island he acquired considerable worldly experience, as a clerk (until 1847) in the mercantile house of Tyng & Company, ship-brokers and commission merchants; as a revolutionary agitator and propagandist assisting Narciso López and others from 1848 to 1851; and as a partial editor of the Cuban-owned commercial and anti-Spanish paper, *El Faro Industrial de la Habana,* from August 1850 to September 1851. As a result of this editorial activity, he was tried by court martial on Oct. 16, 1851, imprisoned by the Spanish authorities, and sent to serve eight years at hard labor at Ceuta on the north coast of Africa. From this embarrassment he was freed, by the beginning of 1852, through the intervention of the American minister and his wife at Madrid, and he promised never to return to any Spanish possession. A year later, 1853, he presented to the State Department—though he never pressed it—a claim against Spain for a sum which he felt represented the extent of damage to his Cuban periodical and the cost of the balm for his wounded pride and reputation.

In the middle of 1852 he was back in New York, but he soon went to New Orleans where he actively aided John A. Quitman [*q.v.*] and the Cuban filibusters and vociferously declared for Cuban annexation to the United States. He remained there until 1855, when he again returned to New York. Using his journalistic experience in Cuba and New Orleans, he was able to obtain a position on the *New York Herald,* for which paper he traveled in Mexico and South America until 1859. During the Civil War he was connected with the Southern Associated Press, with headquarters at Atlanta. By this time he had married Rebecca Mary, widow of Michel Branamour Menard [*q.v.*], founder of Galveston, Tex.

Thrasher's chief reputation rests upon his writing and his editorial work. Besides the Cuban paper already mentioned he was connected as editor or contributor with the *Beacon of Cuba, DeBow's Review,* and the *Picayune* of New Orleans; with the *New York Herald,* Leslie's *Ilustración Americana,* and *Noticioso de Nueva York* of New York City; with the *Civilian* of Galveston; and probably with other periodicals. He was also author of several pamphlets in Spanish and English, including *Cuba and Louisiana* (1854) and *A Preliminary Essay on the Purchase of Cuba* (1859). At New York in 1856 he translated and edited in a garbled fashion Alexander von Humboldt's essay on Cuba, under the title *The Island of Cuba,* omitting the arguments against slavery which so offended his own pro-slavery views. This led in 1865 to a brief journalistic tilt with Von Humboldt.

As an itinerant editor, author, and general adventurer, Thrasher seems not to have been entirely honest in dealing either with his friends or with his enemies, but as a pro-slavery protagonist of the purchase of Cuba, his sincerity

and his enthusiasm cannot be questioned. To his numerous other interests he added in later life a study of spiritualism, and he finally forsook his Baptist faith for this new adventure. He died after a stroke of apoplexy, and was buried in Magnolia Cemetery, Galveston.

[Fernando Ortiz, ed., *Ensayo político sobre la Isla de Cuba por Alejandro de Humboldt* (Havana 1930), vol. II; Herminio Portell Vilá, *Narciso López y su Época,* vol. I (Havana 1930); R. G. Caldwell, *The Lopez Expeditions to Cuba, 1848–1851* (1915); Vidal Morales y Morales, *Iniciadores y Primeros Mártires de la Revolución Cubana* (1901, repr. in 3 vols., 1931); J. F. H. Claiborne, *Life and Correspondence of John A. Quitman* (1860), vol. II; A. C. Quisenberry, *Lopez's Expeditions to Cuba, 1850 and 1851,* being Filson Club Pub. no. 21 (1906); José Gutierrez de la Concha, *Memorias Sobre el Estado Politico, Gobierno y Administración de la Isla de Cuba* (1853), pp. 226–27, 282; *House Ex. Doc. 14,* 32 Cong., 1 Sess.; *Senate Ex. Doc. 5,* 32 Cong., 1 Sess.; documents listed in L. M. Pérez, *Guide to the Materials for Am. Hist. in Cuban Archives* (1907), pp. 70, 71; and *Galveston Daily News,* Nov. 11, 12, 1879.]
A. C. W.

THROOP, ENOS THOMPSON (Aug. 21, 1784–Nov. 1, 1874), jurist, congressman, governor of New York, was the eldest child of George Bliss Throop and Abiah (Thompson). His father, son of John and Mary (Throop) Bliss, had been adopted by a maternal uncle, the Rev. George Throop of Johnstown, N. Y.; there was a tradition that their ancestor, William Throope, who settled in Barnstable, Mass., before 1666, was a son of Col. Adrian Schoope or Scrope, one of the regicides (Fitch, *post*). After the Revolution, George Bliss Throop married the daughter of Enos Thompson, who had moved from New Haven to develop a tract of wild land in Dutchess County, N. Y. The young couple purchased land at the sale of confiscated Loyalist estates, and established a home in Johnstown, and here Enos Thompson Throop was born. The death of his father in 1794 seriously interfered with the boy's schooling, but four years later he obtained permission to enter the law office of George Metcalf, a friend of his mother and at that time district attorney for Montgomery, Albany, Saratoga, and Schoharie counties. Metcalf arranged for Throop to study law, and personally instructed him in the classics. He was admitted to the bar in January 1806. The ensuing March he began to practise at Poplar Ridge, N. Y., but soon removed to Auburn, where he became a partner of Judge Joseph Richardson. This partnership continued until the junior partner, in 1811, was appointed county clerk.

Throop now became very active in politics. A member of the Republican party of that day, he supported the administration's war policy, and in 1814 was elected to Congress largely on that issue. In 1816, however, he was defeated for reelection because of his support of the act to change the pay of members of Congress from six dollars per day to eighteen hundred dollars per annum. He thereupon resigned, and returned to his law practice. In 1823 he was appointed circuit judge—a position which he held until 1828. In that year his friend of long standing, Martin Van Buren [q.v.], who was seeking the governorship, persuaded him to become candidate for lieutenant governor. Both men were elected, and consequently, when in March 1829 Van Buren was appointed secretary of state by President Jackson, Throop became acting governor. In 1830 he was elected to the governorship, but in 1832 he refused to be a candidate for reëlection. He appears to have made this decision primarily because of protests which his opposition to the construction of the Chenango Canal aroused in certain localities. It was through his efforts as governor that the first state insane asylum was founded in New York. In 1833 President Jackson appointed him naval officer at the port of New York, and in 1838 President Van Buren appointed him chargé d'affaires to the Kingdom of the Two Sicilies. In this capacity he served until 1841, devoting his chief efforts to obtaining a better market for American products, particularly tobacco. He returned to the United States in 1843, and until 1846 resided at "Willowbrook," his home near Auburn. He later acquired a large estate in Michigan, where he engaged successfully in farming, but eventually sold this property and spent his last years in New York City and at "Willowbrook." He was married, July 14, 1814, to Evelina Vredenburgh, daughter of Col. William J. Vredenburgh of Skaneateles, N. Y.; they had three children, all of whom died in infancy.

[Cornelia Williams (Mrs. E. T. T.) Martin, *The Old Home* (1894) and "Sketch of the Life of Gov. Throop" in *Cayuga County Hist. Soc. Colls.*, no. 7 (1889); L. M. Sears, "The Neapolitan Mission of Enos Thompson Throop, 1838–1842," in *N. Y. State Hist. Asso. Quart. Jour.*, Oct. 1928; Winchester Fitch, "The Throope Family and the Scrope Tradition," *N. Y. Geneal. and Biog. Record*, Apr. 1905, Jan. 1906; E. S. Martin, *Some Account of Family Stocks Involved in Life at Willowbrook* (1933); J. S. Jenkins, *Lives of the Governors of the State of N. Y.* (1851); C. Z. Lincoln, *State of N. Y.: Messages from the Governors* (1909), vol. III; *N. Y. Herald*, Nov. 2, 1874.]　　R. W. I.

THROOP, MONTGOMERY HUNT (Jan. 26, 1827–Sept. 11, 1892), jurist, was born in Auburn, N. Y., the son of George B. Throop and Francis (Hunt). His education was acquired in Cazenovia Academy, in Geneva and Naples while his uncle Enos Thompson Throop [q.v.] was in the diplomatic service, and at Hobart College, which he left before graduation. He studied law in the office of his uncle Ward

Hunt [q.v.], was admitted to the bar in 1848, and practised in Utica in partnership with Hunt until 1856, at which time he became a partner of Roscoe Conkling [q.v.], who had been a fellow student in Auburn. In spite of temperamental and political differences between the two men this partnership lasted until 1862. Throop played the part of the office lawyer while Conkling presented the arguments orally in trial court. The former, however, frequently argued on appeal cases in which his partner had appeared in the lower court. In 1864 Throop moved to New York City, where he continued his practice. He appears to have had no political ambitions and never ran for public office, but he took a keen interest in the turbulent political controversies of his day. He was a stanch Democrat, rather of the type of Samuel Nelson or Jeremiah S. Black [qq.v.] who found himself unable to justify what he deemed the excesses of the Republicans, but who desired the preservation of the Union and believed that that end might have been achieved by peaceful means. In March 1864 he published a volume, *The Future: A Political Essay,* written late in the preceding year, giving his views on the war and reconstruction. It is a temperate but forceful attack upon what Throop regarded as the unconstitutional practices and policies of the Lincoln administration as well as the presidential and congressional plans for reconstruction then being shaped and discussed. He did not advocate the abandonment of the war but he protested vigorously against the use of coercive measures in the conquered sections of the South and urged that the existence of war does not suspend the ordinary guarantees of the Constitution. He advocated the calling at the close of the war of a national constitutional convention to adjust the governmental system to radically changed conditions, in part by devising a plan for eliminating the ruinous spoils system and by redrawing the line of demarcation between the powers of the federal and state governments so as to prevent the undue expansion of national power at state expense.

In 1870 Throop was made chairman of a commission to revise the New York statutes. This task, of which he performed the major part, occupied seven years and determined the future direction of his interests; it was brought to completion by the publication, in 1877, of *The Code of Civil Procedure of the State of New York,* which superseded *The New Revision of the Statutes of the State of New York: Code of Remedial Justice,* issued in 1876. The rest of Throop's life was devoted to legal authorship and the editorship of codes and compilations of statutes and decisions. His chief publications in these fields were: *A Treatise on the Validity of Verbal Agreements* (1870), projected as two volumes, of which only one was published; various editions of *The Code of Civil Procedure,* with notes; *The New York Justice's Manual* (fourteen annual issues, 1880–93); the seventh edition (1882) of *The Revised Statutes of the State of New York,* frequently reprinted; *Digest of the Decisions of the Supreme Judicial Court of the Commonwealth of Massachusetts, from 1884 to 1886* (2 vols., 1887); and *A Treatise on the Law Relating to Public Officers and Sureties in Official Bonds* (1892).

Throop moved to Albany in 1880 and made his home there until his death. He was peculiarly fitted for his labor in the field of legal scholarship. Throughout the greater part of his life he was almost totally deaf, but he was intellectually alert, a tireless worker, and a thorough linguist. He was an accomplished scholar in the field of medieval Latin and was widely read in history and belles-lettres. On June 22, 1854, he married Charlotte Williams Gridley of Utica. Two sons were born to them, of whom one died in boyhood. Throop's death was due to apoplexy.

[W. D. Edmonds, "Memorial of Montgomery H. Throop," *Asso. of the Bar of the City of N. Y. . . . Twenty-fourth Ann. Report* (1894), also printed separately; *Proc. N. Y. State Bar Asso. . . . 1892* (1893); *N. Y. Geneal. and Biog. Record,* Jan. 1906; *Albany Evening Journal,* Sept. 12, 1892; *N. Y. Times,* Sept. 12, 1892.]   R. E. C.

THULSTRUP, BROR THURE (Apr. 5, 1848–June 9, 1930), artist and painter, known in America as Thure de Thulstrup, was born in Stockholm, Sweden, of a prominent family. He was the son of Carl Magnus Thulstrup, a soldier, a member of the Swedish ministry, and for a time secretary of naval defense, and Hedvig Kristina (Akrell) Thulstrup. His education and his early experience were essentially those of a soldier. Graduating from the National Military Academy in Stockholm at the age of twenty, he went to Paris, where in 1870 he became an officer in the French Foreign Legion. He saw service in Algeria and later in France during the war with Germany in 1871, through which, after being advanced to the rank of captain, he served to the end. Although now a veteran and by inheritance and tradition inclined to army life, he began to study drawing in the French capital, giving particular attention to topographical engineering, and it was in pursuit of this work that he emigrated to Canada in the early seventies. A thorough master of line, the possibilities of color and the temptations of paint and canvas drew him into the field of creative art. In the latter he always claimed that he had no master, belonged to no school, and was self-taught. Since the United States presented a better chance for his artistic endeavors, he moved to Boston and thence to New York, where, on June 3, 1879, he married Lucie Bavoillot. There were no children.

A close student of military history, he naturally turned in that direction in his paintings. He was scrupulously careful about the correctness of equipment, collecting from every available source the proper uniforms for his models; his work, never haphazard, was correct to the smallest detail. He painted numerous pictures of American battlefields, one of his earliest subjects being Pickett's charge at the battle of Gettysburg. The illustrated weeklies of New York soon found out the value of this painter-illustrator, whose work was dependable and always done on time. For a time on the staff of the *Daily Graphic* (New York), he subsequently became a free lance; for many years hardly an issue of *Frank Leslie's Illustrated Weekly Newspaper* or *Harper's Weekly* came out without some of his drawings, or black and white water-colors. Without hesitation he undertook to do illustrations that involved so many figures, so much composition and detail that the task would have appalled most artists. Gifted not only with imagination but with superb health, he could labor for as much as fifteen hours at a stretch. Taking up color again after this period of strenuous and remunerative endeavor, he produced and exhibited a series of historical paintings of American colonial days that later, reproduced in color, had a large, popular sale. In 1898 appeared a book of reproductions, *Drawings by Thulstrup and Others,* and a year later *Outdoor Pictures,* drawings by Thulstrup alone. He illustrated several books, among them Arthur Conan Doyle's *The Refugees* (copyright 1893).

He was saddened by the death of his wife in 1915 (*Vem Är Det?, post*) and as time drew on his eyesight began to fail in a great measure. The market for illustration disappeared, photographic reproduction taking its place; but he maintained a courageous attitude, and held the stanch loyalty and affection of his friends. Elected to the Players' Club of New York in 1889, in his loneliness he found there welcome and comfort. He was a member of the Society of Illustrators, the American Water Color Society, the John Ericsson Society of Swedish Engineers, and a knight of the Order of Vasa, Sweden. He died at St. Luke's Hospital, New York. For the nine years preceding his death he had lived at the Episcopal Home for Old Men and Aged Couples.

[For the names of Thulstrup's parents, see *Svenskt Biografiskt Handlexikon* (1876) and *Nordisk Familjebok* (1933). Other sources include *Who's Who in America*, 1930–31; *Vem Ar Det?*, 1929; *Svenskt Porträttgalleri*, vol. XX (1901), with portrait; P. H. G., Jr., in *Book Buyer*, Sept. 1895; *Players' Bull.*, June 15, 1930; obituary in *N. Y. Times*, June 10, 1930; personal acquaintance.] **J.B.**

THUMB, TOM [See STRATTON, CHARLES SHERWOOD, 1838–1883].

THURBER, CHARLES (Jan. 2, 1803–Nov. 7, 1886), inventor, manufacturer, teacher, was born at East Brookfield, Mass., the son of the Rev. Laban and Abigail (Thayer) Thurber. After attending the local public schools, Thurber was sent to Milford Academy, and subsequently prepared for college in Bellingham, Mass., under a private tutor. At the age of twenty he entered Brown University and graduated in 1827 with the degrees of A.B. and A.M. With the opening of the school year in the autumn of 1827 he returned to Milford Academy as a teacher, in which capacity he served for four years. He then accepted the principalship of the Latin Grammar School in Worcester, Mass., which he retained for eight consecutive years, relinquishing it only when the pressure of outside business required his full attention. Three years prior to giving up his school work, Thurber entered into partnership with his brother-in-law, Ethan Allen, to manufacture firearms in Worcester. Because of Thurber's mechanical ability this partnership proved to be a most effective one. Within three years after it was formed, on Aug. 26, 1843, a patent (No. 3,228) was granted him for a hand printing machine which proved to be the first invention that approximated a typewriter in the modern sense of the word. It was a type-wheel machine and suggested the first principle of the movable carriage in that the letter spacing was effected by the longitudinal motion of a platen, a principle which is the feature of all modern machines. Furthermore, it incorporated a way of turning the paper when a line was completed, as in the present-day machine. Thurber's typewriter did excellent work, but its action was too slow for practical use. Furthermore, the business world was not ready for a writing machine, and none was manufactured. In 1845 Thurber obtained a second patent, No. 4,271. This was for a writing machine rather than a typewriter, for it was intended for the use of the blind and was designed to perform the motions of the hand in writing. Thurber called it a "Mechanical Chirographer." Allen & Thurber's principal business, however, was pistol manu-

facture, and the firm continued in this until 1856, when it was dissolved, Thurber retiring from active work.

During his active career he had served as county commissioner (1842–44), and had been elected a member of the Massachusetts Senate for one year (1852–53). He was also a member of the board of trustees of Brown University for over thirty years, from 1853 until his death. He married Lucinda Allen, sister of Ethan Allen, immediately after his graduation from college. His wife, by whom he had two daughters, died in Worcester in 1852, and some time later Thurber married Mrs. Caroline (Esty) Bennett. From the time of his retirement until his death he lived in Norwich, Conn., Brooklyn, N. Y., and Germantown, Pa. He died in Nashua, N. H.

[C. G. Washburn, *Industrial Worcester* (1917); Charles Nutt, *Hist. of Worcester and Its People* (1919), vol. II; E. W. Byrn, *The Progress of Invention in the Nineteenth Century* (1900); records of the Am. Antiquarian Soc., Worcester, Mass., Brown Univ., and the U. S. Nat. Museum; obituary in *Boston Transcript*, Nov. 9, 1886.] **C. W. M—n.**

THURBER, CHRISTOPHER CARSON (May 19, 1880–May 31, 1930), social worker, was born in Norwich, Conn., the son of Charles Francis and Annie Elizabeth (Cragg) Thurber. After attending the Norwich Free Academy, he entered Trinity College, Hartford, in 1899, but left after one year to do settlement house social work in Danbury, N. H. Thence he went to Canada to work for seven years introducing improved methods of caring for the mental and physical welfare of lumbermen in the woods. From 1910 to 1912 he was employed by the Young Men's Christian Association to do similar work among the soft-coal miners of Pennsylvania and West Virginia. In 1912 he became superintendent of the Home for Homeless Boys at Covington, Va. When the United States entered the World War in 1917, he left this position for work in the army camps with the Red Cross, which eventually made him director of its hospital work in the South, with headquarters at Greenville, S. C. When the war ended, he became social director of the United States Public Health Service at the same place. In 1921 he joined the Near East Relief organization and was appointed head of an orphanage of three thousand boys at Sivas in Eastern Turkey. After the defeat in 1922 of the Greek army in Anatolia by the Turkish forces under Mustafa Kemal Pasha, Thurber took in four thousand additional boys who had become orphans during the deportation and exchange of the Anatolian Greeks. For eight months he contrived to provide food and shelter for his boys, despite the meagerness of his funds and the suspicions of the local government. On one occasion he was arrested by Turkish authorities and so severely bastinadoed that thereafter he always walked with a limp. Eventually he led five thousand of the orphans on foot across the Pontic Mountains to the Black Sea coast. Thence they were taken on American battleships to Constantinople and housed in the Selimiye Barracks, made famous by Florence Nightingale during the Crimean War. While working there among eleven thousand typhus-stricken refugees, Thurber himself contracted the disease, but survived to become director of the Constantinople unit of the Near East Relief. Invalided home in 1924, he underwent three surgical operations and spent nearly a year in hospitals, but was nevertheless able during two years to address more than eleven hundred meetings on behalf of the relief organization, which in 1926 sent him back to Athens as director of its work in Greece. In addition to regular duties connected with administering the orphanages and training the orphans in trades and farming, he undertook the establishment of three working-boys' homes for orphans who had left the institutions and were earning their own living. His single-hearted devotion to his ideal of service, especially during a severe epidemic of dengue fever, his unstinted labors on behalf of Greek refugees, and his engaging personal qualities gained the respect and affection of the Greek people to a remarkable degree. The government of Greece, which had bestowed upon him three decorations, including the Cross of War and the Golden Cross of the Order of the Saviour, buried him with all the honors of a general after a state funeral service in the Cathedral of Athens.

[*Trinity Coll. Bull.*, n.s., vol. XXVII (1930), pp. 68–69; obituaries in *N. Y. Times,* June 3, and in *Hestia* (Athens), June 2, 1930; copies of letters and biog. data furnished by the Near East Foundation of New York, N. Y.]　　　　　　　　　　　　　W. L. W., Jr.

THURBER, GEORGE (Sept. 2, 1821–Apr. 2, 1890), botanist, horticulturist, author, editor, was born in Providence, R. I., the son of Jacob Thurber, a business man, and Alice Ann (Martin) Thurber. For a time he attended the Union Classical and Engineering School of Providence, but was in the main self-educated. He early took up pharmacy, first as an apprentice, then as a proprietor in partnership with Joshua Chapin. He soon developed an interest in chemistry, and for a time he held a lectureship in this subject with the Franklin Society of Providence. Turning to botany for the sources of vegetable drugs, in time he became intimately associated with such emi-

nent scientists as Asa Gray, George Engelmann, John Torrey, and Jean Louis Rodolphe Agassiz [*qq.v.*]. Plant study became an absorbing passion, and he eagerly seized the opportunity, presented in 1850, to serve as botanist, quartermaster, and commissary on the survey of the boundary between the United States and Mexico. For several years he pursued the fascinating, sometimes perilous business of collecting the native flora along the Mexican border. His herbarium assembled there, comprising many species new to scientists, formed the basis of Gray's "Plantae Novae Thurberinanae" (*Memoirs of the American Academy of Arts and Sciences,* n.s., vol. V, 1855). Among the new plants named for their discoverer was the cactus *Cereus thurberi,* subsequently cultivated in the desert regions of North Africa. Thurber held a position in the United States Assay Office in New York (1853–56), was lecturer in botany and *materia medica* at the College of Pharmacy in New York (1856–61, 1865–66), and also lectured on botany at Cooper Union. The New York Medical College in 1859 conferred on him the degree of M.D. In the same year he was appointed to the chair of botany and horticulture at Michigan State Agricultural College (later Michigan State College). In 1863 he returned to New York to become editor of the *American Agriculturist.* Establishing his home on a small farm, "The Pines," near Passaic, N. J., he cultivated an experimental garden which furnished abundant material for the columns of his journal. His unsigned "Notes from the Pines" for years were conspicuous in horticultural literature for the extent and accuracy of their botanical information. His series entitled "The Doctor's Talks," noted for charming simplicity of style, was designed to instruct young people on scientific subjects. Under his editorship the *American Agriculturist* exerted a vigorous progressive influence upon agriculture and horticulture. He gave much attention to the exposure of business and professional frauds. In 1885 ill-health forced him to relinquish the active direction of the journal, but he continued to contribute regularly to its columns up to the time of his death. He died in Passaic, survived by a brother and three sisters, with one of whom he had shared his home. He never married.

He was one of the earliest exponents of agricultural botany. His specialty was the grasses; he collected many specimens and long cherished the ambition, unhappily never realized, to publish a monograph on American grasses. He revised William Darlington's *Agricultural Botany* (1847) under the new title *American Weeds and Useful Plants* (1859), contributed botanical articles to Appleton's *The American Cyclopedia* (16 vols., 1873–76) and the section on grasses to the *Botany* (1880) published by the Geological Survey of California, and supervised the editing of hundreds of rural books published by Orange Judd [*q.v.*]. He was president of the Torrey Botanical Club (1873–80), a life member of the American Pomological Society, a corresponding member of the Academy of Natural Sciences of Philadelphia, and an active member of the New York Academy of Sciences. In 1880, on a trip abroad, he visited many European botanists and horticulturists, and in 1886 he was made a corresponding member of the Royal Horticultural Society of London.

[C. P. Wimmer, *The Coll. of Pharmacy of the City of N. Y.* (1929); W. J. Beal, *Hist. of the Mich. Agricultural Coll.* (1915); *Semi-Centennial Celebration of Mich. State Agricultural Coll.* (1908), ed. by T. C. Blaisdell; L. H. Bailey, *Cyc. of Am. Agriculture*, vol. IV (1912), and *Standard Cyc. of Horticulture*, vol. III (1915); *Garden and Forest*, Apr. 9, 1890; *Am. Agriculturist*, May 1890; *Botanical Gazette*, May 1890; H. H. Rusby, in *Bull. Torrey Botanical Club*, Aug. 12, 1890; obituary in *N. Y. Tribune*, Apr. 4, 1890; information from F. S. Kedzie, Mich. State Coll.]

C. R. W.

THURMAN, ALLEN GRANBERRY (Nov. 13, 1813–Dec. 12, 1895), representative and senator from Ohio, was born in Lynchburg, Va. His father, Pleasant Thurman, was a minister of the Methodist Church; his mother, Mary Granberry (Allen) Thurman, was the daughter of Nathaniel Allen, of Edenton, N. C., the nephew and adopted son of Joseph Hewes [*q.v.*]. In 1819 his parents removed to Chillicothe, Ohio, where Thurman lived until he removed permanently to Columbus in 1853. His education was largely directed by his mother, who was a cultured woman. Thurman attended the Chillicothe academy and in early life acquired a knowledge and fondness for French literature that was rare in his day. When eighteen years of age, he assisted in land surveying and at twenty-one became the private secretary to Gov. Robert Lucas [*q.v.*]. He had already begun the study of law with his uncle, William Allen, 1803–1879 [*q.v.*]; and at Columbus he continued his legal studies with Noah H. Swayne [*q.v.*]. In 1835 he was admitted to the bar and returned to Chillicothe, where he soon formed a partnership with his uncle. For ten years he rode the circuit. As a lawyer he was studious, painstaking in the preparation of his cases, logical in the presentation of his arguments, quick to discover the vulnerable points in those of his adversary, and aggressive. He practised largely in the higher state and federal courts and as early as 1851 was recognized throughout the state as one of its foremost lawyers. On Nov. 14, 1844, he married Mrs. Mary A. Tompkins, the daughter of Walter Dun of Fayette County, Ky. One of their daughters married Richard C. McCormick [*q.v.*]. The same year, 1844, he was nominated and elected as the Democratic candidate for representative to Congress. While a member of the House, he served on the judiciary committee, supported the administration's conduct of the Mexican War, made a vigorous speech in behalf of the claims of the United States to Oregon for 54° 40′, and voted for the Wilmot Proviso. At the end of his term in Congress, he declined to be a candidate for renomination. He practised law until 1851, when he was elected associate justice of the state supreme court under the new constitution. He was chief justice from Dec. 4, 1854, to Feb. 9, 1856. His mind was instinctively judicial, and the decisions he rendered are notable for their clarity of expression, forceful language, and accurate statements of law. At the expiration of his term, he refused a renomination and resumed his law practice in Columbus.

He took a prominent part in the discussions growing out of the slavery controversy. He opposed the repeal of the Missouri Compromise and advocated non-interference by the federal government, so far as slavery in the territories was concerned. He was against the Lecompton constitution for Kansas and supported Stephen A. Douglas for president in 1860. Although he never accepted the doctrine of secession, he questioned the wisdom of employing coercion against a state that had already left the Union. He wanted to preserve the Union; but he believed that an appeal to arms would destroy the Union forever. Throughout the Civil War, he was one of the leaders of the "Peace Democrats" who opposed the federal administration's arbitrary arrests, suspension of the *habeas corpus,* and infringement of the freedom of the press. In 1867 the Democratic party nominated him as its candidate for governor of Ohio against Rutherford B. Hayes. The campaign was fought over the question of negro suffrage and attracted national attention. Hayes was elected by a majority of fewer than 3,000; but the legislature was Democratic; and Thurman was elected by this body to the federal Senate. It was due to Thurman's political strategy that the Democrats elected William Allen as governor in 1873, carried the legislature, and returned Thurman to the Senate.

During his twelve years of service in the Senate he was the recognized leader of his party in the Senate. The "Old Roman," as he was called, was a doctrinaire, strict constructionist, partisan Democrat of the Jeffersonian school. He won for himself a national reputation for his judicial fairness and skill in debate, especially upon questions of constitutional law. Upon entering the Senate he was appointed to the judiciary committee and, when his party obtained a majority in the 46th Congress, he was made its chairman and was also chosen president *pro tempore* in April 1879, owing to the illness of the vice-president, William A. Wheeler. Thurman also rendered valuable service as a member of the committee on private land claims. He is best remembered for his attacks on the constitutionality of the Civil Rights Bill, his opposition to all inflationary measures, and as the author of the Thurman Act relating to the Pacific railroads. He was a member of the electoral commission of 1877 and voted to seat Tilden. In 1881 he was an unsuccessful candidate for reëlection to the Senate. Upon his retirement, President Garfield appointed him one of the American representatives to the international monetary conference at Paris. He traveled extensively in Europe and shortly after his return home he was selected, with Thomas M. Cooley and Elihu B. Washburne [*qq.v.*], to arbitrate the great trunk line railroad companies' difficulties about differential rates. He was a presidential candidate in the Democratic conventions of 1876, 1880, and 1884; and the unsuccessful candidate for vice-president on the Democratic ticket with Grover Cleveland in 1888. He died in Columbus.

[W. U. Hensel and G. F. Parker, *Life and Public Services of Grover Cleveland and Allen G. Thurman* (1888); J. G. Blaine, *Twenty Years of Congress* (2 vols., 1884–86); *Biog. Cyc. and Portrait Gallery of Ohio*, vol. I (1883); E. O. Randall and D. J. Ryan, *Hist. of Ohio* (1912), vols. IV, V; R. C. McGrane, *William Allen* (1925); *Cincinnati Times-Star*, Dec. 12, 1895; Papers in Lib. of Cong., and in Lib. of Arch. and Hist. Soc., Columbus.]   R. C. M.

THURSBY, EMMA CECILIA (Feb. 21, 1845–July 4, 1931), singer, voice teacher, was born in Brooklyn, N. Y., the daughter of John Barnes Thursby, a rope manufacturer of New York City, and his wife, Jane Ann (Bennett) Thursby. John Barnes Thursby was the grandson of the John Thursby who came to New York in 1796 and founded the first rope manufactory in America. Emma Thursby entered the Moravian Seminary at Bethlehem, Pa., with the class of 1857. In 1859 her father died, and it became necessary for her to help toward the support of the family. She accordingly began vocal study under Julius Meyer, a pupil of Mendelssohn, and later with Achille Errani. She rapidly developed a soprano voice of remarkable range—from middle C to F above the staff. From 1865 to 1868 she was engaged as soprano soloist at Plymouth Church in Brooklyn. In

1873 she went abroad for instruction with Lamperti, in Milan, and with San Giovanni, and returned to America to study for a time with Madame Rudersdorff before making her début as a concert singer in 1875 at the Bedford Avenue Church in Brooklyn. For this concert she engaged the services of Patrick S. Gilmore [*q.v.*] and his band. Gilmore was so impressed with Thursby's singing that he engaged her for his summer concerts in New York and for a tour through the United States. Engagements at the Church of the Divine Paternity and at the Broadway Tabernacle in New York followed. At the Tabernacle she came to the attention of Maurice Strakosch, concert manager and brother-in-law of Adelina Patti. He persuaded her to appear in concerts and oratorios under his management and she remained under his direction for seven years.

She appeared in concert with the London Philharmonic on May 22, 1878, and for almost a year sang at the Crystal Palace, the Popular Concerts, and with Leslie's Choir. From London she went to Paris, where her début created a sensation, and then toured the French provinces. In France she received the most flattering offer of her career, a proposal that she appear at the Paris Opéra on her own terms. Thursby, like Jenny Lind, was prejudiced against the opera and the theatre, and it is said that she had promised her friends at Plymouth Church never to be an opera singer. According to a family tradition these same friends were disappointed that she had not accepted the offer when she returned to America expecting approval.

In 1879 she was in America again, appearing with the Norwegian violinist, Ole Bull, on his last American tour. In 1880–81 she toured the Continent, returning to America at the end of 1882. In 1883 she toured the United States and Canada, and during her last full season was the principal soloist for Theodore Thomas [*q.v.*] and his orchestra. Thereafter Thursby appeared in concert at less frequent intervals. She began a scientific investigation of methods of voice training and in 1898 commenced her active career as a vocal teacher. She was the first teacher of Geraldine Farrar and acted as sponsor and adviser to the younger singer throughout Farrar's entire career. Thursby made a tour of China and Japan in 1903 and then definitely retired as a concert artist. Her voice, like Jenny Lind's, has become something of a tradition. She was one of the first American singers to win an international reputation after having won first laurels at home and she was considered one of the greatest Mozart interpreters of her time. Until the year of her death in New York City, her apartment in Gramercy Park was a salon for the gathering of the most brilliant figures in the musical world.

[Records and documents supplied by the family; *Who's Who in America,* 1901–02; *Hist. of Plymouth Church, 1847–1872* (1873); "The Biography of Emma Thursby," reprint from the *Ladies Home Jour.*; Edmund Kennedy, "Emma Thursby: Speranza," *Musical Digest,* Sept. 1930; *Musician,* Aug. 1931; *N. Y. Times,* July 5, 1931.]   J. T. H.

THURSTON, LORRIN ANDREWS (July 31, 1858–May 11, 1931), lawyer, editor, official of Hawaii, a descendant of Daniel Thurston who settled in Newbury, Mass., between 1635 and 1638, was born in Honolulu, the son of Asa Goodale and Sarah (Andrews) Thurston. His grandfathers on both sides—Asa Thurston and Lorrin Andrews [*q.v.*]—were American missionaries. His early education was obtained at a private school and at Oahu College in Honolulu. He then studied law as a clerk in the office of the attorney general of Hawaii; was admitted to practise in the lower courts in 1878; spent two years in sugar plantation work; in 1880 went to New York and studied for two years at Columbia Law School. Returning to Hawaii in 1883, he was admitted to practice before the supreme court and formed a law partnership with W. O. Smith. In 1886 and 1892 he served in the Hawaiian legislature as an elected member. Interested in politics only for its bearing on the problem of good government, he sought a legislative seat only when the need of reform was acute. His convictions that if reform could not be accomplished in any other way revolution must be the remedy, and that the Hawaiian Islands must some day be a part of the United States, serve to explain his political career from 1885 to 1898.

The few reform members of the legislature of 1886—capable and earnest men, of whom Thurston was one of the most active—were unable to drive out the corruption and maladministration which prevailed under the premiership of Walter M. Gibson [*q.v.*], and the revolution of 1887 followed in due course. As one of the leaders in the movement Thurston helped to draft the new constitution, curtailing the royal prerogative, and was appointed minister of the interior. The reform ministry remained in office until 1890 and was then forced out, partly by dissensions among its own members and partly by a rising tide of native Hawaiian opposition zealously fostered by King Kalakaua. During 1890–92 the royalist party grew and old abuses crept back. The legislative session of 1892 was a repetition of that of 1886. In the spring of 1892 Thurston visited Washington to sound out opinion on the subject of annexation, conditioned on its being accom-

plished by peaceful means with the acquiescence of Queen Liliuokalani, who had succeeded to the throne; but at the close of the year he believed neither annexation nor the end of the monarchy to be near at hand. Liliuokalani's attempted *coup d'etat* in January 1893 precipitated the revolution which dethroned her. Thurston was admittedly the outstanding leader in the revolution. He drafted the proclamation of the provisional government and headed the commission sent to Washington to negotiate for annexation. In May 1893 he was appointed Hawaiian envoy to the United States, a post which he held for two trying years. He did not possess a diplomatic temperament and the ill-concealed hostility of President Cleveland and the Secretary of State, Walter Q. Gresham, led him into a breach of diplomatic etiquette which brought a request for his recall. He helped in framing the constitution of the Republic of Hawaii in 1894 and was a member of the commission that negotiated the second treaty of annexation in 1897. He energetically opposed the idea of declaring Hawaiian neutrality during the Spanish-American War.

After annexation had been consummated, Thurston withdrew from political life and resumed his private business career. In 1898 he became principal owner and editorial director of the *Honolulu Advertiser,* which he built up to metropolitan standards. He was enthusiastically devoted to the development of the latent resources of Hawaii, was one of the earliest promoters of the pineapple industry and the tourist business, and both in office and out advocated the building of roads and harbor facilities. There was hardly a public question on which he did not write vigorously and pertinently. In his championship of any cause, he was not much concerned about conciliating opposition, but simply strove to overpower it by the weight of argument. Examples of his numerous contributions to the press are, "The Sandwich Islands: The Advantages of Annexation" (*North American Review,* March 1893), "The Growing Greatness of the Pacific" (*Ibid.,* April 1895), and *A Hand-book on the Annexation of Hawaii* (n.d., *circa* 1897). In 1904 he edited a volume of Hawaiian constitutions and related documents under the title *The Fundamental Law of Hawaii.* His last important public service was in bringing forward (1926) and advocating the cause of a civil government for American Samoa. Thurston was twice married: first to Margaret Clarissa Shipman of Hilo (Feb. 21, 1884), and some years after her death, to Harriet Potter of St. Joseph, Mich. (Apr. 5, 1894). He was survived by his second wife, a son of his first marriage, and a son and a daughter of the second.

[Sources include Brown Thurston, *Thurston Geneals.* (1880); *Who's Who in America*, 1930–31; *Men of Hawaii* (1921); *Oahu College Directory* (1916); G. F. Nellist, *The Story of Hawaii and Its Builders* (1925); A. A. Greene, in *Honolulu Advertiser*, July 2, 1931; obituary, *Ibid.*, May 12, 1931; *Foreign Relations of the U. S.*, *1894*, App. II (1895); *Sen. Report 227*, 53 Cong., 2 Sess.; Hawaiian legislative records, 1886–92; correspondence in Hawaiian archives and in U. S. State Dept. Certain papers of Thurston have been announced for early publication.]   R. S. K.

THURSTON, ROBERT HENRY (Oct. 25, 1839–Oct. 25, 1903), engineer, educator, was born in Providence, R. I., eldest of three children of Robert Lawton Thurston [*q.v.*] and Harriet (Taylor) Thurston. The father was one of the pioneer steam-engine builders of the country and the son, during his early years, spent much time in his father's shops. Persuaded by his high-school principal, Edward H. Magill [*q.v.*], to take a college course in preparation for engineering as a learned profession, he matriculated in Brown University at sixteen and graduated in 1859 with the degree of Ph.B. and a certificate in civil engineering. In the fall of that year he entered the drafting room of his father's firm in Providence and a year later went to Philadelphia as their representative. Here he published his first technical paper, "On the Economy Resulting from the Expansion of Steam" (*Journal of the Franklin Institute*, March 1861). Not very successful in a business way in Philadelphia, he returned to Providence, but within a few months, on the outbreak of the Civil War, volunteered for service as an engineer in the navy, and after examination was appointed a third assistant engineer.

On Aug. 25, 1861, he was called to active service in the U.S.S. *Unadilla*, fitting out at the Brooklyn Navy Yard for duty on the Southern blockade. He was subsequently assigned as a member of the prize crew to the *Princess Royal*, a merchant steamer taken by the *Unadilla* in an attempt to run the blockade, and later, successively, to the *Chippewa*, the *Maumee*, the *Pontoosuc*, and the *Dictator*. In the meantime he had, on examination, been promoted to the rank of second assistant engineer, which rank he held until July 1865, when on examination he was promoted first assistant engineer.

After the close of the war, following a brief delay on waiting orders during which time he married (Oct. 5, 1865) Susan Taylor Gladding, he was assigned in December 1865 to the Naval Academy as assistant professor in the department of natural and experimental philosophy. Upon the death of Prof. A. W. Smith a few months later, he became head of the department. While at Annapolis he devised a successful magnesium lamp for signaling, made a study of fric-

tion and lubrication, and contributed several papers to the *Journal of the Franklin Institute*. Two of these, "Steam Engines of the French Navy" (September 1868) and an account of the British ironclad *Monarch* (April 1870), prepared at the request of the editor, Henry Morton [*q.v.*], gave Morton such a conception of his capacity that in 1871, as president of the newly founded Stevens Institute of Technology, Hoboken, N. J., he called Thurston to help with the organization of that institution as professor of mechanical engineering. Meanwhile, in 1870, on leave of absence from the Naval Academy, Thurston had visited Great Britain to investigate for Rhode Island interests certain metallurgical processes in Wales, and upon his return he published in the *Journal of the Franklin Institute* (January, March, April, May 1871) a series of papers on "Iron Manufactures in Great Britain," which further enhanced his reputation.

After accepting the call to Stevens but before leaving Annapolis, he drew up a plan for a four-year course of instruction in mechanical engineering, designed as preparation for entrance into practice. This plan, dated July 1871, he circulated among engineers all over the country asking for criticism, and it subsequently became the basis for the curriculum at Stevens Institute. The work at Stevens was largely pioneer in character, and precedents and guides were few and uncertain in value. One of his first new measures was the inauguration of a small mechanical laboratory, formally organized in 1875—the first in the country. Seeing an opportunity to combine the training of students in research with the accomplishment of researches of commercial value, he began at once to accept commissions from business firms to assist them in solving problems. The income from this commercial work was applied directly to the purchase of additional equipment for the laboratory and for the shop courses which he inaugurated in 1878. His experience as a boy in his father's shop in Providence had impressed on his mind the importance to an engineer of a practical knowledge of the tools and processes of the machine shop. Both the mechanical laboratory and the shop courses had formed part of his original plan for his course of instruction; he realized them as soon as he could (see his articles, "On the Necessity of a Mechanical Laboratory: Its Province and Its Methods," *Journal of the Franklin Institute*, December 1875, and "Instruction in Mechanical Engineering," *Scientific American Supplement*, Apr. 19, 1884). For his laboratory he designed an "autographic recording testing machine" for testing materials in torsion, and a machine for testing lubricants, both of which he patented. Feeling the need of textbooks for the course on structural materials, one of his fundamental courses, he used the laboratory to gather findings which were ultimately incorporated in *The Materials of Engineering* (3 vols., 1883–84), abridged under the title, *A Text-Book of the Materials of Construction, for Use in Technical and Engineering Schools* (1885).

Thurston's personal energy and his bold and striking measures at Stevens attracted the attention of leaders in engineering and industry and he was soon called upon to serve on important commissions and juries. Thus he was a member of the committee to test steam boilers at the American Institute exhibition of 1871 (*Annual Report,* 1872, p. 66) ; in 1873 he was a member of an international jury and also a United States commissioner at the Vienna exposition, and he was subsequently appointed to edit *Reports of the Commissioners of the United States to the International Exhibition Held at Vienna, 1873* (4 vols., 1876), for which he wrote "Report on Machinery and Manufactures," included in Vol. III. He served as a member of a government commission to experiment with steam-boiler explosions (1871–76), and in 1875 was appointed secretary of the important United States Board to Test Iron, Steel, and Other Metals. Much of the work of the latter board was carried on under his direction in the laboratories of Stevens Institute, and it was in connection with some of these investigations, while studying the physical properties of the alloys of copper and tin, copper and zinc, and copper, tin and zinc, that he developed the three-coördinate solid diagram, exhibiting at a glance any specified physical quality of any relative combinations of these three constituents—a form of diagram which has since become standard for purposes of this character. This device he described at a meeting of the American Association for the Advancement of Science in 1877 (*Proceedings,* vol. XXVI, 1878).

During these years his zeal for work began to outrun his physical and nervous endurance, and between 1876 and 1880 he was forced to accept a part-time schedule. From 1878, some months after the death of his wife, until 1880, he was incapacitated by a breakdown, but regained his health, and during the remaining twenty-three years of his life he lost no time from serious illness. His first wife left one daughter. On Aug. 4, 1880, he was married a second time, to Leonora Boughton of New York. Two daughters were born of this marriage.

In 1885 he resigned his post at Stevens Institute to accept a call by the trustees of Cornell University to undertake as Director the reorganization of Sibley College as a high-grade college of mechanical engineering. He was given full responsibility, including control of appointments, equipment, and instruction, and proved fully worthy of the trust imposed. Under his administration the number of candidates for the degree of M.E. increased from sixty-three in 1885 to 885 in 1903, and the faculty from seven to forty-three. He was successful at once in establishing a department of experimental engineering, a great elaboration of the pioneer mechanical laboratory courses at Stevens. During his eighteen years as director of Sibley College he taught the courses in thermo-dynamics and steam-engineering. He saw the possibility of a great engineering school at Cornell and gave his unremitting efforts to its realization.

In addition to his regular work at the University, he found time to serve as member of the New York state commissions on voting machines and on the selection of a firearm for the National Guard, and of the United States commissions on postal-pneumatic service and on safe and vault construction. He was a member of the leading engineering and scientific societies of America and Europe, notably of the American Society of Civil Engineers from 1871 and of the American Institute of Mining Engineers from 1875; he took a leading part in organizing the American Society of Mechanical Engineers in 1880, and was its first president, serving for two terms; he was three times a vice-president of the American Association for the Advancement of Science.

In his own researches on the reciprocating steam engine, Thurston gave much thought and study to the losses arising from the reaction between the steam and the iron of the cylinder—losses arising from what may be called the cycle of the cast iron, parallel to and at the expense of that of the steam; and many of his papers and certain inventions relate to this phase of engineering. Always a voluminous writer, he was the author of a number of exhaustive treatises and contributed a very large number of papers, on a wide range of subjects, to the transactions of numerous engineering and scientific societies.

He possessed in remarkable degree the capacity for rapid and intensive work; the flow of his ideas was often too rapid for expression. A list of his books and more important papers comprises works on the materials of engineering construction, works on the steam engine and steam boiler, and works of historical, biographical, or philosophical character. His principal publications, most of which went through a number of editions, were: *A History of the Growth of the Steam-Engine* (1878); developed from popular lectures at Stevens Institute; *Friction and Lubrication: Determinations of the Laws and Coefficients of Friction by New Methods and with New Apparatus* (1879); *The Materials of Engineering* (3 vols., 1883–84), previously mentioned; *Stationary Steam Engines, Especially as Adapted to Electric Lighting Purposes* (1884); *A Treatise on Friction and Lost Work in Machinery and Millwork* (1885); *A Text-Book of the Materials of Construction, for Use in Technical and Engineering Schools* (1885), mentioned above; *Steam-Boiler Explosions, in Theory and in Practice* (1887); *A Manual of Steam-Boilers; Their Design, Construction, and Operation* (1888); *Heat as a Form of Energy* (1890); *Reflections on the Motive Power of Heat* (1890), a translation of *Réflexions sur la Puissance Motrice du Feu* (1824), by M. L. S. Carnot; *A Handbook of Engine and Boiler Trials, and of the Indicator and Prony Brake* (1890); *Robert Fulton, His Life and Its Results* (1891); *A Manual of the Steam-Engine: For Engineers and Technical Schools* (2 vols., 1891); *The Animal as a Machine and a Prime Motor, and the Laws of Energetics* (1894). He was also editor for the subjects comprehended under "Engineering" for the *Universal Cyclopædia* and contributed to the *Century Dictionary*, with collaboration in certain fields, the definitions in general technology, "including all branches of the mechanical arts."

It was not, however, through books and papers that his greatest influence was exerted. Hundreds of engineers who passed under his personal instruction, being touched by his loyalty to scientific truth and his high ideals of life and service and carrying into after life the inspiration of his example, were the most influential contribution to his profession of this pioneer in the domain of engineering education.

In his personality and bearing Thurston was gracious, sympathetic, and kindly. His judgments on technical questions were rapid; on matters involving the human element he was likely to be more deliberate in reaching a conclusion. He had the ability to present scientific results with great clearness. As an administrator he had organizing ability of a high order; he respected individuality and did his best to make use of the distinctive capabilities of his subordinates; he was cordial and generous; gave credit liberally, and had the gift of friendship. Under storm and stress he was always cheerful; an appearance of failure never discouraged him. Little, and shaggy of head and beard, with bright, dark eyes,

great personal dignity, and quick, energetic movements, he was affectionately known on the campus as "Bobby" and his steam-engine courses, as "Bobbyology." He died suddenly and peacefully while friends were gathering to celebrate his sixty-fourth birthday, in the midst of his labors and in full possession of his normal strength and mental activities, with apparently many years of fruitful labor yet before him.

[Thurston's autobiography (MS.), written for his family; W. F. Durand, *Robert Henry Thurston* (1929) and memoir in *Ann. Report . . . of the Smithsonian Inst. . . . 1903* (1904); *Trans. Am. Soc. Mech. Engineers*, vol. XXV (1904); *Trans. Am. Inst. Mining Engineers*, vol. XXXV (1905); *Who's Who in America*, 1903–05; F. M. Bennett, *The Steam Navy of the U. S.* (1896); *Morton Memorial: A Hist. of the Stevens Inst. of Technology* (1905), ed. by F. DeR. Furman; W. T. Hewett, *Cornell Univ.: A Hist.* (1905), vol. II; *N. Y. Tribune*, Oct. 26, 1903; personal acquaintance.]   W. F. D.

THURSTON, ROBERT LAWTON (Dec. 13, 1800–Jan. 13, 1874), pioneer manufacturer of steam engines, was born on his father's farm at Portsmouth, R. I., the youngest son of Peleg and Ruth (Lawton) Thurston. He was a descendant in the sixth generation from Roger Williams [*q.v.*], founder of Rhode Island, and in the fifth, from Edward Thurston who was living in that colony as early as 1647. After obtaining a good schooling, he began learning the trade of machinist in the local shop of Pelham & Walcott, having shown since his early boyhood an unusual mechanical talent. In the course of his apprenticeship, about 1821, he attracted the attention of John Babcock, Sr., who was engaged in experimental work on steam boilers. The latter persuaded young Thurston to assist him, and together the two built an experimental steam engine and a "safety tubular boiler" of Babcock's invention, and placed them in a small boat designed for use at Slade's Ferry near Fall River. This apparatus gave such a satisfactory performance that the partners undertook the design and construction of two large steamboats and between 1826 and 1828 completed the *Babcock* and the *Rushlight* for use on the Providence-New York run. The machinery for the former was of their own construction, while that for the latter was built by James P. Allaire [*q.v.*].

After the death of Babcock in 1827, Thurston was employed for a time by the Fall River Iron Company and assisted in the construction of the Annawan mill. His thoughts, however, were wholly taken up with steam-engine building and in 1830 he went to Providence where, in partnership with John Babcock, Jr., he formed the Providence Steam Engine Company for the manufacture of steam engines and power machinery of all kinds. This is said to have been the first establishment for the manufacture of steam engines in New England and the third in the United States. The undertaking was successful from the start, primarily because of the intelligence and practical experience of the partners. In 1838 Babcock retired and the firm became Robert L. Thurston & Company, the business of which Thurston continued to direct alone. Early in the forties, a boiler explosion destroyed several of his factory buildings and several months later came a fire which completely destroyed the plant. Between these two disasters, in 1845, he reorganized the company as Thurston, Green & Company, and soon after the fire rebuilt the plant. One of the first acts of the new company was to purchase the invention of Frederick E. Sickels [q.v.] of the "drop cut-off" for steam engines, which they incorporated in their engines; they were the first manufacturers in either Europe or America to build a standard form of expansion steam engine. Thurston, however, continued to be unfortunate in monetary matters and in 1854 the company was reorganized again as Thurston, Gardner & Company and began the manufacture of the steam engine invented by Noble T. Greene which long remained a favorite form in the field of automatic cut-off steam engines. Thurston brought suit against George H. Corliss [q.v.] for infringement of the Sickels patent and after a long drawn-out trial won a decision, but on appeal the United States Supreme Court decided in favor of Corliss. Although the cost of this lawsuit was extremely heavy, Thurston carried on, but the heavy losses which his company incurred at the beginning of the Civil War, coupled with his advancing age, caused him to retire in 1863 from active participation in the business. He was twice married: first, in 1827, to Eliza Stratton of Portsmouth, who died July 10, 1828. On Jan. 5, 1839, he married Harriet Taylor, daughter of William and Elizabeth (Bailey) Taylor of Little Compton, R. I., who with three children survived him. His elder son, Robert Henry Thurston [q.v.], won great distinction in the profession of mechanical engineering.

[*Providence Daily Journal*, Jan. 14, 21, 1874; Brown Thurston, *Thurston Geneals.* (1880); C. M. Thurston, *Descendants of Edward Thurston* (1868); W. F. Durand, *Robert Henry Thurston* (1929); *Scientific American*, Mar. 7, 1874; R. H. Thurston, *The Hist. of the Growth of the Steam Engine* (1878).] C. W. M—n.

THWAITES, REUBEN GOLD (May 15, 1853–Oct. 22, 1913), librarian and editor, was born in Dorchester, Mass., the son of parents recently from Yorkshire, England, William George and Sarah (Bibbs) Thwaites, and he was educated in the public schools of Massachusetts.

Then going to Wisconsin in 1866, he worked on a farm, taught school, and put himself through a course of college studies. Before the age of twenty he was on the staff of the *Oshkosh Times* and was sent to report the convention at Baltimore in 1872 that nominated Horace Greeley. His desire for college training led him to Yale University in 1874, where he supported himself as a newspaper correspondent, while studying advanced courses in history and economics. In 1876 he became managing editor of the *Wisconsin State Journal,* the leading Republican newspaper at Madison, Wis. There he worked for a decade acquiring a wide acquaintance in the state and a thorough technique in the art of printing, typography, and proof reading that was valuable to his future career.

His fondness for history took him often to the rooms of the State Historical Society of Wisconsin, presided over by Lyman C. Draper [q.v.]. Draper recognized the promise of the young journalist, invited him to become assistant secretary, and on his own retirement at the close of 1886 recommended Thwaites as his successor. He was unanimously elected and assumed his duties on Jan. 1, 1887. The new secretary's first care was to enlarge the society's usefulness by building up its manuscript collection and making it available to the scholars of the University of Wisconsin. He visited the descendants of the French pioneers and obtained many of their papers; then in 1891 the society inherited the vast collection of the Draper Manuscripts. Thwaites arranged seminar rooms for the use of Frederick Jackson Turner, where Turner gathered advanced students for research in the history of the West, now made available in these manuscript sources. It was soon evident that the society must have a larger place than the rooms it had occupied in the Capitol. Thwaites obtained the enthusiastic support of the state's leaders for a joint library building for the state historical society and the university upon the lower campus of the university. To this building he gave such care and attention that it may be called his monument. Dedicated in 1900, the historical library has amply fulfilled its purpose.

Impressed with the need of a new edition of the Jesuit Relations, he collected and translated these, with a corps of assistants, until from 1896 to 1901 there appeared seventy-three volumes of *Jesuit Relations and Allied Documents.* This edition with its fine annotations and translations established his reputation as one of the best historical editors of his day. Continuing his editorial work he brought out the *Original Journals of the Lewis and Clark Expedition* (8 vols.,

1904–05) ; Hennepin's *New Discovery* (1903) and Lahontan's *New Voyages* (1905), two volumes each with bibliographies; *Early Western Travels,* annotated reprints in thirty-two volumes (1904–07) ; the Draper Series (with L. P. Kellogg) from his manuscript material, *Documentary History of Dunmore's War* (1905) ; *The Revolution on the Upper Ohio* (1908) ; *Frontier Defense on the Upper Ohio* (1912). During all these years he produced a yearly volume of the society's *Proceedings* and a biennial volume of the *Collections,* containing source material for the history of the state. As an author he wrote along the lines of his editorial work, bringing out *Father Marquette* in Appletons' Life Series and *Daniel Boone* (both in 1902) ; *A Brief History of Rocky Mountain Exploration* (1904) ; *France in America* (1905) for the American Nation Series. He wrote in 1891 *The Colonies* for the Epochs of American History Series, and several books on Wisconsin history, of which *Wisconsin* (1908) in the American Commonwealth Series remains the standard. His love of nature and travel served as a basis for *Historic Waterways* (1888) ; *Our Cycling Tour in England* (1892) ; *Afloat on the Ohio* (1897).

In addition to editorship and authorship, he was much in demand for lectures, and his executive ability was enlisted for professional service. In 1900 he was president of the American Library Association, and he served the American Historical Association in many capacities. He was a delightful host and guest, a great friend, a lover of nature and of human nature. His wife, Jessie Inwood (Turville) Thwaites, whom he married in 1882, supplemented him in all his activities. They had one son.

[F. J. Turner, *Reuben Gold Thwaites, a Memorial Address* (1914), with bibliog. of writings ; *Who's Who in America,* 1912–13 ; *Review of Reviews* (N. Y.), Dec. 1913 ; *Outlook,* Nov. 8, 1913 ; *Wis. State Jour.* (Madison), Oct. 23, 1913.]   L. P. K.

TIBBLES, SUSETTE LA FLESCHE [See Bright Eyes, 1854–1903].

TIBBLES, THOMAS HENRY (May 22, 1838–May 14, 1928), journalist, social reformer, was the son of William and Martha (Cooley) Tibbles and was born in Washington County, Ohio. It is said that he ran away from home at the age of six and that he was picked up by a party of emigrants who took him to western Missouri. In 1856 he appears to have been a member of John Brown's company in Kansas. According to the legend he was once captured by Quantrill's men and hanged, though friends arrived in time to save his life. He returned to Ohio and for a time attended Mount Union College at Alliance.

In 1861, at Freedom, Pa., he married Amelia Owen. During the Civil War he served on the plains as a guide and scout, and had some employment as a newspaper correspondent. After the war he became an itinerant Methodist preacher, though later he joined the Presbyterians and still later the Unitarians. In 1873–74 he was employed as a reporter on the *Omaha Daily Bee* and in 1876–79 on the *Omaha Daily Herald* (subsequently the *Morning World-Herald*). It was while engaged with the latter paper that he took part in an episode that brought him into general notice. A party of thirty-four homesick Poncas, led by their chief, Standing Bear, had left their new reservation in the present Oklahoma and after a terrible mid-winter journey had arrived among the friendly Omahas late in March 1879. They were arrested by the military, under orders to return them to the reservation. Tibbles, with a fellow reporter, enlisted the help of two attorneys, and on Apr. 30, after a trial in the Federal District Court, the Poncas were freed (*United States ex rel. Standing Bear* vs. *Crook, 25 Federal Cases,* 695). Tibbles, arranging with Standing Bear and with Francis La Flesche and his sister Susette, or Bright Eyes [*q.v.*], of the Omahas to plead the cause of the Indians before the people, conducted a speaking tour which inspired a nation-wide movement in their behalf. His first wife had died in 1879. In 1881, on the Omaha reservation, he married Bright Eyes.

Tibbles was, from their beginning, a zealous supporter of the National Farmers' Alliance and the People's (Populist) party. In 1895, at Lincoln, he took charge of the *Independent,* a weekly organ of the movement, which became nationally influential. In 1904 he was the party's candidate for vice-president. From 1905 to 1910 he edited a weekly newspaper, the *Investigator,* and then returned to the *World-Herald,* where his last newspaper work was done. His wife died on May 26, 1903. At Ute, Iowa, Feb. 24, 1907, he was married to Ida Belle Riddle, who, with two daughters, survived him. He died at his home in Omaha.

Tibbles was an indefatigable writer and besides his newspaper work published three books —*Ponca Chiefs* (1880) ; *Hidden Power* (1881), and *The American Peasant* (1892). He was active also as a stump speaker for the People's party, and as a lecturer on social questions and Indian welfare. He was a large man, somewhat expansive in manner, who made many friends, and who was highly respected for his integrity and for his courageous espousal of unpopular causes.

[*Who's Who in America*, 1920–21; C. Q. De France, in *Nebr.Hist.Mag.*, Oct.–Dec.1932; obituaries in *N. Y. Times, Morning World-Herald* (Omaha), and *Nebr. State Jour.* (Lincoln), May 15, 1928; information from Ida B. Riddle Tibbles.]   W. J. G.

TICHENOR, ISAAC (Feb. 8, 1754–Dec. 11, 1838), lawyer, politician, and jurist, was born in Newark, N. J. Little is known of his parentage and early life. He was graduated at the College of New Jersey (Princeton) in 1775, began the study of law in Schenectady, N. Y., and soon afterward entered the commissary service of the Continental Army. The course of his duties took him to Bennington, Vt., in 1777 and he settled at that place, where he maintained a residence throughout the rest of his long life.

The organization of the new state of Vermont, accompanied as it was by disputes with neighboring states and some internal dissension, offered opportunity for political leadership and constructive service. Tichenor served in the legislature from 1781 to 1785, being speaker in 1783–84. Between 1782 and 1789 he served as agent to the Continental Congress for several sessions and in 1790 was appointed a commissioner for the settlement of boundary and land-title difficulties with New York. He was a member of the council from 1786 to 1791 and of the supreme court from 1791 to 1796, serving as chief justice for two years and resigning to enter the United States Senate.

His service in the latter body was of short duration (Oct. 18, 1796–Oct. 17, 1797), since in 1797 he was elected governor of Vermont. In this capacity he served continuously for eleven years (1797–1807), although the Federalist party to which he belonged was losing ground and in the last part of his service he was usually confronted by Republican legislatures. He was reported by contemporaries to be most attractive personally, his charming manners winning him the somewhat uncomplimentary nickname of "Jersey Slick." His messages to the legislature are free from the monotonous pessimism and vindictiveness of many Federalist documents of the era; if they are overloaded with wise saws and governmental truisms, they also contain sound admonitions concerning economy and the retirement of the public debt. While Tichenor lamented the unfortunate "progress and violence of party spirit" the state under his régime was prosperous and well governed. After a year's enforced retirement, he was reëlected governor for the term 1808–09, his election recording Vermont's bitter opposition to the Embargo, but condemning local instances of violence and disorder which had characterized that opposition. In his message of this year he urged a revision of the

criminal code and a humane administration of the newly founded state's prison.

He was not in the political foreground during the War of 1812 but in 1815 was elected to the United States Senate for a six-year term. Voting for the most part with the Federalists who still remained in the Capitol, he played no prominent part in national affairs. His last years were spent at Bennington. His wife, Elizabeth, died there in 1815, and he left no children.

[La Fayette Wilbur, *Early Hist. of Vt.* (4 vols., 1899–1903); *Records of the Gov. and Council of the State of Vt.*, vols. III (1875), IV (1876); Hiland Hall, *The Hist. of Vt.* (1868); Governor's Messages in *Jour. of the Gen. Assembly*, 1797–1807, 1808–09; A. M. Hemenway, *The Vt. Hist. Gazetteer*, I (1868), 174–75; Isaac Jennings, *Memorials of a Century . . . Bennington* (1869); *Biog. Dir. Am. Cong.* (1928); J. M. Comstock, *A List of the Principal Civil Officers of Vt.* (1918); *Daughters of the Am. Rev. Mag.*, Nov. 1916; *Boston Daily Advertiser*, Dec. 19, 1838.]   W. A. R.

TICHENOR, ISAAC TAYLOR (Nov. 11, 1825–Dec. 2, 1902), Baptist clergyman, educator, missionary secretary, was born in Spencer County, Ky., the son of James and Margaret (Bennett) Tichenor. He was a descendant of Martin Tichenor, said to have been of French extraction, who was in New Haven, Conn., as early as 1644, and was later one of the settlers of Newark, N. J. Martin's great-grandson, Daniel, grandfather of Isaac, moved from New Jersey to Kentucky in 1790. At the age of fifteen Isaac entered the Taylorsville academy, where he was under two able teachers, Moses and David Burbank, graduates of Waterville College, Maine, and there did work that would have admitted him to the junior class of a college. An attack of measles, however, left him with physical infirmities which troubled him for a long time. When he was sufficiently recovered, he engaged in teaching and was for three years connected with the Taylorsville academy, the last year as principal.

In the meantime, at the solicitation of local Baptists, he had begun to preach, and his effectiveness soon won for him the title "boy orator of Kentucky." In 1847 he became agent for the American Indian Mission Association and while traveling about in its interest he was called to the Baptist church in Columbus, Ky., where in 1848 he was ordained. He served here until 1850, then traveled and preached in Texas, was in charge of the church at Henderson, Ky., for a short time, and on Jan. 1, 1852, began a sixteen-year pastorate at the First Baptist Church, Montgomery, Ala. For two years during the Civil War he served as chaplain of the 17th Alabama Regiment—not confining himself strictly to his prescribed duties, for he acquired reputation as a sharpshooter and at the battle of Shiloh went to the front of his regiment and rallied the wavering lines. In 1868 he resigned his church and for some three years lived on his plantation in Shelby County, Ala., engaging more or less in evangelical work. He accepted a call to the First Baptist Church, Memphis, Tenn., in 1871, but the following year returned to Alabama to be the first president of the State Agricultural and Mechanical College, located at Auburn.

During the ten years he was at the head of this institution he laid a broad and firm foundation for its subsequent development. He studied the agricultural, mineral, and manufacturing resources of the state, and in his numerous addresses awakened its people to a greater appreciation of them. He prophesied the industrial development which has since taken place and labored to prepare the way for it. Throughout this period he continued to maintain a position of leadership in the councils of the Southern Baptists, and in June 1882 he resigned his collegiate position and became secretary of the Home Missionary Board of the Southern Baptist Convention, the headquarters of which were at Atlanta, Ga.

For eighteen years he carried on the work of this office with a statesmanship that resulted in great constructive achievements. At the outset his activities did much to preserve for the Southern Convention its natural field, which was being encroached upon by other more aggressive and better equipped Baptist bodies. He inaugurated extensive work west of the Mississippi, took possession of Texas, insisted that the Convention provide its own Sunday school literature and arranged for its publication, initiated educational projects in the mountain regions, and grappled with problems created by growing industrial centers. In 1899 he retired from active work and was made secretary emeritus. His health soon failed and after protracted suffering he died at Atlanta.

He was four times married: first, Dec. 16, 1853, to Monimia C. Cook, who died Feb. 9, 1860; second, in April 1861, to Emily C. Boykin, who died Sept. 7, 1864; third, in October 1865, to Lulah Boykin, who died in 1869; and fourth, to Mrs. Eppie Reynolds McCraw, who died in 1878. By each he had children, four of whom survived him.

[J. S. Dill, *Isaac Taylor Tichenor: The Home Mission Statesman* (1908), contains some of his writings; see also R. B. Teachenor, *A Partial Hist. of the Tichenor Family in America* (1918); J. M. Carroll, *A Hist. of Texas Baptists* (1923); *Annual of the Southern Bapt. Conv., 1903* (n.d.); *Religious Herald* (Richmond, Va.), Dec. 4, 8, 1902; *Atlanta Jour.*, Dec. 2, 3, 1902.]
H. E. S.

TICKNOR, ELISHA (Mar. 25, 1757–June 22, 1821), educator, merchant, was born in Leba-

non, Conn., the son of Col. Elisha and Ruth (Knowles) Ticknor. His earliest education was obtained on his father's farm and in the local district school; later he was sent to the academy conducted by Nathan Tisdale in Lebanon, where he acquired a fair mastery of the classical languages. In 1774, his parents removed to Lebanon, N. H. For the next five years, Ticknor assisted his father in developing his new farm, continuing, in periods of leisure, his preparation for college, and teaching in near-by district schools. Graduating from Dartmouth College in 1783, he was appointed master of Moor's Charity School, Hanover, N. H., but withdrew from this position to open a private school in Boston in October 1785. On Mar. 5, 1788, he was appointed principal of the South Writing School, in Boston. At the end of six years he resigned because of ill health, and in 1795 he ventured into business as a grocer. Within a short time he had acquired a sufficient fortune to enable him to devote himself to the cultivation of his various civic and intellectual interests. On May 23, 1790, he married Elizabeth (Billings) Curtis, widow of Dr. Benjamin Curtis of Boston and daughter of Elijah and Elizabeth (Hartshorn) Billings of Stoughton, Mass. The only child of this marriage was George Ticknor [q.v.], who, according to his own letters, received most of his really worthwhile preparation for college from his father.

While he was principal of the South Writing School, Ticknor published a grammar entitled *English Exercises* (1792) which was widely used in the schools of Massachusetts. In 1798, he was one of the organizers of the Massachusetts Mutual Fire Insurance Company; and in 1816 he founded, with his friend James Savage [q.v.], the Provident Institution for Savings in the Town of Boston, one of the first savings banks in the United States. He was elected selectman of Boston in 1815. Throughout the period of his business life he took an active interest in the work of the public schools. In 1805 he suggested an important innovation in the school system, the establishment of free schools for children under seven years of age. At that time, the town regulations, under which the grammar schools admitted only those who were able to read, virtually excluded from higher education all children whose parents could not provide for their preliminary instruction. Ticknor urged the importance to the town of reducing illiteracy among its citizens and continued to press his suggestion until in 1818 the town of Boston established its first primary school. From 1818 to 1821 he served as a member of the Primary

School Committee Among his activities after his retirement from business was an attempt to establish the popularity of the merino sheep in New England. He imported and kept a large flock on his father's farm, in Lebanon, N. H. For some years his counsel on educational matters was sought by President Eleazar Wheelock of Dartmouth, and he died, as the result of a paralytic stroke, while visiting a member of the Dartmouth faculty in Hanover.

[Wm. Allen, *The Am. Biog. Dict.* (3rd ed., 1857); *Am. Jour. Educ.*, V, 335 (1858), XXVIII, 796 (1878); *Life, Letters, and Journals of George Ticknor* (2 vols., 1876), ed. by G. S. Hillard; *Reports of the Record Commissioners of the City of Boston,* vols. XXV (1894) and XXVII (1896), containing Selectmen's Minutes, 1776–98, vol. XXX (1903), containing Boston Marriages, 1752–1809, and vol. XXXVII (1906), containing Boston Town Records, 1814–22; Justin Winsor, *The Memorial Hist. of Boston,* vol. IV (1881); J. M. Hunnewell, "The Ticknor Family in America," 1919, typescript in Lib. of Cong.; *Boston Daily Advertiser,* June 25, 1821.] R. F. S.

TICKNOR, FRANCIS ORRAY (Nov. 13, 1822–Dec. 18, 1874), poet, physician, was born at Fortville, Jones County, Ga., son of a Connecticut physician, Dr. Orray Ticknor, who had settled in Savannah and there married Harriet Coolidge of Norwich Town, Conn. He was a descendant of William Ticknor who was in Scituate in 1646. After Dr. Ticknor's death in 1823, Mrs. Ticknor removed to Columbus, Ga., where she reared and educated her three children. Francis, after completing his schooling in Massachusetts, studied medicine in Philadelphia and New York, spent a year (1842) in Norwich Town, received the degree of M.D. at the Philadelphia College of Medicine in 1843, and, returning to Georgia, began to practise at Shell Creek, Muscogee County. On Jan. 18, 1847, he married Rosalie Nelson, daughter of Thomas Maduit Nelson of Virginia, an officer in the War of 1812 and subsequently a member of Congress. He and his wife had six sons and two daughters. About 1850 he settled at "Torch Hill," seven miles south of Columbus, and followed the busy existence of a country doctor, finding time nevertheless for such major passions as the cultivation of fruits and flowers (with infrequent articles thereon for the *Southern Cultivator*) and the writing of poetry, such minor ones as music and drafting. The verses which he contributed to newspapers or obscure periodicals won him some local reputation before the war years which saw his nature deepen and his poetic powers develop; but he was careless of literary fame, and, although certain of his pieces had found a place in the anthologies of Southern war poetry, it was five years after his death before an incomplete collection of his work appeared in volume form.

This posthumous publication shows the range of his poetic interests to have been essentially that of his Southern colleagues, but, despite their unevenness and other occasional limitations, even the conventional lyrics about roses and humming-birds reveal a feeling for artistic structure, a graceful prosody, an incisive and effective turn of phrase which are well above the average of the day and which furnish ground for the assumption that with more leisure, more criticism, more encouragement, Ticknor might readily have secured a considerably higher place among the American poets. As it was, he reached full stature only in his poems on martial and chivalrous themes, with their simple and direct narrative, dramatic intensity, and noticeable compactness of style. "Little Giffen," based on an actual incident during Ticknor's supervision of the Confederate hospital work in Columbus, and easily his best-known poem, can bear comparison with any other American heroic ballad, yet such war verses as "The Virginians of the Valley" and "Loyal" (his tribute to General Cleburne) are not markedly inferior to it. His grand-daughter (Michelle C. Ticknor, *post,* p. 152) attributes to him the authorship of the anonymous "The Barefooted Boys," one of the most spirited and memorable of all the Civil War poems, but does not undertake to prove Ticknor's title to this tremendously powerful lyric which may well have come from his pen.

Genial, humane, unselfish, he died in middle life, partly in consequence of his unremitting devotion to duty. The epitaph which he wrote for the title character in his humorous poem, "The Farmer Man," further sums up his own career: "He read the Bible, loved his wife . . . loved God, his neighbor, and his home." Posterity has unduly neglected his work, as did his generation, yet various poets whose names are better known might have learned much from him.

[J. M. Hunnewell, "The Ticknor Family in America," 1919, typescript in Lib. of Cong.; biog. sketch by Michelle C. Ticknor, in *The Poems of Francis Orray Ticknor* (1911); P. H. Hayne, in *Poems of Frank D. Ticknor, M.D.* (1879), ed. by Kate M. Rowland; *Lib. of Southern Lit.,* vol. XII (1907); *Cambridge Hist. of Am. Lit.,* vol. II (1918); S. A. Link, *Pioneers of Southern Lit.* (1899), vol. I, pp. 89–115; Sarah V. Cheney, "Francis Orray Ticknor," 1934, MS. in Duke Univ. lib.; obituary in *Savannah Daily Advertiser,* Dec. 22, 1874.] A. C. G., Jr.

TICKNOR, GEORGE (Aug. 1, 1791–Jan. 26, 1871), educator and author, was born at Boston. He was the son of Elisha [*q.v.*] and Elizabeth (Billings) Ticknor, the widow of Benjamin Curtis, and was a descendant of William Ticknor who came from England to Massachusetts in or before 1646. William Davis Ticknor [*q.v.*] was a cousin. His father, who graduated from Dartmouth College in 1783, was a teacher before becoming a successful man of business in Boston. George's mother had also been a teacher. He was fitted for college in the home circle and received a certificate of admission to Dartmouth before he was ten years old, after an examination which, in later life, he termed "perhaps a farce." He did not enter Dartmouth until he was fourteen, but he was then admitted as a junior.

Graduating in 1807, Ticknor continued with a private tutor the study of Latin and Greek, which he had begun to cultivate at an early age. After reading law in an office for three years, he was admitted to the bar in 1813, but he realized very soon that the law had no real attraction for him and that the ancient classics had a potent hold on his fancy. As the family fortune left ample opportunity for the purpose, it was decided that he should go to Europe for study. After a journey through the Mid-Atlantic states he made a visit to "Monticello," where he was cordially received by former President Jefferson. The latter may then have told him, as he later wrote, about the plans which eventually took form in the University of Virginia. Ticknor set sail for England in 1815. Among his fellow passengers was Edward Everett [q.v.]; these two scholarly youths were probably the first to go from the United States to German institutions of learning for the express purpose of obtaining a university training more advanced than that possible at home.

Ticknor's first visit to Europe lasted four years, and it took him to England, the Netherlands, Germany, France, Switzerland, Italy, Spain, and Portugal. Inspection of the pages of the *Life, Letters, and Journals of George Ticknor* (2 vols., 1876; new ed., 1909) reveals the ease with which this American student penetrated into the aristocratic, literary, scientific, and generally scholarly circles of the different European centers to which his travels led him. Among the scholars, scientists, and men of letters who received him were A. von Humboldt, Byron, Châteaubriand, Humphry Davy, Mme. de Staël, Miss Edgeworth, Goethe, A. W. and F. Schlegel, Scott, Wordsworth, Southey, J. H. Voss, and F. A. Wolf. With many of these notable personages he maintained a correspondence after his return to the United States, and no few of them he saw again on the occasion of later visits to Europe.

At the University of Göttingen, then the leading institution of higher learning in Germany, Ticknor remained in residence for twenty months (1815–17) attending lectures, reading assiduously, and forming invaluable personal relations with his various teachers. He ardently applied himself to the acquisition of a practical command of German and a good knowledge of its literature, but was not overimpressed with the worth of German philosophy. Greek also claimed his serious attention in this center of philological activity, and he would probably have continued his devotion to it but for the invitation which came to him before the end of 1816 to enter upon the duties of the recently founded Smith professorship of French and Spanish at Harvard College, with an added professorship of belles-lettres. "Here," he says in a letter to his father of Nov. 9, 1816, "is at once a new subject of study proposed to me, to which I have paid no attention since I have been here, and which I have not taken into the plan of my studies and travels in Europe. If I am to be a professor in this [Spanish] literature, I must go to Spain" (*Life,* I, 117). His formal letter of acceptance of the post at Cambridge was written by him at Rome on Nov. 6, 1817, so that he spent a year in consideration of the proposal. From April to August 1817 he was in Paris, eagerly improving all opportunities of augmenting his knowledge of French and its literature; and from early October to the end of the spring of 1818 he visited various cities of Italy, spending most of his time in Rome, where he took private lessons in Italian. He passed some four months of 1818 in Madrid and made no little progress in Spanish under the guidance of some able tutors, among whom was the Orientalist J. A. Condé. Then, after a few weeks in Portugal, he sailed for England, en route for his native land. On Aug. 10, 1819, he was inducted into the professorship which he was to hold until 1835.

Interpreting broadly his functions as a professor of belles-lettres, Ticknor proposed to President John Thornton Kirkland [q.v.] a program of lectures which would have permitted him to cover ancient as well as modern literatures, but he was obliged to restrict his attention in large measure to the French, Spanish, and Italian domain. Within this field he found enough to enlist his best endeavors, and, in spite of the coldness and even declared opposition of colleagues committed to a stereotyped curriculum allowing little scope for the teaching of modern foreign languages and their literatures, he won and maintained the interest of a considerable body of the students. Certain of his lectures, framed for the purpose, attracted a notable audience from without the walls of the college. On Sept. 18, 1821, Ticknor married Anna Eliot, a daughter of Samuel Eliot, a prosperous merchant of Boston.

Her fortune, added to that which he had inherited from his father, allowed him to live in ease and elegance for all the rest of his life; but he avoided ostentation, spent his money rather in the acquisition of a large and useful library than in pompous display, and contributed generously to private and public charities.

Dissatisfied with the state of education in Harvard College and encouraged by a few colleagues and alumni, Ticknor proposed certain changes in the curriculum to the governing bodies, the Corporation and the Board of Overseers. "We are neither a university—which we call ourselves," he said in 1823, "nor a respectable high school—which we ought to be" (*Life*, I, 359). He proposed, among other things, a division of the college into departments grouping related studies. The majority of his colleagues, after a brief period of unwilling experimentation on their part, rejected his innovations, but he triumphed to the extent of receiving permission to continue them for his own courses in modern languages. Thus he began a departmental system which was to develop fully under his wife's nephew, President Charles W. Eliot [*q.v.*], and was to be reflected eventually in all the higher institutions of learning in the United States.

In 1826 Ticknor was appointed a member of the Board of Visitors of the United States Military Academy at West Point. Sooner or later he became identified with a number of enterprises of a more or less public nature, such as the Massachusetts General Hospital, certain banking and insurance companies, and the Boston Primary School Board, of which his father had been a founder. His home life was happy. Although two children, a girl and a boy, died at a tender age, two daughters remained to gladden the household. In January 1835, he wrote to a friend: "I have substantially resigned my place at Cambridge, and Longfellow is substantially appointed to fill it. . . . I have been an active professor these fifteen years, and for thirteen years of the time I have been contending, against a constant opposition, to procure certain changes which should make the large means of the College more effectual for the education of the community. In my own department I have succeeded entirely, but I can get these changes carried no further. As long as I hoped to advance them, I continued attached to the College; when I gave up all hope, I determined to resign" (*Life*, I, 399–400).

Released from his professorial duties, Ticknor planned to go to Europe for a prolonged visit, and, accompanied by his wife and his two little girls, he landed at Liverpool, June 25, 1835. The details of this stay abroad are revealed in a manuscript journal of some 1700 quarto pages. The journal of his first visit is no less bulky. This second visit occupied full three years, during which he had the pleasantest of relations with old and new friends, and began an acquaintance with Prince (later King) John of Saxony, which was highly appreciated by that devotee of Dante. At home again by June 1838, Ticknor was to spend the ensuing period in the writing of his *History of Spanish Literature*, for which his earnest studies during his professorial career had well fitted him. He had the advantage of the constant advice of his friend, the historian Prescott, who had profited in no small degree by the counsel which Ticknor had given him when he was writing his *History of the Reign of Ferdinand and Isabella* (1838). With unflagging ardor Ticknor labored for some ten years on the elaboration and coordination of the material entering into his famous work. Having assembled a representative Spanish library through his own efforts and those of foreign friends, he had at hand a goodly array of documents on which to base his estimate of Spanish letters. To an English friend, Sir Charles Lyell, he wrote when the book was finished: "You know our reading public in the United States, how large it is, as well as how craving and increasing; so that you will be less surprised than others that I have prepared my book as much for *general* readers as for scholars" (*Life*, II, 253.)

The first edition of the book was published by Harper & Brothers, New York, in the latter part of 1849; at the same time John Murray brought out a small edition in London. The reception given to the work was immediately favorable both at home and abroad, and the sales exceeded the author's expectations. No captious criticism of recent times can detract from the fact that in it, for the first time, there was produced a truly scholarly survey of the whole range of Spanish letters from their inception to the early nineteenth century. Nothing at all comparable in merit had hitherto appeared in Spain; the accounts given by the German Bouterwek and the Swiss Sismondi, the most considerable antedating his, pale to insignificance in its light. It blazed the way for the investigations of Spanish literature which were carried on so energetically after the midpoint of the nineteenth century, and it remains a monument of American scholarship. Ticknor's other writings are of ephemeral or minor value, but this book shines in no reflected glory and has a brilliancy of execution which suffices to fix permanently its creator's fame. The defects in it which the greatest of Spanish literary critics, Menéndez y Pelayo, indicated (Jaime Fitzmaurice-Kelly, *Historia de la literatura Española . . . con un estudio preliminar por Marcelino Menéndez y Pelayo*, 1900, pp. xiii–xiv) were natural at a time when many original documents that later came to light were unknown. Again, they are to be explained in part as due to the fact that Ticknor, trained as a student of the ancient classics, was largely autodidact in so far as modern literature is concerned, and in part to the no less patent fact that, dealing with an essentially Catholic literature, Ticknor, the New England Protestant, though no intellectual bigot, could not always appreciate at their full worth many of the leading religious writers of Spain. After nearly a century of brilliant literary accomplishment in Spain the *History of Spanish Literature* is somewhat antiquated. Its treatment of the medieval period and of the Renaissance calls for correction and addition; on the other hand, its story of the course of Spanish authorship in the rationalistic eighteenth century retains much of its original worth.

The first edition was followed by one of 1854; then came a third edition, that of 1863, in which Ticknor availed himself of the additions and corrections provided by his European translators and critics. During the remaining eight years of his life he added the supplementary notes and changes which were printed in the definitive edition issued in 1872, shortly after his death. The work was translated and published with critical notes in Spanish (4 vols., 1851–56), German (1852; 2 vols., 1867), and French (3 vols., 1864–72). In 1850, Hawthorne made a visit to Ticknor which he thus recorded: "He has a fine house, at the corner of Park and Beacon Streets, perhaps the very best position in Boston. . . . Mr. Ticknor has a great head, and his hair is gray or grayish. You recognized in him at once the man who knows the world, the scholar, too, which probably is his more distinctive character, though a little more under the surface. . . . Methinks he must have spent a happy life (as happiness goes among mortals) writing his great three-volumed book . . .; writing it, not for bread, nor with any uneasy desire of fame, but only with a purpose to achieve something true and enduring" (*Passages from the American Note-Books of Nathaniel Hawthorne*, 1868, pp. 151–53).

Ticknor became one of the founders of the Boston Public Library in 1852 and, four years later, passed fifteen months in Europe, engaged in the purchasing of books for it with funds provided chiefly by a benefactor, Joshua Bates [*q.v.*].

He presented 2400 volumes to the library in 1860 and a few hundred additional volumes in succeeding years. Finally, by his will, he bequeathed to it his invaluable collection of books relating to the Spanish peninsula, stipulating that not a volume was ever to leave the precincts of the library building.

In 1859 Ticknor undertook the preparation of a biography of his close friend, the historian Prescott; it appeared as the *Life of William Hickling Prescott* (1864). His other writings comprise: a *Syllabus of a Course of Lectures on the History and Criticism of Spanish Literature* (1823); *Outlines of the Principal Events in the Life of General Lafayette* (1825); *Remarks on Changes Lately Proposed or Adopted in Harvard University* (1825); *The Remains of Nathaniel Appleton Haven, with a Memoir of His Life* (1827); *Remarks on the Life and Writings of Daniel Webster* (1831); a *Lecture on the Best Methods of Teaching the Living Languages* (1833); and various articles in the *North American Review* and other periodicals.

The last part of Ticknor's life was uneventful and happy, cheered by the company of his wife, children, grandchildren, and many friends. He died on Jan. 26, 1871, in his eightieth year. He had been elected to numerous learned societies and had received several honorary degrees.

[*Life, Letters and Journals of George Ticknor* (2 vols., 1876), the ed. referred to in this article; new ed., with introduction by Ferris Greenslet (1909); *Proc. Mass. Hist. Soc.*, vol. XII (1873), pp. 13–29; vol. XX (1884), pp. 384–91; C. H. Hart, *Memoir of George Ticknor, Historian of Spanish Literature. Read before the Numismatic and Antiquarian Soc. of Philadelphia, May 4, 1871* (1871); W. H. Milburn, "George Ticknor and a Glimpse of Boston Society in 1854," *Quart. Review of the M. E. Church, South*, April 1893; *Briefwechsel König Johanns von Sachsen mit George Ticknor herausgegeben von Johann Georg, Herzog zu Sachsen, im Verein mit E. Daenell* (Leipzig and Berlin, 1920); George Ticknor's *Travels in Spain*, ed. by G. T. Northup (1913); *George Ticknor: Letters to Pascual de Gayangos* (1927); O. W. Long, *Thomas Jefferson and George Ticknor. A Chapter in American Scholarship* (1933); *Catalogue of the Spanish Library and of the Portuguese Books bequeathed by George Ticknor to the Boston Public Library*, by J. L. Whitney (1879); *Boston Daily Advertiser*, Jan. 27, 1871; correspondence in private hands.]   J. D. M. F.

TICKNOR, WILLIAM DAVIS (Aug. 6, 1810–Apr. 10, 1864), publisher, was born in Lebanon, N. H., the son of William and Betsey (Ellis) Ticknor. An ancestor, William Ticknor, had emigrated from England and settled in Massachusetts as early as 1646. The boy's educational opportunities were confined to those offered by the village school; and at the age of seventeen, with a sum of money derived from the sale of sheep which he had raised on his father's farm, he went to Boston to seek his for-

tune. There he found employment in the brokerage office of an uncle, Benjamin Ticknor. And
there, five years later, his bookish tastes as well
as his marked aptitude for business prompted
him to establish himself as a publisher and seller
of books. The firm which he founded, and in
which James Thomas Fields [q.v.] early became
a junior partner, was variously known in Ticknor's lifetime as Allen and Ticknor (1832–33),
William D. Ticknor and Company (1833–49),
Ticknor, Reed, and Fields (1849–54), and Ticknor and Fields. In addition to taking over the
Atlantic Monthly Ticknor's house published,
with financial success, the works of many of the
leading contemporary writers of England and
America: Tennyson, Browning, DeQuincey,
Leigh Hunt, Hawthorne, Emerson, Thoreau,
Longfellow, Holmes, Whittier, Lowell, and
others. During these years, too, Ticknor was
the directing genius of "the old Corner Book-
store," which was the favorite rendezvous of the
literary men of Boston, Cambridge, and Concord.

In his busy career as publisher, Ticknor found
time for his family, for public service, and for
friendships. He married on Dec. 25, 1832, Emeline Staniford Holt, who bore him seven children, five of whom survived their father. He
was a public-spirited citizen prominent in many
civic and educational enterprises, and an active
member of the Baptist Church. An unimpeach-
able integrity was his leading trait; as an instance, for which he should receive especial
honor, one may cite the fact that at a time when
piratical publication flourished in both England
and America Ticknor was among the first in
America to insist upon full payment for the
works of English authors. Tennyson in a letter
to the son of the publisher in 1889 rightly
praised Ticknor as "one who gave so honorable
an example to his countrymen of justice in the
highest sense" (Caroline Ticknor, *post*, p. 3).

His notable friendship with Nathaniel Hawthorne [q.v.] began about 1850 and continued
without interruption until death. Their relations can be traced in details in the numerous
letters (about one hundred and fifty altogether)
written by the author to his publisher. Ticknor
often accompanied Hawthorne on journeys: to
Washington in 1853, shortly after the inauguration of Franklin Pierce; to Liverpool in the
same year, Ticknor returning to America after
having spent about three months in England and
on the Continent; and to Washington again in
1862, when the two men saw Lincoln and visited
the scene of Bull Run. During these years of
friendship, and particularly while he was abroad,

Hawthorne trusted his publisher implicitly with
the management of his business affairs. On Mar.
28, 1864, Ticknor, apparently robust, set out
with Hawthorne on a southward journey in the
hope of reviving the latter's failing health. In
Philadelphia Ticknor was suddenly stricken with
pneumonia and died on Apr. 10; and Hawthorne's death, which occurred little more than
a month later, was doubtless hastened by the
shock of the loss of this true and faithful friend.

[J. M. Hunnewell, "The Ticknor Family in America," 1919, typescript in Lib. of Cong.; H. W. Boyn-
ton, *Annals of Am. Bookselling, 1638–1850* (1932);
*Letters of Hawthorne to William D. Ticknor, 1851–
1864* (2 vols., 1910, privately printed); Caroline Ticknor, *Hawthorne and His Publisher* (1913); H. M.
Ticknor, in *Memorial Biogs. of the New-England Hist.
Geneal. Soc.*, vol. V (1894), pp. 396–403; obituaries
in *New England Hist. and Geneal. Reg.*, Oct. 1864,
pp. 381–83, and in *Boston Transcript*, Apr. 11, 1864.]
R. S.

TIDBALL, JOHN CALDWELL (Jan. 25,
1825–May 15, 1906), soldier, of Scotch-Irish
and Welsh descent, was born in Ohio County,
Va. (now W. Va.), the son of William and
Maria (Caldwell) Tidball. He graduated from
the United States Military Academy in 1848,
was appointed brevet second lieutenant, 3rd Artillery, and saw service against the Seminoles,
in New Mexico, in the exploration of a route to
California, with the Coast Survey, and with the
Harpers Ferry expedition to suppress John
Brown's raid in 1859.

After the outbreak of the Civil War he took
part in the expedition to Fort Pickens, Fla.,
April–July 1861. Promoted captain in May, he
returned to Washington in command of Battery
A, 2nd Artillery. He served in the Manassas
campaign, and his battery, with that of Henry
Jackson Hunt [q.v.], covered the withdrawal of
the Union forces from Centreville into the defenses of Washington. In September he organized his battery to operate with cavalry. He
was in all of the battles of the Peninsular campaign; after the battle of Mechanicsville, May
27, 1862, he supported Porter's withdrawal to
Gaines's Mill, where he checked the Confederate
envelopment and again assisted the withdrawal.
During this campaign, to avoid causing an alarm,
Tidball initiated the custom of having "Taps"
sounded at a soldier's burial, in lieu of firing vol-
leys.

In the Maryland campaign of 1862 he served
with the cavalry division. At Boonsboro, and
repeatedly at Antietam, the fire of his battery
was a decisive factor, while in the pursuit of the
enemy and subsequent cavalry operations he
again rendered valuable service. He participated
in Stoneman's raid on Richmond (Apr. 13–May

2, 1863) and in the operations in northern Virginia culminating in the battle of Chancellorsville (May 2–4). Experience had taught massed employment of artillery and in June 1863 Tidball was assigned to command a brigade of horse artillery. He ably supported the cavalry corps throughout the Gettysburg campaign. In August, he was appointed colonel of the 4th New York Volunteer Artillery (foot), and assigned to the defenses of Washington.

Reassigned to the Army of the Potomac in March 1864, to command the artillery of the II Corps, he was conspicuous for skill and gallantry at Spotsylvania and the North Anna (May 1864). In July he was appointed commandant of cadets at the Military Academy, but in October rejoined the Army of the Potomac as chief of artillery, IX Corps. On Mar. 25, 1865, when a Confederate force surprised and captured Fort Stedman, a key point in the Union lines before Petersburg, Tidball by a prompt concentration of artillery fire paralyzed the attack and enabled the infantry to recapture the position. A week later he directed the artillery preparation and support of the final assault on Petersburg.

After the war, having received brevets of major-general of volunteers and brigadier-general, United States Army, he reverted to his Regular Army rank of captain. There followed service on the West Coast and in Alaska. He was promoted major in 1867, and was superintendent of artillery instruction at Fort Monroe from 1874 to 1881. During this period he compiled the *Manual of Heavy Artillery Service* (1880). Other writings of his were "The Artillery Service in the War of the Rebellion" (*Journal of the Military Service Institution,* at intervals, July 1891–November 1892) and various official reports included in the *Annual Report* of the secretary of war. He was promoted lieutenant-colonel, 1882, and colonel, 1885. From 1881 to 1884 he served as aide-de-camp to General Sherman, and from 1883 to 1888, as commandant of the Artillery School. He was retired for age, Jan. 25, 1889.

Tidball was an officer of martial appearance and austere manner, back of which was a nature rich in humor and affability. He was twice married: first, in 1853, to Mary Hunt Davis, and after her death, to Mary Langdon Dana in 1870. He was survived by two sons and two daughters.

[J. A. Caldwell, *Hist. of Belmont and Jefferson Counties, Ohio* (1880) ; J. H. Calef. "A Distinguished Horse Artilleryman," *Jour. of the Military Service Inst.,* July–Aug. 1908 ; *Ann. Reunion Asso. Grads., U. S. Mil. Acad.* (3rd ed., 1891), vol. II ; T. F. Rodenbough, *The Army of the U. S.* (1896) ; *Battles and Leaders of the Civil War* (4 vols., 1887–88) ; *War of the Rebellion:*

Official Records (Army) ; H. C. Kirk, *Heavy Guns and Light* (1890) ; *Memoirs of Gen. W. T. Sherman* (1891) ; *Who's Who in America,* 1906–07 ; *Army and Navy Jour.,* May 19, 1906 ; *Newark Evening News,* May 16, 1906.]   T. F. M.

TIEBOUT, CORNELIUS (c. 1773–c. 1830), line and stipple engraver, was born in New York City, the son of Tunis and Elizabeth (Lamb) Tiebout and a descendant of Jan Tibout [*sic*] who came to America before 1656 and in 1660 joined the church in New Amsterdam. As a lad, Cornelius was apprenticed to John Burger, a goldsmith in New York City, and he is said to have begun his experiment in engraving before he was out of his indentures. What is probably his earliest piece of work—a plan of New York —is dated 1789, but before he completed his apprenticeship he had engraved maps, portraits, and subject plates for the *New York Magazine* and for John Brown's *Self-Interpreting Bible.* In 1793 he went to London, where he received training in engraving in line and stipple under James Heath. While he was in the British capital (1795), he engraved and published a stipple portrait of John Jay which has been characterized as "probably the first really good portrait engraved by an American-born professional engraver" (Stauffer, *post,* pp. 271–72).

Having acquired the practical knowledge he needed, Tiebout returned to New York in November 1796, and in partnership with his brother Andrew set up in business as an engraver. On Apr. 20, 1799, he married Esther Young, who bore him two sons and a daughter. Later that year he removed to Philadelphia, which was his home for the following quarter century. He had already made portrait plates for some of William Dunlap's translations from Kotzebue and was now engaged by booksellers to furnish plates, but he also engraved portraits in quarto and in folio. Conspicuous among his larger plates were those of Rembrandt Peale's Thomas Jefferson, a full length, and "View of the Water Works at Centre Square," after the picture by Barralet. Tiebout also engraved plates for Benjamin Tanner [*q.v.*]. A small stipple plate, printed in color, after Sir Joshua Reynolds' "Hope," was another of his early accomplishments. Some of his work is to be found in Mathew Carey's Family Bible (1803–05); in the *Port Folio* (1812); in William Gibson's *Institutes and Practice of Surgery* (1824); and in many of the volumes of William Mavor's *Historical Account of Celebrated Voyages* (1802–03).

In 1817 Tiebout joined Benjamin Tanner and Francis Kearny [*q.v.*] in exploiting Henry S. Tanner's patent (1815) for engraving ornaments on banknotes to make them difficult to counterfeit. The banknote company of Tanner, Kearny & Tiebout existed until 1822, when it succumbed. According to one account (Dunlap, *post*), Tiebout accumulated considerable property but lost most of his savings through investment in a blacking manufactory. He is said to have gone to Kentucky about 1825, where he died, apparently in 1830. His last published plate, a stipple of a picture entitled "Lion and Horse," appeared in *The Casket* for May 1830. In 1928 he was represented in the exhibition of One Hundred Notable Engravers at the New York Public Library.

[William Dunlap, *A Hist. of the Rise and Progress of the Arts of Design in the U. S.* (1834), vol. II; W. S. Baker, *Am. Engravers and Their Works* (1875); D. M. Stauffer, *Am. Engravers upon Copper and Steel* (1907); Mantle Fielding, *Am. Engravers upon Copper and Steel* (1917); *One Hundred Notable Am. Engravers* (N. Y. Pub. Lib., 1928); *The Ancestry and Posterity of Cornelius Henry Tiebout of Brooklyn* (1910).]

J. J.

TIEDEMAN, CHRISTOPHER GUSTAVUS (July 16, 1857–Aug. 25, 1903), professor of law, legal writer, was born in Charleston, S. C., the son of Otto and Caroline Amelia Tiedeman. His childhood and youth were spent in the city of his birth, where he completed his secondary and college education, graduating from the College of Charleston with the degrees of A.B. and A.M. in 1876. The following spring he went to Germany where he attended successively courses at the Universities of Göttingen and Leipzig, coming under the influence of Rudolf von Ihering, Wilhelm Roscher, and Emil Albert Friedberg. On his return to the United States, in the autumn of 1878, he matriculated at the Columbia Law School, being graduated LL.B. the following spring. After a short period of practice, first in Charleston, then in St. Louis, he accepted in 1881 an assistant professorship of law in the University of Missouri; he was made full professor in 1882 and retained that position until 1891. The Phi Delta Phi Legal Fraternity chapter at Missouri bears his name. During this period of his life, in 1885, he married Helen Bruce Seymour. He became a professor at the law school of the University of the City of New York in 1891, remaining with this school until June 1897, when he resigned to pursue his literary activities. When he had completed the text he was then writing, he accepted the position of dean of the Law School of the University of Buffalo, in which capacity he served from May 1902 until his death in 1903.

Successful as Tiedeman was as a teacher, he was probably better known for his writings on legal subjects. Publishing his first text in the early years of his incumbency at the University of Missouri, he continued his literary labors unremittingly, either in revising editions or in preparing new treatises and texts. These were: *An Elementary Treatise on the American Law of Real Property* (1884; 4th ed. 1924); *A Treatise on the Limitations of Police Power in the United States, Considered from both a Civil and Criminal Standpoint* (1886); *A Treatise on the Law of Commercial Paper* (1889); *The Unwritten Constitution of the United States* (1890); *A Treatise on the Law of Sales of Personal Property* (1891); *A Treatise on Equity Jurisprudence* (1893); *A Treatise on the Law of Municipal Corporations in the United States* (1894); and *A Treatise on State and Federal Control of Persons and Property in the United States* (1900), a second edition of his earlier work on the limitations of the police power. He also edited *Selected Cases on Real Property* (1897) and prepared a student's textbook under the title, *A Treatise on the Law of Bills and Notes* (1898). In addition he was a frequent contributor to the legal periodicals of the day.

In all his writings Tiedeman displayed a clarity and accuracy that made his works very popular. By 1897 texts of his were used in thirty-six law schools. Personally he was well liked. He was, in the words of a successor at the University of Buffalo, "a most cultured and thorough gentleman in every sense of the word." He was survived by his wife and four children.

[*Buffalo Express*, Aug. 26, 1903; *Gen. Alumni Cat., N. Y. Univ., 1833–1906* (1906); *Publisher's Weekly*, Sept. 5, 1903; *Who's Who in America*, 1903–05; *The Brief* (Phi Delta Phi), first quarter, 1904; J. F. Tucker, "The Law School of the Univ. of the City of N. Y.," *Intercollegiate Law Jour.*, Dec. 1891.]

L. M. S.

TIERNAN, FRANCES CHRISTINE FISHER (July 5, 1846–Mar. 24, 1920), author, was born at Salisbury, N. C., the daughter of Col. Charles Frederic and Elizabeth (Caldwell) Fisher. Her father was an Episcopalian, her mother a Roman Catholic; she followed the religion of her mother and was confirmed in the Catholic Church by the Rt. Rev. James Gibbons, at the time vicar apostolic of North Carolina. She was educated at home in the mountain town where her family had lived since the earliest settlement. Her youth was saddened by the death of her father, a Confederate officer, who was killed in 1861 at the battle of Manassas. For years she lived in the old home, a columned gray house in a setting of cedars and oaks, with a maiden aunt as her companion. Visits to Asheville were the chief break in her routine of walking, driving, and writing, for she avoided most social relations. She was devoted to her religion and had the Church of the Sacred Heart built on a portion of the family land.

Her first novel, *Valerie Aylmer* (1870), was published under the pseudonym of Christian Reid. Others followed rapidly until she had written nearly fifty. Representative novels of her early period are *Morton House* (copyright 1871), which describes Christmas on a plantation; *A Daughter of Bohemia* (1874); *A Question of Honor* (1875); *The Land of the Sky* (1876), whose scene is western North Carolina; *Bonny Kate* (1878); and *Hearts of Steel* (1883). On Dec. 29, 1887, she married James Marquis Tiernan of Maryland and went with him to Mexico, where he was engaged in mining developments. There she lived most of the time until his death in January 1898, when she returned to Salisbury. Many of her novels of this period have Mexican settings and characters, and make use of Mexican history and legends. Among them are *A Cast for Fortune* (copyright 1890); *Carmela* (1891); *A Comedy of Elopement* (1893); *A Little Maid of Arcady* (1893); *The Land of the Sun* (1894); *The Picture of Las Cruces* (1896); *The Man of the Family* (1897); and *Fairy Gold* (1897). Her later books include *Under the Southern Cross* (1900), a drama, which shows her passionate devotion to the Confederacy and her belief in the right of secession; *A Daughter of the Sierra* (1903); *Princess Nadine* (1908), later dramatized; *The Light of the Vision* (1911); *The Wargrave Trust* (1912); and *A Far-Away Princess* (1914). In 1909 she was awarded the Laetare medal by Notre Dame University. She died at Salisbury. Her fiction has been described as "pellucidly pure" in style, with some dramatic quality and wit in dialogue; yet it lacked real humor and depth of intellectual perception, and, because of its author's aloofness from life, was without wide appeal (Egan, *post*, p. 18).

[*Who's Who in America*, 1920–21; *Cath. Encyc.*, Supp. I (1922); Eleanor C. Donnelly and others, *A Round Table of the Representative Am. Cath. Novelists* (1887); *Ave Maria* (Notre Dame, Ind.), Apr. 17, 1920; Maurice F. Egan, in *America*, Apr. 24, 1920; *Charlotte Observer* (Charlotte, N. C.), June 1, 1909, and Mar. 25, 1920.]　　　　　　　　　　　S. G. B.

TIERNEY, RICHARD HENRY (Sept. 2, 1870–Feb. 10, 1928), Roman Catholic priest and journalist, sixth child of Richard Tierney who came from Thurles, Ireland, and his wife, Bridget Shea, who was brought as a child to America from County Clare, was born at Spuyten Duyvil, New York, where his father was a superintendent in Johnson's Iron Foundry. Reared in a family of eight children, attending local schools at Kings Bridge and St. Francis Xavier's College, New York, from which he was graduated in 1892, Tierney was a good student and a superior athlete of powerful physique. He

was received as a candidate for the Society of Jesus by Provincial Thomas J. Campbell, and made his novitiate in Frederick, Md. Following a period of study at Woodstock, and of teaching in Gonzaga College, Washington, and Holy Cross College, Worcester, Mass., he returned to Woodstock for his theological studies, and was ordained priest by Archbishop John Farley, June 27, 1907. On completion of his tertianship at Linz, Austria, in 1909, he was assigned to teach philosophy and education at Woodstock; an outcome of this experience was his stimulating manual, *Teachers and Teaching* (1914). He had already sent numerous contributions to Catholic magazines, and in January 1914 he joined the editorial staff of the Jesuit weekly, *America,* of which he became controlling editor some two months later.

Through the pages of *America* Tierney became in some minds "the journalistic spokesman of the Catholic Church in the United States" (Talbot, *post*, p. 54). The journal reflected its editor—a man of exceptional ability, abrupt in manner, self-confident, by some considered arrogant, caustic in speech, and liberal in his views. He inevitably made enemies; at times his weekly worried some of the leaders of the Catholic Church—though it received full patronage from Archbishop Patrick Hayes—because of its aggressiveness in controversial matters. Neutral in the World War until the entry of the United States, *America* was a target for both German and Allied propagandists. The champion of the Church in Mexico in the days of Carranza and Villa, it instituted the Mexican Fund for refugees and stoutly opposed the Mexican policy of the Wilson administration. He spoke trenchantly on the Irish question, accepted the Free State despite attacks by extremists, fought Mayor John Purroy Mitchel [*q.v.*] in the New York charities investigation, opposed prohibition although he was personally a total abstainer, and waged a fight against what he regarded as a dangerous federal control of education. At times he may have been irritating, but he was frank in his courageous espousal of an issue. After the World War, he promoted relief work in Europe, especially in Austria. On three occasions, he received papal briefs in commendation of his services as a Catholic leader. Prior to his retirement as the result of a paralytic stroke in 1925, he served in 1922 as a delegate to the International Sodality Conference in Rome, and in 1923 as a delegate to the General Congregational of his Society in Rome. He died at St. Vincent's Hospital, New York, after three years of invalidism.

[F. X. Talbot, *Richard Henry Tierney, S.J.* (1930), a sympathetic study; *Who's Who in America*, 1926–27; *N. Y. Times*, Feb. 12, 1928.]   R. J. P.

TIFFANY, CHARLES LEWIS (Feb. 15, 1812–Feb. 18, 1902), jeweler, the son of Comfort and Chloe (Draper) Tiffany, was born in Killingly, Conn., a descendant of Humphrey Tiffany who was in the Massachusetts Bay Colony in 1660. The boy first attended a district school and then spent two years at an academy at Plainfield, Conn. Meanwhile his father organized a small cotton-manufacturing company, and near his mill started a general store which the boy Charles was set to manage at the age of fifteen. The mill prospered, Comfort Tiffany bought out his partners, and the firm became C. Tiffany & Son. Charles had some more snatches of education at schools near by, then entered the office with his father. In 1837 he followed his schoolmate, John B. Young, to New York City, and the two opened a small stationery and notion store on a thousand dollars capital, loaned by Comfort Tiffany. Their total sales for the first three days amounted to $4.98. They were opposite the City Hall, which was considered rather far uptown. By 1839 they were selling mostly glassware, cutlery, porcelain, clocks, and jewelry. In 1841 the firm became Tiffany, Young & Ellis, and they rented the adjoining room, more than doubling their space. Jewelry, Bohemian glass, porcelain, and similar goods now became their specialties. They had established a reputation for selling articles of beauty and taste, and they strove to better it. Finer grades of English jewelry, and then Italian and Roman jewelry were sought by Young, now the European buyer; they issued an annual catalogue; and in 1848 they began manufacturing jewelry, the revolutionary movements in Europe that year enabling them to buy diamonds at very low prices. During the next few decades they bought some historic gems, the relics of royal and noble houses of Europe—the collection of the Hungarian Prince Esterhazy, for example, and the crown jewels of the Second French Empire. In 1850 a branch was established in Paris, and in 1868 one in London. In 1853 Young and Ellis retired from the firm, and, with the admission of new partners, the business was reorganized under the name of Tiffany & Company, and so continues eighty years after. In 1858 Tiffany procured a large section of the first Atlantic cable which was left after the laying, cut it into short pieces, and made them into souvenirs which were so popular that a detail of police was required to keep the throng of buyers in order. At the outbreak of the Civil War, for a time his store became a depot for military sup-

plies. The New York house gradually moved uptown until it erected its own building on Fifth Avenue. Incorporated in 1868, the company became the greatest jewelry company on the continent, and at Tiffany's death was capitalized at $2,400,000.

For half a century Tiffany was considered the leader of the jewelry trade in America. He was one of the founders of the New York Society of Fine Arts, a patron of the Metropolitan Museum of Art, and a member of the National Academy of Design. France made him a Chevalier of the Legion of Honor (1878) and the Czar of Russia conferred on him the medal Praemia Digno. His company had more than twenty foreign monarchs among its customers. He married Harriet Olivia Avery Young, sister of his first partner, on Nov. 30, 1841. She died on Nov. 6, 1897. Tiffany died in Yonkers, N. Y., survived by four of his six children.

[N. O. Tiffany, *The Tiffanys of America: Hist. and Geneal.* (1901); *Who's Who in America*, 1901–02; G. F. Heydt, *Charles L. Tiffany and the House of Tiffany & Company* (1893); *N. Y. Times*, Feb. 16, 19, 1902; obituaries in *N. Y. Tribune*, *N. Y. Herald*, Feb. 19, 1902.]   A. F. H.

TIFFANY, KATRINA BRANDES ELY (Mar. 25, 1875–Mar. 11, 1927), civic worker, social reformer, was born in Altoona, Pa., the daughter of Theodore N. Ely and Henrietta (Brandes) Ely. Her father, chief of motive power of the Pennsylvania Railroad, was not only an able engineer but a man of great cultivation, a descendant of William Ely who went from the West Indies to Connecticut in 1670. Her maternal grandfather, Dr. Charles von S. Brandes, a Hanoverian, emigrated to America in the 1830's and settled in Erie, Pa., where he is said to have been the outstanding physician and surgeon of a large region. From him Katrina Ely absorbed an especial devotion to liberal ideas and unpopular causes. Educated by tutors and in private schools in Detroit and Bryn Mawr, she entered Bryn Mawr in 1893, where she became at once an outstanding personality by reason of her personal beauty, her boyish spirit of adventure, her athletic skill, her fine intellect, and her love of people. At Bryn Mawr, under such teachers as Franklin Giddings, she developed the absorbing interest in civic, political, and philanthropic undertakings which were to characterize all her later life. She received the degree of A.B. in 1897. On June 24, 1901, she was married at Bryn Mawr to Charles Lewis Tiffany, son of Louis C. Tiffany [*q.v.*].

In New York, where she went to live, she interested herself immediately in city politics, and when woman's suffrage came to the fore she devoted much of her time and her money to it. She became president of the College Women's Equal Suffrage League and recording secretary of the Woman Suffrage Party of New York; she was one of the foremost women speakers and debaters on suffrage, and traveled extensively through the state of New York throughout the suffrage campaign. Later she allied herself more closely with the Democratic party in the state of New York, and more than once took the stump for its candidates. But her interest in party politics did not preclude her enthusiastic support of the New York League of Women Voters, of which she was a regional director at the time of her death. She was a member of the executive board of the Foreign Policy Association (1918–27), one of the founders of the Woodrow Wilson Foundation and a contributor to its prize fund, an enthusiastic worker in the cause of world peace, and a strong supporter of the League of Nations. Soon after her marriage she interested herself in the New York Intercollegiate Bureau of Occupations, which sought to find positions other than teaching for women college graduates. It was largely through her efforts as chairman of the finance committee that the bureau became the important and outstanding institution of its kind in the United States, and served as a model for numerous others. For many years she was a trustee of the New York Infirmary for Women and Children, and treasurer of the Sunnyside Day Nursery. She died in New York, survived by her husband. She had no children. Her friends speak of her sincerity and utter simplicity, of "the cheerful gallantry with which she ... would challenge the inertia or the selfishness of society," of the fact that always "she put truth in the first place."

[M. S. Beach, *The Ely Ancestry* (1902), ed. by G. B. Vanderpoel; *The Hist. of Woman Suffrage*, vols. V–VI (1922), ed. by Ida H. Harper; *Woman's Who's Who of America*, 1914–15; *Bryn Mawr Alumnae Bull.*, Apr. 1927; *News Bull.* (Foreign Policy Asso.), Mar. 18, 1927; *Weekly News of the N. Y. League of Women Voters*, Mar. 18, 1927; obituary and editorial in *N. Y. Evening Post*, Mar. 11, 12, 1927; obituaries in *N. Y. Times* and *World* (N. Y.), Mar. 12, 1927; letters in the possession of Gertrude Ely, Mrs. Tiffany's sister; letters from friends.]					L. K. M. R.

TIFFANY, LOUIS COMFORT (Feb. 18, 1848–Jan. 17, 1933), artist, glass-maker, philanthropist, was born in New York City and was the son of the jeweler, Charles Lewis Tiffany [*q.v.*], and Harriet Olivia (Young) Tiffany. The boy was simply reared, and his formal education took him only through the secondary schools. He early began to show his natural bent by haunting art galleries and studios of leading artists in New York, and presently took up seri-

ous study under the latter—first with George Inness and Samuel Colman [*qq.v.*], later under Léon Bailly in Paris. His first work was in oil and water color. He was accepted in 1871 as an associate of the National Academy of Design. His early training with Inness turned him towards landscape only for a brief time; as years passed, human figures became more and more prominent in his landscapes, and presently the figure was his chief concern. He had an oriental love of color, which was intensified by a visit to the Near East in his youth. Although a member of the American Water Color Society and a participant in its exhibitions for many years, he early in life aroused much acrimonious debate among its members by his advanced methods. In 1877 he and other artists, such as Wyatt Eaton, John La Farge, and Augustus Saint-Gaudens [*qq.v.*], who felt that the National Academy of Design was too narrow and unprogressive, organized the Society of American Artists.

He had already begun to turn his attention to other media than paints. In 1875 he began experimenting with stained glass, and in 1878 established a glass-making plant of his own, the first of several, his factory being destroyed by fire no less than three times. He invented a process of his own for staining glass. Instead of producing a much-leaded mosaic of different colored pieces of glass, or painting the color upon the surface and burning or fusing it in—processes hitherto prevailing in Europe—he worked his pigment directly into the glass and produced draperies or other shadings by forcing a pot-metal glass, while in a molten condition, into wrinkles or folds. He designed several famous windows, but his largest work in this medium was the glass curtain for the National Theatre in Mexico city, a creation weighing many tons, depicting the florid landscape near the city, with its two volcanoes in the background. Having much colored glass left over from such work, he utilized it in the production of vases, bric-à-brac, cigarette boxes, ornamental plaques, wall and floor tiling. This beautiful product, to which he gave the name of Favrile glass, brought him his greatest popular reputation. Between 1893 and 1926 he received numerous prizes and medals, among them the Grand Prix and a gold medal at the Paris Exposition of 1900. He was a Chevalier of the Legion of Honor, and an honorary member of the Imperial Society of Fine Arts of Tokyo, and of the Société Nationale des Beaux Arts of Paris. He also gave no little attention to the designing of jewelry, rugs, and textiles. He owned at one time and another four notable homes, for which he designed grounds, buildings, decoration, and furnishings. In 1919 he established the Louis Comfort Tiffany Foundation for art students, deeding to it his eighty-acre estate and buildings at Oyster Bay, Long Island, as well as his entire collection of paintings, glass, and other art objects, and a $1,000,000 endowment. He built additional studios and living quarters, and every summer thereafter during his lifetime invited artists from all parts of the country to work there. He was vice-president and a director of both Tiffany & Company, jewelers, and the Tiffany & Company Safe Deposit Company. On May 15, 1872, he married Mary Woodbridge Goddard (d. Jan. 22, 1884), by whom he had two sons and two daughters. On Nov. 9, 1886, he married Louise Wakeman Knox (d. 1904), by whom he had one son and four daughters. He died in New York City, survived by a son and a daughter of his first marriage, and three daughters of his second.

[N. O. Tiffany, *The Tiffanys of America: Hist. and Geneal.* (1901) ; *Who's Who in America*, 1932–33 ; L. C. Tiffany, *The Art Work of Louis C. Tiffany* (1914) ; Ethel Syford, in *New England Mag.*, Sept. 1911, pp. 197–208 ; *International Studio*, Dec. 1906, pp. xxiii–xlii ; Samuel Howe, *Ibid.*, Feb. 1908 ; H. H. Saylor, *Ibid.*, Dec. 1908 ; Charles De Kay, *Ibid.*, Oct. 1920, pp. lxxviii–lxxxi ; J. K. Mumford, in *Arts and Decoration*, Feb. 1921 ; obituaries in *N. Y. Herald Tribune, N. Y. Times, Sun* (N. Y.), Jan. 18, 1933.]   A. F. H.

TIFFANY, LOUIS McLANE (Oct. 10, 1844–Oct. 23, 1916), surgeon, was born in Baltimore, Md., the son of Henry and Sally Jones (McLane) Tiffany, and a descendant of Humphrey Tiffany who was in Massachusetts in 1660. His maternal grandfather was Louis McLane [*q.v.*]. Tiffany obtained his academic education at Cambridge University, England, receiving the B.A. degree from Emmanuel College in 1867. He was graduated from the University of Maryland School of Medicine in 1868, with the degree of M.D. It was customary at the time for medical students to enter the offices of professors as office students, and Tiffany became an office student of Nathan R. Smith [*q.v.*]. The influence of this association was lifelong. The year after his graduation he began to teach as demonstrator of anatomy and became professor of operative surgery in 1874, succeeding Christopher Johnston as professor of surgery in 1880. He retained this position until the year before his retirement in 1903.

Tiffany entered upon the practice of surgery in the pre-antiseptic days; he promptly accepted Lister's principle but often questioned the method employed. In the disinfection of the skin he laid great stress on the mechanical effects of soap and water, but did not deny the value of chemical disinfectants. He was always a be-

liever in clean hands, clean field, and clean surroundings. He practised and taught the advantage of sharp rather than blunt dissection, believing that the vitality of the tissues was thus better preserved and the dangers of tension in a wound reduced. Drainage was an important part of his technique and in his early days must have contributed largely to his good results. He was ambidextrous, using the knife first in one hand then in the other—a maneuver that gave a decided flourish to his operations. In many fields he was a pioneer; he is credited with performing the first nephrolithotomy in America, and excised the Gasserian ganglion for trifacial neurology a few months after Frank Hartley [*q.v.*] and F. Krause had performed the same operation almost simultaneously in New York and in Germany. He also performed the first successful gastro-enterostomy in Baltimore in October 1892.

A considerable number of papers in the surgical literature came from Tiffany's pen. As a member of several professional societies, he took an active part in the proceedings and discussions. He was at different times president of the Baltimore Medical Association, the Medical and Chirurgical Faculty of Maryland, the Southern Surgical and Gynecological Association, and the American Surgical Association, and was an honorary fellow of the American College of Surgeons. A man of distinguished appearance, tall, of splendid proportion, with a commanding manner and address, he was an impressive figure in any company. Socially he was a delightful companion but in dispute he was an opponent to be dreaded. For many years he dominated surgical thought as well as surgical practice in Maryland. In August 1871 he was married to Madeline, the daughter of M. Woolsey Borland, of Boston. They had two children, one of whom survived him. After the death of his wife he was married, in January 1879, to Evelyn May Bayly, the daughter of Thomas H. Bayly, 1810–1856 [*q.v.*].

[*Who's Who in America*, 1916–17 ; N. O. Tiffany, *The Tiffanys of America: Hist. and Geneal.* (1901) ; Frank Martin, biographical sketch in H. A. Kelly and W. L. Burrage, *Am. Medic. Biog.* (1920) ; *Hospital Bull., Univ. of Md.*, 1914 ; *Medic. Annals of Md.* (1899) ; *Trans. Am. Surgical Asso.*, vol. XXXVI (1918) ; *Jour. Am. Medic. Asso.*, Oct. 28, 1916 ; Baltimore *Sun*, Oct. 24, 1916.]   A. M.

TIFFIN, EDWARD (June 19, 1766–Aug. 9, 1829), first governor of Ohio, was born in Carlisle, England. His parents, Henry and Mary (Parker) Tiffin, with their five children emigrated in 1784 and settled near Charles Town, Va., now in Jefferson County, W. Va. He studied medicine in England, then attended Jefferson Medical College in Philadelphia, and began practice in Charles Town. In 1789 he married Mary, the daughter of Robert Worthington, a wealthy land-owner of the neighborhood. They had no children. He and his wife became ardent Methodists, and he was ordained a lay preacher by Bishop Asbury in 1792. In the spring of 1798 Tiffin and his brother-in-law, Thomas Worthington [q.v.], with their families and several negroes, whom they had recently manumitted, removed to Chillicothe, Ohio. If he removed to Ohio with political ambitions, he acted opportunely for the Virginia Military District became a political unit that determined Ohio's political history for more than a decade. Short of stature with heavy body and light limbs, a large head, and round, florid face, he was remarkable for his animation and energy; and from 1798, when St. Clair appointed him prothonotary of the territorial court of common pleas, until his death he was constantly in public office. In 1799 and 1801 he was a member of the territorial legislature, and served as speaker in both sessions. Contemporary correspondence points to Tiffin as the leading spirit in the internal organization of the "Chillicothe Junto" that successfully opposed St. Clair. As president of the constitutional convention in November 1802 he determined the membership of committees and was able to prevent any concerted action on the part of the Federalists.

Elected governor almost without opposition in the subsequent state election and reëlected two years later, he took office in March 1803. The constitution of 1802 gave little authority to the governor, but as leader of Ohio Jeffersonians, he exerted considerable influence. Although English-born, he urged that English common-law crimes, as such, should not be recognized by Ohio courts. The requisite legislation was enacted, and hence in Ohio all crimes are, of necessity, statutory. In his second administration he displayed such energy in directing the efforts to capture Aaron Burr's flotilla that his activity was publicly praised by Jefferson. He was elected to the federal Senate on Jan. 1, 1807, to fill the place of Worthington, whose term was about to expire but resigned after adjournment in March 1809. He supported the measures of the administration, including the embargo policy, and served on a number of committees having to do with Western problems; and his advice seems to have carried weight. In July 1808 his wife died. On Apr. 16 of the following year he married Mary Porter, who had recently removed to Ohio from Delaware. Four daughters and a son were born to this second marriage. Although he seems to have desired to retire to his farm and to

his medical practice he could not keep out of politics. He served as speaker of the state House of Representatives in the sessions of 1809–10 and 1810–11. In the controversy involving the right of the state courts to nullify acts of the state legislature on the grounds of unconstitutionality, being a thorough-going Jeffersonian, he was a party to the passage of the "sweeping-resolutions" by which the conservative court was ousted.

When in 1812, Congress created a general land office to be administered by a commissioner, Madison, apparently without solicitation, appointed him to the position. He entered into his new duties with characteristic energy; he brought order out of the chaotic records and surveys and was able, in December 1813, to present a creditable report to the Thirteenth Congress. When the British invaded the capital, he was sufficiently far-sighted to remove his records to a place of safety. However, he longed for his home in Ohio and with the consent of Madison exchanged positions, in the fall of 1814, with Josiah Meigs, surveyor-general of the Northwest and carried on the routine of this office almost to the day of his death. He grew old among his friends who continued to respect his political opinions, his skill as a physician, and his sincerity as a Methodist exhorter. Tiffin, Ohio, was named in his honor.

[Tiffin MSS. in Ohio State Lib., Columbus, and Western Reserve Hist. Soc. Lib., Cleveland; W. E. Gilmore, *Life of Edward Tiffin* (1897); C. G. Comegys, *Reminiscences of . . . Edward Tiffin* (1869); W. T. Utter, "Judicial Review in Early Ohio," *Miss. Valley Hist. Rev.*, June 1927 and "Ohio and the English Common Law," *Ibid.*, Dec. 1929; W. Lang, *Hist. of Seneca County* (1880); *Scioto Gazette* (Chillicothe), Aug. 12, 1829.]

W. T. U.

TIGERT, JOHN JAMES (Nov. 25, 1856–Nov. 21, 1906), clergyman, editor, elected a bishop of the Methodist Episcopal Church, South, six months before his death, was born in Louisville, Ky., the son of John and Mary (Van Veghten) Tigert. His father was a pump maker. Carefully reared by his Methodist parents, the boy obtained his early education in the schools of Louisville, and in 1875 matriculated at the newly opened theological school of Vanderbilt University, Nashville, Tenn. Completing his studies there in two years, he received license to preach in 1877 and the same year joined the Louisville Conference of the Methodist Episcopal Church, South.

For four years he served small churches near his native city, continuing, also, his studies in the Baptist Seminary of Louisville. In 1881 he returned to Vanderbilt as instructor in sub-collegiate courses and candidate for the degree of master of arts. Here he began to show that enormous capacity for work which was to characterize his entire career. His hours during this period were regularly from seven o'clock one morning to one the next. In 1884, having obtained his master's degree, he was appointed professor of philosophy in the University. This relation continued six years. Meanwhile, he had become much interested in history and English, developing a lucid and robust style of writing. In 1885 he published a textbook on logic.

Tigert gave up his professorship in 1890 to engage again in the work of the active ministry. Assigned to a pastorate in Kansas City, Mo., he remained there four years. During this time he continued his studies and wrote much. In 1892 he was the fraternal delegate of his Church to the General Conference of the Methodist Episcopal Church. His address on that occasion, "A Voice from the South," and the personal contacts incident to the visit resulted in a series of friendships with the leaders of the sister denomination which continued throughout his life.

Elected in 1894 to the position of Book Editor, he devoted twelve years to editing, revising, annotating, writing, and publishing books, mainly theological. At the same time, 1894–1906, he edited the *Quarterly Review of the Methodist Episcopal Church, South,* known also during this period as the *Methodist Quarterly Review.* For its columns he wrote voluminously and established contacts with numerous scholars and writers throughout the world. His reviews of books were widely read and had much influence. The list of his published volumes grew; among them were *The Preacher Himself* (1889), *Theism; a Survey of the Paths that Lead to God, Chiefly in the Light of the History of Philosophy* (1901), and *The Christianity of Christ and His Apostles* (1905). In 1894 he published his most important work, *A Constitutional History of American Episcopal Methodism,* and later compiled and edited, with a historical introduction, *The Doctrines of the Methodist Episcopal Church in America as Contained in the Disciplines of Said Church from 1788 to 1808* (2 vols., 1902).

In the General Conference of 1906, such was the esteem in which he had come to be held, that on the first ballot he was elected to the episcopacy. In November of that same year, some six months later, having presided at but a single annual conference, he went to Indian Territory to prepare for another. There while taking one day a hurried wayside luncheon he accidentally swallowed a small bone. It lodged in his throat in such a way that a physician when called was unable to locate and remove it. Blood poisoning followed

and within two weeks, at the city of Tulsa, four days short of his fiftieth birthday, he died. On Aug. 28, 1878, he was married to Amelia McTyeire, daughter of Bishop H. N. McTyeire [*q.v.*], then president of Vanderbilt University, by whom he had three sons and three daughters. Tigert was a large, vigorous man, of great vitality, rarely ill, never tired. In the pulpit and on the platform he was an impressive figure. His voice was powerful, though a little harsh, his vocabulary was affluent, and his sermon themes invariably human and spiritual.

[*Who's Who in America,* 1906–07; *Methodist Quart. Rev.,* Jan. 1907; *Christian Advocate* (N. Y.), Nov. 29, 1906; *Christian Advocate* (Nashville), Nov. 30, 1906; *Nashville American,* Nov. 22, 1906; personal acquaintance.]   G. B. W.

TIKAMTHI [See TECUMSEH, 1768?–1813].

TILDEN, SAMUEL JONES (Feb. 9, 1814–Aug. 4, 1886), governor of New York, presidential nominee, corporation lawyer, was born at New Lebanon, N. Y., the fifth child of Elam Tilden and Polly Younglove Jones. He was descended from Nathaniel Tilden of Tenterden, Kent, who emigrated to New England in 1634 and settled in Scituate, Mass. His father, Elam Tilden, storekeeper, postmaster, and a man of political consequence in his community, was a friend of Martin Van Buren and Silas Wright. During the long ascendency of the Albany Regency, it was not uncommon for Van Buren, Wright, William L. Marcy, Edwin Croswell [*qq.v.*], and others to repair to the Tilden home for conferences. Elam's stock of goods included patent nostrums and drugs. His interest in these dubious specifics amounted to an obsession and led to a morbid interest in his own health. His painstaking descriptions of "symptoms" to Samuel created one of the strangest bonds of sympathy which has ever existed between father and son. These, then, were Samuel Tilden's patrimony: a genuine patriotism, a devotion to the Democratic party based upon tradition and also upon intimate acquaintance with Democratic leaders, and a morbid and introspective interest in his physical health. It may almost be said that he was nurtured on the Constitution and that the writings of Thomas Jefferson were his *Mother Goose.* Certainly his precocity and early environment robbed him of his childhood and, in so doing, perhaps stunted the development of certain social characteristics which would have eased his later life and made him more comprehensible to his contemporaries.

Tilden's formal education was sporadic and disjointed. He spent little time in the village school because of his uncertain health, but was given some private tutoring at home and for a short time attended an academy at Williamstown, Mass., which he left, too, for reasons of health. Following this experience he remained at home for a period of two years and then went in 1832 to New York, where he hoped to continue his preparatory studies and at the same time have access to a higher order of medical skill than was available in his native village. In New York he lived with an aunt, a Mrs. Barnes, who eked out a precarious living by keeping a fashionable boarding house. Tilden found the boarding house atmosphere uncongenial, and much of his time was irritatingly consumed in business transactions for his impractical aunt and his exacting father. He did manage to take a few lessons in elocution and to do a little tutoring. On one of his visits to his home during this period he wrote an article defending President Jackson's veto of the bill for the recharter of the United States Bank. This paper, written by a boy not yet out of his teens, was published by the Democratic party and distributed throughout New York state. On one of these visits to New Lebanon, too, it was decided that he should enter Yale. There was a lengthy discussion of this prospect, as there was of every problem affecting any member of the Tilden family. (For Samuel's own state of mind see a letter written to his father from New York in June 1833, Bigelow, *Life,* I, 31–32.) He entered Yale in June 1834, but left after one term never to return. The diet in commons and the climate were obnoxious, and all connection with this institution was terminated until 1875 when he was given the honorary degree of LL.D. and enrolled with the class of 1837. He returned home and shortly thereafter resumed his residence in New York. He attended the University of the City of New York (later New York University) spasmodically but was concerned mainly for several years with the writing of political treatises, the most noteworthy being a series written for the old *New York Times* (Mar. 23–May 12, 1837) over the pseudonym "Jacksonis Amicus" in which he defended President Van Buren's threat to veto any bill aimed at the abolition of slavery in the District of Columbia (*Writings,* I, 41–54); and two letters for the *Daily Albany Argus* (Sept. 28, Oct. 20, 1837) signed "Crino" and supporting Van Buren's call of a special session of Congress to recommend the establishment of the Independent Treasury. Tilden entered the law school of the University of the City of New York with the first class in 1838 and took the three-year course. At the same time he served a clerkship in the law office of John W. Edmonds [*q.v.*].

He was admitted to the bar at the May term of the supreme court in 1841, and immediately hung out his shingle at No. 11 Pine Street in New York City.

Once launched upon his legal career, Tilden's life became more purposeful and consistent and there was a noticeable decline in "symptoms." The death of his father in 1842 was a severe shock and severed his closest tie with his early life. He entered earnestly into the practice of law, was named corporation counsel of New York City in 1843, and rapidly became a commanding figure in the New York Democracy. The Van Buren-Wright faction of the New York Democracy was demoralized by the nomination of Polk in 1844 and their instinctive reaction was to oppose Polk and by defeating him in New York cause him to lose the election. Tilden at this juncture intervened with temperate counsel and suggested that his friends could place Polk under obligation by saving the state for him and thus the election. Silas Wright, much against his will, was induced to run for governor and to aid in the campaign. Tilden with John L. O'Sullivan [*q.v.*] undertook the establishment and publication of the *New York Morning News.* The state was saved for Polk, but in New York affairs Polk fell under the influence of Marcy and others who were opposed to the Wright faction, and his distribution of federal patronage to Marcy's friends signalized the definite split in the New York Democracy. Marcy led the group known as Hunkers (later Hardshells), who were closely aligned with the Southern Democrats because of their complacent attitude towards the extension of slavery, while Wright, Van Buren, Azariah C. Flagg, Benjamin F. Butler (1795–1858), Tilden and others led the opposition group dubbed Barnburners (later Softshells). This latter faction was committed to free-soil principles, and carried within it the germ of the later Republican party. Tilden did not follow the revolt to that extreme but this schism in the party resulted in his practical divorcement from Democratic leadership until after the Civil War. It is true that at the special request of Governor Wright he served a term in the state legislature in 1846 during which he presented a lucid analysis of the anti-rent disturbances (*Writings,* I, 188–220); that as a member of the constitutional convention of 1846 he distinguished himself in framing legislation to improve state finance; and that he was an unsuccessful candidate for the attorney-generalship in 1855. These activities enriched his political experience without adding appreciably to his political stature.

In his disappointment with the trend of politics Tilden turned his attention and energies to the development of his law practice. He gained his first real prominence at the bar in the case of *Giles* vs. *Flagg,* arising out of frauds in connection with the votes for the comptrollership of New York City in 1855 (*New York Tribune,* Apr. 2–7, 23–25, 1856). In this case he was associated with Charles O'Conor and William M. Evarts in the defense of Azariah C. Flagg. Tilden was given a conspicuous rôle and the resultant publicity added great lustre to his reputation. In 1857 he conducted another spectacular trial involving the murder of Dr. Harvey Burdell and the fraudulent claim of his housekeeper and suspected murderess that by virtue of a secret marriage she was entitled to a widow's third in his estate. In both of these cases Tilden was handicapped by lack of evidence in favor of his own clients and built his arguments on the inconsistencies in the testimony of opposing witnesses.

Following these suits Tilden engaged in a maze of cases of a complex nature, among the most notable of which were *Pennsylvania Coal Company* vs. *The President, Managers and Company of the Delaware and Hudson Canal Company,* and *The Cumberland Coal and Iron Company* vs. *Sherman, Dean and Postley* (O. L. Barbour, *Report of Cases . . . in the Supreme Court of the State of New York,* XXIX, 1860, p. 589; XXX, 1860, p. 553). His peculiar genius, however, seemed to be adapted to that type of litigation and advice incident to the reorganization of railroads. He himself stated that at one time or another more than half of the great railway companies north of the Ohio and between the Hudson and Missouri rivers were his clients. It was in connection with the refinancing and reorganization of railroads and in the acquirement of certain mining interests that he laid the foundation for his enormous fortune which was later augmented as a result of shrewd financing during the period of unstable money which resulted from the Civil War. At his death he possessed one of the largest personal fortunes in America.

Tilden's attitude during the Civil War was one of detachment. He opposed the election of Lincoln and disapproved of the war from the beginning. In a letter to Judge William Kent, printed in the New York *Evening Post* a week before the election of 1860, he pointed out the salient fact that a victory of the Republican party would amount to a practical disfranchisement of the whole South and predicted that it would lead to dire consequences (*Writings and Speeches,* I, 289–330). When war was actually

declared Tilden was called to Washington by Secretary of War Stanton (Bigelow, *Life,* I, 169). At that time he advised Stanton to call out the full military strength of the North immediately and by sheer force of superior numbers to crush the uprising by a swift and devastating stroke. Following this early visit to Washington, Tilden took little part in wartime activities. He rather devoted his energies to encouraging the Democratic party in the maintenance of a "constitutional opposition" to the threat of tyranny inherent in the powerful, centralized government at Washington. He favored President Johnson's liberal reconstruction policy, supported him in his efforts to circumvent the savage onslaughts of the Radicals in Congress, and was a not infrequent caller at the White House.

Tilden was elected from New York City as a delegate to the state constitutional convention of 1867, and the year previous he had succeeded Dean Richmond as chairman of the Democratic state committee, a position which he held for the eight years following. It was in this latter capacity that he prosecuted his titanic labors to oust the "Tweed ring" from New York City. Under the dominance of the predatory and unscrupulous William M. Tweed [*q.v.*] the "ring" controlled city politics absolutely, its insidious influence extended even into the state government, and, fortified by a charter made to its measure, it appeared impregnable. In the face of what many leaders believed to be political suicide, Tilden commenced his fight for good government. It is true that in 1870 the *New York Times* instituted a campaign to expose the rogues in the city government, organizing in 1871 the Committee of Seventy to assist in the movement. None the less, the dissipation of the "ring" was justly regarded as Tilden's personal triumph. He went to the legislature in 1872 to lead the battle for adequate legislation with which to combat the situation in the city, and his legal talent and persistent devotion to the mass of intricate details resulted in the production of the judicial proof which finally convicted the guilty persons. The system adopted by him in tracing misappropriated municipal funds to private bank accounts was closely analogous to that employed by him in the Flagg and Burdell cases. In taking the leading part in the smashing of the "Tweed ring" Tilden was responsible also for reforming and purifying the state judiciary, securing an investigation of certain suspect judges by the Bar Association of the City of New York, which he was partly instrumental in organizing, and the impeachment of two judges. A third judge resigned to escape punishment.

Tilden was active in the campaign of 1868, in which Horatio Seymour was defeated for the presidency, and also in that of 1872 in which, fantastically, Horace Greeley was the Democratic presidential nominee. Tilden's influence in politics was becoming more and more potent within his party, and his valiant fight for reform had made him a national figure. It was logical, therefore, that he should be the Democratic candidate for governor of New York in 1874. He was elected by a plurality of 50,000 over Gov. John A. Dix [q.v.]. During his two years as governor he did heroic work in the arena of state affairs, not however without an occasional gesture to the national gallery. He was swept into office as a champion of reform and reform was the constantly recurring theme in his governmental symphony. He brought about a substantial reduction in state taxes and expenditures as a result of the discovery and elimination of frauds and of economies in administration. His most spectacular stroke for reform was the shattering of the "Canal ring," a group of politicians in both parties bound together by the common ties of dishonesty and avarice, who had grown wealthy and powerful through control of the enormous sums expended in repairing and extending the state canal system. Tilden exposed the fraudulent device of revised estimates under which the "ring" cloaked its predatory activities and then undertook an arduous speaking campaign throughout the canal counties of the state exhorting the electors to return honest men to the legislature to break the power of the "ring" and to support the campaign to exterminate fraud (*Writings*, II, 98–116, 214–33, 296–305). His determined effort to reform municipal financing was frustrated because of one obnoxious item in the proposed amendment to the state constitution which was to give it effect. In his first message to the legislature, he advocated the resumption of specie payments by the national government, and the next week protested, in a special message, against the action of General Sheridan under whose orders a squad of United States soldiers entered the legislature of Louisiana and removed five of its members (*Writings*, II, 60–62, 80–84). His intrepid leadership and championship of reform movements had attracted the attention and fired the imagination of the whole country, and his nomination for the presidency on the Democratic ticket was almost inevitable. When the National Democratic Convention met at St. Louis June 27, 1876, Tilden was nominated on the second ballot. His nearest rival, Thomas A. Hendricks [q.v.], who held "soft-money" views, was named for vice-president. The Re-

publicans nominated Rutherford B. Hayes [q.v.] of Ohio.

The campaign was one of exceptional bitterness. The Democrats made savage onslaughts against the waste and extravagance in the Grant administration and their speeches were liberally sprinkled with intimations or outright charges of graft and corruption against men closely identified with the national administration. The Republicans, resorting to the waving of the "bloody shirt," accused the opposition party of rebel sympathies; attempted to stigmatize Tilden's connection with the railroads and to make an issue of his frail health; and imputed fraud in connection with his personal income tax returns. Because of his bad health and his absorption in his duties as governor, he himself manifested such a secretive aloofness that the campaign committee thought him indifferent (Nevins, *post*, pp. 305–19). On Nov. 7, 1876, a majority of approximately 250,000 of the voters indicated their preference for Tilden, and to this day it is uncertain whether this majority was so distributed as to signify election as well as preference by the people of the country. Following conflicting reports on the morning of Nov. 8, it became apparent from the returns that Tilden was assured of 184 electoral votes and Hayes of 163. The still-doubtful states of Oregon, Louisiana, South Carolina, and Florida, with a total of 22 electoral votes, were claimed immediately by the Hayes managers. There ensued an invasion of the South by representatives of both parties who betook themselves to the scenes of dispute. These "visiting statesmen" of both parties were involved in a frenzied welter of probing, cajoling, and bargaining, of plot and counterplot, and the actual circumstances which governed events must have been even more obscure at that time than they are today. The dispute was finally resolved by the creation of an Electoral Commission resulting from a compromise. It came about, partly through force of unforeseen circumstance, that this body had a majority of one in favor of the Republicans. By a strict party vote the commission declared that Hayes had carried all doubtful states. Tilden claimed his constitutional right, acquiescing in the compromise only as an escape from civil war, and always maintained stoutly that he was wrongfully deprived of the presidency.

Following the disputed election Tilden's political activity was restricted, but he remained to the end of his life a significant figure in national politics. In 1877, accompanied by John Bigelow, he took a trip to England, his previous trip having been made alone in 1873. This peaceful interlude was followed in 1878 by a feverish period in which he was involved in the investigation of the "Cipher Despatches." These were concerned with some questionable negotiations of the "visiting statesmen" of the Democratic party about which Tilden disclaimed any personal knowledge. Also, beginning shortly after his nomination in 1876 and continuing intermittently for approximately five years, he was plagued by a personal income tax investigation set in motion by the government, an effort which spent itself eventually in futility. In 1879 he purchased "Greystone," a magnificent estate at Yonkers, where he spent the remainder of his days. In 1880 and again in 1884 he was mentioned for the presidential nomination but he persisted in his refusal to be seriously considered, basing his refusal on his advanced age and physical infirmities. While Tilden supported the policies of the Cleveland administration, the personal relationship between the two men was none too cordial. In his last years Tilden's infirmities were such that he became almost a recluse and his time was spent mainly in reading and in collecting books for his large library.

Tilden died at the age of seventy-two, a bachelor. In his will he provided that the bulk of his estate, involving some six million dollars, should be administered by a Tilden Trust whose object should be the establishment of a free library for the City of New York. Proceedings were brought by certain of the Tilden heirs to break the will and finally the clause establishing a Tilden Trust was declared invalid by the New York Court of Appeals for indefiniteness of subject (130 *New York Court of Appeals,* 29). The vote of the court was four to three. According to a settlement with the heirs, the Tilden Trust was finally established with a capital of approximately three million dollars and in the end the cherished dream of Tilden to establish a free library for New York City was realized, largely through his generosity and instrumentality.

In appearance Tilden in the prime of life was a man of unimpressive mien. Of medium stature, slight build, nervous and awkward in his movements, he attracted little attention in a group of men. His face was round and boyish, his eyes were large and blue, his hair was a chestnut color, his broad brow of the intellectual type, and his voice weak. Throughout his life he was afflicted with a feeble constitution which curtailed his social contacts. Although inordinately secretive, exasperatingly dilatory, and extremely non-committal, he possessed extraordinary power of concentration, had a logical and analytical mind, was endowed with a marvelous, well-stored

memory, and was favored with a remarkable command of language. It was not his personality but his intellect that made him an outstanding corporation lawyer, a sagacious financier, and a political leader for half a century.

[In addition to the contemporary newspapers and magazines, which devoted considerable space to Tilden's reform activities, his accomplishments as governor and his presidential candidacy, there appeared in 1876 two campaign biographies, a semi-official one by T. P. Cook, and another of less value by W. M. Cornell. John Bigelow, *The Life of Samuel J. Tilden* (2 vols., 1895), presents a full but perhaps too apologetic interpretation. The same author's *The Writings and Speeches of Samuel J. Tilden* (2 vols., 1885), and *Letters and Literary Memorials of Samuel J. Tilden* (2 vols., 1908), form the best printed collection of Tilden's papers. His messages to the legislature are found in C. Z. Lincoln, *State of N. Y. Messages from the Governors* (1909), vol. VI. On the election of 1876, see the *Congressional Record*; *Proceedings of the Electoral Commission . . . 1877* (1877); "Presidential Elections Investigations" (5 vols., 1879), *House Miscellaneous Doc. No. 31*, 45 Cong., 3 Sess.; P. L. Haworth, *The Hayes-Tilden Disputed Presidential Election of 1876* (1906), a full study with Republican leaning; A. M. Gibson, *A Political Crime* (1885), inspired and financed by Tilden and presenting his side of the case; Allan Nevins, *Abram S. Hewitt, with Some Account of Peter Cooper* (1935), containing fresh material on the campaign and election. Contemporary writers of both political parties supply additional information. See also D. S. Alexander, *A Pol. Hist. of the State of N. Y.*, vols. II, III (1906–09); obituaries in *N. Y. Times*, Aug. 5, 1886, and other papers. The large collection of personal papers of Tilden, which he preserved with care, are in the N. Y. Pub. Lib., but under the full authority of his will they are to be thoroughly sorted out by the executors before leaving their custody. A new interpretation of his life, based on the study of his papers, is in preparation by A. C. Flick.]   A. C. F.

TILESTON, THOMAS (Aug. 13, 1793–Feb. 29, 1864), printer, merchant, ship-owner, was descended from another Thomas Tileston who crossed from Cheshire to settle in Dorchester, Mass., in 1634. The younger Thomas was born in Boston, second of the numerous children of Lemuel and Mary (Minns) Tileston. He attended the public schools until thirteen, when the family finances led him to become a printer's devil with the firm of Greenough & Stebbins for thirty dollars a year and board. He chose this trade in the hope of absorbing an education and soon revealed literary ability. When the firm moved to Haverhill, Mass., and acquired the *Merrimack Intelligencer*, Tileston became its editor. At twenty-one he supervised the printing of a revised American edition of the King James version of the Bible and soon bought an interest in the firm. On Apr. 11, 1820, he married Mary Porter of Salem (Nov. 30, 1797–Nov. 9, 1879). They had one son, who died in childhood, and eight daughters.

In 1818 Tileston had joined the swarm of New Englanders who were seeking fortunes in New York City just as it was clinching its leadership over the rival American ports. Haverhill had become an active manufacturing center during the War of 1812, but needed an outlet for its shoes and other products. Tileston formed a partnership with Paul Spofford (Feb. 18, 1792–Oct. 28, 1869), who had started as a country storekeeper, to sell these Haverhill wares on commission. They began by sending these to the West Indies, South America, and Southern ports, and in turn imported coffee, sugar, and other products of those regions. This trading, as in the case of Preserved Fish and Charles Morgan [qq.v.], led to ship-owning, which soon overshadowed their other business. Their yellow house flag with its blue cross appeared over a steadily increasing flotilla. About 1822 Spofford & Tileston became agents for a line of coasting packets to Boston. For their southern trade they chartered vessels at first but soon bought several brigs and schooners, and later built two excellent packets for the Havana trade. In 1846 they built for the New York-Charleston run the *Southerner*, followed in 1847 by the *Northerner*. These have been called "our two first coastwise steamships" (Morrison, *post*, p. 445), the earlier New England steamboats evidently being excluded from that category. Spofford & Tileston later added to their steam fleet the *Marion, Columbia, James Adger*, and *Nashville*, as well as the fast excursion steamer *Leviathan*. They were among the first to send ships to California during the gold rush. When Edward Knight Collins [q.v.] started his famous line of subsidy steamships in 1850, Spofford & Tileston purchased the sailing packets of his "Dramatic Line," later adding the *Webster, Calhoun, Clay*, and *Orient*. Though they were inferior to the Collins and Cunard steamships, these sailing packets, like those of Charles Henry Marshall [q.v.], were operated well into the 'sixties. The firm's southern business, like Charles Morgan's, was seriously interrupted by the Civil War. The Confederates made a privateer of the *Nashville*; the *James Adger* was bought for the naval blockading force; and the other steamships were diverted from Charleston to Havana. The firm refused to transfer any vessels to British registry.

Tileston was also a prominent figure in New York financial circles. He was president of the Phoenix Bank from 1840 until his death, and was a founder (1829) and director of the Atlantic Insurance Company. He was an organizer and for nine years chairman of the New York Clearing House. As early as 1846 his fortune was estimated at $300,000 and Spofford's at $200,000. He was a gifted speaker and a tireless worker. His evenly balanced mind, his sa-

gacity, and his promptness helped to account for his success. His portrait, showing a full, clean-shaven face, bears a superficial resemblance to that of Stephen A. Douglas. He remained active and progressive to the end, and was described, just before his death, as " 'Young America on the shoulders of seventy years' experience'" (*Hunt's Merchants' Magazine*, Feb. 1864, p. 90). He died very suddenly of heart trouble at his home on Fourteenth Street in New York.

[Mary W. F. Tileston, *Thomas Tileston, 1793–1864* (1925), with geneal. tables; *Hunt's Merchants' Mag.*, Feb., Apr. 1864, with portrait; George Wilson, *Portrait Gallery of the Chamber of Commerce of the State of N. Y.* (1890); J. H. Morrison, *Hist. of Am. Steam Navigation* (1903); F. L. Griswold, *The House Flags of the Merchants of N. Y.* (1926), reprinted in *Clipper Ships and Yachts* (1927); M. Y. Beach, *The Wealth and Biog. of the Wealthy Citizens of N. Y.* (1846); *N. Y. Tribune*, Mar. 1, 1864.]   R. G. A—n.

TILGHMAN, EDWARD (Feb. 11, 1750/51–Nov. 1, 1815), lawyer, was born at Wye, Queen Anne Co., Md., the second son of Edward and Elizabeth (Chew) Tilghman. He was the cousin of William and Tench Tilghman [qq.v.], and the great-grandson of Richard Tilghman, a physician who emigrated to Maryland in 1661 from Kent County, England, on the *Elizabeth and Mary*. His father was high sheriff of his county, member of the provincial assembly for many years and one time speaker, officer in the Maryland militia, and a member of the Stamp Act Congress. In 1767 he graduated from the College, Academy, and Charitable School of Philadelphia, now the University of Pennsylvania. On June 24, 1772, he was admitted to study at the Middle Temple in London. During his two years abroad he attended regularly the courts of Westminster Hall, taking extensive notes of the arguments in chancery before the leading jurists, which he later used to advantage before courts as a lawyer. His days in London were spent in serious study and hard work. Upon his return to America he married on May 26, 1774, his first cousin, Elizabeth, the daughter of Benjamin Chew [q.v.]. The youngest of their four children became the mother of William Henry Rawle [q.v.]. The same year he was admitted to the Philadelphia bar, where he continued to practise until his death. Although the Tilghman family in colonial days enjoyed many favors from the Crown, at the outbreak of the Revolution Edward, like his father, threw his lot with the colonials. In 1776 he enlisted as a private soldier with the Philadelphia associators and later the same year at the battle of Long Island was a brigade major attached to Lord Sterling.

However, he soon returned to Philadelphia to continue his practice as a lawyer.

It was in the field of law that he gained distinction. A biographer, also a leading lawyer, credits him with having possessed "the most accurate legal judgment of any man of his day" at the Philadelphia bar (Binney, *post*, p. 51). His severe and rigid training so imbued him with legal principles that he seemed to seize the true result on some perplexing legal question before he had time to prove it. In the field of contingent remainders and executory devices he was recognized as an authority. In addition to being well versed in the law, he was also an advocate of surpassing powers. There was little ornament in his speech; he commanded attention rather by the weight of what he said than how he said it. A wary tactician in managing a case, eloquent in language, a faultless logician, he was highly feared by opposing lawyers. Judges had deep confidence in his opinions and respected his plain and direct reasoning. Before juries his sense of shrewdness, occasional pleasantry, and constant air of sincerity were almost indomitable. He had a persistent aversion to authorship and public office. In 1806 he was proffered the chief justiceship of the supreme court of Pennsylvania by Governor McKean, but he declined the honor and recommended his cousin, William Tilghman, for the post. He was rather short in stature, spare of flesh and delicate, but well proportioned. Possessed of a buoyant spirit and a sharp wit, his cheerfulness invariably brought a luminous circle about him on all occasions. Neither jester nor satirist, he quoted English and Latin poetry frequently and with ease, and he demonstrated the utmost simplicity in dress and manner. Unlike his colleagues he never wore black at the bar nor powdered his hair. His last years of life were darkened by lack of health and the loss of all of his property.

[Horace Binney, *The Leaders of the Old Bar in Philadelphia* (1859) and in *Pa. Mag. of Hist. & Biog.*, Apr. 1890; *Ibid.*, July 1916; J. H. Martin, *Martin's Bench & Bar of Phila.* (1883); *Md. Hist. Mag.*, Dec. 1906; E. A. Jones, *Am. Members of the Inns of Court* (1924); B. A. Konkle, *Benj. Chew* (1932); *Relfs' Phil. Gazette and Daily Advertiser*, Nov. 2, 1815.]   J. H. P.

TILGHMAN, MATTHEW (Feb. 17, 1718–May 4, 1790), Revolutionary leader, member of the Continental Congress, the son of Richard and Anna Maria (Lloyd) Tilghman, was born in Queen Anne County, Md. His paternal ancestry has been traced to Richard Tilghman, a civilian of Snodland, Kent County, England, in the fifteenth century. His grandfather, Richard Tilghman, a surgeon, arrived in Maryland in 1661 on the *Elizabeth and Mary*. For transport-

ing to the province twenty persons of British descent he received a grant of one thousand acres of land. He built the Tilghman "Hermitage" in Queen Anne County, continued the practice of his profession, and acquired other lands by purchase. His son Richard, Matthew Tilghman's father, joined two large landholding families by marrying the daughter of Philemon Lloyd and became prominent in public life as a representative of Talbot County in the Maryland Assembly and as a member of the governor's Council. Matthew Tilghman was the youngest of nine children. His early education was under the direction of Hugh Jones [*q.v.*], and at the age of fifteen he was adopted by his cousin, Matthew Tilghman Ward, who endowed him with the riches of experience and influence acquired from long public service, and a large estate at Ward's Point (now Tilghman's Point) in Talbot County.

Tilghman entered public life in 1741 as captain of a troop of horse organized for protection from Indian incursions on the Eastern Shore. The same year he was appointed an associate justice of the Talbot County court. He was promoted to a justice of the quorum in 1749, continued in that capacity until 1769, and was the presiding justice from 1770 to 1775. He took a seat in the Maryland Assembly in 1751, as a representative of Talbot County, served until 1758, represented Queen Anne County in 1760 and 1761, was returned by Talbot County in 1768, and served until the Revolution. In 1773 and 1774 he was speaker of the Assembly. In recognition of his high standing, the lord proprietor, in July 1768, issued commissions appointing him to a seat in the Council and agent to direct the collection of his territorial revenue. But Tilghman declined. Although a large landholder, he had at no time been friendly to the proprietary interests, and since the British Parliament had undertaken to tax the colonies he cast his lot with the popular cause against both Parliament and proprietor. In June 1768 he served on a committee of the Assembly to draft a remonstrance to the king against the Townshend Acts. He signed the non-importation agreement, adopted on June 22, 1769, as a further protest against those Acts. He presided over the Maryland Conventions, 1774–76, which formed the Association of the Freemen of Maryland, adopted a provisional government with a council of safety and committees of observation and correspondence, and chose delegates to the Continental Congress. He was chairman of the committee of correspondence for Talbot County, was president of the council of safety, and headed every Maryland delegation to the Continental Congress from September 1774 to December 1776. Tilghman was one of the Maryland delegates who first expressed themselves openly in favor of independence and recommended a session of the Maryland Convention with a view to the removal of its restrictions in that particular. He presided over that session and the restrictions were removed, but he was not present in Congress when the Declaration of Independence was passed or when it was signed.

The few remaining years of his public life were devoted chiefly to the organization and operation of a government for the State of Maryland. He was chosen president of the convention that met at Annapolis on Aug. 14, 1776, to draft the first constitution of the state, and served as chairman of the committee elected by that body to prepare "a declaration and charter of rights, and a form of government." He was elected in December 1776 to a seat in the state Senate for a term of five years, was reëlected in September 1781, and for a time served as its president. While senator, he voiced his opposition to the confiscation of British property, and, as president of a special council, afforded military protection to property on the Eastern Shore. Immediately following the declaration of peace in 1783, he closed his public career, retired to "Bayside," his estate in Talbot County, where he resided until his death from a paralytic stroke. On Apr. 6, 1741, he was married to Anna Lloyd, the daughter of James Lloyd, and to them were born three sons and two daughters. The younger daughter, Anna Maria, became the wife of her cousin, Tench Tilghman [q.v.], aide-de-camp of General Washington.

[Christopher Johnston, "Tilghman Family," *Md. Hist. Mag.*, June–Dec. 1906; Oswald Tilghman, *Hist. of Talbot County, Md.* (2 vols., 1915); H. F. Powell, *Tercentenary Hist. of Md.* (1925), vol. IV; *Archives of Md.*, vols. XI, XIV, XLVII (1892, 18595, 1930); *Proc. of the Conventions of the Province of Md. . . . 1774, 1775 and 1776* (1836); *Md. Jour. and Baltimore Advertiser*, May 18, 1790.]   N. D. M.

TILGHMAN, RICHARD ALBERT (May 24, 1824–Mar. 24, 1899), chemist, the fourth son of Benjamin and Anna Maria (McMurtrie) Tilghman, was born in Philadelphia, Pa. He was of the sixth generation from Richard Tilghman, and a grandson of Edward Tilghman [q.v.]. He studied at the University of Pennsylvania, graduating with the B.A. degree in 1841. While in college, he became interested in chemistry and physics. As the laboratory facilities were very meager, he was compelled to seek practical experience in the private analytical laboratory of James C. Booth [q.v.], under whom his active interest in research was sustained and directed. His first scientific paper, presented be-

fore the American Philosophical Society in 1847, was entitled "On the Decomposing Power of Water at High Temperatures" (*Proceedings of the American Philosophical Society*, vol. IV, 1847), and dealt with the question of the hydrolysis of hydrated and anhydrous inorganic salts when exposed to water vapor at elevated temperature. This was the first systematic study of hydration, and was later rewritten to include the action upon fats by water at elevated temperature and various pressure conditions. A hydrolysis was effected, by means of which a pure fat acid and glycerine were obtained. The acid was of high grade and the method was sold to the Price Patent Candle Company of London.

At the time of Tilghman's early activity, the chemical industries in America were not well developed and he did much of his work in Scotland, where he completed a method for the production of caustic soda, based upon hydrolysis, that met with some commercial application. His first practical work was concerned with the manufacture of potassium dichromate and his method was adopted by the Baltimore Chrome Works. The production of gas from coal, and the use of gas as a smokeless, dustless fuel in surface evaporation in chemical operations next absorbed Tilghman, but his idea was somewhat in advance of the time and did not receive the notice it deserved. He also proposed to convert coal into gas at the mines and then pipe it to the market, a suggestion that has since been repeated but not yet put into practice. He spent two years evolving a method, later known as the "sulphite process," for the manufacture of paper pulp. The method was not commercially successful at the time, but his patents covered all the basic principles. With a brother, Benjamin Chew Tilghman, he developed the "sand blast" process for shaping objects made of hard, brittle materials, and manufactured chilled iron shot for sandblasting machinery. He was also a director in the George Richards and Company, Ltd., manufacturers of machine tools, and in the Tilghman Sand Blast Company at Broadheath near Manchester, England.

In 1860 he was married to Susan Price Toland, the daughter of Robert and Rebekah Toland. He lived a quiet life, interested only in his work and his home. The fact that he had much trouble with his eyes, owing to an explosion, led to his avoidance of public affairs. A long and painful illness terminated his scientific and business activities a number of years before his death. He was survived by his wife, two sons, and three daughters.

[Isaac J. Wistar, biographical article in *Proc. Am. Phil. Soc.*, *Memorial Volume* (1900); *Trans. Am. Phil. Soc.*, vol. X, n.s. (1853); Dingler's *Polytechnisches*

Jour., vols. CVI, CXXXVIII (1847, 1858); *Public Ledger* (Philadelphia), Mar. 25, 1899.]   O. L. S.

TILGHMAN, TENCH (Dec. 25, 1744–Apr. 18, 1786), Revolutionary soldier, was a descendant of an ancient family of Kent, England, and a great-grandson of Richard Tilghman, who emigrated to Maryland in 1661. He was the eldest son of James Tilghman, a Provincial Counselor of Pennsylvania, and Anna, the daughter of Tench Francis [*q.v.*], a brother of William, and a cousin of Edward Tilghman [*qq.v.*]. He was born at "Fausley" in Talbot County, Md., and was graduated from the College, Academy, and Charitable School of Philadelphia (now the University of Pennsylvania), in 1761. He entered upon a mercantile career in Philadelphia, but liquidated his business at the approach of the Revolution. He acted as secretary and treasurer, in 1775, to the Continental Congress commissioners to the Six Nations, and his private diary, supplementing his official minutes of these proceedings, is a valuable record of Indian character and the social life of Albany and vicinity— the frontier of the period. He was adopted by the Onondagas, but sagely noted that the customary bowls of punch that he furnished may have been the reason for this complimentary ceremony. On his return to Philadelphia he became captain of an independent company which joined the Flying Camp in 1776. In August he joined the military "family" of General Washington as a volunteer and served continuously as aide-de-camp until the end of the war.

The amount of secretarial work, in addition to military duties, that he performed for Washington was prodigious. Washington's letters to and about Tilghman constitute a most unusual acknowledgment of friendship, of valued services, and a high eulogy of patriotic devotion. Washington successfully urged Congress to grant Tilghman a regular commission of lieutenant-colonel and aide, in place of his volunteer appointment, in these words: "He has been a zealous Servant and slave to the public, and a faithful assistant to me for near five years, great part of which time he refused to receive pay. Honor and gratitude Interest me in his favor, and makes me sollicitous to obtain his Commission" (Papers of George Washington, Letter to Sullivan, May 11, 1781). His selection to carry to the Continental Congress the announcement of the surrender of Cornwallis was the highest military honor in the gift of the commander-in-chief. He was given a horse, properly caparisoned, and a sword, by Congress, on Oct. 29, 1781, in recognition of his services.

Tilghman was married on June 9, 1783, to his cousin, Anna Maria Tilghman, daughter of Matthew [*q.v.*]. After the war he entered into a business association with Robert Morris [*q.v.*], but the hardships encountered during the war caused his death two years later. He was survived by his widow and two daughters. Washington referred to him as a pillar of the Revolution and as having left "as fair a reputation as ever belonged to a human character ..." (Washington Letter Book, volume VII, p. 130, Letter to Jefferson). He was buried in St. Paul's churchyard in Baltimore. The best portrait of Tilghman was painted by Peale, and hangs in the State House at Annapolis.

[Papers of the Continental Congress and the George Washington Papers, Library of Congress; S. A. Harrison, *Memoir of Lieut. Col. Tench Tilghman* (1876), containing his diaries of 1775 and 1781, with certain correspondence; Oswald Tilghman, *Hist. of Talbot County, Md.* (2 vols., 1915); information furnished personally by Harrison Tilghman, of Easton, Md.; Christopher Johnston, "Tilghman Family," *Md. Hist. Mag.*, June–Dec. 1906; *Md. Jour. and Baltimore Advertiser*, Apr. 21, 1786.]   J. C. F—k.

TILGHMAN, WILLIAM (Aug. 12, 1756– Apr. 29, 1827), jurist, was born at "Fausley" in Talbot County, Md., the son of James and Anna (Francis) Tilghman. He was the cousin of Edward Tilghman, the nephew of Matthew Tilghman, the brother of Tench Tilghman, and the grandson of Tench Francis [*qq.v.*]. He was the great-grandson of Richard Tilghman, a physician who emigrated from England to Maryland in 1661. His father, also a lawyer, sat in the Maryland Assembly and, after moving to Philadelphia about 1762, was secretary of the proprietary land office. The boy entered the College, Academy, and Charitable School of Philadelphia, now the University of Pennsylvania, in 1763 and in 1769 entered the college department, from which he was graduated in 1772. For the next four years, 1772 to 1776, he read law in the office of Benjamin Chew [*q.v.*]. In the Revolutionary War, both he and his father were loyalist and late in 1776 retired to the family estate in Maryland. He lived quietly reading law and classical literature and in 1783 was admitted to practice in Maryland. He first entered public life as a member of the Maryland Assembly, 1788, 1789, and 1790. A silent adherent of the federal Constitution rather than an enthusiastic supporter of it, he was a delegate to the Maryland convention for ratification. In 1791 he became a member of the Maryland Senate, but in 1793 he resigned and removed to Philadelphia, where he was admitted to the bar on Sept. 1, 1794. On July 1 of that year he had married Margaret Elizabeth, the daughter of James Allen. They had one daughter. On Mar. 3, 1801,

President Adams appointed him one of the "midnight judges," chief judge of the third circuit court. When this court was abolished in 1802 he resumed his law practice until his appointment in 1805 as president judge of the court of common pleas for the district embracing Philadelphia and the surrounding counties, and he also became a judge of the Pennsylvania high court of errors and appeals. In 1806 he was commissioned chief justice of the Pennsylvania supreme court, over which he presided until his death. As a judge he was careful to remain aloof from the bitter partisanship of Pennsylvania politics. During his tenure the judges of the supreme court prepared for the legislature a report of the English statutes in force in Pennsylvania (see *Digest of Select British Statutes,* 2nd ed. 1817). His chief contribution as a jurist was the incorporation of the principles of scientific equity with the law of Pennsylvania.

His *Address Delivered before the Philadelphia Society for Promoting Agriculture* (1820), of which society he was an active member, reflects his keen interest in agriculture and his experiments on the family estate in Maryland. He was one of the early advocates of a line of canals between the Susquehanna and Alleghany rivers. A firm believer in the development of home industry, for the last ten years of his life he refused to wear any article of cloth not made in the United States. He was president of the American Philosophical Society from 1824 until his death and a trustee of the University of Pennsylvania from 1802 until his death. Slight of frame, unpretentious in manner, his gentle and amiable disposition commanded high respect from members of the bar. He was the author of *An Eulogium in Commemoration of Doctor Caspar Wistar* (1818), which was delivered before the American Philosophical Society. He died in Philadelphia.

[John Golder, *Life of ... William Tilghman* (1829); Horace Binney, *A Eulogium upon ... Wm. Tilghman* (1827) and in 16 *Sergeant and Rawle's Pa. Reports,* 439–56; D. P. Brown, *The Forum,* vol. I (1856); J. H. Martin, *Martin's Bench & Bar of Philadelphia* (1883); Oswald Tilghman, *Hist. of Talbot County, Md.* (1915), vol. II; B. A. Konkle, *Benj. Chew* (1932); *Am. Phil. Soc. Proc.,* "Memorial Vol." I (1900), p. 192; *Univ. of Pa., Biog. Cat. of the Matriculates of the College* (1894); *Md. Hist. Mag.,* Dec. 1906; *Pa. Mag. of Hist. and Biog.* (July 1877, Apr., Oct. 1893); *National Gazette* (Philadelphia), Apr. 30, May 1, 1827.]

J. H. P.

TILGHMAN, WILLIAM MATTHEW (July 4, 1854–Nov. 1, 1924), frontier peace officer, known as "Bill" Tilghman, was born in Fort Dodge, Iowa, the son of William Matthew and Amanda (Shepherd) Tilghman, and a descendant of the Richard Tilghman, of England, who settled in Maryland in 1661. In 1856 the family moved to a farm near Atchison, Kan. His father and elder brother served in the Civil War, leaving the boy as the main support of the mother and four children. He early became an expert in the use of firearms. At the age of sixteen, with three other boys, he made a successful trip to the buffalo country, then thronging with hostile Indians, and in the following year adopted the Fort Dodge (Kan.) region as his home. He became a noted buffalo hunter, was at times a scout operating from Fort Dodge, and at a later time a cattleman. In 1877 he served as a deputy sheriff of Ford County under "Bat" (William B.) Masterson [*q.v.*], and was for a time marshal of Dodge City. In 1878 he was married to Flora Kendal and started a stock ranch on the Arkansas River. He was one of the participants in the spectacular settlers' race that marked the opening of Oklahoma, on Apr. 22, 1889, and obtained a good location in the present Guthrie. In 1891 he took up a claim at Chandler, which he developed into a fine farm. In the same year he was appointed a deputy United States marshal, and though a Democrat, continued to hold the office for about twenty years. The region was for a number of years overrun by outlaw gangs, and it was largely through Tilghman's efforts that they were broken up or exterminated.

In 1910 he was elected to the state Senate, but in the following year he resigned to become chief of police of Oklahoma City, a post he retained for two years. After the death of his first wife, by whom he had four children, he was married on July 15, 1903, to Zoe Agnes Stratton, of an old pioneer family. By the second marriage he had three children. In 1915 he superintended the making of a moving picture, "The Passing of the Oklahoma Outlaws," which for several years he exhibited. He had retired from active business when, in August 1924, the citizens of Cromwell, a "boom" oil town, asked him to become marshal. He accepted, and three months later was assassinated on the street. His body was taken to Oklahoma City, where it lay in state in the capitol, and his funeral was largely attended. His wife and several children survived him.

Tilghman was of powerful build, five feet eleven inches in height. His manner was gentle, he was generous, kindly, and notably fond of children. He had many devoted friends. In personal habits he was abstemious. He was a student and possessed an exceptional knowledge of Western history and a fluent command of the Spanish language. His reputation for courage is not exceeded by that of any other frontiersman of his time, and his skill with a revolver was uncanny. It was in answer to a question by President Theodore Roosevelt, who had eagerly sought his acquaintance, that he explained that the secret of his survival from so many desperate encounters was his ability to fire a sixteenth of a second before the other man, and that this shade of advantage was due to the fact that he represented the law (see Macdonald, *post*, pp. 64–65).

[Information from Mrs. Zoe A. Tilghman, of Oklahoma City; H. R. Stratton, *A Book of Strattons*, vol. II (1918); J. B. Thoburn, *A Standard Hist. of Okla.* (1916), vol. III; A. B. Macdonald, *Hands Up!* (1927); *Muskogee Daily Phoenix*, Nov. 2, 1924.]   W. J. G.

TILLMAN, BENJAMIN RYAN (Aug. 11, 1847–July 3, 1918), governor of South Carolina and United States senator, was born in Edgefield County, S. C., the youngest of the seven sons of Sophia (Hancock) and Benjamin Ryan Tillman. His ancestors, both paternal and maternal, had settled in South Carolina before the Revolution. His father, a farmer who supplemented his income by using his house as an inn for stage passengers, died in 1849; two brothers were killed in war; one died of fever; two others were killed in personal encounters; and in 1856 Tillman's brother George, who had become a lawyer and politician at Edgefield Court House, killed a bystander in a gambling feud and as a consequence served two years in jail. Ben aided his mother in the management of her many slaves, studied in a local private school, and in 1861 entered Bethany, a rustic academy near his home. An apt student of English and Latin, he left school in 1864 to join the Confederate army, but was prevented from carrying out his plan by an illness which incapacitated him for two years and resulted in the loss of his left eye. On Jan. 8, 1868, he married Sallie Starke of Elbert County, Ga., by whom he had seven children. Tillman and his wife lived on a four-hundred acre estate adjoining his mother's property, and for the next seventeen years he gave most of his time to wresting a meager living from his red lands. He participated in the Hamburg and Ellenton Riots of 1876, and aided in the Democratic triumph of that year by frightening prospective colored voters away from the polls. In 1880 he ardently championed the political ambitions of Gen. Martin Witherspoon Gary [*q.v.*] in the Edgefield County Democratic convention, and in 1882 was an inconspicuous figure in the state convention of his party. Up to this time no one dreamed that he was destined to have a conspicuous political career. Careless in manners, unattractive in personal appearance, and possessed of a rasping voice and irascible disposition, he was not even liked by his neighbors.

But in 1885, moved by his reverses as a farmer, he forced himself on the attention of the people of South Carolina. In a speech on Aug. 6 at Bennettsville, he aroused the enthusiasm of the farmers by bluntly asserting that their interests were being betrayed by lawyers and merchants, and by demanding that the state undertake a system of agricultural education. This address was followed by a series of masterful letters to the Charleston *News and Courier* in which he caustically arraigned the rulers of the state and urged the farmers to organize. Although the personal character of his indictments aroused bitter opposition, he was able to organize the Farmers' Association, and in 1886 almost captured control of the state government. Fresh stimulus was given to his agitations by the death of Thomas Green Clemson [*q.v.*] in April 1888, who left a site and an endowment for a proposed state agricultural college. During the following summer, Tillman so awakened the rural masses that he was almost able to name the Democratic nominee for governor, and was able to force the governor and legislature to accept the Clemson bequest. Convinced that he was the only man who had "the brains, the nerve and the ability to organize the common people against the aristocracy" (*News and Courier,* Mar. 28, 1890), Tillman in 1890 became the farmers' candidate for the Democratic nomination for governor. The result of the canvass, which created almost unparalleled excitement, was the nomination of Tillman by the state Democratic convention of August 1890, and his election by a great majority over Alexander C. Haskell, an independent Democrat, in the following November. Tillman was easily reëlected in 1892 after a canvass as turbulent as that of 1890. He served as governor from Dec. 4, 1890, to Nov. 27, 1894.

For a number of years Tillman was complete master of the political fortunes of South Carolina. At his dictation distinguished men long in office—Wade Hampton (1818–1902), Samuel McGowan [*qq.v.*], and Judge William H. Wallace—were replaced by his partisans. When the legislature of 1890 refused to do his exact bidding, he stigmatized it as "dead, rotten driftwood" on "the tide which swept from the mountains to the seaboard" (*Ibid.,* Dec. 30, 1891), and the voters in 1892 enthusiastically gave him a legislative body thoroughly obedient to his will. In 1894 he defeated Matthew Calbraith Butler [*q.v.*] for United States senator, and made John Gary Evans, the youthful nephew of Gary, his successor as governor. The following year, in the face of bitter opposition, he was able to secure a convention which rewrote the constitution of the state as he bade. Moreover, he accomplished constructive reforms. Clemson College was opened in 1893, and two years later Winthrop College, a state controlled normal and industrial school for women. The state railroad commission was given power to fix rates; taxes were equalized and expenditures for public education increased; representation in the legislature was reapportioned and congressional districts were redrawn so as to discriminate against the negroes. The most radical innovation of the Tillman administration was the establishment in 1893 of the state dispensary, a public monopoly over the sale of alcoholic beverages. Tillman also wrote into the constitution of the state a provision for educational and property qualifications that legally disfranchised the negroes. Having aroused the political consciousness of the white masses, he made more effective their participation in politics by securing in 1896 the primary method of nominating state officers.

On his election to the Senate Tillman achieved national notoriety as an extreme champion of Southern agrarianism. "Send me to Washington," he had yelled at the frantic mobs responsible for his election, "and I'll stick my pitchfork into his [Cleveland's] old ribs!" (*Chronicle,* Augusta, Ga., June 18, 1894). The maiden effort of "Pitchfork Ben," as he was now called, was a coarse indictment of Cleveland. Aspiring to the Democratic nomination for president in 1896, he ruined his chances by his violent speech before the national convention. Dark and savage-featured, snapping his jaws together, his hands high above his head, and hissing out a denunciation of Cleveland, he failed to touch the multitude; the nomination went to William Jennings Bryan [*q.v.*]. Tillman followed his efforts at the Democratic convention by a series of addresses in the Senate denouncing the policies of the Republicans. Although he favored naval expansion and the war with Spain, he opposed the annexation of Hawaii and the Philippines, and Roosevelt's Panama policy. Charging that the "armor trust" was making excess profits out of the government, he advocated the establishment of government shops for the manufacture of armor plate for battleships (*Congressional Record,* 54 Cong., 2 Sess., pp. 2556–60). Although this move was defeated, he had succeeded in exposing before an interested public the machinations of the steel magnates. He also presented to the nation the views of Southern extremists on the race question in a series of addresses in the Senate and on the Chautauqua platform. He justified lynching in cases of rape and the use of force in disfranchising the negro, and advocated the repeal of the

Fifteenth Amendment. Toward President Roosevelt he developed a hatred similar to that he had manifested toward Cleveland. This was induced by the President's withdrawal in 1902 of an invitation to a White House state dinner after Tillman had engaged in a personal altercation with John L. McLaurin on the floor of the Senate. Tillman accused Roosevelt of hypocrisy in dealing with the trusts and of dictatorial ambitions. In retaliation the President published documents intended to show that the senator, while trying to forestall alleged illegal purchases of public lands in Oregon, was using his official influence to effect advantageous purchases of Oregon lands for himself. Although fraud was not proved, these disclosures were embarrassing for a professed champion of the public interest against private greed. Personal aversion for the President did not, however, prevent Tillman from championing administration measures which he favored. The most constructive act of his legislative career was the steering of the Hepburn Rate Bill, an administration measure, through the Senate.

After his elevation to the Senate he continued to be a powerful factor in South Carolina politics. With little difficulty he secured his reëlection in 1900, 1906, and 1912; until his death he was able to control the state's vote at the national Democratic conventions; and his advice was always sought by the political leaders of the state. Largely through his influence his nephew, Lieutenant-Governor James H. Tillman, was acquitted in 1903 of the assassination of N. G. Gonzales, an editor who was the impassioned foe of Tillmanism. After engaging on Feb. 22, 1902, on the floor of the Senate in a fist fight with John L. McLaurin, his colleague and former friend, he demonstrated his power by forcing the retirement of McLaurin to private life. But after 1902 his influence in South Carolina affairs gradually declined. A growing conservatism, stimulated by the gratification of personal ambitions, led him to view complacently the return of traditional influences in politics. His irascible disposition led to quarrels with old friends without the gain of more than the stimulated affections of former enemies. In 1908 and 1910 paralytic strokes deprived him of the ability to harangue the people. In 1902 Duncan C. Heyward, a member of an old low-country family, was elected governor. The state dispensary, Tillman's pet institution, grew corrupt, and was abolished by the legislature in 1907; and state-wide prohibition was adopted in 1915. A Tillman-created state supreme court in 1910 decided against him in a contest with his daughter-in-law, a member of the aristocratic Pickens family, for the possession of his two infant grandchildren. In 1912 he was unable to prevent the reëlection of Coleman L. Blease, a Tillman partisan with whom he had quarreled. Tillman is remembered for his constructive achievements, notably Clemson and Winthrop colleges, and the advance of white democracy, but he is also remembered for having overturned honored traditions and for arousing bitter passions. When South Carolinians want to recall a hero from the immediate past, they more often think of Wade Hampton than Ben Tillman.

[See *Who's Who in America*, 1918–19; F. B. Simkins, *The Tillman Movement in S. C.* (1926), which summarizes Tillman's early career; Thornwell Haynes, *Biog. Sketch of Gov. B. R. Tillman of S. C.* (copr. 1894); *Benjamin Ryan Tillman . . . Memorial Addresses . . . in the Senate and House of Representatives* (1919); J. C. Hemphill, ed., *Men of Mark in S. C.*, vol. I (1907); J. B. Knight and August Kohn, in Yates Snowden, *Hist. of S. C.* (1920), vol. V, pp. 101–03, reprinted from *News and Courier* (Charleston), July 4, 1918; files of the *News and Courier*, 1885–1918, and *State* (Columbia, S. C.), 1891–1918; *Independent*, Feb. 27, 1902, p. 527, July 12, 1906, pp. 68–70, Jan. 21, 1909, p. 115; Zach McGhee, in *World's Work*, Sept. 1906; *Current Lit.*, Feb. 1909, pp. 118–21; obituary in *Lit. Digest*, July 27, 1918, pp. 32–36. The Tillman Papers are in the lib. of the Univ. of S. C.]   F. B. S.

TILTON, EDWARD LIPPINCOTT (Oct. 19, 1861–Jan. 5, 1933), architect, born in New York City, was the son of Benjamin White and Mary (Baker) Tilton, and a direct descendant of John Tilton, who emigrated to Lynn, Mass., from England between 1630 and 1640. He was educated in private schools in Mount Vernon and Chappaqua, N. Y. (1870–80), and studied architectural drawing with a private tutor (1879–80). In 1880, after experience in business, first with the firm of R. R. Haydock and later with Corlies, Macy and Company, he entered the offices of the architects McKim, Mead & White. The following year, on their advice, he went to Paris for three years at the École des Beaux Arts. He returned to New York in 1890 and in 1891 formed a partnership with William A. Boring, the firm at first being Boring, Tilton & Mellen, later Boring & Tilton. Long interested in archaeology, in 1895, through William Robert Ware [*q.v.*], Tilton was appointed architect to the group sponsored by the American School of Classical Studies in Athens to excavate the Argive Heræum. Boring and Tilton's first important commission was that for the United States immigrant station on Ellis Island, won by competition and completed in 1900. Largely because of its efficient solution of this complicated problem, the firm was awarded a gold medal at the Paris Exposition of 1900. Other important works of the firm are Tome Institute, Port Deposit,

Md., the Seamen's Institute, New York City, and the Town Hall, East Orange, N. J. After the withdrawal of Boring in 1915 to become director of the Columbia University School of Architecture, Tilton associated himself with Alfred M. Githens, the firm name in 1921 becoming Tilton and Githens.

The public library at Mount Vernon, N. Y., built in 1910, was the first of a long series of buildings with which Tilton's name is especially connected, and the modern public library form (with ground-floor stack space and reading-room above) is in no small measure due to his logical analysis of library problems. His views on control of books and readers, efficiency and directness of service, and open cheerfulness of effect are fully expressed in his "Library Planning" (*Architectural Forum*, Dec. 1927) and "Library Planning and Design" (*Ibid.*, June 1932). During the World War Tilton designed over sixty libraries and over thirty theatres for various army camps and cantonments. Characteristic examples of his work are the public libraries at Somerville and Springfield, Mass., and especially the more recent McGregor Public Library (1925) of Highland Park, Mich., and the Wilmington, Del., library (1930), awarded the Gold Medal of the American Institute of Architects. In the last two the stack and service floor is sunk into the ground in order to secure entrance to the reading-room floor from the street. Both are also characterized by an original handling of classic motives, the wings becoming almost all glass on the sides, with a more solid central entrance. Other important libraries designed by Tilton are the Knight Memorial Library, Providence, R. I., the library of Emory University, Atlanta, Ga., several branch libraries in Washington, D. C., and the library of Girard College, Philadelphia, Pa. In addition, Tilton served as consulting architect to many libraries, and Tilton and Githens were associated with Clyde and Nelson Fritz in the Enoch Pratt Free Library of Baltimore, Md. Notable works of other types include the Central High School, Johnstown, Pa., the Museum of Fine Arts and the Museum of Natural History at Springfield, Mass., and the county administration building for Bergen County, N. J.

Tilton's work is remarkable for its careful study of practical requirements. He was a classicist in taste, inspired in his early work by the Italian Renaissance and in his later work by the work of ancient Greece and Rome, but he was never the copier or the unthinking plagiarist, and in his novel and charming buildings at Highland Park and Wilmington achieved a new synthesis of classic detail and modern needs. He was a man of wide and scholarly interests, and a charming speaker. He was one of the organizers of the Society of Beaux Arts Architects, and for twenty-five years treasurer of the fund for the Paris prize; a member of the Architectural League; a fellow of the American Institute of Architects; a fellow of the Archaeological Institute of America, and its treasurer at the time of his death. In religion he was a Quaker. In addition to his architectural articles he was the author of *The Architecture of the Small Library* (Lansing, Mich., 1911), and "The Architecture of the Argive Heræum" in *The Argive Heræum* (2 vols., 1902–05), by Sir Charles Waldstein and others. He married Mary Eastman Bigelow of Mount Vernon, N. Y., on June 5, 1901, and had a son and a daughter. He died in Scarsdale, N. Y., survived by his wife and his son.

[F. T. Tilton, *Hist. of the Tilton Family in America*, vol. I, no. 1 (1927); *Who's Who in America*, 1932–33; *The Works of Edward Lippincott Tilton* (N. Y., n.d.); I. N. P. Stokes, *The Iconography of Manhattan Island*, vol. V (1926); *Am. Art Ann.*, 1933; obituaries in *N. Y. Times*, Jan. 6, *N. Y. Herald Tribune*, Jan. 7, 1933; information from W. A. Boring and C. E. Tilton.]

T. F. H.

TILTON, JAMES (June 1, 1745–May 14, 1822), army surgeon, was born on a farm in Kent County, Del., at that time a part of Pennsylvania. All records of his parents have been lost, but he is said to have been descended from John Tilton who emigrated to Lynn, Mass., between 1630 and 1640 (Tilton, *post*). His mother, left a widow, sent him to Nottingham Academy at Nottingham, Md. Later after studying with a local physician he entered the newly created medical department of the College of Philadelphia and was given the degree of B.M. with the first class from that school in 1768. His graduation thesis was on respiration. He settled for practice in Dover, Del., but returned to his old school to obtain the degree of M.D. in 1771 with an essay entitled *"De Hydrope."* The outbreak of the Revolutionary War found him a medical practitioner in Dover and a lieutenant of infantry in the local militia. With the organization of the Delaware Regiment in 1776 he was appointed regimental surgeon. He served with the regiment through that year in the battle of Long Island, at White Plains, at Trenton, and until it was virtually wiped out at the battle of Princeton on Jan. 2, 1777. From that time until October 1780 he was in charge of hospitals at Princeton, Trenton, and New Windsor, Md. He wrote scathing reports upon the condition of these hospitals and of the system which made it possible. He devised and later established a hos-

pital group of small well-ventilated log huts, each to accommodate but six patients. A great decrease in hospital mortality followed this innovation. In 1780 he was promoted to senior hospital physician and surgeon, and in this capacity he operated a hospital at Williamsburg, Va., during the Yorktown campaign. With the close of hostilities he returned to his practice at Dover. In the meantime he had been offered and had declined the chair of materia medica in his old medical school, reorganized as the medical department of the University of Pennsylvania in 1779. He served one term (1783–85) in the Continental Congress and several as a member of the state House of Representatives. From 1785 to 1801 he occupied the position of government commissioner of loans for Delaware.

Giving up the active practice of medicine, he bought a farm in the hill country adjoining Wilmington and varied the work of cultivation of his fields by an occasional essay on some agricultural subject. In February 1813, while the country was at war with Britain, he published a small treatise entitled *Economical Observations on Military Hospitals: and the Prevention and Cure of Diseases Incident to an Army*. It was dedicated to Gen. John Armstrong [*q.v.*], secretary of war, and embodied his observations during the Revolutionary War, and repeated his former recommendations regarding the construction and administration of military hospitals. Probably as a result of this book, he was offered the position of physician and surgeon-general of the army, an office created by a reorganization of the staff departments under an act of Mar. 13, 1813. Immediately upon taking office he made a tour of inspection along the northern frontier, where he found such a contempt for all sanitary measures and such direful results as to tax to the utmost his administrative ability. His efforts to remedy these defects and to rehabilitate the medical and hygienic service of the army resulted in the publication of the *Regulations for the Medical Department* issued in general orders of December 1814. This, the most important result of his administration, defined clearly for the first time the duties of medical officers and other sanitary personnel. His office was terminated by an act of Congress of June 1815.

While still in office he developed a malignant tumor of the leg, which materially affected his usefulness to the military service and which resulted in an amputation at the knee in December 1815. Despite his seventy years he withstood the pre-anaesthetic agonies of this operation with stoical fortitude. He passed the remainder of his days in his stone mansion overlooking Wilmington, occupied with the care of his orchard and garden. Physically he was of unusual height and of spare build. He was of a jovial disposition, and though a bachelor he was fond of company. He was exceedingly eccentric in his habits, and in his medical practice was a warm advocate of the use of mercury for practically all acute disease.

[F. T. Tilton, *Hist. of the Tilton Family in America*, vol. I, nos. 1–7 (1928–29); James Thacher, *Am. Medic. Biog.* (1828), vol. II, pp. 129–40; H. E. Brown, *The Medic. Dept. of the U. S. Army* (1873); J. E. Pilcher, *The Surgeon Generals of the Army of the U. S.* (1905), with portrait; F. R. Packard, *Hist. of Medicine in the U. S.* (2 vols., 1931); J. T. Scharf, *Hist. of Del.* (1888), vol. I; Elizabeth Montgomery, *Reminiscences of Wilmington* (1851), pp. 53–57; obituary in *Del. Gazette* (Wilmington), May 17, 1822.]   J. M. P—n.

TILTON, JOHN ROLLIN (June 8, 1828– Mar. 22, 1888), landscape painter, was born at Loudon, N. H., the son of Daniel Tilton. He began his career at a time when there was little opportunity for study and little encouragement for the painter; what knowledge and skill he gained were of his own getting. After a common-school education, he went to Rome in 1852, and lived in Italy for over thirty-five years, traveling again and again to its famous places, visiting the Alps, the Rhine, Spain, Greece and its islands, Egypt, and Switzerland, specializing in pictures of places famous for their historical associations. His studio in the Barberini Palace in Rome was for years a favorite resort for American and English tourists, who were eager to buy pictures of the places they had visited and enjoyed. Many of his landscapes found their way into the collections of the British nobility and gentry. He exhibited "The Palace of Thebes" at the Royal Academy, London, 1873, and his "Lagoons of Venice" and "Komombo" at the Centennial Exhibition, Philadelphia, 1876. He also sent his work to the National Academy, New York, and to the Boston Athenaeum. His "Venetian Fishing Boats" and "Rome from Mount Aventine" belong to the Corcoran Gallery, Washington, D. C. In addition to many medals and honors, he received much extravagant praise on both sides of the Atlantic. The *London Daily News* solemnly announced that he was "the first American painter since Benjamin West to receive special commendation from the President of the Royal Academy" (*The Corcoran Gallery of Art: Catalogue of Paintings*, 1920, p. 90). H. T. Tuckerman found "a ghostly charm" in one of his pictures of the Alps, and went into raptures over some other indifferent performances which he characterized as "most faithfully and artistically rendered," "very attractive,"

"charming," "greatly admired in Rome" (Tuckerman, *post*, p. 558).

Tilton was a prominent example of the American artists who have won fame for themselves by persevering industry. He studied life and nature in many countries, and his paintings of Naples and Venice, of Greece and Egypt were as well known in England and all over Europe as they were in his own country. His wife, Caroline Tilton, published some translations from the Italian. There were two children. Tilton died in Rome. In the winter of 1889, about a year after his death, a sale exhibition of his oil paintings and watercolors was held at the gallery of Leonard & Company, Boston, the collection being composed of two hundred and ninety-six works belonging to his estate; all but thirteen of these were watercolors.

[Tilton's name is given in the records of Loudon, N. H., as John B. Rollins Tilton. For biog. material see H. T. Tuckerman, *Book of the Artists* (1870); J. D. Champlin, Jr., and C. C. Perkins, *Cyc. of Painters and Paintings*, vol. IV (1887); *Atlantic Monthly*, Mar. 1869, Feb. 1881; *Standard* (London), Feb. 5, 1874; *Times* (London), Jan. 8, 1878; *New England Mag.*, Nov. 1895; *Boston Transcript*, Jan. 26, 1889; intro., cat. of sale of Tilton's paintings, Boston, 1889; obituary in *N. Y. Times*, Mar. 24, 1888. Information has been supplied by the registrar of vital statistics and the N. H. Hist. Soc., Concord, N. H.]   W. H. D.

TILTON, THEODORE (Oct. 2, 1835–May 25, 1907), editor, was born in New York City, the son of Silas and Eusebia (Tilton) Tilton. His father kept a store. Both his parents were strict Advent Baptists, and brought the boy up in a religious atmosphere. From the public schools he went to the Free Academy (later the College of the City of New York), where he was a student from 1850 to 1853. He gained some newspaper experience reporting for the *New York Tribune*, and came under the notice and influence of Greeley himself. Ardent, impressionable, devoted to evangelical Christianity, abolition, and other causes, and fluent of speech and pen, he attracted attention both by his tall handsome figure and his impetuous energy. Immediately after leaving school he declined a place on the *New York Herald* because it involved Sunday work, and joined the *New York Observer*, a Presbyterian weekly, instead. One of his regular assignments was to take down in shorthand the sermons of Henry Ward Beecher [*q.v.*]; and on Oct. 2, 1855, he married Elizabeth Richards, a Sunday school teacher of Plymouth Church in Brooklyn, Beecher performing the ceremony. In the following year he quarreled with the *Observer* for its lukewarm attitude toward slavery, and owing in part to the good offices of the Rev. George B. Cheever [*q.v.*], a leader of the religious anti-slavery party in New York, became managing editor of the *Independent,* the Congregationalist journal of Henry C. Bowen [*q.v.*].

In this post he at once made a notable reputation. It is little exaggeration to say that, taking more and more of the control from Bowen and his aide Joshua Leavitt, he temporarily "developed into one of the really great editors of the country" (Hibben, *post,* p. 170). The *Independent* had been distinctly sectarian, its chief contributors clergymen; Tilton made it a journal of broad appeal, numbering Elizabeth Barrett Browning, Whittier, Lowell, Garrison, Seward, and Kossuth among its writers. Losses were converted into profits. He also arranged for the regular publication of Beecher's sermons, thus increasing the preacher's audience and income. The association between the two men became closer than ever. Tilton acted as superintendent of Plymouth Sunday School, and he, Bowen, and Beecher were called "the Trinity of Plymouth Church." When the Civil War fell with ruinous effect on Bowen's mercantile business, Beecher came to his aid late in 1861 by assuming the editorship of the *Independent,* while Tilton remained in his old place. The two used the journal aggressively in the fight for emancipation and a more vigorous prosecution of hostilities; but the arrangement lasted only a year, and when Beecher went to England to plead the Northern cause, Tilton succeeded him as editor-in-chief, holding the place until 1871. He not only kept the *Independent* a successful family magazine but made it an organ of political power, taking a "radical" stand throughout the war and Reconstruction; its circulation increased so remarkably that in 1865 Bowen offered him a partnership. To his house in Livingston Street, Brooklyn, frequently came such famous figures as Greeley, Wendell Phillips, Sumner, Henry Wilson, and Gerrit Smith. Immediately after the close of the war he became one of the most popular figures on the lyceum platform, while he also blossomed out as a writer of musical but unoriginal verse, *The King's Ring* and *The Sexton's Tale, and Other Poems* appearing in 1867. He attracted much attention when he went to Washington to labor for Johnson's impeachment, and when he threw himself into the woman's suffrage cause. His wife for a time edited *Revolution,* a suffragist journal, and both were prominent in the Equal Rights Association. In 1870 he assumed an additional burden in the editorship of the Brooklyn *Union,* also owned by Bowen. He was a national figure.

But this promising career was totally disrupted by the great Beecher scandal. In the summer of 1870 Elizabeth Tilton confessed to her husband intimate relations with the pastor of Plymouth Church. The exact degree of intimacy was disputable, Tilton and his friends being convinced of adultery while Beecher first believed himself accused merely of "making improper solicitations" (*Tilton* vs. *Beecher, post,* III, 50). At first Tilton resolved to shield his wife and keep the matter secret; but unfortunately neither could forget. In a short time several members of the woman's rights group, including Victoria Woodhull [*q.v.*], of whom Tilton had become a blind admirer, knew all about it; so did others in Plymouth Church who did everything in their power to keep the peace and suppress the scandal. Henry Bowen in alarm decided to dismiss Tilton from the *Independent* and the Brooklyn *Union;* he had just described him in a signed article in the *Independent* as "bold, uncompromising, a master among men" (Dec. 22, 1870), but now declared him guilty of moral lapses and unsafe in judgment (Hibben, *post,* p. 248). Beecher acquiesced in this proceeding while asking through an intermediary for Tilton's forgiveness and writing: "I humble myself before him as I do before my God" (*Ibid.,* p. 257). Tilton's friend Frank Moulton came to the rescue by enabling him to start a new magazine, the *Golden Age,* but it proved weak. In April 1872 he sued Bowen for breach of contract. Meanwhile, his charge against Beecher, though not openly pressed, was the subject of smouldering gossip.

Full publicity was ultimately inevitable. On Nov. 2, 1872, *Woodhull and Claflin's Weekly* printed the charges in full. Beecher, unable longer to maintain a dignified silence and forced to try to clear his name, appointed a committee of members and stockholders of Plymouth Church to investigate. It completely exonerated him, as later did a group of Congregational ministers. Under Frank Moulton's restraining hand Tilton had played a longsuffering rôle, trying to shield Beecher while assailed by Beecher's friends; but now his patience was exhausted. On July 20, 1874, he appeared before Plymouth Church and formally lodged a charge of adultery against Beecher. In this crisis the distracted Elizabeth Tilton decided to leave her husband and children and stand by her pastor. Tilton, deserted by his emotional wife, condemned by thousands of Beecher's admirers as a slanderer, charged by Beecher himself with blackmail, found his position desperate. The result was his suit against Beecher for criminal conversation, with damages of $100,000 demanded. Hearings began Jan. 11, 1875, in Brooklyn City Court, lasted 112 trial days, and resulted in a hung jury and a division of public opinion that still persists.

The case left Tilton completely ruined in fortune and reputation. He had sold his share of the *Golden Age* in 1874, and lived by writing and lecturing. In 1883 he left the country never to return, traveling in England and Germany and finally settling in Paris. Books and articles brought him small sums, and he long lived on a pittance on the Île St. Louis, writing poetry and playing chess at the Café de la Regence. Though four years after the trial his wife recanted and declared her husband's charges true (*New York Times,* Apr. 16, 1878), he was never reconciled with her. Among his later books were a wildly improbable romance, *Tempest Tossed* (1874); ballads called *Swabian Stories* (1882); *Great Tom, or the Curfew Bell of Oxford* (1885); *Heart's Ease* (1894); and *Sonnets to the Memory of Frederick Douglass* (1895). Tilton's death in Paris resulted from pneumonia; four children lived to maturity.

[Paxton Hibben, *Henry Ward Beecher: An Am. Portrait* (1927); Lyman Abbott and S. B. Halliday, *Life of Henry Ward Beecher* (1887); Emanie Sachs, *The Terrible Siren* (1929); *Theodore Tilton vs. Henry Ward Beecher* (1874); *The Great Brooklyn Romance; All the Documents in the Famous Beecher-Tilton Case, Unabridged* (1874); L. P. Brockett, *Men of Our Day* (1868); *Evening Post* (N. Y.), May 25, 1907; *N. Y. Tribune* and *N. Y. Herald,* May 26, 1907; J. E. Stillwell, *Hist. and Geneal. Miscellany,* vol. V (1932).]

A. N.

TILYOU, GEORGE CORNELIUS (Feb. 3, 1862–Nov. 30, 1914), amusement park owner and inventor, son of Peter Augustus and Ellen (Mahoney) Tilyou, was born in New York City. His father, a descendant of a pioneer Huguenot family of New York, was a hotel proprietor at Coney Island, the neighboring seaside amusement resort, and thither the family removed when George was three years old. The boy received a part of a common-school education. At fourteen his business career may be said to have begun. That was in 1876, when many inland American visitors to the Centennial Exhibition at Philadelphia went on to New York and down to Coney Island, just for a look at the Atlantic Ocean. George Tilyou set up a stand near his father's hotel, and as souvenirs of their ocean visit sold to these inlanders little boxes of sifted beach sand and bottles of sea water. In the course of one busy excursion day he earned enough money to enable him to enjoy a trip to the Centennial. At seventeen, with a capital of $2.50 invested in business cards, he began a successful career as a Coney Island real-estate operator. He laid out the Island's famous Bowery, a carnival amusement street barred to wheeled vehicles, and built Tilyou's Surf Theatre, the first show-house of importance at the resort. In 1897 he founded his famous Steeplechase Park, which expanded until it covered nearly twenty acres. Twice it was wrecked by fire, and each time restored on a greater and more gorgeous scale.

Tilyou originated most of the fun-making devices used in his amusement enterprises, their various objects being to give the patron nervous thrills as he was whirled or tumbled about, shot down steep slopes, and made to undergo weird experiences in dark chambers, or to subject him unexpectedly to the laughter of others and then give him his turn to laugh at those who followed him. Among the devices which Tilyou patented, built, or perfected were the Human Roulette Wheel, the Human Pool Table, the Bounding Billows, the Earthquake Floor, the Blow Hole, the Eccentric Fountain, the Razzle Dazzle, the Third Degree Regions, the Electric Seat, the Hoodoo Room, the California Bats, the Funny Stairway, the Barrel of Love, the Aerial Thrill, and others. He believed in and always purveyed clean amusements. He became a reformer in politics and was instrumental in the overthrow of John Y. McKane, the notorious political boss under whose rule Coney Island had taken on a distinctly rowdy tone. During this reform movement Tilyou was elected a justice of the peace. In addition to his Coney Island park, he operated at one time or another similar large concessions at Atlantic City, Asbury Park, N. J., Rockaway Beach, N. Y., Revere Beach, Mass., Bridgeport, Conn., St. Louis, and San Francisco, several of these being likewise christened Steeplechase Park. He married Mary Elizabeth O'Donnell of New York in 1893, and she, with three sons (who continued his great amusement business) and two daughters, survived him.

[H. I. Hazelton, *The Boroughs of Brooklyn and Queens, Counties of Nassau and Suffolk, Long Island, N. Y.* (1925), vol. II; *Hist. of Coney Island, List and Photographs of Main Attractions* (1904); *Brooklyn Daily Eagle, Brooklyn Times, World* (N. Y.), *N. Y. Times, N. Y. Herald, N. Y. Tribune, Sun* (N. Y.), and *Coney Island Times,* Nov. 30, 1914; files of the last-named paper.]

A. F. H.

TIMBERLAKE, HENRY (1730–Sept. 30, 1765), soldier, was born in Hanover County, Va., the son of Francis and Sarah (Austin) Timberlake, and the grandson of Joseph Timberlake who emigrated from England to Virginia. After receiving a fairly adequate education, he joined the Patriot Blues for the campaign of 1756 against the French and Indians under George Washington. In 1758 he was appointed to a cornetcy of horse in the regiment of William Byrd III and was in the John Forbes campaign against the French at Fort Duquesne.

Timberlake

He served in 1759 under John Stanwix, who placed him in command of Fort Burd, or Fort Necessity, in Pennsylvania. In the spring of 1761 he was ordered to join the regiment of Colonel Byrd against the Cherokee, then besieging the British Fort Loudoun on Little Tennessee River, and he marched with Adam Stephen to the Holston River. After the peace of Nov. 19, 1761, the Cherokee requested that an officer visit them, and Timberlake, then an ensign, volunteered for this mission, to be accompanied by Thomas Sumter [q.v.]. The twenty-two-day journey to the Indian towns was made by skiff down the Holston and up the Little Tennessee. Timberlake made notes of the courses of these rivers and executed an excellent map of the streams, showing, also, the locations of the towns of the Overhill Cherokee.

After three months with the Cherokee, they returned to Virginia, where they were placed in charge of Outacity [q.v.] and two of his warriors to make a visit to England. In London the Indians drew large crowds to see them, the aristocracy included. Entertained sumptuously at Vauxhall Gardens and other leading resorts, the Cherokee and the two young Virginians were admitted to audience by the King. Timberlake is said to have received a lieutenant's commission as a reward for his services. He married in London and returned to Virginia. In 1764 he conducted overseas a second group of Cherokee warriors. Falling into financial difficulties, he sought to recoup by writing and publishing the *Memoirs of Lieut. Henry Timberlake,* which was published in London in 1765. There he recorded his experiences in the French and Indian War and his observations of the customs and ceremonies of the Cherokee. The book ever since its appearance has been considered by ethnologists as dependable source material. A German translation appeared in J. T. Köhler's *Sammlung neuer Reise-Beschreibungen,* vol. I, pt. 2 (1769), and a French translation by J. B. L. J. Billecocq was published in Paris *Voyages du lieutenant Henri Timberlake* (1796); the poet Robert Southey drew largely from the book in the preparation of his epic, *Madoc* (1805). Timberlake died in London, seemingly before his book came from the press, certainly before he could have profited from its sale.

[*Lieut. Henry Timberlake's Memoirs* (1927), ed. by S. C. Williams, with bibliog. references; bibliog. in sketch of Outacity for London visit of 1762; "The Official Records of Robert Dinwiddie," *Va. Hist. Colls.,* n.s., vol. IV (1884); *Annual Register ... 1765* (1766), pp. 65–66; *Gentleman's Mag.,* Oct. 1765, p. 491; information from Wade H. Fleischer, Northport, N. Y.]
S. C. W.

Timby

TIMBY, THEODORE RUGGLES (Apr. 5, 1822–Nov. 9, 1909), inventor, was born in Dutchess County, N. Y., the son of George W. and Sarah (Johnson) Timby, formerly of Pittsfield, Mass. He grew up on his father's farm, attending the local common schools. During his teens he is said to have invented a form of floating dry dock. As early as 1841 he exhibited at the War Department, Washington, a model and plans for a revolving battery for coast defense, suggested to him by the circular form of Castle William on Governors Island in New York Harbor. He seems also to have conceived of a similar structure for ships of low freeboard. On Jan. 18, 1843, he filed a *caveat* covering the invention of the revolving turret for use on land or water. It appears that in the spring of the same year he sent a model to China by Caleb Cushing [q.v.], the United States minister, and in June exhibited a model to President Tyler and his cabinet. During the fifties he urged the revolving battery on Emperor Napoleon III, but the idea seems nowhere to have received effective recognition until, in 1861–62, it was utilized by John Ericsson [q.v.] as a distinctive feature of his first Monitor. After the *Monitor* had proved successful, Timby, then a resident of Worcester, Mass., was granted two patents on July 8, 1862 (No. 35,846 and No. 35,847), for a revolving battery tower and a revolving tower discharging guns by electricity. In September he received another patent for a revolving battery tower. Ericsson's associates in the business of building Monitors for the government acquired these patents almost at once and thus quieted all claims of infringement. In later years a controversy followed as to credit for the idea of the revolving turret or battery tower, Ericsson arguing that the idea of a revolving fort long antedated the nineteenth century and thus was one of the concepts of military engineering which belonged as common property to the engineering practice of the time, while supporters of Timby pointed to his early *caveat* as proof that credit should go to him. It seems clear that the honor of first publicly urging this form of gun housing on governmental authorities belongs to Timby, while the honor of first using the idea in actual construction belongs to Ericsson, who may or may not have known of Timby's design. In 1857 and 1862 Timby received patents for a barometer; in 1869 he patented a turbine water wheel, and in 1871, a gun carriage; he also devised a process of printing terrestrial globes in colors and a process for quickly ripening coffee. His inventions seem to have brought little financial return, however, and his family was supported in

554

part by the friends who memorialized Congress and the New York legislature in his behalf. During his later years, as a resident of Brooklyn, N. Y., he occupied himself with literary avocations, publishing several small volumes of poems and essays, including *Bridging the Skies* (1883), *Beyond* (1886), *Stellar Worlds and Other Didactic Literature* (1896); *Lighted Lore for Gentle Folk* (1902). In 1844 he married Charlotte M. Ware. He died in Brooklyn.

[*N. Y. Herald,* June 7, 1843; *N. Y. Weekly Evening Post,* June 7, 1843: "The Revolving Tower and Its Inventor," *Harper's New Monthly Mag.,* Jan. 1863; James Parton, *People's Book of Biog.* (1868); W. C. Church, *The Life of John Ericsson* (1890), vol. II; *Famous Am. Men and Women* (1895), ed. by Stanley Waterloo and J. W. Hanson, Jr.; F. M. Bennett, *The Monitor and the Navy under Steam* (1900); Alfred King, "Theodore R. Timby," *Successful American,* Jan. 1902; *Am. Shipbuilder,* Oct. 23, 1902; *Memorial of the Patriotic League of the Revolution to the Fifty-Seventh Cong.* (1902); *Who's Who in America,* 1908–09; Helen Woods, "Timby the Forgotten," *Harper's Weekly,* Feb. 11, 1911; *What Authorities Say about Timby and the Revolving Turret* (1912); *Brooklyn Daily Eagle,* Nov. 10, 1909.]   W. F. D.

TIMKEN, HENRY (Aug. 16, 1831–Mar. 16, 1909), inventor, manufacturer, son of Jacob Timken, a prosperous German farmer, was born near Bremen, Germany. He was one of seven children, and three years after the death of his mother, when he was seven years old, his father emigrated to the United States and settled in St. Louis, Mo. A year later he bought a tract of farm land near Sedalia, Mo., and there young Timken grew up, doing his share of the farm work and attending the country school. He disliked farming, however, and when he was sixteen years old he went to St. Louis and apprenticed himself to one of the leading carriage and wagon manufacturers.

Upon completing his apprenticeship he worked as a journeyman wagon maker for a while and in 1855 established his own carriage factory in St. Louis. That same year he married Fredericka Heinzelmann. His business was successful and within a year or two, in partnership with his father-in-law, he established a branch factory at Belleville, Ill. In 1860, however, afflicted with the gold fever, Timken deliberately gave up his business and went to Pikes Peak to seek his fortune. Six months' prospecting convinced him that carriage manufacturing was more profitable, and returning to St. Louis, he engaged again in that enterprise. Its fortunes were considerably affected during the Civil War by Timken's military services in the home guard, and in the 13th Regiment of the Missouri Militia, in which for three years he was a captain. In 1864, moreover, his plant was destroyed by fire. This he rebuilt after the war and operated it success-

fully until 1887, when he retired and established his home at San Diego, Cal. Seven years later, however, he reëntered the carriage-making business in St. Louis and erected there a model factory, which he conducted in association with his two sons until 1897. He then retired again to his home in California and lived there until his death.

Timken possessed a bent for invention and secured during his life thirteen patents, all but two of which pertained to carriage or wagon improvements. On Nov. 27, 1877, he was granted Patent No. 197,689 for a carriage spring which he introduced to the carriage trade through his own vehicles in 1878. This "Timken Spring" was an immediate success and carried his name and fame over all the world. Demands for it became so great that his carriage plant gradually became a spring-manufacturing plant and yielded him a handsome fortune. The two patents which were not for carriage or wagon improvements were issued June 28, 1898, and were for a tapered roller bearing, which has come into very wide use in recent years and has also done much to make his name widely known. For the production of this product he organized the Timken Roller Bearing Axle Company, with himself as president, and erected a plant at Canton, Ohio, but left the active management to his two sons. During 1896 and 1897 he was president of the Carriage Builders' National Association, at that time the largest and oldest trade association in the country. Besides his manufacturing interests he was the owner of extensive agricultural lands in Kansas and citrus groves in California. His greatest pleasures in his later years were derived from these interests and from travel. He died at the age of seventy-eight years in San Diego and was survived by five children.

[William Hyde and H. L. Conard, *Encyc. of the Hist. of St. Louis* (1899), vol. IV; *Carriage Monthly,* Oct. 1895, Apr. 1909; *Los Angeles Daily Times,* Mar. 17, 1909; Patent Office records.]   C. W. M—n.

TIMM, HENRY CHRISTIAN (July 11, 1811–Sept. 5, 1892), musician, conductor, was born in Hamburg, Germany. He received his musical education from Albert Gottlieb Methfessel (known principally as a composer of partsongs for men's voices), and Jacob Schmitt, and made his début abroad in 1828. In 1835 he emigrated to New York and immediately became active in the city's musical life. He made his first American appearance in a concert at the Park Theatre, and at once gained popular favor. His next venture was an unsuccessful concert tour of New England, after which he returned to New York and became second horn player at the Park Theatre. Later he went South for six months as conductor of a traveling opera troupe. He remained in Baltimore for a time, where he had a position as church organist and gave some concerts with Signora Velané and the baritone, Giuseppe De Begnis. Upon his return to New York, he became trombone player and chorus master of Charles Edward Horn's opera company, which was about to open the National Opera House with *The Pilgrim of Love*. The theatre burned a few months later and Timm secured a position as organist of St. Thomas's Church. Later he became organist at All Souls', where he played for almost eighteen years. He was one of the early members of the Philharmonic Society of New York (founded in 1842), assistant director in its third and fourth seasons, vice-president in its fifth, and president from 1848 to 1863 (seventh to twenty-first seasons inclusive). He died in Hoboken, N. J.

Timm often appeared as piano soloist with the Philharmonic. The New York correspondent of *Dwight's Journal of Music* called him "the most elegant of our pianists" (May 1, 1852), and on another occasion (Nov. 20, 1852) he wrote: "How finely that gentleman plays you need not be told. The deeply melancholy character of the music (Hummel's piano concerto in B minor) was admirably conveyed in the performance of both pianist and orchestra, and was doubly effective from its contrast to the Symphony" (Beethoven's 8th). The same magazine was less flattering in another account: "Later in the evening he (William Scharfenberg) and Mr. Timm played a Grand Duo of Mendelssohn's. . . . It was effective but not striking." William Mason, the pianist, perpetuated the tradition that Timm had such a perfect technique that he could play scales with a full wine glass on the back of each hand without spilling a drop (*Memories of a Musical Life*, 1901, p. 58). As a composer, Timm wrote a Grand Mass for soli, chorus, orchestra, and organ; a number of part-songs; and transcriptions for two pianos of classical works. As an editor, he prepared several editions of works from the standard repertoire.

[In addition to the contemporary sources cited above, see H. E. Krehbiel, *The Philharmonic Soc. of N. Y.* (1892); J. T. Howard, *Our Am. Music* (1931); Theodore Baker, *A Biog. Dict. of Musicians* (1900); *Musical America*, Feb. 24, 1917; F. L. Ritter, *Music in America* (1883); *N. Y. Tribune*, Sept. 6, 8, 1892.]

J. T. H.

TIMON, JOHN (Feb. 12, 1797–Apr. 16, 1867), Roman Catholic prelate, the second of ten children of James and Margaret (Leddy) Timon, immigrants from County Cavan, was born in Conewago, Pa. In 1802 the Timons removed to Baltimore, where the father, who had served apprenticeship to a draper, carried on a successful dry-goods business. Later, they went to Louisville (1818) and finally to frontier St. Louis (1819), where they prospered until the hard year of 1823. John completed his theological studies in the Lazarist seminary at The Barrens. He accompanied John Mary Odin [*q.v.*] of the seminary on missionary circuits through Missouri and into the Indian country, and an intense lifelong friendship between the two resulted. Ordained in June 1825 by Bishop Joseph Rosati [*q.v.*] of St. Louis as a priest of the Congregation of the Mission (Vincentians or Lazarists), he continued in the seminary as a teacher until assigned to the missions of the Southwest with the log church at Cape Girardeau, Mo., as a center. Though a retiring, sensitive little man, hardly five feet in height, his zeal for souls enabled him to brave bigoted hostility and dangerous journeys on horseback over the wild country even into Texas.

Appointed visitor general of the Vincentians in 1835, he handled the community's business, effected a compromise in its conflict with Rosati over properties, built a permanent foundation at Cape Girardeau, refused Archbishop Eccleston's offer of Mount St. Mary's College at Emmitsburg, Md., and visited Europe in 1837 to secure missionaries, one of whom was Michael Domenec, later bishop of Pittsburgh. Refusing an appointment as coadjutor bishop of St. Louis, Timon accepted the more arduous position of prefect-apostolic of Texas with Odin as his vice-prefect. Letters of Cardinal Fransoni, which he transmitted to Acting President David G. Burnet [*q.v.*] were regarded as a papal recognition of Texan independence. Within the space of a few years, he made visitations in Texas and Indiana, journeyed through the Colorado region, represented his community in ecclesiastical councils, aided in founding the first conference of the Society of St. Vincent de Paul in St. Louis (1844), and revised the rules of the Lorentine Sisters. Few priests in the Mississippi Valley were as well known, and in 1847 Pius IX selected him for the new diocese of Buffalo, concerning the creation of which he was quite ignorant. Consecrated in New York on Oct. 17 by Bishop Hughes who regarded him as the humblest man he had ever known but rather lacking in force, Timon lost no time in undertaking his new burdens.

His most annoying problem was removed when the rebellious trustees of St. Peter's Church succumbed before an interdict. A prelate who would give his clothes to beggars and carry destitute babies to orphanages was naturally a founder of eleemosynary institutions. Among those he established were three orphanages, including one for German children; a hospital under the Sisters of Charity; Providence Lunatic Asylum; a home for mutes; a Magdalen asylum; and the first American Catholic institution for unmarried mothers. With more vigor than success, he urged the right of inmates of county institutions to have the service of a priest and to be freed from attendance at Protestant exercises (see *Buffalo Daily Republic,* June 5, 1858). As an educator, he established Niagara Seminary under the Lazarists (1848) and St. Joseph's College in Buffalo (1849), which was unsuccessful until assigned to the Christian Brothers (1861); aided the Franciscans at Allegany; and promoted the American College in Rome. Despite Know-Nothing threats, he dedicated his Cathedral of St. Joseph in 1855, for which he made collections in Europe and in Mexico. During the Civil War he was an ardent militarist who favored waging the war with sufficient energy to enforce an early peace and who took active steps to end the local draft riots (see *United States Catholic Historical Society, Historical Records and Studies,* vol. I, 1900, pp. 189–90). In 1862 he published *Missions in Western New York and Church History of the Diocese of Buffalo.*

Timon attracted non-Catholic attention by his unostentatious piety, charity, and civic interest. His self-sacrificing spirit was apparent in his death from erysipelas contracted during a visit to the hospital. Bishop Francis P. Kenrick [*q.v.*] preferred him for the see of Baltimore and when he himself was translated to Baltimore urged Timon for Philadelphia. He exerted a marked influence in Rome as a papal prelate and as an invited guest on various occasions.

[C. G. Deuther, *The Life and Times of Rt. Rev. John Timon* (1870); R. H. Clarke, *Lives of the Deceased Bishops of the Catholic Church in the U. S.,* vol. II (1888); *Cath. Encyc.*; J. E. Rothensteiner, *Hist. of the Archdiocese of St. Louis* (1923); F. E. Tourscher, *The Kenrick-Frenaye Correspondence* (1920); files of *Western New York Catholic,* especially Apr. 1867; *N. Y. Freeman's Jour.,* Apr. 27, 1867; *Catholic World,* Apr. 1871; *Buffalo Commercial Advertiser,* Apr. 17, 1867.]
R. J. P.

TIMOTHY, LEWIS (d. December 1738), printer, was the son of a French Protestant who had taken refuge in Holland at the revocation of the Edict of Nantes. In Holland he learned the printing craft and married Elizabeth ———. He arrived in America in September 1731 with his wife and four children (*Pennsylvania Archives,* 2 ser., vol. XVII, 1890, pp. 29, 31, 32),

and by October had settled in Philadelphia, advertising himself in the *Pennsylvania Gazette* of October 14, 1731, as "Mr. Louis Timothée, Master of the French Tongue." In June 1732 he was connected in an editorial capacity with Benjamin Franklin's *Philadelphische Zeitung,* the first German-language newspaper in America. In November 1732, some time after the demise of the very short-lived *Zeitung,* he became librarian of the Philadelphia Library Society. In 1733 he was working for Franklin as a journeyman printer. On Nov. 26, 1733, there was effected a partnership agreement between Franklin and Timothée whereby the latter was to conduct a printing business at Charlestown, S. C., as successor to Thomas Whitmarsh, Franklin's former partner in Charlestown, who had died the preceding September. On Feb. 2, 1734, Timothée revived the *South-Carolina Gazette,* which had ceased publication on the death of Whitmarsh. In April 1734 the printer anglicized the spelling of his name to Lewis Timothy.

Timothy was the printer of the most ambitious and important production of the colonial press of South Carolina, the two-volume collection of *The Laws of the Province of South-Carolina* (1736), compiled by Nicholas Trott, LL.D. The printing of this work, of about eight hundred pages, was Timothy's principal occupation from December 1734 until early in 1737 (see McMurtrie, "The First Decade," *post,* p. 442, for a discussion of the date). In its production the printer was generously subsidized by the provincial government. In addition to the monumental *Laws,* Timothy has left record of only some eighteen pieces of printing, other than the issues of his newspaper, for the five years of his activity at Charlestown; of these printed works, only eight are now known from surviving copies. They include legislative acts, tracts on the smallpox, an almanac, a sermon, an essay on currency, and *A Collection of Psalms and Hymns* (1737), the earliest Wesley collection (McMurtrie, "A Bibliography of South Carolina Imprints," *post*).

Timothy died in December 1738 and was buried on the thirtieth of that month (A. S. Salley, Jr., *Register of St. Philip's Parish, Charles Town, S. C., 1720–1758,* 1904, p. 174). He was survived by his widow, Elizabeth Timothy, and six children, of whom one, his son Peter, became his active successor in the printing business. Benjamin Franklin, in his *Autobiography,* said of Lewis Timothy and his wife: "He was a man of learning, and honest but ignorant in matters of account; and, tho' he sometimes made me remittances, I could get no account from him, nor any satisfactory state of our partnership while he lived. On his decease, the business was continued by his widow, who, being born and bred in Holland, where, as I have been inform'd, the knowledge of accounts makes a part of female education, she not only sent me as clear a state as she could find of the transactions past, but continued to account with the greatest regularity and exactness every quarter afterwards, and managed the business with such success, that she not only brought up reputably a family of children, but, at the expiration of the term, was able to purchase of me the printing-house, and establish her son in it" (Smyth, *post,* vol. I, pp. 344–45).

When Lewis Timothy died, just five years of the six-year partnership agreement with Benjamin Franklin had expired. "At the expiration of the term," Peter Timothy became the owner of the business and so continued, with some interruptions, until 1781. In that year he was taken prisoner by the British to St. Augustine and was drowned at sea. In addition to his printing, he was active in public affairs, especially during the Revolutionary War. His widow, Ann Timothy, continued the printing business until her death in September 1792, and was succeeded then by her son, the happily named Benjamin Franklin Timothy, with whom the Timothy dynasty of printers seems to have ended.

[In addition to Benjamin Franklin's account of Timothy, A. H. Smyth, ed., *The Writings of Benjamin Franklin,* vol. I (1905), pp. 345 ff., see *Pa. Mag. of Hist. and Biog.,* Jan. 30, 1906, pp. 104–06, which contains the partnership agreement between Franklin and Timothy; D. C. McMurtrie, "The First Decade of Printing in the Royal Province of S. C.," *Trans. Bibliog. Soc.* (London), 2 ser., vol. XIII (1933), and "A Bibliog. of S. C. Imprints, 1731–1740," *S. C. Hist. and Geneal. Mag.,* vol. XXXIV (1933), nos. 11–30; Isaiah Thomas, *The Hist. of Printing in America* (2nd ed., 1874), vol. I, p. 342, vol. II, p. 170; and A. H. Hirsch, *The Huguenots of Colonial S. C.* (1928), pp. 239–42.]

D. C. M.

TIMROD, HENRY (Dec. 8, 1828–Oct. 6, 1867), poet, was born in Charleston, S. C., of racially varied, middle-class stock. His paternal grandfather, Heinrich Dimroth, emigrated to Charleston from Germany in 1765, and, after amassing property as a merchant tailor, set up as a planter. His third wife was his Scotch-Irish housekeeper, Susannah Hargan; their son, William Henry, a bookbinder of uncommon character and intellect who achieved local recognition through his literary abilities, died in 1838 as a consequence of his services in the Seminole War, leaving his family in straitened circumstances. From him Henry Timrod inherited poetic temperament and a vein of impracticality; from his English-Swiss mother, Thyrza Prince, to whom "a walk in the woods . . . was food and drink, and the sight of a green field was joy inexpressible,"

the sensitive city-born child derived his deeply seated love of nature. A normally active boy, despite his slightness and his bookish inclinations, he was educated in the Charleston schools, where began his life-long intimacy with Paul Hamilton Hayne [*q.v.*]; although modest, diffident, and slow of speech, he proved ambitious and quick to learn. At eighteen he entered Franklin College (later the University of Georgia), in Athens, where he applied himself diligently to belles-lettres and the classics, in his leisure hours composing verses to the face of "every pretty girl" whom he met. Temporary ill-health and chronic want of means forced his withdrawal after two years, and, returning to Charleston, he began to read law in the office of James L. Petigru [*q.v.*]. He was not long, however, in realizing how unsuited he was to the law; abandoning it, he renewed his classical studies in order to qualify as a college professor. When no professorship offered, he taught school for a term at Bluffton, subsequently accepting employment as tutor on a Carolina plantation.

For a decade and more the shy and abstracted young poet lived in this cloistered fashion, faithfully if none too effectually instructing his charges, yet finding opportunity to feed "his muse with English song," to commune with nature, or to write verses for the *Southern Literary Messenger* and other periodicals. During his holidays he hastened to Charleston to fraternize —sometimes too convivially—with the little group of litterateurs who clustered about William Gilmore Simms [*q.v.*], joining with them in 1857 to launch the short-lived but valuable *Russell's Magazine,* to which he contributed numerous poems and occasional prose articles. In 1860 Ticknor & Fields published a small collection of his poems, but although favorably received by discriminating readers, North and South, the volume was speedily obscured by the stress of events. Timrod's disappointment was soon engulfed by his tremendous emotion at the approach of hostilities between the sections, a feeling foreshadowed in his memorable nature lyrics, "Spring" and "The Cotton-Boll." In February 1861 he wrote his elaborate and impressive ode, "Ethnogenesis"; he followed this with a series of impassioned and fervent war poems which strongly stirred the South and focussed attention upon him as "the laureate of the Confederacy." From the beginning he had been an artist, self-controlled, careful of form, studious of the exact word, the felicitous phrase; now that he had something other than mid-century commonplaces to say, his powers ripened. "A Cry to Arms," "Carolina," "Carmen Triumphale," "Charleston," and others not only proved popularly effective, but struck a firmer and stronger note than had appeared in his earlier work.

During the first year of the war he remained in Charleston, his health rendering him unfit for military service. On Mar. 1, 1862, he enlisted in Company B, 30th South Carolina Regiment, and was detailed as a clerk at regimental headquarters. After Shiloh he joined the Confederate Army of the West as correspondent of the *Charleston Mercury,* but neither his constitution nor his temperament was adapted to camp life, and he was compelled to withdraw; in December he was discharged from the Confederate service as suffering from incipient tuberculosis. On top of this, the project of certain Charleston admirers late in 1862 of bringing out in England an elaborate illustrated edition of his poems was allowed to lapse, to the "unspeakable disappointment" of Timrod, who saw fame and competence once more elude him. For a brief period, however, the tragedy that was never distant from him lagged behind. In January 1864 he moved to Columbia to become part proprietor and associate editor of the *South Carolinian;* married a month later (Feb. 16, 1864) Kate Goodwin, the English "Katie" of his pleasing and distinctive love lyric, whose brother had married Timrod's sister Emily; and found his happiness brought to a climax by the birth of a son on Christmas Eve. Then, just a year and a day after his marriage, Columbia was burned, and Timrod, his livelihood destroyed, was reduced to abject poverty. Ill, unworldly, inadequately equipped to support even his own small family, he saw added to this household his mother, his widowed sister and her four children. In October died his son, Willie, his "single rose-bud in a crown of thorns," plunging the poet into a grief from which he never recovered. His health began to fail rapidly, accelerated by the lack of medicines and proper food. Not until December did he obtain employment, on a newspaper; at the end of four months he had received nothing for his editorial labors. He sought vainly to establish a girls' school in Columbia; his efforts to market poems in the North were equally abortive. Writing to Hayne in March 1866 he summed up his story for the preceding year as "beggary, starvation, death, bitter grief, utter want of hope" (Hayne, *post,* p. 45). Only through the gradual sale of their belongings and the generosity of similarly impoverished neighbors could his household find sustenance, yet there is no querulousness, no morbidity in his letters: "We have eaten two silver pitchers," he continues, "one or two dozen silver forks, several sofas, innumerable chairs,

and a huge—bedstead!" Small wonder that the desperate poet should exclaim of his verse that he "would consign every line of it to eternal oblivion, for—*one hundred dollars in hand!*" An exhausting clerkship in the governor's office lasted merely a few weeks; an invitation to visit a Northern publisher had to be declined for lack of railroad fare. His visit, in April, to Hayne's home in the Georgia pine barrens served as a welcome anodyne, but was followed shortly by a painful and dangerous operation; while still suffering from its effects he completed his exquisite Magnolia Cemetery "Ode," perhaps the most perfect and enduring of his compositions. In August he visited Hayne again; hemorrhages commenced soon after his return to Columbia; a month later he died. For ten years his grave remained unmarked, although efforts of Hayne, Simms, and other faithful friends to perpetuate his fame eventually bore fruit. In 1873 Hayne (even before collecting his own verses) edited *The Poems of Henry Timrod,* prefacing them with a sympathetic memoir; in 1884 appeared an illustrated edition of "Katie"; and in 1899 the activities of the Timrod Memorial Association (founded 1898) in promoting the standard "Memorial Edition" effected a mild but fairly widespread revival of interest in the man and his work.

Both the restricted range and the small body of his product place Timrod definitely among the lesser gods of song. Yet he was the most representative and, barring Sidney Lanier [*q.v.*], the ablest Southern poet of his century. He knew better than most of his contemporaries what poetry was, just as he surpassed most of them in taste and sheer lyrical power; and, a masterly artificer, he devoted time and patience to the polishing of his measures. His style is regularly crystal-clear, chastened, natural, extraordinarily quotable; if the thought lacks profundity, it is straightforward and sane, showing a "genial breadth" rather than provincialism—even his most fiery war songs soften at the end into a prayer for peace. His address at Columbia, 1863, for the benefit of the Soldiers' Hospital reveals his conviction that the sources of poetry could not be reduced to the element of beauty alone, but that to this must be added power and truth ("A Theory of Poetry," *Independent,* Mar. 28, Apr. 4, 11, 1901; *Atlantic Monthly,* Sept. 1905); there are other aspects of his theory in his essay, "The Character and Scope of the Sonnet" (*Outlook,* July 23, 1904), although his own attempts at this form, while often extravagantly praised, are for the most part mediocre and well below his best work. Vicissitudes of fortune hampered his genius and occasionally affected his writing;

at times he followed too closely in the footsteps of Wordsworth or Tennyson; otherwiles the conventionalities of the plantation tradition led him into oversweetness or a too pronounced didacticism. In the handful of singularly beautiful pieces, however, in which he succeeded in turning "life's tasteless waters into wine" and by which he will be remembered and measured, he made a valuable and permanent contribution to American literature. His ideals, his intense imagination and playful fancy, his spirituality, his wholesomeness, his unmistakable sincerity, even his sentiment, were characteristic of the finer qualities of his section, as was his own high-minded and heroic nature. It was one of the ironies of American literature that so gentle and childlike a spirit should have been the outstanding poet of the Confederacy; it was more than ironic that his output should have been so reduced by tragic circumstance and premature death.

[Timrod's name was entered in his father's day books as Henry H. See G. A. Cardwell, Jr., "The Date of Henry Timrod's Birth," *Am. Lit.*, May 1935; Paul H. Hayne, in *The Poems of Henry Timrod* (1873); H. T. Thompson, *Henry Timrod, Laureate of the Confederacy* (1928), with bibliog.; G. A. Wauchope, *Henry Timrod: Man and Poet* (1915); H. E. Shepherd and A. S. Salley, in *Southern Hist. Asso. Pubs.*, Oct. 1899; W. P. Trent, *William Gilmore Simms* (1892); obituary in *Charleston Daily Courier*, Oct. 9, 1867.]

A. C. G., Jr.

TINCKER, MARY AGNES (July 18, 1831–Nov. 27, 1907), novelist, was born at Ellsworth, Me., the daughter of Richard and Mehitabel (Jellison) Tincker. Educated in the public schools of Ellsworth and at Bluehill Academy, Bluehill, Me., she began teaching at the age of thirteen in the public schools of Ellsworth; later she taught in a Roman Catholic parochial school. At fifteen she began writing and contributed sketches, anonymously, to local newspapers and to magazines. At twenty she embraced the Catholic faith, an action which was profoundly to influence all her later work. She became a volunteer nurse in 1863 and worked in military hospitals in Washington for a short time. Returning to Boston, she began again her anonymous contributions to periodicals, mainly *Harper's Magazine* and *Putnam's Monthly Magazine*. Her first published book, *The House of Yorke*, appeared in 1872, after having been serialized in the *Catholic World* from April 1871 to June 1872. The setting of the story is her home, Ellsworth, during the Know-Nothing times of 1854–55; the atmosphere and the philosophy of the novel are decidedly religious. From 1873 to 1887 she lived in Italy. After that period she lived almost uninterruptedly in Boston until her death,

which occurred in Dorchester, frequently contributing sketches and short stories to magazines, notably the *Catholic World*. She was in poor health all the latter years of her life, doing her writing under serious physical handicaps. She had been a precocious child of wilful temperament, now gay, now melancholy, adjectives which fittingly describe contrasting moods in her novels. In her twenties, when her writings began to reach a larger and more appreciative audience, she felt a strong urge to leave what she thought to be a cramping environment. This feeling, with the personal renaissance caused by her religious ideas, served thoroughly to transplant her in thought from New England to Rome. It would be difficult to overestimate the influence which her religion had upon her writing or her life.

She published eleven novels and books of sketches, among them *By The Tiber* (1881), *Aurora* (1886), *Two Coronets* (1889), *San Salvador* (1892), and *Autumn Leaves* (1899), which contains some verse. Her novels were highly praised by contemporary reviewers for their rich imagination and Christian spirit. The most popular of these, *Signor Monaldini's Niece* (1879), is, indeed, characterized by delicate descriptive touches which serve pleasingly to recreate the atmosphere of Rome, but whatever charm she possessed as a novelist lay in her ability to describe atmospheric lights and shadows, and not in any especial stylistic or imaginative excellence. In this novel appears her one strong social protest, that against the conventional restriction of woman's freedom, especially the freedom of the unmarried woman. In general, her work has had little influence upon later novelists and is well-nigh forgotten.

[There are no adequate biog. sketches. Information has been supplied by Adah A. Tincker of Cambridge, Mass., a relative. Some data may be found in *Who's Who in America*, 1906–07; J. F. Kirk, *A Supp. to Allibone's Critical Dict. of Eng. Lit.* (2 vols., 1891); death notice in *Boston Transcript*, Nov. 30, 1907. Reviews are to be found in *Cath. World*, June 1872, *Nation*, Mar. 13, 1879, and June 9, 1881, and *Lit. World* (Boston), Sept. 27, 1879, and Dec. 11, 1885. The date of birth is from Louise Royal of Belfast, Me., a niece.]

H. S., Jr.

TINGEY, THOMAS (Sept. 11, 1750–Feb. 23, 1829), naval officer, was born in London, England, the son of a Church of England clergyman. In youth he served in the British navy with officer's rating, as evidenced by an order (copy in Personnel Files, United States Navy Department Library) from Admiral John Byron, R.N., July 31, 1771, giving him command of twenty-two men at Chateau Bay, Labrador. Not long thereafter he left the British service (according to family tradition because of differences with a fellow officer), and in 1778 he was master of the brig *Lady Clausen* in trade from Saint Croix, Virgin Islands, to Europe. He was married at Saint Croix, Mar. 30, 1777, to Margaret, daughter of William Murdoch of Philadelphia. Following the Revolution he commanded vessels in the American merchant service, living after 1783 in Philadelphia, and after about 1797 in Kingston, N. J. At the opening of naval warfare with France he was made captain in the American navy, Sept. 3, 1798, senior of five captains added that year, and during the next winter he commanded the *Ganges* and two smaller vessels cruising in the Windward Passage. Here he captured numerous prizes, including the *Vainqueur* (8 guns), taken after a ninety-mile chase. When the British frigate *Surprise* sought to examine his crew for British seamen, he peremptorily refused the demand, declaring the flag a sufficient protection. He had already assured his crew that he would resist search "while he was able to stand at quarters" (Letters, 1798–99, *post*, p. 49). Benjamin Stoddert, secretary of the navy, in a letter of Mar. 7, 1799, informed him that the president highly approved his action. From June until late in the following autumn, after the departure of Commodores Thomas Truxtun and John Barry [*qq.v.*], he was senior officer in the West Indies. On Jan. 22, 1800, he was appointed by Secretary Stoddert, as "being a man of understanding and having seen the navy-yards of England" (Hibben, *post*, p. 25), to lay out and command the new Washington navy yard. Though twelfth in the captain's list and thus not among the nine retained in the Peace Establishment of 1801, he remained superintendent of the Washington yard till 1803, was then temporarily "financial agent," and on Nov. 23, 1804, was recommissioned captain and made commandant of the yard and naval agent —the only instance of the combined functions. In these duties he continued until his death. Until 1814 his yard was the chief naval depot and construction base. Tingey was an indefatigable worker, carrying on the official correspondence largely in his own hand, slow to admit error and quick to defend himself, but never shirking responsibilty. His rules for government of the yard (1808) were adopted for all similar stations on the coast. At the British invasion of Washington in 1814 he received orders, based on a cabinet consultation, to burn the yard, and accordingly set fire to the buildings and shipping at 8:20 P.M., Aug. 24, just as the Capitol was fired by the British. He returned next morning at nine, being, as he wrote to his daughter (Sept.

17, 1814), "the last officer who quitted the city after the enemy had possession . . . and the only one to venture in" next day. The establishment was valued at $678,210 and the loss at $417,745.

Highly respected and of genial, kindly nature, Tingey was prominent in Washington social life, a school trustee in 1805, head of the vestry of Christ Church, and an incorporator of its cemetery (now the Congressional Cemetery), in which he was buried. He was a close friend of Commodore John Rodgers [*q.v.*] and his second in negotiations (1806) for a duel—happily averted—with Capt. James Barron [*q.v.*]. By his first marriage he had three daughters who lived to maturity, one of them the mother of the naval officers Thomas Tingey Craven and Tunis A. M. Craven [*qq.v.*]. He was married, second, Dec. 9, 1812, to Ann Bladen Dulany; and third, May 19, 1817, to Ann Evelina Craven. He died in Washington.

[G. W. Allen, *Our Naval War with France* (1909); F. W. Hackett, in *Proc. U. S. Naval Institute*, Mar. 1907; H. B. Hibben, "Navy-Yard, Washington . . .," in *Sen. Exec. Doc. 22*, 51 Cong., 1 Sess.; W. B. Bryan, *A Hist. of the Nat. Capital*, vol. I (1914); Margaret B. Smith, *The First Forty Years of Washington Society* (1906); C. O. Paullin, *Commodore John Rodgers* (1910); obituary in *Daily National Intelligencer* (Washington), Feb. 24, 1829; correspondence, etc., in Navy Dept. Lib., including Letters and Communications to Comm. Thomas Tingey, 1798–99, Letters and Communications from Mordecai Booth, Aug. 22–Sept. 10, 1814, and Log of the Washington Navy Yard, 1822–30; family data from Lewis D. Cook of Philadelphia.]

A. W—t.

TINGLEY, KATHERINE AUGUSTA WESTCOTT (July 6, 1847–July 11, 1929), theosophist, was born in Newbury, Mass., the daughter of James P. L. Westcott and his wife, Susan Ordway (Chase). Her father, a shipwright, became an officer in the Civil War, and later a hotel proprietor in Newburyport. She was descended from Stukely Westcott, one of the associates of Roger Williams in the founding of Providence Plantations. According to theosophical accounts, she was subject in her childhood to religious visions. She was educated in the public schools and by private tutors and is also reported to have spent two years in a convent in Montreal. While still a young woman, she was married three times: her first husband, Richard Cooke, was a printer; her last, Philo Buchanan Tingley, to whom she was married on Apr. 25, 1888, was a stenographer. Until she was past forty her life was spent in almost total obscurity, but at about that time she emerged in New York City as a spiritualist medium who was also engaged in mission work on the East Side, having thus combined two of the major interests of her life—occultism and philanthropy.

A third major interest—personal power—was soon to be gratified.

She was brought into the theosophical movement by William Quan Judge [*q.v.*], Outer Head of the Theosophical Society in America, over whom she acquired extensive influence. Immediately after Judge's death in 1896, a meeting of the "Esoteric Section" was held in New York City, at which extracts were read from an alleged secret diary of Judge, referring to the remarkable occult powers of a mysterious disciple whom he appointed as his successor. A report of this meeting was sent out by the members of a new "Advisory Council," who also claimed appointment by Judge, and in this report the Society was informed that the identity of the Outer Head would not be made known until a year had passed. Although the papers of Judge on which this action was said to be based were never exhibited, the *coup d'état* passed unchallenged. The new Outer Head was variously described as "Promise," "the Veiled Mahatma," "the Light of the Lodge," and "the Purple Mother," but long before the year was out it was an open secret that the person chosen was Katherine Tingley. At the annual Theosophical Convention in April 1896, she secured the election of E. T. Hargrove (the man chiefly instrumental in putting her forward as Outer Head) as president of the Society, and raised a large sum of money to found a "School for the Revival of the Lost Mysteries of Antiquity." Soon after, she duplicated this success by getting many thousands of dollars from her followers to send a group of "Crusaders" under her leadership on an eight months' trip around the world. After their return, a rift developed between Mrs. Tingley and Hargrove. At the annual convention in April 1898 she unseated the latter by obtaining the adoption of a new constitution which merged the Theosophical Society in a new organization called the Universal Brotherhood and vested absolute power in her as its "Leader and Official Head." This action led to numerous schisms, but she retained control of the central body until her death.

Her abilities lay mainly in the field of organization. During the Spanish-American War she established an emergency hospital for sick and wounded soldiers at Montauk Point, L. I., and was furnished transportation and assistance by the United States government for hospital work in Cuba. In 1904 she led a second theosophical crusade around the world. In addition to the international headquarters at Point Loma, Cal., which included the School of Antiquity, the Theosophical University, Râja Yoga College, a Greek theatre, and a home for orphan children, she

erected a children's summer home at Spring Valley, N. Y., a theosophical institute at Newburyport, Mass., three schools in Cuba, seven theosophical centers in Europe, one in England (at Fleet in Hampshire), and Swedish theosophical headquarters on the island of Visingsoe in Vetter Lake, Sweden. In 1925 she received the Medal of Honor of the German Red Cross. She edited the *Century Path,* a weekly, from 1907 to 1911, when it was superseded by the *Theosophical Path,* of which she was editor until 1929; she also edited the *Râja Yoga Messenger,* a bimonthly, from 1912 to 1929, and published a number of fugitive pamphlets of little importance.

Charges of immorality brought against her institution at Point Loma were answered by Mrs. Tingley through successful libel suits, but in 1925 a verdict against her of $100,000 was upheld by the California supreme court for alienating the affections of Dr. George F. Mohn, a theosophist, from his wife, Irene M. Mohn (*Mohn* vs. *Tingley,* 191 *California,* 470). Thenceforth Mrs. Tingley resided chiefly in Europe, where she lectured every year in Paris and Berlin. On her way to Berlin in June 1929 she suffered serious injuries in an automobile accident near Osnabrück in Westphalia, and though she recovered sufficiently to permit her return to her home at Visingsoe in Sweden, she died there a few days after arrival.

[*Vital Records of Newbury, Mass.* (1911); R. M. Tingley, *The Tingley Family* (1910); J. C. and G. W. Chamberlain, *Seven Generations of the Descendants of Aquila and Thomas Chase* (1928); R. L. Whitman, *Hist. and Geneal. of the Ancestors and Some Descendants of Stukely Westcott* (1932); J. J. Currier, *Hist. of Newburyport* (1906), II, 393; Lilian Whiting, *Katherine Tingley, Theosophist and Humanitarian* (1919); *The Theosophical Movement, 1875–1925* (1925); E. T. Hargrove, *An Occultist's Life,* May 17, 1896, eulogistic pamphlet; E. T. Hargrove, *E.S.T.,* Mar. 1, 1898, denunciatory pamphlet; *N. Y. Tribune,* May 18, 1896; *Theosophy, passim,* 1896–97; A. L. Cleather, *H. P. Blavatsky as I Knew Her* (Calcutta, 1923); *N. Y. Times,* July 12, 1929; *Theosophical Path,* Aug. 1929; *Who's Who in America,* 1928–29.]   E. S. B—s.

TIPTON, JOHN (Aug. 15, 1730–August 1813), soldier, frontier politician, was born in Baltimore County, Md., the son of Jonathan and Elizabeth Tipton and the uncle of John Tipton [*q.v.*]. When he was about twenty years of age he removed to Frederick County, Va., with his father, and settled on Cedar Creek. Sometime before 1753 he was married to Mary Butler, who bore him nine sons. After her death in 1776, he was married on July 22, 1779, to Martha (Denton) Moore, the widow of Dr. James Moore. They had about six children. From John Tipton's numerous progeny stem many of the Tiptons whose names appeared in almost every frontier community of the Shenandoah Valley, the transmontane districts of North Carolina, Tennessee, Ohio, and Indiana. Tipton's services in Virginia extended over a period of more than thirty years. He was instrumental in founding Woodstock, in Dunmore (later Shenandoah) County, was a vestryman and justice of the peace in Beckford Parish, cooperated with John Peter Muhlenberg [q.v.] in organizing the Revolutionary meeting at Woodstock, June 16, 1774, and signed the resolutions drawn up on that day. He served under Andrew Lewis [q.v.] in Dunmore's War and participated in the battle at Point Pleasant in October 1774, became a member of the committee of safety and correspondence and a recruiting officer for his county, and served as a member of the Virginia House of Burgesses from 1774 to 1781. He represented Dunmore County at the Virginia Convention at Williamsburg on May 6, 1776, supported four or five sons as Revolutionary soldiers, and acted as lieutenant-colonel of militia, commissioner, and high sheriff of Shenandoah County during the war.

Late in 1783 he removed to the Watauga settlement in North Carolina (later part of Tennessee), where, after some vacillation, he soon crystallized his political views in opposition to John Sevier [q.v.], and the "State of Franklin." His election from Washington County to the North Carolina Assembly in 1785 precipitated the first conflict with Sevier, then governor of the State of Franklin, and Tipton, as colonel of the Washington County militia, and justice of the court, followed it up by strenuous punitive measures. The two men became bitter and implacable enemies. Innumerable opportunities for clashes rose out of a chaotic situation in which two sets of courts, two sets of local officials, and two "officially" authorized bodies of militia tried to function. Armed raiding parties, first from one side and then the other, carried off the court records and official papers of the opposition, and for three years the community was in a state of civil war. Tipton's side was clearly in the minority; when the petition of William Cocke [q.v.], representing Franklin's case for separate recognition, was refused in the North Carolina Assembly, Franklinites hanged Tipton in effigy. Upon one occasion the two leaders met, and, after long and spirited argument, Tipton finally set upon Sevier, and, as an early historian so quaintly put it, "began to annoy him with his hands clinched ..." (Haywood, *post*, p. 161). A compromise arranged by Evan Shelby [q.v.] on behalf of the conciliatory North Carolina government failed, and strife subsided, with Tiptonites victorious, only after a pitched battle in 1788

at Tipton's fortress-like home near Jonesboro.

The adoption of the federal Constitution brought about the final collapse of the State of Franklin; but Tipton's enthusiasm for a central government was bounded by state lines, and he voted against adoption in the Assembly. His tactics, those of a strong, self-reliant, ambitious, hot-headed, unrelenting dispenser of justice, were nowhere popular, although his long record testifies to the fact that his neighbors respected him highly. Sevierites were ultimately elected to all offices in the Washington district, but Tipton's great native ability and his experience were once more made use of when Tennessee became a territory; he represented his county in the first assembly in 1793, and in 1794 and 1795. He helped to draft the constitution, when Tennessee became a state in 1796, and was a senator in the first and second state legislatures. This was his last public service. He and Sevier were among the first trustees of Washington College at Salem in 1795. He died at his home on Sinking Creek at the age of eighty-three.

[C. B. Heinemann, "Tipton Family" (1934), typescript, Lib. of Cong.; Selden Nelson, "The Tipton Family of Tenn.," *East Tenn. Hist. Soc. Pubs.*, no. 1 (1929); S. E. Massengill, *The Massengills, Massengales and Variants* (1931); N. K. Reid, "Sketches of Early Indiana Senators—(IV) John Tipton," *Ind. Mag. of Hist.*, Dec. 1913; J. W. Wayland, *A Hist. of Shenandoah County, Va.* (1927); S. C. Williams, *Hist. of the Lost State of Franklin* (rev. ed., 1933); John Haywood, *Civil and Pol. Hist. .... of Tenn.* (1823); J. G. M. Ramsey, *The Annals of Tenn.* (1853); *State Records of N. C.*, vols. XVIII (1900), XX–XXII (1902-07); H. E. Carr, *Washington Coll.* (1935); *Tenn. A Hist.* (1933), ed. by P. M. Hamer, vol. I.] M. S. E.

TIPTON, JOHN (Aug. 14, 1786–Apr. 5, 1839), soldier, senator, was born in Sevier County, Tenn., the son of Joshua and Jennett (Shields) Tipton, and a nephew of John Tipton [q.v.]. The family had migrated from Maryland to eastern Tennessee, where Joshua Tipton was killed by Indians in 1793. Fourteen years after his death his widow, with four children, moved to Harrison County, Indiana Territory, where one of the sons operated a ferry across the Ohio River. John Tipton received no formal education, and learned to read and write with meager facility only when he became justice of the peace in 1810. At that time Indiana Territory was on the Indian frontier and Tipton belonged to a company of riflemen that saw service at the battle of Tippecanoe. For several years thereafter he commanded a troop of rangers which harassed the Indians away from the Ohio River frontier. In 1822 he was elected major-general of the 2nd Division of Indiana Militia. Meanwhile, 1816-19, he served as sheriff of the county, and then represented his county in the state assembly until 1823. He was appointed one of the two surveyors to run the Indiana-Illinois boundary line in 1821.

On Dec. 22, 1823, he was appointed Indian Agent for the Fort Wayne district of Northern Indiana, and negotiated important Indian treaties in 1826, 1828, and 1836. He speculated widely in the cheap lands of the state and was a prolific founder of county seats on sites adjacent to generous holdings of his own. In 1831 he was appointed to fill out an unexpired term in the United States Senate, and in 1833 was elected for a full term. In politics he was a Democrat, being a close friend of Jackson and a frequent visitor at the "Hermitage." His senatorial career was not spectacular, since he was not a fluent speaker and was never as adept in the intricacies of national intrigue as in the rough and tumble of local frontier politics. He was hostile to the abolition of slavery, championed Michigan's fight for the "Toledo strip," and took a moderate part in all discussions of Indian and military affairs.

In appearance he was of medium height, sinewy, small featured, with a low wrinkled forehead, and stern grey eyes. His stiff sandy hair stood erect in the Jacksonian manner. He was married about 1818 to his cousin, Jeanette Shields, by whom he had three children. After her death, he was married, in April 1825, to Matilda Spencer, and had three children by this marriage. He completed his senatorial term in March 1839, and died the following month at his home in Logansport, Ind. He was a typical frontier politician, a hard-drinking, hard-hitting Indian fighter, and an adroit land speculator. His "journal" was published in the *Indianapolis News* of Apr. 17, and May 5, 1879, and reprinted in the *Indiana Magazine of History,* volume I, numbers 1 and 2, 1905.

[No adequate account of Tipton exists in printed form, but the Indiana Historical Commission has in preparation a two-volume edition of his letters with a generous biographical preface. For this sketch the author consulted a collection of more than 8,000 original Tipton documents and photostats housed in the Indiana State Library, Indianapolis, Ind. See also, C. B. Heinemann, "Tipton Family" (1934), typewritten manuscript, Lib. of Cong.; *Biog. Direct. Am. Cong.* (1928); M. W. Pershing, *Life of Gen. John Tipton and Early Ind. Hist.* (n.d.); N. K. Reid, "Sketches of Early Indiana Senators—(IV) John Tipton," *Ind. Mag. of Hist.,* Dec. 1913; *Ind. Democrat,* Apr. 17, 1839.]

G. A. B.

TISQUANTUM [See Squanto, d. 1622].

TITCHENER, EDWARD BRADFORD (Jan. 11, 1867–Aug. 3, 1927), experimental psychologist and leader of the "structuralist" school, was born at Chichester, England, son of Alice Field (Habin) and John Titchener, of a family that in several centuries had displayed unusual ability. His early school training was obtained in the Prebendal School at Chichester and at Malvern College. From 1885 to 1889 he was at Brasenose College, Oxford, where he was senior scholar in classics and philosophy, and senior Hulme exhibitioner; in 1889–90 he was research student in physiology. He received the degree of B.A. in 1890. The next two years he spent in Wilhelm Wundt's psychological laboratory at Leipzig, and there in 1892 he won his doctorate. After a short time as extension lecturer in biology at Oxford, in the autumn of 1892 he accepted an assistant professorship of psychology in Cornell University; three years later he became Sage Professor of Psychology. In 1894 he received the degree of M.A. from Oxford. In the same year he became American editor of *Mind,* a position he held through 1921; in 1895 he joined Edmund Clark Sanford as associate editor of the *American Journal of Psychology.* On June 19, 1894, he married Sophie Kellogg Bedlow of Portland, Me., who had been studying history at Cornell. In the summer of 1896 he made his only return to England and the Continent.

During the first eight years of his career at Cornell he published a number of translations: with J. E. Creighton, *Lectures on Human and Animal Psychology* (1894), from the German of Wundt; *Outlines of Psychology* (1895), from Oswald Külpe; with W. B. Pillsbury, *Introduction to Philosophy* (1897), from Külpe; and, with J. H. Gulliver, *Ethics* (1897), from the first volume of Wundt's *Ethik.* He also published two textbooks, *An Outline of Psychology* (1896) and *The Primer of Psychology* (1898). The point of view of these books is orthodoxly Wundtian: the subject matter of psychology is mental processes, and its method analysis by introspection of these processes into elements and attributes. In 1898 he defended the Wundtian type of psychology as "structural" against the "functional" type then coming to the fore, especially at the University of Chicago, which dwelt on the significance of various mental reactions for welfare rather than on the introspective analysis of mental states ("The Postulates of a Structural Psychology," *Philosophical Review,* Sept. 1898).

His most important work, *Experimental Psychology* (2 vols., 1901–05), was a milestone in the progress of psychology. Each volume consisted of two manuals, one for the student, the other for the instructor. The first volume, "Qualitative," dealt with experiments not involving exact measurement; the second, "Quantitative," with more precise psycho-physical work; the student's manuals gave carefully tested directions for experimenting, while the instructor's manuals were mines of erudition on all possible points, historical and theoretical, relating to the interpretation of the experiments. It is characteristic of his loyalty to England (he never gave up his British citizenship) that he presented these books to Oxford for the degree of D.Sc., which he won in 1906. In 1904 he published a translation of the first volume of Wundt's *Grundzüge der physiologischen Psychologie*. Later appeared *Lectures on the Elementary Psychology of Feeling and Attention* (1908); *Lectures on the Experimental Psychology of the Thought-Processes* (1909); *A Textbook of Psychology* (2 vols., 1909–10), dedicated to the memory of his Oxford teacher in physiology, Sir John Burdon Sanderson; and *A Beginner's Psychology* (1915). In 1909 he became research professor in the graduate school, and in 1917 declined a call to succeed Hugo Münsterberg [q.v.] at Harvard. He delivered the Lowell Institute lectures, never published, at Boston in 1911. From 1921 to 1925 he was editor of the *American Journal of Psychology*. The last ten years of his life were relatively unproductive; he was, however, working on a systematic psychology, to be his *magnum opus*, but his death from a brain tumor, after only a few days' illness, came before it was far advanced. His wife, a son, and three daughters survived him. In 1929 some introductory material for his unfinished work appeared, edited by a colleague, under the title of *Systematic Psychology: Prolegomena*.

Titchener's personality was a dominating one. It has been pointed out that his attitude towards his junior colleagues and his students was modelled after the autocracy of Wundt at Leipzig (Boring, *post*, p. 492). Because the American Psychological Association refused to expel one of its members for a mild plagiarism from one of Titchener's translations, he attended only one of its meetings after 1895, and formed a group of his own. It was a point of personal privilege that caused him to relinquish the editorship of the *American Journal of Psychology* in 1925. Yet in his letters he was unassuming, reasonable, and kind. As a lecturer he was unequaled. He could hold an ordinary popular audience spellbound through an hour's discourse on the measurement of sensations. He was versatile—a scholarly amateur of music (he was actually professor of music at Cornell, 1896–98, before its department was organized), a connoisseur of coins. But, although he wrote a classic book on experimental psychology, he made no important experimental discovery. And although he was a

penetrating, if not always illuminating, critic of theory, he made no major contribution to it. So far as his writings show, the most noteworthy change in his views on method as time went on was an inclination towards the use of "phenomenological observation" as a substitute for introspection (see "The Schema of Introspection," *American Journal of Psychology*, October 1912, and "Experimental Psychology, a Retrospect," *Ibid.*, July 1925), but he was not the author of this new method. The originality of his mind was apparently not equal to its remarkable grasp, versatility, and acuteness. But it may truly be said of him that his high conception of psychology as pure science has made his work, and that of his pupils, the strongest bulwark against the flood of applied psychology, educational psychology, and mental testing that has threatened in America to obliterate the science. He held a number of honorary degrees, and was a member of numerous important scientific and philosophical societies.

[*Who's Who in America*, 1926–27; *Brasenose Coll. Reg., 1509–1909* (1909), vol. I, p. 682; E. G. Boring, in *Am. Jour. of Psychology*, Oct. 1927; *Cornell Alumni News*, Aug. 1927, pp. 495–96; obituary in *N. Y. Times*, Aug. 4, 1927; personal acquaintance.]   M.F.W.

TITCOMB, JOHN WHEELOCK (Feb. 24, 1860–Jan. 26, 1932), fish culturist and conservationist, was born in Farmington, N. H., the son of George Alfred and Mary Elizabeth Lemist (Lancaster) Titcomb. He was educated in the public schools and at Phillips Exeter Academy, from which he graduated in 1880. During the succeeding thirteen years he was in the employ of the Howe Scale Company at St. Johnsbury, Vt. In 1891 he was appointed one of the fish and game commissioners of the state of Vermont, and in 1894 he assumed in addition the superintendency of the federal fish hatchery at St. Johnsbury. On Dec. 22, 1896, he was married to Martha Ross of St. Johnsbury, by whom he had a son and a daughter. In 1902 he went to Washington as chief of the division of fish culture of the United States bureau of fisheries, and in this position showed himself to be an efficient and progressive administrator. A year later, at the request of the Argentinian government, he spent a number of months in South America establishing a fisheries service in the Argentine and successfully introducing American fishes. The Peruvian government later requested his services for a similar purpose, but for some reason the trip was not made. When his services with the bureau of fisheries ended in 1909, he returned to Vermont, and again assumed the duties of state fish and game commissioner. From 1916 to 1921 he was state fish culturist for New York.

He intermittently accepted private commissions as well, in the somewhat unusual character of consulting fish culturist. He entered the employ of the state of Connecticut in 1921, and in 1922 became superintendent of its board of fisheries and game. In this position, which he occupied until his death, he achieved real success in demonstrating the possibility of maintaining fishing and hunting in a state having a limited area and a large population. He was president of the American Fisheries Society, 1899–1900 and 1926–27, its librarian for a number of years, and an officer and active participant in the American Game Conference sponsored by the American Game Association. He was always prominent in deliberations having a bearing upon the conservation of wild life, and the vigor with which he supported his own views at times engendered unjustified opposition. He died in Hartford, Conn., survived by his two children.

Titcomb was a fairly prolific writer, most of his work being of a technical, though not strictly scientific nature. Government publications under his authorship comprise six titles, and he wrote extensively for the official reports of the states with which he was connected, and for the transactions and proceedings of the societies in which he had a membership. He also contributed occasional articles to sportsmen's magazines. Among his outstanding publications were a government pamphlet on *Aquatic Plants in Pond Culture* (1909) and a report on a biological survey of Lake George, N. Y. His first consideration was for the welfare of wild life rather than the desires of would-be exploiters of game and fish, and he deserves recognition as a successful conservation administrator during an era when, all too frequently, positions of this nature were political spoils, and were filled by men who had little conception of their responsibilities and limited ability for meeting them.

[The maiden name of Titcomb's mother was Seaverus, but she was known by her stepfather's name. See *Who's Who in America*, 1930–31 ; *Trans. Am. Fisheries Soc.* (1932) ; official records and reports, U. S. Bureau of Fisheries, and fish and game depts. of N. Y., Vt., and Conn.; obituary in *Hartford Times*, Jan. 27, 1932; information from Titcomb's colleagues and from his daughter.]   M. C. J.

TOBANI, THEODORE MOSES (May 2, 1855–Dec. 12, 1933), composer, was born in Hamburg, Germany, the son of Josef Tobani and Marianne (Wède) Tobani. He began the study of the violin at three years of age. In his boyhood he was taken to New York by his family and for a time attended the Rivington Street School in that city. The boy's musical talent was so remarkable that after a few years in America

the family returned to Germany so that Theodore could have the best instruction in music. He is said to have studied composition in Germany under V. Bermuth. In 1870 the Tobanis came once more to America, and the fifteen-year-old Theodore became a violinist at Simpson's Theatre in Philadelphia (*New York Herald Tribune, post*). Two years later, in 1872, he was engaged as first violinist at the Arch Street Theatre in Philadelphia, but he soon left for New York and for six years played at Wallack's Theatre. After that he held positions at the Grand Opera House, the Bijou Opera House, Daly's Theatre, and the Thalia Theatre, all in New York.

It was as a composer and an arranger that Tobani was best known. He composed altogether 5,480 original pieces, some under his own name and others under the pen-names "Theodore Moses," "Florence Reed," and "Andrew Herman," and his orchestrations of the works of other composers were widely distributed and performed. His own compositions were of a semi-classic variety that were never too difficult for the abilities or the comprehension of average performers. They were generally marked by a wistful sentimentalism and pathos which found a ready response when they were written and for several decades later. His first composition (1877) was entitled "The Telephone Galop" because of the interest in the new invention then coming into use. For a piano gavotte called "The Little Nestling" (1883), which was performed 1,100 times during the run of a single play, he received only thirty-five dollars, but in the case of his most popular work, "Hearts and Flowers," he was more fortunate. He received a royalty on every copy sold, and the sale ran into the millions, though the figure 23,000,000 which is sometimes given (*New York Herald Tribune, post*) is a great exaggeration. "Hearts and Flowers" was first published in 1893 as a piano piece, simple enough to be played by those of the most modest attainments. Soon it was transcribed in arrangements for solo instruments and combinations of all sorts, and its popularity became international. It was particularly useful as incidental music to pathetic moments in the theatre, and today whenever those producing a revival of a late nineteenth- or early twentieth-century melodrama seek to be authentic, they select "Hearts and Flowers" for the orchestra to play during sad scenes. Others of Tobani's popular works were "Echoes from the Metropolitan Opera House," "The Spanish Patrol," "Moonlight on the Hudson," "Land of My Dreams," "The White Squadron," "Crack Regiment Patrol," and two Hungarian fantasias. He was the composer of several marches, "The Patriot," "The United States," "Manhattan," and others. His last published composition, "Just a Gem," was issued in 1917, just before the beginning of the "jazz era." Tobani was a genial sort of person with a kindly humor. A distinctive feature of his appearance was a spreading moustache that remained black when his hair became grey. At the time of his death at Jackson Heights, L. I., he was still busy composing, at work on an "Old World Symphony" and a suite, "The Battle of the Marne." His wife, Helena Tobani, died some years before him. He was survived by five daughters and three sons.

[*Metronome*, Apr. 1906; *Musical Courier*, Dec. 23, 1933; *Musical America*, Dec. 25, 1933; obituaries in *N. Y. Times*, Dec. 13, and *N. Y. Herald Tribune*, Dec. 14, 1933; information from Tobani's family.]

J. T. H.

TOBEY, EDWARD SILAS (Apr. 5, 1813–Mar. 29, 1891), merchant, capitalist, was born in Kingston, Mass., the only child of Silas and Betsey (Fuller) Tobey. He was a descendant of Thomas Tobey who was in Sandwich by 1644. His father was a sea captain who died in 1817, and in 1823 his mother married Capt. Phineas Sprague, senior member of the Boston shipping firm of Phineas and Seth Sprague. Tobey became a clerk in the office of the firm in 1827, after having received the usual education of those days in the public schools of Boston and Duxbury. In 1833 he was made a partner, but though he remained one for thirty-three years, his business activities extended far beyond the affairs of the firm. He became an officer of several steamship companies, one of them developing into the Fall River Line; treasurer of the United States Insurance Company and of the Russell Mills, a cotton-duck factory in Plymouth, Mass.; and director of commercial and savings banks in Boston. During the Civil War he was prominent because of his knowledge of shipping and finance. In 1861 Gov. John Albion Andrew of Massachusetts appointed him to a committee to devise defenses for Boston Harbor, and Secretary Salmon P. Chase [*qq.v.*] made him a member of an advisory group to formulate a financial policy for the United States government; in 1863 Secretary Edwin N. Stanton appointed him to a board to discuss means of destroying the Confederate iron-clad *Merrimac,* and he was conspicuous in other ways because of being president of the Boston Board of Trade (1861–63) and of the Boston Young Men's Christian Association.

After the war he continued his connection with commercial and religious organizations. Some of his speeches on public questions were published to give them wider currency: *The Industry of the South* (1865), *American Shipping Interests* (1871), and *The Boston Hydraulic Protector Against Fire* (1873). He was a trustee of Bradford Academy (1863–75) and of Dartmouth College (1863–70), and he indorsed and enlisted support for the founding of the Massachusetts Institute of Technology. He was a member or officer of many bodies concerned with the propagation of religion or the investigation of American history, being himself an orthodox Congregationalist with five generations of American ancestors. In 1866 he was elected to the Massachusetts Senate, serving one term there; in 1869 he was appointed to the board of commissioners of Indian affairs; and in 1875 he was appointed postmaster of Boston (appointment confirmed, Dec. 13, 1875), an office he held until December 1886. However, his distinction arose not so much from the public offices he held as from his wide range of influence in activities for public safety or welfare. On Apr. 5, 1841, he married in Boston Hannah Brown Sprague, his stepfather's daughter, by whom he had ten children. He moved from Boston to Brookline in 1883, and died there, survived by his wife, three sons, and four daughters.

[R. B. Tobey and C. H. Pope, *Tobey (Tobie, Toby) Geneal.* (1905); J. S. Pond, *Bradford: a New England Academy* (1930); obituaries in *Boston Herald, Boston Transcript,* Mar. 30, 1891, and *Brookline Chronicle,* Apr. 4, 1891.]

S. G.

TOD, DAVID (Feb. 21, 1805–Nov. 13, 1868), governor of Ohio, diplomat, and capitalist, was born near Youngstown in Trumbull, later Mahoning, County, Ohio, the son of George Tod [*q.v.*] and Sarah (Isaacs) Tod. Reared on his father's farm, "Brier Hill" he went to the neighborhood schools and later to Burton Academy in Geauga County. He read law in the office of Powell Stone of Warren and was admitted to the bar in 1827. From 1830 to 1838 he was Democratic postmaster at Warren, though his father was affiliated with the Whig party. For one term, 1838–40, he represented in the state Senate a district normally Whig. He became the unsuccessful Democratic nominee for governor in 1844 and again in 1846. Accepting an appointment as minister to Brazil in 1847, he remained there until 1851. His tact and good sense soon cleared away the misunderstandings with that government; but his efforts to stop the African slave trade to Brazil, largely in the hands of Americans, ended in failure because his own government would take no action. Amassing a fortune in the coal and iron business, he was an important figure in the business affairs of

Youngstown; and business interests, rather than politics, occupied his attention through the 1850's. He began to ship coal to Cleveland by canal from his "Brier Hill" mines in 1841 after having personally convinced steamboat owners of its value as fuel. He soon became interested in iron manufacturing and was one of the founders of Youngstown's great iron industry. He was also one of a group of six promoters who built the Cleveland and Mahoning Valley Railroad, and he served as president of the road from 1859 to his death.

In the Democratic convention of 1860 he appeared as a Douglas delegate, was elected first vice-president of the convention, and after Caleb Cushing [q.v.] withdrew assumed the chair. When the Civil War began, his active espousal of the Union cause led to his nomination for the governorship by the Union party, and he was easily elected. He had to deal with such matters as draft evasion and resistance, the activities of the Peace Democrats, the excitement over the Vallandigham arrest, the defense of Cincinnati against Kirby-Smith's threatened invasion in September 1862, and the raid of John H. Morgan across the Ohio in July 1863. His vigorous actions and forceful utterances gave offense in some quarters but stamped him as an executive of energy and decision. He was especially watchful over the welfare of the disabled and wounded soldiers, but in making promotions of officers he incurred some criticism. However, the system, rather than the governor, was principally at fault. When he was defeated for renomination by John Brough, he supported the ticket, though deeply disappointed at the result. He was inclined to blame the national administration for his defeat, and perhaps this was a consideration in causing him to refuse Lincoln's offer of the secretaryship of the treasury in 1864 after Chase's resignation, though he gave the condition of his health and his business affairs as reasons. He was chosen as one of the Republican presidential electors in 1868 but died soon after the election from a stroke of apoplexy. He was survived by his widow, Maria (Smith) Tod, to whom he had been married on June 4, 1832, and by six of his seven children.

[Letters and papers in archives of department of state, in Ohio Arch. and Hist. Soc. Lib., Columbus, Western Reserve Hist. Soc. Lib., Cleveland, and in Lib. of Cong.; G. B. Wright, *Hon. David Tod* (1900) and in *Ohio Arch. and Hist. Pubs.*, vol. VIII (1900); Samuel Galloway, *Eulogy on Ex-Gov. David Tod* (1869); J. G. Butler, *Hist. of Youngstown* (1921), vols. I, III; E. H. Roseboom, "Ohio in the 1850's," thesis in Widener Lib., Harvard Univ.; E. A. Holt, *Party Politics in Ohio, 1840–1850* (1931) and in *Ohio Arch. and Hist. Quart.*, July 1929; G. H. Porter, *Ohio Politics During the Civil War* (1911); L. F. Hill, *Diplomatic Relations between the U. S. and Brazil*

(1932); Whitelaw Reid, *Ohio in the War* (1868), vol. I; *Herald* (Cleveland), Nov. 16, 1868.]   E. H. R.

TOD, GEORGE (Dec. 11, 1773–Apr. 11, 1841), jurist, was born in Suffield, Conn., the son of David and Rachel (Kent) Tod. His father was an emigrant from Perthshire, Scotland. His brother was John Tod and his son David Tod [qq.v.]. Upon graduating from Yale College in 1795 he entered the Litchfield Law School conducted by Tapping Reeve [q.v.]. On Sept. 18, 1797, he was married to Sarah Isaacs, the daughter of Ralph Isaacs, a Yale graduate and merchant of some means, and, admitted to the bar that year, began practice in New Haven. In 1800, after a preliminary visit, he removed to Youngstown, Ohio, where he lived until his death. In August 1800 he was appointed prosecuting attorney of Trumbull County in the Northwest Territory. In the contest that ended in Ohio's statehood he was not active, apparently distrusting the "Republicanism" of the "Chillicothe Junto." He rose rapidly in the esteem of his neighbors and represented them in the state Senate, 1804–06. In January 1807 he was elected judge of the state supreme court by the legislature, a position he had held since the previous April by an interim appointment. In 1807 he and Samuel Huntington [q.v.] upheld the decision of a district court declaring unconstitutional an act of the legislature to grant jurisdiction to magistrates in civil suits involving as much as fifty dollars. This was held by the court to impair the right of jury trial. The state legislature, dominated by Jeffersonians, regarded the decision as a challenge. An attempt was made to remove Tod by impeachment, which failed in 1809 by the narrow margin of one vote and established the doctrine of judicial review in Ohio. The next year the legislature removed him by a strictly political maneuver, when his enemies were able to interpret the constitutional provision for a term of seven years as meaning that his term should close on the seventh anniversary of statehood, that is in 1810.

During 1810–12 he served two terms in the state Senate. In the War of 1812 he saw active service in northern Ohio as major of the 19th Infantry and later as lieutenant colonel of the 17th Infantry in the regular army. In February 1816 he was elected by the legislature as presiding judge of the 3rd district circuit court of appeals, a position he filled with distinction until his retirement to private practice at the end of 1829. Such decisions of his as were printed indicate a lucid, well-trained mind. In politics he was nominally a Jeffersonian and later a Whig but had the conservative inclinations that characterized so many transplanted New Englanders. He took an active interest in the improvement of agricultural methods in the state but was unable to make a financial success of his own farm. It remained for his son David to exploit the coal that underlay the farm. His old age was uneventful, his last political activity being in behalf of the candidacy of Harrison in 1840. He died at his home "Brier Hill," near Youngstown, survived by his widow and five children.

[Papers in Western Reserve Hist. Soc. Lib., Cleveland; some letters and papers in Ohio State Lib., Columbus, and in Lib. of Cong.; F. B. Dexter, *Biog. Sketches of the Grads. of Yale College*, vol. V (1911); *Western Law Monthly*, Aug. 1863; W. T. Utter, "Judicial Rev. in Early Ohio," *Miss. Valley Hist. Rev.*, June 1927; F. W. Bailey, *Early Conn. Marriages*, vol. VII (1906), p. 27.]   W. T. U.

TOD, JOHN (November 1779–Mar. 27, 1830), congressman from Pennsylvania, was born in Suffield, Hartford County, Conn., the son of Rachel (Kent) and David Tod, an emigrant from Scotland. He was the brother of George Tod and the uncle of David Tod [*qq.v.*]. He attended the common schools of Connecticut, and, while still a youth, lived for a time in New York. He studied law in the office of his brother George and about 1802 removed to Bedford, Pa., where he practised very successfully. During 1806 and 1807 he was clerk to the county commissioners of Bedford County. From 1810 to 1813 he sat in the state House of Representatives and was speaker twice. From 1814 to 1816 he was a member of the state Senate, in which he was president for a time. His record in the legislature was one of cooperation with the Democratic majority. Like many of his colleagues from the western counties he urged the adoption of more extensive programs for the construction of roads and canals and for the promotion of manufactures. In 1817 he married Mary R. Hanna. They had three daughters.

He was elected by the Democrats to Congress, where he served from Mar. 4, 1821, until his resignation in 1824. He was a ready debater with a lofty conception of his obligations to his constituents. A member of the committee on military affairs, he was an advocate of an extensive military establishment and in 1822 vigorously urged larger appropriations for fortifications and the ordnance department. If necessary he would have abolished all military bands in favor of appropriations for these branches of the service on the theory that it was "better to part with our fiddlers, than our laborers" (*Annals of Cong.*, 17 Cong., 1 Sess., col. 1632). In 1822, when it was proposed to increase the number of congressmen in the reapportionment bill, he denounced

the idea as "an heretical and pernicious innovation in American politics, supported by no reason, nor recommended by any experience" of the American people. To increase the membership would bring in a "legislative rabble" and would be like increasing a club of debaters ten times over "because speeches are reproductive of speeches, and the more is said the more there remains to say" (*Ibid.*, cols. 926, 930). During 1823–24 he was chairman of the house committee on manufactures and in this capacity worked indefatigably for higher duties and for a wide extension of the protective list. In the debates on the tariff of 1824 he urged higher duties as a military necessity to encourage manufactures for the nation's needs in case of war. Pointing to the danger and disgrace of habitual reliance upon foreign nations for the daily necessaries of life, he saw in the tariff a means of utilizing natural resources, especially hemp, glass, lead, and iron, of finding a market for the raw products of the farmer, and of preventing money from being drained out of the country by foreign nations—a scheme that he thought would, in the final analysis, reduce the cost of commodity prices instead of increase them. He declared that all the devastations and losses of the War of 1812 were nothing compared with the devastations and losses of manufacturing capital under the tariff of 1816 (*Ibid.*, 18 Cong., 1 Sess., col. 1473). In 1824 he was appointed president judge of the 16th judicial district of the state. On May 25, 1827, he was appointed associate justice of the state supreme court. He died in Bedford, Pa.

[W. H. Egle, *Notes and Queries, Hist. and Geneal.* . . . *1900* (1901), pp. 39–41, 47–51; *Hist. of Bedford, Somerset, and Fulton Counties* (1884); *Biog. Directory Am. Cong.* (1928); *Niles' Weekly Register*, Apr. 3, 1830; *The Register of Pa.* (ed. by Samuel Hazard), Apr. 10, 1830.]   J. H. P.

TODD, CHARLES STEWART (Jan. 22, 1791–May 17, 1871), lawyer, soldier, diplomat, son of Thomas [*q.v.*] and Elizabeth (Harris) Todd, was born near Danville, Ky., then a part of Virginia. His father in his later years was associate justice of the United States Supreme Court. After attending Transylvania University (Lexington, Ky.), Charles entered the College of William and Mary and was graduated in 1809. He then studied law with his father in Washington, and later with James Gould and Tapping Reeve [*qq.v.*] in Litchfield, Conn. Admitted to the bar in 1811, he began the practice of law in Lexington, Ky.

On the outbreak of the War of 1812 he volunteered, and was made acting quartermaster in the advance of the left wing of the Northwestern Army. He served on Gen. William H. Harrison's staff, his courage and intelligence winning him steady promotion until in March 1815 he was inspector general with the rank of colonel. When the army disbanded he resumed the practice of law at Frankfort, Ky. On June 16, 1816, he married Letitia Shelby, youngest daughter of Gov. Isaac Shelby [q.v.] of Kentucky; twelve children were born to them. He was secretary of state under Gov. George Madison for a short time in 1816 until the latter's death. In 1817 and 1818 he represented Franklin County in the Kentucky legislature.

In February 1820 President Monroe appointed Todd diplomatic agent in Colombia, where he was to observe conditions with a view to guiding the United States government in its recognition policy; promote friendly relations between the two countries; press for the settlement of American claims against Colombia; and work for the withdrawal of discriminating tariffs against the United States. He carried out his duties in a conscientious manner, was friendly, but also realistic and unsentimental. Becoming convinced that Pedro Gual, Colombian secretary for foreign affairs, was unfairly prejudicing Colombian opinion against the United States, he appealed directly to acting-President Santander and other prominent Colombian officials. Gual was furious. He attacked Todd's integrity and wanted him recalled. Todd gained the confidence of the Colombian people, however, and President Monroe offered him an appointment as secretary of legation in Colombia in 1823. This he declined, and retiring to a farm in Shelby County, Ky., became active in agricultural affairs. As a commissioner to the Presbyterian General Assembly he sustained the Old School when the separation of 1837 took place.

In the presidential campaign of 1840 Todd supported General Harrison, making speeches, writing a campaign biography in collaboration with Benjamin Drake (*Sketches of the Civil and Military Services of William Henry Harrison*, 1840), and publishing the *Cincinnati Republican*. He accompanied Harrison to Washington for his inauguration, and was closely associated with him until his death. President Tyler appointed him minister to Russia on Aug. 27, 1841, which post he held throughout the administration. No outstanding issue arose during his residence at St. Petersburg. In 1846 he retired to his farm in Shelby County where he raised blooded stock and wrote numerous articles for magazines and newspapers. He refused to become candidate for governor in 1848, but took an active part in the presidential campaign in behalf of Taylor. In 1850 he was appointed one of three commissioners to treat with Indian tribes on the Mexican border and drew up the final report. He became interested in the development of Texas resources, and was for a time a Texas railroad official. In his later years he was an editor of the Louisville *Industrial and Commercial Gazette*. At the beginning of the Civil War he offered his services at Washington, but they were declined. He died of pneumonia at the home of his son-in-law, Judge Posey, in Baton Rouge, La.

[For sources, see G. W. Griffin, *Memoir of Col. Chas. S. Todd* (1873); T. M. Green, *Hist. Families of Ky.* (1889); J. R. Witcraft, *The Virginia Todds* (1913); *The Biog. Encyc. of Ky. . . . of the Nineteenth Century* (1878); Lewis Collins, *Historical Sketches of Ky.* (1850); Lewis and R. H. Collins, *Hist. of Ky.* (1874); *Louisville Commercial*, May 20, 1871 (editorial); H. M. Wriston, *Executive Agents in Am. Foreign Relations* (1929). A few personal letters are in the manuscripts division, Lib. of Cong.; diplomatic correspondence is preserved in the archives of the Department of State; selections from Todd's official correspondence while diplomatic agent in Colombia are printed in W. R. Manning, *Diplomatic Correspondence of the U. S. Concerning the Independence of the Latin-American Nations* (1925).]   I. L. T.

TODD, ELI (July 22, 1769–Nov. 17, 1833), physician, a descendant of Christopher Todd who settled in New Haven in 1638, was born in New Haven, Conn., the son of Michael and Mary (Rowe) Todd. His father, who was in the West India trade, died in 1774, leaving a large estate, and thereafter, until he was eight years of age, Eli lived with his great-uncle, the Rev. Jonathan Todd of Guilford, Conn. He prepared for college with the Rev. Elizur Goodrich of Durham, entered Yale College in 1783, and graduated with honor in 1787.

After a voyage to Trinidad, where he suffered an almost fatal attack of yellow fever, he returned to New Haven and studied medicine for two years with Dr. Ebenezer Beardsley. Before he was twenty-one he was practising medicine in Farmington, Conn. There he achieved distinction and was commended by the governor of the state for his courage and devotion during the epidemic of "spotted" fever in 1808, when nearly all those unaffected fled from the town in panic. He spent four years practising in New York, but was persuaded to return to Farmington in 1816. In 1820 he moved to Hartford, where he became the most distinguished consulting physician in the city.

Todd was an early member of the Connecticut Medical Society, of which he was elected vice-president in 1823 and president in 1827 and 1828. In 1812, he was made a member of the society's official committee to investigate the condition of the mentally ill, who were misunderstood and abused. The interest thus aroused was renewed in 1821, and in 1822, largely through his initiative and leadership, a Society for the Relief of the Insane was incorporated. Because his father and a sister had suffered from mental illness, Todd had a special interest in this field. When the movement for a public asylum was begun, he became the leader, and in 1824 was instrumental in raising money to build the Connecticut Retreat for the Insane at Hartford. He became its first superintendent when it opened, Apr. 1, 1824.

The humane Quaker methods used by William Tuke in York, England, were known to Todd, and he instituted the same methods at the Retreat, giving to the institution "a character for the comfort and care of its members not surpassed in this or in any other country" (Woodward, *post*). He was the first to realize the necessity of trained nurses and attendants in the mental hospital, and believing alcoholism to be a form of mental disease, recommended that it be treated as such, and suggested the organization of a home for inebriates. The influence of Todd and the Retreat which he organized was felt throughout America and many countries in Europe. He refused offers of the position of superintendent in Bloomingdale Asylum, New York, and in the Massachusetts State Lunatic Asylum, Worcester, but remained superintendent of the Retreat at Hartford until his death in 1833. Todd was a man of charming personality —sympathetic, understanding, courageous, and of a friendliness which inspired unusual confidence. On Aug. 9, 1796, he married Rhoda Hill, who died in 1825. Three years later, in November 1828, he married her sister, Catherine Hill, who survived him.

[Unpublished material collected by Dr. Henry Barnard, and certain Todd MSS., including "Medical Diary No. 1, 1819" and notes on the spotted fever epidemic, in the files of the Hartford Retreat; C. W. Page, "Dr. Eli Todd and the Hartford Retreat," *Am. Jour. of Insanity*, Apr. 1913, and separately reprinted; W. H. Rockwell, "Biographical Sketch of the Late Eli Todd, M.D.," *U. S. Medic. and Surgic. Jour.*, vol. I (1834); H. A. Kelly and W. L. Burrage, *Am. Medic. Biogs.* (1920); *Boston Medic. and Surgic. Jour.*, Apr. 20, 1836; F. B. Dexter, *Biog. Sketches Grads. Yale Coll.*, vol. IV (1907); J. E. and G. I. Todd, *The Todd Family in America* (1920); *The Seventieth Ann. Report ... of the Retreat for the Insane* (1894); S. B. Woodward, 'Dr. Eli Todd," in S. W. Williams, *Am. Medic. Biog.* (1845); *Columbian Register* (New Haven), Nov. 30, 1833.]   C. C. B.

TODD, HENRY ALFRED (Mar. 13, 1854– Jan. 3, 1925), Romance philologist, editor, was born at Woodstock, Ill., the son of a distinguished Presbyterian divine, the Rev. Richard Kimball Todd, and Martha (Clover) Todd, both of New England descent. His early education

was directed by his father. In 1876 he was graduated from the College of New Jersey (later Princeton University), where for the next four years he taught French. In 1880 he went abroad to continue his studies, first at Paris, then at Berlin, where he followed the courses of Adolph Tobler, at that time the chief German authority on Old French syntax. Going thence to Rome, he worked for one semester under Ernesto Monaci, a leading philologist of Italy, after which he passed to the Central University of Madrid in order to attend, during one semester, the courses of the literary critic Marcelino Menéndez y Pelayo. Returning to Paris in 1882, he spent a year studying Romance philology and literature, as well as Sanskrit, under Gaston Paris, Paul Meyer, Arsène Darmesteter, and Abel Bergaigne. During this time he was commissioned by the Société des Anciens Textes Français—the first American to receive that honor—to edit for its series an Old French text, *Le Dit de la Panthère d'Amours* (Paris, 1883), by Nicole de Margival.

From 1883 to 1891 he was instructor in Romance languages at Johns Hopkins University, Baltimore, where he was awarded the degree of Ph.D. in 1885. During this time he collaborated with A. Marshall Elliott in founding and editing *Modern Language Notes,* of which the first number appeared in January 1886, and in organizing the Modern Language Association of America (1883). He later served as treasurer of the Association (1886–91), member of the editorial committee (1894–95), member of the executive council (1893, 1908–11), and president (1906). On July 30, 1891, he married Miriam, daughter of John S. Gilman, a banker of Baltimore. The following autumn he was called to Leland Stanford University as professor of Romance languages and head of the department. Two years later (1893) he became professor of Romance philology at Columbia University, a chair that he held until his death. He was one of the chief organizers of the celebration held in March 1894 to commemorate the centenary of the birth of Friedrich Christian Diez, the founder of Romance philology; in collaboration with Adolphe Cohn, he founded and edited until his death the Columbia University Studies in Romance Philology and Literature; and in 1909, with three colleagues, he founded at Columbia the *Romanic Review,* a quarterly journal devoted to research in Romance philology and literature, the first of its kind to be established in the United States. With Raymond Weeks, he continued joint editorship of the *Review* until his death. He was a life member of the Institut Français aux États-

Unis; president of the committee on courses and lectures of the Institut; president of the French Union, university branch of the Institut, from 1917; and vice-president of the council of administration of the Musée d'Art Français. In 1919 he was sent to France by the United States government as a member of the *mission de rapprochement*. He died in New York City, survived by his wife, two daughters and a son.

He was author of nearly one hundred books, articles, and book reviews. His chief publications include the following editions of Old French manuscripts: "Guillaume de Dole" (*Publications of the Modern Language Association of America,* vol. II, 1886); "La Naissance du Chevalier au Cygne" (*Ibid.,* vol. IV, 1889), a French poem of the twelfth century; "La Vie de Sainte Catherine d'Alexandrie" (*Ibid.,* vol. XV, 1900); "The Old French Versified Apocalypse of the Kerr Manuscript" (*Ibid.,* vol. XVIII, 1903); "An Unpublished Fourteenth-Century Invocation to Mary Magdalen" (*Studies in Honor of A. Marshall Elliott,* vol.I, n.d.); and, in collaboration with F. C. Ostrander, *Li Romans dou Lis* (1915). After his death his colleagues, friends, and pupils issued the *Todd Memorial Volumes: Philological Studies* (2 vols., 1930), edited by John D. Fitz-Gerald and Pauline Taylor.

[*Who's Who in America,* 1924–25; J. D. Fitz-Gerald, in *Todd Memorial Vols.,* vol. I (1930), with bibliog.; T. F. Crane, in *Romanic Rev.,* July–Sept. 1925; obituary in *N. Y. Times,* Jan. 4, 1925.]   J.L.G.

TODD, JOHN (Oct. 9, 1800–Aug. 24, 1873), Congregational clergyman, author, was a descendant of Christopher Todd, who came to Boston from England in 1637, and was one of the settlers of the New Haven colony. He was born in Rutland, Vt., where his parents Dr. Timothy and Phoebe (Buel) Todd had recently settled. The father died when John was six years old; the mother, who became insane at his birth, lived for many years without recovering her reason. The boy spent his youth in various places and at length lived for a number of years in Charlestown, Mass., attending school in Boston. At the age of eighteen he entered Yale, where, in spite of scant preparation, poverty, and constant ill health, he was graduated in 1822 with honors. While a student of theology at Andover, he began to preach at Groton, Mass., and was called to the pastorate by the orthodox portion of the church. His rejection by the parish led to the formation of a new church, where he was ordained Jan. 3, 1827. Here he continued till 1833, when he removed to Northampton, Mass., to assume the pastorate of a newly established church,

which he persuaded his people to name the Edwards Church, in honor of his favorite New England divine. After a pastorate of three years, he was called to a recently organized Congregational church on Clinton Street, Philadelphia, which was the first church of that order in the city. At the dedication of its new building he preached a sermon, published under the title *Principles and Results of Congregationalism* (1837), which contained such strictures on the other denominations as to cause much feeling. The new enterprise was successful at first, but dissensions and the business depression of the time ultimately caused its failure, and in 1842 Todd was settled over the First Congregational Church in Pittsfield, Mass., where he remained till his death.

When he went to Pittsfield, he was in the full maturity of his powers, and he at once assumed a position of leadership in western Massachusetts and far beyond, both within and without his denomination. In his theological positions he never swerved from the Calvinism of Edwards; but his preaching was seldom doctrinal and his sermons were made attractive by his vivid imagination, apt illustration, and quaint earnestness of speech. The membership of his church was increased by frequent revivals, of which he was an earnest promoter. He was a constant advocate of temperance and a stanch supporter of foreign missions. The Berkshire Medical Society made him an honorary member; he was one of the founders of Mount Holyoke Seminary, and for many years a trustee of Williams College.

He became widely known through his numerous publications. As a student he had written much for periodicals and while at Andover he had been offered two editorships. His *Lectures to Children* (1834) achieved immediate success; 200,000 copies were issued, and it was translated into five foreign languages. His better known and most influential work, *The Student's Manual* (1835), was circulated and translated even more widely, over 150,000 copies being sold in London alone. Among his other books were *The Sabbath School Teacher* (1837); *Truth Made Simple* (1839); *Serpents in the Doves' Nest* (1867); *Woman's Rights* (1867). Of the last two, the former was highly commended by the medical profession and the latter bitterly attacked for its criticism of a rising movement. He was a constant contributor to magazines and periodicals and wrote many sketches, stories, and question books for Bible students. While always solemn in the pulpit, he possessed rare social gifts and was much in demand as an after-dinner speaker. On Mar. 11, 1827, he married Mary Skinner Brace of Newington, Conn., who survived him with five of their nine children.

[J. E. and G. I. Todd, *The Todd Family in America* (1920); *Obit. Record Grads. Yale Coll.*, 1874; *John Todd: The Story of His Life, Told Mainly by Himself* (1876), ed. by J. E. Todd; R. H. Cooke, "Rev. John Todd, D.D.," in *Colls. of the Berkshire Hist. and Sci. Soc.*, vol. III (1899); J. E. A. Smith, *The Hist. of Pittsfield* (1876); Caleb Butler, *Hist. of the Town of Groton* (1848); Mark Hopkins, *A Sermon Delivered at the Funeral of Rev. John Todd, D.D., Aug. 28, 1873* (1873); *Congregationalist*, Aug. 28, 1873; *Pittsfield Sun*, Aug. 27, Sept. 3, 1873; *Berkshire County Eagle*, Aug. 28 and Sept. 4, 1873; *Springfield Daily Republican*, Aug. 25, 1873.]   F. T. P.

TODD, MABEL LOOMIS (Nov. 10, 1856–Oct. 14, 1932), author, and first editor of Emily Dickinson's poems and letters, was born in Cambridge, Mass., the daughter of Eben Jenks and Mary Alden (Wilder) Loomis, and a descendant of Joseph Loomis who emigrated in 1638 to Dorchester. Her father, by profession a mathematician and astronomer, was by temperament a poet-naturalist, a friend of Thoreau, Whitman, Burroughs, and Joaquin Miller. After attending private schools in Washington and Boston, and spending one year in Washington society, Mabel Loomis married on Mar. 5, 1879, David Peck Todd, a brilliant young pupil of Simon Newcomb [*q.v.*], then attached to the United States Nautical Almanac Office. They had one daughter. In 1881 her husband was appointed professor of astronomy and director of the observatory at Amherst College, where Mrs. Todd, young, vivacious, beautiful, with buoyant energy, gave herself without stint to the enrichment of her surroundings. She taught music and painting in two private schools for girls, sang in the village church, and made her home a center for lovers of music and literature. With William Austin Dickinson, treasurer of the college, she worked effectually to promote the tasteful development of both public grounds and private estates; through him also she came to know his secluded poet-sister Emily [*q.v.*]. The Boston Authors' Club originated in her house, and she took a leading part in founding several other clubs, including the Mary Mattoon Chapter of the Daughters of the American Revolution, and the Amherst Historical Society, for which she obtained permanent headquarters and the nucleus of a valuable historical collection. For the college she secured the gift of Observatory House, where she and her husband made their home from 1898 to 1917, and she was instrumental in raising funds for a new observatory. After 1890 she was increasingly in demand as lecturer on astronomy, literature, travel, or local history. She accompanied her husband on as-

tronomical expeditions to Japan (1887, 1896), Tripoli (1900, 1905), the Dutch East Indies (1901), Chile (1907), and Russia (1914), sending back accounts of her experiences for publication in the *Nation,* the *Century,* and other magazines. In 1887 she was the first woman to climb Fuji-san on foot, and on her second trip to Japan she made a pioneer collection of Ainu artifacts, now in the Peabody Museum, Salem. Her publications include a work of popular science, *Total Eclipses of the Sun* (1894); two books of travel, *Corona and Coronet* (1898) and *Tripoli the Mysterious* (1912); *Footprints* (1883), a novelette; *A Cycle of Sonnets* (1896), edited for her friend Cara E. H. Whitton-Stone; an edition of J. D. Steele's *Popular Astronomy* (1899); and *A Cycle of Sunsets* (1910).

Her most memorable service to American letters was begun about 1886–87 when she undertook to prepare for publication the poems of Emily Dickinson. Twelve hundred or more lyrics were found, some of them "copied" with variant readings puzzlingly indicated in the margin, others obscurely scrawled on odd scraps of paper. Mrs. Todd performed single-handed the arduous task of transcribing and arranging these chaotic papers, a work calling for the most sympathetic and conscientious interpretation of the writer's intention. With Col. Thomas Wentworth Higginson [*q.v.*], she brought out two series of *Poems by Emily Dickinson* in 1890 and 1891, and was alone responsible for a third series in 1896. Meanwhile she had collected and edited the *Letters of Emily Dickinson* (2 vols., 1894), enlarged in 1931. Mrs. Todd's correspondence with her co-editor reveals the care she took to establish an accurate text, comparing each poem in proof with the original manuscript and sometimes resisting, though not always with success, Higginson's impulses to "correct" what Emily had written. Her years of hard work brought Emily Dickinson triumphantly before the world and saved the larger portion of the poet's writing from possible loss or slovenly editing. An alienation from the Dickinson family after Austin's death in 1895 unfortunately prevented Mrs. Todd from completing the work and postponed for many years the publication of the remaining poems.

In 1913 she suffered a cerebral hemorrhage, which resulted in a partial paralysis of the right hand. In Florida, where she spent the winters after 1917, she continued to found organizations for social betterment, to write articles, to lecture, and to encourage all efforts toward culture in the youthful city of Miami. Until the day she died from a second cerebral stroke as she was preparing to leave her summer home on Hog Island, Me., her tireless industry was unchecked. On her gravestone in Wildwood Cemetery, Amherst, a carved panel of Indian pipes commemorates her friendship with Emily Dickinson, for whom she originally painted the flowers, and her invaluable services as the poet's editor and earliest interpreter.

[Much autobiog. material is to be found in Mabel Loomis Todd's writings. See also Elias and Elisha S. Loomis, *Descendants of Joseph Loomis in America* (rev. ed., 1908); J. E. and G. I. Todd, *The Todd Family in America* (1920); *Who's Who in America*, 1932–33; M. L. Todd, in *Amherst Graduates' Quart.*, May 1918; Millicent T. Bingham, in *Amherst Record*, Nov. 9, 1932; obituaries in *N. Y. Times*, Oct. 15, and *Springfield Sunday Republican*, Oct. 16, 1932. On the editing of Emily Dickinson's papers, see the prefaces to *Poems of Emily Dickinson* (1891) and *Letters of Emily Dickinson* (1894, 1931); M. L. Todd, in *Harper's Mag.*, Mar. 1930; and manuscript letters in Galatea Coll., Boston Pub. Lib.]   G. F. W.

TODD, SERENO EDWARDS (June 3, 1820–Dec. 26, 1898), agriculturist, journalist, author, was born on his father's farm near Lansingville, Tompkins County, N. Y. He was the seventh child of Josiah Todd, a descendant of Christopher Todd who emigrated from England to Boston, Mass., in 1637 and the following year moved to New Haven, Conn.; his mother, Lucretia (Ingersoll), was the daughter of David and Sarah (Parsons) Ingersoll of Vermont and the great-grand-daughter of Jonathan Edwards [*q.v.*]. Sereno received some education in the rural schools near his home and while working on the farm borrowed and read many books. The Bible he read through annually for over twenty years. In the academies of Groton and Cayuga near by he acquired a little knowledge of the classics. In 1844 he married Rhoda Peck of Greenwich, Conn., and settled on a farm of his own in Tompkins County. Here he remained until 1860, when he sold his land and moved to Auburn, N. Y., where he worked as a mechanic in the implement factory of D. M. Osborne & Company.

While at Auburn he began to contribute to the agricultural press, particularly to Luther Tucker's *Country Gentleman*. Soon he came to be known as an authority on agriculture, and for a time was one of the advisers of Gov. Alonzo B. Cornell [*q.v.*]. In 1865 he became associate editor of the *American Agriculturist* and moved to New York City. The following year he took charge of the agricultural and live-stock department of the *New York Times*. Later he was editor of the home department of the *New York Observer*, editorial writer for *Hearth and Home*, and agricultural editor of the *New York Tribune*, under Horace Greeley. He also held a posi-

tion on the *New York Herald* and edited the *Practical Farmer*. In 1881 his health failed and he retired to a small farm near Orange, N. J., where he lived until his death seventeen years later.

Recognizing that a vast acreage in New York and adjoining states was in need of drainage, he became a stanch advocate of underdraining and patented, Nov. 12, 1872, a power ditching machine for laying title. He stressed the necessity of systematic and economical management, improved methods of cultivation, and better care of live stock. His earliest book was *The Young Farmer's Manual*, the first volume of which was published in 1860 and the second in 1867. In 1868 he published *The American Wheat Culturist* and about the same time issued a privately printed volume later published in enlarged form as *Todd's Country Homes and How to Save Money* (1870). His growing prominence caused Harper & Brothers to engage him to write *The Apple Culturist* (1871), and he is said to have published a book of verse entitled *Rural Poetry and Country Lyrics*.

After the death of his first wife, who left three children, he married, Mar. 19, 1887, Dora Amanda Peterson, by whom he had two sons.

[J. E. and G. I. Todd, *The Todd Family in America, 1637–1919* (1920); L. H. Bailey, ed., *Cyc. of Am. Agriculture*, vol. IV (1909); *Newark Evening News*, Dec. 27, 1898; city directories of Auburn, N. Y., for 1862–63 and 1863–64; S. P. Mead, *Ye Hist. of Ye Town of Greenwich . . . Conn.* (1911); correspondence with a son, David Peck Todd.]   R. H. A.

TODD, THOMAS (Jan. 23, 1765–Feb. 7, 1826), associate justice of the Supreme Court, was born in King and Queen County, near Dunkirk on York River, Va. He was the youngest son of Richard and Elizabeth (Richards) Todd, and a descendant of Thomas Todd who settled in Norfolk County, Va., in 1669. When Thomas was eighteen months old his father died, and although he left a sizable estate, by the law of primogeniture it descended to the eldest son, William, who afterwards became high sheriff of Pittsylvania County, Va. The mother died when Thomas was eleven, having accumulated a considerable estate after her husband's death through managing a boarding house in Manchester. This inheritance enabled the boy to acquire a good elementary education, including a substantial knowledge of Latin, but through his guardian's mismanagement he was soon left without financial resources.

After serving as a soldier for six months during the latter part of the Revolutionary War, he went in 1786 to Danville, Ky. Here he made his home with Judge Harry Innes [*q.v.*], a cousin of his mother, earning his keep by teaching the judge's daughters. At that time the people of Kentucky, then a part of Virginia, were holding numerous conventions for the purpose of devising plans whereby a separation from the parent state might be effected. At the most of these Todd served as clerk. Having studied law evenings by the light of a fire, he began practice, having as capital a horse, saddle, bridle, and thirty-seven and a half cents. At the end of his first term of court he had not only paid his expenses, but had acquired in addition bonds for two cows and calves. He served as clerk of the federal court for the district of Kentucky until the organization of Kentucky as a state in 1792, and then as clerk of the court of appeals until 1801. For some years, beginning in 1792, he was clerk of the Kentucky House of Representatives. In 1801 he was appointed by Gov. James Garrard [q.v.] a judge of the court of appeals, which position he held until 1806, when he was elevated to the chief justiceship. The opinions of the judges of this court were then rendered anonymously, but it is known that many of the decisions dealing with land titles and other property subjects were rendered by Todd. These laid the foundation for the land law of Kentucky. On Mar. 3, 1807, Todd was commissioned by President Jefferson as an associate justice of the United States Supreme Court. Jefferson had asked the representatives in Congress from the states included in the newly created western circuit—Ohio, Kentucky, and Tennessee—to submit nominations, and Todd was either the first or second choice of each (Warren, *post*, I, 299-300).

Though Todd during the nineteen years that he was a member of the Supreme Court rendered not over a dozen opinions, there is ample evidence that his judgment—especially on cases involving land laws—was highly regarded by his colleagues. Most of his time and strength while a justice were devoted to traveling the western circuit, the hardships of which task contributed to his ill health and ultimately to his death. Although of the political faith of Jefferson he was of Marshall's constitutional school, and consistently concurred with his chief in cases involving constitutional doctrine. The only instance of any consequence when he seems to have differed with Marshall was in the Dartmouth College case, and absence from court when the decision was rendered prevented a dissent. His ability and integrity were held in high esteem by Marshall, Story, and others of their kind. He was patient, candid, modest to a marked degree, and known for his many acts of benevolence. Physically, according

to one account (*Western Monthly Magazine, post,* p. 402), his body was "finely proportioned" and his dark face was a "model of beauty and intelligence."

In 1788 Todd married Elizabeth Harris; five of their children lived to maturity, one of whom was Col. Charles Stewart Todd [q.v.], a soldier in the War of 1812 and later minister to Russia. A year after the death of his first wife in 1811, Judge Todd married Lucy Payne, sister of Dolly Madison [q.v.] and the widow of Maj. George S. Washington. Two sons and a daughter were born to this marriage.

[T. M. Green, *Historic Families of Ky.* (1889); J. R. Witcraft, *The Va. Todds* (1913); *Western Mo. Mag.,* July 1836; H. L. Carson, *The Hist. of the Supreme Court of the U. S.* (1902); Charles Warren, *The Supreme Court in U. S. Hist.* (1926); A. J. Beveridge, *The Life of John Marshall,* vol. IV (copr. 1919); G. W. Griffin, *Memoir of Col. Chas. S. Todd* (1873); *Daily Nat. Intelligencer* (Washington), Feb. 20, 21, 1826.]
                       G. W. G.

TOLAND, HUGH HUGER (Apr. 16, 1806–Feb. 27, 1880), surgeon, was born on a plantation at Guilder's Creek, S. C., the fourth child in a family of ten. His father, John Toland, who had emigrated from Ireland, became a wealthy planter and banker, and held a high place in his community; his mother, Mary (Boyd) Toland, of Scotch descent, was a remarkable woman of considerable executive ability. A precocious child, sent to school at four years of age, he soon distinguished himself in studies and athletics. After acquiring a good English education he began to study medicine under the tutelage of a distinguished physician, Dr. George Ross. In 1828 he was graduated in medicine at the head of a class of one hundred and sixty from Transylvania University in Lexington, Ky. After two years of practice in Pageville, S. C., and a winter in Lexington, where he studied French and worked in the dissecting room, he spent two and a half years in Paris under Guillaume Dupuytren, Jacques Lisfranc, and Philibert Joseph Roux. There he met a notable group of American students — George Washington Bethune, Henry Ingersoll Bowditch, Oliver Wendell Holmes of Boston, and William Wood Gerhard, William Pepper [qq.v.], and Joseph Peace of Philadelphia. Although in 1833 he returned to Pageville to resume practice, he soon moved to Columbia, where he married Mary Goodwin, who lived only a few years. Soon he became a dominant surgical leader in his community. His success in operating for the relief of clubfoot and strabismus, and in the use of the lithotomy forceps spread beyond his state, and in 1841 arrested the attention of James Marion Sims [q.v.] of Montgomery, Ala. In 1844 he married Mary Avery, who bore him two daughters.

In 1852, after the discovery of gold in California, he set out for the West. Three days after the arrival of his party his wife died at Stockton. Bringing one of the first quartz mills into the state, Toland bought the Gwin mine in Calaveras County, and tried his luck at mining, but after three months he realized that mining was neither to his taste nor to his profit, and sold out. Saddened by the death of his wife and discouraged by the loss of part of his fortune, in 1853 he moved to San Francisco and gave himself over wholeheartedly to his profession. He was soon appointed chief surgeon to the Marine Hospital and later a member of the staff of the county hospital. For twenty-seven years, even to the day of his death, he played a leading rôle in the practice of surgery, being widely known as the "great surgeon of the Pacific Coast." In 1860 he married Mrs. Mary B. (Morrison) Gridley of San Francisco, by whom he had one son. Four years later he founded at his own expense the Toland Medical College in San Francisco, becoming its president and professor of surgery. The latter position he held until his death. In 1873 he placed the buildings, equipment, and land unconditionally in charge of the regents of the University of California, and they became an integral part of the institution. He died suddenly in 1880, survived by his widow, a stepson, and a son.

Although his teaching and his enormous practice occupied most of his time, he wrote seventy-one articles (mostly discussions of case reports), a large number of which were published in the *Pacific Medical and Surgical Journal,* and a textbook on surgery. His contributions were criticized by some of his contemporaries, but they reveal good judgment, versatility, and sincerity. His lack in style was compensated for by a straightforward description of surgical procedures. Of his surgical ability there can be no doubt. He was a good diagnostician, and for his day a capable and rapid operator. His operations ran the gamut of general surgery. Best known for his lithotomies, he operated for stone in the bladder sixty-four times with a mortality of only two. He popularized the method of Antyllus of the double ligature for the prevention of secondary hemorrhage, and ligated the subclavian artery three times, the brachial six times, the femoral eight times, and the external iliac ten times. Having a thorough knowledge of the fundamental principles of plastic surgery, he performed many operations of this character (see "Rhinoplastic Operation," *Pacific Medical and Surgical Journal,* no. 5, 1863, and

"Skin Grafting," *Western Lancet,* San Francisco, Mar. 1874). His knowledge of bone regeneration was unusual for that period, and his comprehensive article on this subject, "On the Reproduction of Bones" (*Pacific Medical and Surgical Journal,* no. 1, 1858), is illuminating today. Among his other important papers were "Movable Cartilages in the Knee Joint—Operation—Cure" (*Ibid.,* no. 12, 1858), "Two Successful Cases of Ligation of the Femoral Artery for Secondary Hemorrhage" (*Western Lancet,* San Francisco, Aug. 1877), and "Case of Penetrating Gunshot Wound of Abdomen" (*Ibid.,* Oct. 1877). He was a commanding figure, tall, erect, dignified, and deliberate, with an industry, perseverance, and determination that remind one of the indomitable John Hunter.

[Toland's name, which often appears as Hugh Hughes Toland, and the date and place of birth are from the inscription on his tombstone, given in Henry Harris, *California's Medic. Story* (1932), p. 366. See also J. D. B. Stillman, *Cal. Medic. Gazette,* Aug. 1870; H. H. Bancroft, *Chronicles of the Builders of the Commonwealth,* vol. VII (1892); A. B. Stout, in *Trans. Medic. Soc. of the State of Cal.* (1880); W. H. Mays, in *San Francisco Western Lancet,* Apr. 1880; R. A. McLean, in *Western Lancet,* Dec. 1880, highly eulogistic; Emmet Rixford, in *Trans. Am. Surgical Asso.,* vol. XLVI (1928); obituary in *Call* (San Francisco), Feb. 28, 1880.]

                             E. L. G.

TOLMAN, HERBERT CUSHING (Nov. 4, 1865–Nov. 24, 1923), Greek and Indo-Iranian scholar, author, and clergyman, was born at South Scituate (later Norwell), Mass., son of James Turner Tolman and Mary Thomas (Briggs) Tolman. The earliest of the Tolman family in America was Thomas Tolman who came from England before 1640 and settled at Dorchester, Mass. Of Tolman's mother's line in America the first was Walter Briggs who settled in Scituate, Mass., in 1643. Tolman attended grammar school in Hanover, to which the family removed when he was a boy, and high school at Rockland, Mass. In 1884 he entered Yale University. There he distinguished himself in Greek, Latin, and Sanskrit, and in 1888 received the degree of B.A. with high honors. In 1890 he received the degree of Ph.D. at Yale and became assistant to Prof. William Dwight Whitney [*q.v.*]. On Aug. 26, 1891, he married Mary Belden Wells, who with an adopted daughter survived him. He was instructor in Latin (1891–92) and assistant-professor of Sanskrit (1892–93) at the University of Wisconsin; professor of Greek and Sanskrit (1893–94) at the University of North Carolina; and professor of Greek at Vanderbilt University (1894–1923). During his last ten years at Vanderbilt he served as dean of the College of Arts and Science. He also taught for many years in the summer sessions of the George

Peabody College. Numerous honorary degrees were conferred upon him. He studied at the University of Berlin in 1896, at the University of Munich in 1905.

During his years of teaching and administrative duties he was remarkably active in productive scholarship. He published *Eight Books of Cæsar's Gallic War* (1891), with W. R. Harper; *A Grammar of the Old Persian Language* (1892); *The Gospel of Matthew in Greek* (1892), with Alexander Kerr; *A Guide to the Old Persian Inscriptions* (1893); *Greek and Roman Mythology* (1897), with K. P. Harrington, based on Hermann Steuding's *Griechische und Römische Mythologie*; *Herodotus and the Empires of the East* (1899), with J. H. Stevenson; *The Art of Translating* (1901); *Mycenaean Troy* (1903), with G. C. Scoggin; *Ancient Persian Lexicon and the Texts of the Archaemenidan Inscriptions Transliterated* (1908); and a *Cuneiform Supplement* (1910) to the latter. To Tolman should be assigned also the Vanderbilt Oriental Series of nine volumes, for, aside from his own contributions, the whole series found its inspiration in him. In 1912 he was lecturer for the Archaeological Institute of America. He was associate editor of *The World's Progress* (10 vols., 1911). He was a frequent contributor to such periodicals as the *American Journal of Philology*, the *Journal of the American Oriental Society*, and the *American Journal of Archaeology*. The wide recognition of his scholarship was attested by his being invited to contribute to the Madressa jubilee volume published in Bombay in 1914, for which he wrote "The Grave of King Darius at Naksh-i-Rustam."

In addition to his work in ancient languages, Tolman published three books on religious themes: *Urbs Beata* (1902), *"Via Crucis"* (1907), and *Christi Imago* (1915). The last of these consisted of articles written for the *Living Church*, of which he was devotional editor in 1914–15. Though reared a Congregationalist, he became a member of the Protestant Episcopal Church and studied theology while at the University of Wisconsin; in 1895 in Milwaukee he was ordained deacon and priest. While never rector, he served frequently in the pulpit and had temporary charge of churches both in the United States and abroad. From 1904 he was an honorary canon of All Saints' Cathedral, Milwaukee. Tolman was distinguished for the diversity of his gifts; he was described after his death as "a scholar of rare attainments, a teacher by instinct and by training, an administrator of courage and courtesy, a preacher of eloquence and power."

[Jedediah Dwelley and J. F. Simmons, *Hist. of the Town of Hanover, Mass.* (1910); *Who's Who in America*, 1922–23; *Yale Univ. Obit. Record* (1924); *In Memoriam: Herbert Cushing Tolman* (privately printed, 1926); obituaries in *Living Church*, Dec. 1, 1923; *Evening Tennessean and American* (Nashville), Nov. 24, 26, *Nashville Banner*, Nov. 25, and *Nashville Tennessean*, Nov. 25, 1923; information from Mrs. Tolman.]   E. L. J—on.

TOME, JACOB (Aug. 13, 1810–Mar. 16, 1898), merchant, banker, and philanthropist, was born in Manheim Township, York County, Pa., the son of Christian and Christiana (Badger) Thom or Tome. He attended the district schools, and, when he was only sixteen, on his father's death, he went to work on a farm in York County. For the succeeding seven years he held various jobs in the vicinity, even teaching a country school for a season in spite of his meager education. In 1833 he went to Port Deposit, Md., where he made his home for the remainder of his life, except for a brief stay in Philadelphia that winter to study banking. The next year he was engaged as a clerk in a lumber dealer's office. In 1835 David Rinehart, a lumber merchant from Marietta, Pa., proposed a partnership, though Tome had nothing but labor to invest, and on Rinehart's death in 1851 the original capitalization of $5,000 had been multiplied many times. Tome continued to make money in lumber by forming a partnership with John and Thomas C. Bond in 1855. Since Port Deposit was equally well placed for a steamship line, Tome in 1849 organized, with others, a company that ran steamers between Baltimore and Port Deposit. In 1865 a line between Baltimore and Fredericksburg was established. He also interested himself in railroads and continued to profit in both these fields the rest of his life. His success in the field of banking was even more striking. Establishing the Cecil Bank at Port Deposit in 1850 with a capitalization of $25,000, two decades later he owned banks at Elkton, Hagerstown, Md., and Fredericksburg, Va., with a total value of millions. He also owned stock in many other banks of Maryland. His real-estate holdings in Cecil County alone at the time of his death were estimated at one million dollars. His letters are scarce, but such as have been found of a business nature depict an extremely busy yet sagacious man, terse, direct, very strict in his banking methods, and making his point in spite of the handicap of a meager education with the telltale misspellings and grammatical mistakes (Creswell Papers, Library of Congress).

In the political world he was not quite so successful. As a reward for patriotic unionism, he was elected to the Maryland Senate in 1863 and again the following year, gravitating naturally to the chairmanship of the finance committee. In 1871 he was put up by the Unionists as a candidate for governor; but he was defeated by the Democratic candidate, William Pinkney Whyte. His name is best remembered today by the founding of the large school, the Jacob Tome Institute, later the Tome School for Boys at Port Deposit, incorporated in 1889 and opened in September 1894. He contributed largely to the support of Dickinson College at Carlisle, Pa., and was on the board of trustees for many years. He gave to other charities and built the Tome Memorial Methodist Episcopal Church at Port Deposit. At Port Deposit he married, on Dec. 6, 1841, Caroline M. Webb, an aunt of John A. J. Creswell [*q.v.*]. After her death he married on Oct. 1, 1884, Eva S. Nesbitt, of the same place. His children all died in infancy.

[*Sun* (Baltimore), Mar. 17, 1898; *Appletons' Ann. Cyc. . . . 1898* (1899); J. T. Scharf, *Hist. of Md.* (1879), III, 714.]   C. W. G.

TOMKINS, FLOYD WILLIAMS (Feb. 7, 1850–Mar. 24, 1932), Protestant Episcopal clergyman, was born in New York City, the son of Floyd Williams and Eliza (Dunham) Tomkins. He received his early schooling at the Charlier French Institute, New York, and entered Harvard in 1868, graduating in 1872. While in college he supported himself in part by services as an organist; he was always fond of music, and composed several hymns. He graduated from the General Theological Seminary, New York, in 1875, was ordered deacon, and married Ann Maria Grant Cutter. The following year he was ordained priest. After missionary work in Colorado, Wyoming, and the Middle West (1875–83), he returned East and became rector of St. James Church, Keene, N. H., where he remained less than two years. From 1884 to 1888 he was minister in charge of Calvary Chapel, New York City. Thereafter until his death he was rector of important churches in various dioceses: Christ Church, Hartford, Conn. (1888–91); St. James, Chicago (1891–94); Grace, Providence, R. I. (1894–99); and the Church of the Holy Trinity, Philadelphia (1899–1932), where his most notable work was done.

For more than thirty years he was one of the most prominent religious and civic leaders of Philadelphia and one of the best known Episcopal clergymen of the country. This prominence was not the result of any ecclesiastical offices that he held, though he was frequently a delegate to the General Convention of the Episcopal Church; nor can it be attributed to any superlative gifts that he possessed, though he was well equipped for his work both by nature

and by training; it was rather the result of an apostolic zeal dominating him completely and finding expression in whatever he undertook. To its demands he was able to respond with seemingly inexhaustible physical energy, for he was a man of large frame and great endurance, capable of carrying out a daily program of activities that few could equal. His warm evangelistic fervor and his absolute sincerity gave power to his preaching; he was invited to college pulpits and frequently summoned to conduct special services in different parts of the country. He held to the old faith and to the old ways, pleading for loyalty to the Bible, whatever men might say about it, and for the strict observance of the Sabbath, resigning as a director of the Sesquicentennial Exposition, Philadelphia, when the board decided to open it on Sundays. He was active in various organizations, a member of the Civil Service Reform Association and of the Pennsylvania Prison Society, a trustee of the Divinity School of the Protestant Episcopal Church, Philadelphia, and for ten years he served as chaplain of the 1st Regiment, Pennsylvania National Guard. In 1924 he was an honorary vice-president of the World Sunday School Association, meeting at Glasgow.

In the midst of his religious and civic activities he found time for much writing. He contributed to religious periodicals, and for years furnished Sunday School lessons for the Philadelphia *Public Ledger*. His books were published not to display learning, nor to bring renown to the author, but solely to give spiritual aid and inspiration. Like his preaching they glow with fervor and faith, and are eminently practical and helpful. Among them are *Following Christ* (1901), *My Best Friend* (1901), *Beacons on Life's Voyage* (1903), *The Faith and Life of a Christian* (1909), *Helps Toward Nobler Living* (1909), *Prayers for the Quiet Hour* (1910), *Sunshine on Life's Way* (1913). He died of pneumonia in his eighty-third year, survived by a son and three daughters.

[*Harvard Coll.: Class of 1872: Eleventh Report of the Secretary, 1917–1924* (n.d.); *Public Ledger* and *Philadelphia Inquirer*, Mar. 25, 1932; *Who's Who in America*, 1930–31.]   H. E. S.

TOMLINS, WILLIAM LAWRENCE (Feb. 4, 1844–Sept. 26, 1930), teacher of music, was born in London, England, the son of William and Sarah (Lawrence) Tomlins. He began his career as a choir boy in London, and during that period of service was a pupil of George Alexander Macfarren and Eduard Silas. At the age of fifteen he became organist and choirmaster of a London church and at seventeen began conducting oratorio. At eighteen he was made a government inspector and examiner of music teachers in the public schools of England, in the department of theory and harmony. In 1864 he was made one of the examiners of the Tonic Sol-Fa College in London. He married Mrs. Elizabeth (Stripp) Squire in 1868.

Tomlins came to America in 1870, settling in Brooklyn, N. Y. There he attracted the attention of the Mason & Hamlin Company for his remarkable mastery of the harmonium, and in 1875 that concern sent him to Chicago to demonstrate their orchestral organ. Remaining in Chicago, he became during that same year conductor of the Apollo Club, then a male chorus, which in 1876 was changed to a mixed chorus. Tomlins was its conductor for twenty-three years. He began in 1883 to organize classes of school children for choral singing and in this type of work specialized for many years, producing astonishing results. In 1893 he had charge of choral singing at the World's Columbian Exposition, Chicago, for which he trained a chorus of twelve hundred children. Five years later he resigned his position as conductor of the Apollo Club in order to devote his entire time to his work with children. In 1903 he established in Chicago the National Training School for School Music Teachers and in the same year was engaged by the Chicago board of education as instructor of music teachers in the grade schools. Returning to England in 1906, he carried on his work with children for two years, in four different centers, with notable success. He then came back to America and thereafter until nearly the end of his life spent most of his time lecturing and illustrating his ideas throughout the country.

In his teaching of children, Tomlins' original purpose was simply to establish in early life normal habits of musical expression so as to facilitate later musical studies. In time, however, he came to believe that the act of singing is capable of influencing the character of the singer by liberating the moral and spiritual faculties, and thenceforth he endeavored to stimulate the inner life through breathing, rhythm, the song voice, and "a vital, reverent attitude toward the Human Spirit, Nature, and God." Profoundly religious, though not in any orthodox sense, since he could not bring his philosophy within the limits of any creed, he made a definite effort, as part of his instruction, to awaken his pupils to spiritual values. His system became known as "The Tomlins Idea."

Tomlins was the author of *Children's Songs and How to Sing Them* (1884) and editor of *The*

Laurel Song Book (1901). He died in his eighty-seventh year at the home of a daughter in Delafield, Wis.

[*Music*, May 1892, June 1898; *Musician*, Dec. 1930; *Music Supervisors Journal*, Oct. 1930, May 1932; *Grove's Dict. of Music and Musicians, Am. Supp.* (rev. ed., 1930); W. J. Baltzell, *Baltzell's Dict. of Musicians* (rev. ed., 1914); *N. Y. Times*, Sept. 28, 1930; unpub. archives of the Apollo Musical Club; information as to certain facts from a daughter, Miss Christine Tomlins.]

D. A. C.

TOMLINSON, EVERETT TITSWORTH (May 23, 1859–Oct. 30, 1931), author, educator, and Baptist minister, was born at Shiloh, Cumberland County, N. J., the son of the Rev. George Edwin Tomlinson, a prominent Seventh-Day Baptist minister, and his wife, Amanda P. Titsworth. After graduating from the high school in Westerly, R. I., he was a student at Williams College from 1875 to 1877, and in 1881 became principal of the high school in Auburn, N. Y. In 1883 he returned to New Jersey as headmaster of the Rutgers College Preparatory School, a position he held for five years. During this period he published Greek and Latin school texts that were widely used. So successful was he as a teacher that William Rainey Harper [*q.v.*] twice tried to persuade him to accept the principalship of the preparatory school of the new University of Chicago. From 1888 to 1911 he was pastor of the Central Baptist Church in Elizabeth, N. J., resigning that position at last because of the pressure of his literary activities, although he continued to live in Elizabeth. He was one of the executive managers of the American Baptist Board of Education (1898–1912), a member of the board of managers of the American Baptist Home Mission Society (1899–1920), and executive secretary of the Ministers and Missionaries Benefit Board of the Northern Baptist Convention (1911–26). His work in the last capacity has been called the "crowning achievement of his life" (Wright, *post*, p. 3). When he assumed office, the organization was without funds; when he resigned, it had assets of $18,000,000. After his resignation he continued to serve as advisory secretary. He died of heart disease at his home in Elizabeth. He was survived by his wife, the former Anna Miranda Greene, and two sons, his only daughter having predeceased him.

Tomlinson was well known as a writer of books for boys, most of them historical, with the Revolutionary period, the Indian wars, and the Civil War as backgrounds. All his books—and by 1927 he had over a hundred volumes to his credit—went into several editions, and the total sales passed the two million mark. His best known books are *Three Colonial Boys, a Story of the Times of '76* (1895), *Camping on the St. Lawrence, or On the Trail of the Early Discoverers* (1899), *The Fort in The Forest, a Story of the Fall of Fort William Henry in 1757* (1904), *The Young Rangers, a Story of the Conquest of Canada* (1906), *Four Boys in the Yellowstone* (1906), *Four Boys in the Land of Cotton* (1907), *Four Boys on the Mississippi* (1908), *Mad Anthony's Young Scout, a Story of the Winter of 1777–78* (1908), and *Pioneer Scouts of the Ohio* (1924). His own times he used, less successfully, as the setting for *Ward Hill at College* (1899), *The Winner* (1903), *Winning His Degree* (1905), and other stories of American college life. In *Elder Boise* (1901) he attempted, also less successfully, a serious novel. Because he understood boys and girls thoroughly, he did not adopt a condescending attitude towards them. In "The Historical Story for Boys" (*Papers and Proceedings of the Thirty-first Annual Meeting of the American Library Association*, 1909, pp. 270–74) he expressed his belief in the need for accurate use of historical material and in the necessity of maintaining the point of view of a boy. As an historian, he believed that the War of 1812 had been unduly neglected. Although as an historical writer he found it necessary to devote considerable attention to armed conflict, he has expressly stated that he had "no desire to glorify war." He also wrote *A Short History of the American Revolution* (1901), *Young Americans in the British Isles* (1909), a travel-book, and *The Story of General Pershing* (1919). His last work, *The First Twenty Years of the Ministers and Missionaries Benefit Board of the Northern Baptist Convention* (1932), was finished a week before his death.

[*Who's Who in America*, 1930–31; P. C. Wright in Tomlinson, *The First Twenty Years* (1932); *Ann. of the Northern Baptist Convention*, 1932; obituaries in *N. Y. Times, N. Y. Herald Tribune*, Oct. 31, 1931; prefaces to Tomlinson's books; private information.]

H. S. R.

TOMOCHICHI (1650?–Oct. 5, 1739), Indian chief, was born among the lower Creeks, possibly at Apalachicola on the west bank of the Chattahoochee almost directly across the river from Columbus, Ga., in what is now Alabama. Among the various spellings of his name are Thamachaychee, Tomochachi, or even Bocachee. Owing to some unexplained difficulty he left his home after 1721 and with a few Creeks and Yamassee settled at Yamacraw on the Savannah River. He was living there when James Edward Oglethorpe [*q.v.*] and the first Georgia colonists landed in 1733 and began the settlement of Savannah some four miles downstream. With Mary

Musgrove, the half-breed wife of a Carolina trader, as interpreter, he came to an understanding with Oglethorpe and signed the formal treaty on May 21, 1733. Shortly afterward he was reconciled to the other Creek tribes and helped to negotiate a similar treaty with them. The next year, with his wife Scenawki and several other Indians, he accompanied Oglethorpe to England. There he was received by the King at Kensington and by the Archbishop of Canterbury at Lambeth Palace. His portrait, painted by William Verelst, was hung in the room of the Georgia trustees at London and in 1735 an engraving from the painting was published as the frontispiece in Samuel Urlsperger's *Ausführliche Nachricht von den Saltzburgischen Emigranten*. Having seen the sights of London like many a later American tourist, Eton, Windsor, the Tower, Greenwich, and Hampton Court, where crowds of the curious gathered in the great gardens to see him and the other Indians, he sailed for Georgia in October 1734 laden with gifts and mementos, which he distributed among his friends at home with notable generosity. His visit was valuable in advertising Georgia and enlisting British opinion in favor of the colony; and in the remaining years of his life he continued to be friendly to the white settlers and to use his influence in easing those adjustments between the two races which made the early years of colonization exceptionally peaceful for Georgia. Numerous anecdotes bear witness to his possession of a philosophic religious sense that continued to be critical of the Christianity of the Europeans about him and withstood the ministrations of John Wesley and George Whitefield. He died secure in the peace of his forefathers, calmly and benevolently. According to his wish his body was taken down the river to Savannah, where it was buried with distinguished military honors in Percival Square, later the Court House Square.

[C. C. Jones, *Hist. Sketch of Tomo-chi-chi* (1868) and *Hist. of Ga.* (1883), vol. I; T. M. Harris, *Biog. Memorials of James Oglethorpe* (1841); A. S. Gatschet, *A Migration Legend of the Creek Indians* (2 vols., 1884–88); *The Colonial Records of the State of Ga.*, vol. IV (1906), XXI (1910), ed. by A. D. Candler; *London Mag.*, June 1734, p. 605, Mar. 1735, p. 162; *Gentleman's Mag.*, June 1734, p. 329; Aug. 1734, pp. 449, 450; Sept. 1734, p. 505, Oct. 1734, p. 571, Mar. 1740, p. 129.]

K. E. C.

TOMPKINS, ARNOLD (Sept. 10, 1849–Aug. 12, 1905), educator, the son of Henry and Delilah (Williams) Tompkins, was born on a farm eight miles south of Paris, Ill. He received his early instruction in nearby schools, worked on his father's farm, and taught school winters. In September 1868 he matriculated at Indiana University, but overwork forced him to withdraw the following spring. Entering Butler University in 1870 he was again obliged to abandon his studies on account of illness. For two years he taught near Paris and in 1872 became principal of a two-room school at Grand View, Ill. Here on Dec. 23, 1875, he married his associate teacher, Jennie, daughter of John and Martha (Butler) Snyder. To prepare for larger opportunities they alternated in attending the Indiana State Normal School at Terre Haute, one of them teaching while the other was in attendance.

Graduating in 1880, they went to Worthington, Ind., where Tompkins had been appointed superintendent of schools. Two years later he was elected superintendent in Franklin, Ind. He had definite theories as to what a school should be, introduced a system of instruction conforming to them, and in 1883 published *A Graded Course of Study for the Franklin Public School*. This brought him to the attention of schoolmen elsewhere, and in 1885 he was called to take charge of the English department in the normal school of De Pauw University; four years later he became dean of the school. In 1889 Indiana University conferred upon him the degree of A.B. Resigning his position at De Pauw in 1890, he became head of the department of English in the Indiana State Normal School. Here his insistence on greater freedom in the institution brought him into conflict with the officials, and in 1893 he withdrew and entered the University of Chicago, where he remained as a student until 1895. He spent the years 1895–99 at the University of Illinois as professor of pedagogy. In 1899 he was chosen president of the Illinois State Normal University, but remained there only a year, during which time, however, he instituted a complete reorganization of the course of study, making it more flexible and adaptable to students of different degrees of preparation. Called to the presidency of the Chicago Normal School in 1900, he held the position until his death, which occurred at his country home, in Menlo, Ga.

Tompkins believed that the ideal school as he conceived of it was the objective of all educational practice and while he advocated freedom in the employment of method, he considered any method that failed to contribute to the realization of his ideal was thereby discredited. His philosophy is embodied in his publications, which include *The Science of Discourse* (1889), *The Philosophy of Teaching* (1893), and *The Philosophy of School Management* (1895). These works were widely read by teachers and used in training schools. He also published *Literary Interpretations; or a Guide to the Teaching and Reading*

of *Literature* (1896). He was metaphysical in his thinking, but had abilities in presentation that made him a popular lecturer. His theories, together with his inflexible attitude in advocating them, brought him much criticism and made it difficult for him to get along well with his associates.

[*Arnold Tompkins* (1905), pamphlet issued by the faculty of the Chicago Normal School; *Semi-Centennial Hist. of the Ill. State Normal Univ., 1857–1907* (1907); *The Semi-Centennial Record of the Univ. of Ill.* (1918); *School and Home Education*, Sept. 1905; *Who's Who in America*, 1903–05; *Chicago Tribune*, Aug. 15, 1905; date of death from a daughter.]

R. F. S.

TOMPKINS, DANIEL AUGUSTUS (Oct. 12, 1851–Oct. 18, 1914), engineer, manufacturer, and a leading figure in the industrial development of the South, was born and reared on a cotton plantation in Edgefield County, S. C., the son of DeWitt Clinton Tompkins and his wife, Hannah Virginia (Smyly). From his father he derived mental curiosity, imagination, and eloquence; from his mother, practicality, ingenuity, and moral fervor. At sixteen, having passed through old-field schools and the Edgefield Academy, he entered the University of South Carolina, an institution almost wrecked by the Civil War but holding to its tradition of intellectual independence and honorable conduct. Though he did well in his classes, Tompkins found the literary training uncongenial. In the carpenter and blacksmith shops on the plantation he had developed his mechanical aptitude, and what he valued most at the University was his friendship with Gen. Edward Porter Alexander [*q.v.*], profesor of mathematics, who had been chief engineer in Lee's army. Under Alexander's urging, the boy after two years entered the Rensselaer Polytechnic Institute at Troy, New York, to study mechanical engineering. Thus suddenly transferred, he found himself in his element, and during four happy years stood high in his studies and upon his graduation with the degree of C.E. in 1873 was elected grand marshal, the chief office in the gift of the students.

During his vacations he had supplemented his theoretical training with practical work in the mills and machine shops of Troy. Here he came to know Alexander Lyman Holley [*q.v.*], who was introducing the Bessemer process of steel making into America, and he spent the year after his graduation as draftsman in Holley's office in Brooklyn. On going to Europe, Holley got work for Tompkins under John Fritz [*q.v.*] at the works of the Bethlehem Iron Company in Pennsylvania. Here Tompkins insisted upon getting away from the drawing board to perfect himself as a practical machinist, and at the end of five years was a principal reliance of Fritz, who was the instrument of his going to the Schwerte Iron Works in Westphalia, Germany, to set up American machinery. On his return after a year abroad, Bethlehem recognized his importance to the community by electing him a burgess; he had always taken active part in civic affairs, particularly in promoting a building and loan association. He determined, however, to go back to the South, where both discouragements and opportunities were greater, and after two years devoted to construction work in Missouri, in March 1882 he hung out his sign in Charlotte, N. C.: "D. A. Tompkins, Engineer, Machinist, and Contractor."

His beginning was small enough—repairing piping in the local steam laundry, surveying for the streets of the town. He soon secured the agency for the Westinghouse engine, and worked incessantly not only to introduce his engine into such plants as existed, but also to encourage the establishment of new plants which would use his services. In the midst of apathy and poverty, he strove to bring the industrial development of the North to the prostrate South. R. M. Miller, a cotton commission merchant of Charlotte, backed him with capital. Tompkins soon saw the possibilities in cotton-seed oil manufacture; realizing that the mills being bought up by the American Cotton Oil Company were antiquated, he organized the Southern Cotton Oil Company with the assistance of Richard H. Edmonds, editor of the *Manufacturers' Record,* and designed and built eight new mills scattered through the South, in six months in 1886. Many others followed. Tompkins was the complete promoter, furnishing information, incentive, plans, equipment, buildings, and even capital where necessary. He had seen the old South of exclusive agriculture destroy itself in economic exploitation, political strife, and civil war; he held with a tenacious affection and faith to what was good in the old régime, but now demanded that the bad—poverty, unskilled and languid labor, ignorance, sectionalism—should be replaced by thrift, manufactures, education, and national participation. He made innumerable speeches and wrote for every paper that would print his articles—his burden always being that manufactures must supplement agriculture, that the injuries worked by slavery must be done away by industrial enterprise.

He next promoted a wide and successful campaign for the spinning and weaving of cotton, putting forward a plan whereby any community could start a factory and pay in the capital in instalments. Others—such as William Gregg, Francis Warrington Dawson, and Henry Pinckney Hammett [*qq.v.*]—had preceded Tompkins in advocating cotton manufacture in the South, but Tompkins was technically equipped to bring the program to realization. In his industrial crusade self-interest was mixed with public spirit, but the latter was never a cloak for the former. In the interpretation of its economic history, he told the South unpalatable truths, for he was given to straight thinking and candor. He was constantly pointing out the advantage to the South of increasing the value of its raw materials by adding brains and skill to them in manufacturing processes; he published an ingenious little book comparing the value of cotton in the raw state with its value as worked up into various fabrics (*Cotton Values in Textile Fabrics,* 1900). He was himself the president of three cotton mills, and was interested in many more.

Tompkins realized that the economic recovery of the South rested ultimately upon improved education, and to this cause he gave statesmanlike devotion. Particularly he inspired the founding and guided the work of textile schools connected with the state agricultural and mechanical colleges in North and South Carolina and was instrumental in establishing those of Mississippi and Texas. He wrote volumes which served as texts in these institutions and as handbooks for practical mill men. In his own extensive shops at Charlotte he had apprenticeship courses for boys still attending school.

Many of Tompkins' speeches, on every subject from road building to trained nursing, were published in pamphlet form, while the *Charlotte Daily Observer,* of which he was chief owner for a quarter of a century, served him as a mouthpiece. His principal publications were *Cotton Mill Processes and Calculations* (1899); *Cotton Mill Commercial Features* (1899); *Cotton and Cotton Oil* (1901); and *History of Mecklenburg County and the City of Charlotte from 1740 to 1903* (2 vols., 1903). He received national recognition, among other ways, by appointment on the United States Industrial Commission which reported in 1902; here and in subsequent utterances he represented the capitalist interest in an ingenuous manner: he wanted to substitute proprietor paternalism for restrictive labor legislation and trade unionism; on these matters he really lacked information, his own good intent blinding him to the more selfish designs of others. His strong nationalism was thoroughly wholesome, though his protectionism and imperialism were undiscriminating.

Though fond of the society of women, he never married. His last years, spent at his summer home at Montreat, N. C., where he died, were resolutely cheerful in spite of paralysis. He always gave generously to charities and education; his native town of Edgefield, S. C., has a public library built in his honor.

[G. T. Winston, *A Builder of the New South, being the Story of the Life Work of Daniel Augustus Tompkins* (1920); Broadus Mitchell, *The Rise of Cotton Mills in the South* (1921), and "Some Southern Industrialists," in *Va. Quart. Rev.*, Jan. 1929; *Who's Who in America*, 1914–15; H. B. Nason, *Biog. Record of the Officers and Grads. of the Rensselaer Polytechnic Inst., 1824–1886* (1887); *Charlotte Daily Observer*, Oct. 19 1914; date of birth from Winston, supported by family Bible.]   B. M.

TOMPKINS, DANIEL D. (June 21, 1774–June 11, 1825), governor of New York, vice-president of the United States, was born at Scarsdale, Westchester County, N. Y., the son of a Revolutionary patriot, Jonathan G. Tompkins, and of Sarah (Hyatt), and a descendant of John Tompkins who settled at Concord, Mass., in 1640. Named simply Daniel, he is said to have adopted the middle initial "D" to distinguish himself from a schoolmate of the same name. Tompkins was graduated from Columbia College in 1795. He took up the practice of law in New York City and entered politics as a Republican, was a member of the state constitutional convention in 1801 and of the Assembly in 1803, and was elected to Congress in 1804 but resigned to accept appointment as an associate justice of the New York supreme court. This office gave him a wide acquaintance in the state, and his gracious manner, affability, and broad human sympathy made him a popular favorite. He was spoken of affectionately for years as the "farmer's boy." About 1797 he married Hannah Minthorne, by whom he had seven children; this marriage may have aided him politically, for his wife's father, Mangle Minthorne, was a prominent Republican of New York City.

In 1807 Tompkins was selected by the Clinton faction as their candidate for governor to oppose the incumbent, Morgan Lewis [*q.v.*]. He was elected in that year and reëlected in 1810, 1813, and 1816, serving continuously for almost ten years. Though he had won the governorship with the support of DeWitt Clinton [*q.v.*], he soon became Clinton's most able antagonist in state politics. His administration was marked by loyalty to the measures of the government in Washington, including the Embargo of 1807 and the War of 1812, and by liberal reform measures in the interest of the common people of the state. With varying success he urged improvements in the state's school system, liberalization of its criminal code, more humane treatment of negroes and Indians, the complete abolition of slavery, and a reform in the militia system designed to make wealth bear a larger share in the burden of defense. A militia law such as he desired was passed late in 1814, over the bitter protests of the propertied classes (Van Buren, *post*, pp. 55–57), but too late to be of service in the War of 1812. A law which extinguished slavery in the state on July 4, 1827, was passed at his request in 1817. His democratic attitude is suggested by his remark, in a message opposing the multiplication of banks, that "the less wealthy part of the community . . . are generally the most moral, upright and useful members thereof" (*State of New York: Messages from the Governors*, 1909, II, 698). In the spring of 1812 he took the extraordinary step of proroguing the legislature in a vain effort to block the chartering of the Bank of North America.

Tompkins' powers were strained to the utmost during the War of 1812, when, as commander-in-chief of the New York militia, it fell to him not only to supply troops and equipment for the defense of the New York frontiers, but to perform many duties which should have devolved upon officers of the United States. Handicapped by an inadequate staff, a vicious militia system, insufficient funds, a hostile Assembly (till the fall of 1814), and the incompetence of the United States army officers, he probably handled the tasks of war in his area as successfully as any man could have done. Declining an appointment as secretary of state in the fall of 1814, he accepted instead command of the Third Military District, embracing southern New York and eastern New Jersey. New York City was in a panic at the prospect of a British attack. Tompkins succeeded in putting some 25,000 troops in the field about New York City alone and in borrowing, partly on his personal credit, large sums of money for the pay of New York and New Jersey troops and even for the defense of New England and the maintenance of the Military Academy at West Point. For these services he was ill requited. It is not surprising that in the press of his business vouchers had been lost and accounts had fallen into confusion. At the close of the war he was unable to account for all the money that had passed through his hands, and though his integrity was unquestioned and the value of his service recognized, he was technically in default to both New York and the United States. Charges were made against him (Archibald McIntyre, *A Letter . . . to Daniel D. Tompkins*, 1819) against which he published a defense (*A Letter to Archibald M'Intyre*, 1819). Eventually the New York legislature balanced his accounts (1820) and Congress, upon President Monroe's recommendation, authorized the payment to him (1823–24) of over $95,000 for losses which he had incurred in the public service (*Annals of Congress,* 18 Cong., 1 Sess., pp. 788, 828, 1906, 2697, and *passim*), but unfortunately, before these settlements were made, the question of his accounts had been dragged into politics when Tompkins ran again (unsuccessfully) for the governorship in 1820. These financial troubles darkened his last years. He impressed contemporaries as a man broken in health and prematurely aged by overwork and worry, grieving his friends by his intemperance. He served as vice-president of the United States from 1817 to 1825, but was absent much of the time from his post; in 1821 he presided over the state constitutional convention. He died at his home on Staten Island in his fifty-first year.

[Edward Tompkins, Jr., *A Record of the Ancestry and Kindred of the Children of Edward Tompkins, Sr.* (1893); *Public Papers of Daniel D. Tompkins* (3 vols., 1898–1902), ed. by Hugh Hastings; *State of N. Y.: Messages from the Governors* (1909), vol. II; J. D. Hammond, *The Hist. of Political Parties in the State of N. Y.* (2 vols., 1842); D. S. Alexander, *A Political Hist. of the State of N. Y.,* vol. I (1906); "The Autobiography of Martin Van Buren," ed. by J. C. Fitzpatrick, *Ann. Report of the Am. Hist. Asso. . . . 1918,* vol. II (1920); P. J. Van Pelt, *An Oration, Containing Sketches of the Life, Character, and Services of the Late Daniel D. Tompkins* (1843); J. L. Jenkins, *Lives of the Govs. of . . . N. Y.* (1851); Robert Bolton, *The Hist. . . . of the County of Westchester* (2nd ed., 1881), II, 223; *Columbia Univ. Quart.,* Dec. 1906; *N. Y. Evening Post,* June 13, 1825.]   J. W. P.

TOMPKINS, SALLY LOUISA (Nov. 9, 1833–July 25, 1916), hospital head and the only woman to hold a commission in the Confederate States army, was born at "Poplar Grove," Mathews County, Va., of prominent lineage, daughter of Christopher and Maria (Patterson) Tompkins, and grand-daughter of Col. John Patterson who was brevetted by Washington at Monmouth. After her father's death, her family removed to Richmond, where Miss Tompkins devoted freely her time and ample means to philanthropic enterprises. When the Confederate government appealed to the people of Richmond after the first battle of Manassas (Bull Run) in July 1861 to open their homes to the wounded, she obtained the use of Judge John Robertson's residence, fitted it up at her own expense, and maintained it as a hospital until June 13, 1865. The institution found many willing helpers, but to the demure, diminutive, and frail young woman who flitted from bed to bed, medicine chest strapped to her side and Bible in hand, fell the responsibility of directing the hospital routine and procuring the necessary drugs and food. The building was none too large or well adapted to hospital purposes, and often there were few medicines save whisky and turpentine to supplement cleanliness and careful nursing, but the register shows 1,333 admissions between Aug. 1, 1861, and Apr. 2, 1865, with only seventy-three deaths (Freeman, *post,* p. 47)—despite the fact that the authorities, having early noted that her hospital returned a larger number of patients than any other, sent her many of the most desperate cases. When an executive order placed all hospitals under government control, rather than lose the efficient chief of the Robertson Hospital and in recognition of her invaluable work, President Jefferson Davis had her commissioned a captain in the Confederate service, Sept. 9, 1861 (*Ibid.,* p. 14). She returned her pay to the government, but retained the rank that she might issue orders and draw supplies to augment her own liberality in behalf of the sick and wounded soldiers. To the end of her long life she was known as "Captain Sally."

Lacking beauty, she was of dignified and forceful presence, and it was an earnest of her strength of personality and character that after the war she received numberless offers of marriage from men of all ranks in the army. In later years she gave liberally of her means and personal service to the work of the Protestant Episcopal Church, until financial disaster compelled her to become a guest in the Home for Confederate Women, Richmond, upon its establishment. An honorary member of R. E. Lee Camp, Confederate Veterans, at her death she was buried with full military honors. The chapters of the United Daughters of the Confederacy at Gloucester and Mathews Court House, Va., were named in tribute to her.

[Douglas S. Freeman, *A Calendar of Confederate Papers* (1908); *Confederate Veteran,* Feb. 1908, p. 72, and Nov. 1916, p. 521; M. P. Andrews, *The Women of the South in War Times* (1920); Mary N. Stanard, *Richmond, Its People and Its Story* (1923); *William and Mary College Quarterly,* Jan. 1905; obituaries in *News-Leader* (Richmond), July 26, and *Richmond Times-Dispatch,* July 26, 27, 1916.]   A. C. G., Jr.

TOMPSON, BENJAMIN (July 14, 1642– Apr. 10 (?), 1714), author, educator, the son of the Rev. William and Abigail Tompson, was born in Quincy, Mass., then a part of Braintree, five years after his father emigrated from England to the colonies. His mother died shortly after his birth, and he was brought up chiefly in the household of Thomas Blanchard, a neighbor, who moved from Braintree to Charlestown, where Tompson probably studied with John Morley, the local schoolmaster. He graduated at Harvard College in 1662 and, until his father's death in December 1666, lived with him in Braintree. In the next year he married Susanna Kirtland, who bore him nine children. The same year he succeeded Robert Woodmansey as master of the "free school," now the Boston Latin School. In January 1670/71 Ezekiel Cheever [*q.v.*] replaced him, and Tompson taught in Cheever's former position in Charlestown until Nov. 7, 1674. He seems to have had no regular employment again until 1679, when he began teaching in Braintree. He continued in this work until 1699. He taught in Roxbury, at what is now the Roxbury Latin School for three or four years, and then resumed his place in Braintree, probably in 1704, and kept it till 1710. Throughout his life he labored as physician as well as pedagogue, and his interest in medicine grew with the years. The writing of verses, too, took a share of his time. There were printed before his death: *New Englands Crisis* at Boston in 1676 and *New-Englands Tears for Her Present Miseries* at London in 1676, two volumes of verse on King Philip's War, much of the contents being identical; *A Funeral Tribute* to Gov. John Winthrop of Connecticut, a broadside printed in Boston in 1676; *The Grammarians Funeral,* an elegy on Robert Woodmansey, printed as a broadside, probably in Boston, in 1708; "Upon the Elaborate Survey of New-Englands Passions from the Natives," prefixed to William Hubbard's *A Narrative of the Troubles with the Indians* (1677); "Upon the Very Reverend Samuel Whiting" and "Celeberrimi Cottoni Matheri," both in Cotton Mather's *Magnalia* (1702); *A Neighbour's Tears . . . on . . . Mrs. Rebekah Sewall* in Boston in 1710; and "The Translation by Death of . . . Mr. James Allen," in Benjamin Wadsworth, *Death is Certain* (1710). These, and his other verses, left in manuscript, have been collected in H. J. Hall, *Benjamin Tompson . . . His Poems* (1924), except for two which are included in K. B. Murdock, *Handkerchiefs from Paul* (1927).

It is only as a verse-writer that Tompson is remembered, and it is only among his New England contemporaries that he has distinction. He handled couplets competently and is at his best in satire, but his work lacks any truly poetic quality. He displays, however, some signs of literary training and a constant effort to conform to the literary fashions of his time. His writing is of interest because it represents the cultivated standard of achievement in verse in New England in the late seventeenth century, and particularly because it concerns itself specifically for the most part with native material—Indian wars and Puritan divines, colonial fashions, attitudes,

and standards. Subject rather than style makes Tompson's verse a minor landmark in American literary history.

[Hall, *ante,* for best recent biog., bibliog., and critical account; Murdock, *ante,* for correction of Hall's erroneous ascription of one short poem to Tompson, for certain additional material on the Tompson family, and on the poetic background of the colonies in the time; J. L. Sibley, *Biog. Sketches of Grads. of Harvard Univ.,* vol. II (1881); M. C. Tyler, *A Hist. of Am. Lit.* (1879) for critical comment; other references in Hall and Murdock, *ante.*]   K. B. M.

TONDORF, FRANCIS ANTHONY (July 17, 1870–Nov. 29, 1929), seismologist, Roman Catholic priest, was born in Boston, Mass., the son of Joseph and Louise (Musler) Tondorf. After graduating from the Boston College High School he entered the Society of Jesus and spent the next five years in classical studies at the novitiate in Frederick, Md. In spite of his later activities in other fields, his services as a Latin scholar and his skill in the construction of Latin verse in lapidary style were in frequent demand. In 1893 he went to Woodstock College at Woodstock, Md., where he spent two years in the study of philosophy and in 1895 received the degree of A.B. In the years 1895 to 1898 he taught a variety of subjects at Loyola College, Baltimore, and at St. John's College (later part of Fordham University), Fordham, N. Y. At the end of this time he was sent to Johns Hopkins University for graduate work in mathematical physics. There he also did work in general biology and osteology (1898–99) and attended lectures in geological physics (1899–1900). Unfortunately he was not able to stay to finish his work for the doctorate, possibly because he was needed to teach the classics at Fordham the following year. Returning in the fall of 1901 to Woodstock College, he spent three years in the study of theology, was ordained priest, and then was sent to Georgetown University, Washington, D. C., where he remained, except for one year at Poughkeepsie and another at Fordham, until the time of his death. There he was professor of physics (1904–15), professor of biology (1912–29), and at various times also held professorships in astronomy, geology, German, and other subjects. He received the degree of Ph.D. from Georgetown University in 1914.

At Georgetown he founded the Georgetown seismological observatory, which was put into operation in January 1911. Besides carrying on the routine work of the observatory as director (1909–29), he found time to write a large number of popular articles on seismology and to give lectures on the subject, and in this way contributed very materially to the development of seismology in the United States. From 1916 to 1929 he prepared and published for the observatory *The Registration of Earthquakes and Press Dispatches on Earthquakes.* In the fall of 1924 he made a study of the cause of failure of road surfacing, which he showed to be the transverse vibration of traffic. As a seismologist he was widely consulted. From 1913 to 1924 he lectured on physiology at the Georgetown University School of Medicine. As head of the department of physiology he was a most vigorous champion of experimental medicine against the anti-vivisectionists. He published *A Vindication of Vivisection* (1920), to which a supplement was issued in 1922, and once appeared before a Senate committee (Nov. 4, 1929) to testify on the subject. His other publications include *Anniversary Tribute to George Martin Kober* (1920) and *Frank Baker . . . Professor of Anatomy . . . an Appreciation* (1923). He was a fellow of the American Association for the Advancement of Science and of the Royal Astronomical Society, and a member of numerous other scientific associations. He has been described as having "an almost boyish spirit of simplicity."

[*Who's Who in America*, 1928–29; ann. cats. of the Md.-N. Y. Province of the Soc. of Jesus, and of Georgetown Univ.; records of Johns Hopkins Univ.; *Bull. Seismological Soc. of America*, Dec. 1929, pp. 245–46; *Cath. World*, Jan. 1930; obituary in Woodstock Letters, Oct. 1931, and *Evening Star* (Washington), Nov. 29, 1929; personal recollections.]　　F. W. S.

TONER, JOSEPH MEREDITH (Apr. 30, 1825–July 30, 1896), physician, writer, collector, was born in Pittsburgh, Pa., the son of Meredith and Ann (Layton) Toner, descendants of early Irish settlers in that state. He attended the Western University of Pennsylvania, Pittsburgh, and Mount St. Mary's College, Emmitsburg, Md. After two years' study under Dr. John Lowman at Johnstown, Pa., he spent the winter of 1849–50 at Jefferson Medical College, Philadelphia, then for three months attended the Vermont Medical College at Woodstock, from which he received a medical degree in 1850. After periods of practice at Summit and Pittsburgh, and at Harpers Ferry, Va., he settled in Washington, D. C., in 1855. In the meantime he had obtained the degree of M.D. from Jefferson Medical College in 1853.

For many years thereafter he was one of the capital city's leading practitioners, though his strong bent toward historical and literary pursuits caused him virtually to abandon medical practice during his later years. In 1861 he aided the Sisters of Charity in founding Providence Hospital, which he long served as attending physician. He inspired the founding of St. Joseph's Orphan Asylum, and was its physician, in which capacity he served also St. Vincent's Female Orphan Asylum and St. Ann's Infant Asylum. He was on the board of directors of Garfield Hospital and of Columbia Hospital, and for years was consultant and member of the board of managers of St. Elizabeth's Hospital. He took a leading part in the local medical societies and was chosen to the presidency of the American Medical Association in 1873 and to that of the American Public Health Association in 1874.

It is, however, as a writer and collector that Toner is best known. His first book, *Maternal Instinct,* appeared in 1864, and his other early writings, mainly professional, discussed the necessity for vaccination, yellow fever, public health problems, and vital statistics. Later he turned his attention to medical history and biography. He wrote *Contributions to the Annals of Medical Progress and Medical Education in the United States before and during the War of Independence* (1874), *Annual Oration before the Medical and Chirurgical Faculty of Maryland . . . Contribution to the Medical History and Geography of Maryland* (1875), *The Medical Men of the Revolution* (1876), and *Address on Medical Biography* (1876). Subsequently he concentrated his research upon the career and writings of George Washington. He edited *Washington's Rules of Civility and Decent Behavior* (1888), *Journal of My Journey over the Mountains . . . 1747–8* (1892), *The Daily Journal of Major George Washington in 1751–2, Kept while on a Tour . . . to the Island of Barbadoes* (1892), *Journal of Colonel George Washington . . . in 1754* (1893), describing his part in the ill-fated Braddock expedition. He also published "Wills of the American Ancestors of George Washington" (*New England Historical and Genealogical Register,* July 1891); *George Washington as Inventor and Patron of the Useful Arts* (1892), an address; "Some Account of George Washington's Library and Manuscript Records" (*Annual Report of the American Historical Association . . . 1892,* 1894); and "Washington in the Forbes Expedition of 1758" (*Records of the Columbia Historical Society,* vol. I, 1897). He left in manuscript an uncompleted biographical dictionary of deceased American physicians.

Toner's collection of books and pamphlets was the work of years. He began collecting generally, though with an especial interest in medical, historical, and biographical material. Later becoming keenly interested in early American physicians, he sought to build up a library as complete as possible of books, pamphlets, and journals to cover America's contribution to medical history. In 1882 he turned over twenty-seven thousand volumes, together with related pictures, charts, and medals, to the Library of Congress, which has kept his collection intact. He made a subject index of the contents of all American medical journals up to 1870. In 1868 he started a library for the American Medical Association in the Smithsonian Institution; when the collection had reached six thousand volumes and had outgrown its quarters, it was transferred to the Newberry Library in Chicago. In 1871 he founded the Toner Lecture Fund for the Smithsonian Institution which for a number of years provided semi-annual lectures upon medical and scientific progress. He also donated medals for scientific research performed by students of Jefferson Medical College and the medical school of Georgetown University. He was repeatedly offered teaching positions in medical schools, but always set them aside. In 1894 he participated in the founding of the Columbia Historical Society and was chosen its first president. Though a bachelor, he maintained a spacious home on Louisiana Avenue where, among his collections, he dispensed a warm and far-reaching hospitality. His Washington's Birthday receptions were famous. A sympathetic contemporary describes him as the soul of geniality, without brilliancy or depth of learning, but eminent in sincerity of purpose and industry. He died unexpectedly while visiting at Cresson, Pa., and was buried in the family plot at Derry, Pa.

[A. R. Spofford, in *Ann. Report . . . Smithsonian Inst. . . . 1896* (1898); M. F. Morris, in *Records of the Columbia Hist. Soc.*, vol. I (1897); Thomas Antisell, *Biog. Sketch of Joseph M. Toner, M.D.* (1878); C. S. Busey and others, in *Nat. Medic. Rev.*, Dec. 1896; *Evening Star* (Washington, D. C.), Aug. 1, 1896.]

J. M. P—n.

TONTY, HENRY de (1650–1704), lieutenant of La Salle, explorer, and founder of the first settlements in the Mississippi Valley, was born probably at Paris, son of Lorenzo de Tonti, originator of the tontine form of life insurance, who had fled from Naples after taking part in an insurrection. Tonty's mother was Isabelle de Liette (or Desliettes), and he was the eldest of three children, all of whom later came to New France. Henry entered the French army at the age of eighteen and, serving in Italian waters, lost his right hand in the explosion of a grenade. He replaced it with a metal hand, which he wore covered with a glove, and which he sometimes used with great effect upon rebellious Indians; from this he was known as "the man with the iron hand." Tonty was introduced by Prince de Conti to the explorer Robert Cavelier, Sieur de la Salle [*q.v.*] in 1678, when the latter was seeking assistance in France for his exploration projects in North America. Tonty immediately enlisted in La Salle's service, and thenceforth gave him a loyalty and devotion that were La Salle's greatest aids in carrying out his plans. After their arrival in Canada they went at once to La Salle's seigniory at Fort Frontenac on Lake Ontario; thence Tonty was detailed to the Niagara River to superintend the building of La Salle's ship, the *Griffon*, the first sailing vessel on the upper Great Lakes. Tonty went in advance at the time of sailing and was taken on board at the Detroit River. Thence he and La Salle sailed for Michilimackinac, where Tonty again left ship, coasting down the east shore of Lake Michigan to join La Salle at the St. Joseph River. Together they advanced into Illinois and in the winter of 1679–80 built Fort Crèvecœur on Lake Peoria. In the spring La Salle found it necessary to return to Fort Frontenac, and Tonty was left in command in the Illinois country. There his men soon deserted; he was unable to complete his fort; and the summer was filled with difficulties of every sort. Yet he never despaired, and when in the autumn a war party of Iroquois Indians entered the Valley breathing vengeance upon the Illinois, he fearlessly visited their camp to protest their raid upon French-allied Indians. He was seriously wounded, but escaped with his life. Then, finding he could not calm the storm, with five companions he retreated through the Wisconsin woods, living upon roots and gleanings from the deserted Indian villages. Toward the end of the year 1680 he finally reached Green Bay and safety (L. P. Kellogg, "A Wisconsin Anabasis," *Wisconsin Magazine of History*, Mar. 1924, pp. 322–39). After recruiting his health and recovering from his wound, he left for Michilimackinac, which he reached in June 1681 just too late to meet his cousin Daniel Greysolon Duluth [*q.v.*]. La Salle, arriving the next day, was overjoyed at finding Tonty, who he feared had perished in Illinois. Together they returned thither once more, built Fort St. Louis on the Illinois, and gathered there a settlement of French and Indians. In the spring of 1682 they explored the Mississippi, finding its mouth and there taking possession of the whole Valley for France (*Wisconsin State Historical Society Collections*, vol. XI, 1888, pp. 33–35). In the spring of 1683 La Salle left for France to prepare to colonize Louisiana. Tonty never saw his chief again. In France La Salle secured a captaincy for his faithful lieutenant left in Illinois.

It was 1686 before Tonty could undertake a voyage to join La Salle; that year he went down the Mississippi without finding any trace of his leader, and returned unsuccessful. The next year he was called upon by Governor Denonville of New France to lead his Indian forces against the Iroquois. At Fort des Sables he also met his cousin Duluth and returned west with him in the autumn of 1687 (Pease and Werner, *post,* pp. 190–92). At his post in Illinois he found Jean Cavelier, brother of La Salle, and Henri Joutel [*q.v.*], neither of whom revealed to him the fact of La Salle's death. In March 1689 he was still unaware of it, as one of his letters shows (Margry, *post,* vol. III, p. 564), but in September of that year one of his men, whom he had left to found a settlement in Arkansas, brought him news of his beloved leader's assassination. He started south in December to try to find the colonists La Salle had left, but returned unsuccessful. For a decade longer he remained in Illinois, bringing settlers, trade goods, and missionaries from Canada. He was respected and beloved by all, and was the true founder of Illinois. In 1700, hearing of the settlement made by Pierre le Moyne, Sieur de'Iberville [*q.v.*], near the mouth of the Mississippi, he asked permission to join the new colony, and for four years gave his valuable services to Louisiana in exploration and in conciliation of the Indians. He died near Mobile, probably from yellow fever. He never married, and left his property to his younger brother Alphonse.

Tonty's exploits have not been as much noticed as they deserve. He wrote two brief memoirs of his experiences, one covering the years 1678–83 (see Margry, *post,* vol. I), the other covering the years 1678–91 (see Kellogg, *Early Narratives, post,* for a translation, and Pierre Margry, *Relations et Mémoires Inédits pour Servir à l'Histoire de la France dans les Pays d'Outre-Mer,* 1867). A later memoir published under his name in 1697—*Dernières Découvertes dans l'Amérique Septentrionale de Monsieur de la Salle par Chevalier de Tonti*—he declared spurious. He was a modest person, not given to boasting of his undertakings. He has been regarded only as a faithful lieutenant of La Salle; in fact he was himself a great explorer and an able administrator who succeeded where La Salle failed. He secured the respect and confidence both of the Indians and of his men; he was popular with the missionaries of every group; and his courtesy and consideration enabled him to accomplish his ends. As La Salle wrote of him to the Prince de Conti: "His honorable character and his amiable disposition were well known to you; but perhaps you would not have thought him capable of doing things for

which a strong constitution, an acquaintance with the country, and the use of both hands seemed absolutely necessary. Nevertheless his energy and address make him equal to any thing" (quoted in Francis Parkman, *La Salle and the Discovery of the Great West,* 1869, pp. 117–18).

[Tonty's letters and memoirs are to be found in Pierre Margry, *Découvertes et Etablissements des Français dans l'Ouest et dans le Sud de l'Amérique Septentrionale* (6 vols., 1876–86), vol. I, pp. 573–616, vol. III, pp. 551–64, vol. V, pp. 36–38, 62–66; P. G. Roy, ed., *Bulletin des Recherches Historiques,* Jan. 1900, p. 31, Nov. 1931, p. 704, Jan. 1933, p. 62; I. J. Cox, ed., *Journeys of La Salle* (1905), vol. I, pp. 3–61; and L. P. Kellogg, ed., *Early Narratives of the Northwest* (1917), pp. 283–334. See also Benjamin Sulte, "Les Tonty," *Proc. and Trans. Royal Soc. of Canada,* vol. XI (1894), sec. 1, pp. 1–31; H. E. Legler, "Chevalier Henry de Tonty," *Parkman Club Pubs.,* vol. I, no. 3 (1896); C. W. Alvord, *The Illinois Country* (1920); J. C. Parish, *The Man with the Iron Hand* (1913); L. P. Kellogg, *The French Régime in Wis. and the Northwest* (1925); T. C. Pease and R. C. Werner, "The French Foundations, 1680–1693," *Ill. State Hist. Lib. Colls.,* vol. XXIII (1934).]   L. P. K.

TOOLE, EDWIN WARREN (Mar. 24, 1839–May 17, 1905), lawyer, was born at Savannah, Andrew County, Mo., the eldest of ten children. Joseph Kemp Toole [*q.v.*] was a younger brother. Their grandfather, Benjamin Porter, was a soldier in the American Revolution; their parents, Edwin and Lucinda (Porter) Toole, natives of Kentucky, moved to Missouri in 1837. Edwin Warren attended local schools at Savannah and then entered Masonic College, Lexington, Mo., where he graduated in 1860. He began the study of law, but in 1861 enlisted in the Confederate service and became a lieutenant. He was wounded at the battle of Pea Ridge and soon after retired from the army. In 1863 he went to Denver, Colo., and thence to that part of the Territory of Idaho which in 1864 became Montana Territory.

He settled in Virginia City at a time when there was no recognized law, and his first task was to help formulate a system of law for the mining camps. His practice extended to every community in Montana and his reasoning aided much in bringing the decisions of local courts into harmony with each other. In 1865 he moved to Helena which was his home for the rest of his life. In 1871 the Southern Democrats in Montana, over his protest, nominated Toole for delegate to Congress; the Irish Democrats were angry at the defeat of the incumbent, James M. Cavanaugh, and many of them voted for the Republican candidate. Toole was defeated and thenceforth gave his whole attention to the law, making himself preëminent in this profession and maintaining his position of leadership until his death.

He was an expert in legal logic and a compelling advocate before a jury; his appeal to the court was made attractive by a rich voice under perfect control. His greatest case was probably that of *Barden* vs. *Northern Pacific Railroad Company* (154 *U. S.*, 288–349). This suit was over rights claimed by the railway to minerals under the land in its Congressional grant. The grant had reserved minerals, but the Northern Pacific contended that the reservation applied only to mineral lands known to be such at the time. Toole appeared for the State of Montana, and his argument that the mineral reservation was perpetual was upheld by the courts and caused the railroad the loss of about 80,000 square miles of mineral land.

Many of Toole's important cases depended upon the "apex" law, which gave persons holding mining claims the right to follow veins of ore under land belonging to others. In the case of *Montana Company* vs. *St. Louis Mining and Milling Company* (9 *Montana*, 288; 152 *U. S.*, 160), decided in 1890, Toole upheld the law against charges of unconstitutionality. The "apex" law as he expounded it was seized upon by Frederick A. Heinze [*q.v.*] in his fight to control the copper mines of Montana; Toole became his attorney and guided him through his long fight with W. A. Clark and Marcus Daly [*qq.v.*].

Toole's practice was varied and extensive. He appeared in 228 cases in the territorial supreme court, in 169 cases in the supreme court of the state, and in twenty cases in the United States Supreme Court, and was of counsel in many others. His income from his practice was large and for many years he invested profitably in mines and real estate. He gave liberally to organized charities and to anyone who asked for help. He gave his legal services without charge to poor clients and carried a case for one of them against the Northern Pacific to the Supreme Court of the United States. He had many friends and admirers but few intimates. He was never married, and aside from his legal activities he lived almost a recluse. He was a member of no organizations except the United Confederate Veterans and the Democratic party.

[C. P. Connolly, in *Mag. of Western Hist.*, June 1891; *Progressive Men of the State of Mont.* (2 vols., n.d.); Wm. Wallace, in *Contributions to the Hist. Soc. of Mont.*, vol. VI (1907); *Soc. of Mont. Pioneers, Constitution, Members, and Officers*, vol. I (1899); Tom Stout, *Montana* (1921), I, 430, 433; *Proc. Mont. Bar Asso., 1903–14* (n.d.); *Helena Independent*, May 16–18, 1905; *Montana Daily Record* (Helena), May 17–18, 1905; *Butte Miner*, May 17, 18, 1905; *Anaconda Standard*, May 18, 20, 24, 1905.]   P. C. P.

TOOLE, JOSEPH KEMP (May 12, 1851– Mar. 11, 1929), governor of Montana, the ninth

child of Edwin and Lucinda (Porter) Toole and brother of Edwin Warren Toole [*q.v.*], was born at Savannah, Mo. He attended school at St. Joseph, and later entered Western Military Institute, at Newcastle, Ky., where he was graduated in 1868. He studied law in the office of Webb & Barber for a year, and in 1869 went to Helena, Mont. Here he continued his legal preparation in the office of his brother Edwin, was admitted to the bar in 1872, and became his brother's partner.

Toole soon entered politics and became leader of the Montana Democrats. From 1872 to 1874 he served as district attorney. In 1881 he was elected to the territorial council, and, although a new member, was made president of that body. There he began a campaign to secure statehood for Montana and was influential in calling the constitutional convention of 1884 and in drafting the constitution of that year, which Congress refused to recognize. He was elected territorial delegate to the Forty-ninth and to the Fiftieth Congress, serving from Mar. 4, 1885, to Mar. 3, 1889. He continued his efforts to secure statehood for Montana and was active in support of the omnibus bill of 1889 providing for the admission of North and South Dakota, Montana, and Washington as states of the Union. After the enabling act for Montana was passed he became a member of the convention of 1889 that drafted the state constitution and was influential in securing the insertion of guarantees for social and civil rights. He was unsuccessful, however, in his effort to have the legislature free to decide the question of woman's suffrage.

Toole was elected the first governor of the new state and served from Nov. 8, 1889 to Jan. 1, 1893. Since the first legislature was deadlocked, he was obliged for a time to run the state on credit. To the second legislature he submitted an extensive program of administrative organization. He recommended state provision for higher education and further support of public schools, and championed the claims of miners to the minerals underlying the land grant of the Northern Pacific Railway. Refusing to seek reelection, in 1893 he resumed the practice of law. Soon, however, he was engaged in a fight to have the state capital located permanently at Helena, and in 1896 he actively supported Bryan's candidacy for president. In 1900 he was again elected governor and was reëlected in 1904, serving from Jan. 7, 1901, to Apr. 1, 1908, when he resigned on account of ill health. In 1903 the governor called the legislature in special session to provide means to reopen the mines at Butte which had been closed by the Amalgamated

Copper Company as a protest against the domination of the courts by Frederick A. Heinze [*q.v.*]. He supported many political and social reforms and in 1905 the initiative and referendum were adopted.

In addition to possessing unusual political talents, Toole had much personal charm. He was handsome, had attractive manners, and could adapt his conversation and interests to all types of people. Endowed with a deep, rich voice, as a public speaker he aroused the emotions of his hearers to a high pitch. He had a genius for organization and was a successful administrator. An invalid during the last twenty years of his life, he lived most of the time in California; yet his great popularity in Montana survived and his opinion on public affairs was often sought. On May 7, 1890, he married Lily, daughter of Gen. William S. Rosecrans [*q.v.*]; they had three sons.

[*Who's Who in America*, 1928–29; *Biog. Dir. Am. Cong.* (1928); Tom Stout, *Montana* (1921), vol. I; R. G. Raymer, *Montana* (1930), vol. I; *Montana Standard*, Mar. 12, 1929; *Helena Standard* and *Lewiston Democrat-News*, Mar. 12, 1929.]   P. C. P.

TOOMBS, ROBERT AUGUSTUS (July 2, 1810–Dec. 15, 1885), better known as Robert Toombs, senator, Confederate secretary of state, was a talented, forthright, and high-hearted public servant. Given his quality and circumstances, his career must have seemed to him in the main a matter of course, the more so because of its close parallel to that of his lifelong intimate friend, Alexander H. Stephens [*q.v.*]. Toombs was born in Wilkes County in the uplands of eastern Georgia, the fifth child of Robert Toombs, who had been a major in the Revolution and was now a well-to-do cotton planter, and the latter's third wife, Catherine Huling. As a lad he attended the University of Georgia, but withdrew in sequel to an escapade and completed his education in the North, graduating at Union College, Schenectady, N. Y., in 1828. Admitted to the bar in March 1830, he soon acquired a lucrative practice, which was intermitted rather than interrupted by legislative service. Part of his accumulating wealth was invested in a plantation and its corps of slaves in southwestern Georgia, but his home was always in the village of Washington in his native county, where life had a serenity not often disturbed by the storms in public affairs. In 1830 he married Julia DuBose, and they had three children.

Elected to the Georgia legislature in 1837, Toombs had half a dozen annual terms of service (1837–43, except for 1841) in that assembly during a time of severe economic depression. He promptly made himself an outstanding member on the Whig side, insisting upon sound finance in all its aspects, urging the creation of a supreme court for the state, but concerning himself little with federal questions. In 1844 he was elected to Congress, taking his seat at the close of the next year during a lull in the strife between the sections. For two sessions he was an unobtrusive member, speaking only to deprecate projects of aggression by the United States whether directed against Great Britain or Mexico, and to indorse moderate protectionism in the tariff. In this phase of his career he was more a conservative Whig than a champion of the South. As always, he was a careful student of public accounts, an advocate of regular procedure, and a watchdog of the treasury. Increasingly his terse phrasing, his robust eloquence, and his familiarity with current business won him a hearing when he took the floor, while his conviviality, salty comments, and hearty laughter warmed his welcome in a widening circle.

The Southern disquiet at the Wilmot Proviso did not at once bring Toombs into the sectional fray, for he pinned his faith to benign rule by his party. But when Taylor as a Whig president became, under Seward's influence, "a Southern man with Northern principles," and the crisis of 1850 was culminating, Toombs became a leader in the aggressive defense of the South. His "Hamilcar speech," demanding a share in the territorial opportunity, was but one of a series by him which became famous throughout the South: "Deprive us of this right and appropriate this common property to yourselves, it is then your government, not mine. Then I am its enemy, and I will then, if I can, bring my children and my constituents to the altar of liberty, and like Hamilcar I would swear them to eternal hostility to your foul domination. Give us our just rights, and we are ready, as ever heretofore, to stand by the Union, every part of it, and its every interest. Refuse it and I for one will strike for Independence" (June 15, 1850, *Congressional Globe*, 31 Cong., 1 Sess., p. 1216).

Toombs did much in Congress to procure the compromise measures of 1850; and upon the close of the session he, with Stephens and Howell Cobb, canvassed Georgia to procure a ratification of them. When they were ratified by a convention of the state he led the delegates to launch a Constitutional Union party with the maintenance of the compromise measures as its cardinal policy. This party prevailed in Georgia for several years and elected Toombs to the United States Senate. When it dissolved because of lack of response in other states, Toombs with some reluctance joined the Democrats. He gave mild approval to the Kansas-Nebraska Act as "a measure of peace, equality and fraternity" ("Correspondence," p. 342), and then sought to terminate the ensuing disorders by a bill of his own in 1856 providing for the prompt admission of Kansas as a state with whatever constitution a new convention might adopt after a thoroughly policed election of delegates (*Congressional Globe,* 34 Cong., 1 Sess., p. 1439). This bill was adopted by the Senate, against Republican opposition, but was killed in the House. The question of slavery in the territories persisted—trivial in itself because no region remained into which slavery could economically be thrust, but portentous as a touchstone of sectional doctrine and prestige.

Believing that control of the government by the Republican party would menace the security of the Southern régime, Toombs advocated harmony among the Democrats; but when they split in the campaign of 1860 he supported the "Breckinridge and Southern rights" ticket as a gesture of trenchant antagonism to the Republicans. Upon Lincoln's election he considered secession imperative unless, most improbably, the Republicans would sanction guarantees of Southern interests. Having spoken to this effect in Georgia, he supported Crittenden's compromise in the Senate committee of thirteen. Upon the rejection of this by the Republican members he sent broadcast through the press a telegram (Dec. 23, 1860) to his "fellow-citizens of Georgia" urging them to elect secessionists as delegates to a convention already scheduled ("Correspondence," p. 525). Himself chosen among these, he made a farewell speech to the Senate, Jan. 7, 1861 (*Congressional Globe,* 36 Cong., 2 Sess., p. 268), answering the question "What do these rebels demand?" Hastening to Milledgeville where the Georgia convention sat, he took a principal part in the proceedings and wrote the address which the convention adopted to justify its ordinance of secession (*Journal of the Public and Secret Proceedings of the Convention of the People of Georgia,* 1861). As a matter of course he was chosen as one of the delegates from Georgia to meet those of the other seceding states at Montgomery, Feb. 4, to launch a Southern union.

At Montgomery, Toombs was doubtless disappointed at not being made president of the Confederacy when its provisional constitution had been adopted; and he accepted the secretaryship of state with some reluctance, realizing that his talents lay rather in finance. But for the time being his vigor found varied outlets in shaping the permanent constitution and in dashing

about on semi-military errands as well as in writing diplomatic instructions and giving cabinet counsel. His advice, as when he opposed the authorization of Beauregard to reduce Fort Sumter and when he recommended heavy taxation rather than complete reliance upon credit for the conduct of the war, often came to naught. As months passed he grew contemptuous of Jefferson Davis; and subordination in an idle office became unbearable. He therefore applied for a military commission, and in July 1861 was given command of a Georgia brigade on the Virginia front, though still retaining membership in the Confederate Provisional Congress till near the end of the year.

As a general Toombs wanted to fight; and when superior commanders adopted a defensive policy he tried to debate the question and then censured their inaction and that of the government which supported them. It was presumably not merely in private that he said that the epitaph of the Confederate army should be "died of West Point," and of Davis, "We shall get our independence but it will be in spite of him" ("Correspondence," pp. 577, 592). In short, he showed the defects of a political, temperamental brigadier. When at the battle of Malvern Hill his commanding officer, D. H. Hill, reproved him for his tactics with an implication of cowardice, Toombs replied with a challenge to a duel. It was of course declined with an additional reprimand. But on the field of Antietam, where his brigade stanchly held the stone bridge and an enemy bullet shattered his left hand, Toombs proved his bravery and a degree of capacity. In recognition he virtually demanded promotion; and when this was not forthcoming he resigned his commission, saying publicly that he would no longer hold it "under President Davis with advantage to my country, or to you [the brigade], or with honor to myself" (*Ibid.,* p. 612).

Now for a time Toombs had nothing to do but expose the errors and oppressions of the government, censuring the draft of troops, the impressment of supplies, the suspension of *habeas corpus,* and especially the continued reliance upon credit and the partial repudiation of paper currency. With the purpose of making some of his policies effective he sought election to the Confederate Senate, which in a previous year he had declined; but in this candidacy he was defeated. Sherman's advance against Atlanta then gave him a bit of military service again as a divisional adjutant and inspector-general in the Georgia militia; but no glory or contentment was to be had in handling that nondescript array. The collapse of the Confederacy found Toombs at home, where he stayed until a detail of Federal troops approached his house with an order for his arrest. Thereupon, in May 1865, he became a fugitive, finding his way through New Orleans and Havana to London. When the fervor for punishing "rebels" had passed he returned home in 1867, but he never applied for pardon as a means of regaining citizenship of the United States under the Reconstruction laws. He nevertheless rebuilt a large law practice and resumed a strong influence in the public affairs of the state.

In this phase of his career Toombs was a tribune of the people, opposing whether at the bar or on the rostrum the rapacity of corporations and the plunderings of the Carpet-bag government. Avoiding the perfervid in order not to give ammunition to the vindictive wing of Republicans at the North, he steadily strove to hamper and overthrow Radical rule. For a time he saw salvation in the Democratic party alone; but in 1877 he welcomed the program of President Hayes and censured the Northern Democrats for their criticisms: "They fear it may 'split the party.' So much the better if it does. It certainly needs sifting and cleansing. . . . They do not want redress but grievances to complain of. While that may be fun for the children it is death to the frogs. I hope Hayes will put honest men in office at the South and care not a copper for their politics" (*Ibid.*, p. 727). In the same year his labors to reform and modernize the constitution of Georgia bore fruit. He dominated the convention of 1877 which repudiated the Carpet-bag bonds, diminished the prospective effects of negro suffrage, improved the judiciary system, and provided for the control of corporations. At the same time he resisted the inclusion of specific laws in the constitution, saying: "All this convention has to do is to establish a few fundamental principles and leave these other matters to the legislature and the people, in order to meet the ever varying affairs of human life" (Phillips, *post*, p. 271). Two years later he lent a guiding hand in legislation to create a commission to regulate railroad rates (*Ibid.*, p. 272).

Cataracts now began to darken Toombs's eyes, and a domestic affliction to depress his buoyant spirit; his wife died in September 1883, after suffering from a malady of the brain. His indulgence in liquors became habitual, though he had long known that what was moderation for others was excess for him; and he grew negligent of his affairs as well as of his dress. He was now loved not for what he was but for what he had been. When death ended the decrepitude,

his name was already one to conjure with among Georgians.

[P. A. Stovall, *Robert Toombs* (1892); U. B. Phillips, *The Life of Robert Toombs* (1913), containing frequent quotation of speeches; J. C. Reed, *The Brothers' War* (1905), in large part an appreciation of Toombs; U. B. Phillips, ed., "The Correspondence of Robert Toombs, Alexander H. Stephens, and Howell Cobb," in *Annual Report of the Am. Hist. Asso. for the Year 1911*, vol. II (1913); A. C. Cole, *The Whig Party in the South* (1913); R. H. Shryock, *Georgia and the Union in 1850* (1926); obituary in *Atlanta Constitution*, Dec. 16, 1885.]
U. B. P.

TOPLIFF, SAMUEL (Apr. 25, 1789–Dec. 11, 1864), news-dealer, author, was born in Boston, Mass., the son of Samuel and Mindwell (Bird) Topliff, and a descendant of Clement Topliff who settled in New England between 1635 and 1637. His father was a sea-captain, with a fatal inclination to indorse other men's notes, so that the younger Samuel's life was spent, when he was at home from his voyages as supercargo, in straightening out the family finances. When his father was murdered at sea in a mutiny in 1811, the support of the family devolved upon him, and he forsook the sea and his employer, William Gray, a merchant. Joining Samuel Gilbert, he took charge of the books at "Mr. Gilbert's Marine and General Newsroom," then in the Exchange Coffee House in Boston. In 1814 he succeeded Gilbert and changed the name to the Merchants' Reading Room. Two years later he formed a short-lived partnership with Elkanah Cushman, the father of Charlotte Cushman [*q.v.*], selling West Indian goods on Long Wharf. Meanwhile he was selling foreign news from his correspondents to the Boston, New York, and Philadelphia papers, and the nearer New England journals. For this reason Melville E. Stone [*q.v.*] characterized him as the forerunner of the Associated Press (*M. E. S. His Book*, 1918, p. 292). In 1820 he erected a ninety-two-foot signal staff on an island in Boston harbor by which the approach of vessels could be signalled from far down the harbor, and he had two boats which brought news and bills of lading. In the same year he added the Merchants' Hall Reading-Room to his own. In 1824 his brother Benjamin became his partner. For the *New England Galaxy*, Jan. 12, 1821, he wrote the story of Pitcairn's Island and the mutiny of the *Bounty*. The year 1828, and part of 1829, he spent in making the "grand tour" of Europe. He visited Lafayette at Lagrange and met again in Paris his old friend John Cheverus [*q.v.*], archbishop of Bordeaux. His letters home about his adventures have been published as *Topliff's Travels* (1906).

Topliff married in Providence, R. I., on Dec.

2, 1829, Jane Sisson Blackstock (d. 1860), the daughter of a Scotch merchant of Boston, formerly of New York. On the roof of their house in Washington Square, Fort Hill, overlooking the harbor, was a telescope, and a constant watch was kept to augment Topliff's news-gathering facilities. He and his wife were very social, and their chafing-dish and venison dinners were well known. They had five sons and three daughters. In 1830 the Reading Room and the Boston Post Office shared space in the old State House (then called the City Hall). Later the basement was fitted up for the Reading Room. Here it remained until the Topliffs sold out in 1842. When it closed one newspaper commented that "it has sustained the reputation of the best news-room in the country, and it has become as much identified with the merchants of Boston as State Street itself." Topliff served on the Boston City Council (1844–49), was elected alderman in 1855, and in March offered an ordinance for the erection of the first public library. He later refused to run for the state Senate because of his timidity in public speaking. On his death he was characterized as "not only indefatigable in procuring intelligence of every kind, but . . . remarkably accurate" (*Topliff's Travels, post*, p. 30).

[The fullest account of Topliff is given in *Topliff's Travels: Letters from Abroad in the Years 1828 and 1829 by Samuel Topliff* (1906), ed. by Ethel S. Bolton. Other sources are E. S. Bolton, *Clement Topliff and his Descendants in Boston* (1906); Abel Bowen, *Bowen's Picture of Boston* (2nd ed., 1833); obituary in *Boston Transcript*, Dec. 12, 1864; *Sunday Herald* (Boston), Dec. 3, 1911; and Topliff family papers in the possession of the writer.]   E. S. B—n.

TORBERT, ALFRED THOMAS ARCHIMEDES (July 1, 1833–Aug. 29, 1880), soldier, diplomat, was born at Georgetown, Del., the son of Jonathan R. and Catharine (Milby) Torbert. His father was a farmer, a Methodist local preacher, and a bank cashier. After attending the local schools, Alfred entered the United States Military Academy in 1851 and was graduated and appointed brevet second lieutenant of infantry on July 1, 1855. During the next five years he served on the frontier, participating in operations against Indians in New Mexico and in Florida, 1856–57; in the Utah expedition, 1857–60; and in the march to New Mexico, 1860–61; he was promoted second lieutenant in 1856, and first lieutenant, Feb. 25, 1861.

At the outbreak of the Civil War he was assigned to mustering duty in New Jersey; on Sept. 16, 1861, he was appointed colonel of the 1st New Jersey Volunteers, and nine days later, captain in the Regular Army. He commanded his regiment in the Peninsular campaign and took part in the siege of Yorktown, and the battles of West Point, Gaines's Mill, and Charles City Cross-roads. In the second Manassas and Maryland campaigns he commanded a brigade of the VI Corps and was wounded at the battle of Crampton's Gap but rejoined his brigade in time to be present at Antietam. After the battle of Fredericksburg, where he rendered efficient service in covering the withdrawal of the VI Corps across the Rappahannock, he was promoted brigadier-general of volunteers, as of Nov. 29, 1862, and retained command of the same brigade during the Chancellorsville and Gettysburg campaigns.

In April 1864, Torbert was assigned to command the 1st Cavalry Division, which in the Richmond campaign, together with the division commanded by Gen. David M. Gregg [*q.v.*] under Sheridan, covered the left of the army in its successive turning movements. During these operations Torbert defeated opposing Confederate forces at Hanovertown, Matadequin Creek, and Cold Harbor. In Sheridan's Trevilian raid, June 5–21, 1864, Torbert defeated the cavalry division of Gen. Wade Hampton [*q.v.*] at Trevilian Station, but suffered a repulse the next day at Mallory's Ford. In the operations before Petersburg he was engaged in a successful action at Darbytown, July 28, 1864.

In August, Torbert was ordered to join Sheridan's Army of the Shenandoah, and on arrival he was appointed chief of cavalry of the middle military division. During the next four months he maintained contact with the Confederate forces in the Shenandoah Valley and carried out Sheridan's policy of devastation. At the battle of Winchester, Sept. 19, 1864, Torbert's envelopment of the Confederate left secured the victory. He defeated the cavalry under Gen. Thomas L. Rosser [*q.v.*] at Tom's Brook, Oct. 9, and when the army was surprised at Cedar Creek, Oct. 19, Torbert's cavalry and Getty's infantry division were the only units that continued resistance until Sheridan arrived and rallied the disordered forces. In December he conducted a cavalry raid to break up the railroads in western Virginia, but did not accomplish that object. Having previously been several times brevetted for meritorious service, on Mar. 13, 1865, he was brevetted major-general, United States Army.

On Jan. 17, 1866, he married Mary E. Curry of Milford, Del., and on Oct. 31 of that year resigned from the service. In April 1869 he was appointed United States minister to Salvador. He was transferred as consul general to Havana in December 1871, and to Paris in December 1873, resigning in 1878 to engage in a business enterprise in Mexico. In August 1880 he sailed from New York on the steamer *Vera Cruz* in connection with this venture and was drowned when the vessel was wrecked off the Florida coast. His chivalrous conduct in this disaster befitted his gallant career.

Torbert as a subordinate commander was stanch, sure, and victorious. On independent cavalry missions requiring the utmost initiative and audacity he was less successful. His genial and steadfast character was evinced by the esteem in which he was held by his military associates, by the dependability of his troops, and by his popularity in public and private life.

[U. S. Census Records of Sussex County, Del., 1840–1850; G. B. Hynson, *Hist. Etchings of Milford, Del., and Vicinity* (1899); *Hist. and Biog. Encyc. of Del.* (1882); G. W. Cullum, *Biog. Reg. Officers and Grads. U. S. Mil. Acad.* (3rd ed., 1891); *Reunion of the Asso. Grads. of the U. S. Mil. Acad.*, 1881; *Personal Memoirs of Gen. P. H. Sheridan* (2 vols., 1888); *War of the Rebellion: Official Records* (Army); *Battles and Leaders of the Civil War* (4 vols., 1887–88); *Papers of the Hist. Soc. of Del.*, no. 57 (1922); *Daily Gazette* (Wilmington, Del.), Sept., Oct. 1880; *Harper's Weekly*, Oct. 15, 1864; *Army and Navy Jour.*, Sept. 18, Oct. 2, 1880.]

T. F. M.

TORRENCE, JOSEPH THATCHER (Mar. 15, 1843–Oct. 31, 1896), iron manufacturer, was born in Mercer County, Pa., the son of James and Rebecca Torrence, natives of that state. He left home at the age of nine to live with a distant relative. For three years he worked for a blast-furnace operator at Sharpsburg, Pa., then went to Brier Hill, Mahoning County, Ohio, where he learned the blacksmith trade. Until the outbreak of the Civil War he worked around the blast furnaces in this region, becoming an assistant foreman. In August 1862 he enlisted in the 105th Ohio Infantry, but was wounded at the battle of Perryville, Ky., in October, and in January retired from service. He later joined the volunteer forces raised for the pursuit of the Confederate raider John Hunt Morgan [*q.v.*].

After leaving the military service he entered the employ of Reis, Brown & Berger of New Castle, Lawrence County, Pa., operators of rolling mills, blast furnaces, and coal mines. After some five years in charge of the sale of their furnace products, he resigned to go South as an expert rebuilder of iron works. In 1869 he went to Bridgeport, Ill., to build a furnace for the Chicago Iron Company; the following year he became connected with the Joliet Iron & Steel Company; and in 1874 he settled in Chicago as consulting engineer for the Green Bay & Bangor Furnace Company.

From this time forward he was identified with the Chicago region. He was one of the organizers of the Joseph H. Brown Iron & Steel Com-

pany, which about 1881 was sold to the Calumet Iron & Steel Company. He purchased a half interest in the rolling mills at Evansville, Ind., in 1884, and the following year moved the business to Hammond, Ind. In 1886 he helped organize the Chicago & Calumet Terminal Railway Company, the beginning of the elaborate system of belt lines which now surround Chicago. About this time he secured title to 1,000 acres of land in Lake County, Ind., on which the town of East Chicago was developed; he was active in securing a congressional appropriation for the improvement of the Calumet River. Another of the enterprises he promoted was the Chicago Elevated Terminal Railway Company, begun in 1890, to bring main line railroads into the city without grade crossings; he was a pioneer in this work of track elevation.

In 1874 Torrence was commissioned colonel of the 2nd Regiment of the Illinois National Guard, and from 1876 until his resignation in 1881, was brigadier-general. During the riots accompanying the railroad strikes of 1877, he was made civil and military dictator of the city and county and succeeded in restoring order without great loss of life or serious property damage. A Republican in politics, he toured through many states in company with Gen. John A. Logan [*q.v.*] during the Blaine-Logan campaign of 1884.

On Sept. 11, 1872, Torrence married Elizabeth Norton, daughter of Judge Jesse O. Norton of Chicago. They had one child, a daughter. Torrence survived his wife five years, dying in Chicago at the age of fifty-three. He was a man of large physique and capable of great endurance. His expert knowledge of the iron and steel business together with much native sagacity and foresight enabled him to become wealthy, while because of his vision and practical force he left his mark upon the Chicago region.

[*Encyc. of Biog. of Ill.*, vol. I (1892); Joseph Kirkland, *The Story of Chicago*, vol. I (1892); A. T. Andreas, *Hist. of Chicago*, vol. III (1886); A. W. Tourgée, *The Story of a Thousand* (1896); *Chicago Sunday Tribune*, Nov. 1, 1896.]

E. A. D.

TORREY, BRADFORD (Oct. 9, 1843–Oct. 7, 1912), ornithologist, author, was born in Weymouth, Mass., a son of Samuel and Sophronia (Dyer) Torrey. He was a descendant of Lieut. James Torrey who emigrated from England and settled at Scituate, Mass., soon after 1640. He was educated in the public schools of his native town. After graduating from high school, he worked for a time in a local shoe-factory and taught school for several years. He then went to Boston and, after brief connection with two or three business houses, was for sixteen years employed in the office of the treasurer of the American Board of Commissioners for Foreign Missions. From boyhood a lover of nature and an attentive observer of wild life, it was not until these years in Boston that he became especially interested in the study of birds, and then in putting the results of his observation into literary form. His first published writing was an article, "With the Birds on Boston Common," which appeared in the *Atlantic Monthly* in February 1883. Two years later his first book, *Birds in the Bush,* was published. In 1886 he found highly congenial employment as one of the editors of the *Youth's Companion.* He was a member of the staff until 1901; his work was the selection and preparation of the entertaining miscellany pages for which that popular weekly was famous. In this occupation he found leisure for continual observation of bird life, not a little travel, and the writing of a succession of essays, sketches, and books, all dealing in the most charming way with his experiences in the fields and woods. The titles of his published volumes are: *A Rambler's Lease* (1889), *The Foot-path Way* (1892), *A Florida Sketch Book* (1894), *Spring Notes from Tennessee* (1896), *A World of Green Hills* (1898), *Everyday Birds* (1901), *Footing it in Franconia* (1901), *The Clerk of the Woods* (1903), *Nature's Invitation* (1904), *Friends on the Shelf* (1906), which was a book of literary criticism, and *Field Days in California* (1913). He was also the sympathetic editor of the fourteen volumes of the journal of Henry David Thoreau [*q.v.*] which were published in the twenty-volume Walden edition in 1906.

Torrey was not a scientifically trained ornithologist and received no academic recognition. He was, however, as many ornithological authorities have testified, a singularly faithful and accurate field observer, whose careful work has added much to the knowledge of the habits and characteristics of native American birds. He became perhaps the foremost authority on humming-birds during his lifetime. His books are as far as possible from being handbooks of ornithology. Torrey was first of all an essayist, and his writing has the discursive fluency and whimsical humor of the true essayist. His style is graceful, unassuming, almost conversational. He takes his reader delightfully into his confidence, and reveals to him a personality of rare gentleness and charm. He writes not of birds alone, but of nature in all its aspects of beauty, and his books are as attractive to the general reader as to the bird lover to whom they are primarily addressed.

Torrey was never married. His circle of acquaintance was not large, for he lived much by himself, but his friends found in him a rare and sympathetic personality, and a character of unusual gentleness and purity. In his last years he moved, partly for reasons of health, to California. He lived near Santa Barbara, much of the time a solitary life, reminiscent of Thoreau's, in a cabin of which he was the sole occupant. He died Oct. 7, 1912, in a hospital in Santa Barbara.

[F. C. Torrey, *The Torrey Families and Their Children in America* (2 vols., 1924–29); *Who's Who in America,* 1912–13; F. H. Allen, in *Auk,* Jan. 1913; obituaries in *Boston Transcript* and *Evening Post* (N. Y.), Oct. 8, 1912; personal acquaintance, letters, and private information.]   H. S. C—n.

TORREY, CHARLES TURNER (Nov. 21, 1813–May 9, 1846), abolitionist, was born in Scituate, Mass., where his ancestor, James Torrey, had settled soon after 1640. His parents, Charles Turner Torrey and Hannah Tolman (Turner), were first cousins, grandchildren of the Rev. Charles Turner; they both died of tuberculosis in their son's infancy, and he was brought up in the home of his maternal grandfather, Charles Turner, Jr., a substantial citizen and sometime member of Congress. Torrey was prepared for college at Phillips Academy, graduated at Yale (A.B., 1833), and after a few months of teaching entered Andover Theological Seminary in 1834. Here he became an abolitionist and organized a students' antislavery society, but because of failing health withdrew from the seminary and completed his theological training at West Medbury under the Rev. Jacob Ide, whose daughter, Mary, he married on Mar. 29, 1837. Two children were born of this union.

Torrey was licensed to preach by the Mendon Association, Oct. 25, 1836, and on Mar. 22 following was ordained and installed as pastor of the Richmond Street Congregational Church of Providence, R. I., but was not successful as a minister either here or at the Harvard Street Congregational Church in Salem, where he served from January 1838 to July 1839. His interest in anti-slavery politics soon encroached upon his pastoral duties. Sharing in the rising irritation against William Lloyd Garrison [*q.v.*] and his heresies regarding Sabbath observance, civil government, and the rights of women, Torrey organized the conservative abolitionists of Massachusetts in a revolt against Garrison's leadership. In the fall of 1838, the conservatives founded the *Massachusetts Abolitionist,* with Torrey as editor, and a few months later they seceded from Garrison's society, organized the Massachusetts Abolition Society, and appointed Torrey as their agent. In this capacity he was not successful. "It was exceedingly difficult for him to labor with others, either as a pastor, a lecturer, or an editor," remarked a colleague (Lovejoy, *post*, p. 87). He shortly resigned, and in 1841 went to Washington as free-lance correspondent.

While reporting the notorious "Convention of Slaveholders" at Annapolis, Md., in January 1842, Torrey was identified as an abolitionist and on Jan. 14 arrested. The case immediately attracted national interest. The anti-slavery congressmen employed a Boston lawyer to be his counsel, and two Maryland lawyers, T. S. Alexander and Joseph M. Palmer, acted for him without compensation. After four days of widely publicized proceedings, Torrey was freed (Jan. 19). Made momentarily famous by this episode, he was appointed editor of the *Tocsin of Liberty*, later the *Albany Patriot*, but was unsuccessful in this position and after a few months relinquished its editorial care.

"An exceedingly vain, trifling man, with no wisdom or stability," as a fellow abolitionist characterized him (T. D. Weld to his wife, Jan. 18, 1842; *Letters, post*, II, 896), Torrey was unable to sustain these recurrent stresses of notoriety and failure. Moving to Baltimore, he made grandiose plans to engage in business, and at the same time he helped escaping slaves from Virginia and Maryland across the border. Inevitably he was arrested, and once more figured in a notorious trial (Nov. 29–Dec. 1, 1844). This time, however, although defended by the distinguished Reverdy Johnson [*q.v.*], he was convicted and sentenced to six years at hard labor in the Maryland state penitentiary. Once in the jail, his mind gave way, and tuberculosis, long latent in his constitution, caused his death little more than a year after his imprisonment. His body was removed to Boston, and at a great public funeral he was honored as a martyr to the anti-slavery cause.

[J. C. Lovejoy, *Memoir of Rev. Charles T. Torrey* (1847), by a brother of Elijah P. Lovejoy [*q.v.*], the first anti-slavery martyr; *N. Y. Evangelist*, Jan., Feb. 1842; *Letters of Theodore Dwight Weld, Angelina Grimké Weld, and Sarah Grimké* (2 vols., 1934), ed. by G. H. Barnes and D. L. Dumond; W. P. and F. J. Garrison, *William Lloyd Garrison* (4 vols., 1885–89); *Massachusetts Abolitionist*, vol. I; *Biog. Notices Grads. Yale Coll.* (1913); F. C. Torrey, *The Torrey Families*, vol. I (1924); Jacob Turner, *Geneal. of the Descendants of Humphrey Turner* (1852); *The Sun* (Baltimore), May 11, 1846.]   G. H. B.

TORREY, JOHN (Aug. 15, 1796–Mar. 10, 1873), botanist and chemist, was born and died in New York City. His earliest American ancestor, Capt. William Torrey of the parish of Combe St. Nicholas, Somerset, emigrated to America in 1640 and settled in Weymouth, Mass.

His father and grandfather were soldiers of the Revolution serving in the vicinity of New York and settled there at its close. His father, Capt. William Torrey, one of the original members of the Society of the Cincinnati, married Margaret Nichols. John was the second of their ten children. About 1810 William Torrey was appointed fiscal agent of the state prison at Greenwich (later Greenwich Village). Here came—imprisoned for debt, it is said—Amos Eaton [*q.v.*], enthusiast in the natural sciences; he took a fancy to John and inspired him with an interest in science that gave direction to his life work. Much of Torrey's earlier scientific work was in mineralogy, but he must have been at the same time a careful student of botany. He was one of the group of young men at the College of Physicians and Surgeons who, under the stimulating leadership of their professor, Samuel Latham Mitchill [*q.v.*], in February 1817 established the Lyceum of Natural History, forerunner of the New York Academy of Sciences. On May 5 a committee of three was appointed to prepare a catalogue of the plants growing near New York, and on Dec. 22, 1817, *A Catalogue of Plants Growing Spontaneously Within Thirty Miles of the City of New York* (1819) was presented to the Lyceum. Most of the work is shown to have been done by Torrey, and it has always been called "Torrey's Catalogue."

Meanwhile, in 1818, Torrey had received the degree of M.D. from the College of Physicians and Surgeons, and had begun the practice of his profession in his native city, but his real interests lay in other fields. During the next few years he gave special attention to the plants of the northeastern United States, and his published scientific papers and correspondence soon spread his fame. At about this time began the long series of government explorations of the West. Members of these expeditions, as a part of their official duties, collected plants, and nearly all of these, for many years, were turned over to Torrey for study and report. The thoroughness of his pioneer work upon these collections has been amply demonstrated by the studies of later generations of botanists. His first publications in this field were his report on the plants collected by David Bates Douglass [*q.v.*] near the source of the Mississippi in 1820 (*American Journal of Science and Arts*, vol. IV, no. 1, 1821) and his reports on the collection made by Edwin James [*q.v.*] in 1820 (*Annals of the Lyceum of Natural History*, vol. I, nos. 1, 2, 1823; vol. II, nos. 4–5, 1826, nos. 6, 7–8, 1827). Late in 1823 was issued the first part of the first book bearing Torrey's name as sole author, *A Flora of the Northern and Middle Sections of the United States.* Two other parts completed the first volume, but the preparation of an intended second volume was prevented by the pressure of other demands upon his time, and by his growing dissatisfaction with the Linnean artificial system of classification then in general use. A small work, however, issued in 1826 under the title, *A Compendium of the Flora of the Northern and Middle States,* supplied in concise form descriptions not only of the plants actually treated in the first volume, but of those intended for inclusion in the projected second one. On Apr. 20, 1824, Torrey married Eliza Shaw of New York, and they went to live at West Point, where he had been appointed professor of chemistry, mineralogy, and geology in the United States Military Academy. Three years later he returned to New York City as a professor of chemistry at the College of Physicians and Surgeons; in this position he was active until 1855, and he continued as professor emeritus for the remainder of his life. In 1830 he accepted the professorship of chemistry and natural history at the College of New Jersey (later Princeton), which he held concurrently with his professorship in New York for nearly twenty-five years.

It was in 1834 that Asa Gray [*q.v.*] came from western New York to New York City, where he was librarian of the Lyceum and in charge of its buildings and collections for a year, and studied plants with Torrey. The latter was so impressed with the younger man's ability that he invited him to become his associate in the preparation of a work on the *Flora of North America,* of which seven parts, comprising all of one volume and most of another, appeared from 1838 to 1843. Meanwhile Torrey's work upon this publication was more or less hampered by his acceptance in 1836 of an appointment as state botanist, resulting in the preparation of a *Flora of the State of New York* (2 vols., 1843). The necessity of studying the western plant collections, pouring in in increasing numbers every year, finally caused the abandonment of Torrey and Gray's *Flora,* but Torrey continued active botanical study and publication. He reported on the plant collections of Joseph Nicholas Nicollet's explorations of 1836–39, Frémont's first expedition of 1842 and his second of 1843–44; W. H. Emory's military reconnaissance of 1846–47; the Mexican Boundary survey of 1848–54; Howard Stansbury's exploration of the Great Salt Lake region in 1849–50; Lorenzo Sitgreaves' expedition down the Zuñi and Colorado rivers in 1851; R. B. Marcy's exploration of the Red River in 1852; various expeditions connected with the Pacific Railroad surveys of 1853–55, including those of E. G. Beckwith, J. W. Gunnison, John Pope, A. W. Whipple, R. S. Williamson, and J. G. Parke; and J. C. Ives's exploration of the Colorado in 1857–58. All of these appeared in the official reports of the expeditions. In spite of these labors he did not neglect monographic work. His monograph of the *Cyperaceae* appeared as early as 1836; his revision of the *Eriogoneae,* in collaboration with Gray, as late as 1870. And throughout his career he was building up his botanical library and herbarium until they became among the most valuable in America; these he transferred to Columbia College about 1860, and in 1899 Columbia deposited them with the newly established New York Botanical Garden. Many of the specimens are accompanied by Torrey's pencil sketches illustrating their structure as shown by his careful dissections.

In 1839 Torrey was elected a foreign member of the Linnean Society of London, and in 1841 a member of the American Academy of Arts and Sciences. In 1863 he was one of the corporate members of the National Academy of Sciences. When the Assay Office was established in New York in 1853, Torrey accepted an appointment as United States assayer, resigning from the Princeton faculty in 1854, and retiring from active work as a professor at Columbia. He continued in this position for the remaining twenty years of his life. Much of his time, however, continued to be devoted to botanical study. His position as assayer opened the way for occasional travel. He visited California, by way of Panama, in 1865, on a confidential mission for the Treasury Department and was able to see for the first time in their natural surroundings various plants that he had made known to science by herbarium study many years before. He spent part of the winter of 1871–72 in Florida, and the next summer visited California for the second time. On his way east he ascended Torrey's Peak in Colorado, which had been named in his honor several years previously. Within a year after his return to New York he suffered an attack of pleurisy, from the effects of which he never recovered, and a few weeks later, in his seventy-seventh year, he died. He was survived by three daughters and one son.

No account of Torrey would be complete without some reference to his remarkable personality, which endeared him to all who knew him. It was characterized by integrity, sagacity, and studiousness, but above all by a certain ingenuousness and genial friendliness, which increased with age. His early encouragement of

Asa Gray has already been mentioned, and his influence upon the careers of other young botanists was extremely helpful. Late in his life a group of young men gathered about him and established a botanical society named, even during his lifetime, the Torrey Botanical Club. This organization, dating from 1867, established in 1870 the *Bulletin of the Torrey Botanical Club*, the first botanical monthly in America; it was largely instrumental in the establishment of the New York Botanical Garden, and today occupies an honored place among the scientific societies of the world. It is a fitting memorial of Torrey the man.

[F. C. Torrey, *The Torrey Families . . . in America* (2 vols., 1924–29) ; *Bull. Torrey Botanical Club,* Mar.–Aug. 1873, Oct. 1900; *Asa Gray, Sci. Papers* (1889), vol. II ; T. S. Hunt, in *Proc. Boston Soc. Nat. Hist.,* Mar. 19, 1873; W. J. Youmans, *Pioneers of Sci. in America* (1895) ; Marcus Benjamin, in *Proc. Am. Asso. for the Advancement of Sci.,* vol. XLVIII (1889) ; *Botanical Gazette,* Feb. 1883 ; *Proc. Linnean Soc.* (London), 1872–73 ; H. L. Fairchild, *A Hist. of the N. Y. Acad. of Sciences* (1887) ; death notice in *N. Y. Times,* Mar. 11, 1873.]   J. H. B—t.

TOTTEN, GEORGE MUIRSON (May 28, 1809–May 17, 1884), engineer, son of Gilbert and Mary (Rice) Totten, was born in New Haven, Conn. After attending schools in his native town, including the Hopkins Grammar School, in 1824 he entered Norwich Military Academy at Norwich, Vt., which later became Norwich University. Graduating in 1827 during the era of canal building, he at once secured a position as assistant engineer on the Farmington Canal, afterwards used as part of the roadbed of the New Haven & Northampton Railroad. He served in a like capacity on the Juniata Canal in Pennsylvania (1828–31), and on the Delaware & Raritan in New Jersey (1831–35). By this time the railroad was rapidly superseding the canal as the principal means of transportation and in 1835 Totten was employed to assist in the construction of a road from Reading to Port Clinton, Pa.; subsequently he was engaged in similar work in Virginia; in Pennsylvania in connection with the Sunbury & Danville R. R. (1837–40) ; and in North Carolina in connection with the Gaston & Raleigh (1840–43).

In 1843 his first South American commission took him to the harbor of Cartagena in Colombia, where he built the Canal del Dique to connect that harbor with the Magdalena River. Associated with him in this enterprise was another pioneer engineer of the United States, John C. Trautwine [*q.v.*]. In 1850, also in association with Trautwine, he became identified with the construction of the Panama Railroad, conceived at the time of the California gold rush of 1849, when the only methods of getting to the West were to go "the Plains across, the Horn around, or the Isthmus over." As engineer-in-chief of this work Totten spent some twenty-five years on the Isthmus, working under the worst possible conditions as to health and compelled to endure great hardships and privations. When Ferdinand de Lesseps became president of the Panama Canal Company in 1879, Totten was asked to remain on the Isthmus as chief, and the only American member, of De Lesseps' staff. Later he went to Venezuela on railroad work near Carácas, served as consulting engineer in connection with the first Panama Canal project, and on many other canal and railroad works.

Generally known as Colonel Totten, he received numerous honors and was recognized as one of the foremost members of his profession. He was made a member of the American Philosophical Society, Jan. 17, 1851; Napoleon III is said to have presented him with a ring and Gen. Guzman Blanco, president of Venezuela, gave him a gold medal. He was married at Pottsville, Pa., July 12, 1835, to Harriet Seely of Sunbury, Pa., who with two daughters survived him.

[W. A. Ellis, *Norwich Univ.* (1911), vol. II ; "The Panama Railroad," *Harper's New Mo. Mag.,* Jan. 1859; *Engineering News,* May 24, 1884; *N. Y. Times,* May 17, 20, 1884.]   J. K. F.

TOTTEN, JOSEPH GILBERT (Aug. 23, 1788–Apr. 22, 1864), soldier, scientist, and engineer, for whom Fort Totten in New York Harbor was named, was born in New Haven, Conn., the son of Peter and Grace (Mansfield) Totten. His mother died when Joseph was three years old and his father shortly afterward was appointed vice-consul at Santa Cruz in the West Indies. The guardianship of the boy thus fell upon his uncle, Jared Mansfield [*q.v.*], a Yale graduate who was selected in 1802 as the first professor of mathematics at the United States Military Academy. Here Joseph became a cadet, in November 1802, and was graduated and commissioned a second lieutenant of engineers, July 1, 1805, the tenth graduate of West Point. As a cadet he had been outstanding in scholarship, industry, "gentlemanly deportment," and popularity. Immediately upon his graduation he was made secretary to his uncle, who had been appointed surveyor general of the Northwestern Territory, in charge of the first systematic survey of the new states of the Union. In order to pursue the requisite explorations, Totten resigned from the army Mar. 31, 1806, but was reappointed to the same rank and corps two years later. He was promoted first lieutenant July 23, 1810, and captain July 31, 1812.

From the time of his return to the service, he

acted as assistant engineer of the harbor defenses of New York City, with special supervision of Fort Clinton at Castle Garden, and of the defenses of New Haven, New London, and Sag Harbor. At the beginning of the War of 1812, he was made chief engineer of the army on the Niagara frontier, where he rendered conspicuous and active service in harbor and fortress defense, winning the brevet of major, June 6, 1813. For gallant conduct at the battle of Plattsburg he was brevetted lieutenant-colonel, Sept. 11, 1814. There followed more than two decades of service on various engineering boards, in the planning and erection of coast defenses, and the execution of river and harbor improvements, during which time he was promoted major in 1818, lieutenant-colonel in 1828, and colonel, Dec. 7, 1838. With the last commission he was simultaneously made chief engineer of the army and inspector of the United States Military Academy, both of which posts he held uninterruptedly for over a quarter of a century, until his death. When Gen. Winfield Scott [q.v.] undertook the southern campaign in the Mexican War, he took Totten with him as chief engineer and member of his "Little Cabinet." Totten originated the detailed and successful plan of operations at Vera Cruz, and was brevetted brigadier-general as of Mar. 29, 1847, for "gallant and meritorious conduct" at the siege. He was also one of the commissioners at the capitulation.

In 1851 when the Lighthouse Board was legally established, Totten became a member, serving until 1858 and again from 1860 till his death. In this capacity he was instrumental in establishing and maintaining a system of lighting by Fresnel lenses. His name is particularly associated with the lights at Seven-Foot Knoll, off Baltimore, and Minot's Ledge off Cohasset, Mass., difficult works to which he devoted all his energy and talents. For these contributions alone, according to a colleague, Gen. John G. Barnard [q.v.], he is entitled to recognition among the Smeatons, Stevensons, and Brunels as one of the great engineers of the age ("Memoir," post). Between 1851 and 1855 he conducted a series of experiments on the effects of firing heavy ordnance from casemate embrasures. He was chosen as a member of the New York state commission on the improvement and preservation of New York Harbor, and to a similar capacity with the Massachusetts commission on Boston Harbor. In 1859–61 he made a reconnaissance of the Pacific Coast in order to determine its state of defense. During the Civil War he continued to be chief engineer of the army and on Mar. 3, 1863, was made a brigadier-

general. He was active in supervising the defensive works around Washington and was a member of the commission to examine them. He was president of the retiring board for disabled officers in 1861 and a member of the board appointed to regulate and fix the heavy ordnance (1861–62). One day before he died he was brevetted a major-general by Congress "for long, faithful and eminent service."

In addition to his reports on national defenses and his essays on ordnance, he published *Essays on Hydraulic and Common Mortars and on Lime-Burning* (1838), a translation from the French, with added notes of his own, which aided engineering progress materially. His studies in conchology were rewarded by having two shells —the *gemma* and *succinea tottenii*—named for him. In 1829 he was awarded the honorary degree of A.M. by Brown University. He was a regent of the Smithsonian Institution from its establishment in 1846 until his death, and in 1863, a corporator of the National Academy of Sciences.

In 1816 he married Catlyna Pearson of Albany, New York, who bore him three sons and four daughters. Before the close of the Civil War he died suddenly of pneumonia, survived by two daughters. The order of the Secretary of War announcing his death stated that "his military career of more than half a century has been one of continued usefulness and distinguished services."

[J. G. Barnard, "Memoir of Joseph Gilbert Totten," in *Nat. Acad. Sci. Biog. Memoirs*, vol. I (1877), and *Eulogy on the Late Bvt. Major Gen. ʾoseph G. Totten* (1866) ; G. W. Cullum, *Biog. Reg. Officers and Grads. U. S. Mil. Acad.* (3rd ed., 1891), vol. I ; J. H. Smith, *The War with Mexico* (2 vols., 1919) ; W. A. Ganoe, *The Hist. of the U. S. Army* (1924) ; F. B. Heitman, *Hist. Reg. and Dict. U. S. Army* (1903) ; *Army and Navy Jour.*, Apr. 30, 1864 ; *Daily National Intelligencer* (Washington), Apr. 25, 1864 ; Records, Old Files Section, Adjutant General's Office, Washington.]

W. A. G.

TOU, ERIK HANSEN (Oct. 11, 1857–Nov. 14, 1917), missionary, the son of Hans and Helga Serine (Eriksen) Andersen, was born near Stavanger, Norway. After completing his early schooling, he worked as a miller in Tou mill near his home; hence his surname Tou. In 1881 he went to Minneapolis, Minn., to learn more about mills, intending to return to Norway later. Disheartened at the poor prospects for employment, he became a student in Augsburg Seminary, and was graduated with the B.A. degree in 1886, and the degree in theology in 1889. In 1889 he was married to Caroline Elisabeth Knudsen, of Fulton, Iowa, and took up missionary work in Madagascar. They were first stationed at Tulear and St. Augustine, 1889–90, and then

Tou

in Manasoa, on the southwest coast. They were the first missionaries in the region south of the Onilahy River, occupied by the Tanosy tribe.

Tou preached at two main stations and thirteen substations, established a school, in which Malagasy and French were taught, a theological seminary, and two foundling asylums, which were converted to orphanages when the French government took full possession of the island. He advocated, and finally saw realized, a free dispensary and the teaching of scientific agriculture at his station. Much of the flourishing Christian life in southwest Madagascar owed its beginnings to his efforts. He faced an almost impossible task in the midst of an immoral, grossly superstitious tribe, yet, after a few years he claimed that Christianity had done more for the Tanosy than had three hundred years of partial contact with European civilization. The climate was unhealthful, and financial support entirely inadequate. Three of his children and his wife died on the island. In a fascinating book, *Den lutherske Frikirkes Hedningemission paa Madagaskar* (1898), he related his earlier experiences on the island. His later experiences were detailed in articles for the press, and were published in the *Lutheraneren, Luthersk Kirkeblad, Folkebladet, Gasseren,* and, occasionally, in *Skandinaven,* and *Visergutten.* He also wrote for these papers on theological themes and great missionaries of the past, and translated into Norwegian *The Miracles of Missions* (1891), by A. T. Pierson. At his death he left seven volumes of diaries. Other diaries, antedating these, along with records and books, were consumed when his home was destroyed by fire in Madagascar.

With his health much impaired, Tou left Madagascar in 1903 after his marriage to his second wife, Alida Olen, of Benson, Minn., who had worked as a deaconess at Manasoa. He was missionary pastor in Pukwana, S. Dak., from 1904 to 1909, and at Napoleon, N. Dak., until his death. His hardships were many in these sparsely populated regions of extreme summer heat and winter cold. Hard travel, loneliness, poverty, and exposure, shortened his life. He was a faithful pastor and an able expounder of the Scriptures. In the United States he again gathered a valuable working library and his correspondence was extensive. From 1915 he was editor of *Gasseren.* A short time before he died he was made a member of the Lutheran Board of Missions of the Lutheran Free Church. His wife and three children survived him.

[Diary in the possession of the writer; annuals of *Den norsk danske lutherske Konferents, Den forenede norsk lutherske Kirke i Amerika, Augsburgs Venner,*

Toucey

Den norsk lutherske Frikirke; Lars Lillehie, *Augsburg Seminary and the Luth. Free Ch.* (1928); obituaries in *Napoleon Homestead* (Napoleon, N. Dak.), and in *Folkebladet* (Minneapolis, Minn.), Nov. 21, 1917.]

J. O. E.

TOUCEY, ISAAC (Nov. 15, 1792–July 30, 1869), governor of Connecticut, congressman, senator, and cabinet official, was born in Newtown, Conn., the son of Zalmon and Phebe (Booth) Toucey (or Tousey). He was a descendant of Richard Toucey who came from England to Saybrook, Conn., about 1655 and whose grandson, Thomas, was the first Congregational minister of Newtown. After a common-school training, Isaac studied law with Asa Chapman, who later became a judge of the supreme court of errors. Admitted to the bar in 1818, Toucey practised law in the city of Hartford, which was thereafter his place of residence.

From 1822 to 1835 he was state's attorney for Hartford County. In the latter year he became a member of Congress, serving as such until Mar. 3, 1839. He did not speak often, or ever at great length, his most sustained effort being a plea, Sept. 29, 1837, for the postponement of payments on the surplus distribution bill (*Register of Debates in Congress,* 25 Cong., 1 Sess., pp. 1133–35). At the close of his second term, he resumed his practice in Hartford, and again served as state's attorney, 1842–44. In 1845 he was the unsuccessful Democratic candidate for governor; the following year, there being no choice by the people, he was chosen governor by the legislature; in the election of 1847 he was defeated. He had displeased those interested in local railroads by vetoing a bill authorizing the construction of a bridge over the Connecticut River at Middletown, and had aroused ill feelings by declaring that there was a great deal of bribery practised in connection with state elections.

Shortly after his governorship he again became connected with national affairs, serving as attorney-general in Polk's cabinet from June 1848 to March 1849, and for a short time during that period, in the absence of Buchanan from Washington, acting as secretary of state. In 1850 he was elected to the upper house of the Connecticut legislature, and in 1852 was again a member of the lower house. In the latter year he was elected to the United States Senate, and served from May 12, 1852, to Mar. 3, 1857. Here he was more prominent than he had been in the House. In August 1852, while condemning the "higher law" theory embraced by Seward and Sumner, he asked for the enforcement of the fugitive-slave act because it was the law, and because Northern opposition to it amounted to nullifica-

600

tion (*Congressional Globe,* 32 Cong., 1 Sess., App., pp. 1121–22). Two years later he supported the Kansas-Nebraska bill, on the ground that the Missouri Compromise had placed an unconstitutional limitation on states to be admitted from the northern part of the Louisiana Purchase (*Ibid.,* 33 Cong., 1 Sess., App., pp. 313–15). For this stand Toucey was criticized by the *Hartford Times,* a Democratic paper which had usually supported his policies as congressman and as governor.

In 1857 President Buchanan chose Toucey as secretary of the navy. His sympathies were more or less with the South, and he was suspected, perhaps unjustly, of so disposing of the country's naval forces in 1860 as to aid the South in the movement toward secession (See *House Journal,* 36 Cong., 2 Sess., pp. 359, 466–69; *House Report, No. 87,* same session; Report of the Secretary of the Navy in *Senate Executive Document, No. 1,* 37 Cong., 1 Sess.). Toucey's sympathetic attitude toward the South incited some members of the Connecticut legislature to remove his portrait from the gallery of ex-governors, and a resolution providing for the replacement of the portrait, offered in the state Senate in 1863, was defeated. One achievement of the much maligned secretary has received unstinted praise: he supervised the naval expedition to Paraguay, December 1858, consisting of a force of some nineteen vessels and 2,500 men, which was financed with such economy as to be completed without a special congressional appropriation. After his retirement from the cabinet Toucey passed the remainder of his life in Hartford. During the Civil War he supported the cause of the North. In private life he was a likeable man, reserved though not distant in contacts with others. He had a striking personal appearance, somewhat resembling that of Andrew Jackson. His declining years were troubled by the feeble health of his wife, Catharine Nichols, whom he had married Oct. 28, 1827; they had no children.

[Index to Barbour Coll. of Conn. Vital Records, State Library, Hartford; *Biog. Dir. Am. Cong.* (1928); J. H. Trumbull, *The Memorial Hist. of Hartford County, Conn.* (1886), vol. I; W. D. Shipman, "Isaac Toucey," 36 *Conn. Reports,* 587–88; J. B. Moore, *The Works of James Buchanan* (12 vols., 1908–11); *U. S. Democratic Rev.,* Oct. 1859; *Hartford Daily Courant,* July 31, 1869.]					J. M. M.

TOULMIN, HARRY (Apr. 7, 1766–Nov. 11, 1823), clergyman, educator, territorial district judge, was born at Taunton, Somersetshire, England. A ministerial bent in the youth, inherited perhaps from his father, the Rev. Joshua Toulmin (see *Dictionary of National Biography*), was strengthened by intimacy with Joseph Priestley [*q.v.*]. Most of his education, however, was acquired in the book store kept by his mother, Jane (Smith) Toulmin, although he also attended Hoxton Academy. While serving as minister in Monton and Chowbent, Lancashire (1786–92), he aroused popular disapproval because of his Unitarian leanings. Influenced by this feeling and by an interest in America gained from extensive reading, he published, in 1792, three pamphlets favoring emigration to America (Jillson, *post*). A few months later, he accompanied Priestley to the United States, where he became acquainted with Jefferson. The latter and Madison furnished him with letters of introduction, commending him as an instructor of youth "in classical knowledge and other branches of liberal education" (Madison Papers, Library of Congress). Thus armed, he went to Kentucky, where, in February 1794, he was elected president of Transylvania University. Despite opposition, he held the office for two years, and then for eight years was secretary to the Commonwealth of Kentucky. During this period he compiled *A Collection of the Permanent and Public Acts of the General Assembly of Kentucky* (1802), and with James Blair prepared *A Review of the Criminal Law of the Commonwealth of Kentucky* (2 vols., 1804–06). In 1806 he published *The American Attorney's Pocket Book,* and in 1807, *The Magistrates' Assistant,* which may have first appeared as early as 1801.

In 1804 Toulmin was appointed judge of the superior court for the eastern, or Tombigbee, district of Mississippi Territory (later part of Alabama). Thenceforth he was permanently identified with this region, without losing touch with influential friends or former background. Through letter, personal counsel, and legal procedure he sought to restrain lawless borderers and to allay the fears of jealous Spaniards by securing the remission of imposts at Mobile and by softening the resentment aroused by these exactions. In this double task he was only partially successful (Cox, pp. 176, 222, 293). Nor did he fare better in 1807 with Burr's mysterious following; he merely succeeded in arresting a few of that conspirator's associates and in remanding them for trial elsewhere. His purpose was to keep Burr away from the restless settlers on the Tombigbee. He found himself roundly abused—unjustly he thought—as a tool of Gen. James Wilkinson (cf. *Indiana Magazine of History,* December 1929, p. 274).

In 1810 Toulmin's law-abiding course experienced its most severe tests. Insurrection broke out in West Florida and self-appointed leaders of the Tombigbee district hastened to organize the Mobile Society for the purpose of occupying the nearby Spanish holdings. Toulmin, prompted both by President Madison and by Gov. David Holmes [qq.v.], bestirred himself to forestall the attempts. While he supported the claim of the United States to the Mobile region and sympathized with those who protested against Spanish exactions there, he sought in a masterly charge to the grand jury, Sept. 16, 1810, to restrain his fellow citizens from using force and to impress upon them their responsibility for the maintenance of peace. His efforts contributed to break up these illegal attempts but thereby made him extremely unpopular (Cox, pp. 444–54; *National Intelligencer*, Nov. 7 and 13, 1810).

In the following month, Toulmin was still further hampered in his efforts to preserve order by the presence of Reuben Kemper [q.v.]. The latter represented the convention that had wrested Baton Rouge from Spanish control and now sought to incorporate Mobile in the embryo state of West Florida. Toulmin's purpose was to keep the American population above the line from helping Kemper. He also hoped to induce the Spanish authorities to deliver Mobile to the American government (*American Historical Review*, July 1897, pp. 701–02). In neither task did he gain his immediate end. At a critical period in Kemper's movements, however, by arresting that obstreperous leader, he contributed to the defeat of another filibustering project. For this service, Kemper characterized him as a "base Devil, filled with deception and Bloody Rascality" (Cox, p. 470), but later congressional reports failed to support this prejudiced opinion (*American State Papers, Miscellaneous*, vol. II, 1834, pp. 162, 184, 443), while most of the "good elements" of the community appreciated his efforts to uphold a high standard of legal procedure.

Toulmin retained his judgeship until 1819 and during this period did much to straighten out the land claims and other legal tangles in the region. He also edited *The Statutes of the Mississippi Territory* (1807). In 1819 he was a prominent member of the convention that formed a constitution for Alabama, and four years later he compiled *A Digest of the Territorial Laws of Alabama* (1823). Thus he linked his name with three formal state codes. He was twice married, and left children.

[Printed sources include A. J. Pickett, *Hist. of Ala.* (1851), vol. II; I. J. Cox, *The West Florida Controversy* (1918); W. P. Jillson, *A Transylvanian Trilogy* (1932), reprinting Toulmin's pamphlets favoring emigration, with a bibliog. of his writings and of references; *Official Letter Books of W. C. C. Claiborne* (6 vols., 1917), ed. by Dunbar Rowland; Robert Peter, *Transylvania Univ.* (1896), being Filson Club Pub. No. 11; *Daily National Intelligencer* (Washington), Dec. 13, 1823. Unpublished letters of Toulmin's occur in the papers of Jefferson, Madison, and John Breckinridge, and the West Florida Papers, in the Lib. of Cong.; in the Miss. Territorial Archives and the Proc. of the Exec. Council of Miss. Territory, Dept. of State, Washington; and in Claiborne Letters E, Miss. Dept. of Archives and Hist. According to Jillson (*op. cit.*), a manuscript account of the Toulmin family is preserved at Transylvania Univ.]   I. J. C.

TOULMIN, HARRY THEOPHILUS (Mar. 4, 1838–Nov. 12, 1916), Confederate officer, jurist, was born in Mobile County, Ala., the son of Theophilus Lindsay and Amante E. (Juzan) Toulmin. He was a grandson of Judge Harry Toulmin [q.v.], a prominent figure of frontier days. After obtaining his preparatory education in the private schools at Toulminville and Mobile, he entered the University of Alabama in 1852. Although he left this institution in his sophomore year, he resumed his studies in 1856 at the University of Virginia, where he devoted a year to law. Subsequently he became interested in the Civil Law and attended a course of lectures at the University of Louisiana (now Tulane University), studying in the office of a local attorney at the same time. This interest was short-lived for one year later, in 1860, he returned to Mobile where he studied in the office of Col. Robert H. Smith and was admitted to practice before the Alabama bar. The outbreak of the Civil War interrupted his work, and soon after its commencement he was fighting as a private in the Confederate army. He quickly rose from the ranks and by the end of the war held a commission as colonel. During the course of hostilities he was wounded three times, took part in numerous battles, and participated in the campaigns of Dalton and Atlanta.

When peace was restored he resumed practice with Colonel Smith. In 1868 he was chosen presidential elector and two years later was elected for a two-year term to the Alabama legislature. In the meantime, on May 4, 1869, he married Mary Montague Henshaw. In 1874 he again ran for office and was elected for a six-year term as judge for the sixth judicial circuit of Alabama. In 1880 he was reëlected to the same position (although the circuit was somewhat realigned and was then known as the first circuit) but in 1882 resigned to return to his practice. Upon the creation of the federal Southern District of Alabama in 1886, President Cleveland appointed him district judge. His nomination was confirmed by the Senate Jan. 13, 1887, and on Jan. 31 he took the oath of office. He remained in this office until his death.

During his long career on the bench he earned for himself the affection and esteem of the bar, as shown by the genuine expressions of respect vouchsafed him on the occasion of the announcement of his contemplated resignation, a resignation forestalled by death. His decisions were seldom reversed by the upper courts and were at one time complimented by William Howard Taft. Among the first to use the injunction in labor disputes, he applied it in 1893 to prevent striking shop employees from interfering with strike-breakers in the Louisville & Nashville Railroad strike.

It had been an ambition on the part of Toulmin to be a federal judge, and he took pride in his long service. A little over a month prior to his death, on making known his plans to resign, he said: "I am happy that my early ambitions have been realized and I trust that my stewardship will bear the light of day" (*Mobile Register*, Oct. 4, 1916, p. 1). He died in Toulminville, a quarter-mile from his birthplace; his wife survived him.

[See *Who's Who in America*, 1916–17; T. M. Owen, *Hist. of Ala. and Dict. of Ala. Biog.* (1921), vol. IV; *Memorial Record of Ala.* (1893), II, 606; T. W. Palmer, *A Reg. of the Officers and Students of the Univ. of Ala.* (1901); *Mobile Register*, Oct. 4, Nov. 13, 14, 1916; *Montgomery Advertiser*, Nov. 13, 1916. The first three references give year of birth as 1838, the last three, as 1835.]

L. M. S.

TOUMEY, JAMES WILLIAM (Apr. 17, 1865–May 6, 1932), forester, teacher, was born in Lawrence, Mich., the son of Dennis and Mary (Buckley) Toumey. His youth was spent on his father's farm and his early education was in the local schools. He prepared for college at the high school in Decatur, Mich., but taught school for some years before entering the Michigan Agricultural College, from which he graduated in 1889.

He was appointed instructor in botany at the Michigan Agricultural College in 1890. In 1891 he was called to the University of Arizona, where he remained until 1898, having advanced to a professorship in botany. At the same time he also held the position of botanist in the Arizona State Agricultural Experiment Station, and served as acting director of the Station in 1897–98. While in Arizona he made notable investigations in the fields of botany and entomology, with special work on the date palm and on the cacti. He visited England in 1899 to assist in arranging the collection of cacti at Kew.

In 1899 he was appointed superintendent of tree planting in the division of forestry, United States Department of Agriculture. The following year the Yale School of Forestry was established and Toumey became one of the two regular members of the staff. From 1910 to 1922 he

served as dean and during this period he materially enlarged the endowments, physical facilities, and forest properties of the institution. Because of his scholarly attitude and his vigorous personality he played a prominent part in formulating a program of forest education and in building the scientific foundations of the practice of forestry in America. In 1922 he retired from the deanship in order to devote his entire efforts to teaching and research. He possessed exceptional ability to inspire research activities in others and directed basic studies in plant physiology and in ecology as affecting the growth and development of trees and forests. He gave a new emphasis to the importance of soil moisture as one of the factors governing the survival of young trees in the forest.

Toumey was widely known among scholars both in the United States and abroad. His books, *Seeding and Planting in the Practice of Forestry* (1916), revised by Toumey and Clarence F. Korstian in 1931, and *Foundations of Silviculture upon an Ecological Basis* (1928), are standard works. He initiated a series of scientific bulletins at the Yale School of Forestry and he wrote extensively for forestry journals and other periodicals. His writings cover a wide range of subjects, including forestry articles of a popular nature, and though they were dominantly of a scientific character, they include discussions on applied silviculture, forest taxation, watershed protection, forest economics, and public forest policy. Toumey was twice married: first, June 17, 1897, to Constantia H. Blake of New Haven, who died in 1904 leaving a son; second, in 1908, to Nannie Trowbridge of New Haven.

[For sources, see *Science*, June 3, 1932; *Yale Forest School News*, July 1932; *Journal of Forestry*, Oct. 1932; *Who's Who in America*, 1932–33; J. M. and Jaques Cattell, *Am. Men of Sci.* (1927); *Alumni Cat. No. Mich. State Coll. Bull.* (1931); J. M. Cattell, *Leaders in Education* (1932); *N. Y. Times*, May 7, 1932; *New Haven Journal Courier*, May 9, 1932. A list of Toumey's writings is filed at the Yale Univ. Lib.]

H. S. G—s.

TOURGÉE, ALBION WINEGAR (May 2, 1838–May 21, 1905), Carpet-bagger, author, the first and only surviving child of Valentine and Louisa Emma (Winegar) Tourgée, was born in Williamsfield, Ohio. His father was of French Huguenot, his mother of German Palatine descent. At the age of nine he removed with his family to Kingsville, Ohio, and later he lived for two years with a maternal uncle in Lee, Mass. Afterward he attended Kingsville Academy until he entered the sophomore class at the University of Rochester in 1859. He withdrew in January 1861 to teach at Wilson, N. Y., and on Apr. 19 enlisted in the 27th New York Regiment; in

1862, however, he was awarded the B.A. degree. At the first battle of Bull Run he received a spinal wound from which he never entirely recovered, and he said that he there lost the sight of his left eye, but there is considerable evidence that this misfortune had resulted from an accident in boyhood (Dibble, *post,* p. 21). He began to read law, but in July 1862 was commissioned a lieutenant in the 105th Ohio Regiment; at the battle of Perryville he was again injured in the spine. In January 1863 he was captured at Murfreesboro, Tenn., and, according to his own account (Chicago *Daily Inter Ocean,* Feb. 15, 1890), was confined for four months in Confederate prisons. Exchanged, he returned to Ohio and on May 14, 1863, married Emma Lodoiska, the daughter of Harmon and Mary Corwin Kilbourne, who, with one daughter, survived him. Returning to his regiment, he was present at Tullahoma, Chickamauga, Lookout Mountain, and Missionary Ridge. Twice during his military service he was placed under arrest for virtual insubordination, and on Dec. 6, 1863, he resigned and returned to the study of law; he was admitted to the bar of Ohio in May 1864. He taught a short time in Erie, Pa., meanwhile writing for a newspaper, and in the fall of 1865 removed to Greensboro, N. C., where he practised law and organized a nursery company which soon failed.

In 1866 he definitely entered politics. At the Southern Loyalist convention at Philadelphia he attracted widespread attention by a speech notable at once for venom and inaccuracy. In January 1867 he founded the *Union Register,* devoted to Radical policies with respect to the "poor, misguided, and mismanaged South." This paper was forced to suspend in June. In the proceedings of the so-called "carpet-bag" convention of 1868 in North Carolina he took an active and prominent part. He sought vainly to secure the repudiation of the ante-bellum debt of the state, and was instrumental in securing the insertion in the new constitution of a provision for the codification of the whole law in imitation of New York and Ohio; in 1868, with V. C. Barringer and W. B. Rodman, he prepared *The Code of Civil Procedure of North Carolina, to Special Proceedings.* In 1868 also he was elected a judge of the superior court; he served for six years.

As a judge Tourgée was a bitter political partisan, seeking at all times the larger financial rewards and opportunities of a place in Congress, and converting the bench into a stump. But with respect to causes that had no political implications, he became one of the best judges of the Carpet-bag régime. He was utterly careless in

attendance upon courts and won the enmity of the mass of the white people, who doubted his honesty, but, by his personal courage, he excited admiration. He was one of the larger beneficiaries of the corrupt Littlefield and Swepson "ring" for services never publicly named (Hamilton, *Reconstruction,* pp. 430–31). He was one of the most brilliant of the Carpet-baggers in the South, but the mature judgment of many of his contemporaries in North Carolina was that he was unstable and unreliable. In public matters he was not so much immoral as unmoral, while his private life was above reproach.

He served without distinction in the convention of 1875, and the following year became pension agent at Raleigh. In 1878 (Mar. 18–May 28, in Greensboro *North State*) he published anonymously the "C" Letters, which are important in North Carolina political literature, and are marked by a brilliance not often found in his writings. In the same year he was defeated for Congress and the following year he went to New York. In the winter he was for a few months in Denver, and in 1881 he purchased a house in Mayville, N. Y., which was thenceforth his home.

Tourgée made money in a number of ways during Reconstruction, but lost it in hopeless ventures. Constantly dabbling with journalism, he finally attempted more pretentious literary work. In 1874, *Toinette,* which had been written some years before, was published under the pseudonym "Henry Churton." It was later published as *A Royal Gentleman* (1881) under his own name. Other works followed in rapid succession. Besides *A Digest of Cited Cases in the North Carolina Reports* (1879), these were chiefly novels and collections of contributions, chiefly political, to newspapers and magazines. He was for two years (1882–84) editor and chief contributor of a weekly magazine, *Our Continent,* which failed, taking all his savings; he was a regular contributor to the Chicago *Daily Inter Ocean*; he collaborated in an unsuccessful play, based upon the best-known of his novels; and he delivered several hundred public lectures. In 1895 he established in Buffalo *The Basis: A Journal of Citizenship,* which died a year later. The sale of his books steadily declined, and his income had almost reached the vanishing point when President McKinley appointed him consul at Bordeaux, where he remained in declining health until his death. In 1903 he was appointed consul-general at Halifax but never accepted the post.

In spite of the volume of his published work, Tourgée's reputation as a writer rests largely upon one book, *A Fool's Errand* (1879), and that, perhaps, more because it was the first literary effort to deal with Reconstruction than because of its inherent merit, though it has undoubtedly a certain power. None of his other works can be compared with it in quality or popularity. Five of his other novels, *Figs and Thistles* (1879), *Bricks Without Straw* (1880), *A Royal Gentleman* (1881), *John Eax and Mamelon* (1882), and *Hot Plowshares* (1883), dealt directly or indirectly with Reconstruction. All of his novels are conventionally romantic, show little originality, and lack literary finish. His political articles, reflecting the author, are dogmatic and egotistical.

[*Who's Who in America*, 1903–05; *Jour. of the Constitutional Convention of the State of N. C. . . . 1868* (1868); *North Carolina Standard*, 1866–70; *The Sentinel* (Raleigh, N. C.), 1865–74; R. F. Dibble, *Albion W. Tourgée* (1921), containing complete bibliog. of writings; J. G. de R. Hamilton, ed., *The Correspondence of Jonathan Worth* (2 vols., 1909); J. G. deR. Hamilton, *Reconstruction in N. C.* (1914); A. W. Tourgée, *The Story of a Thousand* (1896); Frank Nash, in S. A. Ashe, ed., *Biog. Hist. of N. C.*, IV, 1906, pp. 440–49; obituary in *N. Y. Times*, May 22, 1905.]

J. G. deR. H.

TOURJÉE, EBEN (June 1, 1834–Apr. 12, 1891), musician, founder of the New England Conservatory of Music, was the son of Ebenezer and Angelina (Ball) Tourjée, of Warwick, R. I. The Tourjée family was of Huguenot descent, long settled in Rhode Island. On his mother's side Tourjée was of the Balls of Block Island. At the age of eight he was employed in a local calico mill. Later, having obtained work at the Harrisville, R. I., cotton factory owned by Gov. Eilsha Harris, he attracted the attention of his employer by exceptionally beautiful singing in a church choir, and in his fourteenth year he so effectively played the organ at the wedding of one of the governor's daughters that he was given opportunity for regular instruction in music at Providence and in academic subjects at the East Greenwich Seminary. In 1851, holding a clerkship in a Providence music store, he edited and published the *Key-Note,* which later became the *Massachusetts Music Journal* (Samuel, *post,* p. 1). In 1853 he visited Boston, seeking support for a conservatory of music, but received no encouragement. Thereupon, with almost no capital, he opened at Fall River, Mass., a school which exemplified for the first time in New England the conservatory system of teaching. It quickly enrolled upwards of five hundred pupils, but as it failed to pay its way Tourjée presently removed to Newport, R. I., where he combined private teaching and organ playing. He there married, in October 1855, Abbie I. Tuell. She died in October 1867. His second marriage, in 1871, was to Sarah Lee of Auburndale,

Mass., who with two sons and two daughters survived him. In 1861 he was chosen music director at the East Greenwich Seminary. At the time of the Civil War he gave enthusiastic service as musical organizer of enlistment rallies. Midway during the war he studied music for a short time in Germany. By 1864 the musical department at East Greenwich had outgrown the seminary, and Tourjée reorganized it as the Musical Institute of Providence (later the Providence Conservatory of Music).

In 1867 he transferred his activities to Boston, where in association with Robert Goldbeck he opened the New England Conservatory of Music almost simultaneously with the Boston Conservatory of Music, directed by Julius Eichberg [*qq.v.*]. Tourjée's ability as an organizer became nationally known when he served as first assistant to Patrick Sarsfield Gilmore [*q.v.*] in the management of two great peace jubilees in Boston, 1869 and 1872. His conservatory, meantime, had a rapid growth. Its first class was graduated in 1870. In 1882 Tourjée transferred the school from rented quarters in the Music Hall to the former St. James Hotel, Franklin Square, which he bought, incurring a debt of about $250,000. An indefatigable worker, who inspired the best efforts of other musicians, Tourjée struggled in his last years under intolerable financial burdens. The school was large, its gross income was increased by supplementary activities, such as the summer excursions to Europe which he and Mrs. Tourjée successfully conducted, and yet the deficits persisted. When he sought state aid, such as had been granted to the Massachusetts Institute of Technology, he met with rebuffs, even though the Conservatory had been incorporated as a non-profit-making institution. A frail man, never robust, he became an invalid and directed the school from a wheel chair. Shortly before his death, which occurred in Boston, a directory committee was appointed subject to the final authority of a board of trustees, a plan of management that was continued at the New England Conservatory in later directorships. A bust of Tourjée by W. A. J. Claus is at the Conservatory.

[The best biog. account is that of Elizabeth I. Samuel, in *New England Conservatory Rev.,* June 1913, based on notes supplied by Clara Tourjée Nelson and Lizzie Tourjée Estabrook. See also Nicholas Ball, *Edward Ball and Some of His Descendants* (1891); G. M. Stutsman, in *Musical America,* Aug. 1934; H. M. Dunham, in *The Life of a Musician* (1913); F. W. Coburn, in *Lowell Courier-Citizen,* May 21–June 20, 1934; obituaries in *Boston Daily Globe* and *Boston Transcript,* Apr. 13, 1891. In the lib. of the New England Conservatory of Music are many data.]   F. W. C.

TOUSARD, ANNE LOUIS de (Mar. 12, 1749–May 8, 1817), soldier, was born in Paris, the son of Gen. Charles Germain de Tousard, Knight of Malta, and his wife, Antoinette de Poitevin de la Croix. Upon graduating from the Artillery School at Strasbourg, he was commissioned in 1769 a second lieutenant in the Royal Artillery Corps. After the outbreak of the American Revolution, upon the recommendation of Benjamin Franklin, Silas Deane, American commissioner to France, promised the young officer the grade of captain if he would serve in the American army. Tousard, accordingly, joined the Du Coudray expedition, which arrived at Portsmouth, N. H., on Jan. 25, 1777, but Congress refused to confirm the rank promised by Deane. Tousard later joined Lafayette as aide, serving in the ill-fated Canadian campaign, and in the battles of Brandywine and Germantown. In an engagement in Rhode Island on Aug. 28, 1778, he captured a field piece from the English, sustaining a severe wound in his right arm, which was amputated at his request in order that he might the more speedily return to duty. Congress brevetted him a lieutenant-colonel for his gallantry and voted him a life pension of thirty dollars a month (Oct. 27, 1778).

Following his return to France on account of his wound, he was made a Chevalier of St. Louis and awarded the cross of that order, July 3, 1779, and on Apr. 5, 1780, was commissioned major in the Provincial Regiment of Toul. In January 1784, he was made a member of the Society of the Cincinnati, and in July of that year was commissioned lieutenant-colonel of the Regiment du Cap and went to Santo Domingo, where he served brilliantly against the negro uprising. Here he married, in January 1788, Maria Francisca Regina (Joubert) St. Martin, widow of a rich planter.

When the civil commissioners who had been sent to Santo Domingo by the National Convention of France clashed with Colonel Cambefort of the Regiment du Cap and ordered his arrest, Tousard, on Oct. 19, 1792, announced that his regiment would not permit the deportation of its colonel. He was thereupon accused of counter-revolutionary principles, of correspondence with revolted slaves, and of resistance to orders, and with Cambefort was arrested and shipped to the "bloody prisons of l'Abbaye" in France, where the two remained until they were released on Feb. 4, 1793, through the intercession of the American minister. Tousard then joined his wife and children in the United States, whither they had gone for safety. His wife died at Wilmington, Del., in July 1794, and the next year he married Anna Maria Geddes. Reinstated in the United States Army in February 1795, he was commissioned major of the 2nd Artillery, and became its colonel five years later. During the intervening period he planned and superintended the building of fortifications at Fort Mifflin, Pa., at West Point, N. Y., and at Newport, R. I. He was promoted, Dec. 1, 1800, to inspector of artillery, and the following year moved to West Point where he remodeled the garrison as a military school. In 1802 he went back to Santo Domingo and served under the ill-fated General Leclerc, but returned to France the same year and retired to Soissons on a pension of 2000 francs granted him by the Emperor.

In 1805 he was sent back to America as sub-commissary and chancellor of commercial relations at New Orleans, and was later moved to Philadelphia as vice-consul. In 1809 he was transferred to Baltimore to protect Elizabeth Patterson Bonaparte [q.v.], wife of Jerome Bonaparte, and her son, and in 1811 he was ordered to New Orleans as consul ad interim. He occupied this position until July 1816, when he was relieved by Petry and returned to France. He died in Paris less than a year later.

While he was in prison in 1793 Tousard wrote a pamphlet in his own defense, *Tousard, Lieutenant-Colonel du Régiment du Cap, à la Convention Nationale* (1793), which was translated into English, and appeared in Philadelphia under the title, *Justification of Lewis Tousard Addressed to the National Convention of France* (1793). His only other literary venture was the *American Artillerist's Companion* begun in 1795 at the instigation of General Washington, in two volumes (1809–13), with an added volume of plates executed with his left hand.

[Personal letters and documents in the Hist. Soc. of Pa. (Phila.), in the Lib. of Cong., and in the possession of Tousard's descendants; A. B. Gardiner, *The Order of the Cincinnati in France* (1905); F. B. Heitman, *Hist. Reg. of Officers of the Continental Army* (1893) and *Hist. Reg. and Dict. U. S. Army* (1903), vol. I; L. G. M. duB. de Contenson, *La Société des Cincinnati de France* (1934); Dunbar Rowland, *Official Letter Books of W. C. C. Claiborne* (1917), vol. VI.]   E. L. T.

TOUSEY, SINCLAIR (July 18, 1815–June 16, 1887), head of the American News Company, was born at New Haven, Conn., the son of Zerah and Nerissa (Crane) Tousey, and a descendant of Richard Tousey who settled in Saybrook in 1679. Having lost his parents in early childhood, he had very limited schooling and at the age of ten years went to work in a cotton factory in central New York. Later he was bound out to a farmer in the same section. Becoming dissatisfied, he walked back to Connecticut, and worked first as a farm hand and then as an apprentice to a carpenter. Afterwards he sought to make a fortune by going to New York City, where he began as a grocery clerk. After working as a carrier boy for the *New York Herald,* he became a news agent in New Haven for the *New York Transcript,* and then circulation promoter in Philadelphia for the New York *Sun.* When the opportunities in this field seemed to him still too limited, he went to the Middle West as an agent for a patent medicine company; in 1836 he appears in Louisville, Ky., city directory in that capacity. He is said to have established in Louisville a short-lived penny daily newspaper, the *Daily Times* (*Appletons' Annual* and *Frank Leslie's Chimney Corner, post*), the first of its kind west of the Alleghanies. From 1840 to 1853 he operated a farm in New York but in 1853 he entered the firm of Ross, Jones, and Tousey, wholesale news agents and booksellers, in New York City. Seven years later, through the retirement first of one and then of the other of his partners, he became the sole proprietor of the business, which had grown in volume until it amounted, it is said, to a million dollars a year. At the outbreak of the Civil War he enlisted in the 14th New York Regiment of Volunteer Engineers and served until 1863. In 1864 he published *Life in the Union Army,* an account in verse of the difficulties and hardships of the soldiers, which, together with a long introduction in prose, was frankly critical of army officers and of the War Department. Early in 1864 his business was combined with that of some other companies engaged in the same field to form the American News Company, of which he became president, a position that he continued to fill until his death twenty-three years later.

Tousey joined the Republican party at its inception and took an active part in the anti-slavery agitation. During the draft riots in New York City he had fences and sidewalks placarded with posters bearing the words, "Don't Unchain the Tiger," by which he hoped to warn the rioters against an aroused public opinion. Besides his activities against slavery, his humanitarian interests included membership in the societies for the prevention of cruelty to animals and children, and the chairmanship of the executive committee of the Prison Association, to which he devoted much time and effort. Letters he wrote to his family and friends during a six-months' tour through Europe in 1867–68 were published as *Papers from over the Water* (1869). His letters to newspapers and his articles in magazines he published privately in 1871 under the title *Indices of Public Opinion, 1860–1870.* He was married first to Mary Ann Goddard, second to Amanda Fay. He died in New York, survived by his second wife and four sons of his first marriage.

[T. C. Rose, *The Tousey Family in America* (1916); intro. to Tousey's *Life in the Union Army* (1864); *Frank Leslie's Chimney Corner,* Feb. 24, 1866; obituaries in *Appletons' Ann. Cyc.,* 1888, *N. Y. Times, N. Y. Tribune,* and *N. Y. Herald,* June 17, 1887; information from Tousey's grandson, Sinclair Tousey, Esq., of Garden City, L. I.]   W G. B.

TOWER, CHARLEMAGNE (Apr. 17, 1848–Feb. 24, 1923), diplomat, was born at Philadelphia, Pa., the son of Charlemagne and Amelia (Bartle) Tower, and the descendant of John Tower who emigrated from Hingham, England, to Hingham, Mass., in 1637. After attending the public schools at Pottsville, Pa., he entered Phillips Exeter Academy, graduated from Harvard College in 1872, and spent four years in travel and study in Europe and the Near East. Two years after his return to America he was admitted to the bar, in 1878, and practised in Philadelphia until his father's extensive interests in the Vermilion Range iron ore fields in Minnesota took him to Duluth in 1882. He became president of that road and a director of the Minnesota Iron Company, both of which had been largely financed by his father. The Towers sold a large part of their interests in 1887, and he returned to Philadelphia, where he was active in business, especially coal mining and finance, until 1891. On Feb. 8, 1888, he married Helen Smith of Oakland, Cal. He published *The Marquis de LaFayette in the American Revolution* (2 vols., 1895), and he served as a vice-president of the department of archaeology and palaeontology of the University of Pennsylvania and as trustee from 1896 to 1899.

When McKinley became president, Tower's wealth, reputation for learning, and Republican politics made him a logical candidate for diplomatic honors. His appointment on Apr. 1, 1897, as minister to Austria-Hungary, the first of three major diplomatic appointments, launched him upon a diplomatic career that was useful and creditable but by no means brilliant. During his short two years of service at Vienna, June 1, 1897, to Feb. 9, 1899, he was largely concerned with obtaining the release from military service of naturalized American citizens of Austro-Hungarian birth. In this he was generally successful. On Jan. 12, 1899, he was appointed ambassador to Russia, where he served from his arrival on Mar. 16, 1899, to November 1902. He negotiated, although he did not sign, an agreement with Russia to submit to arbitration on the claims of American sealing vessels that had been seized in the Bering Sea by Russian cruisers. His representations to Russia on behalf of the "Open

Door" in Manchuria were less successful (*Foreign Relations, post,* 1902).

Relations between Germany and Venezuela were approaching the breaking point when he received his appointment as American ambassador at Berlin on Sept. 26, 1902. As soon as he reached his post in December he was instructed by the secretary of state, John Hay, to protest to the German government against the measures it was taking to force Venezuela to pay the German claims and to preserve the rights of the United States in case of blockade of Venezuelan ports. Although some of the most important of the Venezuelan negotiations, which led finally to the submission of the dispute to the new Hague Tribunal, took place in Washington, a major portion of the discussions were conducted through Tower at Berlin. He also negotiated with the German foreign office regarding the obligation of a naturalized American citizen born in Alsace to perform military service in Germany. Although Germany would not admit that the Bancroft treaties of 1868 applied to natives of Alsace-Lorraine, then a part of France, he persuaded the foreign office to declare its readiness to negotiate a new treaty to include natives of Alsace-Lorraine. Other troublesome issues between the United States and Germany, such as the tariff question, were settled at Washington. He resigned on June 8, 1908, and returned to Philadelphia. He was a grand officer of the Legion of Honor of France; he was honored with the grand Cordon of the Order of St. Alexander Newski of Russia; and he received numerous honorary degrees. In 1914 he published *Essays Political and Historical.* He died in Philadelphia.

[*Papers Relating to Foreign Relations of the United States,* 1897–1908; *Harvard College Class of 1872. Third Report* (1878) and *Tenth Report* (1917); *Who's Who in America,* 1922–23; sketch of father and family in *The Charlemagne Tower Collection of American Colonial Laws* (1890), comp. by C. S. R. Hildeburn; *Tower Genealogy* (1891), comp. under direction of Charlemagne Tower; W. W. Folwell, *Hist. of Minn.* (4 vols., 1921–30); Jeanette Keim, *Forty Years of German-American Pol. Relations* (1919); *N. Y. Times,* Feb. 25, 1923.]
E. W. S.

TOWER, ZEALOUS BATES (Jan. 12, 1819–Mar. 20, 1900), soldier and engineer, was of English ancestry, a lineal descendant of John Tower who came to America from Hingham, England, in 1637 and settled in Hingham, Mass.; his parents were Nichols and Ann (Bates) Tower of Cohasset, Mass., where he was born. After his school days he entered the United States Military Academy, graduated at the head of his class in 1841, and was commissioned second lieutenant in the corps of engineers. Prior to

1846 he was engaged principally on the construction of the fortifications at the entrance of Hampton Roads, Va.

In the Mexican War he was on the engineer staff of General Scott and took part in all the operations of Scott's army from the siege of Vera Cruz to the capture of the city of Mexico. His duties were mainly the dangerous tasks of reconnoitering the positions of the enemy and of leading columns of attack. For gallant and meritorious service he received the brevets of first lieutenant, captain, and major, United States Army. He was wounded in leading the storming column at Chapultepec, Sept. 13, 1847. After the war he was superintending engineer on the coast defenses of Portland and Portsmouth, and of harbor works on the New England coast; from 1855 to 1858 he was in charge of the defenses of San Francisco, where he also constructed the custom house and appraiser's store.

Early in 1861 he was directed to assume command of Fort Barancas, near Pensacola, Fla., but when he reached Fort Pickens, on a nearby island, the state troops were already in possession of Barancas. As a volunteer he assisted in organizing the defenses of Fort Pickens and Santa Rosa Island and in repelling the attacks made by the Confederates in October 1861, and aided in making the works proof against the bombardments of Confederate batteries later in the year. For these services he received the brevet of lieutenant-colonel, United States Army, and was commissioned brigadier-general of volunteers. In Pope's Virginia campaign in 1862 he commanded a brigade and took part in the battles of Cedar Mountain and Manassas and in the engagement at Thoroughfare Gap. In the second battle of Manassas, he was so badly wounded that he was incapacitated for further field service. For this campaign he received the brevets of colonel and brigadier-general, United States Army. He recovered sufficiently to return to duty in June 1864, and in July became superintendent of the United States Military Academy. In September of the same year, however, the unsatisfactory condition of the field defenses of Nashville, Tenn., gave the War Department grave concern and Tower was sent to take charge of them; later, at General Sherman's request, he was also made inspector general of fortifications for the Division of the Mississippi. By organizing the quartermaster and railroad employees he was able so to strengthen the fortifications that when Hood appeared in their front with his army he dared not venture an attack. Under the protection of these works General

Thomas was enabled to organize his forces for the attack that destroyed Hood's army. For his services in the war Tower received the brevets of major-general of volunteers and major-general, United States Army.

From 1866 until his retirement, Jan. 10, 1883, as one of the senior officers of the corps of engineers he was an active member of many boards convened to consider projects of river and harbor improvement and of coast defense. After his retirement he lived at Cohasset, Mass., where he died. He never married.

[Charlemagne Tower, *Tower Geneal.* (1891) ; G. W. Cullum, *Biog. Reg. Officers and Grads., U. S. Mil. Acad.* (3rd ed., 1891) ; *Thirty-first Ann. Reunion, Asso. of Grads., U. S. Mil. Acad.* (1900) ; *Memorial of the Mass. Commandery, Mil. Order of Foreign Wars* (1900) ; *War of the Rebellion: Official Records* (Army) ; *Army and Navy Jour.*, Mar. 24, 1900 ; *Boston Transcript*, Mar. 21, 1900.]   G.J.F.

TOWLE, GEORGE MAKEPEACE (Aug. 27, 1841–Aug. 9, 1893), journalist, author, lecturer, was born in Washington, D. C., the only son of Nathaniel Carter and Eunice (Makepeace) Towle. His parents moved to Boston in his childhood, and he attended the public schools there, and Lawrence Academy, Groton, and Day's Academy, Wrentham, Mass. He was graduated from Yale in 1861, studied at the Harvard Law School, and received the degree of LL.B. in 1863, qualifying as a member of the Suffolk County, Mass., bar on Nov. 14, 1862 (Davis, *post,* vol. I, p. 344). He practised law in Boston till 1865, when he became associate editor of the *Boston Post*, and in 1866 he published the first of his many books, a popular work called *Glimpses of History*. In 1866 he was appointed United States Consul at Nantes, France, and in August 1868 was transferred as commercial agent to Bradford, England, where he remained till 1870. In Europe he acquired a command of French that he utilized as a translator of Jules Verne and other popular writers in that language, and gained a knowledge of European politics of which he made literary use. One of his many prominent friends was Charles Dickens, to whose periodical, *All The Year Round,* he contributed many articles on American affairs. In 1870 he published a book, *American Society* (2 vols.), in London.

On returning to Boston in 1870, he acted as correspondent for the London *Athenaeum,* and contributed American notes to the London *Graphic* from 1871 to 1876. He also wrote for a wide variety of American publications. He was managing editor of the Boston *Commercial Bulletin* (1870–71) and foreign editor of the *Boston Post* (1871–76), and he was connected at various times with the *Youth's Companion* and with most of the Boston newspapers as contributor or editor. He published more than twenty volumes, among them *A Brief History of Montenegro* (1877), *Pizarro* (1879), *Beaconsfield* (1879), *Marco Polo* (1880), *Ralegh, His Exploits and Voyages* (copyright 1881), *Drake, The Sea-king of Devon* (1883), *Heroes and Martyrs of Invention* (1890), *Literature of the English Language,* vol. I (1892), and other books on topics of general interest or contemporary prominence. He became known for his ability to present his matter effectively in speech as well as in print. For the Lowell Institute of Boston he gave a series of four lectures on "Famous Men of our Day" (1880–81), eight lectures on "Foreign Governments" (1886–87), and six on "The Era of Elizabeth" (1890–1901), all of which with others of a similar nature, he delivered before many other audiences. In Brookline, where he lived, he served as moderator of the town meeting. He was a member of the Massachusetts Senate in 1890 and 1891 as a Republican, and he took a prominent part in it until illness restricted his activities and prevented his seeking reëlection.

He was physically somewhat striking, having a florid complexion and sweeping side-whiskers of the Dundreary variety; in addition, he was emphatic as well as fluent in his speech, and, perhaps because of his residence in Europe, more effusive in manner than most American men. On Sept. 16, 1866, he was married in Paris to Nellie Lane of Boston, who survived him. He died in Brookline after a long illness culminating in paralysis of the brain, and was buried in Mount Auburn Cemetery. He had no children.

[Published accounts of Towle, which are often erroneous, include *Obit. Record Grads. Yale Univ.* (1900) ; W. T. Davis, *Professional and Industrial Hist. of Suffolk County, Mass.* (1894), vol. I, p. 344 ; *Boston Morning Jour.*, Jan. 7, 1891 ; obituaries in *Boston Herald, Boston Transcript*, Aug. 11, 1893, and *Chronicle* (Brookline, Mass.), Aug. 12, 1893.]   S. G.

TOWLER, JOHN (June 20, 1811–Apr. 2, 1889), writer on photography, college professor, was born at Rathmell, Yorkshire, England, son of George Towler of Sheepwash (baptismal register, Giggleswick parish). Supposedly he prepared at the Giggleswick Grammar School for St. John's College, Cambridge (where he may have been the John Towler, "priest," registered as a non-resident ten-year man, 1836–46), but he received no degree at Cambridge. He went to Karlsruhe, Germany, as "private teacher of his vernacular tongue" (preface to J. L. Hilpert, *A Dictionary of the English and German, and the German and English language,* 1846, vol.

II, p. xiv, of which Towler was co-editor), and there he translated Schiller's poetry and German war-songs into English verse. His edition of *Don Carlos* appeared at Karlsruhe in 1843, and his *Meine Jungendzeit* in the same year. After coming to America, in 1850 he joined the faculty of Hobart College, Geneva, N. Y., where he was professor of modern languages, mathematics, and natural philosophy (1852–68), and professor of civil engineering, chemistry, mathematics, and modern languages (1868–82). In 1855 he received the degree of M.D. from Geneva Medical College, and from 1853 to 1872 served as its dean. In addition to natural philosophy, civil engineering, chemistry, and modern languages, he taught medical jurisprudence, anatomy, pharmacy, and toxicology. He was United States consul at Trinidad, 1882–86, and then retired to do literary work at Orange, N. J. He died at St. Cloud, Orange, N. J. By his first wife, whom he probably married in England, Towler had two sons, who were students at the Geneva Medical College in 1855. By his second wife, Caroline Lili Kaiser, he had two daughters. Towler's red-lined military cloak and long white hair made him a striking figure, and his convivial disposition insured his popularity with friends and students.

Except for his *Guide to a Course of Quantitative Chemical Analysis* (1871), from the German of K. F. Rammelsberg, Towler's American writings were chiefly on photography. He edited *Humphrey's Journal of Photography and the Allied Arts and Sciences* (1862–70) and its annual, the *American Photographic Almanac* (1864–67), besides contributing monthly articles (1868–72) to the *Philadelphia Photographer*. His books on photography were *The Silver Sunbeam* (1864), *The Porcelain Picture* (1865), *Dry Plate Photography; or the Tannin Process* (1865), *The Negative and the Print; or the Photographer's Guide* (1866), and *The Magic Photograph* (1866). Of these books, *The Silver Sunbeam* is the longest and the most important. Photography was in its infancy at the time, and the book probably contributed much to the rapidly increasing use of photographic processes. It presented an introductory history of photography, followed by descriptions of all the known processes, with full directions and formulae. Perhaps the most popular photographic manual of its time, it reached its ninth edition in 1879, and was translated into French, German, Italian, and Spanish. Towler made contributions of his own to photography as well. Among other things he devised a "sky diaphragm" for controlling the influx of light into

the camera (E. L. Wilson, *Wilson's Quarter Century in Photography,* 1887, p. 192), and he is credited with being the first proponent of sodium biochromate for photographic use (J. M. Eder, *Ausführliches Handbuch der Photographie,* vol. II, pt. 2, vol. IV, pt. 2, 1893, where many of his chemical formulae are also quoted).

[See Cambridge Univ. Calendars; *Gen. Cat. of Officers, Grads., and Students, 1825–1897* (1897), Hobart Coll.; J. H. Monroe, *A Century and a Quarter of History; Geneva . . . to Nineteen Hundred and Twelve* (1912); obituary in *Gazette* (Geneva), Apr. 5, 1889, which contains some errors. Other sources include memoir in MS. in the lib. of Hobart Coll.; manuscript diary of Mrs. Martha Pope of Geneva; letters from the Rev. G. W. Dresser of Giggleswick, the Rev. A. D. Barker of Rathmell, F. P. White, Esq., of St. John's Coll., Cambridge, and Caroline Towler Smith, Towler's daughter.]   W. H. S—h.

TOWN, ITHIEL (Oct. 3, 1784–June 13, 1844), architect, was born at Thompson, Conn., the son of Archelaus Town, a farmer, and Martha (Johnson) Town. He was a descendant of William Towne who was in Salem, Mass., as early as 1640. Ithiel's father died when the boy was eight years old. During his youth he worked at house-carpentering and also taught school. Adventuring to Boston finally, he there acquired a knowledge of architecture in a school conducted by Asher Benjamin [*q.v.*], an architect and prolific writer of books on the subject. Little is known of Town's activities during these early years, although he is said, while in Boston, to have contrived a plan for the relief of the Old State House. The important work with which his career began was the construction of Center Church on the New Haven Green. In its construction Town showed familiarity with classical examples of architectural design, and ability both as a designer and as an engineer. He constructed the spire as a unit, on the level and within the tower; when finished, it was raised by an ingenious "windlass and tackle" of his own devising to position on the top of the tower in two and one-half hours. He employed unusual architectural refinements, such as proportioning the orders in the tower so that they would appear of the correct classic proportions when viewed from the pavement below, and giving a slight inward inclination to certain panels in the tower to insure "spring." He was next commissioned, 1814, to design and build Trinity Church, also on the New Haven Green. This was executed in seam-faced local trap rock, with delicate parapets and pinnacles of woodwork, in the Gothic taste, bordering the roof and surmounting the square tower.

His reputation now established, he was called upon to design many public buildings: for New

Haven, a state capitol building and a general hospital; for New York City, the custom house on Wall Street; for Hartford, Christ Church. Other designs of his were those of the state capitol buildings in Indianapolis, Ind., and Raleigh, N. C.; he also designed a number of dwelling houses. During 1827–28, he worked in partnership with Martin E. Thompson [q.v.] of New York. In the exhibitions of the National Academy of Design for those years, Town and Thompson exhibited a number of designs made in common, including "Front Elevation of New Boston Theatre" (1827) and "Design for the Church of the Ascension on Canal Street, New York City" (1828). The diary of Alexander J. Davis [q.v.], in the Metropolitan Museum, reveals that the beautiful, old, Greek-revival asylum building, still standing in the grounds of the Cathedral of St. John the Divine, was designed by Town. About 1829 Town and Davis formed a partnership with offices in New York, and their names are associated in many designs. Though he always maintained his home in New Haven, Town's career is even more associated, both professionally and socially, with New York, where he doubtless found more congenial companionship than in the ultra-religious, academic atmosphere of his home town. His selection by Samuel F. B. Morse as one of the two representatives of architecture, in the founding of the National Academy of Design, shows persuasively Town's outstanding position at that time as a designer and as a man of superior culture.

On Jan. 28, 1820, he was granted a patent for a truss bridge, and from that time forward he was the best known bridge-builder in the country. (See *A Description of Ithiel Town's Improvement in the Construction of Wood and Iron Bridges*, New Haven, 1821.) His returns from this kind of work seem to have been greater than from his work as an architect; from 1820 until his death he apparently had ample funds. He thus possessed the means to gather together in his New Haven residence what for many years was the finest collection of choice books relating to architecture and the fine arts assembled in the United States. The fame of this collection is fully supported by the five catalogues issued after his death for its sale in Boston, Washington, and New York. He traveled extensively in Europe with Morse in 1829–30, envisaged transatlantic steamship navigation, and contributed an unsigned article on the subject to the *American Railroad Journal* of Nov. 24, 1832 (reprinted by J. P. Wright in *Atlantic Steam-ships*, 1838). In 1835 he published *The Outlines of a Plan for Establishing in New York an Academy*

and Institution of the Fine Arts (1835). He also wrote on mathematics and the building of schoolhouses, and published *A Detail of Some Particular Services Performed in America . . . 1776–1779* (1835), founded on manuscript material he bought in England. To him has recently been given credit for designing the very charming obverse of the medal struck in 1838 to commemorate the two-hundredth anniversary of the foundation of New Haven. The greatly inferior reverse of the medal was done by Hezekiah Augur [q.v.]. Town died in New Haven and was buried in Grove Street Cemetery, where his grave is marked by a marble headstone as simple as he was modest and unassuming. He never married, but had a daughter who lived with him and bore his name.

[*Vital Records of New Haven, 1649–1850* (1917), pt. II, p. 803; E. E. Towne, *The Descendants of William Towne* (1901); E. H. Knight, *Knight's Am. Mechanical Dict.*, vol. III (1876); L. C. H. Tuthill, *Hist. of Architecture* (1848); William Dunlap, *Hist. of the Rise and Progress of the Arts of Design in the U. S.* (1834), vol. II; G. D. Seymour, *Researches of An Antiquary, New Haven* (n.d.), and *The Residence and Library of Ithiel Town* (1930), and article in *Art and Progress*, Sept. 1912; archives of National Academy of Design, N. Y.; Rexford Newcomb in *Architect*, Feb. 1929; J. F. Kelly, "Early Connecticut Churches" (MS.); E. F. and E. B. Peters, *Peters of New England* (1903).]   G. D. S.

TOWNE, BENJAMIN (d. July 8, 1793), printer, journalist, was born in Lincolnshire, England, and learned the printer's trade before coming to America. While he was a journeyman printer in Philadelphia in 1766, Joseph Galloway [q.v.] considered placing him, with an apprentice, in charge of a newspaper which he was establishing, but William Goddard [q.v.] was finally selected for this position, and Towne served as a journeyman under Goddard on the *Pennsylvania Chronicle, and Universal Advertiser*. In May 1769, financed by Galloway and his partner, Thomas Wharton, Towne became half-owner and a partner in this enterprise. A public quarrel among the partners brought about revelations which did not help the reputations of any of the four men involved and which ended, in 1770, Towne's connections with the *Chronicle*.

Towne opened a printing house of his own in 1774 and published the first issue of the *Pennsylvania Evening Post*, a tri-weekly, on Jan. 24, 1775. This was the first evening newspaper printed in Philadelphia and the only newspaper that continued to be published in that city through the Revolutionary War. Towne changed sides twice during the war in order to continue publication without moving out of Philadelphia. He started as an ardent Whig and Patriot and succeeded in driving his Royalist competitor,

James Humphreys [*q.v.*], out of business, but the first issue published by Towne after the British army occupied the city in September 1777 shows that he had become a Royalist and was ready to abuse the "Rebels." He published a pro-British paper for seven months, and then the British evacuated the city. He was proscribed for high treason by the Supreme Executive Council of Pennsylvania (proclamation of June 15, 1778; *Pennsylvania Archives,* 4 ser., III, 680), but by this time the fortunes of war had made him a Patriot again, and four days before his proscription was announced he resumed publication with an issue that left no doubt of his new sentiments. The treason charge was dropped (*Ibid.,* 6 ser., XIII, 477), and he published his paper undisturbed. His conduct had made him no permanent friends, however, and his clients apparently changed to other newspapers as these were reëstablished in Philadelphia. The *Evening Post* gradually declined in importance and size and finally died, the last issue that has been located being that for Oct. 26, 1784. Towne made a desperate attempt to revive the dying sheet by changing it to a daily in 1783, but this change resulted after a few weeks in decreasing regularity and frequency of publication.

Little is known of the last years of Towne's life. He is thought to have died poor and there is evidence that he himself hawked the last issue of his paper about the streets, calling "All the news for two coppers." It seems probable, however, that he continued as a job printer after the failure of his newspaper. The census records for 1790 list eight individuals with the firm of "Benjamin Towne & Co. (printer)" and this firm disappears from the Philadelphia city directory with the death of Towne. He died at his home in "Sixth Street near Arch Street" and his remains were interred the following evening "attended by a respectable number of citizens; and most of the typographical profession in Philadelphia."

[Consult: Isaiah Thomas, *The Hist. of Printing in America* (2nd ed., 2 vols., 1874); C. S. Brigham, "Bibliog. of Am. Newspapers," in *Proc. Am. Antiq. Soc.,* n.s., XXXII (1923), pp. 152, 155; *Pa. Archives,* esp. 3 ser., XIV and XVI (1897), 4 ser., III (1900), and 6 ser., XIII (1907); *Minutes of the Supreme Exec. Council of Pa.,* XII (1853), 319, 325; Lorenzo Sabine, *Biog. Sketches of the Loyalists of the Am. Rev.* (1864), vol. II; *Editor and Publisher,* Mar. 17, 1934. The Works of the Rev. John Witherspoon (1802), IV, 397, contains the "Recantation of Benjamin Towne" which was never signed by Towne; William Goddard, *The Partnership: or the Hist. of the Rise and Progress of the Pa. Chronicle &c* (1770), is prejudiced, but the most complete account of the quarrel; the explanations of both sides in the dispute appear in advertisements in the *Pa. Journal*

and the Weekly Advertiser, July, Aug., and Sept. 1770; *The Mail* (Phila.), July 11, 1793, contains an obituary notice. The best file of the *Pa. Eve. Post* is held by the Am. Antiq. Soc. The Phila. Lib. Company and the N. Y. Pub. Lib. have almost complete files of the *Pa. Chronicle.*]
C. M. T.

TOWNE, CHARLES ARNETTE (Nov. 21, 1858–Oct. 22, 1928), lawyer, congressman, was born in Oakland County, Mich., the son of Charles Judson and Laura Anne (Fargo) Towne, and a descendant of William Towne who came from England and settled in Salem, Mass., about 1640. Charles attended local schools until he was ready to enter the University of Michigan in 1875. His progress through college was delayed by ill health and the necessity of earning his living, so that it was not until 1881 that he was graduated. Subsequently, he became a clerk in the department of public instruction at Lansing, read law, and was admitted to the bar on Apr. 16, 1885. After practising in Marquette, he went in 1890 to Duluth, Minn., and five years later became a member of the law firm of Phelps, Towne, & Harris.

Although he had declined a nomination for Congress in 1888 (E. E. Towne, *post,* p. 268), his political career really began in 1894, when he was elected to Congress on the Republican ticket from the Duluth district. An ardent proponent of free silver, he refused the nomination by the regular Republicans in 1896 and ran as an independent, being defeated by a small margin; again, in 1898, he was similarly defeated; in 1900 he refused to be a candidate. During this period he was generally recognized as the leader of the Silver Republicans and was chairman of their national committee from 1897 to 1901. Although a close associate and friend of William J. Bryan [*q.v.*], Towne felt that he could aid the silver cause more effectively by not affiliating himself with the Democratic party. Bryan evidently hoped that Towne would be selected as vice-presidential candidate in 1900 by Democrats, Populists, and Silver Republicans, but, while he was chosen by the two last named, the Democrats turned to a more moderate candidate, Adlai Stevenson [*q.v.*]; whereupon, Towne declined the other two nominations (*Review of Reviews,* August 1900). When Senator Cushman K. Davis [*q.v.*] died, Governor Lind appointed Towne to fill the vacancy until the legislature could elect a successor. That body, however, turned to Moses E. Clapp, and Towne's term lasted only from Dec. 5, 1900, to Jan. 28, 1901.

In 1901 he removed to New York City, where he made his home for the rest of his life. He was a delegate to the Democratic National Convention in 1904, and represented New York in the Fifty-ninth Congress (1895–97). In 1907 he was asked to be personal adviser to the King of Korea, but, as he later declared, "By the time I reached the King of Korea, there was no longer a Korean question. It was a Japanese question, —Japanese and American" (*Michigan Alumnus, post,* p. 94). This brief Korean experience no doubt colored his views thereafter, for he retained a persistent apprehension concerning Japan's future course with respect to the United States. Before leaving Duluth, Towne had become interested in oil properties; this interest continued for the rest of his life and drew him into other financial undertakings. At the same time he continued to practise law, being for a time associated with B. F. Spellman. During the World War he was an active supporter of President Wilson and was a frequent speaker on patriotic occasions. His final excursion into politics was in 1928, when he made an extensive speaking tour in support of Alfred E. Smith, the Democratic candidate for the presidency. Towne died in Tucson, Ariz. He was married twice: first, Apr. 20, 1887, to Maude Irene Wiley of Lansing, who died in 1915; second, Mar. 3, 1917, to Mrs. Alice Reinhart Elkin of New York. He had no children.

[*Who's Who in America,* 1916–17; E. E. Towne, *The Descendants of William Towne* (1901); *Biog. Dir. Am. Cong.* (1928); *The Outlook,* Oct. 13, 20, 1900; *The Forum,* Nov. 1900; *Review of Reviews* (N. Y.), June, Aug. 1900; *The Nation,* Aug. 17, 1916; *N. Y. Times,* Mar. 4, 1917; *News Tribune* (Duluth), Oct. 24, 1928; *Minneapolis Journal,* Oct. 23, 1928; *Mich. Alumnus,* Dec. 1907.]   L. B. S.

TOWNE, HENRY ROBINSON (Aug. 28, 1844–Oct. 15, 1924), engineer, manufacturer, son of John Henry Towne [*q.v.*] and Maria R. (Tevis) Towne, was born in Philadelphia, Pa. He was a direct descendant in the ninth generation from William Towne who emigrated from Yarmouth, England, and settled at Salem, Mass., about 1640. Educated in private schools, he was in his first year at the University of Pennsylvania when the Civil War began, and he thereupon entered the drafting room of the Port Richmond Iron Works, one of his father's companies. He worked there for nearly two years. In 1863 he was put in charge of the erection of machinery made for the Federal government in the navy yards of Boston, Portsmouth, and Philadelphia. From 1864 to 1866, he superintended the erection and installation of all the machinery in the monitors *Monadnock* and *Agamenticus,* both designed by John Ericsson [*q.v.*].

In 1866 he went to Europe, where he traveled and studied engineering under the tutelage of Robert Briggs, an American engineer, and took a special course in physics at the Sorbonne, Paris. Towne and Briggs made numerous engineering investigations; the results of one of these, connected with the transmission of power by belts, they published later in the *Journal of the Franklin Institute* (January 1868). Returning to Philadelphia in 1867, Towne entered the mechanical shops of William Sellers & Company, and while working there was introduced by his father in the summer of 1868 to Linus Yale [*q.v.*] of Shelburne Falls, Mass., who had gone to Philadelphia seeking capital and business management for the manufacture of locks of his invention. Soon afterwards Towne's father brought about the formation of the Yale Lock Manufacturing Company, with Yale as president and Towne as manager. The new company immediately selected a site in Stamford, Conn., and began the erection of a modest factory. The enterprise was but three months old, however, when Yale suddenly died, leaving Towne, then only twenty-four, to carry the burden alone. He conducted the business successfully for many years, relinquishing the presidency of the company in 1916 to become chairman of the board of directors, in which capacity he served until his death.

Towne's great success was due to the fact that he perceived the production advantage in Yale's pin-tumbler lock, which Yale himself considered a minor invention. The tumbler mechanism was contained in a small cylinder separate from the bolt-work case and bulkier part of the lock. This fact permitted, as Towne realized, thousands of locks to be made by quantity production methods, all alike except for the tumbler cylinder, so that any cylinder set to any combination might be added to any bolt case to make the complete lock. Furthermore, the small flat key used offered an advantage over the larger, bulkier key of the ordinary bolt lock. From the day of the founding of the original company, reorganized in 1883 as the Yale & Towne Manufacturing Company, the enterprise had a wide influence on the lock and hardware industry of the United States. In 1876 there was added the manufacture of chain blocks, electric hoists, and later, for a time, large cranes and testing machines. Towne was, in fact, the pioneer builder of cranes in the United States, organizing a department for their manufacture in 1878, and developing a large business, which he sold in 1894 to the Brown Hoisting Machine Company of Cleveland, Ohio. He also undertook, in 1882, the building of the Emery testing machines, which he continued until 1887, when he sold this branch of the business to William Sellers & Company of Philadelphia.

Towne possessed the unique combination of engineering ability and technical training with executive capacity and foresight. He was among the first industrialists of the United States to extend the scope of the engineer to include the economics of engineering and the essential union of production and management. He was an influential member of the American Society of Mechanical Engineers and its president in 1889–90; for five years (1908–13) he was the energetic head of the Merchants' Association of New York; he was a director of the Federal Reserve Bank of New York (1914–19); president of the Morris Plan Company (1914–18); and a director in a number of other banking and industrial institutions. He contributed numerous short papers to technical journals, and was the author of *A Treatise on Cranes* (1883), and *Locks and Builders Hardware* (1905). In his last years he was active in endeavoring to provide a technical museum for New York City. The project was not realized during his lifetime, but he bequeathed a large sum of money, from which gift resulted the establishment in 1926 of the New York Museum of Science and Industry. On Mar. 12, 1868, he married Cora E. White, and at the time of his death in New York was survived by a son.

[E. E. Towne, *The Descendants of William Towne* (1901); *Who's Who in America*, 1924–25; *Trans. Am. Soc. Mechanical Engineers*, vol. XLVI (1925); J. W. Roe, *English and Am. Tool Builders* (1926); A. A. Hopkins, *The Lure of the Lock* (1928); J. L. Chamberlain, *Universities and Their Sons: Univ. of Pa.* (1902), vol. II; J. W. Jordan, *Encyc. of Pa. Biog.*, vol. VII (1916); *N. Y. Herald Tribune*, Oct. 16, 1924.]

C. W. M—n.

TOWNE, JOHN HENRY (Feb. 20, 1818– Apr. 6, 1875), engineer and philanthropist, was born in Pittsburgh, Pa., the eldest son of Sarah (Robinson) and John Towne, a successful business man. He was a descendant of William Towne who emigrated to Salem, Mass., from Yarmouth, England, about 1640. He received the greater part of his education at the Chauncey Hall School, Boston, and his engineering training from the firm of Merrick & Agnew, Philadelphia, Pa. In 1836 he became a junior partner in the firm of Merrick (see Samuel Vaughan Merrick). In 1843 he married Maria R. Tevis, the daughter of Joshua Tevis, a prominent Philadelphia merchant. They had three children, one of whom was Henry Robinson Towne [q.v.].

After the partnership was dissolved in 1849, he engaged in private engineering projects, building gas works in particular, two of which were constructed at New Bedford and Savan-

nah. In 1861 he became a partner of the I. P. Morris & Co., the firm's name being changed to I. P. Morris, Towne & Co. This company owned the Port Richmond Iron Works, a concern with a national reputation for the construction of all sorts of heavy machinery. He was by this time considered an engineer of unquestioned ability, and he became the firm's chief engineer. During the Civil War, he produced the engines for the *Monitor, Monadnock, Agamenticus, Lehigh,* and *Sangamon,* and for the *Itasca, Sciota, Pushmataha,* and *Antietam.* Other engineering achievements included the engines for the federal mint, two huge Cornish Bull pumping engines for the Buffalo water works, and blowing machinery for the manufacture of anthracite iron for such well known firms as the Thomas Iron Company of Hokendauqua, Pa., and the Lehigh Crane Iron Company of Catasauqua, Pa. Small-sized machinery was also built, but the concern's reputation was based upon its ability to construct the finest kind of large and heavy machinery. He died in Paris during a European trip taken, on the advice of physicians, to recover his health.

His life was centered mostly on his engineering works, and he was interested in few outside activities. In 1856 he was appointed a director and vice-president of the North Pennsylvania Railroad Company, later leased to the Philadelphia and Reading Railroad Company. He resigned these offices in 1858, but, while he was connected with the railroad for only a short time, he had been faced with a few of its worst construction, operating, and financial problems. He also held a directorship in the Philadelphia and Reading Railroad Company between 1862 and 1864. He joined the Franklin Institute in 1835, listing his occupation as a machinist, and became a life member in 1842. In his will he provided for the University of Pennsylvania Hospital, of which he was a director, the Pennsylvania Academy of the Fine Arts, and the Academy of Natural Sciences of Philadelphia. To the University of Pennsylvania, of which he was a trustee, he left his residuary estate as an endowment fund for payment of salaries in the department of science. The trustees, as one means of perpetuating his memory, created the Towne Scientific School of the University of Pennsylvania, in which most of the university's engineering courses are given.

[Minutes of the board of trustees of Univ. of Pa., and of managers of Philadelphia and Reading Railway Co.; records of Franklin Institute; *General Cat. of the Southwark Foundry and Machine Co.* (1896), p. 3; *Univ. of Pa., Its Hist. . . . with Biog. Sketches* (2 vols., 1901–02); E. E. Towne, *The Descendants of Wm. Towne* (1901); George Morgan, *The City of Firsts*

(1926), p. 268; E. T. Freedley, *Philadelphia and Its Manufactures . . . in 1867* (1867), pp. 338–42; *Pa. Gazette* (Univ. of Pa.), May 15, 1931; *Press* (Philadelphia), Apr. 8, 9, 1875.]
H. S. P.

TOWNS, GEORGE WASHINGTON BONAPARTE (May 4, 1801–July 15, 1854), congressman from Georgia and governor, was born in Wilkes County, Ga., the son of John and Margaret (George) Hardwick Towns, both natives of Virginia. He attended the county academy and began the study of medicine in Eatonton, Ga., but was forced to give it up, when thrown from his horse and seriously injured. He studied law in Montgomery, Ala., and was admitted to the bar in 1824. Returning to Georgia in 1826, he settled in Talbot County, where he practised law. He served in the lower house of the state legislature, 1829–30, and in the Senate, 1832–34. He was a bitter opponent of protective tariff and of federal aid to internal improvements. While opposed to protection, he also opposed the call of a southern convention and abhorred nullification. He attended the Georgia nullification convention of 1832 and played a leading part in obtaining the resolution asking South Carolina to retrace her steps.

He was elected to Congress in 1834 as a Union Democrat but resigned on Sept. 1, 1836. Reelected he served from 1837 to 1839, when he dropped "Bonaparte" from his name. A man of marked business ability, genial nature, attractive manners, and public popularity, he attained great success at the bar and made a good deal of money. His second wife also brought him a fortune and greatly enhanced his social position. He was a man of principle, although timid and inclined to postpone difficulties; and he was a good fighter once he entered an encounter. He was again elected to Congress in 1846 but was not reelected to succeed himself. He championed military and naval preparedness, defense against the Indians, the interests of the United States in Texas, and the removal of the Cherokee, while opposing protective tariff, federal aid for internal improvements, the Second Bank of the United States, the "American system," and the Wilmot Proviso. In 1847 he defeated Gen. Duncan L. Clinch for governor, and renominated by acclamation he defeated Edward Y. Hill in 1849. During his administration he led the fight for the amelioration of the slave code, obtained the adoption of the *ad valorem* system of taxation and the completion of the Western and Atlantic railroad; and he advocated the use of poll taxes, the revenue from the state railroad, and other revenue for common schools with the hope that Georgia might soon boast that she had no illiterate. He was a stanch supporter of the Mexican War and had, by 1849, become an extreme "fire eater." He obtained from the legislature power to call a state convention, if Congress should pass the Wilmot Proviso or any similar legislation. He called the convention that adopted the "Georgia platform," which became the position of the entire South. He also appointed the Georgia delegation to the adjourned Nashville convention, and he wrote the inscription, "The Constitution as it is, the Union as it was," for Georgia's stone in the Washington monument. Retiring from the governorship, he moved from Talbotton to Macon, Ga., and renewed his law practice. He also ran a cotton plantation with a large number of slaves. He died in Macon. He was married twice: first to the sister of John W. Campbell of Alabama, and second to Mary Jones, the daughter of John Winston Jones [*q.v.*], by whom he had seven children.

[S. F. Miller, *The Bench and Bar of Ga.* (1858), vol. II; *Biog. Directory of Am. Cong.* (1928); R. H. Shryock, *Ga. and the Union in 1850* (1926); Herbert Fielder, *A Sketch of the Life and Times and Speeches of Joseph E. Brown* (1883); L. B. Wylie, *Memoirs of Judge Richard H. Clark* (1898); *Augusta Chronicle*, July 18, 1854; *Federal Union* (Milledgeville, Ga.), July 13, 1847.]
F. M. G.

TOWNSEND, EDWARD DAVIS (Aug. 22, 1817–May 10, 1893), soldier, was born at Boston, Mass., the son of David S. Townsend, an army officer of the War of 1812, and Eliza Gerry, the daughter of Elbridge Gerry [*q.v.*]. He was a descendant of Thomas Townsend who settled in Lynn, Mass., about 1637. He was educated at the Boston Latin School, attended Harvard College for one year, and was graduated from the United States Military Academy at West Point in 1837, as a second lieutenant, 2nd Artillery. He served in the Florida war, and later assisted in removing the Cherokee Indians to what is now Oklahoma. In 1846, he transferred to the adjutant general's department, and for the next fifteen years served on the Pacific coast, and at Washington, D. C. During the winter of 1860–61, he was consulted as to the defense of Southern forts. He recommended that, as the forts were in no condition to resist attack, a nominal defense be made, stipulating only for honorable terms and a free passage to the North for the defenders.

When Lincoln became president, Townsend, now a lieutenant-colonel, became adjutant-general to Winfield Scott [*q.v.*], commander-in-chief. Bowed with age, Scott left the direction of affairs largely to Townsend. President Lincoln frequently visited Scott's office, and formed a lifelong friendship with Townsend. Townsend was responsible for many measures taken in 1861 for the defense of Washington and for the organization and discipline of the newly raised troops. Upon Scott's retirement, Nov. 1, 1861, he became senior assistant in the adjutant-general's department. On Mar. 23, 1862, he became adjutant-general, a position equivalent to what would now be chief-of-staff. In daily contact with the president and the secretary of war for the next three eventful war years, he quietly and efficiently carried out their orders. Wherever possible he effaced himself. He had an expert knowledge of files and office work; he was faithful and reliable, and closely supervised his important department. At the end of the war he was brevetted major-general for his services.

After the war, Townsend issued an order to collect all war papers and by this order was responsible for founding that vast collection published later as the *War of the Rebellion: Official Records.* In 1868, during the difficulties between President Johnson and Secretary Stanton, and the impeachment of the former, Townsend handled a serious situation at the War Department with unusual tact. In 1869, he was appointed adjutant-general by President Grant, after having acted in this capacity for seven years. An improved system of military prisons occupied much of his attention during his term. He retired in 1880, and lived in Washington until his death. He possessed strong religious ideas, and some literary ability, publishing two books, the *Catechism of the Bible—the Pentateuch* (1860), and *Judges and Kings* (1862). In 1884 he published *Anecdotes of the Civil War,* a discreet work with little information in it. He was interested in collecting political papers and heirlooms, and was a member of the Society of the Cincinnati. On May 9, 1848, he was married to Ann Overing Wainwright, a sister of Richard Wainwright, 1817–1862 [*q.v.*]. She, with four of their five children, survived him at his death in Washington.

[A biography is now in preparation by Annette Townsend. Important papers are in the possession of Mrs. Townsend Phillips, N. Y. See Annette Townsend, *The Auchmuty Family of Scotland and America* (1932); G. W. Cullum, *Biog. Reg. . . . U. S. Mil. Acad.* (1891); Samuel Breck, biographical article in *Ann. Reunion, Asso. of Grads., U. S. Mil. Acad.* (1893); *Evening Star* (Washington, D. C.), May 11, 1893.]
C. H. L.

TOWNSEND, GEORGE ALFRED (Jan. 30, 1841–Apr. 15, 1914), journalist and author, was born in Georgetown, Del. His father, Stephen Townsend, who combined carpentry with the profession of itinerant Methodist preacher and at an advanced age gave up both for the study of medicine, and his mother, Mary (Mil-

bourne) Townsend, were both descendants of families long resident in Virginia and Maryland. His first fourteen years were spent in various small towns of Maryland, Pennsylvania, and Delaware, where between 1850 and 1854 he studied in the academic departments of Washington College, Chestertown, Md., and Delaware College, Newark. After 1855 the family was permanently settled in Philadelphia. There Townsend finished his studies at the Central High School, from which he was graduated in 1860. He plunged at once into the newspaper world, first with the *Philadelphia Inquirer,* then with the *Press.* In 1861 he began his connection with the *New York Herald,* which he served first as Philadelphia agent and later as war correspondent. Towards the end of 1862 he went to England, where by lectures and articles, notably in the *Cornhill,* he persuasively advocated the cause of the northern states. On returning to America he became war correspondent for the New York *World,* in which appeared his most vivid reportorial work. His accounts of the final battles and of Lincoln's assassination won him an almost nation-wide recognition. In December 1865 he married Bessie E. Rhodes of Philadelphia, and soon thereafter went abroad to report for the *World* the events of the Austro-Prussian War. After settling in Washington in 1867, he began to contribute, as he continued to do for some forty years, to the *Chicago Tribune,* the *Cincinnati Daily Enquirer,* and many other papers (amounting, in the end, to nearly a hundred), a frequent letter of from two to four columns under the signature of "Gath"—a humorously conceived pseudonym, utilizing his initials, and ironically suggesting the Biblical prohibition concerning the downfall of the mighty, "Tell it not in Gath, publish it not in the streets of Askelon." These letters were mainly occupied with politics and the advocacy of Republicanism, but they included also very perspicacious comments upon almost every event of major importance, and are now peculiarly interesting for their often satirical animadversions upon the social life of the time. Their fearlessness, kindly humor, and wise judgments brought to them a large following, and made of their author one of the most important journalists of the reconstruction era. He assisted Donn Piatt [*q.v.*] in organizing the *Capital* in 1871, but, originally a co-editor of that useful weekly, he was forced by the pressure of his other work to resign after a few weeks.

Washington remained the center of his activities, except for the twelve years following 1880 which he spent in New York, though he lived also for long periods at a country house, built on the battlefield of Crampton's Gap, South Mountain, Md., which he called, with the village that grew up around it, Gapland. He traveled widely both in America and abroad, and gave many popular lectures. The latter half of his life was taken up quite as much with the production of books as with newspaper work. He had always been interested in pure literature and had tried his hand, not very successfully, at a play, *The Bohemians,* as early as 1861, but the majority of his books before 1880 were frankly journalistic. They included such revampings of his ephemeral writings as *Campaigns of a Non-Combatant* (1866), *The New World Compared with the Old* (1869), *Lost Abroad* (1870), *The Mormon Trials at Salt Lake City* (1871), and *Washington, Outside and Inside* (1873), and such hasty venturings into biography as *The Life and Battles of Garibaldi* (1867) and *The Real Life of Abraham Lincoln* (1867). In 1880, however, appeared *Tales of the Chesapeake,* a collection of stories notable for their admirable use of local color. This was followed by a novel, the best of his books, *The Entailed Hat* (1884), a tale involving the kidnaping of free negroes in the days before the war in Delaware and the border counties of Maryland, and remarkable for its careful reconstruction of the period and its vivid presentation of local characters. Its sequel, *Katy of Catoctin* (1886), was less painstakingly executed and was deservedly less popular. Among his varied productions, *Mrs. Reynolds and Hamilton* (1890), deserves mention as one of the first romantic picturings of the great Federalist. His poems are less important. Such volumes as *Poems* (1870), *Poetical Addresses of George Alfred Townsend* (1881), and *Poems of Men and Events* (1899), while showing considerable vigor and a wide range of knowledge, are the works of a prose craftsman unhappily essaying verse. He was an invalid for the last ten years of his life, and died of general debility at the home of his daughter in New York. He was survived by his daughter and a son.

[Biog. material may be found in Townsend's contributions to such newspapers as the *Chicago Tribune,* and in many of his books, notably in *The Entailed Hat.* See also *Who's Who in America,* 1914–15, and obituaries in *N. Y. Times, Evening Jour.* (Wilmington), and *Wilmington Morning News,* Apr. 16, 1914. The Pub. Archives Commission of Del. has supplied certain facts, as have also various of Townsend's friends.]

C. D. A.

TOWNSEND, JOHN KIRK (Aug. 10, 1809–Feb. 6, 1851), ornithologist, was born in Philadelphia, the son of Charles and Priscilla (Kirk) Townsend. He came of an intellectual and cultivated family of Quaker ancestry; a brother, Ed-

ward, was distinguished for his philanthropic work, especially in connection with prisons; while two sisters, Hannah and Mary, were writers. John was educated at the famous Quaker boarding school at Westtown, Pa., where much attention was given to the natural sciences. This training, together with close association with his cousin William P. Townsend and Ezra Michener [*q.v.*], both of whom became local ornithologists, may have been the origin of his passionate interest in birds. He spent much of his early life at West Chester, Pa., collecting specimens, and in the course of preparing them became a skilful taxidermist. On one of these early field trips he secured the unique specimen later named Townsend's Bunting by John James Aubudon [*q.v.*] and still preserved in the United States National Museum.

At the age of twenty-five, with the naturalist Thomas Nuttall [*q.v.*], Townsend joined the overland expedition to Oregon under Nathaniel J. Wyeth [*q.v.*], traveling with a wagon train from Independence, Mo., which point they left on Apr. 28, 1834, to Fort Vancouver, where they arrived on Sept. 16. The following year he visited the Hawaiian Islands, and shortly after his return to Fort Vancouver assumed the duties of surgeon to the post; these he performed from late September until the middle of the following March, in the absence of a regular post surgeon. In December 1836 he sailed for home by way of Cape Horn, but at Valparaiso was overtaken by a severe illness which delayed his arrival at Philadelphia until Nov. 13, 1837. On the overland journey and at several places in the Pacific he had assembled valuable collections of birds and mammals. His new birds from the Oregon country were described by himself in the *Journal of the Academy of Natural Sciences of Philadelphia* (vol. VII, pt. 2, 1837; vol. VIII, pt. 1, 1839) and later pictured in the last volume (1844) of Audubon's *Birds of America,* while his mammals were described and pictured by Audubon and John Bachman [*q.v.*] in their *Viviparous Quadrupeds of North America* (3 vols., 1845–49). In 1839 Townsend published *Narrative of a Journey across the Rocky Mountains to the Columbia River,* a valuable contribution to the history of early exploration in western North America. It was reprinted in part by R. G. Thwaites in *Early Western Travels* (vol. XXI, 1905). Townsend also conceived the idea of preparing a work on the birds of the United States and actually published one part (*Ornithology of the United States of North America,* 1840), now one of the rarest of American ornithological treasures. Lack of financial support and the appearance of the octavo edition of Audubon's *Birds* discouraged him, however, and he abandoned his undertaking.

In 1842 he was in Washington engaged in securing and mounting birds for the National Institute, a sort of forerunner of the National Museum, with its collections housed in the Patent Office, but this position was only temporary and in 1845 he was back in Philadelphia studying dentistry, although he probably never practised. Hoping to restore his health, which had begun to fail, he planned to sail early in 1851 as naturalist on a naval vessel bound around the Cape of Good Hope, but his condition rapidly became worse and he had to abandon the plan. He died, in Washington, in February 1851.

Townsend was elected a member of the Academy of Natural Sciences of Philadelphia in September 1833 and a life member shortly before he died. He was a fluent writer as well as an excellent ornithologist, but was overshadowed in his special field by the dominating personality of Audubon. As it is, he will always be remembered for the discovery of many of the birds and mammals of the northwestern United States, not a few of which bear his name. He married Charlotte Holmes of Cape May Courthouse, New Jersey, whose sister, Harriet, later married William Baird, brother of the ornithologist Spencer F. Baird [*q.v.*]. The Townsends had one son.

[Witmer Stone, "John Kirk Townsend," *Cassinia*, no. VII (1903); J. W. Jordan, *Colonial Families of Phila.* (1911), vol. II; F. H. Herrick, *Audubon the Naturalist* (2 vols., 1917); W. H. Dall, *Spencer Fullerton Baird* (1915); death notice in *Daily Nat. Intelligencer* (Washington, D. C.), Feb. 7, 1851; letters from relatives.]   W. S.

TOWNSEND, LUTHER TRACY (Sept. 27, 1838–Aug. 2, 1922), author, Methodist minister, educator, was born at Orono, Penobscot County, Me., son of Luther K. and Mary True (Call) Townsend, both natives of New Hampshire. In his early boyhood he attended various public schools in central New Hampshire, but at twelve, because of his father's death, he was forced to go to work. At sixteen he had become a fireman on a locomotive. In 1855, however, after spending a year at the New Hampshire Conference Seminary at Tilton, he entered Dartmouth College and in 1859 received the degree of A.B. Three years later he completed the regular course at the Theological Seminary, Andover, Mass. He then enlisted with the 16th New Hampshire Volunteers, XIX Army Corps, and served as private and adjutant in the Department of the Gulf, taking part in some of the severest battles of the Southwest. At the expiration of the period of enlistment he was offered a colonelcy but declined it. He was ordained deacon in the Meth-

odist Episcopal Church on Apr. 10, 1864, and elder on Apr. 1, 1866. From 1864 to 1868 he served churches in Watertown, Malden, and Boston, Mass., attracting wide attention by his ability as a preacher. Though he read his sermons, he did so with such perfect art that he seemed to be speaking extemporaneously. In 1868 he became professor of Hebrew and New Testament Greek in the Boston Theological Seminary (later Boston University School of Theology), transferring in 1870 to the department of church history, and in 1872 to the department of practical theology. Few teachers of practical theology have made a more marked impression than he upon his students; his class lectures were rich in content, admirably organized, and unusually stimulating. In 1893 he resigned in order to devote himself to literary work. Throughout his life, however, he remained active as a preacher and lecturer, serving leading churches in different parts of the country for limited periods of time. In 1897–98 he was associate editor of the *Baltimore Methodist*. He was married on Sept. 27, 1865, to Laura C. Huckins of Watertown, Mass., who died in 1917. He had three daughters, only one of whom survived him. He died in Brookline, Mass. He was somewhat short of stature, dark-skinned, with rather boldly chiseled features, wavy hair and beard, and large dark eyes, overhung with noticeable eyebrows. His appearance was dignified and impressive.

It was as the author of books on a variety of subjects that he was best known. Among them are *The Chinese Problem* (1876), *The Art of Speech* (2 vols., 1880–81), and *Clerical Politics in the Methodist Episcopal Church* (1892). But for the most part he dealt with theological topics. His first and perhaps most widely read book was *Credo* (1869). Others are *Lost Forever* (1875), *Bible Theology and Modern Thought* (1883), *The Story of Jonah* (1887), *The Collapse of Evolution* (1905), and *New Theologies Only Bubbles* (Boston, 1906). As these titles suggest, he was an ardent champion of the older authoritarian type of theology. He read widely and had rare gifts of popular exposition, but he made no significant contribution to theological thought. It is as an effective popular apologist for the traditional evangelical theology that he is chiefly to be remembered.

[*Who's Who in America*, 1920–21; *Gen. Cat. of the Theological Seminary, Andover, Mass.* (1908); L. T. Townsend, *Hist. of the Sixteenth Regiment, N. H. Volunteers* (1897); *Zion's Herald*, Aug. 9, 1922, and *Christian Advocate* (N. Y.), Sept. 7, 1922; M. C. McEldowney, "Life of Luther Tracy Townsend," MS. in the lib. of Boston Univ. School of Theology, containing letters from former students and friends; death notice in *Boston Transcript,* Aug. 2, 1922.] A. C. K.

TOWNSEND, MARY ASHLEY (Sept. 24, 1832–June 7, 1901), author and poet, was born in Lyons, N. Y., the daughter of Catherine Van Winkle and her second husband, James G. Van Voorhis. She attended the district school, and later the academy, in Lyons. She was a frail child, and, perhaps because other pleasures were denied her, became devoted to reading early in life. She is reported to have written a good deal in her extreme youth, but to have burned this juvenile literature while still a child. On Nov. 8, 1853, she was married to Gideon Townsend of Fishkill, N. Y. After a short stay in Lyons, they moved first to Clinton, Iowa, and then, in 1860, to New Orleans, where Mr. Townsend had extensive interests in real estate, banking, and mercantile activities.

Mrs. Townsend's writings had begun to appear in print before her marriage, her first efforts being published in the Fishkill, N. Y., *Standard* in 1850. While visiting a married sister in New Orleans, she began to write for the New Orleans *Delta,* a newspaper. She signed her first contributions "Xariffa," the name under which she was to attract a wide circle of friendly readers. Under the name "Mary Ashley" she wrote for the New Orleans *Crescent.* When she went to New Orleans to live she wrote for the *Delta* a series of essays called "Quillotypes." Another series, also uncollected, was called "The Crossbones Papers." During the winter of 1881 she contributed letters to the New Orleans *Picayune* describing her travels in Mexico. She wrote one novel, *The Brother Clerks,* published in New York in 1857. The scene is laid in New Orleans; the plot is melodramatic, the characterization feeble, and the emotional effects are not always happy. Although the book had some success, the author made no further efforts in extended fiction, but employed her talents more happily in verse.

Her first volume of verse, *Xariffa's Poems,* was published in Philadelphia in 1870. This was largely made up of her newspaper poems, and included her popular success, "Creed," first printed in the *Picayune,* Nov. 1, 1868. *The Captain's Story,* published in Philadelphia in 1874, attracted a good deal of attention. The theme dealt with a supposedly white man who discovered that his mother was a mulatto, and the subject was handled with skill and restraint. Oliver Wendell Holmes praised this poem highly. *Down the Bayou and other Poems,* published in Boston in 1882, was dedicated to Holmes. *Distaff and Spindle,* a collection of sonnets, appeared in 1895.

Easter Sunrise, illustrated by A. Molinary, was the only one of her poems to be published separately in New Orleans. Her verse, widely popular at the time of publication, is sincere and competent rather than inspired.

Mrs. Townsend entered fully into the social and literary life of New Orleans. She was one of the founders of the Quarante Club, and president for seven years. With Mary E. Moore Davis [*q.v.*] she edited an illustrated magazine called *Arts and Letters,* published in New Orleans during 1887. She was frequently called upon to write occasional poems. She enjoyed excellent health, and was noted as a gracious hostess and a brilliant conversationalist. Her husband and her three daughters came first in her life. French and Spanish literature, music, and art, were her chief cultural interests. She was injured in a railway accident in the spring of 1901, and died shortly afterwards at Galveston, Tex., at the home of one of her two surviving daughters.

[*Who's Who in America,* 1899–1900; information from the family; Ella Rightor, critical essay in *Lib. of Southern Lit.,* vol. XII (1907); New Orleans Daily *Picayune,* and *Times-Democrat,* June 8, 9, 1901.]

R. P. M.

TOWNSEND, MIRA SHARPLESS (Sept. 26, 1798–Nov. 20, 1859), philanthropist, the daughter of Jesse and Joanna (Townsend) Sharpless, both descendants of early Pennsylvania settlers, was born in Philadelphia and educated at the Select School. A talent for writing became evident in her youth. Her poems were published in contemporary newspapers and magazines; letters written in her early twenties to her cousin, Edward Darlington, showed shrewd observation and a sense of humor; while the journal kept in her later years is a valuable commentary on the experiences of a public-spirited woman in the middle of the nineteenth century.

On Jan. 23, 1828, Mira Sharpless married Samuel Townsend, a prosperous and philanthropic merchant of Philadelphia. They had six children, of whom four died in infancy. Though a Friend all her life, she did not wear plain dress. Doubtless the dignity and distinction of her personality were enchanced by the handsome silks and fine laces in which her taste found expression. For some years she devoted herself to her family and her hospitable home where, during Yearly Meeting Week, as many as fifty Friends would be entertained. As time passed, however, she developed a strong sense of duty toward the unfortunate and the friendless. In 1847 she helped promote a public meeting of women to consider the abolition of capital punishment. At a later meeting of this group, she proposed a plan that led to the formation of the Rosine Association, which founded the Rosine Home, a place for the reformation, employment, and instruction "of unfortunate women who had led immoral lives" (*Public Ledger,* Philadelphia, May 10, 1931). This is said to have been the first institution of the kind run entirely by women (*Ibid.*). The project attracted wide attention and soon led to the establishment of similar homes in other cities. As she came to believe that this charity was more than local in its character, she took the extreme step of going to Harrisburg in 1854 with a friend, Mrs. Sophia Lewis, and petitioning the legislature for an appropriation of $3,000 for the aid of the Rosine Association. The charm of manner of the two women and their sincere devotion to their cause impressed the legislators so favorably that the bill was easily passed. Until her death Mira Townsend remained treasurer of the Rosine Home and a member of its board of managers. A result of her experiences was a volume entitled *Reports and Realities from the Sketch Book of a Manager* (privately printed, 1855). She served as vice-president of the American Female Guardian Society of New York and some of her verse appeared in its semi-monthly publication, the *Advocate and Family Guardian.*

Together with her sister, Eliza Parker, she founded the Temporary Home, still (1936) in existence, of which she became secretary and a manager. This was "a transient boarding house for respectable women out of employment . . . and where also destitute children can be taken care of until suitable homes can be procured." She was instrumental in bringing the House of the Good Shepherd to Philadelphia, for she believed that Catholic girls could be better cared for by their own church. Among other movements that enlisted her sympathies were those concerned with inebriety and slavery. A room in her home was set aside for those whose friendlessness seemed to require her hospitality, while girls needing such encouragement were employed in her service. She seems to have been indefatigable in her care for the wretched, whether these were suffering from misfortune, oppression, or moral unfitness. "The prison and alms houses," she wrote, "houses of ill-fame and the Rosine and Temporary Homes are my familiar haunts." She died at Philadelphia and was buried in Fair Hill Cemetery.

[Joseph Sharpless, *Family Record of the Sharples Family* (1816); Gilbert Cope, *Geneal. of the Sharpless Family* (1887); J. T. Scharf and Thompson Westcott, *Hist. of Phila.* (1884), vol. II; Troth Papers, vol. I, and Cope Collection, Family Data, vols. LXXII and LXXXI, in Geneal. Soc. of Phila.; *Chester County Times,* Nov. 1859; *Public Ledger* (Phila.), May 10, 1931; *Phila. Daily News,* Nov. 22, 1850: family papers.]
　　　　　　　　　　　　　　　　　A. L. L.

TOWNSEND, ROBERT (Oct. 21, 1819–Aug. 15, 1866), naval officer, son of Isaiah Townsend and Hannah (Townsend) Townsend, was born in Albany, N. Y. He was a descendant of both John and Henry Townsend, brothers who settled in Oyster Bay before September 1661. He entered Union College in 1834, but was appointed a midshipman in the navy, Aug. 4, 1837. The following year he was sent in the *Ohio* to the Mediterranean, where he remained for two years. He attended the naval school at Philadelphia for one year, and was warranted passed midshipman on completion of his course. The opening of the Mexican War found him on the brig *Porpoise,* attached to the squadron of Commodore David Conner [*q.v.*] off the coast of Mexico. In this vessel he participated in the expedition against Tampico (Nov. 14, 1846) and assisted in the capture of a Mexican schooner, the *Ormigo.* He also took part in the siege and occupation of Vera Cruz and San Juan d'Ulúa. After the capitulation of Vera Cruz, he was permitted by his commanding officer to join the army temporarily. He served with it for six months, taking part in the march on Mexico city and its capture. He saw but little active service after the war, and resigned from the navy, Apr. 7, 1851.

Possessed of ample means, he lived in retirement in Albany until 1861, when he offered his services to his government. Appointed acting lieutenant in September, he was assigned to the *Harriet Lane* of the Potomac flotilla. Three months later he was ordered to the *Miami* on blockade duty off North Carolina. The following summer he was reinstated in his regular position in the navy, with the rank of commander. He was now given command of the *Miami,* and rendered most efficient service in patrolling Albemarle and Pamlico Sounds. In July 1863 he was transferred to the *Mississippi* and given command of the steam iron-clad *Essex,* in which he participated in the siege and capture of Port Hudson. As a division commander under Admiral David Dixon Porter [*q.v.*], he also participated in the Red River expedition and in subsequent operations on the Mississippi. Just before the close of the war he was given command of the *Wachusett,* with orders to sail by way of the Cape of Good Hope and join the East India Squadron off the Chinese Coast. On the coast of China he rendered valuable service in protecting the lives of American missionaries and consuls, without injury to the prestige of the native authorities. He died on his ship off Chin-Kiang-Fu of congestion of the brain due to the excessive heat. Three weeks before his death he had been promoted to the rank of captain. Though a man of scholarly tastes, and devoted to his home and family, he did not hesitate to volunteer his services when they were needed. He proved himself a highly capable officer, very popular with his subordinates. He married Harriet Monroe of Syracuse, N. Y., in 1850, and had one son and two daughters. He was the owner of the most valuable private library in Albany.

[Margaret Townsend, *Townsend-Townshend, 1066–1909* (1909) ; *War of the Rebellion: Official Records (Navy)*, 1 ser., vols. III–IV, VI, VIII–X, XIX, XXI, XXV–XXVII ; G. F. Emmons, *The Navy of the U. S.* (1853), p. 82; Joel Munsell, *Colls. on the Hist. of Albany*, vol. III (1870) ; G. R. Howell and Jonathan Tenney, *Bi-Centennial Hist. of Albany County, N. Y.* (1886) ; *Cat. of the Sigma Phi* (1927) ; obituaries in *Albany Evening Jour.*, Oct. 18, 20, and *Army and Navy Jour.*, Oct. 27, 1866 ; manuscript letter and reports in Navy Dept. Archives ; manuscript log of the *Wachusett*, 1865–66 ; U. S. Navy Dept. Registers, 1837–51, 1861–66.]   L. H. B.

TOWNSEND, VIRGINIA FRANCES (1836–Aug. 11, 1920), author, was born in New Haven, Conn., a descendant of Thomas Townsend who emigrated to Massachusetts from England in the seventeenth century. She was the daughter of James and Hulda (Smith) Townsend of New Haven, Conn. During her childhood she was debarred from active life by frequent illnesses, and as a result found her greatest pleasures in books. Before she was seventeen she began contributing stories and poems to the ladies' magazines of the time, notably the *Ladies' Repository* of Cincinnati. At the age of twenty, in 1856, she became associate editor of the *Lady's Home Magazine* published by Timothy Shay Arthur [*q.v.*]. She continued this connection until 1872, supplying the paper regularly with serials, poems, articles, and stories for children, all designed, in accordance with the policy of the magazine, to elevate, inform, and entertain. Her popularity with the readers of the periodical is attested by the fact that for ten years after she ceased to be named as associate editor, she continued to contribute historical sketches and travel articles. In 1857 she published her first book, *Living and Loving*, made up of previously printed stories, and embellished with her portrait engraved by John Sartain [*q.v.*]. During the next three decades she wrote over a score of popular books for girls. Some of these appeared in the Maidenhood Series, others in the Breakwater Series. Characteristic titles are *Amy Deane* (1862), *Janet Strong* (1865), *Only Girls* (1872), *That Queer Girl* (1874), *Lenox Dare* (1881), *A Boston Girl's Ambitions* (1887). Besides these tales she published three works "out

of love and reverence for the past"—*The Battle-fields of Our Fathers* (1864) ; *Life of Washington* (1887), "a woman's way of looking at George Washington"; and *Our Presidents* (1889).

After 1865 she made her home in Massachusetts. In that year she accepted an invitation to act as teacher of rhetoric in the Family School for Young Ladies conducted by Dioclesian Lewis [*q.v.*] in Lexington, an institution designed to "secure the symmetrical development of body, mind, and heart." There she enjoyed a pleasant association with girls from many parts of the United States and became increasingly interested in writing books for their entertainment. Some years later, when Dr. and Mrs. Lewis established a sanitarium in Arlington Heights, she became a member of their household. She resided with them until 1881, and afterwards with their successors. She lived a quiet and uneventful life during her later years, reading, walking, writing, and occasionally staying for months in Boston to be near old friends. She died in Arlington and was buried in Mt. Auburn Cemetery.

[L. C. Moulton, "Sketch of Virginia Frances Townsend," *Arthur's Home Mag.*, Sept. 1858 ; *Cat. and Circular of Dr. Dio Lewis's Family School . . . 1865* (1865) ; C. H. Townshend, *The Townshend Family* (4th ed. 1884) ; *Who's Who in America*, 1912–13 ; date of death from Arlington town records.]   B. M. S.

TOY, CRAWFORD HOWELL (Mar. 23, 1836–May 12, 1919), Orientalist and teacher, was born in Norfolk, Va., the eldest of a family of nine children. His father, Thomas Dallam Toy, a man of influence in the community and of reputation as a scholar, was of English descent. His mother, Amelia Ann (Rogers) Toy, was the grand-daughter of a Revolutionary officer. Crawford prepared for college at the Norfolk Academy and graduated from the University of Virginia in 1856. After teaching English for three years at the Albemarle Female Institute in Charlottesville, he studied theology for one year at the Southern Baptist Theological Seminary in Greenville, S. C., with the intention of becoming a missionary in Japan. The Civil War put an end to this plan, and in October 1861 he entered the Confederate service, first as private in artillery and then as chaplain in infantry. Captured at Gettysburg in July 1863 and exchanged in December, he again entered the army, serving until the summer of 1864. After the war he taught Greek for a year in the University of Virginia, and then spent two years in Germany studying theology and the Semitic languages at Berlin. In 1869 he was made professor of Old Testament interpretation in the Southern Baptist Seminary, which in 1877 removed from Greenville, S. C., to Louisville, Ky.; and during the ten years of his service he earned a wide reputation as teacher and scholar. In May 1879 he resigned his chair because of his inability to accept the doctrine of inspiration of the Scriptures which there and then was insisted upon. Removing to New York, he acted as literary editor of the *Independent* until, in 1880, he was called to Harvard as Hancock Professor of Hebrew and other Oriental languages. He became professor emeritus in 1909. In 1888 he married Nancy, daughter of the Rev. R. M. Saunders of Norfolk, Va. They had no children.

At Harvard Toy ranked as one of the foremost members of the faculty and became widely known through his publications. His *Quotations in the New Testament* appeared in 1884, and in 1890 his *Judaism and Christianity,* a sketch of the progress of thought from the Old Testament to the New. These books show Toy's sound scholarship, the clearness and simplicity of his literary style, and the qualities always characteristic of his work: moderation, independence with modesty, and a remarkable freedom from prejudice. His *A Critical and Exegetical Commentary on the Book of Proverbs* (1899) and *Introduction to the History of Religions* (1913) were achievements for which he was especially fitted by his breadth of view and his didactic habit of mind. The latter work was in the field which absorbed his attention in his later years. He founded a club for the study of the history of religions; and when a volume of essays by his pupils, colleagues, and friends was presented to him after his retirement, it was entitled *Studies in the History of Religions* (1912). He originated two other learned societies at Harvard: the Biblical Club, which met in Boston and included in its membership professors in neighboring institutions, and the Semitic Conference, designed mainly for advanced students. Among Toy's more important publications in the Biblical field were two volumes in the Polychrome Bible series, each entitled *The Book of the Prophet Ezekiel:* the one, a critical edition of the Hebrew text, with notes; the other, a new English translation. These appeared in 1899. He also published valuable articles in the *Encyclopaedia Biblica,* the *Encyclopaedia Britannica,* and the *Jewish Enycyclopedia,* of which he was one of the editors. His contributions to learned journals covered a wide range of subjects. A brief popular *History of the Religion of Israel* (1882) went through many editions.

[*Who's Who in America,* 1918–19; D. G. Lyon, in *Harvard Grads.' Mag.,* Dec. 1919, pp. 266–69, with portrait; S. E. Morison, *The Development of Harvard University, 1869–1929* (1930), with portrait; bibliog.

in *Studies in the Hist. of Religions* (1912); obituary in *Boston Transcript,* May 13, 1919.]   C. C. T.

TRACY, BENJAMIN FRANKLIN (Apr. 26, 1830–Aug. 6, 1915), lawyer, soldier, secretary of the navy, was born near Owego, N. Y., of Irish descent. His grandfather, Thomas Tracy, after living in Vermont and Massachusetts, became one of the first settlers in the southern tier of counties of New York. Benjamin was reared on a farm and was educated at Owego Academy, where Thomas C. Platt [*q.v.*] was a fellow student. After studying in the office of N. W. Davis of Owego, Tracy was admitted to the bar in 1851. Two years later he was elected district attorney of Tioga County as a Whig. In 1854 he organized the Republican party in the county. He was reëlected district attorney in 1856. As an assemblyman, in 1862, he urged full support of the national government in the Civil War.

In the summer of 1862 he recruited two regiments and became colonel of the 109th New York Volunteers. In the Wilderness campaign, though ordered to the rear on account of physical exhaustion, he continued to lead his regiment until the condition of his health forced him to relinquish his command. His gallantry earned for him the brevet rank of brigadier-general and years afterward the Congressional Medal of Honor. During the last months of the war he was colonel of the 127th Regiment (colored troops) and commander of the military prison and recruiting camp at Elmira, N. Y.

In 1866 President Johnson appointed him district attorney for the eastern district of New York, where by a series of able prosecutions he broke up illicit distilling. He drafted the safeguarding provisions of the internal revenue act of 1868, under which federal collections were increased fourfold. In 1873 he resumed his private practice in Brooklyn; he defended Henry Ward Beecher [*q.v.*] in the suit brought against him by Theodore Tilton [*q.v.*] and was unusually successful in cases involving the law of public officers. As a judge of the court of appeals, 1881–82, he rendered decisions on the validity of marriages contracted in other states (90 *N. Y. Reports,* 603) and on the liability of elevated railroad companies for damages for the stoppage of light and air (90 *N. Y. Reports,* 122) which still (1936) stand.

In 1889 he received from President Harrison the appointment as secretary of the navy, which has usually been interpreted as a sop to Thomas C. Platt, though Tracy had the indorsement of both the principal factions of the Republican party of New York. He entered at once on a program for the building of a powerful navy, and and during his administration the *Iowa, Indiana, Massachusetts, Oregon,* and *Brooklyn* were completed or authorized. He organized the naval militia, created the board of construction to correlate the work of various bureaus, and did much to abolish political corruption in appointments and the purchase of supplies at the navy yards. In the cabinet he was responsible for several official interpretations of international law, including the right of asylum in the Barrundia case (see J. B. Moore, *A Digest of International Law*, 1906, II, 851), neutral rights and duties in the Chilean revolution (*Ibid.*, II, 1107–08), and the right of property in seals which became the basis of one of the questions put up for arbitration by the United States in the Bering Sea controversy (see Tracy, in *North American Review,* May 1893).

After his retirement he was counsel for Venezuela in the boundary arbitration with Great Britain. He was chairman of the commission of 1896 which formulated the charter of Greater New York. At Platt's insistence, he became the regular Republican nominee for mayor in 1897, but was defeated by a large majority. His principal avocation was the breeding of trotting horses on his Tioga County farm. In person he was unusually handsome. He had keen powers of analysis, good judgment, and great executive ability. In 1851 he married Delinda E. Catlin; she and their younger daughter lost their lives in the burning of their Washington home in February 1890; a son and a daughter survived him.

[*Who's Who in America*, 1914–15; *The New International Yearbook, 1915* (1916); W. B. Gay, *Hist. Gazetteer of Tioga County, N. Y.* (n.d.); L. W. Kingman, *Our Country and Its People* (n.d.); H. R. Stiles, *The Civil . . . Hist. and . . . Industrial Record of the County of Kings and the City of Brooklyn* (copr. 1884); G. O. Seilhamer, *Hist. of the Republican Party* (n.d.); *N. Y. Times* and *N. Y. Tribune*, Aug. 7, 1915; J. D. Long, *The New Am. Navy* (1903); D. S. Alexander, *Four Famous New Yorkers* (1923); *The Autobiog. of Thomas Collier Platt* (1910); H. F. Gosnell, *Boss Platt and His N. Y. Machine* (copr. 1924); *Hist. of the Bench and Bar of N. Y.*, vol. II (1897); *Bench and Bar*, Jan. 1915.] E. C. S.

TRACY, JOSEPH (Nov. 3, 1793–Mar. 24, 1874), Congregational clergyman, editor, author, was born in Hartford, Vt., the son of Joseph and Ruth (Carter) Tracy, and a descendant of Stephen Tracy who came to Plymouth, Mass., in 1623. After graduation at Dartmouth in 1814 and a period of teaching at Albany, N. Y., and Royalton, Vt., he began the study of the law. When nearly ready for admission to the bar, he changed his life-purpose and turned to the study of theology, with Asa Burton [*q.v.*] of Thet-

ford, Vt., as his preceptor. Ordained June 26, 1821, he assumed the double pastorate of Post Mills and West Fairlee, Vt. In 1829 he became editor of the *Vermont Chronicle,* which immediately took rank as one of the ably edited journals of the country. In 1834 he became editor of the *Boston Recorder,* and the following year, of the *New York Observer.* Appointed secretary of the Massachusetts Colonization Society in 1842, he continued in this office for the remainder of his life, becoming, also, in 1858, director of the American Colonization Society. The outstanding work of his career was in connection with the colonization movement, the object of which was a Christian republic of colonized Africans in Africa. He was active in founding the Trustees of Donations for Education in Liberia, and was chosen as secretary at its first meeting, Jan. 15, 1851. To his energetic measures is largely due the founding of Liberia College, the first missionary college in Africa. For many years he wrote the annual reports of the Massachusetts and American colonization societies, and he also prepared the *Memorial of the Semi-Centennial Anniversary of the American Colonization Society* (1867), containing a comprehensive account of the rise and progress of the colonization movement.

His principal published works are *History of American Missions to the Heathen* (1840); *The Great Awakening; a History of the Revival of Religion in the Time of Edwards and Whitefield* (1842); *Colonization and Missions; a Historical Examination of the State of Society in Western Africa* (1844). In addition, he published several missionary maps and occasional sermons and was a frequent contributor to the press.

Tracy had a clear and logical mind, an unusual memory, and a vast store of knowledge. His literary style was crisp and incisive and he had no superior as a controversialist; yet he was modest and unpretending, with a native delicacy of feeling that kept him from giving offense. While conservative in his theological positions, he was always charitable toward those of opposed beliefs. On June 9, 1819, he married Eleanor, daughter of Rev. Azel Washburn of Royalton, Vt., who died Feb. 14, 1836. Of their eight children, seven survived their parents. His second wife, whom he married June 3, 1845, was Sarah C. Prince of Beverly, Mass., who survived him. He died in Beverly.

[E. E. Tracy, *Tracy Geneal.* (1898); *Vital Records of Beverly, Mass., to . . . 1849* (1907); G. T. Chapman, *Sketches of the Alumni of Dartmouth Coll.* (1867); *Congregationalist*, Apr. 2, 1874; *Boston Traveller*, Mar. 25, 1874; E. A. Lawrence, *Address at the Funeral of Dr. Joseph Tracy* (1874); *Fifty-Eighth Ann. Report*

of the Am. Colonization Soc. (1875); E. M. W. Lovejoy, *Hist. of Royalton, Vt.* (1911), pp. 321, 330, 1015;
Boston Transcript, Mar. 26, 1874.]　　　F. T. P.

TRACY, NATHANIEL (Aug. 11, 1751–Sept.
20, 1796), merchant, philanthropist, patriot, one
of the financiers of the Revolution, was born in
Newbury (now Newburyport), Mass., the eldest son of Capt. Patrick Tracy, who had migrated to Massachusetts from Ireland as a youth, and
his second wife, Hannah Gookin. He was graduated from Harvard College in 1769 and received
the M.A. degree in 1772. He commenced business in Newburyport with his brother-in-law,
Jonathan Jackson, and in 1775 fitted out a fleet
of privateers which sailed out of Newburyport
in August. Between 1775 and 1783 he sent to
sea twenty-four cruisers manned by 2800 men
and captured 120 sail of vessels with 2225 prisoners of war. During the same period, as the principal owner, he sent out 110 merchant vessels, all
but thirteen of which were either captured or
lost before the end of the war. The chief service
of his cruisers was in capturing ammunition and
supplies intended for the British army; his merchant vessels with their cargoes were worth $2,-
733,300. The 120 vessels that were captured
were sold for $4,000,000. In spite of his wealth,
which was considerably increased early in the
war, he died in virtual bankruptcy due to the fact
that as the war continued his fleet was almost entirely captured or destroyed. Of his cruisers only
one remained in 1783. He was further reduced
by the failure of several enterprises, particularly
by a contract to furnish masts for the marine of
France, and as one of the principal creditors of
the Portuguese merchant Gardoqui. He contributed $167,000 in cash, as well as clothing and
food to the government. In addition to Jackson,
he was associated in business with his brother,
John Tracy, another brother-in-law, Joseph Lee,
and a cousin, Capt. Nicholas Tracy.

Among his homes was the brick mansion in
Newburyport (now the public library) built for
him by his father upon his marriage, and in
which he entertained Washington and Lafayette,
the Vassall house in Cambridge, now known as
the Craigie or Longfellow house, once the home
of the poet, and the Spencer-Pierce farm in Newbury, to which he retired and where he died.
During his affluence he is said to have owned so
many houses that he could travel from Newburyport to Philadelphia and sleep under his own
roof every night. He served as deputy to the
Massachusetts General Court, 1781–82, as a state
senator in 1783. He was a charter member of
the American Academy of Arts and Sciences.
On Feb. 28, 1775, he was married to Mary Lee,

the daughter of Col. Jeremiah and Martha
(Swett) Lee, of Marblehead. She, with several
of their eleven children, survived him. Charles,
James, 1777–1867, and Patrick T. Jackson [*qq.v.*]
were his nephews.

[T. A. Lee, "The Lee Family of Marblehead," *Essex
Institute Hist. Colls.,* Jan. 1916–July 1917, and "The
Tracy Family of Newbury," *Ibid.,* Jan. 1921; S. C.
Paine, C. H. Pope, *Paine Ancestry* (1912); J. E. Green-
leaf, *Geneal. of the Greenleaf Family* (1896); T. A.
Lee, biographical sketch in *Harvard Grads. Mag.,* Dec.
1916; J. J. Currier, *"Ould Newbury"* (1896); Marquis
de Chastellux, *Travels in North-America* (1787), vol.
II; F. L. Bullard, *Hist. Summer Haunts* (1912); *Co-
lumbian Centinel* (Boston), Sept. 21, 1796.] R. L. J.

TRACY, URIAH (Feb. 2, 1755–July 19,
1807), representative and senator from Connecticut, was born in that part of Norwich which is
now Franklin, Conn., the son of Eliphalet and
Lucy, or Sarah (Manning), Tracy. He was the
descendant of Thomas Tracy who emigrated
from England to Massachusetts and in 1660 was
one of the proprietors of Norwich. After graduation from Yale College in 1778, Uriah read law
with Tapping Reeve [*q.v.*], was admitted to the
bar in 1781, and began to practise in Litchfield,
Conn. A man of sober carriage, a devout Christian, and a stout Federalist, he won reputation
as one of the state's most eminent and successful
lawyers. A clever politician with a keen knowledge of men, an attractive speaker gifted with
satire and humor, and an impetuous debater, he
was honored by his community with an appointment as state's attorney for Litchfield County,
election to the General Assembly, 1788–1793,
and promotion in the militia to the rank of major-general. Meanwhile, he made a good marriage to Susan, or Susannah, the daughter of
Isaac and Eunice (Gillett) Bull of Hartford, by
whom he had a son and four daughters. He became the father-in-law of James Gould, Samuel
Howe, and Theron Metcalf [*qq.v.*].

He was elected a representative to Congress,
where he served from Mar. 4, 1793, until he was
elected to the Senate in October 1796 as the successor of Jonathan Trumbull. An associate and
confidant of the outstanding Federalists, Hamilton, Ames, Morris, Rufus King, and Adams, he
was a man of influence in the party's counsels
and one of its shrewdest politicians. He attracted attention in a speech against the resolution
for an amendment of the machinery for the election of the president and vice-president (*Mr.
Tracy's Speech in the Senate . . . Dec. 2, 1803,*
1803; reprinted in Williston, *post,* and Moore,
post). His brochure, *Reflections on Monroe's
View of the Conduct of the Executive as Published in the Gazette of the United States under
the Signature of Scipio* (1798), once ascribed to

Hamilton, was an able, cynical, partisan criticism that had force as a campaign document. Long an ill man, he died of dropsy in Washington.

[Letters and photostats in Lib. of Cong.; letters in George Gibbs, *Memoirs of the Admr. of Washington and John Adams* (2 vols., 1846) and in *The Life and Correspondence of Rufus King,* vol. IV (1897), ed. by C. R. King; speeches in Frank Moore, *Am. Eloquence,* vol. I (1857), and E. B. Williston, *Eloquence of the U. S.* (1827), vol. II; F. B. Dexter, *Biog. Sketches of the Grads. of Yale College,* vol. IV (1907); *Biog. Directory Am. Cong.* (1928); *Encyc. of Conn. Biog.* (1917), vol. I; P. K. Kilbourne, *Sketches and Chronicles of the Town of Litchfield, Conn.* (1859); G. H. Hollister, *The Hist. of Conn.* (1855), vol. II; E. E. Tracy, *Tracy Geneal.* (1898); *Conn. Jour.* (New Haven), July 29, Aug. 5, 12, 1807; *Conn. Courant* (Hartford), July 29, 1807.]   R. J. P.

TRAETTA, FILIPPO [See TRAJETTA, PHILIP, *c.* 1776–1854].

TRAIN, ENOCH (May 2, 1801–Sept. 8, 1868), merchant, shipowner, was born probably in Weston, Mass., the son of Enoch and Hannah (Ewing) Train, and a descendant of John Traine who came from England in 1635 and settled in Watertown, Mass. After the death of his father in 1805 his mother married Capt. Levi Bishop of Windsor, Vt. (*Town of Weston: Births, Deaths, and Marriages,* 1901).

During the second quarter of the nineteenth century, Train became one of Boston's most active merchants. He seems to have made a specialty of the Baltic trade, but he also had business connections in South America. His particular distinction, however, comes from the fact that in 1844 he established a line of sailing packets between Boston and Liverpool. Ever since the formation of the Black Ball line in 1817, New York had had a virtual monopoly of the packet service. The only successful outside rival was the Cope line from Philadelphia. Near by Train had as a competitor the Cunard line, which had been maintaining regular steamship service between Liverpool and Boston since 1840. Bostonians were openly skeptical about Train's venture. The most of his earlier ships were criticized as slow; frequently, moreover, the lack of adequate eastbound cargoes in Boston led him to sacrifice regularity of sailings—an essential packet feature—and send his ships to Southern ports for cotton cargoes. He made a shrewd move in 1844, however, when he commissioned Donald McKay [*q.v.*] to build the *Joshua Bates* and then persuaded him to move his shipyard from Newburyport to East Boston. About this time young George Francis Train [*q.v.*], a kinsman, became associated with Enoch as a clerk; later he was Liverpool manager, and finally a partner. During the next nine years McKay built for the Train line the *Washington Irving,*

Anglo-Saxon, Ocean Monarch, Anglo-American, Parliament, Daniel Webster, Staffordshire, Chariot of Fame, and *Star of Empire.* Some of these were clipper ships and at least one, the *Staffordshire,* was diverted from the Liverpool run for a voyage to California and Calcutta. McKay's masterpiece, the *Flying Cloud,* was built for the Trains, but was sold by them to Grinnell, Minturn & Company of New York for $90,000, double the contract price. Altogether, the line owned or chartered at least twenty-four different ships.

The immigration which followed the Irish famine of 1846 gave the line a great impetus and Train aggressively encouraged the bringing of immigrants to Boston, widely distributing advertising in Europe. By arrangements with European and American railroads, through rates from foreign cities to the interior of America were offered. The Train line also did a business, amounting it is said to $1,000,000 a year, in sending remittances from the immigrants in America to their old homes. The line derived its popular name from the "white diamond" which appeared on the red house flag; the ships also carried a large black "T" on their foretopsails.

Two of the Train ships, the *Anglo-Saxon* and *Staffordshire,* were lost off Cape Sable; the *Ocean Monarch* was burned near Liverpool with a loss of 400 lives, and with the general slump in American shipping about 1854 many of the ships found their way into British hands. In 1855, Train was one of the leading incorporators of the Boston & Europe Steamship Company, which never materialized, and the panic of 1857 seems further to have increased his business difficulties.

Train is credited with being one of Boston's public-spirited citizens and his name is associated with the development of Fenway Court. He resided on Mount Vernon Street, Beacon Hill. His first wife was Adeline, daughter of Silas and Nancy Tobey Dutton. Their daughter, Adeline Dutton Train Whitney [*q.v.*], was a well known writer of stories and verse. Train's second wife, whom he married in January 1836, was Almira Cheever (*New England Historical and Genealogical Register,* April 1884, p. 188). His portrait shows a narrow, thoughtful, dignified face, with a high forehead. He died at Saugus, Mass., and was buried in Mount Auburn Cemetery, Cambridge.

[Henry Bond, *Geneals. . . . of the First Settlers of Watertown* (1855), I, 607; R. C. McKay, *Some Famous Sailing Ships and Their Builder, Donald McKay* (1928); G. F. Train, *My Life in Many States and in Foreign Lands* (1902); C. C. Cutler, *Greyhounds of the Sea* (1930); S. E. Morison, *The Maritime Hist. of Mass.* (1921); *Some Merchants and Sea Captains of*

Old Boston (State Street Trust Company, 1918); information in regard to dates of birth and death from supt. of Mount Auburn Cemetery.]　　R. G. A—n.

TRAIN, GEORGE FRANCIS (Mar. 24, 1829–Jan. 19, 1904), merchant, promoter, author, was born in Boston, the only son of Oliver and Maria (Pickering) Train, and a descendant of John Traine who settled in Watertown, Mass., in 1635. Oliver was a merchant who moved from Boston to New Orleans, and whose last traceable act was to send his son back to Boston by sea and alone, the child's mother and his three sisters having been victims of a yellow fever epidemic. Train was finally delivered to his maternal grandmother in Waltham, and on her farm he lived until he was fourteen, attending the district school and, for three months only, an academy in Framingham. In 1843 he left his home to escape being apprenticed and found employment in a grocery store in Cambridge. A year or more later a relative, Enoch Train [*q.v.*], called to inquire about him, and the next day George betook himself to his visitor's shipping-office in Boston and demanded employment there. His insistence overrode all objections, and he was soon actively engaged in the management of the business.

Enoch Train had established a packet line to Liverpool and had recently commissioned Donald McKay [*q.v.*] to build a ship for him. Commissions for other ships followed and young Train acquired some prominence in connection with them. It was he, according to his own account, who ordered for the firm, in 1848, the building by McKay of the famous *Flying Cloud,* which the Trains sold at a huge profit. In 1850 he was sent to England as manager of the Liverpool office. Three years thereafter he went to Melbourne, Australia, where he established a shipping firm, and is said to have earned commissions amounting to $95,000 in the first year. He now began to show an increasing tendency to become associated with the sensational and spectacular. Leaving Australia in 1855, he toured the Orient, the Levant, and Europe, establishing connections in Paris with the entourage of Queen Maria Cristina of Spain, from whose banker he later secured funds to build the Atlantic and Great Western Railroad in Ohio. On his return to America in July 1856, the *New York Herald* printed many columns by him, and during the next eighteen years he wrote extensively, producing such books as *Young America in Wall Street, Young America Abroad, in Europe, Asia, and Australia,* and *An American Merchant in Europe, Asia, and Australia,* all published in 1857, and *Spread-Eagleism,* a collection of his speeches with press accounts of the writer and his books, which appeared in 1859. In addition, he issued innumerable pamphlets, leaflets, and fugitive pieces. In the late fifties and early sixties he was in England seeking capital for American railroads, and endeavoring to promote the construction of street railway lines in Liverpool, London, and Staffordshire; after the outbreak of the Civil War he also made stirring speeches in behalf of the Union.

His return to Boston in 1862 was signalized by his being put in jail—one of numerous such experiences—for disturbing a public meeting. He continued to attract attention by his financial undertakings and other spectacular activities: he espoused the Fenian cause; built an elaborate villa in Newport; announced himself a candidate for the presidency in 1869 and made speeches in his own behalf for the next three years except when otherwise engaged; joined the French Communists in 1870 and was expelled from France; and the same year made a trip around the world in eighty days. He championed the cause of Victoria Woodhull [*q.v.*] after her arrest for the character of her published charges against Henry Ward Beecher [*q.v.*], and printed in his paper, *The Train Ligne,* passages from the Bible demonstrating that Victoria's language was well within Biblical limits. This publication resulted in his arrest for obscenity, and he was confined in the Ludlow Street Jail for several months, refusing to avail himself of means of release. Against his protest, his counsel entered the defense of insanity, on which he was discharged. A sheriff's jury then found him sane and not subject to confinement in an asylum. The case is of interest historically, because it marked the beginning of the campaign against obscenity carried on by Anthony Comstock [*q.v.*].

After the above episode in his career, Train's status was somewhat equivocal, and his business activities were curtailed. He still attracted notice from time to time, however, by trips around the world and sensational lectures. In his last years he seldom spoke to any adult, but lived quietly and frugally at the Mills Hotel in New York, spending much of his time among children. His autobiography, *My Life in Many States and in Foreign Lands* (1902), shows a willingness on his part to claim full credit for the success of any enterprise with which he was at all connected. In spite of his eccentricities and mad escapades—he styled himself the "Champion Crank"—Train was a man of no small ability nor unimportant achievements. That his influence on American shipping and

Trajetta

British street railways was considerable is recognized. In his sensational performances, moreover, there was an element of practical joking that gave them a touch of humor and satire. He was tall and dark, and once humorously designated himself an octoroon. On Oct. 5, 1851, at Louisville, Ky., he married Wilhelmina Wilkinson Davis, who died in 1879; they had four children, two sons and a daughter surviving him. He died in New York City.

[In addition to Train's autobiography, see *Who's Who in America*, 1903–05; D. C. Seitz, *Uncommon Americans* (1925); Heywood Broun and Margaret Leech, *Anthony Comstock* (1927), pp. 108–14; *Bookman*, Mar. 1904; *Outlook*, Jan. 30, 1904; *Harper's Weekly*, Feb. 6, 1904; *Times* (London), Jan. 20, 1904; *Sun* (N. Y.), Jan. 20, 1904; *Evening Post* (N. Y.), Jan. 19, 1904.]

S. G.

TRAJETTA, PHILIP (c. 1776–Jan. 9, 1854), musician, composer, was born in Venice, Italy, the son of Tommaso Michele Francesco Traetta, an eighteenth-century Italian composer who wrote thirty-four operas and was successively *maestro di capella* to the princesses on appointment of Don Filippo, Infanta of Spain and Duke of Parma; principal of the Conservatorio dell' Ospedaletto in Venice; and *maestro di corte* by appointment of Catherine II of Russia. Trajetta's mother was a Swedish lady whom his father met in St. Petersburg (*Dwight's Journal of Music, post*, p. 130). After his father's death in 1779 Philip's mother placed him in charge of the Jesuits at the Public Studies of Venice, and the boy's education was directed by this group until he was thirteen. Later he was instructed in music by Fedele Fenaroli and a certain Perillo, who gave him a thorough training in counterpoint and fugue. His inherited talents were looked upon at that time purely as a cultural accomplishment, and the boy expected to follow a military career as a profession. His teachers, however, felt that he should continue his musical studies in Naples with Niccolo Piccinni, the prolific opera composer whose followers and admirers waged the historic controversy with the admirers of Gluck. His friendship with Piccinni, who was suspected of republicanism, led him into political difficulties and cost him the influence he needed to have his works produced. He subsequently joined the patriot army that fought against King Ferdinand IV. When this army was defeated, he was captured, charged with being an enemy and with writing the patriot hymns, and thrown into a dungeon from which he found no escape for eight months. His release was accomplished at last through secret influence, and, provided with a German passport, he sailed for America.

Traubel

In the winter of 1799 he settled in Boston and immediately became occupied as a musician. There he is believed to have written and published *Vocal Exercises* and a "Washington's Dead March." In 1816–18 he appears in New York city directories as "Philip Tragetta, professor of music." He is said to have composed two cantatas, *The Christian's Joy* and *The Prophecy*, and an opera, *The Venetian Maskers*, in New York. After this he became a theatrical manager in Southern cities, introducing to the public a young singer and actress announced as his daughter, Eliza Trajetta, but according to a contemporary account not related to him (*Ibid.*). It is said that Lorenzo Da Ponte [*q.v.*], opera promoter and former librettist to Mozart, brought Trajetta to New York to become a composer for the Manuel García company which in 1825 gave that city its first hearing of Italian grand opera, but that the plan never materialized because the company had disbanded before Trajetta reached New York. Trajetta is said then to have returned to the South and to have lived in comparative seclusion in the mountains of Virginia, enjoying frequent visits from ex-presidents Madison and Monroe, "who held him in high esteem" (*Ibid.*). He was later persuaded by a friend and former pupil, U. K. Hill (F. L. Ritter, *Music in America*, 1883), who appears in Philadelphia city directories as a professor of music, to settle in Philadelphia, probably about 1828, and to establish in the following year the American Conservatorio. He presumably remained in Philadelphia until his death. Others of his works are said to be the oratorios, *Jerusalem in Affliction* (1828), *Daughter of Zion* (1829), both produced in Philadelphia, and the cantatas, *The Nativity* and *The Day of Rest* (1845). He also wrote *An Introduction to the Art and Science of Music* (1829) and *Rudiments of the Art of Singing* (2 vols., 1841–43).

[Trajetta's name sometimes appears in its Italian form of Filippo Traetta. The most complete account of his career and his work appears in *Dwight's Jour. of Music*, Jan. 28, 1854, which reprints an obituary article from the *Evening Bull.* (Phila.). See also death notice in *Phila. Daily News*, Jan. 11, 1854; *Grove's Dictionary of Music and Musicians, Am. Supp.* (1920); and Theodore Baker, *Biog. Dict. of Musicians* (1900). The date of his birth is given in *Dwight's Jour.*, as Jan. 1776, in Grove and Baker as Jan. 8, 1777. The date of his going to Phila. is given by Grove and Baker as 1822.]

J. T. H.

TRAUBEL, HORACE L. (Dec. 19, 1858–Sept. 8, 1919), author, was born in Camden, N. J., the fifth of the seven children of Maurice Henry and Katherine (Grunder) Traubel. He sometimes referred to himself as a "half-breed": his mother, whose home was in Philadelphia, came of Christian parents; his father was a

German Jew who had emigrated to the United States in early manhood and was by trade a printer, engraver, and lithographer. As a boy Horace was shy, puny, and studious. He left school when he was twelve years old, and for the next thirty-two years was successively a newsboy, errand boy, printer's devil, helper in his father's stationery shop, compositor, lithographer, newspaperman, factory paymaster, and bank clerk. After 1902 he was a free-lance journalist. His family became acquainted with Walt Whitman a short time after the poet came to live in Camden in 1873. As Horace grew to manhood he became Whitman's close friend, visiting him every day during his last years and ministering in innumerable ways and with complete fidelity to the old man's comfort and contentment. Whitman made Traubel one of his literary executors, the other two being Richard Maurice Bucke, a Canadian alienist, and Thomas B. Harned, a Camden lawyer, who had married Traubel's sister Augusta.

Meanwhile, Traubel had founded a monthly paper in Philadelphia, the *Conservator,* the first number of which was issued in March 1890. He continued to edit and publish his paper until June 1919. It yielded him a scanty and uncertain income, which he eked out with miscellaneous journalism. All his life he endured poverty heroically that he might be able to say his say about men, books, and ideas. Profoundly influenced by Whitman, he went beyond Whitman in his social thinking, becoming a Marxian socialist and an ardent supporter of Eugene V. Debs [*q.v.*]. He never took an active part in politics, and his communism was more religious, at bottom, than political or economic. His separate publications were *Chants Communal* (1904), translated into German by Otto Eduard Lessing as *Weckrufe* (1907); *With Walt Whitman in Camden* (3 vols., 1906–14); *Optimos* (1910); *Collects* (1915). He edited, also, various writings by or about Whitman and *The Dollar or the Man?* (1900), a volume of cartoons by Homer Calvin Davenport [*q.v.*]. During the latter years of his life he was praised extravagantly by a coterie of disciples, but outside that group his writings were little read. He was the platitudinizer of the American Socialist movement, performing for it a literary function such as Frank Crane [*q.v.*] was performing for more orthodox Americans. His *With Walt Whitman in Camden*, a diary—beginning Mar. 28, 1888—of his visits to Whitman, is neither dull nor unimportant, but it exasperates at times by its merciless record of Whitman's every remark, however casual or commonplace. About three-fifths of the manuscript remains unpublished, though excerpts from it have been printed in various periodicals.

In person Traubel was short and stocky, with blue eyes, mobile, sensitive features, and a great shock of wavy hair. He radiated kindliness and good cheer; to know him was to love him and to wish that he were as great a poet and prophet as his adorers believed. On May 28, 1891, he married Anne Montgomerie of Philadelphia, who with a daughter survived him. During the last months of his life he made his home with his friend David Karsner in New York. He died at Bon Echo, Ontario, of a heart ailment that had afflicted him for several years, and was buried in Camden.

[*Who's Who in America,* 1916–17; *Die Lese* (Stuttgart), Feb. 1913; Mildred Bain, *Horace Traubel* (1913); W. E. Walling, *Whitman and Traubel* (1916); David Karsner, *Horace Traubel* (1919); O. E. Lessing, "Horace Traubel," Jan., Feb. 1920, and "Ein unbekannter Prophet: Horace Traubel," in *Brücken über den Atlantik* (Leipzig, 1927); H. S. Saunders, "Complete Index to the Conservator," typescript, 1920, Lib. of Cong.; *N. Y. Times* and *Pub. Ledger* (Phila.), Sept. 10, 1919. A card in the Union Cat. at the Lib. of Cong. gives Traubel's middle name as Logo; the initial appears in Whitman's will.]

G. H. G.

TRAUTWINE, JOHN CRESSON (Mar. 30, 1810–Sept. 14, 1883), engineer, was born in Philadelphia, Pa., the son of William and Sarah (Wilkinson) Trautwine. As a youth he showed a marked fondness for the sciences, particularly physics and mineralogy, and a part of his education was acquired under the direction of the meteorologist James P. Espy [*q.v.*]. When eighteen years of age, Trautwine entered the office of William Strickland [*q.v.*], the most prominent civil engineer and architect of his day in Pennsylvania. While receiving his technical training here, he performed services in connection with the construction of the Delaware Breakwater and the erection of various public buildings, including the United States Mint.

The development of railroad systems, which was just then beginning, offered special opportunities for a young engineer, and Trautwine was quick to take advantage of them. In 1831 he secured a position on the Philadelphia section of the Columbia Railroad, and was employed on various less important works until 1835, when he was appointed assistant engineer of the Philadelphia, Wilmington & Baltimore Railroad. In 1836 he became chief engineer of the Hiwassee Railroad, then being projected between points in Tennessee and Georgia, and in 1838 established his residence in Knoxville, Tenn., with his bride, Eliza Ritter, daughter of Jacob Ritter, Jr., of Philadelphia. The financial difficulties of the times having seriously affected the construction of this railroad, in 1843 Trautwine returned to Philadelphia.

The following year he sailed for New Granada (Colombia), South America, where for five years he was engaged with George M. Totten [q.v.] in the construction of the Canal del Dique, connecting the Magdalena River with the harbor of Cartagena. At the expiration of that time he went back to Philadelphia, where he was employed for a brief period in surveying work, but late in 1849 left for the Isthmus of Panama to make surveys, in association with Totten, for the Panama Railroad. These he carried on successfully in a tropical region which presented the most difficult problems and innumerable perils to health and life. A copy of the map of the Isthmus which he prepared appeared in the *Journal of the Franklin Institute* (January 1871).

He returned to Philadelphia in 1851, but in April of the year following went back to the Isthmus to seek an inter-oceanic canal route. He spent several months in ascending the Atrato River to its source and in exploring its principal tributaries. Crossing the divide between the Atrato and the San Juan, he descended the latter river to the Pacific, later recrossing the range at several points to locate the lowest section of the divide. He finally decided upon a canal route from the Atrato River at Vigia Cubarador, to Cupica Bay on the Pacific Ocean as "the least inadvisable." In the summary of his report published in the *Journal of the Franklin Institute* (March–May, July–November 1854) he says: "I have crossed it [the Isthmus] both at the site of the Panama Railroad and at three other points more to the South. From all I could see, combined with all I have read on the subject, I cannot entertain the slightest hope that a ship-canal will ever be found practicable across any part of it." In Trautwine's time the causes of malaria and other tropical diseases were unknown, and for this reason it is probable that a canal across the Isthmus could not then have been constructed. His own work, in the face of these and other perils was one of the most difficult and dangerous undertakings upon which an engineer could venture.

In the succeeding years Trautwine was engaged in varied important enterprises. While doing engineering on the Coal Run Railroad in Pennsylvania, he lost an arm, but the loss in no wise lessened his activity. He surveyed the Lackawanna & Lanesboro Railroad (1856); surveyed a route for an inter-oceanic railway in Honduras (1857); planned a system of docks for Montreal (1858), and a harbor for Big Glace

Bay, Nova Scotia (1864); and served as consultant on various engineering problems. After 1864 he appears to have taken life less strenuously, his health having undoubtedly been affected by his previous labors. In 1871 he published the first edition of his justly famous *Engineers' Pocket Book,* a work which was immediately received with unbounded favor by the engineering profession the world over and held its own in competition with other handbooks of similar character for many years. In addition to his reputation as an engineer, he was held in high esteem as a mineralogist, his collection of minerals being one of the best in the country. He died in Philadelphia, survived by two sons.

[*The Jour. of the Franklin Institute,* Nov. 1883; *Phila. Press,* Sept. 15, 1883; "The Panama Railroad," *Harper's New Mo. Mag.,* Jan. 1859.]   F. L. G.

TRAVIS, WALTER JOHN (Jan. 10, 1862– July 31, 1927), champion amateur golfer, was born in Maldon, Victoria, Australia, the son of John Walter and Susan (Eyelet) Travis, and the eldest child in a family of five children. He came of a distinguished family in England and was a direct descendant of Lord Bishop Travis whose tomb is in the Anglican Cathedral at Chester, England. He was educated at a public school and at Trinity College in Melbourne, Australia, and at the age of twenty-three was sent to New York as manager of the New York office of McLean Bros. & Rigg, an Australian importing firm. He was moderately successful in business and, taking a strong liking to the United States, he not long afterwards became a naturalized citizen.

It was in the autumn of 1896 that he first began to play golf, a rather new game in the United States at that time but one that was quickly growing in favor. In 1897 he played in and won his first tournament at Meadowbrook, L. I. He improved rapidly in his skill at the game and within three or four years was the outstanding amateur golf player of the country. He won the national amateur championship of the United States in 1900, 1901, and 1903, and was particularly noted for his skill in putting. His success was considered remarkable in view of the fact that he did not take up the game until he was in his thirty-fifth year, and it is generally recognized that those who are trained to the game from early youth have a great advantage in acquiring correct form and natural swings. To make up for his handicap in such matters, he studied out a plan of play based on the mechanics of the golf swing as they fitted his own physical powers. He wanted to win. He had a keen competitive spirit and a dogged persistence in contests on fairway and green. By unflagging determination and arduous practice he developed a game that, while it was not beautiful to watch, was devastating to his rivals. They hit longer shots from the tee and through the fairway, but the "Old Man," as he came to be called, always hit the ball on a direct line from the tee to the pin, and his putting was deadly. He had no rival in that respect. He became the outstanding amateur player of the United States and capped his career by going to England in 1904 and winning the British amateur championship at the famous Sandwich course, the first time any representative of American golf had performed such a feat. British golfers were startled by the accuracy of his putting and many of them claimed that his success on the greens was due to the "Schenectady" or "mallet-headed" type of putter he used. This led to a formal ruling in Great Britain, that made this type of putter illegal, but the ruling was not accepted in the United States.

Stocky in stature, stern of countenance, and serious in demeanor when on the links, Travis continued in competition for many years, winning many sectional titles though he never again won a national amateur title. He gave up other pursuits and devoted himself entirely to golf, played in tournaments, wrote a book entitled *Practical Golf* (1901), edited and published a golf magazine, *The American Golfer* from 1908, and had a distinguished career as a golf-course architect. He was afflicted with bronchial asthma in later years and died in Denver, Colo., where he had gone for relief. He was married to Anne A. Bent at Middletown, Conn., on Jan. 8, 1890. She, with a daughter and a son, survived him. He was buried at Manchester, Vt.

[Family records and personal acquaintance; A. H. Bent, *The Bent Family in America* (1900); Grantland Rice, "The Marvel of Walter J. Travis," *Am. Golfer*, Sept. 1927; *The Golfer's Year Book* (1930); *N. Y. Times*, Mar. 18, 1917, Aug. 1, 1927.]   J.K.

TRAVIS, WILLIAM BARRET (Aug. 9, 1809–Mar. 6, 1836), commander of the Texas troops at the Alamo, the eldest son of Mark Travis and Jemima (Stallworth) Travis, was born near Red Banks, Edgefield County, S. C. In 1818 the Travis family removed to Alabama and settled in Conecuh County, where the ten children were given such schooling as their father's means and the frontier state afforded. William Barret studied law in the office of Judge James Dellett at Claiborne, and before his twentieth birthday was admitted to the bar and had set up his own law office. While preparing for his profession he had to earn his living by teaching school. On Oct. 26, 1828, he was married to Rosanna Cato, one of his pupils. Two children were born to them, but the marriage was not a

happy one, and Travis, in 1831, left his wife and went to Texas. A reconciliation was never effected and they were divorced in November 1835.

In Texas, Travis settled at Anahuac, the legal port for Galveston Bay and the headquarters of a military garrison commanded by Colonel Bradburn, a Kentuckian in the Mexican service. Bradburn was arbitrary and offensive in his relations with civilians, and by opposing him Travis soon found himself a foremost leader of the "war party," a faction of Texans ever ready to assert their rights and to maintain them by force if necessary. In October 1832, he removed to San Felipe, where he set up a law office and was appointed secretary of the ayuntamiento. He became an ardent leader in local politics. When, in 1835, Santa Anna sent troops to regarrison the fort at Anahuac, abandoned since 1832, Travis raised a company of volunteers and captured and disarmed the Mexican soldiers. Though the mass of the settlers repudiated his action, seeking to avoid trouble with Mexico, they were soon driven to resistance and the Texas revolution began.

During the siege of San Antonio by the Texans in the fall of 1835 Travis performed valuable service in commanding a scouting company. In December he was appointed major of artillery, but was shortly afterward transferred to the cavalry with the rank of lieutenant-colonel. Ordered to reinforce the Alamo, which the Texans had taken in December, he reached San Antonio with twenty-five men—all that he was able to enlist—on Feb. 3, 1836. Ten days later the garrison passed under the joint command of Travis and James Bowie [q.v.], Travis commanding the regulars and Bowie the volunteers. Discord developed between the commanders and the breach was hardly healed when the Mexican forces under Santa Anna arrived on Feb. 23. On the next day Bowie was stricken with typhoid-pneumonia and from that date until the final massacre on Mar. 6, Travis, at the time only twenty-seven years of age, was in full command. Probably all of the 188 men who fought under his orders died without asking for quarter after a desperate struggle. Travis was apparently a man of charming personality and had unusual powers for making friends with men of all conditions. As a lawyer he was fairly well-trained. As a politician he was practical, astute, and youthfully ambitious. He was six feet tall and weighed about 175 pounds. Contemporaries spoke of him as "the gallant Travis," and the adjective in its best sense describes him.

[The fullest treatments of the life of Travis are two graduate theses (manuscript) in the Library of the University of Texas: Ruby Mixon, "William Barret

Travis, His Life and Letters" (1929), and Amelia Williams, "The Siege and Fall of the Alamo" (1931). See also Army Papers; Comptroller Military Service Records, nos. 652, 5926; Governor and Council Papers —all manuscript collections in the Texas State Library; *Tex. State Hist. Asso. Quart.*, Jan. 1901; Henderson Yoakum, *Hist. of Tex.* (2 vols., 1856); John Henry Brown, *Life and Times of Henry Smith* (1887); E. C. Barker, *The Life of Stephen F. Austin* (1925); Amelia Williams, "A Critical Study of the Siege of the Alamo and of the Personnel of its Defenders," *Southwestern Hist. Quart.*, Apr. 1933–Apr. 1934, especially Oct. 1933.]
A. W—s.

TRAYLOR, MELVIN ALVAH (Oct. 21, 1878–Feb. 14, 1934), banker, was born in Breeding, Ky., the son of James Milton and Kitty Frances (Hervey) Traylor. His grandparents, Methodists and Jeffersonian Democrats, had moved to Kentucky from Virginia. The family was poor and Melvin, the eldest of seven children, began ploughing and harvesting corn and tobacco at the age of eight. He attended the country schools until he was fifteen, receiving the equivalent of a sixth-grade education. At sixteen he entered the high school at Columbia, Adair County, where he stayed four months, and then taught school at Leatherwood Creek for two years. In 1896 he campaigned for Bryan. Two years later he went to Hillsboro, Tex., fifty-five miles from Fort Worth, where he studied law, passing the bar examination in 1901. For the next four years he practised law and was also city clerk (1901) and assistant county attorney (1904–05) of Hill County. He started his banking career by acting as cashier of a bank at Malone, Tex., from 1905 to 1907. He then became cashier and later vice-president of the Citizens' National Bank in Ballinger, Tex., and when this was consolidated with the First National Bank he was elected president of the new institution. Most of the depositors were farmers and cattlemen and Traylor mastered the farm and cattle-loan business. In 1911 the Stock Yards National Bank of East St. Louis, Ill., made him vice-president and three years later he was given a similar appointment at the Live Stock Exchange National Bank at the Chicago Stock Yards. He was soon made president of the bank and also of the Chicago Cattle Loan Company (1914–19). During the World War he organized the local campaign for the Treasury certificate of indebtedness, and by that time was recognized as one of the outstanding bankers of Chicago.

Traylor was made president of the First Trust and Savings Bank in 1919 and at the same time vice-president and director of the First National Bank. Six years later he was president of the latter institution. These two banks and the Union Trust Company were consolidated in 1928 under the name of the First-Union Trust and Savings Bank, Traylor continuing as president of the combined institution. In 1931 the Foreman-State National Bank (itself a consolidation) with its affiliated group was absorbed, and the First National became the largest bank in Chicago. Traylor was a man of broad interests, an excellent golf player (president of the United States Golf Association, 1928) and greatly interested in higher education. He was president of the Illinois Bankers Association (1923–24), vice-president (1924–26) and president (1926–27) of the American Bankers' Association, president of the Shedd Aquarium Society, and trustee of Northwestern University, of Berea College, and of the Newberry Library. He was also director in various important corporations.

In 1929 Traylor represented the United States, together with Jackson Reynolds, in organizing the Bank for International Settlements at Basel. His point of view as a financier appears most clearly, perhaps, in a speech which he delivered before the International Chamber of Commerce in Washington, on May 5, 1931, and from which he gained great publicity ("The Human Element in Crises," *Pamphlets on the Economic Crisis of 1929*, vol. IV, 1931, no. 15). He said that financial leaders must take large responsibility for the crash, and proposed as remedies the abolition of the daily settlement and the daily call-money rate, the abolition of floor trading, and the limitation of trading to cash when the amount involved was less than $10,000. "This country," he said, "cannot afford again the wreck and ruin of people of small means which followed the last crash." He was mentioned as a Democratic candidate for the presidency of the United States in 1932. At the time of his death in Chicago, on Feb. 14, 1934, he was chairman of the committee on drought relief for Illinois and of the national committee to plan aid for the drought-ridden farms in the whole country. His wife, Dorothy Arnold (Yerby) whom he had married on June 8, 1906, and two children survived him.

[*Melvin A. Traylor, Homespun American* (privately printed, 1932), a pre-convention biography; "Dr. Traylor's Prescription," *Literary Digest*, May 23, 1931; Frazier Hunt, "The Mountaineer Boy who went Places," *Popular Mechanics Mag.*, Apr. 1933; *Business Week*, June 24, 1931; *Colliers*, Feb. 13, 1932; L. W. Burnham, "Melvin Traylor," *Rev. of Reviews*, Mar. 1932; *Who's Who in America*, 1932–33; *Who's Who in Finance Banking and Insurance*, 1931–32; *N. Y. Times, Chicago Daily Tribune, Chicago Daily News*, Feb. 15, 1934.]
E. L. B.

TREADWELL, DANIEL (Oct. 10, 1791–Feb. 27, 1872), inventor, Rumford Professor at Harvard, was descended from Thomas Treadwell who settled at Ipswich, Mass., in 1638. Born on his father's farm at Ipswich, the son of Capt.

Jabez and Elizabeth (Dodge) Treadwell, Daniel was left motherless at two and orphaned at eleven. Living with a guardian, he attended school until he was fourteen, and was then apprenticed to his eldest brother, who had just set up as a silversmith. After the failure of this brother two years later, Treadwell completed his apprenticeship in Boston with Capt. Jesse Churchill and continued as Churchill's partner for four years. A youth of studious tastes, as soon as he moved to Boston, where a library was available, he commenced a course of reading in history and the English poets.

Although Treadwell became an able silversmith, he cared less for his trade than for experimenting with machinery. Accordingly, when the War of 1812 ruined his business, he zealously went to work with a friend to devise a screw-making machine. Completed in about a year, although in imperfect form, it was put into successful operation in a mill at Saugus, Mass., but with the return of imported screws to the market at the close of the war, this business declined. Treadwell next devised a successful nail-making machine, but was compelled by ill health to seek a less strenuous occupation, and studied medicine for a year and a half with Dr. John Ware [q.v.].

Returning to his mechanical experiments, he centered his attention on the printing press, and by an ingenious application of levers and the "toggle joint" he produced a press in which a treadle operated by the weight of the printer took the place of the laborious hand-lever. He also invented a means of printing on both sides of paper without shifting the sheet. He was unsuccessful in his effort to introduce his press into England in 1819–20, but on his return to Boston, with the financial aid of friends, began to manufacture his presses. Later he applied steam power to the operation of his press, patenting a power printing press on Mar. 2, 1826. "Treadwell's Power Press" was soon installed in all the larger cities of the Atlantic Coast. It was at first used wholly in book printing, but in 1829 was introduced into newspaper work by the *Boston Daily Advertiser*. In this year Treadwell relinquished the business, having made a profit of some $70,000.

Meanwhile, he had made a study of rope making and in 1828 completed a machine for spinning hemp. For the greater part of the next eight years he devoted his time to developing machines for this purpose, securing four basic patents between 1831 and 1835. In 1833, after it had successfully demonstrated his method of manufacturing rope, the company which he organized

was merged in a larger corporation. The "Gypsey," as his machine was called, attained world-wide use, and seventy-six of the machines were still in operation fifty years after they were built.

Treadwell's brief period of medical study with Dr. Ware had brought him into a group of Boston's scientific men; in 1823 he was elected a fellow of the American Academy of Arts and Sciences, and from that year until 1826, with his preceptor and Dr. John W. Webster [q.v.], he edited the *Boston Journal of Philosophy and the Arts*. Chosen vice-president of the Boston Mechanics' Institute in 1827, he began to give a course of lectures on the steam engine and other practical subjects, adapted to the needs of the working man. He became president of the Institute and was awarded the honorary degree of A.M. by Harvard College in 1829, and in May of that year presented a report "On the Practicability of Conducting Transportation on a Single Set of Tracks" to the Massachusetts Railroad Association, describing a system of turnouts he had devised; this system was later adopted by three New England railroads.

In 1834 he accepted the call of Harvard College to the post of Rumford Professor and Lecturer on the Application of Science to the Useful Arts, and in 1835 went to England to observe processes and gather equipment for his lectures, of which he gave about two a week for the next ten years. He served on two commissions (1825; 1837) appointed to investigate the practicability of a water supply for Boston, and on one (1835–36) to examine the state standards of weights and measures; in 1837 he supervised the construction of Gore Hall, to house the Harvard library, and devised a method of heating that building. The Cambridge Scientific Club was organized at his house in 1842. From 1833 to 1839 he was recording secretary of the American Academy of Arts and Sciences, and from 1852 to 1863 a vice-president.

In the later thirties Treadwell turned his attention to an improved cannon. In 1841 he filed in the United States Patent Office a caveat which described a method of cannon contsruction consisting of building up a series of steel rings welded together and reinforced by bands, and in 1842 organized the Steel Cannon Company to manufacture four small pieces ordered by the United States. He was unsuccessful, however, in seriously interesting any government in his product, and this disappointment, together with his conviction, evidenced in a lawsuit against Robert P. Parrott [q.v.] about 1863, that the latter had appropriated his idea, so preyed on his mind that he never regained interest in his earlier activities and for the last ten years of his life lived more or less in retirement in his home in Cambridge, Mass. In his will he made generous gifts to the American Academy of Arts and Sciences and other educational institutions of Boston and provided liberally for the public library of Ipswich. He was survived by his wife, Adeline (Lincoln), daughter of Dr. Levi Lincoln of Hingham, whom he married on Oct. 6, 1831; they had no children.

[T. F. Waters, *Augustine Heard and His Friends* (1916); W. A. Robbins, *Thos. Treadwell of Ipswich, Mass. and Some of His Descendants* (1906); Patent Office records; *Boston Daily Advertiser*, Feb. 28, 1872; *Boston Morning Journal*, Feb. 29, 1872.]

C. W. M—n.

TREAT, ROBERT (1622?–July 12, 1710), colonial governor, was born at Pitminster, Somerset, England, the second son of Richard and Alice (Gaylard) Treat, or Trott. His exact date of birth is unknown; if his epitaph is correct, he was at least two years old at the time of his baptism on Feb. 25, 1624/25. The family emigrated to America and by 1639 was settled at Wethersfield, Conn., where Richard Treat rose to a position of prominence. Although only a youth, Robert took part in the settlement of Milford in 1639–40. Because many early records of the town and of the New Haven Colony are lost, the first steps in his public career cannot be traced. By 1653 he was being regularly elected deputy from Milford to the General Court of the colony and in the following year was chosen lieutenant and chief military officer of the town. From deputy he advanced to magistrate in 1659 and was annually reëlected until 1664, when he declined to serve. In the vain struggle to prevent the absorption of the New Haven Colony by Connecticut under its charter of 1662 Treat took a fairly active part, and, although he represented Milford in the General Assembly of Connecticut in 1665, he remained for some time unreconciled to the union and determined to emigrate. He became the leader of the group from the former New Haven Colony that settled Newark, N. J., and from 1667 until 1672 was deputy from that town to the Assembly of East Jersey. He also served as magistrate and recorder of Newark. But eventually he returned to Milford and was chosen an assistant of Connecticut in 1673. In the meantime his military capacities were gaining recognition. In 1661 he had become captain of the Milford train band and on his return from Newark was promoted to major. In the summer of 1675 he was appointed commander in chief of the Connecticut troops operating against King Philip. Although too far away at the time to prevent attacks upon Northfield and Springfield,

Mass., he took an active part in the defeat of the Indians at Hadley. In the following winter campaign in Rhode Island he again commanded the Connecticut contingent and distinguished himself in the successful attack upon the Indian stronghold. He lacked conventional military training, yet he proved an adept leader in Indian warfare. The colony rewarded his services in May 1676 by electing him deputy-governor, and after the death of William Leete in April 1683 he advanced to the governorship.

His first problem was the settlement of a boundary dispute with New York, which resulted in the loss by Connecticut of the town of Rye. Soon a more serious threat to the colony appeared with the creation of the Dominion of New England. Connecticut refused to admit the validity of the writs of *quo warranto* issued against its charter in 1685 and 1686, and, when Sir Edmund Andros reached New England, Treat followed as long as possible a policy of postponement and delay. But resistance was futile, and at a meeting in Hartford, Oct. 31, 1687, Andros assumed authority over Connecticut. For the second time Treat found a government of which he was an important member absorbed by a more powerful neighbor. Although appointed to the council of the Dominion, he took little part in its administration. Upon the overthrow of Andros at Boston in 1689 Connecticut restored its government under the charter, which, owing largely to Treat's wise management, had never been legally invalidated. He continued as governor until 1698, carrying on the conservative traditions of the colony. In 1692, when Gov. Benjamin Fletcher of New York claimed superior authority over the Connecticut militia, Treat and the Assembly sent Fitz John Winthrop to England to gain recognition of their military independence. The successful accomplishment of this mission brought Winthrop great popularity, and in 1698 he was elected governor. The aging Treat stepped down to the deputy-governorship, where he continued to serve until 1708, two years before his death.

In 1647 or before, he married Jane Tapp, the daughter of Edmund Tapp, one of the leaders in the settlement of Milford. She died in 1703, survived by seven of their eight children. Two years later, on Oct. 24, 1705, he married Elizabeth (Powell) Hollingsworth Bryan, the daughter of Michael Powell of Boston and widow of Richard Bryan, a Milford merchant. Her death occurred in the spring of 1706. According to the standards of seventeenth-century Connecticut, Treat was a wealthy man. He became a large landholder and was an owner or part owner of saw and fulling mills in Milford. Pious and orthodox, he was highly respected in the community, yet gained a reputation for good nature and humor in personal contacts as well as for firmness and wisdom in public affairs.

[Milford Land Records, I, Town Clerk's Office, Milford, Conn.; *Records of the Colony or Jurisdiction of New Haven from May 1653 to the Union* (1858); *The Public Records of the Colony of Conn.*, vols. I–V (1850–70); Records of the Town of Newark, New Jersey, in *N. J. Hist. Soc. Colls.*, vol. VI (1864); Benjamin Trumbull, *A Complete Hist. of Conn.* (1818), vol. I; G. H. Hollister, *The Hist. of Conn.* (1855), vol. I; I. M. Calder, *The New Haven Colony* (1934); E. R. Lambert, *Hist. of the Colony of New Haven* (1838) with several legendary episodes of Treat's early career; J. H. Treat, *The Treat Family* (1893) with "Life and Character of Gov. Robert Treat," by Henry Champion; G. H. Ford, "Robert Treat: Founder, Farmer, Soldier and Statesman," *Papers New Haven Colony Hist. Soc.*, vol. VIII (1914).]   L. W. L.

TREAT, SAMUEL (Dec. 17, 1815–Aug. 31, 1902), jurist, law teacher, son of Samuel Lanceton and Lydia (Sheldon) Treat, was born in Portsmouth, N. H., being descended through Gov. Robert Treat [*q.v.*] of Connecticut, from the Treat (Trott) family of Somerset, England. After receiving a good education in the public high school at Portsmouth and teaching there for one year, he entered Harvard College, where he received the degree of A.B. in 1837. While teaching for four years in private schools, first at Jamaica Plain, Mass., and afterwards at Geneseo, N. Y., he studied law under practising lawyers. In 1841 he went to St. Louis and was admitted to the Missouri bar. Before 1843 he was recognized as an influential member of the Democratic party in that state. Treat himself attributed his early prominence to an encounter with the state leader of the Whig party, Henry Sheffie Geyer [*q.v.*]. The latter had publicly disparaged New Englanders, of whom there was a considerable group in Missouri—some Democrats and some Whigs; Treat publicly defended New England and was afterwards regarded as the political champion in Missouri of that section. Sent as a delegate to the National Democratic Convention of 1848, he was elected secretary. He was also a delegate to the national railroad convention of 1849, held at St. Louis, and introduced the resolution which resulted in a formal petition that the federal government build a telegraph line and railroad from the Missouri River to the Pacific Ocean.

In 1849 Treat became judge of the St. Louis court of common pleas. He served in this capacity until 1857, when he was appointed federal district judge for eastern Missouri by President Pierce. A competent, hard-working, urbane, courageous, respected trial judge, he remained on the bench until failing sight forced his retire-

ment in 1887. He maintained his home in St. Louis until his death, though he spent much of his time in later years with a daughter in Rochester, N. Y., where he died.

In the judicial history of Missouri Treat stands out as the chief expert in admiralty, a branch of federal law significant locally in his time because of the great though temporary importance of steamboating on the Mississippi and Missouri rivers. The advent of the Civil War, with St. Louis becoming a fortified camp and half of Missouri a huge battle ground, brought to his tribunal novel and delicate questions. After the war, by charges to grand juries and by fearless handling of criminal trials, he combatted the spirit of lawlessness which undoubtedly prevailed in Missouri during the era of the outlaw Jesse James [*q.v.*] and the so-called "whiskey ring" of St. Louis. Of his published opinions the most widely cited is *In re McDonald* (16 *Fed. Cases,* 17), decided in May 1861, upholding the jurisdiction of federal courts at that particular time to issue writs of *habeas corpus* to military authorities (see also *American Law Register,* September 1861, pp. 661–95).

In 1853 Treat became one of the incorporators and original directors of Washington University, St. Louis; in 1867, cooperating with Henry Hitchcock [*q.v.*], he helped to organize the law school of that university, and for twenty years he was a member of its faculty as professor of admiralty law. On Aug. 21, 1841 he married Caroline Bryan of Geneseo, N. Y., who with one daughter survived him.

[Sources include: Treat Papers, Mo. Hist. Soc., Jefferson Memorial, St. Louis; J. H. Treat, *The Treat Family* (1893); J. L. Chamberlain, *Universities and Their Sons,* vol. V (1900); Wm. Hyde and H. L. Conard, *Encyc. of the Hist. of St. Louis* (1899), vol. IV; *Proc. of the St. Louis Bar on the Retirement of Samuel Treat* (1887); *Am. Law Rev.,* Mar.–Apr. 1887, Sept.–Oct. 1902; C. C. Allen, "The St. Louis Law School," *Green Bag,* July 1889; *St. Louis Republic,* Sept. 2, 1902; *St. Louis Globe-Democrat,* Sept. 2, 1902. The extension of federal admiralty jurisdiction to the Mississippi River is described in *The Hine* vs. *Trevor* (1866), 71 *U. S.,* 555.]   T. W.

TREAT, SAMUEL HUBBEL (June 21, 1811–Mar. 27, 1887), jurist, was born in Plainfield, Otsego County, N. Y., the son of Samuel and Elsie (Tracy) Treat and a descendant of Matthias Treat, who was a freeman of Wethersfield, Conn., in 1657. After spending most of his early life on his father's farm, young Treat studied law at Richfield, N. Y., where he was admitted to the bar in 1834. Seeking a field for practice, he turned to the West, and journeyed, most of the way on foot, to Springfield, Ill., where shortly before Stephen T. Logan and Stephen A. Douglas [*q.v.*] had settled, to be followed within a few years by Abraham Lincoln.

Treat's rise in the practice in Springfield was rapid, and by 1838 he had more cases on the circuit court docket than any other lawyer. In the following year he was appointed judge of the circuit court, which office he resigned in 1841 to accept appointment as justice of the supreme court of Illinois. He served on the supreme bench for fourteen years, during the last seven as chief justice. In 1855 he resigned to accept the offer tendered him by President Pierce of a federal judgeship for the newly created southern district of Illinois. This position he held for the remainder of his life, a period of thirty-two years.

Treat's opinions are characterized by exact and terse expression, many of them not exceeding a page in length. He was a lover of books and collected one of the finest libraries in the state. With Walter B. Scates and Robert S. Blackwell he compiled and annotated *The Statutes of Illinois* (2 vols., 1858). From early life he was an active and devoted member of the Protestant Episcopal Church; it is said that he never entered a church of another denomination except on public occasions when his presence was necessary. He was a stanch Democrat throughout life but aside from the performance of his judicial duties took little part in public affairs. In appearance he was tall and straight and in later life walked with a slow and dignified step, seldom stopping to greet acquaintances. He was, however, always courteous, quiet, and unostentatious. Though he was regarded as eccentric and had but few intimate friends, his integrity, legal ability, and unusual power to grasp and appraise facts were respected by all. So closely did he attend to his judicial duties that his private affairs suffered, and at his death they were found in a much neglected condition. The only recreation he is known to have cared for was chess, a game which he sometimes played with Lincoln.

In 1837 he married Ann Bennett of Jacksonville, Ill., but they had no children. When he died his only close relative was a married sister.

[*Chicago Legal News*, Apr. 2, 1887; J. H. Treat, *The Treat Family* (1893); John Moses, *Illinois, Hist. and Statistical*, I (1889), 431, 445; *Albany Law Jour.*, Apr. 16, 1887; *Green Bag*, May 1891; Newton Bateman and others, *Hist. Encyc. of Ill.* (1925), vol. I; U. F. Linder, *Reminiscences of the Early Bench and Bar of Ill.* (1879); J. M. Palmer, *The Bench and Bar of Ill.* (1899), I, 35; A. J. Beveridge, *Abraham Lincoln* (1928), I, 212, 506; *Am. Law Rev.*, May–June 1887; *Chicago Tribune*, Mar. 28, 1887.]   G. W. G.

TREE, LAMBERT (Nov. 29, 1832–Oct. 9, 1910), jurist, diplomat, was the second son of Lambert and Laura Matilda (Burrows) Tree,

of Washington, D. C. Two of his great-grandfathers were Revolutionary officers, and both his grandfathers fought in the War of 1812; his father was a postal official in the capital for sixty years. With a background of brilliant social and official life, Lambert Tree grew to manhood. Early schooling under private tutors was followed by two years of law study in the office of James Mandeville Carlisle [*q.v.*] and a year in the law department of the University of Virginia. In 1855 he was admitted to the Washington bar, and the same year moved to Chicago, Ill., where he soon became junior member of the firm of Clarkson & Tree. He met and formed a lasting friendship with Abraham Lincoln, then a practising lawyer.

In 1864 he was elected president of the Chicago Law Institute, and in 1870, judge of the circuit court of Cook County. One of his first duties was to conduct an investigation into charges of corruption of Chicago city officials, which he pressed with such vigor, sincerity, and effectiveness that a dangerous political ring was broken up. Reëlected without opposition, he resigned in 1875 because of ill health and traveled for three years in Europe. Before his return Illinois Democrats nominated him for Congress, but the overwhelming Republican majority in his district made his race hopeless, and four years later he was again defeated. He was delegate-at-large from Illinois to the National Democratic Convention in 1884. In an exciting contest for a seat in the United States Senate in 1885 he lost to John A. Logan [*q.v.*] by one vote.

In July 1885 President Cleveland appointed him minister resident of the United States in Belgium, where one of his first official duties was to present notes announcing United States recognition of the new Congo Free State government. On March 15, 1886, he signed the conventions for the international exchange of official documents, parliamentary, scientific, and literary publications. The rank of the United States representatives in Belgium was raised in 1888, and Tree was made envoy extraordinary and minister plenipotentiary. To King Leopold's expression of gratification the Belgium foreign minister added, "Mr. Lambert Tree during his residence here has won universal good will" (*Papers Relating to the Foreign Relations of the United States, 1888*, pt. 1, p. 50). Late in the same year Tree was appointed envoy extraordinary and minister plenipotentiary to Russia, but resigned after a few weeks at St. Petersburg. He was made a grand officer of the Belgian Order of Leopold and an officer of the French Legion of Honor.

As Democratic member of the United States delegation to the International American Monetary Commission (Washington, 1891), he succeeded in preventing a resolution favoring a common double monetary standard for the Americas. His loyalty to the principle of monometalism led to his breaking with the Democratic party in the free silver campaign of 1896. He was an incorporator of the American Red Cross Society and one of the organizers of its Illinois branch, president of the Illinois Historical Library Board, vice-president of the Chicago Historical Society, and life trustee of the Newberry Library. On Nov. 24, 1859, he married Anna Josephine Magie, only daughter of Haines H. Magie, pioneer Chicago merchant. Two sons were born to them, one of whom died in infancy. Lambert Tree died in New York City, a few days after his 122nd transatlantic voyage.

[J. G. Leach, *Some Account of the Tree Family* (1908); J. S. Currey, *Chicago* (1912), IV, 30–35, and *The Makers of Illinois* (1913), II, 367–71; *Encyc. of Biog. of Ill.*, vol. I (1892); Paul Gilbert and C. L. Bryson, *Chicago and Its Makers* (1929); John Moses and Joseph Kirkland, *The Hist. of Chicago, Ill.* (2 vols., 1895); J. M. Palmer, *The Bench and Bar of Ill.* (1899), I, 492–94; *Who's Who in America*, 1910–11, and previous volumes; *Chicago Daily News*, Oct. 10, 1910; *Chiacgo Daily Tribune*, Oct. 10, 11, 1910; *Chicago Record-Herald*, Oct. 10, 11, 1910; *Papers Relating to the Foreign Relations of the U. S., 1885–89* (1886–90); official correspondence in the archives of the Dept. of State.]   I. L. T.

TREMAIN, HENRY EDWIN (Nov. 14, 1840–Dec. 9, 1910), soldier and lawyer, the son of Edwin Ruthven and Mary (Briggs) Tremain, was born in New York City. He was a descendant of Joseph Truman, who settled in New London, Conn., in 1666. After preliminary education in the public schools he attended the College of the City of New York and was graduated with the B.A. degree in 1860. He then entered Columbia University Law School, but his course was interrupted by service in the Civil War and he received the LL.B. degree in 1867. In April 1861 he enlisted as a private in the 7th New York State Militia. On the return of the regiment from Washington, he resigned to recruit the 73rd New York Volunteers in which he was commissioned first lieutenant in August 1861. Under McClellan and Pope he participated in the Virginia campaigns of the Army of the Potomac and was mentioned for gallantry at Williamsburg and Malvern Hill. Taken prisoner while leading a counter attack at the second battle of Bull Run, he was confined in Libby Prison for a short time. He resumed duty as aide-de-camp to Daniel E. Sickles [*q.v.*], and rendered notable staff service in the battles of Fredericksburg, Chancellorsville, and Gettysburg. He was

also a favorite staff officer of Joseph Hooker [*q.v.*]. In 1864 he accompanied Sickles to the West to inspect all armies in the field. Upon his return he rejoined the Army of the Potomac, and participated as a staff officer in all battles to Appomattox. He was appointed captain in 1862, major and aide-de-camp in 1863, and brevetted lieutenant-colonel on Mar. 13, 1865, "for gallant and meritorious service." He became a colonel in June and a brigadier-general in November 1865. For conspicuous gallantry at the battle of Resaca, on May 15, 1868, when he rode between two brigades of Union troops that were firing into each other, he was awarded the Congressional Medal of Honor. He served in South Carolina until his discharge in 1866.

Immediately after his return to New York in 1868 he began his career at the bar. He was unsuccessful in his candidacy for justice of the court of common pleas in the following year, but maintained an active interest in politics and public law. As special counsel to the United States marshall in 1870 he prosecuted violations of the election laws, and participated in attacks upon the "Tweed ring." From 1873 to 1877 he was first assistant United States attorney in New York, and thereafter appeared as counsel in the federal courts in cases involving revenue law violations. He joined Joshua T. Owen in 1872 in establishing the *New York Law Journal*, a daily devoted to news of the courts. He served as editor for two years, but relinquished the post because of the pressure of his legal duties. He showed deep interest in the associations made by the War. He was president of the Society of the Army of the Potomac, 1902, colonel of the Veterans of the 7th N. Y. N. G., and president of the III Army Corps Union. He was twice president of the National Republican Club and, from 1870 to 1874, president of the alumni association of the College of the City of New York. Besides many papers on law, tariff, and taxation he wrote: *Last Hours of Sheridan's Cavalry* (1904); *Two Days of War* (1905); *Sectionalism Unmasked* (1907); and *Fifty Papers, Addresses and Writings* (1909). He was married to Sarah Brownson, of New York City, on June 1, 1869. They had no children.

[*Who's Who in America*, 1910–11; E. M. Treman, M. E. Poole, *The Hist. of the Treman, Tremaine, Truman Family in America* (1901), vol. I; H. E. Tremain, *A Family Geneal.* (privately printed, 1908); F. B. Heitman, *Hist. Reg. . . . U. S. Army* (1903); *Am. Decorations . . . 1862–1926* (1927); *N. Y. Times*, Dec. 11, 1910.]   D. A. R.

TREMAINE, HENRY BARNES (July 20, 1866–May 13, 1932), manufacturer of mechanical musical instruments, was born in Brooklyn,

N. Y., the son of William Burton Tremaine, and Emeline Cornelia (Dodge) Tremaine. He was a descendant of Joseph Truman who settled in New London, Conn., in 1666. He was educated in the public schools of Brooklyn and at about sixteen entered the employ of Hastings & Company, paper merchants of New York City. In 1888 he joined the Aeolian Organ and Music Company, of which his father was manager, a firm which in 1887 had acquired the business of the Mechanical Orguinette Company. The product of the company was a small mechanical organ, played by a crank that turned a paper music-roll. Tremaine saw immediately that, though the promoters of the organette were offering it as a toy, it had possibilities as a musical instrument, and he accordingly proposed that a better instrument be introduced which would appeal to adults as well as children. In 1890 he succeeded his father as manager. In 1894 he acquired the sales rights of the Vocalion organ, and in the same year a mechanical device for playing it, the Orchestrelle. In 1895 the name of the company was changed to the Aeolian Company, and three years later Tremaine was elected president. When in 1896 the pianola, a mechanical device for playing the piano, was invented, Tremaine acquired it for the Aeolian Company. This led to the formation of the Aeolian, Weber Piano and Pianola Company in 1903. Subsequent activities of the firm included the manufacture of phonographs and records (1913–25), and the development of the Duo-Art (1914), a device similar to the pianola, but one which automatically reproduced the expression and nuances of living pianists in its performance.

Tremaine's ability to anticipate changes in taste was shown not only by his development of mechanical musical instruments but also by his choice of locations for the firm in New York City. He seemed to know what sections would become fashionable shopping centers. When he joined the firm at 831 Broadway, the owners had difficulty in paying the rent. Tremaine insisted that they move (1891) to West Twenty-third Street, where the rent was higher, and the same intuition guided him in subsequent moves. He also gave his business an international aspect by the establishment of foreign branches —London (1898), Berlin (1901), Australia (1905), and Paris (1907)—and furthered musical activities by establishing concert halls in the United States and abroad. Although he labored under severe handicaps of health and during his active career was forced to be absent for more than half of his usual working hours, he possessed a remarkable faculty for judging situations and solving problems in absence. In November of 1930 he resigned the presidency of the Aeolian Company, and became chairman of its board of directors. He died suddenly in Washington, D. C. He was married to Maud Aline Cooke of New York City, Apr. 2, 1890, and had two daughters and a son. He was awarded several foreign decorations, among them the Order of Leopold, the Order of Philip the Magnanimous (Belgium), 1922; the Order of St. Gregory the Great (papal), 1923; and the Order of the Crown of Italy, 1926; he became a member of the Legion of Honor in 1927.

[See E. M. Treman and M. E. Poole, *The Hist. of the Treman, Tremaine, Truman Family in America* (2 vols., 1901); *Who's Who in America*, 1932–33; "The Development of the Player-Piano," booklet issued by the Aeolian Company; obituaries in *Music Trades*, May 1932, and *N. Y. Times*, May 14, 1932. Information has been supplied by relatives of Tremaine and by members of the staff of the Aeolian Company.]   J. T. H.

TRENCHARD, STEPHEN DECATUR (July 10, 1818–Nov. 15, 1883), naval officer, son of Capt. Edward Trenchard, United States Navy, and Eliza (Sands) Trenchard, was born in Brooklyn, N. Y. He was a descendant of George Trenchard who came to America with the followers of William Penn. At the age of eleven, intending to become an Episcopal clergyman, he enrolled at Kenyon College, Gambier, Ohio, an institution conducted by Bishop Philander Chase [*q.v.*]; but on Oct. 23, 1834, he entered the navy as a midshipman. His studies under the Bishop made a lasting impression on him, however, and throughout his career he was known in the service as a deeply religious man. In 1840, after one year's study at the naval school in Philadelphia, he was warranted a passed midshipman. The next four years he served in the Mediterranean, at the end of which time he was assigned to the coast survey. On this duty his ship, the brig *Washington,* was nearly wrecked off the coast of North Carolina and the captain and ten seamen were drowned. The following spring, the brig having been repaired, he sailed with her under Lieut. Samuel Phillips Lee and joined Commodore Perry's squadron off Vera Cruz. The *Washington* took part in the expedition against Tabasco in June 1847, but on July 4 was ordered back to coast-survey duty. Commissioned lieutenant the same year, he was occupied mainly in coast-survey work until 1857. On Aug. 14, 1856, while in command of the *Vixen,* he rescued the sinking British bark *Adieu* off Gloucester, Mass. For this action he was presented with a sword by Queen Victoria, and with a chronometer by the owners and underwriters. He sailed with the *Powhatan* (East India Squadron) on her diplomatic cruise to China and Japan (1857–60). On this cruise Trenchard was Commodore Tattnall's flag-lieutenant, accompanying him on his visit to the British Admiral Hope, and participating in the British action on Peiho River, China, June 25, 1859, where he was wounded.

At the outbreak of the Civil War, he was assigned to the command of the *Keystone State* (Apr. 19, 1861), and three days later arrived at Hampton Roads, where he witnessed the burning of the Norfolk Navy Yard. He assisted in saving the *Cumberland* from capture, and brought off Commodore Paulding and the marine garrison. Three months later he was transferred to the steamer *Rhode Island* with orders to transport supplies to the blockading squadrons. After eighteen months of this arduous duty, his ship, armed for cruiser warfare, was assigned to blockade duty. While towing the original *Monitor* (Dec. 31, 1862), the *Rhode Island* ran into a heavy storm. The *Monitor* foundered, but owing to Trenchard's vigilance and expert seamanship, most of her crew was saved. He was then ordered to cruise off Havana and Key West, keeping a sharp lookout for the Confederate raiders, *Alabama* and *Florida*. Late in 1864 he joined Admiral Porter's great fleet at Hampton Roads and participated in both attacks on Fort Fisher, his men assisting in landing the heavy siege guns and mortars for the army.

He was commissioned captain in 1866, commodore in 1871, and rear admiral in 1875. In 1876 he commanded the North Atlantic Squadron. After the disputed Hayes-Tilden election of that year, he assembled a large fleet at Washington to prevent disturbances. He retired July 10, 1880. He was a strict disciplinarian but was conceded, even by his enemies, to be a highly upright, humane man. He made an admirable record in the Civil War and in the second attack on Fort Fisher played a distinguished rôle. He married Ann O'Connor Barclay in 1848, and had one son, Edward Trenchard, an artist.

[*Army and Navy Jour.*, Nov. 17, 1883; G. F. Emmons, *Navy of the U. S.* (1853); L. R. Hamersly, *The Records of Living Officers of U. S. Navy* (1890); C. C. Jones, *The Life and Services of Commodore Josiah Tattnall* (1878); E. S. Maclay, *Reminiscences of the Old Navy; from Journals and Private Papers of . . . Rear-Admiral Trenchard* (1898); *N. Y. Times*, Nov. 16, 1883; *War of the Rebellion: Official Records (Navy)*; Edward Trenchard, transcript of his father's Civil War record, in Office of Naval Records, Navy Dept.; *The Report of the Supt. of the U. S. Coast Survey*, 1847, 1856; U.S. Navy Dept. archives; Navy Registers, 1834–80; *American Ancestry*, vol. VI (1891).]
L. H. B.

TRENT, WILLIAM (Feb. 13, 1715–1787?), Indian trader and land speculator, was born probably in Philadelphia, Pa., the son of Mary (Coddington) and William Trent who had emigrated from Scotland and become a prominent citizen and officeholder, first in Pennsylvania and later in New Jersey. In 1746 the younger Trent was appointed captain in the Pennsylvania troops raised for an expedition against the French in Canada, and he spent several months in 1746 and 1747 on the New York frontier north of Albany. He attended councils with the Indians at Logstown in 1752, at Easton in 1757, and at Fort Pitt in 1759. While at Logstown in 1752 he was directed by the Virginia commissioners to proceed with Andrew Montour to Pickawillanee, a village of the Twightwee, or Miami, Indians, with presents. He kept a journal of the expedition, which is available in published form (*post*). About this time he was married to Sarah Wilkins. They had six children. He lived in Lancaster and in Carlisle, Pa., and from 1768 to 1784 his home was in Trenton, N. J., where he was a vestryman in the St. Michael's Episcopal Church. In 1754, acting upon the authority of Governor Dinwiddie of Virginia, he raised a force and undertook the construction of a fort at the forks of the Ohio. When, in his absence, the post was captured by the French before its completion and renamed Fort Duquesne, he was blamed (*The Writings of George Washington*, vol. II, 1834, ed. by Jared Sparks, p. 47). In 1758 he accompanied John Forbes's successful expedition against Duquesne, which later became Fort Pitt. During these years, he had also been engaged in the Indian trade. About 1749 he had formed a partnership with George Croghan [*q.v.*], a connection that lasted five years or more. In 1754 he and his associates suffered heavy losses from French and Indian depredations along the Ohio. About 1760 he became a member of the Pennsylvania trading firm of Simon, Trent, Levy & Franks, being stationed at Fort Pitt. Again Trent and his partners suffered severe losses during Pontiac's uprising.

Many years were spent by Trent and others in endeavoring to obtain restitution for the losses of 1754 and 1763, and out of these efforts grew his career as a land speculator. At the treaty of Fort Stanwix in 1768, along with Samuel Wharton and George Morgan [*qq.v.*], he obtained from the Six Nations, by way of compensation, a grant of a vast tract along the upper Ohio that became known as "Indiana." Early in 1769 he accompanied Wharton to England, to try to obtain royal confirmation of the grant. The Indiana enterprise was merged with the larger Vandalia project, involving a still greater extent of territory and the participation of many prominent Englishmen and Americans. The royal authorization was never obtained, and early in 1775 he returned to America, where he endeavored to make good the Indiana claim by establishing the principle of the validity of titles obtained from the Indians by private purchase. Meetings of the Indiana Company were held, and in 1779 he presented its claims before the Virginia Assembly, but without success. He then directed his efforts toward Congress and during the period 1779 to 1783 presented several memorials relating to both the Indiana and Vandalia projects, but to no avail. The enterprise failed and after 1783, little more is heard of Trent. In 1784 he removed to Philadelphia, where he died.

[*Journ. of Captain William Trent from Logstown to Pickawillany, A.D. 1752* (1871), ed. by A. T. Goodman, including biog. sketch; E. F. Cooley, *Geneal. of Early Settlers of Trenton* (1883); Hamilton Schuyler, *A Hist. of St. Michael's Church, Trenton* (1926); C. A. Hanna, *The Wilderness Trail* (2 vols., 1911), also with text of journ.; Gratz papers and manuscript "Opinions Regarding the Grant to Wm. Trent, 1775" in possession of Hist. Soc. of Pa.; *Case*, rare pamphlet in N. Y. Pub. Lib., relating to grant to Trent and other traders, probably printed in London about 1770; *Minutes of the Provincial Council of Pa.*, vol. VIII (1852), esp. pp. 382, 383; *Jours. of the Continental Cong.*, vols. XV (1909), XVIII (1910), XX–XXI (1912), XXIV (1922); A. T. Volwiler, *George Croghan and the Westward Movement* (1926); Max Savelle, *George Morgan, Colony Builder* (1932); date of death from statement concerning date of will in Cooley, *ante*, p. 289.]   W. E. S—s.

TRESCOT, WILLIAM HENRY (Nov. 10, 1822–May 4, 1898), historian, diplomat, was born in Charleston, S. C., the son of Henry and Sarah (McCrady) Trescot. After attending private schools in his native city he graduated from the College of Charleston in 1841. He read law under his uncle, Edward McCrady, and was admitted to the bar in 1843. In 1848 he married Eliza Natalie Cuthbert and devoted the next four years of his life to the practice of law, the management of his wife's estate on Barnwell Island near Beaufort, S. C., and the study of the history of American diplomacy. He was small in stature and noted for the instability of his opinions; but he was impressive in manners and brilliant and voluble in conversation and public speech. His historical works are marked by forcible summaries, calmness of tone, and the elegance of style popular in his generation. He first attracted attention in 1849 by a pamphlet entitled *A Few Thoughts on the Foreign Policy of the United States*. To the controversial literature provoked by the Omnibus Bill of 1850 he contributed *The Position and Course of the South* (1850), an excellent summary of the Southern social and economic view. Two years later his

illuminating *Diplomacy of the Revolution; an Historical Study* (1852) appeared. The same year he was appointed secretary of legation in London. The following year he wrote *A Letter to Hon. A. P. Butler . . . on the Diplomatic System of the United States* (1853), which is still regarded as a valuable contribution of the history of that subject. Returning to South Carolina in 1854, he published his most pretentious and original work, *The Diplomatic History of the Administrations of Washington and Adams* (1857).

In June 1860 he was appointed assistant secretary of state. When South Carolina seceded the following December he resigned, but, remaining in Washington until February as the unofficial adviser of the South Carolina authorities, he played an important part in the negotiations over the Charleston forts. He urged the necessity of caution upon the state authorities and strove with some success to postpone a crisis by endeavoring to prevent the federal government from reinforcing the forts. His "Narrative and Letter" (published with notes by Gaillard Hunt, *American Historical Review*, Apr. 1908) is his own account of those difficult days. During the Civil War he served on the staffs of Gov. Andrew Magrath and of Gen. Roswell S. Ripley and was a member of the Executive Council of South Carolina, an important local body. From 1862 to 1866 he represented Anderson District in the legislature. There he delivered a series of memorial eulogies which, notably the *Memorial of the Life of J. Johnston Pettigrew* (1870), excited wide comment. During the summer of 1861 he acted as an intermediary between the Confederate government and the British and French consuls at Charleston in their effort to obtain the adherence of the Confederate government to the Declaration of Paris respecting privateering (see his *Confederacy and the Declaration of Paris*, 1918, reprinted from the *American Historical Review*, July 1918).

Intermittently for twenty-five years after the war he labored with notable success in Washington as the agent of South Carolina for the recovery of lands seized and taxes levied under the direct tax act of Congress. In 1866 he refused to become a candidate for the federal Senate. Although not affiliated with the Radical party in South Carolina, as an attorney for the Blue Ridge Railroad he defended before the state tax-payers convention of 1871 the scheme to have the state indorse the bonds of that dubious venture. He was one of the counselors for the United States government before the Halifax fishery commission in 1877. Three years later, with James B. Angell and John F. Swift [*qq.v.*], he was sent to China to arrange for the modification of the Burlingame treaty concerning Chinese immigration. The following year he concluded a treaty with the Colombian minister in Washington regulating American rights in the Isthmus of Panama. Later in 1881 Blaine sent him to South America to warn Chile against making excessive demands on Bolivia and Peru as the result of her victories in the War of the Pacific; but when he arrived in Chile he learned that Blaine had resigned and that his original instructions had been published and reversed in order to discredit Blaine's policies. The mission was accordingly a failure. In order to compensate him for this undeserved humiliation he was appointed, along with Ex-President Grant, in 1882 to negotiate a commercial treaty with Mexico. The treaty was approved by the Senate but was never put into operation because of the opposition of the House of Representatives to its free sugar provisions. His last diplomatic service was as a delegate to the Pan-American conference of 1889, in which he participated actively. Shortly afterward he retired because of lack of health to his home in Pendleton, S. C., where he died, survived by his widow and five children.

[Letters in Lib. of Cong.; R. M. Betts, "William Henry Trescot," manuscript biog. in lib. of Univ. of S. C.; biog. sketch by Gaillard Hunt in *Am. Hist. Rev.*, Apr. 1908; R. W. Simpson, *Hist. of Old Pendleton District* (1913); *Appletons' Ann. Cyc. . . . 1898* (1899); W. P. Trent, *Southern Writers* (1905); *Lib. of Southern Lit.*, vol. XII (1907); *News and Courier* (Charleston), May 5, 1898, Aug. 30, 1903; *State* (Columbia), May 5, 6, 1898; information from son, Edward A. Trescot, Pendleton, S. C.]   F. B. S.

TREVELLICK, RICHARD F. (May 1830–Feb. 15, 1895), labor leader, was born on St. Mary's, one of the Scilly Islands. He became a ship's carpenter, worked in a Southampton shipyard, and later, as a seaman, visited Africa, India, China, and the Antipodes. As a youth he became known among his fellows as a debater, agitator, and advocate of the eight-hour day for workers. In Auckland, New Zealand, in 1852, and in Melbourne, Australia, in 1854, he attained prominence in controversies raging about this subject. His wanderings brought him at length, in 1857, to New Orleans, La., where he worked at his trade and became president of the ship carpenters' and caulkers' union, in which rôle he led a successful fight for the nine-hour day.

On the outbreak of the Civil War he settled in Detroit, and in 1864 became the first president of the Detroit Trades' Assembly. That same year he was a delegate to the Louisville Convention which set up the short-lived International

Industrial Assembly of North America. In 1865 he was made president of the International Union of Ship Carpenters and Caulkers. He represented the Detroit Trades' Assembly and the Michigan Grand Eight Hours League at the congress of the National Labor Union in 1867, and in that year was elected a delegate to the International Workingmen's Association, meeting at Lausanne, Switzerland, but could not attend because of lack of funds. In 1869, 1871, and 1872 he served as president of the National Labor Union, the leading labor organization of the day. When, in 1872, it split into two sections, he attended the meetings of both factions. Later he carried on organization work for the Knights of Labor.

Paying his own expenses, Trevellick in 1868 led one of the first successful labor lobbies, pushing through Congress an act instituting the eight-hour day for federal workmen, mechanics, and laborers. With William H. Sylvis and Andrew C. Cameron [*qq.v.*], he led an agitation against subsequent efforts to make proportionate wage reductions. Trevellick also led the fight against the blacklist, from which he himself suffered seriously. He opposed the importation of Chinese labor under contract, and, in 1870 capitulated to the majority in the National Labor Union when it accepted the California idea of complete exclusion of Chinese. He espoused the unpopular idea of abolishing the color-line then generally drawn in labor unions against negro workers. As a leader in the National Labor Union he advocated the relief of the working classes from capitalist exploitation. The collapse of organization after organization never undermined his belief in the general principle of organized labor struggle. With the decline in unionism under employers' attacks after the crisis of 1873, however, he fell under the influence of the Greenback movement, and thenceforth advocated relieving industrial depression by means of inflationary price-boosting schemes. He helped establish the Greenback Party and was a delegate to the convention of 1876 which nominated Peter Cooper [*q.v.*] for the presidency; he also served as temporary chairman of the convention of 1878 at Toledo which formed the National Greenback Labor Party, and as chairman of the convention of 1880 which nominated James B. Weaver [*q.v.*].

His energy was boundless. In 1867–68 he toured the West, making 270 addresses to labor audiences and organizing forty-seven unions. In 1869 he spent 169 days on the road, especially in the industrially backward South and the Pennsylvania anthracite fields. In 1870 he covered sixteen states and helped to establish 200 local unions and three state organizations. His vision may have been narrower than that of Sylvis, but his sense of the need for combined industrial and political activity, his ability for organization, and his oratorical powers made him one of the first great labor agitators of America. In every major industrial center of the country his black beard, fierce eyes, and ringing phrases were well known to workers. He was married, and was survived by four of his five children. He died in Detroit.

[Obadiah Hicks, *Life of Richard F. Trevellick* (1896), which gives day of birth as May 20; J. R. Commons and others, *Hist. of Labour in the U. S.* (1918), vol. II; G. E. McNeill's *The Labor Movement* (1887); T. V. Powderly, *Thirty Years of Labor* (copr. 1889); *Detroit Jour.* and *Evening News* (Detroit), Feb. 15, 1895, which give day of birth as May 2.]   H. S.

TRIMBLE, ALLEN (Nov. 24, 1783–Feb. 3, 1870), governor of Ohio and agriculturist, was born in Augusta County, Va., the son of James and Jane (Allen) Trimble and the grandson of John Trimble who with three brothers emigrated from the north of Ireland early in the seventeenth century and settled at Staunton, Va. When only eleven months old, Allen was taken by his parents to their new home, near the present Lexington, Ky. The father, accompanied by Allen, visited Ohio in 1801 and in 1802 to select lands, and in 1804 he built a cabin in what is now Highland County, Ohio. When he died in the autumn of 1804, Allen removed the family to the new home the next year. In 1808 or 1809 he was appointed clerk of the common pleas court for Highland County and county recorder. At this time he removed to Hillsboro, the county seat. In the second war with Great Britain he served as a colonel in a successful expedition against the Indians on the upper Wabash and Eel rivers for the relief of the garrison at Fort Wayne. Later he commanded a battalion of militia, which was, however, disbanded almost at once. He served in the Ohio House of Representatives, 1816–17, and in the Ohio Senate, 1817–25, of which he was speaker for seven consecutive years. Owing to the resignation of Gov. E. A. Brown to become a federal senator, Trimble served as acting governor in 1822. In this position he appointed a committee on the common schools, whose work established the substantial basis for Ohio's school system. He was defeated in the election for governor in the autumn of 1822 and in 1824. In the legislative session of 1824–25 he was chosen as one of the first canal fund commissioners, authorized to negotiate a loan for building the newly planned Ohio canal system, but resigned in 1825. In 1826

he was elected governor over three opponents by an overwhelming majority. He was authorized by the legislature to select a half million acres of land granted by Congress for canal purposes, and in the summer of 1827 he went with a companion to the Maumee and Sandusky river valleys to examine the region. A supporter of Henry Clay, he was again chosen to the governorship as an Adams-Clay partisan in 1828, although the Ohio Jacksonian electoral ticket was successful in November. Retiring from public life in 1830, he continued to participate in the plans of the National Republican party in Ohio and later in those of the Whig party. A lover of the Union, he became a candidate of the American party for governor of Ohio in 1855, apparently hoping that this organization might help to offset a too ardent sectionalism.

He was instrumental in the establishment of the Ohio State Board of Agriculture, and he served as its president, 1846–48. He was a pioneer in Ohio in the importation of British horses and cattle to improve the domestic breeds. Although modest and apparently guileless, he could be firm and self-reliant when occasion demanded. He found religious satisfaction in the Methodist faith, which he embraced in 1828. He was married twice, in January 1806 to Margaret McDowell, who died in 1809, and to Rachael Woodrow on Jan. 10, 1811. His widow, four sons, and a daughter survived him at his death in Hillsboro.

[Letters in the McArthur Papers, Lib. of Cong.; *Autobiog. and Correspondence of Allen Trimble* (1909) and in *Old Northwest Geneal. Quart.*, July 1906–Jan. 1909; *Biog. Encyc. of Ohio of the 19th Cent.* (1876); E. H. Roseboom, "Ohio in the 1850's," in Widener Lib., Harvard Univ.; *Highland Weekly News* (Hillsboro), Feb. 10, 1870.]   F. P. W.

TRIMBLE, ISAAC RIDGEWAY (May 15, 1802–Jan. 2, 1888), soldier, engineer, was born in Culpeper County, Va. In 1805 his father, John Trimble, moved to Kentucky, and through Isaac's uncle, David Trimble, congressman from Kentucky, the youth received an appointment to the United States Military Academy. Graduating in 1822, he was commissioned a second lieutenant in the artillery. His principal service as a subaltern was on the survey of a road from Washington to the Ohio River. About this time the development of railroads in the United States offered an attractive field to young West Point graduates and many resigned from the army to engage in this work, among them six members of Trimble's class, including himself. His own resignation took effect May 31, 1832, and for three years he was assistant engineer on the Boston & Providence Railroad.

Thereafter, he was chief engineer successively of the Baltimore & Susquehanna Railroad, the Philadelphia, Wilmington & Baltimore, and the Philadelphia & Baltimore Central, and from 1859 to 1861 general superintendent of the Baltimore and Potomac Railroad.

At the beginning of the Civil War he took an active part in obstructing the movement of Union troops to Washington by burning bridges north of Baltimore. In May 1861 he went to Virginia and received a commission as colonel of engineers in the state troops. On Aug. 9, 1861 he was commissioned brigadier-general in the Confederate service and in September was charged with the construction of batteries on the Potomac River to prevent the passage of United States vessels. In 1862 he was assigned to the command of a brigade in the Army of Northern Virginia and was charged with the removal of the stores from the depot at Manassas Junction when the army was withdrawn to meet McClellan on the Peninsula. Trimble's brigade remained on the Rappahannock as a part of Ewell's division. It took part in Jackson's famous operations in the Shenandoah Valley in 1862 and did conspicuous service in the battles of Winchester and Cross Keys. After this campaign it took part in the Seven Days' battles in the vicinity of Richmond.

In the campaign against Pope's army in northern Virginia in 1862, Trimble's command saw action in the battle of Cedar Mountain, the engagement at Hazel Run, and in Jackson's march around Pope to Bristoe Station on the Orange and Alexandria Railroad. Jackson reached this station at dark after a forced march of some twenty-five miles under an August sun. The Union depot of supplies at Manassas Station was about seven miles away, but Jackson was unwilling to order his infantry to proceed any farther that night. When, however, Trimble volunteered to take part of his brigade and advance on Manassas, Jackson gladly acquiesced, and the depot was captured at dawn of Aug. 27 by Trimble assisted by J. E. B. Stuart's cavalry. In the battle of Manassas that followed Trimble was so seriously wounded that he was unable to perform field service for many months. In October of that year when Jackson was promoted to command a corps he recommended that Trimble be commissioned major-general and placed in command of his old division. Trimble returned for duty in 1863 just as the Gettysburg campaign opened, and on June 18 was assigned by General Lee to the command of the troops in the Shenandoah Valley. He led his troops in this campaign as far north as Carlisle, Pa., where he

received orders to return. On the second day at Gettysburg he was assigned to the command of a division in Hill's corps, of which the commander, Gen. William D. Pender, had been seriously wounded. With two brigades he took part in the third day's attack in support of Pettigrew's division on Pickett's left. In this engagement he was seriously wounded, lost a leg, and was left a prisoner when the Confederate army retreated. The Union authorities, remembering the part he had played early in the war in obstructing troop movements and fearing his influence in the important border state of Maryland, did not permit his exchange until February 1865. He was on his way to join Lee when the latter surrendered at Appomattox. After the war he made his home in Baltimore, where he died. "Of all the soldiers whom Maryland furnished to the Southern Cause, General Trimble performed the most distinguished services, obtained the highest rank, and won the greatest name" (Nineteenth Annual Reunion of the Association of Graduates of the United States Military Academy, 1888, p. 68). He was twice married: first, to Maria Cattell Presstman of Charleston, S. C., who died in 1855; second, to her sister, Ann Ferguson Presstman. By his first marriage he had two sons, who survived him.

[G. W. Cullum, Biog. Reg. Officers and Grads. U. S. Mil. Acad. (3rd ed., 1891); Nineteenth Ann. Reunion . . . Asso. Grads., cited above; War of the Rebellion: Official Records (Army); Southern Hist. Soc. Papers, vol. XXVI (1898); G. F. R. Henderson, Stonewall Jackson and the Am. Civil War (1898); Army and Navy Jour., Jan. 7, 1888; Sun (Baltimore), Jan. 3, 1888.]
G. J. F.

TRIMBLE, ROBERT (1777–Aug. 25, 1828), jurist, the son of William Trimble, was born in Augusta County, Va. While still very young he was taken by his parents to Clark County, Ky., where his father acquired a patent to 700 acres of frontier land. Here Robert grew to manhood, clearing ground, cultivating crops, hunting wild game, and fighting Indians. From early boyhood he appears to have been a leader among his fellows, excelling in physical as well as mental activities. In the spring of 1795 he entered Bourbon Academy in Bourbon County, from which institution, a year later, he was compelled to withdraw because of illness. After teaching for a short period he became a student in Kentucky Academy in Woodford County. Upon completing his course there, he began reading law, first under George Nicholas [q.v.] and later under James Brown [q.v.], afterwards minister to France.

In 1800 Trimble entered upon the practice of his profession at Paris, Bourbon County, and thereafter maintained a residence in that town. His practice was uninterrupted, except for one term, 1802, in the state legislature, until the governor made him a judge of the court of appeals in 1807. This position he resigned two years later because the emoluments were insufficient for the support of himself and his family, and for the same reason he declined the chief justiceship of the court in 1810, and another offer of a justiceship in 1813. In the meantime his practice and reputation as a lawyer were growing, and by 1815 he was appearing in most of the important cases arising in his section of the state. From 1813 to 1817 he also served as district attorney and in this capacity was a courageous and vigorous prosecutor. In the latter year he gave up his practice to accept the tender by President Madison of the federal district judgeship for Kentucky, in which position he served until May 9, 1826, when, upon the nomination of President Adams, he was confirmed by the Senate as an associate justice of the Supreme Court of the United States, succeeding his friend and fellow Kentuckian, Thomas Todd [q.v.]. Though a Jeffersonian politically, as a district judge Trimble had insisted upon the supremacy of the federal over the state law. For this reason he was opposed for confirmation as a Supreme Court justice by Senator Rowan of Kentucky, but much to the satisfaction of Marshall and Story, the opposition was able to muster but five votes as against twenty-seven in Trimble's favor. On at least two occasions he was importuned unsuccessfully to become a candidate for the United States Senate, and was twice offered but declined the professorship of law at Transylvania University.

His service on the nation's highest tribunal was curtailed by his untimely death to the brief period of two years, but the vigor, clarity, and statesmanlike quality of the opinions rendered by him during that time mark him as a jurist of high order. Though nearly always in accord with Marshall on constitutional doctrine, he differed with him in the case of *Ogden* vs. *Saunders* (12 *Wheaton,* 212), wherein Trimble wrote one of his ablest opinions, holding that a state insolvency law was not an impairment of the obligation of a future contract between citizens of that state. Marshall dissented. Trimble also thought, contrary to the view of the Chief Justice and a majority of the Court, that such a law could be made to apply constitutionally to the rights of creditors who were citizens of another state. He was married soon after he began the practice of law and had a large family.

Trimble County, Ky., was named in his honor. He died at Paris, Ky.

[Obit. by Joseph Story, in *Columbian Centinel* (Boston), Sept. 17, 1828, reprinted in "Memoir of Judge Trimble," *Am. Jurist,* Jan. 1829, and in *Ky. Law Jour.,* Sept. 1882; H. L. Carson, *The Hist. of the Supreme Court of the U. S.* (1902); Charles Warren, *The Supreme Court in U. S. Hist.* (1922); *Autobiog. and Correspondence of Allen Trimble, Gov. of Ohio* (1909); Lewis and R. H. Collins, *Hist. of Ky.* (1874); *Western Citizen* (Paris, Ky.), Aug. 30, 1828.]   G. W. G.

TRIPP, BARTLETT (July 15, 1842–Dec. 8, 1911), jurist and diplomat, was born at Harmony, Me., the son of William and Naamah (Bartlett) Tripp. After attending the common schools and several academies he taught school and went to Waterville (later Colby) College from 1857 to 1860. His first acquaintance with the West came in 1861 on a trip to California, in the course of which he taught at Salt Lake City, Utah, and worked as engineer on the Central Pacific Railroad. In 1863 he married Ellen M. Jennings of Garland, Me., who died in 1884 leaving one daughter. In 1867 he studied at the Albany Law School of Albany, N. Y., and for two years practised law in Augusta, Me. He then returned to Dakota Territory, with which he had been impressed on his western trip, and practised at Yankton, which was his home the rest of his life. On Nov. 6, 1887, he married Maria Janet (Davis) Washburn, the sister of Cushman K. Davis [q.v.]. His service as a member of the Yankton school board, an incorporator of Yankton College in 1881, and as a member of the board of regents of the University of South Dakota indicate his constant interest in education. A prominent member of the Dakota bar, he served as president of the bar association, was in 1875 made a member of the commission for codifying the laws of the territory (*The Revised Code of 1877,* 1877), and in 1903 served on a similar commission for the codification of the laws of the state (*The Revised Codes, 1903,* 1903). In his later years he became a lecturer in law at the University of South Dakota. Although a Democrat he presided in 1883 over the first territorial constitutional convention, which was strongly Republican in composition. Two years later President Cleveland made him chief justice of the territorial supreme court, and he served from 1885 to 1889. When the legislature of the state of South Dakota met to choose a federal senator in 1891 he seems to have been near to election as the Democratic candidate. The election was, however, settled by a kind of compromise, and James H. Kyle [q.v.] was named.

Tripp's services to the federal government began with his arrival in Vienna on June 1, 1893, as minister to Austria-Hungary to succeed Frederick D. Grant. During the four years before he resigned on June 18, 1897, he was called upon to protest to the Austro-Hungarian government the seizure of numerous naturalized American citizens, natives of Austria-Hungary, for performance of military duty. One of the most important of these cases was that of John Benich in which Tripp persuaded the Austrian government to admit that its administrative officers should accept American passports as *prima facie* evidence of citizenship. Olney was able to say in 1896, in the only annual report ever made by a secretary of state, that friction with Austria-Hungary over citizenship cases had recently diminished greatly. In April 1899 Tripp was made the American member of the Samoan commission that was to undertake provisionally the government of the Samoan Islands then on the brink of civil war. Upon their arrival in the islands on May 13, the British and German members chose Tripp chairman. The report of the commission was rendered in July and his own able report to the secretary of state on Aug. 7, 1899. He urged the importance of Pango-Pango harbor to American interests, and it may be significant that when the islands were partitioned later in the same year the United States received Pango-Pango. After his return to the United States he published *My Trip to Samoa* (1911). He died at Yankton.

[A collection of photographs of events in Samoa during 1899 in the archives of state department; *Who's Who in America*, 1899–1900, 1910–11; obituary in *Report of . . . the S. D. Bar Asso. . . . 1912* (1912); Doane Robinson, *South Dakota* (1930), vol. I; G. W. Kingsbury, *Hist. of Dakota Territory* (1915), vols. II–IV, ed. by G. M. Smith; *Daily Argus-Leader* (Sioux Falls), Dec. 8, 1911.]   E. W. S.

TRIPP, GUY EASTMAN (Apr. 22, 1865–June 14, 1927), industrialist, son of Alonzo K. and Abbie F. (Yeaton) Tripp, was born in Wells, Me.; his father was an attorney. Guy attended the district school in Wells and later, South Berwick Academy, working in a grocery store summers to secure needed funds. When he was eighteen, a friend found a place for him as clerk in the office of the Eastern Railroad at Salem, Mass.; at twenty-five, he was employed by the Thomson-Houston Electric Company as its storekeeper in Boston and subsequently became traveling auditor. In this capacity he visited and studied many public-utility plants, attracting attention by his keenness in appraising the value and possibilities of such properties.

In 1897 he joined the staff, as auditor, of Stone & Webster, then a young engineering firm beginning to build and operate public-serv-ice plants. He rapidly rose to the vice-presidency of both of the two corporations into which, for engineering and management purposes, the business of the firm was divided. When in 1910 the firm was called upon to aid in the reorganization of the Metropolitan Street Railway Company of New York, Tripp acted as its representative. He became chairman of the reorganization committee, and at the auction of the railway's properties in December 1911, he bought them in for the bondholders for about $12,000,-000. His masterly handling of the intricate task of reorganizing this company led in January 1912 to his being chosen chairman of the board of directors of the Westinghouse Electric & Manufacturing Company, a position which he continued to hold until his death. Under his direction the company enjoyed great prosperity, increasing its varied business in all countries of the world. During the participation of the United States in the World War, Tripp was one of the most prominent of all civilians in patriotic service. In January 1918 the government selected him as chief of the production division of the ordnance department with the rank of major, but within ten months he was made a brigadier-general and assistant to the chief of ordnance of the United States Army. Upon his resignation, Nov. 21, 1918, the Distinguished Service Medal was conferred upon him. Thereafter, he continued to cooperate with the War Department in plans for industrial preparedness for possible war. He was for some time a member of the advisory board of the New York ordnance district, and for several years president of New York Post, Army Ordnance Association. In 1923–24 he made a trip around the world to study business conditions bearing upon the great foreign trade of the Westinghouse concerns, and during his visit to Japan he was decorated by the Emperor with the Second Class Order of the Sacred Treasure, the highest honor that Japan confers upon a private citizen.

During the latter years of his life, he spent much time studying the future possibilities of electric development in the United States, believing that power is to be perhaps the greatest factor in progress. He spoke and wrote much on the subject, and worked out in detail an elaborate plan for a great electric system to operate all railroads, street transportation, factories, farms, and homes in the entire country. Among his published monographs are *Proposed Antitrust Legislation* (1914), a speech before the Chamber of Commerce of the United States; *Water Power and Statesmanship* (1923), reprinted from the *New York Times*, Mar. 11, 1923; *Super-Power* as an *Aid to Progress* (1924); *Electric Development as an Aid to Agriculture* (1926). He was a director of nearly a dozen Westinghouse corporations, besides radio companies, banks, and other concerns. On Aug. 25, 1887, he married Mary Elaine O'Connell of Salem, Mass., who with three daughters survived him. He died in New York City.

[*Who's Who in America*, 1926–27; *Am. Mag.*, Nov. 1919; *N. Y. Times, N. Y. Herald Tribune*, and *Sun* (N. Y.), June 15, 1927; *Industrial Management*, July 1927.]   A. F. H.

TRIPPE, JOHN (1785–July 9, 1810), naval officer, was born in Dorchester County, Md. He was a direct descendant of Henry Trippe, prominent soldier and legislator, who migrated from England to Dorchester County in 1663. His paternal grandfather, John Trippe, married Elizabeth Noel, and, according to a son's account, had twenty-one children. One son, William, the father of John, was married to his cousin, Mary Noel, and to this union were born three children. It is not clear what academic training John received, but the superior quality of his official communications to the navy department, after he had reached maturity, suggests that his formal schooling had by no means been neglected. When hostilities occurred between the United States and France, he was residing at Easton, Md. On Apr. 5, 1799, he entered the navy as a midshipman, and during the next two years made extended voyages on the *United States* and the *Experiment*. After the settlement of difficulties with France, he was transferred to the *President* and sent to the Mediterranean, whither a squadron had been dispatched to check the aggressions of the Barbary powers, particularly Tripoli. In 1802 he received a furlough to make a voyage in the merchant service. The following year he was ordered to the *Vixen* as acting-lieutenant, and, on Aug. 3, 1803, sailed for Tripoli, where he joined Commodore Edward Preble's squadron.

In the subsequent assaults upon the enemy, Trippe displayed courage of the highest order. While in command of Gunboat No. 6, Aug. 3, 1804, he ran alongside one of the largest of the enemy boats and boarded her with only ten companions, his own boat falling off before others could follow. There were thirty-six of the enemy, led by a Tripolitan over six feet in height, who, it was said, had sworn upon the Koran that he would never surrender (Goldsborough, *post*, p. 224). Trippe, who was undersized but exceedingly agile, now engaged in a desperate hand-to-hand conflict with this man. His own pike broke, and he was forced to grapple with his antagonist. Both fell; but Trippe, after receiving a total of eleven wounds, finally killed the Tripolitan commander with the latter's own saber. Meanwhile the Americans under Trippe's command subdued the remaining Tripolitans. Some of his wounds were serious, but he nevertheless participated in subsequent attacks. For his outstanding services he received the thanks of Congress, and was voted a sword. He returned to the United States in November 1805.

His later activities included service in the Mediterranean in 1806, duty at Charleston, S. C., relative to the enforcement of embargo legislation in 1808, a mission to Holland on board the *Enterprise* to transact business pertaining to commercial relations in 1809, and the beginning of a voyage to New Orleans in 1810. Near Stirrup Key, on June 24, 1810, Trippe's vessel, the *Vixen,* was fired upon by the British warship, *Moselle*. The *Vixen* was immediately cleared for action, but an engagement was averted when the British commander tendered a written apology for his action. Trippe died at Havana. He was unmarried. Two United States vessels have been named after him: a sloop-of-war and a destroyer.

[Manuscript records, Archives Section, Naval Records and Library, Washington, D. C.; family papers and records collected by E. C. Trippe under the title: "Manuscript Genealogical Records of the Trippe and Allied Families," 1928, at the Lib. of Cong. Useful secondary works are G. W. Allen, *Our Navy and the Barbary Corsairs* (1905); J. H. Brown, *Am. Naval Heroes* (1899); Charles Gaylord, *Am. Naval Battles* (1837); and C. W. Goldsborough, *U. S. Naval Chron.* (1824).]   R. W. I.

TRIST, NICHOLAS PHILIP (June 2, 1800–Feb. 11, 1874), diplomat, was born in Charlottesville, Va., the son of Hore Browse and Mary (Brown) Trist and the descendant of Nicholas Trist who emigrated from Devonshire, England, and died in Louisiana in 1784. He was educated at the United States Military Academy at West Point, although he did not graduate, and in the law office of Thomas Jefferson, whose granddaughter, Virginia Jefferson Randolph, he later married. This family connection and a friendship with Andrew Jackson Donelson, the nephew of Andrew Jackson, established while the two were at West Point, were destined to be influential in his career. He possessed a keen conscience and a high sense of honor. In 1827 he refused to profit by conciliating Jackson, whose campaign biographer wished him to allow Jefferson's name to be used in behalf of the "Hero of New Orleans." Trist thought that Jefferson, if living, would not have allowed his influence to be thus employed. His first appointment, a clerkship in the state department, resulted from Henry Clay's desire to comfort the mother of Trist's wife,

Martha Jefferson Randolph, who was harassed by debt. It was obtained several months before the inauguration of President Jackson; but, doubtless owing largely to the influence of Andrew Jackson Donelson, he retained the post under the new administration, and during a brief period in 1829 appears indeed to have been private secretary to the President. His relationship with Jackson soon developed into mutual admiration. In April 1833 he was commissioned as consul to Havana, a position he held until July 1841. Owing to conditions in Cuba and the character of American shipowners, captains, sailors, and residents in Havana, the duties of this post were heavy and often irritating. Although the consul acted with his usual industry and high regard for duty, he was accused of failure to support the rights of American citizens, of cruelty to American captains, of truckling to the Spanish authorities, and of connivance in the slave trade. An investigation made by Congress and the state department failed to sustain these charges in 1840 (see *House Report 707, 26 Cong., 1 Sess.,* 1840), although it seems to have revealed that citizens of the United States were illegally engaging in the negro traffic. Trist's recall in 1841 was due to partisan politics rather than to any doubt as to his faithful performance of his functions.

Shortly after Polk's inauguration, Trist was called back to the state department as chief clerk; and occasionally, in Secretary Buchanan's absence, he acted as head of the department. The Mexican War soon brought him the greatest opportunity of his public career. Early in 1847 he was sent as special agent to negotiate a treaty of peace. Upon his arrival in Mexico he had an initial quarrel with Gen. Winfield Scott. The general's suspicious nature and the failure of the war department to keep its commander informed of the administration's policy were mainly responsible for the unpleasant episode, and Scott and Trist soon became warm friends. Trist was eager to bring his negotiations to a successful and speedy conclusion in order to save Mexico from collapse and anarchy, but Polk and his cabinet gradually came to regret that they had offered such mild terms. On one occasion Trist allowed his eagerness to induce him to agree to a boundary not warranted by his instructions. His motive was to avoid the termination of negotiations, but his conduct proved too much for the feeble endurance of an administration already irritated by the initial quarrel with Scott and perhaps not unwilling to demand severer terms of peace. In November 1847 he accordingly received his letter of recall. This action by his su-

periors was followed by general consternation in Mexico and pressure on the part of British and Mexican diplomats to have him proceed with his negotiations. The American agent, although knowing that to stay would end his career, soon decided, nevertheless, to yield to pressure in Mexico, and on Feb. 2, 1848, he signed a treaty in strict compliance with his original instructions. The pact was reluctantly received by an embarrassed administration in Washington and finally accepted by both governments. Trist had done what he conceived to be his duty, and Polk dared not refuse to accept the result.

Trist then settled down to unsuccessful legal practice, observing political developments from a distance. He denounced the dogmas of Calhoun, opposed secession, voted for Lincoln, and received from President Grant in 1870 an appointment as postmaster at Alexandria, Va. There he died four years later.

[Trist Papers, 44 vols., in Lib. of Cong.; archives of the state department; L. M. Sears, "Nicholas P. Trist, a Diplomat with Ideals." *Miss. Valley Hist. Rev.,* June 1924; J. H. Smith, *The War with Mexico* (2 vols. 1919); G. L. Rives, *The U. S. and Mexico* (2 vols. 1913); J. S. Reeves, *Am. Diplomacy under Tyler and Polk* (1907); information from Mrs. Harry R. Burke, Rosemont, Alexandria, Va.]   J.F.R.

TROLAND, LEONARD THOMPSON (Apr. 26, 1889–May 27, 1932), psychologist, physiologist, physicist, engineer, inventor, was born in Norwich, Conn., the son of Edwin and Adelaide Elizabeth (O'Brien) Troland. On his father's side he was, it is said, of Dutch ancestry. Graduating in 1912 from the Massachusetts Institute of Technology with the degree of B.S. in biochemistry, he took up the study of psychology under Hugo Münsterberg [*q.v.*] in Harvard University, obtaining the degree of A.M. in 1914 and that of Ph.D. in 1915. As Sheldon Traveling Fellow, he spent the following year in the Nela Research Laboratory of the General Electric Company, Cleveland, Ohio, where he undertook his first researches in physiological optics (flicker and heterochromatic photometry, after-images, Purkinje phenomenon). On his return to Harvard in 1916 one of his first enterprises was an investigation of telepathy in the psychology laboratory, which gave negative results. Already the articles which he contributed to various scientific journals had begun to attract notice. His first book, *The Nature of Matter and Electricity, an Outline of Modern Views,* written in collaboration with D. F. Comstock, appeared in 1917. During the World War Troland was employed by the United States navy in the development of submarine acoustical apparatus. At the same time he was a member of the committee of the National Research Council on vision and aviation psychology, and in 1921 as a member of the Council's committee on physiological optics he wrote a learned monograph on *The Present Status of Visual Science* (1922). From instructor in psychology in Harvard University (1916–22) he was promoted to the rank of assistant professor (1922–29); he later became lecturer on psychology. During these years of ceaseless activity Troland gave advanced courses in psychology in Harvard, lectured on physiological psychology, psychology of motivation, and other subjects, and, most important of all, organized and conducted with consummate skill a series of novel and far-reaching experiments in the psychology and physiology of vision which brought him into prominence in a wide field of pure and applied science, and made his name known in Europe as well as in America. He was an active member of many learned societies and in 1922–23 president of the Optical Society of America. His *The Mystery of Mind* (1926) was followed soon afterwards by *The Fundamentals of Human Motivation* (1928). In addition he contributed nearly forty articles to various scientific journals, besides writing long chapters in several handbooks of psychology.

Troland's university work in pure science was, however, only one part, perhaps the smaller part, of his varied scientific activities. From 1918 to 1925, in addition to his other employments, he was closely associated with the scientific engineering firm of Kalmus, Comstock and Westcott in Boston; at the same time he was also chief engineer of the Technicolor Motion Picture Corporation of California, which maintained an office in Boston chiefly in order to employ Troland's services without compelling him to sever his connection with Harvard. In 1925 he was made director of research, an office which he continued to hold for the rest of his life. He not only developed and improved the old two-color process of color photography, but invented and perfected the modern multicolor process in all its details. He devised nearly all the photographic and mechanical apparatus for colored motion pictures, the patents being issued in his name. Towards the end of 1929 the Boston office of the Technicolor Corporation was closed, and Troland was induced, though with reluctance, to resign his chair in Harvard and move to California in order to be near this organization. At this time (1930) he must have been very much overworked. Two volumes of his *magnum opus, The Principles of Psychophysiology,* had just been published—the first (1929)

on the problems of psychology and on perception, the second (1930) on sensation—and he was then at work on the third volume (1932) on cerebration and action. (The manuscript of the fourth and last volume on the ultimate theory of mind and matter was finished before Troland died but has not yet, 1936, been published.) His constitution was naturally strong and robust, but in California his health gave way under the strain of his incessant labors, and he was advised by his physician to take a rest. Going to Hollywood with his wife for a vacation, he stood one day (May 27, 1932) on the edge of a cliff near the summit of Mount Wilson, posing for a kodak picture. Suddenly he lost his balance and fell headlong into the rocky chasm; he was killed instantly. He was survived by his wife, Florence Rogers Crockford, whom he married on June 28, 1924; there were no children.

Troland was almost equally at home in physics, physiology, and psychology; he was conversant with the problems of biophysics and biochemistry; and withal he was an engineer, mechanical as well as electrical, of extraordinary ability. He had little art of expression either as writer or speaker, although his mind was too clear and logical ever to leave in doubt the meaning he sought to convey. His intellectual powers almost instantly impressed everybody who came into contact with him; it has been said of him that "the theoretical scientists respected him because of his technological achievements, while technologists admired him for his vast fund of theoretical knowledge" (Roback, *post*, pp. 26–27). Affable and courteous in manner, Troland mingled easily with his comrades and yet was a solitary, aloof from all, *facile princeps* among his peers.

[*Who's Who in America,* 1932–33; *Who's Who in Engineering,* 1931; A. A. Roback, in *Sci.,* July 8, 1932; J. P. C. Southall, *Jour. Optical Soc. of America,* Oct. 1932; J. B. Beebe-Center, in *Am. Jour. Psych.,* vol. XLIV (1932); obituary in *N. Y. Times,* May 28, 1932; letter from Dr. E. F. McCarthy, closely associated with Troland at Harvard.]   J. P. C. S.

TROOST, GERARD (Mar. 15, 1776–Aug. 14, 1850), geologist, was born at Bois-le Duc, Holland. His parents, Everhard Joseph Troost and Anna Cornelia van Haeck, were of but limited means, yet he was educated at the universities of Leyden and Amsterdam, devoting himself especially to chemistry, natural history, and geology. From the former institution he received the degree of doctor of medicine and from the latter that of master in pharmacy. He practised as a pharmacist at Amsterdam and at The Hague. He served in the army as a private soldier and later as a health officer and was twice wounded. In

1807, Louis Napoleon, King of Holland, sent him to Paris for further scientific study. There he became a pupil of René Just Haüy and attained the remarkable skill in mineralogy and crystallography that characterized his later work. Between 1807 and 1809 he traveled widely in Europe, collecting minerals for the cabinet of the King of Holland. He was a pupil, probably during this period, of Abraham Gottlob Werner.

In 1809 he was appointed on a Dutch scientific commission to Java, but was captured, taken to a French port, released on his identity becoming known, and proceeded to Paris, where he was made a corresponding member of the Museum of Natural History of France. Early in 1810 he sailed for Philadelphia. The Kingdom of Holland was soon after annexed to the French Empire. Troost then abandoned the idea of going to Java and decided to become an American citizen. He soon established a pharmaceutical and chemical laboratory in Philadelphia and in 1812 was one of the seven founders of the Academy of Natural Sciences in Philadelphia, which for five years he served as its first president.

In 1811 he became interested in establishing at Cape Sable, Md., the first manufactory of alum in the United States. This venture failed within a few years, causing Troost heavy losses. In 1821 he became professor of mineralogy in the Philadelphia Museum and in 1821–22 was professor of pharmaceutical and general chemistry in the Philadelphia College of Pharmacy. Between 1821 and 1825 he made a geological survey of the environs of Philadelphia for the Philadelphia Society for Promoting Agriculture, publishing the results in 1826.

In 1825 he joined William Maclure, Thomas Say, Robert Dale Owen, and C. A. Lesueur [qq.v.] in the "boat-load of knowledge" which floated down the Ohio to Robert Owen's community at New Harmony, Ind., but, disappointed he moved in 1827 to Nashville, Tenn., with the large collections in natural history and geology which he had spent twenty years acquiring. While in Philadelphia he had made frequent scientific excursions into New Jersey and New York, and from New Harmony had visited the Missouri lead mines. From Java alone he had over 400 species of mounted birds. Later he acquired so much more material that his museum at Nashville became the most notable west of the Appalachians. His meteorites have since been acquired by Yale University.

From his election early in 1828 until his death, Troost was professor of geology and mineralogy, and for most of that time of chemistry and natural philosophy, also, in the University of Nash-

ville; from 1831 to 1850 he was also state geologist of Tennessee and did much to make known the mineral resources of that state. Becoming interested in Indian archeology, he made extensive collections from Tennessee mounds and graves. His last important work, a monograph on the crinoids of Tennessee, remained unpublished for many years but was at length reworked and published by the Smithsonian Institution (Elvira Wood, *A Critical Summary of Troost's Unpublished Manuscript on the Crinoids of Tennessee,* United States National Museum Bulletin 64, 1909).

Troost was a member of many of the learned societies of both Europe and America and was a frequent contributor to their publications. His interests ranged over practically all the known sciences. The bibliography of his writings (Glenn, *post,* pp. 90–94) contains articles on geology, natural history, chemistry, ethnology, mineralogy, and crystallography. Kindly and courteous, he had the polish that characterized the literary and scientific circles in which he moved in Paris; he was an excellent teacher, a good classical scholar, and widely read in science; he was probably most able in chemistry and mineralogy. Because of the long delay in publishing his work on fossil crinoids he lost much of the honor prompt publication would have brought him.

He was twice married: first, Jan. 14, 1811, to Margaret Tage, who died Aug. 3, 1819; and second, to a Mrs. O'Reilly. He left two children, both of the first marriage.

[Philip Lindsley, "The Life and Character of Professor Gerard Troost, M.D." (discourse, Oct. 2, 1850), in *The Works of Philip Lindsley,* vol. I (1859); L. C. Glenn, "Gerard Troost," in *Am. Geologist,* Feb. 1905; H. G. Rooker, "A Sketch of the Life and Work of Dr. Gerard Troost," in *Tenn. Hist. Mag.,* Oct. 1932; *The First Century of the Phila. Coll. of Pharmacy* (1922); G. P. Merrill, *The First One Hundred Years of American Geology* (1924); *Popular Science Monthly,* June 1894; *Nashville True Whig,* Aug. 17, 1850.]

L. C. G.

TROTT, BENJAMIN (*c.* 1770–*c.* 1841), portrait painter in miniature and oil, was born probably in Boston, Mass. He first set himself up as a painter in 1791 in New York. Several years later he moved to Philadelphia, which was his headquarters for many years, to make miniatures after the portraits of Gilbert Stuart [q.v.]. With his friend Elkanah Tisdale he lived in Albany for a time about 1796 (Dunlap, *post,* vol. I p. 354). He devoted 1805 to a horseback tour of the "western world beyond the mountains" (*Ibid.,* vol. II, p. 99). In 1812 he exhibited at the Pennsylvania Academy, receiving glowing attention from the press. He was painting in Charleston,

S. C., in 1819. Following an obscure marriage made in Philadelphia he went to Newark, N. J., in 1823 to obtain a divorce, and lived there painting for several years. The three years following 1829 he spent in New York because, as Dunlap says, he felt he had lost his public in Philadelphia. In 1833 he moved to Boston. His last residence was in Baltimore, where he went in 1839; he appears in the Baltimore directory for 1840–41 as "B. Trott. Portrait and miniature painter. Office cor. St. Paul and Fayette Streets."

William Dunlap [*q.v.*] says Trott "was of the full medium height, thin, with a prepossessing countenance" (*Ibid.*, vol. II, p. 101). He lived his life as a man with a grievance, his sense of inferiority centering about the painter's technical problems. Possibly from being self-taught, he lacked the authority of a system and always imagined other painters possessed secrets he did not know. Dunlap once saw him experimenting on a miniature by Walter Robertson, half obliterating it in his efforts to discover the secret of its brilliance, making his way "beneath the surface like a mole, and in equal darkness" (*Ibid.*, vol. II, p. 98). He refused to exchange miniatures with Edward Greene Malbone [*q.v.*], suspecting some mischievous plan. Yet he was a close friend of David Edwin [*q.v.*], the engraver; he won the confidence and admiration of Stuart, who is said to have enjoyed his blunt and caustic manner; and he is said twice to have shared a house with Thomas Sully [*q.v.*] in Philadelphia (*Ibid.*, vol. II, p. 100). Dunlap's analysis of Trott's personality is confirmed by examples of the artist's work, such as the Joseph Anthony miniatures, which show him insecure in his method and lacking in confidence.

His earliest style is unknown. The first examples known, which date from 1795, were painted with broad free strokes, with studied concentration on the face, with attractive and lifelike color. Much of the ivory was left showing through, and the backgrounds as a rule were light. The characteristics by which any of Trott's best miniatures may be recognized are those which prevail in this period. It is likely that Stuart's influence upon his style was a determining one, but he evolved from this a manner of his own which is distinguished by his talent for characterization. He gave nearly all his sitters the same easy half-front pose and eliminated any but the most necessary details of costume. One flaw fairly common to his drawing was the lengthening of the neck line; the elongated collar is very nearly a Trott signature. By 1819 the principal change in his style is a broader stroke and more slapdash application. The painterly

quality which distinguishes his work from that of the earlier miniaturists, with their engraver technique, became extremely marked in this period. From then on his powers began to decline. In 1828 his stroke was smaller and much constrained. Trott achieved fine clear color, profiting from frequent chemical experiment. Though his transitions and combinations of color were not so subtle as Malbone's, the effect of naturalness is much the same. Like Malbone he is unmistakably American in his palette. The works of Trott from his best period, around 1805, compare favorably with fine miniature painting in England and France. In his own country half a dozen of his miniatures are excelled only by Malbone's. About fifty of his miniatures have been identified but none of his oil portraits. Among his sitters were Nicholas Biddle, Robert Morris, Charles Wilkins, and Sally Waln.

[Almost the only source for Trott's life is William Dunlap, *A Hist. of the Rise and Progress of the Arts of Design in the U. S.* (3 vols., 1918), ed. by F. W. Bayley and C. E. Goodspeed. H. B. Wehle and Theodore Bolton, *Am. Miniatures, 1730–1850* (1927), contains the best modern account and reproduces many of the miniatures. See also *Cat. of an Exhibition of Miniatures . . . 1720–1850* (1927), *Metropolitan Museum of Art*; and Jean L. Brockway, in *Antiques*, Aug. 1931, where miniatures not in Wehle and Bolton are reproduced.]
J.L.B.

TROTT, NICHOLAS (Jan. 19, 1662/63–Jan. 21, 1739/40), South Carolina jurist, was appointed, by the Lords Proprietors, naval officer and attorney-general of that part of the Province of Carolina which lay south and west of Cape Fear, Feb. 5, 1697/98, and arrived at Charlestown (Charleston) on May 3, 1699. An English lawyer of great learning, he can probably be identified with the Nicholas Trott, Jr., who was attorney-general in Bermuda, 1696–97, but should not be confounded with Governor Nicholas Trott of the Bahamas, who appears to have been his cousin. This governor, who was removed from office, married a daughter of Thomas Amy, one of the proprietors and, becoming one himself, made Nicholas Trott of Carolina his deputy. The latter, elected a member of the Commons House of Assembly in 1700, was made speaker. However, the House being dissolved by Governor Blake, Trott was arrested and held to bail for seditiously denying and disowning the governorship of Blake on the ground that he was without commission; Chief Justice Moore found this a sufficient reason for Trott's arrest, but the electors of the province disregarded it and elected him a member of the new Commons House by the highest vote cast for any one. Nominated again for speaker, he failed of election. The record of proceedings, however, reveals Trott as the aggressive leader of the faction in the province which ruled it for the twenty years following it. A man of great learning and unwearied industry, a sincere supporter of the Church of England and the proprietary government, he rose to the office of chief justice (Mar. 5, 1702/03) and to membership in the Council. In 1714 the proprietors gave him the exclusive right to appoint the provost marshal of the province, and made his presence necessary for a quorum of the Council and his consent necessary to the ratification of its acts; but in 1716 this grant of extraordinary power was revoked on protest from the Assembly.

Upon the overthrow of the proprietors' government, it has been claimed that he retired from public life, thereafter devoting himself exclusively to legal and historical pursuits, but as late as 1729 he claimed the office of chief justice. He had published *Clavis Linguæ Sanctæ* in 1719, and *The Laws of the British Plantations in America, Relating to the Church and the Clergy, Religion and Learning,* in 1721. As early as 1714, Trott was engaged on his monumental work, *The Laws of The Province of South Carolina* (2 vols. in one, 1736), the publication of which was refused by the provisional government most unreasonably. In the last year of his life he devoted himself to his explication of the original Hebrew text of the New Testament, finishing one folio. After the death of his wife, Jane, who was buried Feb. 23, 1726/27, he had married, on Mar. 4, 1727/28, her sister, Sarah (Cooke) Rhett (*Register of St. Philip's Parish,* pp. 23, 158). The latter was the widow of Col. William Rhett and the mother of William Rhett, who had married Trott's daughter Mary.

[J. H. Heyward, *Nicholas Trott. A Sketch* (n.d.), which is too eulogistic; A. S. Salley, Jr., "Judge Nicholas Trott," *State* (Columbia, S. C.), Mar. 18, 1923, the best account, quoting obituary in *S. C. Gazette,* Feb. 2, 1740; A. S. Salley, Jr., *Register of St. Philip's Parish, Charles Town, S. C., 1720–1758* (1904); *S. C. Hist. and Geneal. Mag.,* Jan. 1903, July 1920; Edward McCrady, *The Hist. of S. C. under the Proprietary Government* (1897), and *The Hist. of S. C. under the Royal Government, 1719–1776* (1899), fairer to Trott in the latter than in the former; J. B. O'Neall, *Biog. Sketches of the Bench and Bar of S. C.* (1859), vol. I, a brief, unfavorable account with a reprint of a charge to the grand jury; *Calendar of State Papers. Colonial Series, America and West Indies, 1699–1702, 1712–15, 1719–20* (1908–33).]   T. D. J.

TROUP, GEORGE MICHAEL (Sept. 8, 1780–Apr. 26, 1856), representative and senator from Georgia, governor, son of George and Catherine (McIntosh) Troup, was born at McIntosh's Bluff on the Tombigbee River in that part of Georgia that became Alabama. His father was born and educated in England, served as an officer in the British army, but spent his later years as a successful merchant in Georgia. His cousin was William McIntosh [q.v.], a Creek chief. About 1782 Troup was taken by his father to "Belleville," the home near Savannah, Ga., where he grew up. Tutored at home, he later studied at Erasmus Hall, Long Island, N. Y., where he was prepared for college by Peter Wilson [q.v.]. He graduated from the College of New Jersey (Princeton) in 1797. He studied law in Savannah and was admitted to the bar. Probably in 1801 he was elected to the state legislature and reëlected twice from Chatham County. In 1804 he removed to Bryan County but returned to Savannah within a year or two. Elected to the federal House of Representatives, he served from Mar. 4, 1807, to Mar. 3, 1815. A consistent supporter of the Jeffersonian program, he won the confidence of the Democratic administrations. He was a bitter opponent of the Yazoo claims and the recharter of the federal bank. He supported the Embargo as a resistance measure and voted against its repeal. Ready for war in 1807, in 1809 he opposed non-intercourse because he believed New England favored compromise; and as a vigorous advocate of preparedness he was willing to incur a debt up to a billion dollars to build a navy and raise an army. He was elected to the federal Senate and served from Nov. 13, 1816, until he resigned on Sept. 23, 1818.

Defeated as the Crawford candidate for governor in 1819 and 1821, he was elected in 1823 and reëlected in 1825. He advocated public education, a state supreme court, a state program of roads, canals, and railroads, a state penitentiary, combining hard labor and solitary confinement, and the repeal of the law for the sale of free persons of color. His most conspicuous work as governor, however, had to do with the Creek Indian controversy (see sketch of William McIntosh). He openly defied President Adams' orders and called upon the people of the state to stand by their arms in defense of the sovereign power of the state, and thereby secured the cession of all the Creek lands.

Again elected to the federal Senate he served from Mar. 4, 1829, until November 1833, when he resigned. Continuing to be a strong State-Rights Democrat, he voted against the bonus bill, the tariff, and the bank recharter. He upheld the right of nullification but thought South Carolina unwise in acting alone. He urged legislative remonstrance against the tariff, and Southern non-consumption as a remedy. In 1830 he openly advocated secession if the federal policy of aggression was not abandoned. He attended the State-Rights convention at Milledgeville in 1832 and was nominated for the presidency. He accepted but refused a similar nomination by South Carolina. He retired from the Senate in 1833 to devote his time to the care of his six plantations; but he was consulted by the State-Rights party on all important issues and gave his views in public letters that were generally accepted by the press and the people. He favored annexing Texas in 1844 and opposed the compromise of 1850. Lack of health prevented his attending the Nashville Convention, but he wrote a public letter advocating military schools, arsenals, armories, and powder manufactories as the only means whereby Southern rights could be safeguarded. He was married, first, on Oct. 30, 1803, to Anne St. Clare McCormick, the daughter of James McCormick of Louisville, Ga., who died the next year. On Nov. 8, 1809, he was married to Anne Carter, the daughter of George Carter of Alexandria, Va. They had six children. He died and was buried at his plantation "Rosemont" in Montgomery County, Ga.

[*Biog. Directory Am. Cong.* (1928); E. J. Harden, *The Life of George M. Troup* (1859); L. L. Knight, *Georgia's Landmarks, Memorials and Legends* (2 vols., 1914) and *Reminiscences of Famous Georgians*, vol. II (1908); *Men of Mark in Ga.*, vol. II (1910), ed. by W. J. Northen; George White, *Statistics of the State of Georgia* (1849); C. S. Wylly, *Annals and Statistics of Glynn County, Ga.* (1897); *Times and Centinel* (Columbus, Ga.), May 7, 9, 1856.]   F. M. G.

TROUP, ROBERT (1757–Jan. 14, 1832), soldier, jurist, and agent of the Pulteney estate, was probably the son of Robert Troup, commander of the privateer *Sturdy Beggar* (see *New York Historical Society Collections,* Publication Fund Ser. vol. XXX, 1898), who married, May 22, 1737, Elinor Bisset (*Names for Whom Marriage Licenses Were Issued . . . Province of New York,* 1860). This Robert, who died in 1768, mentioned a son Robert in his will (*Archives of the State of New Jersey,* 1 ser. XXXIII, 1928, p. 438). Graduating from King's College in 1774, Troup studied law, first in the office of Thomas Smith of Haverstraw, N. Y., and subsequently under John Jay [*q.v.*]. At the beginning of the Revolution he obtained a lieutenancy in the Continental Army, then stationed on Long Island. Shortly afterward he was appointed aide-de-camp to Brig-Gen. Timothy Woodhull. When Howe prepared to capture New York, Troup with three other officers was captured at Jamaica Pass while attempting to reconnoiter the enemy (Aug. 27, 1776). After a period of confinement in the prison ship *Jersey* and in the Provost Prison, New York City, he was exchanged (Dec. 9, 1776) and joined the army in New Jersey. On Oct. 4, 1777, he was

promoted to a lieutenant-colonelcy "as a reward of his merit and services in the American army" (*Journals of the Continental Congress,* vol. IX, 1907, p. 770), and attached to the staff of Gen. Horatio Gates. He participated in the battle of Stillwater and was present at the surrender of Burgoyne (Oct. 17, 1777). In February 1778 Congress created the board of war, of which Troup was appointed secretary. When the board was dissolved (1779), Congress made him secretary to the board of treasury (May 29, 1779–Feb. 8, 1780). Returning to civil life, he completed his law studies with William Paterson [*q.v.*], one of his fellow students being Aaron Burr [*q.v.*]. Troup practised law at Albany and New York, was elected to the state Assembly, and in 1796 was appointed judge of the United States district court of New York.

In 1794 he became interested in land speculation and invested a considerable portion of his fortune in western New York. Charles Williamson [*q.v.*], agent for the Pulteney interests in this region, was spending large sums for improvements designed to attract settlers, and for a while Troup had visions of handsome profits. The lands failed to sell readily, however, and some of those who bought were not able to make payments. In 1800 Sir William Pulteney became uneasy and requested Williamson's withdrawal from the agency. Since Williamson held the lands in his own name, Troup was employed to facilitate the transfer and between December 1800 and March 1801 he secured a series of deeds conveying the Genesee Tract to Sir William and his associates. Pulteney now offered the agency to Troup and for the next thirty years his name was intimately connected with the Genesee country, during which time a large portion of the Pulteney lands were sold and settled. In 1814 he became a permanent resident of Geneva, although he still spent much of his time at Albany, where he assisted or hindered legislation which might affect his special interest. Keenly watchful of western welfare, he was one of the early promoters of the Erie Canal (*A Letter to the Honorable Brockholst Livingston . . . on the Lake Canal Policy of the State of New York,* 1822).

A friend to strong central government, Troup gave valuable help in the campaign to secure the adoption of the Federal Constitution in New York. He was a warm personal friend of Alexander Hamilton; in fact, few enjoyed more intimate acquaintance with the prominent men of his day. He was a conservative in politics with small liking for republicanism or Republicans. The more he saw of "the progress of Jacobinism," the more he realized the need of setting up a college for the training of the clergy of the Episcopal Church (C. R. King, *post*, V, 37; Troup to King, June 1, 1807). He therefore gave his support to the founding of Geneva (later Hobart) College. He died in Laight Street, St. John's Square, New York City.

[Troup Papers, Rochester Hist. Soc.; Pulteney Papers, Canandaigua Hist. Soc.; Rufus King Correspondence, N. Y. Hist. Soc.; C. R. King, ed., *The Life and Correspondence of Rufus King* (6 vols., 1894–1900); Geneva *Gazette*, Hobart College; G. S. Conover, "Kanadesaga and Geneva" (MS., Hobart College); G. S. Conover, *The Genesee Tract* (1889); L. C. Aldrich, *Hist. of Ontario County, N. Y.* (1893), ed. by G. S. Conover; R. H. Greene, "King's College and its Earliest Alumni," *N. Y. Geneal. and Biog. Record*, Apr. 1896; Orsamus Turner, *Hist. of the Pioneer Settlement of Phelps and Gorham's Purchase and Morris' Reserve* (1851); *Memoirs of Long Island Hist. Soc.*, vol. III (1878); A. C. Parker, *Charles Williamson, Builder of the Genesee Country* (1927); Morgan Dix, *A Hist. of the Parish of Trinity Church in the City of New York* (4 vols., 1898–1906); D. R. Fox, *The Decline of Aristocracy in the Politics of N. Y.* (1919); P. D. Evans, "The Pulteney Purchase," *Quart. Jour. of the N. Y. State Hist. Asso.*, Jan. 1922; John Schuyler, *Institution of the Soc. of the Cincinnati . . . N. Y. State Soc.* (1886), pp. 313–14; *N. Y. Evening Post*, Jan. 14, 16, 1832.]   J. G. V–D.

TROW, JOHN FOWLER (Jan. 30, 1810– Aug. 8, 1886), printer, bookseller, and publisher, was born in Andover, Mass., the son of Lieut. John Trow and Martha (Swan). He was graduated from Phillips Academy, Andover, Mass., with the class of 1831, and entered the employ of his brother-in-law, Timothy Flagg, of the printing concern of Flagg & Gould, later the Andover Press. Here he acquired a knowledge of printing in the oriental languages, for the firm, having received a donation of Greek and Hebrew type, was doing such printing under supervision of members of the Andover Theological Seminary faculty. On Apr. 14, 1832, Trow established the *Nashua Herald* at Nashua, N. H., with S. J. Bard as editor and himself as printer. The newspaper was not successful, however, and was discontinued on July 11, 1832.

Removing to New York City in 1833, he first appears in the city directories as a printer in 1834. In that year he formed a partnership with John T. West under the firm name of West & Trow, which continued until 1837. Thereafter he seems to have conducted the business alone until 1844, when he became associated with Jonathan Leavitt and carried on a book shop as well as his printing establishment. This connection was broken in 1849. In 1866 the firm of John F. Trow & Company, printers and publishers, was formed; for most of the time from 1873 to his death Trow was an official of the Trow City Directory Company, and from 1877, of Trow's Printing & Bookbinding Company.

He is best remembered for his publication of *Trow's New York City Directory*, compiled until 1878 by Henry Wilson, which was first issued in 1852–53. The John Doggett, Jr. and Charles R. Rode series of New York directories, begun in 1842, were being published when the Wilson-Trow directory was launched, but after the issue of 1854–55 this series was discontinued, leaving Trow's alone in the field. It continued under its original name until 1925, many years after Trow's death. In 1847 he began printing and publishing *Wilson's Business Directory of New York City*, which appeared annually thereafter until 1884, when it became *The Trow City Directory Co.'s (Formerly Wilson's) Business Directory of New York City*. Another publication, first issued by John Doggett, Jr., and later printed by Trow, was *Wilson's New York City Co-partnership Directory*.

In his directories Trow advertised himself as a printer and stereotyper, doing every type of book and job printing. In 1853 he issued a volume entitled *Specimen Book of the Letterpress, Stereotyping, and Wood-cut Printing Establishment of John F. Trow, 49 Ann Street, New–York*. He is credited with being one of the first to introduce electrotyping into the printing business, and honors were conferred upon him for the excellence of his work. He published the *New York Citizen and American Republican*, later *New York American Republican*, a daily paper, from Jan. 1, 1844, to its discontinuance in 1845. He was also the author of *Alton Trials: of Winthrop S. Gilman, Who Was Indicted . . . for the Crime of Riot Committed on the Night of the 7th of November, 1837* (1838). On Aug. 12, 1834, Trow married Catharine Swift, daughter of Dr. Nathaniel and Sarah Abbott Swift of Andover, Mass., and they had five children, four of whom survived him. His death occurred at the home of a daughter in Orange, N. J.

[*Vital Records of Andover, Mass.* (1912); E. E. Parker, *Hist. of the City of Nashua, N. H.* (1897); Harrison Ellery, *The Memoirs of Gen. Joseph Gardner Swift* (1890); manuscript records of the Trow family; records of Phillips Acad., Andover, Mass.; *N. Y. Herald*, Aug. 9, 1886.]   A. J. W.

TROWBRIDGE, AUGUSTUS (Jan. 2, 1870– Mar. 14, 1934), physicist, was born in New York City, the son of George Alfred and Cornelia Polhemus (Robertson) Trowbridge, and a descendant of Thomas Trowbridge who came to Dorchester, Mass., about 1636. Augustus entered Columbia University in 1890, but left in 1893 to take a position with the World's Columbian Exposition at Chicago. On Sept. 20 of that year he married Sarah Esther Fulton of New York. After finishing his work at the Fair, he

went to Germany, where he studied physics at the University of Berlin, receiving the degree of Ph.D. in 1898.

Returning to the United States soon thereafter, he became instructor in physics at the University of Michigan, leaving there in 1900 to accept the position of assistant professor at the University of Wisconsin; three years later he was promoted to a full professorship. In 1906 he accepted a similar position at Princeton, which he held until his resignation shortly before his death. In 1928 he became dean of the graduate school and fulfilled the duties of that office with notable success from that time until June 1932, when failing health compelled him to relinquish it. During his lifetime he carried on important research work and published between twenty and thirty articles, some of them in collaboration with other scholars, which appeared in various scientific publications. His studies were chiefly in the field of radiations, including the theory and behavior of the coherer.

In 1903 as a member of the International Congress of Applied Chemistry in Berlin, he began that phase of his activities for which his career was chiefly noted, those of an able administrator and director of organizations for the advancement of science. He was secretary of the physics section of the International Congress of Arts and Sciences, St. Louis, in 1904; a member of the National Academy of Sciences and in 1921 chairman of its division of physics; and chairman of the division of physical sciences and member of the research fellowship board of the National Research Council, 1920–21. In 1925 he obtained leave from Princeton in order to go to Paris as the director for science of the International Education Board of the Rockefeller Foundation, in which connection he was charged with the distribution of many millions of dollars, designed to restore the scientific institutions of Europe and to revive scientific work. His service in behalf of the advancement of science abroad was later recognized by his appointment as a Knight of the Order of St. Olav (Norway).

During the World War he was attached, 1918, to the staff of General Pershing as a member of the intelligence department, with the rank of lieutenant-colonel. His principal work was with the flash and sound ranging service of the army, the function of which was to locate the position of enemy guns either from the flash when fired, if that could be seen, or from the report. The French had devised a method of such location which the British had developed, and all the information acquired was put at Trowbridge's disposal. With the aid of this, American officers,

through the incorporation of automatic devices, were able to develop, in the Palmer Physical Laboratory, equipment by which an enemy's gun at its normal range could be located within forty to forty-five seconds after it was fired. At the end of the war Trowbridge's services were recognized by the award of the Distinguished Service Medal (United States), the Distinguished Service Order (Great Britain), and appointment as an officer of the Legion of Honor (France).

Trowbridge combined an unusual knowledge of the world and its peoples with a gift for languages. The combination made it possible for him to carry on readily the conferences required by the negotiations of the International Education Board, and while in the military service, to act as a liaison officer for the staffs of the allied armies. After resigning his professorship at Princeton in June 1933, he went to Europe, hoping to benefit his health, but died in Taormina the following March, survived by his wife and two sons.

[F. B. Trowbridge, *The Trowbridge Geneal.* (1908); *Who's Who in America,* 1932–33; *Princeton Alumni Weekly,* Mar. 23, 1934; *N. Y. Times,* and *Evening Star* (Washington), Mar. 15, 1934.]   H. M.

TROWBRIDGE, EDMUND (1709–Apr. 2, 1793), jurist, son of Thomas Trowbridge by his second wife, Mary (Goffe), was born in Cambridge, Mass. He was a descendant of Thomas Trowbridge of Taunton, Somerset, England, who came to Dorchester, Mass., about 1636 and about 1638 moved to New Haven, Conn. Down into middle life Edmund bore the name Goffe, after his uncle, Col. Edmund Goffe, whose adopted child and heir he was. About 1766 he appears to have resumed his surname of Trowbridge. He graduated from Harvard in 1728 and subsequently became prominent at the Massachusetts bar. Commissioned attorney-general in 1749, he held this office until his appointment as judge of the superior court in 1767. In 1759 John Adams referred to him as commanding "the practice in Middlesex and Worcester and several other counties," adding, "He had power to crush, by his frown or his nod, any young lawyer in his county" (*Works, post,* IV, 6). Isaac Parker [*q.v.*], later chief justice of the Massachusetts superior court, characterized him as "perhaps the most profound lawyer of New England before the Revolution" (Warren, *post,* I, 51).

While Trowbridge's arguments before the superior court do not appear to have met with more than average success, his skill as a special leader is evinced by the forms of his pleadings which were incorporated into later books of practice.

Trowbridge

His opinions on the bench were notable for their impartiality and penetration. His disagreement with the rule laid down by the majority on an earlier occasion in *Baker* vs. *Mattocks* (*Quincy*, 69, at p. 74), to the effect that the province statute of 1692, by which lands descended to all the children, did not extend to estates tail but left them as at common law, was an example of clear thinking and in accord with earlier precedent (cf. R. B. Morris, *Studies in the History of American Law,* 1930, pp. 96–97). His colleague, Thomas Hutchinson [*q.v.*], who was not a professionally trained lawyer, appears to have leaned heavily upon him for legal advice. In 1765 they issued a joint opinion in which they denied that justices of the peace were empowered to grant writs of assistance, but conceded the legality of the latter when issued by the superior court (*Quincy,* 439). A moderate conservative and attached to Hutchinson at this time, Trowbridge refused spiritedly to enter a *nolle prosequi* against the Berkshire rioters in 1766 (Adams, *post,* II, 204). His fairness and impartiality were manifest in the Boston Massacre trial in 1771. An expert in real property law, Trowbridge wrote a tract on mortgages, one of the few known colonial studies in private law (appended to 8 *Massachusetts Reports;* 1818). While borrowing much from Coke on Littleton and from Bacon's *Abridgment,* he was quite critical of Mansfield's contributions to this subject.

On the eve of the Revolution Trowbridge was a moderate sympathizer with the Loyalist point of view, and on this account was dropped from the Council in 1766 (Adams, II, 195). Nevertheless, he expressed strong resentment at the appointment in 1771 of Foster Hutchinson to the probate court, manifesting a traditional Puritan hostility to the judicial powers of the Anglican Church (*Ibid.,* II, 284). Again, in 1774, he was frank to concede that, in the light of the English Constitution, the Massachusetts House of Representatives had the power to impeach the judges, asserting that this power was "essential to a free government" (*Ibid.,* II, 331; X, 239). Somewhat gloomy in manner and a notorious hypochondriac, Trowbridge counted among his large circle of friends such Revolutionary leaders as John Adams and Joseph Hawley. Surrounded by relatives and associates active in the Patriot cause, he maintained a strict neutrality during the conflict. He received an offer of safe conduct from the Committee of Public Safety and retired from his Cambridge home, taking up his residence with the Parsons family in Byfield, whither he took his famous law library, probably the finest in New England at that time. Here The-

ophilus Parsons [*q.v.*] studied with him and gained the legal foundation for his later career. Among other leaders of the bar who studied law in his office were James Putnam and his nephew and heir, Francis Dana [*q.v.*]. On Mar. 15, 1737/38 Trowbridge married Martha, daughter of Jonathan Remington; there were no children. He died at Cambridge at the age of eighty-four.

[F. B. Trowbridge, *The Trowbridge Geneal.* (1908); Theophilus Parsons, *Memoir of Theophilus Parsons* (1859); Lorenzo Sabine, *Biog. Sketches of Loyalists of the Am. Revolution* (1864), II, 362–64; L. R. Paige, *Hist. of Cambridge, Mass., 1630–1877* (1877), pp. 671, 672; W. T. Davis, *Professional and Industrial Hist. of Suffolk County, Mass.* (1894), I, 216; Emory Washburn, *Sketches of the Judicial Hist. of Mass.* (1840); C. F. Adams, *The Works of John Adams,* vols. II (1850), IV (1851), X (1856); Charles Warren, *Hist. of the Harvard Law School* (1908), I, 51, 129; John T. Morse, "Bench and Bar in Boston," in Justin Winsor, *The Memorial Hist. of Boston,* vol. IV (1881).]
R. B. M.

TROWBRIDGE, JOHN (Aug. 5, 1843–Feb. 18, 1923), physicist, educator, was born in Boston, the son of John Howe Trowbridge and Adeline (Richardson) Whitney Trowbridge, and a descendant of Thomas Trowbridge who came from Somersetshire, England, to Dorchester, Mass., about 1636. Though at his birth the family was in comfortable circumstances, a reverse of fortune compelled John while still a youth to use his considerable artistic talent as a means of earning money, and he painted a number of pictures which found a ready sale. Graduating from the Lawrence Scientific School of Harvard University in 1865, with the degree of S.B., he taught mathematics at Harvard for a time, served in the physics department of the Massachusetts Institute of Technology, 1868–70, and then returned to Harvard as assistant professor of physics. Ten years later he became full professor, and from 1888 until his retirement in 1910 was Rumford Professor of Science and director of the Jefferson Physical Laboratory.

One of the first of American teachers to encourage students in original research in physics, Trowbridge was largely responsible for changing the method of instruction of the Harvard department from the old system of set lectures, demonstrations, and textbook assignments, to the modern plan of laboratory practice, research, and encouragement of constructive thought. Imbued with the spirit of progress, he possessed vision and furthermore had the ability to recognize and give scope to the capabilities of other men. Keeping abreast of developments elsewhere, he planned for, worked for, and finally in 1884 secured for Harvard a physics building with genuine laboratory features, though the first director of this laboratory was his senior, Prof. Joseph

Lovering [*q.v.*]. It was under Trowbridge's influence and guidance, however, that the Jefferson Laboratory gradually acquired a physical equipment and a working staff which made it notable. This achievement, together with the assistance he gave to younger investigators, must be regarded as his great contribution to the progress of science.

Trowbridge was an associate editor of the *American Journal of Science* from 1880 to 1920, and published therein numerous brief contributions, including notices of work done by others. He also published often in the *Proceedings* of the American Academy of Arts and Sciences (Boston), of which he was president from 1908 to 1915. He was interested particularly in spectrum analysis and the conduction of electricity through gases, and many of his papers were contributions in these fields. In 1910 he retired from the directorship of the Jefferson Laboratory and from the Rumford Professorship.

Trowbridge was quiet and gentle, almost melancholy in manner, and except when he encountered intentional opposition was generous, almost too yielding; in the face of opposition, however, he could display considerable tenacity. His sense of humor was ordinarily concealed, but could not be ignored, and he was by nature quite as much an artist as a man of science. He wrote easily, producing besides his scientific papers a number of books combining fiction and science, which he illustrated with pencil sketches of his own. His published volumes include *The New Physics* (1884); *The Electrical Boy; or the Career of Greatman and Greatthings* (1891); *Three Boys on an Electrical Boat* (1894); *What is Electricity?* (1896); *The Resolute Mr. Pansy* (1897); and *Philip's Experiments; or Physical Science at Home* (1898). He married, June 20, 1877, Mary Louise, widow of Thomas W. Gray and daughter of Seth Turner Thayer. There were no children of this marriage. Trowbridge survived his wife sixteen years, dying in Cambridge in 1923.

[E. H. Hall, "Biog. Memoir of John Trowbridge" (1931), with portr. and bibliog., in *Nat. Acad. Sci., Biog. Memoirs*, vol. XIV; *Science*, June 1, 1923; *Am. Jour. Sci.*, June 1923; S. E. Morison, *The Development of Harvard Univ. . . . 1869–1929* (1930); F. B. Trowbridge, *The Trowbridge Geneal.* (1908); *Who's Who in America*, 1922–23; *Boston Transcript*, Feb. 19, 1923; personal acquaintance.]   E. H. H.

TROWBRIDGE, JOHN TOWNSEND (Sept. 18, 1827–Feb. 12, 1916), author, was born on his father's farm in Ogden Township, Monroe County, N. Y., the eighth of the nine children of Windsor Stone and Rebecca (Willey) Trowbridge, and seventh in descent from Thomas Trowbridge of Somerset, England, who emigrated to Dorchester, Mass., about 1636. Except for weak eyes he was a healthy boy, fond of hunting, fishing, ball playing, and kite flying, but his real business, even then, was with literature. A list of foreign words and phrases in his spelling book tantalized his imagination, and the brief extracts from the poets in Goold Brown's grammar exercised a charm that he never forgot. A cousin bequeathed him her French grammar, dictionary, and reader, and with them he taught himself French. A few years later he taught himself to read Latin. By the age of thirteen he was writing verse. Five Byronic stanzas by him on "The Tomb of Napoleon" were printed in the *Rochester Republican* when he was sixteen years old, and while attending the academy at Lockport, 1844–45, he contributed the newscarriers' New Year address to the *Niagara Courier*. After a brief experience as a school teacher in Du Page County, Ill., and at Lockport, he went to New York in 1847, at the age of twenty, determined to make a career as a writer. His confidence was justified. He had a gift for story-telling and was practical, industrious, and quick to learn. Mordecai Manuel Noah [*q.v.*] gave him kindly advice and helped him to find a publisher for his first stories. He was fortunate in other ways also, especially in his friendship with a French family, in whose household he lived the greater part of a year. Boston, however, was still the literary center of the country, and thither he removed in 1848. It remained his headquarters for the rest of his long life.

After a few years of journalism and hack writing for Benjamin Perley Poore [*q.v.*] and some lesser men, Trowbridge began his literary career with a novel, *Father Brighthopes* (1853), which he published over the pseudonym of Paul Greyton. Its success resulted in a series of related stories and the eventual abandonment of the pseudonym. Fifty years later he closed his career, formally but not quite completely, with a volume of collected poems (*The Poetical Works of John Townsend Trowbridge*, 1903), and an autobiography, *My Own Story* (1903). During the half century intervening, he wrote with remarkable steadiness, neither idling nor overworking, producing in all some forty volumes of fiction; a few plays adapted from his novels; several volumes of verse; a descriptive work, *The South: A Tour of its Battlefields and Ruined Cities* (1866), and some miscellaneous matter. He contributed constantly to *Our Young Folks*, the *Atlantic Monthly*, and the *Youth's Companion* and occasionally to other magazines. He was a contributing and consulting editor of

Our Young Folks, 1865–70, and managing editor, 1870–73. The genre that he made peculiarly his own was a boys' story sufficiently mature in substance to be about equally interesting to adults. Few American novelists have had so large and loyal a public. He himself regarded his fiction as good journeyman's work but thought that he would be remembered for his poetry.

He was married twice: on May 9, 1860, to Cornelia Warren of Lowell, who died Mar. 23, 1864; second, on June 4, 1873, to Sarah Adelaide Newton of Arlington. He had two children by the first marriage, one dying at birth, and three by the second. He was a discriminating admirer of Walt Whitman and a sane friend. Of other Boston men of letters, he was on especially friendly terms with Holmes and Longfellow. He twice made extended visits to Europe. His home, from 1865 until his death, was in Arlington, Mass., eight miles from Boston. He died there in his eighty-ninth year.

[In addition to Trowbridge's autobiog., see *Who's Who in America,* 1914–15; F. B. Trowbridge, *The Trowbridge Geneal.* (1908); A. E. Winship, "Authors as I Have Known Them: J. T. Trowbridge," *Jour. of Educ.,* Mar. 16, 1916; *N. Y. Times,* Feb. 13, 1916.]

G. H. G.

TROWBRIDGE, WILLIAM PETIT (May 25, 1828–Aug. 12, 1892), engineer, scientist, educator, was born in Troy, N. Y., a descendant of Thomas Trowbridge who settled in New Haven, Conn., early in the seventeenth century, and the son of Stephen Van Rensselaer and Elizabeth (Conkling) Trowbridge. His early education was obtained in rural schools, but at the age of sixteen years he was able to fulfil the requirements for entrance to the United States Military Academy, where he stood at the head of his class throughout the four-year course. Graduating in 1848, he was made brevet second lieutenant of engineers. During the last year of his course, he had acted as assistant professor of chemistry, and after his graduation he spent two years in the astronomical observatory, preparing himself for service in the United States Coast Survey; he was commissioned second lieutenant on Nov. 30, 1849. His first assignment was on the Atlantic coast, where he was engaged in the execution of the primary triangulation of the coast of Maine; subsequently, he was engaged in surveys of the Appomattox and James rivers in Virginia.

Proceeding to the Pacific coast in 1853, he was occupied during the succeeding three years in conducting astronomical, tidal, and magnetic observations along the coast from San Diego to Puget Sound. He was promoted to a first lieutenancy in the corps of engineers on Dec. 18, 1854; but, upon returning from the West in 1856, he resigned from the army to accept a professorship of mathematics in the University of Michigan. In the course of a year, however, he was persuaded to accept a permanent appointment as assistant superintendent of the Coast Survey. The *Reports of the Superintendent of the Coast Survey, Showing the Progress of the Survey During the Years 1857–1861* (1858–62) reveal the nature of Trowbridge's employments at this period. They cite observations on the winds of the Pacific coast; arrangement of Gulf Stream observations; investigation of the laws of motion governing the descent of the weight and line in deep-sea soundings; a review of the origin, cost, and progress of foreign geodetic surveys; description of an apparatus devised by Trowbridge for determining ocean depths and obtaining specimens of the bottom; results of experiments made with an instrument, also devised by Trowbridge, to register depths in soundings, and distance as a log at sea. In 1860 he was selected to install the self-registering instruments of the permanent magnetic observatory established at Key West for the purpose of recording the variations in the direction of the magnetic needle, and also the intensity of the earth's magnetic force in terms of the fundamental units of space, mass, and time.

The following year preparations for warfare became of concern to his office, and, by recourse to the official records, he produced detailed descriptions of the harbors, inlets, and rivers of the coasts of the Southern states for the use of the navy; this task finished, he proceeded to execute a hydrographic survey of Narragansett Bay in relation to the project to establish a navy yard there. Soon after the beginning of the Civil War, he was placed in charge of the army engineer agency at New York City for supplying materials for fortifications, and for constructing engineering equipage for armies in the field; at the same time he was superintending engineer of the construction of the fort at Willets Point, of the repairs to Fort Schuyler, and of the works on Governors Island.

In 1865 he accepted the vice-presidency of the Novelty Iron Works, New York City, which position he held until 1871, when he became professor of dynamic engineering in the Sheffield Scientific School at Yale; from 1877 to the close of his life he was professor of engineering in the School of Mines of Columbia College. He lent impetus to the advancement of engineering education and to the application of science in place of empiricism in engineering. While at Yale, he served as a member of the New Haven board of harbor commissioners, as a commissioner for

the building of the capitol at Hartford, and as adjutant-general of Connecticut; while at Columbia, he was a member of the commission to examine and report upon the construction of the capitol at Albany. He was the author of designs for a cantilever bridge across the East River at Blackwell's Island, N. Y. (see his *Proposed Plan for Building a Bridge across the East River at Blackwell's Island,* 1868), and of treatises entitled *Heat as a Source of Power ... An Introduction to the Study of Heat Engines* (1874), and *Turbine Wheels* (1879), besides important contributions on various subjects to the *Transactions of the New York Academy of Sciences.*

From 1878 to 1884 he was councilor of the New York Academy of Sciences, and from 1885 to 1889, a vice-president; he was also prominent in the American Association for the Advancement of Science, and a member of the National Academy of Sciences. On Apr. 21, 1857, he was married, in Savannah, Ga., to Lucy, daughter of Samuel Breck and Theresa (Halsey) Parkman. He died in New Haven, Conn., survived by his wife and six children.

[F. B. Trowbridge, *The Trowbridge Geneal.* (1908); *Twenty-fourth Ann. Reunion, Asso. Grads. U. S. Mil. Acad.* (1893); G. W. Cullum, *Biog. Reg. Officers and Grads. U. S. Mil. Acad.* (3rd ed., 1891); *Nat. Acad. Sci. Biog. Memoirs,* vol. III (1895); *New Haven Evening Reg.,* Aug. 13, 1892.] G. W. L.